Genealogical and Family History of the State of New Hampshire

Yours truly Benj Chase

[illegible]

VOL. IV

ILLUSTRATED

[illegible]
NEW YORK [illegible]
[illegible]

GENEALOGICAL AND FAMILY HISTORY

OF THE

STATE OF NEW HAMPSHIRE

A RECORD OF THE ACHIEVEMENTS OF HER PEOPLE IN THE MAKING OF A COMMONWEALTH AND THE FOUNDING OF A NATION

COMPILED UNDER THE EDITORIAL SUPERVISION OF

EZRA S. STEARNS

EX-SECRETARY OF STATE; MEMBER AMERICAN ANTIQUARIAN SOCIETY, NEW ENGLAND HISTORIC-GENEALOGICAL SOCIETY, NEW HAMPSHIRE STATE HISTORICAL SOCIETY; CORRESPONDING MEMBER MINNESOTA STATE HISTORICAL SOCIETY; MEMBER FITCHBURG HISTORICAL SOCIETY

ASSISTED BY

WILLIAM F. WHITCHER

TRUSTEE NEW HAMPSHIRE STATE LIBRARY, MEMBER NEW HAMPSHIRE STATE HISTORICAL SOCIETY AND NEW ENGLAND METHODIST HISTORICAL SOCIETY

AND

EDWARD E. PARKER

JUDGE OF PROBATE, NASHUA

VOL. IV

ILLUSTRATED

THE LEWIS PUBLISHING COMPANY

NEW YORK CHICAGO

1908

NEW HAMPSHIRE

FARNSWORTH Of English origin are all the families of Farnsworth in the United States. The name is derived from one of the two places in Lancashire, England, called Farnworth. One of them is in the parish of Prescott, not far from Liverpool, and the other is in the parish of Dean, a few miles northwest of Manchester, in the hundred of Salford. The name is thought to be taken from the latter place.

The word is Saxon and derived from fearn, meaning fern, and Wearth, a place, a farm, an estate; and signifying a place or farm where ferns grow. The greater number of the English families spell their name Farnworth, and so did the early settlers of this family in America, but as the writers and recorders of those early times spelled it ffarneworth, ffernworth, ffearneworth, ffarnot, ffearnoth, and finally Farnsworth, the Farnsworths themselves finally adopted the last form, which is now uniform orthography in America. The pronunciation in early times in this country was probably as if spelled Farnoth.

(I) Matthias Farnsworth, by occupation a weaver, first appears of record in Lynn, Massachusetts, where he was a resident in 1657, but he had probably already resided there some years at that date. When he came to this country is unknown. He was a farmer and had a farm near what is now Federal street, on which he lived until 1660 or 1661, when he removed to Groton. There he shared in the distribution of lands with the other proprietors. The records show that Matthias had the following uplands: His houselot, ninety acres, more or less, lying on both sides of the mill highway, bounded on the north by the side hill by "James his brook," &c.; six acres and a half, more or less, lying on Indian hill; eighteen acres, more or less, bounded west by Mill road; seventy-one acres, more or less, lying on the other side of the Mill road. His meadows: In south meadow, fourteen acres, more or less, bounded on several points by the town common; six acres, more or less, near the mill; five acres and a half, more or less, near the mill; two acres and a half, more or less, at Half Moon Meadow; in all something over two hundred and twelve acres of virgin soil.

The first of the lots described was the one on which he built his log house. This was undoubtedly burned by the Indians when nearly the whole town was destroyed by them, March 13, 1676. A number of settlers were killed, the others escaped to Concord, and on March 17 removed in sixty carts what was left of their portable property. In the spring of 1678, Matthias Farnsworth with his family, including his three eldest sons, who were then of age, returned to his clearing in the woods and rebuilt his house and began anew. This latter house stood until 1820, when it was torn down to make room for improvements. Here he lived until his death, January 21, 1689. He was admitted a freeman of the Colony, May 16, 1670, and made his will January 12, 1689, being then seventy-seven years of age.

Matthias Farnsworth was a prominent member of his church, of which he was one of the early members, and a leading citizen of the town. He was one of the council of eleven held in Groton, in May, 1664, to consider certain "uncomfortable differences that had been amongst them about Church Government." He filled many offices in the town, the most important of which were those of constable and selectman. He held the office of constable, whose duties then were the collection of rates and taxes for the settlement as late as 1684, when he was seventy-two years old.

He was probably twice married, but nothing is known of his first wife, by whom he probably had three children. He married (second), Mary, daughter of George Farr, of Lynn, Massachusetts. She survived him many years, seems to have been a householder in 1692, made her will December 5, 1716, and died between that date and March 7, 1717, when her will was proved. The children of Matthias Farnsworth were: Elizabeth, Matthias, John, Benjamin, Joseph (died young), Mary, Sarah, Samuel, Abigail, Jonathan and Joseph.

(II) Benjamin, third son and seventh child of Matthias Farnsworth, was born in 1667, and died in Groton, August 15, 1733, aged sixty-six years. He built a house and lived on the east side of the road running on the westerly side of the broad meadow. He owned a large stretch of land west of the meadow, and southerly of the road from Farmer's Row, across the meadow to the First Parish Meetinghouse. His house was standing till 1830. He held the office of selectman and other town offices. He and his wife were church members, and their children were baptized. He married, in 1695, Mary Prescott, born February 3, 1674, in Lancaster, Massachusetts, daughter of Jonas and Mary (Loker) Prescott. She died October 28, 1735, aged sixty-one. They had Mary, Martha (died young), Benjamin, Isaac, Ezra, Amos, Lydia, Aaron, Martha, Jonas and Deborah.

(III) Aaron, eighth child and fourth son of Benjamin and Mary (Prescott) Farnsworth, was born August 29, 1709, and died in July, 1769, aged sixty years. He married (first), March 29, 1739, Hannah Barton, who died about 1743; married (second), 1744, Sarah ——, who died about 1747; married (third), 1749, widow Elizabeth Parker, who died December 12, 1766, aged forty-seven. Married (fourth), June 16, 1767, Sarah Bennett, born in 1723. After his death she married a Bolton, and died June 24, 1822, in the one hundredth year of her age. The children of Aaron and Hannah (Barron) Farnsworth were: Zaccheus, Sybil (died young), Mary, Hannah, Eunice, Samuel, and Esther; by second wife, Sarah and Aaron; by third wife, Elizabeth (Parker) Farnsworth, Timothy and Sybil.

(IV) Mary, third child and second daughter of Aaron and Hannah (Barron) Farnsworth, was born in Groton, March 29, 1732, and died September 19, 1796. She married, March 2, 1767, Colonel Osmyn Baker (See Baker I).

McLANE The McLane family is of Scottish descent. Those emigrating to New Hampshire came from the county of Argyle. The Clan McLane was located at Loch Buoy. The family seems to have been honorable and distinguished, Sir John McLane, to whom the present family traces its lineage, having rank with the nobility, claiming descent from a younger branch of the family of Charles the Pretender. Those earliest there seem to have possessed the sterling virtues characteristic of those who originally settled in Londonderry, and on their arrival came among them before finally locating. They were strong in their religious convictions and intensely patriotic. Captain Obadiah McLane, who settled in Goffstown, was a fellow-clansman and a prominent officer in the Revolution, who was given the special duty of looking after the Tories and deserters, and had with them some romantic and desperate encounters.

(I) Sir John McLane married, and had among other children a son Daniel.

(II) Daniel, son of Sir John McLane, was a soldier in the army of Charles the Pretender at the battle of Culloden, April 16, 1746. He married Molly Beaton, by whom he had among his children two sons, Malcolm and Hugh.

(III) Malcom, son of Daniel and Molly (Beaton) McLane, was born in the parish of Lear Castle, Argyle county, Scotland. He emigrated to this country in 1775, landing in Boston. He spent some time among his countrymen in Londonderry and New Boston, and finally located in Francestown in 1784, buying of Hugh Morrill the place next north of the Haunted Lake. He married Isabell, daughter of John and Jenny (Carmichael) Livingston, by whom he had the following children: Jane, born May 1, 1780, died December 7, 1852; John, born March 6, 1784; Daniel, born October 10, 1787, married Mary Starrett; Nancy, born April 2, 1789, died June 26, 1819; Niel, born February 6, 1791, never married; Mary, born October 9, 1792, died March 9, 1873; Isabel, born April 4, 1794, died January 21, 1881; Archibald, born May 26, 1796, died unmarried, December 17, 1852.

(IV) John, eldest son and second child of Malcom and Isabell (Livingston) McLane, was born in New Boston, March 6, 1784. He settled on a farm in Francestown, near his father, where he resided till 1822, when he removed to Newport, and some time after to Fairlee, Vermont, and died there August 8, 1851. He was a prominent man, and in Fairlee was honored with election to town offices, and represented the town in the legislature. He was also for a time associate judge of the court in Caledonia county. He was a man of positive convictions, clear-headed, capable, and highly respected by all. He married, August 24, 1815, Elizabeth McCollom, who died in New Boston, September 30, 1882, aged ninety-one years. Their children were: Neil, born January 19, 1816, married, October 14, 1849, Sarah C. Kelso, of New Boston; Alexander, born January 16, 1817, married, in 1850, Betsey Church, of Kirby, Vermont; John; Charles, born April 28, 1819, married (first), Rebecca Bailey, and (second), in 1852, Edwina Powell; Rodney, born July 18, 1820, married, November 17, 1853, Adeline Farley, of New Boston; Mary, born October 11, 1822, married, in 1851, James Lyford, of Canterbury; Nancy J., born in Newport, April 30, 1823; George Waterman, born April 30, 1824, married, November 19, 1848, Philena Renyon, of Plainfield; Elizabeth, born in Newport, June 29, 1825, died in Fairlee, Vermont, March, 1842; Clarissa, born August 5, 1827, died August 15, 1849; Helen, born July 31, 1828; Sarah, born in Sunapee, July 22, 1830; Marion, born in Sunapee, July 4, 1833, died December, 1853; Robert E., born in Grafton, October 23, 1834, married Emma Burton, of Athol, Massachusetts.

(V) John, third son and child of John and Elizabeth (McCollom) McLane, was born in New Boston, April 14, 1818. He received his education in the district schools. His occupation was that of carpenter and farmer. He went to Boston, Massachusetts, and for five years ran a store for himself, and then returned to New Boston and worked in a door shop. He built himself a house where he afterwards resided. Politically he was a Republican, and religiously a Presbyterian. He was a member of the Independent Order of Odd Fellows. He died August, 1900. He married, November, 1850, Hannah E. Whipple, by whom he had James Neil, and perhaps other children.

(VI) James Neil, son of John and Hannah E. (Whipple) McLane, was born in New Boston, November 8, 1858. He was educated in the public schools. After leaving school he learned the trade of blacksmith, and worked at it for fourteen years. He was then engaged in carrying on the lumber business for three years. Afterwards he went into partnership with his brother Reid in running a grist mill, and carrying on the feed business. He has also handled some real estate. In politics he is identified with the Republican party. Denominationally he is a Presbyterian. He is a member of the Independent Order of Odd Fellows, and has filled the chairs. He has been selectman, and represented his town in the legislature in 1902. He has also been a road agent. He married, September 22, 1881, Rebecca H., daughter of John and Mary (Crombie) Andrews, of New Boston. She received her education in the district schools and Francestown Academy, from which she graduated. Afterwards she went to Boston and took a course in training for a nurse. She is a member of the Presbyterian Church. The children of Mr. and Mrs. McLane are: Francis, born in 1883; Alice W., born in 1885, married Waldren Stevens; child born February 22, 1888; John W., born October 19, 1892; a daughter, born January 25, 1895; a son, born August 9, 1897.

AMES Several persons of this name came to Massachusetts Bay Colony in the early days of its existence, and from one of these ancestors an untraced line no doubt runs to this family.

(I) James Ames was born November 16, 1741, and died January 30, 1827, aged eighty-six years. His children were: Jacob, Peter, James, Caleb, Mary and Comfort. (Mention of Caleb and descendants appears in this article.)

(II) James (2), son of James (1) Ames, was born about 1780, and died in Gilford. He owned and cultivated a farm of one hundred and fifty acres of land. He was a cooper by trade, and also worked at farming during the latter part of his life. In politics he was a Democrat, and in religion a Free Will Baptist. He married Catherine Thompson, a native of Gilford, by whom he had four children: James Thompson, Morrill, Mary and Susan.

(III) James Thompson, eldest child of James (2) and Catherine (Thompson) Ames, was born in Gilford, 1821, and died in Gilmanton, 1886, aged sixty-five. He was educated in the common schools, and learned the cooper's trade. For some time he lived in Gloucester, Massachusetts, where he worked at his trade. He returned to Gilmanton where he engaged in farming up to the time of his death. In early life he was for a few years engaged in mercantile pursuits at West Alton. He was a Free Will Baptist and a Democrat, and lived up to his profession in both. He married Catherine Glidden, who was born in Alton, 1821, and died in Peabody, Massachusetts, in 1881, aged sixty. She was the daughter of Noah and Polly Glidden, of Alton. The children of James (3) and Catherine (Glidden) Ames were: Gorham B., James N., Frank P., and George, the latter dying in infancy.

(IV) James N. (4), second son of James (3) and Catherine (Glidden) Ames, was born in Alton, September 18, 1850. After leaving the common schools in which he was educated, he engaged in farming two years. Subsequently he removed to Salem, Massachusetts, where he ran a meat wagon for sixteen years. After a short stay in Salem, Massachusetts, he removed to Peabody, where he kept a provision store seven years, after which he carried on business in Boston Highlands and subsequently in Malden. From the latter place he came to New Hampshire and took charge of a farm of two hundred and six acres in Gilford, on which are fine farm houses, an orchard and a stock of cattle. Here he is engaged in farming, but his principal occupation is the entertainment of summer boarders, who find here a beautiful and agreeable place for rest and pleasure. Mr. Ames married (first), in November, 1871, Emma A. Dearborn, who was born in Salem, Massachusetts, 1845, daughter of Charles and Mary Dearborn. She died in the winter of 1874, and he married (second) Mary Ellen Hayes, who was born in Alton, Massachusetts, 1855, daughter of Ezekiel and Lydia Hayes. By the first wife there was one child, Hattie, who died young. By the second wife there are four children: Bertram Frank, born July 21, 1877; Thurlow H., August 21, 1879; Maynard J., September 5, 1888; and Morrill Roger, August 5, 1891.

(II) Caleb, son of James (1) Ames, was born in Gilford, October 12, 1782, and died in New Hampton, May 19, 1862, aged eighty. He grew up a farmer, and was educated in the district schools. At the age of twenty-six he removed to New Hampton, where he remained two years. Before his marriage he bought a farm of one hundred acres, which he cleared, and on which he built a log house and barns. He settled on that place about 1809, and was a prosperous farmer. He served a term in the war of 1812, being stationed at Portsmouth. The day before he would have been discharged he learned of the serious illness of one of his children, and set out for home, sixty miles away, walking the whole distance from Portsmouth to New Hampton in a day and a half. Not being present to be mustered out and receive his discharge, he was not able to obtain the pension afterward granted to soldiers of the war of 1812. He married, January 30, 1809, Sally Burleigh, eldest daughter of William and Sarah (Ames) Burleigh (see Burleigh), who was born January 27, 1788, and died May 19, 1862, aged seventy-nine. Their children were: Sarah, William Burleigh, James. (died young), James Marston, Peter B., Almira and Daniel H.

(III) James Marston, fourth child and third son of Caleb and Sally (Burleigh) Ames, was born in New Hampton, July 13, 1817, and died in Bristol, December 28, 1881, in the sixty-fifth year of his age. He left home at twenty-one years of age, and for six years was employed as a quarryman. He then bought the homestead of his father, which he enlarged until he had three hundred acres of land, and he also rebuilt the buildings. In 1866 he removed to Bristol, and settled at what is called the North End on the farm now owned and occupied by his son, where he and his wife spent the remainder of their lives. He was an active, hard-working man, who took good care of his own affairs and felt an interest in matters of public importance. His exemplary habits and success in taking care of his own caused many of his neighbors to come to him in times of doubt or adversity for advice. In religious belief he was a Baptist, and in politics a Democrat. He married, February 17, 1845, Abigail F. Batchelder, born June 8, 1827, daughter of Benjamin and Mary (Spaulding) Batchelder, of Bridgewater. She died January 10, 1886, in the sixty-second year of her age. They had two children: Mary Comfort, who was born in New Hampton, January 7, 1852, and married January 1, 1872, Laurin C. Tilton; and Burleigh M., whose sketch follows.

(IV) Burleigh Marston, first child and only son of James M. and Abigail F. (Batchelder) Ames, was born in New Hampton, March 8, 1848. He lived in his father's family and attended school until about nineteen, and then went to Watertown, Massachusetts, and stayed a year, and then (1867) for six or seven years was a manufacturer of straw board at Bristol. In 1875 he engaged in the manufacture of gloves which he carried on for a time. He owns the paternal homestead which he carries on, and is also a dealer in wood, coal, ice, etc. He has built and sold several houses in Bristol. He is a trustee and vice-president of the Bristol Savings Bank, and a director of the First National Bank of Bristol. He is a Democrat and a Free Baptist. He is a member of Union Lodge, Ancient Free and Accepted Masons, Bristol. He married, February 14, 1869, Mary Ann Locke (see Locke, VII), who was born September 21, 1850, daughter of Orrin and Nancy J. (Favor) Locke, and they have two children: Aletea Elfra, born in Bristol, February 27, 1872, who married Nathan P. Smith, of Plymouth; they have one child, Abby F., born May 12, 1889. Ethel Winnifred, born November 17, 1879, who married (first) Charles E. Spencer; married (second) George P. Fifield; their home is also in Plymouth.

AMES This family name appears early in Massachusetts, whence it spread into New Hampshire; and it is from an early Massachusetts branch of the family that the Ameses of this article have descended.

(I) John Ames is supposed to have moved from Newmarket, New Hampshire, to Parsonfield, Maine, where he died. He was a farmer. He married Elizabeth Neal, and they had six children: Samuel, John, Marston, Catherine, Daniel and Betsey.

(II) Samuel, eldest child of John and Elizabeth (Neal) Ames, was born in 1770, and died in 1861, aged ninety-one years. He settled in Tamworth,

New Hampshire, where he was a farmer for some years; and then moved to Wakefield, New Hampshire, where he died May, 1861. He married Susan Glidden, who was born 1771, and died 1872. Their children were: Betsey, Marston, John, Susan, Jacob, Samuel, and Daniel, all born after 1796.

(III) Marston, second child of Samuel and Sarah (Glidden) Ames, was born in Tamworth, December 25, 1799, and died in June, 1887, aged eighty-seven years. He was taken by his parents on their removal to Wakefield when a mere child. He settled at Ossipee and followed farming. He married in October, 1827, Clarissa Moulton, who was born in September, 1806, daughter of William and Mary Pearl of Parsonfield, Maine. She died August 11, 1876, aged seventy-one years. Their children were: William, born 1828, died young; Mary, born 1832, died 1867; Samuel and William (twins), born April 1, 1834; Martin Luther; John born August 10, 1839; Silas, died young, and David, whose sketch follows.

(IV) David M. Ames, youngest child of Marston and Clarissa (Moulton) Ames, was born in Ossipee, October 21, 1843. At eighteen years of age he began work in a tannery for Joseph Hodgdon and was employed there three years. He then went to Cornish, Maine, and worked at the same business for Albers & Allen six years, and then to Portland, where he was similarly employed two and a half years. Returning to Ossipee he cultivated the homestead two years. In 1877 he removed to Rochester, New Hampshire, and entered the employ of E. G. and E. Wallace, shoe manufacturers, and for ten years past has been foreman of their tanning department. In politics he is a Republican, and he has held the office of councilman of Rochester for six years. He married, February 28, 1866, Mary Cobb, who was born in Limerick, Maine, July 14, 1841, daughter of Joshua and Mary (Cook) Cobb. There were born of this union four children: 1. Sarah C., born February 8, 1867, a graduate of Boston University, class of 1895, since a teacher in Rochester four years, and in Chester county, Pennsylvania, now engaged in educational work in Boston. 2. William Marston, born July 3, 1869, a graduate of Dartmouth, class of 1894, a civil engineer at Berwick, Maine. He married, September 2, 1896, Mabel A. Fogg, born in Springvale, Maine, 1871, daughter of John D. and Phebe A. Fogg, of Springvale, Maine, and they have three children: John D., born May 31, 1897; Marjory, born January 17, 1902; Elizabeth Howland, born February 25, 1906. 3. Howard O., July 8, 1871, died young; 4. Arthur O., July 23, 1878, a graduate of Rochester high school, bookkeeper in New Britain, Connecticut.

QUIMBY This name is not numerously represented in New England or in any part of America, but the quality of its representatives will compare favorably with that of many families of much larger numbers. It has been identified with the development of New Hampshire, and is entitled to honorable mention in connection therewith. It begins at an early period of American history, in settlement of the Massachusetts Bay Colony, and is still continuing in a worthy way along the lines of civilization.

(I) Robert Quinby is found of record in Amasbury, Massachusetts, as a ship carpenter and was there married about 1657 to Elizabeth Osgood, daughter of William and Elizabeth Osgood, of Salisbury. He purchased land in Amesbury the next year, and received grants in 1659 and 1668. He is of record as a "townsman" in 1660, and holding a meeting house seat in 1667. He died about 1677, and it is probable that his death occurred in the Indian massacre at Amesbury, July 7, of that year. His wife was wounded in that massacre but survived. She was appointed administratrix of his estate October 9 of that year. The inventory was made August 27. Their son Robert was appointed to administer the estates of both parents September 26, 1694, and it was not divided until 1700. Their children were: Lydia, William, Robert, John, Thomas, Elizabeth, Philip and Joseph. (Mention of Robert and descendants is a part of this article).

(II) William (1), eldest son and second child of Robert and Elizabeth (Osgood) Quimby, was born June 11, 1660, in Salisbury and resided in Amesbury. He took the oath of allegiance in 1677 and was a member of the training band in 1680. He was living in 1700, and administration upon his estate was granted June 11, 1705. The inventory was presented by his brother Robert. The christian name of his wife was Sarah, but no record of her birth, death or parentage is obtainable. Two children are recorded in Amesbury, namely: Elizabeth and William.

(III) William (2), son of William (1) and Sarah Quimby, was born, October 8, 1693, in Amesbury. He married Hannah Barnard, who was born November 26, 1694, daughter of Joseph and Mary (Jewell) Barnard. They owned the covenant in the Second Salisbury church, February 4, 1728, and had children baptized at that church August 16, 1730, namely: Samuel, Joseph, Enoch and Hannah; and on June 9, 1734, their sons Moses and Aaron were also baptized.

(IV) Aaron, son of William (2) and Hannah (Barnard) Quimby, was born July 22, 1733, and baptized June 9, 1734, in the second Salisbury church. He was among those who asked for the incorporation of Hawke now Danville, New Hampshire, and this town was incorporated February 20, 1760. There were several among the incorporators of the same name, including Moses, who was probably his brother. They removed to Derryfield, now Manchester, whence they went as pioneer settlers to Weare, in 1752, 1753 and 1754, says one account. The "History of Carroll County" states that "Aaron Quimby was one of the incorporators of Weare. one of its first selectmen, served in the old French war, went on the expedition to Canada in 1755, and was a captain in the Revolution, and was promoted to Major." His revolutionary record is as follows: Aaron Quinby's name is on the pay roll of Captain John Parker's company in Colonel Timothy Bedell's regiment of rangers, "raised by the Colony of New Hampshire in defence of the Liberties of America—Joined the Northern division of the Continental Army under General Montgomery, 1775." He was a sergeant, entered the service July 11, and was discharged December 20, after serving five months and ten days, for which he received pay, £12, 16s. and a coat and blanket valued at £1 16s, billeting, 10s, 6d; amounting in all to £15 2s 6d. On the muster roll his age is given as forty-one, occupation husbandman, and he is credited to the town of Weare.

His name appears again on a muster and pay roll of the men raised and mustered in the Seventh Regiment, December 16 and 17, 1776, to be under the command of Colonel David Gilman, Captain Gorden's company, to recruit the American army till March 1, 1777.

The pay roll of Captain Aaron Quinby's com-

Alfred Quimby

the Free Soil party, to which he firmly adhered

number of years. He was naturally ingenious and
of a mechanical bent of mind, and in 1828 he settled

pany of volunteers in Colonel Moses Kelly's regiment in the expedition to Rhode Island, has the following record: Aaron Quinby, captain, entered the service August 6, 1778, discharged August 27, time of service twenty-four days, rate per month twelve pounds, amount of wages, £9 12s, travel out at 8d, home at 8d, one hundred and twenty-five miles, £8 6s 8d, subsistence money £4 16s, total £22 14s 8d. The roll is attested by "Aron Quinby," but the name is elsewhere spelled Quinbee and Quenbe.

Aaron Quimby from Derryfield March 27, 1754, bought lot 37, range 1, Weare, of Jeremiah Bennett, the proprietor who once thought to settle there himself, for £100 old tenor bills of credit and "Emediate settlement made on the lot." He built a good, substantial, large house of hewed logs and a rough log barn. It was on the north road from Oil Mill to South Weare, one-half mile east of the Meadow brook, and the mark of his cellar can now be seen. When the town filled up with inhabitants he opened an inn, probably the first one in Weare, and kept it for a long time. It was a busy house and had some exciting scenes. The first barrel of rum ever in town was loaded by him on a "jumber" and drawn by a horse on the rough path up the Piscataquog and over the hills to his inn. How many got balmy on that first barrel can not now be told. In his bar-room the old logger-head was always kept at a white heat. With it he warmed the flip made of West India rum with some pieces of pumpkin dried on the "lug pole," apple skins and bran in it. This gave it excellent flavor, and lips smacked that tasted it. Half a mug of flip was 3d. He also used it to warm the sling and milk, and sold each for 3d a mug. He was a prominent man in town, and once held the office of coroner of Hillsborough county.

About 1779 he moved to Sandwich, then on the very outskirts of civilization, and bought four hundred acres of Rock Maple Ridge, North Sandwich, (paying in Continental scrip) where he afterward lived, and died December, 1810. He was married (first), October 8, 1753, in Hampstead, to Anna Batchelder, who died about 1765. He was married (second) in Hampstead, March 20, 1766, to Mary Johnson. His first two children were born of the first wife. They were: Sarah, Joseph, Moses, Enoch, Samuel, James, Daniel, Anna, Aaron J., Susannah, Johnson D. and Mary. (Johnson D. and descendants are mentioned at length in this article.)

(V) Enoch, the fourth of Aaron Quimby's twelve children was born in Weare, New Hampshire, March 23, 1769, and died in Sandwich, March 22, 1831. He became an officer in the War of 1812, and was one of the hardest working men and most thriving farmers in Sandwich. In 1792 he married Sarah Libby, by whom he had eleven children, among whom were: John Smith, Joseph L. (Col.), Polly (Mary Johnson), Betsey, Enoch, Nathaniel E., Sally, Moses Dustin.

(VI) John Smith, eldest child of Enoch and Sarah (Libby) Quimby, was born in Sandwich, New Hampshire, March 10, 1793, and died there July 14, 1853. He was one of the leading men in Sandwich and vicinity in his day. Coming into active life when party politics ran high, he became ardent Jackson Democrat, and was intimately associated in politics with such men as Captain Paul Wentworth, Hon. Neal McGaffey, and Captain Randall, until the schism in that party about 1844 or 1845, when he with John P. Hale and others joined the Free Soil party, to which he firmly adhered till his death. Living all his life on a farm, with limited means of education and with no professional training, he was yet a man of affairs, and could with equal facility lead his men in the mowing field without fear of being "cut out of his swath," act as farrier for himself and neighbors, or preside as moderator in town or church meetings, act as counsel, or preside as justice, according to circumstances. He was a captain in the old militia, held many town offices, and represented Sandwich in the legislature in 1843-46-47. He was a man of aldermanic build and fine presence, a genial companion, and firm friend, a strong opponent, fearless, and tenacious of his opinions and rights. For sixteen years previous to his death he was a leading member and zealous supporter of the Free Baptist Church at Centre Sandwich. On January 27, 1814, he was married by Rev. Joseph Quimby to Nancy Marston, of Moultonboro, daughter of John Marston, and granddaughter of General Jonathan Moulton, of Hampton, both men of ability and prominence in the state. The children of this marriage were: Enoch, George M., James M., John M., Mary Ann, Caroline E., Elvira B., Caleb M., Abigail T., Harrison M., Alfred and Sarah.

(VII) Alfred, seventh son and eleventh child of John Smith and Nancy (Marston) Quimby, was born in Sandwich, New Hampshire, December 10, 1833. He was brought up on his father's farm and educated in the public schools of the town. He left home at an early age, going to Lawrence, Massachusetts, where he was engaged as clerk in George P. Cutler's bookstore. By his diligence, courtesy, and faithfulness he soon gained the fast friendship of his employer, remaining with him till the spring of 1861. He then went to Manchester, New Hampshire, where he established himself in the same line of business which he carried on successfully for twenty years. Since his retirement from active business he has dealt in stocks and real estate, in which field he has attained a prominent position. He has been a director in the New Hampshire Fire Insurance Company since the organization of the corporation in 1870, and is one of the only two living organizers. He is also a railroad director, being largely interested in railroad stocks. Mr. Quimby has always been a staunch Republican, and was a member of the legislature in 1878-79. He was married September 10, 1865, to Carrie Augusta Davis, by Cyrus W. Wallace, D. D., first pastor of the Hanover Street Congregational Church, of which Mr. and Mrs. Quimby have always been regular attendants. Mr. and Mrs. Quimby of late years have traveled extensively in this country and spent their winters in California and the south.

(V) Johnson D., youngest son of Aaron and Mary (Johnson) Quimby, was born on his father's forest farm, in (North) Sandwich, April 17, 1782, and died February 22, 1855. He followed farming, was a man calculated to lead, and held a prominent place among his townsmen. He built the Baptist Church in North Sandwich, and was a brigadier-general of militia. He married Mary ———, and they had children: Charles, Grace, Eliza M., George W., Mary B., Eveline B., Lucy M., Dolly H., now Mrs. N. S. Watson, of Dover.

(VI) Colonel George W., second son and fourth child of Johnson D. and Mary Quimby, was born in Sandwich, December 27, 1810, and died in Manchester, October, 1902. He was educated in the common schools, and lived on a farm for a number of years. He was naturally ingenious and of a mechanical bent of mind, and in 1828 he settled in Manchester and entered the employ of the Amoskeag Manufacturing Company as a machinist. He worked at his trade until seventy years of age, being last employed in the Blood Locomotive Works. He inherited the military spirit of his ancestors, served in the militia, and rose to the rank of colonel of the state militia of Sandwich, Nineteenth Regiment, Second Brigade, Second Division, 1840-42. He was a valued member of the Free Will Baptist Church in Manchester, and later of the First Congregational Church, being the oldest member at the time of his death. He was a member of Lafayette Lodge, No. 41, Free and Accepted Masons.

He married, March 6, 1839, Mary Elizabeth Fullerton, who was born September 16, 1816 (still living), daughter of William and Keziah Fullerton. Their children were: Mary Ellen, George W. and Emma Belle. Mary Ellen, only one living, born July 30, 1841, North Sandwich, married, June 6, 1864, Nicholas Nichols, for many years a merchant in Manchester, first in the drygoods, and later in the fur business. For twenty years in the latter part of his life he was assistant assessor of Manchester. He died November 29, 1901. George W., born January 28, 1847, in Manchester, died November 18, 1870. In the Civil war he served as a private in the Twenty-sixth Massachusetts Volunteers. His wife was Martha Fish. Emma Belle, born September 26, 1855, married Henry J. Carr, formerly of Grand Rapids, Michigan, librarian of the state library in Pennsylvania; Emma Belle died September 29, 1882.

(II) Robert (2), second son and third child of Robert (1) and Elizabeth (Osgood) Quimby, was born in Amesbury, and resided in that town, but little of his history appears in the records. No date of his marriage is discovered and the surname of his wife is unknown. Her christian name was Mary, and she was made administratrix of his estate, June 6, 1715, which will indicate approximately the time of his death. The estate was divided in December of that year. The children were: Joseph, John, Mary, Benjamin, Hannah and Anne.

(III) Benjamin, third son and fourth child of Robert (2) and Mary Quimby, was born January 10, 1689, in Amesbury, and resided in that town. He was married on Christmas day, 1722, to Judith Gould, daughter of Samuel and Sarah (Rowell) Gould, of Amesbury, and granddaughter of Nathan Gould, the pioneer patriarch of that name. She was born December 25, 1701, in Amesbury.

(IV) Jonathan, son of Benjamin and Judith (Gould) Quimby, was born August 15, 1726, in Amesbury and resided in that town until 1774, when he settled in Hopkinton, New Hampshire. The record of his marriage is not preserved, but the christian name of his wife was Ruth. They have had three children: Isaac, Benjamin and Mary.

(V) Benjamin (2), second son of Jonathan and Ruth Quimby, was born February 4, 1768, in Amesbury, Massachusetts, and died March 27, 1834, in Unity, New Hampshire. When he was six years old his father removed from Amesbury to Hopkinton, New Hampshire, but it is not certain how long he resided there. Benjamin and an older brother Isaac lived in Deering for many years, and finally moved to unity in 1813. Benjamin (2) Quimby married Kezia Beckford. She was born January 10, 1773. Their eight children were: Dorothy, Michael (died in infancy), Benjamin, Joseph, Michael, Kezia, Silas and Larenda. Two of the sons, Michael and Silas, became Methodist clergymen. Michael Quimby, born in Deering, September, 1805, was a preacher in the New Hampshire conference from 1832 until his death in March, 1843. Silas, the fifth son of Benjamin, was a member of the same conference for a long term of years. He received only the usual advantages of the district schools of his day, but he was a clear thinker and became an indefatigable student. He occupied some of the best pulpits in his conference, and was considered a strong, enthusiastic and logical preacher. He died in West Unity, January 25, 1885, aged seventy-four years. He left one son, Silas, who is a prominent clergyman in the New Hampshire conference, a man of liberal education and broad culture.

(VI) Benjamin (3), second son of Benjamin (2) and Kezia (Beckford) Quimby, was born October 18, 1800, probably in Deering, New Hampshire, and died May 4, 1859, in West Unity, in which town he had lived the greater part of his life. He was a sturdy, industrious farmer, and accumulated a good property for those times. He married March 23, 1826, Percis Gee, daughter of Asa and Rhoda (Otis) Gee, and a descendant of Solomon Gee, who was a citizen of Lyme, Connecticut in 1730. She was born December 12, 1805, and died May 29, 1871. Their children were: Milan W., Francis L., Melissa D. and Wilbur B.

(VII) Francis L., son of Benjamin (3) and Percis (Gee) Quimby, was born in West Unity, December 25, 1827, where he resided until his removal to Claremont in 1899. Mr. Quimby was one of the most prosperous farmers in his community, and a highly esteemed citizen. He was always ready to bear his share of public burdens, and was honored with various offices of trust by the citizens of his native town. He is a Methodist, and at the time of his removal from Unity had been an official in the church for fifty years. In politics he is a Republican. At an advanced age he is still young in heart and takes an active interest in whatever movements make for righteousness in civic affairs and for the advancement of God's Kingdom in this world. May 22, 1849, Francis Quimby married Lydia Johnson, daughter of Amos and Huldah (Green) Johnson. She was born January 8, 1825, in Weare, New Hampshire. Her parents were Quakers, hence she was of that faith at the time of her marriage. She later joined the Methodist Church, of which her husband was a member. She was a woman of superior quality of mind and great force of character, thus bearing evidence of the worthy ancestry. May 25, 1899, Mr. and Mrs. Quimby celebrated their golden wedding in the same house where they began their married life. One of their sons came twelve hundred miles in order to be present at the rare anniversary, and as it proved to be the last meeting of the children in their old home, for a few weeks later witnessed the removal of their parents from the farm in West Unity to the new home in Claremont village. Here Mrs. Quimby died May 21, 1906. Their six children, all born in West Unity, were: Irving Wesley, Adella L., George E., Lewis J., Herbert F. and Emerson A.

Irving Wesley was born May 20, 1851. He passed his life in his native town, and died in the house so long occupied by his father, November 13, 1905. This was the first death to be recorded in the family for a period of fifty-five years. Mr. Quimby was a man of good abilities, stern integrity and quiet tastes, never desiring public office. He married Josie Reed, of Acworth, who survives him. Adella L., only daughter of Francis L. and Lydia (Johnson) Quimby, was born December 16, 1853. She was

Col. Geo. W. Quimby

JESSE G. MAC MURPHY.

show that his wife's Christian name was Sarah. Their children were: Sarah, John, Benjamin, Elizabeth, Jacob, Mary, Thomas and Stephen. (Mention of Thomas and descendants forms part of this article).

(II) Benjamin, second son and third child of John and Sarah Brown, was born about 1647, in Hampton, and was a farmer residing in the southeastern part of the town, in what is now Seabrook, on land received from his father. He was married, in 1679, to Sarah Brown, daughter of William and Elizabeth (Murford) Brown, pioneer settlers of Salisbury, Massachusetts. She was born April 12, 1658, in Salisbury. Their children were: William, Sarah, Benjamin, Elizabeth, John, Jacob, Stephen, Mary, Thomas and Jeremiah.

(III) Thomas, ninth child and sixth son of Benjamin and Sarah (Brown) Brown, was born May 21, 1699, in Hampton, and resided in that part of the town now Seabrook, where he died in November, 1765. He was married May 2, 1729, to Mehitabel, daughter of Joseph and Mehitabel (Hobbs) Towle, of Hampton. Their sons were: Joseph, Benjamin, Thomas and John.

(IV) Joseph, eldest child of Thomas and Mehitabel (Towle) Brown, was born about 1730, in Seabrook, and resided in Kensington, where he was married, September 30, 1754, to Phebe Neal. Their children were: Molly, Dorothy, Betty, Abigail, John, Nancy and Nathaniel.

(V) Nathaniel, youngest child of Joseph and Phebe (Neal) Brown, was born June 1, 1777, in Kensington. He resided at Newburyport for a number of years after his marriage; but finally left there in 1814 and removed to Chester, New Hampshire, and resided on the Elliott place. He married Mary Sleeper, of Newburyport, who was born March 16, 1779. Their children were: John Sleeper, Nathaniel, Simon, Mary, Sarah S., Elizazeth E. and Charles H.

(VI) Nathaniel, second son and child of Nathaniel and Mary (Sleeper) Brown, was born in Newburyport, Massachusetts, September 2, 1799, and accompanied his parents on their removal to New Hampshire. He was a farmer and blacksmith, and made a specialty of the manufacture of edge tools. He married Sarah, daughter of William and Sarah (Hall) Graham, of Pembroke. She was educated at Pembroke Academy, and taught school before marriage. She was a member of the Methodist church. The children of this union were: Sarah, Ann, Mary J., Belinda, Abbie F., William G., Elizabeth, George E., Simon H. The first two died unmarried. Abbie F. married Simon Prescott. William G. is mentioned below. George E. married Malone Davis, and Julia Spiller; Simon H. married Ella Kimball.

(VII) William Graham, sixth child of Nathaniel (2) and Sarah (Graham) Brown, was born in that part of Chester (now Auburn), November 19, 1838, and was educated in the common schools, and also by private teachers. He worked three years at the shoemaker's trade, and afterward learned the nursery business and carried it on six years in Auburn. He now owns and cultivates a farm of seventy-five acres, and is engaged in market-gardening. He enlisted in Company K, First New Hampshire Artillery, in 1864, and served a year as a drummer, being discharged in 1865. In local political faith he is a Republican, and has been selectman ten years, and was elected to the legislature in 1895, serving in the session of 1896-7. He is a Methodist, and has been Sunday school superintendent twenty years. A member of Chester Post, Grand Army of the Republic, and also of Massabesic Grange No. 127, Patrons of Husbandry, and is past chaplain. He married (first), 1867, Mary A. Neal, who was born in Candia, February 21, 1839, and died June 21, 1897. She was the daughter of Peter and Mary (McDuffee) Neal, of Candia. He married (second), April 10, 1900, Ella F. Hanson, who was born in Manchester, October 13, 1847, daughter of Wyman and Mary (Martin) Hanson, of Manchester. Mrs. Brown was educated in the common schools and at Manchester Business College, and taught fifty-two terms of school. For twelve years she was a member of the school board. She is a member of Massabesec Grange, Patrons of Husbandry, and has passed the chairs. She is also a member of the Methodist Church.

(II) Thomas, fourth son and seventh child of John and Sarah Brown, was born July 17, 1657, in Hampton, and passed his life in that town. He married Abial Shaw, eldest child of Joseph and Elizabeth (Partridge) Shaw. She was born in October, 1662. Their children were: Thomas, Joseph, Sarah, Elizabeth, Ebenezer and Josiah. (Mention of Josiah and descendants appears in this article).

(III) Ebenezer, third son and fifth child of Thomas and Abial (Shaw) Brown, was born about 1696, in Hampton, and resided in what is now Kensington. He was married (first), November 27, 1724, to Sobriety, daughter of Josiah and Elizabeth (Worthington) Moulton. She was born August 14, 1694, but no record of her death appears. The name of Mr. Brown's second wife was Mary Flanders. He died October 20, 1780. His children were: Thomas, Ebenezer (died young), Margaret (died young), Martha, Mary (died young), Nathan, Richard, Margaret, Ebenezer, Abial, James, Jeremiah, Stephen and Mary.

(IV) Jeremiah, seventh son and twelfth child of Ebenezer and Mary (Flanders) Brown, was born July 16, 1745, in Kensington. He was an early settled in Loudon, New Hampshire, where he died May 24, 1838. He was married August 6, 1787, to Betsey Prescott, daughter of Captain James Prescott, at Loudon. (See Prescott VIII). They were the parents of six children namely: Mary, Betsey, Sally, Abigail, Sophia and Jeremiah. Mary married Amos Barton, of Epsom; Betsey married John Sargent, of Loudon; Sally became the wife of Osgood Ring, of Cheltenham; Abigail married Abraham Sanborn, of Pittsfield; and Sophia wedded Mark Prescott, of Chichester.

(V) Jeremiah (2), sixth and youngest child of Jeremiah (1) and Betsey (Prescott) Brown, was born in Loudon May 21, 1806. He resided in Loudon, and was engaged in farming until 1853, when he removed to Concord, where he lived the remainder of his life. For years he had charge of the work of repairing the streets of Concord, and did his work in a skillful and efficient manner. He was a Republican in political sentiment, and attended the Baptist Church. He married Mary Jane, daughter of Samuel and Mary (Thompson) Batchelder, of Loudon, by whom he had five children: Elizabeth Ann, Sarah Jane, George A., Jeremiah Warren and Warren. Sarah Jane married, December, 1853, Jonathan Lane, of Concord; Elizabeth, Jeremiah W. and Warren died young.

(VI) George A., third child and oldest son of Jeremiah and Mary Jane (Batchelder) Brown, was born in Loudon, April 14, 1836, and acquired his education in the common schools of Loudon and Concord. At the age of eighteen he entered the wagon factory of Abbott & Downing, where he learned the wheelwright's trade. This firm has a remarkable record for selecting and keeping competent employes, and Mr. Brown's period of service with them exceeded that of any other man. For fifty-two years after he began to learn his trade, he was continuously in the employ of this company. His unusual record is a very high testimonial of his qualifications as a workman, and his strict and undeviating attention to one employment. Mr. Brown was an accomplished artist, and painted numerous pictures of merit from an artistic point of view. He died February 6, 1907. In politics he was a Republican. He married (first), Grace Young, and (second), Lizzie Coffin, who was born in Concord. By the first marriage there was one son, Fred Irving Brown, who died some years since.

(III) Josiah, youngest child of Thomas and Abial (Shaw) Brown, was born November 15, 1701, in Hampton, and lived at Hampton Falls and Kensington. He married (first), January 1, 1724, Elizabeth Toule, daughter of Philip and Zipporah (Bracket) Towle. She was born December 9, 1699, and died about the end of the year 1733. Mr. Brown was married (second), December 5, 1744, to Mary Bradbury. His children were Zipporah, Caleb, Josiah (died young), Elizabeth, Josiah, Benjamin, Hannah, Mary, Rebecca and Samuel.

(IV) Caleb, eldest son and second child of Josiah and Elizabeth (Toule) Brown, was born March 3, 1726, at Hampton Falls, and resided in Kensington. No record of his marriage appears, and it seems impossible to discover the maiden name of his wife. Her christian name, however, was Lydia; and record of the birth of three of their children appears. It is probable that there were several others, as a period of twenty years elapsed between the birth of the eldest and that of the youngest. They were: James, Elizabeth and Caleb.

(V) James, eldest child of Caleb and Lydia Brown, was born September 17, 1755, in Kensington, and settled in the town of Weare, New Hampshire, as a very young man. Tradition says he came there before the Revolution. He located in the North Range near the northeast corner of Weare, New Hampshire, and moved over the townline into Henniker about 1800. He died August 23, 1842. He was a soldier in the Revolutionary war, and served in Rhode Island and at Saratoga. He was married, December 8, 1779, to Anna Emery, who was born July 2, 1761, daughter of Caleb and Susannah (Worthley) Emery. (See Emery, V.) James and Anna (Emery) Brown had three children: (1) Lydia, born February 16, 1780, married John Newton; (2) Susannah, born February 21, 1783, died unmarried; (3) Moses, born November 2, 1785, died April 26, 1858.

(VI) Moses, only son of James and Anna (Emery) Brown, was born in Henniker, November 2, 1785. He was a farmer like his father before him. He died April 26, 1858. He was a man above his fellows in many ways, and was held in high esteem for his business ability. He was selectman ten years, moderator seven years and representative in the New Hampshire legislature nine years. He married Abigail Folsom, of Deering, and lived in Henniker. She died October 17, 1863. Their children were: (1) Anna, born February 20, 1810, died unmarried, October 16, 1843; (2) Jesse, born April 22, 1812, died unmarried January 4, 1874; (3) David Folsom, born October 29, 1813; (4) Josiah, born October 14, 1818, physician in Lynn, Vermont, died October 15, 1868; (5) James Brackenbury, born September 7, 1826, died June 23, 1896.

(VII) David Folsom, son of Moses and Abigail (Folsom) Brown, was born in Henniker, October 29, 1813, died June 11, 1890. As a young man he taught school, teaching two years in Martha's Vineyard. For a period of twenty-eight years he was engaged in the mercantile business in New London, Weare Center and Hillsborough Bridge, New Hampshire. In 1864 he moved to Concord, New Hampshire, and bought the "Ben Gage" shoe store, where he was for a number of years engaged in the shoe business under the firm name of Brown & Moore. He was very much interested in the Methodist Church, and in the cause of education. He married Betsey Jane Butler, of Hillsborough Bridge, November 27, 1845. They had one child, James Butler, born September 23, 1848.

(VIII) James Butler, only child of David Folsom and Betsey Jane (Butler) Brown, was born in Weare, New Hampshire, September 23, 1848. He learned mercantile business in the store of his father, and that of his uncle, James S. Butler, of Hillsborough Bridge, and early in life engaged in trade and became a successful merchant in Wentworth, New Hampshire. He is a stirring business man, with a good deal of public spirit. For twenty-seven years he has been postmaster. He is a prominent Mason, and has attained the thirty-second degree in that ancient and honorable fraternity. In politics he is a Republican. He and his family attend the Congregational Church. He married, May 22, 1872, Eva M. Merrill, daughter of Russell Merrill, of Warren, New Hampshire. They have three children: Harry James, born March 2, 1873, is mentioned at length below. David Russell, born June 9, 1879, graduated from the University of Vermont, medical department, in 1902. He was married September 21, 1904, to Mary Wheeler Northrup, of Burlington, Vermont; he is a physician in Danville, Vermont. Bessie Jane, born August 24, 1881, was married November 20, 1905, to Charles Ayers Young, of Lisbon, New Hampshire.

(IX) Harry James, son of James B. and Eva M. (Merrill) Brown, was born in Wentworth, New Hampshire, March 2, 1873; attended the public schools of Wentworth, and the high school of Concord, New Hampshire, graduating from the latter in the class of 1891. He entered Dartmouth College in the fall of that year, and graduatel with the class of 1895 with the degree of B. S. After leaving college he read law in the office of Leach & Stevens, in Concord, New Hampshire, entering the law department of Columbian University in Washington, D. C., in the fall of 1895, from which in 1897 he received the degree of LL. B., and later in 1899 that of LL. M. While in Washington he was employed in the department of agriculture, in the Section of Foreign Markets, where he was engaged during the day, and attended law school in the evening. He was admitted to the bar in July, 1899, and began to practice the same year in Concord, New Hampshire. He is now well established in general practice and has a constantly increasing clientele. A Republican in politics, he was elected a member of the common council of Concord in 1904. He is a thirty-second degree Mason, belonging to the Masonic bodies located in Concord, and to the Consistory in Nashua, New Hampshire, and also belongs to Capital Grange, located in Concord.

BROWN Thomas Brown, a member of the Brown family of Hampton, a sketch of whose earlier generations appears in this work, was born May 23, 1780, probably in

Hampton or Stratham, and died October 24, 1848. He moved to Deerfield, and in 1826 or 1828 to Wilmot. He married (first), November 4, 1806, Rebecca Bartlett, who was born May 23, 1780, probably in Stratham, and died July 24, 1807; (second), September 26, 1809, Rachel Smith, who was born probably in Stratham, August 14, 1788, and died September 1, 1853. The children of Thomas and Rebecca were: Rebecca (died young), Smith, John, Rebecca, Thomas, Joseph G., James, Ruth and Asa.

(II) Joseph Goodhue, sixth child and fourth son of Thomas and Rachel (Smith) Brown, was born in Deerfield, March 25, 1820, and died at Wilmot Center, March 20, 1896. He was a farmer by occupation. He was taken by his parents to Wilmot when eight years of age. After that time he lived in Wilmot, mostly in the northern part of the town, until the time of his death. In 1843 he was converted at a campmeeting to the Methodist faith, and was ever afterward a strong adherent to its doctrines, for many years being a class leader. In politics he was a Democrat. April 24, 1845, he married Mary Ann Vinton, of Cornish, born May 26, 1823, and died October 3, 1891, aged sixty-eight years. Their children were: Lucy Amelia, died young; Lucy Jane, born August 6, 1851, married Horace Pingree in 1893, and died at Wilmot, June 1890; Helen A., born September, 1854, died February, 1901; Mary Emma, born January 12, 1855, now living at Wilmot; Ernest, the subject of the next paragraph.

(III) Ernest, fifth and youngest child of Joseph G. and Mary Ann (Vinton) Brown, was born in Wilmot, December 14, 1869. He was educated at the Kearsarge School of Practice at Wilmot, and the New Hampshire Seminary at Tilton. He engaged in newspaper work some time before attaining his majority, and has spent about twenty years in that line of employment. He worked on the Franklin *Transcript* four years; the Nashua *Daily Telegraph* five years; was foreman of the Nashua *Daily Press* three years; was editor of the Franklin *Journal Transcript* a short time; for five years was foreman of the composing room of the Nashua *Telegraph;* night editor of the Lowell *Daily Mail* one year; and since March, 1905, has been editor and manager of the Rochester *Record*. He is a Mason, a member of Ancient York Lodge, No. 89, Free and Accepted Masons, of Nashua, a charter member of Granite State Commandery, No. 196, Ancient and Independent Order Knights of Malta, Nashua, of which he is past commander; as a member of the Grand Commandery of Maine and New Hampshire he has filled various offices in that body, being elected in June, 1907, to the position of grand generalissimo, placing him in line for the position of grand commander in 1908. He married, November 5, 1899, Ella May Blackmun, born April 12, 1866, daughter of William J. M. and Jennie (Lamoy) Blackmun, of Nashua. Mr. and Mrs. Brown are members of the Methodist Church, and are active Christian workers. They have one child, Dorothea Eleanor, born November 5, 1902. Mrs. Brown is descended as follows:

(1) Luke Shurman Blackmun was born in Connecticut, June 12, 1775, and about 1800 moved to northern New York, where he obtained title to a large tract of wild land at Mooers. There he was an early settler, and there he passed many years of his life in clearing and making improvements on his farm. His name was originally Blackman, but in order that he and his descendants might be distinguished from all the other Blackmans he had the cognomen changed to Blackmun. He married, December 13, 1797, Sally Foster, daughter of Rev. John Foster, who was born April 21, 1780. Their ten children were: Delia, Polly, Judith Foster, Sally Ann, Luke Sherman, Andrew Josiah, Lydia Amelia, William Sherman, Martha Ann and David Savage.

(2) William Sherman, eighth child and third son of Luke S. and Sally (Foster) Blackmun, was born December 15, 1816, and died in 1874, aged fifty-eight years. He married, February 20, 1838, Philena Manning, born at Franklin, Province of Quebec, September 3, 1818, died at Mooers, in 1873. She was the sixth child of John and Phebe (Latten) Manning. They had ten children: Andrew Perkins, Cyrus Judson, William John Manning, Calvin Luther, Richard Lattin, Elizabeth Philena, Delia Sweet, Sarah Nelly, Elbert Foster and Emma Jane.

(3) William John Manning, third son and child of William S. and Philena (Manning) Blackmun, was born January 4, 1844, at Mooers, New York. He married Eliza Jennie Lamoy, and their children are: Ella M., John M., Philena J. and Reuel A. Ella May, born April 12, 1866, married Ernest Brown, now of Rochester.

The family of Lamoy is small and a comparatively newly settled one in the United States, the ancestor, Philip Lamoy, having settled here since the independence of the United States was established.

(1) Philip Lamoy was born in France, February 29, 1784, and died July 3, 1852. He was brought to this country when four years old, and resided near Plattsburg, New York. He died not far from Plattsburg, where he was visiting, from drinking too much water. He married Jeanne Paul, born September 10, 1782, died April 2, 1847. She is said to have been the daughter of Robert Paul, of the same family of which John Paul Jones, the famous Revolutionary sea captain, was a member, but the exact genealogical connection is not known by the present members of the Lamoy family. By his first wife, whose name is not known, Mr. Lamoy had one child, Mary. By his third wife, Jeanne Paul, he had: Philip, Margaret, Julia and William.

(2) Philip (2), eldest child of Philip (1) and Jeanne (Paul) Lamoy, was born in Plattsburg, New York, October 13, 1816, and died in Chazy, New York, October 11, 1901. He married, February 7, 1841, at Whitehall, New York, Charlotte Eaton Switzer, born February 5, 1818, at Warren, Massachusetts, died at Chazy, New York, December 13, 1897, aged eighty. The Switzers were and are a well known family of Northern New York. Philip (2) and Charlotte E. (Switzer) Lamoy had eleven children: Eliza Jennie, Mary Cornelia, Timothy Thomas, Sarah Elizabeth, Francis Henry, Julia Ann, Charlotte Caroline, Philip Charles, Albert Bently, William Joseph and Antoinette Aurelia.

(3) Eliza Jennie, eldest child of Philip (2) and Charlotte E. (Switzer) Lamoy, was born February 15, 1842, at Rutland, Vermont, and married, May 15, 1866, William John Manning Blackmun, of Mooers, New York. Came to Nashua, New Hampshire, December, 1888.

(Second Family.)

BROWN The families of this name are numerous and of different ancestral stocks, but the same has furnished many men prominent in the business, political, religious and social circles of the various states.

(I) Richard Brown, the immigrant ancestor of a prominent branch of the Brown family, is first of record in Newbury, Massachusetts, as early as 1635.

and probably is the Richard Brown who came from England in the ship "Mary and John" in the year 1633. He married (first), Edith ———, who died in 1647, and (second), February 16, 1648, Elizabeth (Greenleaf) Badger, daughter of Edmund Greenleaf, and widow of Giles Badger. He died April 16, 1661.

(II) Joshua, son of Richard and Edith Brown, was born April 10, 1642, in Newbury, where he spent his life and died in 1720. He married, January 15, 1669, Sarah Sawyer, daughter of William and Ruth Sawyer, born in Newbury, November 20, 1651. They had seven children.

(III) Deacon Joseph, son of Joshua and Sarah (Sawyer) Brown, was born in Newbury, October 11, 1669, and followed the vocation of trader. About 1700 he removed from Newbury to Amesbury, Massachusetts. He died in 1732, leaving a will in which he provided a legacy to the First Church of Amesbury, of which he was a deacon. He left a widow Sarah, and five surviving children. His youngest son, Dr. Simeon Brown, married Hannah Young, daughter of Henry Young, and lived in Kingston, and subsequently in Haverhill, Massachusetts. Among the children of Dr. Simeon Brown was Henry Young Brown, a captain in the French and Indian war, who received a grant of land in recognition of conspicuous service, and was the founder of Brownfield, Maine.

(IV) Joshua (2), son of Joseph and Sarah Brown, was born in Amesbury, about 1702, and for twenty years was a tailor in that town. In 1745 he bought the homestead in Kingston of his brother, Dr. Simeon Brown, and removed to that town, where he was a merchant and accumulated a good estate. He died in Kingston, April 23, 1756. He married in Salisbury, December 8, 1726, Joanna Morrill, born in Salisbury, February 17, 1708, daughter of Jacob and Elizabeth (Stevens) Morrill. She married (second) before 1762, Jonathan Brown, of Kensington. A record of the birth of six children of Joshua and Joanna Brown is found in Salisbury and a record of the baptism of three appears in the church records of Kingston.

(V) Joseph (2), son of Joshua and Joanna (Morrill) Brown, was born April 28, 1733, and baptized in Salisbury, Second Church, May 13, 1733. He accompanied his father's family on its removal to Kingston in 1745, when he was twelve years old. He was a resident of the latter place until 1760, and was one of the petitioners for the division of Kingston and the incorporation of Hawke, now Danville. His homestead was in the north part of the new town. He was a worthy citizen and an active business man. He signed the association test in 1776, and was a soldier in the Revolution. In 1781 he removed from Hawke to Andover, where he died April 6, 1812. He married in Kingston, December 29, 1757, Elizabeth Sawyer, baptized 1738, daughter of Joseph and Dorothy (Brown) Sawyer. She died July 13, 1813. Children: 1. Joseph, born in Kingston, March 31, 1759, died in Andover, July 29, 1843. 2. Isaac, born in Hawke, May 24, 1761, died in Andover, March 31, 1812. 3. Moses, baptized in Hawke, November 3, 1765; lived in Andover. 4. Nathaniel, baptized in Hawke, May 27, 1770; lived in Franklin. 5. Henry, baptized in Hawke, February 14, 1773. (See forward).

(VI) Henry, son of Joseph and Elizabeth (Sawyer) Brown, was baptized February 14, 1773. He was a farmer in Bridgewater, occupying the Woodman farm on the river road. He died in 1834. He married Lovie Ladd, a sister of Theophilus Ladd, of Augusta, Maine. They had four children: 1. Hannah, born about 1800, died 1862. 2. James, born July 3, 1805. 3. Child, died September 29, 1818. 4. Mary Potter, born September 12, 1816; married Seth Spencer.

(VII) James, son of Henry and Lovie (Ladd) Brown, was born July 3, 1805, in Andover. He was a farmer and a respected citizen of New Hampton, and later of Bridgewater, and a deacon of the Second Baptist Church of Bridgewater. In 1867 he removed to Bristol. After the death of his wife he had a home several years with his son, John H. Brown. He died in Plymouth, at the home of his son, Manson S. Brown, January 17, 1898. He married, November 18, 1830, Judith Blaisdell Harran, daughter of John and Nancy (Pressey) Harran, born in Bridgewater, January 12, 1807, died June 12, 1883. The father of John Harran left Ireland when a young man, and came to America and was a Revolutionary soldier from Massachusetts. They had nine children: 1. Mary Elizabeth, born in Bridgewater, December 5, 1831; married Dudley Marshall. 2. Joseph Harran, born in New Hampton, December 19, 1833. 3. Manson S., born in Bridgewater, November 29, 1835. 4. John Henry, died in infancy. 5. Hester Ann, born in Bridgewater, January 25, 1839; married Melvin A. Dame. 6. Hannah Angeline, born in Bridgewater, July 31, 1841; married John D. Harris; died in Ipswich, Massachusetts, April 5, 1893. 7. Josephine G., born in Bridgewater, February 5, 1844; married William H. Abel; died June 20, 1869. 8. Lavinia G., born April 13, 1847; married William H. Abel; died August 7, 1870. 9. John Henry, subject of following paragraph:

(VIII) General John Henry Brown, fourth son and ninth and youngest child of James and Judith (Harran) Brown, was born May 20, 1850, at Bridgewater, New Hampshire. He acquired his primary education in the common schools, and at the age of sixteen he was apprenticed to the machinist's trade in Greenville, Rhode Island, and went with his employers from that place to Bennington, Vermont, continuing his apprenticeship through a period of three years. Having saved his earnings he now took up further studies at the New Hampton Literary Institution, where he continued nearly two years. On account of the ill health of his parents he returned to his home in Bristol, and was employed in a shop and store and in various ways until 1873. He established a small store in Bristol, which he conducted a few years, and subsequently became associated with James T. Sanborn in the lumber business, and their undertakings developed on an extensive scale. They operated a mill in Bristol, and did a large business in lumber jobbing in other sections of the state, and also in Vermont and Canada. Upon the death of Mr. Sanborn, Mr. Brown, being not in robust health, discontinued the business. He was subsequently in the railway mail service for about a year, and was appointed postmaster at Bristol under President Arthur, serving four years. For a period of seven years he served as chairman of the board of selectmen of Bristol; was deputy sheriff, and in 1891 represented Bristol in the state legislature. In the same year he was appointed freight and claim agent of the Concord & Montreal railroad, and after the lease of that road to the Boston & Maine railroad, he was claim agent for that road in New Hampshire, removing to Concord in 1895. In 1904 he was appointed postmaster at Concord and resigned his position with the railroad company. He is a director of the First National Bank of Concord. He was commissary general on the staff of Governor Busiel, 1895, and 1896; has been a member of the

John H. Brown

Republican state committee for twenty-six years; and for four years, 1900 to 1904, was chairman of the Republican city committee of Concord. In 1900 he was a presidential elector, and was a delegate to the Republican national convention in St. Louis, 1896, being one of the original McKinley men. He is a member of the Wonolancet, Commercial and Webster clubs of Concord, and of the Derryfield Club, of Manchester. General Brown is a member and past master of Union Lodge No. 79, Free and Accepted Masons, of Bristol, a member of Pemigewasset Chapter No. 13, Royal Arch Masons, of Plymouth, Mount Horeb Commandery, Knights Templar, and Bektash Temple of the Mystic Shrine, of Concord. He owes his popularity and prominence in commercial and political affairs to his natural ability and his genial and companionable disposition. He was married, June 10, 1872, to Marietta Sanborn Lougee, born September 22, 1849, in Sanbornton, a daughter of Deacon Joseph and Sarah (Cram) Lougee.

(Third Family.)

BROWN This name was very early planted in New England, in various localities, and has numerous representatives scattered throughout the nation. The line herein traced was very conspicuously identified with the colony of Rhode Island in its inception and other later periods down to the present day.

(I) Rev. Chad Brown, one of the most honored representatives of the name, came from England in the ship "Martin" in July, 1638. His name appears as a witness to the nun-cupative will of a passenger, who died on the voyage. About this time occurred the "Anabaptist" heresy, and many of the Boston colonists removed to the Providence Plantation. It is probable that Mr. Brown was among these, for his tombstone erected by the town of Providence bears the record that he was "exiled from Massachusetts for consciences' sake." By some authorities the date of his arrival is erroneously fixed as early as 1636, but the most probable date seems to be the autumn of 1638, when Roger Williams and twelve others executed what is known as the "initial" assigning of lands, acquired by purchase from the Indians. Mr. Brown at once became a leader in the colony, and when after a few months the restless Williams found that the church would not implicitly accept his teachings and again seceded, Mr. Brown was chosen as his successor. He was formerly ordained elder in England, in 1642, and assumed that office on his return and was in reality the first elder of the oldest Baptist Church in America. Prior to his ordination serious dissensions had arisen in the Colony involving a quarrel with Massachusetts, and Mr. Brown was appointed a member of the committee to make peace. His influence in shaping the early tendencies of the Colony was marked, and it is probable but that for his resolute character and judicious management some of the restless spirits that composed the Colony would have come to blows on numerous questions of civil and religious import. So successful was he in adjusting these quarrels of his flock that the honorable title of "peacemaker" was popularly accorded him, and more than a century after his death (in 1792) the town of Providence voted a modest sum of money to erect a stone over his grave in the north burying ground whither his remains were removed at that date. In his history of the Baptist Church, Hague speaks of him as follows: "Contemporary with Roger Williams, he possessed a cooler temperament and was happily adapted to sustain the interests of religion just where that great man failed. Not being affected by the argument of the seekers he maintained his standing firmly in a church, which he believed to be founded on a rock of eternal truth, even the word of God which abides forever." From the little that can be now learned of his character and record it is plain that he was highly esteemed as a man of christian spirit and of sound judgment. He lived in a community where individual influence was needed as a substitute for well-established laws, and he won that commendation which the Saviour pronounced when he said: "Blessed are the peacemakers for they shall be called the children of God."

In 1640, the first established code of laws for the Colony, which was adopted and continued in force until the arrival of the charter three years later, was written by a committee consisting of Robert Cole, Chad Brown, William Harris and John Warren. To this report or agreement Chad Brown's name is the first signed and it is followed by forty others. It is probable that he wrote the draft. Rev. Chad Brown died probably in 1665.

(II) Elder John Brown, the eldest son of Rev. Chad Brown, was born in England, in 1629-30, and accompanied his father when he went to Providence, being at that time about eight years of age. About 1665 he was chosen a member of the town council and was a deputy governor of the Colony, and was afterwards elder in the First Baptist Church of Providence. He resided at the north end of the town, northward of the house of Elisha Brown. He married Mary Holmes, daughter of Rev. Obadiah Holmes, who was the second pastor of the First Church in Newport, Rhode Island.

(III) Rev. James Brown, son of Elder John and Mary (Holmes) Brown, was born 1666, in Providence, and died there October 28, 1732. He lived at the northend where his father had lived, and was pastor of the First Baptist Church. The various annals represent him as a man of great piety and power for good in the church and community. He married Mary Harris, daughter of Andrew and granddaughter of William Harris, of Providence.

(IV) Elisha Brown, son of Rev. James and Mary (Harris) Brown, was born May 25, 1717, in Providence, where he resided and died April 20, 1802. He was a member of the general assembly for many years, and was deputy governor of the Colony from 1765 to 1767. He married (first), Martha Smith, a descendant of John Smith, the miller; and (second), Hannah (Barker) Cushing, widow of Elijah Cushing, and daughter of James Barker.

(V) Elisha (2) Brown, son of Elisha (1) and Martha (Smith) Brown, was born June 1, 1749, in Providence, Rhode Island, and continued to reside there throughout life, dying in March, 1827. He was a successful merchant of good standing in his native city. He married, April 24, 1774, Elizabeth Bowen, of Rehoboth, Massachusetts.

(VI) John Brown, son of Elisha (2) and Elizabeth (Bowen) Brown, was born January 20, 1784, in Providence, Rhode Island, and was a prominent merchant in that city, where he died. He married Elizabeth Daggett, of Seekonk, Rhode Island, and they had five sons, all over six feet tall except Colville D., who was five feet and eight inches.

(VII) Colville Dana Brown, son of John and Elizabeth (Daggett) Brown, was born July 4, 1814, in Providence, Rhode Island. He began existence about the close of the second war with Great Britain, and was reared in an atmosphere fully charged with

New England patriotism. He was employed in the cotton mills as a printer until 1860, when he was appointed to a position in the government commissary department. After the war closed he was appointed superintendent of Capitol grounds at Washington, D. C., a position he held for thirty years, until his death, January 2, 1898, in Providence, Rhode Island. He was a Whig until the formation of the Republican party, when he became an ardent supporter of that party. He married, 1840, Mary Eliza Rhodes (see Rhodes ancestry), and their children were: John Colville, Robert Dana, Mary Eliza, Elisha Rhodes, Lizzie Ellen, Carrie Mitchell, Emily Louise and Charles Nichols.

(VIII) Elisha Rhodes Brown, third son and fourth child of Colville Dana and Eliza (Rhodes) Brown, was born in Providence, Rhode Island, March 28, 1847. The family removed to Dover, New Hampshire, when he was a lad and here he was educated in the public schools. He began his business life as a clerk in the dry goods store of Trickey & Bickford, Dover, where he remained four years. In 1867 Mr. Brown entered the Stratford National Bank as teller, and from that time until the present (1907) he has been actively connected with that and its sister institution, the Strafford Savings Bank. The first named was established in 1803 and ran as a state bank until 1865, when it organized under the national banking laws and became a national bank. The Savings Bank was organized in 1823. Both are highly rated and successful institutions. Mr. Brown was also a director of the National Bank, and in 1876 was advanced to the position of cashier. In 1897 he was elected president, the position he now worthily occupies. In 1883 he became a trustee of the Strafford Savings Bank, and in 1891 was elected president. Besides his active connection with the banks, Mr. Brown has been closely identified with many other important enterprises and public institutions. He was a director in the Manchester & Lawrence railroad, Dover & Winnepiseogee railroad, West Amesbury Branch railroad, Eastern New Hampshire railroad and others. He is now a director in the Cocheco Manufacturing Company, and Concord & Portsmouth railroad. In fact during his forty-four years of business life in Dover every worthy and legitimate public enterprise has had his hearty support. On February 5, 1889, Governor Sawyer and Council appointed Mr. Brown one of the commissioners for New Hampshire at the celebration of the Centennial of the Inauguration of General Washington in New York City. Politically Mr. Brown supports the men and measures of the Republican party. He is a member of the Congregational Church of Dover, as is his family. He is a member of the Independent Order of Odd Fellows, of Dover. He stands very high in the Masonic order, being a member of Strafford Lodge, Free and Accepted Masons; Belknap Chapter, Royal Arch Masons; Orphan Council, Royal and Select Masters, and St. Paul's Commandery, Knights Templar, all of Dover. In Scottish Rite Masonry he has all the degrees up to and including the thirty-second degree, and is a member of the New Hampshire Consistory of Nashua.

Elisha R. Brown married Frances Bickford (see Bickford), October 18, 1870. Their children are: 1. Alphonso Bickford, born January 23, 1872. He graduated from Yale College in 1894, choosing medicine as his profession; he entered the Harvard Medical College, graduating in 1897, after which he passed two years in the Boston City Hospital, thoroughly qualifying as a general practitioner. He located at Newburyport, Massachusetts, where he practiced six years, until his death, October 17, 1906. He married October 3, 1899, Edith Lawrence, daughter of Mayor Huse, of Newburyport, who was also editor of the *Newburyport News*. They had one daughter, Elizabeth Lawrence Brown, born July 6, 1903. Dr. Brown was a member of the Dover Congregational Church, and at the time of his death was president of the Newburyport Young Men's Christian Association. He was a man of commanding physique, thoroughly versed in his profession, and greatly beloved by those who enjoyed his friendship. 2. Harold Winthrop, born November 8, 1875. He is a graduate of Harvard College, and holds the responsible position of treasurer of the Strafford Savings Bank. He married, June 15, 1899, Catherine Van Hovenberg, of Eau Claire, Wisconson, a graduate of Smith College. 3. and 4. Raymond Gould and Philip Carter, born August 27, 1885. Both are graduates of Harvard College. Raymond G. is now attending Harvard Law School, and Philip C. the Boston School of Technology.

Mr. Brown's residence is on Silver street, Dover, where he has a well chosen library of choice literature, historical works having the preference. His collection of steel engravings is very large, and among the thousands of engravings are reproductions of the best work of the great masters in art.

Elisha Rhodes Brown descends through his mother, Mary Eliza (Rhodes) Brown, from (1) Roger Williams, the famous Baptist minister. Roger Williams was born in Cornwall county, England, about 1600, came to Massachusetts Bay in 1630, being banished therefrom, and became the founder of Providence, Rhode Island, 1636. He was a captain of the militia and governor of Rhode Island. He helped organize the first Baptist Church of Providence, and it is disputed whether he or the Rev. Charles Brown was the first pastor. He died in 1683, and his remains now rest under a monument in Roger Williams' Park, Providence. His wife died in 1676.

(2) Mercy Williams, daughter of Roger Williams, was born in Providence, Rhode Island, July 15, 1640, and there she died. She married Resolved Waterman.

(3) Waite Waterman, daughter of Resolved and Mercy (Williams) Waterman, was born in Providence, Rhode Island, 1668, and died in Warwick, Rhode Island. She married John Rhodes, son of Zachary Rhodes, a land proprietor and deputy of Warwick to the general assembly, 1663-64-65. John Rhodes was born in Warwick, 1658, married Waite Waterman, February 12, 1685, died in Warwick, August 14, 1718. He was a leading lawyer of the colony, and King's attorney for several years.

(4) Major John Rhodes, son of John and Waite (Waterman) Rhodes, was born in Warwick, Rhode Island, Nevember 20, 1691. He married Catherine Bolden, of Warwick, January 29, 1714, and died in Warwick, 1776. He was an officer in the Colonial army and deputy in the general assembly.

(5) Captain Charles Rhodes, son of Major John and Catherine (Bolden) Rhodes, was born in Warwick, Rhode Island, September 29, 1719. He married Deborah, daughter of Peter Green, January 31, 1739, and died in Cranston, Rhode Island, 1777. He was a sea captain and later a Baptist minister. Deborah Green, born February 4, 1720, the great-great-grandmother of Mary Eliza Rhodes, mother of Elisha Rhodes Brown, was the daughter of Peter Green, born January 20, 1682, died June 5, 1728, of Warwick, who was the grandson of John Green, who was deputy governor of Rhode Island several years, and a man of distinction and influence in the

E. R. Brown

E. R. Brown

Colony. His father was one of the earliest settlers of Warwick, to which place he came from Salisbury, England. The Green family is one of the most distinguished and powerful in Rhode Island. It has had a member in every session of the general assembly from the founding of Warwick in 1642. The general in the Revolution who was second only to General Washington, Nathaniel Green, was of this family.

(6) Captain Peter Rhodes, son of Captain Charles and Deborah (Green) Rhodes, was born in Warwick, Rhode Island, February 24, 1741, and died in Warwick, 1823. He married Hesta Arnold, daughter of Simon Arnold, March 22, 1761. Captain Peter Rhodes was a sea captain, was a private soldier in the "Pawtuxet Rangers" in the Revolutionary war, and was second officer of the guard ship "Pigot" that was stationed at Narragansett Bay and at one time was in chief command.

(7) Captain James Peter Rhodes, son of Captain Peter and Hesta (Arnold) Rhodes, was born in Warwick, Rhode Island, July 11, 1773, died at Cranston, Rhode Island, December 26, 1832. He was a sea captain. He married Sarah, daughter of Zebedee Hunt, of Pawtuxet, Rhode Island, August 16, 1795.

(8) Captain Elisha Hunt Rhodes, son of Captain James Peter and Sarah (Hunt) Rhodes, was born in Cranston, Rhode Island, July 28, 1805, died at sea, December 10, 1858. He was a sea captain, and made his home in Pawtuxet, Rhode Island. He married Eliza Ann Chace, daughter of Dudley and Mary (Durfee) Chace, of Fall River, Massachusetts, June 17, 1823.

(9) Mary Eliza Rhodes, daughter of Captain Elisha Hunt and Eliza Ann (Chace) Rhodes, was born in Pawtuxet, Rhode Island, April 22, 1834, married Colville Dana Brown (see Brown, VII), in 1840, died in Dover, New Hampshire, March 8, 1864.

(Fourth Family.)

BROWN The early record of the Massachusetts colony contains mention of several of this name, and descendants of various American ancestors are now found scattered through New England. The line herein traced has pioneers in New Hampshire, and is still represented in the state by living citizens of mental and moral worth.

(I) Henry Brown (sometimes spelled in the records Browne) was born about 1615 and was among the early residents of Salisbury, Massachusetts, where he received land in 1640-41-42 and was made a freeman in 1649. He was a commoner in 1650, and appears on the records of the Salisbury Church in 1677, of which he was a deacon. His name appears on most of the early Salisbury lists. By trade he was a shoemaker. His brothers, William and George, were also early residents of Salisbury. He died in Salisbury, August 6, 1701. His wife's name was Abigail, and they were members of the Salisbury church in 1687. She survived him a few days more than one year, dying August 23, 1702. Their children were: Nathaniel, Abigail, Jonathan, Philip, Abraham, Sarah and Henry.

(II) Philip, third son and fourth child of Henry and Abigail Brown, was born December, 1648, in Salisbury, and was a tailor, residing in that town. He was admitted to the Salisbury church, June 10, 1688, and died July 21, 1729. He was married June 24, 1669, to Mary, daughter of Isaac and Susanna Buswell, of Salisbury. She was born August 29, 1645, in Salisbury, and died November 27, 1683. Their children included a son who died at the age of eight days, Susanna, Mary (died young), another son died at three days, Abigail, Mary, Sarah, George, Phoebe and Hannah.

(III) George, third son and eighth child of Philip and Mary (Buswell) Brown, was born July 1, 1680, in Salisbury, and was admitted to the first church of Salisbury, July 30, 1704. His intention of marriage was published April 10, 1705, to Elizabeth Eastman, daughter of John and Mary (Boynton) Eastman, at Salisbury. She was born September 26, 1685, in that town. Their children were: Abigail, Sarah, Phoebe, Ruth, Elizabeth, Philip, David and Hannah. His will was made May 29, 1740, at which time his wife was living, and was proved February 5, 1753, indicating his birth about the beginning of the latter year.

(IV) Philip (2), eldest son and sixth child of George and Elizabeth (Eastman) Brown, was born June 29, 1718, and was baptized four weeks later, July 27, 1718, at the First Salisbury Church. He continued to reside in that town until his death, December 28, 1798. He married (first), Abigail Baker, who died July 29, 1755, and he married (second), February 8, 1756, Hannah Thompson, who died February 1, 1776. He survived his second wife nearly twenty-three years. Among their children were sons: Philip and Jeremiah. (Mention of Jeremiah and descendants appears in this article).

(V) Philip (3), son of Philip (2) and Abigail (Baker) Brown, was born August 6, 1753, in Salisbury, and became one of the early settlers in Loudon, New Hampshire, where he died August 11, 1833. When a young man he went to East Kingston, where he learned the trade of cabinet maker with Thomas Batchelder, and with him removed to Loudon in the early settlement of that town. They bought land together and cleared it, and Brown engaged in farming and also kept a hotel in the village. His building was the third in the village and is now standing and used as a dwelling. His grandson still preserves a communion cup which was used by Deacon Thomas Batchelder, the first deacon of the First Churrch of Loudon. Philip (3) Brown was married January 16, 1775, to Elizabeth, daughter of Deacon Thomas Batchelder, who was born August 3, 1753, in East Kingston, and died October 6, 1812, in Loudon. Subsequent to her death Mr. Brown was married to Nancy Wedgewood, who was born March 28, 1769, and survived him, dying January 5, 1838. His children were: Thomas, William, David, Levi, Philip, Timothy, Asa and Eliphalet, besides Joanna, who died at the age of three years.

(VI) Levi, fourth son and child of Philip (3) and Elizabeth (Batchelder) Brown, was born November 7, 1784, in Loudon, and died in that town January 4, 1858. He was quite extensively engaged in lumbering and cleared off one hundred and twenty-five acres of heavy timber. In 1810 he began building a house into which he moved as soon as it was completed, having been married during its construction, and continued to reside there throughout his life. He was a member of the Congregational Church. He was a strong opponent of slavery, and was very active in the period preceding the Civil war in the agitation for the abolition of that evil. He was the nominee of the Free Soil public for representative when that party was very little in favor in New England, and received thirty votes. He was subsequently a Whig and one of the founders of the Republican party. He was married January 8, 1810, to Mary Morse, who was born April 15, 1785, and died April 30, 1817, a daughter of Henry Morse. He was married (second), to her sister, Sally Morse, who was born January 18, 1797, and died March 23,

1872. His children were: Anson W., Joanna E., Mary M. and John.

(VII) John, youngest child of Levi and Mary (Morse) Brown, was born June 9, 1820, in Loudon, and still resides in that town. He has always lived in the house in which he was born, and his active life was chiefly devoted to agriculture. When a young man he learned the carpenter trade and engaged to some extent in building in the village of Loudon. He has devoted some attention to stock raising and made a specialty of full blood Devon and Ayrshire. His farm has been noted for its large oxen and is now devoted chiefly to dairying. He added to the original domain cleared by his father until he was the possessor of two hundred acres of land and the farm now includes one hundred and seventy-five acres, a portion having been sold off for village lots. The farm is at present conducted by his son who usually keeps a dozen cows. Mr. Brown was a member of the Congregational Church of Loudon until it was disbanded, and was long a warden of the society. He is a remarkably well preserved man for his years and reads without the aid of glasses. He was married, December 23, 1840, to Anne Batchelder, daughter of True Batchelder. (See Batchelder, VII). They were the parents of two sons: Alvah Leroy, the elder, is now upon the homestead farm and has three children. The second, John Warren, mentioned below.

(VIII) John Warren, second son of John and Anna (Batchelder) Brown, was born in Loudon, April 19, 1860. He attended the public schools of his native town and continued to reside there until 1882, when he went to Lebanon and entered the employ of Messrs. Mead, Mason & Company as a clerk, retaining that position for five years. Going to Brattleboro, Vermont, he was for a short time employed in the office of *The Household Magazine*, and returning to Lebanon in September, 1888, he engaged in the furniture business under the name of J. W. Brown & Company, having as a partner, Mr. Oscar W. Baldwin. He continued in business until the death of Mr. Baldwin in 1905, and since that time has occupied a responsible position in the office of the Baxter Machine Company in Lebanon. He is a member of Mascoma Lodge, Independent Order of Odd Fellows, and also of the Centre Congregational Church. In politics he is a Republican. He married Alice M. Baldwin, daughter of Oscar W. and Annie M. (Choate) Baldwin, of Lebanon. Mr. and Mrs. Brown have one son, Oscar Choate Brown, who was born in Lebanon, October 29, 1893, and is now attending the Vermont Academy at Saxtons River, Vermont.

(Fifth Family.)

BROWN The following line of Browns, which includes some of the most successful men in the state, is apparently unrelated to others of the same name whose history has previously been written. The first two or three generations of this family spelled their name with an "e," which was dropped about the beginning of the eighteenth century.

(I) Charles Browne, the immigrant ancestor of this line, was one of the first settlers of Rowley, Massachusetts, where he married, October 4, 1647, Mary Acie, of Rowley. He died in 1687, and was buried December 16, while his wife died four years earlier and was buried on December 12. Their daughter, Mary, died in 1683, the same year as her mother. Charles Browne's will mentions eight sons: Beriah, Gershom, deceased; William, John, Samuel, Ebenezer, Nathaniel and Joseph.

(II) John, fourth son of Charles and Mary (Acie) Browne, was born February 5, 1653-4, probably at Rowley, Massachusetts. He lived in his native town, near the Newbury line. In 1706 he requested to be dismissed from the First Church in Rowley to become one of the founding members of the church in Ryfield Parish, which included a part of the territory both of Rowley and Newbury. In 1690 he was the executor of the will of his grandfather, William Acie. On August 31, 1685, John Browne married Abigail Browne, daughter of John and Sarah Browne, who was born in Newbury, Massachusetts, October 24, 1665. There were eleven children. John Browne's will was dated in 1721, and was probated in 1722, which indicates the year of his death.

(III) Samuel, eldest son of John and Abigail (Browne) Browne, was born at Rowley, Massachusetts, July 20, 1686. In 1722 he purchased of his sister Hannah and his brother Joseph, then of Boston, their rights to the estate of their father, John Browne, then deceased. He lived several years in Ryfield Parish and the town of Rowley. He was collector of the parish and a prominent citizen of the latter place. On February 11, 1711, he was excused from military service on account of a lame hand, and on July 17, 1724, he was again excused, "provided he keep arms and ammunition to show when required." In 1729 he removed from Rowley to Littleton, Massachusetts, and with his wife was admitted to the church in Littleton from Ryfield Parish. In 1736 he was constable at Littleton. In 1743 he moved from that town to West Dunstable, now Hollis, New Hampshire, where he was prominent in church and town affairs, and was one of the committee to arrange for the ordination of Rev. Daniel Emerson. Samuel Browne's name appears frequently in the registry of deeds in connection with the purchase of valuable tracts of real estate. On May 17, 1716, Samuel Browne married Elizabeth Wheeler, daughter of Josiah and Elizabeth Wheeler, of Salisbury, Massachusetts, who was born July 12, 1695. They had nine children: John, who died young; Mary, Josiah, John, whose sketch follows; Hannah, who married Samuel Farley, of Hollis; Sarah, Susannah, Martha, who married Eleazer Cummings, and removed, after 1760, to Maine; and Samuel. Samuel Brown the father, died February 25, 1755, probably at Hollis, and his will, which was probated on June 18, of that year, names his son Josiah as executor. The widow, Mrs. Elizabeth Browne, was living in 1758.

(IV) John, third son and fourth child of Samuel and Elizabeth (Wheeler) Brown, was born probably at Rowley, Massachusetts, and was baptized at Byfield by Rev. Moses Hale, March 29, 1724. When a youth of nineteen he moved with his people to Hollis, New Hampshire, and six years later he settled in the neighboring town of Monson, now a part of Amherst, New Hampshire, where he lived for sixteen years, serving as selectman during three years of that period. In 1762, in company with his brother Josiah, who had been a lieutenant in the French and Indian war, and five other pioneers, he traveled north along the Merrimack and Pemigewasset rivers till they reached what is now Plymouth. Here they chose locations, built log cabins, and began to clear the land for farms. In the spring of 1764 they took their families into the wilderness. The names both of John and Josiah Brown appear among the grantees or proprietors of the new town, and John Brown was taxed there till 1774, being taxed the next year as a non-resident. He was one of a committee of arrangements for the ordination of Rev. Nathan Ward, of Plymouth. John Brown

1872. His children were: Anson W., Joanna E., Mary M. and John.

(VII) John, youngest child of Levi and Mary (Morse) Brown, was born June 9, 1820, in Loudon, and still resides in that town. He has always lived in the house in which he was born, and his active life was chiefly devoted to agriculture. When a young man he learned the carpenter trade and engaged to some extent in building in the village of Loudon. He has devoted some attention to stock raising and made a specialty of full blood Devon and Ayrshire. His farm has been noted for its large oxen and is now devoted chiefly to dairying. He added to the original domain cleared by his father until he was the possessor of two hundred acres of land and the farm now includes one hundred and seventy-five acres, a portion having been sold off for village lots. The farm is at present conducted by his son who usually keeps a dozen cows. Mr. Brown was a member of the Congregational Church of Loudon until it was disbanded, and was long a warden of the society. He is a remarkably well preserved man for his years and reads without the aid of glasses. He was married, December 23, 1840, to Anne Batchelder, daughter of True Batchelder. (See Batchelder, VII). They were the parents of two sons: Alvah Leroy, the elder, is now upon the homestead farm and has three children. The second, John Warren, mentioned below.

(VIII) John Warren, second son of John and Anna (Batchelder) Brown, was born in Loudon, April 19, 1860. He attended the public schools of his native town and continued to reside there until 1882, when he went to Lebanon and entered the employ of Messrs. Mead, Mason & Company as a clerk, retaining that position for five years. Going to Brattleboro, Vermont, he was for a short time employed in the office of *The Household Magazine*, and returning to Lebanon in September, 1888, he engaged in the furniture business under the name of J. W. Brown & Company, having as a partner, Mr. Oscar W. Baldwin. He continued in business until the death of Mr. Baldwin in 1905, and since that time has occupied a responsible position in the office of the Baxter Machine Company in Lebanon. He is a member of Mascoma Lodge, Independent Order of Odd Fellows, and also of the Centre Congregational Church. In politics he is a Republican. He married Alice M. Baldwin, daughter of Oscar W. and Annie M. (Choate) Baldwin, of Lebanon. Mr. and Mrs. Brown have one son, Oscar Choate Brown, who was born in Lebanon, October 29, 1893, and is now attending the Vermont Academy at Saxtons River, Vermont.

(Fifth Family.)

BROWN The following line of Browns, which includes some of the most successful men in the state, is apparently unrelated to others of the same name whose history has previously been written. The first two or three generations of this family spelled their name with an "e," which was dropped about the beginning of the eighteenth century.

(I) Charles Browne, the immigrant ancestor of this line, was one of the first settlers of Rowley, Massachusetts, where he married, October 4, 1647, Mary Acie, of Rowley. He died in 1687, and was buried December 16, while his wife died four years earlier and was buried on December 12. Their daughter, Mary, died in 1683, the same year as her mother. Charles Browne's will mentions eight sons: Beriah, Gershom, deceased; William, John, Samuel, Ebenezer, Nathaniel and Joseph.

(II) John, fourth son of Charles and Mary (Acie) Browne, was born February 5, 1653-4, probably at Rowley, Massachusetts. He lived in his native town, near the Newbury line. In 1706 he requested to be dismissed from the First Church in Rowley to become one of the founding members of the church in Ryfield Parish, which included a part of the territory both of Rowley and Newbury. In 1690 he was the executor of the will of his grandfather, William Acie. On August 31, 1685, John Browne married Abigail Browne, daughter of John and Sarah Browne, who was born in Newbury, Massachusetts, October 24, 1665. There were eleven children. John Browne's will was dated in 1721, and was probated in 1722, which indicates the year of his death.

(III) Samuel, eldest son of John and Abigail (Browne) Browne, was born at Rowley, Massachusetts, July 20, 1686. In 1722 he purchased of his sister Hannah and his brother Joseph, then of Boston, their rights to the estate of their father, John Browne, then deceased. He lived several years in Ryfield Parish and the town of Rowley. He was collector of the parish and a prominent citizen of the latter place. On February 11, 1711, he was excused from military service on account of a lame hand, and on July 17, 1724, he was again excused, "provided he keep arms and ammunition to show when required." In 1729 he removed from Rowley to Littleton, Massachusetts, and with his wife was admitted to the church in Littleton from Ryfield Parish. In 1736 he was constable at Littleton. In 1743 he moved from that town to West Dunstable, now Hollis, New Hampshire, where he was prominent in church and town affairs, and was one of the committee to arrange for the ordination of Rev. Daniel Emerson. Samuel Browne's name appears frequently in the registry of deeds in connection with the purchase of valuable tracts of real estate. On May 17, 1716, Samuel Browne married Elizabeth Wheeler, daughter of Josiah and Elizabeth Wheeler, of Salisbury, Massachusetts, who was born July 12, 1695. They had nine children: John, who died young; Mary, Josiah, John, whose sketch follows; Hannah, who married Samuel Farley, of Hollis; Sarah, Susannah, Martha, who married Eleazer Cummings, and removed, after 1760, to Maine; and Samuel. Samuel Brown the father, died February 25, 1755, probably at Hollis, and his will, which was probated on June 18, of that year, names his son Josiah as executor. The widow, Mrs. Elizabeth Browne, was living in 1758.

(IV) John, third son and fourth child of Samuel and Elizabeth (Wheeler) Brown, was born probably at Rowley, Massachusetts, and was baptized at Byfield by Rev. Moses Hale, March 29, 1724. When a youth of nineteen he moved with his people to Hollis, New Hampshire, and six years later he settled in the neighboring town of Monson, now a part of Amherst, New Hampshire, where he lived for sixteen years, serving as selectman during three years of that period. In 1762, in company with his brother Josiah, who had been a lieutenant in the French and Indian war, and five other pioneers, he traveled north along the Merrimack and Pemigewasset rivers till they reached what is now Plymouth. Here they chose locations, built log cabins, and began to clear the land for farms. In the spring of 1764 they took their families into the wilderness. The names both of John and Josiah Brown appear among the grantees or proprietors of the new town, and John Brown was taxed there till 1774, being taxed the next year as a non-resident. He was one of a committee of arrangements for the ordination of Rev. Nathan Ward, of Plymouth. John Brown

Alson L Brown

was a practicing physician, though he probably never graduated from a medical school. He was twice married and had ten children in all, of whom seven were by the first wife. She was Keziah Wheeler, daughter of James Wheeler, who was born in Concord, Massachusetts, March 10, 1726-7, married October 9, 1744, and died October 31, 1760, leaving seven children. They were: Silas, who married Lucy Wheeler, lived at Plymouth, New Hampshire, and died in the Continental service, December 31, 1777; John, who married Abigail Phillips, and was a prominent citizen at Thornton, New Hampshire; Keziah, who married William Hobart, of Campton, New Hampshire; Abigail, who married Samuel Shaw; Phineas, Rebecca and Elizabeth, who married Nehemiah Phillips. On February 18, 1761, Dr. John Brown married his second wife, Martha Jewett, daughter of Ezekiel and Martha (Thurston) Jewett, of Rowley, Massachusetts, and sister of Rev. David Jewett, of Candia, New Hampshire. They had three children: Martha, Sarah and Stephen Thurston, whose sketch follows. Dr. John Brown died May 6, 1776, and his widow survived him nearly twenty-one years, dying March 5, 1797.

(V) Stephen Thurston, youngest of the ten children of Dr. John Brown, and only son and third child of his second wife, Martha Jewett, was born at Plymouth, New Hampshire, April 18, 1766, being the second male child born in that town. He bought sixty-five acres of land in what was afterwards known as the Locke neighborhood in Bristol, this state, and there built a log cabin and brought up a family of ten children. Mr. Brown was a man of ability and sterling integrity, belonging to the sect of Quakers in whose faith, and according to whose forms he reared his large family. On December 18, 1788, Stephen T. Brown married Anna Davis, of Goffstown, New Hampshire, and their children were: John, a soldier in the War of 1812, who married Sally Ingalls, and died in Michigan at the age of ninety-two; Anne, who married Isaac Swett and lived in Bristol, New Hampshire; Samuel, who married Susanna S. Dolloff, and lived in Bridgewater, New Hampshire; Joseph, whose sketch follows; Enos, who married Lavina Heath, and lived in Bridgewater; Martha, who married Daniel Simonds, of Bristol, New Hampshire; Sally, who married Jacob Colby, of Weare, New Hampshire; Hannah Locke, who married William Colby, of Bow, New Hampshire; Stephen, who died at the age of eighteen; Mary Ann, who married Jeremiah B. Warner; Michael, who died young; Asenath, who married Calvin Fuller, and lived in New Boston, New Hampshire. Stephen T. Brown died in the family of his daughter Martha (Mrs. Daniel Simonds) at South Alexandria, New Hampshire, May 4, 1839, aged seventy-three years. His widow died at the home of his son Samuel in Bridgewater, New Hampshire, May 23, 1851.

(VI) Joseph, third son and fourth child of Samuel Thurston and Anna (Davis) Brown, was born March 3, 1796, at Bristol, New Hampshire. He was a lumber dealer and manufacturer. He built the first saw mill the largest establishment of the kind in that neighborhood, at Moore's Mills on the Pemigewasset river, five miles above Bristol village. For fourteen years he did a large business at this place, turning out masts, spars, factory beams and the like, which were rafted to Newburyport and Boston by river and canal. He would have acquired a handsome property, but the location of his business was unfortunate, and freshets persistently carried away his dams. He and his wife surrendered everything to their creditors, giving up all they had, according to the old fashioned ideas of honor and justice. In 1843 he moved to Campton, put up a sawmill, and for forty years was engaged in lumbering and farming, living on a fine farm in Thornton during the years of this period. Mr. Brown was an early Abolitionist, a man of high principles, firm convictions and advanced ideas. He predicted the invention of the telephone more than half a century before it came into use. He was brought up a rigid Sabbatarian, according to strict Quaker rule; and he never diverged from the habits of that sect; but in early life he became a Universalist, and later a Spiritualist. In 1825 Joseph Brown married Relief Ordway, daughter of Stephen and Mary (Brown) Ordway, of Salisbury, Massachusetts. She was born in 1803, and her mother belonged to a prominent family in Bow, New Hampshire. Mr. and Mrs. Brown had nine children: Alson Landon, whose sketch follows; Stephen, who served in the Fortieth Massachusetts Volunteers, and died in the army at Folly Island, South Carolina, in November, 1863, aged thirty-four. Mary Ann, who married Hanson S. Chase, and lived in Plymouth, New Hampshire; Amos, who marriel Annie M. Peebles, and was a prosperous lumber merchant at Seattle, Washington; Warren G., whose sketch follows; Relief, who married Elijah Averill, Jr.; John O., born and died in 1841; Joseph, who served in the Fifteenth Regiment New Hampshire Volunteers, and died August 11, 1863, aged twenty-one; Laura Augusta who married George W. Merrill of Campton, New Hampshire. Of these nine children, all lived to adult life except John O. who died in babyhood, and the two soldiers, Stephen and Joseph, who were sacrificed on the altar of their country in 1863. Joseph Brown died at Whitefield, New Hampshire, March 26, 1884. having attained the goodly age of eighty-eight years. His wife died at Campton, May, 1867, aged sixty-four years.

(VII) Alson Landon, eldest child of Joseph and Relief (Ordway) Brown, was born at Bristol, New Hampshire, April 9, 1827. At an early age he acquired a practical knowledge of lumbering from his father with whom he served a long apprenticeship in hard work and exposure to the elements. When twenty-two years of age he received two hundred dollars as capital with which to begin business for himself. He married that year and bought his father's place in Campton, and a half interest in the mill, becoming manager of the latter. He continued in this work for twelve years, or until 1861, when he resold his share to his father who returned to Campton and put up a fine set of buildings. Alson Brown then moved to a large interval farm across the river where he engaged in agriculture till 1872. Meanwhile he carried on lumbering in company with his father till 1864, when Warren G. Brown bought the interest of the latter. From that time the two brothers were associated in business, which eventually became the great Brown Lumber Company, of Northern New Hampshire. This business is mentioned more fully in the sketch of Warren G. Brown. In 1872, Alson Brown moved to Whitefield, which was his home during the last twenty years of his life. He was a Republican in politics, and represented Whitefield in the legislatures of 1881-2. He was a member of the constitutional convention of 1876, and a delegate to the Republican national convention at Chicago in 1880, which nominated James A. Garfield. He was a delegate to nearly all state conventions after the age of thirty. He became a Free Mason in 1860, and belonged to White Mountain Lodge, Whitefield; to North Star Chapter and North Star

Commandery, Lancaster; and to Omega Council, Plymouth. He was also a member of St. John's Lodge, No. 58, Independent Order of Odd Fellows, of Whitefield. Mr. Brown was a man of integrity and remarkable business ability kind of heart quick to act and faithful in the performance of every duty. He was held in high esteem by his workmen, who presented him with a beautiful gold watch and chain oh the occasion of his silver wedding. On September 11, 1849, Alson Landon Brown married Mary A. Currier, daughter of William and Sophia Currier, who was born in Ashland, New Hampshire, June 27, 1832. They had eight children, of whom five lived to maturity: A daughter, born and died November 11, 1850; William Wallace, born February 22. 1852, married (first), Louisa Veasey; (second), Belle Follansbee, and lives in Wentworth, New Hampshire; Oscar Alson, born January 21, 1854, married Ada Page, and lives in Whitefield; Charles Fremont, born September 7, 1856, died August 23, 1863; George Landon, born May 5, 1860, died September 5, 1860; Alice Sophia, born November 14, 1861, married Edward Ray, and lives in Whitefield; Joseph Walter, born May 3, 1864, married (first), Katie Howland, and (second), Annie Martin, and lives in Whitefield; Etta Condelle, born May 17, 1869. married Emery Appleton Sanborn, now deceased, and lives in Jamaica Plain, Massachusetts; married (second), Professor Fred L. Thompson. Alson Landon Brown died at Whitefield, January 28, 1892, at the comparatively early age of sixty-four years. His widow survives him (1907) at the age of seventy-five years.

(VII) Warren G., fourth son and fifth child of Joseph and Relief (Ordway) Brown. was born at Bristol, New Hampshire, July 27, 1834. He was educated in the common schools, and at sixteen he was a rugged lad with great physical strength and a determination to assist his father in caring for the family. He helped to lift the mortgage from the farm by cutting timber, working in the mills and driving logs. From 1855 to 1857 he was employed in various ways in the lumber business, going "on the drive. to Lowell, and working for his father and brother Alson at their mill at West Campton. In 1857, inspired by dreams of the Golden West, he went as steerage passenger to California, and in December of that year arrived at Puget Sound, Washington territory, and began cutting logs for the Puget Mill Company at one dollar per thousand. In 1860, after three years' continuous labor, he had saved between five and six thousand dollars. Coming back to his native state on July 1, 1860, he bought his father's farm of four hundred acres at Thornton. In 1864 he sold his place in Thornton, and in connection with his brother Alson L., formed the firm of A. L. and W. G. Brown, the nucleus of the great Brown Lumber Company. In 1864 the Brown brothers built mills at Rumney, which they operated till 1870, when they moved their plant to Wentworth, constructed large mills at the foot of Orford and Wentworth ponds, and did business there for many years. In. 1867 they bought a large tract of timber near Bellows Falls, Vermont, and Walpole, this state, and did a rushing business for two years, or until they had exhausted the supply, when they moved to Littleton. In 1869, Warren G. Brown went to Whitefield to superintend affairs. They took the building of the defunct White Mountain Lumber Company, and at once put in machinery for cutting eight millions feet of lumber yearly, and in 1872 enlarged their plant so they could cut fifteen millions feet yearly. In 1869 there was no railroad nearer than Littleton, and the firm gave Mr. Lyon, president of the White Mountain railroad, four thousand dollars to use in extending the tracks from Wing Road to Whitefield. In June, 1870, the firm began the construction of a private railway to transport timber from their land in Carroll, where they owned between eight and nine thousand acres, to their mills in Whitefield. This was called the John's River railroad and was extended from time to time as their business required. In 1878 they obtained a charter for the Whitefield and Jefferson railroad, which was opened to Jefferson Meadows in July, 1879, and has since been extended to Berlin.

On September 1, 1874, Brown's Lumber Company was organized with a capital of half a million dollars. The Browns, Alson L. and Warren G., have always owned a controlling interest, but associated with them at different times have been Nathan R. Perkins, of Jefferson; Dr. Aaron Ordway, of Lawrence, Massachusetts; Ossian Ray. of Lancaster; Charles W. King, of Lunenburg, Vermont; and A. G. Folsom. Their plant is the largest and most complete of the kind in New England. In 1882 a complete system of electric lighting was introduced, enabling them to run at full time the entire year. They put up their own telephone system in 1881, and they have owned big stores at Whitefield and Jefferson Meadows since 1879. They have factories for the manufacture of mouldings, floorings and finishings of all kinds, and for the making of fine furniture from birch, ash and bird's eye maple. They own enormous tracts of pine and spruce timber lands, and their annual sales have sometimes reached half a million dollars. To Warren G. Brown must be given the credit of first suggesting the use of the yellow fir of the Pacific coast for spars and masts in the Atlantic shipyards. This fir soon established a reputation, and the Brown firm has furnished masts for the English, French and Chinese navies. In 1875 the Brown brothers built a ship of fifteen hundred tons at Newburyport, Massachusetts, which cost one hundred and twenty thousand dollars when ready for sea. The next year this ship, the "Brown Brothers," brought the first cargo of Pacific spars to Atlantic ports. Six other cargoes were afterwards brought at a cost of over a quarter million. Warren G. Brown has had special charge of this work, and he has been several times to the Pacific coast. He sees great changes in the state of Washington, which, when he first went there in 1857, had seven thousand white inhabitants and twenty-one thousand Indians.

Mr. Brown began political life by voting for John C. Fremont, and was connected with the Republicans until he became interested in the Greenback party, which made him its candidate for governor in 1878 and 1880. He represented Whitefield in the state legislature of 1872-3, was a delegate to the National Greenback convention in 1880 and was a delegate to the convention that organized the Union Labor party in February, 1887. Mr. Brown is active in temperance work, a strong believer in Spiritualism, and is a Master Mason of the local lodge. Mr. Brown is a man of democratic plainness, honesty of purpose, strict integrity and originality of mind. He is now retired from active business. Warren G. Brown has been twice married, but his first wife lived but two years and a half, and his children are all by the second marriage. In March, 1861, Warren G. Brown married Ruth B. Avery, daughter of Stephen and Hannah (Mitchell) Avery, who was born in Campton, New Hampshire, and died in Thornton in September, 1863. On

Warren G. Brown

BROWN LUMBER COMPANY.
(WHITEFIELD MILLS.)

November 2, 1865, he married Charlotte, daughter of Ephraim and Eliza (Broad) Elliott, who was born in Brownfield, Maine, January 11, 1848. Amos Broad, Mrs. Brown's maternal grandfather, was an Englishman, who became quite noted as a hotel keeper and man of affairs in Westbrook, Maine. Her father, Ephraim Elliott, a native of Thornton, New Hampshire, for many years conducted the hotel at Waterville, New Hampshire, one of the choicest spots in the White Mountains. Mrs. Brown is a woman of practical ability, and an able help-meet in every way. Warren G. and Eliza (Elliott) Brown had four children: Josephine Ruth, born at Campton, June 22, 1867; Dasie A., born at Whitefield, September 22, 1870; Carl Eliott, born at Whitefield, September 10, 1878; Kenneth Warren, born at Whitefield, September 8, 1883; Josephine R. Brown married Milford M. Libby, and lives in Whitefield. Carl E. Brown is located in Idaho. The other children live in Whitefield.

(Sixth Family.)

BROWN There are many families of Browns in this country, and the name is especially numerous in Connecticut, where the little town of Torrington gave to the world the most famous of the family, John Brown, "whose soul is still marching on." The present line has an ancient and honorable record, but it has not been traced to the earliest American ancestor, because of the impossibility of finding the parentage of Deacon Isaiah Brown, of Stratford, Connecticut, with whom the record begins.

(I) Deacon and Captain Isaiah Brown was born in 1713, and lived at Stratford, Connecticut, where he took the freeman's oath in 1736. He must have been a man of prominence, for titles meant something in those days. He was one of the original proprietors of Stratford, New Hampshire, which was named for the Connecticut town, but Deacon Brown never settled there, leaving the pioneer work for his eldest son to carry out. Many of the river towns in New Hampshire and Vermont owe their beginning to Connecticut enterprise, because it was an easy matter for the inhabitants of the Nutmeg state to push up the river. In January, 1735-36, Deacon Isaiah Brown married Ann Brinsmade, daughter of Zachariah Brinsmade, of Stratford, Connecticut, and their children were: Hannah, Ann, Sarah, James, whose sketch follows; Betty, Samuel, Rhoda, Nathan, who died young; and Isaac, born March 19, 1755. Deacon Isaiah Brown died in 1793, at the age of eighty, and his widow died in 1788, at the age of seventy-two.

(II) James, eldest son and fourth child of Deacon Isaiah and Ann (Brinsmade) Brown, was born in February, 1744, probably at Stratford, Connecticut. With seven other men he began the settlement of Stratford, New Hampshire, in 1772, and at the meeting of the proprietors in December of that year, each of these men was awarded the sum of three pounds in payment for his pioneer work during the preceding summer. James Brown called the first town meeting in Stratford, and was one of the leading men in the new community. Being the son of a Congregational deacon, he brought religious books in his saddle-bags, and the early Sunday services were held at his house. In 1800, when the first church was organized, which happened to be the Methodist, he became a member, and was ever an active worker for the cause of religion. James Brown was a commissary general during the Revolution, and had charge of the fort at Stratford, which stood on the land where his great-grandson, William Riley Brown, now lives. This fort was built of logs fourteen inches square, and was situated on the Connecticut, commanding an extended view up and down the river. The early settlers were greatly harassed by the Indians, who came down from the North, and received a bounty of twenty dollars a head for every able-bodied man they captured. This fort had an underground tunnel to the cellar of Mr. Brown's house. Looking out of the door of his home he saw a moose crossing the Connecticut river, and taking his flint lock gun pointed it and shot the moose, killing him with the first shot; when dressed it weighed seven hundred pounds. On another occasion, while fishing in the river where the water was about twenty feet deep, seeing a salmon too large for his hook and line, he attached a manure fork (three tines) to the end of the fishing pole and speared the fish, which weighed forty pounds. In 1775 James Brown married Hannah, the sixteen-year-old daughter of Joshua Lamkin, another Stratford pioneer, and they had a family of nine children. This was the first marriage to occur in the new settlement, and their eldest child Anna, born March 17, 1776, was the first baby born in the new settled town. James Brown died in 1813, aged sixty-four, and his widow died in 1836, aged seventy-seven.

(III) Samuel F., son of James and Hannah (Lamkin) Brown, was born at Stratford, New Hampshire, about 1790. He was a man of prominence, was selectman in 1818-19-35, and probably at other times, but the town records between 1820 and 1835 have been lost. He was representative in 1835, and also served as sheriff of Coos county. His early death at the age of forty-six cut him off in his prime, and at a period when he was in high favor with his townspeople. Samuel F. Brown married (first) Judith Smith, and they had three children: Samuel C., James B. (mentioned with descendants below), and William R. He married (second), Caroline Bishop. Children: Helen, Rollin, John H., Loyal, Henry and Alonzo.

(IV) Samuel C., son of Samuel F. and Judith (Smith) Brown, was born at Stratford, New Hampshire, February 18, 1811, on the farm which the family have owned for generations. He was educated in the common schools, and became a prosperous farmer. He was a Democrat in politics, and held all the town offices, and represented Stratford in the legislature of 1877-78. He attended the Methodist Episcopal Church. Samuel C. Brown married Sophia, daughter of Thomas Curtis, of Stratford. They had seven children. The three now living are Samuel F., who is a farmer in Stratford, New Hampshire; Cora B., married Dewer Rich, of Woodsford, Maine; and William Riley, whose sketch follows. Samuel C. Brown died June 8, 1871.

(V) William Riley, son of Samuel C. and Sophia (Curtis) Brown, was born in Stratford, New Hampshire, in the same house as his father, April 2, 1844. He was educated in the common schools, at the academy at Lancaster, New Hampshire, and at Newbury Seminary, Newbury, Vermont. For eleven years he taught school during the winters and farmed summers. For fifteen years he was a drover, taking cattle to the Boston market. For several years he was in trade at Stratford Hollow, but he now devotes his entire attention to farming. He has been justice of the peace since the age of twenty-one. He is a Democrat in politics, and was selectman for ten years, a member of the legislature in 1887-88, just ten years after his father, and served on the school board for six years. He attends the Methodist Episcopal Church. October 8, 1872, William Riley Brown married Ella, daughter of John and Caroline (Richardson) Bishop, of Lisbon, New Hampshire. They have three children: Everett C., born January 18, 1879, who has sales stables at Groveton, New Hampshire; Loyal P., born March 28, 1881, who is a merchant at Orange, Massachusetts; and Howard B., who is a student at Tilton Seminary, Tilton, New Hampshire.

(IV) James B., son of Samuel and Judith (Smith) Brown, was born at Stratford, in 1818. He was a merchant and lumber dealer in Northumberland, where he participated actively in public affairs as a Democrat, held all of the important town offices and represented his district in the state legislature. His death occurred in 1882. He married Ellen Patterson, of Lunenburg, Vermont, who died in 1881. She was the mother of six children, namely: Eliza, Cora, Rollin J., Gertrude, Maude and Mabel. Of these Cora and Rollin J. are the only survivors.

(V) Rollin James, third child and only son of James and Ellen (Patterson) Brown, was born in Northumberland, February 14, 1858. He began his studies in the public schools, continued them at the Plymouth (New Hampshire) high school, and concluded his education at St. Johnsbury (Vermont) Academy. He was associated with his father in business until the latter's decease, after which he went to Lancaster and entered the employ of the Thompson Manufacturing Company as bookkeeper. He subsequently became a stockholder in the concern, and in January, 1907, was elected its treasurer. In politics he acts with the Democratic party, and from 1888 to the present time has served with ability as town clerk. He formerly attended the Unitarian Church, but now worships with the Congregationalists. In 1888, Mr. Brown married Helen F. French, daughter of Elijah French, of Stratford. They have no children.

(Seventh Family.)

BROWN This name has been variously represented in New England from the earliest colonization of the country; and in Westminster, Massachusetts, the early seat of the family of this article, the members were so numerous, the branches so various, the records so fragmentary and heterogeneous, that it has been found impossible not only to trace any one family to its original progenitor, but also to connect the different families with each other to any great extent.

(I) Nicholas Browne, son of Edward Browne, of Inkburrow, Worcestershire, England, settled first at Lynn, Massachusetts, and early removed from there to Reading, where he appears to have owned two places. He was a man of comfortable means as appears from the fact of his sending his son John, in 1660, to England to look after certain property, to which he had become heir. He died in 1673. His wife's name was Elizabeth, and their children were: John, Edward, Joseph, Cornelius, Josiah and perhaps Elizabeth.

(IV) Jonathan Brown was no doubt a descendant of Nicholas Browne, and resided in Westminster. He married Mehitable Hay. Her father, James Hay, was an original proprietor of No. 2, drawing in the first division of lands lot No. 106, near Wachusetville.

(V) Jonathan (2), son of Jonathan (1) and Mehitable Brown, probably located on the lot No. 106 mentioned above, occupying a house built some years before by Benjamin Gould. He was first taxed in 1764, and in 1769 a public school was kept in his house. January 3, 1771, he purchased of Joseph Lynde, of Charlestown, lot No. 105, lying directly south of the Hay lot, which was long known as the Brown estate, more recently owned by Asaph Carter and his son Edward R. On his way from Reading to Portsmouth, Mr. Brown seems to have sojourned a while in Leominster, where he married Huldah Hawkes. He died March 14, 1820, aged eighty years. She died January 1, 1818, aged seventy-five. Their children were: Jonathan, Benjamin, Joseph, died young; Huldah, Sally, Joseph and John.

(VI) Jonathan (3), eldest child of Jonathan (2) and Huldah (Hawkes) Brown, was born in Reading, August 20, 1765, and died in Gardner, July 24, 1840, aged seventy-five. He removed to and resided in Gardner on a farm in the east part of that town, where his grandson Charles (?) lately lived. He married Beulah Jackson, daughter of Elisha and Beulah (Taylor) Jackson. She died November 24, 1839, aged sixty-seven. Their children were: Jonathan, John, Charles (died young); Elisha, Charles, Sally (died young), Sally, Benjamin B., Lucy and Nancy.

(VII) Charles, fifth son and child of Jonathan (3) and Bertha (Jackson) Brown, was born in Gardner, Massachusetts, March 12, 1800, and died in Boston. He settled in Boston, where he was for many years successfully engaged in the retail grocery business, and took part in the public affairs of the city. In 1847 he served as alderman. He married Susan Morehead. The children born to them were: Susan, married O. H. Underhill. Mary E., married Edward J. Brown. Abbie, married R. G. Davis. Charles S., mentioned below.

(VIII) Charles Severence, son of Charles and Susan Morehead Brown was born in Boston, November 18, 1844, and was educated in the common schools of that city and at Chauncey Hall. In 1872 he engaged in the carriage service, to which he has given his unremitting attention ever since that time, and now employs a hundred horses and many vehicles in his business, which has steadily grown from the beginning. He has a summer home in New Ipswich, New Hampshire, where he passes the summer months. In politics he is an independent. He married (first), Frances Partridge, who was born in Boston, daughter of Adrian Partridge. He married (second) Ruth Miller, daughter of Ephraim Miller, of Temple, and granddaughter of General James Miller. Two children, Albert Edwin and Susan, were born to the first wife; and one, Philip, to the second.

BROWN In the United States there are several ancient families bearing this name, and from among them many men of prominence have arisen. The surname is of the class called complexion names, and was assumed by its first bearer from his complexion or the color of his hair.

(I) Samuel Brown was a farmer in Andover, Vermont. He was one of the principal citizens of the town, and was selectman, town treasurer several times, and representative in the state legislature several terms, holding office as late as 1808 or thereabout. He had three children: Abraham, Ebenezer and a daughter. He lived to be nearly ninety years old, and died about 1830, with his mental faculties unimpaired.

(II) Ebenezer, son of Samuel Brown, was born in what is now Andover, Vermont, and was a lifelong farmer. He lived in Cornish and West Windsor, then a part of Windsor. About 1825 he removed from there to Windsor Village, where he remained until about 1840, when, some of his older children having settled in New York, he and his wife went to them and spent their remaining years in that state. Mr. Brown died in the early fifties, aged about seventy-three, his wife having preceded him, dying in 1846, aged about fifty. Both died and were buried at Fonda, Brodalbin, New York. He married Lucy Walker, a native of Plainfield, New Hampshire, daughter of Nathan and Abigail (Ames) Walker, and they had eight children: Selinda, Adaline, Lorenzo E., Madison, Horace Ames, Persis, Luman and Stillman.

(III) Horace Ames, third son and fifth child of Ebenezer and Lucy (Walker) Brown, was born in Cornish, New Hampshire, October 3, 1823. He received very little education in the public schools which he attended but a brief time, but by constant study and attention to the defects in his early schooling he afterward largely compensated for what he was then unable to obtain, his life occupation having constantly furnished to him opportunities for education that no other trade could have done. January 18, 1837, he became an apprentice to the printer's trade in the office of the *Democrat-Statesman*, at Windsor, Vermont. After a year and a half of service there he went to Claremont, New Hampshire, and worked on the *National Eagle*, four years, of which time he was two years a journeyman. From that employment he went to the Claremont Manufacturing Company, a concern of importance at that time, which manufactured paper, and printed and bound books, taking large contracts for work of this kind from individuals and firms in New York city and elsewhere. Here he worked intermittently from 1844 to 1847, and completely mastered the details of the business. In company with the late Joseph Webber he published for a time the *Northern Intelligencer* at Claremont. With the suspension of this publication he returned for a brief period to the *National Eagle*, and in 1852 proceeded to Concord. There he entered the employ of McFarland and Jenks, proprietors of the New Hampshire *Statesman*. This firm afterward sold out to the Republican Press Association, which later became the Rumford Press Company. From 1852 until March 1878, he was pressman and foreman of the pressroom, doing as opportunity afforded, more or less composition. From 1878 to 1882 he devoted his time to municipal affairs. Returning to his old employment at the latter date he took charge of the stone work or preparation of the forms for press, for fifteen years, and for six years more was employed on composition. January 18, 1907, he completed seventy years as a printer, and established what is believed to be a record for New England. He was a thorough master of the art in every branch, and the men employed in the office ever found him a stanch friend and a wise counsellor. On the occasion of his having in 1887 completed fifty years of service as a compositor his typemates in Concord presented him with an elegant gold watch and chain inscribed: "1837-1887. From Black Art Friends to Horace A. Brown."

Mr. Brown's political affiliations were first with the Whig party, and he cast his first vote for Henry Clay in 1844. In 1856 he cast his ballot for John C. Fremont, the first Republican candidate for the presidency, and has ever since been a Republican. Mr. Brown was made assessor in Concord in 1866, and served that and the following year. Subsequently he was alderman, and also filled the office of highway commissioner. He was elected to the legislature from ward 4, in 1875-76, and elected mayor of Concord, and served from March 18, 1878, to November, 1880. By a change in the law governing this office his last term covered a period of twenty months instead of one year as under the old law.

Mr. Brown was an industrious worker, an exemplary citizen, and a leading layman in church circles, and prominent in the choir of his church. While at Claremont, Mr. and Mrs. Brown joined the Episcopal Church by baptism. In 1857 he was elected secretary of the Episcopal diocese of New Hampshire, and filled that place from that time until his death, a period of fifty years, by successive annual reëlections. In 1863 he was made junior warden and in 1865 became senior warden of St. Paul's Church, and filled the latter office at the time of his death. He was elected a member of the standing committee of the Episcopal diocese of New Hampshire in 1861, and was secretary of the same from 1897, to his death. He was a lay reader in the diocese since 1857. While in Claremont (1852) he became a member of the church choir, and on his removal to Concord took a place in the choir of his church at that place, which he held at his death, making a continuous service of fifty-five years in that office. When seventy-eight years of age he was elected a delegate to the triennial convention of the church in the United States, and enjoyed equally with much younger men the trip to San Francisco and return as well as the great church gathering. In 1884 he delivered the historical address at the twenty-fifth anniversary of building the St. Paul's edifice.

He was also a prominent man in the fraternal secret societies. November 25, 1845, he joined Sullivan Lodge, No. 12, Independent Order of Odd Fellows, of Claremont, of which he was soon after noble grand. In 1851 he was representative to the Grand Lodge, which held its sitting at Concord that year. From 1868 to his death he was a member of Rumford Lodge, No. 46, of Concord. In 1880 he became a member of Penacook Encampment, No. 3, of which he was a past chief patriarch. In 1883 he was elected grand master of the Grand Lodge of New Hampshire, and served one year, and in 1886 was sent as representative to the Sovereign Grand Lodge. He was a Mason in Blazing Star Lodge, No. 11, of Concord, in 1867, and was worshipful master of that body four years—1871-2-3-4. He subsequently was department grand master, and became a member of Trinity Royal Arch Chapter, No. 2, of which he was later high priest, and still later grand high priest of the order in the state. He was made a member of Horace Chase Council, No. 4, Royal and Select Masters, and became a member of Mount Horeb Commandery, Knights Templar. Of this organization he was prelate from 1884 until his death. In 1889 he delivered the historical address at the celebration of the one hundredth anniversary of Blazing Star Lodge, Ancient Free and Accepted Masons.

Horace A. Brown married in Claremont, May 29, 1845, Sarah S. Booth, born in Claremont, New Hampshire, February 8, 1825, daughter of Colonel Hosea and Nancy (Downs) Booth. Jabez Downs, maternal grandfather of Sarah S. Booth, was born in Connecticut, and served in the war of the Revolution. He died at Claremont, New Hampshire, from a wound received while serving in that war. His body was removed from Claremont to Concord by H. A. Brown, and now lies in Blossom Hill cemetery. Hosea Booth was born in Lempster, New Hampshire, and his wife was born in Windsor, Vermont, Colonel Hosea Booth was an officer in the American Revolution. The children of Horace A. and Sarah S. (Booth) Brown were: Edwin O., who died young, and Frank Eugene, whose sketch follows. Horace A. Brown died at the Margaret Pillsbury Hospital, after a long illness, October 31, 1907.

(IV) Frank Eugene, son of Horace A. and Sarah S. (Booth) Brown, was born in Claremont, July 15, 1850, and was taken by his parents to Concord two years later. He completed the course in the public schools of Concord, and graduated from the high school in 1868. In August of the same year he entered the employ of the Concord Railroad Company at Concord, as superintendent's clerk. He held that position and other clerkships until March 1, 1883, when he was appointed general ticket agent for the Concord Railroad Company, with office at Concord. Upon the consolidation of the Concord & Boston, and Concord & Montreal Railroad companies, he was appointed general passenger and ticket agent of the Concord & Montreal railroad, and upon the leasing of the road of that corporation to the Boston & Maine Railroad Company, he was appointed assistant general passenger and ticket agent with office at Concord. He was been clerk of the Mount Washington Railroad corporation many years and now holds that position. He is also a director and general passenger agent of that corporation. Frank E. Brown has now (1906) lived in Concord fifty- four years; for thirty-eight years of that time he has been continuously in the service of one railway company and its successors. He is one of the oldest railway officers, in point of service, in New Hampshire, and one of the most efficient and most favorably known men of that class in New England. His cheerful and tactful manner and prompt and expeditious disposition of railway business have made him friends from ocean to ocean, and from the Gulf of Mexico to the frozen north. He is a man of pleasing personality, a true and steadfast friend, and a good neighbor. He is a Republican and has indulged in politics to a small degree, and has been a representative in the state legislature, but has not sought further official positions. Born of Episcopalian parentage he was baptized and brought up in that faith. For many years he was organist of St. Paul's Episcopal Church, and organized and directed the first vested choir in that church in Concord. He is at present organist and choir director in the First Baptist Church. He has a talent for musical composition, and has written several anthems and songs. He is a member of Blazing Star Lodge, Free and Accepted Masons of Concord.

He married (first) Evelyn Hazeltine, daughter of James H. Hazeltine, of Concord. She died in 1888. He married (second), Annie Baker Dietrich, daughter of John and Ann (Baker) Dietrich. She is a lady of superior musical talent, sings in the choir of the Congregational Church, and is one of the best known lady vocalists in the state. Two sons were born to the first wife: Frank W. and Charles Walker. Frank W. is a civil engineer in the office of the state engineer at Concord. He married, 1898, Bessie Farwell, daughter of ——— Farwell, of Montpelier, Vermont. Charles W. is a clerk in his father's office.

BROWN This family is not connected with other families of the name which have previously been written about. The Browns are so numerous that no one has ever undertaken to make a genealogy of the family; hence it has been impossible to trace this line further than four generations.

(I) Aaron Brown was born in Marlow, New Hampshire. It is said that his father was a general in the Revolutionary army, and commanded New Hampshire troops at Bunker Hill. The only Browns in New Hampshire regiments recorded on the rolls as participating in this battle as officers are James Brown, first lieutenant, Fourth Company, Third Regiment, commanded by Colonel James Reid, and Josiah Brown, first lieutenant, Sixth Company, Third Regiment. There is nothing to show which of these Browns, if either, was the father of Aaron. In early life Aaron Brown removed to Acworth, New Hampshire, where he lived for a short time. Later he went to Putney, Vermont, remaining for two or three years, and finally moved to Syracuse, New York, where he lived until his death. He was a carpenter by trade. Aaron Brown married Polly, eldest child of Isaac and Mary (Wheelock) Gates, of Acworth, New Hampshire. Her father settled in that town in 1781. Aaron and Polly (Gates) Brown had three children: Aaron (2), whose sketch follows: Polly, who married Alden Gee, of Marlow, New Hampshire; Isaac, who married (first) Mary Newton, and (second) Sarah A. Bliss.

(II) Aaron (2), eldest child of Aaron (1) and Polly (Gates) Brown, was born at Alstead, New Hampshire, March 4, 1795. He attended the schools in Acworth and Lempster, New Hampshire. He was a farmer and lived in Acworth till late in life, when he removed to Alstead, New Hampshire, where he died. He was a Democrat in politics, and attended the Universalist Church. He married Eady, daughter of John and Polly (Cockle) Watts, of Hollis, New Hampshire. They had ten children: Eady Diana, married (first) Captain George Lewis, of Marlow, and (second) Orlando Newton, of Claremont. Mary Urana, married Amos Fletcher, of Hollis. Isaac married Frances L. Bundy, now living in Fowler. Samuel, died young. Martha Melissa, married Samuel Savory, of Newbury, New Hampshire. John Cockle, whose sketch follows. George R., studied at Tufts College; read law with Edmund Burke, at Newport, New Hampshire. Maria L., married Moses Moulton, of Manchester, New Hampshire. James H. married Mary Ellen Whittemore, and lives at Hillsboro Bridge, New Hampshire. Emily A., died young. Aaron (2) Brown died at Alstead, New Hampshire, January, 1884. His wife died in 1874.

(III) John Cockle, third son and sixth child of Aaron (2) and Eady (Watts) Brown, was born at Acworth, New Hampshire, June 10, 1831. He was named after his maternal great-grandfather, John Cockle, who at the age of sixteen was taken by a press gang from a ball-room in England, and impressed into the British army. He was in the first regiment sent to Boston at the outbreak of the Revolution, and deserted to the Continental army. He served through the war and went east at its close. John Cockle Brown attended the public schools of Acworth and Alstead. In 1852 he went to Sheffield, Ohio, where he remained a year, engaged in farming. He came back to New Hampshire, but in 1855 he went to Ohio again, remaining till 1857. This time he, with two partners, built a "fore and aft" boat, and freighted timber to Buffalo and other points whence it was shipped by the Erie canal to New York City. The panic of 1857 caused a suspension of this business, and Mr. Brown was obliged to return home. He farmed in Langdon, New Hampshire, for about four years, and then came to Walpole, where in company with George H. Holden he conducted a meat market for about two years. He then bought a farm in that town and returned to agriculture. Mr. Brown owns about one hundred and thirty acres of land, and has made a specialty of raising cattle, Merino and Southdown sheep and Morgan and other thoroughbred horses.

He is a Democrat in politics, and represented his town in the legislature in 1876 and 1877, and for a third time in 1889. He has been selectman, supervisor, road agent, and has served on the school committee for three years. He attends the Unitarian Church.

He married, February 28, 1862, Jeannette, daughter of Levi Snow (2), of Wilmington, Vermont. She was born in Wilmington, February 22, 1839. They had five children: Annette, born December 6, 1862, married Erwin S. Bowman, and lives in Boston. Orr W., born June 1, 1867, died February 14, 1904. Ashton Burton, February 18, 1873, lives at Jamaica Plain, Massachusetts, and is in the grocery business. Florence Maud, May 3, 1876, lives at home. Harry Brigham, lives at Jamaica Plain, and is in business with his brother, Ashton B.

BROWN The family of Browns of which this article treats is descended from early residents of Dunbarton, who settled in the wilderness of what is now Hillsborough county, before the Revolution. The imperfect manner in which the early records were kept precludes the possibility of tracing the family to the immigrant ancestor.

(I) Barton B., son of Barton Brown, a native of England, was born in Concord, New Hampshire, 1810, and died in Dunbarton, 1865, aged fifty-five years. His mother died when he was a child, and he was adopted by a family by the name of Wallace, of Concord, with whom he lived until twenty-one years of age. He was educated in the public schools, and brought up as a farmer, which line of work he followed throughout his active career. In politics he was a Democrat, and in religious faith a Baptist. He married Susan P. Goodwin, born July 17, 1816, daughter of Alpheus and Ann (Hammond) Goodwin. She is living at the present time (1907), aged ninety-two years. Her mind is clear and her memory retentive, and she tells of the incidents of the reception of La Fayette at Hopkinton, New Hampshire, in 1823, as if they were the happenings of yesterday. She was a Methodist in early life, but is now a member of the Baptist Church. The children born to Barton B. and Susan P. (Goodwin) Brown were: Wilbor, who was one of Berdan's sharpshooters; he died in Andersonville prison. Eldridge C., resides in Dunbarton, New Hampshire. Annie S., deceased. Susan F., deceased. Alpheus, deceased. Parker Richardson, see forward.

(II) Parker Richardson, sixth child and fourth son of Barton B. and Susan P. (Goodwin) Brown, was born in Dunbarton, May 25, 1855. He was educated in the public schools of Dunbarton, Weare and Grafton, and Pembroke and Canaan academies. He was reared on his father's farm, and at the age of fifteen engaged in the grain business as a clerk for E. P. Prescott & Company, at Concord, continuing until 1880. He then went to Manchester and was a clerk for J. S. Kidder & Company, later with C. R. Merrill, and subsequently this became the firm of Freeman & Merrill. Later the firm dissolved, after which H. H. Freeman formed a partnership with H. H. Merrill, and Mr. Brown was with them until he bought out the business of Freeman & Merrill, 1895, and he conducted the business successfully until 1900, when he sold it to his son, Arthur S. Brown. During this time Mr. Brown and O. M. Titus, as partners, built the Milford railroad from Milford to Manchester. Mr. Brown is a Republican, and attends the Baptist Church. He was an orderly sergeant in the State Capital Guards from 1877 to 1880. In 1888 he became a member of the Amoskeag Veterans, and since 1893 has been color sergeant of that organization. With the Guards he was present at the laying of the corner stone of the Bennington (Vermont) Monument, 1877; at the dedication of this monument, 1888; at the World's Columbian Exposition in Chicago, 1893, and in fact attended all the affairs of this organization since becoming a member. He was a member of Queen City Lodge, No. 32, Knights of Pythias; Lodge No. 146, Benevolent and Protective Order of Elks; Uncanoonuc Court, No. 1962, Independent Order of Foresters, and Ben Franklin Lodge, No. 1, American Mechanics. Parker R. Brown married, in Manchester, Angie Straw, born in Manchester, 1856, daughter of Daniel Felch and Lucretia Ann Straw. She died in 1885 (see Straw). They had one child, Arthur Straw Brown, of whom later.

(III) Arthur Straw, only child of Parker R. and Angie (Straw) Brown, was born in Manchester, April 3, 1879. He was educated in the common and high schools of Manchester and at Bryant & Stratton's Business College. He learned the flour and grain business while assisting his father in that line. At the age of twenty-one he purchased his father's business, which he has since conducted with success, and has now one of the leading flour and grain stores in Manchester. He is a thirty-second degree Mason, and a member of the following named Masonic bodies: Washington Lodge, No. 61; Mount Horeb Royal Arch Chapter, No. 11; Adoniram Council, No. 3, Royal and Select Masters; Trinity Commandery, Knights Templar, and Edward A. Raymond Consistory, Sublime Princes of the Royal Secret, the last named of Nashua. He is also a member of Bektash Temple, Ancient Arabic Order Nobles of the Mystic Shrine, of Concord, and is a call member of the Manchester Fire Department.

Arthur S. Brown married, November 6, 1900, in Manchester, Ina Grace, daughter of Dana Elmer and Anna Maria (Stewart) Brown, of Hillsborough, and granddaughter of Stephen A. Brown, formerly a prominent citizen of Hillsborough, and a leading Mason of the state. Mrs. Arthur S. Brown has taken an active part in the Rebekahs, and is now (1907) a vice-grand of that order. Both Mr. and Mrs. Brown are active members of Ruth Chapter, No. 16, Order of the Eastern Star, Mrs. Brown having been treasurer for two years, 1906 and 1907.

BROWN James Brown, a native of Westteny, England, and a jack-spinner by occupation, married Sarah Curtis, and reared a family of seven children, namely: Ham, William, Jeremiah, Sarah, Caroline, Ann and Oxford.

(II) Jeremiah, third son and child of James and Sarah (Curtis) Brown, was born in England, in 1809. He was educated in a school conducted under the auspices of the Established Church of England. Having served a long and arduous apprenticeship in a woolen mill, he acquired unusual proficiency in both the carding and spinning departments, and eventually became an overseer in a large manufactory of woollen goods. In 1854 he came to the United States, and locating in Franklin, New Hampshire, was employed as a spinner in that town for two years, and at the expiration of that time he returned to England, where his death occurred about 1881, at the age of seventy-two years. He married for his first wife Eva Reeves, who died in 1842, and he was again married two years later to Mary Wickton. He was the father of six children: Adam, Martin, Mary, Jane, Sarah and George, all of his first union.

(III) George, youngest son of Jeremiah and Eva (Reeves) Brown, was born in England November 11, 1836. After concluding his attendance at the public schools he was employed in a woollen mill for two years, and having accompanied his father to America he remained on this side of the ocean. He resided in Franklin for two years, going from there to Portsmouth, where he remained two years, and for the ensuing seven years he worked in the Amesbury Mills, in Amesbury, Massachusetts. Some forty years ago he purchased a farm in Candia, and has ever since resided in that town, devoting the greater part of his time to agricultural pursuits. Politically he is a Republican, and in his religious faith he is an Episcopalian. In 1854 he was united in marriage with Eliza Martin, daughter of James and Ann (Sawyer) Martin, of England. Mr. and Mrs. Brown are the parents of three children: 1. James H., born in 1855. He is a farmer in Candia. He married first Annie Pettingill, and they had a daughter Emma, who married George Smith, and who had two children. He married second, Mary Leach, and they had three children: Walter, Mary, Clara. He married third, ———. 2. Jane, born 1857, married Thomas Clough, of Lakeport, and they had two children, Ethel and Frank, both of whom married, and each has two children. 3. George E., born 1863, a farmer in Candia; married Grace Kimball, and they have two sons, George and Alfred.

BROWN (I) Moses Brown, who was born in Landaff, New Hampshire, in 1824, went to reside in Colebrook, this state, during his boyhood, and was reared upon a farm in that town. He was an industrious farmer, an upright, conscientious man, and a most estimable citizen. His interest in the moral and religious welfare of the community was frequently manifested, and for many years he served as a deacon of the Christian Church. He married Abigail Stevens, daughter of James Stevens, of Colebrook, and had a family of six children, three of whom are now living, namely: William M., a resident of Lancaster; Irving Charles, a clergyman of Salisbury, Massachusetts; and Elmer F., who is again referred to in the succeeding paragraph. The others were: Abbie, Dencie and Ida.

(II) Elmer Frederick Brown, M. D., youngest son and child of Moses and Abigail (Stevens) Brown, was born in Colebrook, July 16, 1868. His early education was acquired in the public schools and at the Colebrook Academy, and after the completion of his studies he taught school, tilled the soil and was otherwise employed for some time. His professional preparations were pursued at the Baltimore (Maryland) Medical College, from which he was graduated in April, 1897, and in the following June he located in Groveton, where he has ever since been engaged in the general practice of medicine.

Although not active in politics, Dr. Brown is interested in civic affairs, especially in all matters relative to public education, and has served with ability for three years upon the school board of Colebrook. He is a member of the New Hampshire State and the Coos County Medical societies, the American Medical Association, the Independent Order of Odd Fellows, and the Independent Order of Foresters. He united with the Methodist Episcopal Church at East Colebrook, in 1894.

PHILLIPS The name is spelled in a variety of forms, and is of ancient and classical origin, being derived from the Greek *Philos-hippos*, or horse lover. In Wales and other parts of Great Britain its use as a surname has continued for a long period, evidently for five hundred years, and perhaps much longer.

Families and individuals of this name began to emigrate from the Old World at a very early date in the history of this country, as early as 1630, and some a little earlier, and located at different points near the seacoast, but more especially in New England. From that time to the present they have continued to multiply and spread, by natural causes and by emigration, until now they are to be found in every state from Maine to California. A recent writer has said: "A Phillips crossed the water with John Winthrop, and from him descended a long line of ministers, judges, governors, and councilors—a sterling race, temperate, just, and high-minded." The Phillips here referred to is Rev. George Phillips, of Watertown, Massachusetts, from whom are descended five divisions of this family, so marked by long continued residence in particular localities, that they might well be designated as distinctive branches. From this "earliest advocate of the Congregational order and discipline," have sprung men who have stood at the head of great financial institutions, honored each of the learned professions, and taken front rank as patriots, leaders and benefactors of mankind. As promoters of learning they stand in the front rank of the earlier New England history. Hon. Samuel Phillips, Hon. John Phillips and Judge Samuel Phillips founded Phillips Academy at Andover, which was incorporated by an act of the legislature in 1780, being the first academy so incorporated in America. Six months later Dr. John Phillips, of Exeter, secured the incorporation of Phillips Exeter Academy. "In Brechin Hall at Andover, the library of the theological school, in the great halls of the academies at Andover and Exeter, and in Memorial Hall at Harvard College, one may see hanging upon the wall portraits of one and another man and woman of this family, which belongs among the untitled nobility of New England, representing the best element of life there—not that which always dwells in the brightest glare of publicity, but that which directs and shapes the current of public opinion."

(I) Rev. George Phillips, the first minister of Watertown, Massachusetts, son of Christopher Phillips, of Rainham, was born about 1593, at Rainham, St. Martins, near Rougham, in the hundred (or district) of Gallow, county of Norfolk, England. He graduated as B. A. from Gonville and Cains College, Cambridge, 1613, and received the degree of M. A., 1617. "He gave early indications of deep piety, uncommon talents, and love of learning, and at the university distinguished himself by his remarkable progress in learning, especially in theological studies for which he manifested an early partiality." He was settled for a time in the ministry in Suffolk county, but suffering from the storm of persecution which then threatened the non-conformists of England, he determined to leave the mother country and take his lot with the Puritans. He embarked for America on April 12, 1630, in the "Arabella," with his wife and two children, as fellow-passengers with Governor Winthrop and

Sir Richard Saltonstall, and arrived at Salem on June 12. Here his wife soon died, and was buried by the side of Lady Arabella Johnson, both evidently being unable to endure the hardships and exposure incident to a tedious ocean voyage. He soon located at Watertown, and without delay settled over the church in that place, which was called together in July. At the court of assistants, August 23, 1630, it was "ordered that Mr. Phillips shall have allowed him 3 hogsheads of meale, 1 hogshead of malte, 4 bushells of Indian corn, 1 bushell of oat-meale, halfe an hundred of salte fish." Another statement from the same source says 'Mr. Phillips hath 30 ac of land grannted him vpp Charles Ryver on the South side." His first residence was burned before the close of the year. There is a tradition that his later residence is still standing "opposite the ancient burial ground, back from the road." He continued to be the pastor of this church, greatly respected and beloved, till his death fourteen years after his arrival. He died at the age of fifty-one years, July 1, and was buried July 2, 1644. "He was the earliest advocate of the Congregational order and discipline. His views were for a time regarded as novel, suspicious and extreme, and he, with his ruling elder, Mr. Richard Brown, stood almost unaided and alone, until the arrival of Mr. John Cotton, maintaining what was and still is the Congregationalism of New England. It is not now easy to estimate the extent and importance of the influence of Mr. Phillips in giving form and character to the civil and ecclesiastical institutions of New England." His name appears on the list of those who were admitted freemen, May 18, 1631, which is the earliest date of any such admission. His inventory amounted to five hundred fifty pounds, two shillings and nine pence, a sum, allowing for the difference in commercial value between that time and the present, equivalent at least to seven or eight thousand dollars. His library was valued at seventy-one pounds, nine shillings and nine pence. He married (first) a daughter of Richard Sargent, and (second) Elizabeth, probably the widow of Captain Robert Welden. She died in Watertown, June 27, 1681. The children (by the first marriage) were: Samuel and Elizabeth; by the second marriage; Zerobabel, Jonathan, Theophilus, Annabel, Ephraim, Obadiah and Abigail.

(II) Rev. Samuel (2), oldest child and only son of Rev. George Phillips, was born in England, 1625, probably at Boxstead, in the county of Suffolk, graduated at Harvard College, 1650, settled in Rowley in 1651, as colleague of Rev. Ezekiel Rogers. "He was highly esteemed for his piety and talents, which were of no common order, and he was eminently useful both at home and abroad." He married, in October, 1651, Sarah Appleton, born in Reydon, England, 1629, daughter of Samuel Appleton. He died April 22, 1696, "greatly beloved and lamented," and his widow died July 15, 1714. Her funeral sermon was preached by her grandson, Rev. Samuel Phillips, of South Andover, in which he said, "She was an early seeker of God, and spent much of her time daily in reading the word and in prayer. She took care of her children's souls. She was always humble and penitent, and as she lived, so she died, depending on Christ for righteousness and salvation." Their remains repose in the ancient burying ground at Rowley. Some of their descendants have been among the most distinguished of New England people for their intellectual talents, piety, benevolence, and public services. Their eleven children were: Samuel, died young; Sarah, Samuel, George, Elizabeth, died young; Ezekiel, George, Elizabeth, Dorcas, Mary and John.

(III) Samuel (2), third child and second son of Samuel (1) and Sarah (Appleton) Phillips, was born in Rowley, March 23, 1658, and removed to Salem where he followed the occupation of goldsmith, and died October 13, 1722, aged sixty-five. He married (first) May 26, 1687, Mary Emerson, daughter of Rev. John and Ruth (Symonds) Emerson, of Gloucester, and granddaughter of Deputy Governor Samuel Symonds of Ipswich. She died October 4, 1703, aged forty-two. He married (second) 1704, Mrs. Sarah (Pickman) Mayfield. Children all by the first wife, except the eighth: Patience, died very young; Samuel, Sarah, Mary, Ruth, Elizabeth, John and Patience.

(IV) Rev. Samuel (3), second child and eldest son of Samuel (2) and Mary (Emerson) Phillips, was born in Salem, February 17, 1690, graduated from Harvard College 1708, and died in Andover, June 5, 1771. He was the minister of the church at the south parish, the present "Old South Church," Andover, for sixty years, where he commenced to preach in 1710, and was ordained October 17, 1711, the same day the church was organized, and continued till his death. "In his individuality, simplicity, decision, energy, strength, and pristine hardiness of character, he abated nothing from the spirit of his worthy ancestors. He was, like them, also a model of industry, and frugality, and resolute self-restraint, and order in all that he did. His portrait bespeaks a man of authority, born to command, and knowing his birthright; and such was he in an eminent degree, a conscious and acknowledged leader wherever he was known." He married, January 17, 1712, Hannah White, daughter of John White, Esq., of Haverhill, deacon of the church and captain of the company of the town. It was her practice to accompany her husband on his parishional calls, at which time he rode on horseback, with his wife seated on a pillion behind him. She died January 7, 1773. Their five children were: Mary, Samuel, Lydia, John and William, the subject of the following sketch.

(V) Hon. William (1), third son and youngest child of Samuel (3) and Hannah (White) Phillips, was born in Andover, July 6, 1722, and died January 15, 1804, aged eighty-one. At the age of fifteen years he went to Boston and became an apprentice to Edward Bromfield, Esq., a highly respectable merchant of that town, son of Hon. Edward Bromfield, for many years one of His Majesty's council in the province of Massachusetts Bay, and a great-grandson of Rev. John Wilson, the first minister of Boston. At the termination of his apprenticeship he married, June 13, 1744 (old style), Abigail Bromfield, eldest daughter of his late master, and engaged in mercantile pursuits, in which he was very successful. By this marriage a great-grandson of the first minister of Watertown was united with a great-granddaughter of the first minister of Boston. He was for many years a deacon of the Old South Church, and was repeatedly elected representative and state senator. "He took a decided and active part in the proceedings which preceded and attended the Revolution; was on many of the committees appointed by the town of Boston in those trying times, and often contributed liberally of his estate to promote the measures which issued in the establishment of our independence. He was one of the committee sent to demand of Governor Hutchinson that the tea should be sent back to

England; was rejected as a councillor by Governor Gage, was a member of the convention for framing the constitution of the commonwealth, and that of adopting the constitution of the United States. Upon the outbreak of the Revolution he moved his family to Norwich, Connecticut, where they remained while the British had possession of Boston, occupying the Arnold mansion, the same house in which the traitor Benedict Arnold was born." He gave by his last will five thousand dollars to Phillips Academy, Andover. The children of William and Abigail (Bromfield) Phillips were: Abigail, William, died young; William, Sarah, died young; Hannah, died young; Hannah, Sarah and Mary.

(VI) Lieutenant Governor William (2), third child and second son of William (1) and Abigail (Bromfield) Phillips, born in Boston, March 30, 1750, died in Boston, May 26, 1827. He was deacon of the Old South Church, representative, and from 1812 to 1823 lieutenant-governor; from 1804 until his death in 1827 president of the Massachusetts Bank; presidential elector at large in 1820, when the vote of the state was cast for Mr. Monroe. To the already very liberal endowments of Phillips Academy, Andover, he added the sum of fifteen thousand dollars, and gave ten thousand dollars to Andover Theological Seminary. His generous gifts distributed among about a dozen worthy objects, amounted to sixty-two thousand dollars. "He came into possession of an ample fortune, to the management of which, and to the duties of his family and of friendship, to the service of the public, and to deeds of benevolence, he was thenceforth chiefly devoted. He was eminently a domestic man, fond of retirement, and of the society of his family and intimate friends. Yet he was not averse to the calls of public duty." The Rev. Dr. Wisner in preaching his funeral sermon said, "Scarcely a measure has been adopted or an association formed in this vicinity for the improvement of the physical, the intellectual, the moral or the spiritual condition of men, which has not received his co-operation and liberal support." He married, September 13, 1774, Miriam Mason, born June 16, 1754, third daughter of Hon. Jonathan Mason of Boston. She died May 7, 1823, "greatly lamented." He died May 26, 1827. Their children were: William Wilson, died young; Jonathan, died young; Jonathan, Miriam, Edward, Abigail Bromfield and William.

(VII) William Phillips was born October 13, 1791, in Boston. He married Betsey Granger and resided in Lynn, Massachusetts, where she died November 17, 1878.

(VIII) Harriet Phillips, daughter of William and Betsey (Granger) Phillips, was born April 12, 1815, in Lynn, and became the wife of Ira Gove (see Gove, VII).

COLBY This is a name intimately associated with the early history of New Hampshire, being found in many localities in the pioneer periods, and is still prominent in business, social and professional affairs throughout the state

(I) The founder of the family in America was Anthony Colby, who came with Rev. John Winthrop's colony in 1630, his name being the ninety-third on the list of church members. He came from the eastern coast of England, and was one of the many driven by persecution to seek a home in the New World. He is found of record in 1632, at Cambridge, Massachusetts, where he married Susannah, supposed to have been a daughter of William Sargent. He removed to Salisbury in 1634, and in 1647 he sold his house and two-acre lot to William Sargent, and settled on the west side of the Powow river, in what is now Amesbury. He was recorded as a "planter," and received land in the "first division," in 1640 and 1643; was one of the first commoners of Amesbury, where he received land in 1654 and 1658, and his widow in his right in 1662 and 1664. He died in Salisbury, February 11, 1661. His widow Susannah, married (second) William Whitridge (or Whitred) in 1663, and was again a widow in 1669. She died July 8, 1689, "or thereabout." The children of Anthony and Susannah were: John, Sarah, a child died young, Samuel, Isaac, Rebecca, Mary, and Thomas. (Isaac and Thomas, with descendants receive extended notice in this article.)

(II) John, eldest child of Anthony and Susannah Colby, was baptized at Boston, September 8, 1663. He was a "planter" of Amesbury, where he was an original commoner in 1654, and received land in 1658-59-62-66-68. He married at South Salem, January 14, 1656, Frances Hoyt, and died February 11, 1674. His widow married December 27, 1676, John Barnard. Their children were: John, Sarah, Elizabeth, Frances, Anthony, Susannah, Thomas, Mary and Hannah.

(III) John (2), eldest child of John (1) and Frances (Hoyt) Colby, was born in Salisbury, November 19, 1656, and died in Amesbury, April 6, 1719. He received "children's land" in 1659, and a "township" in 1660. He was a soldier in King Philip's war, was in the Falls fight under Captain Turner, May 18, 1676, was in the "training band" in 1680, and was known as "Sergeant." He took the oath of allegiance and fidelity, December, 1677. He married (first), December 27, 1675, Sarah Eldridge; (second), before 1700, Sarah Osgood, and (third), February 8, 1715, in Amesbury, Ruth, widow of Robert Ring. Her children were: John, Joseph, Sarah, three children unnamed, died in infancy, Judith and Hannah.

(IV) Joseph, the second son and child of John and Sarah (Eldridge) Colby, was born in Amesbury. He lived in Amesbury, East Parish, and Hampstead, New Hampshire. "Mr. Joseph Colby" owned the covenant and was baptized June 27, 1731, at the first Amesbury Church. "He was administrator of his father's estate, and of the gift to himself and brother of certain land in Amesbury." In 1718 he sold to his brother's widow his right and title to said land, bought land in Hampstead, New Hampshire, where he soon after settled and lived the remainder of his life. Mary, wife of Joseph Colby, with others, was dismissed from the First Haverhill Church, to form a church at Hampstead, May 31, 1752. Joseph Colby married (first) in Amesbury, November 22, 1704, Anne Bartlett, who died October 24, 1721; (second) in Amesbury, August 1, 1722, widow Mary Johnson, of Haverhill. Joseph Colby died in 1753 or 1754, and the inventory of his estate was made May 23, 1754. His children, eighteen in number, were: Benaiah, Joseph, Nathan, Judith, Hannah, Martha, Ann, John, Mary, Sarah, Theophilus, Lydia, Dorothy, John, Philbrook, Susanna, Edmund and Mary.

(V) Philbrook, fifteenth child of Joseph and third son and eighth child of Joseph and Mary Colby, was born in Amesbury, March 16, 1735, was a "blacksmith," and lived in Haverhill, Massachusetts, and Weare, New Hampshire. He was a soldier in the French and Indian war, and is also credited with serving two or three enlistments in the Revolutionary war, after which he removed to Weare, New Hampshire. He married (first) at Haverhill,

July 13, 1758, Susanna Bradley, who was admitted to the First Haverhill Church, August 2, 1778; and (second) Ruth Lufkin. His thirteen children were: William, Samuel, Susanna, Mary, Daniel, Jeremiah, John Bradley, Benjamin, Jonathan, Joseph, Polly, Sally, and Rhoda, the last six children being by the second wife.

(VI) Benjamin, eldest child of Philbrook and Ruth (Lufkin) Colby, removed to Weare probably with his father's family. He married Priscilla Hogg, and they were the parents of six children: Lydia, Sally, John, Hiram, David and Anna.

(VII) John (3), eldest son and third child of Benjamin and Priscilla (Hogg) Colby, was born in Weare, in 1813, and died at the house of his son-in-law, Levi C. Woods, in Concord, July 31, 1886, aged seventy-three years. He was a farmer in Weare and Henniker. He married Orpha Metcalf, born in Croydon, who died at the residence of her daughter Helen P., in Somerville, Massachusetts, March 28, 1892, aged eighty-one years. The children of this union were: Robert, Samuel, Belinda D., Matilda A., Helen P., George P., Nancy and James B.

(VIII) Belinda D., third child and eldest daughter of John and Orpha (Metcalf) Colby, born in Deering, July 7, 1839, married Levi Cobb Woods (see Woods, II).

(II) Isaac, third son of Anthony and Susannah Colby, was born July 6, 1640, in Salisbury, in which town he was a "planter," and died in Amesbury, 1684, between March 29 and April 15. His estate was divided in 1725. He had a meeting-house seat in Amesbury in 1667. He married Martha Jewett (sister of Deacon Ezekiel Jewett), who survived him forty-six years and died July 13, 1730, in Amesbury. Their children were: Anthony, Elizabeth, Martha, Sarah, Rebecca, Dorothy, Isaac and Abraham.

(III) Anthony, of Haverhill, eldest child of Isaac and Martha (Jewett) Colby, was born January 24, 1670, married (first), October 23, 1701, Mary Currier, who died April 8, 1719. He married (second), December 4, 1721, Elizabeth West, who died June 25, 1738, a daughter of Thomas West of Bradford. The Haverhill records bear mention of the following named children: Anthony, Elijah, Richard and Isaac, whose sketch follows.

(IV) Isaac (2), fourth son and child of Anthony and Mary (Currier) Colby, was born in Haverhill, March 23, 1712, and married, April 25, 1733, Sarah Davis, both being according to the record "of Haverhill;" she died June 3, 1755. He married (second), April, 1757, Hannah Colby, of Amesbury. The children, born in Haverhill, of the first wife, were: William and Anthony, twins, died young; Elizabeth, Sarah, William Davis, Anthony, Isaac, Benjamin, Mary and Martha, twins, and Abigail.

(V) Benjamin, eighth child and sixth son of Isaac and Sarah (Davis) Colby, was born in Haverhill, July 14, 1750, and died in Sanbornton, New Hampshire, November 9, 1816, aged sixty-six. He was the "first of his name" in Sanbornton, though he probably did not settle earlier than his brother Isaac, or till after his marriage, 1773. He bought the farm, lot No. 10, second division, on the north slope of Colby Hill, and there built his original house, and kept it many years as one of the first taverns. He also built another house which was occupied by his son Benjamin. He was a prominent man in the town, was a captain in the militia, and in 1782 was selectman. He married (first), in Haverhill, October 19, 1773, Elizabeth Hunkins, probably a daughter of John Hunkins. She died November 22, 1806, aged sixty-six. He married (second) widow Sarah (Eastman) Carter, of Concord. The children, all by the first wife, were: Sarah, died young; William, died young; Benjamin and William.

(VI) Benjamin, third child and second son of Benjamin and Elizabeth (Hunkins) Colby, was born in Sanbornton, July 5, 1778, and died February 6, 1856, aged seventy-seven. He was a school teacher for thirty-four consecutive years, mostly in Sanbornton, after 1800, and was favorably known as "Master Colby." He married, January 11, 1804, Polly Woodman, who was born in Sanbornton, April 23, 1784, daughter of Rev. Joseph and Esther (Whittemore) (Hall) Woodman. Her father was for thirty-five years pastor of the Congregational Church of Sanbornton. She died June 14, 1861, aged seventy-seven. The children of this union were: Eliza Esther, Sally Chase, Albert, Ethan, Jonathan Wilkins, Hannah Taylor, Benjamin Marion, Jeremiah Hall Woodman, Charles Woodman, Aaron Whittemore, died young; and Aaron Woodman.

(VII) Ethan, fourth child and second son of Benjamin and Polly (Woodman) Colby, was born in Sanbornton, August 29, 1810, and died in Colebrook, March 28, 1895, aged eighty-five. He went to St. Johnsbury, Vermont, in 1829, as a clerk for Moses Kittredge, and afterwards was in company with Mr. Kittredge till 1836, when he went to Littleton and into trade with Cyrus Eastman, as Colby & Eastman. In 1838 Mr. Colby sold out and went to Colebrook and commenced the mercantile business in company with his old partner, Moses Kittredge, but at the end of five years purchased the entire business and remained in trade at the same place till 1856, when he sold out to George W. Brackett and retired. He bought the Chamberlin farm on which stood the Chamberlin Tavern, and was engaged in agriculture until his death. The most of the farm is now in blocks and streets and constitutes a part of Colebrook, and one of the streets is called Colby in honor of Mr. Colby. He was a positive man in his ideas, and a liberal supporter of the church. In politics he was first an old-line Whig, and after the dissolution of his party a Republican. He was postmaster for several years. He represented Colebrook in the legislature in 1861, and the next year was a member of the governor's council from district No. 5. He declined several offices on account of his health, including that of sheriff of Coos county "upon unanimous recommendation," in 1856, and that of commissioner on the board of enrollment, from Hon. E. M. Stanton, secretary of war, 1863. He married, March 29, 1843, Mary Chamberlin, who was born April 6, 1819, and died November 18, 1900, daughter of Edmund and Polly Chamberlin, of Colebrook. They had three children: Edward Chamberlin, Charles and Sarah. Sarah Colby, born May 10, 1852, married Melrose V. Knight (see Knight) of Colebrook, and resides on the old homestead.

(II) Thomas, youngest child of Anthony and Susannah Colby, was born in Salisbury, March 8, 1651, and died before March 30, 1691. He took the oath of allegiance and fidelity in December, 1677. He married, September 16, 1674, Hannah, daughter of Valentine and Joanna (Pindor) Rowell (see Rowell, II), born in Salisbury, January, 1653, and they had five children: Thomas, Hannah, Isaac, Abraham and Jacob. After the death of her husband Hannah Colby married (second), probably about 1691, Henry Blaisdell. (Mention of Jacob Colby and descendants appears in this article.)

(III) Thomas (2), eldest son and child of Thomas and Hannah (Rowell) Colby, was born in Amesbury, July 1, 1675. According to records he served as snowshoe man in 1708, and from the same source it is learned that the Christian name of his wife was Frances, but her maiden surname is wanting. He died June 4, 1741, and his estate was divided the following year. His widow was still living in 1748. Their children were: Ezekiel, Sarah, Judith, Orlando, Thomas, Frances, Hannah, Nathaniel, Anne, Abraham and Willebee. (Mention of Abraham and descendants forms part of this article.)

(IV) Ezekiel, eldest child of Thomas (2) and Frances Colby, was born April 12, 1699, in Amesbury, and resided in the west parish of that town, where he was described as a yeoman. His will was made May 18, 1756, and proven May 4, 1756, showing that he was possessed of considerable foresight and had care for his family. He was married, December 24, 1724, to Mary Elliott, daughter of John and Naomi (Tuxbury) Elliott, of Amesbury, granddaughter of Edmund Elliott, of that town. She was born August 4, 1699, and was living in 1732. Ezekiel Colby and wife owned the covenant and were baptized March 19, 1727, in the Second Amesbury Church. Their children were: Daniel, Ezekiel, John, Elliott, Mary and Anne.

(V) Elliott, fourth son and child of Ezekiel and Mary (Elliott) Colby, was born May 22, 1735, in Amesbury, and lived in early life in the west parish of that town. He served in the French war of 1758. He removed to Warner, New Hampshire, about 1780, and died in that town February 20, 1811. He was married (first) June 17, 1760, in the Second Amesbury Church to Judith Sargent, daughter of Stephen Sargent, of Amesbury (see Sargent, IV). Mr. Colby was married (second), November 30, 1782, to Hannah Smith. The records of the Second Amesbury Church show that Elliott Colby and wife renewed the Covenant in 1761, and that the latter was received to full communion June 12, 1763, and was dismissed to Warner, January 30, 1780. There were ten children of the first wife and two of the second, namely: Naomi (died young), Ezekiel, Stephen, John, Elliott, Judith, Naomi, Anna, Molly, Phineas Kelley, Pearson Smith and Daniel.

(VI) Naomi, third daughter and seventh child of Elliott and Judith (Sargent) Colby, was born December 18, 1773, in Amesbury, and was baptized the following day at the Second Church of Salisbury. She became the wife of Benjamin Badger, and resided in Warner, New Hampshire (see Badger, VI).

(VI) Phineas, youngest child of Elliott and Judith (Sargent) Colby, was born in Warner June 24, 1780. He learned the carpenter's trade, which he followed in Deerfield, this state, for a time, and in 1810 removed to a farm in Candia, where he resided for the rest of his life, applying himself to his trade as well as to agriculture. His death occurred in 1850. He served as a selectman, and was otherwise quite prominent in local public affairs, acting in politics with the Democratic party. His religious affiliations were with the Congregationalists. He was first married in 1798 to Patty Jenness, daughter of Thomas Jenness of Deerfield, and she died in 1810, having borne him three children—Phineas, Thomas J. and Sally. In 1811 he married for his second wife the Widow Emerson of Candia, who bore him two sons, Asa and Jonathan E.

(VII) Thomas J., second child and youngest son of Phineas and Patty (Jenness) Colby, was born in Deerfield, in 1807. He began the activities of life as a carpenter, following it until 1829, when he went to Topsham, Vermont, and he died in that town at the age of thirty-nine years. In 1829 he married Mary Dolber, daughter of John and Lydia (Robie) Dolber, of Candia, New Hampshire, and she survived him many years, dying there in 1897, at the advanced age of ninety years. Both were members of the Congregational Church. They were the parents of two sons—John D. and George.

(VIII) John Dolber, eldest son of Thomas J. and Mary (Dolber) Colby, was born in Topsham, October 22, 1830. After concluding his attendance at the public schools, including the Manchester high school, he engaged in the milk business, and continued in it for eight years. He was subsequently engaged in lumbering in Candia for some time, drove a team regularly between New Boston and Francestown for a period of ten years, was for seven years in the railway service in Boston, and for the ensuing fifteen years was in the employ of the Lawrence Manufacturing Company at Lowell, Massachusetts. In 1896 he returned to the old Colby homestead in Candia, for the purpose of taking charge of the farm and caring for his mother during her last days, and he is still residing there. In politics he is a Republican, and for two years was chairman of the board of selectmen in Candia. He is a member of Rockingham Lodge, Free and Accepted Masons, and of the local Grange, of which he has been secretary for four years. In religious faith he is a Congregationalist, a member of the society, and treasurer and clerk.

On September 6, 1854, Mr. Colby married Keziah Patten, daughter of Francis and Rebecca (Knight) Patten, and five children have been born to them: Mary R., born April, 1857, married Charles Eastman, of Littleton, and died, 1900; Ella F., born 1859, died 1869; Thomas J., born 1865, died in infancy; Emma B., born 1868, married B. F. Stephenson, of Lowell, one child, Paul Colby; Grace, born 1873, married Eugene Elliott, of Lowell, one child, Frank G.

(IV) Abraham, tenth child and fifth son of Thomas (2) and Frances Colby, was born in Amesbury, East Parish, about 1720, and baptized January 25, 1736, and was living in the same parish in 1751. He married, March 23, 1742, Elizabeth Blaisdell, fourth daughter and tenth child of Jonathan and Hannah (Jameson) Blaisdell, of Amesbury. He was an early resident of Bow, New Hampshire, where he purchased, August 16, 1768, of John Leavitt, of Stratham, part of lots three and four, in range 14, and settled thereon, with his five sons. The tract included one hundred and twenty acres, and the purchase price was forty-five pounds, lawful money, equivalent to about one hundred and fifty dollars at that time. This land was on Wood Hill, and is held now by his descendants. The father was then about fifty-three years of age, and two of his sons were of legal age. He continued to reside there until his death, in 1809, at the age of ninety-four years. His children were named: Sarah, Elijah, Willaby, Anna, John, Hannah, Thomas, Eli and Jonathan. Eli was killed at the battle of Bennington, in his nineteenth year. The first child died young, and the others married and settled in Bow, where their posterity are now numerous.

(V) Willaby, second son and third child of Abraham and Elizabeth (Blaisdell) Colby, was born February 28, 1745, in Amesbury, Massachusetts, and became the pioneer of the family in coming to Bow. On attaining his majority he pushed into the wilderness on a tour of investigation, and he selected the land on Wood Hill, in Bow, where his father and the entire family subsequently settled. He returned to his Massachusetts home and at once began making preparations for settling in the new location. One of the first steps in this preparation was the taking of a wife, and Sarah Sargent, of Newport, became his bride. When they removed to the new home in the year 1768, she rode on horseback, carrying in her arms their infant child, born in the fall of 1767. He built a log house, which was soon succeeded by a frame building that was occupied after him by his son, Philip. He was skilled in the use of carpenter's tools, and was well adapted to building, being able to climb with ease and without fear over any frame. In July, 1777, Mr. Colby was one of eight who marched from Bow, under Captain Benjamin Bean, to the relief of Ticonderoga. On arriving at Charlestown, New Hampshire, they learned that the fort had been evacuated, and returned after a service of seven days. In 1774 he purchased of Benjamin Noyes lot No. 5, in the fourteenth range, comprising one hundred acres, which was called "Nottencook." This land he divided between his sons, James and Philip. He was one of the committee to pass upon the completion of the church building in 1792, and was selectman in 1796-97. He died October 30, 1829, aged eighty-five years. His first wife, Sarah (Sargent) Colby, died April 22, 1796, aged fifty-four years, and he married (second), in 1797, Molly Sargent, of Pembroke, daughter of Sterling and Lydia (Coffin) Sargent (see Sargent, V). The second wife was the mother of two of his children. The entire family included: James, Hepsebeth, Sarah, Philip, Merriam, Judith, Sarah, Polly and Willaby.

(VI) James, eldest child of Willaby and Sarah (Sargent) Colby, was born October 27, 1767, in Newton, New Hampshire, and was brought to Bow while a babe in arms. He inherited and acquired the skill of his father in building operations, and they built many of the best dwellings in the town. In 1790 he purchased thirteen acres of land, and next year added twenty acres, with a house, all on Wood Hill. He died February 15, 1829, and was survived by his wife until December 18, 1848, when she was seventy-five years of age. He was married in 1789 to Susanna, daughter of James Stewart, of Dunbarton. She was born 1773, in Salem, this state, and was the mother of the following children: Willaby (died young), Aaron, Willaby, Levi, Abiah, Lucinda, Susan, James and Charles Sargent.

(VII) Aaron, the second child and son of James and Susanna (Stewart) Colby, was born in the town of Bow, April 15, 1792. He enlisted in September, 1814, for the defense of Portsmouth, New Hampshire, and was in the service about three months. He married, December 25, 1817, Edith, daughter of John Rowell, of Bow. She was born July 30, 1795. He followed farming in the town of Bow until 1838, when he purchased a farm at Potter Place in the town of Andover, New Hampshire, and resided there until 1867, when he sold out and purchased the Hoag farm in the town of Bow, where he and his wife resided until their death. He died January 18, 1877. His wife died March 15, 1877. Their children were: Harrison, born April 11, 1820, and Sylvanus R., January 29, 1829. The latter moved to Ohio in 1852, and was killed on the Ohio & Pennsylvania railroad, September 14, 1853; he was buried in Salem, Columbiana county, Ohio.

(VIII) Harrison, eldest son of Aaron and Edith (Rowell) Colby, was born in the town of Bow, New Hampshire, April 11, 1820, married, November 28, 1843, Judith E. Whitaker, daughter of Joseph and Nancy (Elkins) Whitaker. She was born October 25, 1819. Their children were: Clemantine L., born in Andover, New Hampshire, April 23, 1845, and Anthon W., born in Andover, December 7, 1850. Harrison Colby died May 5, 1905, in Concord, aged eighty-five years.

(IX) Anthon W., second child and only son of Harrison and Judith L. (Whitaker) Colby, was born in the town of Andover, New Hampshire, December 7, 1850. He left Andover for Vineland, New Jersey, in December, 1865, where he resided until the fall of 1869, when he returned to Bow to care for his aged parents. He married, August 28, 1873, Jessie L. Brown, who was born in Bow, New Hampshire, July 3, 1856. Mr. Colby was in the employ of the Concord railroad for several years. Commencing in 1870 he carried the mail from Concord to Dunbarton and Bow, eight years. He was the first postmaster at Bow Mills, and since 1888 has been employed in the state house at Concord.

(X) Eva M., only child of Anthon W. and Jessie L. (Brown) Colby, was born in the town of Bow, New Hampshire, June 10, 1874. She married, June 28, 1893, David Waldo White, of Concord, New Hampshire (see White, V). They are the parents of the following named children: Lloyd David, born May 29, 1894, died May 10, 1897; Una Goodell, August 21, 1895; Irene B., September 14, 1898.

(III) Jacob, youngest child of Thomas (1) and Hannah (Rowell) Colby, was born in Amesbury, April 13, 1688, and lived in Amesbury, East Parish. He married (first), in Amesbury, April 9, 1711, Hannah Hunt, born March 23, 1688, fourth daughter of Edward and Ann (Weed) Hunt; (second), at Amesbury, November 11, 1724, Elizabeth Elliot, born in Amesbury, November 11, 1691, third child of John and Naomi (Tuxbury) Elliot. A Mrs. Elizabeth Colby died in Amesbury, February 5, 1737. Their children were: Bekius, Jacob, Edmund, Valentine and Thomas Elliot.

(IV) Valentine, fourth son and child of Jacob and Elizabeth (Elliot) Colby, was born in Amesbury, May 29, 1728, baptized June 13, 1736, in Amesbury, died about 1812. His will was dated November 2, 1805, and probated January 4, 1813. He married (first), August 20, 1747, Hannah Kimball; (second), February 1, 1788, Elizabeth Lowell, of Amesbury, who survived him. His fourteen children, probably all by the first wife, were: Valentine, died young; Judith, Rhoda, Valentine, died young; Hezekiah, Rhoda, Thomas, David, Hannah, Elizabeth, Valentine, Jonathan, Levi and Molly.

(V) Levi, eighth son and thirteenth child of Valentine and Hannah (Kimball) Colby, was an early resident of Warner, where he married and raised a family of children.

(VI) Valentine, son of Levi Colby, was born in Warner, in 1764, married Sally Osgood, and raised a family there.

(VII) Levi Osgood, son of Valentine and Sally (Osgood) Colby, was born in Warner in 1818. He was well educated for his day and time, was a farmer and a member of the Congregational Church. Originally a Democrat, he became a Republican in

1855, and adhered to that faith the remainder of his life. He married Mary Durrell, born in Bradford, in 1823, daughter of Nicholas and Polly (Batchelder) Durrell. Nicholas, son of Eliphalet Durrell, of Northwood, was born in 1777, and died in 1844, reputed the wealthiest man in Bradford. Polly Batchelder was a daughter of Deacon Simon Batchelder, of Northwood.

(VIII) Frederick Myron, first child of Levi O. and Mary (Durrell) Colby, was born in Warner, December 9, 1848. His early years were spent in labor on his father's farm, and in obtaining his education in the common schools of Warner, New London Academy, and the Commercial College at Concord. Mr. Colby was born a poet and has found pleasure and profit in indulging the Muse and writing stories. Professionally he is an undertaker and embalmer, and incidentally he has administered upon various estates, in all of which occupations he has been successful. He is the author of "The Daughter of Pharaoh," "Brave Lads and Bonnie Lasses," "Boy Kings and Girl Queens," and "Poems of Heart and Home." Always a Democrat he has been placed in various positions of honor and trust by his fellow citizens. He has been a member of the Warner board of education six years; town treasurer four years; postmaster five years; and member of the Democratic state committee from 1890 to 1904. He is a member of the New Hampshire Licensed Embalmers' Association, of which he was secretary from 1902 to 1905; is one of the trustees and treasurer of the Pillsbury Library; treasurer of Pine Grove Cemetery Association, member of the New Hampshire Antiquarian and New Hampshire Historical societies, and an honorary member of the Manchester Press Club. He married in Warner, December 24, 1882, Hannah Maria George, born in Warner, daughter of Gilman C. and Nancy (Badger) George, of Warner. Gilman C. George, born in 1820, died September 12, 1894, was a son of James and Hannah (Church) George, and a descendant of James George, who settled in Haverhill, Massachusetts, in 1653. He was a captain in the state militia in 1843-44, town clerk from 1868 to 1872, and selectman from 1885 to 1888. He was master of Warner Grange, president of the Kearsarge Agricultural Association, and was the first worshipful master of Harris Lodge, No. 91, Ancient Free and Accepted Masons, of Warner.

COLBY The Colbys of this article are descended from Anthony Colby (or Colebie), the immigrant, an account of whom precedes this, but the generations preceding those given below have not yet been definitely ascertained.

(I) Thomas Colby was born in Maine, in 1777, and died in Franconia, New Hampshire, March 30, 1855. He married Polly Knapp, born in Saulsbury (now Franklin), New Hampshire, in 1798, and died in Franconia, New Hampshire, in 1826. They had children: 1. Thomas, born in Belgrade, Maine, 1805, was killed by blasting stone at Milford, New Hampshire, in 1827. 2. Lucy, born in Belgrade, Maine, January 20, 1810, died in Franconia, New Hampshire, December 20, 1893. 3. Enoch Libby, see forward. 4. Clarke, born in Franconia, 1817, died in 1835. 5. John, born in 1812, died in 1844. 6. Mary A., born in Franconia in 1819, died there in 1859. There were three other children who died in infancy.

(II) Enoch Libby, son of Thomas and Polly (Knapp) Colby, was born in Belgrade, Maine, May 11, 1814, and died in Lancaster, New Hampshire, December 21, 1875. When he was two years of age he was brought by his parents to Franconia, New Hampshire, and there he resided until 1850. His education was limited to an attendance of eleven weeks in the common schools of the district. He worked on the farm of his father until he had attained his majority, and then learned the carpenter's trade, which he followed until 1850. About 1840 he removed to Colebrook, New Hampshire, in which town he held the office of deputy sheriff for two years. He removed to Lancaster in 1854, and the following year was one of the corporators of the Lancaster Manufacturing Company. In the same year he was one of the corporators of the Coos Mutual Fire Insurance Company, and at the first meeting of the proprietors he was elected a member of the board of directors. At the meeting of the stockholders, September 1, 1863, he was again elected, and on the same day was elected president, and held that office until his death. He also served the company for a long time as one of its solicitors. He was elected to the board of fire wards in 1856, and was re-elected in 1861-62-64-65-66-67-68. He became sheriff in 1857, and held that office for a period of ten years. He was appointed deputy sheriff in 1867, and served in that office for ten years. He and his son, Charles F., were proprietors of a harness shop in 1875, doing business under the firm name of Enoch L. Colby & Son. He was a Democrat until the "Know Nothing" party arose, which he joined, but upon the organization of the Republican party he affiliated with that, and ever afterward was a staunch upholder of its principles. He was a delegate to the national Republican convention at Baltimore, Maryland, 1864, when Lincoln was nominated for a second term. He was also a deputy United States marshal for some time during the civil war, and filled minor offices of trust and responsibility. Mr. Colby was a man of sturdy character, and practical good sense, and had he received a liberal education would undoubtedly have made his mark in the world. He was brought up in the Baptist religion, but later in life united with the Episcopal Church.

Mr. Colby married, July 24, 1842, Lucy Ann Jane Fletcher, born at Charlestown, New Hampshire, December 27, 1823; died at Lancaster, New Hampshire, September 25, 1900. She was the daughter of Ebenezer and Peady (Smith) Fletcher, and a lineal descendant of Robert Fletcher, of Concord, Massachusetts, who came from England in 1630 with Richard Saltonstall and Governor Winthrop. On the paternal side her ancestors were English, on the maternal, Irish. Ebenezer Fletcher, son of one of the heroes of Bunker Hill, was born May 17, 1775, and died at Colebrook, New Hampshire, August 22, 1843. He removed to Pittsburg, New Hampshire, in 1811, where he was one of the first settlers, and there erected a frame dwelling house, a grist and saw mill which were standing until recently, and bore his name. He also expended considerable money in developing the country in various other directions. He married at Charlestown, New Hampshire, Peady Smith, and they had children: 1. Lucretia Eliza, born September 6, 1804; married Cyrus Eames; died at Green Bay, Wisconsin, September 21, 1844. 2. Hiram Adams, born at Springfield, Vermont, December 14, 1806; married, May 24, 1834, Persis Everett Hunking; died at Lancaster January 30, 1879. 3. Kimball Batchelder, born September 13, 1810; died at Lancaster November 4, 1894. 4. Mary Nassau, born February 28, 1813; married Archalaus Cummings; died at Colebrook in 1902. 5. Lucy Ann Jane, mentioned above. Mr.

Frederick Myron Colby.

Sincerely yours
George H Colby

and Mrs. Colby had children: 1. George Henry, see forward. 2. Charles Frederick, born July 14, 1846, at Colebrook; was a druggist at Lancaster; died November 17, 1902. 3. Frank Arthur, born at Colebrook November 4, 1852; a physician who served as staff surgeon in the Egyptian army in 1875; died at Berlin, New Hampshire, July 14, 1896. 4. John Irving, born December 24, 1856; was a drug clerk; died in Somerville, Massachusetts, June 17, 1904.

(III) George Henry, eldest child of Enoch Libby and Lucy Ann Jane (Fletcher) Colby, was born in Colebrook, New Hampshire, December 27, 1844. He received his education at the Colebrook and Lancaster academies, and learned the art of printing in the office of *The Coos Republican*, at Lancaster, and later with the Riverside Press, Cambridge, Massachusetts. Prior to going to Cambridge he had served one year as postal clerk in the store of Royal Joyslin, and three years with E. & T. Fairbanks & Company, at St. Johnsbury, Vermont; had failed in an attempt to establish himself in the book trade in Lancaster; and had read law for one year in the office of Ossian Ray, of Lancaster. He established *The Fairfield Chronicle* in May, 1869, a weekly newspaper published in Fairfield, Somerset county, Maine, which he managed as editor and sole proprietor for a period of ten years, and then disposed of it to a syndicate of Fairfield citizens. He then returned to Lancaster, and in the summer and fall of 1879 visited Europe, traveling extensively, and upon his return devoted six months to travel in the United States. He assumed charge of the mechanical department of three newspapers in July, 1880, owned by Thomas G. Thrumm, in Honolulu, Hawaiian Islands. One of these papers was *The Press*, a weekly newspaper of considerable influence among the business residents and planters, and which was founded for the purpose of advocating the annexation of the islands to the United States. When this object had been attained the paper suspended. *The Kukoa* was published in Kanaka, the native language of the islanders, and had a circulation of five thousand weekly. It exerted a great influence among the native population. *The Friend* was a monthly missionary journal, edited and owned by Father Damon. After nearly two years devoted to the newspaper and job printing business at Honolulu, Mr. Colby ascended the volcano of Kilauea, and traveled about the islands. He then visited Australia, and returning east in May, 1883, opened a book store in Lancaster, where he has been prosperously located for almost twenty-five years, thus making a splendid contrast to his failure in this direction in his earlier years. During this time he has made a trip to the island of Jamaica; spent a winter in Mexico; three times visited Europe; in 1906 traveled to Japan as the invited guest of Hon. H. W. Denison, the legal adviser of the Japan Foreign Office, and in that land spent a month in continuous travel. He returned in 1907, on his way visiting Siam, China, India and the Mediterranean, spending some time at Naples, and not omitting to visit Pompeii and Rome, thence home by Gibraltar and the Azores. Upon his return he delivered free lectures, by invitation, to about twenty audiences in the various towns of Coos and Grafton counties. Mr. Colby is a notable man of business, and carries about fifty thousand volumes in his stock, which is the largest number carried by any house of this kind in the state. He has been an intelligent observer during his travels, is an interesting writer, a lover of books, modest and unassuming in his manner, liberal in his views and tenacious of his convictions. He is a firm believer in public libraries and schools, and has done much to further the interests of these institutions. His religious views are those of the late Robert G. Ingersoll; he is an advocate of women's rights; and is a believer in cremation after death. He has been a lifelong Republican, of the Abolition type, but has never sought nor held public office. He is a member of Fairfield Lodge of Free and Accepted Masons, and of the Royal Arch Chapter of Oakland, Maine.

Mr. Colby married (first), July, 1867, Margaret Harrington, a Roman Catholic, of Littleton, New Hampshire, by whom he had a son who died in infancy. He married (second), in 1871, Mrs. Martha A. (Small) Gilmore, of Fairfield, Maine, who bore him two children, both of whom died in infancy. He married (third), October 2, 1884, Miss Julia Lizette Hastings, born November 18, 1842, daughter of Lambert and Maria (Holton) Hastings, of St. Johnsbury, Vermont. Mrs. Colby is a most estimable woman, and has been a fitting helpmate to her talented husband. She is a member of the Congregational Church in Lancaster. They have no children.

BURBANK There is a tradition that the family name Burbank is of ancient German origin, but whether much importance attaches to vague tradition of this character is questionable, although certain renditions of the name as discovered in old English records bore semblance and possible relation to the names known to be of German origin. In "Doomsday Book" the name Burbank is found just once in a list of ten thousand land owners in Great Britain, but that of Bowerbank, which is one of the various forms of expressing the name of some of the same family as the Burbanks, is found in several counties in England. It also appears as Borebancke, Bowbank and Burbancke, and some of these crossed the Atlantic with early immigrants and have found permanent lodgement in American nomenclature. It is believed, however, that the original of all these renditions is Bowerbank, a name well known both in England and in America, but it does not follow that the Burbanks and the Bowerbanks are in any way related; nor is the subject one of vital importance to the peace and well being of the American Burbanks who have been known in New England history for almost three centuries.

(I) John Burbank, the immigrant ancestor of a numerous progeny, settled in Rowley, Massachusetts, where he was made a freeman May 16, 1640, and was granted a house lot on Bradford street in 1643. The christian name of his (first) wife was Ann, and the second was named Jemima, but nothing appears to show the family name of either. The latter died March 24, 1693, having survived him nearly twelve years. He died 1681, "Aged and Decreped." His will was made April 5th of that year, and was probated on the tenth of the same month. In this instrument he mentions his wife, Jemima, sons John and Caleb, and daughter Lydia Foster. Three of his children, Timothy, Lydia and Mary, died young.

(II) Caleb, second son of John Burbank, was born May 19, 1646, in Rowley, Massachusetts, where he lived. The time of his death is approximated by the dates of executing and proving his will, which were February 15, 1688, and March 25, 1690. In it he mentions "my honored and aged mother."

He was married May 6, 1669, to Martha Smith, born February 5, 1648, daughter of Hugh and Mary Smith. She survived him and was married (second), July 3, 1695, to John Hardy, of Bradford. The children of Caleb Burbank were: Caleb, John, Mary, Timothy, Martha, Eleazer, Samuel and Ebenezer.

(III) Eleazer, fourth son and sixth child of Caleb and Martha (Smith) Burbank, was born March 14, 1682, in Rowley, and settled in Bradford, Massachusetts. The christian name of his wife is known to have been Lydia, although it appears in one place as Hannah in the Bradford records. She survived him and died June 26, 1771, in her eighty-seventh year. Their children were: Daniel, Eleazer, Caleb, Sarah, Nathan, Moses, Martha, John, Lydia, and Abraham. (Mention of Abraham and descendants appears in this article).

(IV) Moses, son of Eleazer and Lydia Burbank, of Bradford, was born February 6, 1717, in that town, and was one of the earliest settlers of Boscawen, New Hampshire. The year of his settlement was 1733, and after coming to the town he married Sarah Emery, believed to have been a sister of Edward Emery, the latter also being one of the pioneers of Boscawen. The children of Captain Moses and Sarah were: Moses, born June 26, 1741, married Sarah Danforth; Samuel, August, 1745, married Eunice Pettengill; Nathaniel, December 14, 1747, married Mary Durgin; Molly, February 22, 1749, married Cutting Noyes and lived in Boscawen; David, July 4, 1754, died November 4, 1815; Wells, August 8, 1756, and was a school teacher; Sarah, September, 1758, married Benjamin Blanchard; Betty, December 1, 1760, married Benjamin Bolter; Eleazer, January 19, 1763, married Abigail Burbank.

(V) David, fourth son and fifth child of Captain Moses and Sarah (Emery) Burbank, was born July 4, 1754, and died November 4, 1815. He built and lived in the parsonage on Boscawen plain, and removed from thence to Bashan, where he was a farmer, and still later to "Schoodic," in Warner, where he died. His first wife was Mary Little, daughter of Enoch Little, and by whom he had eight children. His second wife was Dorothy Lowell, who bore him two children. The children of David Burbank by both marriages were: Sarah, born February 9, 1779, married Moses Smith, of Salisbury, New Hampshire; Abigail, born March 20, 1780, died July 18, 1816; Abraham, born November 16, 1781, died January 14, 1856; Eliezer, born January 1, 1785, married Drusilla Flanders, of Boscawen; Little, born February 2, 1787, died November 17, 1870; Jesse, born June 13, 1790, died in the United States navy; Enoch, born July 20, 1793, moved to Michigan; Judith, born July 10, 1798, married Benjamin Carter of Boscawen.

(VI) Abraham, third child and eldest son of David and Mary (Little) Burbank, was born in Boscawen, New Hampshire, November 16, 1781. He learned the trade of blacksmith from his father, and carried on business with Jesse Little on Little hill. He was adept in making axes, giving them a shape and weight much preferred by woodchoppers and of such keen temper that "Abe Burbank's axes" were known all through the region and found ready sale with the merchants, much to the profit of the maker. He afterwards settled on a farm in Bashan and carried on lumbering. His operations in this direction became quite extensive, and at one time, in company with his son Friend, he had mills on Blackwater river, Knight's meadow and on Pond brook, and nearly every mill in Boscawen was at one time employed in sawing his lumber, which was rafter down the Merrimack river to Lowell and Boston markets. He was much respected by his fellow townsmen, and was repeatedly elected to represent them in the state legislature. He was a cheerful supporter of religious and charitable organizations, and always alive to every measure proposed for the public welfare. Abraham Burbank was twice married. His first wife was Mary Call, and his second Polly Jackman, daughter of Benjamin Jackman, of Boscawen. He had five children by his first and seven by his second marriage, viz: Friend Little, born June 29, 1806; Joanna Call, born March 5, 1808, died February 19, 1843; Mary Little, born November 16, 1809, married Woodman Jackman, of Boscawen; Sophronia Gerrish, born August 25, 1812, died February 22, 1847; Judith Call, born November 2, 1815, married J. Warren Jackman, and died November 21, 1847; George Washington, born June 29, 1819, died May 16, 1873; David Emory, born May 16, 1822; Bitfield Plummer, born March 1, 1824, died in California in 1860; Abraham Pettingill, born November 2, 1825, married Augusta Runnels, of Boscawen, and removed to California; Azro Sheridan, born August 29, 1827; Ezekiel Webster, born June 16, 1829, married (first) Martha A. Pillsbury, of Boscawen, (second), Emelie Hunkins, of Sanbornton, and died on the Mississippi river in 1863, during the civil war; Amanda Jane, born June 11, 1831, married Horatio N. Webber, of Boscawen.

(VII) Friend Little, eldest son and child of Abraham and Mary (Call) Burbank, was born in Boscawen, New Hampshire, January 29, 1806. His principal occupation in life was lumbering, which he began with his father and continued it long after the latter had passed from the field of business activity. He also took an earnest interest in town affairs, and was selectman in 1844, 1846 and 1848, and represented his town in the state legislature in 1852 and 1853. He married Dorothy Jackman, daughter of Joshua Jackman, of Boscawen, and had five children: Lucretia Little, born May 21, 1840, died August 10, 1861; William Wirt, born September 13, 1842; Joanna Clough, born June 22, 1846, died December 23, 1848; Irvin Abram, born April 18, 1854; Almon Friend, born October 17, 1857. (Irvin A. and descendants receive mention in this article).

(VIII) William Wirt, eldest son and second child of Friend L. and Dorothy (Jackman) Burbank, was born September 13, 1842, in that part of Boscawen which is now Webster. Beginning at the age of four years he attended the common schools of his native town, and afterwards studied at Elmwood Literary Institute. In 1865 he became partner in the lumber business with his father, the firm name being F. L. Burbank & Son. After a period of fifteen years this connection was dissolved in 1880, and he continued business alone two years, after which time he formed a partnership with his brother Irvin A., and since that time the firm of Burbank Brothers has continued business and has engaged quite extensively in the manufacture of boxes and other enterprises connected with lumbering business in their district. Mr. Burbank is a man of much executive ability, and is ready in grasping opportunities and pushing business advancement. He was one of the originators of the Kearsarge Telephone Company, and has been its president since its incorporation. For more than a quarter of a century he has served as one of the directors of the Merrimack County Fire Insurance Company. Mr. Burbank is a courteous gentleman, and his ability and integrity have led them to select him for many important official positions. For fifteen years he was selectman of the town, was moderator twelve years, town treasurer three years, and representative in the state legislature in 1881. He is a steadfast and straightforward Republican in politics. He joined the First Congregational Church of Webster in 1858, and has been superintendent of its Sunday school for thirteen years, and clerk of the church since 1895. He has for many years been a member of Harris Lodge, No. 91, Ancient Free and Accepted Masons of Warner, New Hampshire, and is a past master of that body. He is a charter member of the Daniel Webster Grange, and was its first master, serving five years in that position, and has also filled the lecturer's chair. He is a charter member of Merrimack County Pomona Grange, and a past master of that body. He was president of the New Hampshire Grange Fair Association two years, and was four years superintendent of its fair.

Mr. Burbank was married, September 26, 1865, in Penacook (then Fisherville), to Ellen Maria Dow, daughter of Enoch Hoyt and Judith Walker (Chandler) Dow, of Concord. Judith W. Chandler was a daughter of Captain John (5) Chandler, (See Chandler VII, Rolfe VIII, and Hoyt V). Mr. Dow was a selectman of that town in 1837 and 1840, and was captain in the Third Infantry Militia from February, 1832, to February 19, 1835. He was engaged in the lumber business. He was a son of Moody and Joanna (Hoyt) Dow. Moody was a son of Ebenezer and Elizabeth (Wilson) Dow, and Ebenezer was a son of John and Elizabeth (Moody) Dow. Mrs. Burbank was educated in the schools of Concord, and Elmwood Literary Institute at Boscawen. She is the mother of four daughters, all born in Webster. Ellen Lucrecia, the eldest, was educated at Penacook Academy, the high school at Warner, and the New England Conservatory of Music in Boston. She is the wife of Samuel Howard Bell, a pharmacist of West Derry; Sarah Chandler, the second, died in her twenty-third year; Alice Mabel was educated at Pembroke Academy and Wellesley College and became the wife of William Bradford Ranney, now residing in Penacook; Annie Florence, the youngest, was educated at the Concord High School, Framingham Normal School and the Teachers' College of New York City, and is head of the household science department at Northfield Seminary, Northfield, Massachusetts.

(VIII) Irvin Abram, second son and fourth child of Friend Little and Dorothy (Jackman) Burbank, was born in the town of Boscawen, New Hampshire, April 18, 1854, and for the last thirty and more years has been engaged in active business pursuits. His early life was spent at home, and he was given a good education in the town schools and the academies at Warner and Penacook. After leaving school he began work with his father and older brother in their lumbering and milling enterprises, anl in 1882 he became partner with his brother in the same line. This partnership has continued to the present time, and the members of the firm are numbered among the prosperous and substantial business men of northern Merrimack county. Mr. Burbank is always a busy man, but has found time to devote to public affairs in his home town, having served in various offices of a political character, and represented the town of Webster in the state legislature in 1903. He is a Republican in politics, attends the Congregational Church, is trustee of the Webster Public Library, and member of the order of Free and Accepted Masons. He married, October 24, 1883, Ellen A. Little, who was born August 19, 1863, a daughter of Sherman and Mary A. (Austin) Little (see Little VII) of Webster, New Hampshire. Mr. and Mrs. Burbank have three children: Lucretia L., born December 15, 1884; Henry Irvin, born January 6, 1886; Ray C., born December 31, 1887.

(IV) Abraham, youngest child of Eleazer and Lydia Burbank, was born November 18, 1727, in Bradford, Massachusetts, and died there September 9, 1775, in his forty-eighth year. He was married April 25, 1753, to Abigail, daughter of Robert and Rebecca Savory. She was born April 1, 1733, and died less than a month after her husband, October 6, 1775, in her forty-fourth year. The records of Bradford show only two children, Eliphalet and Abigail.

(V) Captain Eliphalet, son of Abraham and Abigail (Savory) Burbank, was born June 22, 1760, in Bradford, Massachusetts, and passed his life in that town. He was married in January, 1781, to Susanna, daughter of Jedediah and Sarah (Stickney) Barker. She was born December 21, 1763. No record of either appears. Their children were: Sarah, Abraham, Abigail, Jedediah, Susanna, Eliphalet, John and Barker.

(VI) Barker, youngest son of Captain Eliphalet and Susanna (Barker) Burbank, was born in Bradford, Massachusetts, September 8, 1795, and died December 23, 1867. He settled in Shelburne, New Hampshire, where he had a large farm, and was for many years the most prominent man in all that region. He was a practical farmer, a successful merchant, and a lawyer of considerable ability. His dwelling was a large two-story house erected by him about 1840, which, now somewhat modernized, stands in the center of an ampitheatre of rare and peculiar beauty. He married Polly Ingalls, daughter of Fletcher and Mercy (Lary) Ingalls, and raised a family of fourteen children: Mercy Ingalls, Robert Ingalls, Mary Ann, Emerline, Alcander, Sarah F., Martin L., Deborah C., Edward P., Barker L., Parker C., Buchanan B., Helen and Helen Mar.

(VII) Edward Payson, son of Barker and Polly (Ingalls) Burbank, was born in Shelburne, January 14, 1832. He was a prosperous farmer and resided in Shelburne until a few years ago, when he moved to Gorham, New Hampshire, where he now lives in retirement and comfort. He held all the principal town offices except that of treasurer, and served two terms in the legislature. He married Mary Smith, who was born August 22, 1834, and who was the daughter of Potter and Sarah Smith of Shelburne, New Hampshire. They had six children: Edward Adelbert, Elmer Ellsworth, Nelson F., Abraham Lincoln, Sarah Myrtilla, and Barker L.

(VIII) Edward Adelbert, eldest child of Edward Payson and Mary (Smith) Burbank, was born in Shelburne, New Hampshire, August 30, 1859. He was educated in the public schools of Lewiston, Maine, which he left at the age of sixteen years and began to learn the trade of tinsmith. In 1881 he became a journeyman tinsmith and then removed to Richmond, Maine, where he worked till 1883, and then he moved to Bethel, Maine, and then to South Paris, Maine, then to Mansfield, Pennsylvania, where he was in business two years; then to Port Chester, New York, two years; Gorham, New Hampshire, one year, and in 1888 settled in Berlin, New Hampshire, where he has since resided. He had charge of the plumbing and heating department of Hodgdon & Crowell works until 1901, and then he formed a partnership with Lyman U. Cole, under the firm name of Burbank & Cole, and engaged in the hardware business. In 1902 he bought his partner's interest, and since then the firm name has been the Burbank Company, with Mr. Burbank at the head of the business. He has been a prosperous business man, and he is a stockholder in the City National Bank of Berlin. His place of business was burned at the time of the Clement Opera House fire, January 4, 1905, and he lost a large amount, but he got to work at once and secured new quarters and was able to hold his business. A little later he bought out one of the older business houses, which gave him additional trade. He never was much interested in politics, but devoted much of his spare time to secret societies, holding high offices in several. He is a member and a past grand of Berlin Lodge, No. 89, Independent Order of Odd Fellows, and was for several years secretary. He served as district deputy grand master for Coos district, and was instrumental in forming Berlin Encampment, No. 35, Independent Order Odd Fellows, and was the first chief patriarch and was afterward appointed district deputy grand patriarch. He mustered Canton City of Berlin No. 19, Patriarchs Militant, Independent Order Odd Fellows, and was elected the first captain. He was afterward appointed bannerett on staff of the department commander, serving in that capacity for six years. He assisted in forming Maida Rebekah Lodge, No. 75, Independent Order Odd Fellows, and was voted the Decoration of Chivalry by the department council for his services in the cause of Odd-fellowship, being the first voted to any chevalier in the state. He was charter member of and assisted in forming many other orders and held high offices in each. He belonged to the Knights of the Maccabees, Royal Arcanum, Red Men, Uniform Order Pilgrim Fathers, Golden Cross, and Independent Order of Foresters, and was a past chief ranger and deputy supreme chief ranger for several years. He formed the New Hampshire Brigade of Royal Foresters, and was their first brigadier-general. He represented the state of New Hampshire at the dedication of the Foresters Temple at Toronto in 1896. He was the first captain of Mt. Washington Division No. 1, Knights of the Maccabees, and for several years was organizer for Maine and New Hampshire of the Uniform Rank Knights of the Maccabees. He is a member of Industry Lodge, No. 2, Knights of Pythias, of Lewiston, Maine, and was a charter member of Starr King Commandery, No. 21, Lancaster, New Hampshire, Uniform Rank Knights of Pythias, and got a discharge to become a charter member of Androscoggin Commandery, No. 28, Uniform Rank Knights of Pythias, at Berlin, and was elected second lieutenant; shortly after being elected was appointed battalion adjutant of the Third Battalion, second regiment of the New Hampshire Brigade. He was a charter member of Berlin Lodge, No. 618, Benevolent Protective Order of Elks, and its second exalted ruler, and was elected as delegate to the national convention at Salt Lake City. He was a member and past master of Sabatis Lodge, No. 95, Ancient Free and Accepted Masons, of Berlin, New Hampshire, a member and past patron of Starr King Chapter, No. 32, Order Eastern Star, a member of North Star Royal Arcanum Chapter of Lancaster, New Hampshire; Evening Star Council, Royal and Select Masters, of Colebrook, New Hampshire; Edward A. Raymond Consistory, thirty-second degree, Sublime Princes of the Royal Secret, of Nashua: Bektash Temple, Ancient Arabic Order Nobles of the Mystic Shrine, Concord. He is also a member of the Sons of the American Revolution, gaining that privilege from Captain Eliphalet Burbank, who served in the Continental army. He married, February 13, 1880, Minnie G. Dingley, of Lewiston, Maine, who was born July 19, 1859, in Lawrence, Massachusetts. She was the daughter of George and Carrie (Black) Dingley, of Lawrence, Massachusetts, and a distant relative of Governor Nelson Dingley, of Maine. They have three children: Arthur F., Eva G. and Lester H.

LANE This name is of the class called locative surnames, that is, those showing where the person lived, "John atte Lane," "William at Lane," are often found in English records of four hundred years ago, and show that the person named lived in a narrow street. Lane is of English origin, but for hundreds of years has been found in all four quarters of Great Britain.

Among the early settlers of New England there were at least a dozen named Lane. There is a tradition that William Lane of Boston had two brothers, cordwainers in Beverly, or Gloucester, Massachusetts, and in Maine, were nephews of William Lane, of Dorchester, Massachusetts, who in 1635 came from Norfolk county, England, whose two adult sons, Andrew and George, settled in Hingham, Massachusetts. The Lane family of this article is notable for the number and local prominence of its members in military affairs, three generations having been captains in the revolutionary war. Since the revolutionary period the Lanes have been equally prominent in the pursuit of peaceful occupations.

(I) William Lane, referred to above as of Hingham, was probably an old man when he came to this country with his sons, and is found at Dorchester as early as 1635. In 1637 he received several grants of land there amounting in all to eight acres. He was among the seventy-one accepted inhabitants of the town in 1641, and on December 7 of that year he relinquishel his grant to Thompson's Island for the purpose of a public school. The first public school in America was established at Dorchester, in 1639, and William Lane with others relinquished their grants on Thompson's Island that it might be devoted to school purposes. He was evidently a man of means and a very good citizen who enjoyed the esteem of his fellows. His last years were spent in the home of his daughter Mary, who was the widow of Joseph Long, and he died in 1658. His will was dated December 28, 1650. The inventory amounted to £82, 10 shillings and 8½ pence, and the daughter was made residuary legatee after paying bequests of £32. His children were Elizabeth, Mary, Annis, George, Sarah and Andrew.

(II) George, elder son of William Lane, was born in England, and was one of the early planters of Hingham, Massachusetts. He was among the thirty proprietors of that town, and on September 18, 1635, drew his house lot of five acres, situated on the main street, which is now North street. His lot is described as "No. 21, from the cove on the north side of the road to Fort Hill." In the next three divisions his land was increased to twenty acres besides thirteen acres in the common lands. He was a shoemaker by trade, and was evidently prominent in the community as shown by his rating of six pounds, six shillings and eight pence for the building of the new meeting house, which rate was laid October 9, 1680. Upon the assignment of seats in the new building he was assigned to "seate under ye pulpit" and his wife to a "sitting in the fore seate for the women in the body

Chester L. Lane

of the meeting house." He died June 11, 1688, and was survived nearly eight years by his widow, who passed away March 26, 1695. She was Sarah, daughter of Walter and Mary (Frye) Harris, and died in Dorchester, Massachusetts. Walter Harris came to America in 1632, and was about twenty years at Weymouth, Massachusetts, and died in Dorchester, November 6, 1654. He was survived by his widow less than three months. The children of George and Sarah Lane were baptized in Hingham, namely: Sarah, Hannah, Josiah, Susanna, Elizabeth, John, Ebenezer, Mary and Peter.

(III) John, second son and fifth child of George and Sarah (Harris) Lane, was born January 20, 1648, in Hingham. He was known in that town as "John Lane, shoemaker," to distinguish him from John Lane, carpenter, of the same town. He served as constable of Hingham in 1689. About 1694 he removed to Norton, Massachusetts, and settled on the boundary between that town and Attleboro. It is apparent that he owned land in Attleboro, as he was taxed one pound for the town debt, there in 1696, and was chosen grand juryman March 22, 1697. In 1710 he was rated in Norton for building the first meeting house, and was on a committee in 1711 to secure the incorporation of the precinct of Norton. He died in that town November 23, 1712. His gravestone gives his age as sixty-two years, which would make him born about 1650. He was married (first), June 18, 1674, to Mehitable, daughter of Jonathan and Jane Hobart. She was born in Hingham, July 4, 1651, and baptized when two weeks old. She was seated January 5, 1682, "in the fift seate next ye pew of the wife of John Lane, shoemaker." She died February 15, 1690, in Hingham, in her thirty-ninth year. John Lane married (second), about 1693, Sarah Briggs, who was admitted to the church in Norton, on profession of faith in 1718, and died November 12, 1727, aged eighty-three years. John Lane's children are recorded in Hingham, Rehoboth, Attleboro and Norton; baptisms are in the Rehoboth church records. By his first wife there were: Samuel, Priscilla, Mary, Asa, and a child who was drowned September 16, 1692. By Sarah Briggs he had Ephraim, John, Benjamin, Sarah, Meletiah and Elizabeth.

(IV) Ephraim, sixth child of John Lane and eldest child of his second wife, Sarah, was born June 24, 1694, in Rehoboth. He was admitted to full communion with the church in Norton, in 1715, and was tithingman in 1719. He was married, January 10, 1717, to Ruth "Shepperson," who united with the church in Norton, in 1718. She was a daughter of John and Eliza Shepherdson, of Attleboro, Massachusetts. They have many descendants in Norton and vicinity. Their children were: Ephraim, Elkanah, Ruth (died in infancy), Ruth, Jonathan, Abigail and Samuel.

(V) Elkanah, second son and child of Ephraim and Ruth (Shepherdson) Lane, was born April 1, 1719, in Norton, and was baptized on the thirtieth of the November following. He removed with his two sons and daughter to Swanzey, New Hampshire, previous to the Revolution. There he joined the Minute Men under Captain Joseph Hammond, April 21, 1775, and marched at sunrise, April 25, for Concord and Lexington, Massachusetts. The town paid him for fifteen days' service at Cambridge, Massachusetts, and for five days in the militia at another time, one pound, nine shillings and three pence. He was a member of the committee of correspondence and inspection for Swanzey, under the Continental Congress. He was selectman of Swanzey in 1785, and as such certified on June 11 that James Green was wounded at the battle of Bunker Hill and was worthy of attention from the general court. Mr. Lane died in Swanzey, December 6, 1811, in his ninety-third year. He was married June 10, 1742, by Rev. Joseph Avery, to Hannah Tingley, of Attleboro, Massachusetts, who died September 15, 1772, aged fifty-two years. Their children were born in Norton, namely: Hannah, Elkanah, Luke, Ruth, Samuel and Abigail.

(VI) Samuel, third son and fifth child of Elkanah and Hannah (Tingley) Lane, was born January 9, 1759, in Norton, Massachusetts, and removed with his father to Swanzey, New Hampshire. He was a Revolutionary soldier and marched to Ticonderoga, October 21, 1776, and served until November 16, a period of twenty-six days. He was then about seventeen years old. He was among those mustered at Walpole, New Hampshire, in May, 1777, being then eighteen years old, and enlisted in June in Grigg's company, Alexander Scammel's regiment, Continental troops, June 4, 1777. After this service he received the town's bounty of ten pounds, sixteen shillings and eight pence. He was selectman of Swanzey in 1792. He was married, June 15, 1785, to Eunice, daughter of Elisha Scott. She was born June 15, 1766, and died November 28, 1825. Mr. Lane lived for a time in Winchendon, Massachusetts, and removed thence to Northfield in that state in 1807. He died January 26, 1845. His children were: Samuel, Elijah, Elisha, Ezekiel, Luther and Lucy. (Ezekiel and children are mentioned in this article).

(VII) Elijah, second son and child of Samuel and Eunice (Scott) Lane, was born October 2, 1788, in Swanzey, twin of Elisha. Both lived and reared families. He was a member of the Congregational Society of Swanzey from December 26, 1809, and resided in that town. He died there May 16, 1851. He was married, January 29, 1815, to Fanny Scott, of Winchester, who died March 14, 1871. Their children were: Maria P., Luther Scott, Elliott W., Fanny F., Ebenezer F. and Eunice F.

(VIII) Ebenezer Frink, third son and fifth child of Elijah and Fanny (Scott) Lane, was born November 20, 1824, in Swanzey, and lived on the same farm in that town for thirty-five years. He was married August 14, 1850, to Hannah Porter, daughter of Chester Lyman, who was commissioned captain in the war of 1812 by James Madison, president. She was born May 21, 1829, and died May 22, 1886. Their children were: Henry C., Edgar W., Hattie M., Chester L. and Maria F.

(IX) Chester Lyman, third son and fourth child of Ebenezer F. and Hannah Porter (Lyman) Lane, was born April 9, 1857, in the family homestead in West Swanzey. He was educated in the public schools of the town and early took employment in the pail factory of George F. Lane & Son, where he continued for ten or twelve years. He purchased a farm on the border of East Swanzey village, where he now resides, and is numbered among the successful farmers of the town. He also engaged in the lumber business, and in 1900 with George Whitcomb and Levi Fuller purchased the pail and bucket factory in East Swanzey, in which he had been employed as a boy and young man. He has been active in conducting the town affairs and served for several years efficiently as road agent. He has served as selectman and was representative in the state legislature in 1903-04, serving on the insurance committee. He is a member of the Grange, of the Knights of the Golden Cross, is a member of Monadnock Lodge, No. 8, Free and Accepted Masons; Cheshire Chapter, Royal and Select Masters; and Hugh DePayen Commandery, Knights Templar. He was married, September 27, 1879, to Emma Florence, daughter of Nathan and Emily B. (Harris) Newell. She was born January 30, 1862, in Bloomington, Illinois, and is the mother of the following children: Ralph Waldo, Florence S. (deceased), Zora Alice, Lora Agnes, Chester E., Earl N., Raymond L. and Kenneth P.

(VII) Ezekiel, fourth son and child of Samuel and Eunice (Scott) Lane, was born September 28, 1790, in Swanzey. He was one of the most prosperous agriculturists of Swanzey, and his farm of three hundred and fifty acres was located some three miles east of Swanzey Centre. His interest in local public affairs, as well as in all other matters relative to the general welfare of the town, was frequently emphasized, and his citizenship was of a character well worthy of emulation. In politics he was a whig. He died May 16, 1851. On February 3, 1814, he married Rachel Thayer Fish, who was born in Swanzey, July 27, 1796, daughter of Farnham Fish. They were the parents of Farnham Fish, born March 15, 1816; George Farrington, February 21, 1818; Alonzo Franklin, December 28, 1819; Ezekiel Francis, April 27, 1823; Elisha Frederick, who will receive further mention presently; Alpheus Ferdinand, July 3, 1828; Ezra Fish, December 14, 1830; Rachel Caroline, April 1, 1833, married (first), Alonzo Mason, and (second), J. Woodward; Nathaniel Fayette, February 21, 1839, was killed in the Civil war; and Sarah Josephine, January 8, 1842, became the wife of Adoniram Judson Van Armun, of Hartford, Vermont, June 8, 1862. The two first born of this family died in infancy, and the mother of these children died in Keene, May 17, 1880.

(VIII) Elisha Frederick, seventh son and child of Ezekiel and Rachel Thayer (Fish) Lane, was born in Swanzey, April 29, 1826. Having acquired a good education, which was concluded in Hancock, New Hampshire, he was for some time engaged in educational pursuits, teaching schools in Warwick, Massachusetts, Swanzey Factory and East Swanzey. In 1849 he became associated with his brothers Alpheus F. and Ezra F. in purchasing and operating a mill privilege in Marlboro, this state, and for a period of seven years was engaged in the manufacture of wooden-ware. In 1857 he was appointed deputy sheriff, and two years later established his residence in Keene. In 1861 he was named by the secretary of the treasury, Salmon P. Chase, as United States assessor, retaining that office for two years, when he was advanced to the responsible post of deputy collector for Cheshire county and continued as such until the war taxes were abolished. In 1870 he was elected sheriff of Cheshire county, in which capacity he served with unquestionable energy and fidelity for three years, or until the successful predominance at the polls of the opposing political party. He then became interested in railway enterprises, manufacturing industries and the development of real estate. He was one of the promoters of the Ashuelot railroad, after it had passed into the hands of a trustee, retaining his shares in that corporation long after its sale to the Connecticut River Railroad Company, and was a director and treasurer of the first-named company, the Connecticut River, Vermont Valley and Sullivan County railways. When the Connecticut River road was absorbed by the Boston and Maine system he disposed of his interests in railway enterprises. He has erected two large business blocks in Keene, which bear his name, and has a third building of a similar character in process of construction. He is president of and principal stockholder in the Lancaster Shoe Company (incorporated), has been a director of the Keene National Bank for the past forty years, of which he served as president, and in various other ways has actively participated in forwarding the business interests of Keene. Mr. Lane's contributions to the substantial growth and development of Keene have not been confined to his numerous personal building operations. He was an especially active factor in causing the erection of the Young Men's Christian Association building (and the payment of its debt); the museum, and indeed the best part of the business portion of Keene was built under the impetus of his wise judgment and knowledge. Politically he is a Republican. He is an advanced Mason, being a member of the Blue Lodge, Chapter, Council and Commandery. As a member of the First Congregational Church he is prominently identified with religious work, and was largely instrumental in organizing the local Young Men's Christian Association. In concluding this brief outline of Mr. Lane's busy and successful life it is both just and proper to add that his high personal character, public-spirited generosity and long continued interest in behalf of the welfare and prosperity of Keene, have won the genuine admiration and esteem of his fellow citizens, and although he has reached the venerable period of an octogenarian, it is their sincere hope that his removal from their midst may prove to be an occurrence far remote from the present.

On March 15, 1849, Mr. Lane married Susan M. Fish, who died March 31, 1867, and September 15 of the following year he married for his second wife Harriet P. Wilder, whose birth took place in Keene, April 4, 1836. Hubert E., the only child of his first union, was born March 19, 1854. The children of his second marriage are: Henry W., born April 2, 1871; Susanna Grace, born September 15, 1876; and Harriet M., born July 6, 1879. The family homestead, which occupies a most desirable location on lower Main street, possesses considerable historic interest, as it is the original site of the first meeting house ever erected in Cheshire county.

(Second Family.)

LANE

(I) William Lane, above referred to as of Boston, the earliest of this line of whom we have record, was a cordwainer of Boston in 1650. His first wife was Mary, who had four children: Samuel (died young), Samuel, John and Mary. His second wife was Mary Brewer, and she had four children: Sarah, William, Elizabeth and Ebenezer. (William and descendants are noticed in this article).

(II) Captain John, son of William and Mary Lane, was born in Boston, February 5, 1654. In 1674 John Lane was a cordwainer in Boston. In March, 1675, when twenty-two years old, he was a soldier in King Philip's war, in the same company where his brother Samuel served under Captain Poole. There is no further trace of this John Lane, unless he is the John Lane who lived a while in Hampton and then became Captain John Lane, of York county, Maine. In November, 1692, when he married in Newbury, Massachusetts, he was Mr. John Lane. Ten years later he is called Captain John Lane, and so afterwards. In 1699, December 10, John Lane of Newbury, gave a deed of land to John Frost, of the Isle of Shoals. About 1708 "Captain Lane is mentioned among the brave men of the garrison." He afterwards served as captain

E. F. Lane

The Lewis Publishing Co

EUGENE LANE.

in the province of Maine, and in 1717 was commander at Fort Mary, Winter Harbor, near Biddeford, at the mouth of Saco river, where he died and was buried about 1720. John Lane married, November, 1693, Johannah Davinson, and by her had: Abigail, John and Mary, and probably Jabez and other children.

(III) Captain John (2), son of Captain John (1) and Joanna (Davinson) Lane, was born in Hampton, March 1, 1702. He entered the military service early under his father, was a lieutenant, and at the death of his father became captain. He served in various places in Maine, and became famous in fighting the Indians. In a report to Lieutenant Governor Dummer, dated York, 21 April, 1724, Colonel Thomas Westbrook says with regret, that "Lieutenant John Lane has been so imprudent as to suffer his men to kill sundry creatures belonging to the people of the County of York. He did not deny the fact, and made satisfaction to the people." He lived at York, Biddeford, Broad Bay, St. George, etc. In the French war, which commenced in 1744, the Indians burned his house, and "he enlisted a company under Colonel Harmon and met them in battle at Norridgewock." "When the province granted bounties for scalps he was out all the winter of 1744-45, after the St. Johns Indians." He was captain of a company in the expedition against Louisburg under Sir William Pepperill, and after the surrender was mustered out in June, 1745. He was soon after taken sick, sent to Boston, and was unable to serve again till April, 1746, when he was given command of a company on the eastern frontier, but he suffered a relapse and did not recover for many months, being at his home in York with his wife and three small children, suffering from sickness and poverty, so that in February, 1748, he received seven pounds from the general court, and again in April, 1749, the legislature voted five pounds for his relief, and on December 7, 1749, four pounds. In the next war against the French and Indians he was at Boston in April, 1758, with a company of Biddeford men, and served in the expedition against Crown Point. But a return of this company, dated October 11, 1756, reports Captain John Lane Sr. as dead, and the command as devolving on his son, John Lane Jr. It is supposed that he died in the service of his country, at the age of fifty-four, and was buried not far from Crown Point, Essex county, New York. He married, about 1733, Mary, daughter of Peter Nowell, of York, Maine, and had five children: John, Henry, Joanna, Daniel, and Jabez. His three sons, John, Daniel and Jabez, were "splendid looking men, possessed of great physical powers and personal bravery. They inherited the military spirit of their father, and each of them became a captain in the revolutionary war."

(IV) Captain Jabez, fifth child and fourth son of Captain John and Mary (Nowell) Lane, was born in Wiscasset, Maine, September 21, 1743, and died at Buxton, April 30, 1830. He resided in Buxton, one mile from the Lower Corner, on a farm, and was often engaged in "lumber operations." His name in 1754 appears on the roll of his father's company as "a son under age, not twelve years." The muster roll of Captain Jabez Lane's company is dated January 1, 1777, and he served through most of the revolutionary war. In early youth his taste for military affairs was cultivated in the company where his father commanded at Crown Point, where his eldest brother John was lieutenant, at the age of twenty, and his brother Daniel a private at the age of sixteen. Colonel Isaac Lane once met a southern gentleman in Washington City, who said that his father, an officer in the revolutionary army at the south, once fought a duel with a Captain Lane from the east. That "it was at a dinner given by the officers; that when they had become excited over their wine, his father said something derogatory to the Yankees, and Captain Lane slapped him in the face, and a challenge followed. Captain Lane was wounded in the side, and his father in the leg." Colonel Isaac concluded that if it was either of the three Buxton captains, it must have been Captain Jabez, for neither of the others would have kept it secret for so long. After his return to Maine, one Saturday afternoon, when Captain Jabez and "a goodly number of citizens were met at his store, drinking rum and molasses, telling stories, swapping horses, and so forth, Colonel Isaac related the story of the duel. Captain Jabez, at the close of the story, removed his clothes and showed a scar, left by the wound, on his side." He was a quiet man and remained on the farm where he settled in 1772, until his death. He married, August 27, 1772, Sarah, daughter of Joshua Woodman, who died March 11, 1825. They had ten children: Samuel, Jabez, Polly, Joshua, John, Captain Stephen W., Mehitable M., Rufus K., Silas Nowell, and James.

(V) Joshua, fourth child and third son of Captain Jabez and Sarah (Woodman) Lane, was born June 5, 1782; and died October 5, 1860, at Waterboro, Maine. He was a farmer and resided at Buxton. He married, October 21, 1799, Elizabeth, daughter of Jonathan and Priscilla (Davis) Rinnery, of Buxton, born November 28, 1780, who died April 28, 1846. They had ten children: Sarah W., Alvin Bacon, Rufus K., Priscilla Ann, Henry J., Joshua C., Jonathan R., Mary R., Amanda Elizabeth and Jonathan R.

(VI) Joshua Charles, fourth son and sixth child of Joshua and Elizabeth (Runnery) Lane, was born at Buxton, Maine, August 4, 1823. He has been long a resident of Limerick, where he has been a merchant, banker, and influential citizen. He was treasurer of the Savings Bank at Limerick for twenty-three years, and of the Limerick National Bank for seventeen years. He is a Democrat, and has taken a lively interest in politics, having filled the offices of selectman, representative in the state legislature, delegate to the National Convention in 1894, etc. He was trustee of the Phillips Limerick Academy, and president of the board of trustees. He is a Universalist, a member of the Masonic fraternity and of the Odd Fellows. He married, 1849, Martha A. Staples, born in Limington, 1826, died in Limerick in 1903. They adopted two children: Eugene, born in Limerick, December 25, 1856, and Alice M., born in 1870.

(VII) Eugene, adopted son of Joshua C. and Martha A. (Staples) Lane, was born in Limerick, Maine, December 25, 1856, and educated in the common schools and Limerick Academy. At the age of fifteen he went to Augusta, where he learned the printer's trade in the office of the *Gospel Banner*. Two years later he had so fully mastered the details of the business that he was placed in charge of the *Banner's* entire printing establishment, which at that time was the largest Universalist denomination and book publishing house in the country. This place he filled four years, and then engaged in newspaper work at Limerick and Cornish, Maine.

Mr. Lane came to Suncook in 1881 and entered the newspaper field. In April, 1883, he came into possession of the *Suncook Journal*, and with commendable enterprise and energy endeavored to give the community a sprightly, newsy, weekly paper, and meet promptly the demands of the public for job work. To furnish greater facilities for increasing business, he added a cylinder press in 1884. He conducted this paper till October, 1894, when he sold the plant and it was removed from the town. Mr. Lane has contributed to other papers in the state, and for several years was the local representative of the Associated Press. He was appointed postmaster at Suncook in 1898, and served in that office four years. In politics he is a Republican, and for twenty-two years past has been a member of the town council, serving all that time as its clerk. He has served two terms as town clerk, and in 1893-94 represented Pembroke in the New Hampshire legislature. He married, May 17, 1883, Meta G. Gault, daughter of Andrew and Abby (Davis) Gault, of Pembroke, born January 5, 1860. They have had three children: Dean G., born February 20, 1884, died August, 1884. Hazel, born May 2, 1889, died June 17, 1906, and Gladys, born October 29, 1891.

(II) William (2), second child and eldest son of William (1) and Mary (Brewer) Lane, born October 1, 1659, was a tailor by trade. He joined the North Church, Boston, in 1681, and in 1686 removed to Hampton, New Hampshire, where he settled on a grant of ten acres. He built a one-story house near the meeting house and the spot where the old academy stood. He is said to have been "a devout and godly man," living a quiet and humble life, respected by those who knew him. He died at the home of his son Joshua, February 14, 1749, aged about ninety years. He married, June 21, 1680, Sarah, daughter of Thomas and Sarah (Brewer) Webster, born January 22, 1661, died January 6, 1745, aged eighty-five years, and they had seven children: John, Sarah, Elizabeth, Abigail, Joshua, Samuel, and Thomas.

(III) Deacon Joshua, fifth child and second son of William (2) and Sarah (Webster) Lane, was born June 6, 1696, and was killed while standing on his door-step after a shower, June 14, 1766, aged seventy years. He and his wife joined the church in Hampton, March 10, 1718. Here he resided on a farm on the road to North Hampton, one-half mile north of the present railroad station, and carried on the trade of tanner and shoemaker. He married, December 24, 1717, Bathsheba, daughter of Samuel and Mary Robie, born August 2, 1696, Old Style, died April 13, 1765. They had sixteen children, eight sons and five daughters of whom lived to become useful members of society. He had sixty grandchildren before his death. His children were: Deacon Samuel, Mary, Joshua (died young), William, Joshua, Josiah (died young), Major John, Sarah, Bathsheba, Isaiah, Deacon Jeremiah, Ebenezer, Abigail, Elizabeth, Josiah and Anna. (Mention of Joshua, John and Jeremiah and descendants occurs in later paragraphs of this article).

(IV) Deacon William, third son and fourth child of Deacon Joshua and Bathsheba (Robie) Lane, was born January 1, 1723, and baptized on the tenth of the following February, in Hampton. He was a tanner and shoemaker by occupation, and his estate continued in the family for many years, being occupied in very recent years by his great grandson. He died December 20, 1802, but a few days short of eighty years of age. He was married, February 13, 1746, to Rachel, daughter of Thomas and Rachel (Sanborn) Ward, of Hampton. Their children were: Noah (died young), Abigail, Ward, William, Noah, Thomas and Jeremiah. (Noah and descendants are noticed in this article).

(V) Ward, second son and third child of Deacon William and Rachel (Ward) Lane, was born June 1, 1751, in Hampton, and died there June 24, 1837. He was also a shoemaker, and settled on the North Hampton road. His house was standing until the latter part of the past century. He was married, April 28, 1774, to Mehitable, daughter of Samuel and Abigail (Towle) Fogg, of Hampton. She was born July 13, 1755, and died August 21, 1839. Their children were: Abigail, Samuel Fogg, Rachel, Daniel Ward, Dearborn, Thomas, Mary, William, Anna and John.

(VI) Daniel Ward, second son and fourth child of Deacon Ward and Mehitable (Fogg) Lane, was born March 7, 1780, and died July 4, 1865, in Hampton. He was a farmer by occupation, and was succeeded by his youngest son, who was still living in recent years. He married Lydia, daughter of Josiah and Hannah (Towle) Towle, of Hampton. She was born April 3, 1783, and died December 18, 1849. Their children were: Joseph Stacey (died young), Oliver (died young), Joseph Stacey, Asa, Thomas, Shuabel, Sarah, and Oliver.

(VII) Oliver, youngest child of Daniel Ward and Lydia (Fogg) Lane, was born January 14, 1828, in Hampton, where he died. He was a blacksmith by trade, and was employed many years on the railroad. He married Sarah A., daughter of Sewall and Nancy (Blake) Brown. She was born August 26, 1830, and died September 2, 1891. Their children were: Mary Abbie, Lydia Ann, Julia Etta, Sarah Augusta, Lizzie Florence and Nellie Gertrude.

(VIII) Sarah Augusta, fourth daughter of Oliver and Sarah A. (Brown) Lane, was born January 22, 1860, in Hampton, and was married July 23, 1887, to Walter E. Darrah, of Concord (see Darrah, V).

(V) Deacon Noah, fourth son and sixth child of William and Rachel (Ward) Lane, was born in Hampton, January 30, 1756 or '57. He settled upon a farm in Deerfield, where he became closely identified with the Congregational Church, and was for many years a deacon. He married Mehitable Burnham, who died in 1846, aged ninety-one years. The twelve children of this union were: Molly, Lieutenant Edmund Churchill, William, Sarah, Rachel, Thomas Robie, Noah, Simeon and Levi (twins), Joshua, John and Samuel, all of whom were born in Deerfield except the first born.

(VI) Joshua, seventh son and tenth child of Deacon Noah and Mehitable (Burnham) Lane, was born in Deerfield November 26, 1794. He was a shoemaker, and followed that trade in connection with farming. The last years of his life were spent in Manchester, and he died there August 12, 1849. February 28, 1822, he married Jane Batchelder, who was born in Deerfield, October 22, 1796; died January 12, 1880. She became the mother of six children: Erastus, born March 16, 1823; Mehitable Jane, August 12, 1824; Thomas A., the date of whose birth is recorded in the succeeding paragraph; Abigail Ann, February 8, 1831; Sarah Elizabeth, June 1, 1833; and Adoniram Judson, October 30, 1835.

(VII) Thomas Alvin, second son and third child of Joshua and Jane (Batchelder) Lane, was born in Deerfield, June 17, 1827. In early life he followed the shoemaker's trade in Deerfield, but subsequently was employed in cotton mills, and later in the manufacture of rifles in Springfield, Massachusetts. After leaving Springfield he came to Manchester and took from Governor Straw a forty thousand dollar contract for making the trimmings of guns then being manufactured in the last named city. Later he was a partner with his brother, Adoniram Judson, in a grocery business, in Manchester, and in the same place was for nearly thirty-five years engaged in a steam-fitting business. In 1885 he purchased the farm in Bedford upon which his son Fred now resides. His religious relations were with the Universalists, and in politics he was a Republican. He was a Mason of high rank, affiliated with Lafayette Lodge, Ancient Free and Accepted Masons; Mount Horeb Chapter, Royal Arch Masons; Adoniram Council, Royal and Select Masters; Trinity Commandery, Knights Templar; Edward A. Raymond (now New Hampshire) Consistory, Sublime Princes of the Royal Secret, and has attained the thirty-second degree, Scottish Rite. He was an accomplished musician, and a member of the Manchester Cornet Band, one of the famous bands in the state. May 4, 1847, he married Hannah Maria, daughter of Charles and Deborah (Baker) Smith, of Knox, Maine. Of the five children of this union, four lived to maturity. Frank Alvin is the subject of the next paragraph; Inez A.; Scott Weston, born October 29, 1854, married Mary S. J. Kittridge, and has one son, Edwin Scott; Fred Forest is mentioned at length in this article; Judson Ellsworth, born May 11, 1861, married Grace W. Farrington, and died April 28, 1893, leaving two children: Natalie Augusta and Thomas Arthur. Mrs. Hannah M. Lane died January 2, 1896. She was a member of the Methodist Episcopal Church.

(VIII) Frank Alvin, eldest son of Thomas A. and Hannah M. (Smith) Lane, was born in Manchester, New Hampshire, October 22, 1849, and was educated in the public schools of that place. While his father was engaged in the manufacture of guns with the Amoskeag Manufacturing Company, Frank A. learned the trade of machinist. At the expiration of three years he went to Lowell, Massachusetts, where he accepted a position with the Rollin White Arms Company, and was engaged in the manufacture of revolvers for a period of six months. He then went to Providence, Rhode Island, with his father, returning to Manchester, and in 1871 with him commenced a plumbing and steam fitting business, among the first in that city. He remained in the employ of his father and rose to the position of foreman and superintendent. This concern was later incorporated and was known as the Thomas A. Lane Company, and Frank A. was the manager, a position he filled very capably for a period of fourteen years. After the death of his father the corporation went out of business in February, 1906, since which time Mr. Lane has lived in retirement. His political affiliations are with the Republican party, and he had served as alderman for two years. He is connected with the following fraternal organizations: Lafayette Lodge, No. 41, Free and Accepted Masons; Mount Horeb Chapter; Adoniram Council; past commander of Trinity Commandery; Edward A. Raymond Consistory, thirty-second degree; the Nobles of the Mystic Shrine; and the Benevolent and Protective Order of Elks. He is an attendant at the Universalist Church. He married, October 22, 1868, Susie E. Martin, born in Hooksett, daughter of Gilman and Nancy (Darrah) Martin, who had two children; Gilman Martin spent his life in Hooksett, and died at the age of seventy-three years; his wife died at the age of seventy-five. Mr. and Mrs. Lane have had one child: Inez A., born March 18, 1874. She was educated in the public schools, and married Ernest A. Smith, of Manchester, a member of the firm of Smith Brothers Piano Company, dealers in musical instruments. They have children: Lane E. and Elliott.

(VIII) Fred Forest, third son and fourth child of Thomas A. and Hannah M. (Smith) Lane, was born in Manchester, November 8, 1857. He was educated in the public schools of his native city, graduating from the high school, after which he served an apprenticeship at the steamfitter's trade, under the masterly direction of his father. With him he came to Bedford in 1885 and engaged in dairy farming, which has ever since been his principal occupation. He is also extensively interested in the lumbering business, and has also dealt in real estate. He is prominently identified with public affairs, having served with ability as highway agent for six years, supervisor for four years, also on the board of selectmen two years. He is a Master Mason, and a member of the local grange, Patrons of Husbandry, and of the Royal Arcanum. In politics he is a Republican, and he attends the Presbyterian Church. On September 1, 1876, Mr. Lane was united in marriage with Mary Frances Stevens, daughter of John and Elvira (Smart) Stevens, of Raymond. Of this marriage have been born four children: Grace Maria, born March 8, 1878; Gertrude May, born October 26, 1881; Bertha, born September 16, 1894, and a son who died in infancy. Grace Maria married, March 18, 1895, Ora Kilton, of Bedford, and has two children—Earl, born February 4, 1897, and Francis G., born October 31, 1906. Gertrude M. married, April 24, 1906, Charles F. Shepherd, of Bedford. Before her marriage she held a responsible clerical position in Manchester.

(IV) Joshua (2), fourth son and fifth child of Deacon Joshua (1) and Bathsheba (Robie) Lane, was born July 8, 1724, died January 13, 1794. He was a farmer, carpenter and cabinet-maker, a superior workman. He resided in Hampton till about 1762, when he removed to Poplin (now Fremont), near to Epping, to the Sanborn farm, plain and meadow, occupied in 1890 by John M. Fitts, his great-great-grandson. He was a member of the Congregational Church in Hampton, and removed his relations to the church in Epping, under the care of Rev. Josiah Stearns, whose son John married his daughter Sarah. Joshua Lane was a man of sterling integrity and unsullied Christian character. He was careful in keeping the Sabbath, and regular in observing family worship, and the public worship of the Sabbath. He married, December 16, 1747, Ruth Batchelder, born in Hampton, November 23, 1727, died June 14, 1812, in her eighty-fifth year. She descended from the Rev. Stephen Batchelder. It is said of her that though independent and outspoken in her opinions, she was an able helpmeet to her husband, revered and loved by her children, and esteemed highly by her neighbors. There were born of this marriage three children: Mary, John and Abigail.

(V) John, second child and eldest son of Joshua and Ruth (Batchelder) Lane, was born at Poplin, October 24, 1750, and died March 12, 1823, aged seventy-three years. He settled in Candia in 1775, on a farm about a mile from the village, on the North road, where Ezekiel Lane afterward resided. Besides being a farmer he was a carpenter and cabinet-maker and land surveyor. He used a compass box and tripod of his own manufacture. He furnished soldiers' supplies in 1778, one hundred and eighty-eight pounds, and took an active part in town affairs as moderator, justice, selectman and representative for fourteen successive years, 1806 to 1820. For many years as town clerk he used to "cry" candidates for matrimonial honors, in meeting on the Sabbath. He was a man of much influence in town affairs, and was retained in office until the time of his death. He regularly maintained family devotions, and was a constant attendant and supporter of public worship. He married, November 30, 1775, Hannah Godfrey, born in Poplin, November 19, 1755, daughter of Joseph and Susanna (Morrill) Godfrey. The farm of Hon. Ezekial Godfrey and his son Esquire Joseph was the best one in the neighborhood. Esquire Joseph did the most town business, and was the richest man in town. The Lanes and the Godfreys lived on adjoining farms, and John and Hannah were intimately associated from childhood. Hannah Godfrey Lane was characterized by marked intelligence and common sense, great sweetness of temper and cheerful Christian grace. Owing to conscientious doubts respecting the rite of baptism, she did not make a public profession of religion till 1838, in the eighty-third year of her age, when she united with the Congregational Church. After her husband's death she lived on the homestead with her son Deacon Ezekial. She died October 15, 1845, in the ninetieth year of her age. John and Hannah Lane had eleven children: Ruth, Susanna, Joseph, Josiah, John, Hannah, Joshua, Ezekial, Sally, Dr. Isaiah, and Abigail. Eight of these children settled in Candia.

(VI) Esquire John (2), son of John (1) and Hannah (Godfrey) Lane, was born October 15, 1783, and settled on the North road, about one-quarter of a mile west of the homestead. He was a good farmer, and possessed the confidence and esteem of his fellow citizens, whom he served for many years as selectman, representative, justice of the peace, land surveyor, town agent, etc. In 1823 he united with the Congregational Church; was an extensive reader, and a teacher and superintendent of the Sunday School forty years. As a justice of the peace throughout the state he was often and largely employed, and by his excellent advice frequently saved a resort to law. On April 28, 1851, he died instantly of apoplexy, aged sixty-seven years. November 12, 1811, he married Nabby, daughter of Colonel Nathaniel and Sarah T. Emerson, born in Candia, July 9, 1786 (see Emerson, V). She was a lady of quiet tastes, and admirable discretion and ability in her household. She survived her husband fifteen invalid years in great patience and Christian fortitude, dying June 25, 1866. Their children received a thorough education. They were: Richard Emerson, Sarah Tilton, Hannah Godfrey, Abby Emerson, Emily and Lucretia.

(VII) Lucretia, sixth child and fifth daughter of John and Nabby (Emerson) Lane, was born November 13, 1828, studied at the academies in Henniker and Pembroke, and was a teacher in Manchester. January 1, 1854, she married Francis Brown Eaton, son of Peter and Hannah H. (Kelly) Eaton, born in Candia, February 25, 1825, a distinguished journalist of Manchester, Boston, and Washington D. C. (See Eaton.)

(IV) John, sixth son and seventh child of Deacon Joshua and Bathsheba (Robie) Lane, was born in Hampton, New Hampshire, February 14, 1726. He joined the Hampton church, October 23, 1748, but later removed to Kensington, New Hampshire, where he was selectman. He also made return of the census there in 1773. He appears to have been a man of dignity and standing in the community. On August 24, 1775, he was chosen by the Provincial congress first major in Colonel J. Mounton's third regiment of militia. He married, December 28, 1749, Hannah Dow, who was born September 20, 1727, and died September 10, 1775, aged forty-eight years. They had eight children: Samuel, born December 17, 1750; John; Hannah, died unmarried; Comfort, died young; Mary, married William Harner; Joshua; David; and Joseph, born February 26, 1789. Major John Lane died at Kensington, March 21, 1811, aged eighty-five years. (Joshua and descendants are mentioned in this article.)

(V) Samuel Lane, eldest son and child of John and Hannah (Dow) Lane, was born December 17, 1750, and died August 5, 1811. He was one of the earliest settlers in what is known as the Lane neighborhood on the south side of Salmon brook mountain in Sanbornton. His occupation was that of tanning, at which he carried on quite an extensive business, and it is said to have been his invariable custom when a poor man lost any domestic animal to tan the hide without charge and give the loser a dollar. He was a lifelong member and for many years deacon of the Congregational Church. He was town clerk first after Daniel Sanborn. On February 9, 1774, Samuel Lane married Judith Clifford, who died December 6, 1825. Their children were: Samuel, Hannah, Simon, Jeremiah, Ebenezer, John, David, Judith and Timothy.

(VI) Hannah, eldest daughter and second child of Samuel and Judith (Clifford) Lane, became the wife of Nathan Plummer (see Plummer, II).

(V) Joshua, third son and sixth child of Major John and Hannah (Dow) Lane, was born at Kensington, New Hampshire, August 28, 1782. After his marriage he lived first at Kensington, then at Rochester, and finally settled at Sanbornton, New Hampshire, in 1798. He built the first house on the Sanborn road, where J. T. Durgin now lives, which place he made over to the widow of his brother Joseph in 1813. He then built on the place where his descendants have since lived to the fourth generation. He had the town clerk's office for twenty successive years in both these houses. He was a fine penman, and drew the plan of the town, as originally laid out, which is now in the town clerk's office. He also made the surveys for Sanbornton and at least seven other of the neighboring towns for the famous Carrigain map. This map, which was not published until 1818, though the plans were made ten years earlier, was the work of Colonel Philip Carrigain, of Concord, the witty and accomplished secretary of state, 1805-1809. "Master Lane," as he usually was called, had an important part in this valuable work. He gained his title from his school-teaching. He had learned the shoemaker's trade, but for twenty-one years in succession kept the school in the present Sanborn district in Sanbornton. Beside his draughting, he has left behind him another prized memorial in the shape of a diary, which he kept for nearly forty years. He began his "Memorandum of Daily Occurences" when he went to keeping house, November 13, 1788, and continued it till within four days of his death, which occurred September 1, 1829, at the age of sixty-seven. Joshua Lane married at Kensington, July 9, 1788, Huldah Hilliard, who was born July 5, 1768, and died of palsy, April 1, 1850, in her eighty-second year. They had five children: John, born April 2, 1789; Julia, who married Levi Lang; Joseph Hilliard; Joshua, Jr., who died at the age of seven years; and Charles, mentioned below in this article, with descendants.

(VI) Joseph Hilliard, second son and third child of Joshua and Huldah (Hilliard) Lane, was born August 10, 1793. It is not certainly known whether his birthplace was Kensington or Rochester,

New Hampshire, as his parents lived in both towns. They moved to Sanbornton, which became their permanent home, 1798. He was at first a farmer and teamster, but after his second marriage he kept the hotel at Sanbornton Square. It was here that his early death occurred at the age of fifty. Mr. Lane was twice married. On June 12, 1814, he married his first cousin, Polly or Mary Lane, daughter of David and Judith (Philbrick) Lane, of Sanbornton. They had six daughters: Catherine, Judith A., Mary, Pauline Moulton, Huldah, Hannah Perkins. Mrs. Polly (Lane) Lane died June 6, 1830, of consumption. On June 6, 1832, Joseph Lane married (second) Caroline Chase Kimball, daughter of Joseph and Rachel (Chase) Kimball, who was born in Sanbornton, January 13, 1804. After her husband's death she moved back to the farm, where she delighted to entertain her grandchildren during the summer. She had a happy, cheerful disposition, and was a woman of great activity and industry. She lived to the advanced age of ninety, and did much good during her long life, leaving pleasant memories to be cherished by her descendants. Joseph H. and Caroline Chase (Kimball) Lane had three sons: Joseph H. (2), whose sketch follows; Andrew Louis and Joshua.

(VII) Joseph Hilliard (2), eldest son and child of Joseph Hilliard (1) Lane and his second wife, Caroline C. (Kimball) Lane, was born in Sanbornton, New Hampshire, August 11, 1835. When a boy he went to live with his mother's sister, Mrs. Louisa H. Hardy, at Groveland, Massachusetts, and he was educated at the Groveland Academy. In 1851 he came to Concord, New Hampshire, and went to work for the Abbott-Downing Company, at that time the most noted firm of carriage builders in the country. He learned his trade of wheelwright there, and stayed with them for a period of thirty-two years with the exception of the interval between 1866 and 1869 when he had an establishment of his own in Roxbury, Massachusetts. While with the Abbott-Downing Company Mr. Lane helped to build the famous Deadwood coach, which after years of active service on the plains became familiar to the public through Buffalo Bill's exhibitions. In 1883 Mr. Lane went into the undertaking business with Hamilton A. Kendall, under the firm name of Kendall & Lane. He continued in this until his death, which occurred instantly from heart disease on March 30, 1895. Mr. Lane was a member of the First Baptist Church. He was a Republican in politics, and was often asked to represent his ward in official life. He was councilman for two terms, first in 1879 and second in 1881-82. He served as alderman two terms, 1883-84 and 1885-86. In 1889 he represented ward six in the legislature. He was a member of White Mountain Lodge, Independent Order of Odd Fellows; Blazing Star Lodge, Ancient Free and Accepted Masons. In the days of the old Volunteer Fire Department, Mr. Lane belonged to the Merrimack, Number Three, Hand Engine Company, and at the time of his death he was foreman of the Hook and Ladder Company. Mr. Lane was a man of upright character, and was held in high esteem by all who knew him. He was happy in his home and was a devoted husband and father. On November 23, 1854, Joseph H. Lane (2) married Ann Allison, daughter of James and Catherine Allison of Windsor, Nova Scotia. Mrs. Lane is a member of the First Baptist Church, and has been a resident of Concord for more than half a century. A woman devoted to her home and family, her activities have been largely within the domestic circle, but her benevolence has been widespread and she has blessed all who have come within the circle of her influence. Joseph H. (2) and Ann (Allison) Lane had three children: Caroline J., Edward H., and Louis A., the subject of the succeeding paragraph. Caroline Josephine, the eldest child and only daughter, was born November 8, 1855. She was graduated from the Concord high school in 1878, and on August 20, 1878, was married to William Wallace Elkin, of Concord. Mr. Elkin was born in Brooklyn, New York, and was the son of Henry and Jane (Burgum) Elkin, of Birmingham, England. Mr. Henry Elkin became a sugar planter in Cuba and was the first manufacturer to introduce machinery for grinding cane; this work had previously been done by ox power. Mr. and Mrs. William W. Elkin have one son, Henry Shadrach. Mrs. Elkin is a woman of refined and cultivated tastes with an ardent love of nature. Active in church and club work, diligent in domestic duties, she has always found time for study and out-door life. Possessed of great social charm and a sunny disposition, she is beloved by all who know her. Edward Hamlin, eldest son and second child, was born June 2, 1860. He is a silversmith at the Durgin factory in Concord. He married Minnie J. Burgum, of Concord, a niece of Mrs. Jane (Burgum) Elkin.

(VIII) Louis Andrew, second son and youngest child of Joseph Hilliard (2) and Ann (Allison) Lane, was born at Concord, New Hampshire, August 23, 1862. He was graduated from the Concord high school in 1882. He was first employed at the National State Capital Bank in Concord, but at the end of the year he left this position to become private secretary to Charlamagne Tower, of Philadelphia. Mr. Tower developed the great iron mines about Lake Superior and built the Duluth and Iron Range railroad. His son and namesake is now minister to Austria. Mr. Lane remained with the elder Mr. Tower three years or until the death of the latter. This position was a liberal education in itself, and Mr. Lane has always greatly prized the opportunities that it afforded. After Mr. Tower's death, Mr. Lane returned to Concord, and entered the employ of Norris & Crockett, afterwards J. C. Norris & Company, as bookkeeper, holding this position for twelve years. After a brief rest he contemplated studying medicine with his cousin, Dr. Henry E. Allison, the noted alienist, at that time superintendent of the Asylum at Fishkill-on-the-Hudson. His health being hardly equal to the demands of such a career, Mr. Lane decided to adopt his father's profession, and in 1897 was graduated from the United States College of Embalming in New York City. He began business at Concord in December of that year. He has been especially successful in his chosen practice, and his establishment is one of the largest north of Boston. In 1901 he was graduated from the Massachusetts College of Embalmers. In 1899 he founded the Licensed Embalmers' Association of New Hampshire, and was its secretary for several years, but was obliged to give up this position on account of the demands of his own business. Mr. Lane is a man of fine sensibilities and sympathetic nature, which render him peculiarly adapted to his chosen work. He attends the First Baptist Church of Concord. He is a Republican in politics, but never has had time to hold office. He belongs to many fraternal organizations. He is a member of White Mountain Lodge, Independent Order of Odd Fellows, in all its branches. He belongs to Horace Chase Council, Royal Arch Chapter, Blazing Star Lodge, Ancient Free and Accepted Masons. He belongs to the Concord Lodge, Knights of Pythias, also the Grand Lodge of New Hampshire. He has been past chancellor and district deputy of the Concord Lodge. He is a member of Capital City Grange and of Aroosagunticook Tribe, Improved Order of Red Men.

On December 27, 1897, Louis A. Lane married at Alexandria, New Hampshire, Harriet Laycock, daughter of John and Martha (Berry) Laycock, formerly of Bradford, England. Mrs. Lane was born in Bradford, December 27, 1875, and came as a child with her parents to Canada. They afterwards moved to Lawrence, Massachusetts. She then went to Tuscaloosa, Alabama, where her brother Arthur had an orange plantation, and in 1896 was graduated from the Tuscaloosa Female College. She comes of a family gifted in music and elocution, and at the time of her marriage was preparing to enter the Boston School of Oratory. Her brother, Professor Craven Laycock, is the present professor of Oratory at Dartmouth College. Mrs. Lane joined the Methodist Church at Lawrence, Massachusetts. Her father was a local preacher of that denomination in England. Mr. and Mrs. Louis A. Lane have two children: Joseph Hilliard (3), born September 25, 1898, and Martha Allison, born February 11, 1904, both at Concord.

(VI) Charles, fourth son and youngest child of Joshua and Huldah (Hilliard) Lane, was born February 11, 1799, at Sanbornton, New Hampshire. He served his time in a store at Concord, New Hampshire, and later established himself in business at Sanbornton Square. He early engaged in the newspaper and book publishing business, editing the paper which he issued. In 1837 he published an elegant Family Bible, which would have done credit to a city establishment. He was an acknowledged leader in the affairs of the town, and did much for the prosperity of the Square. His newspaper was the first ever issued in Sanbornton. In 1841 he removed to Laconia, New Hampshire, where he purchased and edited the *Belknap Gazette* for several years. He was clerk of the Boston, Concord & Montreal railroad from its organization till his death. He was United States marshal for New Hampshire under the administrations of Van Buren and Jackson. He also served the state as representative and state senator. In later years he did a large business as insurance agent and adjuster. When the Montreal railroad was built, he settled all the land damages between Concord and Woodsville, New Hampshire. "Physically speaking, he was a man of fine and commanding presence, with a large frame, surmounted by a head whose Websterian proportions and strong features betokened great intellectual ability. His rare gifts, combined with a genial and sunny disposition, won him hosts of friends." He was prominent in Masonic circles, and at his death, March 6, 1876, in Laconia, after a four years' invalidism from paralysis, special trains brought large Masonic delegations from Concord, Plymouth and other places. Charles Lane was twice married. His first wife was Pauline (Moulton) Lane, of Concord, New Hampshire, whom he married at Bradford, Massachusetts, August 3, 1822. She died of consumption, March 17, 1838, leaving him two children: Charles Parker, a printer, who died July 9, 1876, in Haverhill, Massachusetts, aged fifty-three; and Edwin Jonathan, a dry goods merchant and manufacturer of Boston, Massachusetts, who married Asenath Smith, of Lowell, Massachusetts. They had two children, Paulina, who married Edward Wasfield, of Boston, and Josephine, who married Charles S. Spaulding, of Brookline, Massachusetts. Colonel Charles Lane's second wife was Sarah Jane, eldest of the ten children of Rev. Abraham and Nancy (Conner) Bodwell, of Sanbornton. They were married August 6, 1838. She was a woman of superior qualities of mind and heart. Her father was a graduate of Harvard, and for forty-six years was pastor of the Congregational Church at Sanbornton. Her brother, Dr. Joseph Conner Bodwell, was a graduate of Dartmouth, became a clergyman in England, and later returned to this country where he filled pulpits in Massachusetts, and finally became a professor in the Theological Seminary at Hartford, Connecticut. Mrs. Sarah J. (Bodwell) Lane died at Laconia, November 11, 1880, leaving three children: George Bodwell, mentioned below, Jennie Frances, who married A. Henry Waitt, of Boston, and James Willis, who lives at Sour Lake, Texas.

(VII) George Bodwell, eldest child of Colonel Charles Lane and his second wife, Sarah J. (Bodwell) Lane, was born in Sanbornton, New Hampshire, August 5, 1841. He was educated in the common schools of Laconia and at Gilford Academy. He then entered the dry goods store of John Prentiss Tucker, of Concord, New Hampshire, where he was clerk for ten years. Mr. Tucker's wife was Hannah (Whipple) Tucker, a niece of Chief Justice Salmon P. Chase. After leaving Concord Mr. Lane acted as travelling salesman for a Boston firm, his route took him through the state of Maine; he continued in this occupation until 1860. In 1862 he enlisted in Company H, Twelfth Regiment, New Hampshire Volunteers; he helped recruit the regiment at Laconia. He was appointed regimental mail clerk for the territory between Point Lookout and Washington, and in 1864 was made commissary sergeant. In 1865 he returned to Laconia and subsequently took the position of bookkeeper in the Gilford hosiery mill, remaining for three years. Later he was engaged in the insurance business with his father. He was register of deeds for Belknap county for two years, and town clerk for Laconia, six years. In 1894 he was appointed by Colonel Thomas Cogswell, of Gilmanton, to a position in the pension office at Concord. He subsequently became chief clerk, which office he still holds. In politics he is a Democrat, and he attends the Congregational Church. George B. Lane married, November 18, 1870, Mrs. Mary Jane (Davis) Webber, daughter of Samuel Davis, of Lakeport, New Hampshire, where she was born May 25, 1841. They have one child, Ada Florence, born March 15, 1877.

(IV) Deacon Jeremiah, seventh son and eleventh of the sixteen children of Deacon Joshua and Bathsheba (Robie) Lane, was born March 10, 1732, and died June 21, 1806, aged seventy-four. He was a man of some means and of excellent standing in the community where he resided. His name is on petitions to Governor Wentworth relative to delinquent taxpayers in May, 1772. In March of the following year he made a statement to Governor Wentworth and the general assembly respecting a dispute in a parish of Hampton Falls, and October 1, 1762, he was one of a committee to determine the boundaries between Salisbury and Andover, then called Stevenstown and New Britain. He was very pious, a man of fair speech, active as a deacon in the church, and delivered the address at the funeral of his father which was printed under the title of "A Memorial and a Tear of Lamentation." Jeremiah Lane married, January 18, 1759, Mary Sanborn, who was born May 24, 1736, daughter of Lieutenant Joseph Sanborn. She died August 17, 1818, aged eighty-two. Their children, born at Hampton Falls, were: Mary, Sarah, Joshua, Jeremiah, Simeon, a son, and Levi.

(V) Jeremiah (2), fourth child and second son of Deacon Jeremiah (1) and Mary (Sanborn) Lane, was born in Hampton Falls, January 20, 1768, and died July 18, 1848. He was a farmer and settled in Chichester in 1792. He and his second wife were members of the Congregational Church. He married (first), December 29, 1791, Eunice Tilton, who was born November 26, 1764, and died January 18, 1811; and (second), December 31, 1811, Hannah Tucke, who was born October 2, 1776, and died May 13, 1848. By his first wife he had children: Benjamin, Jeremiah, Joshua, a son, Eunice, Polly, Betsey and Joseph; and by his second wife: Anthony Knapp, Moses Garland and Hannah Sarah.

(VI) Moses Garland, second child of Jeremiah and Hannah (Tucke) Lane, was born August 26, 1814, and died October, 1895. He was named for his great-uncle, Lieutenant Moses Garland, who was a Revolutionary soldier and fought valiantly at the battle of Bunker Hill. He resided on the homestead in Chichester, then removed to Pittsfield. He and his wife were members of the Congregational Church. He married, November 29, 1839, Sophia Ann Sanborn, daughter of Captain James Sanborn, of Epsom. She died in Pittsfield, August 9, 1856. They had six children: Elizabeth A., born April 6, 1841, married, January 24, 1866, David K. Swett, of Pittsfield. Charles H., see forward. Abbie M., born February 22, 1847, married, December 5, 1872, George P. Woodman, of Manchester. James T., died young. Helen A., born August 2, died October 30, 1853. Walter B., born March 21, 1855, died April, 1880.

(VII) Charles H., second child and eldest son of Moses G. and Sophia Ann (Sanborn) Lane, was born in Chichester, October 9, 1843, and while he was still a boy his parents removed to Pittsfield. He attended the public schools in that town and in Concord, and was subsequently a student at Pittsfield Academy. For many years he was a builder and lumber dealer. After marriage he resided in Concord, and then removed to Pittsfield, which has since been his home. Beginning life with a small capital he has acquired a large property and become prominent as a contractor and builder, banker and dealer in real estate. Quiet and retiring in manner, he has ever been interested in promoting the growth of Pittsfield and has done much toward that end. He constructed most of the large buildings and managed the most difficult carpenter work of the town. He possesses not only mechanical skill but much ingenuity, and has invented several useful appliances. He was among the first in the organization of the Pittsfield Acqueduct Company, of which he was superintendent fifteen years, and is still a director. For a time he was superintendent of the Pittsfield Gas Company, and is yet a member of its directorate. He is a trustee of the Farmers' Savings Bank of Pittsfield, a director in the Pittsfield National Bank and a director from its organization to the present time in the Merchants' National Bank of Dover. He is a loyal Republican, has never sought or filled an office, but has been ever ready to assist in his party's progress and in the cause of temperance. He is a deeply religious man by nature, an active member of the Congregational Church, and for years has been its treasurer and one of its wardens. He is a charter member of Corinthian Lodge, No. 82, Free and Accepted Masons, of Pittsfield, and of Suncook Lodge, No. 10, Independent Order of Odd Fellows, of Pittsfield.

He married (first), in Pittsfield, January 2, 1868, Almira Lorena Perkins, who was born August 3, 1845, daughter of Oliver Lowell and Abigail (Sanborn) Perkins, of Pittsfield. She died February 24, 1897, aged fifty-two. She attended the same schools that Mr. Lane did, and subsequently taught school. She was a fond mother, a lady of culture, and took much interest in the education of her family. The children of Charles H. and Almira L. (Perkins) Lane, were: Willis H., died aged seven years. Katie Rena, died at the age of three years. Winifred, born April 30, 1875, married, June 26, 1895, Charles C. Goss. Ethel, born July 2, 1880, died December 29, 1884. Mr. Lane married (second), Ella (Chesley) Martin, a woman active in the educational interests of the town.

(Third Family.)

LANE Many early immigrants of this name are found among the seventeenth century settlers of America, and most of them reared large families and have numerous descendants. The present line is derived from James Lane, of Casco Bay, Maine, and is unrelated to that sprung from William Lane, of Boston, whose grandson, Deacon Joshua Lane, was a prominent citizen of Hampton, New Hampshire. The Hampton Lanes and their descendants are already well represented in the biographies of this work.

(I) James Lane, born in England, son of James Lane, was a craftsman and perhaps a member of the guild of turners, London, in 1654. That same year he had joint ownership with his brother, John Lane, in real estate at Rickmansworth, Hertford county, which had been received from their parents. James Lane had paid debts on the property and was thereby depleted in pocket. Perhaps with a view of bettering their circumstances, the brothers Job, James and Edward Lane, came to America and settled in Malden, Massachusetts, about 1656. Soon after Edward Lane went to Boston and Job to Billerica, Massachusetts, but James Lane had more of the pioneer spirit, and finally pitched his tent at Casco Bay, Maine. Here he acquired large tracts of land and gave his name to a point and an island off the east bank of Royall's river, which they still bear. Tradition says that Lane's Island is the place where the Indians planted corn, held councils and buried their dead. In 1665-66 James Lane was "sergeant of ye companye," the Westcustigo military organization, formed on the plan of the London train-bands to which the immortal John Gilpin belonged. As chief officer Sergeant Lane would be armed with halberd, sword and pistol. James Lane is supposed to have had a wife, Ann, and certainly had a daughter by that name. He afterwards married Sarah White, daughter of John and Mary (Phips) White. Sarah White had interesting antecedents, and was the half sister of Sir William Phips, the royal governor of Massachusetts. Her mother Mary was the widow of James Phips when she married John White and she had twenty-six children by the two husbands. James Lane died intestate, leaving six children who shared his estate. These were: Ann, who married Richard Bray; John, whose sketch follows; Samuel, who had a wife Abigail; Henry, who died at Boston, June 4, 1690; Job, who married Mary Fassett; and James. Sergeant James Lane was killed in a fight with the Indians, but the date cannot be ascertained. It was probably between 1675 and 1678, because a deposition from his son John says that they lived at Casco Bay until driven thence by the "first warr." A massacre of four adults and three children occurred there September 12, 1675, and on August 11, 1676, Falmouth (which later developed into Portland) was attacked and thirty-four persons killed or captured. All the settlements in that region were abandoned for a time. The inventory of the estate of Sergeant James Lane was made in 1680, and among the items are: "Lincewulse, 34 shillings; puter, 14 shillings; 3 bras cetles at 20 shillings." There is a goodly amount of cloths of various kinds, beside bed and table linen, but the only kitchen furniture mentioned beside the kettles are one porridge pot and a pair of tongs and pot-hooks.

(II) John, eldest son and second child of Sergeant James Lane, was born in 1652 in England. It is not known whether his mother was Sarah White or her predecessor Ann; probably Sarah White. When he was past eighty years of age, John Lane deposed that he lived at Casco Bay, Maine, until driven out by the second Indian war. He continued to live on the Maine coast for some years after leaving Casco Bay, because he was at Cape Elizabeth in 1680, and at Purpooduck Point in 1687 and 1689. Soon after he went to Gloucester, Massachusetts, which became his permanent home. It was from him and his family that the village of Lanesville on Cape Ann takes its name. John Lane's name is attached to many deeds conveying tracts of land in the vicinity of Gloucester. He also possessed large estates in Maine, both by inheritance and purchase. There was great confusion about the titles to land in the latter place, and in 1700 the general court of Massachusetts established a commission to examine into the matter. In these records John Lane was accounted among the old planters of Westcustigo, and there are many depositions extant signed by his name. John Lane was connected with the First Church in Gloucester before 1703, and was an original member of the Third Church, Annisquam, when it was organized in 1728. About 1680 John Lane married Dorcas Wallis, daughter of John and Mary (Shepard) Wallis, of Cape Elizabeth, Maine. They had eleven children, five born at Cape Elizabeth and six at Gloucester: James, born in 1682, married (first), Ruth Riggs, (second), Judith Woodbury; John, married Mary Riggs; Josiah, married Rachel York; Dorcas, married William Tucker; Sarah, married Thomas Riggs; Hephzibah, married Caleb Woodbury; Mary, married (first), Thomas Finson, (second), Joseph Thurston; Joseph, married Deborah Harraden; Benjamin, whose sketch follows; Deborah, died in her twenty-seventh year; and Job, married Mary Ashby. John Lane died January 24, 1737-38, aged eighty-six years. His widow, Dorcas (Wallis) Lane, died February 2, 1754, in her ninety-third year. They are both buried in the Lanesville cemetery near Gloucester, Massachusetts.

(III) Benjamin, fifth son and ninth child of John and Dorcas (Wallis) Lane, was born in Lanesville, Gloucester, Massachusetts, July 25, 1700. He spent his life in Gloucester where at different times he bought several tracts of land in addition to what he inherited from his father. On January 6, 1725-26, Benjamin Lane married Elizabeth Griffin, a descendant of Samuel and Elizabeth (York) Griffin. They had sixteen children: Thomas, Benjamin, whose sketch follows; Elizabeth Jonathan, John, Lydia, Hezekiah, David, Daniel, Dorcas, Joseph, Joshua, Lois, Nathaniel, Rebecca and Peter. Benjamin Lane died March 12, 1773, aged seventy-two years, and his widow Elizabeth died of asthma, September 11, 1779, aged seventy years.

(IV) Benjamin (2), second son and child of Benjamin (1) and Elizabeth (Griffin) Lane, was born at Gloucester, Massachusetts, November 23, 1727. In 1752 he bought land in Gloucester, Massachusetts, and in 1770 moved to New Gloucester, Maine, which was largely settled by emigrants from the former town. In 1782 he bought the "most Easterly Corner Pew" in the meeting house at New Gloucester. His name appears in connection with several transfers of real estate in that region. On October 28, 1749, Benjamin (2) Lane entered intentions of marriage with his second cousin, Hannah Lane, daughter of Samuel and Mary (Emmons) Lane, of Gloucester. She was the mother of his ten children: Nathaniel, Benjamin, mentioned below, Eliphalet, Zephaniah, Hannah, John, Samuel, Joshua, Susanna and Betty. Two of the sons served in the Revolution. In 1778 John Lane, at the age of nineteen, was killed in an engagement with a British ship mounting twenty guns, being the first man from Gloucester, Massachusetts, to lose his life in the Continental cause. In May, 1780, Joshua Lane was mustered with Captain Isaac Parson's New Gloucester company, Colonel Prince's regiment, under General Wadsworth for eight months' service at Thomaston, Maine. On September 23, 1780, when Benjamin (2) Lane was in his fifty-third year, he entered intentions of marriage with Mrs. Sarah Pool, a young widow of twenty-two. He died about 1805, and his widow lived till March 30, 1840, when she died at the age of eighty-two.

(V) Benjamin (3), second son and child of Benjamin (2) and Hannah (Lane) Lane, was baptized at Gloucester, Massachusetts, December 1, 1752. When a youth he moved with his people to New Gloucester, Maine, finally locating at Poland, that state, where he bought land in 1796, and at later times. Benjamin (3) Lane had two wives, but it is probable that the seven children were all by the first marriage. On July 3, 1775, Benjamin (3) Lane married Sarah Davis, who was baptized and admitted to the church in Annisquam, Massachusetts, on September 27, 1778, on the same day that her eldest child was baptized. The seven children of Benjamin (3) and Sarah (Davis) Lane were: Benjamin (4), whose sketch follows; John, Sally, Oliver, Nehemiah, Rebecca and Zenas. On March 26, 1816, Benjamin (3) Lane married Elizabeth Norwood. He probably died in 1841, at the age of eighty-nine, for his will was proved in January, 1842.

(VI) Benjamin (4), eldest child of Benjamin (3) and Sarah (Davis) Lane, was born at Gloucester, Massachusetts, January 14, 1777. He lived with his parents in Poland, Maine, and in 1815 for the sum of five hundred and twenty-five dollars he bought a tract of one hundred acres in Minot, Cumberland county, Maine, which became his permanent home. His name appears in connection with several other transfers of real estate up to 1846. On August 9, 1798, Benjamin (4) Lane married Hannah Downing, and they had eleven children: Palfrey, Jacob, Phebe, John Barnard, Richard, mentioned below, Rebekah, Sally D., Hannah, Benjamin, Nathan D. and Hannah P. Benjamin (4) Lane died of cancer at Auburn, Maine, October 4, 1846, aged sixty-nine years. His widow died April 18, 1867, aged eighty-seven years.

(VII) Richard, fourth son and fifth child of Benjamin (4) and Hannah (Downing) Lane, was born in Minot, now a part of Auburn, Maine, on May 4, 1806. In 1832 he moved to Whitefield, New Hampshire, which, with the exception of a few years spent in Carroll, this state, became his permanent home. He was a farmer and lumberman, and a respected citizen. He attended the Free Baptist Church, was a Republican in politics, and served as selectman for one year, and also acted as captain of a militia company. In the fall of 1851 Richard Lane went to California, engaged in farming, but returned home in the spring of 1853. On September 2, 1833, Captain Richard Lane married Hannah, daughter of Asa and Sarah (Barnes) King, of Whitefield, and they had eleven children: Benjamin Franklin, whose sketch follows; Asa King, Albert Winch, Richard (2), Caroline Adelaide, who died at the age of eight years; Augustus Henry, Hannah Lewella, John Barnard, Edward Austin, Charles Irwin (twins), and Effie Jean. Of these children, two became physicians, Hannah Lewella and Charles Irwin. Hannah L. Lane was born August 27, 1847, received the degree of M. D. from Boston University in Boston, was for a time physician at Snell Seminary, Oakland, California, and is now established at Berkeley, that state. Charles I. Lane was born November 27, 1854, received his degree of M. D. at Hahnemann Medical College in Philadelphia, studied abroad, became a successful physician at Concord, New Hampshire, and died April 13, 1883. Dr. Lane was a man of fine qualities of mind and heart, and his untimely death cut short a promising career. During his last illness he was married to Frances Kendrick Adams, of Concord, to whom he had been engaged. On January 22, 1907, Mrs. Frances K. Lane became the second wife of Rev. Daniel C. Roberts, D. D., vicar of St. Paul's Episcopal Church at Concord. Three of the sons of Captain Richard and Hannah (King) Lane served in the Civil war, and one died from the effects of wounds. Albert W. Lane, born June 19, 1838, and Richard (2) Lane, born April 11, 1840, both enlisted for one year, September 21, 1864, in Company L, First Regiment, New Hampshire Heavy Artillery, and were mustered out June 15, 1865, each having attained the rank of corporal. Albert W. Lane now lives in Plymouth, New Hampshire; and Richard (2) Lane died April 10, 1907. Augustus H. Lane, born May 19, 1844, enlisted August 22, 1862, was mustered into Company E, Fourteenth Regiment, New Hampshire Volunteers, on September 23, 1862, and was discharged disabled, October 24, 1864, at Jefferson Barracks, Missouri, and died September 17, 1866, at the age of twenty-two years. Of the other children of Captain and Mrs. Richard Lane, Edward A., born November 27, 1854, is a lawyer at Pittsfield, New Hampshire. On May 24, 1882, he married Anne A. Barter, daughter of Lewis Barter, of Concord, who had been educated at Wellesley College. Effie Jane Lane, born December 10, 1856, was educated at Wellesley College and married James Edson Noyes (now deceased), late of Tilton, New Hampshire. They lived at Redlands, California. Captain Richard Lane died at Whitefield, October 12, 1884, aged seventy-eight years, and his widow died April 15, 1896, aged eighty-one years.

(VIII) Benjamin Franklin, eldest child of Captain Richard and Hannah (King) Lane, was born at Whitefield, New Hampshire, April 28, 1834. He was educated in the schools of his native town and at Derby Academy, Derby, Vermont. He taught school for twelve years in various places near his home, and has served on the board of education in Whitefield for nine years. From 1856 to 1862 he was in the ice business in New York City. In the latter year he came home and bought a farm in Whitefield, where he has lived ever since. He owns one hundred and sixty acres of land, and makes a specialty of milk. B. F. Lane has been deacon of the Free Will Baptist Church for twenty years, and was superintendent of the Sunday school for ten years. Deacon Lane is a Republican in politics, and was selectman for 1871-72-73, 1881-82-83-84 and 1898. He represented Whitefield in the legislatures of 1874 and 1875. Deacon Lane inherits the excellent qualities that have distinguished this family for generations. He is a valuable citizen of his native town, one of those who makes the world better by living in it. On November 20, 1861, Benjamin Franklin Lane married Julia A. Farr, daughter of Gilman and Triphena Farr, of Littleton, New Hampshire. They have had four children: Bert R., born January 16, 1865, lives in Brookfield, Missouri; he married Sada Westgate, children: Mabel, Olivette, Alice, deceased; Benjamin Franklin and Ralph. Carrie, born April 6, 1867, married, November 18, 1891, William H. Sawyer, son of Eli Sawyer, of Littleton, New Hampshire. They have lived since their marriage at Concord, New Hampshire, where Mr. Sawyer is a lawyer of standing, and an active worker in temperance and other good causes. They have five children: Howard, Helen, Marion, Robert and Murray. Mabel F., born April 11, 1879, is a teacher in Whitefield. Minnie, died in infancy.

NOYES Commencing with the Plymouth Colony, in 1620, New England had many emigrants from the mother country in the early part of the century, and most, if not all, from the same cause. Under James I. and Charles I. all forms of worship which died not conform to those of the established church (Anglican) were strictly prohibited; and all "Non-Conformist," as they were called, were rigorously persecuted, and many fled to Holland and America. Catholics and Puritans suffered alike under that bigoted church. Puritan ministers were driven from their livings by the hundred, and flocked to Holland, their old shelter, and to America, a newly discovered refuge. Between 1627 and 1641, during the persecutions of Laud, New England received most of its early settlers, and this persecution was no doubt the cause of the emigration of James and Nicholas Noyes and those who came with them. The weight of authority seems to indicate that the family of Noyes is descended from one of the nobles of William the Conqueror of England in 1066. William des Noyers, one of these nobles, whose name rendered into English is William of the Walnut trees, was a prominent figure. The name des Noyers by first dropping the article became Noyers, and later was corrupted to Noyes.

(I) Rev. William Noyes was born in England, in 1568, and died in Cholderton, in the county of Wilts, England, before April 30, 1622. He matriculated at University College, Oxford, November 15, 1588, and was admitted to the degree of B. A., May 31, 1592. He was instituted rector of Cholderton, a place about eleven miles from Salisbury, in 1602, and served in that position until his death. The inventory of his estate was made April 30, 1622, and his widow appointed administratrix May 28, 1622. He married, about 1595, Anne Parker, born 1575, and buried at Cholderton, March 7, 1657. Their children were: Ephraim, Nathan, James, Nicholas, a daughter name not known, and John.

(II) Deacon Nicholas, fourth son and child of Rev. William and Anne (Parker) Noyes, was born in England in 1615-16. Rev. James and Deacon Nicholas Noyes, brothers, in March, 1633, embarked for New England in the "Mary and John" of London, with their cousin, Rev. Thomas Parker. No record has been found of the place and date of the landing of James and Nicholas, but it was probably on the bank of the Mystic river, as the records show that they settled in Medford in 1634, and that they moved to Newbury the following year. On arriving they sailed up the Parker river (then called the Quascacunquen) to a point a short distance below where the bridge now stands. Tradition says that Nicholas was the first to leap ashore. He walked forty miles to Cambridge to qualify as a voter when he was made a freeman, May 17, 1637. He was a deputy to the general court at Boston from Newbury, December 19, 1660, May 28, 1679, May 19, 1680, and January 4, 1681. He was chosen deacon of the First Parish, March 20, 1634, and died November 23, 1701, at Newbury. His will was made July 4, 1700, and proved December 29, 1701. The personal estate was £1,531, and the real estate was £1,160. "In 1652 many were brought before the court for not observing the sumptuary laws of 1651. The records say 'Nicholas Noyes' wife, Hugh March's wife, and William Chandler's wife were each prosecuted for wearing a silk hood and scarf, but were discharged on proof that their husbands were worth two hundred pounds each. John Hutchins' wife was also discharged upon testifying that she was brought up above the ordinary rank.'" Nicholas Noyes married, about 1640, Mary Cutting, daughter of Captain John Cutting (a ship master of London), and Mary his wife. John Cutting in his will mentions Mary, wife of Nicholas Noyes. Their children were: Mary, Hannah, John, Cutting, Sarah, Timothy, James, Abigail, Rachel, Thomas, and three who died young. (James and descendants are mentioned in this article).

(III) John, eldest son and third child of Deacon Nicholas and Mary (Cutting) Noyes, was born in Newbury, January 20, 1645. He was made a freeman January 9, 1674. He was a house carpenter, and lived in what was afterward known as the "farms district." There he built a substantial house in a style unusual for a farm house in those early days. The front hall is wainscoted, and a handsome staircase, with elaborately carved balusters, then fashionable for first-class mansions, leads to the second story. The kitchen fireplace was huge even for that period, and an ox could have been roasted whole in its capacious recess. This house, built in 1677, was owned by Noyes in 1879. John Noyes died in Newbury, intestate, in 1691, and his widow and son Nicholas were appointed administrators, and made their account September 28, 1694; the personal estate was £309 and the real estate £246. He married in Newbury, November 23, 1668, Mary Poore, of Andover. Their children were: Nicholas, Daniel, Mary, John, Martha, Nathaniel, Elizabeth, Moses and Samuel.

(IV) Samuel, youngest child of John and Mary (Poore) Noyes, was born in Newbury, February 5, 1691. He went to Abington with his brother Nicholas, about 1712. He was elected selectman in 1719, and town clerk in 1726. He was the progenitor of more descendants of the name than all his five brothers. He married Hannah Poore, in 1714, and died November 16, 1729. Their children were: Samuel, Daniel, Mary, John, Benjamin, Abigail, Jacob and Ebenezer.

(V) John (2), fourth child and third son of Samuel and Hannah (Poore) Noyes, was born in Abington, April 7, 1720, and died May 30, 1770. After the death of his father, his uncle, Samuel Poore, of Rowley, was appointed his guardian, 1736. He settled in Pembroke, New Hampshire, at what was then called "Ox Bow." He was the progenitor of the large branch of the family from the fourth generation, having eight sons who had seventy-five children. After his death his son Benjamin was appointed administrator of his estate, which consisted of the home in Bow, valued at £115; an island in the Merrimack river, £9; house and farm in Pembroke, £170; personal property, £92. He married, June 11, 1741, Abigail Poor, and they had eight sons: Benjamin, John, Samuel, Daniel, Enoch, Aaron, Moses and Nathan. (John and descendants receive mention in this article).

(VI) Benjamin, eldest son of John (2) and Abigail (Poor) Noyes, was born April 29, 1742, in Bow, New Hampshire, and died March 16, 1811. He served in the Revolutionary war as an ensign in Colonel Moses Nichols' regiment in the expedition to Rhode Island in August, 1778. He probably settled in Vermont after the close of the war. He married Hannah, daughter of Benjamin Thompson, and their children, born in Bow, were: Abigail, Clement, Hannah, Thomas, Judith, Mary, Benning, Jane, Elizabeth, Phoebe and Sally, beside three who died in infancy.

(VII) Judith, third daughter and fifth child of Benjamin and Hannah (Thompson) Noyes, was born October 15, 1777, in Bow, and became the wife of Robert Thompson, who died in 1803, leaving two children. She subsequently married a Currier. (See Thompson, VI).

(VII) Mary (Polly), fourth daughter and sixth child of Benjamin and Hannah (Thompson) Noyes, was born June 11, 1779, in Bow, and died May 26, 1858, in Peacham, Vermont. She married Truman Martin. (See Martin, IV).

(VI) John (3), second of the eight sons of John (2) and Abigail (Poor) Noyes, was born in Bow, New Hampshire, March 13, 1744. He was a captain in the Revolutionary army. He married Mary Fowler, and died October 7, 1825. Their children were: Abigail, John, Sarah, Abner, Jacob, Nancy, Isaac C., Mary, George and Martha.

(VII) Nancy, sixth child and third daughter of John (3) and Mary (Fowler) Noyes, was born in Bow, June 29, 1779, and married John Robinson.

(VIII) Nancy, daughter of John and Nancy (Noyes) Robinson, born November, 1808, in Bow, was married November 25, 1840, to Samuel Dakin. (See Dakin, II).

(III) James, fourth son and eighth child of Nicholas and Mary (Cutting) Noyes, was born May 16, 1657, in Newbury, Massachusetts, and resided in that town. In the records of the town he is styled lieutenant-colonel. He was the first discoverer of limestone in the colony at Newbury, and this discovery is said to have created much excitement at the time, which was quite natural. In 1683 he married Hannah Knight. In his will he bequeaths to his eldest son his silver-headed staff and hilted rapier. His children, born in Newbury, were: Rebecca, Joseph, Hannah, Nicholas, Nahum, Benjamin, Mary and James.

(IV) James (2), youngest child of James (1) and Hannah (Knight) Noyes, was born August 19, 1705, in Newbury, and resided in that town and in Atkinson, New Hampshire. He was probably a soldier in the French and Indian war and was also a sergeant in the Revolutionary army, serving from September 27 to October 31, 1777. He was married in 1729 to Sarah Little, and their children were: Enoch, Sarah, Mary, James and Nathaniel.

(V) James (3), second son and fourth child of

James (2) and Sarah (Little) Noyes, was born March 31, 1745, in Atkinson, New Hampshire, and resided in that town where he died in 1831. He was married in 1770 to Jane Little, and they were the parents of a daughter and a son, Polly and Henry.

(VI) Polly, only daughter of James (3) and Jane (Little) Noyes, was born March 15, 1771, in Atkinson, New Hampshire, and became the wife of Enoch (2) Little. (See Little, V).

CHASE The annals of North America are frequently embellished by this name, which has been borne by statesmen, jurists, soldiers, clergymen and others honored in the various walks of life. New Hampshire has been highly honored by many prominent in the councils of the nation, and its annals may well give prominence to the name.

(I) For many years the earliest known ancestor of the American family of this name was Aquila Chase, who was among the founders of Hampton, New Hampshire, and he was said to be from Cornwall, England, by several antiquarians whose authority was tradition. A long search has established beyond a reasonable doubt that he was from Chesham, in Buckinghamshire, some thirty miles northwest of London. The family is said to have been of Norman origin, and it has been suggested that the name was formerly LaChasse. In the old English records it is spelled Chaace and Chaase, and in the fifteenth and sixteenth centuries it was modified to the present form most in use—Chase.

Matthew Chase, of the parish of Hundrich, in Chesham, gives his father's name as John, and the father of the latter as Thomas. As the name of Matthew's wife is the first female found in the line, this article will number Matthew as the first. His wife was Elizabeth, daughter of Richard Bould.

(II) Richard, son of Matthew and Elizabeth (Bould) Chase, married Mary Roberts, of Welsden, in Middlesex. He had brothers, Francis, John, Matthew, Thomas, Ralph and William, and a sister Bridget.

(III) Richard (2), son of Richard (1) and Mary (Roberts) Chase, was baptized August 3, 1542, and was married April 16, 1564, to Joan Bishop. Their children were: Robert, Henry, Lydia, Ezekiel, Dorcas, Aquila, Jason, Thomas, Abigail and Mordecai.

(IV) Aquila, fourth son of Richard (2) and Joan (Bishop) Chase, was baptized August 14, 1580. The unique name of Aquila is found nowhere in England, before or since, coupled with the name of Chase, which makes it reasonably certain that this Aquila was the ancestor of the American family. Tradition gives the name of his wife as Sarah. Record is found of two sons, Thomas and Aquila, the latter born in 1618. It is generally believed that William Chase, the first of the name in America, was an elder son, and that the others came with him or followed later. The fact of their being minors would lead to their absence from the records of the earliest days of William in this country. Some authorities intimate that Thomas and Aquila were employed by their uncle, Thomas Chase, who was part owner of the ship "John and Francis," and thus became navigators and so found their way to America. This theory is strengthened by the fact that Aquila was granted a house lot and six acres of marsh by the inhabitants of Newbury, Massachusetts, "on condition that he do go to sea and do service in the Towne with a boat for foure years." (Aquilla and William and descendants receive mention in this article).

(V) Thomas, assumed by some authorities to be elder son of Aquila (1) Chase, of Chesham, England, was born, probably about 1615, in England. He was in Hampton, New Hampshire, as early as 1640, and died there in 1652. He married Elizabeth, daughter of Thomas Philbrick, of Newbury, and probably lived in that town for a short time. His widow Elizabeth administered his estate. She was married (second), October 26, 1654, to John Garland; and (third), January 19, 1674, to Henry Roby. She died February 11, 1677. Thomas Chase's children were: Thomas, Joseph, James, Isaac and Abraham.

(VI) James, third son and child of Thomas and Elizabeth (Philbrick) Chase, was born 1649, in Hampton, where he resided. He was married November 2, 1675, to Elizabeth, daughter of Henry Green, and they had four daughters.

(VII) Abigail, second daughter and child of James and Elizabeth (Green) Chase, was born August 27, 1681, and married John (2) Chase (q. v.), a grandson of Aquila (2).

(V) Aquila (2), son of Aquila (1) Chase, settled in Newbury, Massachusetts (that part which is now Newburyport), about 1646. He was formerly in Hampton (now part of New Hampshire), where he and his brother Thomas received grants of land in June 1640, along with fifty-five others. As owner of a houselot he was listed among those entitled to a share in the common lands, December 3, 1645. This he subsequently sold to his brother, as shown by town records, after his removal to Newbury. His wife, Ann Wheeler, was a daughter of John Wheeler, who came from Salisbury, England, in September, 1646. According to the county records Aquila Chase and his wife, with her brother David Wheeler, were presented and fined "for gathering pease on the Sabbath." They were admonished by the court, after which their fines were remitted. Mr. Chase died December 27, 1670, aged fifty-two years. His widow was married June 14, 1672, to Daniel Mussiloway, and died April 21, 1687. Aquila's children were: Sarah, Ann, Priscilla, Mary, Aquila, Thomas, John, Elizabeth, Ruth, Daniel and Moses. Mary became the wife of John Stevens. (See Stevens, II). (Mention of John, Daniel and Moses and their descendants forms part of this article.)

(VI) Thomas, second son and sixth child of Aquila (2) and Anna (Wheeler) Chase, was born July 25, 1654, in Newbury, Massachusetts, and made his home in that town throughout life. He subscribed to the oath of allegiance there in 1678. His will was made August 3, 1732, and proved on the twenty-fifth of February following, indicating his death to be near the end of the former year. He was a carpenter and resided near the road leading to Amesbury Ferry. He was married (first), November 22, 1677, to Rebecca Follansbee, who died before August 2, 1714. On that date he was married to Elizabeth Mooers. All of his children except the youngest were probably born of the first wife. They were: Thomas, Jonathan, James, Aquila, Ruth, Mary, Josiah, Rebecca, Nathan, Judith and Elizabeth. (Mention of Jonathan and Nathan and descendants appears in this article).

(VII) Thomas (2), eldest child of Thomas (1) and Rebecca (Follansbee) Chase, was born September 15, 1680, in Newbury, where he resided. His will was made December 10, 1748, and proved March 1, 1756. He probably died about the close of 1757, at the age of seventy-seven years. He married Sarah Stevens, daughter of Deacon Thomas and Martha (Bartlett) Stevens, of Amesbury. Their children were: Thomas, Abel, Jonathan, Roger, Sarah, Elizabeth, Josiah and Abigail.

(VIII) Abel, second son and child of Thomas (2) and Sarah (Stevens) Chase, was born February 25, 1702, in Newbury, where he passed his life and died January, 1778. He was twice married, but no record of his first wife appears. The christian name of his second wife was Sarah.

(IX) Abel (2), son of Abel (1) and eldest child of his second wife, Sarah Chase, was born September 11, 1732, and died November 15, 1787, at the age of fifty-five years. He married Judith Gale, daughter of Isaac and Judith (Sargeant) Gale, of Sutton, Massachusetts. She was born April 12, 1734, and survived her husband more than seventeen years, dying February 10, 1805.

(X) Abel (3), eldest child of Abel (2) and Judith (Gale) Chase, was born October 29, 1754, in Sutton, Massachusetts. He was married September 24, 1779, to Hannah Bond, daughter of Jonas and Hannah (Hicks) Bond, of Sutton; she was born March 13, 1757.

(XI) Jonas, third child of Abel (3) and Hannah (Bond) Chase, was born August 20, 1783, in Sutton, Massachusetts, and died in 1827, in Sutton north parish, now Millbury, Massachusetts. He married Lavinia Boyden, and they had five sons: Jonathan, Ira, Leonard, whose sketch follows, Abel and Albin Bond.

(XII) Leonard, third son of Jonas and Lavinia (Boyden) Chase, was born August 7, 1811, in Milbury, Massachusetts, and died June 7, 1868, in Milford, New Hampshire. He received a common school education and the knowledge thus acquired was supplemented by a course at Andover Academy and by a two years' course at Yale, from the latter institution being forced to retire on account of impaired health. Shortly afterward he took up his residence in Milford, New Hampshire, and began the manufacture of agricultural implements, which proved highly remunerative. He took an active and prominent part in the affairs of his adopted city and state, and served as state representative, senator and member of the governor's council, in all of which capacities he rendered efficient and valuable service. He was an anti-slavery man, was one of the come-outers of the Congregational Church, and a member of the Free and Accepted Masons. Mr. Chase married (first), in 1834, Mary I. Dickey, of Milford, New Hampshire, daughter of Adam and Mary (Gordon) Dickey. She died December 16, 1842. Their children are: Mary I., widow of the late Elbridge Wason, of Brookline, Massachusetts. Hannah L. Cornelia Elizabeth, married Charles B. Tuttle. She died December 25, 1893. Mr. Chase married (second), March 21, 1844, Susanna Williams, born May, 1807, in Groton, Massachusetts, and died in 1869. She had one child, Frank W., born December 8, 1844, died May 14, 1906.

(VII) Jonathan, second son of Thomas and Rebecca (Follansbee) Chase, was born in Newbury, Massachusetts, in 1683, and died at Stratham, New Hampshire, in April, 1740. He was one of the principal proprietors of Sanbornton, New Hampshire, and married, in 1703, Joanna Palmer, of Bradford, Massachusetts.

(VIII) Jonathan (2), second son of Jonathan (1) and Joanna Palmer) Chase, was born at Newbury, September, 1707, and died at Stratham, New Hampshire, in 1744. He married Lydia Rollins. (Mention of their son, Nathaniel, and descendants appears in this article.

(IX) Jonathan (3), eldest son of Jonathan (2) and Lydia (Rollins) Chase, was born at Stratham, May 1, 1730, and died in Loudon, September 18, 1808. He was active in promoting the settlement of several New Hampshire towns and also in land speculation. He married, in 1749, Anne Taylor.

(X) Edward, second son of Jonathan (3) and Anne (Taylor) Chase, was born in Stratham, November 24, 1754, and died in Canterbury, June 19, 1814. May 30, 1775, he enlisted in the Second New Hampshire Regiment, commanded by Colonel Enoch Poor, and on September 23, 1776, re-enlistel in Colonel Thomas Tash's regiment, New Hampshire Continentals. He married, in 1779, Polly Moore, of Stratham.

(XI) Levi, eldest son of Edward and Polly (Moore) Chase, was born in Canterbury, April 8, 1782, and died there April 12, 1854. He married, June 8, 1808, Sally Page, of New Sharon, Maine, a descendant of Robert Page, of Ormsby, county of Norfolk, England. Their children were: Charles, of Grafton, New Hampshire, selectman and jurist; William Plummer, a Free-will Baptist clergyman; Uriah, mentioned below; and Levi Badger, of Sturbridge, Massachusetts, who served in the Civil war, compiled the Plympton genealogy and is the author of a history of Sturbridge.

(XII) Uriah, third son of Levi and Sally (Page) Chase, was born in Canterbury, September 28, 1819, and received his education at Gilmanton Academy. He entered the ministry of the Free-will Baptist church, and was licensed to preach by the New Durham quarterly meeting held in May, 1843. Thenceforth he labored as an evangelist until March 14, 1850, when he was ordained at East Parsonfield. His principal pastorates were at Limington, Raymond, Brixton, Parsonfield, Shapleigh, Hollis and Waterboro, Maine, and Alton, Belmont, Andover, Wolfboro, Nottingham, Strafford, Barrington, Epsom and Raymond, New Hampshire. He was a powerful preacher, with a reputation as an orator. His poetical works, which were published in three volumes under the nom-de-plume of William Canterbury, attracted much attention. He died in Waterboro, Maine, August 1, 1888. He married, October 25, 1855, Harriet Ann, daughter of John and Susan (Weeks) Kimball, of Northfield, New Hampshire. She died in Andover, November 18, 1862, leaving one son, John, born July 16, 1855, now a merchant in East Parish, Maine. Mr. Chase married, February 17, 1863, Lizzie Guilford, of Saco, Maine, and they have two children: Mary Nettie, born January 19, 1864; and Charles L., mentioned below. Miss Chase attended the North Parsonfield Academy and the Auburn high school, graduating from Bates College. She secured a free scholarship by winning the first prize awarded a woman in declamation. She was principal of Gilmanton and Proctor academies, and is president of the New Hampshire Equal Suffrage Association. She is a brilliant lecturer, and her services in the cause are in great demand. The degree of Master of Arts was conferred upon her by Bates College.

(XIII) Charles L., only son of Uriah and Lizzie (Guilford) Chase, was born July 15, 1865, at Strafford Ridge, New Hampshire, and attended the North Parsonfield Academy and the Auburn and Gorham high schools, graduating from the latter. He was afterward a pupil at the Main Central Institute. He taught two years and was afterward engaged in real estate in Boston, where he remained fifteen years. He now resides in Concord and is a member of the firm of Chase & Bailey, real estate brokers. He belongs to the Knights of Pythias, the Good Templars, the Sons of Temperance and the Grange. He is a Republican of the staunchest sort and a member of the Free-will Baptist church. He has been twice married. His first wife was Meda Tarbox, of Hollis, Maine, and his second, Margarette, daughter of John Otterson, a shipbuilder of Bath, Maine. Mr. and Mrs. Chase have two children: Ralph W. and Royal E.

(IX) Nathaniel, son of Jonathan (2) and Patience (Heath) Chase, was born April 5, 1750, probable in Hampton or Pittsfield, New Hampshire. In March, 1773, he married Sarah Sanborn, daughter of Reuben and Elizabeth (Ward) Sanborn, who was born at Hampton in 1755. Reuben Sanborn lived both at Hampton and Epsom, New Hampshire, and was prison keeper in 1755. Nathaniel Chase lived both at Seabrook and Pittsfield, New Hampshire.

(X) Jonathan (3), son of Nathaniel and Sarah (Sanborn) Chase, was born in Pittsfield, New Hampshire. He lived in that town the greater part of his life, and was a farmer, drover, stone contractor and bridge builder. On February 25, 1805, Jonathan (3) Chase married Abiah Hanson, daughter of Solomon Hanson, and they had ten children: Nathan, Lydia, Hanson S., whose sketch follows, John, Mary, Nathaniel E., Rouhamia, Elizabeth, Lavinia and James. Mrs. Chase died about 1835, and the father placed the younger children in the care of the Canterbury Shakers. Jonathan (3) Chase died at Canterbury, New Hampshire.

(XI) Hanson Sylvester, second son and third child of Jonathan (3) and Abiah (Hanson) Chase, was born April 7, 1823, at Portsmouth, New Hampshire. During his childhood his parents removed to Pittsfield, where he learned the old fashioned shoemaker's trade of True Tucker. He continued in this work five or six years, and then returned to the Shaker village in Canterbury and engaged in driving one of the wagons used in selling the wares and produce of the Community. He continued in this occupation, which took him all through northern New Hampshire, and even into Canada, until he was twenty-eight years old. In 1850 he moved to West Campton, where he lived on a farm for twenty-three years. At the same time he was engaged in lumbering and in buying and shipping hemlock bark. While at West Campton he was road commissioner and also served on the school board. In 1873 he came to Plymouth, building the house where he now lives. Mr. Chase is a man of force and character, and though past fourscore is still active. On May 23, 1850, Hanson S. Chase married Mary Ann Brown, daughter of Joseph and Relief (Ordway) Brown, who was born in Bristol, New Hampshire, November 10, 1830. They had four sons: James Whitcher, Warren Green, Irving Hanson, whose sketch follows; and Edward Averill. Mrs. Chase, a woman of unusually vigorous mind and body, and a kind friend to the sick, died October 21, 1898. Mr. Chase was a Quaker by birth, but they attended the Universalist Church in Plymouth. Of the sons of this couple, James W., born July 6, 1851, at West Campton, died at Plymouth, August 30, 1874. Warren G., born March 30, 1854, is in the lumber business with his brother, whose sketch follows. Edward Averill, born May 15, 1869, graduated from the Plymouth high school in 1888, and is now the editor and proprietor of the *Plymouth Record*.

(XII) Irving Hanson, third son and child of Hanson Sylvester and Mary Ann (Brown) Chase, was born at West Campton, New Hampshire, November 18, 1859. He was educated in the schools of Campton and Plymouth. He then engaged as clerk for his brother, Warren G. Chase, in the meat and grocery business, at Plymouth. At the end of three years, finding the need of an out-door life, he went to carpentering at which he worked for a year. From this it was an easy transition to the lumber business. The brothers, Warren G. and Irving H. Chase, bought a small timber tract on the Ellsworth branch of the Pemigewasset river, where they built a waterpower sawmill, which they conducted for thirteen years. They finally accumulated about seven thousand acres of timber land, and in 1894 they sold the property to George B. James, of Boston. The Chase brothers operated portable sawmills for two years and in 1898 built a small mill on the site of their present property in Plymouth. This was burned out at the end of a year, but they immediately rebuilt on a much larger scale, and are now conducting an extensive business. The motive power is a stationary engine of two hundred and fifty horse power, and the mill in one day will turn out more lumber than the early mills could have produced in a year. The pine logs are drawn by team from Plymouth and the adjoining towns, while those from remote points are shipped by rail. The firm gives employment to fifty and sometimes eighty men, and daily produces thirty thousand feet of dressed lumber. The greater part is recut and sold for packing cases. The firm also owns a sawmill on the Connecticut river at North Thetford, Vermont, which they purchased in 1901 from the citizens' Bank of St. Johnsbury, Vermont. They also own and run three portable sawmills which are operating in different parts of New Hampshire and Vermont. Besides his regular business, Mr. Chase also deals quite extensively in real estate. He is a Republican in politics, and a member of Plymouth Lodge, No. 66, Independent Order of Odd Fellows. He is a trustee of the Universalist Church in Plymouth. On December 7, 1881, Irving H. Chase married Minnie Elliott, daughter of Ephraim and Lucy (Broad) Elliott, who was born in Thornton, New Hampshire, April 7, 1862. They had two children: Mildred, born April 30, 1883, married, July 25, 1907, J. Frank Drake, secretary of Board of Trade, Springfield, Massachusetts; and Richard V., born June 4, 1888, who is now a student at Worcester Academy, and will enter Dartmouth College in the fall of 1907.

(VI) John, third son and seventh child of Aquila (2) and Ann (Wheeler) Chase, was born in Newbury, November 2, 1655. He married (first), May 23, 1677, Elizabeth Bingley; and (second), Lydia ——. The children by the first marriage were: William, John and Philip; by the second wife: Charles, Jacob, Abraham, Phebe, Mary, Lydia and Elizabeth.

(VII) John (2), second son and child of John (1) and Elizabeth (Bingley) Chase, was born in Newbury (?) August 26, 1684, and lived in Hampton, New Hampshire. He married Abigail, daughter of James Chase (q. v.), and they had five children: James, Elizabeth, Elihu, John and Hannah. (Mention of John and descendants appears in this article).

(VIII) Elihu, second son and third child of John and Abigail (Chase) Chase, was born September 7, 1705, in Hampton, New Hampshire, where he died November 30, 1794. He was married December 9, 1730, to Mary Swain, of Hampton. Their children were: John, Elizabeth, Elihu, William, Solomon, Zaccheus, Rachel, Abial, Lydia, Miriam, Anna, Asa and Patience. (Mention of Elihu and descendants follows in this article).

(IX) John (3), eldest son of Elihu and Mary (Swain) Chase, was born in Kensington, New Hampshire, where he lived and died. He married Lydia Green, and they were the parents of six children, who settled in Weare, New Hampshire, namely: Nathan G., Judith, David, Pauline, Abraham and Theodate.

(X) Theodate, daughter of John and Lydia (Green) Chase, was born July 6, 1773, in Kensington, and became the wife of Enoch Paige, (see Paige, VI), and subsequently of Aaron Foster, and died in 1862.

(IX) Elihu (2), second son of Elihu (1) and Mary (Swain) Chase, was born May 8, 1743, in Hampton, and resided in Kingston, New Hampshire. He was married July 14, 1773, to Sarah (Gove) ——, widow of —— Green. They were the parents of four sons: Samuel, Asa, Ezra and Hosea.

(X) Asa, second son and child of Elihu (2) and Sarah (Gove) Chase, was born February 14, 1777, in Kingston, and resided in that town. He was married February 14, 1790, to Huldah Fowle, daughter of Jonathan and Miriam (Martin) Fowle. She was born January 26, 1775, and died October 22, 1858. Their children were: Elihu, Sarah, Hannah, Jonathan and Asa (the last named is mentioned with descendants in this article).

(XI) Elihu (3), eldest child of Asa and Huldah (Fowle) Chase, was born March 11, 1800, in Kensington, and resided in Springfield, New Hampshire. He was married November 26, 1822, to Betsey Russell, of Wilton, New Hampshire. She was born May 25, 1796, daughter of Aaron and Phoebe (Gilbert) Russell of Wilton, and died February 24, 1888, in Springfield. Their children were: Betsey Ann, who became the wife of Seth Chellis Sargent. She died July 3, 1907; Hosea B., who was born and resided in Springfield up to 1888, and is now a resident of Newport; Daniel, who died in boyhood; and Elihu (IV). The last named went west, where he had a successful business career. He met his death by accident when in middle life.

(XII) Hosea Ballou, elder son and second child of Elihu (3) and Betsey (Russell) Chase, was born October 31, 1826, in Springfield, New Hampshire. He was a leading agriculturist of Springfield, and represented that town in the state assembly in 1877 and 1881. He was married January 22, 1852, to Evelyn H. Kidder, who was born April 12, 1835, daughter of Thomas and Ruth (Mudgett) Kidder, of Sunapee, New Hampshire. Their children are: Waldo Sumner, Herbert Anderson, and Olin Hosea. Mr. and Mrs. Chase are members of the Christian Church. (Mention of Olin H. appears in this article.)

(XIII) Waldo Sumner, elder child of Hosea B. and Evelyn (Kidder) Chase, was born October 14, 1855, in Springfield, New Hampshire. He is a machinist by trade, which he follows in Franklin. He was married (first), January 15, 1875, to Helen Frances Adams, who was born 1855 and died October 29, 1882. Mr. Chase was married (second), December 26, 1885, to Nina Matilda Wallace, who was born April 5, 1868, daughter of William and Dinah (Marsh) Wallace, of Grantham, New Hampshire, who now reside in Franklin. Mr. Chase has one child, Daniel Adams, born July 24, 1876.

(XIII) Olin Hosea, youngest son and child of Hosea B. and Evelyn (Kidder) Chase, received his primary education in the public schools of Springfield, and subsequently attended the high school of Newport, from which he was graduated with the class of 1892. The following year he entered the employ of *The Republican Champion*, a well-known and prosperous weekly journal of Newport, and in 1904 purchased the plant and continues to conduct the newspaper named, and in conjunction therewith also conducts a job printing establishment. In 1904 Mr. Chase was elected town clerk, and has been re-elected each year since. Mr. Chase was one of the original members of Company M, Second Regiment, New Hampshire National Guard, organized in January, 1898. He was first sergeant of his company. This regiment served for six months, being stationed at Chickamauga Park, Georgia, during this period. Sergeant Chase was promoted to a second-lieutenancy. Upon the return of his regiment from the south, and its being mustered out of the national and into the state service, Lieutenant Chase was commissioned captain. He retired therefrom in 1903. Mr. Chase is a member of the Mt. Vernon Lodge, No. 115, Ancient Free and Accepted Masons; Chapter of the Tabernacle No. 19, Royal Arch Masons; Columbian Council (Clarmont) Royal Select and Master Shriners; Sullivan Commandery (Clarmont) Knights Templar; Bektash Temple (Concord), Ancient Arabic Order Nobles of the Mystic Shrine; and Aurora Chapter, No. 33, Order of the Eastern Star. Mr. Chase is past master of his lodge, high priest of the chapter, and worthy patron of the Eastern Star.

(XIII) Herbert Anderson, second son and child of Hosea B. and Evelyn (Kidder) Chase, was born September 28, 1862, in Newport, and resides in that town. He was married September 20, 1884, to Phoebe Russell, who was born September 20, 1865, daughter of William and Mary Ann (Whipple) Russell, of Sunapee, now residing in Newport. His children are: Earl Herbert, born October 17, 1886, and William Hosea, January 18, 1889.

(XII) Elihu Franklin, fourth child of Elihu (3) and Phoebe (Russell) Chase, was born November 17, 1833, in Newport, and died in that town May 21, 1883, in his fiftieth year. He was married (first), September 15, 1859, to Ella M. Sherman, of National, Iowa. She was born March 22, 1844, and died August 8, 1881. Mr. Chase was married (second) January 26, 1882, to Caroline S. Amerine, who was born January 4, 1855, in Hocking county, Ohio. In 1854 he went from New Hampshire to National, Iowa, where he continued until 1877. From that time until his death he resided in Sac City, Iowa. All his children were born of the first wife, namely: Beecher, April 6, 1862; Elihu Burrett, October 21, 1865; Althea, December 8, 1870; Martha, March 1, 1875; Bertha, August 26, 1879.

(XI) Sarah, elder daughter of Asa and Huldah (Fowle) Chase, was born 1802, and was married November 29, 1827, to Nathan S. Trow, of Springfield, New Hampshire. He was born November 28, 1804, and died October 15, 1885. They resided at Mitchell, Iowa, and were the parents of three children: Elihu, the first, born July 11, 1828, died April 20, 1895; Anthony Chase, born July 14, 1833; Jonathan, born March 15, 1806, married Mary Messer, of New London, New Hampshire.

(XI) Asa (2) Chase, third son and fifth child of Asa (1) and Huldah (Fowle) Chase, was born April 19, 1812, and was married June 12, 1836, to Mary Ann Abbott, daughter of Theodore and Mary (Burpee) Abbott (see Abbott, ——). She was born April 11, 1816, and died February 15, 1885. Their children were: Marshall Tram, Willard Winter, and James Albin. Marshall Tram was born September 16, 1837, and resides in Wilmot, New Hampshire. He was married June 1, 1873, to Betsey Ann Robey, who was born April 14, 1845, daughter of John and Betsey (Roundy) Robey of Sutton, New Hampshire. The youngest, James A.,

was born July 23, 1841, and died January 8, 1886. He resided in Sunapee, and was a soldier of the Civil war. He enlisted October 20, 1861, in Company G, Sixth New Hampshire Volunteers, and was wounded August 29, 1862, at the second battle of Bull Run, and was discharged April 20, 1863, at Providence, Rhode Island, and re-enlisted September 6, of the following year in Company C, Twenty-fourth Regiment Veteran Reserve Corps. He was discharged November 14, 1865, at Washington, D. C. He was married May 17, 1868, to Betsey Almira Smith, who was born May 12, 1848, daughter of John B. and Almira (Felch) Smith. Their children were: Grace Bell, Nellie May and Arthur Emerson. The last named died at the age of eleven years.

(XII) Willard Winter, second son of Asa (2) and Mary A. (Abbott) Chase, was born April 18, 1839. He received his education in the common schools, and was reared on a farm. At the age of twenty-four years he bought his grandfather's farm in Springfield, and made great improvements upon the property in the course of time. In 1871, in company with his partner, Alfred Martin, he bought mill property at George's Mills, in Sunapee, and for eleven years they continued to operate the mill with success. In 1880 Mr. Chase began the erection of "Pleasant Home," one of the most popular hotels on Lake Sunapee. This he leased in 1904 to the present proprietors. In connection with the house he is the owner of thirty acres of land, on which he produced most of the supplies for the table in the hotel. He kept six cows and produced all the milk, butter, cheese, fruit and vegetables for summer use, beside other supplies. He is a member of New London Grange, Patrons of Husbandry; of Mont Vernon Lodge, Ancient Free and Accepted Masons, and Tabernacle Chapter, Royal Arch Masons, of Newport. He was one of the organizers and is vice-president and director of the Sunapee Mutual Fire Insurance Company, which is now carrying some $350,000 in risks. Mr. Chase is the holder of the first policy issued by the company. In 1856 he was baptized and became a member of the First Christian Church of Springfield, and was soon after made deacon, and has held that office forty years, having been connected for the last twenty-five years with the George's Mills Church, whose house of worship was erected in 1897, largely through his aid and influence. For eight years he was superintendent of the Sunday-school in Springfield. He is a liberal contributor to home and foreign missions, and is especially interested in that work in Japan. Mr. Chase received a patent on a receiving aperture for ash bins and similar vaults and tanks. It is calculated for insertion in a wall or other permanent location, and is so constructed that the opening will remain either open or closed as the wish of the operator, by its own gravity, and at the same time, while open, serve as a conduit for the material to be sent through the aperture. This has never been placed upon the market. Mr. Chase has done much for the community in which he lives, and especially in the way of encouraging summer visitors, and his ambition to make the place a popular resort has succeeded well. It is well known to people in New York and Philadelphia, as well as Boston and various points in New Jersey, who make it their place of recreation during the summer season. Since disposing of the hotel he has erected another fine set of buildings and continues to board a few of his old patrons. In all his undertakings and efforts he has been cheerfully and efficiently aided by his good wife, who has contributed no small part to the accumulation of the competency which they now enjoy. He was married January 3, 1870, to Laura Ann Morgan, who was born July 6, 1846, daughter of William and Mary (Fuller) Morgan, of Springfield, New Hampshire. They have one child, Dura Alfred Chase, who was born March 26, 1871, in Springfield. He is an industrious and capable young man, and is making his way in the world. He was married September 4, 1895, to Harriet Augusta George, who was born November 25, 1869, daughter of Daniel A. and Miriam D. (Blood) George. Her great grandfather, Jonathan George, was the first settler in this locality, and for him George's Mills was named. Mr. Chase is the owner of "Pleasant Home," and also conducts a livery business. He has two children: Maurice George and Harold Dura.

(VIII) John (3), third son and fourth child of John (2) and Abigail (Chase) Chase, was born September 18, 1708, and resided in Seabrook. His will was proved September 25, 1776. He married, March 27, 1729, Anna Runlet (or Rundlett); and they had Thomas, John, Daniel, James, Charles and Jacob.

(IX) Thomas, second son and child of John and Ann (Rundlett) Chase, was born in Seabrook, July 23, 1731, and died September 19, 1787. He married, in 1758, Mary Dow, by whom he had six children: Nathaniel, Amos, Charles, Edward, Rachel, and Winthrop.

(X) Nathaniel (4), eldest child of Thomas and Mary (Dow) Chase, was born November 9, 1753, and died in Henniker, September 19, 1747. He married, September 27, 1780, Mary Brown, of Hampton, and immediately removed to Henniker, where he had already, before his marriage, made a clearing on the south side of Craney Hill. He went there first, taking his axe, a bag of meal, and a cow. He built himself a "bough house," and commenced his clearing, presuming he had no neighbors nearer than Weare. One day, as he started for Weare to grind his axe, he heard the sound of axes to the westward of him. He at once resolved to know whence the sound came, and was delighted to find within a mile of him the Ross brothers, settled on a clearing; what was still better, they had a grindstone, upon which he ground his axe, thus saving a journey to Weare. The children of Nathaniel and Mary (Brown) Chase were: Winthrop, Abraham, Hannah, Nathaniel, Jonathan, Charles, Mary, Peace, Nathaniel and Sarah (mention of Jonathan and descendants forms part of this article).

(XI) Abraham, second son and child of Nathaniel and Mary (Brown) Chase, was born in Henniker, May 17, 1783, and died March 30, 1861. He lived many years upon the hill in the northwesterly part of the town, know as "Wadsworth Hill." The latter part of his life he resided in Henniker village. He married, first April 3, 1811, Keziah Peaslee, of Deering, daughter of Humphrey and Phebe Peaslee. She died February 15, 1819, and he married, second, October 28, 1824, Fanny Smith, daughter of Bezaleel Smith. The children of the first wife were Hannah and Humphrey; and those by the second wife were: Mary R. and Frances M.

(XII) Hannah, eldest child of Abraham and Keziah (Peaslee) Chase was born December 21, 1811, and was married, December 21, 1837, to Dutton Woods (see Woods, VI).

(XI) Jonathan, fourth son of Nathaniel and Mary (Brown) Chase, was born in Henniker, April 4, 1788, and died October 20, 1864. He settled on what is called the old "Craney Hill" farm, consisting of about two hundred acres, and was a prosperous farmer. May 14, 1817, he married Patience Peaslee, who died February 18, 1868.

(XII) Eli, second son of Jonathan and Patience (Peaslee) Chase, was born in Henniker, August 15, 1820, and died February 8, 1898. He grew up and received his education in the district schools of his native town. Early in life he moved to Weare and settled on the farm now owned by his son. He was a Democrat in politics and served as selectman of the town. He was a member of the Society of Friends until his marriage, when he was declared out of it by marrying outside the Society. March 20, 1842, he married Hannah A. Brown, of Henniker.

(XIII) Horace Oscar, only son of Eli and Hannah A. (Brown) Chase, was born at North Weare, September 1, 1852. Owing to the delicate health of his father, he, at the age of twelve years, assumed the duties and cares of the farm, thus early in life developing a natural ability for active business. He attended the schools of his native town and the academies of Francestown and Contoocook; laboring on the farm in summer and attending school in winter; his was a very strenuous young life. At the age of eighteen years he bought and operated with profit, lumber lots, being probably the youngest lumber dealer in the state. He continued this active life for many years, and at the present time has increased his farm from one hundred to seven hundred acres. Under his supervision the land has been brought to a high state of cultivation and to-day is one of the most productive farms in the town. The extent of his cattle industry is indicated by the fact that the government compelled him to kill ninety-two animals in 1903 on account of the foot and mouth disease. He also has a bearing orchard of one thousand trees and about two thousand young Baldwin trees coming along. He is a charter member of Weare Grange, No. 276, acting as steward of the same in 1899 and 1900; his wife was lecturer in 1899, 1900 and 1901. In politics he is a stanch Democrat, having occupied nearly every office of trust in town. Appraiser of real estate; supervisor of check list and served nine years as selectman, being chairman of the board longer than any other man in one hundred years. He was a representative of the town in the state legislature in 1902 and 1903. In 1906 he built the first piece of Macadam road ever constructed in town, and has always been closely identified with all the important affairs of the town and prominent in all things pertaining to its progress and welfare.

On May 1, 1884, he was married to Ida S. King, daughter of Jonathan and Irene Peasley King. Mrs. Chase is a very enterprising woman, taking an active part in the literary work of the town and a prominent member of the Grange. She was graduated from the Milford high school. They have two daughters: Florence Irene and Mildred Roanna. The elder was educated in the Manchester high school and New Hampshire Literary Institute, the younger in the Nashua high school. Florence I. is a musician of considerable ability and both are successful teachers in the public schools.

(VI) Daniel, fourth son and tenth child of Aquilla (2) and Anne (Wheeler) Chase, was born in Newbury, December 9, 1661, and died February 8, 1707. He married, May 25, 1683, Martha Kimball, who survived him, and married (second), 1713, Josiah Heath. The ten children of Daniel and Martha were: Martha, Sarah, Dorothy, Isaac, Lydia, Mehitable, Judith, Abner, Daniel and Enoch.

(VII) Daniel (2), third son and ninth child of Daniel (1) and Martha (Kimball) Chase, was born October 15, 1702. He was one of the proprietors "of the common and undivided land in the township of Rumford," formerly Penacook, now Concord, New Hampshire, where he settled before March 1, 1733, and died before March 16, 1775, the date of the proving of his will. His name was attached to a proprietors' order to their clerk to call a meeting of said proprietors, January 18, 1737. He was one of the guard in the garrison around Timothy Walker's house in 1746; was a petitioner with others for military protection for a certain grist-mill, 1748; was surveyor of highways 1734; was one of Captain Joseph Eastman's company, in Colonel Joseph Blanchard's regiment, which was raised for the expedition against Crown Point, mostly in service from April to October, 1755; and was a signer of the remonstrance against the petition of certain persons to annex the Gore to Canterbury, 1760. He married (first), January 3, 1723, Mary Carpenter; (second), February 12, 1726, Elizabeth Collins. (Mention of David, supposed to be their son, and descendants, Isaac and descendants appears in this article).

(VIII) Jonathan, son of Daniel and Elizabeth (Collins) Chase, was born in Concord, March 1, 1733. He was a reputable citizen of Concord, and a member of Captain Joseph Eastman's company in 1755, and was surveyor of highways in 1766. He married Sarah Stickney, born in Concord, October 14, 1737, daughter of Jeremiah and Elizabeth Stickney.

(IX) Samuel, son of Jonathan and Sarah (Stickney) Chase, was born March 10, 1761. He married Molly Stanley.

(X) Horace, son of Samuel and Molly (Stanley) Chase, was born in Unity, December 14, 1788. He graduated at Dartmouth College in 1814. The same year he went to Hopkinton and entered the law office of Matthew Hervey. In 1837 and 1842 he was moderator of town meetings; in 1824 and 1825 and again from 1829 to 1835 town clerk; from 1826 to 1835 town treasurer; in 1829 a representative to the general court; from 1830 to 1832 assistant clerk of the house of representatives; from 1829 to 1850 postmaster; from 1843 to 1855 judge of probate for Merrimack county, publishing in 1845 the *Probate Directory*.

Horace Chase was made a Mason in Blazing Star Lodge, No. 11, of Concord, in 1815. He was initiated May 23, passed August 15 and raised October 17, 1815. He was made a Royal Arch Mason in 1817, and a Knight Templar in 1826. In the autumn of 1818 he removed to Cheshire county, where he resided until July, 1821. In 1819 he was elected worthy master of Corinthian Lodge, No. 28, then working in Newport, and in 1820 represented that lodge in the Grand Lodge, when he was honored with the appointment of district deputy grand master. In 1821 he was appointed grand lecturer, and in 1822 again appointed district deputy grand master, to which office he was reappointed in 1823 and in 1829, 1847, 1848 and 1849. In 1850 he was elected deputy grand master, and in 1851 and 1852 was elected most worthy grand master. In 1854 he was elected grand secretary, and annually re-elected to that office, in which he served seventeen consecutive years. In 1850 a committee was appointed by the grand lodge to "confer upon a uniform system of lectures and work, and report to the grand lodge at the next annual communi-

HORACE O. CHASE.

cation." Mr. Chase was appointed chairman of that committee, having associated with him three other distinguished Masons: John Christie, Daniel Balch and John J. Prentiss. The following year the committee made a report to the grand lodge, recited the lectures and exemplified the work, which was accepted, approved, and adopted by the grand lodge, with scarcely one important alteration or amendment; and notwithstanding an attempt was afterward made to substitute another work for it, that work as originally reported, with trifling and immaterial alterations, to this day remains the standard and only authorized work in this jurisdiction. In 1858 the grand lodge decided to reprint its early proceedings, and intrusted to Mr. Chase the preparation of copy, which for many years could be obtained from manuscript records only. He superintended the publication of these, and in 1860 presented the grand lodge a bound volume embracing the proceedings for fifty-three years, from the formation of the grand lodge in 1789 to 1841 inclusive. In 1869 he had completed a second volume containing the proceedings from 1842 to 1856 inclusive. Judge Chase held office in the grand lodge thirty-four years, and to him the Masonic order in New Hampshire is greatly indebted for its prosperity. He died in Hopkinton, March 1, 1875, and his funeral on the 6th was largely attended by Knights Templar and Masons of different degrees, and by numerous citizens not Masons. His life was long and useful and active, and the good works he did are yet remembered by many who knew him.

He married (first), December 24, 1818, Betsey Blanchard, daughter of Stephen and Betsey (Estabrooks) Blanchard, of Hopkinton, by whom he had four children: Mary Elizabeth, Samuel Blanchard: Horace Gair and Charles Carroll. Mrs. Chase died June 28, 1843, and on June 5, 1844, Judge Chase married (second), Lucy Blanchard, her sister, who died December 22, 1848. November 15, 1849, Judge Chase married (third), Ruhama Clarke, widow of Daniel W. Clarke, of Manchester, and daughter of Joseph and Anna (Wilson) Cochran, of New Boston, who survived him and resided in Hopkinton.

(IX) Daniel, a grandson of John (2) and Abigail (Chase) Chase, married Esther Shaw, and they were the parents of "Hunter John."

(X) John, son of Daniel and Esther (Shaw) Chase, settled in the town of Weare previous to the Revolution. He was famous for his skill in hunting when wild animals were abundant in the forests of that town, and by reason of his prowess as a hunter he came to be known as "Hunter John." He married Sarah Morrill, of Salisbury, Massachusetts, and by her had four sons and three daughters: Chevey, Charles, David, John, Hannah, Rhoda and Sally Chase.

(XI) Charles, second son and child of John and Sarah (Morrill) Chase, was for many years a prominent business man in the town of Weare. For a long time he was in trade at Weare Center and afterward built the mills on Center brook and lived there until the time of his death. He married (first), Fanny Whittle, and (second), Mrs. Nancy Peterson. By his first wife he had five children: Harriet, Charles, Samuel W., Fanny and Cosmus; and by his second wife two children: Rhoda and Israel P. Chase.

(XII) Israel P., youngest son and child of Charles Chase, was born in Weare, New Hampshire, March 1827, and died at Hillsborough, New Hampshire, May 26, 1890. In early life he was a printer and when twenty-two years old left the "case" and went to the gold fields of California, voyaging around Cape Horn. He was numbered with the famous forty miners, but after sharing the vicissitudes of a miner's life for a few months returned home by way of the Isthmus of Panama. Later on he took up the study of medicine as a disciple of the Hahnemannian doctrine and completed his professional education at the old Cleveland Homoeopathic Medical College, Cleveland, Ohio, the second institution of its kind in the country. He practiced a year in Richmond, Virginia, and in 1856 settled in the town of Henniker, New Hampshire. In 1871 he removed to Hillsborough Bridge, and lived there until his death. In 1890, in association with his only son, James P. Chase, he established *The Messenger*, and continued the publication of that newspaper until the death of his son in 1876. Dr. Chase married Frances S. Vose, of Francestown, New Hampshire. She was born September 7, 1831, and died July, 1890. They had three children. James P. Chase, their only son, was born in Richmond, Virginia, February 2, 1856, and died in Hillsborough, New Hampshire, November 1, 1876. He was a young man of much promise, had many friends and was considered one of the best practical printers in Hillsborough county. Emma Frances Chase, their elder daughter, was born in Henniker, New Hampshire, July 7, 1859, and married, February 23, 1891, Charles William Thompson (see Thompson III). Alice Pearson Chase, their younger daughter, was born in Henniker, New Hampshire, August 28, 1862, and married Ira P. Smith, of Boston, Massachusetts. They have one daughter, Emma G.

(VI) Ensign Moses, eleventh and youngest child of Aquila (2) and Ann (Wheeler) Chase, was born December 24, 1663, in Newbury, Massachusetts. He was married November 10, 1684, to Ann Follonsbee, and settled in what is now West Newbury, on the main road, about one hundred rods above Bridge street (present). A large majority of the Chases in the Uniter States are said to be his descendants. He died September 6, 1743. Ann Chase was admitted to the Newbury Chuch in 1698, and died April 15, 1708, at the birth of a son. Her tombstone at the old "Plains" graveyard in Newburyport, Massachusetts, which has this date, is the oldest one known bearing the name of Chase. Mr. Chase was married (second), December 13, 1713, to Sarah Jacobs, of Ipswich. Mr. Chase's will was made July 3, 1740, in which he mentions his grandson but no wife, from which it is inferred that he survived his second wife. His children were: Moses (died young) and Daniel (twins), Moses, Samuel, Elizabeth, Stephen, Hannah, Joseph and Benoni. (Samuel, Joseph and Daniel and descendants receive extended mention in this article).

(VII) Moses (3), third son and child of Moses (2) and Ann (Follansbee) Chase, was born January 20, 1688, in Newbury, Massachusetts, now West Newbury, and died September 17, 1760. He lived on the east half of the homestead. He married, October 12, 1709, Elizabeth, daughter of Rev. Thomas and Mary (Perkins) Wells, of Amesbury, granddaughter of Thomas Wells, the settler, who came over in the "Susan and Ellen" in 1635, and settled at Ipswich. She was born December 17, 1688, in Amesbury, and died May 31, 1755. Their children were: Wells, Moses, Seth, Humphrey, Elizabeth, Eleazer, Anne (died young), Daniel, Anne, Rebecca and Abigail.

(VIII) Moses (4), second son and child of Moses (3) and Elizabeth (Wells) Chase, was born July 1, 1713, in Newbury, Massachusetts, and died on the old homestead where he had lived, October

9, 1789. He married, December 9, 1736, Judith Bartlett, daughter of Captain Richard and Margaret (Woodman) Bartlett, who was born in Newbury, March 10, 1713, and died February 18, 1785. They had ten children: Wells, Rebecca, Elizabeth, John, Judith, Waters, Stephen, Enoch, Joshua and Moses.

(VIII) Isaac Chase, son of Daniel Chase, of Amesbury, was born in Amesbury, about 1732, and between 1763 and 1773, removed with his two brothers, Abner and Daniel, to Warner, New Hampshire, where he settled and became a leading man in the town. He often served as moderator of town meetings, and as a selectman. He was also one of the early representatives of the "classed towns."

(IX) Isaac (2), son of Isaac (1) Chase, was born in Amesbury, Massachusetts, in 1764, and removed with his parents in childhood to Warner, and was a life long farmer in that town.

(X) Henry, son of Isaac Chase, was born in Warner, July 17, 1800. He was a farmer and resided in Warner. He married Hannah Palmer, who was born in Warner. She was the daughter of Timothy Palmer, an early settler of Warner. Eight children were born of this marriage and grew up.

(XI) Daniel Aquilla, son of Henry and Hannah (Palmer) Chase, was born in Warner, December 31, 1839. He was educated in the common schools of Warner, and at Phillips Andover Acadamy. In 1850 he removed to Boston and went into the employ of the Roxbury Distilling Company. In 1858 he entered into the business of distilling for himself in Charlestown, and carried on that business until after the close of the war of the Rebellion. He then went west and started the largest rum distillery in the world at Louisville, Kentucky, which he operated, employing many men and turning out annually a product of thousands of barrels. making a large revenue to the government. In politics Mr. Chase was a Republican, and was a stalwart supporter of the party and a liberal contributor to its success in pecuniary contributions. He was a member of the Republican Club, the Home Market Club, the Society of Colonial Wars, and the Society of Sons of the American Revolution. He was a member of the Masonic order and attained the thirty-second degree, and also of the Independent Order of Odd Fellows. He married Mary L. Hoxie, daughter of Benjamin and —— Hoxie, of Maine.

(IX) Wells, oldest child of Moses (4) and Judith (Bartlett) Chase, was born in Newbury, now West Newbury. Massachusetts, September 9, 1737, O. S., on the old Chase farm where his father and grandfather were born and where his great-grandfather settled and died. At the age of sixteen he was apprenticed to learn the trade of house carpenter. In the year 1754 he enlisted under Governor Shirley, who went up the Kennebec to keep order among the Indians, taking twenty days' provisions, his arms, ammunition and blanket on his back. In 1758 he went into the army during the French war, marched to Lake George, and was in the battle of Ticonderoga under General Abercrombie. He was married, February 2, 1760, to Sarah, daughter of Samuel and Mary (Illsley) Hovey and in 1771 moved to Chester, now Auburn, New Hampshire. settling on a fifty-acre lot purchased from Joseph Basford, in a region that had been but little, if any, improved by the pioneers. He died December 28, 1824. His wife was born September 8, 1737, O. S., and died October 5, 1814. Their children were: Benjamin Pike and Hannah. The latter died at an early age.

(X) Benjamin Pike, oldest child of Wells and Sarah Hovey) Chase, was born on "meeting-house hill," in Newbury, Massachusetts, now West Newbury. June 28, 1762. His school privileges were fair for that time, one of his teachers being the eccentric master, Simeon Chase, a widely known instructor of the period. When he was nine years of age the family moved to Chester, New Hampshire (now Auburn) after which time his school advantages were very limited. It may be assumed that the occasion of the removal from the fertile valley of the Merrimac was the state of the family exchequer as the amount of money necessary to purchase a garden spot in Newbury would pay for many acres of rocky land in the Chester woods. As indicating the necessity for economy it may be noted that in the construction of the house on account of the scarcity of nails, some of the floors were laid with wooden pins which may be seen today. The house is still in good condition and good for another century of use but has recently passed out of the name of Chase. Under this roof his father and mother, three wives, two children and himself died, and with one exception. He was a man of strong individuality, philosophical, practical, of sterling integrity, and was often intrusted with public duties, serving as tax collector for town and parish, selectman and deputy sheriff. He united with the Presbyterian Church in 1814. in 1819 was chosen ruling elder, and in 1825 visited his two sons living in Maryland and attended the general assembly of the church as a delegate. From 1840 to 1850 he annuallly visited for several weeks his son, Stephen, then professor of mathematics at Dartmouth College, where he indulged to the fullest extent his taste for reading scientific and other works. At the age of eighty-nine he visited the widow of the professor, who had died a few months previously. He was social in his feelings, and greatly enjoyed making and receiving visits. When the temperance cause was first agitated in Chester, in 1829, he declined to enter into it, and its interference with the social drinking custom was one of his objections, but when he found that the drunkards were citing him as an example, he abandoned the use of all intoxicating drinks, and was a strong and consistent advocate of total abstinence the rest of his life. He early became interested in the anti-slavery movement and aided in forming a society in Chester in 1835, and continued a firm advocate of the freedom of speech and the press, and the same laws and privileges for both white and black. He was not of robust physique, being rather tall and slight of frame, yet he usually was blessed with good health, doubtless resulting largely from his active and temperate habits. He did not complain of the pains usually incident to old age, and sat up all the day before his death. He was up and dressed the next morning, but soon laid down and passed away as quietly as going to sleep, March 16, 1852, lacking but three months of ninety years. As showing the great vitality of the family it can be said that the average age at death of seven children was eighty-four years and two months, and of nine, over seventy-six years, two of the eleven children having lived but a short time.

The children by the first wife were: Moses and Wells; and by the second: John, Stephen (died young), Sarah, Benjamin, Molly and Pike; and by the third: Anna and Stephen. (The last with descendants is mentioned in this article).

(XI) Benjamin (7), sixth child and fifth son of Benjamin Pike and Anna (Blasdell) Chase, was born in that part of Chester which is now Auburn,

B. Pike Chase

Benj. Chase, Jr.

[illegible] died May 5, 1880, aged nearly [illegible] twenty-six years of his life [illegible]. His education, as [illegible] eight weeks [illegible] in a house [illegible] by sixteen feet [illegible] and [illegible], with [illegible] and warmed [illegible] which lay out in the snow [illegible]. The writing [illegible] were planks [illegible] fastened to the wall of the house [illegible] inserted in [illegible] with legs [illegible]. Three terms [illegible] schools taught [illegible] his school days [illegible] of his own [illegible] the common [illegible] of three,' in [illegible] and chalk." In [illegible] writes [illegible]: "In 18[illegible]6 I [illegible] from Stephen [illegible], Esq., an English [illegible] Geometry, Trigonometry and Surveying, [illegible] house, but [illegible] for the pleasure of it and [illegible] practical advantage [illegible]. In the summer of 1826 [illegible] had a controversy [illegible] to settle it [illegible] Chester [illegible] library and got [illegible] contained rules for [illegible] eclipses. I [illegible] thing to know [illegible] elements are [illegible] a geometrical [illegible] is made, [illegible]. I had to copy the [illegible] calculated the eclipses [illegible] of the [illegible]. I had no [illegible] than a [illegible] dividers [illegible] I had to [illegible] dividers. These studies, pursued [illegible]. In 1828 Stephen [illegible] surveying [illegible] took it up and [illegible] the [illegible] and [illegible] trade."

[illegible] a descendant [illegible] generations of clock-mak[illegible] inherit[illegible]. In 1825 he [illegible] wright, which [illegible] the remainder [illegible] during those years he [illegible] in the sawmills and grist [illegible] his time. He also [illegible] and finished the house [illegible] his marriage, and [illegible] to the end of his life.

[illegible] story [illegible] in Pres[illegible] Mr. [illegible] to [illegible] the genealogy [illegible] descending [illegible]. This he [illegible] for his own [illegible] collected more [illegible] lines, making very thorough [illegible] estate and probate records, and [illegible] of old Newbury, Cornish, New Hamp[illegible] and other places, and thus locating the resi[illegible] many of the earlier generations. Dr. John [illegible] of Taunton, Massachusetts, did much [illegible] at the same time, and the [illegible] of their labors is now [illegible] with the

[illegible] 1876, [illegible] and [illegible] children [illegible] practical school [illegible] wright in [illegible] Hampshire [illegible] had the [illegible]

Benj. Chase Jr.

July 7, 1799, and died May 5, 1889, aged nearly ninety. "The first twenty-six years of his life were spent on his father's farm. His education, as stated by him, was limited to about eight weeks each winter, after the age of twelve, at the common school, kept in a house fifteen by sixteen feet, rough boarded and ceiled, with three windows of nine panes each, a smoky chimney, and warmed by burning green wood, which lay out in the snow until needed. The writing desks were planks or boards, one edge fastened to the wall of the house and the other supported by legs inserted in auger holes, and stools with legs for seats. Three terms previously, in summers at private schools taught by a woman, made up the sum of his school days. Before going to any school he had of his own volition, and practically unaided, mastered the common school arithmetic as far as the 'rule of three,' in the absence of a slate, using a board and chalk." In his reminiscences he writes further: "In 1816 I borrowed from Stephen Chase, Esq., an English work on Geometry, Trigonometry and Surveying. and went through that in the school house, but without a teacher, just for the pleasure of it and without the least idea of any practical advantage. I also studied navigation. In the summer of 1816 my brother John and my father had a controversy on some point of astronomy, and to settle it father went to Chester to the town library and got Ferguson's Astronomy, which contained rules for calculating new and full moons and eclipses. I thought that it would be a pleasant thing to know how to do it. From the tables certain elements are obtained, and then a geometrical projection is made. As the book must be returned I had to copy the tables, and now have them. I calculated the eclipses for several years, and have several of the projections now. I had no other instruments than a two foot Gunter scale and a pair of brass dividers. If I wished to draw a circle I had to tie a pan to one leg of the dividers. These studies, pursued merely for the pleasure of them, have proved of great practical utility to me. In 1818 Stephen Chase, who had done all of the land surveying for many years, failed in health and I took it up and did much for several years, which prepared me to write and make the map for the History of Chester. These studies also prepared me to understand the science of the millwright's trade."

His son writes of him: "Being a descendant on his mother's side of two generations of clock makers, he was a mechanic by inheritance. In 1825 he found temporary employment as a millwright, which led him into that line of business for the remainder of his most active life, and during those years he made many improvements in the sawmills and grist mills that were in use preceding his time. He also procured the necessary tools and finished the house which became his residence on his marriage, and was his home to the end of his life.

"When the story of the Chase fortune in England was proclaimed, about 1846, Mr. Chase, though giving no credence to the report, became interested to look up the genealogy of his ancestry and the different lines descending from Aquila. This he made complete for his own line and collected much more for connecting lines, making very thorough search of real estate and probate records, and making maps of old Newbury, Cornish, New Hampshire, and other places, and thus locating the residences of many of the earlier generations. Dr. John B. Chace, of Taunton, Massachusetts, did much work in the same line at the same time, and the product of their labors is now deposited with the New England Historic-Genealogical Society in Boston, awaiting a master hand to complete and publish them.

"In 1864 he began the work of compiling the History of Chester, New Hampshire, 1719-1869, with a map of the original proprietors' lots, devoting to the work the time not occupied in his regular vocation. This was published as a volume of seven hundred pages in 1869, and is regarded as one of the best of town histories.

"Mr. Chase was a man of sturdy frame and great earnestness of purpose. One of the rules of his life was the scriptural injunction, 'Whatsoever thy hand findeth to do, do it with thy might.' Another was, 'I first endeavor to ascertain my duty and then do it.' He knew no idle hours. Pushing his business in working hours, he devoted all others but those for sleep to intellectual and social enjoyment. Though doing a great amount of laborious work in his occupation as millwright, he so kept an even balance of physical and mental effort, that his strength was well preserved and his mind clear until near the end, at two months less than ninety years. Though mathematical and philosophical in his tastes, his character was well rounded out by the development of moral and literary qualities. In his early manhood he heard a discourse on the subject of total abstinence from intoxicating liquors, and at once not only adopted that principle in his practice but confined himself mainly to water as a beverage the remainder of his life.

"When the doctrine of immediate emancipation of the slaves was proclaimed by William Lloyd Garrison, it was embraced by Mr. Chase, as well as that of non-resistance and woman's rights, and he often contributed articles on those subjects to the *Liberator* and the *Herald of Freedom*."

He married, March 2, 1826, Hannah Hall, who was born February 18, 1789, and died February 25, 1876, aged eighty-nine years. daughter of Moses K. and Lucretia (Currier) Hall, of Chester. Their children were: Caroline, Louise and Benjamin. Caroline (8), born September 14, 1828, married, December 16, 1847, Charles, son of Joseph Chase. (See Chase XI).

(XII) Benjamin (8), son of Benjamin (7) and Hannah (Hall) Chase, was born August 18, 1832. He grew to manhood on the paternal estate in Auburn. attending the district school in his boyhood and youth. Subsequently he attended for several winter terms a select school at Lee, New Hampshire, where he profited by the instruction of that magnetic and progressive educator, the late Moses A. Cartland. With only brief interruptions he aided his father in the work upon the home farm and in the millwright business until his twenty-first year. Early recognizing his distaste for agricultural pursuits he was encouraged by his father in a free use of the mechanical tools in the home workshop, and developed much skill in that line so that at the early age of fifteen he began to engage in mechanical work by the day. At the termination of his period of schooling he gratified the craving to go to sea that is felt by many a country lad and made a voyage before the mast from Boston to Mobile, Alabama, and thence to Liverpool, England, which experience he now considers was a very practical and beneficial graduation into life's higher school. On his return he continued further mechanical service in conjunction with his father until 1855, after which he was employed as a millwright in various textile manufactories in New Hampshire and Massachusetts until 1867, when he laid the foundation of a manufacturing business in Derry which has had an unpretentious but uniform and sound growth, and at the end of nearly forty years' occupation of its distinctive field has been recently incorporated as The Benjamin Chase Company, its progenitor being the president of the company. As a manufactory of certain specialties in wood it is the largest and best equipped concern in existence with a world-wide demand for its products, and the intricate and delicate pieces of mechanism which make up the plant's installation are the creation of the proprietor's inventive genius and industry, being all the product of his own brain. Of Mr. Chase personally it can be said without exaggeration that he would be a man of note in any community on account of his varied abilities, his sterling characteristics and his works in every good purpose. A man of extremely retiring disposition and averse to office-holding he is nevertheless sought out by his townsmen for counsel and suggestion in matters of public concern and is extensively known throughout southern New Hampshire. Of late years he has spent the winter months in travel, Havana, Alaska, the Orient and Mexico having been visited, and the rewards of an active and well-spent life are now being enjoyed. He married, June 17, 1875, Harriett Davenport, daughter of Jared and Thankfull (Story) Fuller, of Dunbarton, who was born August 8, 1833. They have one daughter, Harriett Louise, born January 22, 1881. She is a graduate of Abbott Academy, Andover, Massachusetts, in the class of 1903, married Dr. Charles E. Newell, of Derry, January 22, 1907, and resides in Derry.

(XI) Stephen, oldest child of Benjamin Pike and Mary (Chase) Chase, his third wife, was born in Chester, now Auburn, New Hampshire, August 30, 1813. As a boy he was exceedingly precocious, learning the alphabet before he was two and one-half years old, and at four years having read through the New Testament. At the age of twelve he was sent to the Pinkerton Academy at Derry, which was then under the charge of Preceptor Abel F. Hildreth, a most thorough instructor. When fitted for college he, on account of his youth, remained at home on the farm a year or two before resuming his studies, and finally at the age of sixteen entered the sophomore class at Dartmouth College, and graduated in 1832. He entered the Theological Seminary at Andover, Massachusetts, but soon engaged in teaching in Virginia, where he remained a year, going thence to Baltimore, Maryland, for the year 1834. He then accepted a situation in the academy at Gorham, Maine, from whence he returned to the Andover Seminary, but after a brief stay accepted the appointment as principal of the academy at South Berwick, Maine, where he first met the young lady who later became his wife. In the spring of 1838 he was appointed tutor in Dartmouth College, and in June of the same year professor of mathematics, which position he held until his death. Although mathematics was his profession and his favorite science, he was well versed in several languages, as well as the various subjects under discussion in the scientific world. In religion he was orthodox without austerity, bigotry or superstition, being ready to examine any subject and to receive whatever there was evidence to sustain. He early engaged in the temperance and anti-slavery reforms. He had a great thirst for knowledge for its own sake and had a mind to grasp whatever came within its reach. He was of a very social nature, and won the esteem of all who knew him. Though rather frail in constitution he had, by judicious care, maintained a good degree of health until in the later years. In addition to his duties he had prepared a treatise on algebra which was published in 1849 and used as a text book in the college for many years. By this extra work he had run too near the margin of his strength. His health failed several months before his death, but though no serious apprehension was felt as to the immediate result, the vital forces failed and he died, suddenly to his friends, and lamented by all who knew him, January 7, 1851. He married Sarah Thompson, daughter of General Ichabod Goodwin, of South Berwick, Maine, August 31, 1838. She was born December 8, 1809, and died August 17, 1890. They had two sons: Frederick, born September 2, 1840, and Walter Wells, born May 28, 1844.

(XII) Frederick, oldest child of Stephen and Sarah T. (Goodwin) Chase graduated at Dartmouth College in 1860. He was assistant professor of chemistry for a short time, and then taught school in Chattanooga, Tennessee. Returning to Hanover, he read law in the office of Daniel Blaisdell, Esq., until his appointment to a position in the second auditor's office in the United States treasury in 1861. In August, 1864, he was transferred to the office of the secretary of the treasury. In October, 1866, he began to attend the Columbia College Law School in Washington, and graduated in June, 1867, with the degree of LL. B. and took up the practice of law in Washington. In the spring of 1874 he returned to Hanover, where he resided until his death, January 19, 1890. He was elected treasurer of Dartmouth College, and was appointed judge of probate for Grafton county in 1876, both of which positions he held during the remainder of his life. He was also a director in the Dartmouth National Bank and a trustee of the Dartmouth Savings Bank, and a member of the constitutional convention of 1889. He delivered the historical address at the centennial of the Phi Beta Kappa Society of the college in 1887. He was greatly interested in local history, and had been engaged for several years in the preparation of a "History of the Town and College," a labor which he prosecuted with zeal and enthusiasm. The first volume was practically completed and appeared soon after his death, and is considered a work of rare excellence and a monument to the indefatigable and thorough work of the author. It is a source of great regret that the untimely end of the author left the second volume incomplete. He married, November 9, 1871, Mary Fuller Pomeroy, of Detroit, Michigan, daughter of Dr. Thomas Fullet and Mary Anne (Hoadly) Pomeroy. They had six children: George Hoadly (died young), Stephen, Theodore, Mary Hoadly, Frederick and Philip Hartley. The sons are all graduates of Dartmouth College, the alma mater of their grandfather and father. Stephen gained the championship of the world in high hurdling while in college.

(VII) Samuel, fourth son and child of Moses (2) and Ann (Follansbee) Chase, was born May 3, 1690, in Newbury, and died there July 24, 1743. He was married December 8, 1713, to Hannah Emery, and they had eight children, namely: Francis, Amos, Hannah, Mary (died young), Anna, Samuel, Mary and Betty.

(VIII) Francis, eldest child of Samuel and Hannah (Emery) Chase, was born in Newbury, August 18, 1715, and died in Newtown. He married Sarah Pike, and settled in Newtown (now Newton, New Hampshire), at that time a frontier settle-

Samuel Chase

ment. They had twelve children: Hannah, Samuel, Amos, Francis, Joseph, Abner, Simeon, Sarah, Betty, died young, Daniel, Betty and Ruth.

(IX) Colonel Samuel, eldest son and second child of Francis and Sarah (Pike) Chase, was born in Newbury in 1739, and settled in Litchfield, New Hampshire, and died there May 17, 1816. He was a distinguished citizen of Litchfield. He was selectman of that town 1768-69-75-76-77-83 and 1787, and every following year to 1795, inclusive, making a service of fifteen years in all. He was a delegate to the provincial congress in 1775, and a representative in 1780. He was a lieutenant of the militia in 1775, and soon afterward was captain of the Litchfield company, but the dates of his commissions are not preserved. December 11, 1776, Captain Samuel Chase was promoted to major of the Sixth Regiment, of which Moses Nichols, of Amherst, was the colonel. In 1777, for the relief of Ticonderoga, Captain Daniel McQuaid led a company of volunteers, and among them was Major Samuel Chase, as appears on payroll, but the fact is when Captain McQuaid reached home two days later, there was a second alarm, and Major Chase with a few men marched to Charlestown, where they were ordered home. In 1778 he served as major in Colonel Kelley's regiment, which was in service in Rhode Island. December 25, 1784, Samuel Chase was commissioned lieuenant-colonel of the Fifth Regiment of militia. of which Noah Lovewell was colonel. January 25, 1790, he was commissioned colonel of the Fifth Regiment. March 19, 1791, his resignation was accepted by the governor and council. April 12, 1781, the committee of safety, representing the legislature, appointed Lieutenant Colonel Chase an agent to rent and have custody of the confiscated lands of tories of Hillsborough county. He filled this position several years. He married, November 1760, Mary Stewart, of Newton, New Hampshire, and they were the parents of the following named children: Samuel, Ebenezer, Daniel, Robert, Polly, died young, Francis, died young, Francis, Polly, Simeon and Anna.

(X) Major Francis, sixth son and seventh child of Colonel Samuel and Mary (Stewart) Chase, born in 1775, and died in Litchfield in September, 1854, was a store keeper, miller and farmer. He married, 1813, Dorothy Bixby (see Bixby VII), born October 16, 1777; died October 9, 1861. They left the following children: Lydia, Samuel, Francis and Margaret, whose sketch follows.

(XI) Margaret, second daughter and fourth child of Francis and Dorothy (Bixby) Chase, was born in Litchfield, in 1819, and died September 20, 1899, aged eighty years. She married, December 29, 1843, Isaac McQuesten (see McQuesten V).

(XI) Samuel, youngest child of Major Francis and Dorothy (Bixby) Chase, was born in Litchfield, August 29, 1815. He was educated in the district schools and at Hopkinton Academy, and taught school winters for a time. He also worked on the river, was a lumberman, and later owned and tilled a farm. He was a Democrat in politics, and was representative in the New Hampshire legislature two terms from Litchfield and once from Nashua and was a member of the Constitutional convention of 1876. and was also selectman in Litchfield. He married, December 2, 1849, Susan White, born in Litchfield, April 24, 1825, daughter of John and Susanna (Dickey) White, of Litchfield. They had seven children. The first died in infancy, unnamed. Addie M. married Frank Mitchell, of Manchester, and lives in California. Margaret A. married David S. Leach, of Litchfield. Mary W., died young. Ernest S. married Lula Colony, and lives in California. John W. married Gertrude Russell, of Lewiston, Maine, and lives in Worcester, Massachusetts. Charles H. is unmarried; and now lives with his mother, and is engaged in the milk business. Samuel Chase died January 27, 1882.

(VII) Joseph, eight child and sixth son of Moses (2) and Ann (Follansbee) Chase, was born September 9, 1703, in Newbury, Massachusetts. now West Newbury, and lived on the west half of the homestead farm. He was married September 7, 1724, to Mary Morse, who died in 1792 (see Morse, (III). Mr. Chase passed away in November, 1784. aged eighty-one years. He was the father of ten children. (Mention of his tenth child, Moody, and descendants follows in this article).

(VIII) Jacob, eldest son of Joseph and Mary (Morse) Chase, was born December 25, 1727, in Newbury, now West Newbury, Massachusetts. In 1751 he settled on additional lot No. 52 in Chester, New Hampshire, and became an active and prominent citizen of the town. He served often as moderator of the town, and was very active during the Revolutionary period. One item of credit in the selectmen's account for 1780 is the record of a gift to the town by Jacob Chase, Esq., of one hundred and fifty-seven pounds and ten shillings. He married, November 7, 1751, Prudence, daughter of Benjamin (1) and Rebecca (Ordway) Hills. She was born February 12, 1726, and died May 1, 1775, leaving children, Sarah, Stephen and Josiah. He married (second), Dolly Colby, widow of David Worthen. She died in 1815.

(IX) Sarah, daughter of Jacob and Prudence (Hill) Chase, became the wife of Moses Richardson (see Richardson, V).

(IX) Stephen (5), second child and elder of the two sons of Jacob and Prudence (Hills) Chase, was born March 27, 1759, and died February 18, 1819. He succeeded to the homestead where his father had lived. Benjamin Chase, in his "History of Chester," says of him: "Stephen Chase, Esq., came on the stage of active life about the time that Samuel Emerson. Esq., left it, and in some respects filled about the same sphere. He was noted as a land surveyor for more than thirty years, and made the survey and plan of Chester for Carrigan's Map, which is remarkably accurate. He wrote a very large portion of the deeds and wills, and administered on the estates of his time, and held the office of selectman many years. In Esquire Emerson's day, he was a kind of oracle, and nearly all the small disputes were referred directly to him. But things changed, and in Esquire Chase's day there was more litigation, and he was the justice to try the causes, or one of the arbitrators. Although not a finished workman, he had quite a mechanical genius, making carts, plows and other tools, and plastered houses. From 1784 to near his death he kept a diary, filled largely with his labors on the farm. and other business, which shows him to have been a very industrious man: and in it are also entered the births, marriages and deaths and many of the interesting events of the time, from which I have drawn many facts otherwise lost." He married. January 3, 1787, Rhoda Blake, of Hampton, who died in Chester, August 15, 1845. They had ten children: Susanna, Joseph, Stephen, Polly, Jacob, Dolly. Rhoda, Sally (died young), Sally and Henry Franklin. The last named receives mention below in this article).

(X) Joseph (6), second child and eldest son of Stephen and Rhoda (Blake) Chase, was born August 2, 1789, and died September 14, 1841. He followed agriculture, and resided in Chester. He married, November 4, 1817, Mehitable, daughter of Major Benjamin and Nabbe (Emerson) Hall. She was born January 6, 1794, and died June 4, 1882. Seven children were born to them:

(XI) Charles (7), second son and child of Joseph (6) and Mehitable (Hall) Chase, was born on his father's farm in Chester, December 14, 1820, and died May 17, 1892. He was an intelligent and successful farmer, a man of sound judgment whose advice was much sought, an upright and strictly temperate man and a highly esteemed citizen. He was a staunch Republican but not a politician. Although of a retiring disposition he was elected selectman many times and was chairman of the board for five years. He married, December 16, 1847, Caroline Chase, who was born September 14, 1828, eldest child of Benjamin and Hannah (Hall) Chase (see Chase, XI). She died August 11, 1849, leaving an only child, John Carroll, whose sketch follows. His second wife was Amelia J. Underhill and the third Amanda Underhill, daughter of John and Molly (Chase, 7.) Underhill, of Auburn. By them he had five children, the youngest and only surviving one being Charles B. (8), born July 11, 1867, now a resident of Derry and officially connected with The Benjamin Chase Company.

(XII) John Carroll (8), only child of Charles and Caroline (Chase) Chase, was born in Chester, July 26, 1849. He grew up on his father's farm, attended the district school and Chester Academy, entered Pinkerton Academy in 1865, and graduated in 1869, quite a portion of the intervening time being spent in teaching. He also attended the Massachusetts Institute of Technology, being a member of the class of 1874. His professional career as civil engineer was begun in the office of the late Joseph B. Sawyer, of Manchester in 1869, from whence he followed Mr. Sawyer to the force in charge of the construction of the city water works system, of which Colonel John T. Fanning was the chief, where he was employed for nearly four years. After that period he was professionally engaged upon the Boston Water Works and elevated railway systems of New York city. Under the civil service regulations he entered the New York custom house, and after nearly two years of service resigned the assistant cashiership in the naval office, in 1881, to accept the position of superintendent of the Clarendon Water Works, Wilmington, North Carolina, which position he held until 1898—seventeen years, during a large portion of the time being engaged in the general practice of his profession. He was also for several years city surveyor of Wilmington, and from 1893 to 1897 was the engineer member of the state board of health. In 1898 he returned to New Hampshire and settled in Derry. He is a member of the American Society of Civil Engineers, the American Public Health Association, the New England Water Works Association, the Boston Society of Civil Engineers and several other kindred organizations, and is the author of numerous reports upon engineering topics. He is much interested in genealogical work, is a member of the New England Historic-Genalogical Society and many family associations, and president of the Chase-Chace Family Association, one of the largest organizations of the kind in the country. Since 1904 he has been a member of the board of trustees of Pinkerton Academy, of Derry, and as such was the first alumnus to be honored by an election to that place in almost thirty years. He has served since 1901 as secretary of the trustees and chairman of the executive committee, and is also secretary of the Alumni Association. He is a trustee and treasurer of the Taylor Library and the president of the Nutfield Savings Bank. Since coming to Derry he has been interested in manufacturing and is now the treasurer and general manager of The Benjamin Chase Company, makers of various specialties in wood. He is a member of the New Hampshire, Technology and Boston City Clubs of Boston. He is a member of St. Mark's Lodge, No. 44, Free and Accepted Masons, of Bell Royal Arch Chapter, No. 25, of which order he is a past high priest; Mt. Nebo Council, No. 15, Royal and Select Masters, being its present illustrious master, and of Plantagenet Commandery No. 1, Knights Templar, of North Carolina, being a past commander and a member of the Grand Commandery of that state, of which he has been deputy grand commander, and was for seven years chairman of its committee on foreign correspondence. He is also a member of Hillsborough Lodge, No. 2, Independent Order of Odd Fellows, of Manchester, into which he was initiated in 1872; and of Cornelius Harnett Council, No. 231, Royal Arcanum, of Wilmington, North Carolina, of which he is a past regent. He is also a member and past patron of Ransford Chapter No. 3, Order of the Eastern Star, of Derry.

He married, October 21, 1871, Mary Lizzie Durgin, of West Newbury, Massachusetts, who was born there May 16, 1852, daughter of Samuel and Lydia Ann (Emery) Durgin, of West Newbury. They have two daughters: Carolyn Louise, who graduated from Pinkerton Acadamy in 1895, and from Wellesley College in 1900; and Alice Durgin, who is also a graduate of the same institution, the former in 1901, and the latter in 1906. A son, Benjamin (9), born in 1876, lived only a few months. Carolyn Louise (9), married Raffaele Lorini, M. D., of Coronado, California, August 25, 1906, and resides in Coronado.

(X) Henry Franklin, youngest child of Stephen and Rhoda (Blake) Chase, was born in Chester, August 30, 1808, and resided on the Captain John Underhill place. He died at Westminister, Vermont, March 20, 1867. He married Abigail Mitchel, and their daughter, Anna Maria, married Julius Nelson Morse (see Morse, X). Mrs. Annna Maria (Chase) Morse was one of the original members of the Joseph Badger Chapter (Marlboro, Massachusetts), Daughters of the American Revolution. Mr. Julius N. Morse left a valuable library of well selected books about five hundred of which his widow presented to the New Hampshire library and some of which were given by her to the Keene library.

(VIII) Moody, tenth child of Joseph and Mary (Morse) Chase, was born October 7, 1744, in West Newbury. He settled in that part of the ancient town of Chester which is now Auburn, New Hampshire, purchasing part of the homestead of Joseph Basford, and there passed his life, engaged in farming. He was married, October 25, 1768, to Anna, daughter of John Webster, of Hampstead, New Hampshire (see Webster, IV). She died December 4, 1701, and he was married April 19, 1792, to Abigail (Worth), widow of William Rogers. He died July 27, 1808, and was survived many years by his widow, who passed away December 9, 1826. His children, all born of the first wife, were: John W., Mary, Joseph, Jacob, Moody, Samuel, Caleb, Anna, Elizabeth, Thomas and Hannah.

(IX) Joseph, second son and third child of Moody and Anna (Webster) Chase, was born April 4, 1774, in Chester (now Auburn) and lived on

gust 2, 1789, and died Septer
lowed agriculture, and resid
ried, November 4, 1817
Major Benjamin and N
was born January 6,
Seven children were

(XI) Charles (
seph (6) and M
on his father's
and died Ma
successful f
advice w
tempera
was a
thou
sel
b

John C. Chase

Wm M Chase

re, through six terms from 1858 to

egan the study of law at Concord
1859, with Hon. Anson S. Mar-
[illegible]ly studied with Hon. William
[illegible] admitted to practice
[illegible] the supreme judi-
[illegible]cord. At the open-
[illegible]ame associated with
[illegible] style of Marshall &
[illegible] under this arrange-
[illegible] Marshall in 1874. Mr.
[illegible] with Hon. J. Everett
ed the office of chief
al court of this state,
ered by the retirement
iness five years later.
ociate, Mr. Chase con-
n name of Chase &
as associate justice
in 1891. Ten years
ke the jurisdiction
erior courts—and
e supreme bench,
ined.
bench, Justice
ice of the law,
nnected were
During this
eference to
e and, in-
numerous
ved their
manage-
igation.
conse-
ok an
feree
no
ac-
n-
e

part of the homestead. In 1816 he moved to Canaan, Grafton county, this state, where he died September 6, 1820. His wife, Nancy, was a daughter of Major Jesse Eaton, of Chester. (See Eaton, V). She was born September 30, 1775, in Chester, and died January 19, 1857, in Hanover, New Hampshire. Mr. Chase was an industrious farmer, and moved to Canaan to improve his prospects, but was cut off in the midst of an active career by an attack of colic, at the early age of forty-six years. His children were longlived and useful citizens. Jesse and Moody died in Ohio; David resided in Lowell, Massachusetts; Asa, the fourth, was a carpenter, spent his life in Hanover and Lebanon, New Hampshire, and died in Springfield, Massachusetts; Joseph and Nancy were twins, and both lived to be about ninety years of age, the former exceeding that number, dying in Lowell, Massachusetts. The latter married (first), a man named Currier and (second), Moody Chase, a relative. She died in Lyme, a town adjoining Canaan. Horace receives notice in a following paragraph. Eben was a harness-maker, and died in Nashua. Sally became the wife of Uriah Lary and lived in Canaan.

(X) Horace, sixth son and seventh child of Joseph and Nancy (Eaton) Chase, was born March 18, 1809, in Chester, and was only seven years old when his parents moved to Canaan. He was early deprived of his father's care and was accustomed to labor in his own behalf at the beginning of his career. He was employed as a farm laborer, and in time became a farmer on his own account. Being incapacitated largely by asthma, he was forced to give up farming, but continued to labor as long as he was able, at intervals. A man wholly without guile, he never harbored a dishonest thought, and strove to sustain himself and family by honest toil. Always a worker up to and even beyond the limit of his powers, he seemed to enjoy hard work and, no doubt, shortened his days by overexertion. After he left the farm he worked with his father-in-law, who was a blacksmith and operated a shop in Canaan, until his death, which occurred January 3, 1878. He was a regular attendant of the Methodist Church, and lived up to its teachings throughout his time. Mr. Chase was married to Abigail Staniels Martin, who was born June 26, 1818, in Pembroke, New Hampshire, and died March 29, 1901, in Concord. She was a daughter of William and Mary (Staniels) Martin, both descendants of early New Hampshire families. (See Staniels). William Martin was a descendant of Nathaniel Martin, who came from county Donegal, Ireland, and settled in Derry, New Hampshire. Robert Martin, father of William, served in the Revolutionary army, having enlisted several times from Pembroke. Two sons were born to Horace and Abigail (Martin) Chase, namely, William M. and Henry Martin. The latter died at Lowell, Massachusetts, in 1901. A sketch of the elder follows.

(XI) William Martin, elder son of Horace and Abigail (Martin) Chase, was born December 28, 1837, in Canaan, and passed his early years in that rural region, where the simple life prevailed. The foundation of his education was laid in the country school house of the time, after which he attended Kimball Union and Canaan Union academies. He entered the class of 1858, in the scientific department of Dartmouth College, in 1856, and graduated with the class, receiving the degree of Bachelor of Science. While in college he taught district schools in winter, and after graduating was instructor in mathematics and the sciences at Henniker Academy, New Hampshire, through six terms from 1858 to 1860.

Mr. Chase began the study of law at Concord while teaching, in 1859, with Hon. Anson S. Marshall, and subsequently studied with Hon. William P. Weeks, of Canaan. He was admitted to practice August 21, 1862, at the session of the supreme judicial court then in session at Concord. At the opening of the following year he became associated with his former preceptor under the style of Marshall & Chase, and continued to practice under this arrangement until the death of Mr. Marshall in 1874. Mr. Chase then associated himself with Hon. J. Everett Sargent, who had just resigned the office of chief justice of the supreme judicial court of this state, and this connection was severed by the retirement of Judge Sargent from business five years later. With Frank S. Streeter as associate, Mr. Chase continued practice under the firm name of Chase & Streeter until his appointment as associate justice of the supreme court of the state in 1891. Ten years later two courts were formed to take the jurisdiction of that body—the supreme and superior courts—and Judge Chase was continued upon the supreme bench, in which position he has since remained.

Previous to his elevation to the bench, Justice Chase was engaged in a general practice of the law, and the firms with which he was connected were busily and prosperously employed. During this activity the policy of the state with reference to railroad corporations underwent a change and, instead of encouraging a competition among numerous small and independent corporations, allowed their consolidation under a substantially single management, resulting in much controversy and litigation. In this and other litigation of large financial consequence, Mr. Chase's firm were employed and took an active part. He was also largely employed as referee in various controversies, and it is probable that no other in the state heard so many cases in that capacity as long as he was in business. During a considerable portion of the time he was a member of the committee appointed by the court to examine candidates for admission to the bar. Of his work as judge it is proper to say that he has labored diligently to carry forward the work of the court, giving his best energies unceasingly to that end, and that his appointment to the bench of the new supreme court is ample evidence that his work has been successful and acceptable to the people of the state. In 1889 Justice Chase was appointed chairman of the commission created by the legislature to revise, codify and amend the statutes of the state, and the report of this commission was adopted in 1891 by the legislature as the Laws of New Hampshire. In collaboration with his son he compiled and edited an edition of the public statutes and session laws in force January 1, 1901, which has been received favorably by all interested.

While active in large affairs, Mr. Chase has given of his time to the service of his home town, in various ways and to the best interests of the state, along various lines outside of legal matters. He was trustee of the New Hampshire State Library and New Hampshire Normal School several years, and has been a trustee of Dartmouth College since 1890. For twenty years he was a member of the board of education of the Union district of Concord, and its president during the latter part of the term; was fourteen years a member of the board of water commissioners of the city of Concord. He was elected an honorary member of the Phi Beta Kappa Society of Dartmouth College in 1883, and received from the college the degree of Master of Arts in 1879, and Doctor of Laws in 1898. He is a member of the New Hampshire Historical Society and the New England Historic-Genealogical Society.

Mr. Chase has been a director of the First National Bank of Concord since 1875, and was its president two years, and was trustee and vice-president of the Merrimack County Savings Bank several years. His political affiliations have been with the Democratic party, but he has disapproved of the policies advocated by its leaders regarding finance and other subjects in late years, and is considered a conservative Democrat. His religious home is in the Congregational Church. While not a church member, he is a regular attendant upon its religious worship and accepts the teachings of Christ as the best rule of life, by which his walk is ordered.

Mr. Chase was married March 18, 1863, to Miss Ellen Sherwood Abbott, daughter of Aaron and Nancy (Badger) Abbott, of Concord. (See Abbott, VI). The only offspring of this marriage is a son, Arthur Horace Chase, who was born February 16, 1864, in Concord. He graduated from Dartmouth College in 1886, was admitted to the bar of New Hampshire in 1889, practiced law six years, and has been state librarian ten years.

(V) William, said to be one of the three sons of Aquila (1) Chase, born in England, came to America with his wife Mary and son William, in company of Governor Winthrop, in 1630. He thought of going to Scituate, but finally changed his purpose and went with a party to Cape Cod and settled in what is now Yarmouth. He died there in May, 1659. The widow of William Chase was found dead the same year her husband died, and an inquest decided that she died a natural death. The children of William and Mary were: William, Mary and Benjamin.

(VI) William (2), eldest child of William (1) and Mary Chase, was born in England about 1622. He came to America with his parents, and lived in Yarmouth. His children were: William, Jacob, John, Elizabeth, Abraham, Benjamin and Samuel.

(VII) Abraham, fifth child and fourth son of William (2) Chase, married Elizabeth ——, and they had ten children: Josiah, Abraham, Phineas, Henry, Elizabeth, Mary, Tabitha, Johanna, Experience and Melicent.

(VIII) Henry, fourth son and child of Abraham and Elizabeth Chase married (first), January 17, 1735, Mary Tripp, and (second), November 13, 1747, Sarah Durfee. By the second wife there were Moses and other children.

(IX) Moses, son of Henry and Sarah (Durfee) Chase, was born about 1756. He was killed by the collapse of a shed early in 1834. He married Lydia Kimball of Penacook. She was fatally injured in a runaway near Horse Hill two years after the death of her husband, and died two weeks after the accident. Their children were: Eliza, Lydia, Moses, Catherine, Reuben, Clarissa, Baruch, Fidelia and Timothy.

(X) Reuben Kimball, second son and fifth child of Moses and Lydia (Kimball) Chase, was born in Hopkinton, September 5, 1800, and died in the town of Hopkinton, September 3, 1871. He was a farmer. He married Betsey Ryan, born in New Hampshire. She died in Manchester. They had children: Edward, James, Orrin, Matilda and Frank E.

(XI) Orrin, third son and child of Reuben and Betsy (Ryan) Chase, was born in Hopkinton, March 22, 1843, and has always resided in that town. In 1862 he enlisted in Company D, Sixteenth New Hampshire Volunteers, and served nine months in the war of the Rebellion, being stationed at New Orleans in the Department of the Gulf. He was discharged at the expiration of his term, and was unable to work for a year following his return home. He engaged in farming for a short time, and then operated a saw mill for the Northern railroad now the Boston & Maine. While thus engaged the head came off the saw, and Mr. Chase was struck and severely cut in many places, and still carries the scars made by the injuries. Subsequently he was employed as a laborer on the railroad. One day while cutting a railroad rail a chip struck him in the eye and destroyed it. Mr. Chase is a member of the Grand Army of the Republic, and a Democrat. He married, September 3, 1870, Hetty M. Badger, born in Warner, October 1, 1847, daughter of Sargent E. and Emily (Foster) Badger. Their children are: Fred J., Harry A., Lena M. and Walter B. Fred married Emma Hardy, of Warner, daughter of Ira and Celia (Getchel) Hardy. Harry married (first), Emma J. Hook, of Hopkinton, daughter of James Hook of Hopkinton. She died July 3, 1896, and he married (second), Lilla Burgess, of Claremont, daughter of Amos and Martha Burgess. They have one daughter, born December 17, 1902. Walter married Sadie Hannaford, of Manchester. They have one daughter, Lena, who married, April 21, 1898, Delmar W. Hastings, of Hopkinton, son of Alfred and Susan (Perry) Hastings. They have one son, Floyd Delmar, born January 5, 1901.

(VII) Daniel, eldest son of Moses and Ann (Follansbee) Chase, was born September 20, 1685, in Newbury, now West Newbury, Massachusetts. He moved to Littleton, Massachusetts in 1725, and thence to Sutton, same state. He was married January 6, 1706, to Sarah, daughter of George March, of Groton, same state. Subsequently, he moved to Sutton, where he died April, 1768. His children were: Samuel, Daniel, Anne, Joshua, Judith, Nehemiah, Sarah, Caleb, Moody and Moses.

(VIII) Samuel, eldest child of Daniel and Sarah (March) Chase, was born September 28, 1707, in Newbury, now West Newbury, and married Mary Dudley. He settled with his family in Cornish, New Hampshire, being one of the founders of that town. He died August 12, 1800. His children were: Samuel, Jonathan, Dudley, Sarah, Elizabeth, Solomon, Anne and Mary.

(IX) Dudley, third son and child of Samuel and Mary (Dudley) Chase, was born August 29, 1730, and died April 13, 1814. He was married August 23, 1753, to Alice Corbett, and had a distinguished family of sons, namely: Salmon, Ithamar, Baruch, Heber, Dudley and Philander. The first was an eminent lawyer of Portland, Maine. The fifth graduated from Dartmouth, with honors in 1791, and was a leader of the Vermont bar, United States senator, and chief justice of Vermont. The youngest was one of the most distinguished members of the Episcopal clergy, Bishop of Ohio from 1818 to 1831, when he resigned; founder and first president of Kenyon College; and Bishop of Illinois in 1835, and founder of Jubilee College. A daughter, Rachel, became the wife of Dr. Joseph A. (1) Denison of Bethel and Royalton, Vermont. (See Denison, VIII).

(X) Ithamar, second son of Dudley and Alice (Corbett) Chase, was born September 27, 1763, in Sutton, and engaged in farming in Cornish, New Hampshire, until 1815, when he removed to Keene. Three years previously he had engaged in the manufacture of glass, which proved his financial undoing. He died at Keene in 1817. He was married

June 26, 1792, to Janey Ralston, of Keene, daughter of Alexander and Janey (Balloch) Ralston. She was born July 26, 1773, in Charlestown, Massachusetts, whither her parents came from Falkirk, Scotland, about 1772. In 1775 they moved to Keene, where Alexander Ralston died aged sixty-four years, March 29, 1810. His widow passed away in 1883, in Cornish, and was buried in Keene. Mr. Ralston was a distiller and inn-holder, and the "Ralston Tavern" is historic. The Ralston family was one of consequence, its members being handsome, cultured and enterprising. Two of Ithamar Chase's sons, Alexander Ralston, and Salmon Portland, achieved distinction.

(XI) Salmon Portland, son of Ithamar and Janey (Ralston) Chase, was born January 13, 1808, in Cornish, New Hampshire, and was one of the most noted sons in that state, prolific of brainy men. He inherited from two strong families those traits which made him a leader among men and brought him into prominence in the service of his country, and in the regard of his countrymen. His early life was that of a farmer's son, the district school providing his education until he was nine years old. After the death of his father he was sent to Windsor, Vermont, where he continued his studies. At the suggestion of his uncle, Bishop Philander Chase, he was sent in 1820 to Worthington, Ohio, where he had a home in the family of the Bishop, and received instructions in a collegiate school under the latter's charge. When Bishop Chase became president of Cincinnati College in 1822, his nephew accompanied the family thither, and continued his studies in the college. In 1823 Salmon returned to his mother's home in Keene, and soon engaged in teaching at Royalton, Vermont. He matriculated at Dartmouth, in 1824, and graduated with the class of 1826. An expedition to the South in hope of finding an engagement as tutor in some private family proved unsuccessful, and he applied to his uncle Dudley Chase for an appointment in the public service at Washington. That gentleman told him he had seen one nephew ruined by an appointment, and refused to aid him in that way. Young Chase soon found employment in a private school, and shortly became a law student with Attorney-General William Wirt. He was admitted to the bar of the District of Columbia in 1829, and continued his school one year longer. He then went to Cincinnati where he was admitted to the Ohio bar. Here he began a codification of the statutes of the state, and with copious annotations and a sketch of the development of the state made three volumes. This work superseded all previous works of the kind, and made the fame of the author, whose law practice at once assumed importance. His employment by the LaFayette and United States Banks gave him a knowledge of financial matters, and was an excellent preparation for the future United States Treasurer. He became deeply interested in the fugitive slave agitation, and was employed in cases brought under the slave law. His pleadings and writings on this subject became influential and were widely used by the anti-slavery agitators throughout the country. In 1846 he was associated with William H. Seward before the supreme court of the United States, in the case of Van Zandt, and argued that the question of reclaiming slaves in a free state was an interstate matter and not a federal question. Up to this time Mr. Chase had taken no partisan stand in politics, and he now became a leader of public sentiment toward the formation of a new party. In 1841 he called the convention that organized the Liberty party in Ohio, and two years later, when the Liberty party met in convention at Baltimore for the nomination of a presidential candidate, he was a member of its committee on resolutions. He opposed the radical proposition to support the third clause of the constitution if applied to the case of a fugitive slave, but it was adopted by the convention, after being rejected by the committee. Mr. Chase was a leader in the movement for a convention of "All who believed that all that is worth preserving in republicanism can be maintained only by uncompromising war against the usurpation of the slave power, and are therefore resolved to use all constitutional means to effect the extinction of slavery within the respective states." At the resultant meeting in Cincinnati in 1845, in June, Mr. Chase was chairman of the committee on platform, and prepared the address, urging the necessity of a political organization with the overthrow of the slave power as its basic idea. In 1848 he prepared a call for a convention in Ohio which was signed by over three thousand voters, and resulted in the convention at Buffalo in the same year, at which Mr. Chase presided, and nominated VanBuren and Adams on the Free Soil ticket. In 1840 the Democrats and the Federal Whigs united in the election of Mr. Chase to the United States senate. In 1853 he withdrew from the Democratic party on account of its position on the slavery question, and in the same year prepared a platform for the independent party at Pittsburg, which was adopted. In the senate he opposed the compromises with slavery interests and labored diligently for amendments to the fugitive slave law, but he was in advance of his time, and found himself in the minority. He sought to prevent the intervention of Federal authorities in the affairs of the states, to uphold individual State rights, and economy in the administration of finances. He favored free homesteads to settle cheap postage and public improvements. In 1855 Mr. Chase was elected governor of Ohio by the elements opposing the Nebraska Bill and the administration, and two years later he was re-elected by the largest vote ever given for governor in that state. In 1850 his name was proposed by Ohio as a presidential candidate, and again in 1860, at the National Republican Convention at Chicago, he received a nomination and forty-nine votes were cast for him on the first ballot. When the votes of Ohio were needed to secure the nomination of Abraham Lincoln they were promptly turned over to him. In that year Mr. Chase was again elected United States senator, and he resigned the position in 1861, to acept a portfolio in President Lincoln's cabinet. As Secretary of the Treasury he rendered conspicuous service in establishing the war loans and a substantial financial system which made a successful prosecution of the Civil war possible. Through the suggestion of Mr. O. B. Potter, of New York, he issued the greenback, which was universally accepted by the people, and secured the ultimate unity of a great nation. Mr Chase left the Treasury department June 30, 1864, at which time the national debt amounted to $1,740,690,489. On December 6 of the same year he was named by the president as chief justice of the national supreme court, and the nomination was immediately confirmed by the senate. He presided at the impeachment trial of President Johnson in March, 1868. In 1855, Dartmouth, from which he had graduated at the age of eighteen, conferred upon him the degree of Doctor of Laws. His public service was ended by a stroke of paralysis in June, 1870, and he died May 7, 1873, in New York City.

CHASE Following is the record of the descendants of John Chase, a native of Maine, who was an untraced descendant of that branch of the Chase family of Maine whose ancestor was the Aquila Chase, of Chesham, England, who settled about 1640 in Hampson, and previous to 1646 in Newbury, Massachusetts.

(I) Enoch, son of John Chase, was born in Portland, Maine, about 1775. When about eight years of age he went to Hopkinton, New Hampshire, where he became a farmer when he attained manhood. He was a man of good business ability, well thought of by his townsmen, and was collector of taxes from 1818 to 1820, and again in 1824; and selectman from 1820 to 1823. He married Mary Morse, of Newbury, Massachusetts, 1796, and they were the parents of ten children: Charlotte, Enoch J., Daniel D., Thomas, Hannah, Abner, Ambrose, Jacob, Elbridge G., and Sally.

(II) Enoch J., eldest son and second child of Enoch and Mary Morse Chase, was born in Hopkinton, June 25, 1801, and died October 17, 1879, aged seventy-eight. He was a farmer and lumberman, and lived many years in the Blackwater district. He also lived a number of years in Concord, and for a time in Wilmot. He was selectman in Hopkinton in 1843, 1853, and 1854, and representative in 1862 and 1863. He was a stirring business man and a prosperous citizen. He married first, Sarah H. Holmes, who was born in Utica, New York, November 26, 1791, and died December 6, 1832, aged forty-one years. She was the daughter of Dr. Joshua Holmes, of Utica, New York. He married second, Nancy Johnson, of Salisbury, who was born in 1797, and died 1875, aged seventy-eight years. The children of the first wife were: Lucinda H., Horace J., Mary Jane, and Harvey; and of the second: Nancy A., George W., and Malinda B.

(III) Harvey, youngest child of Enoch J. and Sarah H. (Holmes) Chase, was born in Hopkinton, April 3, 1829. With the exception of nine years in Concord and two in Chichester, he has always lived on the old homestead in Hopkinton, which now contains six hundred acres. He is a farmer and lumber dealer. He has inherited the personal qualities that distinguished his father and grandfather, and is a keen trader and a man of good judgment. He was a member of the board of selectmen of Concord in 1852 and 1853, a councilman in 1854, and representative from Hopkinton in 1879. He married, March 17, 1853, Martha R. Bennett, who was born in Freedom, July 9, 1834, daughter of Charles and Olive E. (Crockett) Bennett. They are the parents of children: Mary Jane, Georgia Persis, Fred Harvey, and Mattie Olive.

(IV) Fred Harvey, third child and only son of Harvey and Martha R. (Bennett) Chase, was born in Hopkinton, August 21, 1868. He was brought up to a knowledge of farming and lumber dealing, and obtained his education in the common and high schools of Warner. At the age of twenty he became a dealer in lumber, and has ever since been successfully engaged in that line. He is prominent in the industrial, financial and social circles of his native town. He married, March 10, 1897, in Concord, Lillian Jackman, born August 29, 1871, daughter of Enoch and Elizabeth (Moody) Jackman, of Concord. They have one child, Martha Elizabeth, born March 26, 1901.

KINGSBURY Kingsbury, signifying primarily, "King's castle," and later, "King's town," was at first, the designation of a fortification for defensive purposes. As was common in the days of English castle-building, a town grew up about the kingsburg or bury and took the same designation, the name being spelled in the reign of King Egbert, 800 A. D., Kynggesberie, Kyngesburg and Kinggesburie. Still later, when some emigrant left the place called Kingsbury, he took that name for his surname, and from him it has been handed down to the latest generations of his descendants. The Kingsburys had among them liberal minded and adventurous men who could not abide the religious oppression of their times in England, and in the hope of enjoying greater liberties in the new world, came to Massachusetts Bay Colony. The ancestors of the family in America are: Joseph, John and Henry. The traits of character of this family, as given by one who knows are: Remarkable attachment to agricultural pursuits; from the first settlement in America they lived in the common, temperate style of New England farmers, yet with patriotic ferver, and love of military tactics. Noble-hearted, industrious, ingenuous, intelligent, of the strictest integrity, disdaining the low arts of dissimulation, shunning the ways of vice and walking in the paths of virtue and piety—'a reticent nature having a personal holy of holies into which few are admitted"—reverent, cherishing love of God, family and country with "the courage of their conviction," the word faithful defines the most marked characteristic of a Kingsbury.

(I) Joseph Kingsbury, the ancestor of many of that name in America, was born in England, where he was also married, but we know the date of neither of these events. He came to New England, and settled in Dedham, Massachusetts Colony, in the year 1628; was made a freeman in 1641, and died about 1676. He, like all citizens of that day, was an owner, and probably a tiller of the soil. In April, 1638, the town took land for a burial place, still in use, from the south end of his hamlet, exchanging other land for it, and soon after took an acre of land from the end of his lot for a church. In the forming of the church in 1638, Joseph was one of the ten men considered most suitable to be "an original member," but through the jealousy of some of the company, he and three others of the ten first mentioned were not included in the number of constituents. His wife, who is described as "a tender-hearted soule full of fears and temptations, but truly breathing after Christ," was received in the fellowship of the Dedham church in the winter of 1638-9 without making a public recital of her experience; but by giving good satisfaction in private and by publicly assenting to the relation made for her. Joseph, however, became a member April 9, 1641. Joseph Kingsbury married Millicent Ames, in England. She survived him. Their children were: Sarah, Mary, Elizabeth, Joseph, John, Eleazer, and Nathaniel.

(II) Nathaniel, youngest of the seven children of Joseph and Millicent (Ames) Kingsbury, was born in Dedham, March 25, 1650, was a freeman of Massachusetts in 1677, and died October 14, 1694. He married, in Dedham, October 14, 1673, Mary Bacon, daughter of John and Rebecca (Hall) Bacon, and they had five sons and one daughter: Nathaniel, James, Timothy, John Daniel and Millicent.

(III) Deacon Daniel, fifth son and child of Nathaniel and Mary (Bacon) Kingsbury, born in Dedham, November 11, 1688, died in Wrentham, April 27, 1754. He removed to Wrentham, and spent the greater part of his life there. He was chosen the first deacon, March 8, 1739, of the First

Congregational Church, in that part of Wrentham which was called "Western Precinct," and in 1778 was incorporated under the name of Franklin. He married, December 29, 1713, Elizabeth Stevens (or Stephens) of Dedham, who died July 12, 1764. They were the parents of two sons and two daughters: Daniel, Stephen, Elizabeth and Mary.

(IV) Daniel (2), eldest child of Daniel (1) and Elizabeth (Stevens) Kingsbury, born March 11, 1715, and died in Franklin, March 25, 1783. He married (first), November 3, 1737, Beriah Mann, born April 25, 1717, who died May 12, 1755; and (second), October 19, 1755, widow Abigail Adams, who died October 22, 1759. By the first marriage there were eight sons and one daughter: Nathaniel, Lydia, Daniel, Samuel, John, Timothy, James, John and Theodore, and by the second marriage: Twins, unnamed; Peter and Benjamin.

(V) Lieutenant Daniel (3), second son of Daniel (2) and Beriah (Mann) Kingsbury, was born in Wrentham, Massachusetts, October 6, 1742. In 1759 he settled in Keene, where he became one of the leading citizens, holding many offices of honor and trust, and was a member of the building committee for the first Congregational Church in Keene. He was a member of the provincial congress, New Hampshire, 1775-76, and after the adoption of the state constitution was a member of the state legislature for twenty-one consecutive years. He was a member of committee of safety, April 12, 1776 and lieutenant in the Revolutionary war under Captain Howlett, 1777. He died in Keene, New Hampshire, August 10, 1825.

(VI) Daniel (4), son of Daniel (3) and —— Kingsbury, was a merchant in Plainfield, New Hampshire, where he died June 12, 1819. He married Hannah Bailey.

(VII) Almira, only child of Daniel (4) and Hannah (Bailey) Kingsbury, was born March 6, 1799, in Keene, and was married March 6, 1814, to Austin Tyler (see Tyler, VI).

HARRIS

The Welsh custom of adding to a name the father's name in possessive form to distinguish one from another of the same Christian name, was the origin of this patronymic. In the short four centuries that surnames have prevailed in Great Britain time has sufficed to make many changes and modifications in the form of all classes of words, and names are no exception to the rule. In the Welsh vernacular, William was "David's," Harry was "John's," and David was "William's," and thus we have Davy's (Davis), John's (Jones), William and Harris, all among the most common of Welsh names. The Harris family of whom this article gives some account was among the earliest in New England, has contributed much to the advancement of this region and of the nation, and is now found in connection with all worthy endeavor. It has been especially active in the fields of invention and pioneer development. Almost every state has found the name among those of its pioneer settlers, and it has spread from the Atlantic to the Pacific.

(I) Thomas Harris, born in Deal, Kent county, England, died in Providence, Rhode Island, June 7, 1636. He came to America with his brother William in the ship "Lyon," from Bristol, England, December 1, 1630. On August 20, 1637, or a little later, he and twelve others signed the following compact: "We, whose names are hereunder, desirous to inhabit in the town of Providence, do promise to subject ourselves in active or passive obedience to all such orders or agreements as shall

be made for public good of the body in an orderly way by the major assent of the present inhabitants, members incorporated together into a town of fellowship, and such others whom they shall admit unto themselves, only in civil things."

On July 27, 1640, he and thirty-eight others signed an agreement for a form of government. On September 2, 1650, he was taxed £1. In 1652-3-4-5-6-7, 1661-2-3, he was commissioner; in 1654, lieutenant; 1655, freeman; 1656, juryman. Bishop's "New England Judged," published in London, in 1703, has the following with reference to July, 1658:

"After these came Thomas Harris from Rhode Island into our colony who Declaring against your Pride and Oppression, as we would have liberty to speak in your meeting place in Boston, after the priest had ended. Warning the people of the Dreadful, terrible day of the Lord God, which was coming upon that Town and Country, him, much unlike to Nineveh, you pulled down and hall'd him by the Hair of his Head out of your meeting, and a hand was put on his mouth to keep him from speaking forth, and then had before your Governor and Deputy, with other Magistrates, and committed to Prison without warrant or mittimus that he saw, and shut up in a close room, none suffered to come to him, nor to have provisions for his money; and the next day whipped with so cruel stripes without shewing any law that he had broken, tho' he desired it of the Jaylor, and then shut up for Eleven Days more, Five of which he was kept without bread (Your Jaylor not suffering him to have any for his Money and threatened the other Prisoners very much for bringing him a little water on the day of his sore whipping) and all this because he could not work for the Jaylor and let him have Eight Pence in Twelve Pence of what he should earn; And starved he had been in all probability, had not the Lord kept him these Five Days, and ordered it so after that time that food was so conveyed him by night in at a Window, by some tender People, who tho' they came not in the Profession of Truth openly, by reason of your Cruelty, yet felt it secretly moving in them and so were made Serviceable to keep the Servant of the Lord from Perishing, who shall not go without a reward. And tho' he was in this State of Weakness for want of Bread, and by torturing his body with cruel whippings, as aforesaid, and tho' the Day after he was whipped, the Jaylor had told him that he had now suffered the Law, and that if he would hire the Marshall to carry him out of the Country he might be gone when he would; Yet the next Sixth Day in the Morning before the sixth Hour, the Jaylor again required him to Work, which he refusing, gave his weak and fainting body Two and Twenty Blows with a pitched rope; and the Nineteenth of the Fifth month following, Fifteen cruel stripes more with a three-fold-corded whip knotted as aforesaid. Now upon his Apprehension, your Governor sought to know of him who came with him (as was their usual manner) that so ye might find out the rest of the company, on whom ye might Execute your Cruelty and Wickedness, and your governor said he would make him do it; but his Cruelties could not. Nevertheless they soon were found out (who hid not themselves but were bold in the Lord) viz: William Brend and William Ledd, etc."

In 1664-66-67, 1670-72-73 he was deputy to the general court; in 1664-65-66-69 member of the town council, and on February 19, 1665, he drew lot 7, in the division of the town lands. In May, 1667, he as surveyor laid out the lands. August 14, 1676, he was on a committee which recommended certain conditions under which the Indian captives, who were to be in servitude for a term of years, should be disposed of by the town. April 27, 1683, he made the statement that about 1661, being then a surveyor, he laid out a three acre lot for his son Thomas, at Pauqachance Hill, and a twenty-five acre lot on the south side, etc. June 3, 1686, he made his will, which was proved July 22, 1686, his son Thomas being appointed executor, and his sons-in-law, Thomas Field and Samuel Whipple, overseers. Thomas Harris married Elizabeth ———, who died in Providence, Rhode Island. Their children were: Thomas, Mary and Martha.

(II) Thomas (2), only son and eldest child of Thomas (1) and Elizabeth Harris, died February 27, 1711, always lived in Providence, Rhode Island. February 19, 1665, he had lot 49, in a division of lands. In 1671-79, 1680-81-82-85, 1691-94-97, 1702-06-07-08 and 1710, he was a deputy of the general court: and in 1684-85-86, member of the town council. July 1, 1679, he was taxed 8s. 9d., and September 1, 1687, 14s. 9d. June 21, 1708, he made his will, which was proved April 16, 1711, the executors being his wife Elanthan and his son Henry. He married, November 3, 1664, Elanthan Tew, born October 15, 1644, died January 11, 1718, daughter of Richmond and Mary (Clarke) Tew, of Newport, Rhode Island, and they had nine children: Thomas, Richard, Nicholas, William, Henry, Amity, Elanthan, Joab, and Mary. (Mention of Nicholas and descendants appears in this article).

(III) Richard, second son and child of Thomas (2) and Elanthan (Tew) Harris, was born October 14, 1668, in Providence, Rhode Island, and resided in Providence and Smithfield. He deeded to his son Richard, in 1725, one hundred acres of land in the latter town, and died there in 1750. He married (first a daughter of Clement and Elizabeth King, and his second wife Susanna, born in 1665, was the widow of Samuel Gordon, and a daughter of William and Hannah (Wicks) Burton. She died in 1737. His children, all born of the first marriage, were: Uriah, Richard, Amaziah, Jonathan, David, Preserved, Amity, Dinah and Elnathan.

(IV) Richard (2), second son and child of Richard (1) and ——— (King) Harris, was born in Smithfield, Rhode Island, and settled in that town. He was married (first), December 15, 1723, to Lydia Sprague, of Attleboro, Massachusetts. The date of her death does not appear, but the christain name of his second wife was Dorothy. His children of the first marriage were: Mary, Jeremiah, Lydia, Uriah, Richard, Annie, David, Anthony and Amity (twins). One child, Tabitha, born 1738, came of the second marriage.

(V) Anthony, fifth son and seventh child of Richard (2) and Lydia (Sprague) Harris, was born June 5, 1736, in Smithfield, Rhode Island, and removed thence about 1760, to Richmond, New Hampshire, where he was a pioneer settler, and reared a large family. He was the first settler on lot twelve in range five in that town, and died there March 20, 1817, at the age of eighty-one years. His wife, Ruth Broadway, was probably a native of Rhode Island. She survived him nearly thirteen years, dying January 8, 1830. They were married January 1, 1761. Their children were: Thomas, Eunice L., Mercy, Anna, Lydia, Jeremiah, David B. (died young), David B., William B., Caleb, Luke, Linday and Delila. The eldest daughter, Mercy, became the wife of David Ballou, a pioneer of Richmond and they were the parents of the celebrated Hosea Ballou, one of the first Universalist preachers in America.

(VI) Jeremiah, second son of Anthony and Ruth (Broadway) Harris, was born May 8, 1768, in Richmond, New Hampshire, and died September 16, 1849, in Springfield, Pennsylvania, in his eighty-second year. As a young man, he evinced much of the pioneer spirit for which New England has been famous, and probably resided temporarily in various places. His wife, Priscilla Cole, was the daughter of Barnabas and Asenath Cole of Amenia, New York. Barnabas Cole was a revolutionary soldier of New York, and passed his last years in Coneaut, Erie county, Pennsylvania. During the first years of their married life Jeremiah and Priscilla (Cole) Harris lived near Prescott, Ontario, on the Rideau river. He was subsequently a resident for some years of Henderson, Jefferson county, New York. He settled ultimately in Springfield, Erie county, Pennsylvania, where he cleared up land and was a fairly prosperous farmer. He was a very earnest believer in the doctrines of Universalism, and did all in his power to urge others to believe in the same faith. He took little part in public affairs, and gave his attention to the development of his farm and the care of his large family. His eldest son Silas settled near Twin Valley, Wisconsin, where he died, and his descendants are now distributed over several western states. Barnabas located in Ohio, and there died, leaving descendants. Levi died when a young man. Jeremiah spent some years in Wisconsin in the pioneer days of that state, and ultimately settled at Webster City, Iowa. His descendants are now living there and at Denver, Colorado. Caleb was among the early settlers of Illinois, and is 1838 located in LaGrange, Wisconsin. His descendants are now living in that state, in Nebraska and Utah. Luke resided near the old homestead in Pennsylvania, and there died, leaving several daughters in that vicinity. Annanias lived for many years in Springfield, and then settled at Twin Valley, Wisconsin, where his descendants are now living. There were two daughters, Sarah and Melissa. The latter died unmarried; the former became the wife of Charles Perkins Ellis and passed most of her adult life in LaGrange, Wisconsin, near her brother. She left three children: Priscilla Rumina, James Alfred and Charles Elliott. The daughter is the wife of John E. Menzie, and resides on the homestead in LaGrange. The younger son resides in Duluth, Minnesota. The elder has been for a quarter of a century connected with the preparation of work similar to this, and has been privileged to prepare a considerable portion of this work, including this article.

(III) Nicholas, third son and child of Thomas and Elanthan (Tew) Harris, born in Providence, April 1, 1671, died March 27, 1746, married Anne Hopkins, daughter of Thomas and Mary (Smith) Hopkins, and had ten children: Nicholas, Thomas, Christopher, Anne, Zerviah, Mary, Sarah, Amity, Joseph, and Jedediah.

(IV) Nicholas, eldest child of Nicholas and Anne (Hopkins) Harris, born October, 1691, died May 18, 1775. He married Hannah Blake, and settled in Wrentham, Massachusetts. They had nine children: John, Erastus, Nicholas, Joseph, Oliver, a son who settled in Hardwick, a daughter who married Ellis Medway, a daughter who married a Blake, and a daughter who married a Carpenter, and settled in Keene, New Hampshire.

(V) Erastus, second son and child of Nicholas and Hannah (Blake) Harris, settled in Medway, Massachusetts. He left some writings showing that

Ezra S. Harris

A. E. Harris.

he served as a non-commissioned officer in a regiment of foot, raised in Massachusetts, for one year, in "His Majesty's Service," commanded by Colonel Frye, and for that time was located in Acadia (Nova Scotia) in 1759 and 1760. Afterward he was an orderly sergeant in the American army during the revolutionary war, in a regiment stationed in Boston and Cambridge. Nothing regarding his wife is known. He had five children: Hannah, Bethuel, Rebecca, Erastus and William.

(VI) Bethuel, eldest son and second child of Erastus Harris, born August 14, 1769, died July 21, 1851, settled in Harrisville, New Hampshire. He married Deborah Twitchell (see Adams VII), January 1, 1794, or 1795, and they had ten children; all born in Harrisville: Cyrus, Milan, Almon, Lovell, Calmer, Charles Cotesworth, Pinckney, Sally, Lydia and Lois.

(VII) Deacon Almon, son of Bethuel and Deborah Harris, was born at Nelson, New Hampshire, August 29, 1800. He seems to have learned well the trade of his father. In 1821, when he was twenty-one years old, he took a place as a worker in a woolen mill at Watertown, Massachusetts, and resided there five years. His next work was in Marlow, Cheshire county, New Hampshire, where he built mills for sawing lumber, grinding grain, carding wool, and dressing cloth. He resided here until 1832, when he removed to a farm in Winchester, Cheshire county. Farming, however, was not to his taste, and he abandoned it after a three year trial, and returned to Nelson, and again engaged in the manufacture of woolen goods, and continued in that business until 1847. The village of Fisherville was growing rapidly and attracting considerable attention at that time to its water power. Mr. Harris was one of the manufacturers who went there, and he bought land and water power of the Gage family, and erected the Dustin Island Woolen Mills, near the island made famous by the exploit of Hannah Dustin many years before. These mills have been successfully operated by him, his sons and his grandsons from the time of their erection until now. They were a material addition to the village, and have ever since been an important factor in the prosperity of the village. A man of Mr. Harris's marked ability in taking the initiative in erecting and his success in conducting mills made him the foremost man in the community where he dwelt. He was universally respected, esteemed and trusted, and was often called to attend to the public affairs of the town. He was selectman, and later representative of the town of Boscawen in the New Hampshire legislature, 1864-65. His political faith was Republican. He was a member of the Congregational Church for forty-four years, and was for many years one of its deacons and superintendent of its Sunday school. He died September, 1876. He married, June 26, 1826, Phoebe, daughter of Ezra Sheldon, of Nelson, born March 15, 1801, who survived him until September 3, 1883. They had three sons: Ezra Sheldon, born November 27, 1827; Bethuel Edwin, born May 18, 1829; and Almon Ainger, born December 29, 1832.

(VIII) Ezra Sheldon, son of Almon and Phoebe (Sheldon) Harris, was born at Marlow, November 27, 1827, and died March 22, 1893. He was educated primarily in the schools of Marlow and Nelson, and later in the high school of Fisherville, taught by D. B. Whittier, in the brick school house on the Boscawen side of the river, and at New Ipswich Academy, New Hampshire. Wool carding and cloth dressing were things that he partially learned in his youth in school vacations about his father's mill at Nelson, and fully mastered afterward at Penacook. After serving a long apprenticeship he and his brother were taken into the business by their father, and the firm's name became A. Harris & Sons. After the death of Deacon Harris in 1876, the sons continued the business under the name of E. S. Harris & Company, until 1882, when Sheldon bought the interest of his brother Almon and continued as sole proprietor until his death in 1893. In a biographical sketch in Brown's "History of Penacook," the following summary of his character is found: "Mr. Harris was a man of marked ability in his own line of business, thoroughly skilled in all its various branches, and widely known throughout the state in mercantile and manufacturing circles. Under his management there were many important improvements made in the machinery and processes of manufacture, so that he kept the business fully up to the times, and maintained an enviable reputation for the goods manufactured at his mills. Mr. Harris was a man of upright moral character and correct habits, of a quiet, unostentatious disposition, but genial and courteous at all times. He had in a marked degree that desirable quality of mind known as mental equilibrium. In his relations to the workmen in his factory, he was liberal, considerate and just, and was respected and beloved by them to a greater degree than is usual in such relations. As a citizen Mr. Harris was universally esteemed by the whole community, and was called to serve in various offices in the town, and was honored with an election as representative of Boscawen in the state legislature. In his earlier years of residence in Penacook, Mr. Harris gave some attention to music. He had a very fine bass voice, and sang for several years in the choirs of the Baptist and Congregational churches. He was also a prominent member of the Fisherville Cornet Band, organized in 1858, in which he played a tuba. He was one of the early members of Horace Chase Lodge, No. 72, Ancient Free and Accepted Masons, and took much interest in the work of that organization." In 1890 he built a large and handsome residence on Tremont street, which he lived but three years to enjoy. It is now occupied by his widow and three of his children, and is one of the most attractive and desirable houses in the village. Mr. Harris married (first) June 30, 1860, Cassandra A. Greene, daughter of Nathan B. and Lucy (Carr) Greene, of Penacook, born April 2, 1837, by whom he had one daughter, Grace Greene, now the wife of Guy H. Hubbard; and one son, Robert Lincoln. Mrs. Harris died November 5, 1865, and Mr. Harris married (second) October 12, 1867, Sarah A. Greene, sister of his first wife, born June 30, 1844. Of this union there were three children: Harry Sheldon, born August 24, 1867; Almon Greene, born January 24, 1870; and Lucy Cassandra, born November 3, 1875.

(IX) Almon Greene, youngest son af Ezra Sheldon and Sarah A. (Greene) Harris, was born in Boscawen, January 24, 1870, and his residence has always been in that town. He attended the schools of his native town until he had prepared for high school, and then passed the curriculum of the Concord high school, graduating with the class of 1888. He subsequently attended Commer's Commercial College in Boston, where he obtained his business education. Returning to his home he entered his father's mill and began to learn the business, but more of his time was devoted to office business than to the mechanical processes of the industry. After the death of Ezra S. Harris, his heirs incorporated the business as the Dustin Island Woolen Mills, of which Almon G. Harris became treasurer, and since that time the office department and the financial management of the concern have been in his hands. He is treasurer of the Penacook Electric Light Company, director in the Concord State Fair Association, in the Eastern Fire Insurance Company, and the State Security and Accident Company. In politics he is a Republican, and has given due attention to local public matters and has served several years on the board of selectmen of Boscawen, and in other public places. He was elected a representative from Boscawen to the New Hampshire legislature in 1903 and again in 1905. Mr. Harris was made a member of Horace Chase Lodge, No. 72, Ancient Free and Accepted Masons, of which he is a past master, and in 1905 was appointed deputy grand master of the fourth Masonic district. He is also a member of Trinity Royal Arch Chapter, No. 2, of Concord; Horace Chase Council, No. 4, Royal and Select Masters, of Concord; Mount Horeb Commandery, Knights Templar, of Concord; and Edward A. Raymond Consistory, of Nashua. He received the thirty-second degree of the Scottish Rite. He is a charter member of the Union Club of Penacook; member of the Wonolancet Club of Concord; and the New Hampshire Club of Boston. For several years he has been a prominent member of the Patrons of Husbandry. In religious matters he affiliates with the Congregational church. He possesses a fine voice, and has for years sung in choirs and quartette clubs.

(II) John, sixth son of Henry Adams, came to Boston from England, with his wife and daughter, and settled in Cambridge. They had eight children.

(III) John, fourth child of John Adams, was born in Menotomy (now Arlington), May 1, 1655, settled in Framingham. He married Hannah Brent, and they had three children.

(IV) John, eldest child of John and Hannah (Brent) Adams, was born at Framingham, March 12, 1684. and resided on the "homestead" in Framingham. He was chosen deacon in 1726. He married Elizabeth Goddard, of Roxbury, June 27, 1706, and they were the parents of nine children.

(V) Joseph, eighth child of John and Elizabeth (Goddard) Adams, born in Framingham, August 12, 1728, removed to Dublin, New Hampshire, and resided there. He married three times. His first wife was Prudence Pratt, youngest daughter of David Pratt, of Framingham. He was the father of thirteen children.

(VI) Sarah, seventh child of Joseph and Prudence (Pratt) Adams, was born in Framingham, and baptized May 26, 1754. She married Abel Twitchell, a soldier of the revolution, who died at Harrisville, New Hampshire, March 8, 1837. They were the parents of eight children.

(VII) Deborah, second child of Abel and Sarah (Adams) Twitchell, born in Sherborn, August 14, 1776, died October 30, 1855, married Bethuel Harris, of Medway, January 1, 1795. (See Harris VI).

HARRIS

Sufficient data has not been obtained to connect this branch with the family of either Thomas or John Harhis, from one of whom it probably sprang.

(I) Mark A. Harris was born in Sandwich. He was extensively engaged in agricultural pursuits, and was a mechanic of merit. He married Betsey Swain and they had three children: Alvah, Elbridge, and Isaac, the subject of the next paragraph.

(II) Isaac, third son of Mark A. and Betsey (Swain) Harris, was born in Sandwich, and died in Gilford. He was a farmer. He married Mary Weeks, daughter of Thomas Bedex Weeks, of Sandwich. Three children were born of this union: Mark, who is the subject of the next paragraph; Filinda, who married Leonard Barton; and Ann, who married Daniel A. Maxfield.

(III) Mark, eldest child of Isaac and Mary (Weeks) Harris, was born in Sandwich, August 2, 1846. His early years were passed on his father's farm, and he acquired a practical knowledge of agricultural operations as he grew to manhood. He began to farm on his own account in Sandwich, where he remained until 1891, when he bought a farm of one hundred acres near Lake Winnipesaukee, in Gilford, where he has since resided. He is a thriving, progressive citizen, and makes his occupation profitable. He is a Baptist and a Democrat. He married Lucinda Taylor, daughter of Cyrus and Mary Taylor. They have five children: William B., born September 3, 1879; Eva W., August 5, 1888; Lewis F., April 4, 1892; Arthur C., June 3, 1899; and Evelyn, April 17, 1903.

(Second Family.)

HARRIS

The Harrises are among New England's most distinguished families. In old England a long line of ancestors preceded the immigrant, and on this side of the ocean the system of equality and civil liberty, which the short-sighted rulers of the mother country could not suppress, enabled them to expand their inherent intelligence and thereby gratify their desire to benefit mankind in one form or another. They early acquired prominence in various fields of usefulness, and are still to be found in the front rank of intellectual workers.

(I) John Harris resided in Ottery, St. Mary, Devonshire.

(II) Thomas, son of John Harris, was baptized at Ottery, August 26, 1606. (Perhaps John Harris, head of the third family of this article, was one of his sons.)

(III) Thomas (2), son of the preceding Thomas (1) Harris was baptized in the same place, July 30, 1637, and arrived in Boston about the year 1675. He belonged to the established church in England, but shortly after his arrival he united with the Old South Church, then recently organized, and retained his membership for the remainder of his life, which terminated January 8, 1698. The Christian name of his wife was Rebecca, and he left but one son.

(IV) Benjamin, son of Thomas (2) and Rebecca Harris, was born in Boston, October 21, 1694, and died there in his twenty-eighth year, January 25, 1722. He married Sarah Cary, who bore him a son, Cary.

(V) Cary, son of Benjamin and Sarah (Cary) Harris, was born in Boston, February 10, 1721. He engaged in the manufacture of hats, but his business career was necessarily of short duration, as he died in 1750, prior to his thirtieth birthday. He married Mehitable Crowell. They had a son, William.

(VI) William, son of Cary and Mehitable (Crowell) Harris, was born in Boston, July 7, 1747. Possessing superior intellectual attainments which had been developed by a careful education, he accepted at the age of twenty years the mastership of the public writing school in Charlestown, and retained it until the suspension of public education at the breaking-out of the revolutionary war. Alarmed for the safety of his family, who were domiciled in the immediate vicinity of the hill soon to be made famous as the scene of the first decisive battle for the cause of national independence, he removed them to Chockset, now Sterling, Massachusetts, and joined a regiment of patriots as captain and paymaster. He died while in the Continental service, October 30, 1778, and was buried with military honors. In describing the huried flight of the young schoolmaster, Dr. Nathaniel L. Frothingham writes as follows: "Just before the Battle of Bunker Hill, when his son Thaddeus was not quite seven years old, with a few necessary articles of clothing, such as they could easily carry, they set out for the interior, Thaddeus with his twin sisters, and the father and mother each carrying a child in their arms. By the burning of Charlestown he not only lost his occupation, but also a new house which he had erected and furnished with the savings of several years, thus finding himself reduced from a state of competency to a condition of poverty." He obtained temporary employment as a teacher in some of the country towns, but it was unprofitable and uncertain, owing to the general depression caused by the war, and he at length accepted a commission in the army. While on a visit to his family at Chockset he was seized with a violent attack of fever which proved fatal, and he left them in indigent circumstances. William Harris married Rebekah Mason, daughter of Hon. Thaddeus Mason, originally of Charlestown, and afterwards of Cambridge. Mr. Mason served both the commonwealth and Middlesex county in various positions of responsibility and trust, notably as clerk of the court of sessions and that of common pleas, retaining the latter office for a period of fifty-four years. He was graduated from Harvard with the class of 1728. He, too, suffered severely by the burning of Charlestown, losing an elegant mansion as well as other valuable property, and, with many others, he took refuge in Cambridge. His death occurred in 1802, at the advanced age of ninety-five years. Rebekah (Mason) Harris was the mother of five children. She married for her second husband Samuel Wait, of Malden, who was able to provide a comfortable home for herself and younger children, and she died February 2, 1801. (Possibly Thomas Harris, mentioned later in this article, was one of the sons).

(VII) Rev. Thaddeus Mason, eldest child and son of William and Rebekah (Mason) Harris, was born in Charlestown, July 7, 1768. The untimely death of his father practically threw him upon his own resources at the age of ten years, and he accepted any honorable employment that was offered him. In 1779 he attracted the attention of Dr. Ebenezer Morse, a former minister who had been forced to abandon preaching on account of being suspected of Toryism, and was residing in Boylston, Massachusetts, supporting himself by practicing medicine and preparing boys for college. This generous and sympathetic man gave him a place in his study beside his own son, directing his collegiate preparations without remuneration, and young Harris supported himself by stripping ash and walnut clefts for the manufacture of brooms, and the making of axe-handles and other implements. His cherished idea of going to college was relinquished for a time, owing to the objection of his mother, who advised him to learn a trade instead, but an accident cut short his mechanical career and he was at length enabled, through the assistance of interested friends, to gratify his ambition, entering Harvard College in July, 1783. For a time he resided at the home of Professor Williams, but later a waitership in the commons hall entitled him to free board, and he was graduated with the class of 1787 in company with John Quincy Adams, afterwards president of the United States, Judge Putnam, Judge Cranch and several other men of note. Upon leaving college he became a teacher in a school at Worcester, Massachusetts, and while residing there was offered the position of private secretary to General Washington, but was prevented from accepting that honorable appointment by an attack of small pox. During his junior year at college he united with Rev. Timothy Hilliard's church in Cambridge. After his recovery from the malady just mentioned he decided to enter the ministry, and at the suggestion of President Willard returned to Harvard for the purpose of pursuing his theological studies. He was "approbated to preach" by the Cambridge Association in June, 1789, prior to his twenty-first birthday, and after laboring in Brookline, Massachusetts, for a time, was in 1793 ordained to the pastorate of the church in Dorchester, which he retained for a period of forty-three years, resigning in 1836. Two years later he united with the First Church in Boston, whither he removed from Dorchester, and his death occurred there on Sunday morning, April 3, 1842, at the age of seventy-three years, eight months and twenty-seven days. He received the degree of Master of Arts at Harvard in course (1790), delivering the valedictory oration in Latin at commencement; was appointed librarian of Harvard in 1791, and was made a Doctor of Divinity by his alma mater in 1813. In 1810 he visited Europe. During his pastorate in Dorchester he could not have spent many idle hours as he labored in many fields of usefulness outside of his profession, devoting much time to public education and to several learned societies, with which he was connected, and also to literary work. His best known publication is entitled "The Natural History of the Bible." He was one of the founders of the Antiquarian Society, a member of the Massachusetts and New York Historical societies, the American Academy of Arts and Sciences, the Humane, Massachusetts Bible, American Peace, the Massachusetts Historical societies, and a corresponding member of the Georgia Historical Society and the Archaelogical Society of Athens, Greece. For a number of years he officiated as chaplain and secretary of the Grand Lodge of Massachusetts, Ancient Free and Accepted Masons, which presented him with a silver vase in 1816.

January 28, 1795, Dr. Harris married Mary Dix, daughter of Dr. Elijah and Dorothy Dix, of Worcester. She was a lady of superior intelligence and unusual force of character. Of this union there were eight children, five of whom lived to a mature age, namely: Thaddeus William, M. D., who is referred to at length in the succeeding paragraph; Mary Dorothy, Clarendon, John Alexander and James Winthrop.

(VIII) Thaddeus William, eldest son of Dr. Thaddeus Mason and Mary (Dix) Harris, was born in Dorchester, November 12, 1795. He pursued his collegiate preparations in Dedham and Bridgewater, Massachusetts, entered Harvard in his sixteenth year and took his bachelor's degree in 1815, having as classmates Jared Sparks, afterward president of that university; Professor Convers Francis, John Graham Palfrey and Theophilus Parsons. His preliminary medical studies were directed by Dr. Amos Holbrook, of Milton, Massachusetts, and after graduating from the Harvard Medical School in 1820, located for practice in that town. The life of a physician was, however, uncongenial to him and therefore became one of absolute drudgery from which he longed to escape. Receiving the appointment of librarian of Harvard in 1831, he eagerly accepted it and thenceforward his energies were devoted to the interests of the university, both in the official capacity, which brought him back to it, and developing its department of natural sciences. During his term of service as librarian, which covered a period of twenty-five years, Dr. Harris was largely instrumental in increasing the number of volumes from thirty thousand to sixty-five thousand, and witnessed the removal of the library from old Harvard Hall to Gore Hall, its present repository. His work as librarian led him into various fields of investigation intimately connected with it, and among his most important efforts in this direction was a special study of the early voyages to this country and the settlements along the coast. He is best known, however, for his unceasing labors in the field of natural history and as the father of American entomology. As early as 1820 he began his researches relative to botany as applied to materia medica, and also to entomology and kindred subjects. The study of the character and habits of insects was never lost sight of, but was merely held in abeyance by his official duties and to be taken up and carried forward at every opportunity, and his progress in that science remains to-day as a fitting monument to his memory. His elaborate entomological collection, now possessed by the Boston Society of Natural History, represents the patient labor of many years, and that body, of which he was a leading member, published his entire list of papers in its transactions, numbering one hundred and forty-four. Besides the above he was a member of the Massachusetts Historical and Massachusetts Medical societies, the American Academy of Arts and Sciences, and the Society for the Promotion of Agriculture; a corresponding member of the Academy of Natural Sciences, Philadelphia, of the London Entomological Society; and an honorary member of the Historical Society of Pennsylvania. He died in Cambridge, January 16, 1856. He married, in 1824, Catherine Holbrook, daughter of Dr. Amos Holbrook, of Milton, previously mentioned. Among the children of this union was Charles.

(IX) Charles, son of Dr. Thaddeus W. and Catherine (Holbrook) Harris, was born in Cambridge, Massachusetts, October 2, 1832. His educational opportunities were excellent, and having acquired a knowledge of civil engineering he followed that profession in the state of Ohio and in Boston from 1850 to 1864. For the succeeding eighteen years he was superintendent of streets for the city of Boston, and for twenty years following acted as New England representative of the Barber Asphalt Paving Company. He has since been living in retirement, spending his declining years at his home in Cambridge. In addition to his business ability, which was eminently superior, he possesses intellectual attainments of a high order, and as a gentleman of culture he occupies a prominent position in the exclusive social circles of the University City. He is a thirty-second degree Mason and a member of the Massachusetts Consistory. His religious belief is in accord with the teachings of Emanuel Swedenborg, and he is a member of the Church of the New Jerusalem, Cambridge. He married Sarah Elizabeth Hovey, and reared two children: Thaddeus W., who is referred to at length in the succeeding paragraphs; and Marion, who became the wife of Dr. William W. Pearce, and resides in Waukegan, Illinois.

(X) Thaddeus William Harris, Ph. D., son of Charles and Sarah E. (Hovey) Harris, was born in Cambridge, January 19, 1862. He took his bachelor's degree at Harvard University with the class of 1884, receiving that of Master of Arts in 1885, and he remained there as instructor some nine years, taking the degree of Doctor of Philosophy in 1890. His taste and capacity for educational pursuits were so predominant in his character as to cause him to enter that field of usefulness in preference to the various other professional walks for which he is super-abundantly qualified, and accepting the responsible position of superintendent of the public schools of Keene, in 1894, he thereafter performed his official duties with unusual energy and ability up to his retirement in 1905.

During his residence in Keene Dr. Harris has interested himself in educational matters apart from his legitimate duties, being at the present time a trustee of the Keene Public Library, and acting for 1904 as president of the New England Association of School Superintendents. He also participates actively in religious work as senior warden of St. James (Protestant) Episcopal Church, and as a director of the Young Men's Christian Association. His ancestors, included among which were physicians, ministers, and merchants, were all men of marked ability, and his intellectual attainments and executive ability are therefore in some measure inherited.

He married, June 20, 1894, Winifred Parker, who was born June 18, 1867, daughter of Charles H. and Abby J. (Rockwood) Parker. She is a descendant of (I) John Parker, born in England, September 4, 1575, through (II) Thomas, the immigrant, (1609-1683) (see Parker); (III) Hananiah (1638-1724); (IV) John (1664-1741); (V) Andrew (1693-1776); (VI) Thomas, (1727-1799); (VII) Ebenezer, of Lexington, (1750-1839); (VIII) Quincy (1775-1828); (IX) Ira (1814) and (X) Charles H., who was born in Providence, Rhode Island, March 22, 1839, and died in Cambridge, August, 1895. The latter served in the civil war with the Twenty-first Regiment, Massachusetts Volunteer Infantry, and attained the rank of lieutenant. It is quite evident that her ancestry is the same as that Rev. Theodore Parker, the famous preacher of a half century ago. Dr. and Mrs. Harris have two sons—Thaddeus William, born October 1, 1895, and Charles Parker Harris, born December 28, 1898.

HARRIS The families of Harris in the United States are very numerous, and can not be traced to a common ancestor, as many distinct emigrations of persons bearing the name appear to have taken place at a very early period in the history of New England. Previous to 1640 many of the name were in New England, and were among the early settlers of different towns.

(VII) Thomas Harris, who was born in Massachusetts, died in Hudson, New Hampshire, in 1856, aged eighty-three years. For years he was employed as a sail maker in Salem, Massachusetts. He removed to Hudson, New Hampshire, several years before his death, and was there engaged in agriculture. He was a Democrat in political sentiment. He married (second), in Hudson, Lydia Colburn, of Hudson, he had five children: Eliza, Thomas, William, a daughter (died young) and Albert, the subject of the next paragraph.

(VIII) Albert, youngest child of Thomas and

Lydia (Colburn) Harris, was born in Salem, Massachusetts, November, 1811, and died in Hudson, November 19, 1875. He was educated in the common schools of his native town, and worked on his father's farm in Hudson until he was of age, and then bought the place adjoining, where he spent his remaining years. In his early manhood he was a Whig, but when the questions of slavery and rebellion were agitated he became a Republican and a supporter of Abraham Lincoln and his measures. He married Sarah F. Wellman, who was born at Washington, New Hampshire, daughter of Thomas Wellman, of Washington, New Hampshire; she died, and he married (second) Amanda Stuart of Hudson. There were seven children by the first wife: Edward P., lives in Topeka, Kansas; Catherine, died in youth; Myron W. lives in Amherst; Lydia Frances, married George W. Connell, of Hudson; Henry Albert, the subject of the next paragraph; Harriett A., married O. B. Robinson; Charles Austin, married (first) Georgiana Hill, and (second) Leah Boothby, of Lowell, Massachusetts, and lives in Lowell. Mary F., the only child of the second wife, was born April 15, 1856, and married George W. Bartlett, of Goffstown.

(IX) Albert Henry, who often writes his name Henry A. Harris, third son and fifth child of Albert and Sarah F. (Wellman) Harris, was born in Hudson, October 27, 1842. He attended the public schools of Hudson and Lowell until he was eighteen years of age, and worked at farming and taught school two terms before the outbreak of the rebellion. August 28, 1862, he enlisted in Company L, First Maine Cavalry, and served two years and nine months, being discharged May 28, 1865. He took part in many battles and minor engagements, some of the most important of which were the Wilderness, Spottsylvania, Mine Run, and Appomattox, being present at General Lee's surrender. In his campaigning he had two horses shot under him.

After the war he returned to Littleton, Maine, where he taught school four winters and carried on a farm the remainder of the time. In 1870 he returned to Hudson and engaged in agriculture two years, and then removed to Merrimack, and was station agent of the Boston & Maine railroad at South Merrimack for five years. The next five years he lived on a leased farm and then (1886) bought the place he has since occupied. Mr. Harris has so deported himself as to command the confidence and respect of those who know him, and by them he has been placed in all of the offices of the town but representative. He is a trustee of the public library, was chairman of the school board nine years, and built the school house at Reed's Ferry, and has been a member of the board of selectmen three years. He is a member of John H. Worcester Post, Grand Army of the Republic, of Hollis, and of the Order of the Golden Cross, of which he is a past commander. He is a Republican in the principles for which he fought in the dark days of the rebellion. He is a member of the Union Evangelical First Church of Merrimack.

He married, first, May 9, 1866, Dora F. Hill, who was born in Littleton, Maine, May 1, 1851, daughter of Bradford and Hannah J. (Delaite) Hill of Littleton, Maine. She was a member of the Christian Church (Disciples), a lady of intelligence, and taught school a number of terms before her marriage. She died September 26, 1891, and he married (second) January 5, 1893, at Nashua, Fanny E. Brown, who was born in Amherst, September 25, 1855, daughter of William E. and Elizabeth G. (Cragin) Brown, of Merrimack. She was educated in the public schools of Manchester and at Magaw Institute. She subsequently taught school in Merrimack for sixteen successive years, and was regarded as one of the most successful instructors in that region. She is a member of the Union Evangelical Church. The children of the first wife were: Viola W., died young; Albert H., born February 16, 1876, married Nellie F. Patterson, daughter of George E. and Anna Patterson, of South Merrimack; and Leroy E., born November 21, 1877, married Carolyn Francisco, of New York.

(Third Family.)

HARRIS This is an old New England family, originating in England or Wales, and has furnished many excellent citizens in New Hampshire. It is identified with the earliest pioneer period along the Merrimack river, and is still conspicuous in business circles of the region.

(I) John Harris, progenitor of many of the name in New England is found of record in Charlestown, Massachusetts, as early as 1658, when he was granted two parcels of land. He married Amy Hills, daughter of Joseph and Rose (Dunster) Hills. Her father was a woolen draper, who came from Malden, England, and lived in Charlestown and Newbury, Massachusetts. Her mother was a sister of President Dunster of Harvard College. John Harris' sons were: Samuel, John, Thomas and Joseph.

(II) Thomas, third son of John and Amy (Hills) Harris, was born March 18, 1664, in Charlestown, and was a tailor residing in that town, where he died about 1747. He married, February 25, 1686, Hepzibah Crosswell, who was born May 20, 1668, daughter of Thomas and Priscilla (Upham) Crosswell, of Charlestown. Their children were: Thomas, Hepzibah, Silence, Ebenezer, William, John, Abigail, Rachael and Elizabeth.

(III) Ebenezer, second son and fourth child of Thomas and Hepzibah (Crosswell) Harris, was born June 11, 1698, in Charlestown, and died in Dunstable, New Hampshire. He was a tailor by occupation, and settled in Chelmsford, Massachusetts, where he resided until about 1745, when he removed to Dunstable. The land records show that he purchased land there about that time. He married Elizabeth Spalding, who was born January 17, 1700, in Chelmsford, daughter of Joseph and Elizabeth (Colburn) Spalding. Their children were: Ebenezer, Hepzibah, Hannah and Thomas, born in Chelmsford, and probably others born in Dunstable.

(IV) Ebenezer (2), eldest child of Ebenezer (1) and Elizabeth (Spalding) Harris was born June 12, 1731, in Chelmsford and was a child when he removed with his parents to Dunstable. He served from that town as a soldier of the Revolution. His wife's name was Dorcas, but no record of his marriage is found. It is known that his daughter Silence was born in Dunstable, September 29, 1755, and his son Thomas, March 29, 1757. He was still living in 1783.

(V) Ebenezer (3), second son of Ebenezer (2) and Dorcas Harris, was born July 24, 1759, in Dunstable, and died in Merrimack, March 17, 1843, aged eighty-four. He married Rebecca Hills, who was born in Nottingham West, March 6, 1762, and died March 20, 1852, aged ninety. Ten children were born of this union: Rebekah, June 26, 1782, died January 16, 1874. Esther, July 16, 1784, died October 10, 1857. Reuben, May 2, 1786, died April 23, 1835. Rhoda, February 21, 1788, died April 25, 1872. Ebenezer, June 1, 1790, died March 20, 1869. Anna, December 11, 1793, died December 26, 1883. Hannah, April 7, 1795, died January 5, 1878. Oliver, May 19, 1798, died May 11, 1803. Pauli, March 22, 1801, died August 23, 1888. Robert, March 15, 1807, see forward.

(VI) Robert, son of Ebenezer (3) and Rebecca (Hills) Harris, was born in Merrimack, New Hampshire, March 15, 1807, died in Nashua, September 1, 1889. He was a farmer and resided in Nashua. He married, March 7, 1837, Mary Glines, who was born in Franklin, New Hampshire, October 4, 1816, died January 30, 1899. She was the daughter of William and Naomi (Hancock) Glines, and a descendant of the pioneer Glines settler of Londonderry; she is also of the same stock as John Hancock. There were nine children born of this union: Mary M., June 10, 1838. Alonzo, June 29, 1840, died August 6, 1842. Harvey W., May 23, 1842, died December 6, of the same year. Orin B., May 11, 1845, died September 16, of the same year. George A., March 26, 1846, died August 17, 1870. Lucius L., July 5, 1848. Frank M., July 5, 1851, died August 3, 1892. Ida F., November 8, 1855, died aged seven years, and Ira F., November 8, 1855.

(VII) Ira Francis, youngest child of Robert and Mary (Glines) Harris, was born November 8, 1855, in Nashua. Previous to the age of sixteen years he was a student in the public schools of his native town, after which he went to Jamaica Plain, Massachusetts, and remained a short time. He next took up his residence at New Albany Indiana, and was employed for some time in the navigation of the Ohio river, acting as assistant pilot. In 1875 he returned to Nashua and took up the study of dentistry in the office of Dr. L. F. Lock, where he read two years. At this time he was offered an advantageous position in the Indian Head National Bank and accepted. His duties were so faithfully discharged that he was made assistant cashier in 1886, and after nine years' further service became cashier in 1895. This position he has since held and has become interested in many of the business and social institutions of his native city. He is secretary of the First Congregational Church Society and of the Fortnightly Club. He is treasurer of the local and also of the State Board of Trade, has administered on a number of important estates, and is interested in various business enterprises of the city. He is recorded among the prosperous and most substantial citizens of his native town. Mr. Harris has been an extensive traveler, is a keen observer, and his contributions to literature have been gratefully and happily accepted by the public. His illustrated lectures on the Merrimack Valley, Colonial Homes, Historic Nashua, and other subjects, have delighted many audiences. Mr. Harris is a cultivated gentleman, whose manners are pleasing; whose heart is large, and he is respected and honored by a large circle of friends. He naturally became affiliated with fraternal orders, and is now a Knight Templar Mason, who has attained the thirty-second degree.

He was married in Nashua, June 7, 1881, to Mary C. Proctor, who was born August 29, 1852, daughter of Joseph B. and Sarah J. Proctor of Nashua. (See Proctor, VII). Mrs. Harris is registrar of Nashua Chapter, Daughters of the American Revolution, and is an active member of the Woman's Club of Nashua and other social organizations.

(Fourth Family.)

HARRIS Among the prominent citizens of Portsmouth, this state, are representatives of the line herein traced, of whose ancestry very little is known. The first of whom record now appears was Abel Harris, who resided in Portsmouth.

(II) William Coffin, son of Abel Harris, was born November, 1767, in Portsmouth, New Hampshire. He married Mary Johnson and resided in that town.

(III) Captain Thomas Aston, son of William Coffin and Mary (Johnson) Harris, was born June 13, 1824, in Portsmouth, New Hampshire. Introduced to the active matters of life at an early age, the wide awake lad developed a passion for the sea, which nothing could dispel or divert. His first voyage was to India in the ship "Mary and Susan," commanded by Captain William F. Parrott, a voyage which he heartily enjoyed, and so beneficial that thereafter he was "in all seas." In 1847 he sailed from Norfolk with government stores for California, and arrived at Monterey, February 6, 1848, when the gold fever was at its height. The republic of California was an accepted and wide-awake fact in those days, and of which Mr. Harris received a tangible reminder early in the summer of 1890 in the shape of a handsome flag, one of the original banners of the infant republic. It is of white bunting, ten feet long and four feet wide, with a broad stripe of red on the lower edge, a red, five-pointed star in the field (the star of the republic); in the center of the white a large California bear, walking, known as "Nahl's bear," and underneath the legend "California Republic." This souvenir is very valuable, and of course highly prized by the fortunate receiver. Captain Harris returned to the United States the longest way, via China, and soon after returned to San Francisco arriving in 1850. As is generally known there is a society in that state known as the California Pioneers. A "forty-eighter" is eligible to what is termed a Golden Bear membership, a forty-niner to a Silver Bear, but a pioneer of '50 has no status in the association. Gold and silver badges are indicative of these ranks. Captain Harris was the possessor of the golden trophy and this certificate:

This is to certify that Thomas Aston Harris, who arrived in California, February 6, 1848, is a member of the Society of California Pioneers.

(Signed) EDWARD KRUSE, President.
(SEAL) W. H. GRAVES, Secretary.
San Francisco, California, May 20, 1890.

About this time Captain Harris entered the service of the Pacific Mail Steamship Company, where he remained a considerable time. On returning east he built a vessel for the Russian government, during the Crimean war, an armed steamer, the "Astoria," and sailed thence under the American flag. On arriving at Sitka her name was changed to "Alexander." The vessel made a grand record, and was the same one sent to take Hon. William H. Seward to Sitka when he went there to inspect his purchase for the United States government. While there Captain Harris was urged to take a high position in the Russian navy, and the rank and privilege of a nobleman, but it was satisfaction to believe that the Yankee nobility was good enough for the Portsmouth sailor, and the proffer was gratefully and gracefully declined. At the close of the Crimean war he returned to the United States, arriving in February, 1857. He remained only a few months, however, when in the latter part of that year he sailed for San Francisco in the United States light house steamer "Shubrick," and delivered the vessel, and remained there nearly two years, when he returned. Captain Harris then took charge of steamer "Pei Ho," an armed vessel built for Russell & Company, to open trade with Japan.

Ira Evans.

Reaching Hong Kong, the ports of Japan having been opened by treaty, the vessel was sold to the French government for a despatch boat. He then returned to the United States overland late in 1860, arriving in the midst of the John Brown trouble at Harper's Ferry. Imbued by the excitement. Captain Harris took a trip south, going as far as Texas to see how matters were looking and to ascertain the sentiments of the people. After thoroughly acquainting himself with southern affairs he returned north and entered the United States navy as acting master, his commission dating from May, 1861. On April 27, 1863, he was advanced to acting volunteer lieutenant "as a reward for gallant conduct in the face of the enemy," the official record states. The event referred to was the capture of a battery of six guns at Hill's Point, on the Nansemond river, in Virginia. In this action was a detachment of eight companies of the Tenth New Hampshire Volunteers, Captain George W. Towle and Captain James Albert Sanborn, both of Portsmouth, in command. In April, 1865, he was promoted to acting volunteer lieutenant-commander, and served in that capacity until the close of the war. and was honorably mustered out and discharged October 24, 1865. Captain Harris' first government ship was the "Penguin," of which he was executive officer. His other commands were, in the order named, the "Henry Andrews," "Stepping Stones," "Newbern" and "Lillian," of the North Atlantic Squadron, and the "Preost" and "Abeona," of the Mississippi Squadron. On leaving the United States service he resumed service with the Pacific Mail Steamship Company, and was in command on the Atlantic coast until 1867, whence he went to Acapulco, Mexico, as agent of the company there. Two years later he was transferred to Hong Kong in a similar capacity, and remained there nearly five years. when, and only because of impaired health, he was obliged to come home. On leaving Hong Kong he was presented by the guild of merchants, and with great ceremony, a testimonial made of white satin with handsomely embroidered border and inscribed in golden letters, with the fulsome compliment of the Chinese people. This missive measures four feet by three feet, and attractively framed, has for years held the chief place of honor upon the wall in the captain's library. The change of climate having effected a considerable improvement in his health, he returned to Japan as general agent of the Pacific Mail Steamship Company for Japan and China, with headquarters at Yokohama. In 1876 he was ordered home by medical survey, too long residence and continual overwork having completely prostrated a physique perfect in every point, and for which change of climate and rest were imperative. There was protest but no escape from the plain alternative, and the wanderer, having acquired a competency, returned to Portsmouth, which ever held the dearest corner in his heart and for whose welfare and progress he had undivided interest. Captain Harris was prominent in organizations, and among these was a member of Saint John's Lodge, No. 1, Ancient Free and Accepted Masons, of Portsmouth, the Massachusetts Commandery, Loyal Legion, and a comrade of Storer Post, No. 1, Grand Army of the Republic, of Portsmouth. His gift to the latter organization of a large and centrally located burying ground for soldiers and sailors at Harmony Grove Cemetery, is a memorial to the patriotism and thoughtfulness of the comrade which will be as enduring as time. For many years Captain Harris was a director in the New Hampshire National Bank; and on the resignation of Edwin A. Peterson as president, was unanimously chosen his successor. He was an able, far-seeing financier, and devoted the latter years of his ever active life to its interests. His interest in young men was particularly noticeable, and in the most unostentatious ways, helped many to enter upon successful business careers. Captain Harris was a writer of much force and attractiveness, and was never happier than when seated at his desk, though unfortunately for the community he modestly kept his literary light almost completely hidden. He was a gentleman of culture; had positive convictions; the tenderest sympathies; possessed the most courtly grace; was a fine conversationalist, and had the deepest attachments. Of him it can truthfully be said that he was personified nobleness. Captain Harris married Mary Elizabeth Langdon Pickering, daughter, of John Pickering, esquire, of Portsmouth. (See Pickering). She was born April 14, 1835, in Portsmouth, New Hampshire.

WHEELER There are several families bearing this name distinct, at least as far as connection in this country is concerned, and all are very good stock and found in the early records. The name has figured creditably in both militia and civic annals through many generations, and now has living in New Hampshire some very worthy representatives.

(I) George Wheeler, immigrant ancestor of those herein traced, was born in 1600, in Salisbury, England, and was one of the founders of Concord. Massachusetts, where he located before 1640, and was made a freeman in 1641. He died there between January, 1685, and June, 1687. He was twice married, but no record of his first wife is obtained. His second wife, Katherine, died June 2, 1685. He had five children born in England and three in Concord, namely: William, Thomas, Ruth, Elizabeth, Hannah, Sarah, John and Mary. (John and descendants are mentioned in this article.)

(II) William, eldest child of George Wheeler, was born 1630, in England, and was consequently nearly ten years of age when the family settled in Concord. He died there December 31, 1683. We can easily conceive that his childhood was passed amid rude surroundings and that he bore a part in the struggles of subduing the forests and making a home. He was married in Concord, October 30, 1659, to Hannah Buss (mistakenly printed Beers in some instances), daughter of William and Anna Buss. She was born February 18, 1642. Their children were: Hannah (died young), Rebecca, Elizabeth, William, Hannah, Richard, John and George.

(III) George (2), youngest child of William and Hannah (Buss) Wheeler, was born 1670, in Concord, where he lived through life and died July, 1737. He was married, August 14, 1695, to Abigail Hosmer, daughter of Stephen and Abigail (Wood) Hosmer. She was born November 6, 1669, and died December 27, 1717. Mr. Wheeler married (second), December 3, 1719, Abigail Smith, who was born July 21, 1684, in Sudbury, daughter of Thomas and Abigail Smith. She died between October 3 and December 30, 1728. He had sons James and Peter, who lived in Concord and Bedford, Massachusetts, and in Hollis, New Hampshire. His other children were: Tabitha, Abigail, Jemima, Daniel, Ephraim and Simon.

(IV) James, eldest son of George (2) and Abigail (Hosmer) Wheeler, was born September 5, 1702, in Concord, and lived in that part of the town which was included in Bedford when the latter town was incorporated in 1729. Thus his younger children were born in Bedford, while the older ones were born in Concord and all on the same farm. His wife Mary is supposed to have been a Minot. Their children were: Mary, Keziah, Lydia, James, Elizabeth, Daniel, Azuba and Thaddeus. (Mention of the last named, with descendants, appears in this article.)

(V) Daniel, second son of George (2) and Abigail (Smith) Wheeler, was born April 23, 1736; married February 9, 1757, Amy Morse. He died at "Patch Corner," Hollis, between January 1, 1775, and April 19, 1775. Their children leaving their native place soon after their father's death, there have been no descendants of Daniel Wheeler living in Hollis for more than one hundred years. His widow married, April 7, 1779, Samuel Leeman, whose first wife was Love Wheeler, a daughter of Peter Wheeler and cousin of Daniel Wheeler, her first husband. She had no children by Leeman. After the death of her second husband she lived with her children, alternating between Benjamin, Jacob, Lydia and Daniel. She came to Benjamin's home in Concord, New Hampshire, May 26, 1803, and died at her son Jacob's home in Bow, New Hampshire, November 30, 1821, and is buried in the Bow cemetery, just south of Turee Pond, beside the grave of her son Jacob. Children of Daniel and Amy (Morse) Wheeler: Lydia, born in Monson (now a part of Hollis) November 24, 1757. Abner, born in Monson, April 14, 1760. Jacob, born in Monson, March 5, 1763. Daniel, born in Monson, March 18, 1765. Benjamin, born in Hollis, August 18, 1768; see forward. Hannah, born in Hollis, about 1772, died 1862, aged about ninety.

(VI) Benjamin Wheeler, born August 18, 1768, married Polly Fitch, of Bedford, Massachusetts, born October 23, 1770, died April 27, 1818, in Concord, New Hampshire. He married (second) Hannah Clement, born May 17, 1770, in Salem, New Hampshire. He died December 11, 1848. She died October 20, 1852, in Concord. She had no children. Polly Fitch was a daughter of David Fitch, a descendant of Zachary Fitch, the emigrant, and of kin with John Fitch for whom Fitchburg, Massachusetts, was named. Her father, David Fitch, was in Captain James Moore's company of the Bedford militia and the Concord and Lexington fight April 19, 1775, with the British force of eight hundred troops sent from Boston to seize some military stores. In the battle the English lost two hundred and seventy-three soldiers and the Americans less than one hundred. The British commander, Major Pitcairn, was mortally wounded, and soon after died in the Province Tavern, which stood on the west side of Washington street, Boston, nearly opposite the Old South Church.

In youth Benjamin Wheeler lived with his oldest sister, Lydia, who married Benjamin Winship, of Lexington, Massachusetts, and was there at the time and a witness of that battle, during which a British soldier came into their shay-house, and finding a halter there committed suicide by hanging himself. Between one hundred and forty and one hundred and fifty British soldiers committed suicide during the Revolution.

During his early manhood he lived in Bedford, Massachusetts, working on the farm and in the old grist mill on the Shawsheen river, owned and carried on by his father-in-law, David Fitch, and while in his employment he learned the business of miller and farming, also habits of industry, thrift and good morals. This homestead and mill privilege, owned and occupied by succeeding generations of the Fitch families for one hundred and seventy-five years, was recently sold. After reaching the age of some twenty-five years he married Polly, oldest daughter of David Fitch and Mary Fowle, and moved to Woburn, Massachusetts, in 1794, and leased the farm of Squire Jonathan Simpson for the term of three years, where his son Benjamin Jr., the father of the writer of this sketch, was born.

On April 1, 1798, he, in company with Nathaniel Wyman, leased for one year the grist mill and farm of one hundred and thirty acres of Duncan Ingraham, commonly known as the Belknap farm, where his daughter, Mary Fitch Wheeler, was born. On April 7, 1800, he leased the farm of Samuel Carter in Lincoln, Massachusetts. On October 24, 1801, he came to Concord, New Hampshire, and purchased a farm of thirty-four acres with buildings, for the sum of five hundred dollars, of Ebenezer Dustin, known as the Jacob Towle place. It was occupied at this time by Moses Noyes, a revolutionary soldier. He moved to this place, now known as "Wheeler's Corner," South street, early in the year 1802, bringing with him his effects on an ox-wagon built in Lexington, Massachusetts, by the grandfather of the late Major Lewis Downing. There were additions made to the original purchase by himself and son Benjamin, Jr., so that at the time of his death in 1848 there were one hundred acres in one body, excepting the passage of South street through it. Besides, they owned some seventy acres of wood and timber land in the nearby town of Bow. This old homestead, with two additional sets of buildings and about thirty acres of adjoining land, are now owned by his grandson, Giles Wheeler. The children of Benjamin and Polly (Fitch) Wheeler were: 1. Benjamin Wheeler, Jr., born November 26, 1795; see forward. 2. Mary Fitch, born June 6, 1799, Woburn; died January 13, 1852, Concord, New Hampshire; baptized October 23, 1842, by Rev. E. E. Cummings; admitted to First Baptist Church, Concord.

(VII) Benjamin (2) Wheeler, son of Benjamin (1) and Polly (Fitch) Wheeler, was born November 26, 1795, in Woburn, Massachusetts; married, September 18, 1828, Eliza Ordway, born December 11, 1808, in Haverhill, Massachusetts. He died June 4, 1870. She died September 11, 1881, in Concord, New Hampshire. He was drafted in the war of 1812, but his father could not well spare him from the farm, and provided a substitute. He served in the state militia, Sixth Company, Eleventh Regiment, Third Brigade; appointed ensign October 10, 1826; promoted to first lieutenant, July 21, 1827; promoted to captain, August 31, 1832; discharged March 31, 1834. Like all other children of his day, he had small advantages for schooling. The school where he attended was just south of and near the Orphans' Home of St. Paul's School, about two and a half miles distant from his home. Both were baptized; his wife October 2, 1842; he died October 16, 1842. Received into the First Baptist Church, Concord, October 23, 1842, under the ministrations of the late Rev. Ebenezer E. Cummings, D. D. The children of Benjamin (2) Wheeler and Eliza Ordway were:

(VIII) John Clement Wheeler, born October 11, 1829, died April 21, 1894, on the old homestead at "Wheeler's Corner," Concord, New Hampshire, unmarried. He lived here nearly his entire life engaged in farming. In early manhood he was more or less employed as a stone-setter on the bridge piers on Merrimack river, and was for a time employed on the United States General Postoffice, Washington, D. C. He was named for his (step) grandfather John Clement, a revolutionary soldier from Salem, New Hampshire.

(VIII) Giles Wheeler, born August 7, 1834; married, January 30, 1858, Sarah W. Abbott, born October 18, 1835. She died December 1, 1902. She was the daughter of Charles Abbott and his wife Sarah R. Carter, both being descendants of emigrants who settled in Concord in 1727—Nathaniel Abbott and Ephraim Carter, prominent in town affairs in their day and generation. No better woman ever lived than Sarah W. Abbott Wheeler.

Giles Wheeler lived on the old homestead at "Wheeler's Corner" until twenty years of age, attending school in winter terms of some ten or twelve weeks each, in the little red school house eighteen by twenty feet, generally known as the "Iron Works" district, but officially in the town district system as district No. 18; and in addition to that attended two terms of a private school kept in town, one term kept by Professor Hall Roberts, in the Athenian Hall, and one term by Rev. George S. Barnes, in the Natural Historical Hall. On leaving this school, May 7, 1853, he began learning the carpenter's trade, serving three years with Colby & Dow. On completion of this term of service he took the contract to build the present "Iron Works" school house for the sum of seven hundred and twenty-five dollars, and continued work at his trade until 1861, when he went to Plymouth, Massachusetts, to superintend a manufacturing business, remaining there three years. While there he was drafted for military service in the civil war, in both Concord, New Hampshire, and Plymouth, Massachusetts, under the same call for recruits. Having no taste for roosting on the fence or sleeping on plowed ground, he procured a substitute, a Yankee, William Gilson, a native of Pelham, New Hampshire, who had already been in the army for nine months, who was ready and willing to rough it again; took his place, fought, bled and died vicariously for his principal.

Returning to Concord, January 2, 1864, he resumed work at his trade, and in 1865 and 1866 built his present residence, where he ever after lived. He was engaged in the lumbering business with Mark T. Ladd two years, and in October, 1873, went into the office of Edward Dow, architect; continued in the business with him until the summer of 1885, when he received the appointment of superintendent of construction for the erection of the Concord post office and United States court house. After its completion he continued as building agent and superintendent of the high school house on School street, the Kimball and Franklin school houses, Margaret Pillsbury hospital, State Library building, Soldiers' Memorial Arch, and several business blocks on Main street, and occasionally making plans for buildings. He has held commissions as justice of the peace for some thirty years, and has been a member of the police commission of Concord from the beginning, and serving as clerk of the board; has attended every meeting of the board to date (1907). He has also served as administrator and executor in the settlement of many estates. He has been nominated for every political office in his ward, also for mayor and state senator, but being a "wicked Democrat," has fortunately always escaped an election. He is also the compiler of these genealogies and historical sketches, and the last living descendant of Daniel Wheeler, Sr., bearing the name of Wheeler, and has no descendants.

(VIII) Isaac Fitch Wheeler, born April 18, 1836; married, December 8, 1867, Harriet E. Ordway. He died March 24, 1902. His wife died June 8, 1907. His middle name was from his grandmother's people, the Fitches of Bedford, Massachusetts. His entire life was that of a quiet, unobtrusive, uneventful, industrious farmer, and was spent on the old homestead at "Wheeler's Corner." He lived at peace with all the world, owing no man anything, and died very suddenly of apoplexy in his own home. Universally lamented, he left behind him

"Far worthier things than tears—
The love of friends, without a single foe.
God's finger touched him and he slept.
Oh friend, say not good night,
But on some brighter shore bid us good morning."

(VIII) Albert Francis Wheeler, born March 15, 1839; died October 29, 1844.

(V) Thaddeus, youngest child of James and Mary Wheeler, was born December 16, 1742, in Bedford, Massachusetts, and was a pioneer settler of Hollis, New Hampshire, where he was a farmer. He was married in that town October 17, 1769, to Elizabeth Farner, and their children were: Elizabeth, Thaddeus, Minot, Theodore, Amos, James and Benjamin.

(VI) Minot, second son and third child of Thaddeus and Elizabeth (Farner) Wheeler, was born May 16, 1777, in Hollis, and settled about the beginning of the nineteenth century in Royalton, Vermont, where he was for many years an inn keeper. He was married, April 28, 1800, in Brookline, New Hampshire, to Sarah Farley, who was born June 3, 1781, in Brookline, being a twin of Elizabeth. She was a daughter of Benjamin and Lucy Farley, and granddaughter of Samuel and Hannah Farley, pioneer settlers of Hollis. Benjamin Farley was born March 11, 1756, in Hollis. Minot and Sarah (Farley) Wheeler were the parents of ten children.

(VII) Howe, son of Minot and Sarah (Farley) Wheeler, was born and reared in Royalton, Vermont, at a period when the country was new and the sorrowful experiences of the Revolutionary days were still fresh in the minds of the people. This town was burned and several of its citizens massacred by Indians during the Revolution, and the wife of Howe Wheeler belonged to one of the families that suffered most severely during that inhuman disaster. She was Amy Parkhurst, of Royalton, and a woman of strongly defined character who preserved the New England traditions in their strongest form. Mr. Wheeler spent his declining years in Worcester, Vermont, where he died in the winter of 1869-70.

(VIII) Elisha, son of Howe and Amy (Parkhurst) Wheeler, was born in Calais, Vermont. He was a farmer and at one time resided in Cambridge, Massachusetts. He married Elizabeth Cheney, daughter of Joseph Cheney, of Bradford, New Hampshire, and had a family of nine children, five of whom are now living, namely: Mary L., widow of George G. Fox, of New Boston. Elizabeth, wife of E. I. Barker, of Nashua. Susannah, wife of D. D. Dickey, of Hancock. Nathaniel N., who resides in Nashua. William W., also a resinent of that city.

(IX) William Wallace, son of Elisha and Elizabeth (Cheney) Wheeler, was born in Cambridgeport, Massachusetts, August 4, 1846. His preliminary studies were pursued in the public schools, and he completed his education at the Francistown (New Hampshire) Academy. When eighteen years old he entered the employ of D. A. Gregg, of Wilton, this state, and subsequently going to Nashua he obtained the position of shipping clerk with Messrs. Spaulding and Stearns, flour and grain merchants. In 1884 he joined the Nashua police force, and having proved himself a man of unusual ability and worth as well as a most efficient officer, he was promoted to the rank of captain during the administration of Mayor John Spalding. He was later made deputy marshal and on January 1, 1905, was advanced to the position of marshal, in which capacity he is now serving. As the official head of the police force he has not only realized the expectations of his personal friends and supporters, but is regarded by the citizens in general as an able public officer, possessing a requisite amount of executive ability for any emergency which may arise, and his efforts in preserving the customary peace and good order of the city are heartily approved and appreciated. In politics Marshal Wheeler acts with the Republicans, but is absolutely free from partisan prejudice. He is an Odd Fellow, affiliating with Granite Lodge, No. 1, and in his religious belief is a Baptist, being a member of the Crown Hill Church. For his first wife he married Anna E. Lane, daughter of David C. and Sarah (French) Lane, of Meredith, New Hampshire. His present wife was before marriage Minnie E. Eastman, daughter of John and Margaret (Quinlin) Eastman, of Milford. His children, all by his first union, are: Lillian, wife of George G. Sadd, of Nashua. David S., corresponding clerk for the Boston & Maine Railway Company. Harry A., an operator in the employ of the Consolidated Wireless Telegraph Company at Atlantic City, New Jersey.

(II) John, who may have been a son of George Wheeler, was a native of Concord, Massachusetts, and passed his life in that town, where he was prominent in town affairs and a deacon of the church. He died September 27, 1713. He was married, December 27, 1678, to Sarah Stearns, who was born January 14, 1662, daughter of Isaac and Sarah (Beers) Stearns, of Lexington. Their children were: Joseph, Ebenezer, Thankful, John, Sarah, Abigail, Thomas, Jonathan and Nathan.

(III) John (2), third son and fourth child of John (1) and Sarah (Stearns) Wheeler, was born February 6, 1684, in Concord, and continued to reside in that town as late as 1721; probably passed his entire life there. He was married March 8, 1711, to Dorothy Hosmer, of Concord. Their children, born in Concord, were: John, Dorothy (died young), Josiah and Dorothy.

(IV) Josiah, second son and third child of John (2) and Dorothy (Hosmer) Wheeler, was born March 29, 1718, in Concord, and lived in that town. He was married, February 1, 1741, to Mary Lee, who was born November 9, 1724, in Concord, daughter of Dr. Joseph and Ruth Lee. She died March 11, 1799, having survived her husband, who died about 1790. Their children were: Josiah, Nathan, Mary, Anna, Abigail, Hepzibah, Dorothy and Thomas.

(V) Nathan, second son and child of Josiah and Mary (Lee) Wheeler, was born January 9, 1745, in Concord, Massachusetts, and was an early settler of Temple, New Hampshire, where he was a farmer and died May 7, 1834. He was an active member of the church, and served as tything man in 1785. He married Lydia Adams, who was born August 15, 1757, in New Ipswich, New Hampshire, daughter of Ephraim and Lydia (Kinsman) Adams. She died in October, 1800. Their children were: Nathan, Lydia and Josiah. (Mention of Josiah and descendants forms a part of this article.)

(VI) Nathan (2), eldest child of Nathan (1) and Lydia (Adams) Wheeler, was born in Temple, October 20, 1781, and died October 1, 1881, aged one hundred years, lacking twenty days. He was a merchant in Lyndeborough and Temple, and a leading man in both communities. For many years he was a deacon in the Congregational Church; in 1815 he was Captain Wheeler; in 1836 Nathan Wheeler, Nathaniel Kingsbury and men of that class gave character to the "Temple Lyceum and Forensic Society;" he kept a record of events that was of much assistance to a historian of the town of Temple in compiling its history; and was a public man whose services were required in town affairs of Temple for many years. He served as tything man for years, and was moderator fourteen years, between 1824 and 1849, inclusive; and was selectman in 1844. He married Rachel Cummings, who was born in Temple, in 1784, and died in Temple, September 1, 1841, aged fifty-seven years. The children of this union were: Nathan C., Ephraim A., Luther, George T., Lydia, John, a son died in infancy, and Isaiah, whose sketch follows.

(VII) Isaiah, sixth son and eighth child of Nathan (2) and Rachel (Cummings) Wheeler, was born in Temple, February 7, 1824. After acquiring a practical education in the common schools and at the Academy of New Ipswich, he took charge of his father's farm which he later inherited, and taught school winters and engaged in agriculture the remainder of the year. There he resided until 1885, when he removed to Greenville, where he now resides. In both Temple and Greenville Mr. Wheeler has been a man of influence and has taken a part in public affairs and served in the legislature as a representative of each town. He is a member of the Congregational Church, and has served as deacon. He has a long and honorable record as a citizen, a christian gentleman and a business man. He married, in Temple, February 17, 1848, Elizabeth Fisk Gutterson, who was born in Milford, April 18, 1823, and died in Greenville, May 21, 1873. She was the daughter of Josiah and Phebe (Buss) Gutterson, of Milford. Four children were born of this marriage: Lydia J., died in youth Lizzie A. Walter M., who is a fruit grower, and resides at Grand Junction, Colorado. Charles T., who resides in Greenville. He married, October 16, 1894, Lena Kimball, and they have two children: Doris and Elsie.

(VI) Josiah, third and youngest child of Nathan and Lydia (Adams) Wheeler, was born in Temple, May 11, 1786, and died in Lyndeborough, October 4, 1874. He was a cabinet maker by trade, and settled in Lyndeborough. He was a man who took an interest in public affairs, and was town treasurer He married (first), December 31, 1811, Dolly Shattuck, who was born September 1, 1788, and died August 14, 1845; (second), April 29, 1846, Dorothy (Whiting) Killan, who was born March 14, 1795, and died December 4, 1870. His children, all by the first wife, were: Dolly, who married Henry I. Kimball. Lydia, who married T. D. Rand. Josiah K., the subject of the next paragraph.

(VII) Josiah Kimball, son of Josiah and Dolly (Shattuck) Wheeler, was born in Lyndeborough, July 15, 1822, and educated in the common schools of Lyndeborough and at Francestown Academy. At the age of twenty-one years he went to Lowell, Massachusetts, where he followed the trade of pattern maker, principally in the employ of the Hamilton Corporation, cotton goods manufacturers, and was with them about ten years. When, having saved

J. K. Wheeler

enough from his earnings to buy a farm, he settled in Hudson, where he purchased a farm of one hundred and thirty acres on which he now resides. Although eighty-five years old, Mr. Wheeler is still able to look after his farm. He is a Republican, and represented Lyndeborough in the New Hampshire legislature in the early seventies. He married (first), November, 1849, Abby Anna Marsh, who died June 12, 1865; and (second) Abbie Ann Wilson, December 28, 1865, who was born in New Ipswich, July 28, 1836, daughter of Mathias S. and Laura (Morgan) Wilson, of New Ipswich. They have an adopted daughter, Inez Moffatt, born in Monson, Massachusetts, February 2, 1876, who is a music teacher.

(Second Family.)

WHEELER Among the numerous settlers of this name who located in Concord, Massachusetts, in its primitive period were several bearing the name of Thomas and also a large number of Johns. All of them appeared to be good citizens, so that the descendants of any may feel proud of their progenitors. Captain Thomas Wheeler, of Concord, rendered valuable military service to the colony, but appears to have left no sons who survived the period of youth. The point in England whence these people migrated cannot be obtained, and neither can the identity of the original ancestor be established.

(I) Sergeant Thomas Wheeler, sometimes referred to as Thomas Wheeler, Senior, probably passed his adult life in Concord, Massachusetts. His wife's name was Sarah and their children, born between 1649 and 1673, were: Sarah, Joseph, Mary (died young), Thomas, Ann, Elizabeth, Timothy, Mary, Rebecca and Ruth.

(II) John, second son and third child of Thomas and Sarah Wheeler, was born February 18, 1655, in Concord, and there resided and died September 27, 1713. He was married, December 27, 1678, to Sarah Stearns, who was born January 14, 1662, daughter of Isaac and Sarah (Beers) Stearns, of Lexington. Their children were: Joseph, Ebenezer, Thankful, John, Sarah, Abigail, Thomas, Jonathan and Nathan.

(III) Jonathan, fifth son and eighth child of John and Sarah (Stearns) Wheeler, was born April 19, 1696, in Concord, and lived there until after his children were born. About 1745 he removed to Sutton, Massachusetts, where "After long weakness he died July 10, 1779, aged about 84." His wife's name was Sarah and their children were residents of Sutton, namely: Rebecca, Sarah, Nathaniel, Hannah, Olive, Jane, Milicent, Jonathan and Abel.

(IV) Nathaniel, eldest son and third child of Jonathan and Sarah Wheeler, was born February 5, 1724, in Concord, and removed in youth to Sutton. He lived in that town ten or more years after his marriage, and probably died there in 1756. He was married in Sutton, December 29, 1748, to Hannah Marsh, who was born October 9, 1729, in Sutton, daughter of John and Abigail Marsh, of Bellingham, Massachusetts. Their children were: Sarah, John, Nathaniel and Seth. The widow of Nathaniel (1) Wheeler married, June 26, 1759, Simeon Chamberlain, of Sutton, by whom she had three children: Simeon, John and Abigail. She died January 8, 1791.

(V) Nathaniel (2), second son and third child of Nathaniel (1) and Hannah (Marsh) Wheeler, was born April 10, 1754, in Sutton, Massachusetts, and was twenty-two years of age when with his younger brother he left the family home in Sutton and made his way into the wilderness regions of Sullivan county. Thy settled in Croydon a little more than ten years after the town was chartered and less than ten years after the first settlement under the charter had been made. By reason of his long connection with the church in Croydon Nathaniel was known as Deacon Wheeler. He married, in 1774, Mehitabel Haven, daughter of James Haven, Jr., of Framingham, Massachusetts. She was born October 23, 1756, and died March 1, 1831. They had nine children. He died July 2, 1840, at the age of eighty-seven years. His name is mentioned in the Croydon records as a soldier of the Revolution, and the church records show that he was chiefly instrumental in building the once flourishing church at Northville, in the town of Newport, of which he was a worthy member and deacon for many years. He was decided in his religious views, and of his time and means gave liberally to the support of the church and the work of the gospel. The children were: Hannah, Mehitable, Nathaniel, John, Simeon, Abigail, James, Sarah and Anna.

(V) Deacon Seth, youngest son of Nathaniel Wheeler, of Sutton, and brother of Deacon Nathaniel Wheeler, of Croydon, came with his brother to the town in 1775 and settled on what in later years became known as the M. C. Bartlett farm. He afterward located at Dryden, New York, and died there.

(VI) Colonel Nathaniel (3), son of Deacon Nathaniel (2) and Mehitabel (Haven) Wheeler, was born May 10, 1781, and died July 13, 1864. He married Huldah Whipple, daughter of Aaron Whipple, and granddaughter of Moses Whipple, the latter of whom was born in Grafton, Massachusetts, and came to Croydon in 1766, with his three sons—Thomas, Aaron and Moses, and one daughter, Jerusha. He was one of the first three settlers in Croydon. Huldah (Whipple) Wheeler died in 1833, leaving seven children, and after her death Colonel Wheeler married Lucy F. Freeman, of Lebanon, New Hampshire, whom he survived only a short time. There were no children of his second marriage. Colonel Wheeler's farming operations were extensive and his lands and stock always were well cared for and in good condition. For many years he kept one of the largest and best dairies in the town, which was noted for the number and quality of its dairying interests. He took an active part in military and political affairs, and in the war of 1812 was the first man in the town to volunteer as a private, although at that time he held a commission. In the state militia he was subjected to successive promotion until he had in 1817 obtained the coloneIcy of the Thirty-first New Hampshire Regiment. He was first elected selectman of Croydon in 1815 and served in that office eight years, and in 1816 he represented his town in the general assembly. For more than fifty years he was a Free and Accepted Mason. He had lived at Lebanon, New Hampshire, several years after retiring from active pursuits and died in that town. Colonel Wheeler's seven children were: Griswold W., Anna, William P., Edmund, Morrill, John and Lucy P.

(VII) Griswold Whipple, eldest son of Colonel Nathaniel and Huldah (Whipple) Wheeler, was born in Croydon, New Hampshire, February 22, 1808, and died June 7, 1865. He was educated at Kimball Union Academy, studied medicine with Dr. Willard P. Gibson, of Newport, New Hampshire, and graduated from the medical department of Dartmouth University with the degree of M. D. After spending about one year at Hopkinton, New Hampshire, and a year at Covington, Kentucky, he settled at Perryville, the county seat of Perry county, Missouri, and for the next twenty-five years was the leading man of his profession in all that region. While attending to his professional duties he found time to master the German and French languages, and gave much attention to the natural sciences, especially chemistry, geology and botany, to which he was passionately devoted. His clear and logical mind and love of study and observation, combined with his great industry, gave him a high standing as a professional and scientific man. His attachment to country life was so strong that no inducement could prevail upon him to remove to the city, and he declined a professorship in the St. Louis Medical College. Dr. Wheeler never married. A large share of his time and of his earnings was devoted to deeds of benevolence.

(VII) William Plummer, son of Colonel Nathaniel and Huldah (Whipple) Wheeler, was born in Croydon, New Hampshire, July 31, 1812, and died May 10, 1876. He lived at home on the Wheeler farm in the south part of the town until he was about thirteen years old, and then went to live with his uncle, James Wheeler, in Newport. He remained there until about 1836, and after the death of his uncle was for a time engaged in business as a harness maker. He pursued his studies in the academy at Newport and afterward attended Kimball Union Academy, remaining there about three years, then took up the study of law, first at Keene, New Hampshire, later at Harvard Law School, and still later in Boston, Massachusetts. In 1842 he was admitted to practice in the courts of New Hampshire, and soon afterward opened an office for general practice in Keene. He was a member of the Cheshire county bar until the time of his death. He was solicitor for Cheshire county ten years, and in 1851 was appointed justice of the court of common pleas, which he declined, and afterward was several times offered a seat on the bench of the supreme court, which honor he as often declined, preferring the general practice of the courts. In 1855 and again in 1857 he was a candidate for congress in the third district of New Hampshire. He was a trustee of the State Reform School and also of the State Agricultural College. In the latter institution he took a deep interest, and it was largely through his efforts that that institution was located at Hanover and made a department of Dartmouth University. At the time of his death Mr. Wheeler was president of the Keene Savings Bank, and was prominent among those who organized the Protestant Episcopal Church of Keene. He received the degree of A. M. from Dartmouth in 1842, and the honorary degree of LL. D. from Harvard University in 1850. He married, November 19, 1849, Sarah D. Moulton, of Randolph, Vermont, born March 4, 1825. Their children were Alice and William Wheeler.

(VII) Edmund, third son of Colonel Nathaniel (3) and Huldah (Whipple) Wheeler, was born in Croydon, New Hampshire, August 28, 1814, and died in Newport, New Hampshire, August 21, 1897. His education was acquired at Kimball Union Academy, and in 1833, after leaving school, he went from Croydon to Newport, where he entered the employ of his brother William who was a harness maker and dealer in saddlery. After six years of this association William sold his interest in the business to his brother and turned his attention to the profession of law; and Edmund from 1839 to 1866 carried on the business alone, and in partnership association with Granville Pollard, until 1866, and then retired to devote his attention to literary pursuits. In 1867 he published the "Croydon Centennial," a work of nearly two hundred pages including a short history of the town of Croydon, its settlers and its centennial celebration. In 1878 he issued his "History of Newport," a six hundred page volume in which is reviewed the history of that town from the time of its settlement in 1766 to the year of publication, with an appendix of valuable genealogical records. In 1870 and 1871 Mr. Wheeler was contributor to the *Granite State Journal* and *Aurora of the Valley*, and in 1872 a regular contributor to the columns of the Boston *Advertiser*. In this connection it is interesting to note that in 1878 a large number of citizens of Croydon, his native town, entered Mr. Wheeler's residence in Newport, and with speeches and other ceremonies appropriate to the occasion, presented him with an elegant gold-headed cane as a token of respect and an appreciation of his services as the historian of that town.

For many years Mr. Wheeler was a conspicuous figure in the political history of Sullivan county, and incidentally of the state of New Hampshire. At one time he was an adjutant in the state militia, and for two years a member of the staff of Governor Williams. He took an active interest in the movement to maintain the old state militia system, which was abandoned just before the outbreak of the Civil war. He was a member of the state legislature in 1851 and again in 1852. During the session of the year last mentioned he was chairman of the committee on incorporations and a member of several important special committees, and also took an active part in the discussion of all leading measures before the house. In 1863-64 he was a candidate for the office of county treasurer, and in 1878 a candidate for a seat in the state senate. Locally he was a director of the Sugar River Bank and of the First National Bank of Newport, an earnest friend of education and a firm advocate of the union of the Newport village schools under a single head. He was a member of the board of the Union School District several years after its organization in 1874, and later on was president of the Newport board of education, and for years a member of its school board. The formation of the district suggested by him the new town hall of 1872; he also originated from material removed in erecting "Wheeler's Block" in 1858-59, a betterment of the village sidewalks, and suggested the naming of the village streets in 1875 by a committee of which he was a member, and the improvement made in the original cemetery of the town by James Buell. Many of the leading incidents in the literary, political and social life of Newport, though carried into effect largely by others, found their inception in him. He gave largely to the introduction of the telegraph and railroad to the town, and to industrial and other enterprises intended for its welfare. He was one of the board of trustees of the Newport Savings Bank.

Mr. Wheeler married (first), September 21, 1851, Susan Chittenden Rossiter, of Claremont, New Hampshire, born May 2, 1819, died March 2, 1856, daughter of Sherman and Olive (Baldwin) Rossiter, of Claremont (see Rossiter). Married (second), June 25, 1863, Augusta L. Sawyer (see Sawyer), born August 31, 1839, died March 25, 1886, daughter of Joseph Sawyer, Jr., of Newport, New Hampshire. By his first marriage Mr. Wheeler had one

Wm P. Wheeler.

Edmund Wheeler

son, George Baldwin, born Newport, February 4, 1854, a practical printer and newspaper man, now one of the publishers of the *New Hampshire Argus and Spectator*. By his second marriage Mr. Wheeler had two daughters, Grace, born November 10, 1867, died December 28, 1870, and Anna L., March 8, 1872, died August 5, 1872.

WHEELER is an ancient occupative surname corresponding to wheelwright, and designated the person who made wheels. Its use as a surname probably dates from the fifteenth century, perhaps earlier.

(I) Whitcher Wheeler was born about 1774, probably in Goffstown, where he was a farmer. He married Lydia Cheney, and they had nine children: Joseph, Sallie, Lydia, Dolly, Susan, Jane, Lavinia, Betsey and George W., whose sketch follows.

(II) George Washington Wheeler was born in Goffstown, where he acquired the schooling then and there furnished in the common schools. When a young man he went to Bow where he resided for the remainder of his life, and pursued the vocations of carpenter and farmer. When twenty-eight years old he built the Methodist Church at Bow Bogg, which is still standing. He married Betsey Morgan, a native of Bow, and they had twelve children: John, Daniel, Allen, Jesse, Cyrus C., Eli, Susan M., Rufus H., Oliver, Wesley L., Ann and Asenath. The first four were born in Dunbarton, the next three in Goffstown, and the others in Bow.

(III) Cyrus Colby, fifth son and child of George W. and Betsey (Morgan) Wheeler, was born July 6, 1839, in Dunbarton, and educated in the public schools of Bow. When a young man he joined his brothers, Rufus H. and Oliver, who had preceded him, and engaged in the general merchandise business in Shelly, Michigan. In 1849 he gave up that employment and returned to Bow and bought a farm of seventy acres which he still resides upon, and is engaged in raising various kinds of fruit for market. He is a Republican in politics, and has served three years since 1898 as selectman, one year as chairman. He is a member of the Methodist Episcopal Church. He married Myra Julette, and they have one child, Florence, born February 24, 1874. She married Samuel Sargent and lives in Bow (see Sargent, IX).

(III) Wesley Luther, tenth child and seventh son of George W. and Betsey (Morgan) Wheeler, was born in Bow, December 3, 1849. He attended school in Bow, and at Pembroke Academy. His whole life has been spent in Bow, residing on a farm of three hundred acres near Bow Centre, where he was engaged until 1905, then moving to Bow Mills, where he has since lived, directing the cultivation of his farm from there. Besides attending to his agricultural tasks he has done teaming and at different times has worked about saw mills. Since his removal to Bow Mills his sister Susan M. has resided with him. Mr. Wheeler is a man of sterling character and progressive ideas, a good farmer and reputable citizen. He is a member of Bow Grange, No. 189, and of the Methodist Episcopal Church.

WHEELER This family name is not among those of the grantees of New Ipswich, 1749, nor on the ministers' rate for the year 1763, yet in 1774 the list of taxpayers shows the names of John Wheeler, Jonas Wheeler, Jonas Wheeler, Jr., and Seth Wheeler.

(I) Samuel Wheeler was a private on the pay roll of Captain Stephen Parker's company, in Colonel Moses Nichol's regiment, and General Stark's brigade of New Hampshire militia, which company marched from New Ipswich (and joined the Continental army under General Gates at Stillwater) July 19, 1777. This company was actively engaged throughout the day at the battle of Bennington, August 17, of the same year.

(II) George W., son of Samuel Wheeler, was born in New Ipswich, April 8, 1812, and died January 30, 1891, aged seventy-nine years. He was a farmer, and devoted considerable attention to dairying, supplying a milk route for fifty years. He was also engaged in the manufacture of potash. He married, December 4, 1834, Elvira Blanchard, who was born in New Ipswich, July 21, 1814, and died there January 3, 1876, aged sixty-two years, daughter of Levi and Hannah (Blanchard) Blanchard. Two children were born of this union: Clara E., who married George T. Raymond, now a resident of Florida; and George S., whose sketch follows.

(III) George Samuel, only son of George W. and Elvira (Blanchard) Wheeler, was born in New Ipswich, April 30, 1840. His education was obtained in the common schools of the locality and New Ipswich Appleton Academy. On the death of his father he became the possessor of the old homestead where he makes a specialty of raising poultry and bees, and is also engaged in the milk business. He has made farming profitable, and in addition to his New Hampshire farm has an orange grove in southern Florida where he spends his winters.

WHEELER Several families of this name settled in New Ipswich, some before the Revolution, and others at later periods. Those who first made their homes here were probably of the same family stock.

(I) Richard (2), son of Richard (1) Wheeler, was born about 1792 in New Ipswich, and died 1882, aged ninety years. He was a thrifty tiller of the soil, a member of the Congregational Church, and a man of influence in his neighborhood. He married Rebecca Wilson, died 1882, daughter of Supply and Susannah (Cutter) Wilson, of New Ipswich. Her father was born in Woburn, Massachusetts, in 1750, and in 1769 settled in New Ipswich, where in 1777 he married the widow of John Cutter. Seven children were born of this union; sons were: Joseph A., Augustus C., Charles and George H.

(II) Charles, son of Richard (2) and Rebecca (Wilson) Wheeler, was born in New Ipswich, October 27, 1832. He grew up on his father's farm, and resided there until he was twenty-five years of age. He then commenced to operate a saw and grist mill on the branch of the Souhegan river, which he has ever since continuously carried on. Since 18— his two sons, Charles and Edward, have been associated with him in the business. He also cultivates a farm. Mr. Wheeler is a man of pleasant address, has always been highly respected in the community in which he has spent his entire life, and has been honored with various official positions. For twenty-four years he has been a member of the Congregational Church, and ten years of that time he has been one of its deacons. He was first elected selectman in 1866 and between that time and the present (1907) has filled that office seventeen years. He was elected to the legislature in 1881 and in 1901.

He married, August 20, 1862, Nellie E. Shepperd, who was born in Worcester, Massachusetts, daughter of Hiram, Jr., and Elizabeth Shepherd. Two children were born of this union: Charles S. and Edward R.

GOVE The Gove family was very early in New Hampshire, being located at Hampton, and was subsequently numerously represented in the town of Weare. It was first planted in Massachusetts, and has supplied many useful citizens of this and other states, the descendants of those residing in New Hampshire being widely scattered throughout the country by this time. Its associations are honorable and its record worthy of emulation. It is an ancient name, being found in the state papers in London as early as 1541, and is common in some parts of England at the present time.

(I) The American founder of the family, John Gove, was born, 1601, in England, and was an early resident of Charlestown, Massachusetts, arriving there some time before April 28, 1646. His wife Sarah was also born in 1601, and accompanied him. He was a dealer and worker in brass, as appears by his will and schedule of personal property. He must have died in middle life, as his wife subsequently married John Mansfield and removed to Lynn, Massachusetts, where he died. She died in Hampton, New Hampshire, March 4, 1681, aged eighty years. Her children were: John, Edward and Mary.

(II) Edward, second son of John and Mary Gove, was born in England in 1630, and came with his parents to Massachusetts. He resided in Salisbury, Massachusetts, as early as 1657, and purchased a right of commonage there. He sold his land and settled in Hampton, New Hampshire, in 1665, and was a prominent citizen of that town. In 1683 he was a member of the assembly which was dissolved by Governor Cramfield. The dissolution of the assembly created much resentment among the the people of New Hampshire, and Gove headed a movement to overthrow the government. This he surrendered without bloodshed, and with ten others, including his son John, was tried for treason and convicted. He received a sentence of death, and his estate was seized as forfeit to the crown, the others being pardoned. Gove was sent to England, and was kept a prisoner for three years in the Tower of London, after which he was pardoned and his estate restored to him in 1686. He was the progenitor of a numerous family. He was married, about 1660, to Hannah, daughter of William and Johanna (Bartlett) Titcomb, of Newbury, Massachusetts, formerly of North Banks England. He resided in Salisbury, Massachusetts, as early as 1657, when he bought a right of commonage there. He sold land there in 1665, and moved to Hampton, New Hampshire. In March, 1665, while still living in Salisbury, he bought of Eliakim Wardwell a dwelling house and about thirty acres of land in Hampton, "with one share in the Cowe Comons," also a grant of fourscore acres of land at the New Plantation, with the privileges thereto belonging. He died, May 21, 1691. His children were: John, William, Hannah, Mary, Abial, Penuel, Abigail, Ebenezer, Edward, Jeremiah, Rachel, Ann and Sarah. (Ebenezer and descendants receive extended mention in this article).

(III) John (2), eldest child of Edward and Hannah (Titcomb) Gove, was born September 19, 1661, in Salisbury, Massachusetts, and died in Hampton about 1737. He was a joiner by trade, and was among the petitioners for a church and school to be established at Hampton Falls, soon after the settlement of that parish. He was among those convicted of treason on account of the Gove Rebellion, and subsequently pardoned and restored to citizenship, in April, 1686. He settled in Seabrook. The Christian name of his wife was Sarah, and their children were: Mary, John, Hannah, Jonathan and Sarah.

(IV) John (3), eldest son of John (2) and Sarah Gove, was born May 29, 1689, in Hampton Falls, and died March 23, 1759. He was married, March 24, 1720, to Ruth, second daughter of Edmund and Abigail (Green) Johnson. She was born February 24, 1695, and died in 1737, in Hampton Falls. Their children were: Edward, Daniel, Obadiah, Ruth, Jonathan, David and Patience. Edward and Daniel settled in Seabrook. Obadiah in Kingston, and Jonathan and David are supposed to have settled in Enfield, New Hampshire. (Obadiah and David and descendants receive notice in this article).

(V) Daniel, second son and child of John (3) and Ruth (Johnson) Gove, was born May 8, 1722, in Hampton, and lived in that part of the town now Seabrook. He died there August 23, 1761, aged thirty-nine years. He married Rebecca Hunt, and their children were: Stephen, Daniel, Johnson (died young), David, Johnson and Edmond.

(VI) Daniel (2), second son and child of Daniel (1) and Rebecca (Hunt) Gove, was born March 3, 1749, in Hampton. He came to Weare in 1773 and began to clear lands for the preparation of a farm. He spent two summers here, and in the spring of the third year removed to Weare, where he lived the remainder of his life. He died in 1786. His house was built on the hill east of the Friends meeting house, on lot 32. He married Miriam Cartland. Their children were: Moses, Levi, Lydia, Eunice, Daniel Peletiah, Joseph, Enoch and Miriam.

(VII) Daniel (3), third son and fifth child of Daniel (2) and Miriam (Cartland) Gove, was born April 12 1783, in Weare, and passed his life in that town. He lived for some time at Clinton Grove, and afterwards on lot 72 in range 2. He was a tanner and shoemaker by occupation. He died April 25, 1869. He married Elizabeth Paige, daughter of Eliphalet and Rachel (Chase) Paige of Weare. She was born in 1788, and died 1874. Their children were: Eliza, Paige E., Richard and Alvah.

(VIII) Paige Enoch, eldest son and second child of Daniel (3) and Elizabeth (Paige) Gove, was born February 22, 1818, in Weare, where he passed his life. He was an attendant at the common schools of his town, afterwards attended the Friends' School at Providence, Rhode Island, from which he was graduated and he early began the trade of shoemaker from his father. For some years he worked at this in Weare, then went to Lynn, Massachusetts, where he was employed in a shoe-shop, continuing for several years. He returned to Weare and engaged in farming, and also continued work at his trade for intervals, and so continued until his death, which occurred August 24, 1893, in Manchester. He was an earnest Republican, and held several minor town offices. He married (first) Clarissa Twiss, (second), Mary P. Peaslee, and (third), Harriet Moody. His first wife was the mother of two daughters: Angeline E., who became the wife of Augustus W. Collins, of Weare, and Abbie E., who died young. The children of the second wife were: Edwin, (died young), Clara V., became the wife of Charles Pike, of Lowell, Massachusetts; died November 21,

1903; one son who died at the age of twenty years. Daniel N., who receives further mention below. Almena M., married Elbridge Peaslee, of Weare. Freeman P., who resided in Manchester till time of his death, March, 1907.

(IX) Daniel Norris, second son and fourth child of Paige E. Gove, and third child of Mary (Peaslee) Gove, was born August 6, 1854, in Weare, and passed his early years in that town. He attended the district school adjacent to his home and Clinton Grove Academy. On leaving school he worked one year in a wood turning shop in Gardner, Maine, and subsequently removed to Lowell, Massachusetts, where he was employed for one year as a clerk in a dry goods store. He removed thence to Manchester, New Hampshire, where he entered the employ of Holton & Sprague, afterward Charles F. Sprague, dry goods dealers, and continued several years with them. Finding the confinement of the business detrimental to his health, he left the store and established a livery boarding stable, which he has ever since conducted with success. Like his ancestors he is an earnest supporter of the Republican principles. He is a member of the Queen City Lodge, Knights of Pythias, of Manchester, of the Royal Arcanum, Ancient Order United Workmen, Workmen's Benefit Association, and the New England Order of Pilgrims. He is also a member of the First Congregational Church at Manchester. He was married, January 2, 1878, to Susan M. Downing, who was born March 29, 1855, in Weare, daughter of Oscar and Susan (Cochran) Downing, of that town. She died December 23, 1904, leaving a daughter, Clara May Gove, who was born December 10, 1878, in Weare, and resides with her father. She was graduated from Manchester high school, class '98. For the past four years she has been directress of sewing in the public schools of Worcester, Massachusetts, with three assistants. When not engaged in teaching she resides with her father in Manchester. She is also a member of the First Congregational Church of Manchester.

(V) Obadiah, third son of John and Ruth (Johnson) Gove, married Mary Dow and had children.

(VI) Elijah, son of Obadiah and Mary (Dow) Gove, married Swan Jewell and had children.

(VII) Daniel, son of Elijah and Swan (Jewell) Gove, married Anna Davis and had children.

(VIII) Levi, son of Daniel and Anna (Davis) Gove, married Mary Rand. Levi was born in the town of Gilford, New Hampshire, August 15, 1824, received his education in the town schools and afterward made farming his life occupation. In politics he was a Democrat. He married Mary Rand, September 2, 1855. They had children.

(IX) Ansel Fred, son of Levi and Mary (Rand) Gove, was born in the town of Gilford, January 21, 1866, and was educated in the public schools and New Hampton Business College, graduating from the latter institution. In business life he has followed the example of his ancestors and is a farmer, cattle raiser and lumber dealer, and his efforts have been rewarded with gratifying success. He is past master of Mt. Belknap Grange, No. 52, Patrons of Husbandry, and a member of Chocoma Lodge, No. 5, Independent Order of Odd Fellows, Lakeport, and has served continuously as selectman of Gilford since 1902, being now chairman of the board. On October 31, 1893, he married Julia A. Weeks, a popular teacher, daughter of William H. and Mary I. (Potter) Weeks, who came of an

old Gilford family and one of the respected families of New England.

(IX) Charles H., son of Levi and Mary (Rand) Gove, was born in Gilford, New Hampshire, May 14, 1859, and was educated in the common schools of that town. After leaving school and in the year 1887 he started a general blacksmithing and repair shop in Gilford, and in connection therewith has built up a successful business in the manufacture of wagons, carts, sleighs, etc. He married, February 2, 1884, Ora A. Sawyer, daughter of Levi D. and Mary A. (Dane) Sawyer. Mr. and Mrs. Gove have one child, Willis A. Gove, born May 22, 1888.

(V) David, son of John (2) and Ruth (Johnson) Gove, was born May 10, 1731, in Hampton Falls, in which town he resided for a time. He removed to Seabrook, and from there in the spring of 1781 to Weare, New Hampshire, where he died February 4, 1799. He was married, December 21, 1757, to Martha, daughter of Nathan Hoag, of Newton, Massachusetts. His widow survived him nearly thirty years, dying January 4, 1829, aged ninety-one years. Their children were Hannah, Abigail and Josiah. The first married David Green and the second Elisha Green, and all resided in Weare.

(VI) Josiah, only son of David and Martha (Hoag) Gove, was born June 27, 1773, in Seabrook, New Hampshire, and removed with his parents before he was eight years old to Weare, where he grew up. He settled on the west side of lot 30 in the Middle Range, on part of his father's homestead, which has continued in the family almost uninterruptedly to the present day, and is now owned by a prominent attorney of the name residing in Boston. He was married, December 5, 1799, to Rebecca, daughter of Ebenezer and Mary (Green) Breed, of Lynn, Massachusetts, and Kensington, New Hampshire, respectively. She was born November 20, 1777, in Weare, and died August 19, 1866, in her eighty-ninth year. Mr. Gove died May 18, 1850. Their children were: Albert, Ira, Otis, William and George. The first resided in Lynn, Massachusetts, and died there. The second is the subject of the succeeding paragraph. The third died at the age of thirty years, in Weare. William was employed about thirty years in the pension office at Washington, District of Columbia, where he died. George died at the age of thirty years.

(VII) Ira, second son of Josiah and Rebecca (Breed) Gove, was born July 4, 1805, in Weare, where he grew up. Early in life he went to Lynn, Massachusetts, where he engaged in the manufacture of shoes and became proprietor of a custom shop, which he operated at that time about one year. He then became foreman of the factory of Samuel Boyes at that place, and continued in this capacity three years. Subsequently he engaged in manufacturing on his own account, but on account of the financial panic of 1837 he was obliged to suspend operations in 1839, and in 1840 he went to Painesville, Ohio, where he built a steam flouring mill and continued its operation four years. His health becoming impaired on account of the climate of that new region, he returned to Lynn in 1844, and in 1846 removed to Weare, where he settled on the homestead farm. Here he again engaged in the manufacture of shoes, and also continued farming for some time. Thence he again went to Lynn, and engaged in the manufacture of shoes with good success, but in a short time his health began to fail and he was compelled to return to the home farm in Weare. Here he became associated with his son in the manufacture of shoes, which he continued until 1870, and then retired on account of his advanced age. His last years were spent with his daughter in Claremont, New Hampshire, where he died December 23, 1891. He became affiliated with the Masonic order in Lynn, and was a member of the fire department of that city while residing there. In religious faith he was a Universalist. He was among the founders of the Republican party, casting his vote in support of his convictions, and serving two terms in the state legislature, as representative of the town of Weare. He was married, November 29, 1831, to Harriet Phillips, who was born April 12. 1815, in Lynn, Massachusetts, daughter of William and Betsey (Granger) Phillips of that city. She died November 17, 1878. Brief mention of their children follows: Harriet Ella married Eben M. Colby, resided in Chicago, and died in Weare, January 1, 1872; their daughter Helen is the wife of Robert McKean, of Manchester. George Ira resided on the home farm, was associated with his father in the manufacture of shoes, and now resides at Grasmere. Maria Augusta is the widow of Sewall L. Fogg, residing in Manchester (see Fogg, VI). Helen Elizabeth, born in Painesville, Ohio, is the wife of Rowland R. Kelley and resides in Williamstown, Massachusetts. Rebecca Breed, also born in Painesville, married Josiah Gove, resided at Claremont, and died there, February 2, 1904.

(III) Ebenezer, fourth son and eighth child of Edward and Hannah (Titcomb) Gove, was born June 23, 1671, in Hampton, and lived in the south part of the town, now Hampton Falls. He was married, December 20, 1692, to Judith Sanborn, who was born August 8, 1675, in Hampton, daughter of John and Judith (Coffin) Sanborn. Their children were: Jeremiah, Edward, Sarah, Judith, Ebenezer, Lydia, Enoch, Nathan, Mary and Rachel.

(IV) Edward (2), second son and child of Ebenezer and Judith (Sanborn) Gove, was born May 29, 1696, in Hampton, and resided in that part of ancient Hampton which is now Seabrook. He first married Bethiah Clark, who was born 1697, and died April 19, 1727. He was married (second), January 16, 1728, to Mary Moulton, who was born December 16, 1706, daughter of Daniel and Mary Moulton. She died October 20, 1793. Edward Gove's children were: Elizabeth, Nathaniel, Ebenezer, Judith, Hannah, Winthrop, Mary and Abigail.

(V) Nathaniel, eldest son and second child of Edward (2) and Bethiah (Clark) Gove, was born June 20, 1721, in what is now Seabrook. He removed to Kingston, where he was a prominent man, active in town affairs and served as selectman. He was married, September 14, 1743, to Susannah Stickney, who was born April 10, 1724, daughter of Moses and Sarah (Wardwell) Stickney, of Newbury, Massachusetts. They had twelve children, among whom were: Nathaniel, who moved to Deering and later to Vermont, Abraham, Edward and Michael.

(VI) Abraham, son of Nathaniel and Susannah (Stickney) Gove, settled in Deering, New Hampshire, where he signed the association test in 1776. He was the owner of considerable land and was frequently employed in town affairs. He was married, October 2, 1772, by Rev. Samuel Perley, of Seabrook, to Mary Nudd. They were the parents of the following children: Sarah, Nanna, Jonathan, Abraham, Samuel, Mary, Betty, Polly, Lydia, Ebenezer, Benjamin and Jemima.

(VII) Abraham (2), second son and fourth child of Abraham (1) and Mary (Nudd) Gove, was born 1780, in Deering, and settled early in life in Henniker, New Hampshire, upon the farm well known by his name in the easterly part of the town. He was a worthy citizen and an excellent farmer. He married Nancy Jones, and they had eleven children: Jeremiah, Louisa, Sophia, Mark, Alfred, Wyer, Lydia, Mary, Jeannette, Harriet and Charlotte. Abraham Gove died May 26.

(VIII) Jeremiah, eldest of the eleven children of Abraham (2) and Nancy (Jones) Gove, was born in Henniker, New Hampshire, November 22, 1804. He was educated in the common schools there, and was a general farmer in Henniker, Hopkinton and Warner. In politics he was a Democrat. He married Clara Rowell. They had three children: Mary Etta, who died young. Newton, who is a farmer in Contoocook, and Charles. The family attend the Methodist Church.

(IX) Charles, youngest of the three children of Jeremiah and Clara (Rowell) Gove, was born in Warner, New Hampshire, February 12, 1842. He was educated in the common schools. He has a farm of eighty acres, finely located, and carries on a dairy business. In politics he is a Democrat. He is an Odd Fellow, belonging to Central Lodge, No. 87, and has been through all the chairs. He has also served on the school committee. He has been twice married. His first wife was Annie T. Shepherd, and they have one child, Frank B. Gove, born December 28, 1870. Charles Gove married (second), Annie Maria Olsson, daughter of Captain Olaf and Mattie (Anderson) Olsson, who was born in Gutenberg, Sweden, July 4, 1848. They were married December 5, 1875. Mr. and Mrs. Gove are Christian Scientists.

GILMAN

The earliest discovered records of anything like the name Gilman are connected with Wales. Cilmin Troed-dhu (i. e. Kilmin with the black foot) of Glynllison in Uwch Gwir Vai, in Caer-yn-Arvonshire, lived in the year 843, in the time of Roderick the Great, with whom he came out of the north of Britain. He bore argent, a man's leg couped, sable. The Glyns of Glynllison are descended from Cilmin, whose name is also spelled Kilmin. This Cilmin was head of one of the fifteen noble tribes of North Wales, and there appears to be good reason to believe that he was one of the ancestors of the Gilmins of England, Ireland, and America. The American branch of the family, the largest of all, are the descendants of Edward Gilman, of Hingham, England. In the sixteenth century and previously the name was variously spelled: Gilmyn, Gilmin, Gylmyn, Gylmin, Gyllmyn, and sometimes Guylmyn.

Religious persecution, the cause which expelled the first emigrants from Old England, sent Edward Gilman and his family to Massachusetts; and from this one family has sprung a multitudinous progeny.

The family of Gilman is not one furnishing a few brilliant exceptions to a long list of common place names. Its members appear generally to have been remarkable for the quiet home virtues, and rather to have desired to be good citizens than men of great name. To an eminent degree they appear to have obtained the esteem and respect of those nearer to them for sound judgment and sterling traits of character. Thus in the towns in which they have dwelt their reputation is high. Other names were more prominent in New Hampshire for a time; some men performed more conspicuous services, or underwent more extraordinary trials; "but the sturdy phalanx of Gilmans did more," says their genealogist, "to keep up the steady course of the colony, the province, and the state (in America) certainly till 1815, than any two or three other families together."

(I) From the parish register of Caston it is found that Edward Gilman married, June 12, 1550, Rose Rysse, who survived her husband and proved his will, which was dated February 5, 1573, on July 7, in the same year. By his will he devised his houses and lands in Caston to his eldest son, John, and his other estates, lands, at Saham Toney being mentioned, were divided between his other three sons and his five daughters. The widow married (second), at Caston, April 3, 1578, John Snell, and was buried at Caston, October 3, 1613. As the parish registers of Caston commence in 1539, the date and place of birth of Edward Gilman are not known. The children of Edward Gilman and Rose Rysse, his wife, were: John, Edward, Robert, Lawrence, Margaret, Katherine, Rose, Jane and Elizabeth. (Mention of Robert and descendants forms part of this article.)

(II) Edward (2), second son of Edward (1) and Rose (Rysse) Gilman, was born in Caston. Rev. Robert Peck, of Hingham, England, led a party of one hundred and thirty-three men, women and children from England to America. They embarked in the ship "Diligent" of Ipswich, Captain John Martin, which left Gravesend, April 26, and arrived at Boston, Massachusetts, August 10, 1638. Among those who composed the Pilgrim band were Edward Gilman, with his wife, three sons, and two daughters, and three servants. He settled in Hingham, where he was admitted freeman December 13, 1638. In 1641 a tract of land eight miles square then called Seekonk, now Rehoboth, was granted to Edward Gilman and others by the Plymouth Colony. In 1643 his estate was three hundred pounds. His name does not appear on the records of that town after 1646. In 1647 his name appears in Ipswich, and September 18, 1648, Edward Gilman, Jr., sold to his father, Edward Gilman, the farm given him by his father-in-law, Richard Smith. Edward Gilman and his sons removed to Exeter, New Hampshire, and there Edward died June 22, 1681. He married in Hingham, England, June 3, 1614, Mary Clark. Their children were: Mary, Edward, Sarah, Lydia, John and Moses; and from these sons the Gilmans of New Hampshire have descended.

(III) Edward (3), eldest son and second child of Edward (2) and Mary (Clark) Gilman, was baptized at Hingham, England, December 26, 1617. He came to America with his parents, and in 1647 removed to Exeter, New Hampshire, probably from Ipswich, and finding suitable sites for saw mills and plenty of timber, he entered into an agreement with the town, November 4, whereby he was accepted as a townsman and given privileges to enable him to build mills. In accordance with this agreement he erected mills upon a spot which has ever since been improved as a mill privilege. His father-in-law, it appears, has presented him with a place at Ipswich, which he sold to his father in 1648. He is described as active, enterprising and judicious, and immediately became a popular and leading man of Exeter. In 1648 he was on the committee to treat with a Mr. Thomson "to come to Exeter to be our minister," and if he would not come to engage some other, with the advice of the elders of Boston, Charlestown, and Roxbury. In 1650 he was one of the committee who signed the agreement with Mr. Samuel Dudley "to inhabit Exeter and be a minister of God's word unto us until such time as God shall be pleased to make way for the gathering of a church, and then he shall be ordained the pastor or teacher, according to the ordinance of God." In 1641 he was one of a committee "to make an agreement with Hampton and Dover about the bounds or to petition the general court if they can't agree." Grants of land were repeatedly made to him by the town, the last of which was May 10, 1652, and upon the same day his father and brother Moses were, "upon their request," accepted as townsmen. His brother John was connected in business with him at one time. In 1653 Edward went to England for mill gearing, and never returned, having been lost at sea. His widow administered on his estate in 1655. He married, after he came to America, a daughter of Richard Smith, of Ipswich, formerly of Shropham, Norfolk, England, and they had five children: Edward, Joshua, Charles, John and Daniel.

(IV) Edward (4), eldest child of Edward (3) and ——— (Smith) Gilman, was born 1648, died 1692. He married, December 20, 1674, Abigail (probably daughter of Antipas) Maverick. Their children were: Edward, Antipas, Maverick, Abigail, Catherine and Elizabeth.

(V) Edward (5), eldest child of Edward (4) and Abigail (Maverick) Gilman, was born October 20, 1675. He married Abigail Folsom (see Folsom, VII), and had children: Edward, Antipas, Jonathan, Maverick and Mary.

(VI) Antipas, second son and child of Edward (5) and Abigail (Folsom) Gilman, born 1705, lived in Brentwood, and subsequently removed to Gilmanton, where he died January, 1793, aged eighty-eight. He married Lydia Thing, and they had eight children: Abigail, Antipas, Samuel, Edward, Jonathan, Deborah, Benjamin and Nathaniel.

(VII) Samuel, second son and third child of Antipas and Lydia (Thing) Gilman, was born March 8, 1732, and resided in Gilmanton. He died of camp fever, May 7, 1776. The first town meeting was held in his house, July 31, 1766. He married Hannah Tilton, born July 9, 1730, and they had twelve children: Samuel, John, Betsey, Peter, Hannah, Levi, Lydia, Nathaniel, Anna, David, Dolly and Hetty.

(VIII) Levi, fourth son and sixth child of Samuel and Hannah (Tilton) Gilman, was born in Gilmanton, and with his elder brother Samuel settled, about 1790, on the south side of Gunstock, or Meeting-house Hill, in Gilmanton, now Gilford, where he engaged in farming. Levi Gilman had children: William, Levi, Samuel, Benjamin, Dorothy, Polly, Hope, and probably others.

(IX) Samuel, third son and child of Levi Gilman, was born on his father's farm in Gilford, where he lived the life of a well-to-do farmer. He married a Miss Beedie, and their children were: Lyman W., Eliza, Lydia, Morrill, Anna and Albert C.

(X) Lyman Walker, eldest child of Samuel and ——— (Beedie) Gilman, was born in Gilford, October 4, 1821, and died in Laconia, February, 1890, aged sixty-eight. He grew up on a farm and had the usual common school education. He learned the carpenter's trade and was employed for a time in Boston, then returned to New Hampshire and went into the employ of the Randlett Manufacturing Company, now the Laconia Car Company, where he worked at carpentry. Here he kept pace with the business, was overseer of one shop and later of two. The amount of labor necessary to the discharge of his duties overtaxed his strength and he resigned, and the work was afterwards performed by two overseers. After leaving the Randlett Company he engaged in the business of carriage building on his own account, for a time, but later returned to the employ of the car company, where he was employed the remainder of his active life. He was first a Whig in politics, then during the continuance of the Know Nothing party he was a member of that organization, and on the rise of the Republican party he became a member of that. He was an early member of Winnipiseogee Lodge, No. 7, of which he was later noble grand. He was an upright citizen and a useful member of the community. He married, August 17, 1843, Dorothy Emeline Morrison, born December 12, 1819, died September 13, 1903, daughter of Benjamin and Dorothy (Gilman) Morrison, of Gilford, and they were the parents of six children: Josephine E., Augusta F., Edward F., Frank L., died in infancy; Luella L., and Frank L., next mentioned.

(XI) Frank L., youngest child of Lyman W. and Dorothy E. (Morrison) Gilman, was born in Gilford, now Laconia, September 29, 1858. He obtained his education in the common schools, and then entered the Laconia passenger depot, where he learned telegraphy, and became telegraph operator and ticket agent, holding these positions from 1876 to 1880. In the summer of 1881 he went to Old Orchard Beach, where he was telegraph operator until October, and then went to Boston, where he was employed in the Western Union Telegraph Company's office on State street, until July, 1882. Resigning that place at that date he returned to Laconia and became assistant postmaster under Perley Putnam, holding that position during Mr. Putnam's term, and the first six months of the term of Mr. Putnam's successor, Nathaniel Edgerly. In October, 1887, Mr. Gilman resigned and for the next year or two was collector for the *Laconia Democrat*, clerk for George R. Leavitt in the wood and coal business, and agent for the Singer Manufacturing Company. In the fall of 1888 he was elected register of probate for Belknap county, took charge of the office in July, 1889, and served till the end of his term in 1891. In the latter year he was made assistant postmaster, and filled that place until October, 1895. He was elected tax collector of the city of Laconia in 1895, and again in 1896, and performed the functions of that office, acting at the same time as agent for the New York Life Insurance Company. July 2, 1897, he was appointed by President McKinley postmaster of Laconia. In 1902 was re-appointed by President Roosevelt, and in 1906 was re-appointed again, and is now continuing on his third term. Mr. Gilman is a very methodical man, thoroughly competent, honorable, honest, and prompt in the discharge of his duties. He has never failed to give satisfaction to all reasonable people in the offices he has filled. His general success and popularity might be attributed to the characteristics enumerated, but there is another which has contributed more than any of these to his success. He is even tempered and suave—always a gentleman.

He is a member of Mount Lebanon Lodge, No. 32, and Union Royal Arch Chapter, No. 7, Ancient Free and Accepted Masons; of Winnipiseogee Lodge, No. 7, Independent Order of Odd Fellows; Laconia Encampment, No. 9, of which he is a past chief patriarch, and of Canton Osgood, No. 5, of which he is a past captain. He is a member of Belknap County Fish and Game League, and has served as president and member of the board of managers of the First Free Baptist Church Society of Laconia.

Frank L. Gilman married (first), in Manchester, New Hampshire, December 31, 1881, Ruth W. Barber, of Lewiston, Maine, born in Sherbrooke, Province of Quebec, in 1858, daughter of Horace and Julia Barber. She died April 6, 1883, leaving one son R. Frank Gilman, born March 19, 1883, now (1906) a clerk in the Laconia postoffice. Mr. Gilman married (second) Emma J. Jones, born August 22, 1863, daughter of Chadwick B. Jones, of Epsom. She died February 8, 1901.

(II) Robert, third son of Edward and Rose (Rysse) Gilman, was baptized in Caston, July 10, 1559, and was buried there March 6, 1631. The Christian name of his wife was Mary and his children were: Robert, Edward, Lawrence and John.

(III) Edward, second son of Robert and Mary Gilman, was married in Old Hingham to Mary Clark. With his wife, five children and three servants he sailed from Gravesend, April 26, 1638, in the ship "Diligent," John Martin, master, which arrived at Boston, August 10, following, and the family settled in Hingham, Massachusetts. Other children were born after their arrival, making ten in all. Those who lived to maturity were: Edward, John, Moses, Mary, Sarah and Lydia.

(IV) Moses, third son of Edward and Mary (Clark) Gilman, was baptized at Hingham, England, March 11, 1630. He was in Exeter, New Hampshire, with his father as early as May 10, 1652, and land was granted him in that part of the town which was afterward incorporated as New Market. He figured prominently in public affairs, frequently serving as a selectman, and in 1697 was succeeded in that office by his son, Moses, Jr. His death occurred prior to August 6, 1702, on which date his will was probated, and his descendants are known as the New Market branch of the family, some of whom settled in Sanbornton. He married, in Hingham, Massachusetts, Elizabeth Hersie, daughter of William Hersie, Sr., of that town, and his children were: Jeremiah, Elizabeth, James, John, David, Joshua, Caleb, Moses, Mary and Judith. From the establishment of New Hampshire as a royal province to the present day this family has been identified with civic affairs. John Gilman was one of the original councillors in President Cutt's commission. Colonel Peter Gilman was one of the royal councillors in 1772, while Nicholas Gilman was a councillor in 1777, and again in 1788 under the state government. Hon. John Taylor Gilman was chosen chief magistrate of New Hampshire eleven times in succession, and served as governor in all fourteen years. The latter's brother Nicholas served in both the national house of representatives and the senate. Rev. Nicholas and Rev. Tristram Gilman were graduated from Harvard in 1724 and 1757 respectively.

(V) Captain Jeremiah, eldest child of Moses and Elizabeth (Hersie) Gilman, was born August 31, 1660. He married Mary Wiggin, daughter of Andrew, and granddaughter of Governor Thomas Wiggin. Her mother was Hannah, daughter of Governor Simon Bradstreet, and great-granddaughter of Governor Thomas Dudley. Mrs. Gilman was admitted a member of the church at Hampton, April 4, 1697, as there was no minister at Exeter. Their children were: Jeremiah, Andrew, Simon,

Frank L. Gilman

Israel, Thomas, Benjamin, Ezekiel, Hannah and Joseph. (Benjamin and descendants are noticed in this article.)

(VI) Andrew, second son and child of Captain Jeremiah and Mary (Wiggin) Gilman, was born in 1690, in that part of Exeter now called Newmarket. When nineteen years old, May 8, 1709, Andrew Gilman, his elder brother Jeremiah, William Moody and Samuel Stevens were captured by the Indians at Pickpocket Mill in Exeter, and taken to the shores of Lake Winnepiseogee. Moody, one of the men, escaped, was recaptured, roasted to death, and eaten by the cannibals. The brothers were separated. Andrew was told that Jeremiah had been killed and eaten, and as he never returned to Exeter the story was for a while believed. It is now asserted that after a tedious captivity he escaped to the Connecticut river, and settled near its mouth. Andrew, after remaining some time in captivity, returned to his friends and lived in Brentwood. After his son Winthrop settled in Gilmanton he made him a visit, and went to the lake to see the place where the Indians had camped. Everything, even these, looked familiar to the liberated captive. He died some twenty years after the death of his second wife. His property seemed to have been considerable, being inventoried at six thousand nine hundred and eighty-five pounds and sixteen shillings. He married (first), January 27, 1715, Joanna Thing, of Exeter, and (second) Bridget Hilton, daughter of Colonel Winthrop Hilton of New Market. She died November 10, 1736. The children of the first wife were: Abigail, Jeremiah, Joanna, Deborah and Mary. By the second wife: Winthrop, Elizabeth, Anna and Andrew.

(VII) Captain Jeremiah (2), eldest child and second son of Andrew and Joanna (Thing) Gilman, was born in Brentwood, June 3, 1719, and died May 1, 1791. He was an officer in the colonial wars prior to the Revolution, and during that war captain of a militia company in Colonel Stickney's regiment, of General Stark's brigade, and with his company took part in the battle of Bennington. At this time he was fifty-eight years old. After two hours desperate fighting the British intrenchments were carried, and Captain Gilman was said by his soldiers to have been one of the foremost over the breastworks, where after a fierce hand to hand conflict the struggle was terminated by the rout of the enemy. As early perhaps as 1776 he removed with his family to Wakefield, and built his house just opposite "the Old Maids' Tavern," and resided there until his death. He married Sarah Kimball, daughter of Caleb and Sarah Kimball. Their children were: Andrew, Mehitable, Joanna, Bridget, Sarah, Jeremiah, Lydia, Anne and Abigail.

(VIII) Bridget, daughter of Captain Jeremiah and Sarah (Kimball) Gilman, was born November 4, 1748, and married, August 26, 1773, Samuel Hall (see Hall, IV).

(VI) Benjamin, sixth son of Jeremiah and Mary (Wiggin) Gilman, resided in Exeter, and married Elizabeth Thing, daughter of Samuel and Abigail (Gilman) Thing, and granddaughter of Councillor John Gilman, an illustrious son of Edward (3).

(VII) Jonathan, son of Benjamin and Elizabeth (Thing) Gilman, was born December 25, 1720, in that part of ancient Exeter which is now Brentwood. In 1767 he became the first settler, and was the most prominent citizen of Wakefield, New Hampshire, where he was a selectman and filled other positions of responsibility. He is probably the Jonathan who died at Sandwich, March 28, 1801. He married, December 1, 1746, Mehitabel Kimball, daughter of Caleb and Mehitabel (Porter) Kimball, of Exeter. Their children were: John, Caleb, Samuel, Jonathan, Benjamin, Mehitabel and Porter.

(VIII) Porter, youngest child of Jonathan Gilman, was born June 6, 1762, in Brentwood, and settled in Brookfield, New Hampshire. He married, April 3, 1786, Hannah Hall, and their children, born in Brookfield, were: Polly Pike, Avery Hall, Abigail Hall, Asaf, Alvah, Sally, Caleb and Hannah.

(IX) Avery Hall, eldest son and second child of Porter and Hannah (Hall) Gilman, was born April 26, 1790, in Brookfield, and resided in that town, which he represented in the legislature. He was a farmer. He was married, May 7, 1816, in Brookfield, by the Rev. Asa Piper, to Sally Savage, of that town.

(X) Asaph, son of Avery Hall and Sally (Savage) Gilman, was born in Wakefield, New Hampshire, September 20, 1818. In 1864 he moved to Dover, New Hampshire, and bought the farm where his son now lives. He followed farming until his Gilman, died December 25, 1898, aged sixty-nine, daughter of Theophilus and Sarah L. Gilman, of Wakefield. Of this marriage one child was born, Joseph L., whose sketch follows.

(XI) Joseph L., only child of Asaph and Sarah M. (Gilman) Gilman, was born in Wakefield, New Hampshire, December 20, 1862. He was educated in the common schools and at Franklin Academy. He always remained on the farm with his father, and gave his attention to agricultural pursuits; he has also been engaged in driving cattle, and has dealt quite extensively in horses. Mr. Gilman is a Republican in politics. He married, June 20, 1889, Sarah M. Hussey, daughter of Moses and Sarah (Hadford) Hussey, of Dover. She was born February 20, 1856, and died January 9, 1906.

(VIII) Stephen Gilman, a descendant probably in the fifth generation of Edward of Caston, the emigrant, through the latter's son Moses, was born in Kingston, New Hampshire, but the date of his birth has not yet come to light. He served as a cavalry officer in the Revolutionary war, and after leaving the service he engaged in farming at East Unity, New Hampshire, where he died about the year 1830. His first wife was before marriage Annie Huntoon, and September 5, 1793, he was married a second time to Dorothy Clough, who died about 1850. He was the father of twenty-one children, nine of whom were of his first union, and the others were of his second marriage. The majority of them settled in the Unities, East and West, and a lake in that locality takes its name from the family. (Benjamin and descendants receive mention in this article.)

(IX) Emerson, born July 25, 1794, eldest son of Stephen and Dorothy (Clough) Gilman, was a native of East Unity, and resided there until 1837, when he went to Lowell, Massachusetts. He was a clothier and operated hand-looms prior to the application of machinery to that industry. He subsequently moved to Milford, New Hampshire, whence he removed to Nashua in 1844, and in 1854 he went to reside in Groton Centre, Massachusetts, where his death occurred in October of the latter year. His wife was before marriage Delia Way, born August 11, 1801, and he had a family of eight children, namely: Mary A., born October 24, 1819; Hannah F., December 18, 1823; Virgil C., May 5, 1827; Dorothy A., June 23, 1831; Horace W.,

December 6, 1833; Emerson, Jr., February 6, 1837; Abby F., May 19, 1842; Osman B., June, 1831. Only five of these grew to years of maturity. (Mention of Horace W. and descendants appears in this article.)

(X) Virgil Chase, third child and eldest son of Emerson and Delia (Way) Gilman, was born in East Unity, May 5, 1827. He was educated in the public schools including the high school, and acquired his early business training in Nashua. In 1851 he engaged in the manufacture of paper as a member of the firm of Gage, Murray & Company, who made a specialty of printer's cards, also embossed and marble papers, and from this concern, which enjoyed a most successful career, both industrially and financially, developed the present National Card and Glazed Paper Company. After severing his connection with the paper-manufacturing industry he engaged in agricultural pursuits with a view of recovering his health, which had become somewhat impaired owing to his close application to business. Being an expert penman, as well as one of the most accurate bookkeepers and accountants in southern New Hampshire, he was secured by the Nashua Savings Bank at its organization to open its first set of books, and for some time he acted as cashier's substitute at the Pennichuck's Bank. For nearly twenty years dating from 1876 he was treasurer of the Savings Bank, and he was long a director of the Indian Head National Bank. His business interests were both various and important, and in all probability covered more ground than did those of any of his contemporaries, and he not only invested freely in home and nearby enterprises but used his influence in the building up of Nashua as an industrial center and contributed many convincing articles on the subject to the press, which served to give capitalists a most favorable impression of the outlook. He was president of the Peterboro railroad, and of the Nashua Saddlery Hardware Company, and a director of the Underhill Edge Tool Company, the Amoskeag Axe Company, the Nashua Iron and Steel Company and other successful enterprises, each of which profited in no small measure from his business sagacity and sound judgment in financial matters. His interest in farming was never permitted to grow lukewarm, and his successful achievements in almost every branch of agriculture acted as an incentive in the neighboring tillers of the soil. He was especially interested in the raising of poultry, being among the first to develop the far-famed Plymouth Rock fowl, and was awarded a bronze medal at the Centennial Exposition in 1876 for an unusual fine exhibit. For many years he was a trustee of the New Hampshire Agricultural Society and frequently did yeoman duty at agricultural and horticultural exhibits, local, state and national.

During a long period Mr. Gilman served upon the board of education; was for upward of twenty-five years secretary and treasurer of the board of trustees of the Public Library, the establishment of which he zealously promoted; was mayor of Nashua in 1865; was a member of the lower house of the state legislature in 1879, serving as chairman of the committee on banks and strongly opposing the taxation of church property; was elected to the state senate for the year 1881, being honored with the chairmanship of the judiciary committee, which at that time enjoyed the somewhat unique distinction of not having in its makeup a single member of the legal profession, and in spite of this fact it discharged its duties in a most able and judicious manner. In marked contrast to the majority of public officials his elections invariably were the direct outcome of the office seeking the man. One of his favorite pastimes was his active connection with the Governor's Horse Guards, and he was an honorary member of the Foster Rifles. He was a leading member of the First Congregational Church and its society, participating actively in its work, serving as a director, treasurer and president of its Sunday school, and contributing liberally toward the building fund of the present church edifice. In 1893 Dartmouth College conferred upon him the honorary degree of Master of Arts in recognition of his generosity in founding a scholarship fund there for the use of indigent students. The record of his life work was in every way an honorable one, and on April 28, 1903, he was called hence, respected and esteemed by the entire community, by whom his passing away was sincerely regretted. In 1850 Mr. Gilman married Miss Sarah Louisa Newcomb, daughter of Gideon and Sarah (Abbott) Newcomb, of Roxbury, New Hampshire. Of this union there were two children: Harriette Louisa, born October 21, 1853, married January 14, 1875, Charles W. Hoitt, judge of the Nashua municipal court (see Hoyt, VIII); and Alfred Emerson, born February 16, 1857, died September 29, same year.

(X) Horace Way, son of Emerson and Delia (Way) Gilman, was born in East Unity, December 6, 1833. In early boyhood he went to Lowell and attended school there, and in early manhood moved to Nashua, New Hampshire, and attended Crosley's school. He began the activities of life as a school teacher in Nashua, and later removed to Boston and served in the capacity of clerk in a drug store. He then returned to Nashua and become associated with the Gilman Brothers Manufacturing Company, manufacturers of cardboard. The business this firm conducted was one of the first of its kind in the country. He sold out his interests and went to Albany and organized the Albany Card & Paper Company, of Albany, New York, with Mr. John Dobler, and in the sixties sold out to Mr. Dobler and then returned to Nashua. The Albany Card and Paper Company is still in existence and very prosperous. When he returned to Nashua he purchased an interest in the firm of Gage, Murray & Company, cardboard manufacturers, the Nashua Card & Glazed Paper Company. He was its treasurer from its inception up to the time of his retirement, a period of thirty years, during which time the company was most successful, never losing the semi-annual dividend, which at one time reached as high as sixty per cent. per annum.

Mr. Gilman was not only a prominent figure in the business circles of Nashua, but evinced an earnest interest in the moral and religious aspect of the city as well, having for years devoted much time to the welfare and advancement of the Methodist Episcopal Church, of which he served as treasurer, trustee and superintendent of the Sunday school; he also represented the laity in the conference and attended the centennial celebration of that denomination at Baltimore, Maryland. His desire for the propogation of church work was only equalled by his interest in the general welfare of his fellowmen, and his death, which occurred March 24, 1894, removed from the business and religious circles of Nashua an upright, conscientious man, a zealous christian worker and one of its most successful business men. In politics he took no active part, except he was elected a member of the State Constitutional Convention in the year ——. He was prominently identified with the Masonic Order, in

Virgil C. Gilman

which he had advanced to the thirty-second degree.

Mr. Gilman married, in 1854, Miss Adeline W. Marsh, of Hudson, New Hampshire. She bore him four children, two of whom are living, namely: Colonel E. M., see forward; and William V., who manages the wholesale business in New York City of the Reversible Collar Company of Boston.

(XI) Colonel E. M. Gilman, treasurer and manager of the Reversible Collar Company of Boston, Massachusetts, was born in Nashua, New Hampshire, September 26, 1862. He went to local schools and graduated from the high school in Nashua. Later he graduated from Bryant & Stratton's Business College, Boston, Massachusetts. In 1884 he went to Wichita, Kansas, and engaged in the banking business. He served as bookkeeper of the Citizens' Bank, and after nine months service in that capacity returned east as general manager of their loan department, and in about four years he sent back nine million dollars to invest in farm mortages in Kansas. He severed his connection with this concern in 1891, and then returned to Nashua, New Hampshire, and re-entered his father's business. April 1, 189—, he went to Springfield, Massachusetts, and took the vice-presidency and general managership of the Springfield Glazed Paper Manufacturing Company, which position he held for about six years. He was then induced to accept a position as general manager of the Reversible Collar Company of Boston, in 1897, which position he now holds. He was elected treasureer January, 1905. This company was organized in 1862, incorporated 1866, capital three hundred and fifty thousand dollars, and employs about two hundred hands. He is a Republican in politics. In 1889 he was elected to civic government in Nashua, New Hampshire. He was appointed aide-de-camp on the staff of Governor Goodall, with rank of colonel. He was also elected to civic government while in Springfield. He is a member of the Boston Yachting Club, is fond of automobiling and other sports. He resides in Brookline, Massachusetts. Colonel Gilman married Mary F. Wallis, of Nashua, New Hampshire, daughter of James F. Wallis. They have one son, Francis D., now (1907) seventeen years of age, in sophomore class at Harvard University, having entered college at the age of sixteen. Mrs. Gilman is a member of the Daughters of the Revolution and several other noted clubs and societies.

(IX) Benjamin Gilman, probably a son of Stephen and Dorothy (Clough) Gilman, is supposed to have been born in Unity.

(X) Stephen, son of Benjamin Gilman, was born in Unity, and followed the calling of a farmer. He married Diantha, daughter of David Harding, and among their children was a son, Stephen W., mentioned below.

(XI) Stephen W., son of Stephen and Diantha (Harding) Gilman, was born in Croydon, August 19, 1858, and was brought up by his maternal grandparents. He was educated in the Croydon district school with the exception of one term at the Kimball Union Academy. He states that, in his youth, he considered himself an expense to his ancestors, and that he decided to remain on his uncle's farm until the age of twenty-one, giving his labor in return for his board and clothing. Upon attaining his majority he left the farm with a capital of twenty-five dollars, and for a time worked in a pistol factory in Springfield, Massachusetts, becoming an efficient mechanic. For twelve years he was employed by the government in the Springfield armory, and during the latter six years established himself in business, conducting a variety store in that city and becoming the owner of a comfortable home. In 1899, on account of his uncle's failing health, he disposed of all his interests in Springfield and returned to the homestead. Shortly after his return his uncle died, and Mr. Gilman is now the owner of the farm which consists of about two hundred acres. On his return to Croydon he opened the general store which he now owns, and which had been closed about seventy-five years. The business is now flourishing. In 1900-01 he represented his town in the legislature, and since 1900 has held the office of town clerk. He has also served as librarian, justice of the peace and notary public. He is a member of Hampden Lodge, Independent Order of Odd Fellows, Springfield, Massachusetts, and serves as superintendent of the Sunday school of the Congregational Church of Croydon. He married, in 1880, in Springfield, Massachusetts, Carrie I. Allen Stearns, who died in 1888, leaving no issue. Three of her brothers were professional men, one a prominent attorney of Boston, Massachusetts. Mr. Gilman married, in 1901, Mary C., daughter of William Pernett, of Ansley, Have Ferry, Lunenburg, county, Nova Scotia.

PRAY The original spelling of this name in England was Pre, which is indicative of a French origin. A natural love for the sea, which seems to have prevailed among the American branch of the family, caused many of them to become mariners, and some of them won distinction in the Colonial service.

(I) Quintin Pray, founder of the family in America, was born probably in South of Scotland about the year 1595, and emigrated in 1640 (perhaps previous to that date), first settling in Lynn, Massachusetts. He was an iron-worker. From Lynn he removed to Braintree, Massachusetts, and his death occurred in the last-named town June 17, 1667. The christian name of his wife, who survived him, was Joan, and his children were: Richard, born in 1650, died in 1693. John, see succeeding paragraph. Hannah, the date of whose birth does not appear in the records (was living in 1691). Dorothy, born in 1644, died December 11, 1705.

(II) John, elder son of Quintin and Joan Pray, was born about the year 1635. He resided in Braintree and died there in 1676. May 7, 1657, he married Joanna Dowman, who was appointed administratrix of his estate October 31, 1676, and she subsequently married Daniel Livingstone, with whom she went to live in York, Maine, taking her three youngest children with her. Her second husband was killed by the Indians August 20, 1694. Her second account as administratrix was rendered July 7, 1699, and signed Joanna Livingstone, late Pray. As the wife of John Pray she became the mother of nine children, namely: John, born July 11, 1659, died young. Ephraim, born about 1661, married Elizabeth, daughter of John Hayden, and resided in Braintree. Hannah, born March 4, 1663, died December 12, 1664. Hannah, born March 16, 1665, became the wife of James Bell, of Taunton, Massachusetts. Richard, born May 3, 1667, died prior to 1699. Samuel, the date of whose birth will be given presently. Joseph, born about 1671, married Mary Grant. John, born February 10, 1673, died prior to 1699. Dorothy, born about 1675, became the wife of Daniel Forbush.

(III) Samuel, fifth son and seventh child of John and Joanna (Dowman) Pray, was born in Braintree, May 16, 1669. He began to follow the sea at an early age and became a master-mariner. He was captain of the brigantine "William and Andrew," owned by Colonel Pepperell and named for his two sons. He resided on Gunnison's Neck, Kittery, Maine, and land was conveyed to him in 1700 and 1703. He married Mary Fernald, daughter of Thomas and Temperance Fernald, of Kittery, and died in 1708, as, according to the records, his wife Mary was granted power to settle his estate October 9 of that year. It is quite probable that her death occurred in or prior to 1722, as on May 10 of that year her son Samuel was ordered by the court to act as administrator of the estate of his father. Their children were: Samuel, who will be again referred to. Mary, who became the wife of Samuel Stacy, November 2, 1721. Hannah, who was married to Thomas Rand, of Newcastle, May 24, 1722. John, who was married in Portsmouth, June 2, 1709, to Joanna Jose. A daughter who became the wife of Robert Mendum.

(IV) Samuel (2), eldest son and child of Samuel and Mary (Fernald) Pray, was born in Kittery or the immediate vicinity, but the date of his birth cannot be found. As a member of Captain Samuel Newmarch's company, he participated in some of the important Colonial military operations under Sir William Pepperell, and his son Ebenezer and cousin, William Pray, were enrolled in the same company. He resided in Kittery, and on November 17, 1726, married for his first wife Alice Mendum, daughter of Jonathan and Sarah (Downing) Mendum, of York county, Maine. She died April 20, 1757. His children were: Ebenezer, born October 24, 1728, married Elizabeth Gunnison. Samuel, born April 19, 1731, married Susanna Dunn. Joshua, born February 14, 1733; married Ruth Gunnison. John, who is referred to in the next paragraph. William, born March 16, 1740. Joseph, born August 6, 1742. Nathaniel, born March 29, 1747. Samuel Pray (2) died in January, 1762.

(V) John, fourth son of Samuel and Alice (Mendum) Pray, sea captain, was born in Kittery, February 14, 1736. He married Mary Orr, daughter of John and Eleanor (Dennett) Orr, and of this union there was but one child. John Orr was an officer of the frigate "Alliance."

(VI) Captain Samuel, only child of John and Mary (Orr) Pray, was born in Kittery, December 3, 1789. From his native town, he removed to Portsmouth, New Hampshire, and was a sea captain and ship builder. During the second war with Great Britain (1812-15) he was engaged in privateering. December 14, 1814, he was made prize master of a British ship with orders to take her to Portsmouth, but was shortly afterwards overhauled by a British seventy-four gun frigate, which recaptured his prize, and with the American prize crew he was sent to Dartmoor prison in England, and was in that prison when the prisoners were fired upon. He was subsequently released and returned to America. He married (first), April 23, 1809, Lucy Fernald, who was a daughter of Daniel and Hannah (Manson) Fernald, and who died October 27, 1826. She bore him six children: Adeline, born September 16, 1812, married James Neal, and died October 8, 1845. Sarah Ann, born July 29, 1814, married Nathaniel K. Walker, and died April 6, 1875. John Samuel, born August 3, 1816, mentioned below. Lucy Maria Fernald, born June 28, 1821, married Charles Gerrish, and died September 5, 1864. Margaret Wooster, born July 15, 1825, married James M. Salter, and died July 5, 1881. William Fernald, born May 13, 1823, died Dayton, Ohio. Samuel Pray married (second), Ellen Brown, September 6, 1827, and their children were: Julia Ann, born November 12, 1829, died April 12, 1903. Charles Henry, born January 10, 1832, drowned off Cape Horn, September 30, 1860. Lavina Ellen, born June 11, 1835, married Edwin A. Gerrish, and died December 17, 1891.

(VII) Captain John Samuel, eldest son of Captain Samuel and Lucy (Fernald) Pray, was born in Kittery, August 3, 1816. Like his father he became an efficient master-mariner, and for a number of years was engaged in the West India and cotton trade. In 1849 he made a voyage around Cape Horn to San Francisco, and during the Civil war was a ship owner in Portsmouth and New York. He was a trustee of the Portsmouth Savings Bank, director of the Portsmouth National Mechanics' & Traders' Bank, served as president of the Portsmouth Atheneum, and was a prominent member of the Unitarian parish. His death occurred August 21, 1889. He married Rosalina A. Tisdale, November 17, 1849, who died December 4, 1877, and their children were: Elizabeth Shattuck, born November 23, 1851, married Charles K. Wadham, and died April 9, 1906. Samuel, born July 9, 1854. Frank Wendell, born April 20, 1857, married Elizabeth M. Calder. John Wesley, born July 11, 1858, married Elizabeth Seeley. Maurice, born November 15, 1861, died January 8, 1878. Lucy, born February 5, 1863, died May 31, 1863. Mary Cambridge, born February 26, 1867. Henry Thornton, born January 6, 1870, died August 14, 1870.

(VIII) Captain Samuel, eldest son of Captain John S. and Rosalina A. (Tisdale) Pray, was born in Portsmouth, July 9, 1854. After attending the Portsmouth high school three and one-half years, he adopted a seafaring life, and shipping before the mast in New York on the ship "Yosemite" he sailed to San Francisco, thence to the far east, being two years and a half on the voyage. His second voyage, a Mediterranean voyage, was in the Portsmouth ship "Semiramis," commanded by the late Captain Edwin A. Gerrish, of Portsmouth. In 1878, when twenty-four years old, he superintended the building of and later took command of a clipper bark, the "Harvard," and later commanded the ship "Gov. Goodwin," and was a successful ship master, making long and exceedingly prosperous voyages. Retiring from the sea, he became quite extensively interested in shipping, and at the present time is the Boston representative of the American Hawaiian Steamship Company. Captain Pray is an advanced Mason, a member of Dalhousie Lodge, West Newton, and a Knight Templar. He is a trustee of the Boston Marine Society and a member of Massachusetts Society Sons of American Revolution. He married, February 1, 1881, Emma S. Barnard, of Franklin, New Hampshire, daughter of Daniel Barnard, who was at one time attorney-general of that state. Captain and Mrs. Pray reside in West Newton, Massachusetts, and have one daughter, Dorothy, born December 11, 1893.

WHITE The great number of persons in the New England and western states whose surname is White are descended in most instances from John White, of Salem, Massachusetts, 1638, or from William White, of Ipswich, Massachusetts, 1635. Both were progenitors of a multitude of descendants, and number among them many of the most active and prominent participants in the social, religious and civil affairs of the communities and commonwealths in which they have lived.

Noah White

(I) The present article deals with the descendants of William White, who came from Norfolk county, England, landing in Ipswich, Massachusetts, 1635. Shortly afterward he settled in Newbury, where he became an influential citizen, and later was a pioneer in Haverhill, being one of the first company of twelve settlers. His name is mentioned as one of the six grantees of land at Pawtucket by the two Indians, "Passaquo and Saggahew," November 15, 1642, and he was one of the thirty-two landholders in Haverhill in that year. He was one of the selectmen chosen in the town at a meeting held October 29, 1646, and is listed as one of those who shared in the second division of ploughland laid out June 7, 1652, his portion being seven acres. He died September 28, 1690, aged eighty years. His widow soon afterward moved to Ipswich, where she died in 1693. Mr. White settled on the farm owned in 1861 by James D. White, and we find that he owned a farm in Newbury in 1650. Soon after the church was gathered he became a member, and was one of its firmest pillars. He had the honor of the town very much at heart, and was esteemed by its citizens and was frequently intrusted with its most important business. He left one son, John.

(II) John, only child of William White, married, at Salem, August 25, 1662, Hannah French. He died January 1. 1668-69, aged twenty-nine years, leaving one son, John.

(III) John (2), only son of John (1) and Hannah (French) White, was born March 8, 1664. He married, October 24, 1687, Lydia Gilman, daughter of Hon. John Gilman, of Exeter, and had many sons and daughters, "whose descendants," says an old record, "are exceedingly numerous." Another account says "Said John and Lydia had sons: William, Samuel, Nicholas, Timothy (graduate of Harvard College, 1720), James and John; and daughters: Mary, Hannah, Elizabeth, Abigail, Lydia, and Joanna." John White died November 20, 1727.

(IV) Nicholas, third son of John and Lydia (Gilman) White, was born in Haverhill, December 4. 1698, and died at Plaistow, New Hampshire, October 7, 1782. By his first wife, Hannah Ayer, whom he married in 1722, he had five children, and by his second wife, Mary Culf, he had ten children.

(V) Noah, third child of Nicholas and Hannah (Ayer) White, was born February 15, 1728, and settled at Coos, New Hampshire. He married Sarah Sweet, by whom he had nine children

(VI) Nathaniel, the eldest child of Noah and Sarah (Sweet) White, was born April 10, 1752. His first wife was Betty ———, who bore him three children. After her death he married Rebekah Foord, by whom he also had three children, the youngest of whom was Samuel. In 1790 he removed with his family to Lancaster, New Hampshire, where he spent the remainder of his life. He served in the revolutionary war, and his wife Rebekah received a pension. He died April 28, 1809. He was public-spirited and benevolent, and was held in high esteem as a man and a citizen.

(VII) Samuel, youngest child of Nathaniel and Rebekah (Foord) White, was born September 14, 1787, at Bradford, Vermont, and died June 4, 1854, at Concord, New Hampshire. When three years old he accompanied his parents in their removal to Lancaster, where he grew to manhood. April 2, 1810, he married Sarah Freeman, by whom he had nine children. In February, 1848, he moved to Concord, where he spent the remainder of his life. His wife died December 30, 1857.

(VIII) Nathaniel, oldest son of Samuel and Sarah (Freeman) White, was born at Lancaster, New Hampshire, February 7, 1811. He received the kind and amount of education incident to most boys at the time and in the locality where he grew up, with the exception that his religious education and training, owing to his mothers' tender care, were far above those of the average boy. At fourteen years of age he went to Lunenburg, Vermont, where he entered the employ of a general merchant, and spent about a year. General John Wilson, of Lancaster, about that time assumed the management of the Columbian Hotel at Concord, and young Nathaniel White took a position in the employ of the General, whose wife was a woman of many noble qualities. Knowing that their son was going to a place where he would be under good influences made the young man's parents the more readily consent to this arrangement. On his arrival at Concord, April 26, 1826, Nathaniel White had a solitary shilling in his pocket, but by saving the perquisites that came to him about the hotel he accumulated in the five years he was there the sum of two hundred and fifty dollars. He kept a strict account of the salary he earned and turned it over to his father. In 1832 he borrowed money to start in business. This was the only loan he ever received or asked for business purposes. With his savings and this loan he purchased for one thousand dollars an interest in the stage line between Concord and Hanover, driving the stage himself. In one year he was free from debt, and a short time later he purchased the stage route between Concord and Lowell. In 1838 he became a partner with Captain William Walker Jr. in establishing the express business, making the weekly trips to Boston, where he personally attended to the delivery of all packages, goods or money intrusted in his care. He was eminently adapted to this business, paying great attention to details, even the smallest thing, and thus he was an ideal expressman. Upon the opening of the Concord railroad in 1842 he became one of the original members of the express company then organized to deliver goods throughout New Hampshire and Canada. Soon after, Mr. White bought Captain Walker's interest, and was the principal owner with B. P. Cheney. They sold to the American Express Company in the spring of 1880. The business was long conducted under the name of the United States & Canada Express Company, and has continued in successful operation to the present day, and to Nathaniel White's business capacity it has been greatly indebted for its remarkable financial success.

Mr. White was strongly attracted to Concord from the time he became a resident of the city until his death. To him it is indebted for many of the beautiful structures which make it an attractive city. In the founding of benevolent and charitable institutions he was one of the foremost, taking a deep interest in the establishment of the New Hampshire Asylum for the Insane, the State Reform School, the Orphans' Home at Franklin, to which he gave a generous endowment, and of the Home for the Aged at Concord.

In 1852 Mr. White was chosen by the Whig and Free-Soil parties to represent Concord in the state legislature. He was an Abolitionist from the start and a member of the Anti-Slavery Society from its inception. He extended his aid to negroes escaping from slavery in the south, and the attic of his house and the hay mows of his barn harbored many a negro on his way to Canada and freedom. In 1875 Mr. White was a candidate for governor on the Prohibition ticket. In 1876 he was sent as a delegate to the Cincinnati Republican convention which nominated Rutherford B. Hayes for the presidency. In 1880 he was placed by his party at the head of the list of candidates for presidential electors. As far back as 1846 Mr. White purchased four hundred acres of land lying about two miles from the state house, in the southwestern part of the city, and gave much of his attention to farming, making his estate one of the most highly cultivated in the state. He also had a beautiful summer retreat at Sunapee Lake. In addition to his large interest in the express company and his farm, he was interested in real estate in Concord and Chicago, in hotel property in the mountain districts, in railway corporations, in banks, in manufacturing establishments, and in shipping. He was a director in the Manchester & Lawrence, the Franconia & Profile House, and Mount Washington railroads, and in the National State Capital Bank. He was a trustee of the Loan and Trust Savings Bank of Concord, of the Reform School, Home for the Aged, the Orphans' Home, and other private and public trusts. Mr. White was a man of noble character. As a child he grew up under christian influences; as a young man he was honest, honorable, free from vices, prudent, economical, temperate, diligent in business, energetic and well-liked; as a man he was strong, firm, reliable in every way, tactful, successful, and one who was sought out to care for the interests of others because he had succeeded so well in the management of his own affairs. Mr. and Mrs. White were among the foremost members of the Universalist Church of Concord, and he was ever striving to spread the faith that was in him. Among the liberal contributors to Tufts College, he was the friend of education and every liberal movement, and ever cherished a keen interest in the welfare of mankind. He did more than any other one man to retain the capital at Concord, both giving land and contributing in cash to buy land of others.

Mr. White was married November 1, 1836, to Armenia S. Aldrich, who was born November 1, 1817, in Mendon, Massachusetts, a daughter of John and Harriet (Smith) Aldrich (see Aldrich, VI). Mrs. White has always been interested in the movement for woman suffrage and every effort for the improvement of the condition of her sex. She was a warm friend of Frances E. Willard and other workers in the field of human advancement, whose warm regards have ever been hers. On the maternal side Mrs. White's ancestry includes the Pilgrims of the "Mayflower"—Edward Doty, Francis Cooke, and Stephen Hopkins, also Mr. Hopkin's second wife, Elizabeth, and their daughter, Damaris, who both came with him to Plymouth. Mrs. White's mother, whose maiden name was Harriet Smith, was a daughter of Samuel Smith and his wife Hope Doten, who married at Plymouth, Massachusetts, May 3, 1791. The "Doty-Doten Genealogy" shows that Hope Doten, born in 1765, was a daughter of James and Elizabeth (Kempton) Doten, and was descended from Edward Doty and his wife, Faith Clark, through John and Elizabeth (Cooke) Doty, Isaac and Martha (Faunce) Doten, and Isaac and Mary (Lanham) Doten, Isaac being father of James and grandfather of Hope Doten. Mrs. White's maternal grandmother, Elizabeth, wife of John Doty or Doten, was the daughter of Jacob Cooke (son of Francis) and his wife, Damaris, daughter of Stephen Hopkins and his wife Elizabeth.

Nathaniel and Armenia S. (Aldrich) White were the parents of seven children: John A., Armenia E., Lizzie H., Annie Frances, born May 22, 1852, died November 9, 1865; Nathaniel, Seldon F., born July 13, 1857, died April 24, 1858; and Benjamin C. They also adopted and reared a daughter Hattie S., who is now the widow of D. P. Dearborn, M. D., late of Brattleboro, Vermont.

(IX) Colonel John A. White, eldest son of Nathaniel and Armenia S. (Aldrich) White, was born March 31, 1838, died November 26, 1899. He married, October 5, 1869, Elizabeth Mary Corning. She died in May, 1873, leaving no children. He married (second), August 31, 1881, Ella H. Corning, a cousin of his first wife. Arnold White, of Concord, New Hampshire, born October 20, 1883, is the only child of this union.

(IX) Armenia E. White, born March 22, 1847, married Horatio Hobbs, who died April 24, 1889. He left two children: Nathaniel White Hobbs, born November 1, 1873; and Annie White Hobbs, born July 28, 1875.

(IX) Lizzie H. White married, October 12, 1881, C. H. Newhall, of Lynn, Massachusetts. She died December 12, 1887.

(IX) Nathaniel White, Jr., born June 8, 1855, and died October 4, 1904, was a citizen of Concord. He was general manager of the farm and other properties left by his father, and was a director of the Mt. Washington Railway Company. He married, November 17, 1881, Helen Eastman, daughter of Charles S. and Charlotte (Bedlow) Eastman. They had two children: Nathaniel Aldrich, born November 19, 1883; and Charlotte, July 21, 1889.

(IX) Benjamin Cheney White was born June 16, 1861. He is a resident of Concord, and is a director of the State Capital Bank, the Concord & Montreal railroad, and manager of the White Opera House, Concord. He married, January 12, 1887, Mabel M. Chase, of Concord, daughter of James H. and Augusta S. (Lamprey) Chase. They had two children: James Chase, born August, 1890, died October 5, 1895; and Rose Aldrich, born June 5, 1895.

(Second Family.)

WHITE The branch of the White family with which this narrative is concerned traces its descent from Robert White, a native and resident of Scotland, and a Presbyterian in religion. His two sons, Robert and James, came to America from northern Ireland about 1729, first locating in Lancaster, Massachusetts. Prior to 1740 they located in the town of Pembroke, New Hampshire, where they resided the remainder of their lives, and were farmers by occupation. Robert White took a deed of his right in Suncook of Benjamin Prescott, of Groton, Massachusetts, March 10, 1732, and deeded one-half of the same to James White, April 10, 1733. Both probably located soon afterward on lot number 54, first division, Robert on the southerly and James on the northerly half.

(I) James White, above mentioned, married in Scotland a Miss McAllister, and their children were: Isaac, Mary Moore and Jane.

(II) Isaac, eldest child and only son of James and ——— (McAllister) White, was born in Pembroke in 1736. He resided on the homestead upon which his father located, and followed farm-

ARMENIA S. WHITE.

ing. He sold this farm to Samuel Kimball, and bought another on the street, February 10, 1773, and subsequently sold it to John Head, of Bradford, Massachusetts. About 1778 he settled in Bow, on land now occupied by his descendants. His first house stood on the site now occupied by the school house in district No. 3, known as the White district. December 15, 1765, he married Mary Moore, of Pembroke. She was born in March, 1739, and died March 29, 1838; he died in August, 1806. Their children were: 1. Margaret, born October 1, 1766; married Moody Dow, of Concord, New Hampshire. 2. Mary, born July 11, 1768; married Jonathan Cavis, of Bow. 3. James, born April 21, 1770; married Polly Alexander, November 28, 1779. 4. Robert, born May 7, 1772; marrier Sarah Frye. 5. Mary Ann, born May 21, 1774; married Jonathan Farmer, June 15, 1797. 6. John, born May 9, 1776; died unmarried. 7. Isaac, born November 6, 1778; married Elizabeth Ryder. 8. David, born March 22, 1781; married Betsey Carter. 9. Nancy, born September 21, 1783; married Chauncey Newell. 10. Daniel, (mentioned at length in this article). 11. Susan, born July 12, 1789; married Wells Carter. 12. Betsey, born June 2, 1792; married a Mr. Cavis, and resided in Bow.

(III) David, eighth child and fifth son of Isaac and Mary (Moore) White, was born March 22, 1781. He resided in the town of Bow, and was a farmer by occupation. He married, July 16, 1807, Betsey Carter, daughter of Colonel John Carter (see Carter, VI), of Concord, and died June 29, 1833. His children were: 1. Lucy Carter, born May 1, 1808, died November 14, 1835. 2. Rev. John Brown, born March 10, 1810; married (first), Mary P. Merriman, and (second), Elizabeth R. Wright, and died in Greenville, Illinois. 3. Robert Davis, born March 5, 1812; married Mary Shute, of Bow, and lived and died in that town. 4. Uella, born July 7, 1814, died August 1, 1814. 5. Emily, born July 13, 1816; married John Albin. (See Albin, II). 6. Judith Coffin, born October 16, 1819; married, February 10, 1842, William Albin (see Albin, II). 7. David, mentioned below. 8. Henry Kirk, born September 3, 1830, died December 2, 1809, in Bow.

(IV) David (2), seventh child and third son of David (1) and Betsey (Carter) White, was born in the town of Bow, New Hampshire, April 11, 1826, and his education was received in the public schools of his native town. While he was a resident of Bow he followed farming, and was also interested in the lumber business. Later he located in Concord, where he continued in the latter occupation. He was a member of the Universalist Church in Concord. In politics he supported the principles and policies of the Democratic party. He married, December 29, 1853, Charlotte Page, daughter of Jeremiah and Mehitable (Shute) Page. She was born January 29, 1832, and died August 4, 1876, surviving her husband, who died August 17, 1875. They were the parents of two children: 1. David Waldo, born June 30, 1864. 2. Una Gertrude, born in Concord, October 2, 1869; married Richard C. Goodell; she died April, 1895, in Antrim, New Hampshire.

(V) David Waldo, eldest child and only son of David (2) and Charlotte (Page) White, was born in the city of Concord, New Hampshire, June 30, 1864. He received his education in the public schools of his native city, in Tilton Seminary, and in Dartmouth College, from which he graduated in the class of 1887. After his graduation he entered the employ of the Lake Shore railway, in the engineering department, and subsequently was appointed to the position of engineer of the Concord street railway. In 1899 he purchased the flour, feed, hay and lime business of F. Coffin, in Concord, which he has successfully conducted to the present time. He is owner of the family homestead in Bow, where he with his family passes the summer months, their residence being in the city of Concord during the remainder of the year. He takes an active part in community affairs. He is a Republican in politics, and in 1902 was elected as a representative in the legislature from the town of Bow. He is a member of various fraternal and social bodies—Blazing Star Lodge, No. 11, Ancient Free and Accepted Masons; White Mountain Lodge, No. 5, Independent Order of Odd Fellows; and Bow Grange, No. 189, of which he has been master. He married, June 28, 1893, Miss Eva May Colby, daughter of Anthon W. and Jessie Louise (Brown) Colby (see Colby, VII). She was born June 10, 1874. Their children are: 1. Lloyd David, born in Concord, May 29, 1894, died May 10, 1897. 2. Una Goodell, born in Concord, August 21, 1895. 3. Irene Bernice, born in Concord, September 14, 1898.

(III) Daniel, tenth child and sixth son of Isaac and Mary (Moore) White, born in Bow, March 22, 1786, died March 16, 1826, was a blacksmith and stoneworker, and lived in Bow. He married, July 13, 1815, Mary Carter, of Bow, born May 3, 1793, died January 11, 1847, daughter of Moses and Molly (Robinson) Carter (see Carter, VI), who lived near the old "Iron Works" southwest of the present city of Concord. Their children were: William, born in 1816, died October 13, 1826; Curtis, Mary Ann, born June 20, 1821, died March 9, 1852, unmarried; and Daniel C., born October 6, 1822, died about 1903 in Alton, Illinois.

(IV) Curtis, second son and child of Daniel and Mary (Carter) White, was born in Bow, April 4, 1819, was educated in the common schools, and for a time worked on a farm. In 1851 he settled in Concord and learned the carpenter's trade, and worked at that in Concord and vicinity for twenty years. He subsequently became a wheelwright, and followed that occupation for ten years in Concord. In the days of the Whigs he was a member of that party, and soon after it gave place to the Republican party he became a member of the latter organization. Mr. White's thoroughly upright character and pleasant personality made him many friends, and put him in many offices of responsibility and trust. When a young man he was a lieutenant in the militia. In 1846 he was paymaster of the Eleventh Regiment, New Hampshire Militia (sometimes called the "Bloody Eleventh," filling that office one year. He served one year as a member of the common council, and two years as alderman of Concord. In 1861 he was elected to the board of selectmen, and is now (1906) on the board, having filled the place twenty-two years in the time since his first election, and is still performing the functions of that office. He has been twenty-six years an assessor of Concord, and for four terms of five years each he was justice of the peace, and quorum for the state.

Mr. White is an Odd Fellow, first becoming a member of White Moutain Lodge, No. 5, and afterward a charter member of Rumford Lodge, No. 46, where he passed the chairs. He is also a member of Penacook Encampment, No. 3, of which he is a past chief patriarch, and a member of the grand lodge and grand encampment of the state. When the Knights of Pythias was a young organization Mr. White became a charter member of Concord Lodge, No. 8, and was elected past chancellor, without passing the subordinate chairs. At the second meeting of the grand lodge of the Knights, he was made past grand chancellor of the order without having previously filled offices in the grand body. At the meeting of the grand lodge in 1882 he was elected grand master of the exchequer, and has held the office since by virtue of repeated re-elections. Mr. White professed the Baptist faith in 1862, and is now a member of the First Baptist Church of Concord. He married, March 29, 1853, Hannah Buntin, of Bow, daughter of Benjamin and Lydia (Hackett) Buntin. She was born May 7, 1826, and died June 16, 1888. They had one child, Anna, born November 12, 1856. who married, December 8, 1880, Josiah Eastman Fernald (see Fernald, VIII).

WHITE This family does not appear to be connected with the Whites whose history has been previously written. Undoubtedly the present line is descended from one of the six early immigrants of the name, but the family is so numerous that it has been impossible to trace the early antecedents of this branch.

(I) Samuel White was born in Ossipee, New Hampshire, toward the close of the eighteenth century. He died in 1873, aged eighty-six years. He married Philena Tibbetts, a native of the same town.

(II) Allen Gannett, son of Samuel and Philena (Tibbetts) White, was born at Ossipee, New-Hampshire, in 1821. He attended various schools, and then engaged in teaching for several years. He made quite a local reputation in this profession, and was unusually successful in insubordinate districts, which had the name of not allowing a master to complete the term. Becoming tired of this occupation, he went into the store of Moses Merrill at Centre Ossipee as clerk, later entered into partnership with Mr. Merrill, and finally went into business for himself, which he successfully conducted until his death. He was for several years superintendent of schools at Ossipee. He was a strong Democrat, and an energetic worker in the Free Will Baptist Church. Mr. White married Elizabeth R. Lougee, who was born in Parsonfield, Maine. They had seven children: Orlando L., Clara Bell, Charles Allen, whose sketch follows; George Belmont, Augusta Amanda, Herbert Elmore and Scott Lougee. Allen Gannett White died at Moultonville, June 29, 1873, and his wife is still living.

(III) Charles Allen, second son and third child of Allen Gannett and Elizabeth (Lougee) White, was born at Ossipee, New Hampshire, September 1, 1854. He attended various schools, and afterwards a private high school, which he left at the age of sixteen to go to work in his father's store. Afterwards he was employed in a shoe factory. At the age of twenty-three he fitted himself to enter a business college, but before he began his course bought a half interest from his brother, Orlando L. White, who had a general store. Together they bought the W. H. Wiggin property, and moved into the store. About two years after this partnership was formed Orlando L. White died, and Charles A. White took his youngest brother, Herbert E. White, into the business, still keeping the old firm name of O. L. and C. A. White. Twenty years from the day they moved into the store they sold out the stock to S. O. Huckins, who leased the building for three years, during which time Mr. Charles A. White took charge of the local section of the Telephone Company. At the expiration of the lease Mr. White resumed business, and Mr. Huckins moved into his new store alone, but still continued the old firm name. In politics Mr. White is a Democrat, and was postmaster under Cleveland. He has always held some town office, and was selectman in 1884-85-86, and again in 1894-95-96. He has been supervisor of elections, and was a member of the school board for years. He is a member of Ossipee Valley Lodge, No. 74, Ancient Free and Accepted Masons, and on the night of his promotion to Master Mason was elected warden, and six months from that night was elected master. He has held various chairs in the Knights of Pythias, and is also a member of the Grange. In 1887 Charles Allen White married Emma Josephine Palmer. daughter of Frank and Emily Palmer, of Ossipee. They have one child, Kenwood, born February 2, 1902.

(I) Timothy White, an industrious farmer and conscientious member of the Second Advent Church in Ossipee, New Hampshire, was born in that town in 1803, and died in Madison, New Hampshire, 1879. Perhaps the best years of his active life were spent in Madison, where he occupied a position of considerable influence and where he was several times elected selectman, but declined to qualify and serve in that office. He had previously held the same office in Ossipee, and while not averse to its duties in Madison the farm and its successful cultivation were of greater importance to him. His lands comprised about three hundred and fifty acres, and were always well tilled, well stocked, and had good buildings. His wife, Mary (Clark) White, was born in Parsonfield, New Hampshire, in 1809, and died in Madison in 1878. Their four children were: Mary, who died in infancy. David, born in Ossipee and died in Madison. Lorenzo, born in Ossipee, and resides in Rochester, New Hampshire. Sylvester, see forward.

(II) Sylvester, youngest of the children of Timothy and Mary (Clark) White, was born in Ossipee, New Hampshire. April 25, 1833. In early life he was a farmer, and later on became a shoemaker and worked at that trade, but did not give up farming entirely. He resided for a time in Northwood, but now resides in Gossville, New Hampshire. He married, 1857, Elizabeth J. Gerrish, who was born in Deerfield, New Hampshire, and died while visiting in Nottingham, New Hampshire, in 1900. Sylvester and Elizabeth J. (Gerrish) White had one child, Edgar F. White, now of Epsom, New Hampshire.

(III) Edgar F., only son and child of Sylvester and Elizabeth J. (Gerrish) White, was born in Madison, New Hampshire, December 2, 1858, and received his education in the schools of that town and Northwood, New Hampshire. Like his father, he also became a shoemaker and together with working at his trade carried on a general shoe store. His stock at one time was worth five thousand dollars, and was destroyed by fire, causing him a serious loss, as he carried an insurance of only about fifteen hundred dollars. Worse than all else, his health failed, but not his ambition, and he next turned his attention to farming and teaming until he again became strong. He also ran the stage between Northwood and Epsom for some time, and afterward moved into the town last mentioned and set up a shoe shop. Still later he leased a hotel in Epsom, conducts it successfully, and purchased the property in 1901. Since he came to live in Epsom Mr. White has engaged in lumbering in connection with his other enterprises, and also has carried on a livery business. Notwithstanding his early losses by fire and poor health his business life has been successful, and now he is in comfortable circumstances. He is a Granger, and in politics a Republican. He is inclined to be liberal in his religious views, although brought up under the influences of the Second Advent Church. On September 22, 1882, Mr. White married Annie M. Verity, who was born in Andover, Massachusetts, May 25, 1859. They have four children: Myrtle F., born in Rochester, New Hampshire, October 30, 1884, married J. Arthur Griffon, September 1, 1906. Elsie S., born in Madison, December 30, 1889. Ervin, born in Madison, August 26, 1894. Earl, born in Northwood, January 8, 1896.

WHITE The White family of this article is of Irish extraction and has attained to the third generation in America. Its members have shown the impetuous energy common to the Celtic race, and some of them, though born poor, have outstripped many citizens born to wealth and influence.

(I) William White was born in Ireland about 1836, and when twenty-five or thirty years of age came to America and settled in Somersworth, New Hampshire, where he was a laborer. He died October 1, 1879, aged forty-two years. He married, in 1868, Mary O'Brien, who was born in Ireland, now living in Dover, aged sixty-nine years, daughter of Michael and Julia (Canty) O'Brien, by whom he had six children: Mary C., Michael J., John P., William F., James and Julia. Mary C. was born March 16, 1869, and lives in Dover. Michael J. is mentioned below. John P., born September 17, 1873, lives in Dover. William F., born September, 1875, lives in Dover. Rev. James, born September, 1877, was ordained to the priesthood in the Roman Catholic Church by Archbishop Bruchesi, of Montreal, Canada, December, 1905, and is now assistant pastor of St. Ann's Church, Manchester, New Hampshire. Julia, born May 22, 1880, resides in Dover.

(II) Michael Joseph, second child and eldest son of William and Mary (O'Brien) White, was born in Somersworth, March 2, 1871. At the age of ten years he accompanied his parents on their removal to Dover, where he has since resided. His education was obtained in the public schools of Somersworth, which he left at ten years of age for Dover, where he attended the public school three months, and at the evening schools which he attended for a time. Immediately after going to Dover he became a back boy in the Cocheco Mills. After a term of service in that capacity he learned mule spinning and worked at that occupation until 1905.

At the age of fifteen he became a member of the Knights of Labor, and a year later became a charter member of Local Lodge No. 1, of the Boot and Shoemakers' International Union. In 1889 he became a member of the Mule Spinners' Union, and subsequently filled all the offices of the local union, being elected president at the age of eighteen, and holding that position through several serious difficulties, one of which was a strike lasting five months. In 1895 he was elected member of the executive board of the Mule Spinners' National Union, where he served until 1899. In that year he was elected vice-president of the organization and in 1902 was chosen president and served four years, retiring in 1906, and being made a life member of the order. He was one of the organizers of the United Textile Workers of America, and was a member of its executive board until he retired in 1906. Since 1896 he has been prominent in Democratic local political circles, and for four years was a member of the Democratic state committee. In 1906 he was elected mayor of Dover, and is but the second Democrat who has filled that office since the organization of the city. Mayor White has risen from a humble position to a place of honor and trust, and is a well-known and popular citizen. He has filled many positions of honor and trust. From childhood he has been identified with the Catholic Total Abstinence Union of America.

DODGE This name has been traced to a remote period in England, and has been very widely distributed over the United States, beginning with the earliest settlement of the New England colonies. It has been distinguished in law and letters, in divinity, in war, in politics and in every leading activity of the human family and is still identified with the progress of events in New Hampshire and other states. It has turned out from Harvard nineteen graduates, from Yale a dozen, from Dartmouth ten, from the University of Vermont ten, from Columbia College eight, Union College six, Andover Theological Seminary five, Bowdoin College five, University of Wisconsin five, Brown University three, Colby University three, Williams College two and Middlebury College one. The records of the Colleges of Heraldry in England show that a coat of arms was granted to Peter Dodge, of Stockworth, county of Chester, in 1306, and later a patent to John Dodge, of Rotham, in the county of Kent, in 1546. It is declared that he was descended from Peter Dodge of Stockworth. The name is found frequently in various sections of England, and in the sixteenth and seventeenth centuries there were Dodges of honorable character and connection in the counties of Cheshire, Kent, Norfolk and Down. On the eleventh of May, 1629, there sailed from the harbor of Yarmouth, England, the "Talbot," a vessel of three hundred tons and the "Lion's Whelp," a neat and nimble ship of one hundred and twenty tons, and they arrived at Salem, Massachusetts, on the twenty-ninth of the June following. This marks the arrival of the first of the name of Dodge in America.

(I) John Dodge and his wife, Marjorie, resided in Somersetshire, England, where the following children were born to them, namely: William, Richard, Michael and Mary. An examination of the parish registry of East Coker, Somersetshire, England, discloses the records of the births of these children. It is also learned that Richard Dodge was in 1633 a duly admitted tenant by entry hold of land in Helyar Manor in East Coker, that this manor came into the possession of its then owner about 1616, and that Richard came there from St. Badeaux, Devonshire, about four miles from Plymouth, in that year. (Mention of Richard and numerous descendants forms part of this article).

(II) William, eldest child of John and Marjorie Dodge, settled in Salem, Massachusetts, in 1629. There is a tradition that he was about at his majority at that time, and that he came over on a tour of investigation and that he returned to England for his wife. Her name has not been discovered. It has been erroneously given as Elizabeth Haskell but there are proofs that she was the wife of another William in England. This William Dodge was known as "Farmer" William, and he died between 1685 and 1692. The standing of "Farmer" William in the community is indicated by the fact that he was repeatedly elected or appointed to public offices, such as selectman, grand juryman, trial juryman and on committees in the services of town and church interests, laying out roads, etc. There are also evidences that he was on the best of terms with his pastor, Rev. John Hale, and that he and his sons were sturdy supporters of good morals in every way. In May, 1685, he conveyed his homestead to his son, Captain William, and otherwise disposed of his real estate by deeds. His homestead is on the east side of Cabot street and south of Herrick street, in Salem. His children were: John, William, and probably Joshua. The last named was killed in the Narragansett war, in 1675. (William (2) and descendants receive extended notice in this article).

(III) Captain John, eldest son of "Farmer" William Dodge, was born in 1636, and lived in Beverly, where he owned a mill at the head of Beverly Cove. He served against the Narragansetts in 1675 and probably earned his title in that service, and was chosen representative to the general court in 1693-96 and 1702, and was frequently on the grand and petit juries and on various town and parish committees, and was one of the most useful and prominent men on the colonies. In 1710 he gave thirty-three acres of land in Wenham to his grandson John, the son of John, and otherwise disposed of real estate. He was married (first), April 10, 1659, to Sarah Proctor and (second) to Elizabeth, widow of John Woodberry. She survived him and died January 6, 1726, aged ninety-four years. He died in 1723. His children were: John, William, Sarah, Hannah (died young), Hannah, Martha and Jonathan.

(IV) Jonathan, youngest son of Captain John Dodge, was born between 1675 and 1680, and died in Beverly, about February, 1756. After the death of his older brother, William he took a lease of the lands formerly owned by their father for a term of seven years and ultimately became their owner. He lived on the Salem side of Beverly Cove until about the time of his father's death, when he moved to the Beverly side and there continued the remainder of his life. He was a warm friend of Rev. John Hale, and was a prosperous and influential citizen of the town. He held numerous offices, such as juryman, constable and fence viewer. The inventory of the estate made December 17, 1756, enumerates one hundred and fifty-seven acres of land, and as a total footing 1,822 pounds and five shillings. He was married December 17, 1702, to Elizabeth Goodhue, of Ipswich, who died July 26, following. He married (second) May 15, 1705, Jerusha Rayment. She was a widow and had a daughter Hannah at that time. Their children were: Francis, Peter (died young), George, William, Elizabeth, John, Jonathan and Peter.

(V) John, fifth son and sixth child of Jonathan and Jerusha Dodge, was baptized August 24, 1718, in Salem, and died February 9, 1779. He resided in Beverly, and was probably a farmer. He was married (intention published March 14, 1740) to Hannah Fowler, of Ipswich. He died at Wenham, March 10, 1807, aged eighty-eight years. His will was made one day before his death and was proved on the first of the following month, in which are mentioned his wife, Hannah, three sons, two daughters and a granddaughter, Hannah Masters. The inventory of his estate amounted to 11,435 pounds, 18 shillings. The Beverly records give seven of his children, namely: Ruth, Charles, Jerusha, John, Hannah, Lucy and Jonathan.

(VI) Deacon John (3), second son and fourth child of John (2) and Hannah (Fowler) Dodge, was born May 19, 1747, in Beverly, and resided in Wenham, near Wenham Lake. He died there May 1, 1825, aged seventy-seven years. He is also known by the title of lieutenant. He was married December 1, 1768, to Mehitable Batchelder, of Beverly, who died December 28, 1789-90, aged forty-two years. He was married (second) (published July 2, 1791) to Sarah Raymond, of Beverly. She survived him more than fifteen years and died September 24, 1840, in Chichester, New Hampshire. She was the mother of the last two of his children, the first wife being the mother of ten. They were: John, Lucy, Uzziel, Jerusha, William, Samuel, Mary, Aretas, Havilah, Elezaphan, Mehitable and Sarah.

(VII) Elezaphan, second son and tenth child of Lieutenant John and Mehitable (Batchelder) Dodge, was born December 26, 1789, in Wenham, and died April 4, 1857, in New Boston, New Hampshire, where he settled in 1817. He joined the Congregational church at Wenham, September 30, 1817, and was for a long time deacon of the Presbyterian church in New Boston. He purchased a tract of land in New Boston, which is now occupied by his grandson, on which he made a substantial and permanent home and was a successful farmer. He married (first) a remote relative, Anna Dodge, daughter of Peter and Sarah (Dodge) Dodge, whose ancestry may be carried forward as follows:

(4) Peter, youngest child of Jonathan and Jerusha Dodge, was baptized October 12, 1724, in Beverly, and died September 14, 1796, in Wenham. He lived not far from Wenham Pond and was twice married. His first wife being Sarah, daughter of Mark, who was a son of Edward and grandson of Richard Dodge (II), and (second) Elizabeth Batchelder (a widow), daughter of Benjamin and Christina (Trask) Cressy. They were published December 20, 1761, and were married at Danvers, January 6, 1762. She was baptized September 6, 1736, and died June 21, 1821, in her eighty-fifth year. She was the mother of seven of his nine children, who were baptized in Wenham, namely: Sarah, Peter, Elizabeth, Mary, Martha, Mehitable and Jonathan.

(5) Peter (2), eldest son and second child of Peter (1) and Elizabeth (Cressy) (Batchelder) Dodge, was born November 10, 1764, in Wenham, Massachusetts, and died Frebuary 3, 1844. He married Sally Dodge, who was born December 4, 1778, daughter of Simeon and Abigail (Dodge) Dodge, of Beverly, and died April 4, 1822, aged fifty-two years. They were the parents of two daughters.

(6) Anna, elder daughter of Peter (2) and Sally (Dodge) Dodge, was born June 1, 1796, and married Elezaphan Dodge, as above noted, March 1, 1817. Their only child was Peter, who was killed June 29, 1862, at the battle of Gaines Mills, Virginia. Mr. Dodge married (second) Lavinia Dodge, daughter of Antipas and Jerusha (Dodge) Dodge. She was born March 1, 1797, and died 1891. Her children were: Anna, Elnathan, Uzziel, Willard, Mary Ann, Edwin, Allen, Lendell, Sarah Jerusha and Maria Lavinia.

(VIII) Lendell, sixth son and eighth child of Elezaphan Dodge, and eighth child of his second wife, Lavinia Dodge, was born May 28, 1838, in New Boston, New Hampshire, where his life was passed. He received the common school education of his time and locality, and when a young man was employed for a time at Nashua. On his return to his native town he engaged in farming on a farm of two hundred acres, this being the old homestead and where he still resides, having been in the family now (1907) for over ninety years and where the special subject of this sketch, his son, William O., still resides and where three generations have been born. The farm is devoted chiefly to dairying, and he was also actively interested in lumbering. He is an attendant of the Presbyterian church, and an ardent Republican in political principle. He is respected by his townsmen and active in the support of schools and has served on the school board. He was married December 25, 1871, to Ellen Lamson, daughter of William and Orindia (Odell) Lamson, of Mont Vernon. She was educated in the Academy at Mont Vernon and was a teacher two years. She is a member of the Presbyterian church and both Mr. and Mrs. L. Dodge are members of the New Boston Grange, in which Mr. Dodge has held several of the principal official stations. They were the parents of five children, of whom three died in infancy. The surviving are William O., and Edwin H., resides in Bradford, New Hampshire, a farmer, formerly a member of the firm of Martin & Dodge, of New Boston.

(IX) William Osborne, elder son of Lendell and Ellen (Lamson) Dodge, was born September 26, 1872, in New Boston, and has resided in that town all his life. He attended the district school and the high school of that town, and upon attaining manhood turned his attention to agriculture and is associated with his father in farming. He is extensively engaged in dairying and has a farm of two hundred acres in New Boston and one hundred and sixty in Derry. He is a progressive farmer and endeavors to keep abreast of the times, and is an active member of the local Grange, in which he has filled the principal chairs, having served three times as master. He was six years a trustee of the cemetery and is a member and officer of the Presbyterian church. In politics he supports the principles and policies of the Republican party, and has been selectman three years, two of which he was chairman. He was married November 27, 1895 to Cora Fiske, daughter of Henry Fiske, of New Boston. She was educated in the district and high schools, and has been active in Grange work, filling several of the offices of the Grange, and is also a member of the Daughters of Rebekah. She is also active in the work of the church. They are the parents of one child, Carolyn E., born July 25, 1905.

(III) Captain William (2), second son and child of William (1) Dodge, was born September 19, 1640, and died 1720. He inherited his father's homestead and resided in Beverly, and was a "malster." He was made a freeman in 1683, was deputy in 1689, and representative in 1690. He was in the war against the Narragansetts in 1675, and acquired distinction for courage and skill. In Hubbards' narrative an account is given of his bravery and success. In this expedition Josiah Dodge, who is supposed to have been a brother of Captain William, together with John Balch and Peter Woodbury, were killed at Muddy brook, while fighting under Captain Lathrop. In the historic controversy about the bell of Bass River Church (first church of Beverly) which was captured at Port Royal, in 1654, William Dodge and Thomas Tuck, Senior, with military spirit took the bell and put it to its intended use. Captain Dodge was almost continuously in service upon some town or parish committee, and the records are replete with mention of his services, extending from the period over 1670 to 1708. He was married (first) to Mary Conant, widow of John Balch, who was drowned. He was married (second) May 26, 1685, to widow Johanna Larkin, daughter of Deacon Robert Hale, of Charlestown. She died August 18, 1694, aged forty-seven years, and he married (third) in 1698, Mary Creatty, who died about February 1, 1702. She was the widow of Captain Andrew Creatty, of Marblehead. His first six children were born of Mary Conant, his first wife, and the remainder of the second wife, Johanna (Hale) Dodge. Their names are as follows: William, Mary, Joshua, Hannah, Elizabeth, Sarah, Robert and Rebecca (twins), Josiah and Elisha. Mary Conant was a daughter of Roger Conant (see Conant), who bequeathed to his daughter, the wife of Captain Dodge, £5 and the same sum to each of her five children.

(IV) Robert, third son of Captain William Dodge, and eldest child of his second wife, Johanna (Hale) Dodge, was born October 9, 1686, in Beverly, and died January 1, 1764. He was a prosperous farmer, residing in North Beverly. Three of his sons were coopers, one a cordwainer and another a joiner. At the age of twenty-four years he was chosen surveyor of highways, and subsequently held many other town offices. He was buried with his wife at the old churchyard of the Second Church, where their gravestones are still in a perfect state of preservation. He married Lydia Woodbury, daughter of Isaac and Elizabeth (Herrick) Woodbury, of Chibaco Parish. Their intentions were published June 26, 1709. She died April 6, 1759, in her sixty-eighth year. Their children were: Isaac, Rebecca, Caleb, Lydia, Johanna, Elizabeth, Robert, William (died young), Nicholas and William. (The last named receives further mention in this article).

(V) Nicholas, fifth son and ninth child of Robert and Lydia (Woodbury) Dodge, was born April 16, 1728, in North Beverly, and was a farmer in Boxford, Massachusetts. In December, 1762, he sold the farm in Boxford to William Seers, of that town, which included a fraction over seventeen acres, with the buildings thereon, which had been deeded to him by his father in April of the same year, 1762. In March, 1763, he bought in Boxford forty-four acres and a fraction, with buildings thereon for the sum of £200. In October, 1775, he sold the same with some small pieces in addition for £240 and moved to Londonderry, New Hampshire, where he died between June 10,, 1780, and June 15, 1785, the respective dates of the making and proving of his will. He was dismissed from the Second Church of Beverly, September 2, 1764, and probably joined some other church at that time. His will indicates that he was possessed of a considerable estate in Londonderry. He gave to one of his sons, £12 and a half of his farming tools. To his widow he gave the use of half of all his personal estate and buildings and the use of the land, which was bequeathed to a son and daughter until they became of age. He was married March 3, 1752, to Experience Woodbury, who probably survived him. Their children were: Nicholas, Caleb, Anna, Mary, Ebenezer, Lydia and Isaac.

(VI) Isaac, youngest child of Nicholas and Experience (Woodberry) Dodge, was baptized August 2, 1767, in Boxford. He received by will one half of the house, barn and farming tools of his father in Londonderry, and all of the livestock at the decease or marriage of his mother and a part of the paternal homestead, his sister, Lydia, receiving the remainder of thirty acres. He died in Londonderry, and appointed his wife and friend, Benjamin Woodbury, as sole executors. His wife was Mary

Austin, of Salem, Massachusetts, and their children were: Isaac, Caleb, Samuel, Moody and Benjamin.

(VII) Caleb, second son and child of Isaac and Mary (Austin) Dodge, was born February 2, 1793, in Londonderry, and grew up there in attendance of the district school during his boyhood. He became a carpenter and cabinet maker and was also engaged in farming. He sold his farm in Merrimack and removed to Manchester. He was married in Londonderry to Theresa Garvin, daughter of Moses Garvin. They were members of the Congregational Church. Mr. Dodge was in early life a Democrat in politics, but the issues preceding and arising at the time of the Civil war turned him from that allegiance and he became an enthusiastic Republican. His children were: Mary Jane, Isaac, Eliza Ann, Margaret W., Hazen G. and Charles M. Six besides these died in infancy.

(VIII) Hazen G., second son of Caleb and Theresa (Garvin) Dodge, was born August 24, 1837, in Merrimack, New Hampshire, and was educated in the common schools of that town and the Manchester high school. At the age of nineteen years he quit the schoolroom and engaged in carpenter work with his father and became adept at the trade. At the outbreak of the Civil war he enlisted in September, 1861, in Company I, Seventh New Hampshire Regiment, and was in active service for three years and three months, participating in many important battles. At the close of the war he was employed for three years in the mills at Manchester, and then settled in Merrimack, where he engaged in farming and lumbering. In 1867 or '68 he purchased a farm near Baboosic Pond; he sold this farm in 1886; in 1887 he purchased the farm on which he now resides and is successfully engaged in agriculture. He is a steadfast supporter of the Republican principles and policies. He was married October 10, 1861, to Anna L. Fisher, who was born March 4, 1840, in New London, daughter of Levi and Fanny (Wilkins) Fisher, of that town. Mrs. Dodge is identified with the Congregational church. They have one son, Edwin H. Dodge, who was born December 4, 1867, in Merrimack, and was educated in the district school, Nashua public school and McGaw Institute at Reed's Ferry, and is a machinist by occupation. He married Veda Blake, of Hudson, March 2, 1900, and they have two daughters: Hazel V., born March 13, 1901, and Anna G., born February 27, 1907.

(V) Deacon William (3), sixth son and tenth and youngest child of Robert and Lydia (Woodbury) Dodge, was born at North Beverly, Massachusetts, and was baptized January 2, 1732. He was a joiner and cabinet maker in his native town, and was a deacon of the Second Church there. William (3) Dodge was twice married, and had twelve children in all. His first wife was Mary (Baker) Dodge, to whom he was united November 14, 1752. She died in 1761, leaving four children: William, Simeon, whose sketch follows; Anna and Lydia. On August 1, 1764, he married his second wife, Mary (Trask) Dodge, died April 25, 1812, aged seventy-six years. They had eight children: Edward, Levi, Nabby, Mary or Polly, Joanna, Ezekiel, Pyam and Mercy. Deacon Dodge died June 3, 1810, aged seventy-nine years. He and his second wife are buried in the cemetery adjoining the church at North Beverly.

(VI) Simeon, second son and child of Deacon William (3) Dodge and his first wife, Mary (Baker) Dodge, was born March 26, 1755, in Beverly, Massachusetts. He took part in the fight at Concord and Lexington, and followed the British back to Boston. The pursuit was close, and he saved his life by taking refuge in a cellar. Afterwards he served for three years in the Revolutionary war, beginning February 13, 1777, and continuing till the same date in 1780. He was in Captain Billy Porter's company, Colonel Benjamin Tupper's regiment. Soon after 1781 Simeon Dodge moved to Francestown, New Hampshire, where he lived till his death, nearly fifty years later. On December 31, 1780, he married Mary Balch, of Beverly, Massachusetts, and they had ten children: Simeon, Joshua Balch, Mary, Ruth, Lydia, Sarah, Anna, William, whose sketch follows; Samuel Davis and Baker. Simeon Dodge died at Francestown, New Hampshire, December 25, 1827.

(VII) William (4), third son and seventh child of Simeon and Mary (Balch) Dodge, was born at Francestown, New Hampshire, August 15, 1795. In 1823, in company with his early wedded wife, he moved to Whitefield, this state, where he became the first merchant in town. He built the third house in the village, still standing at the north end of the bridge, and in the south part of this building he opened his store. The next year, 1824, mail facilities were established in the new settlement, and Mr. Dodge was appointed postmaster, which position he held under successive administrations until his death, thirteen years later. In addition to his other activities he carried on the manufacture of pot or pearl ash for many years. Mr. Dodge was a man of liberal education, and he at once became an influential citizen. He was town clerk for seven consecutive years, was superintendent of "schooling," and was representative to the New Hampshire legislature for the years 1834-35-36. All his official life was distinguished by marked ability and strict conduct, and he was an active promoter of the cause of education. William (4) Dodge married Eunice Newell, of Mason, New Hampshire, who was born January 20, 1804. They had seven children. Eunice, born July 15, 1825; Amorensa M., born July 19, 1827, died May 11, 1838; William Franklin, whose sketch follows; Mary Viola, born February 1, 1831, died in infancy; Piam, born October 16, 1832, who died in babyhood; Levi W., born July 21, 1834; and Henry C., born July 30, 1836. Levi W. Dodge married Carrie Webb, and lived in Syracuse, New York, where he was agent of a coal company. He had strong literary tastes and wrote the "History of Whitefield" and other works. Henry C. Dodge married (first) Lizzie Southworth, and (second) Susan Colby Spooner, and was a successful business man in New York City, and a deacon in the Baptist Church. William (4) Dodge died at Whitefield, November 6, 1837, at the early age of forty-two. Had his life been spared he would undoubtedly have become one of the leading men in Coos county. His widow married Joseph Colby, and lived till 1884, dying at the age of eighty years.

(VIII) William Franklin, eldest son and third child of William (4) and Eunice (Newell) Dodge, was born at Whitefield, New Hampshire, November 7, 1829. In early life he was engaged in the starch business in his native town, but in 1861 he bought his present estate, a tract containing one hundred and fifty acres, now containing seventeen hundred acres, fifteen hundred of which is timber land, and the remainder is devoted to farming purposes. Sixty head of horses and cows are kept on the place. The original dwelling was a farm house, but in 1869, attracted by the beauty of the scenery, boarders began to appear. The result is the present Mountain View House, containing one hundred rooms and all the appliances of a first class hotel. It is situated thirteen hundred feet above sea level, and commands magnificent views of the Franconia and Presidential ranges, and of the mountains in Vermont. The surrounding grounds have been fitted up in a manner to enhance their natural beauties, and the place is one of the most attractive in the entire White Mountain region. William F. Dodge is a deacon in the Free Will Baptist Church, and a man who stands high in the community. He belongs to the Blue Lodge Masons. He is a Republican in politics, and served as selectman and town clerk for many years, and as representative in the New Hampshire legislature for two terms. He has often been engaged in the settlement of estates. William F. Dodge married Mary Jane, daughter of William and Rebecca Eastman, whose father was one of the first settlers of Whitefield. They have had three children: A daughter died in infancy; Van Herbert, whose sketch follows; and Charles Eben, born June 1, 1861, who is engaged in the manufacture of typewriter ribbons at Syracuse, New York. He married Ida Bray, of Whitefield, and has two daughters, Beulah and Mary.

(IX) Van Herbert, elder son and second child of William F. and Mary J. (Eastman) Dodge, was born at Whitefield, New Hampshire, March 21, 1859. He was educated in the public schools of his native town, and at New Hampton Institution, this state. He went to Providence, Rhode Island, in 1870, and was cashier in a store for three years. In July, 1873, he returned to Whitefield, which became his permanent home. He is co-proprietor with his father in the Mountain View House, also one of the owners in the Whitefield Farm Company, and is interested with his brother in manufacturing at Syracuse, New York. In the winter he is extensively engaged in lumbering, as the family own a thousand acres, and the business gives employment to the horses which are used for livery at the hotel in the summer. Mr. Dodge is a Republican, but is now too busy to give time to politics, though he served several terms as selectman in his youth, beginning in 1883, and was chairman of the board for three years. In 1897 he was made director of the Whitefield Savings Bank and Trust Company, and was elected president in 1904. He is a member of the Blue Lodge Masons, and attends the Free Will Baptist Church. On May 1, 1888, Van Herbert Dodge married Alice Stebbins, daughter of Schuyler and Joanah (Turner) Stebbins, of Newbury, Vermont. They have one son, Frank Schuyler, born January 5, 1889, who entered Dartmouth College in the fall of 1907.

(II) Richard Dodge, ancestor of a very large progeny scattered throughout the United States, appeared at Salem, Massachusetts, as early as 1638, and "desired accommodations." It is shown by the records of East Coker, in England, that he resided and came from there. As immigrants were admitted to the colonies only by applying to the town and obtaining leave, it is probable that Richard and his family came in 1638, and it is also probable that he left England without royal permission. After living for a while on the land of his brother William, he settled on "Dodge Row" in North Beverly, not far from Wenham Lake. The house which Richard Dodge built was near the present North line of Beverly. He evidently gave his attention chiefly to farming. He was a loyal church member and one of the most liberal contributors to the support of the gospel. He and his wife were members of the Wenham Church before 1648, under the pastorate of John Fiske. He was also interested in the progress of education, and his name appears first in a list of twenty-one subscribers to Howard College in 1653, while the next largest sum was one fourth as much as his. The cemetery of "Dodge Row" is on land which he dedicated for that purpose and this grant was subsequently conferred by his grandson. He died June 15, 1671, leaving an estate valued at one thousand seven hundred and sixty-four pounds and two shillings, a very considerable property for that time. He gave to each of his three sons a good farm valued at over one hundred pounds. He made liberal provision for annual payments by the sons to the support of their mother. His wife's name was Edith and she survived him seven years, dying June 27, 1678, at the age of seventy-five years. The inventory of her estate indicates that she was possessed of considerable property. Their children were: John, Mary, Sarah, Richard, Samuel, Edward and Joseph. (Richard, Samuel and Joseph, and descendants, receive further notice in this article.)

(III) John, eldest child of Richard and Edith Dodge, was baptized December 29, 1631, in England, and died in 1711. He was mentioned in the will of his grandfather, John, who died in 1635, Somersetshire, England. He probably came to Salem with his father, in 1638. He settled in what was then included in Beverly, but but was later annexed to Wenham. He built a saw-mill on Mill river at Wenham Neck, which was not used until about 1822, and received from his father's estate about eighty acres lying about this mill and five acres of meadow on the same side of Longham brook where his house stood near what was then the north line of Beverly. He deeded his homestead to his son, Andrew, May 5, 1708, consisting of forty acres and other lands in the vicinity. Lieutenant John Dodge was a man of more than ordinary standing in the community. He was often elected selectman of the town, and served in almost every public capacity where good sense and integrity were desired and also served as deputy to the general court. There are many evidences that he was a strong advocate of temperance and good morals generally. The town record of Beverly from 1667 to 1702 are replete with reference to the various public services of Lieutenant John Dodge. He served on every sort of committee, to lay out lands and make rates to seat inhabitants in the new meeting house, to prosecute town claims and in various other capacities. His wife Sarah (surname unknown) died February 8, 1706, aged sixty years. Their children were: Deliverance, John, Josiah, Sarah, Ebenezer, Mary, Deborah and Andrew. (Mention of Josiah and Andrew and descendants appears in this article.)

(IV) John (2), eldest son and second child of John (1) and Sarah Dodge, was born April 15, 1662, in Beverly, and died January 18, 1704, in his forty-second year. He lived in Wenham, probably not far from his father. Both his parents and the father of his first wife were witnesses of his will, dated July 7, 1703, and all the signatures are still preserved in the original document in the probate office at Salem. The inventory of his estate amounted to four hundred and fifty-three pounds, with debts at thirteen pounds. His first wife Martha, daughter of Thomas and Martha Fisk, died December 29, 1697, and he was married (second) April 11, 1698, to Ruth Grover, of Beverly. The first wife was the mother of four of his children, and the other of five, namely: Phineas, Amos,

Martha, Elizabeth, Nehemiah, Ruth, Sarah, John and Mary.

(V) Phineas, eldest child of John (2) and Martha (Fiske) Dodge, was born May 23, 1688, in Wenham, and died in that town July 19, 1759, in his seventy-second year. He was a prosperous man and his estate was appraised at six hundred and forty-eight pounds. By the will of his father he was to have that part of the paternal homestead joining upon the town common and Thomas White's land, estimated at thirty-six acres, and was to pay his mother twenty shillings a year while she remained a widow. He married (first) (intention published December 15, 1712), Martha Edwards, who died March 31, 1734, at the age of twenty-nine years. He married (second), September 21, 1736, Sarah Whipple, of Danvers, who died May 27, 1769. She was executrix of his will. His descendants are very numerous. His children were: Phineas, John, Jeremiah, Abner, Solomon, Martha, Amos, Ebenezer, Benjamin, Israel and Stephen.

(VI) Solomon, fifth son and child of Phineas and Martha (Edwards) Dodge, was born June 18, 1721, in Wenham, and died January 16, 1812, in Topsfield. He was living in Andover in 1747, and from about that time until 1754 was an inn holder in Boxford. From that time until his death he lived in Topsfield, and was a much respected citizen. He was chosen deacon December 18, 1776, and declined to serve. He was again chosen June 26, 1781, and was excused in 1797. He was married (first), December 30, 1742, to Hannah Green, who died October 7, 1788, aged seventy-four years. He married (second) (intentions published January 12, 1791) widow Martha Dodge, of Ipswich. She was admitted to the church in Topsfield, in November, 1799, and died August 30, 1804, aged sixty years. His children, all born of the first wife, were: Sarah (died young), Daniel (died young), Solomon, Sarah, Daniel and Hannah.

(VII) Solomon (2), second son and third child of Solomon (1) and Hannah (Green) Dodge, was born August 13, 1747, in Andover, Massachusetts, and died May 4, 1799, in New Boston, New Hampshire. He was a lieutenant of the militia, was a farmer and an energetic and industrious man, and had many excellent qualities. He was married at Topsfield, January 23, 1772, to Sarah Dodge, daughter of Amos and Hannah (Green) Dodge, of Beverly. She was born August 20, 1752, and died in New Boston, December 23, 1845. She was at that time the wife of Jacob Hooper, of New Boston. In January, 1778, Solomon and his wife deeded a piece of land in Long Hill Parish, in Beverly, to Jacob Edwards, of Boxford, and this probably indicates the time of their removal to New Boston. His children were: Amos, Solomon (died young), Solomon, Hannah, Daniel (died young), Daniel, Sally, Alice, Phineas and Aaron.

(VIII) Solomon (3), third son and child of Solomon (2) and Sarah (Dodge) Dodge, was born August 1, 1774, in New Boston, and died there March 16, 1853, in his seventy-sixth year. He was deacon of the church and a genial and broad-minded man, commanding the confidence and esteem of the community. He remained on the homestead of his father, where his buildings were burned October 21, 1829, and these were rebuilt with the assistance of his kindly neighbors. He was married, May 25, 1805, to Elizabeth, daughter of Benjamin Dodge. She was born January 13, 1783, and died December 6, 1840. Their children were: Lydia, Solomon, Sarah, Hannah (died young), Amos, Hannah, Benjamin, Israel and Anne.

(IX) Solomon (4), eldest son and second child of Solomon (3) and Elizabeth (Dodge) Dodge, was born February 27, 1808, and died March 11, 1881, in New Boston, in his seventy-fourth year. He was a farmer by occupation and attended the Baptist Church. He was prominent in town affairs, and in early life was a Democrat. He was among those who early came to the support of the Republican party because of the espousal of the cause of human freedom. He married Mary, widow of Charles Buston. She was born February 20, 1803, and died 1868. Their children were: Margaret E., deceased; Solomon, resides in Andover; Charles Franklin, William Batchelder, in Washington, D. C.; Julian Percival, died in war of Rebellion; Edwin Buxton, resides at Wilmot, New Hampshire; Albert Ernest, deceased.

(X) Charles Franklin, second son and third child of Solomon (4) and Mary Dodge, was born in New Boston, July 2, 1838, and was educated in high school and Colby Academy at New London, New Hampshire. He was engaged in lumbering and farming with his father until the death of the latter, and is now occupied in dairying and general farming, having one of the finest farms in his town, and he has taken a number of premiums at different fairs. His farm is admired by all lovers of fine farms, being composed of rich hills and beautiful fertile valleys. From the top of the hills rising in the rear of his house a magnificent view can be had of the surrounding country for twenty-five miles in all directions. Mr. Dodge is a Republican in politics. He served three years on the school board and two years as selectman. He married, December 26, 1878, Emma J. Wallace, daughter of John M. and Abbie (Bartlett) Wallace, of New Boston. She was a high school student and taught school several terms; she attended the Baptist Church. They are the parents of five children: Jessie E., a graduate of the Normal School, a teacher in a school in Providence, Rhode Island. Winifred, a graduate of the Normal School, was a teacher in the schools of Melrose. Mary A., attended art school in Boston, and has been a teacher of drawing, now (1907) assistant in drawing in the schools of Gardner. Grace W., attended the Boston Conservatory of Music, and is now teaching school. Julian R., who died in infancy.

(IV) Josiah, second son and third child of John and Sarah Dodge, was born June 4, 1665, and died January 19, 1715, in his fiftieth year. His gravestone is now shown in the cemetery at "Dodge's Row." He lived on a small farm on Longham brook, in Wenham, and operated a tannery and had an interest in a saw and grist mill. In the date of purchase of the estate of Robert Caflin, which he acquired in 1695, 1698 and 1701, he was termed a tanner. In October, 1713, he sold to William Dodge, of Wenham, one third of the cornmill, one third part of the materials and irons of the old saw mill with all parts and contents of the building to the same and one third part of the dam privilege of the same on Longham brook. In 1709 he was one of the selectmen of Wenham, and probably held other offices. He was married, December 18, 1690, to Lydia Fisk, and married (second), Sarah Fisk, who died March 17, 1730, in her sixtieth year. The division of the estate indicates that it exceeded £367. in value. His children were: Sarah, Johanna, Josiah, Thomas, Rebecca, Mary, Anna, Jemima, John, Abigail (died young) and Abigail. (Thomas and descendants receive further mention in this article).

(V) Josiah (2), eldest son and third child of Josiah (1) Dodge, was born August 16, 1698, in

J. W. Dodge

Wenham, and was a tanner and farmer, living in that town until 1743. That he was a large land-holder is shown by the records of deeds in Essex and Worcester counties. In January, 1743, he and his wife sold for £45 ten acres of marsh in Ipswich. Six days later they sold for £792 twenty-four acres, with a house in that town. He had previously sold for £250 twenty-five acres with house and barn in Ipswich and Wenham, and for £352 fifty-two acres in three pieces in the same town. On the twenty-seventh of the same month he bought for £380 sixty acres of land in Lunenburg, and on the first of April following he paid for two hundred and sixteen acres with two houses and two barns in that town the sum of £2,600 old tenor. In January following he bought thirty-eight acres more, for which he paid £75, and in this conveyance he is styled gentleman, residing in Lunenburg. In March, 1756, he bought for £87 sixty acres with a mansion house, barn and appurtenances, which he sold a year later for £125. In April, 1748, he sold forty-four acres with buildings in Lunenburg for £600 old tenor. In November, 1749, he sold to his son Josiah for £200 (inflated paper currency) ten acres, a part of the sixty acres which he bought in March, 1746. Other papers on record indicate that he owned a tract on which his house stood with two barns, a saw saw mill, grist mill, tan yard, tan house, cidermill, corn house and the frame of a new house. Between 1760 and 1768 he made various deeds to his sons and numerous conveyances appear upon the records, many of them being to his children. He was married January 27, 1718, to Prudence, daughter of William and Prudence (Fairfield) Dodge, of Wenham. A quit claim deed made March, 1772, does not contain her name from which it would appear that she was not then living. His children were: Josiah, Reuben, Eli, Tabitha, Zebulon, Sarah, William, Seth, Prudence and Thomas. (Eli and descendants are noticed in this article).

(VI) Reuben, second son and child of Josiah (2) and Prudence (Dodge) Dodge, was born in Wenham, January 21, 1721, and died in Lunenburg, June 15, 1762. He probably moved to Lunenburg about 1743, where he resided the remainder of his life. The inventory of his estate was filed November 29, 1762, and his father Josiah was appointed administrator. The estate was reported May 9, 1763, insolvent. In March, 1768, Josiah Dodge and his wife Prudence for one hundred and twenty-five pounds six shillings, four pence, deeded thirty acres of land in Lunenburg to Jesse, Brewer, Levi, Tabitha, Zadok, John P. and Ruth Dodge, all minors except Jesse. Reuben Dodge married, March 9, 1742, Ruth Perkins. Their children were: Reuben, Jesse, Mary, Tabitha (died young), Brewer, Levi, Tabitha, Zadok, Esther, John Perkins and Ruth.

(VII) Levi, sixth child and fourth son of Reuben and Ruth (Perkins) Dodge, was born in Lunenburg, November 21, 1751, and was a patriot soldier in the Revolution, serving as a private in Captain Josiah Stearn's company, Colonel Ephraim Doolittle's regiment, as shown by records dated Cambridge, July 10, 1775, and Winter Hill, October 6, 1775. He married Keziah Stanley.

(VIII) Maria, daughter of Levi and Keziah (Stanley) Dodge, was born in Lunenburg, Massachusetts, and married Hiram Hardy. (See Hardy).

(VI) Eli, third son and child of Josiah (2) and Prudence (Dodge) Dodge, was born January 2, 1723, in Wenham, and probably moved to Lunenburg the same time as his father. In July, 1767, he deeded thirty acres of land in that town to his father and perhaps moved away. He was married (intention published July 25, 1741), in Wenham, to Abigail Gillings, of that town, and their children, all born in Lunenburg, were: Eli, Rebecca, Isaac, Abigail and Prudence.

(VII) Isaac, second son and third child of Eli and Abigail (Gillings) Dodge, was born March 17, 1748, in Lunenburg, and lived in that town and Groton, Massachusetts, and died in the latter town in March, 1807. He married Elizabeth Blood, and their children were: James, Asahel, Maria, Nancy, Lavina, Lucy.

(VIII) James, eldest child of Isaac and Elizabeth (Blood) Dodge, was born February 21, 1795, in Lunenburg, and lived in Keene, New Hampshire. About 1850 he was employed in the cooperage at Keene, where he remained four or five years, and was subsequently a carpenter up to the time when he retired from active life, and died August 28, 1872, in Keene, in his seventy-eighth year. He was married, March 14, 1827, to Randilla Bundy, who was born July 22, 1802, in Westminster, Vermont, and survived her husband nearly twenty years, dying December 30, 1891, in Keene. Her children were: Evaline, Lucy A., Edwin, Charles, Harriet, Frederick, James W. and Herbert.

(IX) James William, fourth son and seventh child of James and Randilla (Bundy) Dodge, was born April 13, 1845, in Keene, and was educated in the common and high schools of that town. At an early age he was employed as clerk by the Cheshire Railroad Company and so continued from 1860 to 1873, at which time he was appointed general freight agent of the road. After holding this position for seventeen years this was consolidated with the Fitchburg railroad and he was appointed division superintendent, in which position he continued about one year and a half and then resigned. He was soon invited to become assistant general freight agent of the Fitchburg railroad with headquarters at Boston, which he accepted and held a little less than two years. On account of ill health he was compelled to resign this position and has been on the retired list since that time. He has taken an active part in the management of public affairs in Keene, and was a member of the city council during the first year of its existence as an incorporated city. He is an attendant of the Unitarian Church. Mr. Dodge served as trustee of the Guarantee Savings Bank, and Cheshire Provident Institution. He was one of the initial subscribers to the Electric Light Company, and subsequently was an active factor in causing the merging of that institution with the local Gas Company and was one of the original directors of the Keene Gas & Electric Light Company. He was married April 25, 1865, to Ella E. Perley, who was born May 20, 1848, in Gardner, Massachusetts. She is a daughter of Asa P. Perley, who was born June 4, 1824, in Templeton, Massachusetts, a son of Asa Perley, who was born October 4, 1797, in Gardner, Massachusetts, and died September 3, 1867, in Baldwinville, Massachusetts. Mr. Dodge's mother was Lucy Ann Austin, and was born March 4, 1826, in Surrey, New Hampshire. Mr. and Mrs. Dodge had two children, Cora Ella, born, in Keene, June 13, 1867, died September 11, 1867; and Walter Fred, born in Keene, July 28, 1869, died October 15, 1869.

(V) Thomas, second son and fourth child of Josiah and Lydia or Sarah (Fisk) Dodge, was born November 30, 1700, in Wenham, Massachusetts, and died September 18, 1736, in that town. He was probably a farmer. His estate was valued at £2,005 and 13 shillings. He was married (intention published March 21, 1724), June 23, 1724, to Sarah Porter, of Wenham. She was born January 6,

1706, and died 1795, aged eighty-nine years. Her father, John Porter, was born 1668, and died March 8, 1753. He mother, Lydia Herrick, was born 1663, and died February 12, 1738. Thomas Dodge's wife survived him and was granted administration of his estate, November 15, 1736. Ten years later she was appointed guardian of Israel and Benjamin Dodge, minors, and of Thomas Brown, Junior, and of all the children of Thomas Dodge. Her children were: John, Lydia, Benjamin, Israel (died young), Sarah and Israel.

(VI) Israel, youngest child of Thomas and Sarah (Porter) Dodge, was baptized April 14, 1736, and lived in Wenham. He was a soldier of the Revolution. He was married in Wenham, March 27, 1758, to Abigail (Elliott) Larcum, and their children were: Israel, Lydia, Francis, Ichabod and probably others whose births are not recorded in Wenham.

(VII) Ichabod, third son and fourth child of Israel and Abigail (Elliott) (Larcum) Dodge, was born 1770, and baptized March 31, 1771, in Wenham. He removed to Claremont, New Hampshire, where he died October 31, 1822. He was married in Wenham, May 23, 1774, to Mehitable Swett, who was born May 25, 1765, in that town, daughter of Josiah and Prudence (Dodge) Swett, of Wenham, later of Claremont, before 1797.

(VIII) Isaac, son of Ichabod and Mehitable (Swett) Dodge, was born June 13, 1797, in Claremont, and lived in that town where he was a farmer. About 1850 he removed to Chester, Vermont, and one of his sons is now living in that state. He was married, December 25, 1822, in Claremont, to Eliza Long, who died July 19, 1830.

(IX) Abraham, son of Isaac and Eliza (Long) Dodge, was born February 18, 1834, in Claremont, New Hampshire, and removed, before attaining his majority, with his father to Chester, Vermont, where he still resides. He has been a lumberman and farmer and is now probably retired in Chester. He was married, March 10, 1857, to Augusta B. Sargent, who was born August 6, 1831, daughter of Edward Dodge and Johanna Atwood Sargent. Their children are: Edward Sargent, Frank O. and Caroline Augusta.

(X) Frank Oak, second son and child of Abraham and Augusta B. (Sargent) Dodge, was born October 15, 1860, in Chester, Vermont, and was educated in the common schools of that town. He worked upon his father's farm until he was nineteen years of age, and then began learning the blacksmith trade with E. A. Hall, of Chester, where he continued about two years. In 1882 he removed to East Swanzey, New Hampshire, and opened a blacksmith shop which he continued to operate about four years, at the end of which period the shop was burned. Removing to Keene he worked a short time for George Russell, and then returned to West Swanzey, and in company with A. H. Freeman opened a shop which they continued to operate a short time. At the end of a year and a half Mr. Dodge bought the interest of his partner and has continued to the present time in the successful operation of a general blacksmith business. He is a member of the Independent Order of Odd Fellows, and takes an intelligent interest in the progress of events about him. For the past eighteen years he has served as constable of the town of Swanzey. He was married (first), to Alma J. Ballou. He married (second), April 14, 1901, Mary R. Stebbins, who was born April 17, 1883, in Keene, New Hampshire. His children, born of the first wife, are Guy F. and Ralph.

(IV) Andrew, eighth child and fourth son of Lieutenant John and Sarah Dodge, was born in Wenham, in 1676, and died February 17, 1748, in the seventy-second year of his age, and was buried in the cemetery at Dodge's Row. He was a carpenter and lived at North Beverly. In 1708 he received from his father a deed of about fifty acres of his homestead. He held some town offices, and in 1713 was appointed on the building committee for constructing the new meeting house at North Beverly for the Second Church there about to be organized. His will was made November 2, 1747, and by it he disposed of over one thousand pounds in money. He had previously given his sons parcels of land. He married (first), May 26, 1686, Hannah Fisk, of Wenham, who died December 2, 1703, in her thirtieth year. He married, in 1704, Sarah, daughter of Daniel and Sarah (Porter) Andrews or Andrus. She died June 6, 1734, in the sixtieth year of her age. He married (third), June 14, 1736, Ellinor Edwards, of Wenham. His children by the first wife were: Hannah and Andrew; by the second wife, Daniel, Thomas, Sarah, Bartholomew, Hannah and Amos. (The last named is the subject of a later paragraph in this article).

(V) Andrew (2), second son of Andrew (1) and Hannah (Fisk) Dodge, was born in North Beverly, Massachusetts, November 26, 1703; married, January 27, 1725, Lydia Bridgman, of Windham, Connecticut, and settled in that town. His will was proved June 23, 1741. He enlisted in the ill-fated expedition of Admiral Richard Vernon against the Spanish possessions of South America, and was killed at Cartagena, in March, 1741. He received a gift of a farm at Windham from his father by deed dated May 13, 1725. Children: Andrew, born February, 1726, died young; Hannah, April 12, 1728; Irena, March 29, 1729; Lydia, May 23, 173—; Andrew, born April 4, 1732, died young; Rufus, March 22, 1734; Andrew, February 21, 1735, died young; Abel, February 9, 1736; Sarah, March 10, 1737; Andrew, February 14, 1738-39; Isaac, February 25, 1739-40, mentioned below.

(VI) Isaac, son of Andrew Dodge, was born in Windham, Connecticut, February 25, 1739-40; married, October 20, 1762, Sarah Utley, born October 25, 1746, daughter of Hon. Jeremiah Utley. From his birth until the close of the Revolutionary war he lived in Windham. He was sergeant in the Windham Company on the Lexington alarm, April, 1775, in Colonel Israel Putnam's regiment. He sold out his property at Windham after the war and removed to Lempster, New Hampshire, then a wilderness, and cleared a farm for himself. He died there October 20, 1806. Children, all born at Windham: Abel, emigrated to New York state. Daniel, born July 28, 1767, mentioned below; Isaac, born 1770; Trephenia, married Leonard Dow; Daughter married ——— Rogers; Daughter married ——— Burnham; Eunice, married ——— Cooper.

(VII) Daniel, son of Isaac Dodge, was born in Windham, Connecticut, July 28, 1767, died August 29, 1837, in Hanover, New Hampshire. He married, December 31, 1793, Nabby Wright, of Hanover; (second), February 20, 1798, Sally Wright, who died June 20, 1797. He left Lempster, New Hampshire, and settled on a farm at Hanover, about 1785, where under many difficulties he brought up a family of ten children, meeting the struggles of life, we are told, with great fortitude and courage. Children, born at Hanover: 1. Omri, born January 10, 1795, died December 27, 1826, at Hancock, Vermont; married Lydia Darling; was an able and successful physician. 2. Daniel, born July 3, 1796, married Judith Gates; was a physician at West Chazy, New York.

where he died June 12, 1864. 3. Nabby, born March 19, 1799, died October 1, 1726. 4. Harvey Bingham, born August 10, 1801, married Eliza A. Beckwith; graduate of Colby University in 1827; pastor of Baptist Church in West Plattsburgh, New York; was missionary in the counties of Clinton, Essex and St. Lawrence, New York, in 1831-32; was pastor at Farmersville, New York, in 1833; at Greene, New York, 1834-36; in 1836 became pastor of a new church at Fort Covington, New York; pastor at Parma, New York, in October, 1839, and at Newton Falls, Ohio, in 1841; removed to Garrettsville, Ohio, in 1842, and accepted a call to return to his first church in Plattsburgh in 1844; died at Schuyler's Falls, November 11, 1866; married, January 13, 1830, Ann Eliza Beckwith, a descendant of Roger Williams. 5. Alfred, born September 24, 1803, died October 23, 1880. 6. Sally, born December 6, 1805, married, July, 1839, Laban Chandler; died at Enfield, New Hampshire, March 1, 1893; "In a marked degree she possessed weight of character, and exerted a decided influence in the home, the church, and the community; at the same time she was of so mild a type, as to win a general esteem and love." 7. Cyrus, born September 13, 1807, died June 4, 1854. 8. Uminos, born August 7, 1809, died August 6, 1858. 9. Isaac, born March 1, 1812, died in Hamilton College, April 14, 1835. 10. John Wright, born September 4, 1815, mentioned below.

(VIII) John Wright, son of Daniel Dodge, was born in Hanover, New Hampshire, September 4, 1815. He was educated in the district schools of his native town, and lived until 1847 on the old homestead. Then he became a clerk in a Hanover store, and subsequently engaged in trade on his own account for fifteen years. He then began to manufacture flannels in Enfield, New Hampshire, and in 1883 became one of the owners of a factory at Bristol, New Hampshire, and this concern became in 1887 the property of a corporation under the name of Dodge-Davis Manufacturing Company with a capital of $150,000, and the manufacture of flannels was continued with great success. A few years before his death, Mr. Dodge retired from active labor and spent his last years at his attractive home in Enfield. He died there February 13, 1897. He was essentially a self-made man of the best type. He began life with no capital and some inherited obligations to discharge, and built up one of the best woolen mills in New England, acquiring a fortune and conferring great benefits upon the community in which he lived and conducted business. He was a thoroughly public spirited citizen and was held in high esteem by his fellow-citizens in town and state. Though a Democrat in politics he was often honored by the Republican district in which he lived by election to the state legislature. He has used his means freely in objects of public benefaction, and at the same time was generous with his less fortunate relatives. Gave $5,000 for a free bed to the town of Hanover, in the Mary Hitchcock Hospital. He was kindly, modest and sympathetic in disposition, but characterized by great force and energy, far-sighted sagacity in business, integrity and honest of purpose. Above the average in stature and weight, he had a striking physique.

He married, July 1, 1855, Clementine Chandler Whipple, widow, who was born November 12, 1818, and died March 6, 1893, daughter of Henry H. Chandler. Children: 1. Son, born January 21, 1857, died October 12, 1857. 2. Fannie L., born April 30, 1859, married, January 13, 1886, Rev. Walter Dole, a Universalist clergyman, a native of Northfield, Vermont. Children: John Walter Dole, born at Enfield; Mary Clementine Dole, born at Enfield; Robert H., born at Revere, Massachusetts.

Rev. Walter Dole, D. D., husband of Fannie Louise Dodge, was born in Northfield, Vermont, August 26, 1851. He graduated at Norwich University in 1870, and from Meadville Theological School in 1874, then took a course in The Boston School of Oratory. He has had a pastorate of three years in Bethel, Vermont, including Gaysville and Stockbridge, three years in Barre, Vermont, ten years in Northfield Vermont, and nine years in Enfield, New Hampshire. The basis on which he stands and works is thus stated: "I believe in the One Holy Church Universal, whereby the Children of Men are to realize their oneness with God, the fulness of divine Manhood, and the Spirit of Eternal Brotherhood, by making the Christ the controlling type of life."

(IV) Amos, eighth child and fifth son of Andrew and Sarah (Andrews or Andrus) Dodge, was born in North Beverly, August 20, 1717, and died February 27, 1755. He resided in Beverly and was buried in Dodge Row. He married, October 9, 1751, Hannah Green, of Salem. She was appointed after his death administratrix if his estate, which was valued at eight hundred and forty pounds, ten pence. She married (second), May 30, 1765, Matthew Wyman, of Woburn, a blacksmith, and lived in Beverly in 1767. Two children were born to Amos and Hannah: Sarah, and Amos, whose sketch follows next.

(V) Amos (2), only son of Amos (1) and Hannah (Green) Dodge, was born in Beverly, July 11 or 21, 1754, was baptized July 20, 1755, and died May 9, 1792. He was a carpenter in 1776, when he sold his share of his father's estate in Beverly. In the same year he receipted to Matthew Eymar for twenty-five pounds, ten shillings, the balance due from his mother as guardian on account of the estate of his father. He appears to have lived in Wenham after his marriage. He married (first), October 29, 1775, Hepzibah Dodge, who died June 19, 1777, in her twenty-first year. He married (second), May 15, 1778, Lydia Batchelder, of Wenham, who was born April 9, 1756, and died August 23, 1836, aged eighty years. By the first wife there was one child, Stephen; by the second wife: Zadok, Hepzibah, Amos (died young), Hannah, Lydia, Sally and Stephen.

(VI) Zadok, eldest son of Amos (2) and Lydia (Batchelder) Dodge, was born March 31, 1780, and died June 9, 1860. Zadok and his father, Amos Dodge, went to Antrim, New Hampshire, in 1814, to purchase farms. Zadok bought the place next west of South Village, begun by James Dinsmore in 1779. He settled on this place in the spring of 1815. He married May 1, 1806, Lydia Hadley, of Andover, Massachusetts, who died August 8, 1820, aged fifty-two. He married (second), Sally Lowe, of Greenfield, who died November 10, 1867, aged seventy-six. He had two children by the first wife, Hepzibah and Alvah, whose sketch follows.

(VII) Alvah, only son of Zadok and Lydia (Hadley) Dodge, was born in Wenham, Massachusetts, February 8, 1811, and died in Antrim. He was a carpenter by trade and lived on the old homestead till 1850, when he moved to the South Village of Antrim. He married, in 1836, Lydia Elliott, who died in 1852, aged thirty-five. He married (second), September 20, 1855, Alice W. Carr, of Antrim. The children of the first wife were: Jennie M., Anna S., Hattie M., Charles H., Hiram D. and Fostina M., and by the second one child, Katie A.

(VIII) Fostina M., sixth child of Alvah and Lydia (Elliott) Dodge, was born in Antrim, November 17, 1851, and married November 5, 1873, Henry H. Barber (see Barber).

(IV) William, youngest child of Richard (2) and Mary (Eaton) Dodge, was born 1678, in Wenham, where he died October 20, 1765, aged eighty-seven years. He spent a long and prosperous life in that and acquired a large amount of land, which he distributed among his sons. In 1703 he received from his father a homestead and land near the north line of Wenham. In January, 1723, he received a deed of six acres from his father-in-law. In 1752 he distributed his lands to four sons, the fifth, Isaac, having been provided for, and removed from the town some years previously. He married Prudence, daughter of Walter Fairfield, Senior, in 1699. She died August 5, 1737, and he subsequently married Mrs. Abigail Giddings, of Hamlet Parish. In the record of his death he is called Lieutenant Dodge. His children were: Prudence (died young), Prudence, Richard, William, Isaac, Tabitha, Jacob, Abraham, Skipper and Sarah.

(V) Richard (3), eldest son and third child of William and Prudence (Fairfield) Dodge, was born September 8, 1703, in Wenham, and died there May 11, 1778, in his seventy-fifth year. He was a surveyor as well as a farmer, and was a prominent figure in the community. Numerous deeds on record show that he was an extensive purchaser of lands and that he also sold some. He probably lived until 1750 on a tract of sixty acres of land, which he purchased with the buildings of Joseph Edwards, in 1740. At the time that he sold this, 1750, he bought of John Lowe the homestead, which had formerly been the home of Daniel, father of David Dodge, and the homestead of his grandfather. Richard, inherited by him from Richard (1), the immigrant. In May, 1752, Richard (3) received by deed from his father a homestead and some small pieces of land and three-fourths of his father's interest in the stream and mills of Wenham. This was on the Longham side and on lands which had been continuously held by the Dodges from the earliest period. At the time of receiving this deed his father was seventy-four years of age, and it is probable that Richard (3) then took possession of and operated the farm. He subsequently gave and sold to his brothers and sons extensive tracts of land. Among these was a gift of twenty acres to his brothers, Jacob and Skipper. His will was made April 20, 1778, and proved on the sixth of the following July. His inventory amounted to £5,716 and 18 shillings. The currency in which this was reckoned was at that time very much depreciated and this was an abundant fortune for those days. In 1724 he married Mary, daughter of Deacon John Thorne, of Ipswich, who probably survived him as she is mentioned in his will. Their children were: Abraham, Tabitha, Richard, (died young, Mary (died young), Mercy, Prudence, Richard, John, Mary, Sarah, Simon or Simeon and Nicholas.

(VI) Simon or Simeon, fifth son and eleventh child of Richard (3) and Mary (Thorne) Dodge, was born January 14, 1740, in Wenham, and died in that town June 25, 1815. It is said of him: "As a husband he was kind, as a father, he was most tender and as a Christian he was one of the most pious of his day. He was happy in his sickness. He died in his chair." He had made his will three years before his death, and the inventory of his estate after his death shows its value to be three thousand dollars. He was married November 16, 1769, to Abigail Dodge, of Beverly. Their children were: Obadiah (died young), Mary, Edward, Polly, Sally, Obadiah, Deacon Richard, Benjamin and Stillman.

(VII) Stillman, youngest child of Simon or Simeon and Abigail (Dodge) Dodge, was born December 7, 1792, and resided in Wenham during the early part of his life. He was a cabinetmaker by occupation, and came to his death, March 3, 1831, by an accident while assisting in the construction of a bridge. He married Sally Highlands, and they were the parents of five children, namely: Sarah, Simon Barnet, Marion, James Stillman and Francis Green Macumber.

(VIII) James Stillman, son of Stillman and Sally (Highlands) Dodge, was born June 15, 1825, went to Blackwater when a small boy and there attended the district school until about nine years of age. At this time he began to work on a farm and was practically self-supporting thereafter. About 1840 he went to Lowell, Massachusetts, where he was employed by the McFarland Brothers, dealers in ice, and continued twelve years with them. In 1852 he went to California and engaged in teaming, hauling goods into the mountains for the mines in mule teams. He stayed there two years and then returned to New Hampshire and settled in Webster, where he built a sawmill and operated it fourteen years. At the end of this time he removed to Norwich, Vermont, where he purchased a grist mill and this was destroyed by fire after he had operated it two years. He then purchased a grist mill at Lebanon, New Hampshire, which he operated two years and sold to go from there to Chelmsford, Massachusetts, where he was employed for five years as manager of grist mill. He next removed to Sheldon, Vermont, where he engaged in the lumber and grain business until his death, May 31, 1895. He was married, October 4, 1846, to Huldah M. Brooks, of Lowell, Massachusetts, daughter of Amos Dodge and Hannah (Kemp) Brooks, and they became the parents of the following children: Elizabeth, who became the wife of George L. Thompson, and died 1891; Henry Stillman, who died 1863; Frank Everett, mentioned at length below, and Charles Arthur, who died in his fourth year.

(IX) Frank Everett, second son and third child of James Stillman and Huldah M. (Brooks) Dodge, was born March 21, 1856, in Lowell, Massachusetts, and attended the public school there and Phillips Academy of Haverhill, Massachusetts. After leaving school he was employed three years as a bookkeeper by Henry Du Bois and son in New York City, from 1872 to 1875. He then removed to Minneapolis Minnesota, and was employed by a lumber firm for eight years, after which he returned to New Hampshire and was associated with his father in business until the latter's death. In 1900 he went to Contoocook, New Hampshire, where he has since been engaged in the operation of a saw mill. Mr. Dodge is an intelligent gentleman, who takes a keen interest in the progress of events and has been chosen by his fellows to some responsible positions. While residing in Sheldon, Vermont, he was three years a member of the school board and was also representative in the state legislature in 1898. He is now serving a second term on the school board in Contoocook. He is a member of the Masonic Order and is affiliated in politics with the Democratic party. He was married December 22, 1889, to Blanche Morse, daughter of John Morse. She died in May, 1892, leaving a daughter, Bessie M., who was born October 25, 1890. He was married (second) November 7, 1894, to Annie McFeeters, daughter of William and Ann (Todd) McFeeters. She is the mother of three children, born as follows: James William, January 31, 1897; Charles Franklin, October 18, 1899, and Catherine Elizabeth, September 26, 1901.

(III) Richard (2), second son and fourth child of Richard (1) and Edith Dodge, was born in Beverly, Massachusetts, in 1643, and died in Wenham April 13, 1705. He was a farmer and lived in the south part of Wenham. He also owned a large farm in Ipswich, which he gave to his eldest son Richard, and had land near Chibocco Lake in Ipswich. He owned a cider mill and press, and from the careful provision for its use, which he made in deeds to his sons, it would seem that they all lived in the same vicinity. About two years before his death he divided his property among his children, giving his "negro man" Mingo, to the eldest son. On the 31st of May, 1705, Richard, Daniel, William and Mary joined in a deed of four and one-half acres of marsh land in "Chibocco," Ipswich, to John and Martha Davidson to carry out what they alleged to be the purpose of their father. He married, February 23, 1667, Mary Eaton, born 1641, and died November 28, 1716, aged 75 years. He and his wife were buried at North Beverly, where their grave-stones still remain. Their children were: Richard, Mary, Martha, Daniel and William.

(IV) William, third son and fifth child of Richard and Mary (Eaton) Dodge, was born 1678 in Wenham, where he died October 20, 1765, aged eighty-seven. In the record of his death he is called Lieutenant William Dodge. He acquired a large amount of land, which he distributed among his sons. In 1703 he received from his father a deed of homestead and land near the north line of Wenham. In 1722 he received a deed of six acres from his father-in-law, Walter Fairfield, Senior, which had been conveyed to his sons, Walter Fairfield, Junior, and Nathaniel, on condition that they should supply his wants. In 1752 he distributed his land to four of his sons, the fifth, Isaac, having been provided for, and moved to Boxford and thence to Sutton some years before. He married, 1669, Prudence, daughter of Walter Fairfield. She died August 5, 1737. He married (second), Mrs. Abigail Giddings, of Hamlet parish. His children were: Prudence (died young), Prudence, Richard, William, Isaac, Tabitha, Jacob, Abraham, Skipper and Sarah.

(V) Richard (3), third child and eldest son of William and Prudence (Fairfield) Dodge, was born September 8, 1703, in Wenham, and died there May 11, 1778. Richard was a surveyor as well as a farmer, and was a conspicuous figure in the community. Some twenty-five deeds of land to him are on record, and a less number from him. In 1740 he bought of Joseph Edwards about sixty acres of land with buildings, where he probably lived until March, 1750, when he sold that place to Benjamin Edwards and his son Benjamin. At the same time he bought of John Low, the homestead which he had recently bought of David Dodge, the inheritance from his father, Daniel Dodge, and had been the homestead of his grandfather, Richard, inherited by him from his great-grandfather, Richard, the emigrant. In May, 1752, he received from his father, for love and affection, a deed of homestead including some small pieces, and three-fourths of his father's interest in stream and mills in Wenham. This is supposed to be the same mill described in a deed dated October 16, 1713, from Josiah Dodge and his wife, Sarah, to William Dodge, husbandman of Wenham, and father of Richard. His father William being seventy-four years old when he surrendered his homestead to his son, Richard, he probably took possession and carried on the farm. In December, 1768, he gave his son, Captain John, a forty-acre farm, and on January 2, 1769, he sold to him for two hundred pounds several pieces of land in Chebacco, and on the same date to his son, Richard, Junior, for one hundred and sixty pounds, several other pieces. In 1766 Richard and his prosperous brother, William, of Ipswich, thinking their brothers Jacob and Skipper had not been so well dealt with as their father intended, gave them a twenty-acre piece in Ipswich, which their father had received from his father Richard, in 1703. In 1775 Richard and his wife, Mary, deeded to Jacob Dodge for two hundred pounds their lands in Gloucester, some thirty-five acres, and a share of a house.

His will was dated April 20, 1778, and proved July 6, 1778. It mentions his wife Mary, sons Richard, John, Simon and Nicholas, daughters Mary Orne and Sarah Hubbard Dodge, and his brothers Jacob and Skipper. His inventory amounted to five thousand seven hundred and sixteen pounds, eighteen shillings. He married, in 1724, Mary, daughter of Deacon John Thorne, of Ipswich; she was living in 1775. Their children were: Abraham, Richard (died young), Mary (died young), Mercy, Prudence, Richard, John, Mary, Sarah, Simon and Nicholas.

(VI) Captain Richard (4), third son and seventh child of Lieutenant Richard (3) and Mary (Thorne) Dodge, was born December 9, 1738, in Wenham, and died June, 1802. He was a farmer in Wenham. He was a captain in Colonel Samuel Gerrish's regiment in 1775. Of his company Robert Dodge was first lieutenant and Paul Dodge second lieutenant. He was also captain of a company of volunteers from third regiment of militia from Essex county, raised under resolve September 22, 1777, and served from September 30, to November 7, 1777, when they were discharged at Cambridge. In the will of his father, dated April 20, 1778, the son is styled major. His own will, dated March 8, 1801, and proved June 7, 1802, mentions his wife Lydia, daughter Polly Patch, Sally Baley, Mary Lee, Lucy Stadley, son John Thorne's daughter, Bulcey Taylor. Son John Thorne Dodge, executor. He married, (intention published) November 27, 1757, Lydia Dodge. She died October 9, 1813, aged seventy-eight years. Their children were: William, Lydia, Mary, John Thorne, Sally, Mary Thorne and Betsey.

(VII) John Thorne, second son and fourth child of Richard (4) and Lydia Dodge, was born April 2, 1764, in Wenham, and died February 26, 1851, aged eighty-six years, ten months and twenty-four days. When only twelve years old he accompanied his father, Richard, and two uncles to the battle of Bunker Hill and remained in that vicinity until after the British evacuated Boston. After that he continued in service as servant, guard and steward until the close of the war then nineteen years old. His mother Lydia was sister of Colonel Robert Dodge, of Hamilton, a family renowned for patriotic service from the earliest history of the colony. He married, September 25, 1786, Elizabeth Dodge. She died January 21, 1851. Their children were: William, Betsey (died young), Thorne, Lydia, Betsey, Nancy Asenath (died young), and Asenath.

(VIII) Lydia, second daughter of John Thorne and Elizabeth (Dodge) Dodge, was born July 14, 1792, and was married, January 10, 1813, to Levi (2) Folsom, of Tamworth, New Hampshire (see Folsom, X).

(III) Samuel, third son and fifth child of Richard Dodge, was born 1643, in Ipswich, where he died April 13, 1705. He was the owner of various parcels of land and houses as indicated by the disposition of his property in his will. This was dated June 26, 1705, and was proven on the day preceding the following Christmas. The inventory of his estate amounted to £1,501 and 13 shillings. To his wife he gave half his personal estate and the use of the other half until his youngest son became of age. His wife Mary was a daughter of Thomas Parker, of Reading, Massachusetts, and died August 6, 1717, aged seventy-three years. Their children were: Samuel, Joseph, Ananiah, Ann, Antipas, Mary, Amy, Deborah, Jabez, Parker and Samuel.

(IV) Antipas, fourth son and fifth child of Samuel and Mary (Parker) Dodge, was born September 7, 1677, in Ipswich, and lived in that town. In 1705 he received by the will of his father one-fifth of the latter's land and the house he then lived in. He probably died in April, 1707, and his widow was appointed administratrix of his estate on the fifth of the following month. This was valued at £205. He was married in 1699 to Johanna Lowe, who became after his death the second wife of Joseph Hale, of Boxford (their intention of marriage being published September 19, 1708). In 1715 he became guardian of her son Joshua. The children of Antipas Dodge were: Joshua, Johanna and David.

(V) David, second son and third child of Antipas and Joanna (Lowe) Dodge, was born in 1704, in Ipswich. He married Martha Esgate in Lowell, and seems to have resided in various places. Their children were: Susanna, Joanna, Mary, Antipas, David, Samuel, Parker and James.

(VI) Antipas, eldest son and fourth child of David and Mary (Esgate) Dodge, was born March 5, 1738, probably in Brookfield, and received from his father a deed of one hundred acres of land, being the third lot, second range, south of the Piscataquog river in Goffstown, and here he settled. On April 15, 1803, he bought of Jonathan Taylor, of Stoddard, lot 28, range 3, in that town, consisting of eighty acres which bordered on the town of Washington. He probably lived on this land from that time until about 1830, when he returned to Goffstown. His last days were passed in Pembroke, where he died July 4, 1834. He is said to have been a very strong man and unusually active up to the time of his death. He rendered much service to his country during the Revolutionary war and a record of the same is hereto appended. His first wife's name was Anna, and he married (second), Molly Arwyne. He had six children: Martha, Mary, James, Margaret, Antipas and Abijah.

"Antipas Dodge, of Watertown, also given as of Ware and Brookfield, Massachusetts, was a private in Captain Thomas Wellington's company, Colonel Asa Whitcomb's regiment. His name is on the muster roll dated Camp at Ticonderoga, November 27, 1776. He enlisted October 1, 1776, and is reported re-engaged November 16, 1776, in Captain Brewer's company, Colonel Brewer's regiment, but to remain in Colonel Whitcomb's regiment until December 31, 1776. His name is also on the return of men raised to serve in the Continental army from Fourth Company, Colonel Converse's (4th Worcester Co.) regiment sworn to by Lieutenant Jonathan Snow, at Brookfield, February 20, 1778. His residence was given as Ware. He engaged for the town of Brookfield (also given as New Braintree), and joined Captain Harwood's company, Colonel Nixon's regiment, for a term of three years. He is also enumerated as a private in Major's company, Colonel Ebenezer Sprout's regiment; continental pay accounts for service from January 1, 1777, to December 31, 1779. His residence is given as Watertown, and he was engaged for the town of Watertown. His name also appears in Captain Brewer's company, Colonel Brewer's report on the muster returns dated Camp Valley Forge, January 23, 1778, and his residence given as Brookfield; enlisted for the town of Brookfield, and was mustered in by the state muster master. He is also on the descriptive list of deserters from the corps of guards, as returned by C. Gibbs, major commandant, dated Headquarters, Morristown, New Jersey, May 22, 1780; age twenty years; statue five feet six inches; complexion dark; occupation hatter; engaged for town of Watertown for the term of the war; deserted February 8, 1780. It seems that after arduous service for between three and four years he went home, as many others did, and failed to return to his command."

(VII) James, eldest son of Antipas Dodge, was born in May, 1770, and died in January, 1855. He married (first), Jerusha Leach, of Goffstown; (second), Margaret Gordon, of Windsor, and (third), ——— Johnson, of Meredith. His children were: Jerusha, John, James, Mary, Maria and Daniel Gordon, the subject of the next paragraph.

(VIII) Daniel Gordon, son of James and Margaret (Gordon) Dodge, was born in Goffstown, March 29, 1812, and died in Windsor, June 14, 1873. He was a farmer, and for a few years practiced medicine according to the theory of the Thompsonian school. He married Elvira Hunt, of Hancock, who was born October 21, 1813, and died December 9, 1871. Their children were: David Daniel, born in Goffstown; John Gordon, born in Windsor; Sarah Martha, born in Goffstown; and Perley Hunt, born in Windsor.

(IX) David Daniel, eldest child of Daniel G. and Elvira (Hunt) Dodge, was born October 20, 1840. He was educated in the district school of Windsor. At the age of five years he went to Windsor with his father, and at his majority took charge of the farm of an aunt, his mother's sister, Sarah Hunt, who died January 11, 1871, and left her property to him. In 1873 he removed to Pembroke and bought a farm on the "street" near Bow Lane, where he has since resided. He married, March 9, 1871, Mrs. Lucy Lavina Hall, daughter of Samuel Murdough, of Hillsboro, and widow of Charles G. Hall, of Hillsboro. She was born in Hillsborough, March 7, 1842. They have had two children: Lula Elvira (died young) and Perley Daniel, the subject of the next paragraph.

(X) Perley Daniel, only son of David Daniel and Lucy Lavina (Murdough) (Hall) Dodge, was born in Pembroke, August 9, 1876. He resides upon and cultivates the farm on which he was born. He is like his father a Democrat in politics. He married, November 10, 1873, Azelie Lemay, born in St. Croix, Province of Quebec, November 10, 1874, daughter of Joseph and Eleanor (Pereest) Lemay, who settled in Manchester, New Hampshire, 1876. Joseph Lemay was born in 1837. His wife died in Manchester in 1901, aged sixty-four years: Perley D. and Azelie Dodge have three children: Arthur F., born February 23, 1901; Lucy E., March 23, 1904; Henry, March 26, 1906.

(III) Joseph, seventh and youngest child of Richard and Edith Dodge, was born in Beverly in 1651, and died August 10, 1716, aged sixty-five. He was a farmer in Beverly, near his father on Dodge's Row. He was one of the executors of his father's estate, and received a liberal share jointly with his brother Edward. They held this property under an oral agreement until February, 1709, when they put their division in writing. His executors were his sons Jonah and Elisha. He married, February 21, 1672, Sarah Eaton, of Reading, who died December 12, 1714. Their children were: Abigail (died young), Joseph, Noah, Prudence, Abigail, Jonah, Elisha, Charity and Nathaniel.

(IV) Jonah (3), sixth child and third son of Joseph and Sarah (Eaton) Dodge, was born in Beverly, August 29, 1683, died probably in 1754 at the age of seventy-one, and was buried in Dodge Row cemetery. He was a farmer and a weaver. His father, on May 3, 1716, gave his sons, Jonah and Elisha "all my lands both upland and meadow ground and salt marsh" in Ipswich each to have the house he now lives in, and the land immediately about it, all else to be equally divided. Said Jonah and Elisha Dodge to pay Nathaniel Dodge an equivalent in money and goods for his share, and to give their father a decent burial. Jonah Dodge married, March 27, 1707, Sarah Friend, of Wenham. She died in 1760. Their children were: Sarah, Jonah, James and Jacob.

(V) Lieutenant Jonah (4), eldest son and second child of Jonah (3) and Sarah (Friend) Dodge, was born in Beverly, November 18, 1710, and died in Bluehill, Maine, March 8, 1788, in the seventy-eighth year of his age. He moved to Bluehill, Maine, in June, 1784. Jonah Dodge, weaver, of Beverly, and wife, April 24, 1784, deeded to Thomas Appleton, yeoman, of Ipswich, for eighty pounds twelve acres in Ipswich, adjoining Manchester, five acres of woodland in Manchester, and four acres in Wenham, and for three hundred and fifty pounds seventy-six acres in Beverly, with buildings at Long Hill. He married (first), at Wenham, February 22, 1738, Mary Edwards, who was born March 11, 1719, and died in Beverly, July 30, 1761; (second), March 29, 1770, Sarah Thorndyke, widow of Hezekiah Thorndyke, of Boston, and daughter of a Mr. Prince. She was born December 21, 1731, and died April 12, 1809. His children by the first wife were: Jonah, Abraham, Benoni, Abner, Mary, Abigail, Benjamin, Sarah and Abraham; and by the second wife: John Prince and Reuben, whose sketch follows.

(VI) Reuben, youngest child of Lieutenant Jonah and Sarah (Thorndyke) Dodge, was born in Beverly, Massachusetts, February 19, 1773, and died at Blue Hill, Maine, December 16, 1830, aged fifty-seven years. He lived at Bluehill. His children scattered to various places: San Francisco, Minneapolis, Marengo, Illinois, and to places in New Hampshire and Massachusetts. He married, January 16, 1799, Sally Peters, who was born February 2, 1780, and died September 19, 1850. Their children were: Addison, Charlotte, Lucretia, Elvira, Sally P., Addison, July P., Mary, Reuben G. W., Mary P., Almira E., Emily W., and Harriet.

(VII) Almira E., eleventh child and eighth daughter of Reuben and Sally (Peters) Dodge, was born in Bluehill, Maine, September 14, 1813, and died November, 1891, aged seventy-eight years. She married William D. Clark (see Clark).

JEWETT The record of the Jewett family in America begins with the settlement of Rowley, Massachusetts. In 1638 about sixty families led by Rev. Ezekiel Rogers came from Yorkshire, England, and began the settlement of Rowley early the following season. Among these pioneers were the brothers Maximilian and Joseph Jewett, men of substance from Bradford, Yorkshire, England, and they were the ancestors of all the Jewetts in this county, a large family, which included many members of distinction in various walks of life. The most widely known person bearing the name is undoubtedly Miss Sarah Orne Jewett, the author, of South Berwick, Maine. In ancient records the name appears as Juet, Juit, Jewit, and in various other forms; but in all cases the spelling preserves the pronunciation. Owing to the fact that no genealogy has been compiled, it has been impossible to trace this record of this branch farther than three generations.

(I) Edward Jewett was a resident of Bradford, in the west riding of Yorkshire, England, where he was a clothier. His will was dated February 16, 1614, and proved by his widow July 12, 1615. He was married in Bradford, October 1, 1604, to Mary daughter of William Taylor. Their children, baptized in Bradford, were: William, Maximilian, Joseph and Sarah, perhaps others who died young. (Mention of Joseph and descendants forms the closing part of this article.)

(II) Deacon Maximilian, second son and child of Edward and Mary (Taylor) Jewett, was baptized December 31, 1609, in Bradford, England. He came to Rowley, Massachusetts, with the Rev. Ezekiel Rogers in 1639, and was made a freeman there May 13 of the following year. He had a two-acre house lot in 1643 on Bradford street. He was a leading man in the affairs of the town, and was several times its representative in the general court. He was also very early a deacon of the church. He was accompanied on his journey to Massachusetts by his wife Ann, who was buried November 9, 1667, and he married (second) August 30, 1671, Ellen, widow of John Boynton. He died October 19, 1684. His will is on file at Salem, Massachusetts, among the Essex county papers. It disposes of considerable amount of property, indicating that he was a man of substance. His widow Ellen was married for the third time, June 1, 1686, to Daniel Warner, Sr., of Ipswich, whom she survived, and died in Rowley, August 5, 1689. The children of Maximilian Jewett, all by his first wife, were: Ezekiel, Hannah, Mary, Elizabeth, Faith, Joseph, Sarah (died young), Sarah and Priscilla. (Mention of Joseph and descendants appears in this article.)

(III) Deacon Ezekiel, eldest of the children of Deacon Maximilian Jewett and his wife Ann, was born in Rowley, Massachusetts, January 5, 1643, and died September 2, 1723. He was chosen to succeed his father as deacon of the church in Rowley, and was ordained October 24, 1686. He married, first, February 26, 1663-64, Faith, daughter of Francis Parrat. She died October 15, 1715, in her seventy-fourth year, as is indicated by her gravestone. He married, second, October 23, 1716, Elizabeth, widow of John Jewett. His will, dated February 16, 1722-23, proved November 4, 1723, mentions "my now wife" and a marriage contract; son Francis to have "my Bradford land;" son Thomas "my Boxford land;" sons of Maximilian, Nathaniel and Stephen, and daughters Sarah Bailey and Elizabeth Nelson (Essex Probate, 13:363). After the death of Deacon Jewett his widow Elizabeth married,

December 2, 1723, Ensign Andrew Stickney, son of William Stickney. Mentioned in the order of birth the children of Deacon Ezekiel Jewett and his wife Faith Parrat were as follows: Francis, Thomas, Ezekiel (died young). Ezekiel, Maximilian, Ann, Sarah, Elizabeth, Nathaniel and Stephen.

(IV) Francis, eldest child of Deacon Ezekiel and Faith (Parret) Jewett, was born March 15, 1665, in Rowley, Massachusetts, and settled in Bradford, same state, and died September 19, 1751, in that town. He was married June 20, 1693 to Sarah Hardy, who was born March 25, 1673, daughter of John Hardy of Bradford. Their children were: Samuel, James (died young), Mary (died young), Ezekiel, Mary, Sarah, Nathaniel, James, Esther and Anne.

(V) Samuel, eldest child of Francis and Sarah (Hardy) Jewett, was born April 26, 1694, in Bradford and probably removed in his old age to New Hampshire, where some of his children were settled. No record of his death appears in Bradford. He was married there October 24, 1718, to Ruth Hardy, who was born June 15, 1699, in Bradford, a daughter of Jacob and Lydia Hardy. Their children were: Lydia, Samuel, Jacob (died young), Sarah, Mehitable and Jacob.

(VI) Samuel (2), eldest son and second child of Samuel (1) and Ruth (Hardy) Jewett, was baptized February 20, 1726, in the first Congregational Church at Bradford, and settled on attaining manhood, in Hollis, New Hampshire, where he died December 29, 1791, in his sixty-sixth year. His wife's name was Sarah, but there is no record of her family name. They were the parents of eight children: Sarah, Mary, Ruth, Samuel, Esther, Jacob, John and Lucy.

(VII) Samuel, fourth child and eldest son of Samuel and Sarah Jewett, was born in Hollis. New Hampshire, January 1, 1756, and lived in that town a little more than twenty-five years. At the outbreak of the Revolution he enlisted in Captain Reuben Dow's company of minute men which marched from Hollis April 19, 1775, on the occasion of the Lexington alarm, and on October 6 of the same year was enrolled as a member of the same company, all Hollis men, in Colonel Paul Dudley Sargeant's regiment. which took part in the battle at Bunker Hill. His name also appears on the muster roll of Captain Daniel Emmons' company of militia which marched from Hollis for Ticonderoga, New York in June, 1777, and proceeded as far as Walpole, New Hampshire, a distance of sixty-five miles, when the men were ordered home, arriving in Hollis July 4. On the following day, the company was again ordered to march and proceeded as far as Cavendish, New Hampshire, a distance of one hundred miles, and there met the troops under Colonel Bellows on their retreat. In September. 1777, Mr. Jewett was enrolled for service in Colonel Gilman's regiment of New Hampshire militia raised for the Northern Continental army, and on the muster roll of September 8 of the same year was a sergeant in Captain Zebulon Gilman's company of Colonel Stephen Evan's regiment which marched to New York and joined the Continental army under General Gates in the historic battle of Saratoga (Stillwater), and in which the British under Burgoyne received their first decisive check. In this campaign Sergeant Jewett was in service three months and eight days. In connection with his service as a soldier of the Revolution it is said that Samuel Jewett offered his enlistment at the very beginning of the war. At the time he was nineteen years old. small of stature, but of strong build and possessed much physical and moral courage. He was so small indeed that some doubt was expressed in respect to his eligibility on that account, and when he was called upon to pass under a pole in order to ascertain his height he raised up on tiptoe and thus succeeded in passing the required physical examination.

In 1782 Samuel Jewett and his younger brother Jacob left Hollis and took up their residence on a tract of land given them by their father in what now is the city of Laconia, where they were the first permanent white settlers. The region then was entirely new and the land was overgrown with great forest trees, and wild animals were numerous. The brothers built log houses near each other and felled the first trees on the site of the mills on the Gilford side of the river. On one occasion, it is said, Samuel lost his only axe in the hollow of a tree and to procure another was compelled to go to Hollis on foot, a distance of about seventy miles. His land was half of a tract of two hundred and fifty acres, and sometime after he had made a sufficient clearing he erected a substantial frame house and brought a good farm under cultivation. Samuel Jewett lived to attain the age of eighty-three years, and his wife was seventy-five years old at the time of her death. Her family name was Smith, of the Smiths in that part of Gilmanton which now is the town of Gilford. Their eight children who grew to maturity were Sarah, who married Samuel Philbrick; Polly, who married Gilman Bennett; Effie, who became Mrs. Hackett; Ruth, who married Isaac Osgood; Hannah, who married Thomas Craft; Samuel, who received a part of his father's farm bordering on the river and whose wife was Sally, daughter of John Crosby; Smith, who married Statira Glines. and John.

(VIII) Smith, fifth child and third son of Samuel (2) and Athia (Smith) Jewett, was born in Gilford, now Laconia, July 21, 1793, and died in Laconia, February 17, 1868. He was a farmer and carpenter. and resided in what is now the town of Laconia until 1841, when he removed into the village of Meredith Bridge, where he resided until his death. He married Statira Glines, who was born in that part of Northfield, now Tilton, May 20, 1799, and died January 24, 1890. They had ten children: Jeremiah S., Statira A., Edith A., Louise A., John G., Samuel B., James W., Mary A., Sarah E., and Albert H. C.

(IX) Jeremiah Smith, eldest son of Smith and Statira (Glines) Jewett, was born in Meredith. November 25, 1822. He attended the schools at Meredith Bridge and Gilford Academy. He was employed on a farm and worked at carpentering with his father until 1845, and was then employed as a surveyor by the Boston, Concord & Montreal railroad two years. From 1848 to 1862 he was employed in the railroad repair shops at Lakeport. The latter part of that period he was foreman. After leaving the railroad employ he formed a partnership with Ira Merrill under the firm name of Merrill & Jewett, and for three years they were engaged in the general merchandise business at Warren. Mr. Jewett then bought his partner's interest and carried on the business another year, at the end of which time Mr. Merrill re-entered the firm which took the name of Merrill, Jewett & Company, and continued the business two years longer. J. S. Jewett and E. B. Eaton, as Jewett & Eaton, were the successors of this firm; and finally J. S. Jewett became sole proprietor and continued the merchandise business the thirteen years following, and then sold to George Clark. He then went back to agriculture, which he enjoys, and has been a farmer in a small way until the present time. Mr. Jewett became a member of the Methodist Episcopal Church in 1857 or 1858, and in 1874 he joined tne New Hampshire Conference, and in 1878 was ordained to preach, and afterward acted as a supply at Wentworth, North Groton, Swiftwater and Warren. In politics he is an ardent Republican. He married, in Warren, February 15, Harriet Merrill Farnum, who was born in Warren, December 30, 1830, and died April 6, 1904. Her parents were Joseph and Betsey (Merrill) Farnum. Of this marriage there was one child, Martin W., who was born in Lakeport, January 24, 1855, and died in Warren, January 12, 1873.

(IX) John Glines, second son of Smith and Statira (Glines) Jewett, was born September 4, 1829, in that part of the present city of Laconia which then was known as Meredith Bridge. He received his education in the Laconia public schools and Gilford Academy, and after leaving school devoted part of his time during a period of ten years to teaching; and he also worked at the trade of a carpenter. In 1855 he went to South America, returned in 1857 and for the next twenty years taught school and was employed in the Laconia car works. In 1876 he was appointed justice of the police court in Laconia, served in that capacity nearly sixteen years, and then resigned. In April, 1891, he was appointed by President Harrison, postmaster of Laconia, holding that office until May, 1895, when he resigned and retired from active life. For almost forty years Judge Jewett was prominently identified with the civil and political history of his native town and county, and as early as 1858, the next year after his return from South America, he was appointed superintendent of the school committee of Gilford. In 1859 he was collector of taxes and in 1860 was selectman, holding that office three years, and in 1863 was recruiting officer for the town of Gilford. In 1867 and '68 he represented his town in the legislature, and while a member of the house served on its committee to apportion the state tax. For nearly twelve years he was a member of the Laconia board of education and for two years registrar of probate of Belknap county.

Colonel Jewett (he is perhaps best known by that title) is and for many years has been identified with the best interests of Belknap county in many other ways than mentioned in preceding paragraphs. He prepared the city charter of Laconia and secured its enactment by the legislature. He is a director of the Laconia National Bank, Laconia Building and Loan Association, Laconia Land and Improvement Company, the Standard Electric Time Company, and the Masonic Temple Association. Mr. Jewett married, June 30, 1880, Annie L. Bray, of Laconia. She was born in Bradford, England, January 6, 1860, daughter of George and Ann Bray, of Laconia, and formerly of Bradford, England. Colonel and Mrs. Jewett have one child, Theo. Stephen Jewett, born December 24, 1891.

On December 11, 1855, Mr. Jewett married Caroline Elizabeth Shannon, born in Gilmanton, New Hampshire, May 3, 1837, daughter of Stephen and Ann Prescott (Chase) Shannon, of Gilmanton. (See Shannon, VII). Mr. Jewett died at his home in Laconia, September 16, 1903. His children are: Stephen Shannon, attorney and counsellor at law in Laconia. John Bradbury, born October 21, 1863; married April 6, 1886, Ella LeBarron, born June 3, 1864, daughter of James S. and Lucy Holmes LeBarron, of White River Junction, Vermont; three children: John R., Forest B. and Edward S. Shannon. Katie Belle, born April 27, 1872; married April 27, 1892, Dr. Kitson Brüce, born January 6, 1860, son of Lewis K. and Margaret Kitson Bruce, of Boston; residence, New York City; one child, Thomas Kitson Bruce.

Stephen Shannon was born in Laconia, New Hampshire, September 18, 1858, and acquired his literary education in the public schools of that town and the academy at Gilford, New Hampshire. In 1876 he began the study of law in the office of Charles F. Stone, of Laconia, and in March, 1880, was admitted to practice in the courts of this state. In 1879 he had completed the prescribed course of law studies and was prepared to present himself as a candidate for admission to the bar, but was obliged to defer that action one year and until he attained his majority. Having come to the bar Mr. Jewett at once began his professional career in his native town of Laconia and practiced alone until 1889, when he became partner with William A. Plummer, a relation which has since been maintained. His practice is large and he is known as one the strongest trial lawyers at the Belknap county bar; and in connection with professional employments he has for twenty-five and more years been prominently identified with the political history of his county and the state, and has a wide acquaintance with public men and affairs throughout New England.

His services in official capacity may be summed up about as follows: Engrossing clerk of the New Hampshire legislature, 1883; clerk of the supreme court for Belknap county 1884; assistant clerk of the New Hampshire house of representatives, 1887 and 1889; aide-de-camp on the staff of Governor Goodell, 1889-91; clerk of the New Hampshire house of representatives, 1891 and 1893; representative from Laconia and speaker of the house, 1895; representative and member of the judiciary committee of the house, 1897; state senator and chairman of the judiciary committee in the upper house, 1899; secretary of the New Hampshire state Republican committee, 1890-91; chairman, 1892-96; city solicitor of Laconia, 1893-1901; 1903 onward; chairman of the New Hampshire delegation to the Republican National convention at St. Louis, Missouri, 1896; state senator, 1899-1901; member of the governor's council, 1907.

(III) Joseph (2), second son and sixth child of Deacon Maximilian and Ann Jewett, was born about 1665 in Rowley, and was an ensign in the military service. The church record of his death made by the Rev. Jedidiah Jewett is as follows: 1735, My Grandfather, Joseph Jewett in the 81 year of his age. October 29." He was married March 2, 1677, to Rebecca, daughter of William Law. She died December 26, 1729, in her seventy-fourth year. He married (second) in Bradford, January 20, 1732, Mary Gage of that town. Her will, dated July 8, 1738, and proved some three years later, mentions her as "Being advanced in years to a great age." The children of Ensign Joseph Jewett were: Jonathan, Aquilla, Priscilla and Rebecca.

(IV) Jonathan, eldest child of Joseph (2) and Rebecca (Law) Jewett, was born March 11, 1679, and baptized five days later in Rowley. He was a tanner by trade, and resided on Bradford street, in Rowley. The record of his death, as entered by his son in the church record of Rowley, is as follows: "1745. My Father, Jonathan Jewet, July 26." His will was dated July 4, 1745, and proved September 23 following. He bequeathed to his sons, Joseph and Benjamin, lands in Nottingham, New Hampshire. He was married January 24, 1700, to Mary, daughter of John Wicom. She died January 21, 1742, while visiting in Exeter, New Hampshire. He was married (second) in Newbury, December 27, 1742, to Rebecca (Hale) Poore, widow of Jonathan Poore, of Newbury, old town. She survived him nearly fifteen years, dying March 16, 1760, in the seventy-seventh year of her age. His children, all born of the first wife, were: Joseph, Benjamin, Jedidiah, Jacob, Mehitabel, Mark, Moses, James and Sarah.

(V) Joseph (3), eldest child of Jonathan and Mary (Wicom) Jewett, was born July 31, 1700, in Rowley, Massachusetts, and was baptized there six days later. On attaining manhood he settled in Stratham, New Hampshire, and there married Anne Wiggin, daughter of Jonathan and Mary Wiggin, of Stratham. He was one of the sixty grantees of Sanbornton, New Hampshire. He died May 24, 1765, aged sixty-four years. His children were: Jonathan, Joseph, Anne, Hannah, Mehitabel, Phoebe, Jacob, Paul and Andrew.

(VI) Jacob, third son and seventh child of Joseph and Anne (Wiggin) Jewett, was born May 1, 1743, in Stratham, New Hampshire, and continued to reside in that town through life. He married Deborah ——, and their children were: Anne, John, Betty, Mary, Joseph and Aaron.

(VII) Aaron, youngest child of Jacob and Deborah Jewett, was born January 2, 1781, in Stratham, and resided in the town of Wentworth, New Hampshire, where he operated wool carding and saw mills. He was an old line Democrat in politics, and a sub-warden of the Universalist Church. He married —— Clark, who was a native of Manchester, New Hampshire, and died in that town. They had five children: Jenny, Alpha Clark, Sally, Anna and Parson.

(VIII) Alpha Clark, second child and elder son of Aaron Jewett, was born in 1826, at Wentworth, New Hampshire. He was educated in the common schools, and then became a wool carder, which occupation he followed till 1881. In that year he took up the trade of glove cutting, which he continued till his death. He was a Republican in politics, and attended the Universalist Church. He married Hannah Flanders, daughter of Peter Flanders, who was born in 1823. They had three children: Alonzo Whipple, mentioned below; Charles A.; and Martha.

(IX) Alonzo Whipple, eldest child of Alpha Clark and Hannah (Flanders) Jewett, was born at Wentworth, September 17, 1839. He was educated in the common schools of that town, and then learned the trade of wood turning, at which he worked till the Civil war broke out. He enlisted in the Twelfth Regiment, New Hampshire Volunteers, and was in the battles of Chancellorsville, Gettysburg, and Cold Harbor. At Richmond he was promoted to the rank of First Lieutenant, and soon after to that of quartermaster. At the close of the war he returned to Laconia, New Hampshire, and started in the ice, coal and wood business, which he still continues. He is a Republican in politics. He belongs to the G. A. R., and is a master Mason of the local lodge. He married Annaette Locke, born in 1840, at Bristol, New Hampshire, and died in 1873. They had three children: Alonzo, Harry, and Kate.

(II) Joseph, third son and child of Edward and Mary (Taylor) Jewett, was baptized in Bradford, England, December 31, 1609. He probably settled in Rowley, Massachusetts, as early as 1639. He was freeman May 22, 1639, and had a two-acre houselot on Bradford street in 1643. His will was proved March 26, 1661. The original, now much worn, is on file in the probate office in Salem. He was buried February 26, 1660. He married (first), October 1, 1634, Mary Mallinson, in Bradford, England. She was buried April 12, 1652, and he married (second), May 13, 1653, Ann, widow of Bozoan Allen, of Boston; Bozoan Allen died September 14, 1652, was buried February 8, 1660. Her will, dated February 5, 1660, proved May 2, 1661, mentions: "One hundred pounds that I have in my own dispose" to be divided among these four of my children, viz.: John Allen, Ann Allen, Isaac Allen and Bossom Allen; "that covenant betwene Mr. Joseph Jewett and me." Children by Mary were: Jeremiah, Sarah, Hannah, Nehemiah, Faith (died young) and Patience, twins. Children by Ann were: Mary (died young), Joseph and Faith.

(III) Nehemiah, second son and fourth child of Joseph and Mary (Mallinson) Jewett, was born April 6, 1643. He lived a short time in Lynn, as shown by the following extract from the Rowley church record: "July 2, 1676, Mr. Nehilmiah Jewett had not procured his dismission from Lynn Church which he had joyned many years since when he lived with his uncle Purchas at the Ironworks." He was a farmer, and owned a farm in Ipswich described as being "next west of his brother Jeremiah's." He was well educated and very prominent in the affairs of Essex county; most of the wills and deeds of his townsmen from 1675 to the time of his death were drawn by him. He died January 1, 1720, aged seventy-seven years lacking three months. His will, dated December 10, 1719, proved January 9, 1720, mentions: wife (unnamed), sons Nehemiah, Joseph, Benjamin and Daniel Dow; grandsons Benjamin, son of Benjamin Jewett, Nehemiah and Joseph, sons of Joseph Jewett, Purchase, son of Nehemiah Jewett, Samuel, son of Thomas Varnum, and Nehemiah Skillion. He married, October 19, 1668, Exercise, daughter of John Pierce, of Lynn. She died in Ipswich, November 13, 1731. The children of Nehemiah and Exercise Jewett, born in Ipswich and baptized in Rowley, were: Mary, Thomas (died young), Joanna, Nathan (died young), Mercy (died young), Nehemiah, Joseph, Mehitabel (died young), Mehitabel and Benjamin..

(IV) Joseph (2), fourth son and seventh child of Nehemiah and Exercise (Price) Jewett, was born September 14, 1685, in Ipswich, and baptized in Rowley, September 20, the same month. He died in Pepperell, 1751, aged sixty-six years. He lived in Ipswich, on part of the farm that was his father's, until 1720, when he removed to Groton. He, of Groton, by deed dated November 25, 1720, conveys to Ammi Rhummi Wise, of Ipswich, a common right in Ipswich. He married, January 1, 1707, Jane, daughter of Edward and Jane (Pickard) Hazen, of Rowley, where she was born October 11, 1685. Their children, born in Ipswich, were: Joseph, Exercise, Edward, Nehemiah and Jedadiah. Children born in Groton were: Jane, Benjamin, and perhaps a daughter Hepsibah.

(V) Benjamin, fifth son and seventh child of Joseph (2) and Jane (Hazen) Jewett, was born November 30, 1724, in Groton. He married, December 31, 1754, Sarah Flagg, in Groton, Massachusetts. Their children, born in Groton, were: Sarah, Benjamin (died young), Hepsibah, Hannah, Eleazer, Benjamin and Ruth, born January 3, 1767.

(VI) Benjamin (2), younger son of Benjamin

(1) and Sarah Jewett, was born April 27. 1765, in Groton, Massachusetts, and resided a short time in Hollis, New Hampshire. At the age of twenty-four years, in 1789, he settled in that part of Gilmanton now Gilford, New Hampshire. The spot was a wilderness, and there he cleared a farm and reared his family. Tradition says "he was a drummer boy in the Revolution." His name does not appear on the Revolutionary Rolls of New Hampshire, but Benjamin Jewett, of Pepperell and Ashby, Massachusetts. appears as a drummer on the Massachusetts Revolutionary Rolls, and is credited with over two years' service. He was a Christian, and an early member of the Congregational Church in Laconia. He was married February 15, 1791, in Hollis, by Rev. Daniel Emerson, to Rebecca Boynton, of Hollis. She was born in Hollis, November 20, 1765. and died June 28, 1843. Their children were: Rebecca, Benjamin, Sally, John B., Moses, Hannah and Mehitabel.

(VII) Benjamin (3), son of Benjamin (2) and Rebecca (Boynton) Jewett, was born in Gilford, July 16, 1795, and died March 23, 1879. He was educated at Gilmanton Academy, and taught school several years, and then opened a general store in Gilford Village, which he conducted for a number of years. Subsequently he returned to the home farm and spent the remainder of his life there. He was a Whig in politics, and filled the office of justice of the peace. He was a Congregationalist in religion, and clerk of the church of that faith in Laconia. He married (first), December 17, 1820, Sally Sleeper, of Gilmanton; and (second). November 7, 1831, Maria French, of Gilmanton, who was born January 7, 1800, and died September 21, 1875. By his first wife he had one child, John Quincy Adams, and by the second, three children: Sarah Maria, Rebecca Melcher. and Benjamin Quincy, whose sketch follows.

(VIII) Benjamin Quincy, youngest child of Benjamin (3) and Maria (French) Jewett, was born in Gilford, August 2, 1838, died February 13, 1890. He was educated in the public schools and at Gilford Academy, and after leaving school took charge of the farm which his grandfather settled, and devoted his life to agriculture. He was a respected member of the Laconia Congregational Church, and a strict observer of the Sabbath. In politics he was a Republican. He was much interested in the order Patrons of Husbandry, and was instrumental in starting Mt. Belknap Grange, which was one of the first organized in this section. and of which he was a charter member, continuing active in its work till the time of his death. He married (first), June 1, 1865, Huldah Maria Brown, who was born in Loudon, September 30, 1840, daughter of Richard and Sally Brown, of Loudon. She died September 15, 1870. He married (second), December 25. 1871, Mary Page Price, who was born in Gilmanton, August 22, 1836. The children of the first wife were Benjamin Richard and John Young; by the second, Harvey Austin, and Edwin Price, the subject of the next paragraph.

(IX) Edwin Price, son of Benjamin Q. and Mary Page (Price) Jewett, was born in Gilford, February 21, 1877. He was educated in the public schools and at Tilton Seminary and New Hampshire State College, graduating from the latter school with the class of 1901. After leaving college he entered the employ of the Walker-Gordon Laboratory Company, Boston, New York and Philadelphia, producers of sanitary and modified milk. He remained with this firm about two and a half years, being for the most of this time assistant superintendent of their largest farm, located in New Jersey, and producing milk for the select trade of New York and Philadelphia. Owing to failure in health he was obliged to give up this work and he then returned to the homestead, the same place which his great-grandfather cleared more than one hundred years before, where he has since resided. He is a Republican in politics, and in religion a Congregationalist.

POWERS The family name of Powers is from the old Norman name "Le Poer," as old in England as the time of William the Conqueror, one of whose officers bore that name in the battle of Hastings. From that time on the name has borne an honorable place in the history of England. The immigrant ancestor of this family came to Massachusetts in early Colonial times, doubtless as a refugee from the religious oppression in England of the Stuarts. The name Powers is of Norman origin and the martial qualities of some members of this family entitle them to the credit of belonging to a race which has produced many brilliant soldiers.

(I) Walter Powers, born in Essex, England, in 1639, came to New England, and later settled on a tract of land then in Concord, now in Littleton, Massachusetts. His house was on the north side of Quagony hill and near Magog pond. where he died February 22, 1709. He was married in Malden, March 11, 1661, to Trial Shepard, who was born December 19, 1641, daughter of Deacon Ralph and Thanks Shepard, of Malden. Their children were: William, Mary, Isaac, Thomas, Daniel, Increase, Walter, Jacob and Sarah. (Daniel and descendants are mentioned in this article).

(II) William, eldest child of Walter Powers, was born March 16, 1661, in Concord, Massachusetts. and died there March 16, 1710. He inherited the homestead on which he resided. He married Mary Bank, daughter of John and Hannah Bank, of Chelmsford. Their children were: John, William, Experience, Mary, Samuel (died young), Samuel, Lemuel, Ephraim, Walter and Benjamin.

(III) William (2), second son and child of William (1) and Mary (Bank) Powers. was born in 1691, and was married March 16, 1714, to Lydia Perham, who was born October 20, 1693. His children included Lemuel, William and Stephen.

(IV) Lemuel, son of William (2) and Lydia (Perham) Powers, was born in 1714, and died in 1792. Despite his age, he served as a soldier in the Revolution. He was a cooper by trade, and resided in Grafton and Uxbridge, Massachusetts. His estate was administered by William Powers, of Grafton, probably his brother. He was married. January 14, 1742, to Thankful Leland, daughter of James and Hannah (Larned) Leland. She was born August 16, 1724, and died in 1809. Their children were born in Grafton, from 1742 to 1765, namely: Deliverance, Ezekiel, Lydia, Prudence, David, Rev. Lemuel, Sarah, Thankful, Colonel Samuel and Mary. Soon after the death of her husband the widow, Thankful (Leland) Powers, removed to Croydon, New Hampshire, where several of her children were then located.

(V) Colonel Samuel, fourth son and ninth child of Lemuel and Thankful (Leland) Powers, was born 1762, in Uxbridge. He was a soldier of the Revolution and, after the triumph of the colonies in that struggle, was among the earliest settlers of Croydon, New Hampshire, and was an influential citizen and popular with his fellows. . He died of spotted fever in 1813. He was married in 1784, to Chloe Cooper, of Croydon, and his children, twelve in number, included: Olive, Obed, Solomon L., Judith, Ara, Larned and Samuel.

(VI) Larned, son of Colonel Samuel and Chloe (Cooper) Powers, was born April 20, 1808, in Croydon, New Hampshire, and was among those who early settled in the neighboring town of Cornish. His wife was Ruby Barton, of a noted Croydon family, daughter of John A. Barton, a prominent citizen (see Barton). Larned Powers died in Cornish in 1896. Ruby Barton was born July 9, 1808, and died in Cornish in 1900. They were the parents of four children: Caroline Matilda, Erastus Barton, Alice Victoria and Samuel Leland, all of whom are still living. Larned Powers was a man of strong character and the highest integrity. He was public-spirited, and took a lively interest in political matters, although he declined to be a candidate for office. He was what was commonly termed a "Jackson Democrat," and fully believed in the principles of the party. He was one of the best farmers in the county, and kept thoroughly in touch with the progress of agriculture. Both he and his wife were greatly interested in education, Mrs. Powers having been a school teacher in her earlier years. Both their daughters were educated at Kimball Union Academy, and for a number of years followed the profession of teaching. Their son, Erastus Barton, fitted for college at Kimball Union Academy, and graduated at Dartmouth in the class of 1865, being valedictorian of that class, and receiving one of the highest ranks in scholarship that has ever been awarded at Dartmouth. He graduated from the Harvard Law School in 1867, and is now engaged in the practice of law in the city of Boston. He has been a great student all his life, and is regarded as a critic of high rank in literature.

(VII) Samuel Leland Powers, youngest child of Larned and Ruby (Barton) Powers, was born October 26, 1848, in Cornish, where his boyhood days were passed. He was fitted for college at Kimball Union Academy and Phillips Exeter Academy, and graduated at Dartmouth in the class of 1874. Among his classmates who have acquired distinction are Frank N. Parsons, chief justice of the supreme court of New Hampshire; General Frank S. Streeter, one of the leaders of the bar in that state; Edwin G. Eastman, for the last twelve years attorney general of New Hampshire; John A. Aiken, present chief justice of the superior court of Massachusetts; Honorable Samuel W. McCall, who for many years has represented the Harvard College district of Massachusetts in congress; the late William H. Davis, an eminent clergyman in the Congressional Church; and many others who have achieved prominence outside of New England. Mr. Powers studied law first with William W. Bailey, Esq., at Nashua, New Hampshire, later at the law school of the University of the City of New York, and with Very & Gaskill, of Worcester, Massachusetts, in which office he was at the time of his admission to the bar in November, 1875. He formed a partnership in January of the following year, with his classmate, Congressman McCall, opening an office in Boston, which partnership continued for one year. Later he became associated with Colonel J. H. Benton, of Boston, with whom he remained for four years; he then formed a partnership with his brother, under the name of Powers & Powers, which continued until 1889, at which time he became general counsel for the New England Telephone and Telegraph Company. Later on he went into partnership with Edward K. Hall and Matt B. Jones, which partnership continued until 1903, at which time Mr. Jones left the firm to become the general counsel for the New England Telephone and Telegraph Company. The present law firm is known as Powers & Hall, and is one of the large and successful law firms in Boston.

Mr. Powers was married, in 1878, to Evelyn Crowell, of Dennis, Massachusetts. They have one son, Leland, who was born July 1, 1890, and at the present time is a member of the sophomore class at Dartmouth. Mr. Powers removed to Newton in 1882, where he has since resided. He has been a member of both branches of the city government and of the school board of that city. In 1890, in response to a public demand, he became a candidate on the Republican ticket for congress from the Eleventh Massachusetts District, receiving a unanimous nomination and being elected by a majority of some 13,000. He accepted a re-election, serving in the fifty-seventh and fifty-eighth congress, but declined another re-election, although he was strongly urged to accept it, and returned to the practice of his profession in 1905. In the fifty-seventh congress he was a member of the committees on judiciary and the District of Columbia, and was selected as one of five members to draft the trust legislation of the second session of the fifty-seventh congress. He was selected as one of the house managers to prosecute the impeachment of Judge Swayne before the United States senate in 1904. While in congress he took an active and prominent part in the debates of the time. He was instrumental in forming what is known as the Tantlus Club, that being an organization of the new Republican members of the fifty-seventh congress, and continued as president of that organization during his two terms in congress.

He is president of the Middlesex Republican Club, the largest political organization in Massachusetts, and vice-president of the Massachusetts Republican Club, a member of the University Club of Boston, of the Newton Club and the Hunnewell Club, of Newton, and is connected with various military organizations, he having formerly been an active member in the militia of the state. He is a Unitarian in religion, attending the Channing Church at Newton. He spends his summers at Meredith, New Hampshire, on the shores of Lake Winnipesaukee, where he has a camp, and has at all times shown great interest in the affairs of his native state. He is a member of the board of trustees of Dartmouth College, in which he takes the greatest interest. He is an owner in the large farm which was tilled for so many years by his father in Cornish, New Hampshire, and intends to retain it for the family for many years to come.

(II) Daniel, son of Walter and Trial (Shepard) Powers, was born in Concord, May 10, 1669. He owned a tract of land one mile wide and extending the whole length of the township of Littleton. He married (first), April 8, 1702, Elizabeth Whitcomb, who was a daughter of Jonathan and Hannah Whitcomb, of Lancaster. Jonathan Whitcomb died in 1700, and his widow, Hannah, was killed by the Indians at Lancaster in 1702. Elizabeth Powers died about 1711, and Daniel married (second) Martha Bates. There were five children by the first marriage, and eight by the second marriage: Daniel, Jonathan, Oliver, Peter, (known as Captain Peter, of Hollis) Hannah, William, Sepheran, Timothy, Jarahmael, Martha, Abijah, Tryphena and Increase.

(III) Jonathan, second son and child of Daniel and Elizabeth (Whitcomb) Powers, was born in Littleton, October 13, 1704. He lived in that part of Lancaster which is now Sterling. He served six weeks in scouting service in July and August, 1748, following the attack by the Indians upon Lunenburg, and the capture of John Fitch and his family, and in 1755 was a volunteer in Captain Peter Powers' company of Colonel Josiah Brown's regiment, at Crown Point. In a petition in 1756 for compensation he records his experience in the service: "Jonathan Powers enlisted himself a private under the command of Captain Jeduthan Ballding in Colonel Brown's Regiment to go in the expedition against Crown Point the Last year. * * * I was taken sick at Lake George and so continued for thre wekes and after recovering some small strength I was embarked in a wagon and got Down to Albany with much Deficulty and thare Taried thre Days and then I being Verry desirous of Giting hom, atempted a tryel and Traveled as my strength would bare untill I got to Kingston, and sent Home for Horse and man to come to my assistance being unable to proceed any further I had got so weke." Appended to this statement are the items of expense attending a sickness at home of three weeks. He also served in the war of the Revolution in Captain Dow's company at Bunker Hill. In "The History of Hollis," pg. 206, is a copy of the "Great Return." It contains the names of all the soldiers from Hollis. In this list is the name of Jonathan Powers as serving in the Continental army in 1775 at the battle of Bunker Hill and Cambridge eight months. He received twenty-four cents per day. He was the oldest soldier of his company, recorded in several places. He was over seventy years of age at the time, but gave his age as "sixty." He died before the close of the year 1775. He was married (first) November 1, 1750, to Lois Blood, and they settled at Pine Hill, a section of Old Dunstable, a few rods east of the Hollis line, where he cleared off the forest and built their home. His first wife died in 1763, and he was married (second) November 28, 1764, to Susannah Willoughby. There were nine children of the first marriage (four died in infancy), and eight of the second, namely: Lois, Bridget, Betsey, Jerusha, Jonathan, John, Susannah, David, Anna, Lucy, Jonas, Joseph and Rebecca. (Mention of John and David and descendants forms a part of this article).

(IV) John, eldest of the eight children of Jonathan Powers and his second wife, Susanna Willoughby, was born March 9, 1766. He married Hannah Brooks, of Hollis, New Hampshire, November 28, 1793. They had six children: John, born August 25, 1796; Nathan, mentioned below; Noah, born November 13, 1802; Isaac, born October 4, 1804; Ira, born September 22, 1807; William P., born April 24, 1813. John Powers died at Hollis, New Hampshire, November 6, 1815, at the age of forty-nine.

(V) Nathan, second son and child of John and Hannah (Brooks) Powers, was born December 8, 1798. He was a man upright in character, honest in all his dealings, progressive and decided in his opinions. He was engaged in the stove business in Peterboro, New Hampshire, and later, with his son, John A. Powers, came to Milford, New Hampshire, where the two conducted a successful business for many years. Nathan Powers married Rhoda C. Butterfield on December 16, 1820. They had four children: John Alvin, mentioned below; Lydia Ann, born December 31, 1823; Charles Brooks, born February 27, 1826; Albert Smith, born March 2, 1834. Nathan Powers died in January, 17, 1851, at the age of fifty-three years.

(VI) John Alvin, eldest son and child of Nathan and Rhoda (Butterfield) Powers, was born March 9, 1822, at Townsend, Massachusetts. When a young man he lived in Peterboro, New Hampshire, where he learned his trade. In 1844 he came to Milford, New Hampshire, with his father. The two were engaged in business together till 1851, when the death of his father compelled a change. In 1856 John A. Powers was associated with John Dickey in the manufacture of tinware and baskets. After the death of Mr. Dickey, Mr. Powers carried on the business alone. He enlarged it each year until 1870, when he built what was at that time the largest business block in Milford. He was a man who had the confidence and esteem of all. His purse-strings were always open to all deserving and worthy poor and to all charitable objects. The poor heaped blessings upon his head which others knew little about. He commanded the love and respect of all who knew him. He was a successful and reliable business man, and one who took an active part in all matters pertaining to the general welfare of the town and its inhabitants. He was among the first to adopt improvements, and he always advocated advancement. He served the town in several responsible positions, and always discharged his duties thoroughly, faithfully and honestly. For thirty-seven years he was engaged in business at Milford, New Hampshire, and upon his death the town lost one of its most respected citizens. John A. Powers was twice married. He married, September 24, 1846, Lucy J. Conant, of Lyme, New Hampshire. They had one child—George A., born June 28, 1848. Mrs. Lucy (Conant) Powers died September 20, 1851. He married (second) February 1, 1862, Sarah L. Spalding, daughter of Asaph S. and Hannah (Colburn) Spalding, of Hollis, New Hampshire. To this union three children were born: Ella M., born August 19, 1865, Frank W., born April 3, 1868, and Fred C., born February 20, 1871. John A. Powers died October 30, 1881, at the age of fifty-nine years.

(VII) Ella M., only daughter and eldest child of John A. and Sarah C. (Spalding) Powers, was born at Milford, New Hampshire, Agust 19, 1865. After attending the public schools in that town she went to Colby Academy, New London, New Hampsire, where she completed the four years' course in two years' time. When nineteen years of age she went to New York, where she successfully conducted a private school of which she was principal for five years. At the same time she pursued an advanced course in music at the Metropolitan College of Music in New York City. During her years of teaching, Miss Powers became a regular contributor to eight educational and teachers' journals. Over five hundred articles written by her have been published. The subjects which claim her attention are literature, science and history. Miss Powers has done much to foster a love for our song birds among the children of the public schools. She was the first to advocate and publish exercises for the observance of Bird Day in the schools. For many years her books of exercises relating to the school observance of Thanksgiving, Christmas, Washington's Birthday, Arbor Day and Memorial Day have been published.

Miss Powers has composed nearly one hundred children's songs, which have been published. In many instances she has not only composed the words and the music, but with pen and ink sketches illustrated the words of the songs. She has written and also assisted many writers in the preparation of books on art, biography and literature. These have been adapted for school use as supplementary reading for the grades. She is widely known in educational circles of this country, and her remarkable versatile talents have been fittingly recognized by her publishers and by honorary memberships to various literary and educational organizations in the country. Besides writing her own manuscripts, doing the work of editing, proofreading and revising, she is often engaged upon works of review or in preparing manuscripts of others for the press.

In 1899 Miss Powers became principal of the Sanborn School of New York City. In 1900 she began a series of school-readers, seven in number, covering the entire course of reading in the nine grades of our public schools. Few women, alone, have attempted such an exhaustive work. These readers are called the Silver-Burdett Readers, from the name of the publishers, Silver, Burdett & Company of New York City.

When not engaged in the pleasures of travel, music and art, Miss Powers may be found living quietly in the little New England town of Milford among her rare books and her music. Her motto has always been "Accomplish something," and she has lived up to this teaching. She is at present engaged upon a series of histories to be used in the public schools.

(IV) David, son of Jonathan Powers, and eighth child of his second wife, Susan Willoughby, was born June 4, 1770, in Dunstable, New Hampshire, and died April 7, 1849, in Hollis, this state. His birthplace was just outside the present town of Hollis, where his father was then living. About 1814 he removed to Barnard, Vermont, where he resided until shortly before the birth of his last child, when he returned to Hollis, New Hampshire, and died in that town, as above noted. He was among those who went to the defense of Portsmouth in 1814. He married (first) Mary Messer, and after her decease, married (second) Lydia Adams, of Dunstable, New Hampshire. The children of the first marriage were: David, Charlotte, Mary, Rebecca; and those of the second were: Lydia Spaulding, Myles, Hannah, Susan Wood, Harvey A., Luther Adams, Salome, William Willoughby, Calvin Page, Sarah Jane and Silas Curtis.

(V) Harvey A., son of David Powers, and fifth child of his second wife, Lydia Adams, was born February 17, 1817, in Barnard, Vermont, and died in Hollis, New Hampshire, June 10, 1882. He was educated in the district schools. He went to Abington, Massachusetts, where he manufactured shoes six years. From there he removed to Hollis, New Hampshire, where he was engaged for a number of years in the business of contractor and builder, and bought a farm upon which he passed his last years. He was a member of the Baptist Church and of the Grange, and voted the Democratic ticket. He married March 7, 1839, in Hollis, Sarah Adeline Colburn, who was born in Hollis July 31, 1820, and died in Hollis in 1896. She was the daughter of Robert and Kasiah (Wright) Colburn, of Hollis, and was a member of the Baptist Church and the Grange. Their ten children were: Francena, a daughter unnamed, Alphonso H., Erwin, Ozro E., Luray C., Marcellus J., Perley A., Llewellyn S., and Jesse B.

(VI) Alphonso Harvey, third child and eldest son of Harvey A. and Sarah Adeline (Colburn) Powers, was born in Abington, Massachusetts, April 27, 1843. He was educated in the public schools, the Nashua High School and the State Normal School at Bridgewater, Massachusetts, graduating from the last named institution with the class of 1870. He taught school the following nine years, filling positions in Crosby's Institute at Nashua, N. H., in the Boston Asylum and Farm Schools for Boys, on Thompson's Island, Boston Harbor, and at Dedham and Bridgewater, Massachusetts. From Bridgewater he removed to Hollis, New Hampshire, and subsequently to Litchfield, where he bought a farm of one hundred and eighty-three acres in March, 1879, and engaged in agricultural pursuits. He has put numerous improvements upon the place, among which is a barn forty by seventy-two feet in dimensions, built in 1876. Mr. Powers' natural integrity and ability, and his education and experience have qualified him to serve his fellow citizens acceptably, and he has been placed in various offices of honor and trust, the duties of which he has faithfully discharged. He has been chairman of the board of selectmen three years; town clerk eleven years; town treasurer two years; superintendent of the public schools seven years; member of the school board three years; trustee of the public library three years; representative in 1887, and was appointed a justice of the peace for Hillsborough county in 1897 by Governor Ramsdell, and a justice of the peace and quorum for the state by Governor John McLane in 1906, which commission he now holds. He has been town correspondent for the Nashua Daily and Weekly *Telegraph* since 1887. He married, September 22, 1883, at Litchfield, Frances L. Tufts, who was born in Litchfield, February 15, 1849. She is the daughter of Thomas and Martha (Worthley) Tufts, of Litchfield. She was educated in the public schools and at Adams' Female Academy, East Derry, and at the Convent in Manchester. While at school in Litchfield she was one of her husband's pupils. The farm upon which Mr. and Mrs. Powers reside was her father's homestead.

GAGE The family of Gage, which is of Norman extraction, derived its descent from De Gaga, Gauga, or Gage, who accompanied William the Conqueror into England in 1066, and after the conquest was rewarded with large grants of land in the forest of Dean, and the county of Gloucester, adjacent to which forest he fixed his abode and erected a seat at Clerenwell, otherwise Clarewell. He also built a large mansion house in the town of Chichester, where he died, and was buried in the abbey there; and his posterity remained in that country for many generations, in credit and esteem, of whom there were barons in parliament in the reign of Henry II. An epitome of the line of descent of Gage is as follows:

(I) John Gage, the first of the name from whom descent is traceable, was born about 1408.

(II) John (2) Gage, the son of John (1), married Joan Sudgrove.

(III) Sir John (3), son of John (2) and Joan

A. K. Powers.

(Sudgrove) Gage, married Eleanor St. Clere. He was knighted in 1454, and died September 30, 1486.

(IV) William, son of Sir John (3) and Eleanor (St. Clere) Gage, was born in 1456. He married Agnes Bolney.

(V) Sir John (4), son of William and Agnes (Bolney) Gage, was born in 1480. He was made a knight May 22, 1541, and died April 28, 1557, aged seventy-seven. He married Philippa Guilderford, and left four sons and four daughters.

(VI) Sir Edward, eldest son of Sir John (4) and Philippa (Guilderford) Gage, was created a knight by Queen Mary. He married Elizabeth Parker, and had nine sons and six daughters.

(VII) John (5) Gage, Esq., eldest son of Sir Edward and Elizabeth (Parker) Gage, was thirty years old at the time of his father's death, and heir to fifteen manors, with many other lands in Sussex and otherwheres, but having survived all his brothers, and dying without issue, the estate descended to his nephew.

(VIII) John (6), nephew of John (5) Gage, succeeded to his uncle's estates, was made a baronet March 26, 1622, and died October 3, 1633. He married Penelope, widow of Sir George Trenchard, by whom he had nine children, four sons and five daughters.

(IX) John (7), second son of John (6) and Penelope Gage, was of Stoneham, in Suffolk, and died in Bradford, Massachusetts, November 8, 1705. He came to America with John, the son of Governor Winthrop, and landed in Salem, June 12, 1630. In 1633 John Winthrop, Jr., John Gage and ten others were the first proprietors of Ipswich. In 1664 he removed to Rowley, where he died in 1673. Throughout his life, both in Ipswich and in Rowley, he was a prominent and highly esteemed citizen "and held responsible offices of trust and fidelity." His first wife's name was Anna. She died in Ipswich in June, 1658, and in November of the same year he married Sarah, widow of Robert Keyes, who, by one account, survived him, though by another he married (third), February, 1663, Mary Keyes, who died December 20, 1668. He left seven sons and one daughter.

(X) Daniel (1), second son of John (7) Gage, is the first of the Gages mentioned in the records of that part of "Old Rowley" which is now Bradford. He married May 3, 1675, Sarah Kimball, by whom he had eight children, three sons and five daughters.

(XI) Daniel (2), eldest son of Daniel (1) and Sarah (Kimball) Gage, was born March 12, 1676, and died in Bradford, March 14, 1747. About 1697 he settled in the extreme northwest corner of Bradford, on the banks of the Merrimack, and established Gage's Ferry, or "the Upper Ferry," on the main road to Methuen. He married, March 9, 1697, Martha Burbank, who died in Bradford, September 8, 1741. They had thirteen children: Mehitabel, Josiah, Martha, Lydia, Moses, Daniel, Sarah, Jemima, Naomi, Esther, Amos, Abigail, died young, and Mary.

(XII) Moses, second son and fifth child of Daniel (2) and Martha (Burbank) Gage, was born in Bradford, May 1, 1706. He succeeded to the farm at the Ferry, and lived and died there. He married Mary Haseltine, April 12, 1733. Their children were: Moses, Sarah, James, William, died young, Richard, died young, Abigail, Mary, William, Richard and Thaddeus, who is the subject of the following sketch.

(XIII) Thaddeus, tenth and youngest child of Moses and Mary (Haseltine) Gage, was born in Bradford, April 17, 1754, and died in Sanbornton, New Hampshire, May 11, 1845, aged ninety-one. He moved to Sanbornton, New Hampshire, probably soon after his marriage, and settled in what is now the town of Franklin, on the west slope of the hill between New Boston and the present river road, where he passed the following seventy years of his life. He married (first), November 30, 1775, Abigail Merrill, of Bradford, who was born in 1756. She died in Sanbornton in December, 1789, aged thirty-three; and he married (second), July 29, 1790, Molly Bean, born April 17, 1761, who died May 13, 1831, aged seventy. The children of the first wife were: Richard, Mary, Daniel, Moses, Lydia and John, twins, died young, and Mehitabel; and those of the second wife were: William, Haseltine, Rhoda, David B., Betsey B., James, John and Polly.

(XIV) William Haseltine, eldest child of Thaddeus and Molly (Bean) Gage, was born in Sanbornton, March 21, 1791, and died in Boscawen, September 26, 1872, aged eighty-one. In 1804 he moved to Boscawen, where he remained until his death, sixty-eight years later. He married, January 25, 1814, Molly B., daughter of Bradbury Morrison, of Sanbornton. She died February 15, 1833, and he married (second) Sarah, daughter of Samuel Sargent, of Canterbury. The children of the first wife were: Sophronia, Eloander Wood, Isaac Kimball, Asa Morrison, Phebe Prescott and Rosilla Morrison. By the second wife there was one child, Polly Rosilla.

(XV) Isaac Kimball, third child and eldest son of William (2) H. and Molly B. (Morrison) Gage, was born in Boscawen, October 27, 1818, and died September 10, 1894. He married, October 27, 1842, Susan G., daughter of Reuben Johnson, and they had: Frederick Johnson, Mary Morrison, Charlotte Hubbard, Lucy Kimball, and Isaac William.

(XVI) Georgiana Judith, second child and eldest daughter of Isaac K. and Susan G. (Johnson) Gage, was born in Boscawen, January 16, 1848, and married Abiel W. Rolfe. (See Rolfe VIII.)

(XV) Polly Rosilla, only child of William H. and Sarah (Sargent) Gage, was born in Boscawen, August 1, 1838, and married Samuel R. Mann. (See Mann V.)

PRESCOTT The name of Prescott is of Saxon origin, meaning priest's house. There are two American ancestors, both among the earliest settlers of this country. John Prescott came to Boston and Watertown, Massachusetts, in 1640. He was a great-grandson of James of Standish in England. Jones, the ninth and youngest child of John, the original immigrant, lived in Groton, Massachusetts, and was the grandfather of Colonel William Prescott, born in that town, the hero of Bunker Hill. William B. Prescott, the historian, was a grandson of Colonel William Prescott. The arms of this branch of the family are three owls, argent, on a sable shield. The crest is an arm, erect, *gules*, with an ermine cuff, holding a pitch pot or hand beacon. These emblems seem singularly appropriate for a family whose descendants number a Revolutionary hero and a scholar.

James Prescott, the ancestor of the New Hampshire family, settled in Hampton, that state, in 1665. His father was a second cousin to John of Watertown; and James was a great-great-grandson of James of Standish, with whom the line begins.

The two American branches are of the same original stock, although they bear different coats of arms.

(I) James Prescott, a gentleman of Standish in Lancashire, England, was ordered by Queen Elizabeth in 1564 to keep in readiness horsemen and armor. He married a daughter of Roger Standish, Esquire, of Standish, and they had six sons: James, mentioned below; Roger, Ralph, Robert, William and John. (Mention of Roger and descendants forms part of this article.)

(II) James (2), eldest son of James and —— (Standish) Prescott, married Alice Molineaux. For his bravery and military prowess he was created lord of the manor in Dryby, in Lincolnshire, and was afterwards known as Sir James. A new coat-of-arms was granted with the title. This emblem is entirely different from that borne by the Massachusetts branch. The main features are two leopards' heads, *or*, on an ermine field; the crest rising out of a ducal coronet, *or*, is a boar's head and neck, *argent*, "bristled with the first." In untechnical language this means, when the symbol is painted, that the coronet should be of gold and the boar's head of silver with bristles of gold. The motto is "Vincit Gui Patitur." Sir James Prescott died March 1, 1583, leaving two children: John and Anne.

(III) John, son of Sir James and Alice (Molineaux) Prescott, was born at Dryby, where he lived. He married and nothing further is known of him except that he had two sons, William and James.

(IV) James (3), younger son of John Prescott, married, and had several children, four of whom are recorded: Mary, baptized in 1631; John, baptized in 1632; Anne, baptized in 1634; and James, who came to America.

(V) James (4), son of James (3) Prescott, of England, was baptized in 1642-3. He came from Dryby, in Lincolnshire, to what is now Hampton Falls, New Hampshire, in 1665. At that time the region was a part of the "Old County of Norfolk," Massachusetts. He began a farm, now one of the best in the state, where he lived till he moved to Kingston, New Hampshire, in 1725. He was admitted a freeman in 1668, which means that he was a church member; was transferred to the church in Hampton Falls in 1712, at which time the town was incorporated, and was transferred to the church at Kingston, September 25, 1725. In 1668 James Prescott married Mary Boulter, daughter of Nathaniel and Grace Boulter, of Exeter, New Hampshire. She was born in that town May 15, 1648, and was one of ten children, most of them daughters. On the death of her two brothers, Nathaniel and John, the family name became extinct. James Prescott was a man of prominence and standing in the community. Although he did not move to Kingston till 1725, three years before his death, he was one of the original proprietors when the town was granted by Lieutenant Governor Usher in 1694. Another proprietor at the same time was Ebenezer Webster, ancestor of Daniel. The two men were chosen a committee to run the line between Hampton and Kingston in 1700. James Prescott was moderator of the proprietors' meeting at Kingston in 1700 and 1701; and he received many grants of land, both in Kingston and Hampton. James Prescott moved from Hampton Falls to Kingston in 1725, where he died November 25, 1728, aged about eighty-five years. Mary, his widow, died at Kingston, October 4, 1735, aged eighty-seven years, four months and twenty days. James and Mary (Boulter) Prescott had nine children: Joshua, born March 1, 1669; James; Rebecca, married Nathaniel Sanborn; Jonathan, married Elizabeth ——; Mary, married Jabez Coleman; Abigail and Patience (twins). Abigail married Richard Bounds; John married Abigail Marston; Nathaniel married Ann Marston, sister to Abigail. (James and descendants are noticed in this article.)

(VI) Joshua, eldest child of James (4) and Mary (Boulter) Prescott, was born March 1, 1669. There is no record of his death or marriage or the name of his wife, and the names of only a part of his children are known. He removed from Hampton Falls to Kingston as early as 1725, as he was one of the members of the church when first gathered or organized there, September 29, 1725. His name appears as that of an inhabitant of Hampton Falls in 1722. In 1727 he and his son Latham are found to be inhabitants of Kingston. He resided a part if not all of the time after leaving Hampton Falls in that part of Kingston which since 1738 has constituted the town of East Kingston. Family tradition says that he did not marry until thirty-eight or forty years of age, which the date of the birth of his children seems to confirm. His children were: Nathan, Joshua, Mary, Edward, Annie, Reuben, Patience, John, a daughter, a daughter, a daughter, a child died in infancy.

(VII) Joshua (2), son of Joshua (1) Prescott, was born about 1713. About 1763 he moved from East Kingston to Chester, New Hampshire, where he died July 12, 1785. He served six months in the expedition against Crown Point in 1758. His term of enlistment began in April and ended in October. He was in the company of Captain Trueworthy Ladd, of Exeter, which constituted part of the regiment commanded by Colonel John Hart, of Portsmouth. He signed the association test in Chester in 1776. He married (first) Abigail Ambrose, and had four sons and four daughters. She died and he married (second) Mary Moulton, about 1763, and had five sons. The children by the first wife: Joshua, Stephen, John, Abigail, Sarah, Dorothy, Dominicus, Lucretia; by the second: Daniel, Moulton, Asa, Joseph and Edward.

(VIII) Lieutenant John, third son and child of Joshua (2) and Abigail (Ambrose) Prescott, was born about 1744, and died in Sandwich at the age of about eighty. In 1767 he removed to Sandwich, New Hampshire, where he was one of the pioneer settlers of the town, and there he and his family suffered many great hardships and privations. After residing in Sandwich for years he removed to Holderness, and afterward returned to Sandwich. He signed the association test in 1776. He married, in 1766, Molly Carr, who was born February 26, 1747, and died in Holderness in March, 1823, aged seventy-six. Their fifteen children were: Parker, Joshua, John, Eliphalet, Stephen, Bradbury, Polly, Sally, David, Judith, Ruth, Asa, Abigail, Anna and Benjamin.

(IX) Polly, seventh child and eldest daughter of John and Molly (Carr) Prescott, was born in 1777, and married (first) Benjamin Graves, and (second) Benjamin Mooney, of Sandwich, where she died in November, 1865, aged eighty-eight. (See Mooney III.)

(VI) James (5), second son and child of James (4) and Mary (Boulter) Prescott, was born September 1, 1671. He married, March 1, 1695, Maria Marston, daughter of William (2) and Rebecca (Page) Marston. She was born November 16, 1672. They were both admitted to the church October 10, 1697. James Prescott married for his second wife, June 17, 1746, widow Abigail Sanborn. She was the daughter of Edward Gove, one of the first settlers of Hampton. James Prescott was her third husband, and like his two predecessors was a deacon of the church. Abigail (Gove) Prescott's first husband was Philemon Dalton, whom she married in 1690, and her second, Benjamin Sanborn, whom she married in 1724. James (5) Prescott was a farmer, and lived near his father on the west side of the road leading from the Hampton Falls Academy to Exeter. He bore the title of sergeant, and was chosen constable in 1707. He was at Port Royal six months from March to September, 1701. James (5) and Maria (Marston) Prescott had eight children: Jeremiah, married Hannah Philbrick; Samuel, mentioned below; Elisha, married Phebe Sanborn; Sarah, married Joseph Lowell, of Newburyport, Massachusetts; Lucy, married Joseph Sanborn; Ebenezer; James, married Dorothy Tilton; Rebecca, married Caleb Towle, Jr. (Ebenezer and descendants are mentioned in this article.)

(VII) Samuel, second son and child of James (5) and Maria (Marston) Prescott, was born March 14, 1697. He married Mary Sanborn, daughter of Joseph and Mary (Gove) Sanborn. She was born July 28, 1697. They were married December 17, 1717, and were admitted to the church July 13, 1740. They lived on a farm at Hampton Falls. Samuel Prescott appears to have been a man of substance, and prominent in the affairs of the town. He served several years as selectman, town clerk and in other official capacities. He also acted as one of the scouting party "above the frontier." This party went out in 1724 to the region above Dover and Rochester, then on the edge of the wilderness. It is supposed that they were sent against the Pequawket Indians, who had their headquarters where Fryeburg, Maine, now is. Samuel Prescott died of fever at Hampton Falls, June 12, 1759, aged sixty-two years and three months. Samuel and Mary (Sanborn) Prescott had five children, all sons: Jeremiah, Samuel, John, Joseph and William. All of these sons except Samuel, who died young, had a notable military record. Jeremiah and John served in the French and Indian war; Jeremiah took part in the expedition against Crown Point and John assisted in the capture of Louisburg. Joseph and William took part in the Revolution, and each attained the rank of major. Joseph was in the battles of Bennington and Ticonderoga and at the surrender of Burgoyne; he was a member of the New Hampshire provincial congress, which met at Exeter in 1775. (William is mentioned in a later paragraph, with descendants.)

(VIII) John, third son of Samuel and Mary (Sanborn) Prescott, was born at Hampton Falls, December 12, 1723, and baptized November 12, 1724. He settled in Epping and in 1745 joined a military company which was raised and commanded by Sir William Pepperell. He signed the association test in 1776. His death occurred in Epping, May 2, 1785. He was first married November 27, 1746, to Hannah Rundlett, who was born November 2, 1728, daughter of Jonathan and Rachel Rundlett, of Epping, and died March 16, 1766. For his second wife he married Mrs. Rebecca Tilton, widow of Samuel Tilton, of Deerfield, and a daughter of Hon. Benjamin Prescott. She survived her seond husband and was married for the third time to Nathan Gove Prescott, of Epping, July 7, 1789. She died in 1794, aged sixty-eight years. The nine children of John Prescott, all of his first union, were: Jonathan, Rachel, Mary, Lucy, Samuel, John, Dudley, Hannah and Leah.

(IX) Samuel, second son and fifth child of John and Hannah (Rundlett) Prescott, was born in Epping, October 30, 1755. He settled on a farm in Pittsfield, New Hampshire, and resided there for the remainder of his life, which terminated July 4, 1819. December 3, 1777, he married Molly Drake, who was born October 30, 1757, daughter of Simon and Judith Drake, of Epping, and her death occurred May 24, 1829. She was the mother of twelve children: Sarah E., born June 17, 1779, died at the age of twenty years; Josiah, July 31, 1780, died September 14, 1846; Hannah, April 8, 1782; Leah, December 5, 1784, died June 14, 1847; Samuel Washington, who will be again referred to; Mary, July 26, 1788; Ann, July 1, 1790; Theodate, April 11, 1792, died December 26, 1847; Martha Brown, May 3, 1794; John, February 29, 1796, died January 4, 1862; Abraham, March 7, 1798, and Sarah, October 19, 1800.

(X) Samuel Washington, second son and fifth child of Samuel and Molly (Drake) Prescott, was born August 4, 1786. Locating in Guilford, New Hampshire, he became a prosperous farmer and resided there until his death, which occurred May 23, 1833. He was married July 30, 1812, to Mary Brown, who was born September 30, 1792, daughter of Enoch Brown, of Pittsfield. She died in Lake Village, December 30, 1858. Of this union there were eight children: Enoch Brown, the date of whose birth will be given presently; Mary Jane, born December 6, 1814; Hannah Brown, December 15, 1816; Elizabeth Ann, February 2, 1819; Sarah Plummer, April 7, 1821; Samuel W., August 2, 1823; John Oliver, September 9, 1825; and Leah Lane, September 27, 1828.

(XI) Enoch Brown, eldest child of Samuel W. and Mary (Brown) Prescott, was born in Pittsfield, New Hampshire, February 12, 1813. He resided in Lake Village, where he followed the blacksmith's trade, and he died June 30, 1881. December 4, 1839, he married Hannah Gove Thing, who was born June 25, 1817, daughter of John and Susan Thing. She became the mother of four children: John Freeman Thing, born January 27, 1841; Susan Ada, April 18, 1850, died February 28, 1877; True Enoch, who is mentioned at greater length in the succeeding paragraph; and Cora Ellen, January 30, 1857, died September 4, 1857. John F. T. Prescott was married in 1871 to Laura T. Robinson, of Laconia, who died April 12, 1882, and of this union there was one son, Edgar T., born March 19, 1877, died December 2, 1879.

(XII) True Enoch, second son and third child of Enoch B. and Hannah G. (Thing) Prescott, was born in Lake Village, June 1, 1852. Having studied preliminarily in the public schools he attended the New Hampshire Conference Seminary at Tilton, and concluded his education with a business course at the Manchester Commercial College. As a young man he engaged in the insurance business at Laconia, and has followed it continuously for more than thirty years, being at the present time one of the best known insurance men in the state. The Melcher and Prescott Agency, of which he is the financier. represents some of the strongest and most reliable companies in the world. Its sphere of action practically covers the entire field, including fire, life, liability, accident, fidelity and health. In politics Mr. Prescott is a Democrat, and he served as postmaster at Lakeport under President Cleveland. He is a thirty-second degree Mason, belonging to all of the subordinate bodies, including the commandery, and also affiliates with the Independent Order of Odd Fellows. He was married November 23, 1886, to Adâ May Garmon, second child and eldest daughter of Charles B. and Laura A. (Philbrick) Garmon, of Laconia, who reared four children: Frederick C., Ada M., Frank A. and Lillian E. Mr. and Mrs. Prescott occupy one of the handsomest pieces of residential property in Laconia. They have one son, Edgar B., who was born April 30, 1888; at this date (1907) a student in Dartmouth College.

(VII) Ebenezer, sixth child and fourth son of James (5) and Maria (Marston) Prescott, was born in Hampton Falls, December 3, 1705, baptized March 3, 1706, and died in 1750, aged forty-five. He resided in Hampton Falls, on the farm his father and grandfather, the immigrant, had first cultivated. He married December 15, 1726, Abigail Tilton, who was born May 20, 1706, daughter of Samuel and Meribah (Shaw) Tilton. They had: Samuel, Sarah, James, Josiah, Abigail, Mary and Meribah.

(VIII) Captain James (6), second son and third child of Ebenezer and Abigail (Tilton) Prescott, was born December 5, 1733, baptized January 20, 1734, and died February 27, 1813, aged seventy-nine years. He lived and died in Hampton Falls. He was many years selectman and moderator, and captain in the militia. He served two terms of enlistment in the Revolutionary Army. He enlisted first September 8, 1777, and served as a lieutenant in Captain Moses Leavitt's company, Colonel Abraham Drake's regiment, which constituted part of the force sent to reinforce the Northern Continental Army at Stillwater, September, 1777. He was discharged December 15, 1777, after serving three months and eight days. He enlisted a second time, July 10, 1781, being one of the force sent to West Point, and was discharged December 22, after five months and three days' service. He resided on the farm where his father and grandfather lived before him. He and his wife were admitted to the church July 18, 1756. He married, January 1, 1756, Mary Lane, born December 6, 1734, daughter of Samuel Lane. She died May 24, 1718, in her eighty-fifth year. The eleven children of this marriage were: Ebenezer, Mary, Samuel, James, Betsey, Jesse, Abigail, Josiah, Sally, Susannah and Levi.

(IX) Betsey, fifth child and second daughter of Captain James (6) and Mary (Lane) Prescott, was born in Hampton Falls, June 11, 1765, and died May 24, 1838, aged seventy-five years. She married, August 6, 1787, Jeremiah Brown, of Loudon. See Brown, IV.)

(VI) Jonathan, third son and fourth child of James (4) and Mary (Boulter) Prescott, of Hampton, New Hampshire, was born August 8, 1675, probably in that part of the town now known as Hampton Falls. He saw some military service in the Colonial wars. In 1696 he labored for ten days at Fort William and Mary at Newcastle, New Hampshire, and in 1710 was one of a scouting party under Captain John Gilman. He settled in that part of Hampton which in 1737 became Kensington, and was one of the petitioners for the new town. Here he was admitted to the church March 5, 1749, in his seventy-fourth years. Jonathan Prescott married Elizabeth ——, but her last name and the date of her marriage are unknown. She was admitted to the church, August 29, 1708. They had six children: Captain Jonathan, who took part in the capture of Louisburg; Jeremiah; Benjamin, who is mentioned in the next paragraph; Abigail, who married Nathaniel Locke; Joseph, who served under his elder brother at Lockhard; and Mary, who married Benjamin Hilliard, of Hampton. Jonathan Prescott died at Kensington, New Hampshire, January 6, 1755, in his eightieth year.

(VII) Benjamin, third son and child of Jonathan and Elizabeth Prescott, was born November 2, 1700, probably at Hampton Falls, New Hampshire. He was admitted to the church there March 18, 1733. On October 16, 1728, he married Mehitabel Dalton, daughter of Philemon and Abigail (Gove) Dalton, who was born September 25, 1713. They had seven children: Philemon, whose sketch follows; Abigail, who married Green Longfellow; Benjamin, married Abigail Currier; Sarah, married David Bachelder and lived in Saco, Maine; Elizabeth; John, married Esther Rollins, of Epping, New Hampshire; and Mehitable. John Prescott, the youngest son, died in the service of his country. He lived at Raymond, New Hampshire, and when the Revolution broke out he left his young wife and infant son, six months old, and hastened to Bunker Hill, where he was killed.

(VIII) Philemon, eldest child of Benjamin and Mehitable (Dalton) Prescott, was born January 13, 1729. He was admitted to the church March 2, 1760. About 1751-52 he married Elizabeth Taylor, who was born in 1732. They had eleven children: Bradstreet; Susannah, married Major Joseph Prescott, of Sanbornton, New Hampshire; Elizabeth, married (first) —— Clough, and (second) —— French; Martha, married Eliphalet Merrill, of Deerfield, New Hampshire; Eunice; Rachel; Mary, married Ezekiel Morse, of Pembroke, New Hampshire; Abigail, married Moody Emery, of West Newbury, Massachusetts; Hannah, married Stephen Prescott, brother of her sister Susan's husband, and lived in Sanbornton, New Hampshire; Mark, whose sketch follows; and Nancy, married Jacob Thompson. Both Philemon Prescott and his wife died in early middle life. He died June 12, 1774, aged forty-five and one-half years; she died August 15, 1772, at the age of forty.

(IX) Mark, second son and tenth child of Philemon and Elizabeth (Taylor) Prescott, was born May 30, 1771. He was a farmer in Kingston, New Hampshire. On August 23, 1795, he married Polly Bean, daughter of Richard Bean, of Brentwood, New Hampshire, who was born October 27, 1776. They had six children: Richard Bean, married Mary S. Pervers; Dr. Benjamin Taylor, who became a dentist in Boston; Mark Hollis, married Priscilla Bartlett, of Kingston, and moved to Ottawa, Illinois; Lewis Franklin, married Elizabeth S. Webber; Harriet Maria, married Samuel Huse Swett, and George Washington, whose sketch follows. Mark Prescott died at Kingston, January 19, 1817, at the early age of forty-six, in consequence of being thrown from a horse the previous evening. His widow survived him some thirty years, dying at Kingston, November 12, 1848, aged seventy-two.

(X) George Washington, youngest of the six children of Mark and Polly (Bean) Prescott, was born at Greenland, New Hampshire, March 22, 1813. He was educated in the common schools at Kingston and at South Hampton Academy. For several years he was a successful teacher at Kingston and Brentwood, New Hampshire, and at West Newbury, Massachusetts. He was town clerk at Newton, New Hampshire, and superintendent of schools for a considerable period. He was an active worker in the Methodist Church, and used to select verses of scripture and write interesting sermons and articles for *Zion's Herald*, the denominational

D. S. Prescott.

paper. For several years he was superintendent of the Methodist Sunday school in the town of Kingston. George Washington Prescott married Mary Griffin Johnson, of North Monmouth, Maine, daughter of Thomas Johnson. She still survives (1907), and lives in Haverhill, Massachusetts, with her youngest daughter. Mr. and Mrs. G. W. Prescott had four children: George W. (2); Lewis Franklin, whose sketch follows; Mary Anvellah, born November 12, 1858, married John L. Webster; and Ida Frances, born April 19, 1861, who lives in Haverhill, Massachusetts. George Washington (2) Prescott was born September 27, 1852. He was graduated with honors from the medical department of Dartmouth College, receiving the prize for anatomy, he was a very studious man. He died in 1875, just at the dawn of a promisinng career. His father, George W. Prescott (1) died January 19, 1883.

(XI) Lewis Franklin, second son and child of George Washington (1) and Mary Griffin (Johnson) Prescott, was born September 16, 1855, at Newton, New Hampshire. He was educated in the common schools of Kingston and at the old academy there. He served an apprenticeship of three years as a carriage painter at Kingston, New Hampshire, and later he owned a carriage manufacturing and repair shop in that town. In 1892 he became superintendent of the Kimball carriage factory at Manchester, New Hampshire, which position he still retains. July 4, 1878, Lewis Franklin Prescott married at Newton, New Hampshire, Bessie A. Marden, who was born at Kingston, New Hampshire, September 10, 1859. She was one of the three daughter of Ebenezer K. and Margaret (Hoitt) Marden, of Candia, New Hampshire. Mr. and Mrs. Lewis F. Prescott have three children: Mabel Lillian, George F. and Florence Myrtle. Mabel L., was born September 16, 1879, married Henry Milbourne and has one daughter, Doris M., born July 1, 1902. George F., was born August 21, 1883, and married, April 18, 1906, Ethel Louise Colby; they live at Manchester; have one one son, Sherwood F., born March 3, 1907. Florence M., was born February 27, 1891, and lives at home.

(VIII) William, youngest of the five sons of Samuel and Mary (Sanborn) Prescott, was born June 21, 1728, at Hampton Falls. He married, on November 22, 1750, his cousin, Susanna, daughter of Joseph and Susanna (James) Sanborn, descended from one of the first settlers of Hampton. She was born April 18, 1728, and died March 28, 1800. They had nine children. Elizabeth, married Daniel Davidson, who was in the battle of Bunker Hill; they moved to Vermont. Elisha, married (first), Mehitabel Swain, and (second), Hannah Belknap; he served throughout the Revolution, and moved to Vershire, Vermont, where he died. Susanna, married Lowell Land, and lived at Sanbornton, New Hampshire. Mary, married (first) William Thompson, and (second), Jeremiah French; they lived in Sanbornton. Samuel, mentioned below. William, married (first), Deborah Welch, of East Kingston, New Hampshire; (second), Sarah, widow of John Forest, of Northfield, New Hampshire; (third) Jane, widow of Dr. George Kazar, of Northfield. William Prescott was a celebrated ploughmaker, making the ploughs wholly of wood, as was the custom of that time. He and his first wife, Deborah, were the parents of Dr. William Prescott, the naturalist and antiquarian, and the author of the Prescott Genealogy. Lucy, married Jonathan Chase, of Stratham, New Hampshire, and died at Alexandria, New Hampshire, at the home of her son, Levi. Joseph, married Rachel Cass, of Sanbornton, where he died in his eighty-sixth year. Levi, married Sarah Cass, of Sanbornton, where he died in his seventy-third year.

William Prescott lived first at Hampton Falls where all his nine children were born. He built the spacious two-story house, which in 1870 was occupied by John Prescott Sanborn. In 1780 Major Prescott sold this place and moved to Sanbornton, New Hampshire, then a new and remote section of the state. Several of his children married and died there. Major Prescott and his wife were admitted to the church at Hampton Falls, April 12, 1752, soon after their marriage. He took an active part in the Revolutionary struggle. In 1778 Captain Prescott, as he was then, commanded a company raised from the regiment of militia under Colonel Jonathan Moulton. They were ordered to proceed to New York to join the American army there. The company was placed in the regiment commanded by Colonel Tash, and when cold weather came on they went into winter quarters at Peekskill. He subsequently was raised to the rank of major. He died at Sanbornton, New Hampshire, September 28, 1811, in his eighty-fourth year.

(IX) Samuel, second son and sixth child of Major William and Susanna (Sanborn) Prescott, was born at Hampton Falls, February 18, 1760. He married, in October, 1784, Mehitabel, daughter of David and Betsy (Bickford) Bean, who was born July 9, 1762. He lived in Sanbornton as a farmer and died there October 25, 1826, in his sixty-seventh year. His widow survived him nearly twenty years, and was burned to death in her own house, January 20, 1844, in her eighty-second year. They were the parents of seven children: David Bean, killed in his twenty-third year, April 8, 1808, by accidentally falling under the water-wheel of a saw-mill. Jonathan Bean, mentioned below. Mehitabel, married Eliphalet Lloyd, Jr. Rhoda, married William Scott Hannaford, and lived at Sanbornton Bridge, now Tilton, New Hampshire. Samuel, married Nancy S. Hannaford, and lived at Peterboro, New Hampshire. Betsey, died on her twelfth birthday, November 13, 1814. Eliza Bean, married Ezra Lawrence Merriam, of Ashburnham, Massachusetts.

(X) Jonathan Bean, second son and child of Samuel and Mehitabel (Bean) Prescott, was born August 31, 1788. He married Phebe, daughter of Bradbury Morrison, who was born in Sanbornton, July 27, 1793, and died December 24, 1853. He was a carpenter and farmer and lived at Sanbornton, Upper Gilmanton, and Franklin, New Hampshire, where he died October 6, 1842. They had eight children: Emeline P.; Sabrina, married Lorenzo D. Colby, and lived at Franklin; Anna; Phebe, married Theophilus Stevens; Polly G., married John L. Colby; David Sanborn, mentioned below; Nathan Morrison, married his cousin, Rosetta Morrill Haley, and went to St. Anthony, Minnesota; and Bradbury Morrison, who married Annette S. Bachelder and lived at Franklin.

(XI) David Sanborn, eldest son and fifth child of Jonathan and Phebe (Morrison) Prescott, was born at Franklin, New Hampshire, April 26, 1822. He studied medicine with Dr. D. W. Knight, of Franklin and graduated from the Dartmouth Medical College in 1849. He began the practice of his profession at Temple, New Hampshire, the first of January, 1850. He came to Laconia, New Hampshire, upon the death of Dr. Joseph Knowles, whose widow he married October 5, 1853. Her maiden name was Olive Jane Ladd. She was the daughter of Jonathan and Betsey (Lawrence) Ladd, and was born at Laconia, June 7, 1824. Her father was a merchant in Laconia. Dr. David S. Prescott was a Democrat, and a member of the Congregational Church. He was a successful and respected physician. He died at Laconia, February 25, 1874, leaving no children. Mrs. Prescott, who is still living at the age of eighty-two, is a member of the Congregational Church. She had a brother, Lucian Augustus Ladd, born at Laconia, August 18, 1821. He married Mary Jane Smith, who was born at Gilmanton, New Hampshire, October 25, 1825. They have four living children: Charles Smith Ladd lives at Oronogo, Missouri; he married Lilia A. Good, and has six children. Ann Frances Ladd, married Abbott Lawrence, a lawyer of Chelsea, Massachusetts. Frederick Young Ladd, married Phebe Murray, has children, and lives at Beechwood, Massachusetts. Clara Jane Ladd, the youngest, lives at home.

(II) Roger, second son and child of James Prescott, resided in Shevington, in the parish of Standish. His will was dated September 26, 1594, and he was buried in the church at Standish. He married (first), 1563, Elizabeth, whose surname is unknown. She soon died and he married (second), August 20, 1568, Ellen (?) Shaw, of Standish. The issue of the first marriage were: Helen and Lawrence; and of the second: Anne, and Ralph, the subject of the next paragraph.

(III) Ralph, only son of Roger and Ellen (Shaw) Prescott, was baptized 1571-2. He resided at Shevington, in the parish of Standish, and was co-executor of his father's will. His own will, dated November 7, 1608, was proved January 24, 1609. He married Ellen, who was co-executor of her husband's will. The children of Ralph and Ellen were: Helen, Roger, Alice, Cecilia and John, whose sketch follows.

(IV) John, youngest child of Ralph and Ellen Prescott, was baptized at Standish, 1604-5, and died in Lancaster, in 1683. The "Prescott Memorial" says: "He sold his lands in Shevington, parish of Standish, in Lancashire, to Richard Prescott, of Wigan, and removed to Yorkshire, residing for a time at Sowerby, in the parish of Halifax, where several of his children were born. From conscientious motives, and to avoid persecution he left his native land, his cherished home in Yorkshire, to seek an asylum in the wilderness of America. He first landed at Barbadoes, in 1638, and became an owner of lands. In 1640 he came to New England, landed at Boston, and immediately settled in Watertown, where he had large grants of lands allotted to him, but in 1643, he associated himself with Thomas King and others for the purpose of purchasing of Sholan, the Indian sachem of the Nashaway tribe of Indians, a tract of land for a township, which tract was to be ten miles in length and eight in breadth. The purchasers entered into an agreement to appear and begin the plantation at a special time. The deed of Sholan was sanctioned by the general court, but there were many circumstances which combined to retard the growth of the plantation, all the associates but Mr. Prescott refusing or neglecting to fulfill their contracts, though choosing to retain their interest in the property purchased. It is stated by Mr. Willard that one only of the associates, John Prescott, the stalwart blacksmith was 'faithful among the faithless.' He turned not back, but vigorously pursued the interests of the plantation till his exertions were crowned with success." The name of the settlement at Nashaway was settled May 28, 1653, N. S., and the territory incorporated as Lancaster in honor of Mr. Prescott, that being the name of his native county in England. Mr. Prescott is said to have been the first settler of the new town, though three others, perhaps persons he had sent ahead, were there tilling the soil when he made his settlement. In answer to a petition of the inhabitants of the plantation, six prudential managers of the town were appointed by the general court, of whom, John Prescott is named first. Mr. Prescott was a genuine and influential member of the original Puritan stock of New England and like many of his contemporaries, he was a man of marked character, devoting his time to mechanical and agricultural pursuits, which were well calculated to fit and prepare him for the trials and hardships incident to and inseparable from the early settlers and pioneers of the wilderness of America. He was a man of strict integrity and of great energy and perseverance, and at an early period became a leading spirit, and a prominent and influential man among the pioneers. He took the oath of fidelity in 1652, and was made a freeman in 1669. By occupation he was not only a farmer, but both a blacksmith and a millwright. In November, 1653, he received a grant of land of the inhabitants, on condition that he would build a "Corn Mill," that is, a mill to grind "grain." He built the mill in season to commence grinding May 23, 1654. The erection of a saw mill soon followed. "The town voted that if he would erect one he should have the grant of certain privileges and a large tract of land lying near his mill, for him and his posterity for ever, and to be more exactly recorded when exactly known. In consideration of these provisions 'Goodman Prescott' forthwith erected his mill." "Its location was on the spot where the Lancaster Manufacturing Company has extensive works. The people from all the neighboring towns came to Prescott's grist mill. The stone of this mill was brought from England and now lies in fragments in the vicinity of the factory." Lancaster, in common with other frontier towns, suffered greatly from Indian depredations whenever there was a war between the mother country and France. In 1675 eight persons were killed in Lancaster; and in 1676 fifteen hundred Indians killed or took prisoners more than fifty persons. Among the killed were two sons-in-law and two grandsons of Mr. Prescott. The white settlers then left the town, and did not return until 1679, when the Prescotts were among those who came back to the ruins of their former homes. John Prescott was a strong, athletic man of stern countenance, and wherever he had any difficulty with the Indians he clothed himself in a coat of mail, helmet, cuirass and gorget, which he had brought from England, and thus arrayed never failed to prevail over the savages. Various stories are told of his encounters with his red foes. John Prescott married, January 21, 1629, Mary Platts, at Wygan, in Lancashire. Her family appears to have been subsequently of the parish of Halifax, in Yorkshire. The children of John and Mary (Platts) Prescott were: Mary, Martha, John, Sarah, Hannah, Lydia, Jonathan, and Jonas, whose sketch follows.

(V) Captain Jonas, ninth child and fourth son of John and Mary (Platts) Prescott, was born in Lancaster, Massachusetts, in June 1648, and died December 31, 1723, aged seventy-five. He settled in Groton, where he or his father for him, built the mill in the south part of the town, now within the limits of Harvard, which is still called "the old mill." At a town meeting held in Groton, November 19, 1673, it was voted that "By agreement of the town Jonas Prescott is to grind the town's corn for the town every second and every sixth day in every week." At a town meeting in Groton, June 13, 1681, liberty was granted to Jonas Prescott to set up his corn mill at Stony Brook, "an agreement between Jonas Prescott and the town of Groton, that he, the said Prescott, have liberty to set up a sawmill at Stony Brook on conditions that he furnish the town at six pence a hundred (feet) cheaper than they are sold at any other sawmill, and for town pay, and that the town be supplied before any other person." This privilege was to continue or cease at the pleasure of the town. He bought land in Groton until he became one of the largest land holders in the town. In addition to being a farmer, miller and sawyer, he was a blacksmith, and upon the re-settlement of the town after its destruction by the Indians in 1676, he built mills and a forge for the manufacture of iron from the ore at Forge Valley, so called, which was then in Groton, but is now in Westford. He was a man of elevated rank and much influence in the community. He was town clerk in 1691; a member of the board of selectmen for several years; and representative to the general court in 1699 and 1705. He was also a captain in the militia and a justice of the peace. He married, December 14, 1672, Mary, daughter of John and Mary (Draper) Loker, of Sudbury. She was born September 28, 1653, and died October 28, 1735, aged eighty-two years. Their children were: Mary, Elizabeth, Jonas, Nathaniel, Dorothy, James, Sarah, Abigail, Martha, Susannah, Deborah and Benjamin.

(VI) Captain Jonas (2), third child and eldest son of Jonas (1) and Mary (Loker) Prescott, was born October 26, 1678, and died September 12, 1750, aged seventy-two. He resided at Forge Village, which has been included in Westford since 1730. He enlarged and improved the works on Stony Brook, which his father established, by erecting additional forges for reducing the iron ore, as well as for other purposes. Upon the petition of himself and others a part of Groton, including "Forge Village," was in 1730 set off from Groton to Westford. The water privilege and works on Stony Brook at Forge Village have been owned, held and occupied by the Prescott family since their purchase of the land from Andrew, the Indian. Jonas (2) was a captain in the militia, a justice of the peace, and in 1720 a representative in the legislature. He married (first), October 15, 1699, Thankful Wheeler, of Concord, who died November 1, 1716. He married (second), April 30, 1718, Mary Page, who was born in 1687, and died July 19, 1781, aged ninety-four. The children, all by the first wife, were: Ebenezer, Jonas, Thankful, Mary, Sarah and Dorcas.

(VII) Ebenezer, eldest child of Jonas (2) and Thankful (Wheeler) Prescott, was born July 19, 1700, and died December 1, 1771, aged seventy-one years. In 1730 he and his brother Jonas, Ebenezer Townsend and others petitioned the general court to be set off from Groton to Westford, which petition was granted that year. He married, May 24, 1721, Hannah Farnsworth. Their children were: Ebenezer, Oliver, Sarah, Joseph, David, Hannah, Rebecca and Eunice.

(VIII) Deacon Oliver, second son and child of Ebenezer and Hannah (Farnsworth) Prescott, was born May 5, 1725, and died January 1, 1803, in the seventy-eighth year of his age. He settled as a farmer at Westford, Massachusetts, where for many years he was deacon of the church. He married, June 8, 1749, Bethia Underwood, who was born September 27, 1729, and died in Harvard, October 1, 1813, aged eighty-four. They had twelve children: Susanna, Hannah, Benjamin, Betsey, Bethia, Oliver, Polly, Phebe, Lucy, Mary, Abraham and Isaac.

(IX) Colonel Benjamin, third child and eldest son of Deacon Oliver and Bethia (Underwood) Prescott, was born March 15, 1754, and died in Jaffrey, New Hampshire, in 1839, aged eighty-five. In 1774 he removed to Jaffrey, New Hampshire, which was then almost in a state of nature, with improvements few and far between. Being in a new country and far from the towns and larger settlements, with roads mere bridle paths, and sometimes without roads, spotted trees alone indicating the way, he and his family for years suffered many hardships incidental to pioneer settlement in the remote wilderness. While acting as a spy the day previous to the battle of Bunker Hill, he was captured by the British, but made his escape the same day. He was a farmer, and for forty years an innkeep. In religious belief he was a Baptist, and was one of the constituent members of the Baptist Church in Jaffrey, of which he was a lifelong pillar. He was a man of much energy and activity, and being highly esteemed for his integrity, uprightness and sound judgment, was a man of much influence. He represented the town of Jaffrey in the New Hampshire legislature, to which he was elected in 1790, 1796 and from 1809 to 1817, inclusive, in all eleven years. He married, December 5, 1775, Rachel Adams, of Chelmsford, Massachusetts, who was born August 9, 1757. Their nine children, all born in Jaffrey, were: Benjamin (died young), Benjamin, Oliver, Rachel, Eldad, Nabby, John Adams, Susannah and Bethiah.

(X) Eldad, fifth child and fourth son of Colonel Benjamin and Rachel (Adams) Prescott, was born in Jaffrey, November 18, 1786. He lived in the village of Squantum in Jaffrey, and was a farmer, having a farm of two hundred acres of the best land in the town. He was a member of the Baptist Church, and a prosperous and highly respected citizen. He married, March 27, 1816, Clarissa Hunt, who was born in Acton, Massachustts, October 4, 1791, and died in Jaffrey, September 20, 1826, daughter of Paul and Betsy Hunt, of Jaffrey. He married, (second), June 10, 1829, Betsey Hunt, sister of his first wife, who was born July 5, 1793, and died October 1, 1752. The children of the first wife were: Eldad Austin, Benjamin, Oliver Parkhurst and Oren; by the second wife: John, Henry and Addison.

(XI) Deacon Oren, fourth and youngest child of Eldad and Clarissa (Hunt) Prescott, was born in Jaffrey, March 24, 1823, and died November 25, 1884, aged sixty-one years. He attended the public schools of Jaffrey and Hancock high school, and afterward taught some years in Rindge. After his first marriage he bought a farm of one hundred acres near the village of East Jaffrey, and there resided till his death. He was a member of the Baptist Church from childhood, and his interest in religious affairs was almost the greatest interest he had in life. He was a member of many church committees, and was a deacon of the church and superintendent of the Sunday school for years. He married (first), June 16, 1846, Martha L. Adams, of Rindge, who was born April 10, 1827, daughter of Jacob and Martha Adams, and died June 25, 1850; (second), June 8, 1852, Caroline Almeda Nutting, who was born January 12, 1834, daughter of William T. and Grata (Chadwick) Nutting, of Jaffrey. She died April 30, 1861, and he married (third), February 11, 1862, Louisa J. Plumer, daughter of Jesse T. Plumer, of Goffstown. One child, Martha E., was born of the first wife. She died March 1, 1863, aged thirteen. By the second wife there were three children: Oren Elliott, Julius Elwood and Caroline Maria. Oren Elliott resides on the old homestead; Julius E. is the subject of the next paragraph. Caroline M. married Wayland H. Goodnow, of Jaffrey, and died October 6, 1890.

(XII) Julius Elwood, second son and child of Oren and Caroline A. (Nutting) Prescott, was born in Jaffrey, March 7, 1856. He attended the common schools and the Conant high school of Jaffrey until he was eighteen years of age; he then became a clerk in the store of W. L. Goodnow & Company, of Jaffrey, and filled that position twenty-one years. He then bought an interest in the firm, which became Goodnow Brothers & Company, which style it still retains. By a wise and economical use of his means Mr. Prescott, who is a man of sterling character and fine executive ability, has become one of the leading citizens of his town. Besides his duties in the mercantile establishment he has many others to discharge. He owns considerable real estate; is second vice president and a trustee of the Monadnock Savings Bank of Jaffrey, and is a director of the Monadnock National Bank. He is treasurer of the Cemetery Association, and a trustee of the funds of the Baptist Church. He married, in East Jaffrey, New Hampshire, October 24, 1882, Ada L. Pierce, who was born in Roxbury, Massachusetts, June 1, 1857, daughter of Benjamin and Lucinda (Stratton) Pierce (see Pierce, IX). Two children, Beulah and Olive, were born to them both of whom died young.

FOSTER The first that is known of the name of Foster was about the year 1065, A. D., when Sir Richard Forrester went from Normandy over to England, accompanied by his brother-in-law, William the Conqueror, and participated in the victorious battle of Hastings.

The name was first Forrester, then Forester, then Foster. It signified one who had care of wild lands; one who loved the forest, a characteristic trait which has marked the bearers of the name through all the centuries that have followed. The Fosters seem to have located in the northern counties of England, and in the early centuries of English history participated in many a sturdy encounter with their Scottish foes. The name is mentioned in "Marmion' and the "Lay of the Last Minstrel." From one of these families in the seventeenth century appears the name of Reginald Foster. Tiring of the tyrannic rule of Charles I, he came to America and settled in Ipswich, Massachusetts, in about the year 1638. He was a prominent figure in the early days, as the colonial records show.

During its existence the Foster family has been a hardy, persevering and progressive race, almost universally endowed with an intense nervous energy; there have been many instances of high attainments: a bearer of the name has been, ex-officio, vice-president of the Republic (Hon. Lafayette G. Foster, president, pro tem., of the senate during Andrew Johnson's administration); another Hon. John W. Foster, of Indiana, was premier of President Harrison's cabinet; another, Hon. Charles Foster, of Ohio, was the secretary of the treasury. Many have attained high positions in financial life, and many have gained prominence in military affairs. The record of Major-General John G. Foster through the Mexican war and the war of the Rebellion, stamped him as a soldier without fear and without reproach. Professor Bell is the reputed and accredited inventor of the telephone, but before that distinguished man had ever conceived the plan of electric transmission of the human voice, Joseph Foster, of Keene, New Hampshire, a mechanical genius, had constructed and put into actual use a telephone embodying practically the same working plan as the Bell machine. Query: Could it be possible that Joseph Foster's telephone afforded the suggestion to Professor Bell? The Foster family has an authentic record covering a period of nearly one thousand years. It has furnished to the world its share of the fruits of toil; it has contributed its share to enterprise and progress. Wherever it appears in the affairs of men it bears its crest; the iron arm holding the golden javelin poised towards the future.

(I) Reginald Foster came from England at the time that so many emigrated to Massachusetts, in 1638, and with his family was on board one of the vessels embargoed by King Charles I. He settled in Ipswich, in the county of Essex, with his wife, five sons and two daughters; where he lived to extreme old age, with as much peace and happiness as was compatible with his circumstances in the settlement of a new country. The names of his five sons who came with him from England, were: Abraham, Reginald, William, Isaac and Jacob. (Mention of William and descendants appears in this article). One of the daughters who came with him from England married (first), a Wood, and after his death she married a Peabody. His other daughter married a Story, ancestor of Dr. Story, formerly of Boston, and of the late Judge Story. It is remarkable of this family that they all lived to extreme old age, all married, and all had large families from whom are descended a very numerous progeny settled in various parts of the United States.

(II) Abraham, oldest son of Reginald Foster, was born at Exeter, England, in 1622; came with his father in 1638 and settled in Ipswich, where he married Lydia Burbank and had children: Ephraim, Abraham, Benjamin, Ebenezer, Mehitabel and Caleb. (Caleb and descendants are noticed at length in this article).

(III) Abraham (2), second son of Abraham (1) Foster, was born October 16, 1659. Few facts relative to him are known.

(IV) Samuel, son of Abraham (2) Foster, was born or subsequently settled in Reading, and lived in the westerly part of that town, where he "owned much land." The town records of Ipswich have the following entry: "December 17, 1699. Abraham Foster, a soldier, wounded in the public service is to receive £8 out of the public treasury for smart money." He died in 1762 "at an advanced age," says his will, which was written in the month before his death. Samuel's sons Jonathan, Benjamin and Samuel, were soldiers in the French and Indian wars, 1745-1759. He married, 1701, Sarah Roberts, daughter of Abraham and Sarah Roberts, and they had children: Abraham, Samuel, Ebenezer, Jonathan, Benjamin, Sarah and Elizabeth.

(V) Abraham (3), eldest child of Samuel (1) and Sarah (Roberts) Foster, was born at Reading in 1703, and died in 1753. He married, in 1733, Susannah Hartshorn, and had children: Susannah, Abraham, Daniel, Sarah, David, Elizabeth and Edmund.

(VI) Edmund, youngest child of Abraham (3) and Susannah (Hartshorn) Foster, was born at Reading, April 18, 1752; and died March 28, 1826.

WILLIAM L. FOSTER.

He graduated at Yale in 1779, and was ordained pastor of the church at Littleton in 1781. He was a freshman at Yale when the battle of Lexington was fought, April 19, 1775, and afterward wrote an account of the engagement. He was a minuteman and accompanied Major Brooks, subsequently governor, and took a very active part in the exciting events of that day, being close in at some of the hottest fighting, and seeing Major Pitcairn fall wounded from his horse. Resuming his studies, he completed his college course, and after his ordination was pastor of the church at Littleton from 1781 until his death in 1826, a period of forty-five years. In Drake's "History of Middlesex County," it is said of Edmund Foster: "Left an orphan when seven years old, he worked his way through Yale college. Harvard and Yale conferred honorary degrees on him." Bancroft's "History of the United States" mentions his presence at the battle of Lexington. He was a member of the Massachusetts house of representatives, 1813-14, and of the senate 1815, and of the constitutional convention of 1820. He was a conspicuous member of the last named body, of which ex-President John Adams was president, and made the closing prayer at the invitation of the presiding officer. The history of the convention contains many of his speeches. Members of the same body were Daniel Webster and Joseph Story.

Abraham and Daniel, brothers of Rev. Edmund Foster, were also soldiers of the revolution. Three of Rev. Edmund Foster's sons (Edmund, William Lawrence and Charles) were commissioned officers in the army during the war of 1812. Edmund being captain; William first lieutenant, and Charles second lieutenant in the same company, in the Ninth Regiment Infantry, under command of Colonel Winfield Scott. In the battle of Lundy's Lane, Edmund and William were wounded. It was related (by the father) that after the battle was over some one asked Charles what he thought when he saw his brothers fall. Charles' reply was: "It looked like an opening for a promotion."

Rev. Edmund Foster married, October 29, 1783, Phebe, daughter of Rev. William Lawrence, of Lincoln. Their children were: Edmund; William Lawrence; Sophia; Charles (died young); Love; Charles; Susannah; Sarah; John; Harrison; Sarah Bass; Mary Ann; and Abel Lawrence.

(VII) John, ninth child and sixth son of Rev. Edmund and Phebe (Lawrence) Foster, was born at Littleton, November 23, 1796, and died February 7, 1854. When a young man he removed to Keene, New Hampshire, where he resided till his death. He was a Whig in politics, and a leading man in his party and in the community. He held the offices of sheriff and register of deeds, and was cashier of Ashuelot Bank, and held other positions of trust. He married Sophia, daughter of Josiah Willard at Westminster, Vermont. She died at Fitzwilliam, New Hampshire, April 19, 1832. Their children were: Sarah; William Lawrence; and Susan Eunice.

(VIII) William Lawrence, second child and only son of John and Sophia (Willard) Foster, was born at Westminster, Vermont, June 1, 1823, and died August 13, 1897. When ten years old he accompanied his parents in their removal to Keene, where he attended the public schools and Keene Academy. Subsequently he attended at Hancock, Walpole, and entered Harvard Law School, graduating therefrom in 1845. In that year he was admitted to the bar at Keene, and was postmaster of that city from 1845 to 1849. In the years 1849 and 1850 he was assistant clerk, and in 1851 and 1852 clerk of the New Hampshire senate. In 1853 he removed to Concord and formed a law partnership with John H. George, which continued until 1857. He continued in the practice of law until elevated to the bench. From 1850 till 1856 he was reporter of the supreme court of New Hampshire, was colonel on Governor Dinsmore's staff in 1849, and served under his successor till 1851; was representative from Ward Four, Concord, in the legislature in 1863; and was United States commissioner in 1864. He served as judge of the supreme judicial court of New Hampshire from 1869 to 1874, and from 1876 to 1881. In the interum between 1874 and 1876 he was chief justice of this court. He was made clerk of the Northern railroad in 1853; was made a member of the standing committee of the Episcopal Church in 1858, and trustee of that church in 1868, and was serving in these positions at the time of his death. In 1864 he received the degree of Master of Arts from Dartmouth College.

He was a Democrat until the outbreak of the rebellion in 1861, and after that time a Republican and a sturdy supporter of the Union. Judge Foster was a man of much natural ability, the heritage from ancestors distinguished for mental stamina, steadfast perseverance, energy, and those two rarer qualities of good judgment and sound common sense. At an early age he learned the value of time, and cultivated the habit of improving each moment. In youth he was a close student; in manhood a busy worker. As a lawyer he was alert, quick to see the advantage of his client, a hard worker, and a man who lived up to the amenities of his profession. Naturally gifted with power to influence others, he found public life agreeable, and devoted many years to public affairs with more advantage to the state than profit to himself. As an officer he was above reproach, ever faithful to duty, realizing his responsibility and never shirking it. As a judge he was careful and deliberate in forming his opinions and firm in maintaining them. Never assuming a position he was not prepared to maintain with ample evidence, his decisions and opinions are highly valued by his successors, both at the bar and on the bench. Judge Foster married at Hopkinton, January 13, 1853, Harriet Morton, daughter of Hamilton and Clara Perkins. She was born February 17, 1834, and died April 30, 1899. Their children were: Clara, Elizabeth Bradley, Mary Bartlett, William Hamilton, and Roger Elliot.

(IX) William Hamilton, fourth child and eldest son of William L. and Harriet M. (Perkins) Foster, was born at Concord, August 27, 1861. He was educated at St. Paul's School, and received the degree of Master of Arts from Dartmouth College in 1884. He has filled the position of instructor at St. Paul's School from 1884 to the present time (1906). He married, June 28, 1888, at Exeter, New Hampshire, Alcina, daughter of Hon. Nathaniel and Alcina (Sanborn) Gordon. They have one child, Harriet Evelyn, born at Concord, April 6, 1890.

(III) Caleb, youngest child of Abraham (1) and Lydia (Burbank) Foster, was born at Ipswich, Massachusetts, November 9, 1677. His home was in Ipswich. In 1700 he had a seat assigned him "behind ye pulpit" in the meeting house recently built. He married, June 2, 1702, Mary Sherwin, of Ipswich. They had nine children: Lydia, born May 14, 1703, married Nathan Dresser; Jonathan, mentioned below; Sarah, died young; Caleb, married Priscilla Buxton; Stephen, married Rebecca Peabody; Mary, died unmarried; Sarah; Philemon; John, baptized November 10, 1717. Caleb died January 25, 1766, aged eighty-nine years. In his will he does not mention Philemon or John, so it is presumed that they died before their father.

(IV) Jonathan, second son and child of Caleb and Mary (Sherwin) Foster, was born at Ipswich, Massachusetts, November 30, 1704. He lived at Ipswich. He was twice married. His first wife was Jemima Cummings. They were married January 1, 1733, and had five children: Affe, born December 4, 1734; Philemon, married Ruth Perley; Apphia; Jemima; Olive, born August 20, 1744, married Amos Chapman. On December 17, 1751, Jonathan Foster married his second wife, Dorcas Porter, at Topsfield, Massachusetts. They had seven children; Jonathan, born September 16, 1753; Moses, mentioned below; Dorcas, married Daniel Ellsworth, of Rowley; Mary, died unmarried; Cabel, married Hepsibah ———; Mercy, married Isaac Plummer, of Newbury; Salome, born November 4, 1766, married (first) Nathaniel Foster, and (second) Nathaniel Gould, and lived in Topsfield. Jonathan Foster died in May, 1779.

(V) Moses, second son and child of Jonathan and Dorcas (Porter) Foster, was born at Ipswich, Massachusetts, December 18, 1755, in the Line Brook parish. He was scarcely of age when the Revolution broke out, and he saw some hard service. He was one of the Ipswich men who marched to Lexington, Massachusetts, April 19, 1775, and he took part in the desperate assault against Quebec the last of December of that same year. He also was in service in Rhode Island during the last five months of 1778. In 1787 he purchased seventy-six acres of land on high ground, south of the Souhegan river, then in Amherst, New Hampshire, but now incorporated in the southern part of Milford. The region was then an unbroken forest. Moses Foster married, April 30, 1789, in Topsfield, Massachusetts, Mary Fuller, daughter of Timothy Fuller, of Middletown, Massachusetts. Timothy Fuller was the second cousin of the grandfather of Margaret Fuller, Countess d'Ossoli, who was also named Timothy. Moses and Mary (Fuller) Foster had four children: Moses, mentioned below; Isaac Plummer, born November 5, 1792, married Harriet Brooks; Timothy Fuller, born January 11, 1798, died January 31, 1835; John, born November 13, 1798, died September, 1838. Moses Foster died September 3, 1800, in Milford, New Hampshire. Some time during 1801 his widow married Philip Butterfield.

(VI) Moses (2), eldest of the four children of Moses (1) and Mary (Fuller) Foster, was born December 25, 1790, at Milford, New Hampshire. He lived in Milford all his life, at first in the house left him by his father, which he enlarged, and relinquished to his son, Deacon John E. Foster, who has since celebrated his golden wedding there. In 1847 Moses Foster moved into the village of Milford to the home where he spent the remainder of his days. He was a carpenter and farmer, and belonged to the Baptist Church. He was twice married. His first wife was Fanny Coggin, daughter of Joseph and Betsey (Herrick) Coggin, of Mount Vernon, New Hampshire. She was born April 27, 1799, and died May 9, 1842. They had four children: Joseph Coggin, born April 11, 1818, became a noted Baptist minister and editor, married (first) Abigail Ann Eaton; second, Julia Ann Gould; Reuben Fuller, born January 19, 1821, married Sarah Elizabeth Ames, of Hollis, New Hampshire; John Everett, born May 17, 1824, married Sophia P. Farley; Moses Freeman, whose sketch follows. Moses Foster's second wife was Diana Wallingford, daughter of Benjamin and Hannah (Needham) Wallingford. She was born in Dublin, New Hampshire, August 27, 1811, and was married September 27, 1842. They also had four children, of whom but one lived more than a few days. The children were: Diana, born and died September 5, 1845; Benjamin F., whose sketch follows: George Wallingford, born June 20, 1848, died July 7, 1848; Diana Wallingford, born July 3, 1849, died July 12, 1849. Moses Foster died April 4, 1873, at Milford, New Hampshire. (The last named receives mention in this article.) Mrs. Diana Foster died July 29, 1881.

(VII) Benjamin Franklin, elder son and second child of Moses and Diana (Wallingford) Foster, was born at Milford, New Hampshire, October 8, 1846. Of his mother's four children he was the only one who lived to maturity. He was educated in the common schools. His first occupation was that of photographer. In 1882 he left this business and engaged in undertaking, which business he conducts at the present time. He learned the details with Lewis Jones & Son, of Boston. Mr. Foster has been president of the New England Undertakers' Association, and also of the New Hampshire Embalmers' Association. For the past twenty-one years (1907) he has been the auctioneer of the town. In politics he is a Republican; he was a member of the state legislature in 1905. He has been a member of the board of health since 1891. He is prominent in fraternal organizations. He is a Mason and belongs to King Solomon Chapter, No. 17, of Milford, and to St. George Commandery, of Nashua, New Hampshire. He is an Odd Fellow, and is Past Chancellor and Past Patriarch of Prospect Hill Encampment. He also belongs to the Granite State Grange, to the Red Men, and to the Camera Club of Milford. Benjamin Franklin Foster has been twice married. His first wife was Celia Frances Peabody, daughter of Ezra Brown and Adelaide (Millin) Peabody, of Milford. Mrs. Celia (Peabody) Foster was a descendant of Reginald Foster, and was born in New Boston, New Hampshire, August 23, 1845. One child was born of this marriage, Harriet Maria, August 3, 1873. She married Willis H. Parker, of Milford. Mrs. Celia P. Foster was department president of the Woman's Relief Corps of New Hampshire. Mr. Foster married for his second wife, Louise R. Anderson, daughter of James and Rebecca (Crosby) Anderson, of Milford. There are no children by the second marriage.

(VII) Moses Freeman, youngest of the four sons of Moses and Fanny (Coggin) Foster, and a descendant of Reginald Foster, was born January 6, 1832, on Federal Hill in Milford, New Hampshire. He was educated in the public schools of Milford, including the high school, and also at the Hancock Literary and Scientific Institute at Hancock, New Hampshire. He first learned the printer's trade, but in the spring of 1849 he entered the employ of the Souhegan Manufacturing Company, where he remained three years. He then went into the cotton mills at Chicopee, Massachusetts, and later to Holyoke and Indian Orchard, Massachusetts; then to Cannelton, Indiana, where he was overseer. After this he went to the Pemberton cotton mills of Lawrence, Massachusetts, and in March, 1858, to Augusta, Georgia. For eight years he was overseer of carding at the cotton factory in Augusta, and this period included the trying times of the civil war. While in Augusta he was conscripted into the Confederate service, but he could be of more service in the cotton mill than in the field; so he was detailed to stay where he was. In 1866 he moved to Cincinnati, Ohio, and was superintendent of the Franklin factory for one year. In the spring of 1867 he came back to Milford, where he built a permanent home near the place of his birth. For one year he was agent of the Richard Kitson machine works at Lowell, Massachusetts. He then became associated with William C. Langley & Company, of New York, and removed to South Carolina to look after their cotton mill property. He organized the Langley Manufacturing Company at Langley, South Carolina, and spent eighteen years there, first as agent and afterward as superintendent. On April 11, 1886, he resigned as superintendent at Langley, and came back to Milford. He then assisted in organizing the Denison Cotton Manufacturing Company of Denison, Texas. The mill was one of the first in that state, and operated about twenty-five hundred spindles and five hundred looms. In 1903 Mr. Foster drew out his investment and returned to Milford to enjoy a well-earned leisure. He was one of the pioneer cotton manufacturers of the South. He became master of the business early in life, and has been uniformly successful in his various undertakings. He spends his summers in Milford, and his winters in Augusta, Georgia.

Mr. Foster was selectman of Milford in 1889, and has always shown a warm attachment for his native town. While in Augusta, Georgia, during the civil war, he joined the Masons. He belongs to Benevolent Lodge, No. 7, in Milford; to King Solomon Chapter, No. 17, of Milford, and to the St. George Commandery of Nashua, New Hampshire. He is also a member of the Commercial Club of Augusta, Georgia. He married, September 13, 1860, Adelaide Lutheria Doane, daughter of Zenas Rebecca (Carlton) Doane, of Lawrence, Massachusetts. They have one child, Fanny Doane Foster, born April 16, 1862. She married, January 6, 1897, Ralph C. Bartlett, of Milford, New Hampshire. They have one child, Millicent Doane Bartlett, born April 11, 1904.

(II) William, third son and sixth child of Reginald and Judith Foster, was born 1633, and was a yeoman. He resided in Ipswich, and later in Rowley, Massachusetts. He was received as an inhabitant of the latter town in 1661, and settled in that part known as Rowley Village, and which subsequently became the town of Boxford. Before removing to Rowley he purchased of Joseph Jewett a seventy-two portion of the village lands, for which he paid eleven pounds thirteen shillings and four pence. Jewett died before the deed was passed. He was one of the petitioners for the incorporation of Boxford, and the petition was granted June 5, 1685. Subsequently he was a member of the committee appointed on the part of the two towns to settle the boundary. He was married May 15, 1661, in Ipswich, to Mary, daughter of William and Joanna Jackson, of Rowley. She was born February 8, 1639. Their children, all born in Rowley, were: Mary, Judith, Hannah, Jonathan, William, Timothy, David, Samuel and Joseph.

(III) William (2), second son and fifth child of William (1) and Mary (Jackson) Foster, was born in 1670 in Rowley Village, settled in Andover in 1697-8, and there died August 29, 1755, in his eighty-sixth year. He was a weaver, and followed that occupation through life, bequeathing his loom to his son Asa in his will. He was first a member of the North Parish in Andover, and was one of the thirty-five who were dismissed therefrom in 1711 in order to form the South Church. He was married (first) July 6. 169—, to Sarah, daughter of John and Sarah Kimball, of Boxford. She was born September 19, 1669, and died November 6, 1729. He was married (second) November 13, 1744, to Margaret Gould, who survived him. His children were: Sarah, Mary, John, Hannah, Lydia and Asa, all born of the first wife. (Mention of Asa and descendants is made in this article.)

(IV) Captain John, eldest son and third child of William (2) and Sarah (Kimball) Foster, was born in Andover, September 27, 1701, and died there June 17, 1773. He was a yeoman and a considerable landholder. In the "History of Andover" he is styled captain. He appears to have been a man of some influence, and with his brother Asa was appointed on a committee to instruct the representative at the general court to enter a protest against the Stamp Act. Again in 1768 the two brothers were on a committee to frame resolutions to induce the inhabitants to "ignore extravagance, idleness and vice, and promote manufactures, industry, economy and good morals in the town, and discountenance importation and the use of foreign superfluities." He married Mary Osgood, January 13, 1725. She died April 6, 1772. Their children were: William (died young), John, William, a son, John, Mary, Isaac, Gideon, Obadiah, Solomon and Osgood.

(V) Obadiah, ninth child and eighth son of John and Mary (Osgood) Foster, was born in Andover, May 25, 1741, and died July 25, 1780. He married, May 30, 1769, Hannah Ballard. She was published May 15, and married June 1, 1792, to Joshua Chandler. The children of Obadiah and Hannah were: John, Obadiah, Hannah and Frederick.

(VI) John (2), son of Obadiah and Hannah (Ballard) Foster, was born in Andover, Massachusetts, March 3, 1770, and died in Warner, New Hampshire, in 1846. It is written of him: "He possessed a quick and sound judgment, great energy of character, and rare virtues; he was mild, frank and determined in action, his influence was widely felt in every community in which he lived." In 1830 he removed with his family to Warner, New Hampshire, where he passed the remainder of his life. He married (first) in 1799, Mary, daughter of Samuel and Mary Danforth, who died November 27, 1802. Married (second) Lucy, daughter of Benjamin and Experience Hastings, 1803; she died September 10, 1842. Married (third) Mrs. Sally Morse Couch, January 25, 1843.

(VII) George Foster, fourth son and youngest child of John (2) and Lucy (Hastings) Foster, was born in Hudson, New Hampshire, September 23, 1821. In 1830 his parents removed to Warner with their family, and it was there that he passed his youth and early manhood. With such education as a bright boy could acquire from the district school of seventy years ago, he started out on the journey of life. Gifted by nature with dauntless courage, ambition, and intelligence of a high order, the young man soon made himself known and felt among his fellowmen. Beginning in business life, first as a peddler, and then as a keeper of an all-round country store at Davisville, he gradually worked into the lines of trade toward which his tastes inclined, those of farming, dealing in wood and buying, manufacturing and selling all kinds of lumber. At the age of thirty-eight he went to Weare, New Hampshire, living there until

1868, when he removed to Bedford, New Hampshire, having purchased the homestead farm of Adam Chandler, Esq. There he resided until his death, March 21, 1881. In Bedford were passed the brightest and happiest days of his life. Engaged in a lucrative business, happy in his family circle, happy in the cultivation, development and improvement of the broad acres of his grand estate, possessed of a host of devoted friends, he was justly proud of the success which had brought all these blessings around him. Genial, hospitable, and generous to a fault, George Foster never lost a friend and seldom made an enemy. His character was cast in the puritanic mold of his forefathers, pure and simple in his habits, gentle and sympathetic in his manners, he was a man whom to know was to love. His business, social and political conclusions were formed quickly but accurately, and once found were as fixed as the eternal hills. He was strong in his likes and dislikes, he loved his family and his friends, he loved truth and justice and humanity, and he hated sham and hypocrisy, and denounced them in all their forms in unmistakable language. As there still lingers among those who were his associates many memories of kind words and generous deeds, there also remains recollections of his apt and cutting repartee and scathing criticism. As a fitting tribute to his ability and sterling integrity he was twice elected to the state senate of New Hampshire, first in 1872 and again in 1873.

Mr. Foster married, in 1847, Salome F. Little, of Salisbury, who was born in Boscawen, August 9, 1825, and died in Bedford, December 12, 1897. Her father was Eliphalet Little, an old time farmer and shoemaker; her mother was Meele, daughter of Moses Fellows, of Salisbury, one of the heroes of the Revolution. Her loving and generous heart and cheerful disposition, added to mental endowments of a high order, made her in every sense a fitting companion for her worthy husband. Mr. and Mrs. Foster were buried in Warner, and the epitaph carved on the stone above their last resting place seems a fitting and comprehensive tribute to the character of both:

"They made the world better by living in it."

Their children were: Lucy A., Sarah M., John, George S., Charles E., Herman and Lucy Mary. Lucy A. was born February 6, 1848, and died May 30, 1855. Sarah M., wife of Edmund B. Hull, was born April 25, 1850, and now lives on the River road, in Bedford. During her residence in the town she has been a central figure in all its social and literary affairs; for a long time she was a teacher in the public schools of the town, retiring from her vocation after her marriage, but she has ever since taken a lively interest in its educational affairs. Their children are Harry F., born July 24, 1878, died January 29, 1907. Grace E., October 14, 1880. John is mentioned below. George S., born July 8, 1857, died August 15, 1882. He was a sturdy young man of great promise. He married Etta F. Moulton. Children: Ethel D., wife of Leslie Ellis; she was born February 10, 1881, and is the mother of two children: Lottie Foster, born June 19, 1900; Leslie A., August 16, 1901; George S., born April 20, 1882. Charles E., born June 12, 1860, married Bertha Cheney, granddaughter of James Gardner, who lived all his life in Bedford. They now reside in Manchester. Children: Electa Little, born May 20, 1896, died January 19, 1901; Charles R., October 17, 1897; Jennie Salome, June 28, 1899, died January 29, 1901; Burton S., January 12, 1901. Herman, born August 3, 1863, married (first) Nancy E. Barr, daughter of David Barr, of Bedford. Children: George Reginald, born December 14, 1888; Lucy Salome, September 25, 1893, died April 26, 1893. Married (second) Mary A. Woolsey, of Livingston Manor, New York; they now reside in Boston. Children: Robert W., August 7, 1899, died same day; Dwight W., June 22, 1900, died December 16, 1901; Amy W., January 21, 1902. Herman Foster is a graduate of Emerson School of Oratory, class of 1896, and is now engaged in the real estate business. Lucy Mary, married Burton Stewart, and they now live in Brockton, Massachusetts.

(VIII) John (3), third child and eldest son of George and Salome F. (Little) Foster, was born in Warner, New Hampshire, March 5, 1852. He was graduated from Manchester high school in 1872, entering Dartmouth College the same year, and was graduated with the degree of A. B. in the class of 1876. Shortly after the completion of his college course, he entered the law office of Hon. James F. Briggs, of Manchester, and upon the completion of his legal studies was admitted to the bar in 1878, and opened an office in Manchester, where he conducted a successful practice until 1890, when on account of ill-health he relinquished his duties as an active practitioner and has since, by way of recreation, added some valued productions to New Hampshire literature. Among his popular metrical efforts are: "The Old Stone Wall;" "The Old Time Dog and Gun;" "The Old Time Stage Coach;" "The Tiger Lily;" "The Abandoned Farm;" "The Old Hoyt School-house;" "The Old March Meeting Day," and "Hayseed." The last mentioned was read at the Henniker Old Home Day celebration in 1906. His last and best contribution is the one entitled "The Triumph of the Anglo-Saxon Race." He also prepared and read as a memorial at the thirtieth anniversary meeting of his class at Dartmouth College, June 25, 1906, "Springtime and Autumn," which received glowing commendation from the press and warm approval by members of his class. Mr. Foster in all his productions evinces the true poetic instinct. A lover of nature and nature's God, he has woven into the warp and woof of his songs the sentiments of a heart which pulsates with love, loyalty and devotion. Many of his best efforts have been memorials to departed friends and cheering quaint verses to those who have been his friends and companions from boyhood. Mr. Foster was elected to the legislature to represent the town of Bedford on the Republican ticket in 1879 and served with credit to himself and his constituency. He married in Manchester, February 18, 1881, Mary Lizzie McCrillis, who was born in Manchester, June 5, 1854, daughter of John B. and Mary (Kilgore) McCrillis. She was graduated from the Manchester high school in 1872, in the same class with Mr. Foster. She is an artist of high repute, and her work in both oil and water color has been received with much favor by the public.

(IV) Captain Asa, youngest child of William (2) and Sarah (Kimball) Foster, was born June 16, 1710, in Andover, and passed his life in that town, where he died July 17, 1787. He owned one hundred and sixty acres of land in Canterbury, New Hampshire, besides large tracts of upland and meadow in Andover. On March 8, 1776, he was appointed one of the members of a committee of the town on correspondence, inspection and safety. His estate was valued at eight hundred and thirty pounds, sixteen shillings and seven pence. He was married (first), Octobr 26, 1732, to Elizabeth,

John Foster

daughter of John Abbott. She was born in 1712, and died July 4, 1758. His intention of marriage to Lucy Rogers was published December 10, 1763. She died October 17, 1787, surviving him exactly three months. His children were: Asa, Abial, Daniel, David (died young), David, Elizabeth, Jonathan, Sarah and Lucy. (Mention of David and descendants appears in this article).

(V) Abial, second son and child of Captain Asa and Elizabeth (Abbott) Foster, was born August 29, 1733, in Andover, Massachusetts, and was an early resident of Canterbury, New Hampshire. He was a clergyman. Owing to mutilation of the records, the full name of his wife cannot now be learned. Her christian name was Hannah, and the first two letters of her family name were Ba——. The records of Canterbury show three children born to them, namely: Hannah, William and James. There were undoubtedly others.

(VI) Abial (2), was undoubtedly a son of Reverend Abial and Hannah Foster, born probably about 1767. He was married February 25, 1796, in Canterbury, to Susannah Moor. The records of Canterbury show Susannah Foster, born February 7, 1775, and another April 9, 1775. No parentage is given, and this is probably two records of the birth of the same person, supposed to be the wife Abial (2). Their children were: Polly, Abial, one whose christian name is not given (supposed to be Simeon B. born April 23, 1800), Susannah, Nancy, Joseph, Elizabeth, Augusta Caroline, Martha Jane, Sarah, Catherine (died young), Catherine and one still born, recorded June 1, 1817.

(VII) Simeon B. Foster was a native of Canterbury, where he lived the life of a plain honest farmer whose chief concerns were in getting an honest living and properly bringing up a family. He died in Canterbury, November 26, 1880. He was first a Whig and in his later years a Republican and his party elected him to the office of selectman and collector. He was married, April 18, 1826, to Polly S. Hill, who died in 1870, aged sixty-five years. They had ten children; Myron C. Harrison, Alonzo, John, Fidelia, Melissa, Emma, Melinda, Nancy, Lyman.

(VIII) Myron C., eldest child of Simeon and Polly S. (Hill) Foster, was born in Canterbury, February 7, 1829, and has followed the same vocation as his father. In politics he is a Republican. For some years he was town tax collector. He is a member of the Baptist Church, and for many years had been one of its deacons. While the Civil war was in progress he served about five months as a contract nurse. He married, January 1, 1854, Lucinda M. Pear, who was born April 1, 1833, in Cambridge, Massachusetts, daughter of George and Nancy (Carter) Pear, of Cambridge. They have had three children: Lizzie, deceased; George, a miller at Contoocook; Lyman B., whose sketch follows.

(IX) Lyman Beecher Foster was born in Canterbury, October 30, 1867, and is youngest child of Myron and Lucinda M. (Pear) Foster. He was educated in the public schools. At eighteen years of age he went into the employment of J. H. Jackman as a clerk in a store at Penacook, where he continued eighteen months; he then took a similar position in a co-operative store in Penacook, where he served seven years; subsequently he clerked for E. J. Young in East Concord, five years, and Philbrick & Hill, of Tilton, five years. In 1904 he bought a grocery stock in Farmington, where he has since been in business. He is a member of Contoocook Lodge, No. 26, Independent Order of Odd Fellows, of Penacook, in which he is a past grand; a member of Penacook Encampment, No. 3, of Concord, and of Wily Canton, Patriarchs Militant, of Concord. He married Annibeck P. Wyman, who was born October 29, 1868, a daughter of Daniel and Annie (Webster) Wyman, of Concord.

(V) David, fifth son of Captain Asa and Elizabeth (Abbott) Foster, was born September 25, 1737, in Andover, and settled in Canterbury, New Hampshire. He was married, November 24, 1760, to Hannah Kittredge, and their children, on record in Canterbury, were: Daniel, Hannah, Simeon, Betsey, Jonathan, Dorcas, Abiah, Abigail, Ruth and Jeremiah. The record states that these children were born in Andover. (Mention of Joseph and descendants forms part of this article).

(VI) Daniel, eldest child of David and Hannah (Kittredge) Foster, was born June 29, 1761, in Andover, and resided in Canterbury, New Hampshire. Nothing in the public records shows his marriage of children. The family records give the birth of the next in order, who was probably a son of Daniel Foster, but nothing now appears by which this can be conclusively determined.

(VII) Daniel Kittredge Foster was born in 1793 at Canterbury, New Hampshire, a town which gave birth to Stephen Foster, the Abolitionist, and to others of the name who have wrought well for the public service. He became a teacher and farmer at Chichester, this state. On November 20, 1823, Daniel Kittredge Foster married Lydia Lane, second child of Simeon and Sarah (Morrill) Lane, who was born in Chichester, May 2, 1799. Her mother died when she was but an infant, and her father married again and had a large family; hence Lydia was adopted by Joshua and Lydia (Blake) Lane, who might properly be considered her parents, as they brought her up and left her their property. Daniel K. and Lydia (Lane) Foster had five children, all sons: Joshua Lane, whose sketch follows; Joseph Addison, born in 1825 or 6; Daniel Kittredge, born December 10, 1827; Lucius Augustus, born November 20, 1831, and Rinaldo Brackett, born March 5, 1836. Daniel K. (2) Foster was a school teacher of note in his day. Daniel K. (1) Foster died October 11, 1869, and his wife died in February, 1875, each at the age of seventy-six years.

(VIII) Joshua Lane, eldest child of Daniel Kittredge and Lydia (Lane) Foster, was born at Canterbury, New Hampshire, October 10, 1824. When about three months old his parents moved to Chichester, this state, to reside with Joshua Lane, and there on the Lane homestead he was reared. From his father he obtained excellent private instructions, and he also attended the district schools till old enough to enter Pittsfield Academy in the neighboring town, where he remained four years. He then spent two years at Gilmanton Academy, this state, and then returned to Pittsfield, where he completed his academic education. He remained on the home farm for a few years, but being of a mechanical turn he learned the builder's trade, at which he worked for two or three years. He then pursued the study of architecture under Professor Benjamin Stanton, of New York City, and for about ten years, ending with the financial panic of 1857, he practiced his profession in Concord. During that time he designed many churches, court-houses and school-houses throughout the state, one of the most notable being the old red brick court-house at Concord, dedicated in 1857, whose stately portico and lofty walls were for more than half a century an imposing feature of the North End. Meanwhile Mr. Foster had been a frequent contributor to the press, and when the building business was brought to a standstill, he was urged to enter the editorial field. In 1858 in connection with Dr. Joseph H. Smith, he bought the *Dover Gazette*, and with Edwin A. Hills, Dr. Smith's son-in-law, he formed a partnership under the firm name of Foster & Hills. Mr. Foster conducted the paper for three years, when he sold out to his partner, and returned to his architectural profession for a short time, during which he resided in Manchester, this state. But the ruling passion proved too strong, and in January, 1863, at the solicitation of leading Democrats of the state, he went to Portsmouth, where no Democratic paper was then published, and started the *Weekly States and Union*, and in 1868 began the issue of the *Daily Times* of that city. In June, 1870. he sold these papers to Thayer & Guppy, two of his employees, and removed to New Haven, Connecticut, where he published the *New Haven Lever* for a time, but not long afterward he returned to Dover, where he began the publication, January 20, 1872, of *Foster's Weekly Democrat*, with which his name is indelibly associated. This paper made a sensation by the vigor and pungency of the editorials and locals, and *Foster's Daily Democrat* was issued on June 18, 1873. Mr. Foster soon gained a reputation that was not confined to New Hampshire, and his writings, which were always couched in pure Anglo-Saxon, were quoted by newspapers in all parts of the land. Mr. Foster did not hesitate to differ with his party when matters of principle were involved, but the honesty of his motives and the brilliance of his writings were so convincing that the paper became an ever increasing success. In 1885, soon after the inauguration of President Cleveland, the paper came out squarely against his administration and boldly espoused the Republican cause, which it has ever since maintained with all its old-time ability. Mr. Foster's habit of thinking for himself, his wide reading, ample vocabulary and dogged grip were sure to attract attention to anything he uttered, while his fidelity to conviction commanded respect even from those whose ideas diverged most widely from the opinions of the radical editor. Mr. Foster never cared to hold political office, though he represented his party repeatedly in state and other conventions. He was, however, elected for three successive terms of seven years each as a member of the board of trustees of the Dover Public Library, and was holding this office when he died.

On July 30, 1848, Joshua Lane Foster married Lucretia A. Gale, daughter of Bartholomew and Abby (Morrison) Gale, of Upper Gilmanton, now Belmont, New Hampshire. Four children were born of this union: Lucia Ella, who married Mercer Goodrich, formerly of Portsmouth, but afterwards of Lynn, Massachusetts; George J., whose sketch follows; Ena Veille, who married Frederick J. Whitehead, of Dover; and Charles G., whose sketch follows. Mrs. Goodrich died February 25, 1905, leaving a husband and three brilliant sons. Mr. and Mrs. Foster were permitted to celebrate their golden wedding, which was a notable event, largely attended by prominent people. Mr. Foster lived a year and a half after this event, dying January 29, 1900, at his home in Dover. Mrs. Foster lived till May 6, 1905, dying at the age of seventy-nine years.

(IX) George J., elder son and second child of Joshua Lane and Lucretia (Gale) Foster, was born at Concord, New Hampshire, February 13, 1854. He was educated in the public schools of Portsmouth, completing his course of study by four years in the high school. He early manifested financial tact and ability, and when his father settled in Dover and started the weekly and then the daily *Democrat*, he placed his son in charge of the business management. That no mistake was made is shown by the complete pecuniary success of the enterprise. Mr. Foster is an attendant of the Methodist Church, and a Republican in politics. He has been a member of the school committee since 1883, and was made chairman of the board in 1903, a position which he still holds. He represented his ward in the New Hampshire legislature of 1893, and was mayor of Dover in 1906. In all of his public career his course of action has been governed by fidelity to public interests, and by a desire to reduce expenditures and keep down taxation. On July 22, 1880, George J. Foster married Anna C. Clark, daughter of Seth H. and Clarissa Clark, of Dover. By this union there have been two sons and one daughter: Bertha Florence, born August 3, 1883; graduated from Wellesley College, 1906. Arthur, born March 27, 1885; Frederick, born December 9, 1887.

(IX) Charles Gale, second son and third child of Joshua Lane and Lucretia (Gale) Foster, was born at Dover, New Hampshire, July 11, 1859. When he was a child his parents moved to Manchester, and after a brief residence there went to Portsmouth, removing from thence in the year 1872 to Dover, where Charles Gale resided up to the time of his death. On account of the frequent removals of his parents he attended the public schools of various New England cities, and acquired a practical education. In 1876 he began work in the office of the *Democrat*, and in the course of his connection with it worked his way up through all positions to the editor's chair. This proved an excellent school for him, as it has done for many other newspaper men, and the paper continued to speak for itself each day, carrying a powerful influence for good throughout Strafford county. Since the death of the father, several years ago, Charles Gale and his brother, George J., conducted the paper. He served in the common council in 1896-97, having been elected on the Republican ticket, and filled the position of president in the latter year. He was an attendant of the First Congregational Church of Dover. He was also prominent in fraternal circles, having been a past noble grand of Wecohamet Lodge of Odd Fellows, one of the oldest in the state, a trustee of the organization at the time of his death, past chief partriarch of Quochecho Encampment, and past commander of Canton Parker, Partiarchs Militant. Mr. Foster married, August 3, 1883, Mabel Clement, daughter of Benjamin and Sarah Clement, of Dover, New Hampshire, who bore him four children: Walter H., born September 14, 1887, a member of the class of 1909, Dartmouth College. Philip C., born February 19, 1892, a pupil in the Dover high school. Arthur and Doris J., died in infancy. Charles Gale Foster died at his home, 47 Central avenue, October 27, 1907, and in his death Dover lost one of its most prominent and useful citizens.

(VI) Joseph, fourth son and fifth child of David and Sarah Foster, was born September 22, 1779, in Canterbury, and settled very early in life in Alexandria, New Hampshire, where many other members of the Foster family resided. He was educated in the district schools and in late life went to Merrimack, and there lived until his death. He was by occupation a farmer, in religious belief a Congregationalist, and in politics a Democrat. His wife's name was Lydia Petty. Their children

Joseph H. Foster

were: Malinda, Phebe, Thomas J., Sylvia, Wilson, John L., Irine and Lydia.

(VII) Thomas Jefferson, first son of Joseph and Lydia (Petty) Foster, was born in Alexandria, December 20, 1819, and died in Amherst, May 3, 1892. He got his education in the district schools. He was a blacksmith and a farmer, and did some lumbering. He lived in Merrimack after 1845. He was a member of the Grange, and an ardent temperance man. In politics he was a Democrat. November 26, 1846, he married Hannah C. Junkins, who was born February 19, 1821, and died January 7, 1904. She was the daughter of Henry and Mary (Miller) Junkins, of Merrimack. They were the parents of three children: Joseph H., mentioned below; George W., born July 25, 1858, married, May 15, 1890, Ida F. Wheeler; Charles W., born September 17, 1863, married, December 26, 1887, Edith A. Gilman.

(VIII) Joseph Henry, eldest child of Thomas J. and Hannah C. (Junkins) Foster, was born in Merrimack, November 2, 1851, and has always resided in the house in which he was born. He was educated in the common schools and at Mont Vernon, completing his studies at the latter place at the age of twenty-two. Returning to his home he worked for his father until 1881, when he purchased the farm of one hundred and thirty-six acres which he has since successfully cultivated. He is engaged in general farming and the milk business. He is a Democrat. He has been a member of the school board six years, tax collector two terms, and selectman two terms. In matters pertaining to farming he is a leader, and for eight years has been a member of Thornton Grange, No. 31, Patrons of Husbandry. He is also a member of Souhegan Lodge, No. 98, Independent Order of Odd Fellows. He married, at Milford, November 13, 1878, Charlotte E. Converse, born in Amherst, December 21, 1856, daughter of Charles and Elizabeth (Fuller) Converse of Amherst. She was educated at Mont Vernon. Mr. and Mrs. Foster are members of the Christian Science Church. They have one daughter, Mary Lizzie, who was born February 16, 1880. She married, April 24, 1901, Bertie L. Peasley, of Bedford, New Hampshire, and has four children: Edith May, born April 22, 1902; Fred William, born April 18, 1903; Alice Mabel, November 4, 1904; and Hellen R., June 2, 1906.

Nathan Foster was born February 26, 1783, in Amesbury, Massachusetts, and was married, October 5, 1805, to Hannah, daughter of Francis Davis (see Davis, VI). She was born August 6, 1781, and died June 6, 1857. They were the parents of nine children: Francis Davis, died in Warner, in 1891; William S., died in 1889; John S., died 1894; Richard S., subject of the following paragraph; Mary Ann, who became the wife of Henry H. Hariman, and died 1899; Elizabeth, the wife of Josiah Trask, died 1893; Jonathan, died in his twenty-third year; Henry, died 1894; Judith, died 1892.

(II) Richard Straw, son of Nathan and Hannah (Davis) Foster, was born December 27, 1813, in Warner. He was educated in the common schools of that town, and early in life learned the trade of stone cutting. For several years he was employed in this capacity in Quincy, Massachusetts, and having been industrious and prudent in the care of his earnings was in a position to secure for himself a permanent home. About 1843 he returned to his native town and lived with his parents, while still continuing to devote a portion of his time to stone cutting. He was an active and influential citizen and held numerous offices. He was a Republican in politics, and was a leading member of the Baptist Church, in which he served as deacon and treasurer, and was also superintendent of its Sunday school. He married Elizabeth K. Pickett, daughter of Thomas and Sophia Pickett. She died January 7, 1902. She was the mother of three children: Sarah, Clarence, and Annette F. The last named became the wife of William A. Sawyer.

(III) Clarence, only son of Richard S. and Elizabeth K. (Pickett) Foster, was born June 5, 1848, in Warner, where he grew up and attended the public schools. Early in life he went to Beverly, Massachusetts, and was employed in a shoe factory. In 1876 he returned to Warner, and since that time he has been engaged in operating a large farm, which is devoted to the general purposes of agriculture. He is the owner of much valuable timber. Mr. Foster is a member of Warner Grange, No. 90, in which he has held several offices and is now master. He is an attendant of the Baptist Church, and is the present librarian of the local society. In politics he is a Republican. He is a member of the Independent Order of Odd Fellows, in which he has passed through the principal chairs, and has been for the past twenty years secretary of his lodge. These facts sufficiently indicate that he is an intelligent and progressive man and enjoys the confidence and esteem of his fellow citizens.

He was married, May 11, 1880, to Clara A. Tyler, who was born in Hopkinton, August 3, 1855, daughter of Lucius H. and Sarah A. (Hall) Tyler, of Hopkinton, New Hampshire. She died February 2, 1899, leaving two children. She was an active church worker, and was a highly esteemed and respected woman. The children are: Mabel L., born April 26, 1881; and Howard T., born April 22, 1890.

(Second Family.)

FOSTER This branch of the Foster family traces its descent from Andrew, who apparently has no connection with Reginald, usually considered the first American ancestor. The Andrew Foster line, though not as numerous as that of Reginald, is quite as ancient, and in some respects it has a more thrilling history.

(I) Andrew Foster was born in England about 1579. His name appears among the first settlers of Andover, Massachusetts, who came about 1640. He was made a freeman in 1669. He had twelve grants of land, most of them in the extreme southerly corner of the town, near Wilmington and around Foster's Pond, which was doubtless named for him. "Andrew Forrester, or Forster, of Andover, with his neighbors, Andrew Allen and Joseph Russell, were all members of the Scotch Charitable Association, once the St. Andrew's Society, formed in Boston as early as 1656, to aid the war prisoners of Cromwell's fights and other unfortunates from Virginia and along the shore who used to walk to Boston to get passage home." It is probable that Andrew Foster was twice married, both times in England. The name of his second wife was Ann, who survived him. The names of five children are recorded. He was seventy-three years of age when his youngest child was born. Andrew Foster died in Andover, May 7, 1685, and the town records read "aged one hundred and six years." His will was proved June 30th of that year. He left property inventoried at five hundred and four pounds. His widow died December 2, 1692. Mrs. Ann Foster was executrix of her husband's will, which proves that she had acknowledged integrity and business ability. Nevertheless, seven years later, she fell a victim to the witchcraft craze which cursed that time and neighborhood. She was examined four times, and through pious frenzy and overwrought nerves, was led to confess herself a witch. She said that she rode on a stick with Martha Currier to Salem village, where they met three hundred other witches. The testimony of herself and her fellow victims has been fully preserved. Mrs. Foster was imprisoned for twenty-one weeks, and would have been hanged had not death granted her a merciful release. Her son was forced to pay the keeper of the jail the sum of sixteen pounds and ten shillings before he could have the dead body of his mother. This sum, twenty years later, after the frenzy had abated, was restored to him and his sister by the Salem authorities. The children of Andrew Foster, so far as recorded were: Andrew. born about 1640, married Mary Russa; Abraham, born about 1648, married Ester Foster, daughter of Deacon Samuel of Chelmsford; Sarah, born about 1645. married, October 15, 1667, Samuel Kemp, of Chelmsford or Billerica; Hannah, married October 15, 1667, Hugh Stone; Mary, born July 9, 1652, married August 5, 1673, Lawrence Lacey. The history of the two younger children is tragic. Hannah (Foster) Stone was murdered by her husband, April 20, 1689. The details are fully given in Cotton Mather's Magnalia. It is intimated that the man was under the influence of strong drink at the time. The murder was the first that ever occurred at Andover, and it made a profound impression throughout the region. The youngest child, Mary (Foster) Lacey, like her mother, was accused and condemned as a witch. She died June 18, 1707.

(II) Andrew (2), the eldest recorded child of Andrew (1) Foster, was born at Andover, Massachusetts, about 1640. He was made a freeman in 1690. He married, June 7, 1662, Mary Russa, daughter of John and Margaret Russa, of Andover. They had six children: Abraham, whose sketch follows; Hannah, born July 16, 1668, married Thomas Astie; Mary, born November 28, 1670, died young; Mary, born June 10, 1673, married Ebenezer (Lovejoy); Sarah (twin), born May 25, 1677, married Benjamin Johnson, of Andover; Esther, born January 14, 1680, married her first cousin, Simon Stone, of Andover, son of Hugh and the murdered Hannah (Foster) Stone. Andrew Foster died in 1697, only five years after the death of his mother. His son, Abraham, was appointed administrator of his estate June 14, 1697. The inventory amounted to one hundred and twenty pounds, less than a quarter of his father's. His widow died April 19, 1721.

(III) Abraham, fourth child and only son of Andrew (2) and Mary (Russa) Foster, was born at Andover, Massachusetts, May 25, 1677. He spent his life in that town. June 29, 1703, he married Mary Johnson Lovejoy, daughter of William and Sarah Lovejoy, who was born in 1678, and died February 21, 1749. Abraham Foster survived his wife nearly five years, dying December 15, 1753. They had seven children: Hannah, born March 12, 1704, died young; Abraham, born in November, 1705, mentioned in the next paragraph; Sarah, born September 3, 1708, married, September 21, 1730, Jacob Preston, of Andover, and moved to Windham, Connecticut; a daughter born October 2, 1710, died young; Isaac, born June 26, 1712, died young; Hannah, born June 13, 1716, married February 16, 1738, John Russell; Jacob, born June 17, 1717, married Abigail Frost.

(IV) Abraham (2), eldest son and second child of Abraham (1) and Mary (Lovejoy) Foster, was born at Andover, Massachusetts, in November, 1705. He lived at Andover and Lynn, Massachusetts. He was published (married) to Sarah Frost, February 2, 1729. They had seven children. Abraham Foster died September 15, 1743, at the early age of thirty-seven. His widow afterwards married November 29, 1758, her husband's cousin, Andrew Foster. Her eldest son, Abraham, had died in February of that year, leaving to his mother six tracts of land in the heart of the town, which had been bequeathed him by his grandfather, Abraham Foster. Mrs. Sarah (Frost) Foster was admitted to the church in Andover from that in Boxford, September 26, 1760. The date of her death is not recorded. Abraham and Sarah (Frost) Foster had seven children: Abraham, born December 1, 1730, died February 1, 1758; Joshua, whose sketch follows; Jonathan, born April 24, 1734, became ward of Deacon Joseph Abbott, November 21, 1748, married Lydia Haggett, February 2, 1758; David, born July 31, 1737, married Molly Foster; Sarah, born September 28, 1739, died unmarried; Daniel, born October 13, 1741, died December 26, 1754; James, a posthumous child, born September 29, 1743, married Hannah.

(V) Joshua, second son and child of Abraham (2) and Sarah (Frost) Foster, was born at Lynn, Massachusetts, July 17, 1732. His father died young, and May 14, 1747, when Joshua was fifteen years of age, his uncle Jacob was appointed his guardian. Joshua married, May 26, 1756, Lydia Peabody, born in 1738. About 1764 Mr. Foster moved from Andover to Temple, New Hampshire, being the first of his family to move from Massachusetts. Of the five children, three were born in Andover, and the two youngest in Temple. Joshua Foster was a Revolutionary soldier, and is recorded as serving in Captain Drury's company, which was enrolled at Temple, April 19, 1775. In a deed of that period Joshua Foster is recorded as a joiner; in another deed he is called a yeoman. Joshua and Lydia (Peabody) Foster had five children: Joshua, whose sketch follows; Daniel, born March 10, 1759, married and died without children, was a Revolutionary soldier, and was drowned in the Kennebec river in Maine, aged seventy-five years; Lydia, born December 30, 1761, married Ensign John Foster of Hancock, New Hampshire; Betsey, born December 22, 1768, married Samuel Kilham, of Lyndeboro, New Hampshire; Sarah, born February 1, 1765. Joshua Foster, the father, died in August, 1776, aged forty-four. His widow died in 1806.

(VI) Joshua (2), eldest son and child of Joshua (1) and Lydia (Peabody) Foster, was born at Andover, Massachusetts, July 5, 1757. He was a Revolutionary soldier. He served in Captain Joseph Parker's company, Colonel Enoch Hale's regiment, July 1776; and was a member of Captain Robert Fletcher's company, same regiment, in August, 1778. He married, is 1806, Lucy Tenney, daughter of Benjamin and Ruth (Blanchard) Tenney; she was born in Temple, New Hampshire, October 26, 1779. They had six children: Sarah, born July 4, 1807, died unmarried, June 29, 1834; Daniel, born July 10, 1809, married Hannah Jones; Joshua, whose sketch follows; Benjamin Tenney, born July 8, 1818, married Abigail Howard; David Peabody, born September 4, 1815, married Mrs. Mary (Massa) Bartlett; Emily Blanchard, born February 14, 1818, died November 12, 1823. Joshua Foster, Jr., lived at Temple, New Hampshire, where he died October 22, 1823.

(VII) Joshua (3), second son and third child

of Joshua (2) and Lucy (Tenney) Foster, was born at Temple, New Hampshire, August 6, 1811. He was a successful farmer and stock dealer. He attended the Congregational Church, and sang in the choir for many years. He was a Republican in politics, and served as selectman for several terms, part of the time as chairman. In 1857 he was one of the committee who had charge of the hundredth anniversary celebration of Temple, New Hampshire. He had a local reputation as a vocalist, and took a lively interest in everything that pertained to the welfare of the town. Joshua Foster, in 1835, married Mary Heald, daughter of Daniel Heald of Temple, New Hampshire. He died September 4, 1890. They had six children: Emily, born June 30, 1837; Hannah A., born October 13, 1840; Oliver Heald, mentioned below; Eugene E., born August 15, 1843, married Francilla Upham; twin children, born February 7, 1845, died in infancy.

(VIII) Oliver Heald, second son and third child of Joshua and Mary (Heald) Foster, was born in Temple, New Hampshire, January 16, 1842. His boyhood was spent in his native town. He was educated in the common schools and at Appleton Academy, New Ipswich, New Hampshire. He was graduated from Bryant & Stratton's Commercial College, at Manchester, New Hampshire, in April, 1866. For a short time he was engaged in teaching, then in Carpentering. In 1867 he and his brother, Eugene Edward, established themselves in the provision business at Temple under the firm name of Foster Brothers. In 1872 they removed to Milford, where for twenty-five years they carried on a wholesale and retail business in meats and provisions. The brother died May 24, 1897, and Mr. Foster subsequently conducted the business alone, retaining the firm name. He retired in 1903. Like most of his ancestors Mr. Foster has seen military service in defense of his country. He was but nineteen years of age when the Civil war broke out, but towards its close he enlisted for three months in the Lafayette Artillery of Lyndeboro, New Hampshire. He was assigned as a private to garrison duty at Portsmouth, New Hampshire. He is a Republican by birth and education, and served as one of the selectmen in Temple, New Hampshire, for two years, and in Milford, New Hampshire, for four years. In 1892 he was elected representative to the state legisature. Mr. Foster is prominent in fraternal organizations. He is a member and past commander of Oliver W. Lull Post, No. 11, Grand Army of the Republic, of Milford. In the order of United American Mechanics he is past counsellor; and he is past sachem in the Improved Order of Red Men. He is a member of Benevolent Lodge, No. 7, Ancient Free and Accepted Masons, also of King Solomon Royal Arch Chapter, No. 17, of Milford. He is a Mason of the thirty-second degree, and belongs to the Saint George Commandery, Knights Templar, of Nashua, New Hampshire, and to Edward A. Raymond Consistory. He belongs to Puritan Chapter, No. 29, Order of the Eastern Star of Milford. He is a member of the Sons of the American Revolution. For seventeen years he was a member of the Milford Cornet Band. He is a trustee of the Milford Savings Bank. He belongs to the Congregational Church, and sang in the choir for many years. He was also a teacher in the Sunday school, and at one time served as superintendent.

December 31, 1874, Oliver Heald Foster married Hannah Elizabeth Wallace, daughter of Charles R. and Elizabeth R. (Lovejoy) Wallace of Milford. She was born February 4, 1853, and was educated in the Milford schools and at Maplewood Academy, Pittsfield, Massachusetts. Her father was a store keeper, and for eight years was town clerk up to his death in 1857. Mrs. Foster is a descendant of Captain Augustus Blanchard and of Captain Hezekiah Lovejoy, of New Hampshire, and of Sergeant Benjamin French of Massachusetts, all of them active in the Revolution. Her relatives were in the civil war, and she was active in societies at home during that time. Mr. and Mrs. Foster are the parents of four sons: Oliver W., born January 28, 1878; Arthur J., born July 23, 1879; Elmer J., born July 8, 1883; George R., born May 21, 1887. Oliver W. graduated from Dartmouth College in 1900, and from the Tuck School of Administration and Finance in 1901. He is now (1907) in charge of the Argentine Department for the American Trading Company, of New York. He married, in June, 1907, Mabel R. Lang, of Brooklyn, New York. Arthur J. married Emma L. Woodwell, August 3, 1903, and lives at Newburyport, Massachusetts. Elmer J. married Pearl O. Bugbee, August 5, 1903, and lives at Milford, New Hampshire. George R. is a member of the Milford high school.

MELLEN The name is that of a family, small in point of numbers, descended from a Scotch ancestor, and well known for the steady habits and good character of its members. It has been well known in mercantile pursuits, and is at present conspicuous in railroad operations.

(I) Simon Mellen, who is supposed to have been a son of Richard Mellen, of Charlestown, was born about 1635, was of Charlestown, 1660, Malden, 1668, Watertown, 1686, and settled, 1687, in Framingham, and built a house at what was afterward called Mellen's Neck. His wife, Mary, died in Framingham, June 1, 1709, aged seventy. Their six children were baptized at one time in Watertown, December 5, 1686.

(II) Thomas, son of Simon and Mary Mellen, was born in Malden, August, 1668. He and Simon, his father, were foundation members of the church of Framingham. His wife's name was Elizabeth. They lived in Framingham, where their seven children were born.

(III) Richard, son of Thomas and Elizabeth Mellen, was born in Framingham, November 10, 1701, and lived on the homestead of his father. In 1771 he sold two hundred acres of land, two houses and two barns. His wife was Abigail, and their children were: Josiah, William, Richard, Samuel and Mary.

(IV) Samuel, fourth son and child of Richard and Abigail Mellen, was born in Framingham, October 15, 1732. He lived in Framingham until after 1764, and removed to Warwick before 1770. He married Submit Stone, born in Framingham, June 30, 1738, daughter of Joseph and Lydia (Parkhurst) Stone. They had seven children: Martha, Ezra, Gilbert, Samuel, Joseph, Amory and Luther.

(V) Ezra, second child and eldest son of Samuel and Submit (Stone) Mellen, was born in Framingham, May 7, 1752. In his childhood the family removed to Warwick. In the revolution he served in Captain Elihu Lyman's company, of Colonel Elisha Porter's regiment, which was raised in 1779 for the defense of Connecticut. The regiment was stationed at New London. He married and had a family of six children: Samuel, Amory, Gilbert, Ezra, Luther and Polly.

(VI) Amory Mellen, second son and child of Ezra Mellen, born in Warwick, Massachusetts, in 1776, died in Alstead, New Hampshire, April 28, 1858. He was a hatter by trade and spent the most of his life in Alstead and Claremont, where he carried on his business with the assistance of two or three journeymen. He married (first) Lois Woods, and after her death he married (second) Candace Kingsbury, born in Alstead, 1790, died in Claremont, July 2, 1840, daughter of Samuel Kingsbury, of Sanbornton. They had four children: John Franklin; George Kingsbury, Charles Harvey and Louisa Emmeline.

(VII) George Kingsbury, second son of Amory and Candace (Kingsbury) Mellen, born in Alstead, August 10, 1821, was educated in the public schools, which he left at twelve years of age and went to Claremont, where he performed such work as he was able to get until he was seventeen. He then learned the hatter's trade, and went to Boston where he followed his trade from the age of twenty-one till twenty-nine, when he went to Lowell and was employed there five years, and in 1855 removed to Concord, New Hampshire. There he went into partnership with his father-in-law who had a short time before settled in Concord, and under the firm name of C. H. Sanger & Company, dealers in hats, caps and gentlemen's furnishings, they carried on business until 1881, when Mr. Mellen took the business and continued it until he retired from trade in 1893. Mr. Mellen was in business in Concord for thirty-eight years, and was always known as an upright and progressive citizen. He is now (1906) an unusually well preserved man of eighty-five years, with mind and memory better than those of many men much younger than he. He married in Lowell, Massachusetts, November 28, 1850, Hannah Maria Sanger, born in Middlesex, May 2, 1832, died in Concord, April 6, 1904, daughter of Charles H. and Hannah Jaques (Littlehale) Sanger, natives of Watertown and Middlesex, Massachusetts. Five children were born of this marriage: Charles Sanger, in Lowell, August 16, 1851, now president of the New York, New Haven & Hartford railway, married Marion B. Foster; Marietta, in Lowell, August 20, 1853, married Samuel Butterfield, and died in Concord, November 22, 1904; Walter Amory, in Concord, September 11, 1858, died September 22, 1859; Frank Warren, December 5, 1859, died May 18, 1864; Cora Candace, June 27, 1867, married Herbert G. Abbott, and resides in Concord.

TUCKER The report of visitation in the county of Kent, England, for the years 1619-20-21, preserved in the Harlein Manuscripts, contain the earliest known record of the Tuckers, and mention several ancestors in direct line of the founder of the family in America. The information contained in those manuscripts was verified some twenty years ago by Deacon John A. Tucker, of Milton, Massachusetts, who visited Milton-next-Gravesend, where he was given access to the registry of baptisms by the rector of the ancient Church of St. Peter's and St. Paul's. This registry reaches back as far as the year 1558, and in it Deacon Tucker found the records of the baptism of his early ancestors, thus proving that the information obtained from the Harlein Manuscripts is absolutely correct.

(I) Willielmus Tucker, of Thornley, county of Devon, married "Jona" (or Josea) Ashe, and had sons George, Thomas and John.

(II) George, son of Willielmus and "Jona" (Ashe) Tucker, married Maria Hunter, of Gaunte, and had five sons: George, Nicholas, Tobias, Mansfield and Daniel.

(III) George (2), gentleman, son of George (1) and Maria (Hunter) Tucker, resided in or near Milton-next-Gravesend, in Kent. He married (first), Elizabeth, daughter of Francis Stoughton, and she bore him one son, George. For his second wife he married Maria Darrett, and had John, Elizabeth, Maria, Robert and Henry Tucker.

(IV) Robert, second son and fourth child of George (2) and Maria (Darrett) Tucker, was born at Milton-next-Gravesend, in 1604. He is supposed to have come from New England with a company of colonists from Weymouth, England, under the guidance of the Rev. Dr. Hall, and was in Weymouth, Massachusetts, in 1635. From the latter place he went to Gloucester, where he served as recorder for a time, but returned to Weymouth and held some of the town offices. He finally purchased several lots of land on Brush Hill, Milton, Massachusetts, some one hundred and seventeen acres in all, bordering on land which his son James had previously acquired, and it is quite probable that he had settled there permanently prior to the incorporation of the town in 1662. For several years he represented Milton in the general court, was town clerk for many years and as the first town records are in his handwriting, he was doubtless the first to hold that office. The answer of the general court to the petition for incorporation bears the date May 7, 1662, and is signed Robert Tucker, recorder. He was active in the church and a member of its committee, and was spoken of as Goodman Tucker. His death occurred in Milton, March 11, 1682, and his interment took place on the 13th. He married Elizabeth Allen, and had a family of nine children, namely: Sarah, James, Joseph, Elizabeth, Benjamin, Ephraim, Mannasseh, Rebecca, and Mary. Sarah became the wife of Peter Warren. Elizabeth became the wife of Ebenezer Clapp. Rebecca married a Fenno, and Mary married Samuel Jones.

(V) Ephraim, fourth son and sixth child of Robert and Elizabeth (Allen) Tucker, was probably born at Weymouth, in 1652. Jointly with his mother he was appointed to settle his father's estate. He was admitted a freeman in 1678, served as a selectman and town clerk in Milton, and was chosen a deacon of the church July 31, 1698. September 27, 1688, he married Hannah Gulliver, and their children were: Ephraim, Stephen, Lydia and Hannah.

(VI) Stephen, second son and child of Ephraim and Hannah (Gulliver) Tucker, was born in Milton, April 8, 1691. He settled in Preston, Connecticut. On August 3, 1716, he married Hannah Belcher, of Milton, and was the father of: Stephen (died young), another Stephen, William, Ephraim and Lydia. The mother of these children died February 28, 1745.

(VII) William, third son and child of Stephen and Hannah (Belcher) Tucker, was born in Preston, May 28, 1737, and died there November 5, 1819. He was married, June 4, 1767, to Esther Morgan, who was born in Preston, March 24, 1744, daughter of Captain Daniel and Elizabeth (Gates) Morgan. She died October 2, 1818. Their children were: Stephen, Susan (died young), Elizabeth, Hannah, Susan and William.

(VIII) William (2), youngest son and child of William and Esther (Morgan) Tucker, was born in Preston, January 26, 1782. For a number of years he was engaged in the cotton manufacturing

DARTMOUTH COLLEGE

business at Norwich, Connecticut, and his death occurred July 11, 1839. On May 5, 1814, he married Sarah Morgan, who was born April 21, 1787, daughter of Daniel and Elizabeth (Lord) Morgan. She died November 4, 1845, having been the mother of seven children, namely: Henry, Mary, Betsey, Daniel M., Sarah, Hannah M. and George.

(IX) Henry, eldest son and child of William and Sarah (Morgan) Tucker, was born in Griswold, Connecticut, January 8, or February 16, 1815. He entered Amherst College but did not graduate, preferring to engage in business, and becoming associated with his father in the textile industry at Norwich, he succeeded the latter as proprietor. He continued in the cotton manufacturing business at Norwich until 1885, when he went to Sandusky, Ohio, thence to Chicago and from the latter city to Brooklyn, New York. His last days were spent in Hanover with his daughter, Mrs. D. C. Wells, and he died in that town in 1905. He was in early life a Whig in politics, and later a Republican. In his religious belief he was a Congregationalist, and as a young man he united with the church in Norwich. He was first married, September 4, 1837, to Sarah White Lester, of Griswold, who was born in December, 1817, daughter of Joseph and Martha (Coit) Lester. She died September 20, 1846, and on December 5, 1849, he married Julia H. Doolittle. She was born June 28, 1830, and died in 1860. The children of his first union are: William Jewett, now president of Dartmouth College, who will be again referred to. Elizabeth Coit, born July 28, 1844, died September 29 of that year; and Edward Jewett, born August 28, 1846, died February 22, 1863. Of his second marriage there is one daughter, Sarah Elizabeth, who was born March 18, 1854, and on June 2, 1887, became the wife of Professor D. C. Wells, of Bowdoin College.

(X) William Jewett, D. D., LL. D., eldest child of Henry and Sarah W. (Lester) Tucker, was born in Griswold, July 13, 1839. Upon the death of his mother in 1846 he was taken into the home of her sister, the wife of the Rev. William Reed Jewett, then pastor of the Congregational Church in Plymouth, New Hampshire, and was subsequently adopted into the family, receiving the legal right to insert the name of Jewett in his baptismal name. He prepared for college at the Kimball Union Academy at was graduated at Dartmouth with honor in the class of 1861. After devoting two years to teaching at Columbus, Ohio, he entered the Andover, Massachusetts Theological Seminary, from which he was graduated in 1866. From 1867 to 1875 he was pastor of the Franklin Street Congregational Church, Manchester, and from the latter year to 1879 he occupied the pulpit of the Madison Square Church, New York City, resigning that pastorate in order to accept the chair of sacred rhetoric at the Andover Theological Seminary, retaining that post until 1893, when he was unanimously elected president of Dartmouth College, and has ever since directed the affairs of that well known seat of learning.

While at Andover he founded the Andover Home, a Social Settlement in Boston, now known at the South End House. He was also one of the original editors of the *Andover Review*, the editorial writings of which Review gave rise to the "Andover Case." He was the Phi Beta Kappa orator at Harvard, 1892; lecturer in the Lowell Institute, 1894; Lyman Beecher lecturer at Yale, 1898; lecturer on the Morse foundation at Union Theological Seminary, 1902; and on the Earle foundation, Berkeley Divinity School, Berkeley, California, 1904. He is the author of "From Liberty to Unity," 1892; "The Making and Unmaking of the Preacher," 1899, etc. He received the degree of Doctor of Divinity from Dartmouth and the University of Vermont, and the degree of Doctor of Laws from Yale, Williams, Wesleyan, and Columbia.

Dr. Tucker's first wife, whom he married June 22, 1870, was Charlotte Henry Rogers, and she died September 15, 1882, leaving two daughters: Alice Lester, born June 27, 1873, wife of Professor Frank H. Dixon; and Margaret, born August 22, 1878, wife of Nelson P. Brown, Esq. On June 22, 1887, he married for his second wife Charlotte Barrell Cheever, daughter of Rev. Henry P. Cheever, of Worcester, Massachusetts. Of this union there is one daughter, Elizabeth Washburn, born June 4, 1889.

(Second Family.)

TUCKER is an old English occupative surname and means weaver. The ancient Tucker families of New England are from several ancestors not known to be related to each other. This family was early planted in Massachusetts and New Hampshire.

(I) Morris Tucker, whose christian name in ancient records is often writter Maurice, of Salisbury, Massachusetts, and Tiverton, Rhode Island, is of record as a "cooper." He was a householder in Salisbury in 1659, took the oath of allegiance and fidelity there in 1677, and became a freeman in 1690. He and his wife signed the Bradbury petition in 1692. He was of Salisbury in 1694, and of Tiverton, February, 1700. He probably moved to the latter town in 1699, as he deeded his real property there to Samuel Joy on February 3 of that year. On May 7, 1694, he deeded ten acres to his son James, for ten pounds. He married (first), October 14, 1661, Elizabeth Stevens, born in Salisbury, February 4, 1642, and died October 16, 1662, daughter of Sergeant John and Katherine Stevens; and (second), 1663, Elizabeth Gill, born January 8, 1646, daughter of John Gill. The only child by the first wife was Benoni. Those by the second wife were: John, Mary, James, Sarah, Joseph, Jabez, Elizabeth, and Morris. (Mention of Joseph and descendants appears in this article). Some of the descendants of this ancestor were Quakers.

(II) Benoni, eldest child of Morris and Elizabeth (Stevens) Tucker, was born in Salisbury, October 16, 1662, and was a weaver, living in Salisbury and later in West Amesbury. He signed the Bradbury petition in 1692; and was a "snow shoe man" in Amesbury in 1708. His will was dated January 14, and proven March 17, 1735. He married Ebenezar Nichols, born August 3, 1664, daughter of Thomas and Mary Nichols, and they had seven children, as follows: Ebenezer, Benjamin, Nathaniel, Elizabeth, Mary, Kathren, Frances, and Ezra.

(III) Ezra, youngest child of Benoni and Ebenezar (Nichols) Tucker, was born in Amesbury, March 27, 1706. He married, January 24, 1727, Bathsheba Sargent, born October 10, 1709, daughter of Charles and Hannah (Foot) Sargent, of West Amesbury, near the town of Merrimack, and they had seven children: Ezra, Mary, Callia, Hittee, Sarah, and Benoni.

(IV) Ezra (2), eldest child of Ezra (1) and Bathsheba (Sargent) Tucker, settled in Henniker, New Hampshire, as early as 1766, and in 1772 purchased a place upon which he moved, and there passed his remaining days. He was a soldier at Crown Point in 1756 and 1758, in the French and Indian war, and was in the Revolution; was commissioned second lieutenant in Captain Emery's company, Colenel Thomas Stickney's regiment, March 5, 1776, and was at the battle of White Plains,

October 28, 1776. He was a prominent man in the town for many years. He died October 26, 1804. He married Hepsibah Pressey, daughter of John and Mercy Pressey, of Kingston, New Hampshire. She died September 22, 1801. Their children were: Ezra, Betsey, Hannah, Jonathan, Phebe, Thomas, David, and three other children of whom there is no record.

(V) Nathan, son of Ezra Tucker, was born in Poplin (now Fremont), October 18, 1764. He settled in Salisbury, New Hampshire, on the west side of the pond, and his farm was recently owned by his grandson, Levi W. Tucker. On March 14, 1782, he married for his first wife Lydia Stevens, and for his second wife he married Mary Welch of Canaan, this state. The children of the first wife were: Rev. Joseph, Hannah, Polly, Caleb, Ezra and Nathan. Those of his second wife were: Lydia, Eliza and Lucinda. (Nathan and descendants are mentioned at length in this article).

(VI) Ezra, third son and fifth child of Nathan and Lydia (Stevens) Tucker, was born March 22, 1793. He went from Salisbury to Grafton, where he resided until his death, the date of which is not given in the records examined. He married Judith Burbank, of Boscawen, and was the father of twelve children: John, Daniel, George W., Lydia, Martha, Oliver, Nathan, Elsie, Alice, Sophronia, Mary and Judith.

(VII) John, eldest son and child of Ezra and Judith (Burbank) Tucker, was born at Salisbury in 1812. When a young man he went to reside in Springvale, Maine, where he was engaged in farming for a short time, and going to Dover, New Hampshire, was connected with the Manufacturing Company for the rest of his life, which terminated May 14, 1852. In 1832 he was married to Eliza Huzzey, of Springvale, who survived him many years and died in 1887. She became the mother of six children: Mary Eliza (who died young), George H., Edward Martin, Sarah J., John and Mary Eliza.

(VIII) Edwin Martin Tucker, M. D., second son and third child of John and Eliza (Huzzey) Tucker, was born in Springvale, April 22, 1839. His early education, which was begun in Dover, included a commercial course at a mercantile school in Boston, and his preliminary medical studies were directed by Dr. L. G. Hill, of Dover. At the breaking out of the civil war he suspended his professional preparations, and on September 5, 1861, enlisted in Battery C, Massachusetts Light Artillery. September 20, 1862, he was severely wounded during an engagement at Shepherdstown, Virginia, and was conveyed to a military hospital in Philadelphia, where he subsequently received an honorable discharge from the service on account of physical disability. Having sufficiently recovered, in 1864 he re-enlisted, was accepted by the examining surgeons, and assigned to duty as hospital steward in the Twenty-fourth Regiment, Veteran Reserve Corps, with which he served until the close of the war. In December, 1865, he was appointed a hospital steward in the regular army by General Grant, and served in that capacity for a period of six years, or until December, 1871, when he resigned in order to complete his professional studies. Prior to leaving the army he was a medical student at Georgetown, District of Columbia, University, and entering the medical department of Bowdoin College in 1872 he was graduated in July of the following year. Locating for practice in Canaan, he found in that town and its environments a most promising field for professional advancement, and availing himself of the excellent opportunities open to him he built up a large general practice, which he has ever since retained. In politics Dr. Tucker is a Republican. He formerly served upon the school board, also upon the board of health and for many years has acted as a justice of the peace. His professional society affiliations are with the New Hampshire State and the White River Medical societies. He was made a Mason at Dover in 1865, and is now a member of Summit Lodge of Canaan, and also of Belknap Chapter, Royal Arch Masons, of Dover. He joined the Knights of Pythias forty-one years ago, and at the present time is a member of Mount Cardigan Lodge of Canaan. He also belongs to Helping Hand Lodge, Independent Order of Odd Fellows, and the Sons of the Revolution, is a comrade of Admiral Farragut Post, No. 52, Grand Army of the Republic, of Enfield, and was in 1895 medical director of the department of New Hampshire. He is an ardent Baptist, a member of the First Baptist Church of Canaan, New Hampshire. Dr. Tucker married Miss Mary Albina Kimball, daughter of Peter and Nancy A. (Adams) Kimball, of Grafton, this state. He has one daughter, Luie Albina, who was born April 28, 1884. Dr. Tucker is of Revolutionary descent. His great-great-grandfather, Moses Burbank, was in the battle of Bunker Hill, and his son, Jonathan Burbank, served from 1776 to the close of the war.

(VI) Caleb, fourth son of Nathan and Lydia (Stevens) Tucker, born in Salisbury, November 6, 1789; died in Wilmot, March 29, 1834, was a substantial and prosperous farmer. He married, December 26, 1811, Dorothy Bean, second daughter of Jeremiah and Mehitable (Garland) Bean, of Salisbury. They had ten children: Samuel Reed (died young), Samuel Reed, Joseph Bean, Mehitable Bean, Mercy, Hannah Hackett, Judith Emeline, Lydia Cox, Charles Walter and Thomas Brown, whose sketch follows.

(VII) Thomas Brown, youngest child of Caleb and Dorothy (Bean) Tucker, was born in Wilmot, August 17, 1830. He attended the common schools until fifteen years old, and then began to serve an apprenticeship at the machinist's trade in Manchester. After a residence of about five years in Manchester he removed to Providence, Rhode Island, where he rose by successive promotions to the position of superintendent of the works in which he was employed. Failing health forced him to give up this place, and he then engaged in mercantile business in Rhode Island until 1857, when he returned to New Hampshire and succeeded Hiram Bell in the management of the old National Hotel at Henniker. In 1859 he returned to his former occupation of manufacturer of fine tools and builder of machinery at Providence, where he remained until ill health again compelled him to give up that business, some years later. He returned to New Hampshire and immediately purchased the Kearsarge House at Warner, which he conducted for the ensuing six years. The seven years following this period he operated the Washington House at Pittsfield, whence he moved to Peterborough, where he pursued the same calling for many years, until he transferred the business to his son. Although compelled by circumstances over which he had no control to relinquish one line of business, Mr. Tucker achieved a success in entertaining the traveling public equal to that which he attained in making machinery. He was a genial and agreeable host, always ready "to welcome the coming and speed the parting guest," and widely and favorably known. His house acquired the reputation of being a model place for the entertainment of the public. In financial matters Mr. Tucker has been successful. He owns valuable land and some of the principal buildings in Peterborough, and has been a director in the savings bank. In politics a Democrat, he took early an interest in public affairs, and has filled various political offices. While residing in Pittsfield he was sheriff, county commissioner, etc. He has been active in local affairs in Peterborough and has filled the office of president of the board of water commissioners. He retired from active business, and is now enjoying the leisure and comforts that a successful life has brought him. He married, in Rhode Island, Susan Ruth Cross Clarke, born in Kingston, 1835, and died September 5. 1901, aged sixty-six years, eight months and three days, daughter of Samuel C. Clarke of Narragansett Pier, Rhode Island. They have one child, whose sketch follows.

(VIII) George Samuel, only child of Thomas Brown and Susan R. (Clarke) Tucker, born in Henniker, New Hampshire, July 12, 1858, was educated in Providence, Rhode Island. His whole life since attaining the required age has been devoted to hotel management. While yet a boy he left school to aid his father in this line of employment, and with the exception of two years spent in completing and managing the new hotel at Dartmouth College, he was associated with his father until the latter retired about 1890. Since that time he has managed Tucker's Tavern with such care and skill as to increase the comforts and the patronage and extend the reputation of that already well known hostelry. Mr. Tucker is an able, energetic and progressive man of the younger generation, abreast of the times in all that pertains to public matters, and as a citizen occupies a prominent place in the community. His political affiliations are with the Democratic party. He is a member of Peterborough Lodge, No. 15, Independent Order of Odd Fellows, of Peterborough, and of Union Encampment, filling all the chairs in the latter. He married in Boston, December 25, 1886, Evelyn Genevieve Barker, born in Exeter, Maine, May 12. 1865, daughter of John and Clarinda (Ginn-Robinson) Barker. They have one daughter, Marguerite Clarke, born July 17, 1888.

(II) Joseph, third son and fifth child of Morris and Elizabeth (Gill) Tucker, was born in Salisbury, February 20, 1672, and died June 30, 1743. On November 27, 1735. he gave his son, Moses, of Kingston, his homestead, which was on the road from "the mills" to Hampton, in consideration of maintenance. This was deeded back by Moses July 13, 1738, and on the same date the father deeded the homestead to his son James, for three hundred dollars in province bills of credit. This deed also included other land. In 1729 the father deeded to James forty acres on which the latter then lived. He married, 1695 (published October 14), Phebe Page, born November 17, 1674, daughter of Joseph and Martha (Dow) Page, of Haverhill. She died December 29, 1736. A Phebe Tucker was admitted to the Salisbury church. June 18, 1718. The children of this marriage were: James, Samuel, Joseph, Moses, Ebenezer, and Phebe.

(III) James, eldest child of Joseph and Phebe (Page) Tucker, born in Salisbury, April 25, 1697, died July 7, 1769, in his seventy-third year, and was buried in the South Plain cemetery. The inventory of his estate exceeded £500. He married, June 15, 1721, Hannah True, born in Salisbury, August 28. 1698, daughter of Deacon William and Eleanor (Stevens) True. She died July 18, 1773. Their children were: Henry, Elizabeth, Jabez, Martha, James, Eleanor, Ebenezer and Henry. (Mention of Ebenezer and descendants appears in this article).

(IV) Jabez, second son and child of James (1) and Hannah (True) Tucker, was born January 6, 1727, and died March 6, 1781. He married in Salisbury, January 5, 1748, Ruth Morrill, born August 27, 1727, in Salisbury, and died December 6, 1819, daughter of Benjamin and Ruth (Allen) Morrill (see Morrill, IV), and they had children: Jabez, Benjamin, Ruth (mother of Ralph Waldo Emerson), Hannah (died young), Molly, Miriam, Micajah, James, John and Hannah.

(V) James (2), fourth son and eighth child of Jabez and Ruth (Morrill) Tucker, was born April 15, 1766, and died in Pittsfield, June 26, 1841. Hannah Cram Tucker, his wife, born March 7, 1769, died February 8, 1842; they had children: Ruth, Jabez, Benjamin, Sally (died early), David, Jonathan, Sally, James, Hannah. Only two, Ruth and Hannah, the oldest and youngest, lived till twenty-one years of age.

(VI) Hannah, daughter of James (2) and Hannah (Cram) Tucker, married John S. Tilton, of Pittsfield, and died in Pittsfield, November 10, 1891, leaving no children. Had one child that died in infancy.

(IV) Ebenezer, son of James (1) and Hannah (True) Tucker, was born on the Tucker homestead in Salisbury, Massachusetts, June 18, 1737, and spent his entire life in that town. He died August 14, 1814. His will, dated April 15, 1814, with that of his father, is now in possession of his grandson, James Tucker, of this sketch. He married (first), December 5, 1758, Mary Adams, and (second), December 6, 1811, Hope Present, of Kensing. New Hampshire. He had children as follows all by his first wife: Sarah, born October 6, 1759. William, December 26, 1760. Stephen, January 12, 1763, died previous to 1814, leaving a son John. Betty, May 4, 1765, married William True. Samuel Adams, May 11, 1767. Ebenezer, January 8, 1769. James, August 21, 1771. Hannah, September 23, 1773; never married. Mary, October 9. 1775, married Moses Gill, died November 23, 1821. Martha, November 2, 1777, married Samuel Huntoon. Benjamin, February 29, 1780, died July 23, 1801.

(V) James (2), seventh child and fifth son of Ebenezer and Hannah (True) Tucker, was born in Salisbury. August 21, 1771, and died June 16, 1842, aged seventy-one years. He succeeded to the ownership of the ancestral homestead, which had been in the Tucker family since 1690, and followed agriculture, the calling of his ancestors, throughout his life. He married, April 24, 1803, Nancy Fifield, who was born in Hampton Falls, New Hampshire, October 9, 1783 daughter of George and Mary (Marston) Fifield, of Hampton Falls. She died April 20, 1852, aged sixty-nine years. Twelve children were born of this marriage. Of these, two died young, and ten grew to mature age. They were: Benjamin, Mary Adams, Ebenezer, Nancy, Clarissa, Ruamy Dodge, Sally Brown. Lavonia, Sophronia and James, who is mentioned below. Benjamin married Betsey Q. Gale; Mary A. married Asa F. Kimball; Ebenezer married Ethelinda Wadleigh; Nancy became the wife of Hiram Collins; Clarissa married Charles Morrill; Ruamy D. married John C. Jewell; Sally B. became the wife of Enoch Morrill; Lavonia married Benjamin S. Blake; and Sophronia, Moses Morrill.

(VI) James (3), fourth son and twelfth child of James (2) and Nancy (Fifield) Tucker, was born in Salisbury, Massachusetts, December 6, 1823. He was educated in the public school and after leaving school served an apprenticeship of three years and four months at the blacksmith's trade at Haverhill. He then worked a short time in Amesbury, and afterward went to North Andover, where he was employed for a year in Miller & Blood's machine shop. During the seven or eight years following he worked in the shops in New Hampshire, being employed successively at Salmon Falls, Great Falls, and Conway. May 8, 1848, he became an employe of the Boston & Maine Railroad Company, and was stationed at Somersworth, New Hampshire, where he remained until November 1, 1855, when he was made foreman of the repair shop of the Northern Division of the Boston & Maine Railroad Company at Sanbornville, in the town of Wakefield, New Hampshire, and has charge of seventy men. He has been in the employ of the Boston & Maine for sixty years, and is now (1908) eighty-four years old, and the oldest man in the employ of the company, yet he is as active as a man of fifty, and can always be found in business hours at his office or about the yards of the place. His geniality and fund of anecdote and humor make him popular wherever he is known. In 1870 he served as selectman of the town of Wakefield. For well on three score years he has been a member of the most ancient of existing fraternal organizations—the Free Masons—having been inducted into Libanus Lodge, No. 49, Free and Accepted Masons, in Somersworth, New Hampshire, May 16, 1854. He was master of Unity Lodge, No. 62 the first eight years of its existence. He is also a member of Carroll Royal Arch Chapter, No. 23, of Wolfeboro, and of Dover Lodge, No. 84, Benevolent and Protective Order of Elks, and an honorary member of all the organizations of engineers. He was a charter member of Songonombe Tribe, Improved Order of Red Men. in 1888. James Tucker married, June 8, 1848, Mary E. Hale, who was born in Haverhill, Massachusetts, March 18. 1822, and died March 2, 1895, daughter of Samuel and Anna (Plummer) Hale. Five children were born of this union: John Chandler, April 21, 1849; died June 3, 1849. Willis Herbert, Frances Hale, James Fifield, and Sophronia. John Chandler was born in Somersworth and died in Haverhill, Massachusetts. 1. Willis H. was born in Somersworth, New Hampshire. 2. Frances H. was born in Somersworth and married William F. Hanson, by whom she has one child, Willis C. Hanson, a locomotive engineer. 3. James F., also born in Somersworth, is also a locomotive engineer. He married Mary F. Brackett. by whom he has eight children: Charles H., Grover C., James C., Willard B., Morris A., Willis F., Harris W. and Mary Elizabeth. 4. Sophronia, born in Wakefield, is the wife of Irving D. Rice, of Sanbornville, by whom she has one child, Dorothy Frances, living, two having died in infancy.

MARSHALL This name is found early in Massachusetts, and has been identified with New Hampshire in a conspicuous way. It has been borne by a very considerable number of men of prominence in this country. A chief justice of the United States Court, an orator and statesman from Ohio, and a prominent lawyer from New Hampshire are among the leading citizens of this name.

(I) John Marshall appears at Billerica, Massachusetts, in 1656-7 but the place of his origin has not yet been discovered. On February 4 of that year he was granted a six acre lot in Billerica. His first allotment of the common lands was twenty acres, lying partly on the township and partly on the commons; bounded by John Sheldon, north; by the commons, east; by Peter Bracket, south; by Mr. Whiting and William Pattin, west; also a parcel of land reserved for "ye ministry on ye west and partly on ye south and partly by East street on the south west." The last bound is a reminiscence of the ancient Andover road, before it was added in 1660 to its present place; and the location is east of the narow gauge railroad line as it runs south from the street. When the road was altered he was allowed a private way across Sheldon's land to reach his own. He received later grants further east and sold his first grant, as above described, to Dr. Samuel Frost. The road running east across Loes' Plain was early known as Marshall's Lane, and a house lot, which was occupied by the family on the east road near the turn of this lane, was standing as late as 1883. According to a deposition made by John Marshall, as found in the Massachusetts Archives, he was born about 1617, the time of his death, November 5, 1702. He was styled in the record Sargeant John Marshall. He was married November 19, 1662, to Hannah Atkinson, who was probably a daughter of Thomas Atkinson, of Concord, Massachusetts. She was born March 5, 1644, and died September 7, 1665. John Marshall married (second) November 27, 1665, Mary Burrage, a daughter of John Burrage, of Charlestown. She died October 30, 1680, aged thirty-nine years, and he married (third) November 30, 1681, Damaris Waite, a widow, of Malden. She was married (third) July 14, 1703, to Lieutenant Thomas Johnson of Andover. John Marshall's children were: John (died young), Mary (died young), Johanna, John, Mary, Hannah, Thomas, Isaac and Mehitabel.

(II) John (2), second son and fourth child of John (1) and Mary (Burrage) Marshall, was born August 1, 1671, in Billerica, and resided in that town where he died January 25, 1714. He was married December 8, 1695, to Unis Rogers, a daughter of John (2) and Mary (Shedd) Rogers, and granddaughter of John (1) Rogers of Watertown, Massachusetts. His children were: Mary, John, Daniel, Unise, Thomas, Samuel, William and Isaac.

(III) Thomas, third son and fifth child of John (2) and Unis (Rogers) Marshall, was born March 28, 1706, in Billerica, Massachusetts, and lived in Tewksbury, where he died September 8. 1778. His first wife, Ruth (surname unknown) died July 5, 1741, and he subsequently married Mary (surname unknown), who died July 7, 1770. He married (third) Phoebe Phelps, widow of Francis P. Pepperell. She died January 15, 1779. Their children were: Thomas, Samuel, Joseph, John, Abel (died young), Jonas, Ruth, Joel, Silas, Rufus, Mary, Daniel, William, Hannah (died young), Hannah and Abel. (Samuel and Joseph and descendants receive mention in this article).

(IV) Thomas (2), eldest child of Thomas (1) and Ruth Marshall, was born November 23, 1729, in Tewksbury, and was one of the foremost citizens of Chelmsford, Massachusetts. He was a man of excellent ability and respected for his upright character and example. He was a soldier in the Revolution and the town records attest his worth thus: "Thomas Marshall died very suddenly much lamented, March 25, 1800." He was married in Chelmsford, February 22, 1753, to Hannah Frost.

(V) Isaac, son of Thomas (2) and Hannah (Frost) Marshall, was born December 25, 1757, in Chelmsford, and was a soldier in the revolution and pensioner. In 1790, he removed from Chelmsford to Pelham, New Hampshire, where his first wife died. He was a farmer in that town where he died November 15, 1840. He married (second) September 5, 1809, Mehitabel Tenney, who was born February 28, 1779, in Pelham, a daughter of Daniel and Elizabeth (Dole) Tenney. She died September 22, 1849.

(VI) Daniel, son of Isaac and Mehitabel (Tenney) Marshall, was born November 9, 1816, in Pelham, where he was a prosperous farmer and a highly respected citizen. He was educated in the common schools, and was raised and spent his life a farmer. He was a member of the Congregational Church in which he was a leader. In politics he was a Democrat, and being a man of natural ability and possessing the confidence of his townsmen, he was elected to various public offices. He was justice of the peace for years, selectman, and representative in 1862-3 in the New Hampshire legislature. Member of the constitutional convention. He was often called upon to give his neighbors counsel and advice, and was frequently employed in the settlement of estates and other probate business. He was married January 9, 1838, to Hannah Jane Campbell, who was born August 3, 1817, in Windham, New Hampshire, daughter of Captain William and Margaret (Hughes) Campbell. They lived to celebrate the golden anniversary of their wedding and nearly ten more years were added to their wedded life. He died September 11, 1897. His widow died March 4, 1907, aged ninety years. They were the parents of five children, and also one, Isaac C., who was adopted. He is now living in Pelham, a retired farmer. Three of these children are living: William O., who lives in Laconia; Louise, who married Edwin Bell, and lives in Lowell; and Moses R., whose sketch follows next.

(VII) Moses Runnel, second son and fourth child of Daniel and Hannah Jane (Campbell) Marshall, was born in Pelham, May 17, 1848. He was educated in his native town and New Hampton Institute and business college., and assisted his father on the farm until he was eighteen years old, leaving school at that time, when he went to Nashua, where he was a salesman in a clothing store for three years until he came of age, when he engaged in the clothing business in Lowell, Massachusetts, where he remained ten years. From Lowell he removed to New Hampshire, and settled in Meredith, and represented that town in the legislature in 1883. The following year he settled in Manchester, and for the next ten years dealt in ice and fuel. In 1898 he bought the interest of the heirs of Aretas Blood in the B. H. Piper Company, of which he is treasurer. This company was organized in 1850, and incorporated in 1890. It employes about twenty men, and manufactures handles, spokes, and base ball bats and other wooden utensils. Mr. Marshall's enterprise and industry have brought him ample financial returns, and his frank and open-hearted manner has made him a wide circle of friends. He married, August 1, 1872, Emily C. Brown, who was born in Nashua, March 2, 1851, daughter of William W. and Caroline (Belterley) Brown of Nashua (See Brown). They have one child, Ethelyn Louise. Mrs. Marshall is a lady of culture and refinement, and is a member of the Daughters of the American Revolution, and one of the board of managers of Molly Stark Chapter of that organization. Ethelyn Louise married Allen E. Cross, of Brooklyn (See Cross family). They have two children. Mr. and Mrs. Marshall attend the Franklin Street Congregational Church.

(IV) Samuel, second son and child of Thomas (1) and Ruth Marshall, was born May 10, 1732, in Tewksbury, Massachusetts. He was an active and useful citizen of Chelmsford, in the same state. His descendants are many and widely scattered. He was married January 2, 1755, to Esther Frost, of Billerica, who was born February 17, 1730, in that town, daughter of William and Elizabeth (Wilson) Frost.

(V) Abel, son of Samuel and Esther (Frost) Marshall, was born September 9, 1764, in Chelmsford, Massachusetts, and lived in that town and in Lyme, New Hampshire. In his last days he returned to his native town and died there. He was married March 11, 1788, to Polly Flint, and their children were: Abel, Micajah, Polly, Hannah, Sally, Samuel, John, Rhoda, Harriet and George.

(VI) Micajah (Macaiah), second son and child of Abel and Polly (Flint) Marshall, was born January 30, 1790, in Chelmsford, and died in Lyme, New Hampshire, May 23, 1882, at the age of ninety-two years. When eighteen years old he removed with his parents to Lyme, where the remaining seventy-two years of his life were spent. He was a well-to-do farmer, and much respected. He was ever a true friend to the poor, and in his long record of years many a deed of charity and whole-souled benevolence is warmly remembered by a large circle of friends. His public enterprise led him to assist in building churches and schoolhouses, and he contributed liberally of his means in every way for the public good. He belonged to no church; but was nevertheless a man of Christian spirit and deeds. At the time of his death he left five brothers and sisters, the oldest of whom was ninety-two and the youngest seventy-three. He married (second), Martha Southard, who survived him. He was the father of sixteen children, none of whom are now living.

(VII) Anson Southard, son of Macaiah and Martha (Southard) Marshall, was born in Lyme, December 3, 1822, and died in Concord, July 5, 1874. His boyhood was passed on his father's farm. In early life he was a child of delicate constitution, but as he grew older he became strong and healthy. At an early age he inclined toward learning and study, and after fitting himself by eighteen months of study at the academy at Thetford, he entered Dartmouth College, from which he graduated with the class of 1848. His first employment after graduation was school teaching. About the year 1849, the town of Fitchburg, Massachusetts, established a high school, and the committee having the selection of teachers in charge chose Mr. Marshall from a large number of applicants. He was a popular and successful teacher, and in after years his pupils spoke of him with enthusiasm and affection. While in Fitchburg he entered the law office of Wood & Torrey, but on account of the duties incumbent on him as a teacher the time he spent in the study of law there was limited. In 1851 he removed to Concord, New Hampshire, where he lived to the day of his death. Entering the law office of President Pierce and Judge Josiah Minot, he made good progress in his studies, and the next year was admitted to the Bar. A partnership was formed with his former college classmate, Henry P. Rolfe, which continued until 1859, and was then dissolved, Mr. Marshall remaining alone until 1863, when William

M. Chase, Esq., became associated with him under the name of Marshall & Chase. This relation continued until the death of the senior partner. Mr. Marshall possessed in a high degree many of the requisites to success at the bar, and to the law he devoted the best years of his life. He was not a learned nor even an unusually well read lawyer, yet very few excelled him in getting at the gist of a case, or in applying the necessary legal principles. He possessed a confidence and courage which helped him to conquer difficulties that others might have deemed insurmountable, and above all a tact that never failed him. He was uniformly courteous not only to the bench and to the bar, but to the witnesses arrayed against him. His knowledge of human nature was large, and he knew almost by intuition which juryman needed his particular attention. But it was as an advocate that Mr. Marshall attracted the notice of the public, for he so invested his arguments with wit and humor, that the court room was sure to be filled whenever it became known that he was to address a jury. His manner of speech was quiet, but he never failed to indulge in invective and sarcasm if the case demanded it, and with these weapons he was counted a most dangerous adversary. He rarely if ever wrote out and committed his speeches, but carefully thought them out as he walked the streets or sat in his home, and this, together with his exceeding readiness both of words and of apt illustrations, often misled his hearers as to the method of his preparation. His law practice constantly increased, and at the time of his death was one of the largest in the state.

It was not in the law alone that Mr. Marshall was a power in the land; he was a factor in politics as well. He was a stalwart Democrat, and his associations were with the leading men of that faith in the state, one of them being President Pierce, and another Judge Minot, one of the wisest counselors of the party at that time. He was elected clerk of the house of representatives, and later was appointed district attorney by President Buchanan, which office he held until the Republican administration was inaugurated in 1861. In the year 1867 he was chairman of the Democratic state committee. At that time the troubles between President Andrew Johnson and the Republican party were at their height, and the Democrats of New Hampshire hoped to profit by Republican dissensions, and elect their candidates. The fight was bitter and hotly contested, but Mr. Marshall and his party were beaten. In the spirited contest between the Northern and the Concord railroads Mr. Marshall was an active factor, and about 1870 was elected clerk of the latter corporation, which position, as well as that of attorney for the company, he held until the time of his death.

He had a great liking for boys and young men, and delighted in giving them advice in regard to their studies and conduct. He was naturally a very bright and witty conversationalist, and in this accomplishment his vast reading was of great service to him. He had a well selected library and in the perusal of books of literary merit he took great delight. His strong memory enabled him to retain long passages from Shakespeare, Milton and others, and these he not unfrequently quoted while in company of his friends, and so accurately that he seldom halted for a word. His love of nature was very strong, and he often sought rest from his labors, and communion with the things of nature, by driving over the country roads and among the woods. It was on one of these outings that he met his death. On July 4, 1874, he drove with his wife and child to the grove at the head of Penacook Lake, where they intended to lunch. Some members of a militia company of Concord were shooting at a target nearby. Hearing the bullets whistling over the heads of his party, Mr. Marshall shouted to the militiamen to be careful. At that instant a bullet struck him in the abdomen, passing through his body. He exclaimed, "I am shot and fatally wounded," and sank down. All was done that could be done to save his life, but he died a few hours later, July 5, 1874.

Mr. Marshall married, April 9, 1861, Mary Jane Corning, born in Londonderry, March 23, 1829, daughter of John C. and Elizabeth (Nesmith) Corning (see Corning III), and they had one son, Anson Southard, Jr., born in Concord, March 29, 1863. He attended the public schools of Concord, fitted for college under the instruction of Moses Woolson and Amos Hadley, and entered Dartmouth College in the class of 1885. He is now practicing law in Concord.

(IV) Joseph, third son and child of Thomas (1) and Ruth Marshall, was born April 3, 1733, in Duxbury, Massachusetts, and died January 27, 1805, in Hillsborough, New Hampshire, where he was an early settler. He married Susannah Walker, who was born January 23, 1747, and died December 22, 1821. Their children were: Asa, Benjamin, Joseph, Ebenezer, Jonathan, John, Betsa, Rufus, Thomas, Moses, Jesse, Sarah, Hannah, Silas and Walker.

(V) Silas, eleventh son and fourteenth child of Joseph and Susannah (Walker) Marshall, was born August 13, 1780, in Hillsborough, and continued to reside in that town where he was a carpenter and farmer. He was married (first) April 29, 1806, to Catherine Houston, of Hillsborough, who died April 27, 1819. He married (second) December 6, 1821, Abigail Robbins, who was born May 3, 1765, and died September 15, 1848, in Hillsborough. The children by the first wife, were: Sarah, (died young), Gustine, Emily, Louisa, Catherine Miller and Caroline Susannah. The children of the second wife were: Asa R., and Sarah C.

(VI) Gustine, eldest son and second child of Silas and Catherine (Houston) Marshall, was born May 15, 1806, in Hillsborough Lower Village and died in Concord, New Hampshire, July 30, 1869. He got his education in the common schools and learned the carpenter's trade under the supervision of his father. They worked at building together for some time, until Gustine removed to Nashua, where he was employed several years as overseer in one of the cotton mills. He then engaged in the dry goods business in Nashua and after a few years, disposed of his general stock and was a successful milliner there. This business was prosperous and was gradually extended until branch stores were opened in three or four of the leading towns of the state. He continued in this line of business until 1861 when he retired from active life. In the fall of 1862 he removed with his family to Concord, where his wife carried on a millinery store for several years thereafter. He was married to Emily Heald, who was born August 16, 1811, in Temple, New Hampshire, and died at Concord, February 26, 1874, in her sixty-third year. She was the daughter of Nathan Heald (see Heald, VI). Four children were born to Mr. and Mrs. Marshall, namely: Sylvester Gustine, Emily Maria, Frances Ellen, and Julia Maria.

(VII) Frances Ellen, second daughter and third

child of Gustine and Emily (Heald) Marshall, became the wife of Edward Stockbridge (see Stockbridge, VII).

WALKER This is a name which has been conspicuous in the entire history of New England and has been especially noted in New Hampshire. It was borne by the first minister of the First Church of Concord, and the line has furnished others equally prominent in jurisprudence, or otherwise honored in both private and public life. The stern virtues which made the early bearers of the name useful and valued citizens of the infant colony of Massachusetts are still evidenced in the life of their posterity, showing the the virility and mental force which characterized them.

(I) Captain Richard Walker, founder of this line, is first found of record at Lynn, Massachusetts, in 1630, when he was ensign of the local military company. As the settlers of that town were English, there is no doubt that he was of the same nativity, but the place of his birth is unknown and its time can only be approximated. The time of his death is indicated by the record which shows that he was buried at Lynn, May 16, 1687, when his age is given as ninety-five years, indicating that his birth occurred about 1592. He was made a freeman in 1634, at Lynn. In 1631 the neighboring Indians threatened the infant settlement, and Ensign Walker was in service on guard. One night he heard a noise in the forest near him and felt an arrow pass through his coat and buff waistcoat. He discharged his gun into the bushes, and it was burst by the heavy charge it contained. He gave the alarm and returned to his post, after which he was again fired at. The next day an assemblage of men made a demonstration which frightened away the marauders for some time. In 1637 Mr. Walker was a member of the committee which made division of the common lands of the community, and in 1638 he received an allotment of two hundred acres, upland and meadow. In 1645 he accompanied Robert Bridges and Thomas Marshall in negotiating with Lord de la Tour and Monsieur D'Aulney, governors of French provinces on the north. As reward for his services in this expedition Lieutenant Walker received four pounds sterling. In 1657 he was one of those who deposed as witnesses against the claim to Nahant of Thomas Dexter, who had purchased it from an Indian for a suit of clothes. In 1678 he was one of the selectmen, then called "the Seven Prudential Men." The name appears in the muster roll of the Honorable Artillery Company of England in 1620. Upon the petition to the general court made by the new troop of Lynn, formed in 1679, that he be its commander (which petition was granted), he is called "Captain Walker." He was by occupation a farmer. His wife, Sarah, was the administratrix of his estate. He had two sons and two daughters, and may have had others. The elder son, Richard, born in England in 1611, was at Reading in 1635, and represented that town several times in the general court. The other receives extended mention below. His daughter Tabitha was married March 11, 1662, to Daniel King; and the other, Elizabeth, married Ralph King March 2, 1663.

(II) Samuel, younger son of Richard Walker, was born in England, and came with his father to New England in 1630. He settled first in Reading, which was originally Lynn Village, and moved thence to Woburn (formerly Charlestown Village), where he is found of record in a tax list of 1655, and again February 25, 1662, having been appointed a surveyor of highways at a town meeting of that date. He was selectman in 1668. He was a maltster, and in 1662 received the first license to sell spirits granted in Woburn. It seems that his good nature at one time overrode his judgment, as it is of record that he was fined ten shillings for selling to a notorious toper, the latter being fined five shillings at the same time for being drunk. That he was a man of character and standing is evidenced by the fact that he was one of a committee of five appointed at a meeting held March 28, 1667, empowered to divide the public lands. For this service the committee received seven acres for themselves, in addition to the several allotments to them as individuals. He died November 6, 1684, aged about seventy. His first wife, whose name is unknown, bore him seven children, namely: Samuel, Joseph, Hannah (died at four months), Hannah, Israel, John, Benjamin. (Mention of Israel and descendants appears in this article). His second wife, Ann, was the widow of Arthur Alger of Scarborough, and daughter of Giles Roberts of that place. She died in Woburn March 21, 1716. She was the mother of Mr. Walker's two youngest children, namely: Isaac and Ezekiel.

(III) Samuel (2), eldest son of Samuel (1) Walker, is entitled successively in the records of Woburn, corporal, sergeant and deacon, and was evidently a man of importance and influence in the town. He served as selectman in 1679 and repeatedly afterwards. After the imprisonment of the tyrant Sir Edmund Andros, who sought to curtail the liberties of the colonists while governor of New England, Mr. Walker was a delegate to the convention held in Boston in 1689 to form a new system of government, and in 1694 was representative of Woburn in the general court. He was made a deacon of the church in 1692 and continued in that office until his death, which occurred January 18, 1703, at the age of sixty-one years. He was married September 10, 1662, to Sarah Reed, of Woburn (daughter of William and Mabel Reed), who bore him six sons and a daughter. She died November 1, 1681, and he was married April 18, 1692, to Abigail, daughter of Captain John Carter, widow of Lieutenant James Fowle of Woburn. His eldest son Edward was killed by Indians in battle at Wheelwright's Pond, Lee, New Hampshire, July 6, 1690. The others were named John, Samuel, Sarah, Timothy, Isaac and Ezekiel. (Mention of Isaac and descendants appears in this article). The daughter, Sarah, became the wife of Edward Johnson, a son of Major William Johnson, and grandson of Captain Edward Johnson, founder of Woburn.

(IV) Samuel (3), third son of Samuel (2) and Sarah (Reed) Walker, was born January 25, 1668, in Woburn, and was married June 1, 1689, to Judith Howard of Concord, Massachusetts. For several years he lived on Maple Meadow Plain, in that part of Goshen, now Wilmington. In 1725 he moved to the southern part of Burlington (then Woburn) and resided in a house which was still standing in the middle of the last century, and in which he died September 28, 1744, in his seventy-seventh year. He was made a deacon of the First Church of Woburn in 1709, and when the Second Church was formed in what is now Burlington, he aided in its organization, and was one of the ten signers of the articles of agreement and church covenant made November 10, 1735. He was one of those who ordained Rev. Supply Clapp as its first pastor, October 29, of that year, and was elected one of the first two deacons November 10 following. He continued in that office until his death, and was buried in the old

Burlington burying ground. His wife, Judith, died November 14, 1724, in her fifty-seventh year, and he subsequently married Mary (Richardson), widow of James Fowle. She survived him four years, passing away October 23, 1748, in her eightieth year. The first wife was the mother of his children, namely: Sarah (married Samuel Buck), Judith (married, first, Ephraim Kendall and, second, Samuel Johnson), Abigail (died at twenty-one), Samuel, Hannah (married Edward Wyman) John (died at two weeks old), John (died one month old), Mary (married Benjamin Johnson), Timothy and Phebe (wife of Noah Richardson).

(V) Rev. Timothy, son of Deacon Samuel (3) and Judith (Howard) Walker, was born July 27, 1705, in Woburn, and died at Concord September 1, 1782. As the first settled pastor of Penacook, later Rumford and now Concord, he exercised a powerful influence upon the community because of his learning and ability and his solicitude for the temporal, as well as the spiritual, welfare of his flock. He was graduated from Harvard College in 1725, at the age of twenty years, and was probably for a time at Penny Cook. That he was known favorably to the people is indicated by the fact that the plantation voted in October, 1729, to raise one hundred pounds for minister's salary and March 31, 1730, to engage Rev. Timothy Walker as pastor. Upon his acceptance it was agreed that the salary should be increased two pounds per year until it reached one hundred and twenty pounds, and a stipulation was made that a reduction should be accepted in proportion to his ability when great age should weaken his powers. It is apparent that the New England fathers were careful, as well as pious business man. This settlement included his right to a proprietary share set aside for the first minister, and the colony kindly voted him one hundred pounds with which to build a house, and this was increased by a further vote of fifty pounds January 16, 1734. He was ordained as pastor November 18, 1730, and was reckoned among the town proprietors for that time. When the second appropriation was made for his house a proviso was made that he réceipt in full for salary to date, this being deemed prudent because of the depreciation in value of silver in which he had been paid. In 1736 he was granted fifty pounds, to secure the clearing of pasture for his use. At the time of his ordination, Benjamin Rolfe, the newly elected town clerk, also a graduate of Harvard, was the only educated man in the settlement beside himself, and they naturally took prominent positions in the management of affairs. Mr. Walker being the senior and looked up to on account of his position, was regarded and respected as the father of the community, as in truth he was. Many of the petitions and other public papers of the time were drafted by him, and he undertook to defend the rights of the town in its lands, which others sought to obtain. Finding no redress before the general court of New Hampshire because of the fact that the grant of Rumford was made by the Massachusetts colony (under th supposition that it was within its jurisdiction), Mr. Walker made three trips to England to lay the matter before the King in Council, between 1753 and 1762. He made many acquaintances among ecclesiastics and public men in these visits, and impressed them so favorably that he won his suit on the last trial in the fall of 1762, and the people of what is now Concord enjoyed their possessions little disturbed by white men thereafter. Up to 1739 the Penacook Indians had been friendly to the settlement, especially regarding Mr. Walker, but the machinations of the French people on the north stirred up Indian animosity and more distant tribes began to threaten disaster. In 1739 a garrison was established about the house of Mr. Walker and at other points, and these were maintained during the King George war. Just before the battle of Bennington, during the revolution, a messenger approached the church while Mr. Walker was preaching, and upon his entrance the preacher asked him if he had any communication to deliver. Being informed that men were desired to proceed at once to the field of danger, Mr. Walker said: "As many of my hearers as are willing to go had better start immediately."

The first home of Mr. Walker was in a log house in the brow of Horseshoe Pond hill, and his frame house was constructed in 1733-4. After various alterations, it is now occupied by his great-grandson. He was a man of medium stature, of fine figure and dignified and pleasing manners. Though not talkative, he was not austere, and sometimes became facetious. Naturally of hasty temper, he held himself under superb control, and never failed to ask pardon if he had injured anyone's feelings. Exact in business and daily life, he was held in high regard by all his flock. With mild blue eye and fair complexion, he wore, in accordance with the custom of the time, large powdered wig, with small clothes and large buckle shoes. The "History of Concord," by his third successor, Rev. Nathaniel Bouton, gives many anecdotes of his life, and other interesting matters not permissible in the limitations of a work of this kind, and herewith follow extracts from that work, touching the teachings of Mr. Walker: "As a preacher, Mr. Walker was instructive and practical, dwelling more on the duties than the doctrines of religion. * * * His style was good for that period, perspicuous and didactic, with but few illustrations, but well supported with quotations from scripture. In his theological views Mr. Walker was 'orthodox,' according to existing standards. * * * In distinction from those preachers who in his day were called 'New Lights,' he was accused of being an Arminian, but called himself a 'moderate Calvanist.' He was highly conservative, as regarded innovations and new measures. * * * At this time all of Mr. Walker's hearers were of one way of thinking in religious matters, and his object was to keep them together and make them steadfast in the 'religion and church order which was very dear to our forefathers.'" During his ministry of nearly fifty-two years he enjoyed vigorous health, and was able to preach nearly every Sunday down to his death, which occurred immediately after he arose on a Sunday morning. The town of Concord erected at his grave a slate slab, which is still standing in the old cemetery.

Of the children of Rev. Timothy Walker, his namesake receives extended mention hereinafter. His wife, Sarah Burbeen, was a daughter of James Burbeen, of Woburn, Massachusetts. She was born June 17, 1701, was married to Mr. Walker, November 12, 1730, and came at once to her wilderness home in New Hampshire, riding on horseback, and accompanied by several other women, wives of settlers. She passed away February 19, 1778, and her body rests beside her husband's. Sarah, their first born died when four years old. Sarah, the third, born August 6, 1739, married Benjamin Rolfe and, after his death, in 1772, Benjamin Thompson, afterward Count Rumford. Their daughter became Countess Sarah Rumford. Mary, born December 7, 1742, married Dr. Ebenezer Harnden Goss, of Concord, and who removed to Brunswick, and later to Paris, Maine. Judith, the youngest, born

HOUSE OF FIRST MINISTER AT CONCORD

December 4, 1744, became the wife of Major Abiel Chandler (see Chandler VI) and lived in Concord, and after his decease became the wife of Henry Rolfe, of the same town.

(VI) Timothy (2), only son and second child of Rev. Timothy Walker, was born June 26, 1737, in Concord and reared on the paternal farm. He is said to have been a favorite among the Indians, who often decorated him with paint and feathers and entertained him at their homes. His father gave attention to his education and sent him to Harvard College when he was fifteen years of age, and he completed the regular course at the age of nineteen years, graduating in 1756. For two years thereafter he taught school at Bradford, Massachusetts, and meantime and subsequently pursued a theological course, partly presumably with his father. He was examined at an association meeting in Haverhill, Massachusetts, and licensed to preach September 11, 1759. During the absence of his father in England, 1762-3, he preached at Rumford and other places. He continued preaching about six years, and invited to settle as pastor at Rindge, but had become immersed in business and never settled in that capacity at any point, though frequently filling the pulpit there and elsewhere for a time. He formed a partnership with Colonel Andrew McMillan in the mercantile business November 25, 1765, and continued one year in trade with him at the southern end of the village of Rumford, after which he kept a store which he opened near his father's residence (at the upper and of the present Main street) until the time of the revolution.

He was zealous in prosecuting the struggle for American liberty and his time was chiefly occupied in the service of his country from the beginning of hostilities. He was a member of the fourth provincial congress which assembled at Exeter, New Hampshire, May 17, 1775. On the third day he was appointed a member of the committee to secure supplies for New Hampshire troops, then in the vicinity of Boston. In August he was sent, with Mr. Ichabod Rawlings, to ascertain the losses sustained by New Hampshire men at the battle of Bunker Hill, and make them compensation, as well as to advance a month's pay to those who had enlisted in the Continental service. These duties were performed to the acceptance of the provincial congress, and the record makes interesting reading, as found in the seventh volume of New Hampshire State Papers. Mr. Walker was commissioned September 5, 1775, as colonel of the third of four regiments of Minute-men raised by New Hampshire, and immediately proceeded to drill his troops and prepare for action when needed. From the fourth to the sixteenth of October he was paymaster of troops under Colonels Stark, Poor and Reid, at Winter Hill, and was again appointed to that duty December 27 by the provincial congress. On June 11, 1776, he was a member of the committee appointed by the house of representatives which succeeded the provincial congress, under a temporary constitution, to draft a Declaration of Independence. This draft was adopted and at once forwarded to the continental congress in session at Philadelphia. Soon after Colonel Walker was placed upon a committee to devise a systematic plan of finance which should pay the indebtedness of the state and provide for impending obligations. When the associated test was sent out by the continental congress, Colonel Walker was among the first to sign and his influence aided in securing the signature of every one to whom it was presented in Concord—one hundred and fifty-six in all. From July 5, 1776, he served to January 20, 1777, on the committee of safety. From December of that year until December, 1779, he was a member of the council, and on March 26, 1777, he was chosen by the legislature as a delegate to the continental congress, and again in 1778, 1782 and 1785, though he never attended. He was delegate from Concord to the constitutional conventions of 1778 and 1781, and on constitutional revision in 1791. In 1777 he became associate justice of the court of common pleas, and continued upon the bench until retired by reason of the age limit, being chief justice from 1804 to 1809, when he retired. He was three times a candidate for governor, being the first Democratic candidate, but was defeated by the overwhelming strength of the Federal party in the state. While participating in the larger concerns of state, he did not despise the affairs of his native town, and was moderator twenty-one years between 1769 and 1809. For nine years beginning with 1769 he was town clerk and was selectman twenty-five years, being chairman of the board all except four. He was instrumental in bringing the legislature, of which he was a member, to meet in Concord in 1782, and was ever ready to advance his home town in every way. He felt an especial interest in the young men of the town, and was wont to aid them with counsel or pecuniary assistance, as the case demanded. His long public service testifies to his ability, powerful character and uprightness, without further comment. He passed away at his home in Concord May 5, 1822, in his eighty-fifth year.

He was married, previous to 1764, to Susannah Burbeen, who was born April 11, 1746, in Woburn, Massachusetts, daughter of Rev. Joseph Burbeen. She died at Concord September 28, 1828, in her eighty-third year. Of her fourteen children, ten grew to maturity, and are accounted for as follows: Sarah, born January 21, 1764, married Major Daniel Livermore; she was a widow fifty years, and died in 1843 at Cambridge, Massachusetts. Charles, born September 25, 1765, was a lawyer and lived in Concord. Timothy, born February 2, 1767, was a farmer in Concord. Esther, the ninth, died unmarried at the age of twenty-five years. Betsey, born April 15, 1780, was the wife of Eliphalet Emery of Concord, and died in 1825. Joseph, born January 12, 1782, resided in Concord. Bridget, born January 1, 1784, married Jotham Stone, and died in Brunswick, Maine, in 1805. Polly, born March 22, 1786, became the wife of Charles Emery of Concord, and after his death of Hon. Francis N. Fiske, of the same place, where she died. Clarissa, born July 27, 1788, married Levi Bartlett, and died in 1845 in Boston.

(IV) Isaac, fifth son of Samuel (2) and Sarah (Reed) Walker, was born November 1, 1677, in Woburn, and was one of the original grantees of what is now Concord, New Hampshire. He was married February 20, 1704, to Margery, daughter of George Bruce, and their children were: Abigail, Isaac, Ezekiel, Timothy, Anne, William, Elizabeth, Mary and Samuel.

(V) Samuel, youngest child of Isaac and Margery (Bruce) Walker, was born August 10, 1723, in Woburn, and lived in Amesbury, Massachusetts. He was among the twenty-one proprietors of "No. 1," now the town of Warner, New Hampshire, who agreed at a meeting in Amesbury, August 9, 1763, to settle in that town. Like many others, he fulfilled this agreement by proxy, and his son Isaac is found among the first settlers of the town.

(VI) Isaac (2), son of Samuel Walker, settled in that part of Warner known as "Schoodac," but soon moved to another location, within half a mile of the first. The Schoodac cemetery is on part of his first farm. He was a soldier of the revolution, going from Warner, in which town he passed his life after that struggle, engaged in agriculture.

(VII) Philip, son of Isaac (2) Walker, was born in 1763 and died in 1848, in Warner, on the paternal homestead. His eldest son, William B., born 1791, died 1872. He had several children, all of whom, except Mary E. Walker, of Concord, are deceased, leaving no issue. Jane, the third child, died unmarried. Sarah, the fourth, married William Trussell, of Boscawen, and died childless.

(VIII) Isaac (3), second son and child of Philip Walker, was born June 6, 1794, in Warner, where he passed his life, and died January 31, 1872. He was a farmer, and always lived on the ancient homestead. He married Mittie Clough, of Warner, and had two sons, Abiel and Reuben. The latter died when about fifteen years of age.

(IX) Abiel, elder son of Isaac (3) and Mittie (Clough) Walker, was born January 15, 1824, on the paternal homestead, where most of his life was passed. When a young man he went to Lowell, Massachusetts, and was employed there some years as a house painter. There he was married May 1, 1850, to Mary Powers, daughter of a Methodist minister of Maine. About 1855 they settled on the old Walker place in Warner, and continued to reside there until the death of Mr. Walker, in December, 1893. His widow subsequently resided with her son in Concord, where she passed away in June, 1903. Mr. Walker was liberal in religious views, and was a firm Republican in politics.

(X) Reuben Eugene, only child of Abiel and Mary (Powers) Walker, now justice of the supreme court of New Hampshire, was born February 15, 1851, in Lowell, Massachusetts, and was a child when his parents removed to Warner. In the common schools of that town he received his primary education, and was subsequently a student at the New London Literary and Scientific Institution (now Colby Academy) and Brown University, graduating from the latter in the class of 1875. He immediately entered upon the study of law with Sargent & Chase, of Concord, and was admitted to the bar in 1878. It is worthy of note that he is now a colleague of one of his preceptors on the supreme bench of the state (see Chase). He formed a partnership with Robert A. Ray, now of Keene, this state, under the style of Ray & Walker, and continued to practice under this arrangement for about five years, after which he practiced alone about eight years, all in Concord. On April 1, 1891, he became associated with Frank S. Streeter, of that city, and this arrangement continued ten years, being ended by the appointment of Mr. Walker as justice of the supreme court, in which capacity he has since served. This is not the first recognition of his worth and legal ability, as he was county solicitor of Merrimack county from 1889 to 1891, and a member of the legislature in 1895, representing Ward Six of Concord. He is one of the authors of "Ray & Walker's Citations," a legal reference work of standard merit. Always an industrious worker, Judge Walker brought to the public service a trained mind, and is still a steady worker, giving undivided attention to the duties of his responsible position and serving his state acceptably and well. In religious faith he is a Unitarian, and he gives unfaltering support to the principles of public policy which seem to him just and best for the general welfare, as promulgated by the Republican party. He was married, in 1875, to Miss Mary E., daughter of Lowell Brown, of Concord. She was born July 22, 1848, and died July 21, 1903. Their only child, Bertha May, born June 18, 1879, resides with her father.

(III) Israel, third son and fourth child of Samuel (1) Walker (twin of Hannah), was born June 28, 1648, in Woburn, where he lived and died. By his wife, Susannah, he had four sons, Israel (died young), Henry, Nathaniel and Israel.

(IV) Lieutenant Henry Walker appears in Hopkinton, Massachusetts, in 1725, when he was one of the selectmen, and also served in that office in 1726, 1727-28-29-30. He was moderator in 1727-28-29-30, and clerk in 1727-28 and 1730. Among those from Hopkinton in the expedition against the West Indies, in 1741, were Henry Walker and Henry Walker, Junior. The latter was the only one from Hopkinton that came back, the rest having perished. There were brobably other sons of Lieutenant Henry Walker, as the records show Thomas, Jason, Israel and Joseph to have been active and prominent citizens, all holding responsible offices repeatedly. With the exception of four years, the first of these was selectman continuously from 1736 to 1749. In 1725 he was on the committee to raise the meeting house. He was town treasurer from 1736 to 1738 and from 1741 to 1752. From 1750 to 1755 he was town clerk. From 1761 to 1768 Jason Walker was treasurer. It is probable that Jason, Israel and Joseph were sons of Thomas, as they succeeded him in turn as selectman and in other town offices. One of these was probably the father of Jacob Walker, noticed below.

(VII) Jacob Walker was among the proprietors of Morristown, Vermont, which was settled by people from Hopkinton and Winchendon, Massachusetts. Heminway's "Historical Gazetteer of Vermont" says that he came from Bennington, Vermont, but the records of that town give no account of him. This makes it appear that he was only a transient resident of Bennington. There can be little doubt that he came originally from Hopkinton. He was the first to locate in Morristown, coming there in 1790. During the first season he boarded with a family located in the adjoining town of Hyde Park, and started out every Monday morning with a week's provisions, spending the time in camp on his land, engaged in clearing away the forest. He returned to Bennington for the winter, and brought his family in the spring. That season was spent upon the land and in the fall they returned to Bennington for the winter. He made a permanent settlement in 1792, and became one of the prosperous farmers of the town. He built a brick house which is still in use, on the west side of the road from Morristown to Morrisville, and cleared up and tilled a large farm.

(VIII) William, son of Jacob Walker, was born July 1, 1814, in Morristown, and died March 20, 1902, in Manchester, this state. He grew up on the paternal farm, attending the local school, and engaged in farming until he was incapacitated for hard labor, being located upon a part of his father's original homestead. By the kick of a horse, several of his ribs were broken, affecting his heart, and he was obliged to abandon farming. He built and operated for several years a mill for extracting the oil of flaxseed. About 1860 he moved to East Andover, New Hampshire, and was employed some time as wheelwright and carpenter. After living a short time in Concord he passed the last thirty-two years of his life in Manchester, where he died as above noted. He was a firm believer in the doctrines of the Advent Church, and a staunch Republican from the organization of that party. His wife, Rhoda Story, was a native of Vermont,

Reuben E. Walker

daughter of Jacob (?) Story. They had only one child.

(IX) Stilman DeWitt, only child of William and Rhoda (Story) Walker, was born July 10, 1847, in Morristown, and was about thirteen years old when the family moved to Andover, this state. He attended the public schools of Vermont and New Hampshire, and was a student at Andover Academy. At the age of seventeen years he began his railroading career as brakeman on a freight train on the Concord railroad, and continued in this service thirty-five years, resigning in January, 1900. For three years he was conductor of a freight train, and was passenger train conductor fifteen years. Having retired from the road, Mr. Walker invested his savings in real estate, and spends his time chiefly in the care of his tenements on South State street, Concord. While in the railroad service he kept up membership in the Order of Railway Conductors, and was for several years a member of the Knights of Pythias. He was among the organizers of the Christian Science Church of Concord, and is one of its most faithful adherents. In politics he is a Republican, but has never given any time to public matters, beyond registering his support of his principles.

Mr. Walker was married, October 7, 1873, to Nettie S. Virgin, daughter of William Virgin, of Concord. She died March 20, 1882, and Mr. Walker was married, in October, 1882, to Mrs. Alma B. Buzzell, widow of Charles S. Buzzell, and daughter of Porter and Lorinda (Reed) Dow, of Walden, Vermont. Charles S. Buzzell was a son of Gilbert Buzzell, one of the oldest residents of Concord. Mrs. Walker's daughter, Genevieve Buzzell, is now the wife of Jesse C. Danforth, of Braintree, Massachusetts. She is a native of Concord, where she is known and appreciated as a talented singer.

(Second Family.)

WALKER (I) A line of Walker ancestry not hereinbefore traced begins, as far as now known, with Archibald Walker, a tailor, who immigrated from Scotland and settled in Province, Rhode Island, where he was as late as 1700. He is reported by tradition to have been a very worthy man. He married Mary Gardner, and had the following children: Charles, Susanna, Abigail, Hezekiah, Nathaniel and Ann.

(II) Nathaniel, third son and fifth child of Archibald and Mary (Gardner) Walker, was born 1708, in Providence, and settled when a young man in Weston, Massachusetts. He was admitted to the church in Weston, 1728. He was a captain and an active man in town affairs. In 1748 he removed to Sturbridge, Massachusetts, where he died February 8, 1783. He was married, March 8, 1732, to Submit Brewer, born July 18, 1709, died in Sturbridge, November 22, 1791, daughter of Lieutenant John and Mary (Jones) Brewer, of Weston. Lieutenant John was a son of John Brewer, of Sudbury, Massachusetts. Nathaniel and Submit Walker were the parents of James, Nathaniel, Phineas, Lydia, Josiah, Submit, Asa, Joel, Mary, Benjamin, Lucy, Benjamin and Beulah. Ten children were born in Weston and three in Sturbridge. Eleven of these children lived to an average age of over eighty-three years. The records of Weston show that the north precinct of the town voted November 10, 1747, to pay two pounds, fifteen shillings and six pence to Nathaniel Walker for work on the meeting house. From this it may be inferred that he was a carpenter.

(III) James, eldest child of Nathaniel and Submit (Brewer) Walker, was born November 15, 1732, in Weston, and was among the first settlers of Belchertown, Massachusetts, where he located in 1755. He served in the French and Indian war in 1757, and was captain of the ninth company of the Fourth New Hampshire Regiment in the Revolution. He was selectman of the town in 1783 and 1786-87. He died in 1806, in his seventy-fourth year. He was married twice, and had eight sons, five of whom resided in Belchertown.

(IV) Nathaniel (2), sixth son of James and Esther (Shummy) Walker, was born April 30, 1770, in Belchertown, where he passed his life, engaged in farming, and reached a great age. He was married, March 4, 1799, to Thankful Morse, and they had children named: Morse, Orimel, Nathaniel B., Appleton, Wayne, Eliza (Blackman), James and Emeline (Chapman).

(V) Nathaniel Brewer, son of Nathaniel (2) and Thankful (Morse) Walker, was born March 13, 1812, in Belchertown, and died in Concord, New Hampshire, January, 1887. He was educated in the common schools of his native town, and afterward learned the trade of silver plater, at which he worked in Albany, New York, and other places, finally coming to Concord from Boston, Massachusetts, about 1843. He bought the interest of Mr. Chandler, of the firm of Blackman & Chandler, the former being a brother-in-law of Mr. Walker, and the new firm took the name of Blackman & Walker, silver platers. Later Leland A. Smith purchased an interest in the firm which then took the name of Jason Blackman & Company. On the retirement of Mr. Blackman in January, 1855, the firm name became Smith & Walker. From that time the firm remained unchanged until the death of Mr. Walker. The business, which at first was confined to silver plating, subsequently included saddlery hardware, which in a few years became the principal feature of the business. During the last year of the firm's existence the business was almost exclusively wholesale. The firm of Smith & Walker was prosperous, and each of the partners possessed a competency before the death of Mr. Walker. He was a Republican and a member of the city council two years. In religious faith he was a Universalist. The only social organization of which he was a member was the Webster Club. His character as a business man was very high, and he was noted for his honesty and integrity.

He married (first) Abby Ellinwood, of Antrim, who died about 1867, by whom he had two children: Edward, who died in Boston about 1901, and Charles H., a graduate of Harvard College, now a physician in Pasadena, California. He married (second), June 2, 1873, Lorinda A. Adams, daughter of Nathaniel and Betsy S. (Kimball) Patch, widow of Stephen D. Adams. She was born in Henniker, September 20, 1834, and had one child by her first marriage: Eugene P. Adams, born in Concord, December 10, 1864. Lorinda A. Patch is a granddaughter of Reuben Patch, a Revolutionary soldier, who resided in New Boston, and soon after 1797 removed to Henniker (see Patch, V).

WALKER The thickening mill has left us several words of familiar import, among which is Walker. Claiming as it does an almost unrivalled position in the rolls of our nomenclature, it reminds us of the early fashion of treading out the cloth before the adaptations of machinery were brought to bear on this phase of the craft. Walker has disappeared as a term of trade, and it is in the directories alone that the name declaring the forgotten mysteries of early English cloth manufacture can be found.

(I) George Walker was born in England. He received a common school education, and by occupation was a gardener. In later life by diligence and skill he became a head gardener. He was a member of the Church of England. His wife's baptismal name was Martha, and they had four children: Hannah, Isaac, William, Betty and George.

(II) Isaac, eldest son and second child of George and Martha Walker, was born in Warwickshire, England, November 22, 1801. After getting such education as he could in the common schools, he worked in coal mines and cotton mills for years. In his later life he accompanied Dinah Murray in preaching tours about the country. He married (first), June 4, 1823, Mary Part; and (second) Maria Anthony. By the first wife he had three children: Samuel, Mary and William; and by the second, six children: Sarah, Martha, Isaac, Anna, George and Lydia.

(III) Isaac (2), third child and eldest son of Isaac (1) and Maria (Anthony) Walker, was born in Derbyshire, England, May 5, 1838. After getting a common school education he worked in a tape factory at Worksworth until he was sixteen years old. In 1856 he left England, and came to America via Liverpool and Boston on the "Wilderforley," landing at the latter place in 1856. In Boston he learned the trade of carriage smith, and later became master mechanic in the rope factory of Soule & Day, where he was employed twenty-five years. In 1903 he removed to Merrimack, New Hampshire, and bought a farm of eleven acres, where he has since resided. Mr. Walker is a member of the Episcopal Church, and has always devoted much of his time and attention to religion and religious subjects. He was licensed as a local preacher in England, and as such preached there. He continued this after settling in Boston, and was the principal assistant of the evangelist Henry Morgan. Since settling in Merrimack he has continued to preach, though now retired. It was through his efforts that the Sunday school at Merrimack was revived. In politics he is a Republican.

He married, in Roxbury, Massachusetts, March 17, 1859, Hannah Ball, who was born in Holland March 14, 1839, daughter of Cornelius and Wilhelmina (Warner) Ball. She is one of thirteen children, only two of whom are now living. They have had six children: Samuel; Willie, died young; Isaac, died young; Charles L.; Anna Marie; and Mary, died young. Mrs. Walker is a member of the Baptist Advent Church.

WALKER The earliest known ancestor of this line was Charles Walker, of Bradford (now Groveland) Massachusetts, who was married August 29, 1773, to a Miss Mary Atwood, of that town. She was born April 15, 1752, daughter of John and Mary Atwood. Their children were: James, David and Jonathan (twins), Betsey and William. No record of his removal has been found, and it is presumed that he lived and died there.

(II) William, youngest child of Charles Walker, was born August 25, 1786, in Bradford, and was married February 25, 1808, at Haverhill, Massachusetts, to Betsey Gay. She was the daughter of a sea captain, and is supposed to have been born in Salem, Massachusetts, tradition giving that as her birthplace. After his marriage William Walker resided for a time in Chester, New Hampshire, whence he removed about 1824 to Amoskeag. During the first year of his residence there he kept a hotel, and later was landlord of a tavern some years at "'Squag," now a part of West Manchester. He was the first landlord of the Amoskeag House, which is still standing at Amoskeag, also now a part of Manchester. In 1830 he moved to Andover Center, where he conducted a tavern until 1835, when he removed to Concord and became the proprietor of the Washington Tavern, and a year later of the Eagle Coffee House, situated on the site now occupied by the Eagle Hotel. This tavern was the most noted establishment of its kind in New Hampshire, and was patronized by the representative people who visited the state capital. He died August 2, 1858, in Concord. Mr. Walker was a capable business man, and fond of good horses. A fine black horse owned by him was bought and presented to General (afterwards President) Pierce, by his admirers in 1847, in the time of the Mexican war. William Walker and Betsey Gay, who was born January 16, 1790, and died March 22, 1862, in Concord, were the parents of Sarah Bradley (died in infancy), William, James Parsons, Nancy Long, born December 19, 1819, who married Cyrus Hill, November 26, 1838, and died October 13, 1897, at Lancaster; and Gustavus.

(III) Gustavus, third son of William and Betsey (Gay) Walker, was born at Amoskeag, May 7, 1830, and died May 5, 1902, aged almost seventy-two years. Before he was a year old his father removed his family to Andover Center, where the next five years of the boy's life were spent. In December, 1835, the family removed to Concord, where William Walker became proprietor of the Washington Tavern, and a year later of the famous Eagle Coffee House, which he conducted until 1849. Gustavus was educated in the schools of Concord, at Hopkinton under the tuition of John O. Ballard, at Portsmouth under Master Harris, at Phillips Andover Academy, under "Uncle Sam" Taylor, and at Northfield Seminary. His familiarity from the age of five to nineteen years with the guests at his father's hotels gave him an extensive acquaintance which proved of much value to him in after years. In 1846 he became messenger for Cheney & Company, who were the successors of his brother William Walker in the express business, continuing in this capacity till the latter part of the year 1849. In the season of 1850 and 1851 he was clerk of the steamer "Lady of the Lake," on Lake Winnipiseogee, built and commanded by William Walker.

March 1, 1852, Gustavus Walker and Hon. David A. Warde formed a partnership and engaged in the hardware business in Concord under the firm name of Warde & Walker. Three years later (1855) Mr. Walker embarked in the same business in the Phoenix block, under his own name, and for thirty-eight years thereafter, was one of Concord's most honored and active merchants. Retiring in 1883 with a competency, he devoted himself to the care of his own property and the estate of his brother William, who had died without issue the year previously. The two properties were extensive and embraced some of the most desirable pieces of real estate in Concord. In his early years Mr. Walker became deeply interested in the question of transportation, and this interest remained through life. To the matter of obtaining for Concord the best possible railway connections he gave his earnest attention. He was largely instrumental in securing the construction of the Peterborough and Hillsborough railroad, and was an ardent advocate of the building of the Concord and Rochester railroad, of which he was president. He was long an active member of the Concord fire department. Mr.

Walker was full of activity and energy; he knew what labor is and delighted to perform it, and enjoy the fruits of his toil. He knew the results of industry; and never forgot that energy and industry directed by good judgment, must win. His life record is an epitome and an illustration of what the exercise of these virtues brings to him who avails himself of them. Naturally honorable, he ever kept in view the fact that an untarnished record is a man's highest recommendation. His life was one of honor and usefulness to the community in which he lived. He married, January 30, 1865, Mary Clintina Butler, born January 31, 1844, in Greenfield, New Hampshire, eldest daughter of John D. and Mary Colby (Burnham) Butler, of Bennington, who survives him. Two children of this marriage died before their majority.

LEAVITT This somewhat numerous family is descended principally from two very early English immigrants, John and Thomas Leavitt. Nothing is known of the time of Thomas Leavitt's arrival in America, or from what part of England he came, although it is probable that he was from Lincolnshire or its vicinity, as were his connections, the Hutchinsons, the Wheelwrights and the Wentworths. He may have been a brother of John Leavitt, the immigrant. In 1639 he was not twenty-one years of age.

(I) Thomas Leavitt, one of the first settlers of Exeter, and a signer of the "Combination" in 1639, removed to Hampton as early as 1644. After his marriage he lived on the Asten homestead, and died November 28, 1696, aged "above eighty." He married Isabella (Bland) Asten, daughter of Joshua and Joanna Bland, of Colchester, England, and widow of Francis Asten, who died a year or two before. She died February 19, 1700. Their children were: Hezron, Aretas, John, Thomas, James (died young), Isabel, Jemima and Heriah, but the order is unknown.

(II) Hezron, son of Thomas and Isabella (Bland) (Asten) Leavitt, who may have been their second child, died November 30, 1712, aged unknown. He married, September 25, 1667, Martha, probably a daughter of Anthony and Philippa Taylor, pioneer settlers, and the first of the name in Hampton. She died in 1716. Their children were: Lydia, John, James, Moses, Thomas, Mary, and perhaps Abigail and Sarah.

(III) Moses, fourth child and third son of Hezron and Martha (Taylor) Leavitt, was born in Hampton, January 30, 1674, and died before 1733. He kept a tavern near the Weare Marston place, which his widow conducted after his death. It was burned in 1733 and rebuilt. He married, December 11, 1700, Mary Carr, who died in 1747. They had six children: Mary, John, Moses (died young), Sarah, Moses and Anna.

(IV) Captain John, second child and eldest son of Moses and Mary (Carr) Leavitt, was born in Hampton, July 24, 1706, and died May 11, 1779. He kept the tavern after his mother, at the old stand till 1751, when by invitation of thirty-six principal inhabitants of North Hampton he removed to "the Hill" and built a tavern near the church. He was a popular landlord, a leading citizen, captain in the militia, and a justice of the peace. He married Abial (Marston) Hobbs, who was born in Hampton, March 23, 1718, and died January 21, 1781. She was the daughter of Thomas and Deborah (Dearborn) Marston, and widow of Benjamin Hobbs. The children of this union were: Benjamin, John, Moses, Thomas, Mary, Deborah, Carr, Simon and Jeremiah.

(V) Benjamin, eldest child of Captain John and Abial (Marston) Leavitt, was born August 27, 1737, and died in 1801. Like his ancestors he was an inn-keeper. He married Ruth Sanborn, who was born in Hampton, September 24, 1740, daughter of Ebenezer and Ruth (Sanborn) Sanborn, of Hampton. They had eight children.

(VI) Ebenezer, fifth child of Benjamin and Ruth (Sanborn) Leavitt, was born March 2, 1771, and did in 1843. He married, 1792, Sally Jewell, who died in 1851.

(VII) William, youngest son of Ebenezer and Sally (Jewell) Leavitt, was born in 1814, and died 1857. He was a moulder and machinist, and in 1850 went to California, in search of gold. Afterward he went to British Columbia, where he died. He married Louisa Dalton.

(VIII) Daniel Eben, son of William and Louisa (Dalton) Leavitt, was born August 4, 1844, in Chicopee, now Springfield, Massachusetts, and died at Wolfboro, New Hampshire, July 26, 1902. He was educated in the common schools of Rye, New Hampshire, and at an early age engaged in the rural peddling business for Frank Jones, of Portsmouth. Later he was employed on the estate of Daniel Pierce, of Portsmouth. Still later he became bookkeeper for Lyman D. Spaulding, ironmonger, for whom he worked three years. He then bought the Oren Bragdon shoe store, which he carried on three years, and then became collector for Frank Jones, brewer. He occupied that position twenty years, until failing health compelled him to retire a few years before his death. In politics he was a Democrat. He was a member of Piscataqua Lodge, Independent Order of Odd Fellows, and also of St. Johns Lodge, No. 1, Free and Accepted Masons, of Portsmouth, and Edward A. Raymond Consistory, Sublime Princes of the Royal Secret, of Nashua, where he attained the thirty-second degree of Masonry. He married, in Portsmouth, April 21, 1868, Ellen Hadley, who was born in Portsmouth, daughter of General Josiah Gillis and Ann Perley Hadley, of Dunbarton.

LEAVITT This family name under the forms Leavitt, Levitt, Levett, is among those found on the early records of New England. Thomas Leavitt was at Exeter, New Hampshire, as early as 1639. John was of Dorchester, Massachusetts, in 1634.

(I) Samuel (2), son of Samuel (1) and Abiah Leavitt, was born in Deerfield, New Hampshire, March 14, 1774. He cleared up a farm in Gilford overlooking Lake Winnepesaukee, on which his descendants are still living. He married and had children.

(II) Samuel (3), son of Samuel (2) and —— Leavitt, was born in Gilford, and was drowned in Lake Winnepesaukee, with his son Jonathan. He married Martha Thurston, and they were the parents of nine children: Jonathan, Smith, Benjamin, Daniel, Mary, Roxanna, Abigail, and two who died young.

(III) Daniel Leavitt, fourth son and child of Samuel Leavitt, was born on the farm settled by his grandfather, May 22, 1833. The death of his father when Daniel was only a few years old left him and his two brothers to manage the farm, while they were yet quite young. But they were counseled by a wise mother and succeeded in their efforts as young tillers of the soil, and Mr. Leavitt is now one of the foremost farmers in his town and resides on the old homestead. In politics he is a Democrat; and in religion a Methodist. He married first, Elizabeth Thompson, and (second), Hannah ——. By the first wife he had two children: Abigail, who married Benjamin Woodman; and Nancy, who married Frank Wilkerson.

CLOUGH This family, very numerously represented in New Hampshire, is among the earliest of the state and among the most widely distributed therein. It is among the first established in Massachusetts and has furnished many leading citizens in both states, as well as in other sections of the United States.

(I) John Clough (sometimes spelled Cluff) was a house carpenter, residing in Salisbury, Massachusetts, and is supposed to have come from England, in the ship "Elizabeth," in 1635. He received land in the first division at Salisbury and again in 1640, and was a commoner and taxpayer in 1650, and he subscribed to the oath of fidelity in that year. He was born about 1613, and died July 26, 1691, in Salisbury. His will was made on the third day of the same month, and was proven in the succeeding November. His first wife, Jane, died January 16, 1680, in Salisbury, and he married (second), January 15. 1686, Martha Cilley: She survived him and was living in 1692. His children were: Elizabeth, Mary, Sarah, John, Thomas, Martha and Samuel. (Mention of Thomas and descendants occurs in this article.)

(II) John (2), eldest son and third child of John (1) and Jane Clough, was born March 9, 1649, in Salisbury, where he was a yeoman, and subscribed to the oath of allegiance and fidelity in 1677. He was on record as a freeman in 1699, and his death occurred April 19, 1718. His will was made more than three years previously. He was married, November 13, 1674, in Salisbury, to Mercy, daughter of John and Mary (Marsh) Page, pioneers of Hingham and Haverhill. She was born April 1, 1655, in Haverhill, and died January 25, 1719, in Salisbury. She was admitted to the Salisbury church September 6, 1691. Her will was made in May, 1718, and proven in May of the following year. Their children were: Benoni, Mary, John, Cornelius, Caleb, Joseph, Sarah, Jonathan, Mercy, Aaron and Tabitha. (Mention of Aaron and descendants appears in this article.)

(III) Joseph, fifth son and sixth child of John (2) and Mercy (Page) Clough, was born October 14, 1684, in Salisbury, and died October 12, 1732, in Kingston, New Hampshire. He was a cordwainer by occupation, and was a resident of Kingston as early as 1711. He was of the constituent members of the church there in 1725, when the Rev. Ward Clark took charge, and his wife Mary was admitted March 20, 1726. They lost a child September 9, 1727, name not given in the Kingston church records. The inventory of his estate was made November 23, 1732, and it was divided in January, 1736, at Concord. He was married, August 11, 1708, to Mary Jenness, who died October 11, 1732. A memoranda in the church records of Kingston indicates that they were the parents of ten children. The names of the following are found: Ezra, Mazey, Joseph (died young), Joseph, Mary, Obadiah, Tabitha, Elizabeth, Love and Reuben. (The last named receives mention, with descendants, in this article.)

(IV) Joseph (2), second son and third child of Joseph (1) Clough, was born July 4, 1717, in Kingston, and had a large family.

(V) Jacob, youngest child of Joseph (2) Clough, was born 1753, and settled in Hopkinton, New Hampshire, and is supposed to be the father of John Clough.

(VI) John Clough was a soldier and died at Portsmouth, about 1819. He married Polly Boyce, who died in Enfield, about 1858. They resided for a short time in a log house in the Otterville district of New London, and had two sons. The first, John, was born in New London, January 31, 1801, and became an eminent physician, practicing for half a century in Enfield and Lebanon. Polly Boyce was a daughter of Lieutenant Peggy and Jeanette Boyce, of Scotch-Irish lineage, from Londonderry, Ireland. Their family bible printed in Edinburgh in 1728, is now treasured by their great-grandson, General Joseph M. Clough, of New London. Lieutenant Boyce held a commission in the war of the revolution, and served at Bunker Hill, and was with Stark at Bennington.

(VII) Hugh Boyce, second son of John and Polly (Boyce) Clough, was born in 1802, in Sunapee, New Hampshire, and in 1840 became a resident of New London, where he had a farm of three hundred acres. He was strong and active in promoting the cause of human liberty, and was an associate in the agitation against slavery of such men as Garrison, Phillips and Pillsbury. He entertained Frederick Douglass at his home in 1842. He often served as a town officer, and died at New London, July 27, 1887, at the age of about eighty-five years. He was married, in 1827, to Hannah, daughter of Zaccheus and Hannah (Hutchins) Messer. She was born November 8, 1808, in New London, and died March 14, 1888. Zaccheus Messer was a son of Lieutenant Samuel and Sarah (Howe) Messer, and was born December 6, 1770, and died January 1, 1855, in New London. Zaccheus and Hannah Messer were the parents of ten children, of whom Hannah was the ninth. Hugh B. Clough and wife were the parents of a son and daughter. Joseph and Hannah A. The last named died before the completion of her fifteenth year.

(VIII) Joseph Mosser, only son of Hugh B. and Hannah (Messer) Clough, was born Jun 15, 1828, in Sunapee, New Hampshire, and was reared from the age of twelve years in New London. His education was chiefly supplied by the common schools, and he spent six months at Norwich University, Vermont, under John Rawson. For three winters he taught in the district schools. After living a few years in Enfield, New Hampshire, he removed in 1848 to Manchester, this state, where he was employed as a machinist, and later was at Suncook and Lowell, in the latter place having charge of the spinning room of the Hamilton corporation for three years. In 1854 he returned to Manchester, and held a similar position in the Amoskeag mills. In the hard times of 1857 he took up his residence at New London temporarily, and there engaged in cutting out the lumber for the addition to the meeting house. His fondness for military affairs seemed innate, and began to be apparent at very early age. At Enfield he was adjutant and captain in the militia, and at Manchester rose from the ranks to be commander of the City Guard. While at Lowell he was a member of the City Guard, commanded by Benjamin F. Butler. It is easy to believe that the son of such sires would be eager to fly to the defense of his country in the hour of danger. On April 26, 1861, he was enrolled as a private in the

GEN. JOSEPH M. CLOUGH.

First New Hampshire Volunteers, and four days later was appointed lieutenant of Company H. On September 10 of the same year he re-enlisted in the Fourth Regiment, and was appointed captain of Company H. He continued in active service until the close of the war, and was engaged in numerous severe battles, including Pocotaligo, Morris Island, Siege of Forts Wagner and Sumter, Petersburg, Bermuda Hundred, Drewry's Bluff, Weir Bottom Church, Cold Harbor, Hatcher's Run, Deep Run, Petersburg Mine, Fort Stedman, and the capture of Petersburg, in March, 1865. He was wounded in the mine explosion at Petersburg, July 30, 1864, and was discharged September 17 following. In less than a month after this discharge he accepted a commission as lieutenant-colonel of the Tenth Regiment, and was the first in command of a regiment until Colonel Livermore was commissioned in January, 1865. In the night attack of Fort Stedman, March 29, 1865, Colonel Clough was again wounded, but continued in the active discharge of his duty until he was mustered out July 29, 1865. Following his wound he was breveted brigadier-general on recommendation by General O. B. Wilcox, then commanding the First Division, Ninth Army Corps, and received his commission at Washington. He was also recommended by General Wilcox and Senator Daniel Clark for appointment as first lieutenant in the regular army, and passed the required military examination, but his determination to continue in the service was changed because of broken health, and he did not accept the commission. At the close of the war General Clough returned to New London, and for thirteen years was employed in the United States railway service, running out of Boston to Lancaster and Saint Albans, Vermont. For seven years from 1877 to 1884 he was commander of the first brigade of the New Hampshire National Guard. He represented the town in the legislature in 1866, and filled the unexpired term of Edwin P. Burpee in 1897. In 1881-2, he represented his district in the state senate. He has a delightful home on Main street, in the village of New London, in which is stored many valuable relics and heirlooms. In the list of interesting and highly treasured of these is the headquarters flag, the second one floated in Petersburg after its capture.

He was married, September 7, 1849, to Abiah Bucklin, who was born October 22, 1828, in Grafton, New Hampshire, daughter of Charles and Choice (Cole) Bucklin, and died December 17, 1873. General Clough was married (second), September 13, 1874, to Cornelia Goss (Smith) Chase, daughter of William P. and Rhoda (Spooner) Smith, and widow of Henry Chase. Her daughter, Minnie Chase, who was born November 10, 1868, was tenderly reared in the family of her stepfather, like his own. She was educated at Colby Academy, and taught in the district schools until her marriage to George K. Burleigh, of Tilton. General Clough's children were: Ella A., who died of tyhpoid fever in her second year, Charles B. and William P. The elder son was a resident of Boston, Massachusetts, where he is held a responsible position, and the younger, William P., born September 13, 1879, married, September 7, 1905, Bertha Roos, daughter of Walter and Harriet (Rice) Roos, of Roxbury, Massachusetts. William P. studied medicine in the medical department of Dartmouth College. His wife is a graduate of the Emerson School of Oratory.

(IV) Reuben, youngest child of Joseph and Mary

Clough, resided in that part of Kingston which is now Sandown, and was a voter in the election of September 24, 1764, which resulted in a division of the town. He was married in Kingston, December 5, 1744, to Love Sanborn, born June 10, 1726, in Kingston, a daughter of Jonathan (2) and Theodate (Sanborn) "Sanborn," of that town. Jonathan (2) Sanborn was a son of Captain Jonathan (1) and Elizabeth (Sherburne) Sanborn, of Kingston, and grandson of Lieutenant John Sanborn, of Hampton (see Sanborn). Reuben Clough was among the early residents at Schoodac in the town of Warner, New Hampshire.

(V) Joseph (2), son of Reuben and Love Sanbourn Clough, was born in Sandown, 1751, and removed with his father to Warner, where he resided. He was a patriot soldier in the Revolutionary war, and the records show that Joseph Clough, of Warner, aged twenty-six, was a soldier in Captain Gordon Hutching's company, Colonel Stark's regiment, in 1775, and was present at the battle of Bunker Hill. His name is on the pay roll of Captain Hutching's company, Colonel John Stark's regiment, date August 1, 1775, where it appears that Joseph Clough, of Warner, private, enlisted May 4, 1775, and had served three months and five days. October 4, 1778, Joseph Clough, of Warner, of Captain Hutching's company, Colonel Stark's regiment, received $4 for regimental coat. Joseph Clough acted as company clerk during his term of service. In the later years of his life he drew a pension from the government.

(VI) Joseph (3), son of Joseph (2) Clough, was born in Warner, November 24, 1793, and died there January 15, 1859. He was a farmer. He married Jane Evans, daughter of Benjamin Evans.

(VII) Joseph Augustus, son of Joseph (3) and Jane (Evans) Clough, was born in Warner, July 31, 1834, and died there December 24, 1887. He was a farmer and carpenter, and resided all his life in Warner. He married Julia Ann Edmonds, who was born in Sutton, daughter of John R. and Judith (Harvey) Edmonds of Sutton, who were the parents of five other children, namely: Jackson, George, Daniel, Helen and Dussilla. Mr. and Mrs. Clough were the parents of two children: George McClellan, see forward, and Persis J., residing in Boston, Massachusetts, unmarried. Mrs. Clough resides in Newport, Rhode Island, and is a member of the Baptist Church.

(VIII) George McClellan, eldest child and only son of Joseph A. and Julia Ann (Edmonds) Clough, was born in Warner, May 28, 1863. He received his education in the common schools of Warner, and at the Simond's free high school, supplemented by private instruction, and as a student he was diligent and attentive. He gave his attention to surveying and teaching. In the former occupation he performed considerable work in Warner and adjoining towns, and followed the latter vocation six years, the first two being spent in the common schools of Wagner, the next two at Canterbury, and the last two at Tilton. In 1888 he became an agent of the Penn Mutual Life Insurance Company, and for eighteen years was in busines in Boston, where he achieved signal success. For a dozen or more years he has been interested in Christian Science, as taught by Mary B. G. Eddy, and as a result of his study and proof of its efficacy as a healing agent and benefactor to mankind he has abandoned all other business and adopted the profession of a Christian Science practitioner. He has prepared a work on life insurance for use in public schools and colleges; this has now been incorporated in a commercial arithmetic published by Ginn & Company, which is in use in the public and commercial schools of a number of states. He has also frequently contributed articles on insurance for various publications. Mr. Clough early became active in the New Hampshire Patrons of Husbandry, and was for two years president of the Somerville Sons and Daughters of New Hampshire. He is the present president of the Simond's Free High School Association of Warner. He resides in Somerville, and is a member of the First Church of Christ, Scientist. Mr. Clough married (first), 1887, Anna G. Gale, of Canterbury, New Hampshire, daughter of Eliphalet and Mary J. Gale, and three children were born to them: Gertrude G., Portia E. and Maurice J. Mrs. Clough died in 1903. Mr. Clough married (second), 1905, Francese W. Riley, daughter of James E. and Kathrine Whitney Riley, of Plattsburg, New York, and they are the parents of one daughter, Kathryn.

(III) Aaron Clough, eleventh child and second son of John (2) and Marcy (Page) Clough, was born in Salisbury, Massachusetts, December 16, 1695, baptized August 4, 1700, and died January 20, 1781. His wife Abigail died January 26, 1743, aged forty-six years.

(IV) Simon, son of Aaron and Abigail Clough, was born about 1740, and was killed at the battle of Bennington, in August, 1777. He settled in Gilmanton, New Hampshire, in 1775, at or about which time several other members of his family came to the locality. He was one of the four Cloughs who signed the test act passed by congress in 1776, while two others of the same family name were among those who dissented from that affirmation on the ground of consciencious scruples against defending their country with arms. Simon Clough was a private in Captain Nathaniel Wilson's company of Colonel Thomas Stickney's regiment in General John Stark's brigade from July 22, 1877, and was one of seven men from Gilmanton who were killed in battle at Bennington. He married, and among his children were three sons, Jonathan, Perley and Joseph Clough.

(V) Joseph, youngest child of Simon Clough, was born at Seabrook, New Hampshire, 1772. He married and had eleven children, Charles, Simon, Judith, Joseph, Rebecca, Nehemiah, Parmelia, Moses, Mary, Isaiah and Jonathan Clough.

(VI) Nehemiah, sixth child of Joseph Clough, was born in Gilmanton, New Hampshire, and died in that town, 1850. He was a soldier from Gilmanton in the second war with Great Britain, and after returning from service was a farmer in his native town. He married Sarah Rowe, who was born, 1796, and died in 1864. Their children were Phebe R., Mary P., Lewis O., Elvira, John P., Sarah B., Julia and Albert N. Clough.

(VII) John P., fifth child and second son of Nehemiah and Sarah (Rowe) Clough, was born in Gilmanton, November 6, 1824, and died in that town October 12, 1893. During his young manhood he gave considerable attention to school teaching in the winter seasons, but his principal occupation was farming. He was a man of influence in town affairs, a consistent member of the Congregationalist Church, and was a member of the school board before the town of Belmont was set off from the territory of Gilmanton. He married, February 7, 1850, Tamson Hayes Winckley (see Winckley), who was born April 25, 1824, and died December 24, 1874, daughter of Francis and Sally (Lougee) Winckley of Strafford, New Hampshire, and by whom he had four children, Elbridge G., Nahum O., Russell W. and Martha Clough. (See Winckley, VI.).

(VIII) Elbridge G., eldest child of John P. and Tamson Hayes (Winckley) Clough, was born in Gilmanton, New Hampshire, January 13, 1852, and for more than twenty-five years had been numbered with the substantial and influential men of that town. His early education was received in public schools of Gilmanton and New Hampton Academy, and after leaving school he went to Manchester, New Hampshire, and found employment in a mill in that city. At the end of about three years he returned home and took the management of his father's old farm, and also for about ten years carried on a meat business in the town. Still later he operated the mail and passenger stage line between Gilmanton and Alton, New Hampshire, and also engaged in lumbering and teaming. Mr. Clough's present farm comprises one hundred and fifty acres and is one of the best cultivated farms in Gilmanton, complete in all its appointments in respect to buildings, stock and management. In addition to farming he is engaged in various other enterprises of a business character, and for many years has been an important factor in the political history of the town, always on the Democratic side. On occasion he has stood as his party candidate for office and in 1896 was defeated for the legislature, the town being generally safely Republican, although the plurality against him at that time was only thirteen votes. However, in 1903 he was again nominated, and was elected to a seat in the lower house of the state legislature. Mr. Clough is a charter member and past master of Crystal Lake Grange of Gilmanton Iron Works and in various other ways is and for many years has been identified with the best interests and history of his town.

He married, December 25, 1873, Emma S. Sargent, who was born in Lowell, Massachusetts, February 20, 1852, daughter of Albert P. and Hannah Sargent, and has seven children, all sons: John, Page, Guy Sargent, Russell Walton, William Everett, Albert Dexter, Clarence Francis and Carl Grosvernor Clough.

(II) Thomas, second son and fifth child of John and Jane Clough, was born May 29, 1651, in Salisbury, Massachusetts, and resided in that town. He subscribed to the oath of allegiance and fidelity in 1677, and was a soldier in the defensive army of the period. With his second wife he was admitted to the Salisbury church, July 27, 1718. He was styled "yeoman" in 1730, and was probably still living as late as 1738. He was married, March 10, 1680, in Salisbury to Hannah, daughter of Samuel Gile. She died December 22, 1683, and he was married (second), in 1687, to Ruth, daughter of Cornelius and Sarah Connor of Salisbury. His children were: Samuel, Thomas, Jeremiah, Ebenezer (died young), Ebenezer, Zaccheus, Isaac, Rebecca, Hannah, Judith and Martha. (Thomas and Zaccheus and descendants receive notice in this article).

(III) Samuel, eldest child of Thomas and Hannah (Dyer) Clough, was born December 5, 1680, in Salisbury and resided in that town. He was called "Sergeant Samuel," probably because of his services in the militia. He died in August, 1728, in his forty-eighth year. His wife's Christian name was Sarah, but her family name is not discovered. She was married (second), March 25, 1730, at the second Salisbury church, to Ezekiel Morrill, who died soon after and she was married (third), January 10, 1734, at the same church to Captain Joseph Taylor, of Hampton. She was living in 1755. Ser-

Wm O. Clough.

geant Clough's children were: Theophilus, Eliphalet, Hannah, Abigail. Samuel, Daniel (died young), Daniel, Sarah, Mehitabel and Miriam. (Daniel and descendants receive mention in this article).

(IV) Theophilus, eldest son of Samuel and Sarah Clough, was born in Salisbury, Massachusetts, November 28, 1703, and was baptized October 19, 1718, at Salisbury Church. He settled in Kingston, New Hampshire, where he was living in 1755. He married at Salisbury (second church), January 4, 1728, Sarah French. Many settlers in Salisbury, New Hampshire, Enfield and vicinity were from Kingston and vicinity. Both the Clough and French families were represented in the settlers at Enfield directly after the Revolution.

(V) Theophilus (2), son of Theophilus (1) and Sarah (French) Clough, was born about 1730. He was a soldier in the Revolution, stationed in 1777 at Fort Washington, and in 1778 took part in the Rhode Island expedition in Captain Joseph Dearborn's company (Chester), Colonel Moses Nichols's regiment. He signed a petition of the noncommissioned officers and privates at Fort Washington in 1777 praying for relief from inadequate pay, etc. Just after the war he settled in Enfield, New Hampshire. According to the federal census of 1790 there were besides himself two adult men in his family and one son under sixteen; also five females (probably four were daughters). Children: 1. Richard, was married and had a family in Enfield in 1790. 2. Henry, mentioned below. Another son and four daughters unknown.

(VI) Henry, son of Theophilus Clough, was born about 1775. He removed in his youth to Enfield, New Hampshire, with the family. His wife was probably a Currier. In 1790 we find in Enfield with families Theophilus, Richard and Jonathan Currier. Henry Clough married and had a son, Theophilus Currier, mentioned below.

(VII) Theophilus Currier, son of Henry Clough, was born about 1800 in Tamworth, New Hampshire, where his parents were then living. He was educated in the district schools of his native town. He operated a woolen mill at Enfield, New Hampshire, for a number of years. When gold was discovered in California he disposed of his business and set out for the new El Dorado with the "Forty-niners." He fell ill on the way and died on the Isthmus of Panama. He was a member of the Universalist Church, and an earnest advocate of temperance reforms. In politics he was a Whig. Children: Edwin A., Angelina B., Emily, Warren Currier, mentioned below.

(VIII) Warren Currier, son of Theophilus Currier Clough, was born in Enfield, New Hampshire, September 25, 1843. He was educated in the public schools of his native town. His father died when he was only six years old and he had to rely largely upon his own efforts for advancement. He engaged in business on his own account in 1869, as a merchant, dealing in boots and shoes and small wares, in Enfield. He enjoyed a large and thriving business for many years, retiring finally in 1906. He was a member of the Enfield Universalist Church; of Social Lodge, No. 50, Free Masons, of Enfield; of St. Andrews Royal Arch Chapter, of Lebanon, New Hampshire; Washington Council, No. 10, Royal and Select Masters; Mount Horeb Commandery, Knights Templar, of Concord, New Hampshire, and Bektash Temple, Mystic Shrine, of Concord, New Hampshire. He is also a member of Titigaw Tribe, No. 38, Independent Order of Red Men, of Enfield. In politics he is a Republican, and he represented the town of Enfield in the legislature in 1905; was town treasurer several years; was postmaster from 1880 to 1885, holding office three years under Cleveland's administration; treasurer of village precinct at the present time; also of the Cemetery Association and of the Universalist Society. He is one of the best known men of the vicinity, and commands the fullest confidence and esteem of his townsmen.

He married, November 14, 1867, Sarah Elizabeth Currier, of Enfield, New Hampshire. She was born February 26, 1845, the daughter of Dennison and Laura Currier, of Manchester, New Hampshire. Their only child is James Currier Clough, born September 19, 1881, at Enfield, educated in the public and high schools of his native town, and at Dean Academy, Franklin, Massachusetts, where he was graduated in 1904.

(IV) Daniel, fifth son and seventh child of Samuel and Sarah Clough, was born July 19, 1718, in Salisbury, and was baptized on the 19th of October succeeding. He resided in Salisbury until after 1753, when he removed to the town of Whitefield, New Hampshire, and was later a resident of Meredith in the same state. His last years were passed in Henniker.

(V) Oliver, son of Daniel Clough, was a native of Meredith and went with his parents to Henniker in early childhood. He enlisted in the Third New Hampshire Regiment, under the command of Colonel Alexander Scammel, for service in the Revolutionary war, and in common with his companions in arms, endured the privations and exposure suffered by the American patriots during the struggle for national independence, and in his declining years he was granted a pension by the Federal government. After his return from the army he settled in Meredith, New Hampshire, and his death occurred in that town November 27, 1847.

(VI) John Kenney, son of Oliver, was born in Henniker. When a young man he went to Maine, and for a time resided in the town of Gray, but in 1842 he returned to his native state, locating permanently in Meredith. He married Ellen Lunt Libbey, a lineal descendant in the seventh generation of John Libbey, who was born in England in 1602, emigrated in 1630, and settled in Scarboro, Maine, where he died in 1682. He was the progenitor of most of the Libbeys of New England. Of this union there were four sons: John F., a resident of Manchester and one of the Hillsboro county commissioners; Edwin H., who is now postmaster at Manchester; Henry B., also a resident of that city; Frank E., who resides in Meredith; and William O., who is referred to at length in the succeeding paragraph.

(VII) William Oliver, son of John K. and Ellen L. (Libbey) Clough, was born in Gray, Maine, July 14, 1840. His preliminary studies in the Meredith public schools were augmented with an advanced course at Rev. Hosea Quimby's Academic School, and at the age of sixteen years he began the activities of life as an errand boy in a jewelry store in Boston, where, in an unusually short space of time, he obtained a clerkship. In 1860 he accepted a position as salesman for the Cape Cod Glass Company, whose headquarters were then located on Milk street, Boston, and he retained his connection with that concern for nine years, or until its suspension in 1869. During his residence in Boston he was an active member of the Mercantile Library Association, serving upon its board of directors for a period of seven years and attending regularly its evening school; also officiating as chairman of its committee on dramatic, declamatory and musical entertainments, and as editor of its paper, *The Tete-a-Tete.* When the Park Street Church Library Association was organized he entered into its work with spirit, serving as its first secretary and its third president. His taste and capacity for journalism developed early in life and was fostered by his connection with *The Tete-a-Tete* and as a contributor to other publications, so that when the Cape Cod Glass Company went out of existence he found no difficulty in profiting by his experience, entering the newspaper field as city editor of the *Nashua Daily Telegraph,* and retaining that posiiton until May, 1892, a period of twenty-three years. After severing his connection with the *Telegraph* he became staff correspondent of the *New Hampshire Republican* and was subsequently its political editor. Purchasing a controlling interest in the *Nashua Daily Gazette,* in October, 1895, he renamed that organ in the following November the *Nashua Daily Press,* and he also changed its political aspect and general policy. Although forced to struggle for existence and compelled at one time to suspend publication, he succeeded in recalling the *Press* to life, placed it upon a substantial basis, and, with the exception of a few months, continued as its editor and manager until the summer of 1905, when he sold his interest to the Telegraph Publishing Company, who were prompt, however, to avail themselves of his services as an editorial writer. Aside from his connection with the local press, he was for twenty-five years a regular correspondent of the *Boston Journal,* under the nom de plume of "Nashoonon," contributed many serials and stories, essays, sketches, etc., to various newspapers and magazines, and edited the biographical section of the "History of Nashua." In political, educational and other matters outside of his profession, Judge Clough took an earnest interest and his efforts in behalf of the city in general, its government and its institutions were both spontaneous and invigorating. From 1876 to 1881 he served as city marshal, was an assessor from 1893 to 1897, and for nearly thirty years was associate justice of the Nashua municipal court. He also served the city for a period of thirteen years as principal of an evening school. When the old-line insurance companies left the state without protection, he readily joined with others in organizing the Indian Head Mutual Fire Insurance Company, of which he was a director and its last vice-president. Another Nashua institution in which he was deeply interested is the Building and Loan Association, and he was one of its most efficient directors. Probably his most valuable service to the city was as associate justice of the municipal court, to which position he was appointed by Governor Cheney in 1878, and he retained it continuously for the remainder of his life, gaining the implicit confidence of the people as a whole, and lawyers in particular, for the care with which he weighed all evidence submitted to him and the impartiality displayed in rendering his decisions. Judge Clough was made a Mason in Columbian Lodge, Boston, and was advanced to the Royal Arch degree in St. Andrew Chapter, that city; was one of the original members of Israel Hunt Council, Royal and Select Masters, and its first illustrious master; was a member of St. George Commandery, Knights Templar; and had attained the thirty-second degree, Scottish Rite. His domestic life was an ideal one, made so by his affectionate nature and kindly disposition, and although suffering from the ravages of an incurable disease during the last two years of his life, he retained his customary cheerfulness to the end, which came on the morning of March 25, 1906. His passing away was not only a severe blow to his family and immediate relatives, but was also keenly felt by the community in general and his journalistic and fraternal associates. He was a leading member and an official of the Church of the Good Shepherd, and his solicitude for the welfare of that parish will be long remembered. On January 16, 1868, Judge Clough was married in Manchester, to Miss Julia Moore, daughter of Jonathan H. and Hannah (Van Sleeper) Moore. She is a lineal descendant of John and Janet Moore, Scotch-Irish immigrants from county Antrim, Ireland, who settled in Londonderry, New Hampshire, about the year 1721. John Moore died January 24, 1774, and his wife died March 8, 1776. Their children were: Deacon William, Elizabeth, Colonel Robert and Colonel Daniel. Colonel Robert Moore, the next in line of descent, was appointed lieutenant-colonel, September 1, 1775, in Colonel Samuel Hobart's regiment of the New Hampshire Continental line. He died in October, 1778. Colonel Robert Moore's youngest son, Robert, was born in Londonderry, New Hampshire, September 20, 1769, and died August 16, 1803. He married Jeannie Rolfe, who was born in Newburyport, Massachusetts, September 22, 1771, and died February 16, 1852. Their son, Jonathan Holmes Moore, was born on Shirley Hill, Goffstown, in June, 1802, and died in Manchester, November 12, 1869; he married Hannah Van Sleeper of Knickerbocker descent, who died August 3, 1858. They were the parents of eleven children, and among them were Hon. Orren Cheney Moore, and Julia, who married Judge Clough, as previously stated. Judge Clough is survived by his widow and two daughters: Charlotte Moore, a graduate of the New Hampshire State Normal School, and now the wife of Chester T. Cornish, of New Bedford, Massachusetts; Christine Rolfe, who is residing with her mother in Nashua.

(III) Thomas (2), second son and child of Thomas (1) and Hannah (Gile) Clough, was born December 9, 1681, in Salisbury. He was a shoemaker by occupation, and resided in that town as late as 1738. probably removing to Kingston, New Hampshire. He is supposedly the Thomas Clough who was married January 15, 1706, in Haverhill, to Mary Gile, daughter of Ephraim and Martha (Bradley) Gile, and granddaughter of Samuel Gile, of Haverhill, a pioneer emigrant who resided in Salisbury. Part of his children are on record in Salisbury, but not all. His estate was administered November 13, 1749.

(IV) Jeremiah, second son of Thomas (2) and Mary (Gile) Clough, was baptized May 28, 1710. On reaching manhood he went to Kensington, New Hampshire. and was there married, February 16, 1738, to Sarah Elkins, by the Rev. Jeremiah Fogg. He was the pioneer settler of Canterbury, New Hampshire, locating there soon after the town was granted, and maintained for many years a garrison for the settlers. The colonial records show that in 1745 he rendered an account of the expenses for provisions, ammunition and wages of himself and ten men in maintaining the garrison, and at the same time presented a bill of ten pounds and six shillings for "medisens and Tendence." Again in 1746 and 1747 he rendered an account which covered a total service for himself and five others of two hundred and ninety-seven days, and the bill for ammunition, provisions and wages amounted to sixteen pounds, fourteen shillings and three pence. Because of his military experience he raised a company for the Revolution, being one of the ten commissioned for that purpose, for Colonel Enoch Poor's regiment, each being required to muster a company of sixty-two able-bodied men. This commission was issued May 24, 1775, and Captain Clough's company was completed on June 13 of that year, composed of men from Canterbury, Loudon, Northfield, Sanbornton, Tamworth, Moultonboro, and one from New Britton, in Hillsboro, making a total of sixty-three men. This company was at Medfield, October 4, 1775, where the men resided for coats promised them by the provincial congress. On account of his age Captain Clough probably did not continue long in the military service, as we find no record of him after that day. The records say that he was justice of the peace in 1776, and a selectman in 1782. In the vital records of Canterbury he is always referred to as "Esq'r Clough." No mention of his wife appears in these records, but his children are named as follows: Jeremiah, Deliverance, Hannah, Thomas, Leavit, Henry, Joseph, Sarah and Abner.

(V) Leavit, fourth son and fifth child of Captain Jeremiah and Sarah (Elkins) Clough, was born July 21, 1751, and died August 13, 1825, in Canterbury, and resided through life in that town. He married Hannah Fletcher, who died January 8, 1782, and he subsequently married Peggy Mason. The children of the first marriage were: Sarah and Leavit.

(VI) Leavit (2), eldest son and second child of Leavit (1) and Hannah (Fletcher) Clough, was born October 30, 1778, and passed his life in Canterbury where he was a farmer. He was married, October 27, 1800, in Canterbury, to Abigail Morrill, of that town. Their children were: Henry, William Patrick, Mary Ann, David Morrill, Miranda, Leavit M., Thomas C., Daniel Webster, Abraham and Isaac (twins), Elizabeth and Martha (twins).

(VII) Colonel David Morrill, fourth child and third son of Leavit (2) and Abigail (Morrill) Clough, was born on his grandfather's farm in Canterbury, June 9, 1805, and died in Canterbury, January 28, 1885, aged almost eighty years. He was educated in the district school and at Gilmanton Academy, attending the latter institution three terms. He learned rapidly and thoroughly, was able to express himself well, and at the age of eighteen began teaching a winter school. This avocation he continued for some years. At the age of nineteen he was commissioned in the state militia. Two years later he was promoted to a captaincy and after five years' service was made a colonel. After the death of his father he had to aid in the settlement of his estate. In 1832 he removed to Gilmanton, where he remained ten years, and then returned to Canterbury, and settled in the vicinity of his old home. In 1848, desirous of determining whether it was expedient to take Horace Greeley's advice and "go West," he made a tour of inspection and discovery through the states of Ohio, Indiana, Illinois and Iowa. After spending several months in this effort he returned with the conviction that New Hampshire offered as many inducements to the farmer as any state in the Union. He bought a little farm near the home of his boyhood, which he improved and sold in 1856. In the autumn of that year he bought the five hundred-acre farm upon which he resided the remainder of his life, a place on the Merrimack Intervale, between the Canterbury and Boscawen stations, the same that his great-uncle, Joseph Clough, once owned. Upon this he expended energy and money, but both were applied with judgment and skill, and in thirteen years the farm he had bought for $4,600 was worth $17,000, and instead of twelve cattle, over one hundred were supported on it. To this he added from time to time as circumstances permitted, outlying places of "sprout land" until he owned about 1500 acres. His average crop of corn on the ear was about 3,000 bushels, and he kept about 120 head of cattle, over a hundred sheep, and six horses.

A man of Colonel Clough's ability and wealth could not escape the notice of his fellow citizens, and in the selection of candidates for office, his name was often mentioned, and not unfrequently appeared on the ballots of his party. In politics he was a Free-Soil Democrat, and attended the national convention which nominated that illustrious son of New Hampshire, John P. Hale, the apostle of freedom and human rights. After the abolition of slavery he gave his adherence to the Democratic party. He served the town of Canterbury as selectman four years, and as representative to the general court two years. The nomination for member of governor's council was given him three times by the Democratic party, and he was elected during Governor Weston's first term. While a member of the legislature, Colonel Clough never lost sight of an opportunity to legislate in favor of the interests of agriculture, and he was an earnest and able advocate for the establishment of the Agricultural College, and was one of its board of trustees for some years. When the order of Patrons of Husbandry was introduced in the state, he was one of the first to perceive the possibilities of such an organization, and gave it his earnest support. He was a charter member of the Merrimack River Grange, and a charter member of the State Grange, of which he was treasurer six years, and on whose executive committee he filled a place for a long time. He was a member of the Merrimack County Agricultural Society, for two years its president and a life member of the New Hampshire Agricultural Society.

He joined the Free Will Baptist Church of Canterbury with his wife, in 1832, and for many years was clerk of the society. He was a life long advocate of temperance and abstained from all intoxicating drinks, including cider, and also from the use of tobacco. Colonel Clough was a champion of the farmers' rights, and an aim and ambition of his life was to dignify the farmers' vocation, and by experiment to develop the science of agriculture in the state. He was possessed of the great elements of success in life: Opportunity, ability, critical judgment, habits of industry and energy. These made him a successful man and a leading farmer upon whom the epithet of "the Corn King of New Hampshire" was right worthily bestowed. As a citizen he enjoyed the confidence and respect of his fellowmen. He was upright in all his dealings, and one in whom the sterling qualities of manhood were always observable, and at the end of a long and useful life he laid down the burden of years mourned by every honest man who had the honor of his acquaintance.

He married (first), October 25, 1828, Almira Batchelder, who was born June 7, 1805, and died November 5, 1851, daughter of Ebenezer Batchelder, of Canterbury; (second), June 17, 1856, Mrs. Caroline (Gibson) Tallent. His children, all by the first wife, were: Anna Maria, who was born in 1830, and died young; Henry Leavitt, February 17, 1834; Mary S., 1836, who died in 1838; Edwin D., 1843; and Charles Newell, the subject of the next paragraph.

(VIII) Charles N., youngest child of David M. and Almira E. (Batchelder) Clough was born January 15, 1850, on the old Ames farm, in Canterbury, which his father then owned. Since 1857 he has lived on the farm he now owns. He lived at home and attended the district school until he was eighteen years of age, when he went to Elmwood and attended the high school, and later to Manchester, where he took a course in a commercial school with the view of entering mercantile life, but yielding to the wishes of his father he returned to the homestead, where he has since resided, devoting his energies to general farming and to the raising of cattle and to dairying. In this latter branch he does a large business, making and selling annually about fifteen thousand pounds of butter. He has considerably improved his farm, and has a handsome residence which he erected in place of the one burned down some twenty years ago. He is a Republican and an attendant of the Congregational Church. He shared his father's interest in the grange, of which he early become a member, and was for twenty years overseer in the State Grange. In 1887-8-9 he was a member of the school board, and selectman in 1896-7. About 1874 he became a member of Horace Chase Lodge, No. 72, Free and Accepted Masons, of Penacook, in which he has filled the senior warden chair. Mr. Clough is a shrewd, farsighted and successful man, and enjoys the respect and confidence of his neighbors and townsmen. He married, January 15, 1874, Emma T. Morrill who was born June 6, 1854, daughter of John B. and ——— (Hoague) Morrill, of Canterbury. They have two children: David M. born May 16, 1879; and Caroline G., born September 4, 1888.

(III) Zaccheus, sixth son and child of Thomas Clough and fourth child of his second wife, was born February 17, 1692, in Salisbury, and was baptized August 5, 1711. He was admitted to the Second Church of Salisbury, January 4, 1734, and later removed to Fremont, New Hampshire, where he died July 30, 1757. He was married, January 21, 1714, to Sarah Page, who was born October 12, 1691, in Salisbury, daughter of Joseph and Sarah (Smith) Page, of Salisbury. John was the son of Onesiphorus and Sarah (Morrill) Page, and grandson of John and Mary (George) Page, of Hingham and Haverhill, Massachusetts. Five of Mr. Clough's children were baptized, April 5, 1724, in Salisbury, Namely: Benjamin, Hannah, Betsey, Jabez and Zaccheus.

(IV) Jabez, second son of Zaccheus and Sarah (Page) Clough, was born about 1722, in Salisbury and was married in Poplin (now Fremont), New Hampshire, September 7, 1749, to Sarah Young. They lived in Fremont, where eight children were born. No record of his death has been found. His wife, Sarah, died in Fremont, March 2, 1807.

(V) Daniel, son of Jabez and Sarah (Young) Clough, was born August 11, 1763, in Fremont. At the age of seventeen years, he enlisted in the Continental army, and served on the quota from Weare, New Hampshire. He was claimed by the town of Hopkinton, but after a hearing before the committee of safety he was credited to Weare. As soon as this matter was settled he was able to draw pay for his services from the town of Weare, which had previously refused to allow him anything. He was a blacksmith, and resided in South Weare, and had a family of several children, only one of whom remained in Weare.

(VI) Daniel (2), son of Daniel (1) Clough, was born 1792, in Weare, and was brought up to his father's trade. He was noted as a player on the violin. He lived in Weare, and died there in 1881. He married Mary Colby, who was born 1791, daughter of Philbrook and Ruth (Lufkin) Colby, of Weare (see Colby V). She died in 1880. They were the parents of twelve children. One, Julia A. Heath, of Dunbarton, is still living.

(VII) Gilman, son of Daniel (2) and Ruth (Colby) Clough, was born February 24, 1825, in Weare, where his earlier years were spent. Early in life he left his native town and settled in Manchester, New Hampshire. His educational opportunities were limited, but he possessed a good constitution and a spirit of energy and industry, and was ambitious to establish himself in life. Soon after he went to Manchester he engaged in the wood and lumber trade, and developed an extensive business. The profits of his trade were judiciously invested in real estate, and he thus became possessed of a competency from the advancement of values and by his wise and judicious management of his estate. He was married, 1848, to Miss Nancy E. Locke, who was born March 31, 1827, in Deering, New Hampshire, daughter of Stephen and Sarah (Peaslee) Locke (see Locke, V). Their only living offspring is Lewis A. Clough, who is now a resident of Manchester.

(VIII) Lewis Augustus, only child of Gilman and Nancy E. (Locke) Clough, was born in Weare, New Hampshire, February 14, 1850. He was educated in the district schools of Weare, and at Pinkerton Academy. The first business he embarked in after attaining his majority was lumbering, and in that business he has ever since remained. He usually owns four of five portable steam sawmills, and with these he prepares for market the timber on large areas which he buys standing. He frequently employs two hundred men for long periods of time, and markets millions of feet of lumber annually. He has resided in Manchester since he was two years old, when his father and mother removed to that place. In politics he is a Democrat, and in religion inclines to Unitarianism, although he is not a member of the church of that denomination. He has made life a success by attending very industriously to his own business, and has accumulated a handsome property. He married, in Manchester, 1875, Nora Burke, who was born in Lebanon, in 1852, daughter of Michael Burke, of Canaan. They are the parents of four children: Blanche E., the wife of Dr. L. M. Farrington, of Brookline, Massachusetts; Harry G., who is mentioned below; Nora Bernice, married Dr. Frank N. Rogers, of Manchester; and Emma Louise, at home.

(IX) Harry Gilman, second child and only son of Lewis Augustus and Nora (Burke) Clough, was born in Manchester, January 17, 1878. His primary education was obtained in the schools of Manchester, his preparatory education at Phillips Andover Academy, and his university course was taken at Harvard, from which he graduated with the class of 1900, when he attained the degree of A. B.. For three years he was engaged in the lumber business, but since 1903 he has devoted himself to caring for his realty holdings in Manchester. In politics he is a Republican. He is a member of the common council of this city. He is a member of the Masonic Order, and belongs to the following named bodies: Lafayette Lodge, No. 41; Mt. Horeb Royal Arch Chapter, No. 11; Andoniram Council No. 3; Trinity Commandery Knights Templar of Man-

William Clough

chester; and Edward A. Raymond Consistory of Nashua. He is also a member of Wildey Lodge, No. 45, Independent Order of Odd Fellows, and Mount Washington Encampment No. 16. He married, December 10, 1902, in Manchester, Lucille Weeks Elliott, daughter of Alonzo and Medora (Weeks) Elliott (see Elliott V).

CLOUGH (I) William Clough was born at Lyman, New Hampshire, in 1795, and followed the carpenter's trade in that town. An attempt to identify his ancestors has thus far proved fruitless, but there is some reason for believing that he was a grandson of William Clough, who served in the French and Indian war, and entering the Revolutionary war without enlistment participated in the battle of Bunker Hill. After the close of the war he went from New Salem to Lyman and located on Clough Hill. He reared six sons, whose names were: Zacheus, Enoch, Bailey, Cyrus, Abner and Jeremiah. William Clough, the cooper, married Betsey Crooks, and she bore him three children, Mary Jane, Mary Ann and William.

(II) William (2), son of William and Betsey (Crooks) Clough, was born in Lyman, April 15, 1824. His boyhood and youth were spent in attending the district school and acquiring a knowledge of agriculture. When a young man he settled upon a farm in Bath, this state, and resided there until 1850, when he went to Charlestown, Massachusetts, and engaged in the trucking business. Selling out his business he became an officer in the Massachusetts state prison, where he remained some two and one half years, at the expiration of which time he returned to his native state. Purchasing a piece of agricultural property in Lancaster known as Prospect Farm, he carried it on for a number of years, erecting new buildings, and making other notable improvements. He finally sold the property to George P. Rowell, of New York City, and it is now owned by the Hon. Samuel McCall, a member of congress from Massachusetts. After relinquishing agriculture he engaged in the real estate business in Lancaster. Mr. Clough was one of the organizers of the Lancaster National Bank and formerly served on its board of directors. He was one of the organizers and president of the Lancaster Works Company. In politics he was a Democrat, and in addition to holding some of the town offices, including that of selectman, he represented his district in the lower branch of the state legislature in 1879. He was highly esteemed both as an upright business man and an able public official, and his death, which occurred October 23, 1896, was the cause of general regret.

Mr. Clough married Elvira Wallace, daughter of Amos P. Wallace, of Franconia, New Hampshire, of Scotch descent. She died in 1890. The only child of this union now living is Mary Clough, who resides in Lancaster.

CLOUGH (I) Simon Clough was a native of Gilmanton, where he was engaged in farming. He married Mercy Elkins, and they had six children: Sarah, Jonathan, Daniel, Frank, Mary and Martha.

(II) Daniel E., second son and third child of Simon and Mercy (Elkins) Clough, was born in Gilmanton, March 23, 1835. His education was obtained in the common schools and at Gilmanton Academy. He taught a term of school at Gilmanton, and about 1856 went to Salem, Massachusetts, where he drove a cart and sold tinware for four or five years. He was an industrious and economical man, and saved a large part of his earnings, with which he purchased a stock of goods and opened a hardware store on his own account in Salem. This he conducted two years, when he became ill of consumption, sold his stock and returned to Alton, New Hampshire, where he died June 18, 1866. He married, at Gilmanton Iron Works, February 4, 1858, Melora S. Avery, born in Cambridge, Massachusetts, May 28, 1835, daughter of David and Apphia (Clough) Avery. They were the parents of one child, Herman W. Melora S., daughter of David Avery, is descended as follows: (1) David Avery was a farmer of Gilmanton, who married and had a family of children, two of whom were John and Lydia. (2) John Avery, son of David, was a native of Gilmanton, and a farmer in Gilmanton and Alton. He married Temperance Nutter, who lived to the age of one hundred years, and died about 1890. Their children were: Joseph, Isaac, David, Mary, Sarah, Belinda and John. (3) David Avery, third son and child of John and Temperance (Nutter) Avery, born in Gilmanton, in 1806, died 1879; he was a farmer in Alton. He married Apphia Clough, born in Alton, August, 1806, daughter of Perley and Mary Clough, and they had seven children: Melora S., Victoria, Gustena, George, a Union soldier who died in New Orleans, in 1862; Myra Elbridge and Emma. Melora S. (Avery) Clough married (second), November 16, 1879, in Concord, Cyrus F. Caswell, who was born in Pittsfield, New Hampshire, February 4, 1816, died January 18, 1892, the son of Stephen and Lydia (Roberts) Caswell. He was a farmer boy, but not caring to till the soil learned the trade of shoemaker, and for many years worked on shoes in his home, having the partly finished portions sent to him from the great shoe factories at Lynn and Haverhill. Later in life he gave up this occupation, and was a switch tender for the Boston & Maine railroad, at Concord. In 1880 he bought a stock of horses and opened a livery stable next to his residence, No. 57 North Spring street, which he conducted till his death, January 18, 1892. He was a man of good habits, steady, honest, industrious, and a member of the Freewill Baptist Church, of Concord. He married (first), Mary Jane Elkins who died, leaving no offspring. He left to his second wife a very comfortable property which she occupies.

(III) Herman W., only child of Daniel E. and Melora S. (Avery) Clough, was born in Salem, June 20, 1861. He attended the common schools at Alton, where his widowed mother lived, and later took two terms in the high school in Farmington, and after removing to Concord, in 1879, attended a private school in that city one year. In 1881 he entered the employ of the Boston & Maine Railroad Company as a switchman, which place he has continuously filled since that time. His political affiliation is with the Republican party. He is a member of the Baker Memorial Church (Methodist) of White Mountain Lodge, Independent Order of Odd Fellows, and of the Order of United American Mechanics. He married, 1891, Annie Johnson, of Farmington, born 1863, daughter of John and Anstress (Varney) Johnson, of Farmington, and they have one child: Edith, born October 11, 1895.

BULLARD The name Bullard is found in the Colonial records as early as 1637, when Benjamin Bullard was in Watertown, Massachusetts, at the division of lands in that town. Between that time and the end of the century various other Bullards settled in New England. Among the early planters no less than seven of the name are found of record. There has been a tradition that they were all brothers, but this is without foundation. George Bullard subscribed to the freeman's oath in 1641, and had land signed him in Watertown as early as 1637. John took the freeman's oath, May 16, 1640, and was a signer of Dedham, June 1, 1636. Isaac was another signer of the same compact at the same time. Nathaniel Bullard was admitted townsman there in 1655. Robert Bullard died at Watertown, April 24, 1639.

(I) William Bullard signed the social compact of Dedham, June 18, 1636. It is quite possible and even probable that the three which signed this document at the same time were brothers or near relatives. William Bullard's wife was received in the church at Dedham in 1639. He took the freeman's oath, May 13, 1640, and was chosen selectman in 1643. He was a respected and prominent citizen, and it is probable that he died not long after 1643, although no record of his death or of the settlement of his estate has been discovered. He left sons who inherited his estate at Dedham and transmitted it to their descendants, who now point at the location of his first habitation. The numerous Bullards of Dedham and some of the adjacent towns are, without doubt, his descendants, but no records have been discovered that afford proof of such descent. Nathaniel Bullard was admitted freeman in 1690, and is supposed to have been a son of William as were also Josiah, Ebenezer and Benjamin.

(II) Isaac, son of William Bullard, resided with his wife, Ann, in Dedham, Massachusetts, where he was admitted to the church June 18, 1665, and died May 11, 1676. His children were: Sarah, Samuel, Judith, Ephraim, Ann, John, Mary and William.

(III) Samuel, eldest son and second child of Isaac and Ann Bullard, was born December 22, 1659, in Dedham, and probably passed his life in that town where his children were born. He was married, January 14, 1683, to Hannah Thorpe, who was born August 19, 1665, daughter of James and Hannah (Newcome) Thorpe. Their children were: Samuel, Hannah, John, Ann, Sarah, Ebenezer, Mary and Abigail.

(IV) Samuel (2), eldest child of Samuel (1) and Hannah (Thorpe) Bullard, was born January 9, 1684, in Dedham, where he died February 10, 1757. His first wife or mother of his children (whose name does not appear of record) died about 1740. He was married (second), September 16, 1742, to Mrs. Rebecca Farmington, who died August 13, 1745. He married (third), June 5, 1746, Mrs. Hannah Holden.

(V) Benjamin, son of Samuel (2) Bullard, was born about 1730, and settled in Sharon, Massachusetts, where he died in 1778, aged forty-eight years. He was a Revolutionary soldier. He was married April 15, 1756, to Judith Lewis, daughter of William Lewis. She died August, 1810, aged sixty-nine years. Their children were: Mary, Benjamin, Oliver, Judith, Zipporah, Louis and Irene. The youngest son settled in Francestown, New Hampshire.

(VI) Oliver, second son and third child of Benjamin and Judith (Lewis) Bullard, was born September 15, 1763, in Sharon, and removed thence to Francestown, New Hampshire. About 1805, he removed from Francestown to Stockbridge, Vermont, and later to Bethel, Vermont, where he died August 13, 1819. He was married March 16, 1786, in Sharon, to Abigail Gay, who was born September 17, 1762, in that town, and died March 22, 1836, in Bethel, Vermont. Their children were: Oliver, Abigail, Betsey, Fanny, Mark, Luke, John, Azubah, Luther, Andes Tailor, Ambrose and Mulfred Dayton. Andes T. Bullard, born in Francestown, 1803, was an able and popular Methodist clergyman.

(VII) Mulfred Dayton, youngest child of Oliver and Abigail (Gay) Bullard, was born June 6, 1808, in Stockbridge, Vermont, and died May 30, 1872, at Lancaster, New Hampshire. He was a Methodist clergyman for thirty-five years, and was a member of the Vermont conference twenty-three years. He was married January 11, 1828, by Benjamin Coleman, Esq., to Lydia Fish Whitaker, daughter of David and Anna (Beech) Whitaker (see Whitaker, III). She was born December 23, 1811, at Windsor, and survived her husband more than fourteen years, dying June 21, 1886, at Montpelier, Vermont. They were the parents of four children: Caroline Matilda, Arial Mulfred, Adeline Dunham and Augusta Jannette.

(VIII) Arial Mulfred, only son and second child of Rev. Mulfred Dayton and Lydia Fish (Whitaker) Bullard, was born December 1, 1830, and died in Lancaster, New Hampshire, October 8, 1881. When about twenty years of age he went to Lancaster, New Hampshire, and there learned the trade of iron moulder. He spent his winters in St. Johnsbury, Vermont, where he was engaged as moulder, until about 1870, and then bought out the iron foundry at Lancaster, which he operated about a year. In 1872 he became a member of the firm of Frank Smith & Company, who carried on milling and dealt in lumber, hay, hardware, etc., and was such until the time of his death. For some years he was a member of the Lancaster Fire company, and a member of the board of fire engineers. He married in Pittsburg, New Hampshire, March 15, 1854, Eliza Jane Haines, who was born in Pittsburg, New Hampshire, November 7, 1836, and died May 18, 1907, daughter of Clark and Adaline Bedell Haines, of Pittsburg. Two children were born of this union: Willie E. and Clara E., who married Charles A. Howe.

(IX) Willie Eugene, eldest child of Arial M. and Eliza J. (Haines) Bullard, was born in Lancaster, December 7, 1855, and was educated in the public schools. In 1876 he became a clerk for Frank Smith & Co., of which firm his father was a member, and was soon after admitted to a partnership. The Lancaster Trust company, a state bank, was incorporated in 1891, and W. E. Bullard was elected a director and secretary of that institution. In 1888 he was elected to the board of fire engineers, and held that position till the close of 1906. In 1882 he was appointed, with George N. Kent and Jared I. Williams, trustee of the Summer Street cemetery, and served until 1890. He has been a trustee of the Methodist Episcopal Church since 1889. He was a member of Company F, Lancaster Rifles, since 1878, and was appointed lieutenant of that organization July 25, 1879, and served three years. He is a member of North Star Lodge, No. 8, Free and Accepted Masons; North Star Royal Arch Chapter, No. 16; North Star Commandery, Knights Templar; and Edward Raymond Consistory, thirty-second degree; Sublime Princes of the Royal Secret. He married, at Lancaster, New Hampshire, March 15, 1877, Mary C. Burns, who was born in Whitefield, New Hampshire, June 22, 1856, daughter of Calvin W. and Elvira (Clark) Burns, of Whitefield. They have three children: Grace Burns, Harold Arial and Mary Claire.

CLARK There is no name more numerously represented in the pioneer settlement of New England than this, and on account of the great number bearing the name, it has been extremely difficult to trace the ancestral lines. They were numerous in almost every New England town, and the line herein given is the first that we have been able to trace with any satisfactory fullness.

(I) Edward Clark is found of record at Haverhill, Massachusetts, as early as 1650. It seems impossible to establish his parentage or the place of his origin. He had a house lot at Haverhill in 1650, and on the division of plow lands over four acres were assigned to him. He was appointed to beat the drum on "Lord's days and lecture days." By occupation he was a carpenter, and probably removed to Portsmouth, New Hampshire, in 1663, and died there 1675. He owned a house and barn and an island where he lived at Portsmouth, and also three acres of land in Little Harbor.

(II) There was a second Edward Clark in Haverhill, who is believed to have been a son of the first. He was born about 1622, and subscribed to the oath of allegiance November 28, 1677. He married (first) Dorcas Bosworth, who died February 3, 1681, and was married (second) November 1, 1682, to Mary Davis, a widow. They had at least two sons, Hanniel and Matthew. There was a Joseph Clark who took the oath of allegiance in 1673, and is supposed to have been another son of Edward (1).

(III) Hanniel, son of Edward and Dorcas (Bosworth) Clark, resided in Haverhill, where administration was granted upon his estate in 1718. He was married August 20, 1678, to Mary Gutterson. Their children were: Mary, Hanniel, Sarah, William, Josiah, Edward, Jonathan, Samuel, Timothy and Elizabeth.

(IV) Jonathan, fifth son and seventh child of Hanniel and Mary (Gutterson) Clark, was born April 23, 1696, in Haverhill. He resided in Haverhill and Amesbury. Administration of his estate was granted to his son Thomas, of Amesbury, May 7, 1753. The inventory amounted to one hundred and thirty pounds. He was married (first) February 23, 1715, to Martha Ela, who lived but a short time thereafter. He was married (second) December 4, 1718, to Priscilla Whitticker. It appears that he married a third time, as the name of his widow appears as Elizabeth. His children were: Amos (died young), Martha (died young), Amos, Jonathan, Thomas, Mary, Priscilla, Martha (died young), Sarah and Martha.

(V) Amos, second son and third child of Jonathan Clark and eldest child of his second wife, Priscilla, was born January 12, 1720, in Haverhill, and settled about 1739 in what is now Hampstead, New Hampshire. This was two years before that region was set off from Haverhill as a part of New Hampshire. He married Sarah Kelly, who was born October, 1718, in Newbury, Massachusetts, daughter of John and Elizabeth (Emery) Kelly. He died in Hampstead in 1783. Three of his children are on record in Haverhill. There were eleven altogether. They included: Judith, Thomas, Moses, Priscilla, Amos (died young), Jonathan (died young), Elizabeth, Amos and Jonathan.

(VI) Morse, second son and third child of Amos and Sarah (Kelly) Clark, was born March 28, 1746, in Hampstead, New Hampshire, and settled in Warner, same state. No record of his marriage appears, but the list of his children gives his wife's name as Molle. Their children were: Judith, Moses, Amasa (died young), Amasa, Jerusha, Amos, Sarah, Lydia, Stephen Bagley and Johnathan.

(VII) Moses (2), eldest son and second child of Moses and Molle Clark, was born July 21, 1770, in Warner, New Hampshire, and passed his life in that town and in the adjoining town of Hopkinton. He was married in Warner, April 14, 1791, to Sarah Kimball.

(VIII) Moses Kimball, son of Moses (2) and Sarah (Kimball) Clark, was born February 20, 1810, in Warner, and resided in Hopkinton. He married Judith Morrill.

(IX) Alvah Augustus, son of Moses Kimball and Judith (Morrill) Clark, was born in Warner, New Hampshire, May 3, 1837. He was educated in the common schools, and was a mill owner and farmer. He was a Republican in politics. He married Harriet Wiggin, daughter of Hemphill Wiggin. They had three children: Anna, born June 7, 1862; Fred Augustus, born March 10, 1864; and Martha, born December 25, 1865. Mr. Clark died January 4, 1895.

(X) Fred Augustus, only son and second child of Alvah Augustus and Harriet (Wiggin) Clark, was born in Warner, New Hampshire, March 10, 1864. He was educated in the district schools and at the Simonds free high school. He has always been in the mill and the ice business. He owns a large mill and makes many shingles, laths and building material every year. He also carries on a general farm. He is a Republican in politics, and has served three terms as selectman. He is a Blue Lodge Mason. He is a member of the Grange, of which he has been overseer. He attends the Congregational church. He married, November 11, 1894, Elsie Colby, daughter of James L. and Abbie (Wright) Colby, of Warner. They have two children: Laura, born July 13, 1894, died January 8, 1904; and Alvah Augustus, born June 29, 1896. Mrs. Clark is an active worker in the Congregational church.

(Second Family.)

CLARK The many families bearing this name render distinctions somewhat confusing and uncertain. The name is undoubtedly derived from an occupation, and arose from the variations in pronunciations in early times. There may have been several who took the surname simultaneously, which arose from the occupation of clerk. The name appears very frequently in the records of Rockingham county, but the data is so fragmentary that it is very difficult to follow any one continuous line.

(I) About the earliest definite record obtainable on the family herein traced locates Jonathan and Zipporah Clark as residents of Stratham, New Hampshire. On July 6, 1715, William Moore deeded to Jonathan Clark, junior, land in Quamscot (which included parts of the present towns of Exeter and Stratham). From this it is probable that Jonathan was a son of Jonathan. The son received a deed May 17, 1743, of land in Barrington from Hunking Wentworth. Other transactions indicate that he was a large landholder. January 8, 1731, he sold to David Davis land granted to him by the town of Exeter, and probably removed to Barrington soon after. He had children: John, Jonathan, Joanna, and Mary, born in Stratham. (Jonathan and descendants are mentioned in this article.)

(II) John, elder son of Jonathan and Zipporah Clark, was born in 1711, in Stratham, New Hampell (died young), Thomas Frazier, George, John Currier, Robert, Martha Mitchell, Helen Margaret and Clara Walker.

(III) Hiram, eldest son and second child of Thomas (2) and Sally (Meloon) Clark, was born April 8, 1822, in Andover, and was nearly of age when the family moved to Plymouth. In early life he was employed several years in a store and glove factory operated by Nathaniel F. Draper, in the lower part of Plymouth. For a time he engaged in the manufacture of gloves on his own account, but soon returned to mercantile pursuits. He was for many years an efficient clerk and salesman in the store of Plummer Fox, at the village of Plymouth. He was town clerk in 1851, and also served as town treasurer, and was frequently employed in the administration of estates. He was an active member and devout supporter of the Methodist Episcopal church. Of genial, kind and generous nature, he made many friends, and was always interested in every undertaking calculated to promote the interests of his home town. He was married, October 8, 1845, in Plymouth, to Betsey Dow Drake, who was born November 4, 1822, daughter of Joseph and Mary (Thompson) Drake, and died May 25, 1889, in Plymouth. Mr. Clark died at the home of his daughter, Mrs. Durrell, in Nashua, February 13, 1899. Their children were: Ellen Augusta, who became the wife of Curtis S. Cummings, of Gloversville, New York; Sarah Irene, wife of Rev. J. M. Durrell (see Durrell); Clara Thompson, wife of Dr. William B. Jackson, of Lowell, Massachusetts.

(IV) Sarah Irene, second daughter of Hiram and Betsey D. (Drake) Clark, was born May 17, 1852, in Plymouth, and received her primary education in the district school of that town. She was a student of Plymouth Academy, of the private school of Samuel A. Burns, and was one of the first enrolled students of the State Normal school. She completed the first course of this institution in 1872, and the second in 1873, and was graduated from the New Hampshire Conference Seminary (now Tilton Seminary) in 1876. She has been a teacher in the public schools, the Castleton (Vermont) Normal School, and Tilton Seminary. She was married, July 23, 1878, to Rev. Jesse M. Durrell, of Boston. (See Durrell, VIII), with whom she has been associated in travels, in studies, and in educational and church work.

(Fifth Family.)

CLARK The Clarks of whom this article treats are pioneer settlers of the "North Country" of New Hampshire, descendants from Massachusetts stock. They have been an active, energetic and intelligent people, industrious in time of peace, but ever ready to defend their country from foreign invaders or native rebels. In a will now in the possession of Benjamin F. Clark it reads: "I Benjamin Clark yeoman of Braintree province of Massachusetts bay in this the reign of our Sovereign Lord and King George the Third do give and bequeath, etc.," naming sons Benjamin, Ebenezer, James and Joseph, and daughter Mary.

(I) Ebenezer Clark, son of Benjamin Clark, was a native of Massachusetts and removed to New Hampshire and raised a family in New Ipswich.

(II) Ebenezer (2), son of Ebenezer (1) Clark, was born in New Ipswich, New Hampshire, November 8, 1774, and died September 11, 1849. He was a farmer there during the active period of his life. He married Mary Sampson, who was born December 22, 1784. They were the parents of a large family: Benjamin, Ebenezer, Jonathan, James, Abraham, Elias, Isaac, Mary, Susan, Abigail, Ruth and Sarah.

(III) Benjamin, son of Ebenezer and Mary (Sampson) Clark, was born in Lexington, Massachusetts, December 11, 1811, and died in Lunenburg, same state, October 2, 1859. In early manhood he was employed in teaming, but later became a farmer. He married, November 4, 1839, Maria Choate, who was born in Lawsville, Pennsylvania, March 9, 1818, and died in Boston, March 6, 1883, aged sixty-five years. She was the daughter of Constantine and Abigail (Choate) Choate, of Enfield, New Hampshire. Three children were born of this union: Ellen Maria, Benjamin F. and Clara Jane. Ellen Maria was born December 2, 1840, and married (first) Joseph H. Pierson, who was killed at the battle of Antietam, September 16, 1862. Left one son, Harry. She married (second) George S. Pitts, now of Conway. Children George F., Kitty and Carl. Benjamin F. is mentioned below. Clara Jane was born in Townsend, Massachusetts, February 13, 1846. She married Judge Henry N. Blake, who was appointed chief justice of the supreme court of Montana under the territorial government, and was elected to that office when the territory became a state.

(IV) Benjamin Franklin, only son of Benjamin and Maria (Choate) Clark, was born in Townsend, Massachusetts, June 25, 1843. He attended the common schools of Lowell and Lunenburg, and at the age of seventeen years entered upon an apprenticeship at the machinist's trade in Fitchburg, Massachusetts. June 28, 1861, he responded to the call to arms in defense of the Union, and enlisted as a private in Company B, Fifteenth Regiment, Massachusetts Volunteer Infantry, Captain Simonds and Colonel Devens being respective commanders of the company and regiment. The regiment was in service on the Upper Potomac, and later took part in the battle of Ball's Bluff, and in the spring of 1862 participated under command of McClellan in the important operations of the Peninsular campaign, including Fair Oaks, the Seven Days' battle, and the second battle at Bull Run. It was later at South Mountain and Antietam, in the latter of which engagements Mr. Clark received a severe gunshot wound in the right eye, which destroyed the sight and caused discharge from the army, November, 1862. Soon after his return home he resumed work in the machine shop in Fitchburg. In 1865 he entered the employ of the United States government as a machinist at the Charlestown navy yard, where he became leading man of the machine shop, and filled that place until 1873. He then entered the employ of the B. F. Sturtevant Company, manufacturers of machinery, of Boston, which for many years manufactured machinery extensively at Jamaica Plain, Massachusetts, and machine peg wood and veneering at Conway, New Hampshire. For twenty years he was manager of their factory at Conway. He retired from active life in 1902. He has been prominently identified with local financial matters, and was president of the Conway Savings Bank for many years, superintendent of the Conway Water Company since its organization, 1890, and is sole owner in the Electric Light Company. He is also a leader in public affairs, having held the office of county commissioner six years, and been twice—1891 and 1893—a member of the lower house of the New Hampshire legislature, where he served on important committees. Polit-

Geo A. Clark

[illegible] publican [illegible]

[illegible]

[illegible] Clark was educated in the common [illegible] of [illegible] and [illegible], and resided under the paternal roof, assisting in the duties thereof, [illegible] she inherited the large estate formerly owned by her father, consisting of sixty acres, including considerable lumber land, and since that time has [illegible]

[illegible] and Mr [illegible]. He married [illegible] T. Wyatt, born in [illegible] 1849. To the [illegible] born, December 14, 1867. She married Dana C. Collins, of Manchester, a commercial traveler, and had two children: Minot Farnham, died October 23, 1901, and Clark W., born May 12, 1898.

CLARK George E., son of Theodore and Frances A. (Fernell) Clark, was born in Orange, New Hampshire, July 25, 1866. After getting what education the public schools afforded, he began in early life to work at agricultural labor and to assist drovers in getting their cattle to the markets at Wilmot, New Hampshire. For three years he drove stage between Potter Place and New London and Bradford. At the age of twenty-one he bought out the livery business of Z. S. Woods, at the old Raymond House Stable, Bradford, which he conducted successfully for eleven years. This business was burned out, and the following year (1888) Mr. Clark removed to Franklin Falls and bought the old Kenrick stable, where he carried on a livery business about three years, and then sold out to H. T. Corser. The following spring he bought out the business of Scott Dudley, which he carried on for nearly a year. In 1904 he formed a partnership with J. F. Fellows and others under the firm name of Fellows, Clark & Company, dealers in lumber, and has since operated in Canada and the states. In May, 1900, in partnership with C. A. French, he purchased the livery business Mr. E. W. Durkey had formerly conducted. This stable, the largest in Franklin, they still conduct. In politics Mr. Clark is a staunch Republican. He was appointed deputy sheriff of Merrimack county under J. F. Fellows, in 1892, and served in that position twelve years, continuously. He served as street commissioner of Bradford one year, and was elected councilman in Franklin Falls, in November, 1905, and has served since. He is a member of Laconia Lodge, No. 876, Benevolent and Protective Order of Elks, of Franklin. He married, in Bradford, June 22, 1893, Ella M. Patch, who was born in Keokuk, Iowa, 1874, daughter of Frank H. and Florence (Baily) Patch, formerly of Bradford, New Hampshire.

CLARK The Rev. Matthew Clark, who was ordained to the ministry in Ireland, and succeeded the Rev. J. MacGregor as pastor of the church in Londonderry soon after 1729, was a man of splendid character and much influence among his people; but whether he or James or Robert Clark, of Londonderry, or any of these prominent citizens of the Scotch colony was the progenitor of the family which is the subject of this article, it is not now possible to determine, on account of the absence of records; but the traditions of the family, which point to a Scotch-Irish ancestry, suggest the probability of such an origin.

(I) William Danforth Clark was born in Derry in 1810, and died in 1883, aged seventy-three. He was a lifelong farmer, and a leading citizen in his town. In his youth he was a Whig, and cast his lot with the Republican party when the questions of slavery and secession agitated the country and rebellion broke out. For forty years he was a dean in the Congregational Church of East Derry. He married Almira E. Dodge, who was born September 14, 1813, and died November, 1891, aged seventy-eight years. She was the daughter of Reuben and Sally (Peters) Dodge. (See Dodge, V). They were the parents of children: Jennie, Frank P., Orpah, Addie, Lizzie, William P., Warren E., Lucy G., Mary, Joshua A. and Charles H., whose sketch follows.

(II) Charles Henry, youngest child of William D. and Almira E. (Dodge) Clark, was born January 30, 1856, in Derry, and educated in the public schools of that town. At eleven years of age he began to earn his own living by working for the neighboring farmers. At sixteen he went to Chester, New Hampshire, where he was employed by one farmer for four years and by another in Hudson, two years. In 1877 he went to Woburn, Massachusetts, where he was employed in a grocery store seven years. He moved to Manchester, New Hampshire, in 1893, and opened a grocery store at the corner of Amherst and Dutton streets, where he has since carried on business successfully. Mr. Clark is a substantial business man and leading citizen in his ward, and has been honored with office by the Republican party, of which he is a staunch supporter. He served three years as councilman of ward three, and in 1902 was elected to the board of aldermen from ward four, and has served four years in that office. He has been a member of the committee on claims and streets, and was in 1906 on the committee of cemeteries, sewers, lands and buildings. He is a member of Wildey Lodge, No. 45, Independent Order of Odd Fellows and of Security Lodge, No. 8, of the Ancient Order of United Workmen. He married, February 22, 1882, in Manchester, Hannah F. Williams, born September 8, 1859, daughter of Augustus and Sarah (Fuller) Williams, of Boxford, Massachusetts. They have seven children: Edith W., Augustus, Harry E., William D., Helen G., Marion M., Richard H. Edith married Harry Alfred Fisher, of Manchester, and has two children, Natalie and William Danforth. Augustus married Abbie Griffin, of Auburn, and resides in Manchester; he has one child, Charles Griffin.

CLARK The surname Clark represents one of the oldest and most respected families of New England, but the period of residence in New Hampshire of the family of that name under consideration here is less than twenty years.

Conrad Clark, of Lakeport, New Hampshire, is a native of Germany and was born February 12, 1862. On coming to America he lived first in the town of North Hero on Lake Champlain in Grand Isle county, Vermont. He located there about 1878, and from there came to New Hampshire and purchased a small farm in Belknap county, near Lakeport, and within the corporate limits of the city of Laconia, where he now lives, and where by industry and economy he has established a comfortable home for his family. On February 24, 1886, Mr. Clark married Emma J. Hazen, who was born in Vermont, February 21, 1862. Six children have been born of this marriage: Wilford E., February 14, 1888. Walter Peter, September 7, 1890. Alice E., July 3, 1897. Ernest B., August 3, 1899. Damson L., May 9, 1901. Nellie M., November 22, 1904.

CLARKE Clarke is the name of one of the earliest of the Massachusetts Bay Colony families, and has furnished to New England and the nation many individuals of prominence. Its members have intermarried with many of the leading families of the Granite State, and to-day the Clarkes of New Hampshire have in their veins the blood of many ancestors eminent in the history of New England.

(I) The town of Newbury, Massachusetts, was settled in 1638 by some principal inhabitants of Ipswich, accompanied by their minister, Mr. Parker, all having previously came from Wiltshire, England. The earliest records of the town are lost, and it has been impossible to find any record of the [illegible] publican [illegible]

[illegible] Clark was [illegible] and [illegible]

[illegible] part and [illegible] and [illegible] nal [illegible], assisting [illegible] the duties thereof. [illegible] she inherited the large estate formerly owned [illegible], consisting of sixty acres, including considerable lumber land, and since that time has [illegible]

[illegible] He mar[illegible] T. Wyatt, b[illegible] 184[illegible] To the [illegible]

ically he is a Republican. He is a member of Mt. Washington Lodge, No. 87, Free and Accepted Masons, of North Conway; of Signet Royal Arch Chapter, of North Conway, and St. Gerard Commandery, Knights Templar, of Littleton, New Hampshire. He was a member of Joe Hooker Post at East Boston, and from there he transferred to Custer Post, No. 47, Grand Army of the Republic, of Conway, and was its first commander.

Benjamin F. Clark married (first), July 19, 1866, Annie M. Norton, who was born in Greenland, New Hampshire, January 30, 1842, and died November 6, 1891, daughter of Captain Robert W. and Abigail (Norton) Norton, of Greenland, New Hampshire. Married (second), September 18, 1894, Sarah Elizabeth, daughter of Hubbard and Sarah Russell, of Malden, Massachusetts. Three children were born of the first wife: Mabel Maria, Charlotte Abigail and Benjamin Franklin. Mabel Maria, born in Boston, October 4, 1869, married Dr. F. D. Lawson, of New York City, a graduate of the Columbia Medical School, who gave up the medical profession to become a musician, and is now a noted tenor. Charlotte Abigail, born in Conway, March 21, 1876, resides at home. Benjamin Franklin, born in Conway, July 29, 1879, graduated from Columbia University with the class of 1902, and is now chief draughtsman of the Taylor Iron and Steel company, of High Bridge, New Jersey.

CLARK The first ancestor (of whom there is any definite information) of this Clark family, represented in the present generation by Miss Claribel Clark, of Lakeport, New Hampshire, was Samuel Clark, Jr., born in Gilford, New Hampshire, followed the occupation of farming, and removed from Greenland or Sandown, New Hampshire, to Lakeport, same state. He married Betsey Clements, who bore him children: Samuel Joseph, John, Noah, Samuel C., Hannah, Caroline, Clementine and two who died in infancy.

Samuel C. Clark, son of Samuel and Betsey (Clements) Clark, and father of Miss Claribel Clark, was born in Lakeport, New Hampshire, 1833, died in same city, March 18, 1897. He received his education in the schools of Laconia and New Hampton, and later pursued a course of reading law, following that profession for many years. He was a man of influence in the community, and was chosen by his fellow citizens to various offices of importance, in all of which he faithfully performed the duties devolving upon him. He served as clerk in the Laconia courts forty years, clerk in the New Hampton, New London and Wolfboro courts seventeen years, clerk and representative of the house of representatives and the legislature, and held office in the Concord, State House. During the war of 1861-65 he served in the capacity of provost marshall. He was a member of the order of Free and Accepted Masons, attaining the third degree. Mr. Clark married Clarissa Hall, born in Dover, New Hampshire, 1837, died in 1901, and two children, twins, were the issue: Claribel and Samuel Claire, born June 11, 1860, at Lakeport, New Hampshire. Samuel Claire served as brigadier quartermaster for ten years, three years of this time under General Patterson, married Octavia M. Gilman, of Hanover, and died in 1902.

Miss Claribel Clark was educated in common schools of Lakeport and Laconia, and resided under the paternal roof, assisting in the duties thereof. In 1902 she inherited the large estate formerly owned by her father, consisting of sixty acres, including considerable lumber land, and since that time has carefully looked after her interests, being a woman of executive ability and clear foresight.

CLARK (I) James Hubbard Clark was born in Kennebunk, Maine, in 1804, and died November 19, 1845, in the forty-first year of his age. He was brought up a farmer, and was engaged in the trade of butcher all his life. He was a self-reliant and reliable citizen, who took an active part in politics, and was sheriff of his county many years. He married Susan, daughter of Paul Twombley, and they had seven children: Martha, died March 18, 1907; she married Nathaniel Richardson. Mary, died August, 1904; she married Alexander H. Downs. Harriet, died June, 1859; she married Jason Dame. James, of New Haven, Connecticut, married Emily Clough. Emeline, married Ansel S. Drew, in Dover, New Hampshire. Ellen, married John C. Frost, in Manchester, New Hampshire. George A., whose sketch follows.

(II) George Albert, youngest child of James H. and Susan (Twombley) Clark, was born in Berwick, Maine, July 26, 1840. He was educated in the common schools, which he attended for a short time each year until he was twelve years old. At the age of five he was left fatherless, and at seven years of age began work in a cotton factory at Great Falls, where he worked as a hack boy in the mule spinning room, fourteen hours a day, at twenty-five cents a day. April 28, 1857, when seventeen years old, he removed to Manchester, New Hampshire, where he began work in the mill May 4, of that year, and has since resided there. Here he was first a mule spinner, then successively doffer, third hand, second hand, overseer, and finally, superintendent for the Manchester Mills. For forty-five years he was in the employ of that corporation, and twenty-seven years of that time he filled the office of superintendent. In June, 1902, he retired with an honorable record, which for length of time covered and efficiency is seldom equalled. In 1904 he was elected on the Republican ticket by the common council for assessor, for a term of six years. When the board of assessors organized after election, he was made chairman, which position he now holds.

August 6, 1862, he enlisted in Company A, Tenth New Hampshire Volunteer Infantry, and went to the front to assist in putting down the Rebellion. He was under fire at Orleans and White Sulphur Springs, Virginia, and December 13, 1862, took part with the regiment in the assault on Fredericksburg, where he was struck by a fragment of shell and seriously wounded, this fragment striking and going through the visor of his cap, taking off the tip of his nose and glancing to the left, passed through the left shoulder. With reference to this wound, Mr. Clark jocosely remarked that he "came near not being hit at all." May 7, 1863, he was discharged on account of disabilities from wounds. For forty years he was an Odd Fellow, being now a member of Mechanics Lodge, and a charter member of Mt. Washington Encampment, No. 16, of which he is past high priest. He is also a member of Washington Lodge, No. 61, Free and Accepted Masons; Mt. Horeb Royal Arch Chapter, No. 11; Adoniram Council, No. 3, Royal and Select Masters; and Trinity Commandery, Knights Templar.

He married (first), January 4, 1860, Sarah F. Farnham, born at Sanbornton Bridge, (now Tilton) New Hampshire, July 29, 1841, daughter of Asa and Martha (Upham) Farnham. She died May 7, 1901. He married (second), April 12, 1905, Annie T. Wyatt, born in Lowell, Massachusetts, April 18, 1849. To the first wife one child, Martha S., was born, December 14, 1867. She married Dana C. Collins, of Manchester, a commercial traveler, and had two children: Minot Farnham, died October 23, 1901, and Clark W., born May 12, 1898.

CLARK George E., son of Theodore and Frances A. (Fernell) Clark, was born in Orange, New Hampshire, July 25, 1866. After getting what education the public schools afforded, he began in early life to work at agricultural labor and to assist drovers in getting their cattle to the markets at Wilmot, New Hampshire. For three years he drove stage between Potter Place and New London and Bradford. At the age of twenty-one he bought out the livery business of Z. S. Woods, at the old Raymond House Stable, Bradford, which he conducted successfully for eleven years. This business was burned out, and the following year (1888) Mr. Clark removed to Franklin Falls and bought the old Kenrick stable, where he carried on a livery business about three years, and then sold out to H. T. Corser. The following spring he bought out the business of Scott Dudley, which he carried on for nearly a year. In 1904 he formed a partnership with J. F. Fellows and others under the firm name of Fellows, Clark & Company, dealers in lumber, and has since operated in Canada and the states. In May, 1900, in partnership with C. A. French, he purchased the livery business Mr. E. W. Durkey had formerly conducted. This stable, the largest in Franklin, they still conduct. In politics Mr. Clark is a staunch Republican. He was appointed deputy sheriff of Merrimack county under J. F. Fellows, in 1892, and served in that position twelve years, continuously. He served as street commissioner of Bradford one year, and was elected councilman in Franklin Falls, in November, 1905, and has served since. He is a member of Laconia Lodge, No. 876, Benevolent and Protective Order of Elks, of Franklin. He married, in Bradford, June 22, 1893, Ella M. Patch, who was born in Keokuk, Iowa, 1874, daughter of Frank H. and Florence (Baily) Patch, formerly of Bradford, New Hampshire.

CLARK The Rev. Matthew Clark, who was ordained to the ministry in Ireland, and succeeded the Rev. J. MacGregor as pastor of the church in Londonderry soon after 1729, was a man of splendid character and much influence among his people; but whether he or James or Robert Clark, of Londonderry, or any of these prominent citizens of the Scotch colony was the progenitor of the family which is the subject of this article, it is not now possible to determine, on account of the absence of records; but the traditions of the family, which point to a Scotch-Irish ancestry, suggest the probability of such an origin.

(I) William Danforth Clark was born in Derry in 1810, and died in 1883, aged seventy-three. He was a lifelong farmer, and a leading citizen in his town. In his youth he was a Whig, and cast his lot with the Republican party when the questions of slavery and secession agitated the country and rebellion broke out. For forty years he was a dean in the Congregational Church of East Derry. He married Almira E. Dodge, who was born September 14, 1813, and died November, 1891, aged seventy-eight years. She was the daughter of Reuben and Sally (Peters) Dodge. (See Dodge, V). They were the parents of children: Jennie, Frank P., Orpah, Addie, Lizzie, William P., Warren E., Lucy G., Mary, Joshua A. and Charles H., whose sketch follows.

(II) Charles Henry, youngest child of William D. and Almira E. (Dodge) Clark, was born January 30, 1856, in Derry, and educated in the public schools of that town. At eleven years of age he began to earn his own living by working for the neighboring farmers. At sixteen he went to Chester, New Hampshire, where he was employed by one farmer for four years and by another in Hudson, two years. In 1877 he went to Woburn, Massachusetts, where he was employed in a grocery store seven years. He moved to Manchester, New Hampshire, in 1893, and opened a grocery store at the corner of Amherst and Dutton streets, where he has since carried on business successfully. Mr. Clark is a substantial business man and leading citizen in his ward, and has been honored with office by the Republican party, of which he is a staunch supporter. He served three years as councilman of ward three, and in 1902 was elected to the board of aldermen from ward four, and has served four years in that office. He has been a member of the committee on claims and streets, and was in 1906 on the committee of cemeteries, sewers, lands and buildings. He is a member of Wildey Lodge, No. 45, Independent Order of Odd Fellows and of Security Lodge, No. 8, of the Ancient Order of United Workmen. He married, February 22, 1882, in Manchester, Hannah F. Williams, born September 8, 1859, daughter of Augustus and Sarah (Fuller) Williams, of Boxford, Massachusetts. They have seven children: Edith W., Augustus, Harry E., William D., Helen G., Marion M., Richard H. Edith married Harry Alfred Fisher, of Manchester, and has two children, Natalie and William Danforth. Augustus married Abbie Griffin, of Auburn, and resides in Manchester; he has one child, Charles Griffin.

CLARK The surname Clark represents one of the oldest and most respected families of New England, but the period of residence in New Hampshire of the family of that name under consideration here is less than twenty years.

Conrad Clark, of Lakeport, New Hampshire, is a native of Germany and was born February 12, 1862. On coming to America he lived first in the town of North Hero on Lake Champlain in Grand Isle county, Vermont. He located there about 1878, and from there came to New Hampshire and purchased a small farm in Belknap county, near Lakeport, and within the corporate limits of the city of Laconia, where he now lives, and where by industry and economy he has established a comfortable home for his family. On February 24, 1886, Mr. Clark married Emma J. Hazen, who was born in Vermont, February 21, 1862. Six children have been born of this marriage: Wilford E., February 14, 1888. Walter Peter, September 7, 1890. Alice E., July 3, 1897. Ernest B., August 3, 1899. Damson L., May 9, 1901. Nellie M., November 22, 1904.

CLARKE Clarke is the name of one of the earliest of the Massachusetts Bay Colony families, and has furnished to New England and the nation many individuals of prominence. Its members have intermarried with many of the leading families of the Granite State, and to-day the Clarkes of New Hampshire have in their veins the blood of many ancestors eminent in the history of New England.

(I) The town of Newbury, Massachusetts, was settled in 1638 by some principal inhabitants of Ipswich, accompanied by their minister, Mr. Parker, all having previously came from Wiltshire, England. The earliest records of the town are lost, and it has been impossible to find any record of the ancestor of this family, Nathaniel Clarke, till his marriage in 1663. In the controversy between religious factions which raged between 1665 and 1669, Nathaniel Clarke and many other prominent men are recorded on the side of Mr. Parker. April 29, 1668. Nathaniel Clarke bought land and was admitted freeman. In 1670 he was chosen "to lay out ye highway to ye Ferry place in Amesbury." In company with William Chandler, May 1, 1684, he was appointed naval officer for the ports of Newbury and Salisbury by the general court, and June 4, 1685, ensign of Captain Daniel Pierce's company at Rowley, vice Archelaus Woodman, discharged. He was the grantee of several pieces in which he is described as "cordwainer." He is called ensign in the Newbury records, and was usually entitled "Hon'ble" when mentioned by his contemporaries. His will is dated "21 day of August Anno Dom. one thousand six hundred and ninety" and disposes of property valued at £714, 19s., including two dwelling houses and barn and seven pieces or lots of land. He was born in 1644, as stated in an affidavit made August 25, 1690. He married, November 23, 1663, Elizabeth, daughter of Henry and Judith Somerby, born November 1, 1646. Henry Somerby was the son of Richard Somerby, of Little Bytham, in Lincolnshire, where his family had been eminently respectable for many generations. The mother of Mrs. Clarke was the daughter of Edmund Greenleaf, who was of Huguenot origin, and one of the earliest and most prominent settlers of Newbury, having come there from Brixham, Devonshire, England, as early as 1635. It is stated that he came from near Torbay, and that may be correct. Greenleaf was a translation of Teuillevert, the original French name of the family. Mrs. Clarke married, August 8, 1698, Rev. John Hale, of Beverley, and died March 15, 1716, aged seventy-one years. The children of Nathan and Elizabeth Clarke were: Nathaniel, Nathaniel, Thomas, John, Henry, Daniel, Sarah, Josiah, Elizabeth, Judith, Mary. (Henry and descendants receive mention in this article).

(II) National (2), son of Nathaniel (1) and Elizabeth (Somerby) Clarke, was born March 13, 1666, and is spoken of as Nathaniel of Newbury. He married, December 15, 1685, Elizabeth, daughter of Dr. Peter and Jane Toppan, and sister of Rev. Christopher Toppan, D. D. She was born October 16, 1665. Her father was sixth in descent from Robert of Linton, near Pately Bridge, in the West Riding of York, where they continue to the present day among the most respectable families of that county. Nathaniel Clarke went with the expedition to Canada, in 1690, and was mortally wounded there on board the ship "Six Friends" in October of the same year. Nathaniel Clarke had two children: Elizabeth, born July 27, 1686, died before October, 1696. Nathaniel, July 29, 1698, died 1754.

(III) Nathaniel (3), only son of Nathaniel (2), and Elizabeth (Toppan) Clarke, was born July 29, 1689, and died in 1754. He lived in Newbury and made numerous conveyances of land. Seven townships were given by the general court to officers and soldiers who were in the Narragansett war, or their lawful representatives. Number one is now Buxton, Maine, and Nathaniel Clarke drew two lots on the division. He died intestate and insolvent, and his son Ebenezer was his administrator. He married, March 7, 1709, Sarah, born November 3, 1692, daughter of Samuel and Sarah Kent Greenleaf, and great-granddaughter of Captain Edmund Greenleaf. Sarah (Kent) Greenleaf was a daughter of John and Mary, and granddaughter of James Kent, who with his brother Richard owned Kents' Island, and much land in Oldtown, and were men of great local importance. Their father was Richard. The children of Nathaniel and Sarah (Greenleaf) Clarke were: Samuel, born April 13, 1710; Elizabeth, October 15, 1711; Sarah, Ebenezer, Stephen, June 9, 1723, died December, 1804; Nathaniel, 1728, died November 7, 1805.

(IV) Nathaniel (4), farmer, of Haverhill, son of Nathaniel (3) and Sarah (Greenleaf) Clarke, was born in 1728, and died November 7, 1805. In 1757 he was a member of the Second Company of Foot, Major Richard Saltonstall, captain, and did all in his power to further the cause of the Revolution by loaning money to the town on several occasions, and by serving in 1780 on the committee to collect clothing for the army. He married, February 8, 1753, Mary Hardy, of Bradford, Massachusetts, born October 8, 1733, died January 13, 1817. Her father, David Hardy, was son of Joseph and Mary Burbank Hardy, and grandson of John Hardy, who with his brother William came to New England, and was assigned land by him, but not taking the place removed to East Bradford and lives on the site where the Marsdon house now is. Mrs. Clarke's mother was Dorcas, daughter of Samuel and Mary Watson Gage, and granddaughter of Daniel Gage, whose father was John Rowley, who is supposed to have been son of John, created a baronet, March 26, 1622, and of Penelope, his wife. Sir John was grandson and heir of Edward Gage, Knighted by Queen Mary. The children of Nathaniel and Mary (Hardy) Clarke were: David, Sarah, Susan, Nathaniel, Greenleaf, Rebecca, Mary, Nathaniel, Paul, Moses, Theodore, Greenleaf. (The last named receives extended mention below).

(V) Nathaniel (5), of Plaistow, New Hampshire, child of Nathaniel (4) and Mary (Hardy) Clarke, was born 1766, died May 19, 1846. When fifteen years old March 12, 1781, he enlisted with the consent of his parents for three years as fifer in Captain Nehemiah Emerson's company, Tenth Massachusetts Regiment. Thomas Page enlisted at the same time as a drummer, and it is said their youth and skillful execution drew the attention of General Washington, to whom Captain Emerson remarked "they were pretty boys," a compliment of which they were ever afterward proud. They were with the same captain till the close of the war, and Nathaniel was wounded at White Plains. He married Abigail Woodman, born August, 1765, died April 3, 1844, and had nine children by her: Susanna, Nathaniel, Nancy, David, Abigail, John Woodman, Mary, Lydia Woodman, Elizabeth.

(VI) Mary, daughter of Nathaniel (5) and Abigail (Woodman) Clarke, born January 21, 1800, died June 6, 1833. Married, July 18, 1822, Isaac Smith, (q. v.) and had three children: Mary Clarke, Isaac William, Nathaniel.

(V) Greenleaf, twelfth and youngest child of Nathaniel (4) and Mary (Hardy) Clarke, was born in Haverhill, Massachusetts, May 5, 1779, and died in Atkinson, New Hampshire, January 12, 1821. He was a farmer, and before his death became an honored and influential citizen. On September 6, 1809, Greenleaf Clarke purchased of Samuel Eaton, of Haverhill, twenty acres and forty rods of land in Haverhill. Afterward he disposed of his property in Massachusetts, and removed to Atkinson, New Hampshire, where he had a large and fertile farm with a substantial house and outbuildings in keeping with it, a short distance northwest of the Atkinson depot. He was a man well liked by his fellow townsmen, and was justice of the peace and selectman. He was a Mason, and past master of his lodge. He married,

March 1, 1810, [illegible] 1789, daughter o[illegible] Cogswell, of [illegible] woman and be[illegible] of Atkinson [illegible] were: Willi[illegible] Moses and [illegible] December [illegible] children, [illegible] Mrs. Cl[illegible] seventy-[illegible]

(VI[illegible] of Gr[illegible] at A[illegible] 189[illegible] bo[illegible] pr[illegible] [illegible]

[illegible] had been nonpartisan, but when the war came Mr. Clarke decided that there should be no neutrals at such a time, and the paper came out boldly for the Union [illegible] Republican par[illegible] [illegible] influence of the daily and [illegible] to the book and job print[illegible] extensive business to which [illegible] was added. Here ma[illegible] were published. Mr. Clarke's litera[illegible] not exhausted by the demands of [illegible] published "The Londond[illegible] History of New Hamp[illegible] [illegible] Almanac and [illegible] of Manchester," and [illegible]

[illegible] that [illegible] to his [illegible] Mr. Clarke had always refused [illegible] office, but was a delegate [illegible] which nominated Mr. [illegible] time to the presidency [illegible] committee of seven [illegible] of Massachusetts, [illegible] of New Jersey, and [illegible] of the *New York Times* [illegible] He was connected with [illegible] of Agriculture, was [illegible] Savings Bank from [illegible] his death; master for [illegible] Grange, No. 3; for tw[illegible] of the Amoskeag Vet[illegible] commander, but declin[illegible] state printer six [illegible] for two year[illegible] the subject [illegible] to the Man[illegible] [illegible] in 1874 he [illegible] in 1879 [illegible] the awards [illegible] from the sale of tickets [illegible] [illegible] hundred [illegible] 1882 [illegible] hundred and [illegible] dollars and thirty [illegible] In February, 1882, [illegible] dollars [illegible] John B. Clarke [illegible] in the state. He was a great lover of horses and was always the possessor of good ones. He was

John B. Clarke

March 1, 1810, Julia Cogswell, born February 20, 1789, daughter of Dr. William and Judith (Badger) Cogswell, of Atkinson. She was an intelligent woman and before her marriage had been preceptress of Atkinson Academy. The children of this union were: William Cogswell, Sarah, Francis, Greenleaf, Moses and John Badger. She married (second), December 12, 1822, Amasa Coburn, and had four children, all of whom except Mary died young. Mrs. Clarke Coburn died January 9, 1860, aged seventy-one years.

(VI) John Badger, youngest of the six children of Greenleaf and Julia (Cogswell) Clarke, was born at Atkinson, January 30, 1820, and died October 29, 1891, at Manchester. He passed the years of his boyhood on his father's farm, and received his primary education in the common schools. He prepared for college at Atkinson Academy, and entered Dartmouth at the age of nineteen. He graduated with high honors in the class of 1843, the only classmate who outranked him in scholarship being the late Professor J. N. Putnam. In his senior year Mr. Clarke was president of the Social Friends Society, and in 1863 was elected president of the Tri Kappa Society. Leaving college he went to Gilford (now Laconia), where for three years he was principal of the academy. While there he began the study of law in the office of Stephen C. Lyford, and continued his studies in Manchester with his brother, William C. Clarke, until his admission to the bar in 1848. The reports that came back to New Hampshire from California inspired Mr. Clarke, as they did thousands of others, with a desire to see the "Land of Gold." February 2, 1849, he started for California, via the Isthmus of Panama, where he was detained eleven weeks, and bought for the Manchester party of forty-three with him, in company with a gentleman of Maine with twenty men, the brig "Copiapo" in which they left the isthmus for California with one hundred and fifty-eight passengers, Mr. Clarke being supercargo. He remained in California a little more than a year, practicing law and working in the mines. Returning, he spent four months in Central America and reached home in February, 1851. His first intention was to open a law office in Salem, Massachusetts, but he shortly returned from there and began practice in Manchester. At the end of a year's time he left the law, in which he was doing well, and at the request of Joseph C. Emerson took charge of the editorial department of the *Daily Mirror*. On account of Mr. Emerson's financial embarrassment the property was sold at auction in October of the same year, Mr. Clarke being the purchaser. The purchase included the *Daily* and *Weekly Mirror* and the job printing establishment connected therewith, of which Mr. Clarke was ever afterwards sole owner and manager. He later purchased the *Daily* and *Weekly American* (in which the *Weekly Democrat* had been previously merged), and the *New Hampshire Journal of Agriculture*. These were all combined with the *Mirror*, and the name of the daily changed to *Mirror* and *American*, and the weekly from *Dollar Weekly Mirror* to *Mirror and Farmer*. Twice after these additions to the *Mirror* and during Mr. Clarke's lifetime it was found necessary to enlarge both the daily and weekly papers. When he bought the *Mirror* the weekly paper had but a few hundred suscribers, but under his management it grew to have a larger circulation than any other paper of its class published in New England outside of Boston. Before the outbreak of the Rebellion the *Mirror* had been non-partisan, but when the war came Mr. Clarke decided that there should be no neutrals at such a time, and the paper came out boldly for the Union, and has ever since been a staunch Republican paper.

The influence of the daily and weekly newspapers brought to the book and job printing department a very extensive business to which a bookbinding establishment was added. Here many works of value were published. Mr. Clarke's literary energies were not exhausted by the demands of his newspapers, and he published "The Londonderry Celebration," "Sanborn's History of New Hampshire," "Clarke's Manchester Almanac and Directory." Clarke's History of Manchester," and several similar works.

Believing that candidacy for office would be detrimental to his influence as a public journalist, Mr. Clarke had always refused to be a candidate for office, but was a delegate to the Baltimore convention which nominated Abraham Lincoln for the second time to the presidency, and was one of the national committee of seven (including Ex-Governor Claflin, of Massachusetts, Ex-Governor Marcus L. Ward, of New Jersey, and Hon. Henry T. Raymond, of the *New York Times*, who managed the campaign. He was connected with the New Hampshire College of Agriculture, was a trustee of the Merrimack Savings Bank from its incorporation in 1858 till his death; master for three years of the Amoskeag Grange, No. 3; for two years lieutenant-colonel of the Amoskeag Veterans, and was twice elected commander, but declined the honor. He was elected state printer six terms; in 1867-68-69-77-78, and in 1879 for two years. Mr. Clarke was deeply interested in the subject of elocution, and for two years gave to the Manchester high school forty dollars a year for prizes in public speaking and reading. In 1874 he offered one hunded dollars a year for five years to Dartmouth College for the same object. In 1879 he proposed to give forty dollars a year for five years for superiority in elocution in the high and grammar schools of Manchester to be divided into four prizes of sixteen dollars, twelve dollars, eight dollars and four dollars, the awards to be made at a public exhibition in the month of January each year, the proceeds from the sale of tickets to which should be invested, and the income from the investment applied for prizes for similar object perpetually. The proposition was accepted by the school board, and the first contest for the prizes was made in Smyth's Hall, in January, 1880, the net proceeds from the sale of tickets being two hundred and forty-five dollars. The succeeding January two hundred and eighty-seven dollars and sixteen cents was realized, and in January, 1882, three hundred and sixty-two dollars and fifteen cents, or a total of eight hundred and ninety-four dollars and thirty-one cents in three years. In February, 1882, Mr. Clarke offered to add to his original forty dollars, twenty dollars a year for the next two years, with the suggestion that the forty dollars be divided into prizes of thirteen dollars, eleven dollars, nine dollars and seven dollars respectively, for the best four of all the sixteen contestants, on the score of merit, and the remaining twenty dollars awarded in general prizes to the contestants adjudged the best in each of the schools represented, excluding all who should have received either of the former prizes awarded. The result of this offer has been a great interest and improvement in reading and speaking in the public schools of Manchester.

Brought up on a farm John B. Clarke was always interested in farming and used his best efforts to improve the breeds of horses, cattle and other stock in the state. He was a great lover of horses and was always the possessor of good ones. He was

John B. C

March ...
1789, ...
Cog...
woman ...
of Ark...
were ...
Mose...
Dece...
child ...
Mrs. ...
sever...
(...
of G...
at A...
1891, ...
boyh...
prim...
pare...
Dar...
with ...
clas...
the...
y...

but when the war came Mr. Clarke decided that there should be no neutrals at such a time, and the

in the state. He was a great lover of horses and was always the possessor of good ones. He was

John B. Clarke.

also fond of blooded dogs, regarding these two genera of animals as man's best and truest servants and friends. He was an enthusiastic sportsman and is said by John W. Moore to have been "a coon hunter without a rival in the state." Believing in the policy of protecting the fish and game of the state he was the prime mover in the organization of the State Fish and Game League, of which he was president.

In 1872 he began seriously to feel the effects that overwork will produce on even the most robust constitution and visited for recreation and recuperation Great Britain, France and Germany and returned much benefited, but thereafter he lived a less strenuous life devoting less time to the cares of business and more to the care of his health. Mr. Clarke, though not a church member, was a frequent churchgoer, and attended the Franklin Street Congregational Church, to the support of which he contributed with the same openhanded liberality with which he gave to every other worthy object that appealed to him for support. A recent biographer in describing him has said, "Physically Colonel Clarke was a fine specimen of robust manhood. He was tall, erect, portly, broad shouldered, and enjoyed excellent health." Mentally he was a many-sided man. He always performed well his part whether as educator, lawyer, gold-seeker and adventurer, sportsman, historian, journalist, citizen or companion and friend, and in the more serious phases of character he shone with lustre of no common kind.

John B. Clarke married, July 29, 1852, Susan Greeley Moulton, of Gilmanton, who died in 1885. He married (second), Olive Rand, who survives him. There were children by the first marriage: Arthur E. and William C., both mentioned at length below.

(VII) Arthur Eastman, the older of the two sons of John B. and Susan Greeley (Moulton) Clarke, was born in Manchester, May 13, 1854. He was educated at Phillips Exeter Academy, and at Dartmouth College, graduating from the latter institution with the class of 1875. After leaving college he entered the office of the *Mirror*, in the fall of 1875, and there familiarized himself with all branches of newspaper work. After mastering the details of the composing and press rooms, he acquired further experience in the job department, and in reading proof; he then became city editor of the *Mirror*, and for a number of years did all the local work alone, but subsequently with an assistant. Later he assumed the duties of general state news and review editor, remaining in this position several years, and then taking charge of the agricultural department and other features of the *Mirror* and *Farmer*, assisting at the same time in the editorial, reportorial, and business departments of the *Daily Mirror*. For four years he was legislative reporter of the paper at Concord, and for one year he served as telegraph editor. In these various capacities he acquired a wide and thorough experience such as few newspaper men possess, and upon the death of his father became manager of both papers and of the job printing and book binding business connected with the establishment, and has since conducted most successfully the extensive concerns of the office, besides doing almost daily work with his pen for both papers.

Mr. Clarke has inherited his father's energy, great capacity for work and executive ability. His versatility is further illustrated by the fact that the Mirror farm near Manchester, widely and favorably known in the agricultural world, is under his supervision. There experiments in branches of rural

economy are conducted, new fruits are tested, the seeds of new varieties tried, and experiments with commercial fertilizers carefully noted.

Mr. Clarke's labors have not all been devoted to newspaper work, nor have his travels all been within his native country. He is a man of broad culture, has traveled abroad extensively, and has embodied his impressions of foreign lands in a most interesting book entitled "European Travels." As a Republican he has been very active in the politics of the state and of the city of his residence. He held the office of public printer of the state of New Hampshire from 1897 to 1901, was a member of the Manchester common council, 1879-80, and represented ward 3 of Manchester in the legislature for two years from June, 1881. He was adjutant of the First Regiment, New Hampshire National Guard, for a number of years was statistician of the department of agriculture for New Hampshire during Garfield's administration, and was colonel on Governor Tuttle's staff. He is a member of numerous associations and clubs. He has been president of the New Hampshire Press Association and the New Hampshire member of the executive committee of the National Press Association, and a member of the Boston Press Club, the Algonquin Club of Boston, the Manchester Press Club, the Coon Club, the Calumet Club of Manchester, and the Amoskeag Grange. He is past exalted ruler of the Manchester Lodge of Elks, ex-president of the Derryfield Club, a member of the Manchester Board of Trade, and a director of the Northern Telegraph Company. He is a member of the Franklin Street Society (Congregational), and president of the Franklin Street Young Men's Association.

Colonel Clarke has been an enthusiastic student of elocution from his school days, and has attained conspicuous distinction in reading and reciting, carrying off high honors at Phillips Exeter Academy and at Dartmouth College. He has gratuitously drilled a number of pupils of the Manchester public schools, who have won first prizes in the annual speaking contests. He has given prizes for excellence in elocution to the schools in Hooksett, and is often invited to judge prize speaking contests at educational institutions. Ever since he became associated with the *Mirror*, he has had charge of its dramatic and musical departments. He has written interesting and valuable interviews with many distinguished players, which have been extensively copied by the press of the country. The first noticably long, analytical and complimentary criticism of the work of Denman Thompson was from the pen of Editor Clarke, Mr. Thompson then being an obscure member of a variety company.

Mr. Clarke has always had a fondness for athletic sports, and has won distinction in many lines. He organized and was captain of a picked team of ball players in Manchester, which defeated the best club in the state for a prize of $100. He is one of the finest skaters, both roller and ice, in New Hampshire. With shot gun, rifle and revolver he is an expert, and holds a record of thirty-eight clay pigeons broken out of forty in the days of the Manchester Shooting Club, a score never before equalled by a Manchester marksman. He held the billiard championship of Dartmouth College, and upon his return to Manchester in 1875 defeated the best players in the city, winning substantial prizes. He is very fond of hunting and fishing and keeps a kennel of fox hounds; for with all his vocations, avocations, and recreations he is a devotee of fox hunting, and in this, as in other things, he excels. He holds the record for the largest brook trout ever taken in Lake Sunapee, seven and three-quarters pounds, and the fish was presented to President McKinley. Colonel Clarke, in April, 1906, purchased a controlling interest in the John B. Clarke Company.

Colonel Clark married, in Cambridge, Massachusetts, January 25, 1893, Martha Bouton Cilley, born in Concord, New Hampshire, daughter of Dr. Nathaniel and Elizabeth Ann (Cilley) Bouton, of Concord, and widow of Jacob G. Cilley, of Manchester. Mrs. Clarke organized the Daughters of the American Revolution in New Hampshire, also the Society of the Colonial Dames of America in New Hampshire, the Woman's Aid and Relief Society in Manchester, the New Hampshire Musical Festival Association, the New Hampshire Audubon Society, the Cambridge (Massachusetts) Shakespeare Club, in all of which societies and clubs she held high offices. She is president of the Animal Rescue League.

(VII) William Cogswell Clarke, the younger son of John B. and Susan Greeley (Moulton) Clarke, was born in Manchester, March 17, 1856. He was educated at the Manchester high school, Phillips Andover Academy, and at Dartmouth College, where he was a student in the Chandler Scientific School. After completing the course at college in 1876 he entered the office of the *Mirror* and *American* and learned the printer's trade. He went to New York City in 1880, and devoted a portion of that year to the acquisition of a knowledge of the business of newspaper advertising. On his return to Manchester he entered the service of the *Mirror* and *American* as a local reporter, and later was promoted to be city editor, a position which he held for about eight years, conducting in the meantime several special departments for the daily and weekly editions of that paper. During these years he made the horse department of the *Mirror* a special feature, and to his efforts in this direction is due the high deputation which that paper justly holds among the horsemen of New England. This department he still conducts, as well as that devoted to field sports, for which he writes under the nom de plume of "Joe English."

From 1884 to 1890 Mr. Clarke was a member of the Manchester school board, and in 1891 served as representative from ward two in the legislature, and was chairman of the committee on fisheries and game. In 1894 he was nominated by the Republicans of Manchester for the office of mayor, and was elected by a large majority, notwithstanding the fact that at the two preceding elections the Democratic candidate had been successful. He was re-elected in 1896, and again in 1898, and in 1900, each year by a handsome plurality, the last time by 2,157 votes, leading the entire ticket, and upon the completion of his term in 1902 had occupied the mayor's chair for a period of eight years, a longer service than that of any of his predecessors, as none of them served three consecutive terms. The years of his mayorship were notable for their public improvements. Five new school buildings were erected, including one for the high school; a steel bridge sixty feet wide and paved with stone blocks was built across the Merrimack river to replace the wooden structure which was carried away by the memorable freshet of 1896; a modern system of street paving inaugurated; the City Hall building was remodeled and refitted; a police patrol system was installed, and is in successful operation. During Mayor Clarke's first term the fiftieth anniversary of the incorporation of the city was fitly commemorated by a celebration which continued for three days (September 7, 8, 9, 1896). Mayor Clarke was the presiding genius of the celebration. From the day when the first plans were roughly sketched down to the hour of the closing exercises, his was the brain that conceived, the mind that directed, the hand that executed. As chairman of the celebration committee he won golden opinions from his fellow citizens for the rare executive ability which he displayed.

In 1900 Mr. Clarke was a delegate-at-large to the Republican national convention at Philadelphia which nominated McKinley and Roosevelt. He was the first delegate from New England to give his support to Theodore Roosevelt for the vice-presidency. He retains connection with the John B. Clarke Company. He is a member of the Derryfield Club, the Manchester Board of Trade, the Amoskeag Grange, the Young Men's Christian Association, and the Passaconaway Tribe of Red Men; and is also a member of the Franklin Street Congregational Society. For a number of years he has been a trustee of the New England Agricultural Society, and vice-president of the New England Trotting Horse Breeders' Association. He was one of the organizers of the New Hampshire Trotting Horse Breeders' Association, and its secretary for three years. He was for several years clerk of the Manchester Driving Park Association, and has represented New Hampshire most creditably on several occasions at the biennial congress of the National Trotting Association. From his youth up he has displayed great interest in athletic sports, and while a collegian took an active part in them. He was captain of the Dartmouth College baseball team in 1876, and at one time held the amateur long distance record of the state for throwing the baseball 358 feet 11 inches. In later years he has taken a deep interest in all field sports, and has made a wide reputation as an accomplished wing shot. By birth and education Mr. Clarke was equipped for the performance of duties of a high order. He is suave and courteous in his manner, a polished and forcible speaker and debater, a graceful and ready writer, a man of high integrity and generous impulses, and of much energy and force of character.

He married, in Manchester, 1879, Mary Olivia Tewksbury, born in Manchester, 1859, daughter of Elliot Greene and Submit Roberts (Scott) Tewksbury, of Manchester. They have two children: John Badger and Mitty Tewksbury, both born in Manchester.

(II) Henry, son of Nathaniel (1) and Elizabeth (Somerby) Clarke, was born July, 1673, in Newbury, and died June, 1749.

(III) Enoch, son of Henry Clark, probably lived and died in Newbury.

(IV) Greenleaf, son of Enoch Clark, resided in Greenland, New Hampshire, and in 1760 signed the petition for the construction of the Newmarket bridge at the new Fields landing. "He was a captain in the Revolutionary war, and on December 2, 1775, was commissioned by the committee of safety to enlist sixty-one men, including two sergeants and three corporals, for the Continental army, to serve until January 15, unless sooner discharged, and as soon as recruited to march them immediately to join General Sullivan's brigade." He married Mary Moody, who was born in December, 1738, died December 21, 1817, and had a family of seven children, namely: Mary, Enoch Moody, Greenleaf, Joseph, Joshua, Sarah and Elizabeth.

(V) Joseph, third son and fourth child of Greenleaf and Mary (Moody) Clark, was born in Green-

Frank B. Clark

land, April 20, 1767, died in 1857. He married Comfort Weeks, who was born November 26, 1773, died in August, 1861. They had several children, a complete list of whom is not at hand. Among them were Ichabod and Mary Moody (and probably Richard, who is mentioned, with descendants, in this article).

(VI) Mary Moody, daughter of Joseph and Comfort (Weeks) Clark, was born in Greenland, August 25, 1795. On January 13, 1814, she became the wife of Samuel Avery, of Wolfboro. (See Avery, VI.)

(VI) Richard, undoubtedly a son of Joseph and Comfort (Weeks) Clark, was born in Greenland, New Hampshire, in 1793. He married a Miss Marston. They had five children: Caleb, David, Betsey, who married John Jones; John and Richard, whose sketch follows. It is said that three of the four sons settled in Canaan, New Hampshire. Many of the descendants of this family are distinguished for remarkable longevity.

(VII) Richard (2), youngest child of Richard (1) and —— (Marston) Clark, was born in 1725. He married Elizabeth Burley. There were six children: Lydia, who married John Scofield (2); Anna, Betsey, Josiah, who is mentioned below; Richard (3), who married Esther Jones, and ——. Richard (2) Clark died in 1815, at the age of ninety years.

(VIII) Josiah, eldest son and fourth child of Richard (2) and Elizabeth (Burley) Clark, was born in 1758. In 1782 he married Pernal Barber, who wrote the *Canaan Town Record* at the age of fifteen. They had five children: Judith, Betsey, Robert, Sally and Josiah. Judith died in 1795. Betsey married John Worth (2). Robert is mentioned in the next paragraph. Sally, born July 1, 1789, married Daniel Blaisdell (2), and had seventeen children. Josiah, born June 9, 1795, lived to be ninety-seven, dying July 3, 1892. He married three women: Betsey Bailey, Sally Gilman and Sally Hazeltine.

(IX) Robert, eldest son and third child of Josiah and Pernal (Barber) Clark, was born August 17, 1787. He was thrice married. His first wife was Betsey Currier. They had nine children: Sophronia, Eliza, Mary, Robert B., who is mentioned below; Josiah, Eleanor, who married David Kimball; Richard, Emily and Betsey. On February 27, 1827, he married Mrs. Eliza Currier, of Lyme, New Hampshire. They had two children: Theda H., born December 11, 1827, who married John Sanford Shepard; and Purnell Elisa, who was born April 29, 1834, married Freeman White, of Boston. In 1852 he married his third wife, Mrs. Mary Flint Wallace.

(X) Robert Burns, eldest son and fourth child of Robert and Betsey (Currier) Clark, was born February 26, 1818, at Canaan, New Hampshire. He was a Republican in politics. He married Elvira G. Stevens, of Canaan, who was born at Wentworth, New Hampshire, July 4, 1818. They had five children: Jemima I., Mrs. Fred Bane; Wyman R., married Mary Buckner, three children; Frank B., mentioned below; Richard O., unmarried; Austin E. Robert Burns Clark died March 2, 1890. His wife died 1869.

(XI) Frank Burns, son of Robert Burns and Elvira G. (Stevens) Clark, was born May 27, 1851, at Canaan, New Hampshire. He was educated in the public schools of his native town, and at Tilton Seminary, Tilton, New Hampshire. He moved to Dover, New Hampshire, in 1885, where he was engaged with J. E. Lothrop Company until 1895, when he engaged in the lumber business. He is a Republican in politics, and has several times been called to serve his party in the New Hampshire legislature. He served two terms as representative from 1899 to 1901, and from 1901 to 1903. He was state senator from the Twenty-second district from 1905 to 1907. He attends the Universalist Church of Dover, of which he is a trustee. He is prominent in fraternal organizations. He is a member of Moses Paul Lodge, No. 96, Ancient Free and Accepted Masons; of Belknap Chapter, No. 8 Royal Arch Masons; of Orphan Council, No. 1, Royal and Select Masters; and of St. Paul Commandery, Knights Templar. He belongs to Aleppo Temple, Ancient Arabic Order Nobles of the Mystic Shrine, of Boston; also the Veritas Lodge, No. 49, Independent Order of Odd Fellows, of Lowell, Massachusetts; and the Olive Branch Lodge, No. 8, Knights of Pythias. Frank Burns Clark married, November 20, 1877, at Claremont, New Hampshire, Lillea M. Davis, daughter of Morris L. and Melissa A. (Benson) Davis. Mrs. Clark was born September 8, 1858, at Burlington, Vermont. She was educated in the public schools of that city and at the academy at Royalton, Vermont. Her father was a contractor and served in the Civil war. Mrs. Clark comes of unusually patriotic ancestry, for her mother had six brothers who fought in the cause of the Union. Mr. and Mrs. Clark have one child, Alice Benson Clark, who was born July 24, 1881, at Claremont, New Hampshire. She was graduated from the Dover high school and from Smith College in 1903.

OSGOOD "Os," as a root word implicative of Deity, has made for itself a firm place in Osgood and other surnames which are as old as the Saxon language. John, Christopher and William Osgood, who do not seem to have been relatives, though they and their families were closely associated, settled in Massachusetts Bay Colony within a short time after the settlement of the Puritans at Plymouth. (William and descendants receive notice in this article.)

(I) John Osgood, born in Wherwell, Hampshire county, England, July 23, 1595, died in Andover, Massachusetts, October 24, 1651, aged fifty-six. He came from Andover, England, and settled in Andover, Massachusetts, before 1645. He had been at Ipswich and Newbury before his settlement at Andover. John Osgood was one of the petitioners who had liberty to begin a plantation at Hampton in 1638. On a leaf in the town records a list is written in an ancient hand, without date, but probably when most of the settlers were living, and may be considered correct: "The names of all the householders in order as they came to town: Mr. Bradstreet, John Osgood, etc." So, John Osgood was the second settler in Andover. He was a freeman in 1639, one of the founders of the church in Andover, October, 1645, and the first representative of the town in the general court in 1651. His will was dated April 12, 1650, and probated November 25, 1651. He was married in England. His wife Sarah survived him more than fifteen years, and died April 8, 1667. Their children were: Sarah, John, Mary, Elizabeth, Stephen and Hannah. Abbott, in "The History of Andover," mentions two more, Christopher and Thomas. (Mention of Stephen and descendants forms part of this article.)

(II) Captain John (2), oldest son of John (1) and Sarah Osgood, was born in England about

1631, and came to America with his parents. He was a captain in the militia, afterward held the office of selectman, and representative in the general court. He died in 1693, aged about sixty-two. He married, November 15, 1653, Mary Clement, of Andover, born about 1637, eighth and youngest child of Robert Clement, an immigrant from England, who came from Coventry, Warwickshire, about 1652 or 1653. She was indicted for witchcraft in 1692, and was living in 1695. They had twelve children, among whom were sons John, Timothy, Peter and Samuel.

(III) Lieutenant John (3), eldest son of Captain John (2) and Mary (Clement) Osgood, was a prominent man in Andover, and held the office of lieutenant and selectman, and died in 1725, aged seventy-one. His sons were: Ebenezer, Clement, John and Josiah.

(IV) Deacon John (4), third son of Lieutenant John (3) Osgood, was born in Andover, Massachusetts, in 1682, and died in Concord, New Hampshire, in 1768, aged eighty-three. His is the fourth name on the petition to Governor Shute, of Massachusetts, 1721, requesting the grant of Penny Cook, and is on another petition for the same purpose to Hon. William Dunmore, lieutenant governor of Massachusetts, in 1725. In 1727 he was elected treasurer "to ye settlers" who were to establish their claims in Penny Cooke, February 28, 1725; he drew lot No. 11 in the lowest range; and in 1727 he drew house lot No. 11 in the "Eleven Lots," containing eight and three-quarters acres. In the statement as to the state and condition of the settlement at Penacook, made October, 1731, it is said of John Osgood that he "had a house built and inhabited. In 1729 he was one of the committee appointed by the settlers of Penacook "to lay our grievances before the general court's committee." His is the first name on the committee appointed by the proprietors of Penacook, June 25, 1729, "to call and agree with some suitable person to be a minister of the town of Penny Cook, and pay him such salary as shall hereafter be agreed upon by the company of settlers." In 1730 John Osgood is first of a committee of seven "to agree with Rev. Timothy Walker, in order to his carrying on the work of the ministry in Penny Cook for the year ensuing." October 14 of that year he was appointed first on a committee "to agree with the Rev. Timothy Walker upon terms for being our minister." As a man's standing in the church was a very certain index of his standing in a community in the days when John Osgood lived, it appears that he was one of the foremost citizens of the infant settlement of "Penny Cook." In the records of the assembly, April 3, 1747, his name appears in reference to his connection in the bloody tragedy of a year before. It was then *voted*, "that there be allowed to John Osgood twelve shillings and six pence for coffins, etc., for the men killed at Rumford last year." He was a deacon in the church and major in the militia. His wife, Hannah, died in 1774, aged ninety. They had sons Josiah, Joseph, John and James, whose sketch follows.

(V) James, son of John (4), died April 16, 1757, aged fifty. He was a proprietor and an early settler in Penacook, and June 19, 1734, was elected one of the three "assessors for the proprietors" (of Rumford, late Penacook). In 1746 there was a garrison around his house. In 1744 he was one of the field drivers. He married Hannah Hazen, daughter of Richard Hazen, of Boxford, Massachusetts. Their children were: Anna, Samuel, Elizabeth, James, Benjamin, Hannah, William, John and Richard Hazen.

(VI) Samuel, eldest son and second child of James and Hannah (Hazen) Osgood, was born in Concord, July 13, 1734, and died March 16, 1774, aged forty. February 16, 1761, John Webster and Samuel Osgood filed a remonstrance with the general assembly, stating that "they had lately purchased the farm commonly called Keith's farm, contiguous to Rumford, of the claimers of the right of John Tufton Mason, Esq., and that it would be more convenient for them to be annexed to Boscawen than to Canterbury, on account of the distance from the meeting house, and the badness of the roads, and not agreeable to their interest, connexions or inclinations" to be annexed to Canterbury. This farm contained three hundred acres, and lay north of the Rumford (Concord) line, on the east side of the Merrimack river. Bouton's History states that he married Jane Webster; Carter's Pembroke says he married, January 4, 1753, Elizabeth ———, who died September 27, 1792. His children were: Lydia, Elizabeth, Sarah, Joseph, Dorcas, John, Thomas and Christopher, whose sketch follows.

(VII) Deacon Christopher, youngest of the nine children of Samuel and Elizabeth Osgood, was born April 25, 1769, and died October 3, 1841, aged seventy-two. He went from Concord to Suncook about 1796. He married (first) November 9, 1793, Anna Abbott, of Andover, Massachusetts, who was born September, 1767, and died December 26, 1827, aged sixty, and (second), February 17, 1829, Anna Abbott, of Deering, who was born October, 1769, and died May 31, 1847, aged seventy-eight. The children, all by the first wife, were: Anne C., Herman Abbot, John Hall, and Ira Ballard.

(VIII) John Hall, third child and second son of Deacon Christopher and Anna (Abbott) Osgood, was born April 23, 1801, and died April 1, 1868, aged sixty-seven. He resided at Suncook. He married, May 13, 1828, Cynthia Stewart, of Lowell, Massachusetts, who died February 22, 1891. Their children were: Cynthia Ann, Alonzo, Melissa, Ellen, James Henry, John Emery, Nancy Jane and Anna Eldusta.

(IX) Nancy, Jane, seventh child and fourth daughter of John Hall and Cynthia (Stewart) Osgood, was born in Suncook, February 28, 1843, and married, November 29, 1860, Thomas Besston Wattles. (See Wattles.)

(II) Stephen, second son of John and Sarah Osgood, was born in Ipswich or Newbury about 1638, and afterward settled in Andover, where he was a farmer. He died January 15, 1691. He married, October 24, 1663, Mary Hooker, and they had children: Stephen (died young), Hooker, Stephen, Joseph and Mary.

(III) Hooker, second son and child of Stephen (2) and Mary (Hooker) Osgood, was born August 24, 1668, and resided in Lancaster, where he died January 29, 1748, aged eighty years. He married, April 26, 1692, Dorothy Wood. Their children were: Hooker, Joshua, Jonathan, David, Benjamin, Moses, Aaron, Dorothy, Elizabeth and Sarah.

(IV) Joshua, second son and child of Hooker and Dorothy (Wood) Osgood, was born September 2, 1694, and died January 31, 1783, aged eighty-nine. He was a farmer in Leominster, but about 1726 bought a farm in Barre, and probably removed to that place at that time. He married, December 20, 1722, Ruth Divall, who died May 28, 1782. Their children were Joshua, Ephraim, Ruth, Sarah, William, Asahel, Abel, Sarah, Manassah, Lemuel and Joshua.

(V) William, fifth child and third son of Joshua and Ruth (Divall) Osgood, was born August 20, 1732, and died February 5, 1801, in Cabot, Vermont. He resided successively in Barre, Massachusetts; Claremont, New Hampshire, and Cabot, Vermont. He married, June 3, 1756, Hepsibah Dunton, who died October 31, 1809. Their fifteen children were: William, Thomas, Levi, Abijah, Mary, Sarah, Amasa, Joshua (died young), Joshua, David, Solomon W., John, Samson, Hepsibeth and Anna.

(VI) William (2), eldest child of William (1) and Hepsibah (Dunton) Osgood, was born in Cabot, Vermont, June 17, 1760, and resided in Newport, New Hampshire, where he died October 4, 1823. His settlement in Newport was on wild land, which he cleared and made a productive farm. He married Priscilla Stone, of Claremont, New Hampshire, who died February 22, 1802, and they had Susannah, William, James, Lemuel, Priscilla, Matthew and Lydia.

(VII) William (3), eldest son and second child of William (2) and Priscilla (Stone) Osgood, was born February 26, 1784, and died February 25, 1866, aged eighty-two years. He resided at Claremont. He married Susannah Field, of Claremont, who died in 1827. Their children were: William, Lois, Joseph W., Lucia, Charles, Matthias and Lyman P.

(VIII) William (4), eldest child of William (3) and Susannah (Field) Osgood, was born in Claremont, in 1809, and died in West Lebanon, October 4, 1859. He was a farmer and miller. He married Eliza Kenney, of Vershire, Vermont, who died July 9, 1863. Their children were: William H., Martha, Mary J., Eliza and Julia.

(Second Family.)

OSGOOD (I) William Osgood, who was born in England in 1609, accompanied John Osgood to New England, sailing in the ship "Confidence" from Southampton, April 11, 1638, and locating in Newbury, Massachusetts. He was the youngest of three immigrants, the others being Christopher and John, and they were undoubtedly brothers. William Osgood was a carpenter and a millwright. In 1640 he settled at the falls on the Powow river, near its junction with the Merrimack, and taking advantage of the excellent water-power he erected the first mills in Salisbury, Massachusetts, which for many years were known as Osgood's mills. He was granted land on each side of the Powow river, extending half a mile back from the Merrimack and embracing a large part of the locality now known as the Salisbury and Amesbury mills. He also acquired other real estate, including his homestead of six acres on Round Hill, Salisbury. His death occurred at Salisbury in the year 1700. The maiden surname of his wife is unknown, but her Christian name was Elizabeth, and the following tradition relative to her family name may be considered by some as throwing a ray of light upon the matter. "After the death of Elizabeth, when the emigrant had become aged, there was a husking in the log house where William lived. In the evening, as the young people became merry, cracking their jokes over the red ears of corn, their merriment awakened in the aged emigrant's mind recollections of his earlier years. The old man, who was in a part of the room by himself, in response to their hilarity, broke out in a sort of musical speech: 'My wife was Betty Cleer and I loved her before I see her.'" William and Elizabeth Osgood had seven children, namely: Elizabeth, Joanna, John, William, Mary, Joseph and Sarah.

(II) John, third child and eldest son of William and Elizabeth Osgood, was born in Salisbury, Massachusetts, August 8, 1647, and died there November 7, 1683. He took the oath of fidelity, with his brother William, December 8, 1677. He married, November 5, 1668, Mary Stevens, daughter of John and Katherine Stevens, of Salisbury. She was bron in 1647. His widow married, August 26, 1685, Nathaniel Whittier. John and Mary (Stevens) Osgood were the parents of six children: Mary, Joseph, William, John, Timothy and Hannah.

(III) William (2), third child and second son of John and Mary (Stevens) Osgood, was born in Salisbury, July 30, 1673, and his death occurred in 1752. He was a farmer, had a large landed estate and was a substantial and influential citizen. His descendants, especially, have maintained the reputation acquired by their ancestor. He married Hannah Colby, daughter of John and Frances (Hoyt) Colby, of Amesbury, and was the father of nine children, namely: Timothy, Judith, Joseph, Mary Daniel, Mehitable, Hannah, Abigail and William.

(IV) Joseph, second son and child of William and Hannah (Colby) Osgood, was born in Salisbury, June 28, 1698, and died December 24, 1781. September 15, 1719, he married Apphia Pillsbury, who was born May 8, 1700, daughter of William, Jr., and Mary (Kenney) Pillsbury, of Newbury, Massachusetts. The twelve children of Joseph and Apphia (Pillsbury) Osgood were: Mary, Henry, Hannah, Reuben, Joseph and Benjamin (twins), the former of whom died young; another Joseph, who died at the age of four years; Apphia (died young), Ruth, Apphia and Joseph (twins), and Oliver.

(V) Reuben, second son and fourth child of Joseph and Apphia (Pillsbury) Osgood, was born in Salisbury, November 21, 1726, and his death occurred in Epping, New Hampshire, (where he settled in 1756), January 30, 1795. On July 18, 1748, he married (first) Mary Brown, of Salisbury, who died in 1753. For his second wife he married, August 5, 1754, Mary True, also of Salisbury, and her death occurred in 1803. He was the father of eight children. Those of his first union were: Samuel, born in March, 1749; Joseph, April 18, 1751; and a daughter who died in infancy. The five children by his second marriage were: True, born April 30, 1755; Reuben, October 20, 1756; William, in 1758; Betsey, March 27, 1760, married in 1772 Ebenezer Page, of Peacham, Walden and Danville, Vermont, and had four children; and Mary True, February 15, 1765, married Abraham Brown, of Salisbury.

(VI) Joseph, son of Reuben and Mary (Brown) Osgood, of Epping, and brother of Samuel and Reuben, was born April 18, 1751, and died April 7, 1809. He married Anna Renlet, of Epping, New Hampshire, who died May 19, 1818. They had seven children: Daniel, True, Rachel, Molly, Jonathan, Anna and Joseph.

(VII) Daniel, son of Joseph and Anna Osgood, of Epping, was born December 15, 1773, and died July 11, 1856. He married Betsey Osgood, daughter of Reuben (2) by his first wife and a sister of Nancy, Polly and Dudley. Daniel and Betsey Osgood had nine children: Melinda, Greenleaf, William C., John Hazen, Nancy, Lucinda, Joseph, Julia Ann and Asa C.

(VIII) William C., son of Daniel and Betsey Osgood, was born in Gilmanton, New Hampshire, November 14, 1812, died in Pittsfield, New Hampshire, July 26, 1869, and is buried in Floral Park cemetery in that town. He married, 1814, Mary C. Dow, died February 25, 1871. They had children: Adelaide M., born March 8, 1840, died September 28, 1865; Henry W., Edwin S. and Frank D. Osgood.

(X) Henry W., second child and eldest son of William C. and Mary C. (Dow) Osgood, was born in Pittsfield, New Hampshire, October 9, 1842, and has been prominently identified with the social and business life of that town for more than thirty-five years. He was educated at Pittsfield Academy, where he attended about one year, and Gilmanton Academy, where he was a student about three years, and where among his classmates were Thomas Coggswell and J. B. Peasley. After leaving school he took up photography and made the first dry plate in Pittsfield, it is still in his possession. His collection of photographic plates and views is large and exceedingly interesting. In connection with his work in this direction he has made frequent trips to Mount Belknap and Catamount and many other places of interest in the mountainous regions. and also in Pittsfield, Gilmanton and elsewhere. He is a lover of nature and an artist by every personal trait. In connection with photographic work Mr. Osgood is proprietor of a large furniture store and business in Pittsfield, having been engaged in that line since 1875. Although business matters occupy much of his time he nevertheless takes a commendable interest in the welfare of his native town, and its institutions. He served nine years as member of the school board, and now is treasurer of the board of trustees of Pittsfield Academy. He also was one of the first board of trustees of Floral Park cemetery, its first superintendent, and has been clerk of the board since it was organized. He is a member of the Congregational Church of Pittsfield, and served several terms as its warden and twenty-five years as librarian of its Sunday school. He was the first member to be initiated after the resuscitation and reorganization of Suncook Lodge, No. 10, Independent Order of Odd Fellows, Pittsfield, New Hampshire, a member of Corinthian Lodge of Free and Accepted Masons, its secretary sixteen years. tyler several years, master four years. and also one of the original members and first trustees of the Masonic Hall Association of Pittsfield.

From the time he was a boy in school, under the instruction of Principal Sawyer of Pittsfield, Mr. Osgood has taken a deep interest in the study of birds and has become an ornithologist of considerable reputation in his locality. This old-time interest never has abated and he frequently lectures on ornithological subjects before high school students and grange meetings. He also is a taxidermist of unusual skill and has done much work in that direction. He find rest and recreation in hunting and fishing, his favorite pastime, and casts a fly with the most expert fishermen; for many years he has been an enthusiastic follower of "Dog, Gun and Rod."

On October 9, 1866, Mr. Osgood married Frances H. Tilton, who was born August 4, 1844, daughter of Levi and Theodate (True) Tilton, of Hampton Falls. New Hampshire. Mr. Tilton was born April 5, 1809, and died March 14, 1899. His wife, Theodate (True) Tilton, was born August 7, 1806, died January 7, 1853, daughter of Nathaniel and Mary (James) True. Mr. and Mrs. Tilton's children were: Frances H., wife of Henry W. Osgood, and Aroline C., born July 17, 1846, a public school teacher and a member of Mr. Osgood's family. Mr. and Mrs. Osgood have had two children: Marion Adelaide, born August 18, 1867, died November 11, 1875, and Annie True, born May 5, 1869.

OSGOOD The Osgoods of old Tamworth, New Hampshire, like nearly all others of the surname in the state, are descended from the same ancestral head and date back in New England to the earliest times of the colonies. The year in which the first representative in Tamworth of the Osgood family to which this sketch relates came there is not known, although some of its descendants are still in that town and others are scattered throughout New Hampshire and other of the New England states.

(I) Samuel Osgood was born in Tamworth in 1821, hence at least one generation of the family before him lived in that town. He was brought up on a farm, but at the age of fifteen years left home and went to Nashua, New Hampshire, engaged in business there several years and then took up his residence in Laconia, where he died in 1877. His wife was Elizabeth (Hyde) Osgood. also a native of Tamworth and by whom he had six children: Frank J., now living in Laconia. George H., born 1844, enlisted in Company K, One Hundredth and Eleventh Pennsylvania Volunteer Infantry, killed July 25, 1864, in battle at Kenesaw Mountain Georgia. Katie J., born 1846, married Frederick Breeman; lives in Laconia. Clara H., born 1849, married Frank Fourtebatt, of St. Paul. Minnesota. superintendent of the Northern Pacific car shops in that city. Ada M., born 1850, married George B. Merrill, of Lynn, Massachusetts; two children, Hollis F. and Harry Merrill. Anna, born 1856, married Albert W. Wilcox, and has one child, Gertrude Wilcox.

(II) Frank Jacob, eldest child and son of Samuel and Elizabeth (Hyde) Osgood, was born in Laconia, New Hampshire, January 3, 1841. and after leaving school began working as a newsboy and was the first boy of the town to do that kind of work. When about seventeen years old he left home and went west, and was a news and train boy on the Chicago, Milwaukee and St. Paul railway. After a short time in the northwest he came back east as far as northwestern Pennsylvania and became landlord of a hotel, continuing in that occupation until the beginning of the late Civil war. In 1861 Mr. Osgood enlisted in Company K, One Hundred and Eleventh Pennsylvania Volunteer Infantry, and on the organization of the company was elected and commissioned first lieutenant. He was promoted captain July 14, 1862, and a little later was promoted to the regimental staff with the rank and commission of major. Still later he was promoted lieutenant-colonel and held that rank at the time of muster out in 1865. After the war Colonel Osgood returned to Laconia and has since lived in that city. He is a member of John L. Perley Post, No. 37, G. A. R., a Republican in politics and was brought up under the influence of the Congregational Church. He married. January 10, 1871, Emma, daughter of Otis and Emma (Robbins) Beman, and has two children: Anna Charlotte, born November 29, 1872, and Lottie May, August 5, 1879, died November, 1892.

FOWLER The known history of this family extends backward more than three hundred years from the present time. It was founded very early in the new colony of Massachusetts, and has many worthy descendants scattered over the United States at the present time. In days when men were taking surnames, those of many were indicated by their occupations. Among these was the bird hunter, or fowler.

(I) Philip Fowler, a cloth worker, was early found in Ipswich, Massachusetts. He was born somewhere between 1591 and 1598, and took the oath at South Hampton, March 24, 1634. He crossed the Atlantic in the ship "Mary and John," and was made a freeman at Ipswich, Massachusetts, September 3, 1634. He continued to reside in that town, and died June 24, 1679. His grandson, Philip Fowler, was appointed administrator of his estate. He married (first), Mary, believed to have been a sister of Samuel Winsley. She died August 30, 1659, in Ipswich, and he was married February 27 following to Mary, widow of George Norton. His children were: Margaret, Mary, Samuel, Hester, Joseph and Thomas. (Mention of Joseph and Thomas and descendants forms part of this article).

(II) Samuel, eldest son and third child of Philip and Mary Fowler, was born about 1618, in England, and came to this country, presumably with his father. He resided in Portsmouth and Salisbury, and was the shipwright. The fact that Samuel Winsley called him cousin makes it apparent that that was the maiden name of his mother. He resided in Salisbury in 1668 and 1680, and in 1669 purchased Louis Hulett's country right in Salisbury. It is probable that he belonged to the Society of Friends. He was brought before the court in April, 1675, for "Breach of the Sabbath in traveling." He died in January, 1711, in Salisbury. The name of his first wife has not been discovered. He was married after 1673 to widow Margaret (Norman) Morgan. His children were: William, Mary, Sarah and Samuel.

(III) Samuel (2), youngest son of Samuel (1) Fowler, was born probably, in Salisbury, and died in that town December 24, 1737. His will had been made almost ten years previously, and was proven six days after his death. He was married December 5th, 1684, in Salisbury to Hannah, daughter of Ezekiel and Hannah (Martin) Worthen. She was born April 21, 1663, in Salisbury and survived her husband. Their children were: Samuel, Hannah, Susanna, Jacob, Mary, Sarah, Ham, Ezekiel, Robert, Abraham, Thomas, Lydia and Judith.

(IV) Jacob, second son and fourth child of Samuel (2) and Hannah (Worthen) Fowler, was born December 10, 1690, in Salisbury and resided in South Hampton, New Hampshire, where he died December 20, 1752. It is probable that he was among those who found themselves in New Hampshire after the establishment of the Province line, in 1741, took some territory from Salisbury. His will was proved December 27, 1752, just one week after his death. He was married May 3, 1716, to Mary Jones, daughter of Joseph and granddaughter of Robert Jones, of Amesbury.

(V) Abner, eldest son of Jacob and Mary (Jones) Fowler, was born in South Hampton, 1757, and died in Hill, April 30, 1833. He resided in Northfield, removed in 1809 to Sanbornton, and in 1822 to Hill, and lived north of Hill village. He served long in the war for independence, and his name appears in various places in the New Hampshire rolls of the Revolution. He was a private in Captain Thomas Simpson's ranging company of Colonel Johnson's regiment at Coos, enlisting October 1, 1776, and serving two months and one day, for two pounds per month pay. Abner Fowler, of Canterbury, was a member of Captain Simeon Steven's company of Colonel Stickney's regiment of Continental soldiers, enlisting in 1777. His name is also on the muster roll of the first company, Captain James Gray's of the Third New Hampshire Regiment, Colonel Alexander Scammel's, which regiment was raised by the state of New Hampshire for the continental service. He was mustered in June 3, 1777, and discharged April 15, 1780. He served as a private until May 1, 1779, when he was promoted to corporal. During his absence in the army his family, like many other families, had no bread winner, and received part of their necessary supplies from the town. His wife, Mary Fowler, signed the following receipt dated February 4, 1780: "The account of articles supplyd by the Select Men for Canterbury to the family of Abner Fowler, a soldier in the service of said town in the Continental army—Total £74 9. 6." Among the articles enumerated are salt at £15 per barrel; rye at £8 per bushel, and corn at £— per bushel, in the depreciated currency of that time. He married Mary Mason.

(VI) Abraham, son of Abner and Mary (Mason) Fowler, was born in Sanbornton, New Hampshire, December 12, 1792, and died in Hill, October 20, 1852. He removed to Hill, probably at the same time his father died, and was a farmer, and kept a tavern north of town. He married Nancy Hodgdon, born June 15, 1798, daughter of Israel and Comfort (Sanborn) Hodgdon, of Northfield. She died June 2, 1885, aged eighty-seven years. Their children were: Isaiah, David, Mary Ann, Comfort S., Israel H., Abner and Nancy Jane.

(VII) David, second son and child of Abraham and Nancy (Hodgdon) Fowler, was born in Sanbornton, October 2, 1818, and died July 11, 1887. He was educated in the common schools and at Plymouth and Franklin Academies. He was a farmer, and occasionally engaged in lumbering. He always resided on the homestead and owned about one hundred and fifty acres of land. He was a member of the Methodist Church of Bristol. He was a Whig, and later a member of the "Know Nothing" party, of which he was a leader, and by which he was elected representative in 1855. Secret meetings were held at his house. When the Republican party rose, he joined it, and was a Republican the remainder of his life. He married (first), Charlotte Dearborn, who was born in Northfield, April 12, 1818, and died in Hill, April 18, 1844. She was the daughter of Shubael and Nancy (Dearborn) Dearborn, of Northfield. She was employed at Peabody & Daniel's Paper Mills for many years before her marriage. He married (second), Abra Ann Dearborn, sister of his first wife, who was born April 28, 1823, and died in Hill, November 24 1860: (third), Caroline H. Norton, who was born in Cabott, Vermont, November 12, 1830, daughter of Moses H. and Temperance (Warner) Norton, of Cabott, Vermont The children by the last wife were: Charles A. (died young); Minnie G., married Oden B. Eaton, and lives in Lakeport; Fred A., mentioned below; Angelo H., graduated from the Franklin high school with the class of 1894, later attended the Waterbury and Green Mountain Seminaries, and resides with his mother and brother on the homestead

(VIII) Dr. Fred Abram Fowler, third child and second son of David and Caroline H. (Norton) Fowler, was born in Hill, September 2, 1869. He obtained his literary education in the common schools and from a private tutor, and in 1897 matriculated at the University of Vermont, where he took the medical course, graduating with the class of 1899. He began the practice of his profession at Hill, and has a liberal patronage. He is a leading representative and was town clerk four years. He is a member of Union Lodge No. 79, Ancient Free and Accepted Masons, of Bristol, and of Saint Omar Chapter, No. 22, Royal Arch Masons, of Franklin; also of Cardigan Lodge, No. 79, Independent Order of Odd Fellows, of Bristol, and St. Andrews Chapter, No. 21, Knights of Pythias, of Franklin Falls. He is a past master of Pemigewasset Grange No. 103, Patrons of Husbandry, of Hill, and is a member of Lake and Valley Pomona Lodge of Bristol. In 1906 he was elected a member of the New Hampshire house of representatives.

(II) Joseph, second son and fifth child of Philip and Mary (Winsley) Fowler, was born in England about 1622, and in 1634 came to this country with his parents in the ship "Mary and John." They settled in Ipswich, Massachusetts, where Joseph grew up and married. His wife was Martha Kimball, daughter of Richard and Ursula (Scott) Kimball. Richard Kimball was the ancestor of nearly all those bearing the name of Kimball in this country. His wife, Ursula Scott, was the daughter of Martha Scott, widow of Hon. John Scott, of Scott's Hall, county of Kent, England, and daughter of Sir George Northup. The Scotts and the Kimballs came over in the same ship. To Joseph and Ursula (Scott) Kimball were born four children: Joseph, born about 1647, married Elizabeth Hutton. Phillip, whose sketch follows. John, married ((first), Sarah ———; (second), Hannah Scott. Mary, married John Briers, of Gloucester. Joseph Fowler was killed by the Indians near Deerfield, Massachusetts, May 19, 1676, on his return from the fight at the Falls.

(III) Philip (2), second son and child of Joseph and Martha (Kimball) Fowler, was born in 1648, probably on October 8, though one record gives the date as December 25. He was adopted by his grandfather, Philip (1) Fowler, of Ipswich, Massachusetts, who brought him up and taught him his trade of cloth worker. On January 20, 1672-73, Philip (2) Fowler married at Beverly, Massachusetts, Elizabeth Herrick, daughter of Henry and Edith (Larkin) Herrick, and granddaughter of Sir William Herrick. Henry Herrick, her father, was born at Bean Manor, England, in 1604. Philip (2) and Elizabeth (Herrick) Fowler had nine children: Philip (died young); Elizabeth, born February 11, 1677-78. Martha (died young). Joseph, married Sarah Bartlett and three other wifes. John, married Mercy Jacob. Benjamin, married Mary Briar and others. Mary, married John Treadwell. Martha, married Lieutenant John March. Philip, whose sketch follows. Philip (2) Fowler, died November 16, 1715, leaving a widow.

(IV) Philip (3), fifth son and ninth and youngest child of Philip (2) and Elizabeth (Herrick) Fowler, was born in October, 1691, at Ipswich, Massachusetts. He married there, July 5, 1716, Susanna Jacob, daughter of Joseph and Susanna (Symonds) Jacob, who was born about 1695. They had sixteen children: Elizabeth, Philip, Jacob, Susanna, Samuel, Martha, Judith, Samuel, Mary, Mary, Symonds, whose sketch follows, Lucy, Ebenezer, Benjamin, Ebenezer and Lucy. Of these children, the two Samuels, the first Mary, both Lucys Ebenezer and Benjamin (twins) and the second Ebenezer, all died in infancy, leaving eight who grew up and married. Philip (3) Fowler carried on the tanning business until he sold out and moved to Newmarket, New Hampshire, in May, 1743, living there till his death, May 16, 1767. His widow survived him six years.

(V). Symonds, fifth son and eleventh child of Philip (3) and Susanna (Jacob) Fowler, was born August 20, 1734, at Ipswich, Massachusetts. When nine years of age he removed with his people to Newmarket, New Hampshire, where he signed the test oath, July 12, 1776. On May 26, 1778, when he was forty-four years old, he moved from Newmarket to Epsom, this state where he spent the remaining half of his life. On July 12, 1756, Symonds Fowler married Hannah Weeks, daughter of Jonathan Weeks, who was born in Greenland, New Hampshire, August 12, 1738. Of this union there were born eleven children: Hannah (died young); Susanna, married John Jenness; Symonds (died young); Hannah, married D. Robinson, and (second), J. Phelps; Abigail married Nathan Libby. Benjamin, whose sketch follows; Sally, married Zebadiah Lovejoy; Samuel, married Betsey Davis; Polly, married Samuel Learned; Esther, married Rev. Asa Merrill; Winthrop, married Abigail Davis. Symonds Fowler died at Epsom, New Hampshire, April 6, 1821, aged eighty-seven years, and his wife died there December 9, 1807, aged sixty-nine years.

(VI) Benjamin, second son and sixth child of Symonds and Hannah (Weeks) Fowler, was born at Newmarket New Hampshire, June 10, 1769. When a youth he removed with his father to Epsom, this state, and after his marriage bought a farm at Pembroke, where he spent the last thirty-seven years of his life. On January 15, 1795, Benjamin Fowler married Mehitable Ladd, daughter of John and Jerusha (Lovejoy) Ladd, who was born in Newmarket, this state, March 9, 1776. Her grandparents were Captain Trueworthy and Mehitable (Harriman) Ladd, of Kingston, New Hampshire. Benjamin and Mehitable (Ladd) Fowler had eleven children: Jerusha, married Chandler Hutchinson. Esther, mentioned below. Mehitable, born May 27, 1798, unmarried. Benjamin, married Hannah Campbell. John Ladd, married Lavina Abbott. Samuel, died unmarried. Polly and David died in infancy. Asa, married C. D. Knox. Clarissa died in infancy. Trueworthy add, married Catharine L. Sargent. Of these children Asa was graduated from Dartmouth College in 1833, became one of the leading lawyers of the state and judge of the supreme court. For more than fifty years he was a resident of Concord, where he reared a large family. Two of his children, William P. and Clara M., of Boston, gave the Fowler Library to the city of Concord in memory of their father and mother. Benjamin Fowler died at Pembroke, July 24, 1832, at the age of sixty-three, and his widow died there twenty-one years later, September 9, 1853, at the age of seventy-seven.

(VII) Esther, second daughter and child of Benjamin and Mehitable (Ladd) Fowler, was born at Pembroke, New Hampshire, March 16, 1797. On October 16, 1816, she married William Abbott (2), son of William and Dorcas (Parker) Abbott, who was born at Pembroke, August 15, 1794. They had five children: Orson, Clarissa, Elvira and Marvetta (twins), and Laura H. Orson married Elizabeth Clark, of Epsom, this state, and for his second wife, Ann Foster. He moved to California, where he died. Clarissa married Aaron Elliot, of Dunbarton, New Hampshire. Elvira died in infancy. Marvetta is mentioned below. Laura H. married Asa R. Chamberlain, and lived in State

Centre, Iowa. Mrs. Esther (Fowler) Abbott died at Pembroke, December 31, 1831, at the early age of thirty-four years. Her husband, William (2) Abbott, lived to complete eighty years, and died there August 23, 1874.

(VIII) Marvetta, third daughter and fourth child of William (2) and Esther (Fowler) Abbott, was born at Pembroke, New Hampshire, May 2, 1823. She was married, June 2, 1846, to William Goss, son of Jonathan Goss, of Epsom, New Hampshire. (See Goss, IV).

(II) Thomas, youngest child of Philip and Mary Fowler, was born about 1636, in Ipswich, and was a resident of Salisbury in 1662 and of Amesbury in 1667, when he had a seat assigned to him in the meeting house there. In December of that year he subscribed to the oath of allegiance at Amesbury. and in 1679 claimed the "township" of common right granted by Amesbury in 1660 to Joseph Peaslee, having purchased it from Peaslee's son in 1667. He was representative to the general court in 1692, and died October 3, 1727, in Amesbury. His will was made in January, 1726, and proved thirteen days following his death. He was married, April 23, 1660, in Ipswich, to Hannah, daughter of Francis Jordan. She died in Amesbury, June 15, 1716. Their children were: Hannah, Thomas. William, John, Margaret, Jane, Jeremiah and Mary.

(III) Jeremiah, fourth son and seventh child of Thomas and Hannah (Jordan) Fowler, was born in Amesbury, and spent his life in that town. He was a "snowshoe man" in 1708, and made his will April 10, 1750. This was proved March 18, 1754, and mentioned his wife Rebecca and children. He was married, January 6, 1707, in Amesbury, to Rebecca Colby, daughter of Isaac and Martha (Jewett) Colby (see Colby, II). She was born before 1684. and was dismissed from the church at Rowley to the Amesbury church in 1714, and was still living in 1750. Their children were: Thomas, Rebecca, Hannah and Elizabeth.

(IV) Thomas (2), only son of Jeremiah and Rebecca (Colby) Fowler. was born January 22, 1708, in Amesbury, where he was still living in 1750, and probably for many years thereafter. He was married, January 17, 1732, to Rebecca Davis, daughter of Joseph and Jemima Davis, of West Amesbury. No record of their children is at hand except that they were the parents of Jeremiah Fowler.

(V) Jeremiah (2), son of Thomas (2) and Rebecca (Davis) Fowler, was born July 27, 1737, in Amesbury, and is found as a resident of Newton, New Hampshire. It is quite probable that he resided in Amesbury and at the adjustment of the province line in 1741 found his home to be in Newton. No record of his marriage appears in either Amesbury or Newton. His wife was Mary Woodward, and they were early residents of Hopkinton, New Hampshire. Mary Woodward was born April 30, 1730, in Warner, New Hampshire, taken captive by the Indians when sixteen years old carried to Quebec, where after three years her father went and bought her back for $18.50. Mr. Fowler died in 1802, leaving five children. She died October 3, 1829, in her one hundredth year.

(VI) David, son of Jeremiah (2) and Mary (Woodward) Fowler, was born September 29, 1761, in Newton, New Hampshire, and must have been a small child when his parents removed to Hopkinton. He was an active and useful citizen of that town where he was a member of the board of selectmen from 1797 to 1799. He married Susan Piper, of that town.

(VII) Joseph, second son of David and Susan (Piper) Fowler, was born in Hopkinton, New Hampshire. He married, in 1806, Nancy Robinson Leavitt, daughter of Jonathan, of Meredith, who served in the Revolutionary war as private, lieutenant and captain. Captain or Lieutenant-Colonel Jonathan Leavitt was a private in Captain Samuel Gilman's company, Colonel Enoch Poor's regiment. 1775; sergeant in Captain Parson's company, Colonel David Gilman's regiment, 1776-77; lieutenant colonel in Joseph Senter's regiment, 1777; lieutenant in Captain Ezekiel Giles' company, Colonel Stephen Peabody's regiment, 1778; captain and lieutenant in Colonel Hercules Mooney's regiment, 1779, New Hampshire Line. Joseph Fowler was a resident of Bristol as early as 1808. He removed to Andover, probably as early as 1825, and died in Lowell, Massachusetts. His wife died in West Boxford, Massachusetts, at the age of ninety-one years. Their children, all born in Bristol, were: Oscar Fitzalon. Amanda, M. F. Worthen, Jonathan, Nancy Leavitt, Joseph Martines and Caroline Matilda Thayer.

(VIII) Oscar F., eldest son of Joseph and Nancy Robinson (Leavitt) Fowler, was born September 3, 1808, and died suddenly while on a visit to his native town (Bristol), August 6, 1876. He removed to Andover with his father, but returned to Bristol in 1836. and carried on the harness maker's trade for many years. But this business represented only a small part of the activities of his life. He was an auctioneer whose fame was not confined to his own state, and his services in this capacity were in constant demand. He was lieutenant-colonel of the thirty-fourth regiment, was postmaster of Bristol for seventeen years, and served as associate justice of the court of common pleas. In politics he was a Democrat, and was very prominent in the councils of that party. Judge Fowler received only the education of the common schools of his day, but he was a man of extraordinary ability and a natural leader in all enterprises that had for their object the advancement of the interests of the community in which he lived. He possessed in a high degree that courtesy of manners that embodies human kindness, and he was a helpful citizen in the best source of the term. He married (first), Abigail, daughter of James and Ruth Smith, of Bath, New Hampshire. She died in Bristol, June 1, 1833, aged twenty-seven years. He married (second), in September, 1834. Louisa M., daughter of Thomas and Susannah Waterman, of Lebanon, New Hampshire. The name of her grandfather. Silas Waterman, appears as one of a company of men who came from Connecticut and made the first settlement north of Charlestown at Lebanon, New Hampshire. It is related of them that "they were a hardy, brave people, tenacious of their principles, of strong minds, carved habits and good common education." Silas Waterman married Silence Peck. Their son Thomas was the first male child born in Lebanon. Mrs. Fowler was a woman of rare dignity of character, and of superior quality of mind. Her neighbor was the one brought to her notice who might be in need. Both Judge and Mrs. Fowler were prominent members of the Methodist Episcopal Church, and among its most devoted and liberal supporters. Their home was always open to the itinerant preachers and meetings were frequently held there. The last few years of their lives Mr.

and Mrs. Fowler made their home with their youngest daughter in Plymouth, where Mrs. Fowler died September 2, 1878, aged seventy years. Their children, all born in Bristol, were: 1. Abbie Smith, born August 12, 1835. married, January 1, 1856, Tristram Rogers, a leading physician who has been many years in practice in Plymouth. Children: Oscar Fowler, born October 21, 1856; died December 10, 1857. Holted Waterman, born March 27, 1859; died March 2, 1880. 2. Harriet Waterman, born October 25, 1837, died April 27, 1861. May 5, 1858, she married Professor Henry Lummis, a well known educator. He was from 1886 up to his death, April 13, 1905, a professor in Lawrence University, Appleton, Wisconsin. The only son of this marriage is Charles Fletcher Lummis, born March 1, 1859, an author of international fame. Among his more important works are "The Awakening of a Nation," (Mexico today), "The Spanish Pioneers," and "A Tramp Across the Continent." He is now editor of *Sunshine Land*, published at Los Angeles, California. Mr. Lummis was appointed Indian commissioner about two years since by President Roosevelt. One daughter Lulie, born December 15, 1860, is now teaching in Quincy Mansion, Wollaston, Massachusetts. 3. Susan Waterman, born December 9, 1839, married, June 16, 1864, John Mason, of Plymouth, who died November 12, 1905. Children: Harry, born June 22, 1865. Walter Webster, July 25, 1867. Susie Elizabeth, born November 7, 1869, died July 30, 1888. Her death occurred June 21, 1895. Both Mrs. Rogers and Mrs. Mason were specially gifted in vocal music, and for many years they were leading singers at musical conventions. 4. George Storrs, born October 11, 1843, married, December 31, 1867, Esther Louise Updegraff. He is a business man, and resided at Fort Wayne, Indiana. He is engaged in railroad business with offices in Washington, District of Columbia. Two children: Florence and Hattie Waterman.

(IX) Charles J., youngest child of Oscar F. and Louise (Waterman) Fowler, was born February 6, 1845, in Bristol, New Hampshire. He was educated in the public schools of Bristol, at Tilton Seminary, and under private tutelage. He entered the ministry in 1871, and for several years labored as a lay evangelist, holding meetings in many sections of New England as well as other states. He was very successful at all points, having extensive revivals in cities like Manchester, New Hampshire, Lawrence and Lowell, Massachusetts. Mr. Fowler was admitted to the New Hampshire Conference in 1883, and served several of the leading churches in that conference, remaining at Grace Church, Haverhill, Massachusetts, seven years. Since 1885 he has labored distinctively as a holiness preacher; in 1894 he was elected president of the National Association for the Promotion of Holiness, which position he still holds. In 1895 he received the degree of Doctor of Divinity from Taylor University, and during that year withdrew from the regular ministry in order to devote his entire time to holiness evangelism. Dr. Fowler has crossed the continent twelve times, and preached in many of the large cities from Maine to California with remarkable success, drawing large numbers and witnessing great revivals. In 1901 he published "Back to Pentecost," and he has been for several years editor of the *Christian Witness*, an advocate of Bible holiness, published in Boston and Chicago. It is a paper of wide circulation and influence, and the leading holiness periodical in the country. February 12, 1874, Mr. Fowler married Emily Peavey, daughter of Hon. John G. and Tamar (Clark) Sinclair, of Bethlehem, New Hampshire. They reside in West Newton, Massachusetts. Their children are: 1. Martha Sinclair, born October 17, 1874, married, October 6, 1898, Andrew S. Woods, of West Newton. Children: Margaret Louise, born December 27, 1900. Edward, December 20, 1903. Katherine, November 10, 1907. 2. Louise Waterman, born February 4, 1880, was married August 26, 1907, to Carl Pickhardt, of Islington, Massachusetts. 3. Harriet R., born April 14, 1883.

FOWLER Several emigrants of this name are known to have been early arrivals in New England, and their descendants are numerous. The family now in hand has resided in New Hampshire for more than a century and a quarter.

(I) Abner Fowler, born March 17, 1753, was residing in Sanbornton during the period of reconstruction which followed the realization of the declaration of independence.

(II) David, son of Abner Fowler, was born in Sanbornton, June 24, 1783. He served as a soldier in the second war with Great Britain (1812-15), being wounded at the battle of Lundy's Lane, and afterwards went from Sanbornton to Hebron. About the year 1846 he moved to North Bristol, where he engaged in lumbering and operating a saw-mill, succeeding his son Blake, who had formerly carried on the business. He was crippled for life through the wound suffered in the battle named. His last days were spent in Alexandria. and his death occurred there at the age of eighty-three years, September 14, 1866. He married, June 16, 1803, Deborah Blake. She died September 5, 1871, aged eighty-six years. Their children were: Blake, Betsey, Abner, Joseph and Mary, who were born in Sanbornton; Deborah Jane and Thomas Lord, who were natives of Hebron.

(III) Rev. Thomas Lord Fowler, youngest son and child of David and Deborah (Blake) Fowler, was born in Hebron, October 10, 1823. In 1845 he opened a general country store at Bristol, where he continued in the trade some five years, and he then turned his attention to the carpenter's trade, which he followed in Alexandria. In 1855 he moved to Seabrook and entered a general store. Prior to locating in Seabrook, and during his three years residence there, he spent his leisure hours in studying theology and kindred subjects, with a view of preparing himself for the ministry, and joining the New Hampshire conference he established the first Methodist Episcopal Church in Marlboro, New Hampshire, of which he officiated as pastor for the years 1859, '60 and '61. Assigned to the church in Chesterfield he labored there for three years or until a severe attack of pneumonia compelled him to suspend his activities. His recovery was slow. and for a considerable length of time he was only able to supply at intervals the pulpits in Westport and Westmoreland. Withdrawing from the ministry, in 1865, he engaged in the manufacture of lumber in Chesterfield, which he relinquished some twelve years later in order to devote his energies to farming. From Chesterfield he removed to Ashuelot, and from the latter place to Westport, where he continued to till the soil for the remainder of his life, which terminated July 10, 1898.

On August 20, 1844, he married for his first wife Mary Hazelton, who died January 16, 1848, and on May 10, following, he married Nancy M. Giles, whose death occurred in 1895. For his third wife he married Mrs. Esther Prince. His children

Herschel J. Fowler.

were: Eugene A., son of Mary (Hazelton) Fowler, and by the second marriage Herschel, mentioned hereinafter; Orrin R., Leforest C., who died in infancy, and Manson L. Fowler.

(IV) Herschel Joseph, son of Rev. Thomas L. and Nancy M. (Giles) Fowler, was born in Alexandria, New Hampshire, April 23, 1849. He went from the public schools to the Newbury (Vermont) Academy, which he left at the conclusion of his first year with the intention of returning, but being offered a position in the drug store of Messrs. Howard & Holman at Keene, he decided to begin the activities of life at once, and was in their employ for two and a half years, or until failing health compelled him to take a season of rest. Upon his return to Keene he entered the employ of Messrs. Whitcomb & Dunbar, but two years later went to Milford, Massachusetts, where he was employed for a time by Captain Barker, and was also engaged in the hat manufacturing business. Going from Milford to Worcester he was employed in the Monroe Organ-Reed Factory for about one year and a half. After making a prolonged visit to his parents he went to Minnesota, in 1873, and spent a year at Medford, that state, in the employ of Le Roy Fowler, a relative. Returning to Chesterfield he purchased his father's lumber mill, which he carried on alone and also with a partner for some time, and in July, 1884, he went to Ashuelot, where he resided five years, during which time he acquired a good knowledge of the box manufacturing business. He next leased of Elisha Munsell a box manufactory at Swanzey Factory, which he operated successfully for three years, and going to Keene at the expiration of that time he engaged in manufacturing what is known as lock-corner boxes at Beaver Mills. In 1904 he established a box manufactory at Keene which was auspiciously inaugurated in a large brick structure two hundred and twenty-four by sixty feet, erected on Island street by Mr. Fowler for that purpose and employing in the neighborhood of seventy operatives. This is now a leading industry of Keene. As a Republican Mr. Fowler has served in the common council, 1897, and on the board of aldermen, and in 1898 and '99 he represented Keene in the lower branch of the state legislature, serving on the committee on manufactures. His fraternal affiliations are with the Masonic Order. He attends the First Congregational Church.

He married (first), September 11, 1876, Ella M. Carpenter, who died May 25, 1887, a daughter, Nellie Maria, born of this marriage, died in May, 1887. His second wife, whom he married February 3, 1892, was Medella Byam. Of this union there are two children: Fred H., born January 2, 1893; and Grace E., February 25, 1896.

HARDY In all probability some man received the epithet of "the Hardy" on account of his bold and resolute demeanor, and in course of time the word which was intended to describe him became his surname and that of his descendants. That this name has not been a misnomer in the case of the Hardys, of Andover, Massachusetts, from whom are sprung the Hardys of this article, is evident from the fact that in one company of soldiers from Andover, that of Captain Benjamin Farnum, a reinforcement to the army near Boston, February, 1776, Eliphalet Hardy was first lieutenant, and five others of the name were privates at the same time. In the same year another member of the Andover family was in Colonel Wigglesworth's regiment, at Albany.

(I) Thomas Hardy, founder of a numerous family, born about 1605, arrived in America in 1633 and was one of the founders of Ipswich, Massachusetts, being among the first twelve who settled there. In 1653 he removed to Bradford, Massachusetts, and aided in forwarding that junior settlement. He died there January 4, 1678, at the age of seventy-two years. His first wife, Lydia, who probably accompanied him from England, was the mother of all his children. His second wife, Ann, survived him more than eleven years and died May 1, 1689. (Mention of his son John and descendants appears in this article).

(II) Thomas (2), eldest child of Thomas Hardy (1), was born in Ipswich or Bradford, about 1650, and resided in the latter town, where he died in 1716. The baptismal name of his wife was Ruth, but there is no record of her family name. She was the mother of his first child. He married (second), Mercy Tenney, who joined the church November 4, 1694, and died in 1716 at Bradford. His children included Thomas, William, James, Ebenezer, Isaac, Hannah and Sarah. The last three were baptized August 26, 1695. (Mention of William and descendants forms part of this article).

(III) Thomas (3), eldest child of Thomas (2) and Ruth Hardy, was born April 2, 1675, and was baptized June 17, 1683. He resided on a farm in Bradford and there passed his entire life. He joined the church there June 26, 1721. He married, January 4, 1722, Martha Hardy, daughter of Joseph and Mary Hardy, born February 17, 1701. Their children were: Gideon, Reuben, Phineas, Ebenezer, Isaac, Phoebe, Martha and Ann.

(IV) Phinehas, third son and child of Thomas (3) and Martha (Hardy) Hardy, was born July 11, 1726, in Bradford, and settled in Hollis, New Hampshire, where he was one of the earliest residents. His name is first found on the tax list of that town in 1752. He was a soldier in the garrison at Portsmouth in 1776, as were four of his sons. He died at Hollis, March 17, 1713, at the age of eighty-six years. He was married at Haverhill, Massachusetts, in May, 1749, to Abigail Gage, of that town. Their children were: Elizabeth, Martha, Phineas, Thomas, Nathan, Jesse, Isaac, Moses and Solomon. (Mention of Jesse and descendants appears in this article).

(V) Phineas (2), eldest son of Phineas (1) and Abigail (Gage) Hardy, went from Bradford to Hollis, New Hampshire, as early as 1752, and cleared a farm from the wilderness. The christian name of his wife was Abigail. He was the father of four sons: Jesse, Phineas, Jr., Noah and Thomas. At the breaking out of the war for national independence he entered the army, and in 1776-77 did garrison duty at Portsmouth, Rhode Island. His four sons were also enrolled in the Continental army.

(VI) Deacon Noah, son of Phineas and Abigail Hardy, was reared to farm life, and upon his return from the army he resumed that useful calling. He removed from Hollis to Nelson, New Hampshire, where he resided for many years, and his last days were spent with a daughter in Antrim, this state. His death occurred December 21, 1835. His wife, who was before marriage Sarah Spofford, died May 9, 1850, aged eighty-five years. His children were: Noah, Betsey, Sally, David, Hannah H., Silas and Lois. Sally became the wife of David Ames, of Hancock, and went to reside in Charlotte, New York. Hannah H. married Benjamin M. Buckminster, in 1819, and died at Antrim-in 1848. Lois became the wife of Henry Kelsey, and died in Newport, New Hampshire.

(VII) Noah, eldest child of Deacon Noah and Sarah (Spofford) Hardy, was born in Nelson, September 16, 1789. He resided on the old homestead farm and followed agriculture until about 1825, when he suffered the loss of one of his lower limbs. He nevertheless continued his activity by taking up the trade of shoemaking, and exercised a general oversight in the management of the farm. He died in Nelson, November 28, 1862. He married Jerusha Kimball, born in Nelson, August 13, 1790, and died there January 11, 1854. The children of this union are: Augustus F., Sylvander W., George G., Abbie M., Noah W, Charles, Caroline M., Silas, Franklin B. and Ezra P.

(VIII) Judge Silas, sixth son and eighth child of Noah and Jerusha (Kimball) Hardy, was born in Nelson, April 3, 1827. Having studied preliminarily in the public schools, he prepared for a collegiate course at the Marlow, New Hampshire, Academy, and was graduated at Dartmouth College with the class of 1855. After teaching school for a year in Foxcroft, Maine, he became a law student at Keene in the office of Levi Chamberlain, under whose preceptorship he remained two years, and he was admitted to the bar in 1858. Since entering the legal profession he has transacted a profitable general law business in Keene, covering a period of nearly half a century, and is still in active practice, being at the present time one of the oldest as well as one of the ablest lawyers in the state. From 1859 to 1864 he served as register of probate; was judge of probate from the latter year to 1874; was a member of the school board for some time; was an alderman in 1884; city solicitor two or three terms; represented Keene in the constitutional convention in 1876 and in the lower branch of the state legislature for the years 1900-01. In his younger days he was an Old Line Whig in politics, but he has supported the Republican party continuously from the time of its formation in 1856. His activities have by no means been confined exclusively to legal and civic affairs, as he has identified himself with most of the public and semi-public institutions of Keene, giving them the benefit of his business ability and sound judgment. He was formerly president of the Cheshire Mutual Fire Insurance Company, and has dealt quite extensively in real estate. Judge Hardy is president of the Winchester, New Hampshire, National Bank. In his religious belief he is a Unitarian.

On December 31, 1863, Judge Hardy married Josephine M. Kingsley, a graduate of Mount Holyoke Seminary, class of 1857. She died June 19, 1871, leaving one son, Ashley K. Hardy, who is now professor of the German language and literature and instructor in old English at Dartmouth College. Dr. Ashley K. Hardy married, in June, 1902, Adelaide, daughter of Rev. Sanford, near Meriden, Connecticut.

(V) Jesse, fourth son and sixth child of Phineas and Abigail Hardy, was born in Hollis, December 19, 1760. He was with his father and three older brothers in the garrison at Portsmouth in the Revolution, and was also one of the sixteen men from Hollis for West Point, who were enlisted in Captain William Barron's company of Colonel Nichol's regiment. He enrolled July 6, 1780, and was discharged October 22, following, after serving three months and sixteen days at £134 per month, with travel allowance of 6s per mile. He married (first), January 3, 1788, Rebekah Bayley; married (second), Rhoda Wood. By the first wife he had two daughters Rebekah and Martha; and by the second wife seven sons: Jesse, Joel, Amos, Eli, Luther, Phineas and Daniel.

(VI) Amos, third son and child of Jesse and Rhoda (Wood) Hardy, was born August 12, 1797, and died in 1881. He was a farmer, and lived in the northern part of town. He commanded the respect and confidence of his townsmen, and was a member of the board of selectmen in 1844-45-46. For many years he was a member of the Congregationalist Church. He married Mary Cummings, born April 2, 1800, daughter of Thomas and Mary Cummings. They had seven children: Francis A., Daniel, Harriette, Edward, William, Horrace and George.

(VII) Edward, third son and fourth child of Amos and Mary (Cummings) Hardy, was born in Hollis, August 6, 1825. After attending the common schools for a time he learned the cooper's trade, and worked at that at Hollis, continuing the business until about 1880. He employed from ten to fifteen men and made pork and beef barrels. In 1880 he bought the farm of one hundred and thirty acres, where he now resides, in the east part of Hollis. Mr. Hardy is a Democrat in politics, and has held the offices of town treasurer and member of the board of selectmen. He is a leading member of Hollis Grange, Patrons of Husbandry, of which he has served as master and twenty-one years as treasurer. He married, November 5, 1850, Louisa M. Wheeler, born in Hollis, March 12, 1827, daughter of James and Dorcas (Moore) Wheeler, of Hollis. She died September 20, 1881. One son was born to them, Charles E., the subject of the next paragraph.

(VIII) Charles E., only child of Edward and Louisa M. (Wheeler) Hardy, was born in Hollis, September 26, 1857, and was educated at Hollis and McGaw Institute, Mont Vernon. He carries on his father's farm and is largely engaged in dairying. He is now a member of the board of education. He was a member of the legislature, 1897, was master of the Hollis Grange two years, is past grand of Amom Lodge, Independent Order of Odd Fellows, of Hollis and secretary and treasurer of the Mutual Fire Insurance Company, of Hollis. He also has extensive interests in Old Mexico. Mrs. Hardy was one of the organizers of the Anna Keyes Powers Chapter, Daughters of American Revolution, of Hollis, and a charter member of the Relief Corps, Grand Army of the Republic. She joined the Hollis Congregational Church when sixteen years of age and has been active in church work for many years. He married, February 20, 1879, Nellie L. Cameron, of Hollis, November 30, 1854, daughter of Henry G. and Rosanna B. (Willoughby) Cameron, of Hollis. They had three children: Edward Cameron, born March 14, 1884, died November 2, 1885. Harold E., born March 20, 1887, now a student in the New Hampshire College of Agriculture and Mechanic Arts. Louisa, born December 9, 1890, now attending the Hollis high school.

(III) William, son of Thomas and Mary (Tenney) Hardy, was born January 11, 1669, in Bradford, where he made his home. His wife's name was Sarah, but no record of their marriage appears in Bradford. Their children were: Sarah, William, Anne, Thomas, Edmund and Susannah.

(IV) Thomas (3), second son and fourth child of William and Sarah Hardy, was born December 14, 1695, in Bradford, and died there "middle aged" December 19, 1736. He was married May 14, 1719, at the First Church in Bradford.

[illegible] Hardy.

January 3, 1788, Rebekah Bayley; married (second), Rhoda Wood. By the first wife he had two

aged December 19, 1736. He was married May 14, 1719, at the First Church in Bradford.

Silas Hardy.

to Deborah Wallingford, who was born in June, 1701, daughter of James and Deborah Wallingford. Their children included Amos, Jonas, Oliver, Rose, Esther, Ezekiel, James and Deborah. There is a tradition that he married the daughter of an Indian chief, by whom he had two children, but this does not seem to be borne out by the records. It is said that some of his descendants displayed marked Indian characteristics.

(V) Jonas, second son and child of Thomas (3) and Deborah (Wallingford) Hardy, was born October 19, 1721, in Bradford, and passed his life in that town, where he died. There is no record in that town of his marriage or death and it is possible that he died in some other place. It appears that his children lived elsewhere, and it is probable that he died at the home of one of these, in New Hampshire.

(VI) Jonas (2), son of Jonas (1) Hardy, was born about 1750 in Bradford, according to family tradition, but no record of his birth appears in that town. He was a private in the Second Foot Company of Bradford, which marched to the defence of Cape Ann, November 30, 1775, under command of Captain John Savory. He died May 13, 1833, in Lebanon, New Hampshire, in his eighty-third year. He resided for some time in what is now Hudson, in Chester, New Hampshire, whence he perhaps removed to Lebanon. Very little concerning the history of his life can now be discovered. He was married in Bradford, August 5, 1773, to Molly Hardy, and was married (second) in February, 1780, in the same town, to Mehitable Hardy.

(VII) Daniel, son of Jonas (2) and Mehitable (Hardy) Hardy, was born in 1782, perhaps in Stoddard, New Hampshire. He lived at Hebron, this state, and at Hyde Park, Vermont, but he is most closely identified with Lebanon, New Hampshire, where the greater part of his mature life was spent. He was a merchant and farmer, and was a self made man of great energy of character. He belonged to the Baptist Church in Lebanon, and brought up his large family according to strict religious principles. Daniel Hardy married Betsey Packard, who was born in Enfield, New Hampshire, and they had a family of fifteen children, of whom five died in infancy or early childhood. The ten who lived to grow up were: 1. Laura. 2. Orinda, married Solomon Heater. 3. Ichabod P., whose sketch follows. 4. Caroline. 5. Julia. 6. Almeda. 7. Rev. Daniel, married Sarah Page. 8. Matilda, married Gardner Briggs. 9. Edwin, whose twin, Edna, was drowned when three years old. 10. Rev. Anthony Colby, married Eliza Martin. The mother of this family was a great reader, and to her is doubtless due in considerable measure the literary tendencies of her descendants. Of the ten children just mentioned, two of the sons became clergymen, Rev. Daniel belonging to the Methodist Church, and Rev. Anthony C., the Methodist and later the Episcopal; and two of the daughters, Laura and Julia, married Methodist ministers. Laura Hardy married Rev. Jonas Scott, an old time exhorter, and was herself gifted in writing and speaking at meetings. Julia Hardy married Rev. Charles Lovejoy, and moved to Kansas, where they endured thrilling experiences in Free-Soil times. She wrote Anti-Slavery articles for the *New Hampshire Statesman* and the *Lebanon Free Press*, and also for western papers. Some of her statements aroused such bitter feeling that she was forced to hide all night in cornfields at the time of Quantrell's Raid. Almeda, who married Noah Barden Stoddard, and lived at Hanover, also wrote for the papers; and Caroline married Horace Hoyt, and became the mother of Horace F. Hoyt, for many years commissioner of Grafton county. Daniel Hardy, the father, died at the home of his son Daniel at Hyde Park, Vermont, during the winter of 1869; and his wife died at the old homestead about 1856.

(VIII) Ichabod Packard, eldest son and third child of Daniel and Betsey (Packard) Hardy, was born July 5, 1808, in Lebanon. He was educated at the old New Hampton Institution, and lived in Groton, Rumney, Lebanon and Hebron, again at Groton, New Hampshire, and was engaged in farming, lumbering and general mercantile traffic. He was a man active in business, eager to promote the public weal, and always ready to help the needy by giving them employment. He was a member of the Christian Church, and his hospitable home was always open to visiting brethren. Large family parties also were in the habit of driving up without warning, and they never failed to find a warm welcome and abundance of good cheer. It was a house where relatives and strangers alike were made to feel at home, and an extra plate at the table was a matter of course. Mr. Hardy was a man of progressive ideas, helped to establish schools in his town, and was one of the earliest members of the Republican party. He died at Groton, New Hampshire, March 17, 1887. On February 2, 1836, at Rumney, Ichabod Packard Hardy married Emeline Mary Webster, daughter of David and Lucy (Hutchins) Webster, who was born at Rumney, New Hampshire, May 1, 1815. (See Webster, VI). Mrs. Hardy, who is still living in her ninety-third year, is a woman of remarkable activity, and does needle-work of exquisite fineness without glasses. She is a granddaughter of Captain Gordon Hutchins, one of the three men from Concord, New Hampshire, who commanded a company at the battle of Bunker Hill. He died the year she was born, and ninety years later she visited his grave at Concord. Emeline (Webster) Hardy was educated at South Parsonfield, Maine, and in early life was a successful teacher, instructing the old-time district schools of fifty or sixty scholars. After her marriage she did all the writing in connection with her husband's business, and became an inspiring companion for her children. *The New York Tribune* was a weekly visitor to the home for fifty years, and many other papers and magazines were read by the family. The house was always a stopping place for visiting ministers, some of whom stayed six weeks at a time. Mrs. Hardy was a helpful neighbor withal, and though she had the care of a large household, she was always ready to respond when sick people needed a "watcher," or a family in affliction called on her to "lay out" the dead.

Ichabod Packard and Emeline (Webster) Hardy had five children: Adeline, David Peabody, Lucy Edwina, Emily Sarah and Ellen Selomy (twins). Of this family two died in infancy. Adeline, the eldest child, who was born April 27, 1837, lived but eight days, while Emily Sarah, one of the twins, died two weeks after her birth. The three children who lived to maturity, not only exhibited unusual intelligence and force of character themselves, but have reared families in which these traits became marked to even greater degree.

(IX) David, son of Ichabod Packard Hardy, was born in Groton, New Hampshire, August 21, 1838. He was a blacksmith by trade, and in his later years engaged in agricultural pursuits in connection with his trade. He was a Republican in politics, held the various local town offices, and a man of excellent judgment, honorable and straightforward, filling the same to the satisfaction of all concerned. He was married, May 1, 1859, in that town to Sarah Diantha Fox, who was born November 1, 1840, in Groton, a daughter of David Page and Sally Spaulding (Powers) Fox, and granddaughter of Daniel Fox, who was born April 20, 1774, and died April 13, 1848. David Page Fox was born May 27, 1811, in Hebron, New Hampshire, and died in Orange, same state, October 28, 1865. He was married February 5, 1835, to Sally Spaulding Powers, who was born April 9, 1809, and died in Hill, New Hampshire, July 27, 1899. The children of David P. and Sarah D. (Fox) Hardy were: Nettie Aldonna, Edward Dana, Ellen Emeline, Mary Adeline, Lucy May and Lizzie Webster (twins).

(X) Nettie A., the eldest daughter, graduated from the academy at Monson, Massachusetts, and was a successful teacher. She married Orin Smith of Stowe, Vermont, and with her husband is active in church work.

(X) Edward D. Hardy, the only son, was graduated from the Thayer School of Civil Engineering, Dartmouth College, and has charge of the filtration plant at Washington, D. C. He married Mary Noud of Washington, and they have three children now living.

(X) Ellen Emeline Hardy, the second daughter, married Dr. Clarendon P. Webster, D. D. S., of Franklin, this state. She is a lecturer and writer, and has made a specialty of ornithology, contributing to the *New York Times* and other journals. She has been president of the Woman's Club at Franklin, and has given stereopticon lectures on her travels and other subjects before different clubs in the state.

(X) Lucy May, daughter of David Peabody and Sarah Diantha (Fox) Hardy, was born August 11, 1872 in Hebron, New Hampshire. She was educated in the village school, formerly known as Hebron Academy, New Hampton Literary Institution and Commercial College, from which she was graduated, and the Ladies' Boarding School at Bishop Hopkins Hall, Burlington, Vermont, which she attended one year, receiving one of the Webb and Vanderbilt prizes. She was married in Hebron, October 1, 1902, to Elbert David Currier, of Andover, New Hampshire (see Currier, III). After marriage she went to Franklin to reside, and with her husband became a member of the Village Congregational Church in Franklin, and was also a member of the Missionary Society and the Ladies' Aid Society connected with the church, and has served as soprano singer and chorister in different choirs in the city. In winter of 1906-07 she was prominent in organizing the Franklin Choral Society, and was elected its secretary. Her vocal instruction covered a period of several years, studying with C. S. Conant, of Concord, New Hampshire, and later going to Boston Fortnightly during winters of 1904-1906 to complete her study. She was a prominent and enthusiastic member of the Audubon Society, and served her turn as secretary and acquired considerable knowledge in bird-lore. Since 1902 she has been a member of the Franklin Woman's Club, contributing her part in literary and musical work. In 1907 she was elected as its president.

(X) Lizzie Hardy became the wife of Elihu Sanborn, of Contoocook, this state, and is a leader in musical affairs in churches of that town.

(IX) Lucy Edwina Hardy, second surviving child of Ichabod P. and Emeline (Webster) Hardy, born July 26, 1840, graduated at the age of fifteen from the classical course at Kimball Union Academy, Meriden, this state. She taught school at Tilton Seminary and Meriden, New Hampshire, and was then married to Professor George I. Cummings, of Harvard University, Washington, D. C. Their only daughter, Lucy Webster Cummings, was graduated from Wellesley College in 1897 (June), was educated in music at Washington, D. C., and married Henry Coburn Sanborn, of Webster, New Hampshire, who was graduated from Dartmouth College, studied in Germany and is now superintendent of schools at Danvers, Massachusetts.

(IX) Ellen Selomy Hardy, third surviving child of Ichabod P. and Emeline (Webster) Hardy, was born at Rumney, New Hampshire, March 2, 1844, and married Rev. Henry P. Lamprey, of Concord, New Hampshire (see Lamprey, VII).

(II) John, son of Thomas (1) and Lydia Hardy, was born 1638, in Ipswich, Massachusetts, and spent most of his life in Bradford. He married, April 2, 1666, Mary Jackman, who died December 2, 1689. The name of his second wife was Martha, but a record of the marriage has not been found.

(III) Joseph, son of John and Mary (Jackman) Hardy, was born February 3, 1674, in Bradford, and lived in that town. He married, April 6, 1698, Mary Burbank, born November 26, 1675, in Rowley, Massachusetts, a daughter of Caleb and Martha (Smith) Burbank (see Burbank, II).

(IV) James, son of Joseph and Mary (Burbank) Hardy, was born April 14, 1699, in Bradford. His early life was passed in Bradford, and he subsequently spent some time in Tewksbury and late in life removed to Andover, Massachusetts. He married, July 4, 1727, Hannah Bailey.

(V) James (2), son of James (1) and Hannah (Bailey) Hardy, was born 1742, probably in Bradford, and lived throughout his adult life in Andover, where he built a house. He died there March 7, 1825. He married Jemima Palmer, daughter of Andrew Palmer, of Andover.

(VI) Benjamin, son of James (2) and Jemima (Palmer) Hardy, was born 1768, in Andover, Massachusetts, and died in Greenfield, New Hampshire, in 1852, aged eighty-four years. In 1779 he removed from Andover to Greenfield, where he purchased a farm, still owned and occupied by his descendants. His original home was the usual log cabin of the time, and his clearing was about sixty acres. He married, November 10, 1794, Phoebe Dane, of a prominent Andover family. She was born 1767, a daughter of William and Mary Osgood Dane. Her brother, William Dane, was a veteran of the Revolutionary war. A daughter of the latter married Samuel Baldwin, of Amherst and Mont Vernon. The children of Benjamin and Phoebe (Dane) Hardy were: John Dane, Benjamin, Hermon, Phoebe, Betsy, Hiram and Hannah.

(VII) Hiram, fourth son and sixth child of Benjamin and Phoebe (Dane) Hardy, was born July 6, 1806, in Greenfield, and died February, 1866, at his native place. He succeeded his father in the occupancy and ownership of the homestead, to which he made additions until it included two hundred and seventy acres. He was an extensive fruit grower and stock raiser. He was a gold seeker, going to California in 1853 and returning in 1857. He was fond of music, and from the age of twelve years until the disbanding of the militia he played the fife in that organization. He was not a member, but attended the Congregational Church. Being deeply interested in public questions, he became a leader of the Democratic party in his town. He held various town offices, was overseer of the poor, selectman a number of times, and representative in the general court in 1865. He married (first) Abigail Dodge, and they had two children: Frances and Charles. He married (second) Maria Dodge, of Greenfield, sister of his first wife, who was born in 1817, and died October, 1893. They were the daughters of Levi and Keziah (Stanley) Dodge, their father being a Revolutionary soldier, and an aide on General Gates' staff. Their children were: Sidney Hiram, Sarah Abigail and Levi Bradley. Sarah A. married Albert H. Hopkins, of Medford, Massachusetts, and has three children: Bertham A., a physician; George W. and Lilian Gertrude.

(VIII) Sidney Hiram, first son and eldest child of Hiram and Maria (Dodge) Hardy, was born in Greenfield, February, 1840. He prepared for college at Kimball Academy, from which he graduated with the class of 1865, and in the autumn of the same year entered Dartmouth College, intending to pursue the scientific course there, but the death of his father obliged him to leave college after he had attended one term. He has always had a fondness for mathematics, in which he excels. Until two years ago he alone carried on the farm, which the brothers now cultivate together. They have two hundred acres of land, raise considerable stock, and do some lumbering. They have an excellent orchard which yields as high as five hundred barrels of apples a year. They pay but slight attention to politics, but vote the Democratic ticket. They attend the Congregational Church.

(VIII) Levi Bradley, second child of Hiram and Maria (Dodge) Hardy, was born in Greenfield, August 31, 1850. He attended high school and Francestown Academy, and is a carpenter and electrician by trade. From 1886 to 1902 he worked at carpentering in Medford, Massachusetts. Since the latter date he has resided on the old homestead. He is a member of Mont Vernon Lodge, No. 186, Independent Order of Odd Fellows, of Medford.

HARDY One hundred Hardys are enumerated among the revolutionary soldiers and sailors of Massachusetts. Persons of this name came early to New Hampshire, and the family was well represented among the sons of the Granite State who fought in the revolution. Deacon Noah Hardy was a revolutionary soldier, and afterward lived in Hollis, Nelson and Antrim. Benjamin Hardy, of Andover, Massachusetts, settled in Greenfield in 1800.

(I) John Hardy was born in Goffstown, and was drowned while attempting to cross the Piscataquog river on a ferry boat. He married Betsy George, who was born in Goffstown and died in Manchester.

(II) Rodney, son of John and Betsy (George) Hardy, was born in Goffstown and died in Hooksett, January, 1876. He was a farmer, but for forty years he was employed as a dyer in the cotton mills. He moved to Hooksett, and spent the remainder of his life there, being employed in the mills for many years, and was sixty-three years old when he died. He married Esther Ayer, who was born in Goffstown, in 1813, and is now (1907) living at the age of ninety-four. They had five children: Ira C., died July, 1905; Rodney; Esta; Elizabeth, who married George Harwood; and John, whose sketch follows.

(III) John, youngest child of Rodney and Esta (Ayer) Hardy, was born in Manchester, March 23, 1845, and has carried on farming for about forty years, and shoemaking fifteen years. He is a Republican in politics, and is a member of the Congregational Church. He married Lydia E. Dow, who was born in Goffstown, June 23, 1847, daughter of Samuel and Lydia (Black) Dow, of Goffstown. Four children were born by this union: Helen, Scott E., Louis J. and Bertha D.

SALTMARSH (I) The name of Saltmarsh is of good old English origin and repute. The first American ancestor was Captain Thomas Saltmarsh, who was born in England, where he was captain in the royal navy. There is a tradition not positively authenticated that he was the son of Captain William Saltmarsh who commanded the ship "Larke," of the royal navy, and who at one time went to the West Indies in the "Jersey." Captain William Saltmarsh died May 28, 1691. Captain Thomas Saltmarsh came to America in the early part of the eighteenth century and settled in Charlestown, Massachusetts. He married Mary Hazen, daughter of Richard and Mary (Peabody) Hazen, of Boxford, Massachusetts. They lived in Charlestown, where their two eldest children were baptized—Mary on June 6, 1731, and Elizabeth on June 10, 1733. About 1734 Thomas Saltmarsh moved to Watertown, Massachusetts, where he was an inn-keeper till 1769. He was constable in 1743; assessor 1741, 1742 and 1745. In 1769 he married a second wife, Mrs. Anne (Stone) Jones, widow of Abijah Stone, and daughter of John Jones of Framingham. He had ten children, all by his first wife. It is probable that the eight younger were born in Watertown. They were: William, born January 20, 1734-35; Thomas, mentioned below; John, born November 29, 1738; Abigail, born May 9, 1740; Deborah, born September 18, 1742; Catherine, born November 2, 1744; Seth, born December 4, 1746; Isaac, born July 28, 1748. William Saltmarsh, the eldest son, was a lieutenant under Captain Jonathan Brown at Lake George in 1758. He married, December 9, 1780, Elizabeth Patterson, and settled on the Susquehanna river, below Owego, New York, where he died at an advanced age. They had eleven children: Alanson, the fifth of these children, was born October 8, 1794. He studied medicine in Vermont, and finally became a wealthy planter at Cahawba, Alabama. He married, May 4, 1826, Mary Ann Beck, eldest daughter of John and Margaret (King) Beck. Mrs. Beck was a sister of Hon. William B. King, vice-president of the United States.

(II) Thomas, second son and fourth child of Captain Thomas and Mary (Hazen) Saltmarsh, was born March 2, 1736-37, probably in Watertown. He married Betsey Abbott, daughter of Edward and Dorcas (Chandler) Abbott, of Concord, New Hampshire. Edward Abbott was one of the original proprietors of that town, and was a grandson of George, who settled at Andover, Massachusetts, in 1743. Betsey Abbott was born August 25, 1743; she married Thomas Saltmarsh in 1759, and she died in 1837 at the age of eighty-four. Her husband died in 1827, in his ninetieth year. They lived in Goffstown, New Hampshire. They had nine children: Mehitable, born in 1762, married James Hoit in 1784, and died in 1814; John, born 1764, at Goffstown, New Hampshire, married Susan Burnham, born 1754; Polly, born 1756, married in 1791, Samuel Vose, born in 1759, at Antrim, New Hampshire; Edward A., mentioned below; Thomas, born 1771, became a physician at Saco, Maine, married Betsey Evans, and died in 1804; Sally, born 1773; Samuel.

born 1775, married Betsey Burnum, born 1780, who died in 1840, he died in 1844 at Goffstown, New Hampshire; Catherine, born 1777, married Thomas Saltmarsh, born 1774, at Gilford, New Hampshire; Isaac, born 1779, married Phebe Stratton, died in 1822, at Antrim, New Hampshire.

(III) Edward Abbott, second son and fourth child of Thomas and Betsey (Abbott) Saltmarsh, was born in 1768, probably in Goffstown, New Hampshire. He married, in 1791, Sally Story, born in 1763. Her father, Nehemiah Story, was a sea captain, and at the time of the Revolution went out as a privateer, and captured several English vessels. He was drowned after the war was over while coming from the East Indies with a cargo of molasses. He owned a gold brooch set with topazes, sapphires and diamonds, probably taken from a captured vessel. This is now in the possession of his great-great-grandson, Rev. Frank N. Saltmarsh, of Alton, New Hampshire. Edward A. and Sally (Story) Saltmarsh had thirteen children: Nehemiah, born 1792, died in the army at Plattsburg, New York, 1813; Aaron, born at Hooksett, New Hampshire, in 1793, married Joan George, and died in 1842; Abbott, Lucy, Betsey, Thomas, Henry, Hazen, Susan, Gilman, Franklin, Sally, Abigail. Mrs. Sally (Story) Saltmarsh died May 19, 1860, aged ninety-seven years.

(IV) Abbott, third child of Edward A. and Sally (Story) Saltmarsh, was born in Goffstown, New Hampshire, November 10, 1795. He lived in Goffstown in his youth, then carried on at the halves the farm of Retire Mitchell, a preacher at Hooksett, New Hampshire. Abbott Saltmarsh later moved to Bow, New Hampshire, where he lived about five years; then lived at West Concord and East Concord, New Hampshire, and came back to West Concord, where he died. When he was living at Bow, he was one of the first in the town who voted the Free Soil ticket. He married, March 12, 1823, Polly Stevens, daughter of John and Lois (Buzzell) Stevens, of Croydon, New Hampshire, who was born June 5, 1803. They had eleven children: Mary, married Captain Albert Abbott, and lived in Concord, New Hampshire; John E., married Abigail D. Abbott, and lived in Concord; Gilman, mentioned below; Hannah, born February 18, 1831, died September 4, 1833; an infant son, born June 23, 1833, died July 24, 1833; Seth, married Sally S. Wales, and lived in Loudon, New Hampshire, and had five children—Alfred, S. Leroy, Minnie, Frank and Albert; Nehemiah, born May 17, 1837, died August, 1897; Alfred and Albert (twins), born February 18, 1840, Alfred died November 23, 1851, Albert is mentioned at length in this article; Amanda, married Luther D. Jones, and lived in Concord; and Emma, born December 1, 1845. Gilman, the third child, and Harriet (Robertson) Saltmarsh had four children: Martha Alice, George Abbott, Harriet Amanda and Frank Nehemiah. All of them taught school. The two sons graduated from college, both of them being Phi Beta Kappa men. George A., graduated from Dartmouth College in 1884, and from the Boston Law School in 1887. He was admitted to the bar in Massachusetts, and is a lawyer in Boston. Frank N. graduated from Dartmouth College in 1893, and from Andover Theological Seminary in 1897. He preached at West Hartford, Vermont, for six years, and in 1903 came to Alton, New Hampshire, where he now ministers to the Congregational Church. Amanda Saltmarsh, ninth child of Abbott and Polly (Stevens) Saltmarsh, married Luther D. Jones. They had two children: Emma A., and Statie. Emma A. Jones married Dr. Marshall Bailey, formerly of Concord, New Hampshire, now physician to Harvard University. Statie married Charles C. Jones, who is employed in the University Press, Cambridge, Massachusetts. Abbott Saltmarsh married for his second wife Mrs. Lois (Stevens) Kempton, widow of Amos Kempton, of Newport, New Hampshire, sister to his first wife. He died January 25, 1876.

(V) Gilman Saltmarsh, third child of Abbott and Polly (Stevens) Saltmarsh, was born in Hooksett, New Hampshire, December 7, 1828. In early manhood he went to Bow and engaged in farming and lumbering, and has ever since resided there. He was for many years an earnest member of the Methodist Episcopal Church, in which he was a local preacher. In politics he is a Republican. He married, in Bow, July 1, 1853, Harriet Emeline Robertson, who was born in Bow, March 26, 1831, daughter of Daniel R. and Harriet (Lawrence) Robertson, of Bow. They have had four children: 1. Martha Alice, unmarried, resides in Concord. 2. George Abbott, mentioned below. 3. Harriet Amanda, unmarried, resides in Bow. 4. Frank Nehemiah, graduated from Dartmouth College in 1893, and from Andover Theological Seminary in 1897. He preached at West Hartford, Vermont, six years, and in 1903 removed to Alton, New Hampshire, where he ministered to the Congregational Church until 1907, and then removed to Gilmanton, New Hampshire. All of the above-mentioned children taught in the New Hampshire schools.

(VI) George Abbott, eldest son and second child of Gilman and Harriet Emeline (Robertson) Saltmarsh, was born in Bow, October 18, 1858. He attended the public schools of Bow and Concord, the seminary at Tilton, took two years private instruction in Concord under the late Amos Hadley, Ph. D., and then entered Dartmouth College, from which he graduated with honors, receiving the degree of A. B. in 1884. He entered the Boston University Law School in 1885, and obtained the degree of B. L. on graduation in 1887. He was immediately afterward admitted to the Suffolk bar and in 1906 to the New Hampshire bar. He was for a time librarian of the Boston Bar Association. He opened an office in Boston soon after his admission to the bar, and ever since then has been engaged in the general practice of his profession, in which he has found success and in which he finds an ever widening field of labor and constantly increasing remuneration. He was for ten years associated in practice with Sherman L. Whipple, one of the most eminent attorneys of the New England bar, and now in connection with his Boston office at No. 18 Tremont street, has an office in Concord, New Hampshire, with John M. Stark. For a number of years he resided in Everett, but since 1900 has made his home in Winchester, with a summer home near Concord, where the family reside several months in the year. He is an attendant of the Congregational Church. He is a member of Palestine Lodge, of Everett, Massachusetts, Royal Arch Chapter, Commandery, Knights Templar, and of the Massachusetts Consistory, of Boston, where he attained the thirty-second degree.

Mr. Saltmarsh married, in Everett, Massachusetts, 1890, N. Gertrude Soulee, who was born in Boston, Massachusetts, February, 1865, daughter of David A. and Lucy M. (Rogers) Soulee, of Everett, Massachusetts. They have four children: Sherman Whipple, George Abbott, Jr., Lucy Marguerite and Roger Wolcott. Harriet Gertrude died young.

George A. Saltmarsh

(V) Albert, eighth child of Abbott and Polly (Stevens) Saltmarsh, was born February 18, 1840, in Bow, New Hampshire. At the age of thirteen he went to live with Nathan Kilburn Abbott and his sisters on the pleasant farm west of Long Pond, in West Concord, New Hampshire. Nathan K. Abbott was one of the old-time school teachers, having taught for twenty-five years in succession. Mr. Saltmarsh was educated in the district schools. He has always been a reader of good literature, and having a retentive memory is able to quote extensively. Nathan K. Abbott died June 14, 1878, and after his death and that of his sisters, Miss Sally and Miss Lois, Mr. Saltmarsh inherited the farm and other property. In 1883 some friends from the city, attracted by the beauty of the location, begged to come as boarders, and every season since then the house has been full of summer people. Mr. Saltmarsh has an invaluable assistant in his niece, Miss Alice who has acted as his housekeeper for many years. Although living on a farm, Mr. Saltmarsh's chief occupations have been in other lines. He has a strong artistic bent, and he receives orders for crayon portraits from all parts of the state. He is unusually successful in catching the likeness of the subject. His mechanical skill is in demand as a repairer of clocks and watches. In politics he is a Republican. He is one of the best known men in his district, and has held many offices. He has been one of the selectmen, and in 1878-79 he was a member of the common council in Concord, being president of that assembly during the latter year. He was alderman from Ward Three during 1883-84. He was a charter member of Capital Grange, founded in 1886, was the first overseer and second master, and has been chorister for many years. He has taken a prominent part in the dramatic entertainments. He has had much to do with educational work, was on the prudential school committee two terms, and since 1888 has served continuously as a member of the town school board, of which he has been chairman since 1894. He has been justice of the peace for the state since 1896. He has been agent for the Grange Mutual Insurance Company for many years. Mr. Saltmarsh has attended the Congregational Church most of his life. The value of his home has been greatly enhanced of late by the immediate proximity of the summer cottages of the New Hampshire State Hospital. This institution has bought a large estate adjoining Long Pond, and encompassing many of the tributary brooks. The grounds have been laid out with taste and skill and constitute one of the finest examples of landscape gardening in the state.

FLETCHER This name has been known in the United States since 1630, and has been borne by many prominent citizens. The Fletchers have generally been leading people in the communities where they have dwelt The name was originally written Fledger, and was the name of the trade of a maker of arrows, or as some think, of affixing the feather to the arrow—fledging it. The French word Flechier has precisely the same meaning, and some have inferred a French extraction. All the traditions concur, however, in making the early ancestors of this family of English or Welsh stock, and Yorkshire, one of the northern countries of England, is named as the spot whence they emigrated to America. The name has been and still is common there. Rev. Elijah Fletcher, of Hopkinton, New Hampshire, born 1747, died 1786, the first so far as known who made genealogical collections of the family, believed that the great ancestor, Robert Fletcher, came from Yorkshire, and that account was gathered when Robert's great-grandchildren were living.

(I) Robert Fletcher settled at Concord, Massachusetts, in 1630, in which year seventeen ships arrived in Massachusetts Bay and at Plymouth. He had three sons, Luke, William and Samuel, and was himself thirty-eight years of age. Concord, the twentieth town incorporated in Massachusetts, was organized in 1635, and his name appears in the earliest records of that town. In the court files of Middlesex county his name frequently occurs as a petitioner for bridges, as juryman, etc. He became a wealthy and influential man, and died at Concord, April 3, 1677, aged eighty-five. His children were: Luke, William, Samuel, Francis and Cary. (Mention of Francis and William, and descendants, appears in this article.)

(II) William, second son of the settler, Robert Fletcher, was born in England, in 1622, and came when eight years of age to Concord, Massachusetts, with his father and his two older brothers. He was admitted freeman, May 10, 1643. In the year 1653 he settled in Chelmsford, Massachusetts, of which he was one of the first inhabitants, and here he was chosen selectman, November 22, 1654. "This first publick meeting was holden at his house." On the court files of Middlesex county his name frequently appears; in 1665, as a petitioner for a road; the same year on a bill of costs for his servant being put in the house of correction, etc. The birth of his daughter Lydia on the Concord records is the first birth of a Fletcher that is recorded in America. His tract of land embraced what is now the city of Lowell. and a part of his land, a farm near the meeting house in Chelmsford, remains as it has been for more than two hundred years in possession of the family, and is now occupied by Gardner Fletcher. He married Lydia Bates, in Concord, October 7, 1645. He died November 6, 1677, and she died October 12, 1704. Their children were: Lydia, Joshua, Mary, Paul, Sarah, William, Esther and Samuel.

(III) Joshua, son of William and Lydia (Bates) Fletcher, was born March 30, 1648, was admitted freeman, March 11, 1689, and died November 21, 1713. He married (first) Grissies Jewell, May 4, 1668, who died January 16, 1682; married (second) Sarah Willy, July 18, 1682. His children were: Joshua, Paul, Rachel, Timothy, John, Joseph, Sarah, Jonathan, Elizabeth and Jonas. (Mention of Joseph and descendants forms part of this article.)

(IV) Joshua (2), son of Joshua (1) and Grissies (Jewell) Fletcher, was born in Chelmsford. He moved to Westford, Massachusetts, and was the head of the Westford branch of the Fletcher family. All of his sons raised their families in that town, but nearly all his grandchildren removed, and he has no representatives there now. He was a deacon in the church. The gravestones of Joshua and his wife may be seen in the east cemetery in Westford, where they lived and reared their numerous family. He married Dorothy Hale, a native of Scotland. He died October 19, 1732, and she died August 20, 1770. Their children were: Joshua, Gershom, Sarah, Elizabeth, Hannah, Esther, Ephraim, Zachariah, Dorothy, Sarah and Eunice. (Mention of Ephraim and descendants appears in this article.)

(V) Gershom, second son and child of Joshua (2) and Dorothy (Hale) Fletcher, was born July 27, 1702, and died June 28, 1779. He appears to have removed from Westford to Groton, Massachusetts, and then to have returned to Westford. He removed in 1773 to Plymouth, New Hampshire, and thence back to Westford, in 1778, where he died. His gravestone is to be seen in the cemetery in Westford. He married Lydia Townsend, who died June 28, 1779. Their children were: Lydia, Esther, Gershom, Olive, Sarah, Mary, Lucy, Martha and Joshua.

(VI) Joshua (3), ninth and youngest child of Gershom and Lydia (Townsend) Fletcher, was born in Westford, Massachusetts, September 24, 1756, and died at Bridgewater, New Hampshire, August 15, 1829. He was a Congregational minister, and preached more than twenty years. He owned a farm in Plymouth, New Hampshire, where he spent most of his life, and followed farming in connection with his ministry, laboring with his own hands, as it was customary for ministers to do in those times. He was a man greatly beloved by all who knew him. He married, 1775, Sarah Brown, who died in 1854, aged ninety-seven and a half years. Their children were: Joshua, Joseph, Gershom, Nathan, Samuel, William, Asa, Amos, Sarah and Daniel H.

(VII) Joseph, second son and child of Joshua and Sarah (Brown) Fletcher, was born in Plymouth, New Hampshire, in 1778, and died at Campton, January 5, 1824. He was a joiner by trade. He married, December 29, 1802, Betsey Webster, born April 30, 1782, died at Rumney, March 16, 1863. Their children were: Betsey, Arthur, Hannah, Joseph, Moore R., Ruth Webster, Sarah B., William W., Charles and George W.

(VIII) George Washington, sixth son and youngest child of Joseph and Betsey (Webster) Fletcher, was born February 2, 1821, at Campton. He lived from the age of five to nineteen with his brother-in-law, David Cheney, on a farm in Groton, New Hampshire. He was educated in the common schools of Groton and at Hebron Academy. When nineteen years old he went to Lowell, Massachusetts, and worked in the cotton mills a short time. From there he went to Natick and worked in a shoe factory. He was a fellow workman with and later on an employee of Henry Wilson, who later was vice-president of the United States. Mr. Wilson failed in the shoe business and at that time was indebted to Mr. Fletcher in a small sum. About fifteen years later the two met on the street in Boston, when Mr. Wilson reminded Mr. Fletcher of his indebtedness and expressed his pleasure to liquidate it, and handed over the amount due to his creditor. Bad health compelled Mr. Fletcher to seek different employment, and he went to Rumney, New Hampshire, and entered into partnership with his brother-in-law, John L. Dearborn. Here he remained six years. About 1855 he began the manufacture of what were called Plymouth buck gloves. This business he carried on until about 1885. Much of the work was done outside of the factory by women who took the materials to their homes and there made up the gloves. Mr. Fletcher retired from business in 1885, and lived at Rumney till his death, March 11, 1890. He was a man who possessed the confidence of his townsmen, and was sent to the legislature in 1862, 1875 and 1876. He cast his first vote for Democratic candidates, but ever afterward was a staunch Republican. He was a Baptist from 1865, and from 1868 to 1883 was a deacon in the Baker's River Baptist Church at Rumney.

He married, April 20, 1845, Hannah R. Avery, daughter of Nathaniel Avery, of Stratham, born November 2, 1820, and died May 5, 1882. There were two children of this marriage—Ellen Webster, born May 20, 1851, married George P. French, of Rumney, and (second) Rev. George W. Clough, a Baptist clergyman, now located at Windsor, Vermont. The second child is mentioned below.

(IX) George Moore, only son of George W. and Hannah R. (Avery) Fletcher, was born at Rumney, December 19, 1852. He received his literary education in the common school and the New London Literary and Scientific Institution, spending one year at the latter school. At the age of twenty-one he formed a partnership with his father in the manufacture of gloves, which continued five years. August 26, 1878, he began the study of law in the office of Hon. Evarts W. Farr, of Littleton, who that year was elected to congress. Here he spent a year, and then entered the law department of the University of Michigan, where he spent two years, graduating in March, 1881, with the degree of LL. B. The following six months he spent in the office of Frederick Hooker, of Minneapolis, Minnesota. After making a visit of some weeks to North Dakota, he returned to Concord and spent six months in the law office of Bingham & Mitchell. In March, 1883, he was admitted to the bar and has since been in the practice of law in Concord. Mr. Fletcher has been a Republican all his life. He was a member of the New Hampshire house of representatives from ward No. 4 from June, 1889, to January, 1891, being elected while the terms were biennial, and having his term shortened by the operation of the law making terms for one year only. He was a member of the committee on revision of statutes and chairman of the committee on engrossing bills. From April 1, 1897, to April 1, 1901, he was solicitor for Merrimack county. January 1, 1902, he was appointed judge of the police court of Concord and still holds that position (1905). He is a member of the Unitarian Church. A member of Blazing Star Lodge, Ancient Free and Accepted Masons. Judge Fletcher is a man of pleasant manners, makes friends and keeps them, and is therefore popular.

Judge Fletcher married, January 19, 1875, Addie C. Spaulding, daughter of George C. and Annette J. Spaulding. They have three sons: Walter H., born August 8, 1877, a graduate of Dartmouth College, class of 1900, principal of Sanderson Academy, Ashfield, Massachusetts; Robert D. and Richard S., twins, born July 31, 1889, now in school.

(V) Ephraim, third son and seventh child of Deacon Joshua (2) and Dorothy (Hale) Fletcher, was born in Westford, March 12, 1710. He enlisted for service in the French and Indian war, departed for the scene of hostilities and was never heard from. In a list of persons in captivity contained in the Massachusetts Archives (Vol. 74) is the name of Ephraim Fletcher, reported as having been captured by the enemy at Oswego in August, 1756, and as there is no official mention of his return his ultimate fate must forever remain a mystery. The christian name of his wife was Hannah, and his first five children were: Joshua, Peter, Lois, Sarah and Ephraim.

(VI) Peter, second son and child of Ephraim and Hannah Fletcher, was born in Westford, January 22, 1736. About the year 1762 he settled in New Ipswich, New Hampshire, and resided there until his death, which took place April 11, 1812. He was a soldier in the Revolutionary war. September 8, 1761, he married Ruth Adams, who was born January 3, 1739, died April 28, 1816, and she bore him nine children, namely: Dorothy, Ruth,

Sincerely,
Everett Fletcher.

[illegible] David, [illegible] James, who died [illegible] James and Lydia.

[illegible] Fletcher, second son and fourth child [illegible] Rhoda (Avann) Fletcher, was born [illegible] Ipswich, [illegible] 1775. He [illegible] but did not confine him[illegible] setting in [illegible] [illegible] he engaged [illegible] lumber, [illegible] a saw[illegible] number of years. In 1824 he re[illegible] Vermont, and subsequently re[illegible] spent the remainder [illegible] The maiden name of his [illegible] Hiram Adams, [illegible] Ann. [illegible] further men[illegible]

[illegible] Fletcher, second child [illegible] Springfield, Vermont, [illegible] education was acquired [illegible] and at the [illegible] New Hampshire. At the age [illegible] his legal preparations, [illegible] five years his studies [illegible] by Ex-Governor [illegible] Cushman [illegible] New York [illegible] New England and [illegible] town. [illegible] to Lancaster [illegible] was open [illegible] practice with [illegible] the remainder of his life [illegible] thirty years [illegible] of the Coös county bar. [illegible] from a [illegible] death occurred [illegible] professional [illegible] that he commanded [illegible] bar, and that [illegible] by varied [illegible] manifested [illegible] Dr. Benjamin [illegible] death occurred [illegible] February 20, 18[illegible] S. Ladd, of the New Hamp[illegible] Emily Eliza, [illegible] December [illegible] 1, 1857; [illegible] born in [illegible] Richard [illegible] Fifth Regiment, New Hamp[illegible] during the Civil War [illegible] referred to [illegible] married William A. [illegible] of [illegible]

[illegible] Everett, third [illegible] fourth child [illegible] Fletcher, [illegible] December 23, 18[illegible] He was [illegible] Lancaster Academy and the Uni[illegible] and his legal [illegible] were [illegible] of Fletcher & [illegible]wood at [illegible] to the Coös county bar in [illegible] his professional career in Lan[illegible] 57, became associated in practice [illegible] under the name of Fletcher & [illegible] continued in business for [illegible]

years, at the conclusion [illegible] entered into [illegible] S. Ladd, previously [illegible] retired from [illegible] of Ladd & [illegible] senior partner [illegible] was continued [illegible] partnership [illegible] As a lawyer [illegible] to his [illegible] [illegible] was a [illegible] at [illegible] [illegible] the [illegible] only [illegible] made [illegible] quite [illegible] [illegible] and [illegible] Fletcher [illegible] [illegible] was [illegible] 1843 [illegible] had [illegible] here [illegible] learned [illegible]

Sincerely.
Everett Fletcher

Peter, Ebenezer, David, Submit, James, who died young, another James and Lydia.

(VII) Ebenezer, second son and fourth child of Peter and Ruth (Adams) Fletcher, was born (probably) in New Ipswich, May 17, 1770. He was a carpenter by trade but did not confine himself exclusively to that calling, and settling in Charlestown, New Hampshire, in 1808, he engaged in the manufacture of lumber, operating a sawmill there for a number of years. In 1824 he removed to Pittsburg, Vermont, but subsequently returned to the Granite State, and spent the remainder of his life in Colebrook. The maiden name of his wife was Peday Smith. She became the mother of five children: Lucretia Eliza, Hiram Adams, Kimball Batchelder, Mary Hasham and Lucy Ann. (Kimball B. and descendants receive further mention in this article.)

(VIII) Hiram Adams Fletcher, second child and eldest son of Ebenezer and Peday (Smith) Fletcher, was born in Springfield, Vermont, December 14, 1806. His early education was acquired in the public schools and at the Kimball Union Academy, Plainfield, New Hampshire. At the age of nineteen years he began his legal preparations, and during the successive five years his studies were directed at intervals by Ex-Governors Hubbard and Williams, General Cushman and John L. Sheaf. After his admission to the bar in 1832 he spent a year in the office of Thomas Gilman Fletcher in New York City, at the expiration of which time he returned to New England and began the practice of law in his native town. A year later he moved to Colebrook, this state, where he created an extensive general law business, and in 1849 he found it advisable to remove to Lancaster, where a broader field of usefulness was open to him. There he continued to practice with pronounced success for the remainder of his life, and for a period of thirty years was regarded as one of the leading members of the Coos county bar. During his latter years he suffered from a serious pulmonary affection, and his death occurred January 30, 1879. A brief biographical article written by one who was familiar with his character and professional attainments states that he commanded the respect of both the bench and the bar, and that his knowledge of law, augmented by varied and extensive reading, was frequently manifested in court. In May, 1834, Mr. Fletcher married Persis Everett Hunking, daughter of Dr. Benjamin Hunking, of Lancaster, and her death occurred in July, 1878. She was the mother of six children, namely: Almira Barnes, born February 29, 1836, became the wife of Judge William S. Ladd, of the New Hampshire supreme court; Emily Eliza, born December 27, 1838, died January 1, 1857; Richard, born in May, 1840, died young; Richard, born May 16, 1844, served in the Fifth Regiment, New Hampshire Volunteers, during the Civil war; Everett, who will be again referred to; and Lucy Ellen, born January 28, 1855, married William A. Holman, of Pittsburg, Pennsylvania.

(IX) Hon. Everett, third son and fifth child of Hiram A. and Persis E. (Hunking) Fletcher, was born in Colebrook, December 23, 1848. He was educated at the Lancaster Academy and the University of Michigan, and his legal studies were pursued in the office of Fletcher & Heywood at Lancaster. Admitted to the Coos county bar in 1870 he inaugurated his professional career in Lancaster, and in 1873 became associated in practice with his father under the name of Fletcher & Fletcher. The firm continued in business for four years, at the conclusion of which time the junior member entered into partnership with Judge William S. Ladd, previously referred to, who had just retired from the supreme bench, and the law firm of Ladd & Fletcher existed until the death of the senior partner in 1891. The firm name, however, was continued unchanged by the succession to partnership of Fletcher Ladd, a son of the Judge. As a lawyer Mr. Fletcher was a worthy successor to his eminent progenitor and it has been said of him that "as one of the best read lawyers in New Hampshire he could quote from memory more genuine law from the statutes than some practitioners could find in a half-day's search. Moreover he was a man of sound judgment, untiring industry and unquestionable integrity." With these qualifications his practice was necessarily extensive. From 1883 to 1886 he served as judge advocate general upon the staff of Governor Hale, and from the latter year until 1892 served as judge of probate for Coos county. It is worthy of note that only one of his decisions was carried to the supreme court on appeal, and his ruling was sustained by that tribunal. At one time when a vacancy existed on the supreme bench his name was brought forward as a candidate, and had the selection been made from the northern part of the state it is quite probable that he would have received the appointment. In politics he was a Republican, and as a member of the state committee he rendered efficient service to his party. He resigned his office of judge of probate in order to devote his time exclusively to his law business, and his practice was brought to an end by his untimely death, which occurred August 18, 1900. Judge Fletcher was a member of all the Masonic bodies, and a thirty-second degree Mason.

On June 9, 1894, Judge Fletcher was united in marriage with Rose Wentworth Davis, born December 6, 1868, daughter of Osborn Davis, of Biddeford, Maine. She was reared in Jefferson. Mrs. Fletcher married for her second husband William H. Chamberlain and resides in Jefferson.

(VIII) Kimball Batchelder Fletcher, second son and third child of Ebenezer and Peday (Smith) Fletcher, was born in Charlestown, New Hampshire, September 13, 1810. He began the activities of life as a farmer in Pittsburg, New Hampshire, whence he moved to a farm in Canaan, Vermont, and in 1857 removed to Lancaster, New Hampshire, where he died November 4, 1894. He was a Republican in politics and took considerable interest in public affairs, holding some of the important town offices. His first wife, who was before marriage Sarah G. Cummings, bore him three children—Ephraim Sumner, born October 24, 1834; Charles Warren, June 30, 1837; and Frederick Goodhue, December 26, 1842. Kimball Batchelder Fletcher was married for the second time at Lancaster in 1843 to Mrs. Mary (Brown) Copp, a widow, who had two daughters by her previous marriage. She bore him two children: Kimball Brown, who will be again referred to; and Mary, who was born December 4, 1851, and died September 26, 1864. Mr. Fletcher's second wife died September 9, 1864, and for his third wife he married, in November, 1865, Mary M. Freeman, of Guildhall, Vermont.

(IX) Kimball Brown, only son of Kimball B. and Mary (Brown-Copp) Fletcher, was born in Canaan, Vermont, November 27, 1849. After the conclusion of his studies in the Lancaster public schools he entered as an apprentice, August 6, 1866, the shops of Thompson, Williams & Company, and learned the machinist's trade. July 5, 1870, he went into the employ of the Grand Trunk railroad in repair shops at Gorham, New Hampshire. November, 1873, he went to Susquehanna Depot, Pennsylvania, in the employ of the Erie railway as machinist on locomotive repairs, but in September, 1874, he returned to Lancaster, New Hampshire. October 9, 1874, he formed the partnership of A. Thompson & Company, and at the death of Mr. Thompson, 1882, the firm name was changed to Thompson Manufacturing Company. That concern was reorganized and incorporated in 1892, and with the exception of a short time spent in Nashua and Boston, Mr. Fletcher has devoted his energies to its welfare and development. He was for eighteen years treasurer of the above company, and at the last annual meeting was chosen president. Mr. Fletcher is a thirty-second degree Mason, being a member of North Star Lodge, chapter and commandery, Lancaster, of Edward A. Raymond Consistory, Nashua. He participates quite actively in religious work, and is chairman of the executive committee of the Congregational Church. He married, November 24, 1880, Nellie Hobson, daughter of S. D. Hobson, of Island Pond, Vermont, and has two children, Esther M. and Robert H.

(IV) Captain Joseph, sixth child and fifth son of Joshua Fletcher, and eldest child of his second wife, Sarah Willey, was born in Chelmsford, Massachusetts, June 10, 1689, and died in Westford, October 4, 1772, aged eighty-three. He settled after marriage in Westford, Massachusetts, where he resided the remainder of his life. He married, November 17, 1712, Sarah Adams, of Concord. She was born in 1691, and died April 24, 1761, aged seventy. Their children, all born in Westford, were: Joseph, Benjamin, Timothy, Thomas, Sarah, Edith, Pelatiah, Joshua, Ruth and Mary.

(V) Deacon Joshua, eighth child and sixth son of Captain Joseph and Sarah (Adams) Fletcher, was born in Westford, November 20, 1731, and died June 10, 1783. He settled about two miles from the place of his birth, in Westford. He married Elizabeth Raymond, and they were the parents of nine children, all born in Westford: Levi, Lyman, Joshua, Paul, Isaac, Elizabeth, Abigail, Patty, and Sally.

(VI) Lyman, second son and child of Deacon Joshua and Elizabeth (Raymond) Fletcher, was born in Westford, June 12, 1758, and resided there, where he died in 1834. He married, in 1794, Louisa Gates, of Ashburnham, who died in 1861. They had eight children: Lyman, Levi, Thomas, Louisa, George Washington, Walter, Hosea, Patty, Paul Raymond, and Sarah.

(VII) Walter, fifth child and fourth son of Lyman and Louisa (Gates) Fletcher, was born in Westford, July 20, 1805, and died in Mason, New Hampshire. He was a farmer. He married, August 31, 1828, Mary Chamberlin. After the birth of his first child he removed to Plymouth, Vermont, whence he removed to Mt. Holly and Weston, Vermont, where his wife died of consumption, May 12, 1841. He married second, Laura Haskell, who was born June 12, 1821, and died April 6, 1863; third, Mrs. ——— Haskell. He spent the last years of his life in Mason, New Hampshire. The children by the first wife were: Samuel Walter, George Washington, and Joseph, and four sons who died young. By the second wife: Henry N., Raymond J., Mary E., Julia A., Judson E., Levi T., Emma E., and George A.

(VIII) Samuel Walter, eldest child of Walter and Mary (Chamberlin) Fletcher, was born in Westford, Massachusetts, January 24, 1829, and died in Bemis, Massachusetts, 1889. He went with his father to Vermont, and in 1848 removed to the east part of Rindge, New Hampshire, where he was engaged for some years in the manufacture of wooden trays. He married and shortly after removed to Bennington, Vermont, where he lived two or three years and then returned to Rindge and settled at "the Center." In 1856 he removed to Haverhill, and thence returned to Rindge. He enlisted in the war of the rebellion, August, 1862, in Company I, Ninth Regiment New Hampshire Volunteers, and was in the battles of South Mountain and Antietam. He was wounded, and discharged after serving nine months on account of disabilities arising from his wounds. For some years preceding 1869 he was engaged the most of the time in the wooden-ware business. About the date last given he formed a partnership with Warren W. Emory, under the style of Fletcher & Emory, and engaged in a general mercantile business at Rindge Centre until 1872. Mr. Fletcher then removed to West Rindge, where the firm carried on a second store. Two years later the partnership was dissolved, and Mr. Fletcher carried on the business alone until 1876, when he removed to Bemis, Massachusetts, where he was engaged in a grocery business until his death, in 1889. In politics he was a Republican, and for several years following his appointment, March 18, 1869, was postmaster at Rindge Centre. He was a member of the Congregational Church Society, and one of its standing committee for several years. He was a man of excellent character and standing, a prosperous business man, a pleasant companion, and a faithful friend. He married first, in Rindge, April 25, 1850, Emily T. Brooks, who was born in Rindge, March 25, 1829, daughter of Joseph and Emily (Taylor) Brooks, of Rindge. She died June 24, 1852, and he married second, November 9, 1852, her sister, Caroline M. Brooks. There was born of the first wife one child, Henry W., and of the second, four children: Frederick Perley, Frank Leslie, Mary Emma, and Irving Taylor. Frederick Perley and Frank Leslie died young. Mary Emma is unmarried, and resides in Allerton, Massachusetts. Irving T. is in the grocery business in Watertown, Massachusetts; he married Effie Green, and has one child, Walter.

(IX) Henry Walter, only child of Samuel W. and Emily T. (Brooks) Fletcher, was born in Rindge, December 8, 1851. He attended the public schools of Rindge, Appleton Academy at New Ipswich, and Bryant and Stratton's Business College in Boston, obtaining a practical business education. After teaching school in New Ipswich and Rindge he became a partner in the firm of Fletcher & Emory, at West Rindge, for fifteen months. He then engaged in agricultural pursuits at Rindge Centre until 1890, and then entered the employ of the Cheshire Improvement Company, a concern in East Rindge, engaged in a variety of pursuits, chiefly farming and brickmaking. After some years of experience he became superintendent of this company, and held that position until 1898, having charge of a force of one hundred or one hundred and fifty men. November, 1899, he purchased the general store of H. E. Wetherbee, at West Rindge, which he has since conducted with a growing and remunerative trade, carrying a general stock of goods. In 1872-3, while in business at West Rindge, he was postmaster, station agent, and express agent. He fills the two last named places now, and was postmaster from 1899 to 1902, resigning the postmastership in the latter year in favor of his son, to go to the legislature. He is a Republican, and has always been active in public business. He has held several minor town offices, and was tax collector two years, selectman six consecutive years, and later two more, and representative 1902-3. Mr. Fletcher's activity in business, liberal and progressive views, and general good fellowship have made him a trusted and influential citizen.

He married in Rindge, 1875, Anna C. Norcross, who was born in Rindge, March 9, 1853, daughter of Joshua and Calista K. (Cooper) Norcross, of Rindge. (See Norcross VIII). They have had four children, three of whom are graduate of the local high school and the Murdock School at Winchendon, Massachusetts. They are: Eva A., Charles W., Sydney N., and Alice, who died young. Eva A. married Dr. F. E. Sweeney, and resides in East Jaffrey; they have two children: Fred Foster and Sydney F. Charles Walter, who attended Dartmouth College one and one-half years, is in the store with his father; he married Stella A. Bemis, of Northboro, Massachusetts, daughter of Justin Waldo and Lizzie Gertrude Bemis, of Northboro, Massachusetts, and resides in West Rindge. Sydney N., a graduate of Bryant & Stratton's Business College of Boston, is employed by the Hotel and Railroad News Company of Boston, and resides in Newton. Massachusetts.

(II) Francis, fourth son of Robert Fletcher, was born in 1636, in Concord, Massachusetts, and remained with his father in that town. He became a large land owner, being the possessor of seventeen lots of land in Concord, Massachusetts, amounting to four hundred and thirty-seven acres. He was admitted freeman in 1677, and in the same year was reported "in full communion with ye church in Concord." In December, 1661, he was one of the signers of a petition to license men to sell wine. He married, August 1, 1656, Elizabeth, daughter of George and Catherine Wheeler. She died June 14, 1704. Their children were: Samuel, Joseph, Elizabeth, John, Sarah, Hezekiah, Hannah and Benjamin.

(III) Corporal Samuel, eldest child of Francis and Elizabeth (Wheeler) Fletcher, was born August 6, 1657, in Concord, and resided in that town, where he was selectman in 1705-07-09-13. He was entitled corporal, which probably arose from his service in the militia. He died October 23, 1744, and was survived three days by his wife. He married, April 15, 1682, Elizabeth Wheeler. Their children, all born in Concord, were: Samuel (died young), Joseph, Elizabeth, Sarah, John, Hannah, Ruth, Rebecca, Samuel, Benjamin and Timothy.

(IV) Timothy, youngest child of Samuel and Elizabeth (Wheeler) Fletcher, was born August 28, 1704, in Concord, where he lived and died. His wife's name was Elizabeth, and their children were: Elizabeth, Timothy, Sarah, James, Joseph, Benjamin, Ephraim and Lydia (twins), Joel and Samuel. (Mention of Ephraim and descendants appears in this article).

(V) James, third son and fifth child of Timothy and Elizabeth Fletcher, was born in Concord, September 23, 1734. He served in the Nova Scotia expedition as a member of Captain Osgood's company, and after his return settled in Chesterfield, New Hampshire. He married and was the father of four children: Ebenezer, Hannah, Joel and Abel.

(VI) Abel, youngest son and child of James Fletcher, settled in Chesterfield. He married Phebe Hildreth, January 18, 1774, and was the father of Samuel, Levi, Silas, Daniel, Luna, Joel, Alpheus, Phebe, David Stoddard and Arad Hunt, the two younger being twins.

(VII) Arad Hunt, youngest son and child of Abel and Phebe (Hildreth) Fletcher, was born August 1, 1800. He was a lifelong resident of Chesterfield. His wife, whose christian name was Bethania Darling, bore him four children: Arad, who will be referred to presently; Rodney, born December 8, 1825; Henry, October 3, 1826, and Elmira, October 13, 1828.

(VIII) Arad, eldest son and child of Arad H. and Bethania (Darling) Fletcher, was born in Chesterfield, May 20, 1823. In early manhood he owned and cultivated a farm located about a half mile west of Chesterfield on the road to Winchester, and he was also employed in Benjamin Peirce's bit manufactory. For sixteen years he acted as superintendent of the Cheshire County Farm in Westmoreland, and he subsequently removed to Keene, residing there for the remainder of his life, which terminated July, 1894. While residing in Chesterfield he served as a selectman for the years 1849-56-59; was a member of the lower branch of the state legislature in 1859-60, and in 1890 was chosen a county commissioner for three years. He married Martha Snow Hall, and reared two sons: Frank A. and Edward Henry.

(IX) Edward Henry, youngest son of Arad and Martha S. (Hall) Fletcher, was born in Chesterfield, September 9, 1851. His early education was acquired in the public schools of Chesterfield and Westmoreland, and he completed his studies at the Brattleboro (Vermont) high school. He was employed at the Cheshire County Farm as assistant superintendent, and when his father withdrew from its management he accompanied him to Keene, where they purchased jointly the old Griffith farm. He has ever since devoted his principal attention to general farming, and is meeting with success. He has served with ability as a selectman, and for the past ten years has been overseer of the poor. His fraternal affiliations are with the Independent Order of Odd Fellows. He attends the Unitarian Church. Mr. Fletcher was one of the original stockholders and a director of the Citizens' Electric Company of Keene, and a member of the board of trustees of Keene Savings Bank.

On April 4, 1876, Mr. Fletcher married Alice Buffum, who was born in Westmoreland, October 17, 1855, daughter of Jewett E. and Clarissa E. (Chickering) Buffum. Mrs. Fletcher is a descendant in the sixth generation of Robert Buffum, who emigrated from Yorkshire, England, to Salem, Massachusetts, in or prior to 1638, and died there in 1679, leaving seven children. Robert, born in Salem in 1650, and died in 1731, married Hannah Pope. Benjamin, son of Caleb, was born in 1686. The maiden surname of his mother was Buxton. Joseph, son of Benjamin, was born in 1717, and resided in Smithfield, Rhode Island. He died in 1796. His wife was before marriage Margaret Osborne. Joseph Buffum, son of Joseph and Margaret, was born in Smithfield in 1754. In 1784 he went to Westmoreland, New Hampshire, settling upon a farm in the southern part of the town, and his death occurred in 1829. He married Sally Haskell, daughter of Elias Haskell, of Lancaster, Massachusetts, and reared seven sons, all of whom, according to information at hand, "were strong mentally as well as physically."

They were Joseph, a graduate of Dartmouth College, a lawyer by profession, members of congress and at one time postmaster in Keene. Jewett, who married Fanny Atherton, of Chesterfield, and settled in Boston. Erasmus, who will again be referred to. William, who married Mary Ann Gordon, of Sterling, Connecticut, and settled in Walpole, New Hampshire. Haskell, who married Salome Wood, daughter of Jonathan Wood. Solon, who died at the age of sixty-nine years. Colonel David Buffum, who married Mary Bellows, daughter of Hon. Thomas Bellows. Erasmus Buffum, son of Joseph and Sally (Haskell) Buffum, was a lifelong resident of Westmoreland and died in 1872. He married Hepsy, daughter of Daniel Thayer, a revolutionary soldier, and was the father of eight children, six of whom grew to maturity: Solon, Sarah, James, Jewett E., Mary and Alba. Solon married Adaline Daul, of New York City. Sarah died at the age of twenty-four years. James, who died in Westmoreland in 1887, married Louisa Howe. Mary became the wife of Lemuel Ingalls. Alba died in New York City. Jewett E. Buffum, son of Erasmus and Hepsy (Thayer) Buffum, was born in Westmoreland, July 5, 1822. He was a prosperous farmer and a prominent resident of Westmoreland, taking an active interest in public affairs, and in addition to serving as a selectman he acted as justice of the peace. In politics he was a Democrat. During the Civil war he was a recruiting officer. He married Clarissa E. Chickering, daughter of Elbridge and Betsey (Gleason) Chickering, and grand-daughter of Timothy Chickering, who went from Massachusetts to Westmoreland. The children of Timothy Chickering were: Luther, Rhoda, Lavinia Thankful, Alvin, Elbridge and Samuel. Elbridge Chickering married Betsey Gleason, daughter of Benjamin Gleason. She became the mother of Caroline, Clarissa E., Ransom, Holland, Elbridge and Shubael. The children of Jewett E. and Clarissa E. (Chickering) Buffum are: Solon E., E. Clayton, J. Colburn, H. Clement, Alice Clara and James Alba. N. B. Triplets were born to them once and twins once.

Alice Clara Buffum, sixth child and eldest daughter of Jewett E. and Clarissa E. (Chickering) Buffum, married Edward H. Fletcher. (see Fletcher IX). One child born to Mr. and Mrs. Edward H. Fletcher, Edith Martha Fletcher, born March 26, 1878.

(V) Ephraim, sixth son and eighth child of Timothy and Elizabeth Fletcher, was born February 5, 1740, in Concord, and died January 1, 1836, in Newport, New Hampshire. He was a soldier in the Patriot army during the revolutionary war, the records showing service as private in the Alarm of April 19, 1775, and in Captain Caleb Whitney's company in 1778. He lived for a time in Sturbridge, Massachusetts whence he removed to Newport, New Hampshire, with three sons, Joel, Ephraim and Timothy. He married Sarah Davenport, (a descendant of the historic Captain Richard Davenport, of colonial fame), who was born in 1740, and died November 4, 1806. Their children were: Sarah, Ephraim, Amos, Polly, Lydia, Timothy, Anna, Joel and Benjamin. (Timothy and descendants receive further mention in this article).

(VI) Ephraim (2), eldest son and second child of Ephraim (1) and Sarah (Davenport) Fletcher, was born November 23, 1767, in Sturbridge, Massachusetts, and settled on the west slope of Oak Hill, in Newport, New Hampshire, his farm bordering on Sugar river, where he died April 27, 1854. He married, February 20, 1794 Jael Mores, born March 22, 1775, died January 3, 1862, in Newport. Their children were: Oliver, Orpha, Quartus, William, Mahala, Polly, Electa, Beulah T., Austin and Lyman. The eldest daughter was three times married, her last husband being Parmenus Whitcomb. At her death she bequeathed several thousand dollars to the Baptist Church of Newport, which very materially aided in the construction of its present beautiful house of worship.

(VII) Quartus, second son and third child of Ephraim (2) and Jael (Mores) Fletcher, was born April 22, 1799, in Newport. Early in life he settled in Cornish, southeast corner of the town, in the neighborhood of Hemp Yard, where he spent his entire life in agriculture. He died April 27, 1874. He married, January 16, 1844, Charlotte Hillard, of Cornish, who survived him and resides with a daughter in Newport. Their children were: Henry L., Luella E., Emma F., and Jael M. The eldest daughter is the wife of Charles M. Emerson, of Newport. (See Emerson, VIII).

(VI) Timothy, third son and sixth child of Ephraim (1) and Sarah (Davenport) Fletcher, was born July 14, 1778, in Grafton, Massachusetts, accompanied his father to Newport, New Hampshire, as above mentioned, and always resided in that town, where he died October 3, 1863, aged eighty-five years. He married, March 27, 1803, Lois Metcalf, born in Franklin, Massachusetts, August 28, 1779, and died April 11, 1878, aged ninety-eight years and seven months. Their children were: Laura F., Aurilla, Samuel M., Cyrus Kingsbury, Nancy, Stillman T. and Benjamin F.

(VII) Aurilla, second daughter and child of Timothy and Lois (Metcalf) Fletcher, was born November 3, 1807, and died June 6, 1862. She married, May 10, 1831, Deacon Austin Kibbey, of Newport. Their children were: William B., Oren C., Lois and Sarah A.

(VIII) William B. Kibbey, who resides in Croyden, married January 11, 1856, Martha Wheeler, of Newport, New Hampshire. She died December 10, 1893, leaving six children: Nellie Aurilla, born in 1857. Leila S., born November 10, 1859. Charles Ellsworth, November 6, 1861. Sarah Frances, born July 11, 1864. Hattie Alice, born March 17, 1870. Fred Burt, born June 17, 1876. Oren C. Kibbey married Lucy Melinda Metcalf, March 16, 1858. Their children are: Milan Austin, born August 8, 1859. Anna Marilla, born June 2, 1861. Herman H., born March 3, 1864. Alma Aurilla, born August 12, 1872. Arthur H., born March 4, 1874; died July 31, 1905.

(VIII) Lois, elder daughter and third child of Austin and Aurilla (Fletcher) Kibbey, was born July 3, 1837, in Newport, and became the wife of Dr. Leonard E. Richardson of that town, whom she survives. (See Richardson, second family, VIII).

FLETCHER The family of this cognomen of which George W. Fletcher is a member, is one of the ancient families of New Hampshire, and has produced many prominent citizens of the state. George W. Fletcher, grandson of John and Betsy Fletcher, child of Josiah S. and Louisa P. Fletcher, was born in London, April 7, 1852. He grew up a farmer boy, attended the common schools until he was prepared to go to a higher school, and then attended Tilton Seminary several terms. At twenty years of age he became a clerk in Concord, where he remained some two years. Then returning home, he soon after engaged in farming interests in Canterbury. In 1882 he bought what was known as the

Stephen A. Frost

PLANT OF SPAULDING & FROST CO., GENERAL COQPERAGE.

FREMONT, N. H.

Kezer farm in Canterbury, where he settled and has since been engaged in general farming, and in providing in summer time, a pleasant resort for about twenty-five persons seeking rest and recreation. Mr. Fletcher is a well informed citizen and [illegible] all matters affecting the welfare of the [illegible] churches, agricultural affairs, and general welfar[illegible] the people of the community in which he resides. He was a member of the First Free Baptist Church, serving as deacon and clerk while he remained in town. He is a member of the board of trustees of Kezer Seminary, Canterbury. In political faith he is a Republican, and has been selectman four years, during one year of which time he was chairman of the board. He married, in Newport, December 21, 1882, Hattie C. Colby, who was born in Grantham, August 27, 1858, daughter of Hiram and Florenda Colby. They have one child, Harold G., born August 10, 1899.

In March, 1907, Mr. Fletcher sold his farm and moved to Concord. He and his family have united with the Curtis Memorial Freewill Baptist Church. He now holds a position with the Page Belting Company as foreman of the assorting department, with residence at 65 South street.

FROST The origin of this name, which is now quite common both in England and America, must in all probability, like many other English family names, remain buried in remote antiquity. It was transplanted in New England early in the colonial period, and one of the original settlers in York county, Maine, bore the name of Frost. The particular family about to be considered, although of English origin, is not however, descended from the ancient Frosts, as it acquired the name by adoption.

(I), Early in the last century a young man by the name of William Drakeford left his home in England, and crossing the ocean settled in Halifax, Nova Scotia. For reasons known only to himself he changed his name to Frost. It is thought that in early life he was a mariner, but his later years were devoted to farming, and he died in Halifax some forty-five years ago. The maiden surname of his wife whom he married in Halifax and who is supposed to have come from the south, was Pelham. Her death occurred in Halifax some twenty years subsequent to that of her husband, and she was buried beside him in what is known as the South East Passage that city. They were the parents of ten children, namely: John Lewis, Joseph, Ann, Hannah, Barbara, Louisa, Eliza, Catherine, Sarah and Elizabeth. (N. B. Apparently these children are not given in the order of their birth). Joseph, who was accidentally drowned some forty years ago, left one son. Some of the daughters are still living in Halifax, and one of them is nearly ninety years old.

(II) John Lewis, son of John William Frost, was born in Nova Scotia, January 15, 1829. As a young man he was a fisherman, but after his marriage he turned his attention to farming, and about 1868 he came to the United States, settling in South Natick, Massachusetts, where he remained two or three years. Returning to the maritime provinces he resided in St. John, New Brunswick, for a period of three years, at the expiration of which time he once more sought a home in the states. He resided for intervals in Shirley, Townsend, Pepperell and Gloucester, Massachusetts, and returning from the latter city to Pepperell, he died there January 3, 1906. He married Mary Ann Winters, born in Halifax in 1836, daughter of William Thomas and Susan (Pengilly) Winters, the former of whom was a native of that city, and his wife came from Devonshire, England. John L. and Mary Ann (Winters) Frost, were the parents of nine children: Jane, Barbara, John (who died young), Charles W., Stephen Alexander, John L., Mary, Annie, and another Mary. The three last named died in early childhood. Jane became the wife of John W. Bartz, of Pepperell, Massachusetts. Barbara, who is no longer living, was the wife of James Stackhouse, of St. John, New Brunswick. Charles W. married Florence Cook, and settled in Fremont, New Hampshire. John L. also resides in Fremont. He married Cora Smith, of Salem, New Hampshire. The mother of these children died in 1880.

(III) Stephen Alexander, third son and fifth child of John L. and Mary Ann (Winters) Frost, was born in Halifax, January 15, 1862. His education was acquired in the public schools of South Natick and Shirley Village, Massachusetts. He began the activities of life in the leather board mill of Messrs. Hill and Cutler at Shirley, but subsequently went to Townsend Harbor, where he entered the employ of Jonas Spaulding (now deceased), a leather board maker and cooperage manufacturer, and with the latter he came to Fremont. Six years later he and Mr. Spaulding became associated in the cooperage business at Gloucester, Massachusetts, under the firm name of Spaulding, Frost & Company, and selling out the plant in that city in 1899 he returned to Fremont, where he organized and incorporated the Spaulding & Frost Company, of which he is secretary, treasurer and general manager. This concern manufactures white pine cooperage of a superior quality, which is used by packers of fish, pickles and other provisions, and transacts a business aggregating in value about two hundred thousand dollars annually. They also manufacture lumber and employ an average force of one hundred and fifty workmen. Their plant is the largest in the state, and covers an area of twelve acres.

In politics Mr. Frost acts independently, and while not an aspirant for public office he has served as town auditor and as a member of the school board. He belongs to Ocean Lodge, Independent Order of Odd Fellows, of Gloucester, Alfaretta Lodge, Daughters of Rebekah, of Raymond, and Fremont Grange, Patrons of Husbandry. Mr. Frost is highly esteemed by his fellow townsmen both as an able business man and public-spirited citizen. In his religious belief he is a Universalist. June 13, 1885, he married Catherine G. Fertig, who was born in Cleveland, Ohio, January 10, 1862, daughter of John and Christina (Lederer) Fertig. Mr. and Mrs. Frost have had four children, namely: Agnes Mary, who died in March, 1892; Lillian Emma, a graduate of Comer's Commercial College, Boston; Lizzie J., and Marion, who died in 1894. Mrs. Frost is a woman of broad intelligence, and a member of the Daughters of Rebekah, and the Grange, and various church societies, and takes an active part in all the affairs of these bodies.

NEWTON The Newton family, which is one the most numerous in New England, is of English origin and was founded in America early in the colonial period. The Goffstown Newtons went there from Worcester county, Massachusetts.

(I) Richard Newton, the immigrant ancestor of the family, arrived in Massachusetts prior to 1645, in which year he was admitted a freeman, and he resided for several years in Sudbury. In company with John How and others he petitioned for the settlement of Marlborough, the incorporation of which they secured in 1666, and removing thither he located in that part of the town which was afterwards set off as Southborough. He lived to be nearly one hundred years old, and his death occurred about August 24, 1701. The christian name of his wife was either Anna or Hannah. These names were frequently bungled in many of our early town records, through the carelessness or ignorance of some one, perhaps the town clerks. She became the mother of six children, and her death occurred December 5, 1697.

(II) Moses, son of Richard Newton, was born in 1646, and resided in Marlborough. October 27, 1668, he married Joanna Larkin, who died December 25, 1713, and on April 14, 1714, he married for his second wife Sarah Joslin. She died November 4, 1723. Moses was the father of eleven children. He distinguished himself in defending the town against the savages during King Philip's war, and in relation to this incident the Rev. Asa Packard wrote the following account: "The Sabbath when Mr. Brimsmead was in sermon (March 20, 1676), the worshipping was suddenly dispersed by the outcry of 'Indians at the door.' The confusion of the first moment was instantly increased by a fire from the enemy; but the God whom they were worshipping shielded their lives and limbs, excepting the arm of one Moses Newton, who was carrying an elderly and infirm woman to a place of safety. In a few moments they were sheltered in their fort, with the mutual feelings peculiar to such a scene. Their meetinghouse, and many dwelling houses left without protection, were burnt. Fruit-trees pilled and hacked, and other valuable effects rendered useless perpetuated the barbarity of the savages many years after the inhabitants returned. The enemy retired soon after their first onset, declining to risk the enterprise and martial prowess of the young plantation."

(III) James, son of Moses and Joanna (Larkin) Newton, was born in Marlborough, January 15, 1683. In 1727, when Marlborough was divided, his property was included within the limits of Southborough, and he died in that town November 29, 1762. He was first married, October 5, 1709, to Mary Joslin, who died May 27, of the following year, and his second wife, whom he married September 8, 1712, was Rachel Greeley.

(IV) Andrew son of James and Rachel (Greeley) Newton, was born in Marlborough August 27, 1713. He settled in the western part of Framingham on the shore of the Hopkinton river, where he operated a forge and a grist-mill for many years or until succeeded by his son. He married Mehitable Bellows, and was the father of Mehitable, Andrew and James.

(V) Andrew (2), son of Andrew (1) and Mehitable (Bellows) Newton was born in Framingham, October 23, 1748. He succeeded his father as the blacksmith and miller of that section, and participated in the exciting scenes common in the villages and hamlets during the Revolutionary war. He married Sarah Marret, daughter of William and Sarah (How) Marret, of Hopkinton and Framingham. The Newtons were connected with the colonial militia just prior to the war for independence, and some of them were afterwards enrolled in the Continental army. A roster at hand of the Southborough company belonging to Colonel Artemas Ward's regiment in 1774 contains the names of Isaac, David, Luke, "Sirus," Eben, Jabez, Ashael and another Isaac Newton.

(VI) William, son of Andrew (2) and Sarah (Marret) Newton, was born in Framingham in 1773. He settled in Shrewsbury, Massachusetts, where he followed the shoemaker's trade in connection with farming and he died in 1850. He married Abigail Newton, perhaps a distant relative, who was born in Worcester, Massachusetts, March 4, 1779, daughter of Benjamin Newton, and reared a large family. Those of his children whose names are at hand are: Thankful, Elizabeth, William, George, Charles, Sarah and Daniel.

(VII) Daniel, son of William and Abigail Newton, was born in Shrewsbury. He resided for a time in Boylston Massachusetts, going from there to Framingham, in 1855, as manager of the town farm, and he subsequently purchased a piece of agricultural property, which he devoted chiefly to the dairying industry. He was also engaged in the lumber business for many years, and attained a comfortable prosperity. In politics he supported the Democratic party and was quite active in civic affairs. He died in Framingham in July, 1898. On April 6, 1837, he married Martha Goddard, who was born in Framingham May 22, 1817, daughter of Captain Nathan and Polly (Bacon) Goddard, and granddaughter of Nathan Goddard, Esq., a well-known lawyer of Shrewsbury, and Framingham in his day. Martha died in August, 1892. She became the mother of five children, namely: Mary B., born in 1840, married Christopher Hunt. Nathan G., who will be again referred to. Lorenzo, born in 1845 (died in 1873). Solomon G. and another child, both of whom died in infancy. The parents were members of the Baptist Church.

(VIII) Nathan Goddard, second child and eldest son of Daniel and Martha (Goddard) Newton, was born in Boylston August 6, 1843. From the Framingham high school he entered the Frost Academy, which he left in 1862 to enlist as a private in Company F, Forty-fifth Regiment, Massachusetts Volunteers, for nine months' service in the civil war. He participated in the battles of White Hall, Kingston, Goldsborough, Deep Gulch, Cross Roads and other engagements. After his return from the army he found employment in a shoe factory in Marlborough, where he remained seven years, and in 1870 he went to Manchester, New Hampshire, where he followed the same occupation continuously for a period of over thirty years. Some five years ago he acquired possession of the Colby farm (so called) in Goffstown, where he now resides, and in addition to a profitable milk business he is engaged quite extensively in lumbering. Politically he is a Republican. In his religious faith he is a Methodist. He is a Master Mason, having joined that order in 1868.

On October 16, 1872, Mr. Newton was joined in marriage with Rebecca Chase Hall, daughter of the late Edward and Rebecca Chase (Harvey) Hall, of Worcester, Vermont. As captain of Company E, Eighth Regiment Vermont Volunteers, her father served under General Butler at New Orleans during the rebellion, and was subsequently killed in action under General Sheridan, in the Shenandoah Valley. Her mother died when she (Mrs. Newton) was three days old, and she was adopted by her uncle, Samuel Hall, of Manchester. She completed her education at the Manchester high school, and prior to her marriage was a school teacher of recognized ability. She is a member of the Methodist Episcopal Church. Mr. and Mrs. Newton are the parents of five children: 1. Maud, R., born October 5, 1874, died January 4, 1878. 2. Walter H., born March 5, 1879, married Ethel

Cooper, of Massachusetts. 3. Arthur S., born February 24, 1881, married Mae Patten, of Goffstown, and their children were: Dorothy M., born 1902; Arthur W., 1904; Vera E., January 2, 1907. 4. N. N. Lyle, born December 20, 1884. 5. Rachel G., born July 12, 1892.

(Second Family.)

NEWTON For more than a century and a quarter the family name of Newton has been closely associated with the history of the town of Newport and the county of Sullivan, and in each succeeding generation from the time of the first settler bearing that surname there have been men of character and action in all that has contributed to the welfare of that part of the state. The learned professiones have claimed some of them and others have turned to business pursuits, but in whatever vocation in life they all have wrought well in building and enlarging on the foundations laid by their ancestors during the last quarter of the eighteenth century.

(I) Christopher Newton, founder of the family of that surname in Newport, was born in Groton, Connecticut, February 26, 1738, and died February 19, 1834, aged almost ninety-six years. He came to Newport about the year 1779 and with his family settled on a farm on the Unity road, afterward the homestead of his son, Erastus Newton, where he died. He was moderator of the town in 1784-85-87-89-1800-02-09-11-14-15-20-22 and selectman in 1884-85. He married, February 26. 1766 (on his twenty-eighth birthday), Mary Giles, of Groton, Connecticut, born November 12, 1745, died May 14, 1821, daughter of Benjamin Giles, of Groton and Newport, one of the early settlers of the latter town and one of the foremost men of New Hampshire for several years and until his death in November, 1787.

Family tradition says that Benjamin Giles was an Irishman by birth, and lived many years in Groton before settling in Newport. He was a man of wealth and education, beyond most of the settlers and soon came to be recognized as the leading man among them. He was not one of the original proprietors of the town, but one of its earliest settlers, and in 1766 was voted one hundred acres of land on condition that he build and maintain a saw mill and a grist mill. In 1767 he was clerk of the first regular meeting of proprietors, and was moderator in 1769 and 1781. He was a thoroughly devoted patriot and during the Revolution was an important member of the provincial councils of the state; and throughout almost the entire revolutionary struggle he was a delegate to the various "provincial congresses" which met to devise means for carrying on the war and forming plans of government. He was a member of the first constitutional convention of the state and a member of the commission appointed to settle the dispute in regard to the boundary between the state of Massachusetts and New Hampshire. It is said, too, that at one time Benjamin Giles was arrested and imprisoned, by authority of His Majesty the King, for alleged seditious acts, and that when it was evening he was rescued by a party of patriots dressed in female attire. In 1775-76 he was representative of the then six classed towns of which Newport was one, also a member of the state senate and at one time a member of the governor's council. In March, 1781, when Newport seceded from New Hampshire, he was a delegate to the general assembly of Vermont and attended the meeting of that body at Windsor.

Christopher and Mary (Giles) Newton had six children, four daughters and two sons, viz: Martha, born April 9, 1768, married Aaron Mack. Mary, born November 29, 1770, married Lemuel Church, a tailor. Margery, born November 2, 1772, married Deacon Jesse Fay, of Alstead. Abigail, born March 13, 1775, married Rev. Orlando Bliss. Erastus, born April 4, 1777, died January 4. 1852; lived on the old homestead; was major of militia; married, November 22, 1801, Betsey Beckwith and had six children. Hubbard, born January 1, 1780.

(II) Hubbard, youngest child and son of Christopher and Mary (Giles) Newton, was born in the town of Newport, New Hampshire, January 1, 1780. His early life was spent on his father's farm. and in later years while occupied with the practice of law he found recreation and material profit in the personal management of his own farm. After a thorough preparatory education he entered Dartmouth College and was graduated with honors in the class of 1804. Having finished his college course he turned attention to the study of law in the office of Samuel Bell, Esq., of Francestown, and in 1806 was admitted to practice and began his professional career in Newport. Later on he practiced five years at Amherst and still later for two years was law partner with his son, William F. Newton, at Claremont. At the end of that time he returned to Newport and afterward devoted attention to his law practice, literary pursuits, editorial work and the care of his farm. In politics Mr. Newton was a Whig of undoubted quality, and in 1830-31 with voice and pen ably championed the cause of Henry Clay and vigorously opposed Andrew Jackson and the Democratic party, whose candidate he was for the presidency. During these years Mr. Newton was editor of the *Farmers' Advocate* and *Political Adventurer*, a weekly newspaper published at Newport by his son, Charles H. E. Newton, who was a practical printer; and in 1832. at the close of the presidential campaign of that year, he assumed editorial supervision of the *Northern Farmer* and *Horticulturist*, a journal devoted to farming interests and horticulture, and with which he was connected until some time in 1833. Besides his editorial labors, Mr. Newton wrote several lectures on various subjects and left on record several interesting poems. Himself a well educated man, he took an earnest interest in the cause of education and was one of the founders and a trustee of Newport Academy, member of the school committee, and also one of the first advocates of temperance on the foundation of total abstinence, delivering many addresses on that subject in Newport and the towns adjoining. He was moderator of Newport seven years and represented the town in 1814-15.

Hubbard Newton married November 25, 1802, Abigail Lyon, born July 4, 1779, died January 21, 1843. Her father, David Lyon, born at Stoughton, Massachusetts, April 11, 1739, settled in Newport in 1790 and kept a store and tavern on the Unity road. He married, in 1777, Abigail Belcher, who bore him two children, Abigail and David. Hubbard and Abigail (Lyon) Newton had eight children, viz: Henrietta M., born April 7, 1806, died September 30, 1876; a woman of education and refinement. Charles H. E., born April 10, 1808, a printer, publisher of the *Farmers' Advocate* and *Political Adventurer* and the *Northern Farmer* and *Horticulturist*, both edited by his father; went from Newport to Mobile, Alabama, where he followed his occupation; removed thence to California, entered the ministery and became a presiding elder of the Methodist Episcopal Church in Oregon. James H., born August 12, 1811, died in

Michigan, January 2, 1847; prepared for college at Newport Academy, and was a teacher by profession. Mary G., born November 14, 1813, died April 12, 1868. Catherine M., born December 5, 1816, died June 25, 1825. William F., born November 23, 1818, a member of the Sullivan county bar since 1843, but now retired from active practice; married, March 23, 1876, Julia, daughter of Dr. David McQueston, of Washington, New Hampshire. Adelia M., born February 1, 1821. Arthur W., born May 10, 1823, died May 16, 1824.

(III) William F., sixth child and third son of Hubbard and Abigail (Lyon) Newton, was born at Newport, November 23, 1818, and has passed almost his entire life in Sullivan county. In early youth he learned the trade of printing and afterward worked at it for a few years. He then took up the study of law in the office and under the direction of his father, and in 1843 was admitted to practice. The scene of his professional life was laid in Sullivan county, where he practiced with gratifying success more than fifty years and where for many years he held the office of clerk of courts, besides having frequently been chosen to other positions of trust and honor. In connection with professional work he also engaged in farming and was one of the earliest growers of strawberries on an extensive scale in his county. During recent years, however, Mr. Newton has retired from the general practice of law and also on account of advanced age has laid aside the cares and responsibilities of public office. He is numbered among the oldest members of the legal profession in New Hampshire, and for many years has enjoyed an extended acquaintance throughout the state.

CHAMBERLAIN This family traces its history back to an ancestor who settled in the primeval forest of Massachusetts when the oldest settlement in that colony was only twenty-one years old. The self-reliant and energetic spirit of this ancestor is still strong in the Chamberlains of the present time.

(I) Richard Chamberlain was of Branitree, Massachusetts, in 1642, and removed to Roxbury where he was baptized, June 4, 1665, with others, Benjamin and Joseph, who both settled in Sudbury. The records show that Richard Chamberlain owned a house and half an acre of land in Roxbury, next to Rev. John Eliot, "The Apostle to the Indians." He died in 1673 and his will was proved on the 15th of April of that year. He left sons, Benjamin and Joseph, and some daughters.

(II) Joseph, son of Richard Chamberlain, born in Roxbury, removed to Oxford with his brother Benjamin and the other settlers in 1713, Joseph then being about sixty-eight years old. He chose his home lot on Bondat Hill, including the "great house," H. 38. In 1712 he sold sixty acres of land, a dwelling house, orchard, and so on, with "all his rights of land or commonages in the town of Sudbury." He was a member of the first board of selectmen, and was a soldier in the Narragansett war. On February 22, 1731, several of his children conveyed to their brother Joseph of Keekamoochang, all their rights in their father's lots laid out or to be laid out to "Ye soldiers which were in ye fight commonly called ye Narragansett or Swamp Fight." His will dated March 4, 1721, names his sons Benjamin and Simon as executors. Valuation three hundred and four pounds, nineteen shillings and six pence. He died August 8, 1721. His wife Hannah had died previously. No record of his family has been found. Nathaniel and Joseph are supposed to have been among the eldest children; Ebenezer, Hannah, Benjamin, Simon and Rebecca were younger.

(III) Nathaniel, son of Joseph and Hannah Chamberlain, was born in Sudbury, at the present village of Wayland, in 1689, and removed to Oxford in 1713. He was one of at least eight children of his father, of whom Nathaniel, Ebenezer and Joseph were of age and took up house lots with the first proprietors of Sudbury. Nathaniel took up his lot adjoining his uncle Benjamin's on the north H. 240, which he sold in 1722. He was a constituent member of the church. He removed to Hatfield about 1722. He was a soldier in Father Rasle's war and was taken prisoner. After his return from captivity he removed to Northfield, Massachusetts. He was a soldier in the Crown Point expedition in 1755 and in Colonel Williams' regiment in 1759. He died November 7, 1780, and the church record of Northfield says "He left a good name behind him." He married, March 31, 1714, Elizabeth, sister of Thomas Hunkins, baptized February 24, 1706, at Boxford, being then adult. Their children were: Richard, Moses, Nathaniel, Elizabeth, Sarah and Mary.

(IV) Deacon Moses, second child and son of Nathaniel and Elizabeth (Hunkins) Chamberlain, was born in Oxford, March 30, 1716. His history for the first thirty-two years of his life is unknown, but in 1748 he bought land in Litchfield, and his name is on the book of the Congregational Church at South Farms, in 1787. The older records have been destroyed. Moses Chamberlain's family settled in Newbury, Vermont, as early as 1772. The names of Moses and Asher Chamberlain are on the roll of Minute Men in 1775, and in Captain John G. Bayley's company guarding and scouting. Remembrance and Moses were in Captain Steven's company, Moses was a private in Captain Samuel Young's company, at Haverhill, in Redels' regiment, also in a "Company raised for the defence of the frontier." He was second lieutenant from June 1, 1778, for one hundred and thirty-eight days, and first lieutenant from December 1, 1778, one hundred and twenty-one days. Moses was sergeant major in Young's company in Bedels' regiment "A company raised for the Expedition against Canada." It is understood that both Deacon Moses and his son Moses served in the war, but which of the foregoing records of service was that of the father and which that of the son cannot now be distinguished. Moses and his wife were members of the Congregational Church, but his title of deacon was held by him before he went to Newbury. He died June 25, 1796. He married Jemima, daughter of Remembrance and Elizabeth Wright, who is believed to have been a sister to the wife of Richard Chamberlain. She died July 30, 1801. The children of this marriage were: Susanna, Azubah, Jemima, Lydia, Remembrance, Moses, Asher and Wright.

(V) Colonel Remembrance, fifth child and eldest son of Moses and Jemima (Wright) Chamberlain, was born December 19, 1747. He owned the farm long known as the Chamberlain farm, north of Bedel's bridge, where he kept a tavern many years. This farm remained in the family three generations. The first record of this branch of the Chamberlain family is the conveyance, November 20, 1772, by Jacob Bayley to Remembrance Chamberlain of Lot No. 2, in Sleeper's Meadow, with the house lot belonging to it, one fifty-acre, and two one-hundred-acre lots. He served in the Revolutionary war in several campaigns, among them

Horace E. Chamberlin

being a service of nineteen days between May, 1779, and May, 1781, in Captain Steven's company; in Captain Frye Bayley's company, in 1781-82, guarding and scouting. He was made first lieutenant by Governor Chittenden, and the original commission is still owned by a descendant. He was made successively, captain, major, and colonel in the militia. In town he was prominent, holding offices, and was a substantial citizen. He and his wife were probably members of the church, joining it before the present records began. He was very particular to keep the Sabbath, and brought up his family in strict Puritan principles. He was a kind and generous man. He married Elizabeth Elliott, widow of Haynes Johnson, and daughter of Edmund and Mehitable (Worthen) Elliott, descendants of Amesbury (Massachusetts) families. After the death of Mr. Johnson she returned to Chester, for fear of Indians and Tories, but came back to Newbury, bringing her three children with her on a horse, fording streams and sometimes compelled to lodge in the woods. She was born in Chester in 1751, and died February 8, 1829. The children of Colonel Remembrance and Elizabeth (Elliott) Chamberlain were: Moses, Azubah, Elizabeth, Mehitable, Remembrance (1), Moody, Remembrance (2) and Olive.

(VI) Moses, eldest child of Colonel Remembrance and Elizabeth (Elliott) Chamberlain, was born in Newbury, November 25, 1777. He was a farmer at Bradford, on the upper plain, where he bought out his Uncle Moses. He married (first) Martha Child, daughter of Cephas and Martha Child, of Woodstock, Connecticut, and West Fairlee. She died in 1839, and he married (second) Mrs. Jemima Peckett. He died November, 1854, and she married (third) a Mr. Morris, of Bradford. The children, all of the first marriage, were: John Elliott, Cephas Child, Martha E., Mary C., Moses Remembrance, Elizabeth, Benjamin F., Elizabeth E., Amanda N. and Azubah A.

(VII) John Elliott, eldest child of Moses and Martha (Child) Chamberlain, was born in Bradford, November 4, 1806, and died October 7, 1886. His education was academical. He was a farmer in South Newbury and held most of the town offices. In 1843 he was a member of the constitutional convention. Being a shrewd man of good judgment and executive ability he improved the opportunity to engage in railroad construction, and with Robert Morse built the White Mountain railroad from Woodville to Littleton, and later with Joseph A. Dodge built the Boston, Concord & Montreal railroad extension from Littleton to the Fabyan House. He was also interested in other enterprises. He married, March, 1831, Laura, daughter of Israel Willard, of Bradford. She was born February 5, 1807, died May 16, 1864. They had six children: George Willard, Horace Elliott, Remembrance Wright, Leona Eveline, Ella Amanda and Charles Wesley.

(VIII) Horace Elliott Chamberlain, son of John Elliott and Laura (Williard) Chamberlain, was born at Newbury, Vermont, November 30, 1834. His primary education was obtained in the public schools, from which he went to the academy at Bradford and Newbury Seminary, where he attended for a considerable time. Having a natural inclination for a business life he entered the railway service in 1856, and was station agent at Littleton, New Hampshire, about seven years. He was then made general agent for the Rutland railroad at Burlington, Vermont, filling that place for a year. The following six years he was general freight agent for the same road. In 1871 he was made superintendent of the Concord railroad, and discharged the duties of that place for nearly twenty years, finally resigning when it went into other hands. A year later he became superintendent of the Concord division of the Boston & Maine railroad and retired in 1900, after serving that road nine years. Since he left the service of the Boston & Maine, Mr. Chamberlin has lived retired, residing in a beautiful mansion on Pleasant street, Concord. He is an independent gold standard Democrat. His life has been too much occupied with business to leave any time for office holding, had he so desired. He is a member of the Unitarian Church of Concord, which he joined in 1886. In 1860 he became a member of Burns Lodge, No. 66, Ancient Free and Accepted Masons, of Littleton, of which he is now a past master. He has also taken the York Rites to and including the Knights Templar degrees, and the Scottish Rites to and including the thirty-second degree.

He married, March 31, 1880, at Laconia, New Hampshire, Nellie M. Putnam, daughter of Perley Putnam, proprietor and manager of the Laconia Car Works, and his wife Ellen M. (Goulding) Putnam, the latter the daughter of an English sea captain. Her mother was Mary (Elvord) Goulding, a native of Ireland. Nellie M. Putnam received an academic education, and in early life joined the Unitarian Church. There are no children of this marriage. Horace E. Chamberlin, born a farmer boy and educated in the less pretentious of our school institutions, had inherited from a respected line of ancestors, strong in body and mind the elements necessary to success. He selected his tasks, put all the energies of his nature into the performance of them, and today after more than half a century of hard work looks back with satisfaction over a long and useful life.

CHAMBERLAIN It is claimed that the family is of French descent and that one Jean or John de Tankerville, a Frenchman, became chamberlain to the King of England, which constituted the origin of the surname of Chamberlain. It is also stated that John Chamberlain, son of the above-mentioned John, emigrated to New England and settled in Boston. These stories, however, are but family traditions, and should be treated accordingly. There were several early emigrants of this name. Henry Chamberlain, who came in the "Diligent" in 1638, and settled in Hingham, Massachusetts, and William Chamberlain, who appears in the Woburn records in 1648, and removed to Billerica, Massachusetts, in 1653, are supposed to have been kinsmen. Thomas Chamberlain was made a freeman at Woburn, May 29, 1644, and resided there until 1655. The christian name of his wife was Mary and his children were: Thomas, presumably born in England; and Samuel, born at Woburn in 1645. (III) Thomas Chamberlain, probably a son of (II) Samuel, married Abigail Hildreth (or Hildrick), of Chelmsford, and had sons John and Samuel. Abigail survived her husband and was married a second time to a Hammond, of what is now Swanzey, New Hampshire. Her sons John and Samuel Chamberlain are believed to have settled in Swanzey, although the available records of that town fail to mention them.

(I) Elisha Chamberlain, of Fitchburg, Massachusetts, held several town offices there between the years 1795 and 1801, including those of selectman and highway surveyor, and was also a member of the school committee. He died in Keene, New

Hampshire, June 11, 1840, in his seventy-eighth year, and Susannah, his widow, died in Swanzey, New Hampshire, May 16, 1846, aged eighty years.

(II) John, son of Elisha and Susannah Chamberlain, was born in Fitchburg, September 10, 1795. In early life he was in the employ of Martin Newton, an extensive lumber manufacturer of Fitchburg in his day, and he later engaged in the same business for himself at Swanzey, also operating a grist mill. In 1850 he retired from business and purchasing a residence at Middletown (Swanzey) resided there for some years. His death occurred in Swanzey, August 28 or 29, 1870. He married (first), March 18, 1820, Nancy Stone, born May 8, 1798, died June 11, 1822; married (second), September 25, 1822, Olive H. Wyman, born March 18, 1792, died April 14, 1826; married (third), late in the year 1826, Sylvia Perry, born September 14, 1797, died October 28, 1852; married (fourth), February 7, 1854, Harriet Ware, daughter of Jacob Ware, of Winchester, this state. His first wife bore him one daughter, Nancy S., born October 2, 1820, married Franklin Holman, died October 22, 1845. The children of his second union are Martha W., born July 7, 1823, married a Mr. Austin, of Newton, Massachusetts; and William B., born April 9, 1826, died April 15, of the same year. Those of his third marriage are: Olive H., born September 9, 1827, became the wife of Albert N. Chase, of Worcester, Massachusetts; John E., born November 29, 1830, died August 19, 1849; Sylvia, born March 11, 1832, died in infancy; William P., who will be again referred to; Sylvia A., born October 5, 1835, married (first) Rev. Albert E. Briggs, (second) Otis B. Wheeler, of Whitingham, Vermont; Sarah J., born September 5, 1837, married Rev. Pearl P. Briggs, a brother of above named minister; and Edmund H., born October 18, 1840. His fourth wife became the mother of three children: Flora E., born January 9, 1855, married George F. Newell; Herbert R., born December 28, 1856; and John S., born in January, 1864.

(III) William Perry, second son and fourth child of John and Sylvia (Perry) Chamberlain, was born in Swanzey July 2, 1833. He attended the public schools of Swanzey and Keene, and concluded his studies at the Keene Academy. His first employment was in a tailoring establishment at Keene, but the possession of a melodious tenor voice and a decided taste and capacity for a musical career, shortly afterwards led him into the concert field. The appearance in 1850 of Jennie Lind, who was the first great European cantatrice to visit the United States, was not only a most important event in the musical life of the Republic but served to stimulate our native singers and instrumentalists to higher artistic aspirations as well, and also inspired the general public to encourage and patronize native talent. Among the most prominent American artists of that day was Ossian E. Dodge, an excellent musician and a composer of merit. Mr. Dodge organized a company of singers and instrumentalists which was known as the Ossian Bards, and while this troup was touring New England in 1853, Mr. Chamberlain was induced much to his gratification to become its first tenor. While with the Bards, which visited the principal cities of the country, he entered the field of original composition and produced an inspiring patriotic song entitled: "Hurrah for Old New England," which acquired widespread popularity. Severing his connection with Mr. Dodge in 1854, he organized the Chamberlain Concert Company, which was inaugurated auspiciously and with which he was identified for a number of years or until 1861, when he withdrew from the concert field permanently. Entering mercantile business at Felchville, Vermont, he conducted a general store under the firm name of Chamberlain & Keyes until 1869, and immediately thereafter entered the shoe business at Keene. He subsequently became associated with Edward Spaulding in conducting a dry goods store, but shortly afterwards disposed of his interest in order to open a new establishment devoted to the same line of trade, and some fifteen years ago he admitted his son-in-law, Frank Huntress, as a partner. Possessing the necessary sagacity for successfuly conducting business on a much larger scale, and realizing that a judicious expansion would increase his purchasing advantages in the wholesale markets, he began the organization of a chain of branch stores, and at the present time is actively interested in dry-goods establishments known as the Chamberlain Syndicate in Vergennes and Rutland, Vermont, Nashua, Winchester and Claremont, New Hampshire, and Fitchburg and Leominster, Massachusetts. These, together with the Keene store, which is one of the best dry-goods emporiums is the state, are all financially sound and therefore in a flourishing condition.

Prior to the incorporation of Keene as a city Mr. Chamberlain served as a selectman, and was elected later to the common council. For the years 1878-79-80 he represented Keene in the lower branch of the legislature, and in 1885 and '86 he was in the state senate. At Concord he devoted his energies to progressive and reform legislation and he labored assiduously and successfully against apparently overwhelming odds to change the character of the "Old Grab Law" (so called), carrying his bill practically alone and finally winning out by nine votes in the senate and three in the house. For a period of nine years was a member of a special railroad commission and rendered excellent services in that capacity. Mr. Chamberlain has been for many years vice-president of the Citizens National Bank. Politically he is a Republican. For the past twenty-six years he has officiated as president of the board of trustees of the Keene Public Library. In Free Masonry he has taken thirty-two degrees, and also affiliates with the Knights of Pythias. He attends the First Congregational Church.

On January 8, 1857, Mr. Chamberlain married Harriet E. Persons, his first wife. She died August 17, 1894, leaving one daughter, Berdia Alia, who is now the wife of Frank Huntress, previously referred to. He was again married, March 16, 1897, to Ellen M. Atwood, daughter of William and Pamelia Atwood, of Keene. Mr. and Mrs. Frank Huntress have three children: William Chamberlain Huntress, born September 5, 1892; Frank Chamberlain Huntress, born August 4, 1894, and Harriet Chamberlain Huntress, born October 12, 1898.

CHAMBERLAIN The Chamberlain family of this sketch is very probably an untraced branch of the family of Chamberlains whose generations are elsewhere given in this work.

Loammi Chamberlain, son of Captain Isaac Chamberlain, was born in Chelmsford, Massachusetts, June 6, 1791, and died in Mason, New Hampshire, November 24, 1853, aged sixty-two years. Early in life he showed a partiality for mechanical occupation and an aptitude for ingenuity in the construction of such tools and utensils as he had occasion to make or mend. He chose to learn a

trade, and was apprenticed to Salathiel Manning, a machinist of Chelmsford. Mr. Manning afterward removed to New Ipswich, New Hampshire, where young Chamberlain completed his apprenticeship in 1812. Soon after he took a contract for building the cards for the Mason Cotton Mills Company, doing the work at the shop of his late master in New Ipswich. When he had finished the cards he went to Mason village and put the carding and spinning machinery in operation. The two or three years next following he was much engaged in setting up machinery and "starting on" mills, in New Ipswich, Milford, and other places.

About the year 1815 Loammi Chamberlain, Roger Chandler and Eleazer Rhoades bought a small mill in New Ipswich, which they fitted up, and there manufactured cotton yarn for two or three years. In 1818 he contracted for water power of the Mason Cotton Mill Company, and built a machine shop. In 1821 he contracted with the Mason Cotton Mill Company "to build, make and put in complete operation sixteen power looms, equal in every respect, to those in the Waltham Factory," and, if necessary, "to buy a loom of the Waltham Factory for a pattern, and then the said company to advance the money for the same, etc." About this period he made a valuable improvement in the power looms then in use. This greatly enhanced his reputation as a machinist, and gave him employment in other states. For several years he carried on quite extensively the manufacture of woolen and cotton machinery, machine tools, and so on, employing at times thirty or forty workmen. In 1846 he sold his machine tools and went into other business. For several years he was engaged in blacksmithing.

About the year 1840, in company with Thomas Pierce, he fitted up the lower cotton mill, which had stood idle since the failure of the Mason Cotton Mill Company, and for a short time manufactured satinets and other woolen fabrics. About this time also he built a saw mill below the village. For several years before his death he was chiefly employed in overseeing his saw mill and his farm. He was a member of the two great fraternal orders, the Masons and the Odd Fellows, in both of which orders he was prominent locally.

Mr. Chamberlain possessed inventive talent and mechanical skill in a high degree. He was one of the busiest and most useful of the ancient citizens of Mason, and gave employment to many persons, some of whom spent many years in his service. He never sought public office, but filled some public positions in the town with honor and ability. He possessed strong powers of observation and great enterprise. He was a good neighbor and a public-spirited citizen, and highly esteemed. But it was in the family circle that his virtues of head and heart were most observable, and there his excellencies were most fully appreciated.

He married, in 1821, Eliza S. Tucker, of Brookline. She survived her husband. They had but one child, James L., whose sketch follows.

(II) James Langdon, only child of Loammi and Eliza S. (Tucker) Chamberlain, was born in Mason, February 16, 1824, and died there. He was educated in the common schools, and, succeeded to the extensive business of his father, which he carried on successfully. In 1857 he erected one of the most extensive and complete flouring mills in the state, which he operated. He married, February 16, 1854, Mary A. Prescott, of Mason.

(III) Ida F., daughter of James L. and Mary A. (Prescott) Chamberlain, became the wife of Herbert J. Taft, of Greenville. (See Taft, III).

SHEDD

Charles Gale Shedd is a lineal descendant in the seventh generation of Daniel "Shed," an early settler in Braintree, Massachusetts, and in the tenth generation of Edmund Doty, the Mayflower Pilgrim. The posterity of both these immigrants have acquired an honorable record for their sturdy patriotism and steadfast devotion to the cause of civil and religious liberty, which constitutes the fundamental basis of our liberal republic, and those of the present generation represent the highest type of American citizenship. The name is unquestionably of remote English origin, and in the early Colonial records it was subjected to the usual variation in spelling, sometimes appearing as Shode.

(I) The family was established in New England by Daniel Shed, who emigrated prior to 1642, in which year his name first appears in the records of Braintree, and he resided in that part of the town which is now Quincy. In 1645 he was granted more land at the mouth of the Weymouth river, on a peninsula which for over a century was designated in the town records as Shed's Neck, and he resided there until 1659, when he removed to Billerica, Massachusetts. His death occurred in the last named town July 27, 1708, at the age of about eighty-eight years. He was twice married, and the christian name of one of his wives, probably the first, was Mary. He was the father of eleven children, two of whom were twins, and one of these was Zachariah, the next in line of descent. (Mention of his youngest son, Nathan, and descendants follows in this article).

(II) Zachariah Shed, third son and sixth child of Daniel and Mary Shed, was born in Braintree, June 17, 1656. He was about three years old when his parents went to Billerica, and he resided there for the greater part of his life, which terminated in Chelmsford, in 1735. He was three times married; his first wife together with two of his children were massacred by the Indians in August, 1692. The maiden name of his second wife is not at hand. His third wife, whom he married July 13, 1702, was Hannah Harris, and she died in Chelmsford, July 4, 1758. The total number of his children was seventeen, eight of whom were of his third union.

(III) Zachariah (2), seventh child of Zachariah (1) and Hannah (Harris) Shed, was born in Billerica, August 27, 1720. He was a carpenter and joiner, and followed that occupation for the major portion of his active life in Chelmsford, where he died February 2, 1784. The family record at hand does not mention the name of his wife, but states that he had five children.

(IV) Captain Ebenezer, fourth child of Zachariah Shed, Jr., was born in Chelmsford, July 10, 1753. Like his father he was a carpenter, but at the age of twenty-two years deserted his bench and with the majority of the young men in his neighborhood espoused the cause of national independence, enlisting April 27, 1775, in Captain John Ford's company, which joined the Twenty-seventh Regiment of the Continental line. He possessed unusual physical strength, and is said to have withstood without injury a hand-to-hand encounter with the enemy at the battle of Bunker Hill. After the completion of his military service he resumed his trade, and subsequently settled in Westford, Massachusetts, died in that town, March 2, 1829. In September, 1780, he married for his first wife, Mary Blood, born April 9, 1757, daughter of Stephen, Jr., and Mary Blood. She died August 13, 1785. May 16, 1793, he married for his second wife Lucy Hartwell, born October 20, 1763, daughter of David and Rachel

(Wortley) Hartwell, of Carlisle, Massachusetts. She survived him nearly twenty years. He was the father of ten children.

(V) Franklin, son of Captain Ebenezer and Lucy (Hartwell) Shedd, was born in Chelmsford, May 25, 1800. Having inherited his father's robust physique he attained a strong and vigorous manhood, and acquired a wide reputation for his muscular prowess. When a young man he engaged in the manufacture of hand-rakes at Plymouth, Vermont, where he resided until 1840, in which year he removed to Mount Holly, same state, and his death occurred in Weston, Vermont, March 30, 1875. He possessed a strong defined character which engendered pronounced opinions in all matters relative to the moral and religious welfare of his fellow-beings, and he not only professed christianity but conscientiously practiced it in his daily life. He was also an earnest advocate of total abstinence from intoxicating liquors, and on every opportune occasion vigorously emphasized his views upon that subject. November 4, 1830, Franklin Shedd married Lydia Kimball, born in Nelson, New Hampshire, November 12, 1804, daughter of Major David and Lydia (Simmons) Kimball. She died May 7, 1889, having been the mother of nine children.

(VI) Captain Charles Wesley Shedd, sixth child of Franklin and Lydia (Kimball) Shedd, was born in Mount Holly, October 21, 1840. He attended school in his native town, and at the age of thirteen entered the employ of M. Tarbell, manufacturer of lumber and hayrakes, with whom he remained for eight years. At the breaking out of the Civil war he and his brother were desirous of enlisting in the army, but the father refused his consent, the sons being under age. However, on the day that he was twenty-one, Charles and his brother joined a company of nine months men organized in the town, Charles with his characteristic energy and patriotic fervor, being the first man to record his name, mounting a table in the recruiting room and urging his young friends to join with him. This body of young men became Company H, Fourteenth Regiment Vermont Volunteers, and Charles Shedd was elected orderly sergeant. The regiment became part of General Stannard's famous Vermont Brigade. The regiment's term of service expired just before the battle of Gettysburg, but with superb patriotism the men went into line in that sanguinary engagement, and on the second day repelled one of the most desperate attacks witnessed on that historic field. After his discharge Sergeant Shedd aided in recruiting the frontier cavalry organized to protect the Canadian border, and with that command performed efficient service.

After the war he became foreman in Batcheller & Son's fork manufactory in Wallingford, and Tarbell's rake factory in Mechanicsville, Vermont. In 1870 he removed to Keene, New Hampshire, where he engaged in business for himself as an upholsterer and manufacturer of spring beds and mattresses. Shortly afterward he entered the employ of the late M. T. Tottingham, then the leading upholsterer, furniture dealer and undertaker in the town, in which business he continued until about 1903, when failing health made it necessary for him to abandon active work, after thirty years constant application. He was intensely interested in military affairs. At the time of the organization of the Keene Light Guard Battalion, and of Company G, Second Regiment New Hampshire Guard, which preceded it, he was one of the first to join, and was elected orderly sergeant of the first company. At the battalion formation he was commissioned first lieutenant of Company H, and was promoted to the captaincy when Captain J. W. Sturtevant became major. Captain Shedd was one of the most efficient in organizing both company and battalion, and was indefatigable in procuring means to perfect the organization and promote its usefulness. At one time he procured the sum of twelve hundred dollars for this purpose. At the time of his resignation, necessitated by failing health, he was the oldest officer in the battalion in period of service. He was an active member of John Sedgwick Post, Grand Army of the Republic, in which he held various offices, and was a charter member and first sachem of Pokahoket Tribe of Red Men. He attended the Unitarian Church. He was a Republican in politics, an earnest worker in many campaigns, and in 1880-81 rendered valuable service in the common council as a representative from the Fourth Ward. On June 12, 1864, he married Sarah Frances Doty, who was born in Wallingford, June 6, 1843, youngest daughter of Elihu and Rhoda (Sayles) Doty, great-granddaughter Jerathmiel Doty, who is said to have served in General Lafayette's bodyguard during the Revolution, and a lineal descendant of Edward Doty, the Mayflower Pilgrim, previously mentioned. (See Doty, VIII).

Captain Shedd died suddenly, at his home, on the evening of February 2, 1907, from apoplexy. He had been out as usual during the day, and was reading the evening paper when stricken. In compliance with his frequently expressed wish, the funeral was private and entirely devoid of display. A local paper (the *New Hampshire Sentinel*) in commenting upon his demise said: "As a man, Captain Shedd was whole-souled and generous to a fault, and was always doing for others, oftentimes aiding those in affliction in a quiet way, or raising money for a worthy object. He had a faculty of making friends wherever he went, and a very unusual faculty for accomplishing whatever he undertook, being a tireless worker, a skillful mechanic, and a good judge of human nature."

(VII) Charles Gale, only child of Captain Charles W. and Sarah (Doty) Shedd, was born in South Wallingford, May 18, 1865. After graduating from the Keene high school he entered the wholesale and retail drug store of Messrs. Bullard & Foster as an apprentice, and having acquired proficiency as a pharmacist, in 1888 he purchased Mr. Foster's interest in the firm, which then was known as Bullard & Shedd. This partnership continued until Mr. Bullard's death. After the death of Mrs. Bullard in 1899 he purchased her interest, organizing a stock company known as the Bullard & Shedd Company, of which he is treasurer, manager and principal shareholder, and is now transacting a profitable business. As a Republican he has figured quite conspicuously in local civic affairs, having served as a selectman and common councilman, and president of the common council and chairman of the board of health since 1903. For several years he has served as chairman of the Ward One Republican Club, and moderator of the ward. In 1900 he represented Keene in the lower branch of the state legislature, serving on the insane asylum committee. He was elected in 1906 to represent the thirteenth district in the state senate. For several years he served as hospital steward of the Second Regiment, New Hampshire National Guard. His fraternal affiliations are with the Masonic order, in which he has taken the highest degree of the Scottish Rite, the Thirty-third degree. He is president of the New Hampshire Society Sons of the American Revolution, a member of the Red Men, Knights of Pythias, Sons

of Veterans, New Hampshire Pharmaceutical Association, and a trustee of the New Hampshire State Sanatorium. He attends the Unitarian Church. On September 23, 1891, Mr. Shedd was joined in marriage with Rhoda Jane Colburn, who was born in Shrewsbury, Vermont, August 17, 1866, daughter of Leonard and Mary (Martin) Colburn. Their children are: Gale Colburn and Paul Wesley, twins, born July 14, 1892; and Charles Herbert, born February 3, 1907.

(II) Nathan, youngest child of Daniel Shedd, was born February 5, 1689, in Billerica, Massachusetts. He married Mary French, of that town, and they were the parents of nine children.

(III) Nathan (2), the eldest child of Nathan (1) and Mary (French) Shedd, was born May 23, 1695, in Billerica, and resided in the adjoining town of Tewksbury, where he was a well-to-do citizen, He was town treasurer for several years, and known by the title of Deacon. He died March 24, 1759. He married a cousin, Hannah Shedd, and they were the parents of eleven children.

(IV) Jonathan, sixth child of Deacon Nathan (2) and Hannah (Shedd) Shedd, was born October 28, 1728, in Tewksbury, where he made his home. He was a very muscular man and industrious, and became well to do. He died March 26, 1801. He married Lydia Kittredge, and they were the parents of five children.

(V) Jonathan (2), eldest son of Jonathan (1) and Lydia (Kittredge) Shedd, was born August 10, 1759, in Tewksbury, and resided nearly forty-seven years in that town, removing then to Norway, Maine. He died in Albany in the latter state, October 3, 1837. He married Abigail Fisk, who was born June 23, 1753, and was the mother of nine children.

(VI) John, fourth child of Jonathan (2) and Abigail (Fisk) Shedd, was born August 14, 1786, in Tewksbury, and lived in Albany, Maine, just outside the town of Waterford. He was married October 9, 1809, to Hannah Fleming, who was born September 18, 1794, in Tewksbury. Both died on the homestead in Albany, he on August 11, 1864, and she September 15, 1870. They were the parents of fourteen children, of whom eleven grew to maturity.

(VII) George, seventh son of John and Hannah (Fleming) Shedd, was born January 27, 1827, in Albany, Maine, and died in the adjoining town of Waterford, January 27, 1893. He married (first), Rebecca Frost, of Albany, Maine. She was descended from an early Massachusetts family as follows:

(I) John Lovejoy, one of the proprietors and earliest settlers of Andover, died in 1690. He married, in 1651, Mary Osgood, daughter of Christopher and Naomi (Hoyt) Osgood, pioneer settlers of Andover. They had two sons and several daughters, most of whom grew up and married.

(II) William, son of John and Mary (Osgood) Lovejoy, was born April 21, 1657, and married Mary Farnum.

(III) Samuel, son of William and Mary (Farnum) Lovejoy, was born April 10, 1693, and married Hannah Stevens.

(IV) Isaac, son of Samuel and Hannah (Stevens) Lovejoy, was born February 9, 1724, and married Deborah Sheldon.

(V) Isaac (2), son of Isaac (1) and Deborah (Sheldon) Lovejoy, was born March 16, 1757. He married, November 12, 1778. Mary Morse, of Methuen, who was born February 12, 1757, and died April 15, 1835. He died December 8, 1832. The children of this union were: Isaac, Bodwell, Mary, William, Lemuel, Phebe, Henry and Anna P.

(VI) Phebe, daughter of Isaac (2) and Mary (Morse) Lovejoy, was born December 5, 1790, and died March 16, 1877. She married Ziba Frost, who was born September 15, 1793, and died November 21, 1860. Their children were: Samuel J., Rebecca and Benjamin F.

(VII) Rebecca, daughter of Ziba and Phebe (Lovejoy) Frost, was born December 22, 1825, and died August 24, 1869. She married George Shedd, May 16, 1852. George Shedd was married (second), in June, 1871, to Saphronia (Brackett) Lamb, of Harrison, Maine. Of the first marriage there were two children: George Horsley and John Ziba; of the second marriage two: Myrtie Nina and Alton Brackett.

(VIII) George Horsley, son of George and Rebecca (Frost) Shedd, was born in Waterford, Maine, February 13, 1853. His preliminary education was obtained in the public schools of Norway, Maine, and in the Norway Liberal Institute. After teaching a few years he entered the Medical School of Maine, from which he graduated in June, 1879. His further medical education was obtained by post-graduate work in New York, Philadelphia, Berlin, and the hospitals of Berne, London. Paris, and Edinburgh. He is a member of the New Hampshire Board of Medical Examiners, of the Conway Board of Health, of his county, state and the Maine Medical Societies, also of the American Medical Association. He is a Mason, being a member of Mt. Washington Lodge and Signet Royal Arch Chapter of North Conway, and of St. Girard Commandery, Knights Templar, of Littleton, New Hampshire. He commenced the practice of medicine in Bartlett, New Hampshire, during the summer of 1879, and in the spring of 1883 moved to Fryeburg, Maine, where he resided until 1891, when he removed to North Conway, where he has since resided and been actively engaged in the practice of his profession. He married, May 15, 1880, Mary Hall, daughter of Soloman Smith and Emily Augusta (Warren) Hall. She decended on the paternal side from Hate Evil Hall, son of one of three brothers who came from England and settled in New Hampshire. Hate Evil Hall (2) was born at Dover, New Hampshire, in 1707, and afterward settled in Falmouth, Maine, where he died, November 28, 1797. He married Sarah Furbish, of Kittery, Maine, by whom he had thirteen children: Dorothy, Daniel, Hate Evil, Mercy, Ebenezer, Abigail, William, John, Jedediah, Andrew, Nicholas, Paul and Silas. Jedediah (3), son of Hate Evil and Sarah (Furbush) Hall, married (first). Hannah Hussey, and (second), Elizabeth Clough. His children were: Peter, Joel, Elizabeth, Aaron, Mercy, Moses, Abigail, David, Jonathan, Ann and Dorcas. Jonathan (4), son of Jedediah, married Mary, daughter of Joshua Smith, who was town treasurer of Norway, Maine, for twenty years. Soloman Smith Hall (5), son of Jonathan and Mary (Smith) Hall, was born at Norway, Maine, June 10, 1821, and died at Waterford, Maine, January 8, 1895. He married (first), November, 1852, Emily Augusta Warren, granddaughter of Abijah Warren, who was born in Taunton, Massachusetts, October 15, 1762, and at the age of thirteen entered active service as minuteman in the battle of Lexington, and served with distinction throughout the Revolutionary war. She was born in Paris, Maine, April 22, 1832, and died in Norway, Maine, August 29, 1861. Of this marriage there were born three children: Mary, Julia and Lizzie E. He married (second), Olivia G. Warren, by whom one child was born: Sidney Smith Hall, now living in Waterford, Maine.

Mary, daughter of Soloman Smith and Emily (Warren) Hall, and wife of Dr. George H. Shedd, was born in Norway, Maine, March 6, 1854. They have one child, George Harold, born in Bartlett, New Hampshire, November 1, 1882. He is a graduate of Harvard University, A. B. 1905, and is now a student in Harvard Medical School. Mrs. Shedd has always been active in educational and charitable work. She is ex-president of the North Conway Woman's Club, of which she is one of the founders; president of the Woman's Educational League; vice-regent of Anna Stickney Chapter, Daughters of the American Revolution, and chairman of the industrial and child labor committee of both the New Hampshire Federation of Woman's Clubs and New Hampshire Daughters of the American Revolution.

John Z. Shedd was born at Norway, Maine, July 8, 1861. During the autumn of 1884 he went to Fryeburg, Maine, and entered Fryeburg Academy, from which he was graduated in 1886. The two following years were devoted to teaching and reading medicine. In 1891 the degree of M. D. was received from the Medical School of Maine, at Brunswick, since which time he has taken several post-graduate courses in New York. In 1891 he began the practice of medicine at North Conway, New Hampshire, where he has since resided and has met with a good degree of success. He is a member of his county, state and the Maine medical societies, as well as of the American Medical Association. Early in his twenty-first years he was made a Mason in Oxford Lodge, Ancient Free and Accepted Masons, Norway, Maine, and during the following year joined Union Royal Arch Chapter in the same town. He later withdrew from these societies to become a member of similar bodies in the town of his adoption, where he has been an active Masonic worker, being past high priest of his chapter, of which he is a charter member. In more recent years he has become a member of St. Girard Commandery, Knights Templar, at Littleton, New Hampshire, and also of Bektash Temple, Nobles of the Mystic Shrine, at Concord, New Hampshire.

Myrtie Nina Shedd was born at Norway, Maine, September 16, 1875. Alton Brackett Shedd was born at the same place, February 17, 1880. About two years after the birth of the latter, the children with their parents removed to Waterford, where they resided until after the death of their father, in 1893. Later, with their mother, they removed to Fryeburg, Maine, where both were graduated from Fryeburg Academy. On September 20, 1899, Myrtie N. was married to Dr. Byron W. McKeen, a native of Fryeburg, and a classmate in the academy. He received his M. D. from the Medical School of Maine, and, after serving one year as house physician at the Maine Insane Hospital, settled in Saxony, Massachusetts, where by his pleasing personality and medical skill he built up a large and lucrative practice. He died of pneumonia, May 7, 1903, at the age of twenty-eight years. Shortly after his sister had become settled in Massachusetts, Alton B. and his mother removed to the same town and household, where they all have continued to reside. Alton B. accepted a position with the Dennison Manufacturing Company at South Framingham, where he has been advanced to becoming the head of one of its departments.

TYLER The name of Tyler has been distinguished in many ways in American history. Beside furnishing a president of the United States, it has been noted in law and literature, in educational and other professional labors. One of its most honored bearers in New Hampshire was long an instructor at Dartmouth College, and other representatives have been honorable and respected business men.

William Tyler probably from Devonshire, England, took the oath of fidelity at New Haven, Connecticut, in 1657. He married Abigail Terrell, daughter of Roger Terrell, of Milford, New Haven Colony. They had ten children. He died in Milford in 1692.

(II) John (1), son of William and Abigail (Terrell) Tyler, was born in 1667 in Weathersfield, Connecticut, and died in Wallingford, Connecticut, in 1741. He married, January 7, 1674, Abigail Hall, daughter of Sergeant Thomas and Grace (Watson) Hall, of Wallingford. There were eleven children.

(III) John (2), son of John (1) and Abigail (Hall) Tyler, was born in Wallingford, Connecticut, January 14, 1710. No date is given of his death. April 7, 1731, he married Phebe Beach, daughter of Thomas and Phebe (Wilcoxen) Beach, of Stratford, Connecticut. There were five children by this marriage.

(IV) Benjamin, son of John (2) and Phebe (Beach) Tyler, was born in Wallingford, February 23, 1733. Colonel Benjamin Tyler came to Claremont, New Hampshire, from Farmington, Connecticut, in 1767, traveling part of the way on snow shoes on the ice of the Connecticut river. That summer he built the first dam across Sugar river at West Claremont. Colonel Tyler is entitled to an extensive sketch in a history of New Hampshire and especially in the town of Claremont, as he did more to open up the resources of the town and the Vermont towns just across the Connecticut river than any other man of his day or since, and has been called "the most sterling man in the first generation of the history of Claremont." His views were liberal, and his interest was always for the advancement of the church, the school and his town. Like many of his descendants he was conspicuous for his progressiveness, liberality and hospitality. In 1768, Colonel Tyler went back to Connecticut, and returned with his family. That year he built the first mill erected in town—a grist mill at West Claremont, near where the Jarvis Mills now stand. He owned all the water power from Fall No. 1 to No. 9 inclusive, on the south and east side of Sugar river; here he built in 1780 the first sawmill in the section. In consideration of Colonel Tyler having built the first mills in town he was given as a premium ten acres of land on the south side of Sugar river opposite the mills. He purchased a tract of land on the north side of Sugar river and eighty acres south of the river. He also bought a tract of what is now Claremont Village, extending from the L. A. Tolles farm to Tremont Square, and south to Summer street. He received as a grant fifty acres of what was called the "big meadow" east of the town. In 1768 Colonel Tyler put a dam across Sugar river a few rods above where the high bridge now stands, and built a smelting and iron working establishment for manufacturing mill irons and other heavy articles from iron which he brought from North Charlestown, obtaining his lime from Weathersfield, Vermont. He did a lucrative business for over twenty years, employing about thirty hands. In 1810 he built and put in operation what was known in those days as the flax mill, the use of which was to prepare flax for the old hand spinning wheel. In 1785 Colonel Tyler built the first mills in the village—the "Old Tyler Mills," Lower Village, both grist and sawmills. He also built the first saw and grist mills that the people had in nearly all the surrounding towns, and also many in northern Vermont.

Colonel Tyler, with two of his sons, bought half of Ascutney mountain, in Vermont, from whence they quarried mill stones with which they supplied the states and Canada for a number of years. Many were the narrow escapes that these energetic first settlers had in getting the large stones down the mountain side. The eleventh patent issued by the United States government in actual series was to Colonel Benjamin Tyler on "a machine for cleaning wheat, etc.," in 1796. During the next few years he with his son John took out six other patents. The crowning work of Colonel Tyler, at the age of over sixty years, was the invention of an improved bucket for a wooden water wheel with an upright shaft called the "rye fly," or tub wheel, for which he secured two patents. one in 1800, the other in 1804. His marked mechanical genius has been transmitted to a long line of descendants. Benjamin Tyler's name appears as a member of the board of selectmen at the "first meeting of the inhabitants of the town of Claremont in the Province of New Hampshire in 1768." He was subsequently re-elected many times, and held many other offices of trust.

The first settlement of the town of Claremont was by a band of Episcopalians, or Church of England people, from Connecticut, several of whom in 1769 addressed "A Memorial of the inhabitants of Claremont, New Hampshire, to the Reverend Clergy of the Church of England, and missionaries of the Venerable Society of P. G. F. P. to be convened at New Milford in the Colony of Connecticut in Trinity week," which was the first step toward organizing Union Church (West Claremont), the oldest Episcopal church edifice in New Hampshire. Benjamin Tyler was one of the signers of this petition. He "contributed £10 and all the timber for the building, and helped to build it with his hands." At the first vestry meeting of the parish in November, 1773, he was chosen warden. and many times after. In 1770 he went by marked trees to Charlestown, New Hampshire, to pilot the Rev. Samuel Peters to Claremont in order that his children might be christened. After the lapse of over a century Benjamin Tyler's descendants of the same name are still communicants of Union Church, the church in the wilderness in whose support he was so zealous that he refused to take up arms against the mother country. Benjamin Tyler's only brother John, after graduating at Yale College, went to London, England, where by the bishop of that city he was ordained in the Established Church and, returning to Norwich, Connecticut, officiated as rector of Christ Church over half a century 1760-1823. He is buried under the chancel of the new church there, which contains a memorial tablet. During the famous "Barber Crusade" in Claremont, when the Rev. Daniel Barber, rector of Union Church, his family and a few others became converts to Catholicism, one of Benjamin Tyler's sons, Noah, (who married Mr. Barber's sister) with his family were of the number. This Noah's son, William Tyler, became a man of note in the Catholic world. Although he died before he was forty years old he reached the distinction of being the first

Roman Catholic bishop of the diocese of Hartford, which See then included the states of Connecticut and Rhode Island.

In 1773, Colonel Tyler built for a home for his family the large house at West Claremont, still standing and but little altered. It was long known as the Mansion House of Colonel Tyler, and many pieces of the handsome carved mahogany with which it was furnished are still in existence. Since its sale seventy-five years ago, by the Tyler heirs, it has been used as a hotel, known as the "Maynard House."

Benjamin Tyler married, at Wallingford, Connecticut, June 26, 1753, Mehitable Andrews, daughter of Elisha and Mabel Andrews. She was a lineal descendant of Lieutenant William Andrews, of Hampsworth, England, who was early at New Haven and died in 1676 at East Hampton, Connecticut. Their children were: Ephraim, married Abigail Pardee; Phebe, married John Hitchcock; Mary, married Nehemiah Rice; Risby, married Elisha Andrews: Patience. married John Strowbridge; Mehitable. married George Hubbard; Sally, married Samuel Sumner; Benjamin, married Anne Smith; Noah, married Abigail Barber; and John, who married Mary Giddings. (Benjamin and John and descendants receive mention in this article). During his lifetime Colonel Benjamin Tyler gave to each of his six daughters a large farm in Claremont. Their land comprised what is now the business section of the town. He died at West Claremont, March 9, 1814, "from which time to this date the family has perhaps been the most conspicuous and aidful of all in developing the resources of this region."

(V) Ephraim, eldest son of Colonel Benjamin and Mehitable (Andrews) Tyler, was born in Farmington, Connecticut, and died in Claremont, New Hampshire, December 16, 1823, aged sixty-four years. On his twenty-first birthday Ephraim Tyler was given by his father one hundred acres of land extending from Main street to Tremont Square, to Summer street, and west to the Lawrence Tolles farm. He also gave him at this time (1780) both the grist and sawmills at the lower village, which he owned and operated during his life time. He built on Sullivan street, which was cut through his farm, the old Tyler homestead still standing, and shaded by the fine old elm trees planted by his hand. Ephraim Tyler married (first), Abigail Pardee, daughter of Benjamin and Hannah (Beecher) Pardee; she was born in New Haven, in 1761, and was a descendant of George Pardee, the Huguenot. who came from Paris at the time of the Huguenot persecution. He was in New Haven in 1645 and engaged to teach the "towne schoole," promising to teach English and Latin. This school was the foundation of what is now the Hopkins Grammar School. Abigail (Pardee) Tyler was also a lineal descendant of Dr. David Yale, LL. D., of Chester, England, and of the Rt. Rev. George Lloyd, bishop of Chester, England, 1604. The children of Ephraim and Abigail (Pardee) Tyler were: Benjamin Pardee, Ephraim, Austin, Miles, Abigail, Lola. Sarah, Marcia, William, Rebecca and Sarah.

(VI) Honorable Austin Tyler, third son of Ephraim and Abigail (Pardee) Tyler, was born in Claremont, January 6, 1790. He is said to have been "the most public spirited son of Claremont." His ambition was to develop and improve the town rather than to aggrandise himself. In 1813 he was commissioned sergeant in the New Hampshire militia, and in 1822, after many years service, he resigned as paymaster of the Fifteenth Regiment, Fifth Brigade, Third Division, New Hampshire Militia, and "was honorably discharged at his own request." He held various offices of public trust. He was deputy sheriff in 1819; selectman for nine years, representative in the New Hampshire legislature in 1827-28 and 1831-32-1835-36-37, and in 1842; state senator in 1838. He compiled and published in 1835 Tyler's "Tax Maker's Book," which was afterward used in nearly every town and city in New Hampshire, and was also used in most of the states of the Union. In 1843 Mr. Tyler placed the picturesque "old stone watering trough" on the West Claremont road, and also rebuilt the same year that highway which is one of the old time corduroy roads. He was one of the most active and influential individuals engaged in organizing in 1832 the Claremont Manufacturing Company, which was the first company organized by citizens of Claremont for manufacturing purposes. Mr. Tyler built as a home for his bride, in 1813, the old colonial house on Mulberry street, since known as the Rossiter house. He later built and occupied the brick house on the corner of Sullivan and Union streets, still owned by his grandchildren. He married, in Plainfield, New Hampshire, March 6, 1814, Almira, only child of Daniel (4) and Hannah (Bailey) Kingsbury, of Plainfield. (See Kingsbury, VI). She was born in Keene, March 6, 1799, and was married on her fifteenth birthday. Their children were: Henry Daniel, Louise, Emeline, Elizabeth Bailey, Frederick Austin, Ellen Almira and Sarah Frances. Austin Tyler died in Claremont, August 12, 1844. The *National Eagle* of August 16, 1844. says: "Hon. Austin Tyler was one of the most active, enterprising and public spirited men in town, the strictest integrity was a prominent trait in his character, and his influence has been extensive in the town where he has always resided." He was an Episcopalian, being a member of the Historic Union Church, where for many years he sang in the choir. His wife survived him, and died in Claremont, December 19, 1867.

(VII) Henry Daniel, eldest son of Austin and Almira (Kingsbury) Tyler, was born August 13, 1815. He was educated at Unity Military Academy, the Rev. Virgil H. Barber Academy, and at Kimball Union Academy, Meriden. He served in the Mexican war; was a volunteer from Massachusetts under Captain Webster, First Regiment, and afterward belonged to the "Army of Acceptation." He died unmarried in San Antonio, Texas, June 16, 1868.

(VII) Louise, eldest daughter of Austin and Almira (Kingsbury) Tyler, was born March 30, 1818. She married, November 14, 1842, Nathaniel Waite Westgate, of Enfield, later known as Judge Westgate, of Haverhill, New Hampshire.

(VII) Emeline, second daughter of Austin and Almira (Kingsbury) Tyler, was born April 21, 1820, and married in September, 1838, Asa Tufts Starbird, of Boston. She died in Dover, Kansas, March 4, 1876.

(VII) Elizabeth Bailey Tyler, third daughter of Austin and Almira (Kingsbury) Tyler, was born September 15, 1822, and died April 26, 1868. She was educated in Dr. A. A. Miners' School at Unity, New Hampshire. She married, May 12, 1853, Samuel W. Howe, of Boston.

(VII) Frederick Austin, second son of Austin and Almira (Kingsbury) Tyler, was born December 10, 1824, and died in Claremont, February 11, 1890. He was educated at Unity, New Hampshire, Military Academy. Mr. Tyler had a very successful business career as a hotel man, being manager of the Pemberton Square House, Boston, of the Washington House, Lowell, Massachusetts, and afterward for many years a member of the firm of Taft, Tyler & Greenleaf of the Flume and Profile Houses, White Mountains. He lived quietly in Claremont after his retirement from business, and from his ample means he assisted many unfortunate people who will long remember him with genuine gratitude. Like his father, Austin Tyler, his integrity was unquestioned.

(VII) Ellen Almira Tyler was born May 29, 1827, and died March 11, 1900. She was a teacher in the Claremont public schools and a member of Trinity Episcopal Church. She married, January 18, 1854, in Trinity Church, John Leonard Lovering, of Quechee, Vermont. (See Lovering, VII).

(VII) Sarah Frances, daughter of Austin and Almira (Kingsbury) Tyler, born in Claremont, New Hampshire, December 27, 1834, educated at Thetford Academy, Thetford, Vermont. Married, December 25, 1855, Joseph K. Egerton, of Quechee, Vermont. She died at Northfield, Vermont, March 9, 1886. Children: Edith Kingsbury Egerton, Frederick Tyler Egerton.

(V) John, son of Colonel Benjamin and Mehitable (Andrews) Tyler, married Mary Giddings.

(VI) John (2), son of John (1) and Mary (Giddings) Tyler, born in Claremont, New Hampshire, March 28, 1818. He was early left an orphan and went to Barre, Vermont, where he learned the trade of millwright. He settled in West Lebanon, New Hampshire, in 1850, and for several years did a large and lucrative business in building mills. He returned to Claremont in 1872, where he was well and favorably known as an inventor and builder, being descended from a long line of eminent mechanics. He was engineer and superintendent in building the Sugar River Paper mill and was principal stockholder and president of the company. He also built the grist and sawmills at the Lower Village. Mr. Tyler was the inventor, 1856, of the iron Tyler turbine water wheel, the first iron water wheel ever made, since which time he has been granted nine patents for improvements on it. These found their way all over the country and some were sent to Europe. For years these wheels were considered the best turbine wheels manufactured, this fact being thoroughly developed some years ago by a comparative and competitive test of the products of other makers of similar wheels. He was also inventor and patentee of Tyler's copper cylinder washer, for washing paper stock. In 1874 he built the reservoir on Bible Hill, putting in an aqueduct system, now known as "Tyler Water Works," which supplied the town with fresh spring water for household purposes. He was much interested in making Lake Sunapee what it is today and opened his purse wide for its improvement; he was a stockholder in the Ben Mere Inn, also of the Woodsum Steamboat Company. He was a far-seeing and sagacious business man and greatly interested in the improvements of his native town. He was a staunch Republican and was a member of the legislature 1891-92 and his record was a clean one. He was a public-spirited, genial man and in his death Claremont lost a worthy citizen. He was a lover of good horses and and in his fine stables could be found always the best blooded and handsomest to be had. He was a most liberal man and no worthy cause was brought to his notice that failed to receive assistance at his hands. He died at his home, November 28, 1896. He is survived by his widow,

John Tyler

who was Miss Anna Maria, daughter of Taylor and Sybil (Lawton) Alexander, of Hartland, Vermont.

(V) Benjamin (2), son of Colonel Benjamin (1) and Mehitabel (Andrews) Tyler, was born in Claremont, February 27, 1771, and died February 17, 1826. He was probably associated with his father in the purchase of one-half of Ascutney Mountain, and later with his brothers John and Noah, succeeded to the extensive business of quarrying mill stones. The farm given him by his father is now a part of the village of Claremont. He married Anne Smith, of Powlet, Vermont. Their children were: Cynthia, John, Benjamin, Benonia, Anna Smith and Maria.

(VI) John (3), son of Benjamin (2) and Anne (Smith) Tyler, was born in Claremont, April 8, 1802. He died January 13, 1886, in the first framed house built in town, where he had lived many years, at West Claremont. He learned the millright trade of his father, and followed it for many years. Mr. Tyler was a representative in the New Hampshire legislature in 1850-51 and warden of Union Church (Episcopal), as his father and grandfather had been before him. He was a man who stood high in the community for his personal worth and ability. John Tyler married (first), November 12, 1830, Mary S. Webster, daughter of Dr. Thomas and Sarah (West) Webster (see Webster, V). He married (second), Jeanette Berry. The children by the first marriage were John Henry, Charles Webster, James Andrews, Mary Anna and Austin. By the second there was one son Hoel. All were born in Claremont. 1. John Henry was born October 12, 1832, and died unmarried, January 29, 1890. He was a merchant, and later in the hotel business in New York City. 2. Charles Webster was born September 17, 1834, and died February 15, 1902. He was a prominent instructor of instrumental music in New York, teaching harp, piano and organ. He married G. A. Simonson. 3. James Andrews, born August 12, 1836, was educated at the public and high schools of Claremont, New Hampshire, and when a young man learned the trade of machinist and worked at this at various places, mainly in Springfield and New York, for about fifteen years. In 1871 he engaged as salesman in the hardware business on a commission basis, and for over thirty years has represented the firm of Herman Baker & Company, of New York. He is a very successful business man. He married Maria Frederika Clement, August 17, 1875. 4. (VII) Mary Anna, only daughter of John (3) and Mary S. (Webster) Tyler, was born July 22, 1843. She was educated in the public schools of Claremont and at a Young Ladies' School in Hanover, New Hampshire. She is an Episcopalian. January 7, 1880, Mary Tyler married Daniel Webb Johnson, for many years a leading citizen and prominent business man of Claremont. (See Johnson, third family, VII). 5. Austin Tyler, born January 16, 1848, died April 21, 1901. He followed the hotel business on Mount Washington and in New York. July 21, 1881, he married Mary Reed Tyler, a distant cousin. She is still living (1906). They had two daughters, Mary Lucy and Sarah Emily, both of whom graduated from Vassar College 1906. 6. Hoel Tyler, only child of John (3) and Jeanette Berry Tyler, was born December 19, 1855. He studied medicine and is a successful physician in Redlands, California (1906).

COLE This name was quite numerously represented in the early settlement of Massachusetts, and there are numerous prolific families bearing the name now scattered throughout the United States. It has been prominently identified with bench and bar, with all the learned professions, and with various occupations in life, contributing no small share to the development and progress of the nation.

(I) William Cole was very early in the Massachusetts Bay Colony, and had a grant of two acres of land at Mount Wollaston, January 23, 1637. In June, 1640, he was granted forty acres at Hampton, and had one share of the common lands there in 1646. He resided for some time at Wells, Maine, and was constable of that town in 1645. He returned to Hampton, and died there May 26, 1662, in his eighty-second year, being then in indigent circumstances. He took the oath of allegiance to the Massachusetts jurisdiction at Wells, July 6, 1653. He married Elizabeth, daughter of Francis Doughty, a merchant of Bristol, England. Dow's History of Hampton states that his widow was named Eunice, and it is quite possible that he may have had a second wife. She was reputed a witch. His children included John, Nicholas, William, and probably others.

(II) Nicholas, son of William Cole, was born in 1636 probably in America, and was but a child when his father settled in Wells, Maine. He signed a petition there in 1656, and was constable in 1658. He was appointed ferryman at Cape Porpoise river in 1664, agreeing to keep the ferry seven years. His children included the following: Nicholas, Jane and Ann.

(III) Nicholas, second son of Nicholas (1) Cole, born 1656, resided at Wells, where he was killed by Indians May 11, 1704. There is no record of his marriage or family.

(IV) Thomas, probably a son of Nicholas (2) Cole, was a resident of Kittery, Maine, where he was married to Martha, daughter of Christian Remick. She administered his estate in 1725. His children were: Daniel, Hannah, Abigail, Asahel, Remick, Jerusha, Charity, Abial and Robert.

(V) Robert, youngest child of Thomas and Martha (Remick) Cole, was born probably in Kittery, and passed his life in that town. He was married (first), November 22, 1726, to Phebe Shepherd. She did not live long, and his second wife was Martha (surname unknown). He was married (third), January 22, 1765, to Mrs. Ann Cottle; and (fourth), in October, 1775, to Mrs. Agnes Weeks, who survived him. His will was made in 1784. His children were: Robert, Ezra, Remick, William, Ichabod, John, Phebe, Mary, Thomas and Simeon.

(VI) Ichabod, fifth son of Robert Cole, and probably child of his second wife Martha, was baptized April 14, 1757, in Kittery, and was married there November 8, 1770, to Elizabeth, daughter of Captain John and Hannah (Fernald) Gowell. She died in October, 1834, aged about eighty-five years. Their children were: John, Gowell, Ichabod, Elizabeth, Nabby, Eli, Mary, Robert, Nancy and William.

(VII) William, youngest child of Ichabod and Elizabeth (Gowell) Cole, was born March 1, 1791, in Kittery, probably in that part which is now Eliot, Maine, and was married in Kittery, May 24, 1820, to Polly Brooks, of Eliot. Their children were: William G., James D., Rose, Mary and Oliver B.

(VIII) William Gowell, eldest son of William and Polly (Brooks) Cole, was born in Elliott, Maine, September 11, 1822. He was a tanner and currier in Portsmouth and Biddeford until about 1866, when his health becoming impaired he engaged in farming in Hampton, New Hampshire, where he has since resided. He filled the office of tax collector of Hampton twenty years, and represented the town in the legislature in 1888. He is a member of the North Church (Congregational) of Portsmouth, and is one of the four original pew owners. He married (first), February 23, 1851, Hannah Toby Brooks, of Elliott, Maine. She died in Portsmouth, April 30, 1860. He married (second), November 16, 1862, Susan Leavitt Page, of Hampton. daughter of Josiah and Susan L. Page. His children by the first wife were: Everett Sumner, who died in 1868, aged fourteen. Myron W., Abbie I., the wife of S. Albert Shaw, of Hampton. (See Shaw, VII). The children of the second are: Anna M., a graduate of Mt. Holyoke College, class of 1888, and now a teacher in Hampton Academy. Ernest Gowell, mentioned below. Hattie L., who died in 1888, aged seventeen.

(IX) Ernest Gowell, second child and only son of William G. and Susan L. (Page) Cole, was born in Hampton. June 16, 1869. After leaving the public schools he attended Hampton Academy, from which he graduated in 1888. In 1891 he graduated from the New Hampshire College of Agricultural and Mechanic Arts, and went into business with J. A. Lane, of Hampton, who formed the firm of J. A. Lane & Company, dealers in general merchandise. Six years later (1897) Mr. Cole sold his interest to Mr. Lane and purchased a similar business at that time owned by J. W. Mason & Co., and has since carried on the business alone. Since 1901 he has been postmaster. He is treasurer of the Hampton Water Works Company, justice of the peace and notary public. In political faith he is a Republican. He is a member of the Congregational Church of Hampton, and has been superintendent of its Sunday school five years. He is a fraternity man, and is a member of Star in the East Lodge, No. 59, Free and Accepted Masons; Rockingham Lodge, No. 22, Independent Order Odd Fellows, of Hampton; Huntoo Encampment, No. 59; and Friendship Lodge. Royal Arcanum. He married, June 16, 1896, at Rochester, Caroline E. Jones, who was born in Rochester, January 23, 1873, daughter of Charles and Maria (Noyes) Jones. They have one child, Ernestine Cole, born June 9, 1898.

(Second Family.)

COLE This name appears in Salem, Massachusetts, as early as 1650; in Boston in 1630-1634; Plymouth, 1634; and another, the earliest in the colonies, that of James, who finally went to Connecticut with Mr. Hooker in 1635. Other settlers bearing this cognomen came early to New England.

(I) Thomas Cole was at Salem in 1650, and is recorded as a husbandman. A Thomas Cole came to Massachusetts in the "Mary and John," March 23, 1633, and was an original proprietor of Hampton, and is mentioned as of that place in 1638, but whether the same individual is referred to in both cases is not certain: His will is dated December 15, 1678, and it was proved April 27, 1679. His widow Ann made her will November 1, 1679, and it was proved May 2, 1681. Their children were: Abraham and John, whose sketch follows.

(II) John, the second son of Thomas and Ann Cole, was born between 1640 and 1650, and was one of the inhabitants of Salem who protested against imposts in 1668. One authority says he moved to Boxford in 1717, and died "very suddenly" in 1737, aged sixty-eight years; another says he was a cooper by trade, and lived in Salem till about 1675, when he removed to Malden, and about 1684 to Lynn, where he died intestate, October 8, 1703. He made a will October 5, 1703, which is endorsed "Will not perfect," and was not probated, as it had but two witnesses. Samuel, the son of John Cole, of Boxford, was appointed administrator of the estate of his widowed mother, Sarah Cole, of Bradford, May 25, 1741. John Cole married, May 28, 1667, Mary Knight, who died before 1675. She was probably a daughter of William Knight. He married (second), between 1675 and 1686, Sarah Alsbee, who was tried for witchcraft at Charlestown, and acquitted February 1, 1693. John Cole's children by the first wife were: John, Thomas, Mary and Hannah; and by the second wife: Samuel and Anna.

(III) Samuel. the fifth child of John Cole, born by his second wife, Sarah (Alsbee) Cole, was born in Lynn, December 27, 1687, and died in Boxford, January 20, 1765. In 1717 he went to Boxford with his father, and for £110 purchased of Ebenezer Burbank the farm on which his posterity resided until about the close of the Civil war. This was the tract of sixty-seven acres laid out to Thomas Lever in 1666. He was taxed in Boxford from 1717 to 1749. His wife Susanna, whom he married between 1710 and 1720, died July 29, 1785, aged ninety-five. Their children were: Samuel. John, Rebecca, Susanna and Mary.

(IV) Samuel (2), eldest child of Samuel (1) and Susanna Cole, was probably born in Lynn, and resided in Boxford, where he died in 1805. He married Bethiah Hardy, of Bradford, October 5, 1738, and they had fifteen children: Daniel, Benjamin, Solomon, Phineas, Mercy, Martha. Rebecca, Eliphalet, Samuel, Margaret, Jesse and David (twins), Bethiah (died young), Simeon and Bethiah.

(V) Solomon, third son and child of Samuel (2) and Bethiah (Hardy) Cole, was born in Boxford, April 1, 1743, and settled in Landaff, New Hampshire, where he died in 1835, aged ninety-two. He married Mehitable Barker, of Andover (published January 8, 1766). Their children were: Timothy, Kimball, Benjamin, Isaac, John, Solomon, Samuel, Asa and Catherine.

(VI) Lieutenant Kimball, second son of Solomon and Mehitable (Barker) Cole, was born in Boxford, Massachusetts, in 1780, and died there in 1822. He was usually called Lieutenant Cole. He married Abigail Runnells (published April 2, 1804). She was born in Methuen, in February, 1780, and died in Boxford, April 7, 1861, daughter of William and Rebecca Runnells, of Methuen. Their children were: Sarah Foster, Rebecca. Ephraim Foster, Mehitable Baker, Abigail, John Kimball and William Runnells.

(VII) Ephraim Foster, third child and eldest son of Lieutenant Kimball and Abigail (Runnells) Cole, was born in Boxford, July 6, 1809, and died there April 23, 1879. He was a farmer and a lifelong resident of Boxford. He married (first), Eliza Spofford, December 10, 1830. She was born in Chester, New Hampshire, and died April 25, 1832. He married (second), March 5, 1833, Sarah Spofford, who was born in Danville, New Hampshire, and died in Boxford, daughter of Benjamin Spofford. He had one child by the first wife, and nine by the second, as follows: Eliza Spofford, William Kimball, George Spofford, John Foster, Charles Warren, Sarah Jane, Arthur E., Joseph Franklin, Wallace W., and Roscoe Kimball. Eliza S. died young; William K., born January 6, 1834, died unmarried in Hillsborough, Iowa, October 23, 1856; George S., born July 2, 1836, resides in Andover, Massachusetts; John F., born January 20, 1841, enlisted in Company F, Thirty-fifth Massachusetts Volunteer Infantry, and was wounded and died in McClellan Hospital, Philadelphia, from the effects of his wounds, June 14, 1864; Charles W., born April 3, 1844, enlisted in Company F, Thirty-fifth Massachusetts Volunteer Infantry, and died of fever at Newport News, March 3, 1863. Sarah Jane, born March 13, 1846, married Melvin T. Wadlin, and resided in North Andover, Massachusetts, now in Methuen, Massachusetts. Arthur E., born September 30, 1848, lives in Orono, Maine. Joseph F., born September 28, 1851, resides in Andover, Massachusetts. Wallace W. is mentioned below. Roscoe K., born February 28, 1861, resides in Andover, Massachusetts.

(VIII) Wallace Woodbury, eighth child and seventh son of Ephraim F. and Sarah (Spofford) Cole, was born in Boxford, Massachusetts, November 19, 1855. He attended the public schools, and remained at home until he was eighteen years old, and then worked a short time in a carriage factory in Amesbury. The five years following he was employed as a carpenter in Andover. In 1876 he removed to Salem, New Hampshire, where he worked for a year as journeyman carpenter, then located on his wife's father's farm and resided there twenty-five years till 1904, then came to his present home at Salem Depot. In 1879 he formed a partnership with Charles A. Dow, under the firm name of Cole & Dow, and engaged in the retail meat business. Subsequently Mr. Cole bought his partner's interest and carried the business on alone up to 1904, when he sold out. In 1899 he became interested in lumbering, and has kept increasing his interests until now he has two portable steam sawmills in Salem and one each in York and Elliott, Maine, and cuts annually several million feet of lumber. He is a man of foresight and good judgment, and has accumulated a large amount of property, much of which is in valuable real estate. Without the advantage of a liberal education, his native ability has been sufficient to win success where better educated men have failed. He is a zealous Republican and a local leader of his party. He has served as chairman of the Republican town committee, has been selectman four terms two of which he was chairman of the board: represented the town in the legislature in 1892-94, and was senator from the Twentieth district in 1905. Was chosen a delegate to the constitutional convention of 1900. He is an attendant of the Methodist Episcopal Church of which he is a trustee. He is also a member of Sprickett Lodge, No. 85, Free and Accepted Masons, of Salem, and has been senior warden a number of years. Member of Salem Grange, Patrons of Husbandry, and treasurer of this a number of years, and also a member of United Order Pilgrim Fathers. He was also treasurer of the public library for a number of years. He married, December 24, 1878, at Salem, Ida Dow Colby, who was born in Salem, daughter of William G. and Frances (Dow) Colby, of Windham. Eight children have been born to them: Mabel, Minnie F., Gertrude C., Clarence W., Edith L., Eva M., William McK. and George W. Mabel, born in Salem, January 26, 1880, married, September 25, 1901, Aaron Alexander, of Windham. They have one child, Everett H. Minnie F. born August 25, 1882, married, September 9, 1903, Fred Weiss, and has two children: Pauline and Donald. Gertrude Colby, born September 16, 1884, married, June 21, 1905, Charles Quimby. Clarence Waldo, born January 20, 1888. Edith Lillian, born May 20, 1891. Eva Mildred, born July 5, 1895. William McKinley, born September 27, 1896. George Wallace, born July 9, 1898.

(Third Family.)

COLE

There are many branches of the Cole, Coles or Cowles family among the early English emigrants to this country. The Hartford (Connecticut) line is descended from James Cole, who was born in England, came to what is now Cambridge, Massachusetts, and in 1635 joined a party which journeyed to the Connecticut valley, under the lead of the Rev. Thomas Hooker, where they established themselves on the site of the present city of Hartford. Another James Cole landed at Plymouth, Massachusetts. He is mentioned in the Plymouth Colony records in the list of freemen of 1633, where the name is spelled Coale. He was the first settler on the eminence known as Burial Hill. He was an innkeeper for thirty years, and in 1644 he was chosen constable. William Cole was among the earliest settlers of Hampton, New Hampshire. His wife Eunice was accused of witchcraft in 1656. She is the "Goody Cole" referred to in Whittier's poem of "Rivermouth Rocks." She died in a little hut in the rear of the present Hampton Academy.

(I) Joseph Cole was born in Plympton, Massachusetts, early in the eighteen century. It is probable that he was descended from the Plymouth (Massachusetts) line, but positive proof is lacking. He was a private in Captain Perkin's company in the expedition against Louisburg. He had previously married Mary ——. He removed to Bridgewater, Massachusetts, where he died. He had ten children: Samuel, married, November 16, 1762, Sarah Packard, of Bridgewater; Ephraim, married Hannah Randall; Joseph, married Betty Southworth; Mary, married June 8, 1758, Colonel Frederick Pope, of Stoughton, Massachusetts; Susanna, married —— Niles; Catherine, married Daniel Littlefield; Elizabeth, married Solomon Smith, of East Bridgewater; Eleazer, mentioned in the succeeding paragraph; Sarah, married —— Worthington; Silence, born in 1755, died young.

(II) Eleazer, fourth son and eighth child of Joseph and Mary Cole, was born April 8, 1747. He married, July 11, 1769, Lucy Shurtleff, of Bridgewater, who was born October 11, 1751. The Massachusetts Revolutionary rolls record him as a drummer in Captain Josiah Hayden's company of minute-men. He enlisted from Bridgewater, April 26, 1775. Later in the year he served as sergeant for three months one week and one day. The company is reported to have been encamped at Roxbury. In after life he moved to Paris, Maine. His final home was in Greenwood, Maine. Eleazer and Lucy (Shurtleff) Cole had seven children, all born in Massachusetts: Calvin, married Betsey Sawn; Phebe, born October 31, 1777, married John Billings; Silence (Tyla), married Gilbert Shaw; Cyprian, is mentioned below: Polly, married Joseph Whitman; Lucy married Lazarus Hathaway, Jr.; Jonathan, married Abigail Whitman.

(III) Cyprian, second son and fourth child of Eleazer and Lucy (Shurtleff) Cole, lived in Greenwood, Maine. He was a colonel in the state militia. He was twice married. His first wife was Lovicy Perham, and his second, Patty Tuell.

(IV) Lar[illegible]enson, son of Cyprian Cole, was born in Greenwood Maine. He was educated in the common and high schools. He owned a large farm in Milton, Maine, where he carried on a successful general farming. In politics he was an active Republican. When the Civil war broke out he was appointed captain of a company, but as he was past forty-five and his mother was still living, he could not serve. He was a deacon in the Baptist Church in Milton, Maine, and was highly respected by all who knew him. He married Lycena Spofford, daughter of ——— and Anna (Fish) Spofford. They had five children: Augusta M., Virgil V., Samuel F., Edmund Chase and Lounaza Chase.

(V) Edmund, third son and fourth child of Deacon Laurenson and Lucinda (Spofford) Cole, was born in Milton, Maine, October 5, 1845. He attended the public and private schools of Milton and adjoining towns, and fitted for college at Norway, and Hebron Academies, Maine. He was a student at Colby University one year, but took the other three at Bowdoin College from which institution he was graduated in 1871 with the degree of A. B. Three years later his *alma mater* conferred on him the degree of A. M. In the fall of 1871 he became the first principal of the Simonds free high school at Warner, New Hampshire, which position he held for three years. He did excellent work in organizing the courses of study and laying the foundation for the subsequent prosperity of the school. In 1874 Mr. Cole began the study of law and continued it for the next three years, in the course of which time he taught one term in Marlow Academy, and three terms at Contoocook Academy, both in New Hampshire. In all he has taught thirty-six successful terms of school, a most creditable record. In the fall of 1878 he bought in Portsmouth the equipment of a printing office, and removed it to Warner. He subsequently began the publication of the *Kearsarge Independent*, whose first issue bears the date of April 4, 1884. The following December he bought the subscription list of the *Hopkinton Times*, published in Contoocook, and changed his paper's name to the *Kearsarge Independent and Times*. He prints and sends out fifteen hundred copies a week. The bulk of the edition goes to Merrimack county, but there are subscribers in several distant states.

In politics Mr. Cole is a Republican, and has held many of the town offices. He has been on the school board since 1871, has been superintendent of the high school, and has been supervisor of the check lists for many terms. He was postmaster during the last year of President Arthur's administration. He is a member of the board of health, president of the trustees of the Pillsbury Free Library, and was for a time a local police officer. He represented the town in the state legislature in 1901. He is chairman of the board of water commissioners. He has been active in establishing the fine water and sewage system and electric light plant for which Warner is noted. He is an efficient member of the fire department. He is a member of Central Lodge, Independent Order of Odd Fellows, and past noble grand; a member of Welcome Rebekah Lodge; a member of the Patrons of Husbandry, and past master of Warner Grange; a member of Kearsarge Division, Sons of Temperance; and a member of the United Order of the Golden Cross, of which he is past commander. He was appointed justice of the Warner police court by Governor McLane and council, and is still acting as such. In religious belief he is a Unitarian. He has been twice married. His first wife was Emma B. Quimby, daughter of Asa and Sally (Colby) Pattee, of Warner. They were married in January, 1877, and of this marriage one child, Sarah Adelaide Cole, was born. Mrs. Cole died September 28, 1882. Seven years later, August 3, 1889, Mr. Cole married Fanny E. Corey, daughter of George H. and Mary H. Corey, of Middlebury, Vermont. They have had four children, the two younger deceased: Edward E., Mary G., Thomas R. and Nada L. Mrs. Cole is active in the Rebekah Lodge, and held the office of noble grand in 1907.

PATTEE This surname is variously spelled in the early records Pettee, Petty, Patty and Pattee. According to family tradition the progenitor was a French Huguenot who settled in the Isle of Jersey with many others of his sect when they fled from France. The members of the Pattee family in Massachusetts and New Hampshire generally have been strong and bright men and women. Their record as pioneers is a most creditable one and they have borne their just proportion of the burdens and responsibilities in the development of the commonwealth of New Hampshire. It was not one of the first among the New England colonists, but it was planted in Massachusetts long previous to the Revolution, and was thoroughly assimilated before that struggle.

(I) Sir William Pattee, ancestor of this family, was a prominent physician, being not only physician to Cromwell under the Commonwealth, but also later to King Charles II. He was one of the founders of the Royal Society of Physicians, and in 1660 was knighted by the king. He was a copious writer on political economy, and is mentioned as an authority in Macaulay's "History of England."

(II) Peter (2), son of Sir William Pattee (1), was born in Landsdown, England, in 1648. In 1669, on account of certain political opinions that he entertained, he found it necessary to take a hasty departure from his native land, and he settled in Virginia. In 1676 or 1677 he left Virginia, possibly on account of domestic unhappiness, as we find him accused of leaving a wife in Virginia, after he had married in Massachusetts, where he sought a new home. Neither the merits of the case nor its disposition appear in the records, but he apparently was not disturbed, for he remained where he had made his home, in Haverhill, Massachusetts, and lived there the rest of his days. In November, 1677, he took the prescribed oath of fidelity and allegiance to the Crown. We are told that he established the first ferry at Haverhill and that the locality still bears his name. Somehow and somewhere he had picked up the trade of cordwainer, as a shoemaker was then designated, and at the annual meeting of Haverhill in the spring of 1677, a year after the application of one William Thompson "to be accepted townsman, to dwell here and follow his trade of shoe-making" had been refused, Pattee made a similar application, and met with a similar refusal. The record of the transaction shows: "Petter Patie making a motion to the town to grant him a piece of land to settle upon, it not being till then known to the town that he was a married man and a stranger, having hitherto accounted of him as a journeyman shoemaker, his motion, according to law, was rejected, and the moderator declared to him before the public assembly that the town doth not own him or allow of him for an inhabitant of Haverhill and that it was the duty of the Grand-jury men to look after him." But this was in line with a general custom in the towns of that period. The very best families, when removing from one town to another, were, according to this custom, "warned out," merely as a precaution, in case of pauperism later, to relieve the town of responsibility, and preventing the acquiring of a legal residence. As a rule no attention was paid to warn-

Edmund C. Cole

Louisa P. Plumer (See Plumer). She is a graduate of the New Hampshire Institution, and is a most intelligent companion and helpmeet of her husband. Mr. and Mrs. Pattee have one daughter, Sara Lewis, born May 13, 1895, at State College, Pennsylvania.

(IV) Peter (2), son of Richard and Susanna (Beale) Pattee, was born about 1705 in Haverhill. The establishment of the province line in 1741 threw his homestead into the state of New Hampshire, but he continued to reside in the same place. In 1745 this was called Haverhill district, and from this region Atkinson and Plaistow were subsequently created. On account of the Indian depredations a company of scouts were organized for service in the Merrimac Valley and in July, 1745, Captain Peter Pattee was in command of a company of cavalry scouts. They were enlisted August 24 and served three days, during which time no doubt the Indians were frightened away. His total remuneration as captain was five shillings and nine pence, of which three shillinsg and nine pence were for wages and two shillings and three pence for provisions, and the balance for ammunition. He was an active and stirring man and possessed of considerable property, as the records of deeds indicate. He married Elizabeth Scribner, of Kingston, New Hampshire. and their children were: Susannah, Muriel, Asa, Rhoda and John.

(V) John, second son and fifth child of Peter (2) and Elizabeth (Scribner) Pattee, was born January 10, 1738, in Haverhill, Massachusetts, and was among the first settlers of Goffstown, New Hampshire, where he passed his life. He was married, October 6, 1763. to Mary Hadley, of Goffstown. At this time there was no church at Goffstown, and their daughter, Martha, was baptized August 5, 1766, in Hampstead. At the same time, Moses, son of Asa Pattee, was baptized.

(VI) John (2), son of John (1) and Mary (Hadley) Pattee, was born February 10, 1771, in Goffstown, where he was a farmer. like his father, and many years justice of the peace. He died March 28, 1829. He married Rebecca Ferren, who died August 3, 1854.

(VII) John (3), son of John (2) and Rebecca (Ferren) Pattee, was born 1795, in Goffstown, where he was a farmer and large landowner. He died October 30, 1832. He was a Universalist in religious faith, and a Whig in politics. He was prominent in the affairs of the town and took an active part in everything that made for progress. At one time he owned all of what is known as Pattee hill in Goffstown. He married Abigail Burnham, and their children were: Jabez B., John C., Sally E., Sabra. Joseph R., Julia and Mitchell.

(VIII) Jabez Burnham. eldest child of John (3) and Abigail (Burnham) Pattee, was born November 5, 1819, in Goffstown, where he continued to reside and conduct a large farm His education was supplied by the district schools, and he was a ready and observing man and was an active and useful citizen. For two years he was superintendent of the poor farm. He engaged in lumbering with success and purchased several tracts of land for a farm in Goffstown, on which he erected substantial buildings and he was one of the first of Goffstown to begin shipping milk to Boston. He attended the Congregational Church. but was a Universalist in belief. He was a Republican in politics, and an active member and one of the charter members of the grange and filled a number of chairs in that organization. He represented the town of Goffstown in the constitutional convention of 1876. He died October 18, 1899. He was married, March 28, 1847, to Lorinda Jones, daughter of Amos and Rebecca (Dimond) Jones, of Goffstown. She died January 21, 1901. She was an attendant of the Congregational Church, and active in grange work. They were the parents of three children: George, Josephine and Loella.

(IX) George, only son of Jabez Burnham and Lorinda (Jones) Pattee, was born September 11, 1850, in Goffstown. He was educated in the district and high schools of his native town, and was from childhood accustomed to the labor of the farm which has been his occupation through life. For one and one-half years in his life he worked in a meat market, and in April, 1874, he purchased a farm of one hundred and twenty-five acres on which he built a new house and is now engaged in dairy farming and shipping milk to Manchester. He is an attendant of the Congregational Church, and a member of the local lodge of Odd Fellows, in which he has filled the principal chairs. He was a charter member and has been active as an officer of the grange, and is a thorough and progressive farmer. With his wife he is affiliated with the Rebekah branch of the Order of Odd Fellows, and he is also a member of the New England Order of Protection, of which he is past grand warden. For six years he served the town as selectman, during five years of which he was chairman of the board, he has also served eight years as supervisor and seventeen years as a member of the school board. and for three years was road agent of the town, and was its representative in the legislature in 1903. He was married, April 2, 1874, to Mary Louise Hazen, daughter of Cyrus and Louisa (Bartlett) Hazen of South Weare. She was an attendant of the Congregational Church and of the Grange. She died December 13, 1882, leaving two daughters, Bertha M. and Ina L. The latter died at the age of sixteen years. Mr. Pattee was married (second), October 22, 1883, to Elizabeth H. Rowe, daughter of Azariah and Elvira (Baker) Rowe, of Goffstown. She died August 5, 1889. She was in early life a teacher, and was an active member of the Congregational Church and of the Grange. She left one son, Carl B. Mr. Pattee was married (third), October 29, 1890, to Julina A. Rowe, sister of his previous wife. She is a member of the Congregational Church and of the Grange and of the Daughters of Rebekah.

(III) Benjamin, son of Peter Pattee, was born in Haverhill, May 13, 1696, and settled there. In 1745 he was the only one of the Pattee family residing and paying taxes in Haverhill.

(IV) Captain Asa, probably son of Benjamin Pattee and certainly grandson of the redoubtable Peter Pattee, was born in Haverhill, in 1738. He settled first at Goffstown, New Hampshire, and at about the close of the Revolution settled in Warner, New Hampshire. He was captain of a company in the old French and Indian war, and was present at the capture of Quebec in 1759 under General Wolfe. Although the town history states that he was a Loyalist, that seems to be a mere assumption because he lived on Tory Hill in Warner after the Revolution. for the Revolutionary Rolls of New Hampshire credit him with service in the Revolution, and his sons Asa and one John Pattee were in his company in 1776. Perhaps later in the war he opposed the course of the patriots. He built the first frame house in the town of Warner, New Hampshire, and it is now called the Dr. Hatch house. For several years he kept a hotel there. He owned the largest farm in the town and raised much stock, cattle, sheep and horses. He became well-to-do, and had the fullest confidence and esteem of his townsmen. He married twice. Children: 1. Asa, Jr., born about 1757, mentioned below. 2. John, born September 2, 1769; succeeded to the homestead at Warner. 3. Daniel, born 1775; settled in Canaan, New Hampshire, father of Mrs. Daniel Bean and Mrs. Jacob Currier. Other children.

(V) Asa (2), son of Captain Asa (1) Pattee, was born about 1757, and settled during the Revolution in Enfield, New Hampshire. He signed a petition for an act of incorporation June 3, 1779. The same land had been incorporated the year before under two charters and two names. He was a soldier in the Revolution from Concord, New Hampshire. in 1775. He was a lieutenant from Enfield of Captain John Parker's company, Colonel Timothy Bedel's regiment, in the northern division of the Continental Army under General Montgomery. According to the census of 1790 two sons under sixteen, and three females were living in his home.

(VI) James, son or nephew of Asa (2) Pattee, was born about 1790 at Enfield, New Hampshire. He settled in that town and was a farmer. Among his children was Wyman, mentioned below.

(VII) Wyman, son of James Pattee, was born at Canaan, New Hampshire, August 28, 1826; died in 1902. He married Mary Jane Burleigh, who was born in Dorchester, New Hampshire, December 10, 1827. He was educated in the common schools of Canaan and at Canaan Academy. He began his business career in the lumber business. He was then for some years in Ottawa, Canada, associated with the firm of Perley & Brown, but before the Civil war had returned to Enfield and engaged in the grain business. He carried on this business in that town for a period of thirty years with much success, acquiring a handsome competence. He attended the Universalist Church. In politics he was a Republican and he was high sheriff of Grafton county, New Hampshire, for eight years; representative to the state legislature from his town and Canaan for several terms; now treasurer of Enfield for a period of twenty years. Child: James Wyman, born July 27, 1864, mentioned below.

(VIII) James Wyman, son of Wyman Pattee (7), was born in Enfield, New Hampshire, July 27, 1864. He was educated in the public schools.

JEWELL The family of this name early settled in New England to escape the religious persecution they were compelled to suffer in England. Many individuals of sterling character traced their descent to the immigrant ancestor.

(I) Thomas Jewell was of Braintree as early as 1639. His will was dated April 10, and probated July 21, 1654. His widow, Grizell, married (second), March 9, 1656, Humphrey Griggs, who died in 1657. She survived him. The children of Thomas and Grizell Jewell were: Thomas, Joseph, Nathaniel, Grizell and Marcy. (Joseph and descendants receive extended mention in this article).

(II) Thomas (2), eldest child of Thomas (1) and Grizell Jewell, was of Hingham and Amesbury. He removed to Amesbury, about 1687, and lived in that part of the town now South Hampton. He married, October 18, 1672, Susanna Guilford, and they had eight children: Mary, Thomas, Ruth, Hannah (died young), John, Hannah, Samuel and Joseph. (Mention of Samuel and descendants forms part of this article).

(III) John, fifth child and second son of Thomas (2) and Susanna (Guilford) Jewell, was born in Hingham, June 29, 1663, and went with his parents when four years old to Amesbury, where he ever after resided. He married, January 9, 1702, Hannah Prowse, born in Amesbury, March, 1676, daughter of John and Hannah (Barnes) Prowse. They had five children: Abigail, Thomas, Hannah, John and Barnes. Hannah (Prowse) Jewell married (second), September 19, 1715, Peter Thompson.

(IV) Barnes, youngest child of John and Hannah (Prowse) Jewell, was born in Amesbury, April 12, 1715. He married, May 13, 1740, Dorothy Hoyt, widow of ——— Jones, born April 22, 1714. (See Hoyt, IV).

(V) Dorothy, daughter of Barnes and Dorothy (Hoyt) Jewell, was born December 20, 1751, and became the wife of Enos (1) George June 28, 1768. (See George, V).

(III) Samuel, third son and seventh child of Thomas (2) and Susanna (Guilford) Jewell, was born February 19, 1688, and died in Amesbury, Massachusetts. He married, November 6, 1712, Sarah Ring, daughter of Robert and Ruth Ring, of Amesbury. She was born October 7, 1691, in Amesbury, and was still living in 1728. The family tradition says that Samuel had a second wife who was the mother of his youngest child, but there is no record of such a marriage. His children were: David, Mary, Sarah, Elizabeth, Ruth, Susanna, Dorothy, Thomas and Timothy.

(IV) David, eldest child of Samuel and Sarah (Ring) Jewell, was born about 1716, in Amesbury, and resided in Stratham, New Hampshire, where he died May 20, 1798. He married Elizabeth Lowe. Their children were: Joseph, David, Daniel, Susanna, Elizabeth, Sarah and Mary.

(V) Joseph, eldest child of David and Elizabeth (Lowe) Jewell, was born May 13, 1741, in Brentwood, New Hampshire, where he passed his life. He married (first) June 24, 1764, Susanna Graves, who died before March 4, 1777. After the last named date he was married to Miriam Currier. All of his children except the last were born of the first wife, namely: Elizabeth, Susanna, Margaret and Anna (twins), Joseph, Simeon and Miriam.

There is a family tradition that he served as a soldier of the Revolution, participating in the battle of Bunker Hill. The records show that Joseph Jewell, of South Hampton, was a lieutenant of Captain William H. Ballard's company, Colonel James Frye's regiment, at Cambridge, October 6, 1675. In the pay roll of Captain John Calfe's company of Colonel Pierce Long's regiment, from December 7, 1776, to January 7, 1777, in the Continental service, stationed at New Castle, appears the name of Joseph Jewell, his pay being forty shillings. In the roll of the same company, entered January 24, 1777, Joseph Jewell's age is given as eighteen years. He drew pay in the second company of Colonel George Reid's second regiment for 1777-78-79; Joseph Jewell is credited with $153.50. In the rolls of men enlisted out of the third regiment of New Hampshire militia by Colonel John Moulton, dated May 19, 1778, appears the name of Joseph Jewell, of South Hampton. The returns of the selectmen of South Hampton, dated February 7, 1780, Joseph Jewell is charged with eighteen pounds, paid April 5, 1777. May 10, 1781, he receipted for fifteen pounds gratuity for service, his wages being eighty-eight dollars. In 1780 he received $68.60 on account of the depreciation of money in which he was paid for service in Captain Samuel Cherry's company of Colonel George Reid's regiment, the Second, of light infantry militia.

(VI) Simeon Jewell, second son and fifth child

of Joseph and Susanna (Graves) Jewell, was born July 20, 1776, in Brentwood. He first settled in Northfield, where he resided upon a farm for several years, and went from there to Sanbornton, New Hampshire, where he died September 10, 1832. He married, in Deerfield, May 19, 1796, Jane French, born in Salisbury, Massachusetts, October 28, 1766, and died in Sanbornton, January 11, 1838. Their children were: John, Milton, Jane and Samuel.

(VII) Milton, second child of Simeon and Jane (French) Jewell, was born in Northfield, July 2, 1803. At the age of eighteen years he began an apprenticeship at the tanner's and currier's trade, and after acquiring a good knowledge of the business worked as a journeyman for a few years in Deerfield. In 1828 he established himself in business at Bow Lake, Strafford, and in 1832 he had the misfortune of losing his property by a disastrous flood. He recovered, however, and continued the tanning and currying of leather and the manufacture of shoes until 1865, when his health failed, necessitating his retirement. He died June 4, 1869. He married Nancy Colley, born in Medbury, New Hampshire, May 3, 1808, and died in Barrington, April 7, 1880. Both were members of the Freewill Baptist Church. They were the parents of nine children, namely: John W., who will be again referred to. Hannah E., who died in childhood. Mary J., wife of W. T. Breston, of Barrington. Asa W., a resident of Dover. Enoch T., Charles M., Sirena T., and Betsey A., none of whom are living. Samuel F., also a resident of Barrington.

(VIII) John Woodman, eldest child of Milton and Nancy (Colley) Jewell, was born in Strafford, July 26, 1831. His preliminary studies in the public schools were supplemented with courses at the Strafford and Gilmanton academies, and while obtaining his education he taught school several winters. He began the activities of life in a textile mill at New Market. He later took a clerkship in a store, which he retained for a year at the expiration of which time he returned to Strafford and took a similar position with Hon. Benning W. Jenness, remaining with him until Mr. Jenness moved to Cleveland, Ohio, when he succeeded him in business. In 1881 he admitted his son, John Herbert, to a partnership under the firm name of J. W. Jewell & Son. This firm continued in business until the death of his son twelve years later, when Mr. Jewell sold out his interests and retired. Mr. Jewell came to Dover in May, 1891, and took charge of the office of the Massachusetts Mutual Life Insurance Company, and in January, 1892, was appointed general agent of the company, which position he holds at the present time. He is also a director and vice-president of the Merchants' National Bank, and a trustee and one of the investment committee of the Merchants' Savings Bank of Dover, New Hampshire.

Mr. Jewell is a lifelong Democrat. In Strafford he was honored by his townsmen with most of the town offices, and represented the town in the legislature. He was sheriff of Strafford county from 1874 to 1876, and a member of Governor Currier's council from 1885 to 1887. While in Strafford he took much interest in assisting the soldiers of the Rebellion, and the widows of soldiers in getting them established on the pension rolls by filling their applications, writing affidavits, and letters to the department at Washington for which he would never take a cent. He made it a rule to fill out the quarterly vouchers for all pensioners in town or out that came to his office, free of charge. For ten years he was postmaster of Strafford under the administration of Presidents Pierce, Buchanan and Johnson. Since 1854 he has served as justice of the peace. In 1903 Mr. Jewell was elected representative to the legislature from ward two in Dover, and re-elected in 1905. This ward has been one of the strongholds of the Republican party. He declined to have his name used for a third time; if he had not, there is little doubt but what he would have been elected again. His fraternal affiliations are with the Order of the Golden Cross.

Mr. Jewell married Sarah Folsom Gale, daughter of Bartholomew Gale, of Upper Gilmanton, now Belmont. The children of this union are: Sarah A., born August 26, 1856, married the Rev. W. W. Browne, of Evansville, Wisconsin, and died in 1898. John Herbert, born September 10, 1859, died in 1893, leaving one daughter, Annie. Mertie Folsom, born September 10, 1863, wife of Herbert Waldron, of Dover.

(II) Joseph, son of Thomas and Grizell Jewell, was born April 24, 1642, probably at Braintree, Massachusetts. He first lived at Charlestown, and kept the ferry between that place and Boston. About 1690 he removed to Stow, Massachusetts, where he owned a grist mill, which as late as 1815 was known as Jewell's Mill. This mill is on the stream which makes the dividing line between Sudbury and Stow. In 1860 the place was occupied as a carpet factory. Joseph was twice married: first, to Martha ——, about 1670. His second wife was Isabel ——, who lived to be over one hundred and three. The Middlesex records show that Joseph died before September 2, 1736, when he would have been ninety-four years of age. Six children trace their parentage to Joseph Jewell: Joseph, Martha, John and James. Between Martha and John were two daughters, whose first names have been lost. One married a Townsend, of Boston, Massachusetts, and the other became the wife of William Skinner, of Stow.

(III) John, second son and fifth child of Joseph Jewell, has left no record of his birth. His death occurred at Stow, Massachusetts, February 5, 1781, at an advanced age. He married Eunice ——, who bore him six children: Silas, Priscilla, David, Daniel, Eunice and William. He may have had a second wife, as the records of Stow state that Elizabeth, wife of John Jewell, died December 14, 1785.

(IV) William, youngest of the six children of John and Eunice Jewell, was born May 1, 1737. He married Lucy Gibson, and they had nine children: Jonathan, Jeduthun, who was a deaf mute; Lucy, William, Levi, Joseph, Timothy, Persis and Rebecca. William (3) died at Stow, Massachusetts, November 15, 1811.

(V) Joseph, fifth son and sixth child of William and Lucy (Gibson) Jewell, was born February 17, 1771. With this member the family came into New Hampshire. He married Polly Frazier, January 10, 1802. They had three children: Abigail, died in infancy; and Lucy and Joseph, who lived and reared families. Joseph (5) died at the early age of thirty-five years, in Hopkinton, New Hampshire, October 17, 1806.

(VI) Joseph, only son and youngest child of Joseph and Polly (Frazier) Jewell, was born in Warner, New Hampshire, March 3, 1806, and died April 17, 1883. His father died when he was but ten months of age, and Joseph was educated in the district schools of Warner. He was very successful in farming, in which occupation he spent his life. He cultivated a tract of one hundred and fifty acres. In politics he was a Republican, but he neither sought nor held public office. He married Rosanna Colby, daughter of Hezekiah and Annie Colby. She was born June 1, 1811, died April 25, 1872. They had

Yours Truly
J. W. Jewell

children: 1. Mary F., born in Warner, January 28, 1836. She married Frank Sargent, deceased, and has four living children: Nellie L., who married Charles L. Cole, had one son; Leon S., who died in January, 1907, while a student at Dartmouth College; Joseph E., married Mabel Colby, deceased, had children: Ruth and Edna; Frank A., married Agnes Goodwin, had children: Linda, Marion, Pearl Agnes and Maud. 2. Joseph H., died in early manhood. 3 and 4. James M. and John F., see forward.

(VII) James M., second son and third child of Joseph and Rosanna (Colby) Jewell, was born in Warner, New Hampshire, October 18, 1843. He was educated in the public schools. He enlisted, in 1861, in Company D, Eleventh Regiment, New Hampshire Volunteers, Colonel Walter Hartman, commanding, and served in this regiment until discharged by reason of disability. After recovering his health he engaged in the grocery business in Manchester, New Hampshire, for several years. He sold this and accepted a position in a reform school in Connecticut, subsequently becoming assistant superintendent of the State Industrial School of Ohio. While returning to his duties after a visit to his home, he received injuries in a railroad wreck, of so severe a nature, as to result in his death at Warner, April 15, 1893. He married Sallie Harvey, of Manchester, and they have no children now living.

(VII) John F., third son and youngest child of Joseph and Rosanna (Colby) Jewell, was born in Warner, New Hampshire, December 29, 1845. He was educated in the district schools of Warner and and in the high school. He first farmed with his father, and later bought a farm of his own which he cultivated successfully. He is a Republican and active in political affairs. He was a selectman for a period of eight years and represented the town in the legislature of New Hampshire in 1895. Ten years later he was elected one of the three commissioners for Merrimack county. He is a member of Central Lodge, No. 67, Independent Order of Odd Fellows, of which he was one of the charter members in 1876, and has held all the offices. He is also a charter member of Warner Grange No. 98, Patrons of Husbandry, which was organized about the same time. He attends the Baptist Church of Warner. He married, May 29, 1869, Nellie, daughter of William R. and Almina Sargent. Mrs. Jewell is active in church work. She was president of the Missionary Society for three years and has taught in the Sunday school. They have had six children: Oscar E., see forward; Gertrude H., born February 14, 1872; Anna M., born January 21, 1874; Almina H., born July 18, 1877; Carl W., see forward; John Everett, born September 16, 1888; married, February 14, 1907, Blanche Greemount, of Warner.

(VIII) Oscar E., eldest child of John F. and Nellie (Sargent) Jewell, was born in Warner, New Hampshire, March 18, 1870. He was educated in the public schools of Warner, and was graduated from the Simonds free high school in 1888. He then went to Manchester, New Hampshire, as a clerk, and later taught in the industrial school at Wilmington, Delaware, for two years. He returned to Warner and started a general store, carrying among other goods a fine line of boots and shoes. He is a Republican in politics and has filled the office of town clerk for eight years. He is now (1907) worshipful master of Harris Lodge, Free and Accepted Masons of Warner, and past master of Warner Grange, No. 90, Patrons of Husbandry. He attends the Congregational Church. He married Kate I., daughter of James and Aphia (Flanders) Bean, of Warner.

(VIII) Carl W., second son and fifth child of John F. and Nellie (Sargent) Jewell, was born January 25, 1878, in Warner, New Hampshire, where he is now engaged in the dairy business and carpentering. He married, December 18, 1906, Maud Blake, widow of Dwight Bailey.

MOODY There is no doubt whatever concerning the identity of the American ancestor of this notable New England family, which has been made all the more famous by reason of the number of its representativas who have entered the gospel ministry, but on account of an error in recording the names of the children of the ancestor some confusion has arisen and has called forth considerable criticism on the part of chroniclers of Moody family history. On this point the author of "Moody Family," writing some fifty years ago, says:

"The indefatigable historian of 'Ould Newbury,' asserts that Mr. Moody had a fourth son, William, and endeavors to prove this assertion by giving the date of his marriage, the names of his children, etc. We regret to be compelled to dissent from so high an authority; but he himself has furnished us with the grounds of our doubt. He says that William was married in 1684, at which time the other three brothers had been married between twenty-five and thirty years. Supposing him to have been born near the time of his father's coming to this country, he must have been at the time of his marriage about fifty years of age. Then again, his death is put down as having occurred in 1730, making him about one hundred years of age. His wife's death is mentioned as having taken place in 1702, aged thirty-eight, rather a young woman to be united to a man of his years."

(I) William Moody, the American ancestor and principal progenitor of the Moody name in New England, came from Wales, England, in 1633, wintered in Ipswich in 1634 and removed to Newbury with the first settlers of that town in 1635. Here he was admitted freeman and received a grant of ninety-two acres of land. There is a tradition that he was a blacksmith by trade, and was the first person in New England who adopted the practice of shoeing oxen to enable them to walk on ice. Whether he ever acquired the enviable appellation of "the learned blacksmith" is a matter of some doubt, but that he was a generous patron of letters seems evident from the fact that so large a number of his immediate descendants entered the learned professions. William Moody's wife was Sarah ———, by whom, according to the best authority, he had three children, Samuel, Joshua and Caleb. Joshua was born in 1632, Caleb in 1637, but the date of Samuel's birth is not known and it is generally supposed that he was born before his father came to New England. Mr. Moody and his sons were persons of considerable note in the civil and ecclesiastical history of Newbury and their names are frequently found in the various committees of the church. Joshua Moody graduated from Harvard College in 1653 and began his ministerial labors in Portsmouth, New Hampshire, in 1658. Caleb Moody married twice and had a large family. He was representative from Newbury in the general court of Massachusetts in 1677-78, and during the administration of Governor Andros was imprisoned five weeks for having spoken in censure of the course of that tyrannical official.

(II) Samuel, probably eldest of the three children of William and Sarah Moody, is supposed to have been born previous to his father's immigration to this country, but writers of the family history give no authentic account of his life. He took the oath of allegiance in 1666 and united with the church in Newbury in 1670. His wife was admitted to the communion in 1674. He died in Newbury, April 4, 1675. He married, November 30, 1657, Mary Cutting, who remarried, June 24, 1679, Daniel Lunt. The children of Samuel and Mary (Cutting) Moody were: Sarah, born November 16, 1658; William, July 22, 1661; John, April 1, 1663; Mary, February 28, 1664-65; Lydia, August 5, 1667; Hannah, January 4, 1669-70; Samuel, December 6, 1671; Cutting, April 9, 1674.

(III) John, son of Samuel and Mary (Cutting) Moody, was born April 1, 1663, in Newbury, Massachusetts, and in the records there is mentioned in 1675 as the second son. He married, before 1693, Hannah ———, by whom he had at least two children, one of whom is believed to have been John. The will of a John Moody is of record in Newbury and probably is that of the elder John, made 1727 and proven 1736.

(IV) John (2), presumed to have been a son of John (1) and Hannah Moody, is also supposed to have been the father of John Moody, of Kingston, although time and continued research may reveal that the premises here assumed are mistaken. It is hardly possible that John the son of Samuel could have been the father of Captain John Moody, of Gilmanton, New Hampshire, but it is settled almost beyond question that John of Kingston was a descendant of William Moody, the ancestor, through his eldest son Samuel.

(V) John (3) Moody, of Kingston, married Mary Gilman, daughter of Jacob Gilman, and had children: David, Dudley, John, Rev. Gilman, Mary (who married Daniel Folsom and lived in Gilmanton), Elizabeth (who married Abraham Folsom), Lydia (who married David Clifford), Dolly (married Humphrey French, and (second) John Cooley), and Sarah.

(VI) Captain John (4), son of John (3) and Mary (Gilman) Moody, was born in Kingston, New Hampshire, January 27, 1739, and died in Gilmanton, New Hampshire, September 15, 1829, aged ninety years. He was quite young when his father died and after that he went to live with the family of Daniel Gilman, his mother's brother. He came to Gilmanton in 1763 and began clearing his land and making preparations for permanent settlement. His nearest neighbor on the south was four miles away and on the north there was no settlement nearer than Canada. Soon after his arrival his camp was burned, with all of his supply of provisions, some of his clothing, and his hat. He was obliged immediately to repair to Kingstop for a new supply, and afterward he was frequently heard to say that his loss at that time was more severely felt than when (1821) his large two-story frame dwelling and nearly all of its contents were burned. In the latter part of the year 1763 he was taken sick, and knowing something of what was about to follow he made a supply of hasty pudding, brought a supply of water from the spring, then lay down in his camp and passed through the course of fever, without a physician or attendance of any kind. Captain Moody was an influential and useful citizen in the town of Gilmanton. He was selectman, captain of militia and an officer of the Revolutionary army. In 1776 he enlisted a company of twenty men and was its captain, and joined the continental army under Washington, serving three months and eight days. His house became the home of his father's family, and his mother, an almost helpless invalid, lived with him until the time of her death.

Captain Moody's first wife was Abigail Swett, a sister of Elisha Swett, of Gilmanton. He married for his second wife the widow Elizabeth White, whose mother, Mrs. Evans, died at Captain Moody's house, as also did her son, William White. After the death of his second wife, December 14, 1821, (age seventy-five), Captain Moody married the widow of Dr. Gale, of Kingston. At that time he was eighty-three and she was seventy-three years old. She was his own cousin, the daughter of Daniel Gilman, in whose family he had been brought up after the death of his own father. The children of Captain Moody were: John, Hannah, Dolly, Elisha, Abigail, David and Peter.

(VII) Elisha, fourth child and second son of Captain John Moody, was born in Gilmanton, New Hampshire, September 28, 1773, and died in that town September 21, 1833, at the age of fifty-nine years. He married, September 16, 1794, Betsey Weymouth, and had twelve children: Peter, Hannah, Dorothy, Elisha, George W., John, Rev. David, Stephen S., Elizabeth, Mary, Job and Daniel.

(VIII) Stephen S., son of Elisha and Betsey (Weymouth) Moody, was born in Gilmanton, New Hampshire, June 25, 1806, and died April 27, 1893.

(IX) Mary H., daughter of Stephen S. Moody, was born in Gilmanton, New Hampshire, December 5, 1830. She married, April 7, 1853, Charles E. Plumer (see Plumer, III), and had three children: Etta J., Carrie E. and William A. Plumer.

MOODY Rev. Joshua Moody was the first minister of the first church of Portsmouth, New Hampshire; was persecuted for his liberal views; was zealous against the witchcraft delusion; and was offered and refused the presidency of Harvard College. Other Moodys were early settlers in New England, but from which of the various worthy immigrants the Moodys of this article are sprung is not certain.

(I) Amos Moody resided in Nobleboro, Lincoln county, Maine, where he was born and died.

(II) Joshua, son of Amos Moody, was born in Nobleboro. He was well educated and of sound judgment. He lived on the original Moody farm. In early life he learned ship carpentry, and in later years besides taking care of his farm he did a considerable amount of contracting and building. For many years he was a justice of the peace. He was very religious, a leader in the construction of the First Baptist Church of Nobleboro, and the chief contributor to the fund which built it. He married Hannah Densmore, daughter of Asa Densmore. There were children of this union: Atwell Alonzo, Thurlow Elwell, Willis Elvin, Louis Alton, Sarah Jane, Frank L. and Mary.

(III) Atwell Alonzo, eldest child of Joshua and Hannah (Densmore) Moody, was born in Nobleboro, March 8, 1850. He worked his way through the public schools, and then engaged in farming in Waldoboro. In a few years he became a retail oil dealer at Jefferson, Maine, and carried on that business three years, till 1868, when taking what money he had accumulated he went to Nevada. After staying some time in Dayton he went to Eureka and engaged in freighting, conveying ore from the mines to the smelters at Eureka, and returning with various supplies for mines. He employed sixteen-horse teams, and being a diligent man and fortunate, he soon had several of these teams and a number of men in his employ. Seeing the necessity of a boarding house at Eureka he built one where he served four hundred dinners daily. It was but a step from freighting to general teaming, and in a short time Mr. Moody went into contract work where heavy teams were required and put in foundations for buildings, constructed streets, and other similar work. Later he acquired a half interest in the Butter-Cup gold mines at Eureka, for the development of which he supplied the capital. This property was soon found to contain a bed of rich ore, and a syndicate, after trying in vain to buy the property, jumped the claim. An ejectment suit was brought by Mr. Moody, and after being carried along for some time the case was tried; but the jury in the face of conclusive evidence in support of the claim of Mr. Moody and his partner, decided in favor of the syndicate. The money spent in developing the mine and in litigation was a serious loss to Mr. Moody. About the time of this disaster he was injured while at work in a mine, and for about a year following he lay in a hospital. So much misfortune left him without means and he returned to the east and engaged in installing woolen and cotton mill machinery, at which he is an expert. Constant handling of this machinery has made him very familiar with its structure, and enabled him to invent some labor and time-saving devices to be used in the operation of it, which he put on the market. Mr. Moody is a member of the following secret orders: Independent Order of Odd Fellows, in which he is a past grand, and was for four years district deputy; Daughters of Rebecca, of Ancient Free and Accepted Masons; Order of the Eastern Star; Knights of Pythias; Improved Order of Red Men; the Ancient Order of United Workmen. He married, in Nobleboro, 1869, Mary Edna Nash, who was born in Nobleboro, April 11, 1850, daughter of Church (2) and Susanna (Brown) Nash, of Jefferson, Maine. To them have been born seven children: Lillian, Grace, Fred. Elvin, Lila Maud, Harry Alton, Ethel Evelyn and Edwin Everett (twins). Lillian, born in Dayton, Nevada, died young. Grace, born in Eureka, Nevada, in 1872, married Joseph F. Starrett, M. D., of Bangor, Maine, where they now reside. Fred. Elvin, born July 19, 1874, in Jefferson, Maine, is married and lives in Cleveland, Ohio. Lila Maud, born March 8, 1876, died August 5, 1900. Harry Alton is the subject of the next paragraph. Ethel Evelyn, born May 26, 1884, at Waldoboro. Edwin E., born May 26, 1884, married Myrtie May, daughter of John and Susan Jane Bragg, of Brookline, Massachusetts, and is now in business in Boston.

(IV) Harry Alton Moody, M. D., fifth child and second son of Atwell A. and Mary Edna (Nash) Moody, was born in Waldoboro, Maine, November 9, 1877. He obtained his literary education in the common and high schools of Warner, Maine, and at Lincoln Academy. In 1897 he became a student in Bowdoin College, and in 1903 graduated from its medical department. He began practice at Greenville, Maine, in 1903, and remained there until 1905, when he settled in Sanbornville, New Hampshire. There his upright character and professional ability have made him an esteemed citizen and a prosperous physician. He is a member of Syracuse Lodge, No. 27, Knights of Pythias, of Sanbornville, and of Lovell Union Grange, Patrons of Husbandry, of Sanbornville. May 29, 1898, he married in Dover, New Hampshire, Mildred Frances Libby, who was born in Saco, Maine, May 27, 1881, daughter of Adin and Clara (Foote) Libby, of Saco, Maine (see Libby, IX).

ELLIOTT This name spelled Eliot, Elliot, and Elliott, appears in the early records of Massachusetts and was borne by many persons in Colonial times. With slight and inconsequential changes in spelling, there were four Elliott families in early New England, namely: Rev. John Eliot, the famous apostle to the Indians, of Roxbury; Ebenezer, of Newton; Edmund, of Amesbury; and Andrew, of Beverly. (Mention of Andrew and descendants forms a part of this article.)

(I) Edmund Elliott was a husbandman or planter of Amesbury, Massachusetts, where his name was frequently mentioned in the records. He was born about 1629, probably in England, and is first found on record among those taxed in Amesbury in 1652. He received land in Salisbury in a division, in 1654, and in Amesbury, in 1659-62-66-68. He subscribed to the oath of allegiance in Amesbury, 1677, and was on record as a resident there in 1680. He died about 1683. His will was executed February 26, 1675, and proved March 17, 1684. He must have served in the Indian war after making his will as it is on record that he executed this will, "When he was going to the war." In case of the death of his wife and son, his property was to go to his nearest relatives in England. The inventory of his estate, made January 2, 1684, shows that it was valued at more than four hundred and eighty pounds. His wife Sarah Haddon was a daughter of Jarrat, or (Jared) and Margaret Haddon, of Amesbury. She was born January 15, 1640, in Salisbury, and after the death of Mr. Elliott and before September, 1685, she married a "young love," and was still living in 1687, as shown by her father's will.

(II) John, only child of Edmund and Sarah (Haddon) Elliott, was born September 25, 1660, in Salisbury. He is described as a yeoman of that town, and took the oath of allegiance in 1677. In 1680 he was a member of the "Training Band." His will was made February 25, and proven on the 19th of the following March, 1733. He was married about 1685 to Naomi Tuxbury. She was born January 18, 1667, in Newbury, and was about eighteen years old at the time of her marriage. Her mention in his will indicates that she survived her husband. Their children were: Edmund, Sarah, Elizabeth, John, Thomas, Mary, Hannah, David and Naomi. (David and descendants are noticed in this article.)

(III) Edmund (2), eldest child of John and Naomi (Tuxbury) Elliott, was born July 30, 1686, in Amesbury, in which town he resided. Thomas Hoyt was appointed as administrator of his estate, April 16, 1733, which would indicate that Elliott was not then living. He was married January 8, 1713, to W. Huntington, daughter of John and Elizabeth (Blaisdell) Huntington, of Amesbury, and granddaughter of William Huntington, a pioneer planter of Salisbury. She was born September 22, 1687 in Amesbury. Their children were: Sarah, Deborah, Hannah, Betty, Edmund and Jonathan, the last two born between 1715 and 1722.

(IV) Edmund (3), elder son and fifth child of Edmund (2) and W. (Huntington) Elliott, was born between 1715 and 1722 in Amesbury, Massachusetts, and became a pioneer settler of Chester, New Hampshire. In 1747 he purchased home lot No. 31 in that town and subsequently became the owner of lot No. 134. He continued to reside there until his death, which occurred October 8, 1789. He married Mehitabel Worthen, who survived him more than sixteen years and died April 11, 1806. Their children were: Jonathan, Elizabeth, Me-

February 2, 1654, to Mary Vivian. Some authorities relate that he had only one son, his namesake. This is probably true of his first marriage, but there were evidently children of the second marriage, because the family is continued in Beverly through names not of record, as among his children.

(II) Francis Eliot, who was probably a younger child of the second wife of Andrew Eliot, was born somewhere about 1670. He settled in that part of Boxford, Massachusetts, which was included in the town of Middleton in 1728. His wife at that time was Abigail (surname unknown). She was the mother of his eight children, and died about 1712. He was married (second), March 28, 1716, to Margaret Knight. His children were: Francis, John, Joseph, Thomas, Abigail, Hannah, Mary and Rebecca.

(III) Francis (2), eldest child of Francis (1) and Abigail Eliot, married Jerucia Walcott, the intentions of marriage being recorded December 3, 1715. He lived in Boxford and in Middleton, and his children were born from 1717 to 1734. They were: Stephen, Abigail, Mary, Jerucia, Francis, Susanna, Experience, Anne and Amos.

(IV) Francis (3), second son and fifth child of Francis (2) and Jerucia (Walcott) Eliot, was born March 15, 1726, in Middleton, Massachusetts, and died, November 19, 1792. He moved after marriage from Middleton, Massachusetts, to New Hampshire, and was one of the early settlers of Souhegan West. He married, August 14, 1753, Phebe Wilkins, who died in December, 1822, aged eighty-four. They had: Amos, Phebe, Andrew, Hannah, Roger, Susannah, Lucy and Sarah.

(V) Deacon Amos, eldest child of Francis and Phebe (Perkins) Elliott, was born June 17, 1755, and died April 7, 1807, aged fifty-two. He was a pious and steady man, having good judgment, and was well liked. For some years he was a deacon in the Congregational Church. He married, May 16, 1781, Martha (Stewart), widow of James Hartshorn, Jr. Their children were: Amos, Betsey, Hannah and Luther, whose sketch follows.

(VI) Luther, youngest child of Amos and Martha (Stewart) Elliott, was born in Amherst, in February, 1794, and died in Amherst, April 1, 1876. He was a cabinet maker, and while in the employ of Thomas Woolson, Jr., he assisted in building the town clock of Amherst, which is still in good working order (1907). He settled in Reading, Massachusetts, in early manhood, and lived there until 1846, when he returned to Amherst and bought a place where he and his wife spent their remaining years. He married, September 22, 1818, Esther Damon, of Reading, who was born in Reading, June 30, 1793, and died in Amherst, February 14, 1891. Their children were: Luther, Augustus, Sylvanus, Lucy and Sarah R.

(VII) Lucy, fourth child and elder of the two daughters of Luther and Esther (Damon) Elliott, was born in Reading, Massachusetts, July 11, 1829, and married, March 3, 1864, William Pratt (see Pratt, II).

ELLIOTT The name of Elliott, or Eliot, was evidently brought into England from France by a distinguished soldier in the Conqueror's army named Aliot. Branches of the family became distributed throughout England, and on the Scottish border, and the river Eliot, or Elot, is said to have derived its name from one of these branches. The families in Devonshire and Cornwall generally spell their name Eliot, while those in Scotland use the double letters. The first of the name in America was the Rev. John Eliot, the distinguished missionary among the aboriginal inhabitants of Massachusetts, who translated the scriptures into their language. Robert Eliot was an early settler on Newcastle Island in Portsmouth harbor, but he had no male children. There were early settled in Scarborough, Maine, named Elliott.

(I) Daniel Elliott, of Limington, Maine, married Lydia Johnson in that town, November 9, 1787, and removed to Parsonsfield, same state, where he cleared a farm in the vicinity of Mudgett's pond. He had a family of ten children.

(II) Daniel (2), son of Daniel (1) and Lydia (Johnson) Elliott, was born in Parsonfield near the close of the eighteenth century. He went to Penobscot county, Maine, in or prior to 1814, and in the latter year was residing in Old Town, the inhabitants of which were then, as now, chiefly engaged in felling trees and manufacturing lumber. He married Susan Gray, and she bore him thirteen children, among whom were: Daniel, born December 2, 1808; Rebecca, November 18, 1811; Francis, February 6, 1814, mentioned below; Susannah, November 13, 1815; John, January 27, 1818; Warren, February 17, 1820; Emily, November 4, 1822; Lafayette, August 4, 1824; Foster, July 4, 1826; Fannie, April 23, 1828; Rebecca, August 14, 1830.

(III) Francis, son of Daniel and Susan (Gray) Elliott, was born at Oldtown, Maine, February 6, 1814. He was a mill-man all his life, retiring from active labor at the age of sixty years. Francis Elliott married Nancy, daughter of Jeremiah and Elsie York, of Sandwich, New Hampshire. There were seven children: Andrew Blake, born November 26, 1838, mentioned below. Elsie Y., April 24, 1840, married Louis F. Smith, of Whitefield, New Hampshire. George M., December 19, 1841. Lucy Ann, July 21, 1843, married Robert W. Morrill, of Whitefield. Eliza Jane, August 29, 1846. Jeremiah, June 16, 1850, resides in Whitefield. Maria, January 21, 1853, married Arthur Bourne, of Jefferson, New Hampshire. Francis Elliott (father) died March 21, 1887, at Whitefield; his wife died October 1, 1889.

(IV) Andrew Blake, eldest child of Francis and Nancy (York) Elliott, was born at Littleton, New Hampshire, November 26, 1838. In early life he was brought by his parents to Whitefield, was educated in the common schools thereof, and at the age of fourteen began earning a livelihood, working on a farm until his marriage, after which he engaged in mill work for a time, and then turned his attention to surveying lumber, wood and bark, which line of work he followed for several years. In 1864 he purchased a farm in Whitefield, which he cultivated in connection with surveying, continuing until 1905, when he retired from active pursuits. He is a Republican in politics, and served as selectman of Whitefield in 1874-75-76-77, and in 1894-95-96. In 1897 he was appointed by the supreme judge to fill out an incompleted term. He has been a member of the town school board for eleven years. He was made an Odd Fellow in 1878, has passed through the chairs of St. John's Lodge, No. 58, and also served as district deputy. He belongs to the Order of Rebekah, and to the Patrons of Husbandry. He has been master and treasurer of Mt. Washington Grange, No. 116, a deputy to the state grange, and a member of the national grange. He attends the Baptist Church. Mr. Elliott married, March 21, 1863, Harriet S., daughter of Daniel Parker. They have had five children: Millie E., born April 29, 1865, married George W. Shattuck, of Whitefield, one child, Helen Woodbury. Ernest H., born February 25, 1867, married Lillian Barnett, one child, Lettie Mary. Amy Ann, died August 1, 1878, aged six years. Eugene Parker, born August 27, 1873, resides at home. Lettie Mary, died August 11, 1878, aged three years.

ELLIOTT The Crusaders had not only a great influence upon the educational, military and commercial features of European countries, but also upon the people's names. As the Crusaders lay before Acre, the remembrance of Elijah and the prophet Carmel must have often recurred to their minds. Elias, in its many forms, once bid fair to become one of the most familiar names in England. Out of the many forms to be found in ancient records are "Ellis," "Elys," "Elice," "Ellice," "Elyas," "Helyas," and its diminutive "Eliot."

(I) William Elliott was born probably near Halifax, Nova Scotia, where he spent his life in farming. He was the son of a British soldier who after his term of service in America received from his government a grant of land on which he settled near Halifax. He was a Presbyterian.

(II) William (2), son of William (1) Elliott, succeeded to his father's homestead and spent his life there as a farmer. He and his wife were members of the Presbyterian Church. He married Jane Blair, daughter of James and Sarah (Cotton) Blair, and they had six children: James B., William, Robert R., Eleanor, Edmund and Jemiah.

(II) James Blair, oldest child of William (2) and Jane (Blair) Elliott, was born in Onslow, Nova Scotia, April 6, 1836, and was educated in the district schools of that town until he was twelve years old. He was then apprenticed to a blacksmith and served five years. At the age of nineteen years he came to the United States, and first worked at Chelsea, Massachusetts. In 1855 he went to Boston, Massachusetts, where he worked as a blacksmith for six months, and then worked in Cambridge. Returning to Nova Scotia, he started a blacksmithing business for himself, and carried it on eleven years. He then returned to Massachusetts and worked at the carpenter's trade one year as a journeyman, and then set up in business for himself, and was in Somerville the six years following. In 1875 he sold his property and removed to Merrimack, New Hampshire, where he has since operated a machine shop. He owns a plot of three acres of land, and on that has a residence which he constructed. He is a member of the Baptist Church, and votes the Republican ticket. He married, October 22, 1857, in Nova Scotia, Elmina Higgins, who was born in Nova Scotia, April 3, 1839, and died November 17, 1884. She was the daughter of John and Mary (Higgins) Higgins, of Onslow, Nova Scotia. They had six children: Richard P., Jennie, William, Hattie, Etta and Mada. Richard P. married M. E. Richardson, of Roxbury. Jennie married Herbert Quimby, of Haverhill, Massachusetts. William married Amy Baker, of Milford. Hattie married Frank Twombley, of Manchester, and Etta married Victor Kohler, of Haverhill, Massachusetts.

ELLIOTT The line of Elliott of this article is of the country about New Bedford, Massachusetts, where for generations it has furnished hardy seafarers to both the merchant marine and the government service. The absence of authentic records has prevented the tracing of any of the earlier members of the Elliott family.

(I) Albert Elliott, son of Joshua and Mercy (Gifford) Elliott, was born January 26, 1813, and died in Tilton, New Hampshire, January 13, 1891. He followed the sea in his younger days, sailing from New Bedford, Massachusetts, upon long whaling voyages to the Arctic ocean, and gradually rising from a position as a man "before the mast" to mate. He lived is various places, among which were New Bedford, Massachusetts; Augusta, Maine, where both his children were born; and Tilton, New Hampshire, to which he removed in 1856, and where he was engaged in the provision business for fifteen years and where his latter years were spent retired from active business life. He and his wife were attendants at the Episcopal Church. He married in Sidney, Maine, October 6, 1842, Adeline Waterman Blackburn, born in New Bedford, Massachusetts, March 3, 1823, daughter of John Carter and Hepsibah Chase (Baker) Blackburn. She died at Tilton, October 29, 1907. They had children: 1. Horatia Anna, married (first) Levi W. Hill, by whom she had one child, who is now the wife of William King, of Tilton, and they have one daughter, Alice Gertrude King. She married (second) Harley A. Brown, deceased, by whom she had one daughter, Hallie. Mrs. Brown resides in Tilton, New Hampshire. 2. Alonzo, see forward.

Mrs. Elliott traced her ancestry to a very ancient family. Francis Baker, son of Sir John Baker, was born in 1611, in St. Albans, Herfordshire county, England; he came to America in the ship "Planter" in 1635. He married Isabel Twining, daughter of William and Elizabeth (Dean) Twining. Francis Baker died in 1696 and his wife died May 16, 1706.

Stephen Dean, the father of Elizabeth (Dean) Twining, came to America in the ship "Fortune" in 1621. He came of a very strong ancestry which can be traced to the year 600. He had children: 1. Nathaniel, born March 27, 1642. 2. John, born May 1, 1648, married Alice Pierce, daughter of Abraham Pierce. 3. Samuel, twin of John, married Mary Pierce, daughter of Abraham Pierce. 4. Daniel, see forward. 5. William, married Mercy ——. 6. Elizabeth, married John Chase, son of William Chase, Jr. 7. Hannah, married ———— Pierce. 8. Thomas, married Bathsheba ————.

(2) Daniel Baker, son of Francis and Isabel (Twining) Baker, was born September 2, 1650. He married, May 2, 1674, Elizabeth Chase, daughter of William Chase, Jr., and had children: 1. Daniel, born 1675, married Mary ————. 2. Shubal, see forward. 3. Elizabeth. born 1678, married Nathaniel Baker, Jr., November, 1705. 4. Hannah, married, March 19, 1714, Joshua Nixon. 5. Thankful, married, January 5, 1728, Jabez Snow, Jr. 6. Tabitha, married, December 19, 1717, Joseph Kelly, son of Jeremiah Davis.

(3) Shubal, son of Daniel and Elizabeth (Chase) Baker, was born in 1676. He married Patience ————. (4) Shubal (2), son of Shubal (1) and Patience Baker, was born March 24, 1710, married, 1733, Lydia Stuart. (5) Shubal (3), son of Shubal (2) and Lydia (Stuart) Baker, was born November 11, 1741, married (first). November 15, 1764, Rebecca Chase; married (second), 1787, Elizabeth Chase. (6) Shubal (4), son of Shubal (3) and Rebecca (Chase) Baker, was born July 10,

1772, married, March 13, 1795, Mercy Smalley. (7) His daughter, Hepsibah Chase, born March 3, 1801, died September 10, 1878, married, July 16, 1820, John Carter Blackburn, born in England, February 1, 1797, died in Augusta, Maine, March 12, 1827, and was the mother of Mrs. Albert Elliott.

(II) Alonzo, only son and second and youngest child of Albert and Adeline Waterman (Blackburn) Elliott, was born in Augusta, Maine, July 25, 1849. At the age of eight years he was taken by his parents to Sanbornton Bridge (now Tilton), where he was educated in the common schools and later at the New Hampshire Conference Seminary. At the age of fourteen years he became clerk in a country store at Tilton, and later went to Colebrook, Coos county, far up in the "North Country." From there he changed to Wentworth, where he continued in the same line of business until September, 1869, when he accepted the position of telegraph operator and ticket seller at Manchester on the Concord, and the Manchester and Lawrence railroads. He succeeded to the position of ticket agent in 1870. Here he became known as the most expert ticket seller and one of the ablest telegraphers on the line. He held this position until 1893, when he resigned in order to engage in the banking and insurance business. His insurance business became very extensive, his agency representing some twenty-five leading fire, life and accident insurance companies. He continued in this line until 1896, during the winter of which year he was thrown from a sleigh and so severely injured that he was unable to attend to business for a year, and at this time sold his insurance business and relieved himself of all business possible.

He was the organizer and one of the incorporators of the Granite State Trust Company, subsequently known as the Bank of New England, of which he was treasurer, and which went out of business in 1898. He was president of the Manchester Electric Light Company, and a trustee and one of the organizers of the Guaranty Savings Bank. He is now (1907) vice-president, director and clerk of the People's Gaslight Company, was secretary of the Citizens' Building and Loan Association and was a director of the Garvin's Falls Power Company. He secured the necessary funds to build the first electric light plant in Manchester; organized the Elliott Manufacturing Company, manufacturers of knit goods, having a capital stock of one hundred and fifty thousand dollars, and employing five hundred operatives, was its first treasurer and is now its vice-president. He has been actively interested in other business organizations, and through his ability to secure the necessary capital has brought to Manchester many of its most important industrial enterprises, including the F. M. Hoyt, Eureka, Cohas, East Side, of which he is president, and West Side Shoe companies, and the Kimball Carriage Company. He is treasurer and director of the Pacific Coal & Transportation Company, which owns large coal deposits at Cape Lisbon, Alaska, and gold mines at Nome, Alaska, also the steamship "Corwin," which has been the first vessel to arrive and to deliver United States mail at Nome in the spring for several years; this is a great event in that section and is also considered of importance in the annals of steamboating and the steamship world. In company with the late Ex-Governor Weston and John B. Varick, Mr. Elliott owned the valuable hotel property known as the Manchester House. He is a tireless and persistent worker, and his labors and influence have contributed materially in making Manchester the business center which it is at the present time.

Mr. Elliott is an Independent Democrat in politics. Feeling that a change of law regarding the liquor question would be a benefit to the state, Mr. Elliott, together with a number of other prominent citizens, endeavored in 1902 to compel the Republican party to nominate a man for governor who would declare himself on this issue. Failing in this, Mr. Elliott was selected and nominated as an independent candidate for governor, and the result of this was the overthrow and repeal of the prohibition law and the enactment of local option, high license law, which was passed by the next legislature. Not only in the state, but in local politics, Mr. Elliott takes an interest, and endeavors at all times to use his influence for the good of the greatest number of people. He became a member of Washington Lodge, No. 61, of Manchester, in 1870, and is also a member of Mount Horeb Royal Arch Chapter, No. 11; Trinity Commandery, Knights Templar; Bektash Temple, Ancient Arabic Order Nobles of the Mystic Shrine; and charter member of the Derryfield Club. He attends the Unitarian Church. Among the most luxurious modern residences in Manchester is "Brookhurst," occupied by Mr. Elliott and his family, situated on the North river road, and built in 1893. The estate surrounding the house includes a part of the original historic Stark farm (which belonged to General John Stark of Revolutionary fame), comprising eight acres and commands a beautiful view of the valley of the Merrimack. Mr. Elliott married (first), 1873, Ella R. Weston, born in Manchester, a daughter of Amos, Jr., and Rebecca J. (Richards) Weston, and niece of Ex-Governor James A. Weston. Mrs. Elliott died in 1876, at the age of twenty-three years. Mr. Elliott married (second), 1878, Medora Weeks, born in Manchester, January 2, 1855, daughter of George W. and Sarah (Mead) Weeks, and they have had four children: Lucille Weeks, who married Harry Gilman Clough, a sketch of whose family is to be found elsewhere in this work. Laura Medora. Mildred Weeks. Alonzo, Jr., a pupil at St. Paul's School, Concord, New Hampshire.

Mrs. Elliott is descended from Leonard Weeks, born in Somersetshire, England; he built the first brick house in New Hampshire, in 1638, and this is now standing in Greenland (see Weeks). He had a son Captain Samuel. Matthias Weeks, son of Captain Samuel Weeks, married Sarah Sanborn.

(4) Josiah, son of Matthias and Sarah (Sanborn) Weeks, was born about 1756, and died in Gilmanton in 1802. He was a shipwright by trade. He sold his property in Exeter, November 8, 1779, and two years later removed to Gilmanton, "near the upper parish Meeting House," where he spent the remainder of his days. He married in Exeter, Abigail, daughter of Dudley James, also of Exeter. She was a descendant in direct line from Governor Thomas Dudley, second governor of Massachusetts (see Dudley). She survived her husband, and March 14, 1812, made a will bequeathing her estate to her two sons: Dudley J. and John.

(5) Dudley J., son of Josiah and Abigail (James) Weeks, was born in Gilmanton, 1788, died in October, 1868. He was a cooper by trade, and served as a soldier in the War of 1812. He married Lucy Sampson, born 1791, died in Boscawen, August 1, 1825, and had children: Mary Jane, Arvilla L., Charles, Elizabeth F. and George W.

(6) George Warner, son of Dudley J. and Lucy (Sampson) Weeks, was born in Boscawen, August 12, 1824, and died in Manchester, Septem-

ber 10, 1903. He was the eighth in line from Edward and Susanna (Fuller) White, of the "Mayflower." Mr. Weeks' grandmother was Rachel (White) Sampson. At the time of the death of his mother he was less than a year of age, and was taken into the family of Rev. Parker O. Fogg, whose wife cared for her motherless nephew until he was about twelve years old. He was known as George W. Fogg. He secured work in the mills of Manchester about 1839. Afterward he went as a sailor in the East Indies for two years, where he met with various adventures. Upon his return he qualified himself for the position of teacher. In this capacity he served in Manchester for some years, then for some thirty years was engaged in the shoe business, and finally turned his attention to the real estate and insurance business. He was a member of the Independent Order of Odd Fellows, having passed all the chairs, including that of noble grand; was also a member of the Free and Accepted Masons, Blue Lodge, chapter, council, commandery and Scottish Rite up to the thirty-second degree. The family were members of the Unitarian Church, in which Mr. Weeks took a prominent part. He took an active interest in school matters, and served for several years as a member of the board. He was a patron of music and the fine arts, a man of considerable literary ability and took an active part in all the affairs of his day. He married, September 27, 1846, Sarah E. Mead, born in Hopkinton, November 13, 1827, died October 25, 1903, daughter of Albigence and Susan Clough (Dow) Mead. They had three children: 1. Laura A., died young. 2. Medora W., married Mr. Elliott, as mentioned above. 3. George Perley, born February 22, 1863, was graduated from Dartmouth College in 1885. He became a shoe manufacturer in Haverhill, and is a Mason. He married Carrie Foote Everett, of Bradford. Mrs. Weeks was of the Goodman Mead family of Dorchester, who came over in 1635. Her grandmother on her father's side was Scilence Atherton, of the old James Atherton and Major Simon Willard stock, of Lancaster, Massachusetts.

KNOWLES This is an old English name which has been identified with the history of New Hampshire from a period very soon after the original settlement within the territory of the present state, and has been honorably connected with the progress and events from that time down to the present. It is now represented by one leading citizen of Barnstead.

(I) The American ancestor of this family, so far as records appear, was John Knowles, a mariner, who settled in Hampton, where he was married, July 10, 1660, to Jemima, daughter of Francis and Isabella (Bland) Asten of Hampton. On March 25, 1666, he bought of Giles Fifield one dwelling-house and house lot containing ten acres, together with six acres of marsh. This house lot lay on the south side of the common in Hampton, and entitled him to two shares of the commonage. This homestead continued in the possession of his descendants down to the seventh generation, and is perhaps still held by them. He became blind during the last ten years of his life, and died December 5, 1705. His children were: John, Ezekiel, James, Joseph, Sarah and Hannah.

(II) Simon, fourth son and child of John and Jemima (Asten) Knowles, was born November 22, 1667, in Hampton. His wife Rachel died November 11, 1696, and he married (second), August 23, 1700, Rachel Joy. Their children were: Simon, Rachel, Joseph, Ruth, Jonathan and Abigail (Jonathan and descendants receive mention in this article.)

(III) Simon (2), eldest child of Simon (1) and Rachel Knowles, was born March 18, 1696, in Hampton, and died in North Hampton, April 22, 1753. He lived for a time in Rye, New Hampshire, where record appears of one child. His wife's baptismal name was Rachel, but her family name is not of record, and only one child is recorded in New Hampshire, namely, Joseph.

(IV) Joseph, only son of Simon (2) and Rachel Knowles, was born December 13, 1727, in Rye, and resided in that town, where he was married March 3, 1748, to Love Brackett. He died November 7, 1823, in Rye. His children were: Simon, Samuel, Deliverance, Love, Rachel, Joseph and John.

(V) Deacon John, youngest child of Joseph and Love (Brackett) Knowles, was born April 8, 1760, in Rye, New Hampshire, and served as a Revolutionary soldier. After that war closed he settled in Centre Harbor, New Hampshire. A petition for the incorporation of that town was signed in June, 1788, but was not granted. A second petition was sent to the general court in 1797, which resulted in the incorporation of Centre Harbor, previously a part of New Hampton, on December 7 of that year. The name of John Knowles was signed to the second petition, and he was probably a resident of that region for several years previously. He was selectman of the town in 1813. No record of his marriage appears in New Hampshire, but his wife's baptismal name is known to have been Phebe. Their children were: Lois, Sally, Isaac, Polly and Joseph.

(VI) Joseph (2), youngest child of Deacon John and Phebe Knowles, was born May 25, 1802, in Centre Harbor, where he lived through life, following agriculture as an occupation. He married Betsey Smith, and they were the parents of four children: Mary Annette, born July 29, 1831, died January 21, 1888; John Haines, May 29, 1833; Orissa Margaret, January 16, 1837; Ellen Nancy, October 27, 1843.

(VII) John Haines, son of Joseph and Betsey (Smith) Knowles, was born at Centre Harbor, New Hampshire, May 29, 1833. In early life he moved to the neighboring town of Meredith, where he was a merchant till 1883, when he began to lose his sight. He is a Democrat in politics, and served several terms as selectman, and represented his town in the legislature of 1883 and 1884. He married Lovisa Merrill, daughter of Jacob and Mary Merrill, of Centre Harbor. They had three children: Herbert Smith, whose sketch follows; Lula, born March 22, 1873, married W. A. Hopkins, of Bridgeton, Rhode Island; Mary Blanche, born July 7, 1888, lives at home.

(VIII) Herbert Smith, only son and eldest child of John Haines and Lovisa (Merrill) Knowles, was born at Meredith, New Hampshire, July 4, 1871. He was educated in the schools of his native town, and at the New Hampton Institution, meanwhile clerking two years in Sanborn's drug store. In 1889, when eighteen years of age, he went to Bethlehem as clerk for C. G. White & Son, and in 1903 he bought out the store from the estate of the former owner. Mr. Knowles is a Republican in politics, and was town treasurer and treasurer of the precinct for several years. He is a trustee and steward of the Methodist Church. He belongs to the Masonic fraternity, and is a member of Littleton Lodge and Lisbon Chapter. On June 26, 1895,

Herbert Smith Knowles married Lillian Foss, daughter of Daniel W. and Ella M. Foss, of Pittsfield, New Hampshire.

(III) Jonathan, third son and fifth child of Simon Knowles and fourth child of his second wife, Rachel Joy, was born August 22, 1710, in Hampton, and lived at Little River. The christian name of his wife was Sarah and they were the parents of Jonathan, Richard, Abigail, Josiah, Sarah and two others, who died in infancy.

(IV) Josiah, son of Jonathan and Sarah Knowles, was born September 10, 1754. He was married, September 9, 1779, to Esther Blake, who was born October 7, 1761. He married (second) Martha Cate, of Epsom, who was born June 9, 1775. He resided in Epsom, and died there in 1840.

(V) Jonathan, son of Josiah and Esther (Blake) Knowles, was born September 24, 1788, in Epsom. He married (first) Peggy Locke, who was born February 22, 1785. He married (second) Ruth Philbrick, who was born September 4, 1788. She died 1843, in Epsom.

(VI) Samuel B. Knowles, son of Jonathan and Peggy (Locke) Knowles, was born September 23, 1811, in Epsom, New Hampshire, and died 1880, in Barnstead. He was educated in the public schools, and was captain in the militia. He was married September 23, 1835, to Olive (Stevens) Bunker. Their children were: Martha, John Henry, Samuel Parker, Jonathan Cyrus and Olive Thompson.

(VII) George Franklin, third son and fourth child of Samuel B. and Olive (Stevens) Knowles, was born January 25, 1849, on the paternal homestead in Barnstead. He attended school only eight weeks, and is wholly self-educated, having been forced to labor for his own support from the age of eleven years. At this time he began to learn the shoemaker's trade with Lewis Swain, but continued only six months. He was next employed for a period of eight months by J. R. Towle, a farmer, and for this service received one hundred dollars in wages. He lived in Northwood four months, and was employed as a teamster at a salary of four and one-half dollars per week. At the age of sixteen he decided to seek for better opportunities, and went to Lynn, Massachusetts, where he was employed at a salary of twelve dollars per week by the Rev. H. M. Brant, who was engaged in the manufacture of shoes as well as in the propagation of the gospel. After a year in this employment Mr. Knowles was engaged by Breed & Drake as a machinist, continuing with this firm two years, at a salary of fifteen dollars per week. He spent the ensuing three years in fitting stock by the piece for P. A. Chase, a shoe manufacturer of Lynn He was subsequently employed as a journeyman by Luther Johnson, with whom he remained a short time at a weekly salary of twenty dollars. Having been industrious and careful of his wages, he now prepared to engage in business upon his own account. Being invited to become a partner with John H. Stevens, he accepted and the firm began a very successful career in the manufacture of shoes. After a time Mr. Knowles sold out his interest to his partner and engaged in the manufacture of women's shoes by contract. In 1883 he patented a lady's sporting shoe and engaged successfully in its production, and when he sold out this business its valuation was placed at thirty-four thousand dollars. Mr. Knowles next took charge of J. R. Towle's shoe factory in Northwood at a salary of five thousand dollars per year, but this engagement lasted only a short time, as he was induced by Governor Tuttle and other citizens of Pittsfield to establish a shoe factory in that town. On November 1, 1891, in company with A. W. Poole, he began business in a new building erected for the purpose in Pittsfield. This building had a ground dimension of one hundred fifty by forty-five feet and was two stories in height. The business soon increased so that they were forced to extend the capacity, and secured two-thirds of an adjoining building, two hundred by thirty-five feet and four stories high. The concern has been in continual operation, keeping up the average output through dull times, and employs an average force of three hundred fifty hands, and the amount of business transacted annually foots up half a million dollars. On account of failing health Mr. Knowles retired from this business and purchased his present farm of one hundred and sixty-five acres in Barnstead, just below the paternal homestead. On this he erected a modern residence with all the necessary outbuildings, and provided water works to supply the same. The buildings are commodious and attractive in appearance, and cost five thousand dollars. Mr. Knowles is a lover of good horses, and has made a specialty of rearing fine stock, and has the finest herd of Jersey cattle in Belknap county. He is extensively interested in lumber operations, and now gives his time chiefly to that business, in which he employs twenty-five men. He has cut from his own farm one and one-half million feet of timber, and his annual cut now amounts to three million, which is sawed in his own mill. He has added to the original farm, and his holdings now include about seven hundred acres. Mr. Knowles is a steadfast Republican in political principle, but has never aspired to any office. He is fraternally associated with Everett Lodge, Knights of Pythias, of Pittsfield. He was married, November, 1896, to Miss Agnes Whitten, daughter of Gustavus Dana and Madeline G. (Porter) Whitten. The former was born in Holderness (now Ashland), October 11, 1835. His wife was of Scotch origin. They were the parents of five children: Mary S., Charles P., Frank B., Agnes and Annie M. Gustavus D. Whitten was the son of Ezra Sawyer and Susan Shackford (Sturtevant) Whitten, the latter born March 21, 1811, in Center Harbor; she was a daughter of Hosea and Sally (Paine) Sturtevant.

COLBATH The early history of the Colbath family is, like that of many another (in truth we might say, most others), shrouded in more or less of doubt and mystery. This is due partly to the fact of few records being kept in early days; partly to changes and wars that brought about the removal or destruction of those heads of families who were capable of handing down orally such valuable information; and to the serious loss by firm of those books and manuscripts in which matter bearing upon and relating to family, church and town history were recorded. Indeed, this latter cause, fire, is the fell destroyer that has blotted forever from the pages of history important and valuable data.

Southgate, in his "History of Scarborough, Maine," published in 1853, writes: "Several brothers bearing the surname Colbath came from England early in the eighteenth century and settled in various parts of New England.

Ridlon, in his "Saco Valley Families," claims that Scotland was the country from which the early Colbaths emigrated. He writes as follows: "The name Colbath, as now spelled in America, has

HOMESTEAD OF JAMES AND OLIVE COLBATH IN 1900

[illegible] YEARS AFTER THEIR DECEASE

HOMESTEAD OF JAMES AND OLIVE COLBATH IN 1900

[illegible] YEARS AFTER THEIR DECEASE

undergone the mutilation common to nearly all surnames dating from an early period. We first find it as Calbreath, and later running through such changes as Galbreth, Galbraith, Colbraith, Kilbreth and Colbroth. The various forms of spelling may be attributed to the fancy of some cadets of the family who, as younger sons, established junior branches in new localities; and to such early scribes as received the pronunciation of names from men of foreign accent.

"The name originated in two Gaelic words, 'Gall' and 'Bhretan,' meaning 'The Stranger Briton,' or as it were, 'Children of the Briton.'"

They were then evidently, descendants of that great, splendid tribe of Brythorn Gauls, or, as the Romans called them, Britons, who invaded and conquered the English Isles some three hundred years before the Christian era, and gave the name of Great Britain to them for all time. Later, when the invading Saxon and Englishman came, they found in these Britons their fiercest foes. More than two centuries of the bitterest war was waged ere they were overcome, and then, only by the ever increasing hosts of the Saxon. Quoting again from Ridlon:

"As intimated, the families bearing these names are of Scottish derivation. The earliest of whom we have found mention were Gillispick Galbrait (1230 A. D.) and Arthur Galbrait (1296 A. D.), who swore fealty to King Edward I. William Galbraith is mentioned as a person 'of good account' in the middle of the fourteenth century. Cadets of the family early intermarried with the lordly houses of Douglass and Hamilton, and through such alliances became possessed of extensive estates in Scotland, where they have continued. During the time of the plantation of Ulster in the north of Ireland by Scottish families (1608-1620), several brothers named Calbreath or Galbraith, who had purchased extensive lands from Sir John Calyuhon, Laird of Luss, removed to that country. These lands, which were called the Manor of Corkagh, were sold in 1664, and two of the brothers, Humphrey and William Galbraith, were retained as agents of Bishop Spottiswood. Another of the brothers was Robert Galbraith. The present representative of the family in Great Britain is John Samuel Galbraith, Esq., magistrate, high sheriff, justice of the peace, and doctor of laws. Heir presumptive his brother, Robert Galbraith. The family seat is Clanabogan, County Tyrone, Ireland."

Nason, the biographer of Hon. Henry Wilson, late vice-president of the United States, says: "Wilson's ancestors, the Colbaths, were of excellent stock, largely from Argyleshire, in Scotland."

Burke's "Encyclopaedia of Heraldry," the great authority in such matters, gives the family coat-of-arms. Bendy of six, argent and azure; on a chief sable, three crosses patee or. The simplicity of these armorial bearings would indicate a very early date; the use of a "chief" presupposes leadership by its bearer; and the pattee crosses point to the bearer being a participant in the crusades to the Holy Land and a member of the order of "Knights Templar."

"And on his brest a bloodie crosse he bore.
The deare remembrance of his dying Lord.
For whose sweete sake that glorious badge he wore.
And dead, as living ever, him adored:
Upon his shield the like was also scored."

—*Spencer.*

(I) So far as known, the earliest appearance of the name Colbath in America is that of John Colbreath, who was one of the Scotch Presbyterians of the "North of Ireland," who petitioned "his Excellency Colonel Samuel Suitt, Gov. of New England," (Gov. Samuel Shute) "to assure his Excellency of their inclinations to transport themselves to his plantation upon obtaining suitable encouragement from him." While many of those names written nearly two hundred years ago (March 26, 1718) are nearly, some quite, obliterated, the name John Colbreath, remains clear and distinct. The handwriting is almost identical with that of the early Colbaths of Newington, now to be found upon legal papers, and gives satisfactory proof that he and George Colbath, (Colbroth, or Colbreath) who was the ancestor—we believe the emigrant ancestor—of the New Hampshire line of Colbaths, were of the same family.

The next apearance of the name is found in Bradford, Massachusetts. "William Nutt, Jane Colbreath, married May 30, 1723." Next we find in a journal kept by Rev. Joseph Adams, who was pastor of the Newington church from November 16, 1715, to the date of his death, May 20, 1783, this entry:

"1725 Sepr 19. Mary Coolbroth owned ye Covenant and was baptized."

"Item. James, Pitman, William & Joseph & Benjamin Sons & Susanna & Mehitabel Daughters wr baptized" "1728 Feb 4. "George Coolbroth owned ye Covenant & was baptized."

We have but one earlier mention of George Colbath—the taxlist of Portsmouth, for the year 1727. shows John and George Colbath as taxpayers. As shown by an old deed, dated July 30, 1730, George Colbath bought land in Newington, of William and Abigail Cotton, of Portsmouth. August 13, 1738, he was granted administration of the estate of his son George Colbath, Jr., in which appointment he is styled "yeoman." April 14, 1752, he sold land in Newington, "with the dwelling house and barn standing thereon," to his son Joseph Colbath, and his wife Mary Colbath joined in the conveyance. Thus we have positive evidence of the existence of eight persons who were sons and daughters of George and Mary Colbath: George, James, Pitman, William, Joseph, Benjamin, Susannah and Mehitable.

It is of interest to note that three of these sturdy sons—Pitman, Joseph, and Benjamin—served their King, under Colonel Samuel Moore, at the siege of Louisburg, in 1745. Later we find one of these sons, Benjamin, a Revolutionary soldier, under Colonel Nathan Hale; he died in the service of his country March 20, 1778. Three sons of Benjamin—John, aged twenty-two years; Downing, aged seventeen years; and Dependence, aged sixteen years—with their father, served their country in her hour of need.

(II) James, second son of George and Mary Colbath, is thought to have been born about 1715. His wife, Olive Leighton, was the fifth child of Thomas and Deborah Leighton, of Newington. Her grandfather was Thomas, who married Elizabeth, daughter of Elder Hatevil Nutter, of Dover, New Hampshire, and her great-grandparents were Joanna and Thomas Leighton (died January 22, 1671), the English emigrants, who were married probably in England.

The children of the marriage of James and Olive Colbath were: Leighton, baptized December 1, 1739; Independance; Hunking, February 17, 1743; Deborah, October 9, 1745; Keziah ———; Winthrop, (the grandfather of the late Hon. Henry Wilson) June 16, 1751; Amy, July 9, 1758; and Benning, born May 28, 1762. (Winthrop and descendants are mentioned in this article).

noticeable that many of the virtues of the early stock are prominent in the later progeny, who with greater opportunities, have accomplished more than was possible for the pioneers and their immediate descendants. "The early records show the Carters of those days to have been prominent in all matters of public interest; the division of land, and laying out of roads, the building of a meeting house, the founding of churches, and the establishment of schools were entrusted to them. Many also were active in the military organizations and duties of their day, so that much of the religious, moral and intellectual culture and prosperity of the communities where they settled is due to the labors of these ancestors."

(I) Rev. Thomas Carter was born in 1610, and graduated at St. John's College, Cambridge, England, with the degree of Bachelor of Arts, in 1629, and Master of Arts, 1633. He came from St. Albans, Hertfordshire, England, in the "Planter," embarking April 2, 1635. He came ostensibly as a servant of George Giddings, because of the difficulty in obtaining leave to emigrate. On his arrival in this country he was admitted an inhabitant of Dedham, Massachusetts,, in September, 1636. He was then a student in divinity. Subsequently he removed to Watertown, Massachusetts, and was ordained the first minister of the church in Woburn, Massachusetts, November 22, 1642. His death occurred September 5, 1684. He preached his first sermon there December 4, 1641, and upon his ordination was presented with a house built for his use. His salary was fixed at eighty pounds annually, one-fourth in silver, and the remainder in the necessaries of life at the current price. In 1674 twenty cords of wood were given him annually in addition. He performed all the duties of his office as pastor for thirty-six years unaided. Afterwards Rev. Jabez Fox became his assistant till the end of life. He was characterized by one who knew him well as a "reverend, godly man, apt to teach the sound and wholesome truths of Christ," and "much encreased with the encreasings of Christ Jesus." Prior to 1640 he married Mary Dalton, who died March 28, 1687. His children were: Samuel, Judith, Theophilus, Abigail, Deborah, Timothy and Thomas. (Thomas and descendants receive notice in this article).

(II) Rev. Samuel, eldest child of Rev. Thomas and Mary (Dalton) Carter, was born August 8, 1640, graduated at Harvard College, 1660, married, 1672, Eunice Brooks, daughter of John and Eunice (Monsall) Brooks, born in Woburn, October 10, 1655, and died minister of the church in Groton, Massachusetts, in the autumn of 1693. Mr. Carter was admitted an inhabitant and proprietor of the common lands by a vote of the town of Woburn, January 4, 1665-66, and sustained at different times several responsible offices in the town—selectman, 1679-81-82-83; commissioner of rates, 1680; town clerk, 1690; and was engaged as teacher of the grammar schools in 1685-86. He owned land on George Hill (Lancaster) given to him by the town, and this land was occupied by his descendants for several generations. He sometimes preached in Lancaster between the years 1681 and 1688. and perhaps resided there a short time. His widow married for her second husband Captain James Parker. After his death she became the wife of John Kendall. Of the time and place of her death we have no information. Children of Samuel and Eunice (Brooks) Carter were: Mary, Samuel (died young), Samuel, John, Thomas, Nathaniel, Eunice, Abigail (died young), and Abigail.

(III) Samuel (2), third child of Rev. Samuel (1) and Eunice (Brooks) Carter, was born in Woburn, January 7, 1677-78, and died in Lancaster, August 30, 1738. He married, March, 1701, Dorothy Wilder, born 1686, daughter of Nathaniel and Mary (Sawyer) Wilder. He lived on the north side of the road that goes up George Hill, a little to the north of the school-house, on the site of a house formerly known as the Captain Ephraim Carter house, his father, Rev. Samuel Carter, having purchased two lots of Captain Henry Kerley in 1688. He was assigned to a garrison on George Hill with his brothers-in-law, Lieutenant Nathaniel and Ephraim Wilder, Thomas Ross, and his brother, John Carter, and lost by an attack of the Indians, July 31, 1704, one cow, one horse, two calves, two swine, and one dwelling house. He was selectman in 1723, and served on various committees for the location of highways and so forth. Samuel and Dorothy (Wilder) Carter were the parents of twelve children: Samuel, Eunice, Nathaniel, Dorothy, Anna, Jonathan, Ephraim, Oliver, Mary, Elizabeth, Prudence and Josiah.

Dorothy, daughter of Nathaniel and Mary (Sawyer) Wilder, became the wife of Samuel (2) Carter, as above noted.

(IV) Nathaniel, second son and third child of Samuel (2) and Dorothy (Wilder) Carter, was born 1706, in Lancaster, and died July 20, 1787, in Leominster. He resided on Bee Hill in that town, on the farm given him by his father. At the first town meeting, July 9, 1740, he was chosen selectman and on December 15 of the same year was made one of a committee to build a meeting house. He was one of the first sixteen to sign the church covenant, when that body was incorporated, September 25, 1743. His son, Elisha, was the first person baptized by the first minister of that church. He was married (first), February 9, 1731, to Thankful Sawyer, daughter of Elisha and Beatrix Sawyer. She was born 1715, and died December 5, 1755. He married (second), July 21, 1758, Dorcas Spofford, of Lunenburg, and died August 6, 1784. His children were: Elizabeth, Nathaniel, Elias, Susanna, Abigail, Prudence, Elisha (died young), Samuel, Elisha, Asa and Thankful.

(V) Susanna, second daughter and fourth child of Nathaniel and Thankful (Sawyer) Carter, was married (intention published December 5, 1757,) to John (2) Joslin (see Prouty, VI).

(IV) Josiah, youngest child of Samuel and Dorothy (Wilder) Carter, was born January 26, 1726, and died in Leominster, February 14, 1812. He married (published May 24), 1745, Tabitha Hough, born 1729, died June 29, 1810. He was but eighteen and his wife sixteen at the time of their marriage. He settled at Leominster, Massachusetts, where he cleared the homestead upon which three succeeding generations were born and reared. He served in the Revolutionary war, attaining the rank of colonel. He was with the army under General Washington in the disastrous campaign in New Jersey previous to the retreat across the Delaware. He died at the age of eighty-four years on the farm his own hands had cleared and in the house his own hands had reared. At the time of his death he had living more grandchildren than he was years old, several of the fourth generation and one or two of the fifth. Inscriptions on gravestones in the old burying ground, Leominster: "In Memory of Col. Josiah Carter, who d. Feb. 13, 1812. AE. 85." "In Memory of Mrs. Tabitha Carter, wife of Col. Josiah Carter, who died June 29, 1810, Aet. 81." They had fourteen children: Tabitha, Tabitha (2), Josiah, Jude, Sarah, Zerviah, Relief, Mary, Abigail, Jacob, Relief (2), James, Relief (3) and Jonah.

(V) James, twelfth child of Josiah and Tabitha

Solon A. Carter,

(Hough) Carter, born December 12, 1768, died at Leominster, May 28, 1853. He married, January 1, 1795, Betsey Hale, born December 21, 1771, died April 20, 1844. He was a farmer, and lived and died on the Carter Hill farm in Leominster. The children of James and Betsey (Hale) Carter were: James G., Betsey, Sarah, Solon, Caroline, Henry, Sophronia, Catherine Hale, Josiah Howe, Artemas, and Julia Maria—in all eleven. James G., the eldest son, graduated from Harvard College in 1820, and was engaged in educational enterprises, being contemporary with Horace Mann, and a co-worker with him in educational matters, notably the establishment of the system of normal schools in Massachusetts.

(VI) Solon, fourth child of James and Betsey (Hale) Carter, was born September 4, 1801, died June 3, 1879. He married, December 4, 1834, Lucretia Joslin, born June 27, 1811. He succeeded to the homestead farm which he cultivated successfully. He was an active participant in the social, religious and civil affairs of his town, being called upon at different times to fill various town offices within the gift of his fellow citizens. The children of Solon and Lucretia (Joslin) Carter were: Solon Augustus, Frances Lucretia, William Withington, Helen Martha and Grace Darling. The second son is a resident of Chicago, Illinois. The elder daughter is the widow of Henry T. Thurston, residing in Boston. The second daughter married John Morse Locke, of Leominster, Massachusetts, where they now live.

(VII) Solon Augustus Carter, eldest child of Solon and Lucretia (Joslin) Carter, was born June 22, 1837, upon the farm cleared by his grandfather. He was educated in the public schools of his native town, and completed his education in the high school at the age of seventeen years. During term-times as well as between terms, he worked on the farm. The winter succeeding his seventeenth birthday he taught a district school in Leominster, and was complimented on his success in the report of the superintending committee. The following winter he taught in Lancaster, and the summer of 1857 he spent in Chicago in the employ of his uncle, Artemas Carter, engaged in the lumber trade, but the panic of that year depressed business to such an extent that he preferred to return home rather than to continue there. The following winter he lived at the old homestead and devoted his attention to teaching school. He became superintendent of the Keene Gas Light Company, in December, 1859, and moved to Keene, where he maintained his residence until 1884, when he removed to Concord, New Hampshire.

In the month of August, 1862, he enlisted in the Fourteenth Regiment, New Hampshire Volunteer Infantry, and was commissioned captain of Company G. He served with his command until July, 1863, when he was ordered upon recruiting service at Concord, where he was assigned to duty as acting assistant adjutant-general upon the staff of Brigadier-General Edward W. Hinks. The following spring General Hinks was assigned to the command of a division of colored troops near Fortress Monroe, and Captain Carter was, at General Hinks' request, by a special order from the war department directed to report to him for assignment to duty. Captain Carter was announced in general orders as acting assistant adjutant-general of the Third (Colored) Division, Eighteenth Army Corps, and remained on duty with that organization until the close of the war, having received a commission from the president as assistant adjutant-general of volunteers, with the rank of captain, July 25, 1864. He participated with his command in all the skirmishes and battles in which it was engaged before Petersburg, on the north of the James, at Deep Bottom, Newmarket Heights, and Ft. Harrison, and in both expeditions to Ft. Fisher and the subsequent campaign to Raleigh, North Carolina. He was subsequently brevetted major and lieutenant-colonel for gallant and meritorious services during the war. In recommending him for brevet commissions Brevet Major-General Charles J. Paine wrote: "Captain Solon A. Carter, late assistant adjutant-general, United States Volunteers, served as assistant adjutant-general of the division which I commanded for about a year, from the beginning of August, 1864. First in front of Petersburg, under constant fire day and night; then across the James, in front of Richmond, taking part in a very severe and successful assault by the division of the enemy's lines on the Newmarket road, September 29, 1864, and in other engagements; later, in both Fort Fisher expeditions, at the taking of Wilmington, and in the march in pursuit of General Johnston's command, never for a moment away from his post, and never neglecting his duties, which often were quite as severe as those of any officer of the division. He was a brave and faithful officer of great merit, and I always exceedingly regretted that he was not promoted. There is not, within my knowledge, an instance of equal desert without a greater reward." After his discharge from the service, Captain Carter returned to Keene and engaged in the furniture trade.

He was a member of the house of representatives from Keene in 1869 and 1870. In June, 1872, he was elected state treasurer, which office he held since that time with the exception of one year (1874-75), receiving the nomination by acclamation and without opposition in successive re-elections. He is an active member of the Unitarian organization, and has served several years as president of the State Association. He is a member of the Military Order of the Loyal Legion of the United States and the Grand Army of the Republic. He has taken an active part in Masonic organizations, having passed the chairs of the Blue Lodge, Royal Arch Chapter and Commandery, and also the chairs of the Most Worshipful Grand Lodge, serving as most worshipful grand master for two years (1878-79), and as right eminent grand commander of the Grand Commandery in 1875. He attained the Thirty-third Scottish Rite, September 19, 1905.

Solon A. Carter married Emily A. Conant, of Leominster, Massachusetts, December 13, 1860. They have two children: Edith Hinks, born January 1, 1864, and Florence Gertrude, February 24, 1866. Edith Hinks Carter, eldest daughter of Solon A. and Emily A. (Conant) Carter, has since her graduation from the Concord high school in 1881, been employed in the state treasurer's office as assistant to her father, having charge of two or more important departments. Florence Gertrude, their second daughter, married, January 7, 1890, Edward Parkhust Comins, of Concord, New Hampshire; died June 8, 1905, at Dorchester, Massachusetts; survived by her husband and daughter Sara, born September 7, 1892.

(II) Thomas (2), youngest child of Rev. Thomas (1) Carter, was born June 8, 1655, in Woburn, and was a husbandman and proprietor, in his father's right, of considerable land in that town. He married Margery, daughter of Francis Whitmore, of Cambridge, in 1682. She died October 5, 1754. Their children, born in Woburn, were: Mary, Thomas, Eleazer, Daniel, Ebenezer and Ezra.

(III) Ebenezer, fourth son and fifth child of Thomas (2) and Margery (Whitmore) Carter, was born September 24, 1695, in Woburn, and lived in

Wilmington, Massachusetts, where he died before March 10, 1746, at which date a committee was appointed to appraise his estate. The whole was valued at three thousand eighty-one pounds, and the estate was administered by his widow, Lydia. It included one piece of forty-four acres with mansion house in the first range of "Great Lots" of Woburn, and another of twenty-three acres in the second range, beside lands in Wilmington. His widow's estate was divided in April, 1775, administration being granted to John Flagg, a son-in-law, to whom the heirs agreed to give the in-door goods in compensation for her care in old age. She was born June 11, 1695, daughter of William and Rebecca Butters, of Woburn; was married to Ebenezer Carter, April 15, 1719, and died February 14, 1775. Of their children, the first six were born in Woburn and the others in Wilmington, namely: Ebenezer, Lydia, Abigail, Ezra, William, Nathan, Rebecca and James.

(IV) Ezra, second son and fourth child of Ebenezer and Lydia (Butters) Carter, was born May 2, 1723, in Woburn, and resided in Wilmington, dying there about 1771. His son, Ezra, was appointed administrator of his estate May 21 of that year. He was married September 5, 1745, to Lydia Jenkins, of Wilmington, who survived him and married (second) John Flagg, who assumed the guardianship of her minor children November 12, 1771. Samuel, who was over fourteen years of age, chose his mother, as a certificate by James Morrill shows, as did also Benjamin, James, John and Moses. Joseph, William and Lydia chose their Uncle Nathan as their guardian. Samuel, Benjamin and James, with their mother's consent, signed a request May 26, 1777, for the appointment of Edward Kendall as their guardian. The children of Ezra Carter were: Ezra, Benjamin, Joel, Ebenezer, Joseph, William, Lydia, Samuel, Benjamin, James, John and Moses. (Mention of Samuel and descendants is a part of this article).

(V) Joel, third son and child of Ezra and Lydia (Jenkins) Carter, was born April 28, 1749, in Wilmington, and passed his life in his native town, where he was a farmer. He was married December 26, 1771, to Sara, daughter of Joseph and Sara Jenkins, of Wilmington. Their children were: Joel, Sara, Lydia, Dolly, Joseph, Hannah, William, Rebecca, Amaziah, Mary and James. (Amaziah and descendants receive extended mention in this article.)

(VI) William, third son and seventh child of Joel and Sarah (Jenkins) Carter, was born April 17, 1787, in Wilmington, Massachusetts, and was an early resident of New Ipswich, New Hampshire. He subsequently resided in Chelsea, Vermont and Warner, New Hampshire, and passed his last days in Lebanon, New Hampshire, where he died November 11, 1875, aged eighty-eight years. He was married March 8, 1813, to Jane Scott, who was born March 11, 1791, and died May 1, 1818, leaving only one child, William (2) Carter. William (1) Carter was married December 31, 1818, to Percis Wood, who was born July 31, 1791, and died May 29, 1866. The children of the second marriage were: Henry W., James H. and Mary Ann. The latter became the wife of T. W. Wyman, of Stanstead, Quebec.

(VII) William (2), only child of William (1) and Jane (Scott) Carter, was born February 11, 1816, in Warner, New Hampshire, and received his education in the public schools of that town. He was early engaged in the mercantile business there and was for many years postmaster and a prominent man in town affairs. He was much respected and esteemed for his integrity and business ability. For a time he was a partner in business with George A. Pillsbury, who was later very prominent as a flour manufacturer in Minneapolis, Minnesota. In addition to other public services, he acted for some time as town clerk. He was a Demorcrat in politics, and an active member of the Congregational Society. He died May 8, 1851, at the age of thirty-five years. He was married January 8, 1840, to Hannah Badger, daughter of Elliott and granddaughter of Benjamin Badger, of Warner (see Badger, VI). They were the parents of two sons. The younger died at the age of twelve years.

(VIII) William Scott, elder son and only surviving child of William (2) and Hannah (Badger) Carter, was born September 28, 1842, in Warner, and received his primary education in the schools of his home town. He fitted for college at Henniker Academy under Professor Thomas Sanborn, a noted educator of his time. He entered Dartmouth College in 1862, but his pursuit of an education was laid aside to serve his country. He enlisted in the fall of 1862 as a private in Company D, Eleventh Regiment, New Hampshire Volunteer Infantry. He was soon appointed commissary sergeant of the regiment. With his regiment he served in Virginia and was present at the battle of Fredericksburg. In the spring of 1863 they removed to Kentucky and were at Vicksburg, Mississippi when that city surrendered, and also at Jackson, Mississippi. Mr. Carter also served at Cairo, Illinois, and in Kentucky, and spent some time in the hospital at Covington, Kentucky, while disabled with chills and fever. In the spring of 1864 he went to Annapolis, Maryland, and was quarter-master for a large body of convalescents located there. He subsequently joined his regiment and participated in Grant's campaign up to the battle of Petersburg. He was discharged in 1865 and returned to the arts of peace, having now reached the age of twenty-three years. He decided to take up a business career and proceeded to Lebanon, New Hampshire. He entered the employ of H. W. Carter, a half-brother of his father, who was conducting a large mercantile business, William S. Carter becoming manager of the store. He continued this for five years and then began business on his own account in a similar line, chiefly gents' furnishings. These he sold by sample for a time, upon the road, and in time admitted a partner in the person of Frank C. Churchill. This relation began in 1877 and after a period of twenty-one years, in 1898, Mr. Churchill withdrew from the firm. Since that time Mr. Carter has been president and active manager of the corporation. Before 1877 the business was confined to wholesale jobbing in gent's furnishings, but now includes the manufacture of shirts, lined coats, overalls and jumpers and similar articles of daily use. In the operation of the business at the present time, five commercial travelers are employed in disposing of the products at wholesale. Mr. Carter is also interested in manufacturing industries at Pawtucket, Rhode Island, and in the south. He is a director of the Lebanon National Bank and a trustee of the Public Library of his home town. He was president of the Lebanon Electric Light Company for a period of eighteen years, until he resigned in 1906. He is active in every movement for the promotion of the welfare of his town and state. Since 1868 he has been a member of the Congregational Church; he is now identified with James B. Perry Post, No. 13, Grand Army of the Republic, and has been department commander of the state in that organization. He is prominent in the Masonic order, being a member of the Franklin Lodge and St. Andrew's Chapter and of the Mount Horeb Commandery, Knights Templar, and Bektash Temple of the Mystic Shrine at Concord. He has served as treasurer of his lodge and chapter for several years. In politics he affiliates with the Republican party; has filled various minor town offices; was a member of the state senate in 1891-92, and was auditor of state treasurer's accounts in 1891. In 1901 Mr. Carter was appointed by Governor Jordan as one of the commissioners sent to Vicksburg, Mississippi, to ascertain and determine the positions of the New Hampshire regiments in the siege of that city. His colleagues were: General S. G. Griffin and Colonel John W. Babbitt. Their action was approved by resolution of the legislature, and an appropriation of five thousand dollars made. On February 10, 1903, Mr. Carter was appointed by Governor Batchelder as chairman of the committee to select a monument to be placed in the National Park at Vicksburg to mark and commemorate the achievement of the three New Hampshire regiments that participated in the siege of that town. Mr. Carter is now president of the Eleventh New Hampshire Building Association with headquarters at the Weirs, New Hampshire. He was married, August 20, 1868, to Theodora Bugbee, who was born January 4, 1847, at Lakeport, New Hampshire, daughter of Orrin and Mary A. Bugbee.

(VI) Amaziah, fourth son and ninth child of Joel and Sara (Jenkins) Carter, was born February 15, 1792, in Wilmington, and settled in Concord, New Hampshire, where he died June 7, 1866. He was married about 1826 to Susan Dodge, of Haverhill, Massachusetts, who survived him six months, passing away December 5, 1866. They were the parents of two daughters, Susan Maria and Sarah Elizabeth. The first died when five years old. The second is the widow of Dustin Watkins Waldron, residing in Concord (see Waldron, IV).

(V) Samuel, eighth child and seventh son of Ezra and Lydia (Jenkins) Carter, was born October, 1758, in Wilmington, and settled in the northern part of Hillsboro, adjoining Bradford, New Hampshire, where he was a successful farmer. He was married about 1792 to Polly Abbott, of Henniker, and died October 3, 1826. His widow survived until March 1, 1855, dying on the farm in Hillsborough, where all their children were born, namely: Jane, Nathan, Samuel, Benjamin, Cyrus, Ira and Lucy.

(VI) Nathan, eldest son and second child of Samuel and Polly (Abbott) Carter, was born January 11, 1796, in Hillsborough, and settled and always lived in West Henniker. He was a carpenter by trade, yet able to do all the work of building and finishing a house, from the foundation to the final painting, and is said to have done more work during his life than any other man in the town. He was also a fine cabinet-maker, and made many cases for clocks in early life. From time to time, as he was able, he purchased contiguous land until he acquired a large farm, which was mainly cultivated by his boys as they became old enough. For nearly fifty years he and his wife were members of the Congregational Church in Henniker. He died June 4, 1880. He was married, November 24, 1819, to Margery, daughter of Aaron H. and Sally (Wood) Wadsworth, of Henniker. She was born September 19, 1801, in that town, and died there January 23, 1892. Her children, born in Henniker, were: William Harrison, Caroline Matilda, Samuel Worcester, Nathan Franklin, Henry Carlton, Harrison and William Frederick. The first two died in early childhood, and the last in his fifteenth year. The third was a farmer in Henniker, where he died. The fourth is the subject of the succeeding paragraph. The fifth was a carpenter and died in Concord. The sixth never married and remained on the parental homestead.

(VII) Rev. Nathan Franklin Carter, third son and fourth child of Nathan and Margery (Wadsworth) Carter, was born January 6, 1830, in Henniker, and fitted for college at Henniker and Kimball Union academies. He graduated from Dartmouth College in 1853, and from Bangor Theological Seminary in 1865. After leaving Dartmouth he was principal of the Highland Lake Institute at East Andover, New Hampshire, in 1853-54, of the Concord high school during the following year, and of the Exeter high school from 1855 to 1864. He was licensed to preach by the Piscataqua Association, April 20, 1859; May 15, 1864; and July 16, 1867. He was acting pastor at Pembroke, New Hampshire, in 1865-66; at North Yarmouth, Maine, for the next two years; and at Orfordville, New Hampshire, from 1869 to 1874. He was ordained as an evangelist at North Yarmouth, Maine, December 19, 1867, and was pastor at Bellows Falls, Vermont, five years, from October, 1874, and eight years at Quechee, Vermont. On account of the failing health of his wife, he gave up an accepted pastorate in Massachusetts, and took up his residence in Concord, New Hampshire, where he has since resided. Meanwhile he has supplied churches in Wilmot, Andover and East Andover, East Concord, Campton, Warner, Quechee, Vermont, and Hopkinton, for periods running up to two years, besides much occasional preaching as opportunity offered. He has been secretary of the New Hampshire Prisoners' Aid Association and of the Central New Hampshire Congregational Club since 1891; a member of the New Hampshire Historical Society since 1890, and was its librarian from 1895 to 1906.

He was married, March 12, 1860, to Harriet Frances, daughter of Major Nathaniel and Harriet (Gilman) Weeks, of Exeter, New Hampshire. She was born July 15, 1833, in Exeter, and died in Concord, October 8, 1890. He was married (second) October 12, 1892, to Harriet Louisa Gale, daughter of Nathaniel and Mary Elizabeth (Lovering) Jewell, and widow of Joseph Gale, of Exeter, where she was born January 9, 1842.

(Second Family.)

CARTER By a remarkable coincidence the founder of this line is of the same name as the clergyman who founded in America the line previously treated. The name must have been frequently found in England at the time of the Puritan emigration, and is readily traced in origin to an occupation. The records contain frequent mention of it at an early day in New England.

(I) Thomas Carter was among the original proprietors of Salisbury, Massachusetts, where he was a planter. He received land in the first division and again in 1640, and is mentioned in the list of commoners in 1650. He was taxed then and in 1652. It is possible that he was at Ipswich before he settled in Salisbury, as a man of that name was made freeman there May 2, 1638. The wife of Thomas Carter, of Salisbury, was named Mary, as shown by his will, which was dated October 30, and proven November 14, 1676. His death must have occurred between these two dates. His children were: Mary, Thomas, Martha (died young), Martha, Elizabeth, John, Abigail, Samuel and Sarah.

(II) John, second son and sixth child of

Thomas and Mary Carter, was born May 18, 1650, in Salisbury, and resided in that town, where he was probably a farmer. He subscribed to the oath of fidelity and allegiance there in December, 1677. He was a soldier and was sent to the defense of Marlboro about 1689. His wife Martha died March 10, 1718, at which time he was living. His children were: Mary (died young), Thomas, Abigail, John, Samuel, Mary and Ephraim.

(III) Ephraim, youngest chld of John and Martha Carter, was born November 2, 1693, in Salisbury, and lved in the northern part of that town. His wife's name was Martha. He was the first of the Carter family in Concord, and appeared there soon after 1740. He came with his family from South Hampton, New Hampshire, and when they started "The neighbors expressed great sympathy for them; gathered around and wept, when they bid them farewell, to go so far into the wilderness." Reaching Sugar Ball hill, they chained the wheels of the cart containing their goods, to get them down the hill safely; transported their goods over the Merrimack in a canoe—swimming the oxen; then fastening bed cords to the tongue of the cart, dragged that across the river. Reloading their goods, the carted them all up to the house. Ephraim Carter and Ezra Carter were in the garrison around the house of Lieutenant Jeremiah Stickney in 1746. Ephraim had a family of five children: Ezra, Daniel, Ezekiel, Joseph and Abigail. The last named is said to have been eleven years old when she came to Concord with her father. (Ezekiel receives mention in a later paragraph of this article.)

(IV) Daniel, second son and third child of Ephraim Carter, was born in Salisbury, Massachusetts, but first settled in South Hampton, New Hampshire, whence he removed to Concord about 1750, after the birth of his eldest child, and settled in what was afterwards known as the Iron Works District. He married Hannah Fowler, a native of Salisbury, Massachusetts, and they had seven children: Ezra, Molly, Daniel, Hannah, John, Moses and Anna. (John and Moses receive further mention in this article.)

(V) Ezra, eldest child of Daniel and Hannah (Fowler) Carter, was born in South Hampton, was brought by his parents to Concord and settled in the West Parish in Concord, where he was a farmer. He married Phebe Whittemore, of Pembroke. Their children were: Ruth, Timothy, Hannah, Rhoda, Ezra, Phebe, Esther, Daniel, Judith and Deborah. Rhoda and Esther became, successively, the wives of Moses Farnum (see Farnum, V). Deborah was the wife of Henry Rolfe (see Rolfe, VI).

(VI) Timothy, second child and eldest son of Ezra and Phebe (Whittemore) Carter, was born in Concord, March 6, 1767, and died February 7, 1843, aged seventy-six years. He resided in the West Parish. He was married June 12, 1794, to Judith Chandler, daughter of Captain Abiel and Judith (Walker) Chandler (see Chandler, VI). She was born October 9, 1770, and died December 28, 1852, aged eighty-two years. Their children were: Abiel Chandler, Ezra, Sarah Rumford and Judith Walker. (Ezra and descendants are noticed in this article.)

(VII) Abiel Chandler, eldest child of Timothy and Judith (Chandler) Carter, was born January 8, 1796, in West Concord, where he passed his life. He was married in 1819 to Patty Farnum (see Farnum, V), and they had the following children: Timothy, Franklin B., Sarah P., Augustine C. and Martha H.

(VIII) Augustine Clark, third son and fourth child of Abiel C. and Patty (Farnum) Carter, was born August 28, 1831, on the old Carter homestead, near Penacook lake, and always lived in the neighborhood of his birthplace. He was a successful farmer, and engaged largely in the timber business in early life. He was considered an expert judge of timber values, and his judgment was often sought by others, on standing timber. He was a regular attendant on church services at the West Concord Congregational Church as long as he was able to be about. He passed away at his home in West Concord, at four o'clock, Sunday morning, February 4, 1906, in his seventy-fifth year. Mr. Carter was a lifelong Democrat, and represented ward three in the legislature in 1874. He was one of the best known and highly respected residents of his ward, and was appreciated by his friends and family as a loving husband and kind father. He was married September 1, 1857, to Sarah E. Restieaux, of Hopkinton, daughter of William and Betsey (Chase) Restieaux. They had two daughters, Lizzie R. Carter and Mattie E., wife of Frank E. Dimond (see Dimond, VII).

(IV) Ezekiel, third son of Ephraim and Martha Carter, was born 1737, in Salisbury, and settled in Hopkinton, New Hampshire. He married Eleanor, daughter of Joseph and Dorothy (Lindsey) Eastman, and they were the parents of Dorothy, David, Sally, Ephraim and Johanna. Ezekiel Carter died October 2, 1804, aged sixty-seven years.

(V) Johanna, youngest child of Ezekiel and Eleanor (Eastman) Carter, was born July 2, 1771, in Hopkinton, and was there married in 1790 to Dr. Benjamin Buzzell, of that town (see Buswell, VI). She died August 15, 1862.

(V) Moses, second son of Daniel and Hannah (Fowler) Carter, was born about 1761, in Concord, and married Molly Robinson. He died March 8, 1833, aged seventy-one years. His children were: William, Daniel, Polly, Alice, Simeon, Moses, Anna, Hannah, Sarah, Jacob C. and Israel Evans.

(VI) Mary (Polly), eldest daughter and third child of Moses and Molly (Robinson) Carter, became the wife of Daniel White (see White, III).

(VII) Ezra, second son of Timothy and Judith (Chandler) Carter, was born in West Concord, December 27, 1798, and died January 28, 1879, aged eighty years. He received his early education in the common schools of Concord; later attended Pembroke Academy, and then commenced the study of medicine with Dr. Moses Chandler, of Concord. He continued his medical studies in Boston, where he had the clinical instruction of Dr. James Jackson; attended lectures in New Haven, Connecticut, and afterwards at Bowdoin College, Maine, from which he graduated in 1824. The obituary notice of Dr. Carter, written by Dr. C. P. Gage, gives so just an account of him that the most of the following account is taken from it.

"He commenced practice in Concord in 1825. In 1826 he removed to the neighboring town of Loudon, but returned in 1828 to Concord, where he continued in the active practice of his profession until within a few years of his death. In 1836 and 1837 he was a representative from Concord in the state legislature, was commissioned justice of the peace in 1837, was physician to the state prison for many years, and held many town and city offices. In 1844 he was president of the New Hampshire Medical Society, in which since 1826 he had been an active and esteemed member."

"As a general practitioner, Dr. Carter stood deservedly high with his professional brethern and with the community. By a judicious course of reading he kept himself well informed in the medical literature of his time. He had a happy faculty of bringing to bear in any given case the results of his reading and experiences, and was always able to sustain his opinion by sound reasons and the best authorities. He early secured, and for a lifetime held, a very lucrative practice. His patrons ranked well in the community as to means and respectability. He was untiring in his investigations of cases; slow, but uncommonly accurate in his diagnoses. From a long and close observance of the modus operandi of drugs, he acquired uncommon skill in selecting and exhibiting remedies. Being endowed with good common sense, much tact and sound judgment, he early gained the reputation of a safe and successful practitioner. In surgery few were better read or had sounder views of that branch of the healing art than he possessed. He treated all cases that fell under his care with remarkable success. At any rate, I do not believe there is a single case of deformity extant to advertise his want of surgical skill, and that is much to say of any man of fifty years' service. For many years he was the leading physician of Concord and its vicinity in obstetrical cases. In the sick room, he was a model physician, quiet, gentle, and soothing."

"Dr. Carter was the most modest and unassuming man I ever met in the profession, never boasting of what he had done or of what he could do, although nature, circumstances, and his own efforts had combined to make him a great physician."

"His well balanced and well stored mind, long experience, strict integrity and watchful care of the interests of his consulting brother, as well as that of the patient, made him a favorite with men of his profession and brought him in frequent counsel with all the well bred physicians of his neighborhood."

He married, May 8, 1830, Abby T. Clark, of Portsmouth. They had two children: Edward Pierce and William Gardner.

(IX) Dr. William Gardner Carter, second child and son of Dr. Ezra and Abby T. (Clark) Carter, was born in Concord, August 8, 1838, and died March 7, 1904. After completing his studies at Pembroke Academy he worked in the book store of his uncle in Portland, Maine, for a time. From there he entered Bowdoin Medical College, but took his degree from Harvard Medical School in 1869. Returning to Concord he succeeded to his father's practice and soon attained popularity as a physician. His professional career was closed about 1889 by reason of failing health, after about twenty years spent in the practice of it. He was one of those bright, cheery persons whose presence is a ray of sunshine in a sick room and is remembered by his former patients with heartfelt pleasure. His retirement did not lessen his interest in the profession and professional work, and during the remainder of his life he kept himself well informed upon matters of interest to the medical world by means of his journals and books, which enabled him to discuss with the fullest professional intelligence the latest methods of treatment. He possessed a broad culture, especially in literature and music, and was a musical critic and performer of fine perception and attainments. While a lad in Portland he was organist in a prominent church, and upon coming to Concord to practice medicine began a term of service as organist at the North Church which lasted as long as his strength would permit him to continue this labor of love. The exercise of his musical talent made many happy hours for him and those around him, both at home and in society. He was a genial, hospitable man and a friend has well said: "Dr. Carter was a man of boundless generosity, and his engaging personality drew around him a group of devoted friends for whom his delightful wit, his broad views of men and affairs, his charming manners and unfeigned solicitude has a constantly increasing allurement. His home was the center of attraction for a rare company of kindred spirits who always found in him a source of keen and delightful companionship." Dr. Carter was married, May 13, 1869, to Miss Harriet Esther Pecker, daughter of Robert Eastman and Esther (Lang) Pecker, of Concord (see Pecker, VI). Mrs. Carter was born October 6, 1846, in the house where she now resides, on North Main street, Concord. She is active in the social and intellectual life of the town, and in club and church work. She is the mother of one son, Robert Ezra Carter, who is now employed in the Boston banking house of E. H. Rollins' Sons.

(V) Colonel John Carter, fifth child and third son of Daniel and Hannah (Fowler) Carter, was born in Concord, New Hampshire, and was a prominent citizen and large property owner there. His residence was on what in 1834 was named Hall street, and owned what was called the Interval Farm in the "Bend of the River" on the southern line of the town. In the war of 1812 he was lieutenant-colonel of a regiment of volunteers enlisted for the northern army, and under the command of General Aquilla Davis, of Warner. Under date of November 11, 1847, the *New Hampshire Patriot* had the following notice: "Died in this town (Concord), November 7, Colonel John Carter, a revolutionary pensioner and colonel in a regiment in the war of 1812, aged eighty-eight years and five months. Colonel Carter was a native of Concord, and at the time of his decease was the second oldest resident of the place. He was always a firm and consistent Democrat, and lover of his country." He married (first) Betsey Brown, and had one daughter, Anna. He married (second) widow Lucy Wells, formerly Cavis. Their children were: Betsey, Wells, John, Nathaniel, Aaron, William M. and Hiram.

(VI) Betsey, second daughter and child of Colonel John and Lucy (Cavis) (Wells) Carter, became the wife of David White (see White, III).

(VI) Hiram, youngest child of Colonel John and Lucy (Cavis) (Wells) Carter, was born in Bow, June 13, 1802. His early life was spent in Bow and on his father's farm on what is now Hall street, Concord. The schooling he received was only such as the district schools of his day afforded, and a part of the time he was obliged to walk three miles to a school house for instruction. His active life was devoted partly to farming and lumbering and partly to matters connected with the navigation of the Merrimack river, which was traversed from Concord to its mouth by boats and rafts by the aid of canals and locks and dams until the completion of the railroad to Concord in 1842. His residence for years was in winter time at the farm and in summer in a house below Concord, near the river. For five or ten years between 1832 and 1842 he was pilot and locktender at Garvins Falls, during the season of navigation, and when other employment was not to be had he devoted his leisure to catching salmon for the market. Between tween 1850 and 1860 he spent five or six years in East Dixfield, Maine, where he was engaged in farming until the death of his second wife, when he returned to Concord. After his third marriage he lived in Pembroke, New Hampshire, where he died November 2, 1890. His political faith was of the

Jacksonian sort of Democracy, and his religious creed was that of the Universalists. He married (first) in Wilton, Maine, June 5, 1823, Sally A. Mayhew, born October 21, 1802, daughter of Nathan and Sally Mayhew. Nathan Mayhew was born December 23, 1778, and he married in Livermore, Maine, June 15, 1800, Sally Mayhew, born March 1, 1773. Their children were: Phebe, Sally A., Thomas, Nathan, Isabel, Samuel, Cordelia and Hannah A. Nathan Mayhew died March 12, 1855, and his wife Sally, June 12, 1844. Sally A. (Mayhew) Carter died July 6, 1846, and Mr. Carter married (second) Hannah A. Mayhew, her sister, born October 18, 1814. She died at East Dixfield, Maine, July 25, 1862, and he married (third) Theodate Brickett, of Pembroke, who survived him, and died February 27, 1896, at Northwood, New Hampshire. The children of the first wife were: Lucy D., Mary A., Amanda M. F. W., Sarah A., George R., Nathan M., Hiram J., Andrew B., Lucy D. and Orin T. The children of the second marriage, all born in Wilton, Maine, were: William Nelson, died young, Nelson N., Albert E., Franklin P. and William Manly.

(VII) Orin T., ninth and youngest child of Hiram and Sally A. (Mayhew) Carter, was born in Concord, February 6, 1843. His early education was acquired in the common school of Dixford, Maine, where he was taken by his father on his removal to Maine. At the age of nineteen he returned to Concord and engaged in the grocery business with C. C. Webster. In 1863 he enlisted in Company A, First Regiment, New Hampshire Heavy Artillery, with which he served until he was discharged. He served two years and two months, stationed at Ft. Constitution, New Hampshire, and at Washington, D. C. After his return from the war he took his former position in Webster's grocery store, where he worked until he started in business for himself as a grocer and fish monger. Later he accepted his brother as a partner, and the firm of Carter Brothers continued the business until ill health compelled Orin T. to relinquish this for some out-door employment. The two years next following he travelled through the rural districts and sold groceries from a wagon. Subsequently the firm of Carter & Pillsbury, dealers in dry goods, was formed, of which Mr. Carter was senior partner. This firm sold out to McQuesten & Company, and Mr. Carter served as an employee of that firm for eight years. He then became a travelling agent and has been engaged in that line of employment for the ten years last past. Mr. Carter is an energetic man and a good citizen, is fond of the company of his fellowmen, and is a member of various fraternal organizations; among which are: E. E. Sturtevant Post, No. 2, Grand Army of the Republic; White Mountain Lodge, No. 5, Independent Order of Odd Fellows; Concord Lodge, No. 8, Knights of Pythias, and Profile Commandery, No. 263, Ancient and Independent Order Knights of Malta. He married, November 24, 1869, at Concord, Nellie A. Pillsbury, born in Concord, November 26, 1850, daughter of Thomas W. and Abigail (Palmer) Pillsbury, of Concord. They have five children: John P., born October 24, 1872; Fred E., June 5, 1874; Katie A., February 28, 1876, died February 4, 1881; Etta M., August 25, 1883, died September 16, 1904; George O., October 9, 1890, died April 4, 1893.

HOBBS Among the early families of New England were three of the surname Hobbs, whose immigration dated to the times of the Puritans of the first half of the seventeenth century. Tradition says they were brothers, and that one returned to his mother country, while the other two—Maurice (or Morris) and Henry remained. . Henry settled in Dover and his descendants removed to what is now North Berwick, where some of them still reside.

(I) Maurice (or Morris) Hobbs was the progenitor of the New Hampshire families of that surname. He was born about 1615, and settled in the town of Hampton, New Hampshire, sometime between the years 1640 and 1645, removing from thence in the latter named year to Rollinsford, where he settled on the bank of the river. He took the oath of allegiance to Massachusetts in the fall of 1648. There is an interesting tradition regarding the immigration of Maurice Hobbs and the circumstances which impelled his action. The story is told by Dow in his valuable "History of Hampton" (New Hampshire) and can be best retold here in the words of that versatile writer: "He (Hobbs) had been paying his addresses to a young lady who, for some cause not mentioned, turned him off, and thereupon he determined to emigrate to America. When the lady knew of it she relented, and knowing he would pass her residence as he proceeded to embark, placed herself in his view, hoping to bring about a reconcilliation. To her grief she found him inexorable; and although she accosted him with the affectionate inquiry, 'Whither goest thou, Maurice,' yet he deigned not to turn his head or look back upon her; and they never saw each other more." Maurice Hobbs married (first) Sarah Estaw, who died May 5, 1686, and she bore him the following children: William, John, Sarah, Nehemiah, Morris, James, Mary, Bethia, Hannah and Abigail. William Estaw, father of Sarah (Estaw) Hobbs, was one of the grantees of Hampton and one of its first settlers. He was made freeman in 1638, and is said to have been a widower when he came to the town. He represented Hampton at the general assembly three years. His children were Sarah and Mary Estaw, the latter of whom married Thomas Marston. Maurice Hobbs married (second) Sarah Swett, June 13, 1678, daughter of Captain Benjamin and Esther (Weare) Swett. She was born November 7, 1650, and died December 8, 1717. Captain Benjamin Swett was a noted character in early Hampton history, and was killed by Indians, June 29, 1677. One son was born of the second marriage of Maurice Hobbs, also Maurice by name.

(II) Maurice (2), son of Maurice (1) and Sarah (Swett) Hobbs, was born in Rollinsford, New Hampshire, September 13, 1680, and died May 7, 1739. He married Theodate, daughter of Nathaniel (2) Batchelder (see Batchelder, III) about the year 1700, and their children were: James, Mary, Sarah, Josiah, Theodate, Morris, Hannah, Jonathan, Esther and Elizabeth.

(III) James, eldest son of Maurice (2) and Theodate (Batchelder) Hobbs, was born March 20, 1701, married Rebecca Hobbs, about the year 1719, and had a son James. (It is possible that Nathaniel, mentioned in this article, was also their son.)

(IV) James (2), son of James (1) and Rebecca (Hobbs) Hobbs, was born January 11, 1729, and died April, 1816. He married, in 1752, Ruth Philpot, who was born December 29, 1731, and they had a son Stephen.

(V) Stephen, son of James (2) and Ruth (Philpot) Hobbs, was born April 10, 1761, and died January 21, 1821. He lived in Berwick, Maine, and in later years several of his children removed to

Industry, Maine. In 1780 he married Abigail Varney, and their children were: James, Isaac, Joseph, George, Stephen, Temperance and Abigail.

(VI) Isaac, son of Stephen and Abigail (Varney) Hobbs, was born August 10, 1787, and died March 2, 1870. He married, October 11, 1818, Elizabeth Chick, who was born September 26, 1790, and died August 31, 1857. They lived in Berwick, Maine, where Isaac was a farmer. They had two children, Nathaniel C. and Charles W., the latter of whom was born in Berwick, April 10, 1824.

(VII) Nathaniel C., son of Isaac and Elizabeth (Chick) Hobbs, was born in Berwick, Maine, January 6, 1822, and for more than twenty years was a school teacher and farmer in that town. He taught school almost continually from the time he was seventeen years old until 1860, and in connection therewith carried on the old home farm which he inherited from his mother. She died in 1857, and in the course of a few years afterward he removed with his family to Dover, New Hampshire, where he has been a member of the board of assessors, holding office for twenty-seven years, and also a member of the school board for many years. Mr. Hobbs married, January 29, 1843, Elmira Littlefield, who has borne him seven children: Charles E., born in Berwick, January 7, 1844, now living in Boston. Ezra A., born in Berwick, December 29, 1845, a physician and surgeon in active practice in Framingham, Massachusetts. Temperance S., born in Berwick, August 11, 1848, married, March 4, 1876, John H. Ingraham, of Dover. Pliny, born in Berwick, November 16, 1850, died May 22, 1905. Justin E., born in Berwick, October 26, 1852, a farmer, now living in Berwick. William L. (twin), born October 8, 1857; and Lizzie (twin), born October 8, 1857, married, December 21, 1881, Charles H. Hobbs.

(IV) Nathaniel Hobbs was born in North Hampton, in 1742, and died in Ossipee, February 18, 1830. He owned property in Hampton which he lost in the early part of the Revolution, and soon after removed with his wife and five children to Ossipee, where he spent the remainder of his life. He married a Miss Leavitt, and had children: Benjamin, Nathaniel, Jonathan, Joseph and Reuben.

(V) Joseph, son of Nathaniel Hobbs, was born in Ossipee in May, 1777, and died there, October 28, 1851. He became a prosperous farmer, and before his death owned four hundred acres of land, a part of which he cleared and otherwise improved; and in connection with agriculture also did a considerable business in lumbering. He was regarded as one of the fathers of the town, and in 1832-33 he represented Ossipee in the state legislature. In politics he was a Democrat. He was familiarly known as "Squire Hobbs." He married Dorothy Cooley, who was born in 1783, and died in March, 1863. Their children were: Samuel D., Lovina D., Annah, Oliver F., Elizabeth, Lucinda B., Wentworth H., Ezra T., whose sketch follows.

(VI) Ezra Towle, youngest child of Joseph and Dorothy (Cooley) Hobbs, was born in Ossipee, September 23, 1827, and died April 25, 1873. He was educated in the public schools of Ossipee, was well instructed in farming by his father, and made agriculture his life work. Not long after his marriage he went to the vicinity of Winona, Minnesota, where he continued farming and lumbering for some years, and then returned to Ossipee, where the remainder of his life was passed. He married, June 1, 1852, Hannah Maria Coggswell, who was born in Portsmouth, November 21, 1830, and died in Ossipee, May 25, 1872, daughter of Rev. Dr. Frederick and Hannah Rogers (Peavey) Coggswell. Their children were: Hannah Evelyn, died young; Frank Pierce, Evelyn Anna, Effie Mary, died young; Child, died young; and Frederick Ezra. Frank P. is mentioned below. Evelyn Anna, born June 10, 1857, graduated from the Winona high school and from the Minnesota State Normal, and subsequently taught in Minnesota and Kansas, in the city of Omaha five years, and in Denver, Colorado, five years. Frederick E., born September 3, 1862, graduated from the State Normal School of Minnesota, the University of Minnesota, and subsequently studied law; after admission to the bar he opened an office in Minneapolis, and has since resided in that city. Since 1896 he has been a judge at one of the municipal courts. He married Evelyn Wait, of Winona.

(VII) Frank Pierce, second child and eldest son of Ezra T. and Hannah M. (Coggswell) Hobbs, was born in Winona, Minnesota, September 6, 1855, and educated in the public schools of Ossipee and Farnworth. While yet a boy he entered the employ of what is known as the Eastern Railroad, which was consolidated with the Boston & Maine railroad. There he served as brakeman and baggage master, and October 31, 1879, was appointed station agent at Wolfborough, and discharged the duties of that position until July 1, 1888. In that year he purchased a livery business which he has since conducted. In June, 1898, he bought the old Belvue House at Wolfborough, which he renamed the Lake Shore. He carried on that hostelry until June, 1899, when he bought the Wolfborough House which he christened "Hobbs is Inn." This is a commodious hotel, accommodating one hundred guests, up-to-date in its furnishings and equipment, charming in its situation and commanding a beautiful and comprehensive view of Lake Winnepesaukee and the surrounding mountains. July 4, 1888, Mr. Hobbs was appointed mail agent on the route between Boston and North Conway, but declined to serve. He was appointed deputy sheriff of Carroll county in 1887, and served twelve years. He was postmaster of Wolfborough from January 31, 1894, until February 3, 1898, during which time the increase of the business of the office caused the salary of the postmaster to be raised from twelve hundred dollars to seventeen hundred dollars a year. In 1898 Mr. Hobbs was a candidate for sheriff of Carroll county, to which office he was elected in November of that year, and he was the only Democrat sheriff in New Hampshire who was then elected, and was also the only Democrat elected in Carroll county. For more than twenty years he has been a member of the Democratic state committee. Besides discharging the manifold duties of the callings enumerated, in which he has been a faithful worker, he has done considerable business as an auctioneer and real estate dealer. He is a stirring, industrious man, popular and prosperous. He is a member of the Morning Star Lodge, No. 17, Free and Accepted Masons; Fidelity Lodge, No. 71; Kingswood Encampment, No. 31, Independent Order of Odd Fellows; and Carroll Lodge, No. 7, Ancient Order of United Workmen, of Wolfborough.

He married, December 6, 1882, Emily S. Evans, of Wolfboro, who was born February 9, 1856, daughter of Otis and Shuab (Libby) Evans, of Wolfboro (see Libby, VII). They have two children: Shuab Maria, born November 21, 1886, a graduate of Brewster Free Academy; and Mary Evelyn, born September 2, 1892.

(VI) Oliver F., second son and fourth child of Joseph and Dorothy (Cooley) Hobbs, lives in Ossipee valley. He married Deborah Jenness, daughter of Joseph and ——— (Weeks) Jenness. They have children: Frank K., Orodon P.

(VII) Frank K., eldest child of Oliver F. and Deborah (Jenness) Hobbs, died June 4, 1896. In early life he was a successful school teacher for twelve years. In 1859 he was a member of the firm of F. K. & W. H. Hobbs, merchants, at Ossipee Valley. September 14, 1864, he enlisted in Company F, Eighteenth New Hampshire Volunteer Infantry, for one year, and was mustered in September 24 as a private. He was appointed sergeant May 1, 1865, and mustered out June 10, 1865. He saw considerable active service, was present and participated in the attack on Fort Stedman, and was in many skirmishes. At the close of the war he engaged in mercantile business in Ossipee. In 1871 he was appointed postmaster and filled that office several years, and was appointed station agent the same year. He was selectman in 1872-73-74, a member of the legislature in 1875-76-78-81-85, and in 1893 was elected to the senate. In politics he was a Democrat. He was made a Mason in Charter Oak Lodge, but left that lodge and became a charter member of Ossipee Valley Lodge, No. 74. He was a member of Thomas Ambrose Post, Grand Army of the Republic, and Ossipee Lake Grange, No. 75, Patrons of Husbandry. He married, January 28, 1868, Sarah A. Atwood, who was born in Orrington, Maine, August 11, 1842, daughter of Benjamin and Lucy (Baker) Atwood. Two children were born to them: Herbert W. and Alice Josephine.

(VIII) Herbert Willis, only son of Frank K. and Sarah A. (Atwood) Hobbs, was born in Ossipee, July 2, 1871, and was educated in the public schools of Ossipee, the Nute high school of Milton, and the Brewster Free Academy, completing his studies at nineteen. He was an enthusiastic athlete, and the energy and determination which made him first in athletics among his fellow students made him a successful business man in a printing establishment at twenty-one. Subsequently he published the *Rochester Leader*. On the death of his father he took up his father's duties as merchant, postmaster and station agent, and has discharged them to the present time with success, besides carrying on his printing establishment. He is a Democrat, and has taken a lively interest in politics since a time previous to his majority. He was a member of the board of selectmen from 1895 to 1899, was re-elected in 1906, and is now (1907) still serving. He is social, and a member of various fraternal societies. He is a member of the Independent Order of Odd Fellows, past chancellor in Knights of Pythias, past sachem of Ossipee Tribe, No. 16, Improved Order of Red Men, and past master of Ossipee Lake Grange, Patrons of Husbandry.

HUTCHINSON This is a very ancient cognomen, and there are various traditions regarding its origin. The most persistent makes the first of the name in England a Norwegian, who came in with William the Conqueror. There is, however, no documentary evidence to confirm such tradition, and the actual origin of the name is lost in the misty ages of the distant past. The name is, however, continuously traced from the year 1282, and from there down the line will be herein given.

(I) Barnard Hutchinson, of Cowlam, county of York, was living in the year 1282, in the reign of King Edward I., but little is known of his personal history. He married a daughter of John Boyville, Esq., but her Christian name is not preserved. They had two sons and a daughter: John, Robert and Mary.

(II) John, son of Barnard Hutchinson, married Edith, daughte rof William Wouldbie, of Wouldbie. No trace of any place of that name can now be found; it probably designated some small landed estate which has since been swallowed up in a larger. They had four children: James, Barbara, Julia and Margaret.

(III) James, only son of John and Edith (Wouldbie) Hutchinson, married Ursula, daughter of Mr. Gregory, of Nafferton. They had five children: William, John, Barbara, a daughter unnamed and Eleanor.

(IV) William, eldest son of James and Ursula (Gregory) Hutchinson, married Anna, daughter of William Bennet, Esq., of Theckley. Their four children were: Anthony, Oliver, Mary and Alice.

(V) Anthony, elder son of William and Anna (Bennet) Hutchinson, married (first) Judith, daughter of Thomas Crosland, and (second) Isabel, daughter of Robert Harvie. He had eight sons: William, Thomas, John, Richard, Leonard, Edmond, Francis and Andrew.

(VI) Thomas, second son of Anthony Hutchinson, is supposed to have married a daughter of Mr. Drake, of Kinoulton, county of Nottingham. He was living October 9, 1550. He had three sons: William, John and Lawrence.

(VII) Lawrence, third son of Thomas Hutchinson, resided at Owlthorpe. His will was proved October 9, 1577, and his wife, Isabel, was living at that time. They had five children: Robert, Thomas, Agnes, Richard and William.

(VIII) Thomas (2), third son of Lawrence and Isabel Hutchinson, resided at Newark, where he died in 1598. He had two sons and a daughter: William, Thomas and Joan.

(IX) Thomas (3), younger son of Thomas (2) Hutchinson, was buried at Arnold, England, August 17, 1618. The Christian name of his wife was Alice, and their children were: John, Isabel, Humphrey, Elizabeth, Robert, Richard and Thomas.

(X) Richard, fourth son and sixth child of Thomas (3) and Alice Hutchinson, was the pioneer of the family in America. He was born in 1602, as indicated by his deposition on file in Salem, Massachusetts. He emigrated to America in 1634 with his wife Alice and four children, and settled in Salem village, now Danvers, in the vicinity of Whipple and Haythorn's Hill. There is some evidence in the town records of Salem that he may have originally settled in the old town. In 1636 he received a grant of sixty acres of land from the town, and on April 3, following he received twenty acres more. In the same year he was appointed on a committee to survey what is now Manchester and Mackerel Cove. On April 17, 1637, it was voted "that in case Ric'd Huchenson should sett up plowing within 2 years he may haue 20 acres more to bee added to his pportion." It seems that there was a great scarcity of plows, there being only thirty-seven in all the settlements. In 1648 Richard Hutchinson bought at Salem village, of Elias Stileman, his farm of one hundred and fifty acres, the consideration being fifteen pounds. The records do not show him to have been much in official station, but he was undoubtedly a man of much force of character and great physical endurance. He was a thorough agriculturist and amassed a large estate. Most of this he divided among his children before the close of his life. He and his wife were members of the First Church of Salem as early as 1636, and he was a strict disciplinarian in religious affairs. He was married (first) December 7, 1627, in England, to Alice, daughter of Joseph Bosworth, of Holgrave. She died before 1668, and he married (second) October 2, of that year, Susanna, widow of Samuel Archard. She died November 26, 1674, and he married (third) to Sarah, widow of James Standish. On the death of the last named Mr. Hutchinson was appointed administrator of his estate. At this third marriage he must have been at least seventy-nine years of age, and was certainly sixty-six at his second. His will was signed January 19, 1769, and proved September 22, 1682, which would indicate that his death occured in the early part of the latter year. His third wife survived him and shortly after his death married for her third husband, Thomas Roots, of Manchester. She was living as late as March, 1684. Richard Hutchinson had seven children by his first wife, Alice, namely: Alice, Elizabeth, Mary, Rebecca, Joseph, Abigail and Hannah.

(XI) Joseph, only son and fifth child of Richard and Alice (Bosworth) Hutchinson, was born in 1633, at North Mukham, England. The date of his birth is indicated by a deposition which is borne upon the same paper as that of his father, made in 1660. He lived on the paternal homestead and acquired most of his property by a deed of gift from his father. This amounted to considerably more than three hundred acres, with orchards, house and barns and numerous meadows. The homestead was situated adjoining the site of the first meeting house in Salem village, which site he had contributed. In 1700 this church was torn down and removed to another spot, and the site reverted to him. Joseph Hutchinson lived through the very memorable period of the witchcraft delusion of 1692. Although he was a man of strong mind and sensible on other subjects, he was led into this folly and was one of the number who complained against others as witches. In 1658 he was chosen constable and tax gatherer. He was on the jury list for 1679, was frequently chosen administrator and overseer of estates, and was often witness to various instruments. During his lifetime he distributed his large property among his children, but there is no will or administration of his estate on record. He died between January and June, 1716, when he was about eighty-three years of age. His first wife was probably a daughter of John Gedney. He was married (second), February 28, 1678, to Lydia, daughter of Anthony and Elizabeth Buckston. She was at that time widow of Joseph Small, who was her second husband, and of whose estate, Joseph was one of the administrators. She was baptized April 27, 1689, and was living in June, 1708. There were five children of the first marriage: Abigail, Bethiah, Joseph, John and Benjamin; and six of the second marriage: Abigail, Richard, Samuel, Ambrose, Lydia and Robert.

(XII) Benjamin, third son and fifth child of Joseph Hutchinson, and youngest child of his first wife, was a native of Danvers and died intestate in 1733. He was a farmer, and lived on that part of the homestead which he received by deed of gift from his father, October 2, 1691. This contained thirty acres, and he afterward acquired considerable land by purchase, contiguous to this, and he also owned a tract of ten acres on the west side of Ipswich river, which he bought August 6, 1713, from his brother Robert. Before his death he settled a snug estate upon each of his remaining children, and disposed of the remainder of his property by sale. While an infant he had been adopted by Deacon Nathaniel Ingersoll, who had previously been bereaved of his only child. He was married (first), before 1690, to Jane, daughter of Walter and Margaret Phillips, who died in 1711. He was married (second), January 26, 1715, to Abigail Foster. He was received into the church May 7, 1699, and his wife on the 28th of the same month. She was the mother of his eleven children. The first, a son, died in infancy. The others were: Benjamin (died young), Hannah, Benjamin, Bethiah, Nathaniel, Sarah, Bartholomew, Jane, Israel and John.

(XIII) Benjamin (2), third son and fourth child of Benjamin (1) and Jane (Phillips) Hutchinson, was born January 27, 1694, in Salem village, and was about eighty-six years old at the time of his death. His will was proved May 10, 1780. He was the first of the family to depart from his native locality and become a pioneer in a new region. He ceased to be taxed in Salem in 1734, and it is probable that he removed to Bedford, Massachusetts, sometime during that year. He and his wife were members of the Salem church, and received letters of dismission to the church in Bedford, November 27, 1737. He had large possessions at Salem village and, after the death of his father, he bought all the other heirs' rights in the estate, with the exception of that of his brother Jonathan, who was then under age. Prior to his removal to Bedford he disposed of all of his property, receiving from Joshua Goodale for his homestead the sum of three hundred pounds. He reserved, however, one-half of his part in the cider mill. This deed was made December 20, 1733. Besides his agricultural pursuits he followed the occupation of cooper. He married, February 7, 1716, Sarah, daughter of John and Mary (Nourse) Tarbell. She was born October 2, 1696. They were the parents of eight children, namely: Nathan, Jane, Benjamin, Sarah, Elizabeth, Bartholomew, Mary and John.

(XIV) Nathan, eldest child of Benjamin (2) and Sarah (Tarbell) Hutchinson, was baptized at the First Church of Salem village, February 10, 1717. He was a farmer and removed with his father to Bedford in 1734. He subsequently settled in that part of Amherst which is now Milford, New Hampshire, where he died January 12, 1795. He married, April 16, 1741, Rachel Stearns, daughter of Samuel and Rachel Stearns (see Stearns, IV). They were the parents of six children: Samuel, Nathan, Benjamin, Ebenezer, Bartholomew and Rachel. (Benjamin and Bartholomew and descendants receive extended mention in this article.)

(XV) Nathan (2), son of Nathan (1) and Rachel (Stearns) Hutchinson, was born in Milford, in February, 1752. He was a farmer. He married, in 1778, Rebecca, daughter of William and Rebecca (Smith) Peabody, who was born in Milford, January 2, 1752, and died February 25, 1826. They had seven children, all born in Milford. They were: Nathan, third, married Lydia Jones, of Milford. Rebecca, married Nehemiah Hayward, Junior. Reuben. Ira, died unmarried in Milford. Olive, married Dr. John Wallace, of Milford. Jonas. Abel, whose sketch follows. Nathan Hutchinson, Junior, died December 26, 1831.

(XVI) Abel, youngest child of Nathan and Rebecca (Peabody) Hutchinson, was born in Milford, New Hampshire, August 1, 1795. He was a farmer, and lived in Milford all his life. He married on January 22, 1816, Betsey, daughter of Isaac and Elizabeth (Hutchinson) Bartlett. She was born in Milford October 26, 1796, and died there August 23, 1873. They had nine children, all born in Milford: Elizabeth D., born June 18, 1816, married Charles A. Burns, of Milford. Abel Fordyce, mentioned below. George Cannin. Jerusha Peabody, married (first) Judson J. Hutchinson, and (second) Dr. Simeon S. Stickney, of Milford. Andrew Jackson. Isaac Bartlett. Helen Augustine, died young. Nathan. Jonas, born January 10, 1840, became a lawyer and judge in Chicago; married, November 14, 1876, Letitia Brown, of Lexington, Kentucky. Abel Hutchinson died in Milford, New Hampshire, February 19, 1846.

(XVII) Abel Fordyce, eldest son of Abel and Betsey (Bartlett) Hutchinson, was born in Milford, New Hampshire, March 20, 1820. He was a merchant, doing business in Milford, and at Waltham, Massachusetts. He married, April 11, 1848, Deborah, daughter of Levi and Rhoda (Griffin) Hawkes, who was born in Windham, Maine, January 22, 1822, and died in Milford, New Hampshire, March 17, 1884. They had four children of whom the three younger were born in Milford: George Edward, born at Lynn, Massachusetts, March 14, 1849, and died at Lynn, April 28, 1851. Ella M., mentioned below. Frederick Sawyer, born February 14, 1854, head waiter in a hotel, died at Saratoga, New York, May 28, 1886. Grace Darling, born November 10, 1864, married, July 10, 1900, Frederick H. Bradford, a salesman, living in Waltham, Massachusetts. Abel F. Hutchinson died at Waltham, Massachusetts, December 2, 1892.

(XVIII) Ella M., elder daughter and child of Abel F. and Deborah (Hawkes) Hutchinson, was born in Milford, New Hampshire, June 12, 1851. She was married to Judge Robert Moore Wallace, August 25, 1874 (see Wallace, VI).

(XV) Lieutenant Benjamin (3), third son and child of Nathan and Rachel (Stearns) Hutchinson, was born June 9, 1754, in Milford, New Hampshire. He lived on a farm near the present railroad crossing. He married Susanna, daughter of William and Rebecca (Smith) Peabody, who was born in Milford, November 4, 1755. They had six children: Benjamin, born August 5, 1777; Sarah, March 16, 1779, lived in Milford, and died November 9, 1865, unmarried; Susanna, April 20, 1781, lived in Milford, and died August 2, 1843, unmarried; Luther, May 2, 1783; Eugene, March 11, 1785, whose sketch follows; Calliope, April 7, 1787, lived in Milford, and died September 25, 1848, unmarried. Lieutenant Benjamin Hutchinson, died September 12, 1832; his widow died August 23, 1834.

(XVI) Eugene, third son and fifth child of Lieutenant Benjamin and Susanna (Peabody) Hutchinson, was born in Milford, New Hampshire, March 11, 1785. He was a farmer. He married, in November, 1812, Susan, daughter of David and Elizabeth Danforth, who was born in Amherst, New Hampshire, July 14, 1787. They had three children, all born in Milford: Eugene, whose sketch follows; Susan H., born February 3, 1816, married, January 4, 1848, George, son of William and Joanna (Hodge) Savage, of Greenfield, New Hampshire, lived in Auburn and Milford, New Hampshire; Eliza, born May 16, 1820, married, September 6, 1842, George W., son of Henry and Hannah (Moore) George, of Goffstown, lived in Manchester, New Hampshire, and died there March 9, 1871. Eugene Hutchinson died in Milford, February 7, 1854, and his widow died about a year later, February 16, 1855.

(XVII) Eugene (2), only son and eldest child of Eugene (1) and Susan (Danforth) Hutchinson, was born in Milford, New Hampshire, March 25, 1813. He lived on the farm once occupied by his father, and now owned by his son-in-law, Charles A. Richardson, till a few years before his death, when he removed to Merrimack, New Hampshire. He was twice married. His first wife was Phebe B., daughter of George and Mary (Wallace) Raymond, to whom he was united, November 28, 1837. She was born in Mount Vernon, New Hampshire, September 13, 1812. They had six children: George Eugene, born January 17, 1839, died May 28, 1859; Henry Pratt, born August 31, 1841, enlisted in Company F, Ninth New Hampshire, was wounded at the battle of the Wilderness May 12, 1864, died May 19, 1864; Abbie Theresa, whose sketch follows: Dana Raymond, born April 1, 1848, a farmer, lives in Merrimack, New Hampshire, married, July 8, 1877, Florie Eliza, daughter of James E. and Susan M. (Beaman) Walch, of Merrimack; Walter Danforth, born April 21, 1850, died December 6, 1874; Delia Caroline, born September 2, 1852, married, July 8, 1877, Clarence E., son of James E. and Susan M. (Beaman) Walch, of Merrimack, and lives in Hudson, New Hampshire. Mrs. Phebe (Raymond) Hutchinson died at Milford, New Hampshire, September 11, 1857. On May 5, 1868, Eugene Hutchinson married his second wife, Lydia A., daughter of William and Lydia (Putnam) Richardson, who was born at Lyndeborough, New Hampshire, February 25, 1830. There were no children by the second marriage. He died at Merrimack, New Hampshire, March 8, 1873. She died in New Mexico, January 12, 1886.

(XVIII) Abbie Theresa, third child and eldest daughter of Eugene and Phebe B. (Raymond) Hutchinson, was born in Milford, New Hampshire, November 7, 1844, married on April 16, 1865, Charles A. Richardson, of Milford, whose Aunt Lydia afterwards became her father's second wife (see Richardson).

(XV) Bartholomew, fifth son and child of Nathan and Rachel (Stearns) Hutchinson, was born in Milford, New Hampshire, February 10, 1759. He was a farmer and lived on the homestead afterwards owned by Edwin D. Searles, on the road to Wilton, New Hampshire. He married, October 14, 1784, Phebe, daughter of Jacob Hagget, who was born in Andover, Massachusetts, in May, 1767. They had thirteen children all born in Milford: Jacob, mentioned below; Lucy, born December 20, 1786, married, June 7, 1804, Reuben Hutchinson, of Milford, died there July 15, 1858; Alfred, born August 27, 1858; Acachy, born November 6, 1790, married in March, 1808, Jonathan Buxton, Jr., of Milford, and died there October 20, 1852; Minerva, born January 31, 1792, married, August 10, 1809, Samuel Henry, of Milford, and died there June 14, 1831; Nancy, born May 19, 1794, married, June 1, 1820, Luther, adopted son of Jonathan Jones, of Milford, and died there October 11, 1821; Augustus, born July 25, 1796, and died in 1800; Rhoda, born July 2, 1798, died March 20, 1822; Alvah, born January 25, 1800, lived in Milford, where he died, July 6, 1826; Myra, born December 24, 1801, married, October 19, 1823, William Darracot, Jr., lived in Milford, and died there December 3, 1837; Eliza, born October 4, 1803, married, February 3, 1823, Holland Hopkins, of Milford, lived there till 1848, when they removed to Illinois, where she died November 17, 1857; Augustus, born August 5, 1805; Albert, born December 8, 1807, lived in Boston, Massachusetts, and in Milford, and died in the latter place August 20, 1834. Bartholomew Hutchinson died at his home in Milford, September 23, 1841. His widow died in Milford, August 27, 1849.

(XVI) Jacob, eldest child of Bartholomew and Phebe (Hagget) Hutchinson, was born in Milford, New Hampshire, February 5, 1785. He lived on the farm now owned by his grandson, Christopher C. Shaw. Jacob Hutchinson was twice married and had four children, all by his first wife. He married, August 27, 1807, Betsey, daughter of Andrew and Elizabeth (Burns) Burnham, who was born in Milford, September 5, 1788, and died January 18, 1839. They had four children: Betsey, mentioned below; Jane, born March 21, 1814, married in October, 1833, Milton V. Wilkins, of Milford, and died there January 23, 1841; Harriet, born November 13, 1817, married, November 23, 1847, Luther S., son of Timothy and Lydia (Bowers) Bullard, of Dublin, New Hampshire, lived in Milford and died there April 26, 1895; Maria, born November 13, 1826, married in April, 1846, Timothy C., son of Jonas and Sarah (Tay) Center, of Wilton, New Hampshire, lived there and died there, August 30, 1854. Jacob Hutchinson married for his second wife, June 2, 1839, Esther, daughter of Phineas and Susan Whitney, who was born in Nashua, New Hampshire, September 29, 1788, and died there February 6, 1867. Jacob Hutchinson died March 23, 1859.

(XVII) Betsey, eldest of the four daughters of Jacob and Betsey (Burnham) Hutchinson, was born in Milford, New Hampshire, March 21, 1808. She married, November 20, 1823, William Shaw, Jr., of Milford, New Hampshire. She died in that town June 22, 1889 (see Shaw).

(XVI) Reuben, second son and third child of Nathan and Rebecca (Peabody) Hutchinson, was born in Milford, New Hampshire, September 9, 1782. He lived on the farm later owned by Charles A. Jenkins in the west part of the town. On June 7, 1804, he married his first cousin, Lucy, daughter of Bartholomew and Phebe (Hagget) Hutchinson, who was born in Milford, December 2, 1786. They had twelve children: Lucy C., born January 17, 1805, died October 15, 1813; Robert, born January 15, 1809; Sophia, born September 12, 1810, married December 30, 1828, James B., son of Jonathan and Sibyl (Sawtell) Farwell, of Milford, where she died February 12, 1878; Sophronia, born August 31, 1812, married (first), March 11, 1847, Abner, son of Nathaniel and Sarah (Upham) Holt, born in Temple, New Hampshire, October 11, 1810, and died July 30, 1851, (second), April 29, 1852, Ira, son of Nehemiah and Mary (Wright) Holt, born in Temple, July 26, 1815. They lived in Milford, where she died May 17, 1872. He died June 19, 1880. There were no children. The other children of Reuben and Lucy (Hutchinson) Hutchinson were: Nathan Randolph, born November 7, 1816, married, November 17, 1842, Abby Maria, daughter of Benjamin, Jr., and Betsey (Tay) Conant, of Milford, removed to Pittsfield, New Hampshire, where he died May 6, 1879; Edmund P., born November 1, 1818; Clifton, born October 11, 1820, died January 15, 1822; Lucy Caroline, born April 8, 1823, married February 14, 1843, Holland, son of Daniel and Elsie (Palmer) Prouty, lived in Milford and died there, May 13, 1891; Clifton, born March 14, 1825, died in October, 1825; Rebecca Peabody, mentioned below; Jeannette, born October 11, 1828, married, February 1, 1848, John, son of Adam and Mary (Gordon) Dickey, of Milford, where he died March 6, 1868; she married for her second husband, February 9, 1882, John, son of John and Roxanna (Leavitt) Marvel, who died November 8, 1888. Reuben Hutchinson, the father, died in the village of Milford, August 25, 1861; his wife died three years earlier, July 15, 1858.

(XVII) Rebecca Peabody, fifth daughter and eleventh child of Reuben and Lucy (Hutchinson) Hutchinson, was born in Milford, New Hampshire, August 13, 1826. On August 27, 1846, she married Christopher C. Shaw, son of her cousin, Betsey (Hutchinson) Shaw, and William (3) Shaw, of Milford (see Shaw, III).

(Second Family.)

HUTCHINSON Like many other families this one has the tradition concerning the "brothers," who came to America. It is substantially that in the time of Ann Hutchinson (1634) two brothers came to America and that one of them soon returned to England, but the other remaining became the progenitor of the family herein written. In following out the proof of the above, it has been traced to Jonathan Hutchinson, a grandson of Timothy, said Timothy being the earliest ancestor to whom we can trace, and this brings us to within two generations of the settler or immigrant ancestor.

(I) Timothy Hutchinson, the earliest ancestor who can now be traced, was residing in Hampton Falls, New Hampshire, in 1710, as appears by a petition of the inhabitants of that precinct, asking to be set off as a separate town, the petition bearing date of May 3, of that year. The earliest date of land purchased by him is November 13, 1718, when he purchased land in that part of Hampton now known as Kensington, which land became his homestead. In the following years his name is frequently on record. The date of his death is unknown, but he was alive as late as 1759, in which year he deeded the homestead to his son Jonathan. His wife Hannah was baptized and admitted to the Hampton Falls church, July 14, 1717, and her death is recorded as of November 21, 1752, and her age seventy years. A list of his children has been made up from various sources as follows: Ebenezer, John, Hannah, Jonathan, Mary, Johnston and Phoebe.

(II) Jonathan, third son and fourth child of Timothy and Hannah Hutchinson, was born in Kensington, and died in Gilmanton, New Hampshire, August 5, 1801. He was a tanner by trade, though in one deed he is described as a cordwainer (shoemaker). He resided in Kensington on the opposite side of the road from the three half shares purchased by his father in 1718. On February 15, 1759 he purchased these three half shares of his father, and in the deed the place is called the "homestead." In 1760 he was a grand juror, and in 1761 sold his farm to Richard Sanborn, Jr., and probably remained in Kensington, for in July of that year his son Levi is born up there. Some time in 1764 he removed to Canterbury, as appears by several deeds. In 1768 he appears in Gilmanton, coming from Loudon, then a part of Canterbury. His name appears among those of Gilmanton who signed the Association Test Paper, but he does not appear to have taken a part in the Revolutionary war. His intention of marriage is recorded as follows in the records of Salisbury, Massachusetts: "Jonathan Hutchinson of Kensington entered his intention of marriage with Theodate Morrill of Salisbury, November 6, 1742." He was married in Salisbury, January 13, 1743. His wife was the daughter of Aaron and Joanna Morrill, born in Salisbury, November 24, 1726, and descended from Abraham Morrill, one of the early settlers of Salisbury. The children of this marriage were: Elisha, Theodate, Jonathan, Dudley, Joanna, Joanna, Susan, Hannah, Levi, Stephen and Elijah. (The history of Stephen and some of his descendants is a feature of this article).

(III) Jonathan (2), third child and second son of Jonathan (1) and Theodate (Morrill) Hutchinson, was born in Kensington, March 20, 1748, and died in Pembroke, May 3, 1830. He was a hatter by trade, residing in Pembroke, on a place still in the possession of his descendants. He married, about 1769, Mehitable (Chandler) Lovejoy, a descendant of John Lovejoy, one of the first settlers of Andover, Massachusetts. She died in Allenstown, March 2, 1835. The children, all born in Pembroke, were: Betsey, Jonathan, Obadiah, and Solomon (twins) and Levi.

(IV) Jonathan (3), second child and eldest son of Jonathan (2) and Mehitable (Lovejoy) Hutchinson, was born in Pembroke, April 24, 1771, and died there January 17, 1843. He was a hatter by trade, and resided in Pembroke, Boscawen and Salisbury. He married Mary Wardwell, born August 28, 1772, died in Merrimack, August 30, 1850. Their children were: Nathaniel P., Chandler H., Pamelia, Herman, Hiram, Hubbard, Jesse, John W., Mary W., Ira, Jeannette W. and Charles K.

(V) Nathaniel P., eldest child of Jonathan and Mary (Wardwell) Hutchinson, was born in Pembroke, November 19, 1794, and died October 4, 1874. He was a farmer and resided on the Hutchinson homestead, which he bought of his Uncle Solomon, April 2, 1818. He was in his earlier life a Congregationalist, but later joined the Methodists, and worshipped in the church which stood on the hill in Pembroke. In politics he was a Democrat. He enlisted in the War of 1812 and served at Portsmouth. March 5, 1820, he married Lydia Smith, born in Danbury, New Hampshire, November 15, 1795, died February 15, 1881. They had two children: Lyman Curtis and Augustus P.

(VI) Lyman Curtis, eldest child of Nathaniel P. and Lydia (Smith) Hutchinson, was born at Pembroke, April 1, 1831, and died there May 14, 1905. He was educated in the common schools and at Pembroke Academy, and was by trade a carpenter. In 1867 he bought the old Hutchinson homestead, and in 1883 built upon the site of the old dwelling an elegant residence, now occupied by his widow. In politics he was a Democrat, and in religious faith, a Congregationalist. He was a man of influence in his neighborhood, a true hearted citizen, a good neighbor and friend, and had the moral courage to profess his sentiments whether they were popular or not. He married, November 29, 1866, Lizzie A. Staniels, daughter of Charles H. and Sarah A. (Farrington) Staniels, of Chichester, born October 10, 1838.

(III) Stephen, eleventh child and sixth son of Jonathan and Theodate (Morrill) Hutchinson, was born July 31, 1764, probably in Canterbury, New Hampshire. He married, March 7, 1792, Elizabeth Sanborn, and they were the parents of five sons: Jonathan, Stephen, David, John and Ebenezer.

(IV) John, son of Stephen and Elizabeth (Sanborn) Hutchinson, was born in Gilmanton, died probably, 1864, in Gilmanton. He was a hatter by trade and lived in Gilmanton and Loudon. During the War of 1812 he was in the military service. He married Betsey Bradbury, born in Meredith, died in Concord, 1879. Their children were: Jonathan M., died in Loudon; Ebenezer B., mentioned below; Eliza Ann, widow of Charles T. Wason, of Concord; Joseph Emerson, of Concord; Ira James, died, 1905, in Concord; Mary Abby, wife of Charles Kendall, of Concord; and Oliver, who died in California several years ago.

(V) Ebenezer Bradbury, second son and child of John and Betsey (Bradbury) Hutchinson, was born in Loudon, April 1, 1831. When eight years old he was taken by his parents on their removal to Gilmanton. After attending school there two years he went to Colchester, Vermont, where he attended school till seventeen years of age. The following year he went to Burlington, Vermont, and there learned the carpenter's trade, remaining in that place till 1852. Removing to Glens Falls, New York, he worked at his trade there four years. In 1857 he went west and spent one year. Removing to Concord in 1859, he was in the employ of White & Brainard, contractors and builders, some years, and then was partner with E. D. Brainard in the same business for four years. At the end of that time, in 1863, he continued in business alone till 1894, when he sold out to Abbott Piper & James, former employes. He attends the South Congregational Church, is a member of White Mountain Lodge, No. 5, Independent Order of Odd Fellows, and is a staunch Republican. In 1883, he was elected to the New Hampshire legislature from ward 6, Concord. He now resides with his daughter in that city.

He married (first), December 31, 1854, Adaline Elizabeth Sabin, born December 31, 1834, at Walden, Vermont, died January 23, 1859, at Concord. She was a daughter of Hiram Sabin, a blacksmith of Walden. He married (second) Mary Frances Brown, born June 13, 1831, in Bow, died March 3, 1903, in Concord, daughter of Jonathan Brown (born about 1805, died March 8, 1888) and his wife, Mary Elizabeth (McCauley) Brown, born May 30, 1811, died May 26, 1900. By the first marriage, Mr. Hutchinson has one child, Ella Martha Hutchinson, born in Loudon, February 13, 1858, married, May 1, 1878, Charles H. Gay, born in Warren, New Hampshire, October 17, 1854, carriage builder in the employ of the Abbott-Downing Company of Concord. They have had two children: Ada Hutchinson, born January 18, 1880, married, March 6, 1901, William Russell Hutton, carpenter, of Concord; Francis, born May 26, 1902, died May 28, 1902.

MORTON The name of Morton, Moreton, and Mortaigne, is earliest found in old Dauphiné, and is still existent in France, where it is represented by the present Comtes and Marquises Morton de Chabrillon, and where the family has occupied many important positions, states the "Genealogy of the Morton Family," from which this sketch is taken. In the annals of the family there is a statement repeatedly met with, that as the result of a quarrel one of the name migrated from Dauphiné, first to Brittany and then to Normandy, where he joined William the Conqueror. Certain it is that among the names of the followers of William painted on the chancel ceiling in the ancient church of Dives in old Normandy, is that of Robert Comte de Mortain. It also figures on Battle Abbey Roll, The Domesday Book, and the Norman Rolls, and it is conjectured that this Count Robert, who was also half-brother of the Conqueror by his mother Harlotte, was the founder of the English family of that name. In the Bayeux tapestry he is represented as of the Council of William, the result of which was the intrenchment of Hastings and the conquest of England. Count Robert held manors in nearly every county in England, in all about eight hundred, among which was Pevensea, where the Conqueror landed, and where in 1087 Robert and his brother Odo, Bishop of Bayeux, were besieged six weeks by William Rufus. Here Camden (1551-1628) found "the most entire remains of a Roman building to be seen in Britain."

When William, Earl of Moriton and Cornwall, son of Robert, rebelled against Henry I, that prince seized and razed his castles, but this one seems to have escaped demolition. In early Norman times this William built a castle at Tamerton, Cornwall, and founded a college of canons, as appeared by the Domesday Book, where it is called Lanstaveton. On the north side of the Gretna in Richmondshire stands an old manor house, called Moreton Tower, from a lofty, square embattled tower at one end of it.

Of the family of Morton were the Earls of Dulcie and Cornwall; Robert Morton, Esq., of Bawtry; Thomas Morton, secretary to Edward III; William Morton, Bishop of Meath; Robert Morton, Bishop of Worcester in 1486; John Morton, the celebrated Cardinal Archbishop of Canterbury and Lord Chancellor of England, 1420-1500; Albert Morton, Secretary of State to James I; Thomas Morton (1564-1659) Bishop of Durham and Chaplain to James II.

Prominent among the English Mortons who early came to America were Thomas Morton, Esq., Rev. Charles Morton, Landgrave Joseph Morton, Proprietary Governor of South Carolina, and George Morton.

(I) George Morton, the first of the name to found a family in America, and the ancestor of former Vice-President Levi P. Morton, was born about 1585, at Austerfield, Yorkshire, England, and it is believed was of the ancient Mortons, who bore for arms: Quarterly, gules and ermine; in the dexter chief and sinister base, each a goat's head erased argent attired or. Crest, a goat's head argent attired or. Hunter, in his "Founders of New Plymouth," suggests that he may have been the George Morton hitherto unaccounted for in the family of Anthony Morton, of Bawtry, one of the historical families of England, and that from Romanist lineage "he so far departed from the spirit and principles of his family as to have fallen into the ranks of the Protestant Puritans and Separatists."

Of George Morton's early life no record has been preserved, and his religious environments and the causes which led him to unite with the Separatists are alike unknown. His home in Yorkshire was in the vicinage of Scrooby Manor, and possibly he was a member of Brewster's historic church; but it is only definitely known that he early joined the Pilgrims at Leyden, and continued of their company until his death. When the first of the colonists departed for America, Mr. Morton remained behind, although he "much desired" to embark then and intended soon to join them. His reasons for such a course is a matter of conjecture. As he was a merchant, possibly his business interests caused his detention, or, what is more probable, he remained to promote the success of the colony by encouraging emigration among others. That he served in some official capacity before coming to America is undoubted. One writer states that he was "the agent of those of his sect in London," and another, that he acted as "the financial agent in London for Plymouth County."

The work, however, for which this eminent forefather is most noted, and which will forever link his name with American history, is the publication issued by him in London, in 1622, of what has since been known as "Mourt's Relation." This "Relation," may justly be termed the first history of New England, and is composed of letters and journals from the chief colonists at Plymouth, either addressed or intrusted to George Morton, whose authorship in the work is possibly limited to the preface. The "Relation" itself is full of valuable information and still continues an authority. Shortly after it was placed before the public, George Morton prepared to emigrate to America, and sailed with his wife and five children in the Ann, the third and last ship to carry what are distinctively known as the Forefathers, and reached Plymouth early in June, 1623. "New England's Memorial" speaks of Mr. Timothy Hatherly and Mr. George Morton as "two of the principal passengers that came in this ship," and from Morton's activity in promoting emigration it may be inferred that the Ann's valuable addition to the Colony was in a measure due to his efforts.

He did not long survive his arrival, and his early death was a serious loss to the infant settlement. His character and attainments were such as to suggest the thought that, had he lived to the age reached by several of his distinguished contemporaries, he would have filled as conspicuous a place in the life of the Colony. The Memorial thus chronicles his decease:

"Mr. George Morton was a pious, gracious servant of God, and very faithful in whatsoever public employment he was betrusted withal, and an unfeigned well-willer, and according to his sphere and condition a suitable promoter of the common good and growth of the plantation of New Plymouth, laboring to still the discontents that sometimes would arise amongst some spirits, by occasion of the difficulties of these new beginnings; but it pleased God to put a period to his days soon after his arrival in New England, not surviving a full year after his coming ashore. With much comfort and peace he fell asleep in the Lord, in the month of June anno 1624."

He married Juliana Carpenter, as shown by the entry in the Leyden Records:

"George Morton, merchant, from York in England accompanied by Thomas Morton, his brother, and Roger Wilson his acquaintance, with Juliana Carpenter, maid from Bath in England, accompanied by Alexander Carpenter, her father, and Alice Carpenter, her sister, and Anna Robinson, her acquaintance."

6
"The banns published 16 July 1612.
23 July
The marriage took place 2 Aug. 1612."

Mrs. Morton married (second) Manasseh Kempton, Esq., a member of the first and other assemblies of the colony. She died at Plymouth, 18 February, 1665, in the eighty-first year of her age, and is mentioned in the Town Records as "a faithful servant of God."

Children of George and Juliana (Carpenter) Morton: Nathaniel, Patience, John, Sarah and Ephraim.

(II) Hon. John Morton, second son of George and Juliana (Carpenter) Morton, born at Leyden, Holland, 1616-7, also came with his parents in the "Ann." He was admitted a freeman of the colony 7 June, 1648, chosen constable for Plymouth in 1654, one of the grand inquest of the county in 1660, elected by the freemen of Plymouth a deputy to the general court in 1662, tax assessor in 1664, selectman in 1666, collector of excise in 1668, and served the town of Plymouth in other important capacities. He removed to Middleboro, in the same county, where he was one of the "famous twenty-six original proprietors and founders," and in 1670 was the first representative of the town to the general court, which office he held until his death (1673). Among his colleagues in the general court in 1662 were his cousin, the Honorable Constant Southworth, Captain Peregrine White, Cornet Robert Stetson and Mr. William Peabody.

Mr. Morton died at Middleboro, October 3, 1673. He married about 1648-49, Lettice, whose surname is unknown. She afterwards became the second wife of Andrew Ring, and died 22 February, 1691. Children of John and Lettice Morton, all born at Plymouth: John (died young), John, Deborah, Mary, Martha, Hannah, Esther Manasseh, and Ephraim.

(III) John (2), the eldest surviving child of Hon. John (1) and Lettice Morton, was born at Plymouth, December 21, 1650. Like others of his family he was well educated, and to his effort is due the establishment of what is believed to be the first absolutely free public school in America, which he "erected and kept" at Plymouth in 1671, "for the education of children and youth." He was succeeded as teacher by Ammi Ruhamah Corlet, a graduate of Harvard, and son of the renowned Elijah Corlet, who, bred at Oxford, was for half a century master of the Latin School at Cambridge, Massachusetts. Mr. Morton died at Middleboro in 1717. He married (first) about 1680, Phebe ——; (second) at Middleboro, about 1687, Mary, daughter of Andrew and Deborah (Hopkins) Ring. Children of John (2) Morton by his first wife: Joanna and Phebe; by his second wife: Mary, John, Hannah, Ebenezer, Deborah and Perez.

(IV) Captain Ebenezer, fourth child of John and Mary (Ring) Morton, was born at Middleboro, 19 October, 1696. He was a prominent citizen, and served in the office of assessor, surveyor of highways, selectman, moderator of the town meeting, and captain of the militia. He died at Middleboro, 1750; married 1720, Mercy Foster, born 1698, daughter of John and Hannah (Stetson) Foster, of Plymouth. She died at Middleboro. April 4, 1782, aged eighty-four. Children of Captain Ebenezer and Mercy (Foster) Morton, all born at Middleboro; Mercy, Mary, John, Ebenezer, Hannah, Deborah, Seth, Sarah, Nathaniel and Lucia.

(V) Ebenezer (2), fourth child of Captain Ebenezer (1) and Mercy (Foster) Morton, was born at Middleboro, August 27, 1726; married there July 23, 1753, Mrs. Sarah Cobb. Children of Ebenezer (2) and Sarah Morton, all born in Middleboro: Mercy, Ebenezer, Phebe. Livy, Priscilla and Sarah.

(VI) Priscilla, fifth child of Ebenezer (2) and Sarah (Cobb) Morton, was born October 4, 1763; married, 1780, Seth Morton, Jr., and died 19 February, 1847.

(V) Seth, seventh child of Captain Ebenezer and Mercy (Foster) Morton, was born at Middleboro, March 11, 1732; died January 30, 1810; married (first) October 10, 1751, Lydia Hall of Sandwich; (second) 1757, Hepzibah Packard. She died in 1820, aged eighty-eight. Children of Seth Morton by his first wife: Phebe, Joshua, Seth; by his second wife: Caleb, Samuel, Lydia, George, Hepzibah, Isaac, Mercy, David and Sarah.

(VI) Seth, (2), third child of Seth (1) and Lydia (Hall) Morton, was born at Middleboro, February 27, 1756, and died December 3, 1805. He was a revolutionary soldier, a private in Captain Nehemiah Allen's company, Colonel Theophilus Cotten's regiment, and served thirty-one days on a secret expedition to Rhode Island in September and October, 1777. He was also a private in Captain Allen's company, of Colonel Jeremiah Hall's regiment. This company marched December 8, 1776, to Bristol, Rhode Island, and was in service ninety-two days. He was also in Captain John Barrow's company, Colonel Ebenezer Sproutt's regiment, serving from September 6 to September 12, 1778; the company marched from Middleboro to Dartmouth on two alarms, one in May, and one in September, 1778. Seth Morton was commissioned, October 28, 1778, second lieutenant in Captain Robert Finney's (Eleventh) company, Colonel Theophilus Cotton's (First Plymouth County) regiment of Massachusetts militia. His residence was always in Middleboro. He married first, November 20, 1783. Rosamond Finney; second, May 21, 1789, his cousin, Priscilla Morton, fifth child of Ebenezer (2) and Sarah (Cobb) Morton, who was born October 4, 1763, and died February 19, 1847. The only child by the first wife was Virtue. The children by the second wife were: Samuel, Phebe, Seth, Hepzibah, Ebenezer, Livy, Lydia and Elias.

(VII) Phebe, second child and eldest daughter of Seth (2) and Priscilla (Morton) Morton, was born in Middleboro, Massachusetts, May 15, 1791. She married in Middleboro, January 14, 1809, Samuel Jennings of Wayne, Maine. (See Jennings V.)

HOWE There were several early immigrant ancestors of this name, but John Howe, of Watertown, Sudbury, and Marlborough, Massachusetts, was one of the earliest if not the first of this name in New England, and his progeny now constitutes a large part of the family of this cognomen in the eastern states. The Howes of America are descended from Abraham Howe of Roxbury and John "How" of Sudbury and Marlboro, Massachusetts, and the Howes of Keene are the posterity of the first-named emigrant. Some of them, notably Elias Howe, the inventor of the sewing machine, have developed remarkable mechanical ingenuity, and several are distinguished for their intellectual attainments and philanthropy.

(I) John Howe, son of John Howe, of Warwickshire, England, was for a long time a resident of Watertown, Massachusetts, in 1638 or 1639 he was one of the first settlers of Sudbury, where he was admitted freeman May 13, 1640, and was selectman in 1642. His name appears on the contract of February 7, 1642, as a member of the committee representing the town with whom John Rutter agrees to build the first meetinghouse erected in the town. He petitioned, in 1656, for the grant of Marlborough, and is said to have been the first white settler on the grant, to which he moved in 1657. He was appointed by the pastor of the church and selectman to see to restraining the youth on the Lord's day. His kindness and honesty gained for him the confidence of the Indians to such an extent that he was often called upon to settle disputes among them. He opened the first public house in Marlborough, and he kept it for several years. His grandson, David Howe, son of Samuel Howe, received of his father in 1702 a grant of one hundred and thirty acres of land, in the "New Grant" territory, on which he built the Red Horse Inn or old "Howe Tavern," the famous "Wayside Inn" of Longfellow. The date of his death is given as 1678, and also as 1687, July 10. By his wife Mary, who survived him twenty years, he had twelve children: John, Samuel, Sarah, Mary died young), Isaac, Josiah, Mary, Thomas, Daniel (died young), Alexander, Daniel and Eleazer.

(II) Isaac, fifth child and third son of John and Mary Howe, was born in Sudbury, August 8, 1648, and died December 9, 1724, aged seventy-seven. He married (first), June 17, 1671, Frances Woods, who died May 14, 1718; (second), December 2, 1718, Susannah Silby.

(III) John (2), son of Isaac and Frances (Woods) Howe, was born in Marlborough, September 16, 1682, and died May 19, 1754, aged seventy-two. He married, November 3, 1703, Deliverance Rice, of Sudbury.

(IV) Benjamin, son of John (2) and Deliverance (Rice) Howe, was born in Marlborough, December 14, 1710, and died October 20, 1757, aged forty-seven. He married, February 4, 1732, Lucy Amsden.

(V) Benjamin (2), son of Benjamin (1) and Lucy (Amsden) Howe, was born in Marlborough, October 17, 1751, and died March 11, 1831, aged eighty years. He married Abigail Howe. (Mention of their son, Winthrop, and descendants appears in this article.)

(VI) Jeroboam, son of Benjamin (2) and Abigail (Howe) Howe, was born in Marlborough, April 1, 1800. During his active adult life he resided in Lowell, where he was engaged in farming and stone contracting. He died there in 1884, aged eighty-four. He married, in Londonderry, Abigail Plummer, who was born in Londonderry.

(VII) George Windsor, eldest son of Jeroboam and Abigail (Plummer) Howe, was born in Lowell, Massachusetts, September 28, 1828, and worked in shoe factories in Marlborough and Fayville, Massachusetts, the greater part of his life, leaving that employment in 1900 to live on a farm in Fayville, where he now resides. He married Clarissa Ann Wyman, who was born in Londonderry, New Hampshire, daughter of Elbridge and Clarissa (Griffin) Wyman, of Londonderry. Four children were born of this union: Warren G., Lizzie C., Nellie F. and Alice C.

(VIII) Warren G., eldest son of George W. and Clarissa (Wyman) Howe, was born in Londonderry, New Hampshire, November 24, 1852, and attended the common schools until he was sixteen years old. He then began work in the L. A. Howe shoe factory in Marlboro, Massachusetts, where he was employed three years, when he began work in the S. H. Howe shoe factory, with whom he continued until 1881, when he removed to Nashua, New Hampshire, and was made foreman of the stitching room of the Estabrook-Anderson Shoe Company and still holds that position, which at the present time (1907) he has filled twenty-six consecutive years. Mr. Howe is a member of the Unitarian Church and endeavors to live up to the teachings of religion and sound morality. He sympathizes with the unfortunate and does what he can to relieve the poor and distressed. He is vice-president of the Protestant Orphanage, and a trustee of the John M. Hunt Home, and in the conscientious discharge of the duties of these offices, finds opportunity to help the deserving and needy. He is a member of Rising Sun Lodge, No. 39, Ancient Free and Accepted Masons, of which he is past master, and Meridian Sun Royal Arch Chapter, No. 9; and of Granite Lodge, No. 1, Independent Order of Odd Fellows; also a member of Governor Wentworth Colony, Order of Pilgrim Fathers.

He married (first), October 31, 1877, at Marlboro, Massachusetts, Winifred M., daughter of William Savery, of Wareham, Massachusetts, who died March 23, 1904. Married (second), September 26, 1906, Emma B. Babbitt, of Craftsbury, Vermont, born January 14, 1867, daughter of Hiram and Emeline (Horner) Babbitt. Children by first marriage: Wyman R., born January 19, 1880, a telegraph operator of Newport, Rhode Island: Marion S., born February 2, 1881; now Mrs. Harry Woodbury, of Hopedale, Massachusetts.

(VI) Winthrop, eighth child and fifth son of Benjamin (2) and Abigail (Howe) Howe, was born in Marlboro, August 12, 1795.

(VII) George Winthrop, son of Winthrop Howe, was born in Pelham, Massachusetts. He was employed in the shoe factories of Marlborough and Grafton, Massachusetts, where he was very useful, as he was a skillful man, familiar with the work in the departments of the business. He married (first) Harriet F. Coburn, daughter of James Coburn, of Warren, Maine; (second) —— Drury, of Grafton, Massachusetts. George W. and Harriet F. (Coburn) Howe, had two children: Everett C., whose sketch follows, and William A. By his second marriage he had one child, Alfred M.

(VIII) Everett Chase, son of George W. and Harriet F. (Coburn) Howe, was born in Marlborough, Massachusetts, April 2, 1871. He was educated in the public schools of Marlborough, where he prepared for college. He entered Harvard University, where he pursued the course of study until he reached the senior year, when he left that institution and began the study of law in the office of William N. Davenport, Esq., of Marlborough. He read there a year and a half, until the outbreak of the Spanish war in 1898, and enlisted in Company F, Sixth Massachusetts Infantry, and went to Porto Rico where he served one year. Returning to the states he resumed the study of law in the office of Albert S. Wait, Esq., and in June, 1901, was admitted to the bar at Concord, New Hampshire. In October following he opened an office in Littleton, where he has since practiced with success. In politics he is a Republican. In 1903-04 he served out an unexpired term as a member of the school board. In 1903 he was appointed special agent of the state license commission, where he served until May, 1906, when he resigned. Mr. Howe married, September 18, 1902, at Newport, New Hampshire, Louise C. Barrett, who was born August 27, 1876, daughter of Frank and Grace E. Barrett, of Newport, New Hampshire. They have one child, Charles F., born in Littleton, June 4, 1903.

(II) John (2), eldest child of John (1) and Mary Howe, was born 1640, in Sudbury, and resided in Marlboro, Massachusetts, where the birth of his children are recorded. It is presumed that he had other children born before his settlement in Marlboro. He was killed by the Indians in Sudbury, April 20, 1676, and his house and buildings were destroyed by the same enemy. He was married January 22, 1662, but the christian name of his wife, Elizabeth, is all that is preserved. Their children born in Marlboro were: John, David and Elizabeth. Others were born in Sudbury (mention of Josiah and descendants appears in this article). His brother, Samuel Howe, was proprietor of the farm in Sudbury, Massachusetts, on which sat the noted Howe Tavern, made famous by Longfellow in his "Tales of a Wayside Inn."

(III) John (3), eldest known child of John (2) and Elizabeth Howe, was born September 9, 1671, in Marlboro, and spent his life in that town. His will was made in 1752, and the inventory of his estate, made in 1754, foots up five hundred and thirty-five pounds, which was a great property in that day. His first wife, Rebecca, died September 22, 1731, and he was married June 18, 1740, to Ruth Eager, who was born December 20, 1694, daughter of Zachariah Eager. His children were all mentioned in his will, namely: Peter, John, Sarah, Ebenezer, Rebecca, Mary, Hannah, Seth, Elizabeth, Eunice and Dorothy. These were all the children of the first wife.

(IV) Peter, eldest child of John (3) and Rebecca Howe, was born May 8, 1695, in Marlboro, and died in that town, October 18, 1778, in his eighty-fourth year. He was married December 24, 1718, to Grace Bush, who was born May 3, 1696, daughter of Abial and Grace (Bennett) Bush, of Marlboro. She died December 10, 1770. Their children were: Ezra, Nehemiah, Kezia, Ebenezer, Mary, Rebecca, Peter, Rhoda and Ruth. Rebecca became the wife of Eliakim Howe and settled in Henniker. They were the parents of Rev. Tilly Howe, who graduated from Dartmouth College in 1783.

(V) Ezra, eldest child of Peter and Grace (Bush) Howe, was born March 22, 1719, in Marlboro, and lived in that town until a few years before the Revolution, when he removed to Henniker, New Hampshire, and there died April 4, 1789. He was a soldier in the French and Indian war. He married Phœbe Bush, who was born March 3, 1729, a daughter of Jonathan and Sarah (Randall) Bush. She died August 11, 1813. Their children were: Sarah, Nehmiah, Phœbe, Eli, Micah, Lydia, Judith, Aaron and Moses.

(VI) Nehemiah, eldest son and second child of Ezra and Phœbe (Bush) Howe, was born March 5, 1752, in Marlboro. In his youth the family removed to Henniker, New Hampshire. He resided for a time in the northern part of that town, and subsequently lived in Lyme and Woodstock, this state, and died in Thetford, Vermont.

(VII) David, son of Nehemiah Howe, was a native of either Woodstock or Lyme, New Hampshire, and settled in Thetford, Vermont, devoting the active period of his life to tilling the soil. Information at hand, which is probably based upon family tradition, states that he was descended from the original proprietor of the old "Howe Tavern" at Sudbury, Massachusetts, made famous by the poet Longfellow, in his "Tales of a Wayside Inn." John Howe, the emigrant, who is thought to have come from Warwickshire, England, was in Sudbury as early as 1639 and took the freeman's oath there in 1640. He was one of the original settlers of Marlboro, Massachusetts. The tavern was opened by the latter's son John in 1666, and for about two hundred years was a noted place of public entertainment. A descendant of the tavern-keeper settled in Henniker, New Hampshire, and was the progenitor in this state of the Woodstock Howes, some of whom became residents of Thetford, Vermont, including the above-mentioned David. David Howe was an active member of the Congregational Church and a lay preacher. Among his children were Henry, Lorenzo and William.

(VIII) William, son of David Howe, was born at Thetford in 1807. He was a blacksmith by trade and followed that calling for many years in his native town, where he died in 1873. He married Sarah Bastoon, of New York City, who was of German parentage. She became the mother of ten children, but four of whom lived to maturity, namely: Almira, who became the wife of Percy Green; Hamilton Tyler, who will be again referred to; Ellen, who is the wife of H. A. Watson of Pacific Grove, California, and Henry, who died about 1888, at Thetford, Vermont. The mother of these children died in 1872.

(IX) Hon. Hamilton Tyler, son of William and Sarah (Bastoon) Howe, was born in Thetford, April 19, 1849. After concluding his attendance at the Thetford high school he served an apprenticeship at the carpenter's trade, which he followed for a short time, and he was also engaged in the manufacture of lumber. In 1871 he went to Oakland, California, where he spent three years in the provision business, and upon his return to Thetford turned his attention to the manufacture of doors, sash and blinds, which he carried on for about fifteen years. Removing from Thetford to Hanover in 1888 he engaged in the livery business, and for a time conducted two establishments, but having disposed of one of these he is at the present time giving his exclusive attention to the Allen street stable, which is well equipped for a general livery and hacking business. He also runs a stage line from Hanover to Lebanon. From 1894 to 1901 he was proprietor of the Wheelock House (now the Hanover Inn). In addition to his livery business he conducts a farm of one hundred and fifty acres. Mr. Howe is one of the most prominent Republicans in western New Hampshire, having presided over the Hanover Republican club for a period of ten years, and he has long and faithfully served the town, county and state in an official capacity. For fourteen years he was deputy sheriff, was moderator at town meetings in Hanover for ten years, and from 1901 to 1905, was a member of the lower house of the state legislature. He is now serving in the state senate from the second district, and in addition to being chairman of the committee on elections is a member of the committees on labor, the revision of the statutes relative to corporations and others. He is past noble grand of Good Samaritan Lodge, Independent Order of Odd Fellows, having occupied for four terms all of the important chairs in that body, and he is a member of Golden Rod Lodge of Rebekahs, Hanover, Morning Star Encampment and Canton Hanover, Patriarchs Militant, Lebanon. He is also a past master of Grafton Star Grange, Patrons of Husbandry, and a member of Mascoma Valley Pomona, and the New Hampshire State Granges. He attends the Congregational Church.

In 1883 Mr. Howe was joined in marriage with Nellie E. Moody, daughter of William E. and —— E. (Wallace) Moody, of Post Mills, Vermont. Mr. and Mrs. Howe have two daughters, Effie N. and Amy E. The former is a graduate of the Thetford Academy.

(III) Josiah Howe, fourth son and sixth child of John (2) and Elizabeth How, was born in 1650, in Sudbury, Massachusetts. He settled in Marlborough, and married, March 18, 1672, Mary, daughter of Deacon John Haynes, of Sudbury. Josiah Howe, died 1711, and his estate was administered by his widow. Subsequently she married John Prescott. Josiah Howe was a soldier in King Philip's war, and was one of those who rallied to the defense of the town when attacked by the Indians. His children were: Mary (died young), Mary (died young), Josiah, Daniel and Ruth.

(IV) Josiah (2), son of Josiah (1) and Mary (Haynes) Howe, was born in Malborough, 1678, settled there, and married, June 14, 1706, Sarah Bigelow. He married (second), November 22, 1713, Mary Marble. The children of Josiah and Sarah (Bigelow) Howe, were: Phineas, Abraham and Rachel. The children of Josiah and Mary

Hamilton L. Howe

(Marble) Howe were: Sarah, Mary, Josiah and Jacob.

(V) Phineas, son of Josiah (2) and Sarah (Bigelow) Howe, was born in Marlboro, December 4, 1707, settled in Shrewsbury, North Precinct, and was admitted to the Shrewsbury Church. His farm was in what is now the town of Boylston. He was married March 22, 1732, at Shrewsbury, where he was living, to Abigail Bennett, who died in Boylston, August 22, 1784. He died there January 4, 1801, aged ninety-three years and twenty days. Their children, all born in North Precinct and baptized in the Shrewsbury Church, were: Phineas, Bezaleel, Silas, Abigail and Elizabeth.

(VI) Silas, third son and child of Phineas and Abigail (Bennett) Howe, was baptized February 13, 1737, and settled in what is now Boylston, then the north precinct of Shrewsbury, where he was a farmer, and where he died October 10, 1817. His wife's baptismal name was Abigail, but her family name is unknown. She died January 18, 1813, aged sixty-nine years. Their children were: Levi, Ephraim, Silas, Abraham, Abigail, Persis, Tamer and one who died in childhood unnamed.

(VII) Ephraim, second son and child of Silas and Abigail Howe, born about 1760, settled in Hollis, New Hampshire, where he cleared up a farm and passed his life. His wife's name was Mary, as shown in the record of their children's birth, namely: Nicholas, Ephraim, Mary, John, Joseph, Sarah, Isaac and Samuel.

(VIII) John, third son and fourth child of Ephraim and Mary Howe, was born October 11, 1782, in Hollis, and was a pioneer, like his father, and settled in Whitefield, New Hampshire, whence he removed in Carroll, same state, in 1828. He lived there till his death, September 25, 1868, at the age of eighty-six years. At the time of his settlement there the country was almost a primitive wilderness, and when he grew up he followed almost the only vocation open to him—farming—and made it his life employment. He had but a limited literary education, but he possessed a large share of good common sense, experience and executive ability, was a good neighbor, and an honest man, and his townsmen put him in various offices where he served to the benefit of the town and to his own credit. He married Sarah Jewell, by whom he had nine children, as follows: Jonas, Louisa, Abagail, Thomas R., Lucy, Mitchell W., Hester, Silas and Eliza.

(IX) Silas, son of John and Sarah (Jewell) Howe, was born in Whitefield, Coos county, New Hampshire, July 14, 1822, and died November 4, 1905, aged eighty-three. He, like his father, grew up on a farm, but fitted himself for the less laborious vocation of school teacher, and followed it for a number of years. He was attentive to his work, and prospered in his farming and had that plenty which makes an independent farmer the most independent man in the world. He was a veteran of the civil war and served from April, 1864, until the close of the war, receiving an honorable discharge. He held various town offices, among which was that of superintendent of schools. He was a staunch member of the Free Will Baptist Church, like his father before him. He married Julia, daughter of David and Betsy Gilman, of Carroll. She was born in Washington, Vermont, July 5, 1829, and still lives in Carroll, (October, 1907), aged seventy-eight years. Nine children were born of this marriage: Ellen, Zeeb, George, Mary, Maria, Ann, Alice L., Laura J. and Sarah J.

(X) Zeeb, eldest son of Silas and Julia (Gilman) Howe, was born in Carroll, August 24, 1850. He remained with his father until seventeen years of age, attending school and doing his part in the performance of the labor on the farm. After leaving home he went to St. Johnsbury, Vermont, and was there employed five years in the Fairbanks shops as a polisher. In 1876 he resumed farming at Carroll, and carried it on until 1889, when he was appointed assistant postmaster at Twin Mountain by William A. Barron, and at the same time was in the employ of Barron, Merrill & Barron as night clerk. In 1897 he received the appointment of postmaster, and held it ten years, until 1907. In politics he is a Republican. He has been town treasurer and clerk for ten years past, and superintendent of the check list for some time. He married, July 23, 1870, Hattie M. Thompson, who was born in Boston, Massachusetts, April 20, 1843, daughter of Isaac and Maria (Woodruff) Thompson, of Carroll. Five children have been born of this union, only one of whom, Stella survives. She married, October 14, 1903, Richard J. Smith, of Carroll.

(Second Family.)

HOWE (I) Abraham Howe, emigrated from England and was admitted a freeman in Roxbury, May 2, 1638. His wife, whom he married in England, and whose maiden name does not appear in the records, died in Roxbury in December, 1645, during a period of mortality described by Eliot as the saddest that town had yet known, and he removed to Boston where his death occurred November 20, 1683. His children were: Abraham, Elizabeth, Sarah, Isaac, Deborah, Israel and probably others.

(II) Abraham, eldest child of the preceding Abraham, was born in England and emigrated with his parents. He was married in Watertown, May 6, 1657, to Hannah Ward, daughter of William Ward and in 1660 became a landed proprietor in Marlboro. His children were: Daniel, Mary, Joseph, Hannah, Elizabeth, Deborah, Rebecca, Abraham, Sarah and Abigail.

(III) Joseph, third child of Abraham and Hannah (Ward) Howe, was born in Watertown, in 1661, and died September 4, 1700. He was a large landholder in Watertown, Lancaster and Marlboro. On December 29, 1687, he was married in Charlestown to Dorothy Martin, who bore him six children, namely: Sarah, Eunice, Bethia, Joseph, Abraham and Jedediah.

(IV) Joseph, fourth child and eldest son of Joseph and Dorothy (Martin) Howe, was born in Marlboro, February 19, 1697, and died there February 18, 1775. February 20, 1722, he married Zerviah, daughter of Captain Daniel Howe; she died December 10, 1723. He married (second), July 12, 1727, Ruth Brigham, daughter of Jonathan and Mary Brigham. Her death occurred October 14, 1781, in her eighty-seventh year. His will was dated July 16, 1770, and probated March 14, 1775. His children were: Zerviah, Joseph, Dorothy, Dinah, Thaddeus, Elizabeth, Samuel, Phineas, Artemas and Miriam.

(V) Joseph, eldest child of Joseph and Ruth (Brigham) Howe, was born February 1, 1728. He was married May 21, 1751, to Grace Rice, who was born in 1730, daughter of Simon and Grace Rice. He died September 26, 1800, and his widow died January 23, 1816. The twelve children of this union were: Lovina, Reuben, Simon, Samuel, Lucy, Eli, Hepsibah (died young), Daniel, Joseph (died young) Miriam, Hepsibah and Joseph.

(VI) Daniel, fifth son and eighth child of Joseph and Grace (Rice) Rowe, was born June 1, 1764. In the spring of 1795 he went from Fitzwilliam, New Hampshire, to Springfield, Vermont, locating in district No. 11, where he cleared a productive farm. He died in Springfield, August 9, 1818. On March 13, 1790, he married Elizabeth Patch, who was born May 3, 1770, and he died May 21, 1862, at the advanced age of ninety-two years. Their children were: Elizabeth, Eli (died young), Hannah, Eli, Daniel and James, who were born in Fitzwilliam; Isaac, Lewis, Achsah and Huldah, who were born in Springfield.

(VII) Lewis, sixth son and eighth child of Daniel and Elizabeth (Patch) Howe, was born in Springfield, July 2, 1804. He was a shoemaker by trade and followed that calling for many years in his native town. He died November 5, 1880. He married, April 6, 1828, Laura Smith, and her death occurred September 12, 1886.

(VIII) Franklin Lewis, son of Lewis and Laura (Smith) Howe, was born in Springfield, 1837. He was an able mechanic, and going to Keene in 1856, entered the employ of the Keene Furniture Company, with whom he remained continuously for a period of forty years. He died in Keene, 1903. He was married to Maria H. MacIntosh, and reared two sons—Frederick E. and George F.

(IX) Frederick Eugene, eldest son of Franklin L. and Maria H. (MacIntosh) Howe, was born in Keene, June 30, 1864. He attended the public schools including the high school and after the completion of his studies he learned wood carving. From 1889 to 1894 he was employed by the Keene Furniture Company, and for the ensuing two years carried on the wood-carving business on his own account. Some ten years ago he purchased the M. White Photograph Studio, and has ever since devoted his time and energies to photography, which has proved an excellent opportunity for the development of his ability as an artist. In politics Mr. Howe is a Republican, and has participated actively in both civic and military affairs, having served as ward clerk, member of the common council two years and of the board of aldermen for the same length of time, and is at the present time acting as moderator in ward four. For two years he was quarter-master sergeant of the Second Regiment, New Hampshire National Guard, and receiving the appointment of regimental quarter-master he served in that capacity continuously with credit for nine years. His efforts in developing the artistic tastes of the community have been attended with good results, and he is now president of the Keene Art Club. He attends the Unitarian Church. He was married to Susie S. Buffum, who was born in Keene, April 19, 1865, and is a representative of a highly reputable family which was established in New England early in the Colonial period.

(1) Robert Buffum and his wife Thomasin, who were of Salem, Massachusetts, in 1638, are supposed to have emigrated from Yorkshire, England, in 1634, and he died in 1679.

(2) Caleb, son of Robert and Thomasin Buffum, was married in Salem, March 26, 1672, to Hannah, daughter of the first Joseph Pope.

(3) Benjamin, son of Caleb and Hannah Buffum, was born in 1686.

(4) Benjamin, son of the preceding Benjamin, was born in 1716. He resided in Smithfield, Rhode Island.

(5) Caleb, son of Benjamin Buffum, was born in 1759, and died in 1803. August 15, 1784, he married Tamer Gaskill, daughter of Jonathan Gaskill. She died and he subsequently married her sister Hannah. She survived him and married for her second husband Stephen Raymond, of Royalston, Massachusetts. Her death occurred in 1856, at the age of eighty-seven years. The children of her first union were: Polly (married Calvin Forbes), Caleb, Silas, James, Elizabeth (married Enoch Metcalf, of Royalston), Benjamin and Gaskill.

(6) James, third son and fourth child of Caleb and Hannah (Gaskill) Buffum, was born in 1792, and died a nonogenarian in Keene. He was a prosperous farmer of Royalston for many years. His first wife was Ruth Bliss, and his second was Frances A. Fifield. His children were: James (died young), Ruth B., Caleb T., Mary B., Sarah A., George B., James, David P., Charles, Emily W., Susan and Caroline.

(7) Caleb Talbot, second son and third child of James and Ruth (Bliss) Buffum, was born in Royalston, June 4, 1820. He completed his education at the Keene Academy, and became a wellknown merchant tailor of that city. For some time he was a member of the city government, and was representative to the state legislature two years. He was also active in benevolent and philanthropic work, and a member of the Humane Society. On April 19, 1843, he married Susan R. Gilmore, daughter of Lewis Gilmore, of Charlestown, this state. She died December 21, 1854. Of this union there was one daughter, Ella A., who died at the age of sixteen years. He was married a second time February 23, 1857, to Sarah A. Stratton, daughter of Asa Stratton, of Greenfield, Massachusetts. She became the mother of two children: Frederick Lincoln, born November 14, 1860, died December 5, 1867, and Susie S., who became the wife of Frederick E. Howe, as previously stated. The children of Mr. and Mrs. Howe are: Reginald F. and Barbara.

(I) Captain Nathaniel Howe was a master-mariner residing in Marblehead, Massachusetts, and died at sea. The name of his wife, whom he married in Marblehead, January 20, 1793, was Mehitable Green.

(II) Captain Nathaniel (2), son of Captain Nathaniel (1) and Mehitable (Green) Howe, was born in Marblehead in 1804. He settled in Hollis, New Hampshire, where he followed agriculture with prosperous results, and was a well-known officer in the state militia, commanding a company which acquired an enviable distinction for unusual proficiency in military tactics. His death occurred, January, 1879. He married Elmira Rideout, daughter of Jonathan and Rebecca (Powers) Rideout, of Hollis, and had a family of six children, namely: Elizabeth R., William, John, Norman, Annie L., and Ellen. Norman was a soldier in the Civil war, Company H., Seventh New Hampshire Regiment, and died in the army.

(III) John Prentiss, son of Captain Nathaniel and Elmira (Rideout) Howe, was born in Hollis, June 2, 1837. He was educated in the public schools of his native town, and reared to agricultural pursuits. From the time of his majority he has been engaged in farming and lumbering, conducting each of these important industries upon an extensive scale, and furnishing employment to a large number of men. His farm, which contains seven hundred acres of fertile land, is one of the largest tracts of agricultural property in Hillsboro county, and its facilities, in the way of improved machinery, appliances, etc., are unsurpassed. As a lumberman he stands foremost among the operators in that section, cutting and hauling a large number of logs annually, and beside furnishing the Nashua Heat, Light and Power Company with its entire supply of poles, he provides the F. D. Cook Lumber Company with large quantities of posts and other material. Politically Mr. Howe acts with the Democratic party.

He takes a profound interest in the moral and religious welfare of the community. He married Olive W. Farwell, daughter of Leonard and Lydia (Williams) Farwell, of Groton, Massachusetts. Mr. and Mrs. Howe have one son, William Farwell Howe, who is principal of the Ames public school at East Dedham, Massachusetts; it has an average attendance of about five hundred pupils.

HALEY This family is of English origin, and the surname, independent of errors in spelling by uneducated scribes, has been found in various forms in various forms, some of which are: Hale, Halle, Halie, Healey, Hally and Haley. Branches of the family were early settled in Kittery and Biddeford; these, as tradition tells, are descended from two distinct heads, possibly brother.

(I) Andrew Haley had a large fishing business in the Isles of Shoals, where he settled in early Colonial days, and from him "Haley's Island" was named. He seems to have been a man of wealth and social standing, and was known as the "King of the Shoals." A sea wall was built by him fourteen rods long, thirteen feet high and fifteen feet wide, to connect two islands and improve his harbor. He bought land in York in 1662 and sold it in 1684. He married Deborah, a daughter of Gowen Wilson, an early and prominent citizen of Exeter and Kittery. She was appointed administratrix of his estate December 2, 1697. They had: Andrew, William, Deliverance, Elizabeth, Deborah, Anna and Rhoda.

(II) Andrew (2), eldest child of Andrew and Deborah (Wilson) Haley, settled on the Haley homestead. He had grants of land in 1692 and 1699. He made his will April 8, 1725, and mentions three sons and three daughters; land and buildings on Spruce creek; reserved orchard for wife Elizabeth. He wrote his name "Hally." He was a wealthy man for his time as is shown by his inventory, returned July 2, 1725, which was £1,176:16:7, with £4:30:0 returned by the executrix June 9, 1727. He married, July 15, 1697, Elizabeth, daughter of Humphrey Scammon. She seems to have lived a widow until 1742, and August 14 of that year she was published to Nicholas Weeks. The children of Andrew and Elizabeth were: Elizabeth, Andrew, William, Samuel, Sarah, John and Rebecca.

(III) John, sixth child and fourth son of Andrew (2) and Elizabeth (Scammon) Haley, was born June 14, 1712. He inherited part of his father's estate at his majority. John Haley and his wife "owned the covenant," September 30, 1744. He married Margaret, daughter of William and Sarah (Eastman) Bryar, as a deed of Alfred shows. Their children were: Joel, Peletiah, Susannah, Dorothy, Milly, Eunice, Tobias, Sarah, Lucy, Robert and Rebecca.

(IV) Robert, son of John and Margaret (Bryar) Haley, married (first), September 10, 1772, Betsey Parker, daughter of Benjamin and Mary (Googin) Parker, who is said to have been his cousin. He married (second), October 15, 1780, Widow Martha (Jones) Hutchings. Four children were born to him: William, Robert, John and Polly. There is no record of his birth or baptism.

(V) Robert (2), second son and child of Robert (1) and Betsey (Parker) Haley, was born in Kittery, Maine, December 22, 1778. He was the founder of the Haley family of Tuftonborough, to which town he removed in 1810. He was killed on the railroad near South Berwick, Maine, February 20, 1845. He married (first), September 5, 1802, Nancy Schillaber, who was born July 25, 1779, and died January 23, 1832. He married (second) Mrs. Sally (Whitehouse) Wiggin. His children, all by the first wife, were: Eliza, Schillaber, William, Abel, twin sons (died young), Parker, Nathaniel, John and Nancy.

(VI) Abel, fourth child of Robert (2) and Nancy (Schillaber) Haley, was born in Rochester, New Hampshire, October 23, 1808, and at two years of age was taken by his parents to Tuftonborough. He died August 3, 1880, at Wolfborough, aged seventy-two, and was buried with Masonic honors. He was educated in the common schools and in the Wolfborough and Tuftonborough Academy. When between fifteen and sixteen years of age he went to Danvers, Massachusetts, where he spent a short time and then returned to his home. For eighteen successive winters he taught school. He owned and carried on a farm, but also did surveying, and most all of the surveying in his time was done by him. He had a good knowledge of law, though not a lawyer, and his advice was sought by many. He settled various estates in Tuftonborough, and for years was one of the trustees of the Wolfborough and Tuftonborough Academy. At eighteen years old he was clerk of the militia company, and later adjutant and inspector. He was a Democrat in politics and held local offices for many years. From 1839 to 1843 he was representative; collector eight years; selectman, 1839 to 1843; moderator for more than twenty years; delegate to the constitutional convention of 1850; state senator in 1850-51; councillor in 1853-54, under the administrations of Governors Noah Martin and M. B. Baker. As further indicative of his business talent and probity it may be observed that while he remained in Tuftonborough he not only almost wholly guided the public affairs of the town, but was the constant advisor of his fellow townsmen in all matter of personal importance, drawing their deeds and their legal documents, and acting as the mutual friend, umpire and peacemaker between many who might be long estranged from each other, but for his kindly and timely mediation. Through all the years of his busy life Mr. Haley was a practical farmer. Enjoying to the full all the comforts, luxuries and contentment of a well stocked farm home and dispensing the bounties of a generous hospitality that never permitted the poor and needy to go away empty handed from his door. His manner of public speaking was of the ornate and flowery kind, but his strong native common sense, his keen judgment of human nature, his treasury of facts garnered from solid reading, his resolute will, his high veneration of justice, and his great argumentative power invariably won for him the admiration and respect even of his opponents in whatever field of controversy he might happen to engage. In 1854 he removed to a farm in Wolfborough and took an active and leading part in the financial affairs of that town. He organized the State Bank of Wolfborough and was elected its first Cashier, and filled that offices for eleven years, until it was merged into the Wolfborough National Bank in 1865. Under the administration of Mr. Haley and his associates the bank was excellently managed and besides paying a semi-annual dividend of four per cent it had an undivided surplus of $10,000 when it went into liquidation, October 24, 1855. Mr. Haley was made an entered apprentice in Morning Star Lodge, No. 17, of Wolfborough and on December 19, 1855, he took the degree of Fellow-craft and Master Mason. In 1857 he was made worshipful master, and served in that office until 1861. About 1830 the charter was returned to the

Grand Lodge, and the lodge remained dormant until 1856, when it was reinstated through the efforts of Mr. Haley. Past Master Haley revived the interest of the members and had its charter restored and he conferred the degree on all candidates received thereafter until 1861. This lodge celebrated its centennial, October 24, 1904, in Brewster Memorial hall with great pomp and ceremony, and Mr. Haley's course was eulogized. He was a member of the Christian Church, and always gave it his strongest support. It was principally through his influence that the church edifice was removed from the country to Wolfboro, where it is now one of the most flourishing religious organizations in the city.

Abel Haley married (first), December 25, 1831, Mrs. Edith (Dodge) Tibbetts, who was born in Beverly, Massachusetts, March 17, 1799, and died in Tuftonborough, June 17, 1850. He married (second) Lucinda C. (Piper) Pinkham, widow of Charles Pinkham, and daughter of John Piper, a revolutionary soldier, who was born January 17, 1760, and died in Tuftonborough in 1830, a lineal descendant in the fifth generation from Nathaniel (born in England in 1630) and Sarah, his wife. John Piper married (first), January 12, 1783, Jemima Hersey, born 1762, and died February 6, 1803; and (second), January 26, 1804, Anna Young, who was born in Wolfborough, August 25, 1777. By the first marriage there were five sons and five daughters. By the second eleven children. Lucinda C., the fifth child of John Piper and Anna Young, born July 24, 1809, died June, 1891, married Abel Haley. Eight children were born to Abel and Edith (Dodge) Haley: Abel (died young), Nancy S., January 6, 1834; Abel S., mentioned below; Lydia C., November 4, 1836; Levi T., mentioned below; James D., mentioned below; Edith D., March 30, 1842; Sarah E., June 1, 1845.

(VII) Abel S., son of Abel and Edith (Dodge) Haley, was born March 30, 1835, in Tuftonborough, and died in Somerville, Massachusetts, April 14, 1891. At the age of sixteen he went to Boston, and that summer and the next he drove a milk wagon, returning to Tuftonborough and attending school winters. In 1855 he entered the employ of Mr. J. B. Severance in Faneuil Hall Market as a clerk He paid close attention to business and afterward admitted as a partner in the business firm, and after the death of Mr. Severance he became the sole proprietor of the business. In 1889, he and R. H. Sturtevant bought our Bird & Company and formed the firm of Sturtevant & Haley, and carried on the meat business together until the death of Mr. Haley. In 1882 Mr. Haley removed his residence to Somerville, where he had just completed a handsome and commodious house, when he died. He had accumulated a property of over one hundred thousand dollars. He was married in 1862, to Laura French, of Newmarket, New Hampshire. He left two children.

(VII) Levi Tibbetts, third son and fifth child of Abel and Edith (Dodge) Haley, was born in Tuftonborough, June 20, 1838, and was educated in the common schools. In 1866 he quit farming, which he had followed to that time, and engaged in the grocery business. Subsequently he was engaged in custom tailoring, and still later conducted a livery stable. He has always had a penchant for public affairs and has been much in office. In politics he is a Democrat. In 1868 he was police officer of Wolfborough and filled that office several years. He was next appointed deputy sheriff under Leavitt H. Eastman, of Conway, and served three years, under a Republican administration. In 1874 Governor James A. Weston appointed him sheriff and he filled that office in 1874-75. In 1878, after the office became elective, he was twice elected and served from 1878 until July 1, 1882. In 1882 he was elected state senator and served full term of two years. Although seventy years of age Mr. Haley is still a very active man and looks carefully after his farming interests and other business. He has a retentive memory, and enjoys talking about men and affairs of long years ago. In 1874 he was made a Mason in Morning Star Lodge and was worshipful master 1869-71, 1875-77. He is also a member of Lake Shore Grange, No. 128, Patrons of Husbandry, of which he has been master, and also of Carroll County Pomona Lodge, of which he was the second master. He is also a member of the National Grange. He married, February 15, 1878, Mary L. Evans, who was born in Wolfborough, 1844, daughter of Otis and Shuah M. (Libby) Evans. (See Libby, VIII.) They have one child, Abel, whose sketch follows.

(VIII) Abel, son of Levi T. and Mary L. (Evans) Haley, was born in Wolfboro, April 19, 1880, and was graduated from Brewster Free Academy with the class of '99. For some years he was a clerk, but is now in the employ of the American Express Company. He was made a Mason in Morning Star Lodge, No. 17, 1901, and is now worshipful master, filing the offices his father and grandfather before him had held, and doubtless there is not another instance in the state where grandfather, father and grandson have all been master of the same lodge. He is also a member of Carroll Royal Arch Chapter, No. 23, Royal Arch Masons, of Wolfboro; Orphan Council, No. 1, Royal and Select Masters, of Dover, New Hampshire; Commandery, Knights Templar, of Laconia; Bektash Pilgrims Temple, Ancient Arabic Order Nobles of the Mystic Shrine, of Concord; and Warren Chapter, No. 10, Order of the Eastern Star of Wolfboro, also a member of the New Hampshire Club of Boston. He passed through all the above degrees and offices when he arrived at the age of twenty-six years.

(VII) James D., fourth son and sixth child of Abel and Edith (Dodge) Haley, born November 17, 1839, at Tuftonborough, New Hampshire, was educated in the town school and Wolfborough and Tuftonborough Academy. Taught school and clerked in a store until he was about twenty-three years of age, then went to New York City and clerked for John P. Huggins, proprietor of the Lovejoy Hotel, New York City, seven years; then clerked in the Grand Hotel, also Fifth Avenue Hotel, having been a hotel clerk in the city of New York about twenty years. Went to Boston about 1884 and there engaged in the meat business, and now owns the stall in the Boston Market where his brother Abel S., had been engaged in the meat business for about thirty-four years. Mr. Haley has made a success of the meat business and has accumulated handsomely. He is a Republican in politics, and has held several local offices at Medford, Massachusetts, where he makes his home. He is a member of Morning Star Lodge, Free and Accepted Masons, of Wolfboro, New Hampshire. He married Clara Coburn, of Boston, and they have three children.

HILTON

It is not absolutely proven who were the first men to make a settlement upon the soil of our state, but that honor, if it does not belong exclusively to the Hiltons, is certainly shared by them. Edward Hilton was one of the company sent by the proprietor of Laconia to make settlement on the Piscataqua river. They expected to cultivate the vine, dis-

ABEL HALEY.

cover mines and carry on the fisheries. Edward with his brother William arrived from London in 1623, and settled at Dover Neck, seven miles from Portsmouth. They had a hard time, and Hilton, being a friend of Governor Winthrop, sought the protection of Massachusetts, in 1641. In 1652 he moved to Exeter, New Hampshire, where he had been granted land some years before. He died in 1671. Edward Hliton's eldest son, Edward (2), married Ann Dudley, daughter of Rev. Samuel and Mary (Winthrop) Dudley, and granddaughter both of Governor John Winthrop and Governor Thomas Dudley, of Massachusetts. Their eldest son, Colonel Winthrop Hilton, became the leading military man in the Province, and was killed by the Indians, June 23, 1710. The descendants of this family are very numerous in the southern part of Maine and New Hampshire, and probably all bearing the name in those regions could be traced to this line, but no genealogy has been written, and the connecting links are lacking.

(I) Edward Hilton was of English birth, but the date and place of his nativity are unknown. Edward and William Hilton were brothers, and came from London to Piscataqua in the spring of 1623. They had been members of the guild of fishmongers, and Edward was selected to take charge of the settlement of Dover which should be supported mainly by fishing. They were sent over by the company of Laconia, and settled at Dover Point. Edward Hilton was from the first a very busy man, and as time passed the amount of his business increased. At first the little settlement at Dover was practically a little republic with Edward Hilton, the company's agent, at its head. He was the first of the "Rulers of Dover," and held office from the spring of 1623 to 1631. He was regarded by the Massachusetts government as the principal man in the Dover settlement, and after its annexation by Massachusetts, which was mainly effected by him, he was depended on to assist in maintaining, and was the first named in the list of magistrates of Dover in 1641, but removed to Exeter shortly afterward. The records of Exeter show that he was settled and had a house in the part of Exeter which is now South Newfields, at least as early as December, 1639. A large grant of land had been made to him by the Exeter authorities, on "4 day of the 1st week of 10th month 1639." In 1653 another grant of about two miles square, comprising the whole village of Newfields, was made to him in regard to his charges in setting up a saw mill. A considerable part of this grant has remained to this day the property of his descendants. He became a leading man in the place, serving as townsman and selectman from 1645 nearly every year up to 1652. In 1657 he was one of the committee of two from Exeter who met a company of three from Dover and "settled the bounds" between the two towns by marking the line, and agreed upon the enjoyment that each town should have, of the border land. He was repeatedly chosen by the inhabitants on various important committees to look after their interests, and was in all respects a useful and valuable citizen. He was assistant judge of the court of common pleas. He has been styled "The Father of New Hampshire." He died early in 1671. He brought a wife with him to America, or soon after married one, who was the mother of his children, but what her maiden name was is unknown. His second wife was Catherine, daughter of Hon. Alexander Shepley, agent of Sir Ferdinando Gorges in Maine, widow of James Treworgie, of Kittery. His children were: Edward, William, Samuel, Charles, Susannah, Sobriety and Mary.

(II) Captain William, second son of Edward Hilton, the settler, is said to be the next in this line of Hilton, but that is not beyond question. He was commander of a company in the militia. He left several children.

(III) Jonathan, son of Captain William Hilton, married his cousin, Sobriety Hilton, daughter of Edward (2), the eldest child of Edward (1) Hilton, and his wife, Ann Dudley. Ann Dudley was born October 16, 1641, and was the daughter of Rev. Samuel Dudley, of Exeter, and granddaughter of Thomas Dudley, the second governor of Massachusetts Bay. Her mother was originally Mary Winthrop, daughter of John Winthrop, the first governor. The children of this union were: Charles, Jonathan, John and Mary.

(IV) Charles, eldest child of Jonathan and Sobriety (Hilton) Hilton, married Hannah Pike, daughter of Robert and Hannah (Gilman) Pike, and they had one child, Charles, the subject of the next paragraph.

(V) Charles (2), only son of Charles (1) and Hannah (Pike) Hilton, was with Benedict Arnold and under the immediate command of Captain Henry Dearborn, for whom he named one of his sons, in the famous march through the woods of Maine to Quebec, and suffered terribly from hunger and cold. The men traversed a country entirely destitute of game, and after eating all their supply of provisions, ate two dogs which accompanied the expedition, and later boiled and ate leather straps and moccasins. Two days after arriving at Quebec, Hilton and others were taken prisoners and suffered from vermin and hunger in captivity. The New Hampshire state papers of the Revolution contain an account of the allowance of twenty-two pounds, eight shillings to Charles Hilton for "Loss at Quebeck." Charles Hilton, the records state, was in the regiment of militia raised to reinforce the Northern Continental army in 1777, and commanded by Nicholas Gilman, Esq. Also Charles Hilton, private, entered, September 15, 1777, Captain Porter Kimball's company, of Colonel Stephen Evans's regiment, which marched from New Hampshire to join the Continental army at Saratoga in September, 1777. He was discharged December 15, 1777, after a service of three months and one day, receiving wages thirteen pounds, thirteen shillings, and an allowance of travel money "out to Bennington home from New Windsor, three hundred miles, four pounds, thirteen shillings and three pence." Charles Hilton removed to East Andover where he settled on a farm, kept a tavern, and became a prominent man. His homestead contained two hundred acres. Besides this he owned at different times between twelve hundred and thirteen hundred acres of land, the twenty-three deeds to which his descendant, Charles H. Hilton, now has. He married Mary Wadleigh, who was the daughter of Benjamin and Hannah (Dearborn) Wadleigh. She was born in 1752. Their children were: Dudley, Elijah, Henry D., Polly, Sally and Charles (twins), and Betsey.

(VI) Captain Henry Dearborn, third child and son of Charles and Mary (Wadleigh) Hilton, was born in Andover, and lived on his father's homestead for a time, and then sold it and removed to Andover Village, where he dwelt the remainder of his life. He married Deborah Clough, who was the daughter of Lieutenant Moses Clough, a Revolutionary soldier, and his wife Molly (Cram)

Clough. They had five children: Dearborn Henry, Polly, Hannah, Isabel, and Charles B., the subject of the next sketch.

(VII) Charles Burdet, youngest child of Captain Henry and Deborah (Clough) Hilton, was born in Andover, April 15, 1818, and died March 30, 1902, aged eighty-four. He attended school and worked at farm labor until he was twenty-one years of age, and then went to Boston, where he was a member of the police force for six or seven years. The two subsequent years he resided in Lowell, and then removed to Concord, where he learned the trade of cabinet maker, and resided about seven years. Returning to his native town, he bought a farm of one hundred acres a mile east of East Andover and resided there until his death. He was an attendant of the Free Will Baptist Church, but not a member. In politics he was a Republican. He married Mary Jane West, who was born in 1820, and died in 1896, daughter of Noah and Hannah (Webster) West, of Salisbury. They had two children: One died in infancy; the other, Charles H., is the subject of the next paragraph.

(VIII) Charles Henry, son of Charles B. and Mary Jane (West) Hilton, was born in Andover, April 29, 1852, and was educated in the common schools. He lives on a farm adjoining the one his father owned, containing four hundred acres. He keeps a large flock of sheep. He raises, buys, and sells stock, and does some slaughtering. In agricultural and in enterprises of public interest he is a leading citizen. In political faith he is a Republican, and has served his town two years, 1891 and 1892, as selectman, has been deputy sheriff of Merrimac county, and for six years was superintendant of the county farm. He married, May 12, 1877, at Franklin, Marcia Frances Nelson, who was born in Danbury, November 7, 1858, daughter of Andrew and Louisa (Withington) Nelson, of Sanbornton.

(I) Ralph Hilton was born in Wells, Maine. He was a merchant in that town in his younger days and later he was engaged in farming. He accumulated quite an amount of land in that region. The latter part of his life he was retired from active duty. He married his cousin, Hannah Hilton. Ralph Hilton died at Wells in 1875.

(II) Eben, son of Ralph and Hannah (Hilton) Hilton, was born at Wells, Maine. He was a stone mason by trade, which line of work he followed all his life in his native town. He had charge of the stone work at the time the Boston & Maine railroad was extended from South Berwick to Portland, Maine. He married Mary Elizabeth Taylor, daughter of Samuel and Louise Taylor. They had six children: Frank W., Lizzie M., Herbert, Lamont, who is mentioned below; Herbert and Arthur E. Eben Hilton died July 26, 1873, at Wells, Maine.

(III) Lamont, third son and fourth child of Eben and Mary E. (Taylor) Hilton, was born February 7, 1864, at Wells, Maine. He was educated in the common schools of his native town, and at the age of twelve worked for two years at farming on Durrell's Island. On January 4, 1878, he was engaged with the Davis Shoe Company, of Kennebunk, Maine, where he remained three years. From here he migrated to Massachusetts, going first to Lynn, where he was engaged with the F. W. Breed shoe factory, and afterwards to Cambridge, where he remained a short time with the Thatcher-Stone Provision Company. He then went back to Lynn and remained one year with the Keene Brothers, shoe manufacturers. For the next dozen years he was engaged in railroad work. He began at Chelsea, Massachusetts, where he was crossing agent for the Eastern Railroad, and then went to Portland, Maine, where he was switchman in the yard. He was afterward promoted to freight brakeman from Portland to Boston, which position he held for five years. He then worked in the grocery business at Wells, Maine, for a short time, and on June 27, 1889, entered the Boston & Maine service as passenger brakeman. He kept this place for one year, or till he was promoted to baggage master, and assigned to the run from Portsmouth, New Hampshire, to Portland, Maine. He held this position for three years, when he was transferred to the Gloucester, Massachusetts, branch, taking charge of the line from Boston to Rockport during the summer season. He was afterward sent to the run from Boston to Portland, Maine, in the capacity of passenger brakeman.

April 2, 1895, Mr. Hilton started on a new line of work. That day he entered the Portsmouth Police force as patrolman. On January 10, 1898, he was promoted to be captain of the night watch, but on account of the close confinement he resigned and went back to the duties of patrolman. In November, 1903, he resigned from the police force and engaged in a general insurance business, representing the Connecticut General Life, the Indemnity of New York, and the United States of New York and Delaware. Mr. Hilton has continued in this business ever since. In April, 1905, he was elected city treasurer of Portsmouth, and on January 1, 1907, was elected city clerk. He is a staunch Republican. Mr. Hilton is very prominent in fraternal organizations. He belongs to the Piscataqua Lodge, Independent Order of Odd Fellows, passing through the chairs in 1896; also to Osgood Lodge, Independent Order of Odd Fellows. In 1901 he took the Grand Lodge degree at Woodville, New Hampshire, and was appointed district deputy grand master of the Portsmouth district, comprising the lodges in Portsmouth, Exeter, Hampton, Newfields and Newton. In October, 1902, he was appointed grand marshal of the Grand Lodge by Grand Master Frank L. Way. In October, 1903, he was elected grand warden, in 1904 elected deputy grand master, and in October, 1905, was elected grand master. In October, 1906, he was elected grand representative to the Sovereign Grand Lodge for a term of two years. He is a member of Union Rebekah Lodge, No. 3, Strawberry Bank Encampment, No. 5, Canton Center, No. 12. He has taken many Masonic degrees. He belongs to the Saint Andrew's Lodge of Masons, the Ineffable Grand Lodge of Perfection, fourteenth degree, to the Grand Council, Princes of Jerusalem, sixteenth degree, to the New Hampshire Chapter of Rose Croix, eighteenth degree, to Edward A. Raymond Consistory, thirty-second degree. Mr. Hilton is a member of the United Order of American Mechanics, Portsmouth Council, No. 8, of Alpha Council, No. 3, Royal Arcanum, and of the Boston & Maine Relief Association. Lamont Hilton married Mary Alice Perkins, daughter of William and Lizzie Perkins, of Portsmouth. They have no children.

FARNUM This is among the early Massachusetts names which have been conspicuous in the settlement and development of New Hampshire, especially at Concord and vicinity. While most of its bearers have been tillers of the soil, they have ever been identified with the work of the church and other moral agencies, and still adhere to the standards of their Puritan ancestors. By many the name is now spelled Farnham.

(I) Ralph Farnum was born in 1603, and sailed from Southampton, England, with his wife Alice, in the brig "James," arriving at Boston, Massachusetts, June 5, 1635, after a voyage of fifty-eight days. He was among the proprietors of Ipswich, Massachusetts, in 1635. His wife was born about 1606, and they brought with them four children, a daughter being born of them here. Their names were as follows: Mary, born 1626; Thomas, 1631; Ralph, 1633; Ephraim and Sarah.

(II) Ralph (2), born 1633, son of Ralph (1) and Alice Farnum, is said by tradition (which is open to question) to have been a native of Wales. He settled in Andover, Massachusetts, where he was a grand juryman in 1679, and was the ancestor of a numerous posterity. He was married October 26, 1658, to Elizabeth, daughter of Nicholas Holt, another pioneer of Andover. She was born March 30, 1636, in Newbury, Massachusetts. He died January 8, 1692, in Andover. His children were: Sarah, Ralph, John, Henry, Hannah, Thomas, Ephraim and James. (Ephraim and descendants receive extended mention in this article).

(III) Ralph (3), son of Ralph (2) and Elizabeth (Holt) Farnham, was born, probably in Andover, Massachusetts, where his parents lived, on June 1, 1662. October 9, 1685, he married Sarah Sterling, and they had ten children: Sarah, Henry, Ralph (4) (mentioned below), Daniel, Abigail, William, Nathaniel, Barachias, Benjamin and Joseph. Of these children, Abigail, the second daughter and fifth child, was married in January, 1714, to James Abbott, of Andover, who became one of the first settlers of Pennycook, now Concord, New Hampshire. (See Abbott, III).

(IV) Ralph (4), second son and third child of Ralph (3) and Sarah (Sterling) Farnham, was born May 25, 1689, at Andover, Massachusetts, but removed when a young man to York, Maine. In 1712-13 by a vote in the York town-meeting he was granted thirty acres of land. Ralph (4) Farnham married at York, Elizabeth Austin, daughter of Captain Matthew Austin, and they had eleven children: Joseph, born June 20, 1713; Ralph, Mary, Matthew, Elizabeth, David, Jonathan, Nathaniel, Paul (mentioned below), Betty and John, born May 26, 1735. Of this family, Betty, the youngest daughter, married Berg, son of Richard Jacques, the soldier who shot Rolle, the Jesuit priest, who incited the Indians to massacre.

(V) Paul, seventh son and ninth child of Ralph (4) and Elizabeth (Austin) Farnham, was born April 20, 1730, at York, Maine. He lived for a time in Lebanon, that state, and afterwards removed to Acton, Maine, where his death occurred in 1820 at the age of ninety years.

(VI) Ralph (5), son of Paul Farnham, was born in Lebanon, New Hampshire, in July, 1756, and afterwards moved to Acton, Maine. He married Mehitabel Bean, and they had seven children, among them John, mentioned below. Ralph (5) Farnham was the last survivor of the battle of Bunker Hill, and as such was introduced to the Prince of Wales, now King Edward VII, on the latter's visit to Boston in 1860. Returning to his home in Acton, Mr. Farnham lived but a short time longer, dying in December, 1860, at the remarkable age of one hundred and four years and five months.

(VII) John, son of Ralph (5) and Mehitabel (Bean) Farnham, was born in Acton, Maine, near the close of the eighteenth century. He married Fannie Wood, and they had five children: Asa, Ezra, James, William and John.

(VIII) Ezra, son of John and Fannie (Wood) Farnham, was born at Acton, Maine, October 10, 1831. After working a few years at the shoemaker's trade he became proprietor of the stage route from Acton Corner, Maine, to South Milton, New Hampshire, which he conducted till the railway was completed. For twenty years afterward he manager a line of teams and stages from Milton Mills to Union, the southern village of the town of Wakefield, in this state. Mr. Farnham was a Republican in politics, and attended the Methodist Church. On June 3, 1855, Ezra Farnham married Harriet A. Hubbard, daughter of Ezekiel and Abigail (Nason) Hubbard, who was born in Acton, Maine. They had one child, John Frank, whose sketch follows. Ezra Farnham died July 26, 1884.

(IX) J. Frank, only child of Ezra and Harriet A. (Hubbard) Farnham, was born in Acton, Maine, April 20, 1860. When but five years of age his parents moved to Milton, New Hampshire, where he attended the common schools and the high school, subsequently taking a course at the New Hampshire Institute, this state. He worked for his father a few years, and in 1884 went to Union, New Hampshire, where he opened a hardware store which he conducted for five years. He then bought the entire interest in the excelsior manufacturing plant, one half of which he had previously owned, and in this factory he has since conducted an extensive and profitable business. Mr. Farnham is a prominent Republican in politics, and has filled many offices in the town, county and state. He served as treasurer of Carroll county for two terms, 1895-96-97-98, and in 1898 was elected to the New Hampshire legislature where he was one of the committee on appropriations and engrossed bills. In 1900, he was chosen state senator and served on the judiciary and railroad committees, and as chairman of the committee on claims and manufacturing. He is prominent in Masonic circles, having reached the thirty-second degree Ancient Arabic Scottish Rite. He belongs to and is past master of Unity Lodge, Ancient Free and Accepted Masons of Union, Columbian Chapter, Royal Arch Masons, of Farmington, this state, Palestine Commandery, Knights Templar, of Rochester, New Hampshire, and has served as deputy grand master of the sixth Masonic district. On November 1, 1877, J. Frank Farnham married Ora E. Cutts, daughter of William F. and Abbie (Sanborn) Cutts, who was born at Milton, New Hampshire. They had two children: Fred H., born at Milton Mills, New Hampshire, December 13, 1878, bookkeeper for Stone & Webster, of Boston; resides in Malden, Massachusetts; married Eva T. Burnham, of Dover. Hazel A., born at Union, this state, December 1, 1897.

(III) Ephraim, fifth son and seventh child of Ralph and Elizabeth (Holt) Farnum, lived and died in Andover. He was married March 20, 1700, to Priscilla Holt, who was probably his cousin, a daughter of Nicholas (2) Holt of Andover. Five of their sons were among the first settlers of Concord, originally called Penny Cook, but the last remained only a short time. Their names were: Ephraim, Joseph, Zebediah, Josiah and James. (Joseph, the second, and descendants receive further notice in this article).

(IV) Ephraim (2), eldest child of Ephraim (1) and Priscilla (Holt) Farnum, was one of the proprietors of Penny Cook, and drew lot No. 15. He was an inhabitant and had a house built in 1731,

Clough. They had five children: Dearborn Henry, Polly, Hannah, Isabel, and Charles B., the subject of the next sketch.

(VII) Charles Burdet, youngest child of Captain Henry and Deborah (Clough) Hilton, was born in Andover, April 15, 1818, and died March 30, 1902, aged eighty-four. He attended school and worked at farm labor until he was twenty-one years of age, and then went to Boston, where he was a member of the police force for six or seven years. The two subsequent years he resided in Lowell, and then removed to Concord, where he learned the trade of cabinet maker, and resided about seven years. Returning to his native town, he bought a farm of one hundred acres a mile east of East Andover and resided there until his death. He was an attendant of the Free Will Baptist Church, but not a member. In politics he was a Republican. He married Mary Jane West, who was born in 1820, and died in 1896, daughter of Noah and Hannah (Webster) West, of Salisbury. They had two children: One died in infancy; the other, Charles H., is the subject of the next paragraph.

(VIII) Charles Henry, son of Charles B. and Mary Jane (West) Hilton, was born in Andover, April 29, 1852, and was educated in the common schools. He lives on a farm adjoining the one his father owned, containing four hundred acres. He keeps a large flock of sheep. He raises, buys, and sells stock, and does some slaughtering. In agricultural and in enterprises of public interest he is a leading citizen. In political faith he is a Republican, and has served his town two years, 1891 and 1892, as selectman, has been deputy sheriff of Merrimac county, and for six years was superintendent of the county farm. He married, May 12, 1877, at Franklin, Marcia Frances Nelson, who was born in Danbury, November 7, 1858, daughter of Andrew and Louisa (Withington) Nelson, of Sanbornton.

(I) Ralph Hilton was born in Wells, Maine. He was a merchant in that town in his younger days and later he was engaged in farming. He accumulated quite an amount of land in that region. The latter part of his life he was retired from active duty. He married his cousin, Hannah Hilton. Ralph Hilton died at Wells in 1875.

(II) Eben, son of Ralph and Hannah (Hilton) Hilton, was born at Wells, Maine. He was a stone mason by trade, which line of work he followed all his life in his native town. He had charge of the stone work at the time the Boston & Maine railroad was extended from South Berwick to Portland, Maine. He married Mary Elizabeth Taylor, daughter of Samuel and Louise Taylor. They had six children: Frank W., Lizzie M., Herbert, Lamont, who is mentioned below; Herbert and Arthur E. Eben Hilton died July 26, 1873, at Wells, Maine.

(III) Lamont, third son and fourth child of Eben and Mary E. (Taylor) Hilton, was born February 7, 1864, at Wells, Maine. He was educated in the common schools of his native town, and at the age of twelve worked for two years at farming on Durrell's Island. On January 4, 1878, he was engaged with the Davis Shoe Company, of Kennebunk, Maine, where he remained three years. From here he migrated to Massachusetts, going first to Lynn, where he was engaged with the F. W. Breed shoe factory, and afterwards to Cambridge, where he remained a short time with the Thatcher-Stone Provision Company. He then went back to Lynn and remained one year with the Keene Brothers, shoe manufacturers. For the next dozen years he was engaged in railroad work. He began at Chelsea, Massachusetts, where he was crossing agent for the Eastern Railroad, and then went to Portland, Maine, where he was switchman in the yard. He was afterward promoted to freight brakeman from Portland to Boston, which position he held for five years. He then worked in the grocery business at Wells, Maine, for a short time, and on June 27, 1889, entered the Boston & Maine service as passenger brakeman. He kept this place for one year, or till he was promoted to baggage master, and assigned to the run from Portsmouth, New Hampshire, to Portland, Maine. He held this position for three years, when he was transferred to the Gloucester, Massachusetts, branch, taking charge of the line from Boston to Rockport during the summer season. He was afterward sent to the run from Boston to Portland, Maine, in the capacity of passenger brakeman.

April 2, 1895, Mr. Hilton started on a new line of work. That day he entered the Portsmouth Police force as patrolman. On January 10, 1898, he was promoted to be captain of the night watch, but on account of the close confinement he resigned and went back to the duties of patrolman. In November, 1903, he resigned from the police force and engaged in a general insurance business, representing the Connecticut General Life, the Indemnity of New York, and the United States of New York and Delaware. Mr. Hilton has continued in this business ever since. In April, 1905, he was elected city treasurer of Portsmouth, and on January 1, 1907, was elected city clerk. He is a staunch Republican. Mr. Hilton is very prominent in fraternal organizations. He belongs to the Piscataqua Lodge, Independent Order of Odd Fellows, passing through the chairs in 1896; also to Osgood Lodge, Independent Order of Odd Fellows. In 1901 he took the Grand Lodge degree at Woodville, New Hampshire, and was appointed district deputy grand master of the Portsmouth district, comprising the lodges in Portsmouth, Exeter, Hampton, Newfields and Newton. In October, 1902, he was appointed grand marshal of the Grand Lodge by Grand Master Frank L. Way. In October, 1903, he was elected grand warden, in 1904 elected deputy grand master, and in October, 1905, was elected grand master. In October, 1906, he was elected grand representative to the Sovereign Grand Lodge for a term of two years. He is a member of Union Rebekah Lodge, No. 3, Strawberry Bank Encampment, No. 5, Canton Center, No. 12. He has taken many Masonic degrees. He belongs to the Saint Andrew's Lodge of Masons, the Ineffable Grand Lodge of Perfection, fourteenth degree, to the Grand Council, Princes of Jerusalem, sixteenth degree, to the New Hampshire Chapter of Rose Croix, eighteenth degree, to Edward A. Raymond Consistory, thirty-second degree. Mr. Hilton is a member of the United Order of American Mechanics, Portsmouth Council, No. 8, of Alpha Council, No. 3, Royal Arcanum, and of the Boston & Maine Relief Association. Lamont Hilton married Mary Alice Perkins, daughter of William and Lizzie Perkins, of Portsmouth. They have no children.

FARNUM This is among the early Massachusetts names which have been conspicuous in the settlement and development of New Hampshire, especially at Concord and vicinity. While most of its bearers have been tillers of the soil, they have ever been identified with the work of the church and other moral agencies, and still adhere to the standards of their Puritan ancestors. By many the name is now spelled Farnham.

(I) Ralph Farnum was born in 1603, and sailed from Southampton, England, with his wife Alice, in the brig "James," arriving at Boston, Massachusetts, June 5, 1635, after a voyage of fifty-eight days. He was among the proprietors of Ipswich, Massachusetts, in 1635. His wife was born about 1606, and they brought with them four children, a daughter being born of them here. Their names were as follows: Mary, born 1626; Thomas, 1631; Ralph, 1633; Ephraim and Sarah.

(II) Ralph (2), born 1633, son of Ralph (1) and Alice Farnum, is said by tradition (which is open to question) to have been a native of Wales. He settled in Andover, Massachusetts, where he was a grand juryman in 1679, and was the ancestor of a numerous posterity. He was married October 26, 1658, to Elizabeth, daughter of Nicholas Holt, another pioneer of Andover. She was born March 30, 1636, in Newbury, Massachusetts. He died January 8, 1692, in Andover. His children were: Sarah, Ralph, John, Henry, Hannah, Thomas, Ephraim and James. (Ephraim and descendants receive extended mention in this article).

(III) Ralph (3), son of Ralph (2) and Elizabeth (Holt) Farnham, was born, probably in Andover, Massachusetts, where his parents lived, on June 1, 1662. October 9, 1685, he married Sarah Sterling, and they had ten children: Sarah, Henry, Ralph (4) (mentioned below), Daniel, Abigail, William, Nathaniel, Barachias, Benjamin and Joseph. Of these children, Abigail, the second daughter and fifth child, was married in January, 1714, to James Abbott, of Andover, who became one of the first settlers of Pennycook, now Concord, New Hampshire. (See Abbott, III).

(IV) Ralph (4), second son and third child of Ralph (3) and Sarah (Sterling) Farnham, was born May 25, 1689, at Andover, Massachusetts, but removed when a young man to York, Maine. In 1712-13 by a vote in the York town-meeting he was granted thirty acres of land. Ralph (4) Farnham married at York, Elizabeth Austin, daughter of Captain Matthew Austin, and they had eleven children: Joseph, born June 20, 1713; Ralph, Mary, Matthew, Elizabeth, David, Jonathan, Nathaniel, Paul (mentioned below), Betty and John, born May 26, 1735. Of this family, Betty, the youngest daughter, married Berg, son of Richard Jacques, the soldier who shot Rolle, the Jesuit priest, who incited the Indians to massacre.

(V) Paul, seventh son and ninth child of Ralph (4) and Elizabeth (Austin) Farnham, was born April 20, 1730, at York, Maine. He lived for a time in Lebanon, that state, and afterwards removed to Acton, Maine, where his death occurred in 1820 at the age of ninety years.

(VI) Ralph (5), son of Paul Farnham, was born in Lebanon, New Hampshire, in July, 1756, and afterwards moved to Acton, Maine. He married Mehitabel Bean, and they had seven children, among them John, mentioned below. Ralph (5) Farnham was the last survivor of the battle of Bunker Hill, and as such was introduced to the Prince of Wales, now King Edward VII, on the latter's visit to Boston in 1860. Returning to his home in Acton, Mr. Farnham lived but a short time longer, dying in December, 1860, at the remarkable age of one hundred and four years and five months.

(VII) John, son of Ralph (5) and Mehitabel (Bean) Farnham, was born in Acton, Maine, near the close of the eighteenth century. He married Fannie Wood, and they had five children: Asa, Ezra, James, William and John.

(VIII) Ezra, son of John and Fannie (Wood) Farnham, was born at Acton, Maine, October 10, 1831. After working a few years at the shoemaker's trade he became proprietor of the stage route from Acton Corner, Maine, to South Milton, New Hampshire, which he conducted till the railway was completed. For twenty years afterward he manager a line of teams and stages from Milton Mills to Union, the southern village of the town of Wakefield, in this state. Mr. Farnham was a Republican in politics, and attended the Methodist Church. On June 3, 1855, Ezra Farnham married Harriet A. Hubbard, daughter of Ezekiel and Abigail (Nason) Hubbard, who was born in Acton, Maine. They had one child, John Frank, whose sketch follows. Ezra Farnham died July 26, 1884.

(IX) J. Frank, only child of Ezra and Harriet A. (Hubbard) Farnham, was born in Acton, Maine, April 20, 1860. When but five years of age his parents moved to Milton, New Hampshire, where he attended the common schools and the high school, subsequently taking a course at the New Hampshire Institute, this state. He worked for his father a few years, and in 1884 went to Union, New Hampshire, where he opened a hardware store which he conducted for five years. He then bought the entire interest in the excelsior manufacturing plant, one half of which he had previously owned, and in this factory he has since conducted an extensive and profitable business. Mr. Farnham is a prominent Republican in politics, and has filled many offices in the town, county and state. He served as treasurer of Carroll county for two terms, 1895-96-97-98, and in 1898 was elected to the New Hampshire legislature where he was one of the committee on appropriations and engrossed bills. In 1900, he was chosen state senator and served on the judiciary and railroad committees, and as chairman of the committee on claims and manufacturing. He is prominent in Masonic circles, having reached the thirty-second degree Ancient Arabic Scottish Rite. He belongs to and is past master of Unity Lodge, Ancient Free and Accepted Masons of Union, Columbian Chapter, Royal Arch Masons, of Farmington, this state, Palestine Commandery, Knights Templar, of Rochester, New Hampshire, and has served as deputy grand master of the sixth Masonic district. On November 1, 1877, J. Frank Farnham married Ora E. Cutts, daughter of William F. and Abbie (Sanborn) Cutts, who was born at Milton, New Hampshire. They had two children: Fred H., born at Milton Mills, New Hampshire, December 13, 1878, bookkeeper for Stone & Webster, of Boston; resides in Malden, Massachusetts; married Eva T. Burnham, of Dover. Hazel A., born at Union, this state, December 1, 1897.

(III) Ephraim, fifth son and seventh child of Ralph and Elizabeth (Holt) Farnum, lived and died in Andover. He was married March 20, 1700, to Priscilla Holt, who was probably his cousin, a daughter of Nicholas (2) Holt of Andover. Five of their sons were among the first settlers of Concord, originally called Penny Cook, but the last remained only a short time. Their names were: Ephraim, Joseph, Zebediah, Josiah and James. (Joseph, the second, and descendants receive further notice in this article).

(IV) Ephraim (2), eldest child of Ephraim (1) and Priscilla (Holt) Farnum, was one of the proprietors of Penny Cook, and drew lot No. 15. He was an inhabitant and had a house built in 1731, as shown by the original report. November 7, 1739, it was "voted, that there shall be a good and sufficient garrison built around the Rev. Timothy Walker's dwelling house, as soon as may be conveniently, at the town's cost," and Ephraim Farnum and others were appointed to build it. In 1746 he was one of ten appointed to the garrison around the house of Henry Lovejoy, in the "West Parrish Village," and March 21, 1747, in garrison around the house of Jeremiah Stickney in Rumford, now Concord. His second settlement was on Rattlesnake Plain, so called, about two miles from the old North meeting house, on the road to Boscawen. His name occurs often in the early records of the proprietors, and he was chosen deacon of the church, August, 1731. How long he served is unknown. He was selectman in 1734. He owned a mulatto boy named Cæsar, who was found in his pig trough when a babe. Mr. Farnum's death occurred in 1775, when he was about eighty years old. He married Molly Ingalls, and they had two sons, Ephraim and Benjamin.

(V) Benjamin, second son and child of Ephraim (2) and Molly (Ingalls) Farnum, was born March 21, 1739, and lived on the south half of the paternal farm, while his brother Ephraim (3) took the homestead and north part of the farm. He married Anna Merrill, and they had fifteen children: Mary, John, Anna, Benjamin, Ephraim, Haynes, Jonathan (died young), Nathaniel, Lydia, Jonathan, Nancy, Abiel, Abigail, Jeremiah and Sarah.

(VI) Ephraim (4), fifth child and third son of Benjamin and Anna (Merrill) Farnum, was born on the old homestead, April 5, 1770, and died at the age of ninety-four years. He succeeded his father in the ownership of the farm, living there all his life. He was an industrious, hardworking man and gave all his attention to the farm. He married Sarah Brown, of Plymouth, New Hampshire, and they had eight children: Nancy, Joseph B., Susannah, Benjamin, Lydia, Luther and George and Harriet (twins).

(VII) Deacon Benjamin, fourth child and second son of Ephraim (4) and Sarah (Brown) Farnum, was born June 1, 1804, on his father's farm, and died January 14, 1892. He attended school in West Concord, obtained a fair education and his life was spent on the ancestral acres. His farm contained three hundred acres, of which two hundred were woodland and the remainder intervale and pasture, and he made a specialty of raising fine stock, and always kept thirty or forty head of cattle. In 1845 he built the largest of the buildings now on the place. He was a Republican and was an alderman of Concord one term. He was appointed deacon of the First Church, (Congregational) of Concord, in 1844, and served as such till his death. He married Emily, daughter of Moses and Rhoda (Carter) Farnum, born July 15, 1803, died in 1885. Their children were: George Edwin, born January 25, 1834, died young; Rhoda Carter, June 30, 1836, died at the age of twenty years; Charles Henry and Cyrus R., mentioned further below; Lewis C., September 28, 1846, married Jane Tiffany and resides in McGregor, Iowa; George Edwin, October 28, 1851, married Josephine Jacobs, and resides in Ames, Iowa.

The lineage of Emily Farnum (wife of Deacon Benjamin) is as follows: (5) Ephraim (3), elder son of Ephraim (2) and Molly (Ingalls) Farnum, was born September 21, 1733, probably in Concord, and succeeded his father on the homestead, dividing the farm with his brother and retaining the paternal residence. He married Judith Hall, of Bradford, Massachusetts, and their children were: Naomi, John, Judith, Sarah, Moses, Esther and Susannah.

(6) Moses, second son and fifth child of Ephraim (3) and Judith (Hall) Farnum, was born October 20, 1769, in Concord, and married Rhoda Carter, daughter of Ezra and Phebe (Whittemore) Carter of West Concord. (See Carter, VI). After her death he married her younger sister Esther, and each bore him three children, namely: Hannah C., Emily, Samuel, Moses H., Lavina and Jennett.

(7) Emily, second daughter and child of Moses and Rhoda (Carter) Farnum, born July 15, 1803, became the wife of Deacon Benjamin Farnum, her second cousin, as above related.

(7) Moses Hall Farnum, fourth child of Moses and eldest child of his second wife, Esther Carter, was born February 3, 1811, in West Concord, and married Judith A. Kilburn in June, 1843. She died February 28, 1868. She was a daughter of Enoch and Betsey (Morse) Kilburn of Boscawen. He filled most of the town offices, before there was a city charter, and has served in the council and board of alderman of the city. He is still living in the house on the site of the one in which he was born, and in possession of his faculties, a most interesting man to meet, having exercised an intelligent observation of events during his long life. The house in which he was born, partly built by his grandfather and partly by his father (in which the latter was born), was burned about 1870, and he built the present house upon the same site. He has four children, namely: Franklin Burke, Ann Elizabeth (see Charles H. Farnum, VIII), Edward Everett and Ralph Perley. The last is a son of the second wife, Ann (Hale), widow of Asa L. Pervier, and daughter of Isaac Hale of Franklin, New Hampshire.

(8) Annie L. (Elizabeth), only daughter and second child of Moses H. and Judith A. (Kilburn) Farnum, born April 15, 1849, is the wife of Charles Henry Farnum, subject of the following paragraph.

(VIII) Charles Henry, third child and second son of Deacon Benjamin and Emily (Farnum) Farnum, was born December 30, 1837, on the ancient Farnum homestead, where his father, grandfather and great-grandfather were born, near Rattlesnake hill, and opposite the village of East Concord. He attended the public schools of West Concord and Concord, and an academy at New London, New Hampshire, leaving school at the age of twenty years. He aided in tilling the paternal acres until he was twenty-three years old, and started out to see something of the world and establish himself in life. In 1860 he went to California, and spent three years in farming at Navata, in that state. For the next five years he was located at Austin, Nevada, where he operated a saw mill and engaged in freighting. Having attained considerable success he felt that he might enjoy a short vacation in visiting the scenes of his childhood. His father being somewhat advanced in years, persuaded him to remain, and he has since been engaged in tilling the home farm, which embraces three hundred acres. It is one of the finest in the Merrimac valley, embracing a large tract of intervale, where a straight furrow of over half a mile may be turned, something typical of the western plains. Like his father, he keeps from forty to fifty head of cattle, including some fine oxen, and a dairy of usually twenty cows. Mr. Farnum is a genial and intelligent gentleman, who has observed men and things in visits to many interesting places, and takes a broad view of the world and its people. By travel and reading he has become well informed on topics of human interest, and is able to carry on his part in conversation with other cosmopolitans. He keeps abreast of the times, and

Benjamin Farnum

Charles H. Parsons

entertains settled opinions on leading questions. A sincere Republican, he supports consistently the policy of his party, and has served as a member of the city council. He supports religious work, as exemplified by the West Concord Congregational Church. Mr. Farnum was married, November 20, 1870, to Annie L. Farnum, daughter of Moses H. and Judith A. (Kilburn) Farnum, of West Concord. She was born in the second house north of her present home, and has spent most of her life in the immediate neighborhood. One daughter born to Mr. and Mrs. Farnum died in babyhood. Surrounded by congenial friends and relatives, they are spending in quiet contentment and enjoyment of the fruits of early industry, a most happy existence.

(VIII) Cyrus Rogers, fourth child and third son of Deacon Benjamin and Emily (Farnum) Farnum, was born in West Concord, July 21, 1842. At the age of eighteen he left school and enlisted, November 22, 1861, in Company F, Second Regiment, United States Sharpshooters, and served until November 26, 1864. He was absent from home three years, and took part in the battles of Antietam, the second Bull Run, the Wilderness, and several engagements of less magnitude. Returning to the Granite State he helped to till his father's acres one year, and then, thirsting for the sort of adventure the West then abundantly afforded, he went to Nevada and engaged in freighting between Austin and other points in that vicinity, across the land of mountains and deserts, at that time often infested with hostile bands of savages. After three and a half years in that wild country he returned to Concord, and in 1869 engaged in the transportation of granite from the quarries on Rattlesnake Hill to the railroad. In 1870 he built a large set of buildings on two acres of the paternal farm where he now lives. Soon after he bought a farm of fifty acres and began to till the soil. Since that time he has acquired forty acres of intervale in Concord and one hundred and twenty-five acres of pasture in Bradford, and has a well tilled and stocked establishment, and carries on mixed farming. For the past eight years he has been road agent of the West Concord district. His political affiliations are with the Republican party. He is a member of Davis Post No. 44, G. A. R., and worships at the West Parish Congregational Church. Mr. Farnum was married, January 4, 1871, to Caroline Elizabeth Clough, born October 26, 1845, daughter of Moses and Esther Kimball (Farnum) Clough, of West Concord. Moses Clough, son of Abel and Alice (Ferrin) Clough was once station agent at West Concord. Mr. and Mrs. Farnum have a daughter and son. Fannie Moore, the elder, born October 28, 1871, married John Dimond, and died August 2, 1903. She had three children—Edna Cornelia, Carl S. and Blanche Farnum. Carl Sumner, born December 26, 1902, now lives with his maternal grandparents. Benjamin H. Farnum, second child of Cyrus R., born November 3, 1875, is unmarried and lives with his parents.

(IV) Joseph, second son and child of Ephraim (1) Farnum, born in Andover, Massachusetts, removed to Penacook when a young man and settled about half a mile north of the east end of Long Pond, where he was the first settler, and where he died November 1, 1792. He had a farm of two hundred acres, and his home was one of the four on Rattlesnake Plain, which stood near the present track of the Concord & Claremount railroad, on the road from West Concord to Hopkinton. He was one of those assigned to duty in 1746 in the garrison around the house of Henry Lovejoy, in the West Parish village. March 21, 1747, he was assigned to duty in the garrison around the house of Timothy Walker. He held numerous offices. He was hogreeve in 1737 and 1739; field-driver, 1742; fenceviewer, 1746; surveyor of highways, 1770-71-80-82; tythingman, 1773-74; and was elected selectman at the first "legal meeting of the freeholders and inhabitants of Concord," held on January 21, 1766. June 23, 1785, Captain Joseph Farnum was appointed one of a "committee to lay out Main street," Concord. He is mentioned as one of those who, like Rev. Timothy Walker, maintained the ancient style of dress, including a cocked hat, after it had generally gone out of use. Captain Joseph Farnum is also mentioned as among "the ancient men who sat in the 'old man's seat'" in the church. He married Zerviah Hoit, daughter of Abner and Mary (Blaisdell) Hoit (see Hoit, IV), and they had ten children: Joseph, Stephen, Betsey, Daniel, Abner, Affia, Zerviah, Mary, Susan and Jacob.

(V) Stephen, second son and child of Joseph and Zerviah (Hoit) Farnum, was born in Rumford (now Concord) August 24, 1742, and resided on the home farm. He was tythingman 1780; surveyor of highways six years, between 1784 and 1800; petit juror, 1792; and constable, 1794. Stephen Farnum, and John his cousin, killed a bear at Horse Hill. While the bear was engaged in defending himself against the dog, Stephen clenched him by the ears and John beat his brains out with a pitch-pine knot. He married Martha Hall, and they were the parents of six children: David, Stephen, Phebe, Isaac, Simeon and Judith. (Mention of Isaac and Simeon appears in this article).

(VI) Stephen (2), second son and child of Stephen (1) and Martha (Hall) Farnum, was born September 20, 1771, and was among the first settlers of Rumford, Maine. He married Susan Jackman, of Boscawen, and had the following children: Reuben, Simeon, George, Stephen, Anson, Lucinda, Susan and Patty. The last named became the wife of Captain Abiel C. Carter. (See Carter, VIII).

(VI) Isaac, third son and fourth child of Stephen and Martha (Hall) Farnum, was born December 1, 1778, and died January 26, 1875, aged ninety-six. He was a successful farmer and a man of influence in Concord. He was a Whig and later a Republican, and was selectman in 1822-23. He bought the machinery for a clock for sixty dollars, which he paid for in wood delivered in Concord at one dollar a cord, cut in sled or eight-foot lengths, which he hauled on a wooden shod sled. ——— Farnum, his brother, made the case of the clock, which is still doing faithful service in the family. A pitch-pipe used by Isaac Farnum in connection with church singing is in possession of his grandson. Isaac Farnum attended the North Church, of which his wife was a member. He married, January 11, 1803, Hannah Martin, whose parents resided by Long Pond. Of this union there were nine children: Esther, married Joseph S. Abbot; Hannah, married Captain Bradbury Gill, and lived in Concord (see Gill, VI); Almira, married Joseph Eastman, and lived in West Concord; David, lived in West Concord; Henry, resided on the old farm; Lucretia, married George W. Brown and resided in West Concord; Phebe M., married William C. Webster and resided in Boscawen; Lucy D., married Andrew Jackson, a resident of Concord; Isaac, died young.

(VI) Simeon, fourth son and fifth child of Stephen (1) and Martha (Hall) Farnum, was born January 14, 1782, in Concord, and resided in his native town. He married (first), Mary Smith of Hopkinton, who bore him three children, namely: Josiah S., Moody (died young) and Mary. After her death, Mr. Farnum married her sister, Clarissa, who was the mother of: Simeon and Clarissa (twins), Moody S., Aaron Q. and Martha A.

(VII) Mary, eldest daughter and third child of Simeon and Mary (Smith) Farnum, was born June 25, 1814, and became the wife of Simeon Abbott in 1837 (see Abbott, VI).

(VII) Martha A., youngest child of Simeon and Clarissa (Smith) Farnum, was born April 8, 1853, and became the wife of George W. Page of Dunbarton. (See Page, VIII).

(V) Abner, fourth son and fifth child of Joseph and Zerviah (Hoyt) Farnum, married (first), Rebecca Merrill and (second), Sally Elliott. The children of the first marriage were: Thomas, John (died young) and Moses. The children of the second marriage were: John, Abner, Jacob, Joseph, Jedediah, Rebecca, Nathan, James, Betsey and Isaac.

(VI) Abner (2), fifth son of Abner Farnum and second child of his second wife, Sarah Elliott, married Mary Martin, and had the following children: Judith, Hiram, Caroline, Daniel, Sarah J. and Abner Doddridge.

(VII) Abner Doddridge, youngest child of Abner (2) and Mary (Martin) Farnum, married Margaret Crosby and had only one child, namely, Abner Doddridge.

(VIII) Abner Doddridge (2), son of Abner Doddridge (1) and Margaret (Crosby) Farnum, was born 1828, in West Concord, where his father was a farmer. He was educated in the public schools of West Concord, and as a young man went to Boston, where he engaged in business. In 18— he went to Billerica, Massachusetts, and was there successfully engaged in the milk business. He was subsequently engaged in the lumber business, and was employed as a carpenter in the ship-yards for many years. He next invested in a steam saw-mill. He located at Mast Yard, New Hampshire, being the first one of the kind in the state. Having lost most of his possessions by fire, he removed to Warner and there engaged in the lumber business. He purchased a farm, on which his son and namesake now lives, and engaged in general farming and was an extensive stockraiser. He still lives on the same farm in Warner. He is an attendant of the Baptist Church, and has always been a Democrat in politics. He was married to Margaret T. Crosby, daughter of Michael C. Bell. She died March, 1887, in Warner. They were the parents of nine children, four of whom are now deceased. Charles, the oldest of those living, is engaged in the milk business in Boston. Alice, the second, is the wife of W. H. Woodward, of Somerville, Massachusetts. Margaret married George Pattee, proprietor of the Yarmouth House, Nova Scotia. Florence May is now a teacher in Mont Clair, New Jersey. Abner Doddridge is the subject of the next paragraph.

(IX) Abner Doddridge (3), second son of Abner Doddridge (2) and Margaret T. (Crosby) Farnum, was born April 16, 1868, in West Concord, and completed his education in the high school of that town. He began his business career in the wholesale house of Dickerman & Company, in Concord, where he continued for three years. He was subsequently employed for one year by the Boston & Maine railroad as a carpenter. On account of the advancing years of his father it became his duty to care for the homestead in Warner, where he is now conducting a successful general farming and lumbering business. He is a Democrat in politics, but has but little to do with public affairs. As the duty of a good citizen he has performed service as road agent of the town of Warner. He is a member of Warner Grange, and attends the Baptist Church. He was married March 31, 1896, to Annie M. Corrigan, daughter of John Corrigan, of Lyndonville, Vermont. She is active in church and benevolent work, and is the willing and competent helpmate of her husband. They are the parents of four children: Harold, Gertrude M., Franklin S. and Abner Doddridge.

GLEASON This line of Gleason, Gleison, Glezen, Gleeson or (as it was sometimes written and pronounced) Leesen, descends from the first of the name in New England. The family has been active in religious and military affairs, in professional life, and all lines of industry.

(I) Thomas Gleason, the immigrant, early took the oath of fidelity at Watertown, Massachusetts, and is named, 1657, on the town records of Cambridge. He was of Charlestown, March, 1666, in the occupation of the "tract of land reserved to Squa Sachem." In 1663 he leased a farm of Captain Scarlett. He died in Cambridge, probably about 1684. By his wife Susanna he had children: Thomas, Joseph, John, Mary, Isaac and William.

(II) Thomas (2), oldest child of Thomas (1) and Susanna Gleason, settled in Sudbury as early as 1665, on the east side of Cochituate pond. On September 29, 1673, he bought by exchange one-half of the Benjamin Rice farm lying between Beaver Dam brook and Gleason's pond in Framingham, Massachusetts, and in 1678 he built near the said pond which took its name from him. He became an inhabitant of Sherborn, October 5, 1678, and died July 25, 1705, his wife Sarah having died July 8, 1703. Their children were: Sarah, Anna, Thomas, Isaac, Patience, Mary and John.

(III) Isaac, fourth child and second son of Thomas (2) and Sarah Gleason, lived in Framingham. On February 18, 1725, he bought eighty acres of land of Jonathan Lamb, where his sons Isaac and Phinehas afterward lived. In 1726 he sold his old place to Daniel How, and opened a tavern. He was one of the petitioners of June 11, 1711, for permission to buy land of the Indians. He was the head of one of the seventeen families set off from Sherborn to Framingham in the boundary controversy settled in 1710. In 1713 he was chosen to have the care of the meeting house, and was voted 19s for such services. He died December 5, 1737. He married, December 11, 1700, Deborah Leland, who was born August 16, 1687, daughter of Ebenezer Leland, of Sherborn. Their children were: Deborah, Isaac, Prudence and Phinehas.

(IV) Isaac (2), second child of Isaac (1) and Deborah (Leland) Gleason, was born in Sherborn, May 17, 1706. He lived in Framingham, and is probably the Sergeant Isaac Gleason who was in Captain Ebenezer Newell's company on the Crown Point expedition; in service from March 27 to June 2, 1756, and again in Captain Nixon's company in the expedition of 1758 against Ticonderoga. He moved to Petersham, and died there in 1777. He married, December 19, 1725, Thankful, daughter of Nathaniel and Elizabeth (Osland) Wilson, of Newton, Massachusetts. She died in Westmoreland, New Hampshire, December 2, 1800, aged ninety-four. They had: Isaac, Elizabeth, Deborah, Simeon, Thankful, James, Joseph, Nathaniel, Benjamin and Fortunatus.

(V) Isaac (3), eldest child of Isaac (2) and Thankful (Wilson) Gleason, was born in Framingham, Massachusetts, August 3, 1726, and lived in several towns in Massachusetts, where his children were born. He finally settled in that part of No. 4 (Charlestown) which is now the town of Langdon, and there died. He married, November 2, 1752, Mary Nixon, who was born December 24, 1733, daughter of Christopher and Mary (Seaver) Nixon. The widow married second, a Sartwell. The children of Isaac and Mary were: Lucia, Dolly, Elizabeth, Eliab, Winsor, Betsey and Thaddeus.

(VI) Winsor, fifth child and second son of Isaac (3) and Mary (Nixon) Gleason, was born February 18, 1762, and died August 8, 1816. He was a farmer in Langdon. He married, January 21, 1787, Sally Gleason, who was born April 7, 1767, and died February 18, 1801, daughter of Isaac and Sally (Curtis) Gleason, of Petersham, Massachusetts. He married (second), July 13, 1803, Martha Follett, who was born August 1, 1776, and died February 28, 1858, aged eighty-two. His children were: Miranda, Sally, Polly, Curtis, Salmon, Winsor, Laura, Joseph Winsor, Huzziel, Horace, Elizabeth and Salmon—nine by the first wife and three by the second.

(VII) Rev. Salmon, youngest child of Winsor and Martha (Follett) Gleason, was born in Langdon, July 9, 1804, and died September 9, 1889, aged eighty-five. He probably acquired his education at Windsor, Vermont. He was ordained deacon at Barre, Vermont, by Bishop Elijah Hadding, June 17, 1830; elder at Lyndon, Vermont, by Bishop Roberts, August 12, 1832. The New Hampshire conference accepted him as elder July 8, 1839. In 1847 he went to Warren from Plymouth, where he was pastor of the Methodist Church for two years. Afterward he moved to East Warren, where he bought a saw mill which he operated until 1858. Subsequently he farmed a short time, and then lived for sixteen years near Mankato, Minnesota. At the end of that time he returned to Warren, and resided there till the time of his death. He was an Abolitionist in the days of the anti-slavery agitation, and a Republican from the formation of the party. He married, December 24, 1828, Jerusha Willard, who was born in Hartland, Vermont, July 20, 1803, and died in Warren, January 9, 1876, daughter of Charles and Hannah Willard, of Hartland, Vermont. The children of this union were: William, Salmon W., George L., Orange S. and Horace W.

(VIII) Orange Scott, fourth son and child of Rev. Salmon and Jerusha (Willard) Gleason, was born at West Plymouth, July 8, 1835. In early life he was in the employ of H. W. Wicks, saw mill operator, and afterward with Mead, Mason & Company, in the same business. In 1887 he began farming in Warren, and has since followed that calling. In politics he is a staunch Republican, and has been overseer of the poor and member of the town building committee. He married, December 7, 1858, Ruth Clifford, who was born February 27, 1832, daughter of Russell and Sarah (Fitts) Clifford. Their children were: Jennie M., died young; Fred C. and Willard Fitts, died young.

(IX) Fred Clifford, second child of Orange Scott and Ruth (Clifford) Gleason, was born in Warren, February 28, 1866, and acquired his education in the common schools of Warren, and at Haverhill Academy. He taught school, clerked for E. B. Eaton & Son five years, and in 1890 engaged in general merchandising, which he has since carried on profitably. He is a strong Republican, and has been postmaster since his appointment in 1897. He has been town treasurer, treasurer of the school board, treasurer of the trustees of the Methodist Episcopal Church, and secretary of the Republican town committee. He organized the Baker River Telephone Company, and is its president and general manager. He is prominent in Masonry and other fraternal secret societies. He is a member of Moosehillock Lodge, No. 63, Ancient Free and Accepted Masons; Pemigewasset Royal Arch Chapter; Omega Council, Royal and Select Masters; St. Gerard Commandery, Knights Templar; Edward A. Raymond Consistory, Thirty-second degree, Scottish Rite Masons; and Bektash Temple, Ancient Arabic Order Nobles of the Mystic Shrine. He is also a member of Waternomie Lodge, Knights of Pythias, of which he is a past chancellor.

He married, September 1, 1892, Etta L. Prescott, who was born October 9, 1865, daughter of Rev. L. W. and Julia (French) Prescott, of Warren. They have one child, Kenneth Prescott, born July 19, 1900.

GLEASON The members of the Gleason family who are now scattered over the United States are descendants of an ancestor whose religious principles brought him to this land; and who for conscience sake left his country and his home and "sought a faith's pure shrine" upon our then bleak and inhospitable shores.

(I) Job Gleason, born 1711, was probably of Scotch extraction and a native of the North of Ireland. He settled early in the eighteenth century near what is now Highgate, Vermont, where he died July 28, 1796, aged eighty-five. By his wife Hannah he had one son, the subject of the next paragraph.

(II) Isaac. son of Job and Hannah Gleason, was born in Vermont, 1776, and removed to the Province of Quebec, Canada, where he married Eunice Loveland, who was born in 1781. He died in 1854, aged seventy-eight. His wife died December 22, 1858, aged seventy-seven. They had two sons, Isaac and Hiram.

(III) Hiram, son of Isaac and Eunice (Loveland) Gleason, was born in Dunham. Providence of Quebec, in November, 1800, and after his marriage moved to Brome, Province of Quebec, and settled there. He was a farmer for years, and then removed to Cowansville, Province of Quebec, where he had a considerable store, and was a man of influence in social and political circles; was mayor of the town, and held other offices. In religious faith he was a Congregationalist. He died in 1878, aged seventy-eight years. He married in Durham, January 15, 1827, Lucinda Wightman, who was born August 18, 1808, and died in 1882, aged seventy-four years. Their eight children were: Hiram Elhanan, Mary Jane, Emily, Roscoe, Isabel, Albert, Ellen and Caroline.

(IV) Hiram Elhanan, eldest child of Hiram and Lucinda (Wightman) Gleason, was born at Brome, May 24, 1852, and died September 7, 1881. At the age of nineteen he removed with his father to Cowansville. There he was in business at first with his father but soon withdrew and engaged in business for himself. He was a shrewd business man, and often saw opportunities for making a profit in other business than that in which he was engaged, and by improving his opportunities he made many profitable ventures. When the lumber about him commenced to command a good price he began to deal in it, and thus made large profits. He was a leading citizen in Cowansville, and was postmaster for years, holding that office at the time of his death. In the "Fenian raid" into Canada in 1869. Mr. Gleason was one of the two hundred volunteer defenders of Misisquoi county, called the "Home Guard," who participated in the battle of Eccles Hill, where the Fenians were repulsed and dispersed. In religion he was a Congregationalist. He married, April 25, 1865, at Cowansville, Province of Quebec, Mary Victoria Stinehour, who was born in Stanbridge, June 10, 1843, and who still makes her home in Cowansville. Their children were: John H., Homer, Edward, Forest, Parkman and Mary.

Mary Victoria Stinehour descends from German ancestry as follows:

(I) Herr Von Christian Wehr, eldest son and heir to the estate and title of his father, Baron Christian Wehr Von Stein, Neukirk, Germany, quarrelled with his father over a girl his father wished him to marry, and left the fatherland and came to America, settling in Albany, New York. He was finely educated, and the master of five languages. In 1770 he made a voyage to Germany, returning the next year. From that time on he lived as a gentleman in Albany until 1777, when his political tenets got him in trouble. Being a "United Empire Loyalist," he was compelled to leave the United States, and went to Canada, where he ever afterward lived, and was made a lieutenant of the royal forces stationed at Canada, October 5, 1783. Shortly after this Lieutenant Wehr, Conrad Best and others petitioned His Excellency Frederick Holdemand, then governor and commander-in-chief in and over the Province of Quebec and territories, for a tract of land east of Misisquoi Bay. This having been granted to others, these petitioners received in 1785 a grant of the greater parts of the counties of Huntington, Misisquoi, Shefford, and Compton, and a township in Sutton. He resided on this grant until well advanced in years, and afterward lived with his son Christian. He cut a great amount of timber from his forest grant and rafted logs down the St. Lawrence to market. On one occasion two large rafts were broken up by the storms of Lake St. Peter, and all the logs were lost. Christian Wehr was the first promoter of the first church in the pioneer days of Misisquoi county, and before it was built Lutheran meetings were held at his house.

(II) Christian (2) Wehr, son of Lieutenant Christian Wehr, was a man of wealth and political influence, and was a colonel in the British military service. He married Katherine, daughter of Conrad Best, who, like the Wehrs, was a United Empire Loyalist and a German gentleman. They lived at St. Armand, Province of Quebec. Seven children were born of this marriage, two sons and five daughters, none of whom died under eighty years of age. One of the daughters. Charlotte Augustus Matilda, was born February 27, 1805, and died at Cowansville, November 26, 1896, aged ninety-two years and nine months. She married John Stinehour, whose sketch appears below.

(I) George Stinehour was a German gentleman who settled in Albany, New York, in 1790. He afterward removed to Highgate, Vermont, and thence to Standbridge, Province of Quebec. He was a man of good standing in the community, and thoroughly imbued with the united empire loyalist principles. He married in Highgate, Vermont, Charity Holenbeck, who died in Highgate, December 5, 1829, in the seventy-second years of her age. He died in Standbridge, February 26, 1844, aged eighty-eight years and ten months. They were the parents of sixteen children.

(II) John, sixth son of George and Charity (Holenbeck) Stinehour, born in Highgate, Vermont, April, 21, 1800, and died May 5, 1865, aged sixty-five, at Cowansville, where he was engaged in agricultural pursuits. He was married in St. Armand, October 17, 1826, by the Rev. James Reed, to Charlotte Augusta Matilda Wehr, and they were the parents of seven children: Harriet Attwood, John Parkman, Charlotte Augusta, Elizabeth, Gertrude, Mary Victoria, Caroline and Jane Adams.

(V) Dr. John Hiram Gleason, eldest child of Hiram E. and Mary Victoria (Stinehour) Gleason, was born in Cowansville, September 20, 1869. He attended the common schools, and later graduated from the Cowansville Academy at sixteen years of age The following year he went to Montreal and matriculated at McGill University, and took a course in chemistry, graduating as a chemist in 1891. He then entered McGill Medical College, and in 1895, after a four year course, graduated with honors as M. D., C. M. After graduation he took a post-graduate course at the Post Graduate College in New York City. In June, 1896, he settled in Manchester, New Hampshire. where he has since resided, and now has a large practice, there being among his patients many of the best people of the city. Soon after going to Manchester he became connected with the outpatient department of the Sacred Heart Hospital, and also with the out-patient department of the Emergency Ward of the Elliot Hospital. He performed the duties of these offices until 1898, when he was appointed surgeon to the Elliot Hospital. In 1903 he took a similar position on the staff of the Notre Dame Hospital and still holds the last named place. Dr. Gleason devotes special attention to surgery, and each year spends two months in medical centers in order to obtain the latest and best ideas relative to the practice of his profession. His skill, manner and conduct as a medical practitioner and a gentleman have made him popular and successful. For three years he has been medical examiner for the Massachusetts Life Insurance Company. He is a member of the British Medical Association, the American Medical Association, the New Hampshire State Medical Society. the New Hampshire Surgeons' Club, the Hillsborough County Medical Association, the Merrimack County Medical Society, the New Hampshire Society for the Prevention of Tuberculosis, and the Manchester Medical Association, of which he is the president. He is also a member of various non-medical societies and clubs, among which are the Manchester Historical Society, the New England McGill Graduate Society, the Derryfield Club, the Cygnet Boating Club, the Manchester Country Club, and the Manchester Driving Club. He attends the Franklin Street Church.

He married, October 17, 1899, Ethel Eastman Simmons. born in New York City, December 26, 1878, daughter of William L. and Julia (Eastman) Simmons, of Lexington, Kentucky, and granddaughter of the late Colonel Arthur McArthur Eastman, of Manchester. Soon after the birth of Mrs. Gleason her mother died, and Mr. Simmons removed to Kentucky, where he was engaged in stock raising until his retirement a few years ago. Mrs. Gleason is an attendant of the Franklin Street Church, and a member of the Society of Colonial Dames of America, and of the Manchester Thimble Club. The children of Dr. and Mrs. Gleason are: Elizabeth Eastman and John MacArthur.

VOSE This name is probably of German origin and was formerly spelled Voose. It became Latinized into Voseius and finally Anglicized into its present form. Two immigrants, said to have been brothers, came from England at an early date, one of whom settled in Massachu-

John H. Gleason

setts and the other in Connecticut. The latter spelled the name Vorse.

(I) Robert Vose came from Lancashire in 1638, and in 1640 purchased a farm in that part of Dorchester which was afterward set off as the town of Milton, where he died in 1683, aged eighty-four years. His wife, whose christian name was Jane, died in 1675. Their children were Henry, Edward, Thomas, Elizabeth and Martha. Of Henry there is no further mention. Edward inherited the homestead in Dorchester. Thomas will be again referred to. Elizabeth, born in 1629, married, in 1657, Thomas Swift, and died in 1675. Martha, married (first), John Sharp, who was killed in King Phillip's war in 1676, and she subsequently became Mrs. Buckminister.

(II) Thomas Vose, third child and youngest son of Robert and Jane Vose, was born in Dorchester in 1641. He resided near the family homestead, and his death occurred in 1708. The maiden name of his wife does not appear in the record at hand. He had a son Henry; Elizabeth, who became Mrs. Crane; Jane, who became Mrs. Lyon; and Thomas, born in 1667, were probably his children.

(III) Henry Vose, son of Thomas Vose, was born in Dorchester in 1663. For his services in a campaign against the Narragansett Indians he received a grant of land in Bedford. His death occurred in 1752. He married (first), Elizabeth Babcock, and married (second), Jemima Tucker. His children, all of his first union, were: Waitstill, Robert, Elizabeth Mary, Martha, Abigail, Joshua, Hepzibah, Beulah and Thomas.

(IV) Robert Vose, second son of Henry and Elizabeth (Babcock) Vose, was born in 1693. He married Abigail Sumner, and was the father of Othniel and Waitstill (twins), Robert, Henry, William (died young), Samuel, William, James, Elizabeth, Abigail, Thomas, Joshua and Benjamin. His eleventh child, Thomas, who acquired the title of honorable by his prominence in civic affairs, went to Robinson, Maine, as manager of the property of Governor Edward Robbins, and established the branch of the Vose family in that state.

(V) Lieutenant James Vose, eighth child of Robert and Abigail (Sumner) Vose, was born in 1734. About the year 1755 he went to Bedford, New Hampshire, accompanied by his brother Samuel, settling first on the river road near the Merrimack line, and later removing to Plummer Hill. The maiden name of his first wife does not appear in the record at hand, but her christian name was Abigail, and they were probably married in Bedford. Their first and second child were each named James, and their other sons were Jacob and Joshua. They also had four daughters, two of whom married Eatons, presumably brothers, another became Mrs. Vickery, and the other became Mrs. Barnes. Samuel Vose, brother of James Vose, married Phoebe Vickery, and had children: Thomas, Samuel, Robert, Frances, John, Roger, Mercy, Phebe. Samuel Vose settled on the river road near Merrimac line. His son John born in 1766, graduated from Dartmouth College, 1795, and was distinguished as an instructor.

(VI) Joshua Vose, fourth child and third son of Lieutenant James and Abigail Vose, was born in Bedford in 1783. In early life he was engaged in teaming between Bedford and Boston. He purchased considerable real estate in Bedford, mostly wild land, and was a prosperous farmer for the remainder of his life, which terminated in 1862. In his religious belief he was a Presbyterian. He was twice married, first to Nancy Shirley, daughter of Thomas Shirley, of Goffstown; second to Mary Houston, daughter of Deacon John Houston, of Bedford. The children of his first union were: Daniel, born in 1808; James, born in 1809; Nancy, born in 1812, died in 1817; and Joshua, born in 1815. Those of his second marriage are: Nancy A., born in 1829, married, in 1857, John O. Parker and resided in Manchester, died November 25, 1904. John Gilman, who will be again referred to. Justin E., born in 1835, died in 1894.

(VII) John Gilman Vose, second child and eldest son of Joshua and Mary (Houston) Vose, was born in Bedford May 26, 1832. After graduating from the West Manchester Academy he engaged in lumbering, but later turned his attention to farming, which he carried on with energy and success on the homestead of his father where he spent the remainder of his life, and died there, and where his widow and family still reside. The homestead settled by their father over one hundred years ago is still in the possession of the family. In politics he acted with the Republican party and was prominent in local civic affairs, serving as selectman for a number of years. His church affiliations were with the Presbyterians and he was an attendant of that body. John Gilman Vose died February 15, 1904. On June 3, 1860, he married Mary Elizabeth Keniston, daughter of Morrill and Sarah (Pherson) Keniston, of Manchester. She became the mother of three children: Joshua, born June 14, 1863, died October 14 of the same year. Mary Frances, born February 17, 1865, married John McAlister, of Manchester, in 1888. Annie Morril, born October 6, 1875. Mary Frances was graduated with honors from the Manchester high school in 1884, and prior to her marriage was a successful teacher. Her children are: Richard Vose, born March 9, 1892; William Roy, born May 7, 1895; John Parker, born October 31, 1897; and Elizabeth, born February 9, 1904. Annie Morril Vose was graduated from Wellesley College with the class of 1898; she is the only college graduate in the town of Bedford. She has taught in the Manchester high school for six years.

(VI) John, fifth son and child of Lieutenant Samuel and Phebe (Vickery) Vose, was born in Bedford, New Hampshire, July 10, 1766. He was graduated from Dartmouth College in 1795, taking high rank in a class which included such men as United States Senator Judah Dana, Congressman Heman Allen, Abijah Bigelow and Luther Jewett, Judge Nicholas Emery and Drs. Samuel Worcester and Thomas Snell. Mr. Vose excelled in mathemathics and philosophy, and his commencement exercise was a "Philosophical Oration on Thunder Storms." After leaving college he became preceptor of the academy at Atkinson, this state, where he remained twenty-one years. This is one of the oldest schools in New Hampshire, and had considerable note in its day. In 1820 Mr. Vose moved to Pembroke, this state, and became principal of the academy there, where he remained eleven years. In 1831, at the age of sixty-five, he returned to Atkinson, where he spent the remainder of his days. In 1801 Mr. Vose was appointed justice of the peace, and in 1815 of the Quorum, and was continued in office till his death. In 1816 he was elected state senator from the third district. He was for many years deacon of the church in Atkinson, and at his death was president of the board of trustees of the academy in that town. He was president of the Merrimack County Temperance Society from its formation till he left the county in 1831; and for many years was one of the vice-presidents of the

American Sunday School Union. "All these trusts," according to Rev. Dr. William Cogswell, "he fulfilled with great propriety, faithfulness and acceptance." Mr. Vose published an oration delivered before the Phi Beta Kappa Society of Dartmouth College in 1805; an oration delivered on the Fourth of July, 1809, at Bedford, New Hampshire; and an oration delivered before the Rockingham Agricultural Society at Derry in 1813. In 1827 he published a "System of Astronomy," containing two hundred and fifty-two octavo pages, and in 1832 a "Compendium of Astronomy" for common schools, issued in 12mo form. These are not merely compilations, but original and valuable works.

On February 24, 1800, John Vose married Lida Webster, of Atkinson, and they had five children. His last illness was a gradual decline, and he died much lamented, April 3, 1840, at the age of seventy-four. He was a modest, exemplary christian gentleman, and at his funeral an appropriate discourse was delivered by Rev. John Kelley, of Hampstead, this state, from Acts 8:2: "And devout men carried Stephen to his burial, and made great lamentation over him."

DOLE The name of Dole is believed to be of French origin, and may have been derived from the ancient city of that name. There is evidence that it was brought into England at the time of the Norman conquest, and was then written De Dole. The emigrant ancestor of the New England Doles, and in fact of nearly all who bear the name in America, was Richard Dole, son of William and grandson of Richard Dole, of Ringsworthy, near Bristol, England. He was baptized in Ringsworthy, December 31, 1622 (O. S.), and at an early age was apprenticed to John Towle, a glover of Bristol. In 1630 he accompanied the Towle family to New England, and in 1639 went with them to Newbury, Massachusetts, continuing in their employ as a clerk for some time after their settlement in that town. Being a young man of activity and enterprise, he embraced the first opportunity to engage in business for himself, and became a prosperous merchant and an extensive landowner. He left at his death, the date of which is unknown, an estate valued at eighteen hundred and forty pounds. His first wife, who died November 16, 1678, was Hannah (Robie) Dole, of Newbury. His second wife was Hannah, widow of Captain Samuel Brocklebank, of Rowley, Massachusetts. His third wife was Patience (Walker) Dole, of Haverhill, same state. His children were: John, Richard, Anna, Benjamin, Joseph, William, Henry, Hannah, Apphia and Abner.

(I) Henry Dole, a descendant of Richard Dole, the emigrant, was born in Newbury, February 4, 1780. At the age of twenty-four years he went from his native town to Limerick, Maine, where he engaged in farming, and resided there for the greater part of his life. His death occurred April 21, 1855. He married Sarah Butler, who was born March 3, 1785, died March 21, 1826, and she bore him eleven children, namely: Albert, Luther, Henry, Almira, John, Ira, Silas, Edmund, Erastus, Phebe and Moses C.

(II) Erastus, eighth son and ninth child of Henry and Sarah (Butler) Dole, was born in Limerick, May 15, 1822. In 1840 he went to Campton, New Hampshire where in company with Moses Cook he engaged in the manufacture of woolen clothing, and a short time later he became associated with his brothers, John and Moses C., in the same line of business under the firm name of Dole Brothers. Ezekiel Hodgdon succeeded John Dole, Henry Cook was also admitted to the firm and at the latter's death the other partners purchased his interest. Erastus Dole continued at the head of the firm of E. Dole & Company for the remainder of his life which terminated August 2, 1902, and he was a successful manufacturer. He served with ability as a selectman and also as town treasurer, represented his district in the lower branch of the legislature, and in politics supported the Republican party. On June 26, 1850, he married for his first wife Samantha Cook, who was born in Campton, January 31, 1822, and died in Lowell, Massachusetts, in August, 1880. His second wife was before marriage Flora E. Hoyt, born in Wentworth, August 25, 1844. His first wife bore him two sons: Moody C. and Herbert E.

(III) Moody Cook, eldest son of Erastus and Samantha (Cook) Dole, was born in Campton, May 17, 1853. Having acquired a good practical education, which was completed at the Kimball Union Academy, Meriden, he entered his father's factory as an apprentice and acquired a good knowledge of the business, including the financial as well as the industrial departments. At the present time he owns a third interest in the enterprise, which is still carried on under the old firm name of E. Dole & Company. This concern manufactures clothing of an excellent quality, and is widely known in that line of trade. In addition to his interest in the above-mentioned enterprise Mr. Dole owns the Campton Electric Light plant and acts as its superintendent. As a Republican he was chosen a representative to the legislature, and for a period of five years served as town treasurer. He is an Odd Fellow and past noble grand of the local lodge. Mr. Dole has been twice married. His first wife was Laura A. Blair, a native of Campton, who died August 29, 1882, and for his second wife he married, April 22, 1886, Lillian F. Merrill, of Thornton, born October 27, 1857, daughter of William and Sarah (Whitney) Merrill. His children, all of his second union, are: Erastus, born March 16, 1889; Florence E., November 28, 1891; Roland, January 7, 1893; Olive, October 24, 1896; Sarah, October 12, 1897; Dorothy, September 27, 1900.

HINMAN The name Hinman is found in England, Ireland and Scotland, and also in Germany, where it terminates with two n's (Hinmann). It has been spelled indifferently with or without the initial H, Hinman and Inman. This article deals with the first Hinman family in New England, its founder being first found in Connecticut, and not in Massachusetts, as most of the early settlers were. Many of this stock have been soldiers, and thirteen of the name from the town of Woodbury, Connecticut, were in the Revolution, including a captain.

(I) Sergeant Edward Hinman was at Stratford, Connecticut, between 1650 and 1652, but when he came from England or in what ship he came is unknown. Family tradition states that Edward Hinman was a sergeant of the bodyguard of King Charles I, and escaped to America in the time of Oliver Cromwell, who sought to do him harm. If he was a member of the King's Guard, he must have been a respectable Englishman, and if he was loyal to his King he was a true and trustworthy man. Sergeant Edward is supposed to have been one of the company of Captain Underhill, whose services were offered to fight the Mohawks and rejected by Governor Stuyvesant. This company was disbanded at Stamford soon afterward, and

Erastus Dole

from Stamford Edward Hinman went to Stratford and located. About 1650 or 1651 he had a house-lot in Stratford. He had several lots of land by division of the town lands, and by purchase, as the record shows. He was a farmer while at Stratford, and an extensive landholder, and took a stand, which is now approved, in the church quarrel at Stratford. He was the first owner of the old tide mill between Stratford and what is now Bridgeport, and some of his descendants have owned the mill and been concerned in milling there ever since. He sold his homestead in Stratford in 1681, and removed to Woodbury, and soon after died, November 26, 1681. He married, about 1651, after he went to Stratford, Hannah Stiles, daughter of Francis and Sarah, who removed from Windsor to Stratford. Their children were: Sarah, Titus, Samuel, Benjamin, Hannah, Mary, Patience and Edward. (Mention of Edward and descendants appears in this article).

(II) Captain Titus, the eldest son of Sergeant Edward and Hannah (Stiles) Hinman, was a military man, and a person of prominence. He was a member of the general assembly in 1715-16-19-20. He married (first), Hannah Coe, of Stamford, (second), January, 1702, Mary Hawkins, of Woodbury. He died April, 1736, aged eighty The children by his first wife were: Ephraim, Joseph, Andrew and Titus; and by the second wife: Ebenezer, Titus, Eleazer, Timothy, Mary, Hannah and Patience.

(III) Joseph, second son and child of Captain Titus and Hannah (Coe) Hinman, was born in June. 1687. He married in November, 1714, Esther Downs, and had children: Ebenezer, Joseph, Tabitha, Esther, Eunice, Mabel, Amos, Elijah, Daniel and Lois.

(IV) Elijah, the third son of Joseph and Esther (Downs) Hinman who attained manhood, was born April 8, 1733, married and removed to Vermont. He had Elijah, Amos and other children.

(V) Elijah (2), eldest son of Elijah (1) Hinman, was baptized in Woodbury, Connecticut, August 22, 1763, and removed with his father's family to Vermont.

(VI) Joseph (2), son of Elijah (2) Hinman, is said to have been born in Canterbury, Connecticut; with more propriety it may be thought that he was was born and resided in Vermont. He was one of the early settlers of Stratford, New Hampshire, where he settled soon after 1800, and was a farmer and also engaged in the manufacture of cloth. He married Diana, daughter of Elijah Blodgett.

(VII) George Washington, son of Joseph (2) and Diana (Blodgett) Hinman, was born in Northumberland, New Hampshire, April 4, 1816, and died in Stratford in 1903, aged eighty-seven years. He was a blacksmith and a millowner, and as there was no village in the town at the time he started in business, he selected a site near the center of the town, and there established his industries which he carried on for a number of years. He was an industrious and energetic man, and attended closely to his own affairs In politics he was first a whig and an Abolitionist, and on the establishment of the Republican party one of its supporters. His party was always in the minority in Stratford and Mr. Hinman consequently held no political offices. He married Mary Ann Curtis, and eight children were born of this marriage: George, now of Groveton; Mary L., who resides in Northumberland: Charles D., a dentist in Portsmouth; Emily H., the wife of Thomas Sweetser; Rose Ann, who married James H. Prince; Frank, deceased; Frederick A., who is mentioned below; and Hattie, who married Abram Bryant.

(VIII) Frederick Albert, seventh child of George W. and Mary Ann (Curtis) Hinman, was born in Stratford, November 6, 1855, and obtained his education in the district schools of that town. Subsequently he became a clerk in a store at Stratford Hollow, on the Connecticut river, where he was employed winters, and during the remainder of the year worked at home on the farm. In 1877 he engaged in agricultural pursuits on his own account, and now owns a farm of about one hundred and seventy-five acres which he cultivates with success and lives independently. In politics he is an Independent Republican occasionally giving his suffrage to a deserving Democratic candidate rather than support an unworthy member of his own party. He has been a member of the Baptist Church, and was superintendent of the Baptist Sunday School for twenty years, resigning that office in January, 1906. Mr. Hinman is a man of strict integrity, regards his word as good as his bond, and is a person whose influence and example have long been for good in the community where he resides. He married, 1902, Abbie Larrabee, of Canterbury, Vermont.

(II) Edward (2) Hinman, youngest son of Edward (1) Hinman, the Pilgrim, and his wife, Hannah Stiles, was born at Stratford, in 1672, and was the only son of Edward (1) who settled at Stratford with his father. By the request of his father he was brought up to a trade by Jehial Preston, of Stratford, with whom he remained until he attained his majority. He drew eighteen acres of land in the land division in Woodbury in 1702; hence, may have been of that town for a short time. He lived and died in Stratford, where all his children were born. He was one of the first Episcopalians in Connecticut, and signed the petition to segregate the churchmen from the Congregationalists in Connecticut about the time that Rev. Mr. Pigot began to preach the doctrines of the Church of England to the people of Stratford. He sustained a high character of integrity and moral worth, and his memory is much honored by his descendants. He married Hannah Jennings and had: Jonah, Hannah, Zachariah, Samuel, Justus, Ebenezer, Sarah, John, Rachel, Ebenezer, Amos and Charity.

(III) Ebenezer, sixth or tenth child of Edward (2) and Hannah (Jennings) Hinman, was born probably October 5, 1709, and died November 18, 1795, aged about eighty-six years (says the record). He moved his family to Woodbury to take charge of the old tide mill and a farm of his grandfather, Sergeant Edward, now the property of his cousin, Captain Timothy Hinman. He married, June 4, 1739 (O. S.), Obedience Jennings, who was born in 1720 and died December 15, 1812, aged ninety-two years. Their children were: Ephraim, Eben, Edward, Sarah, Michael, Philo, Hannah, Betty, Molly, and Ithuel or Bethuel.

(IV) Eben, second son and child of Ebenezer and Obedience (Jennings) Hinman, was born at Stratford, January 25, 1742, and died in 1810. He married Eunice Chatfield, of Derby, Connecticut, who died at the house of her son Elijah, in Otsego county, New York, in 1823. The children of this union were: Sarah, Solomon C., Eunice, Lucy and Elijah.

(V) Solomon Chatfield, second child and eldest son of Eben and Eunice (Chatfield) Hinman, was born in Derby, Connecticut, December 23, 1779. He resided in Southbury, Roxbury, Derby, Bristol, and other places in Connecticut, and then removed to Brunswick, Vermont, but during the Indian troubles in the year 1811 returned to Connecticut, where he remained two years. Going again with his family to the Green Mountain State, he lived a few years in Brunswick, and then settled in Bristol, Connecticut, later removing from that place to Cincinnati, Ohio, and finally to Westchester and Philadelphia, Pennsylvania, where he died December 29, 1861, aged eighty-three years. He married, in Oxford, Connecticut, Urania Hawkins, who was born in May, 1781, and died in Philadelphia, March 6, 1866, aged eighty-four years. They had three children: Daniel B., Harvey, and Havilah Burritt.

(VI) Harvey, second child of Solomon C. and Urania (Hawkins) Hinman, was born in Bristol, Connecticut, September 15, 1803, and was reared and educated partly in Connecticut and partly in Vermont. He followed farming on his own account in Brunswick and Canaan, Vermont, and later removed to North Stratford, New Hampshire. There he lived thirty-five years and a large part of that time kept a tavern. He died there March 20, 1886, aged eighty-three years. He married Harriet Hugh, who was born in Brunswick, Vermont, April 5, 1812, and died December, 1884, aged seventy-four years. She was the daughter of John and Abigail (Hall) Hugh. Their children were: Solomon C., died in infancy; Urania, deceased; Phoebe N., a resident of Stratford; Mary W., deceased; and Havilah B. All were born in Canaan, Vermont.

(VII) Havilah Burritt, fifth child and second son of Harvey and Harriet (Hugh) Hinman, was born in Canaan, Vermont, February 19, 1851, and educated in the public schools of Stratford, New Hampshire, whither his parents had removed when he was twenty-two months of age. In 1867 he entered the employ of the Grand Trunk Railway Company as a clerk, and remained four years and then resigned. At the age of twenty-one he began life on his own account as a farmer, livery man and hotel keeper at North Stratford. For thirty-five years he has carried on a flourishing business, supplying country produce to the various market men. He is extensively engaged in real estate and pulp wood, but still attending to the other lines of business. In politics he is a Democrat, and has taken a prominent part in town affairs and filled various offices. He was collector of taxes of Stratford three years; selectman eighteen to twenty years, and chairman of the board a number of years; representative to the legislature in 1879; delegate to the constitutional convention in 1903; and deputy sheriff of Coos county ten years. He is a member of many fraternities, among which is that of the Masons, in which he has attained the Thirty-second degree. He is a member of Island Pond Lodge, No. 44, Free and Accepted Masons, of Island Pond, Vermont; North Star Royal Arch Chapter, No. 16, and North Star Commandery, Knights Templar, of Lancaster, New Hampshire, and of Edward A. Raymond Consistory, Royal and Select Masters, of Nashua, New Hampshire; also Coos Grange, No. 30, Patrons of Husbandry, of which he is a past master; Stratford Lodge, No. 30, Knights of Pythias, of which he is a past chancellor; Coos Lodge, No. 2533, Knights of Honor, of which he is a past dictator; and grand dictator of New Hampshire. He married, December 28, 1873, Kate M. Barrett, who was born in Canaan, Maine, January 1, 1855, daughter of Levi S. and Hannah (Holmes) Barrett, of Canaan, Maine. Ten children have been born to them: Harvey L., Harriet H., Carrie, died in infancy, Burritt H., John H., Harold P., Mary H., Hazen B., Hal Stearns, died in infancy, and Alice H. Harvey L. graduated from Norwich University in 1894, took a course in Eastman's Business College, Poughkeepsie, New York, was in the employ of the Berlin mills for a time, held a position in the revenue postal service between Island Pond and Portland, Maine, and is now a postal clerk on the Grand Trunk railroad. He married Emily McBride, of Somerville, Massachusetts, and they have one child, Doris H. Burritt H. was a student at Colebrook, New Hampshire, and Exeter, New Hampshire, Phillips Exeter Academy three years, and then at Dartmouth College, from which he graduated in 1904, and after three years' attendance at Michigan University graduated from the law department of the institution in 1907. He is now in the law office of Amy & Hunt, Island Pond, Vermont. John H. graduated from the Stratford high school with the class of 1902, and from Dartmouth in the class of 1908. Harold P. graduated from the Stratford high school in 1906, and is now a student at Dartmouth, class of 1910, Harriet H. was educated in music in California and since October 1, 1905, has been postmistress of Coos, New Hampshire. Mary H. graduated from the Stratford high school in 1906, and is now at Wheaton Seminary, Norton, Massachusetts. Hazen B. is in high school at Stratford, sophomore year. Alice H. is a student in the grammar school at North Stratford.

Kate M. (Barrett) Hinman traces her ancestry on the paternal side to natives of England, from whence they emigrated to this country and were among the first settlers of Concord, Massachusetts.

The first of the family of whom there is authentic record was Nathaniel Barrett, a native of Concord, Massachusetts, from whence he removed to Westford, same state, and continued to reside there until his death, which took place in 1772. He married Mary Winter, of Acton, Massachusetts, who bore him four sons and four daughters, all born at Medford, Massachusetts. The sons were: 1. John, born about 1762, settled in Dublin, New Hampshire, where all his children were born. He removed from there to Maine and died in Dover, that state, about the year 1845. He was a soldier in the Revolutionary army, and was at the taking of Burgoyne. He married Susanna Chalmers, of Boston, Massachusetts, by whom he had three children: William Chalmers, Arathusa and Lucinda. William Chalmers Barrett married Betsey Davis of Fairfield, Maine, by whom he had several children, among whom were John, now deceased, and Charles, who with one or two brothers reside in California. William C. Barrett removed from Fairfield to Dover, Maine, where his death occurred. 2. Nathaniel, Jr., was a soldier in the Revolutionary army, and was at the taking of Burgoyne. He married (first), Lydia Atwood, of Temple, New Hampshire, by whom he had four sons and four daughters, all of whom were born in Temple, in which town he settled. His sons were: Charles, Oliver, Alvin and Nathaniel, Jr. Charles settled in Lowell, Massachusetts, died there, and left a widow and children. Oliver settled in New Ipswich, Massachusetts. Alvin, supposed by his relatives to be deceased. Nathaniel, Jr., resides in Temple, New Hampshire. Nathaniel Barrett married (second), Sybil Spaulding, by whom he had three sons and one daughter. His sons were: Artemas, William and Hiram. Artemas died in infancy. William died in the United States army, August 13, 1862, aged forty-three years. He married Eli:a Russell,

H B Hinman

of Norridgewock, Maine, by whom he had five children, four of whom are now living, one son and three daughters. Hiram, resides in Clinton, Maine; he married Maria Ellis, of Fairfield, Maine, by whom he has three children now living, one son and two daughters. Nathaniel Barrett, second son of Nathaniel Barrett, and father of these children, died December 29, 1853, aged eighty-nine years. 3. Levi, who was a captain in the drafted militia in the war of 1812, and was stationed on the seaboard at Edgecomb, Maine. He also served as justice of the peace. He removed from Templeton, Massachusetts, to Fairfield, Maine, in 1802, and died there October 10, 1851, aged eighty-four years. He married Rebecca Sawyer, of Templeton, Massachusetts, by whom he had two sons and four daughters. The sons, Joseph and Levi, both died unmarried. 4. Joseph, the subject of the following paragraph.

Joseph Barrett, youngest son of Nathaniel and Mary (Winter) Barrett, was born in Westford, Massachusetts, in 1770. He was a captain in the state militia of Maine. He removed from Templeton, Massachusetts, to Dublin, New Hampshire; from thence to Ludlow, Vermont; from thence to Fairfield, Maine; from thence to Canaan, Maine, where he died January 29, 1817, aged forty-seven years. He married and had five sons and two daughters. The sons were: 1. Joseph, born March 7, 1798, in Ludlow, Vermont. 2. Silas, born in Templeton, Massachusetts, August 22, 1800, died in Augusta, Maine, February, 1845, aged forty-five years. He married Ann Moore, an English lady, by whom he had five children, two sons and three daughters; the sons were Franklin, died in childhood, and Silas, now living. 3. Levi, the subject of the following paragraph. 4. John, died in 1813, aged five years. 5. Harrison, born 1814.

Levi, son of Joseph and ——— Barrett, was born in Fairfield, Maine, November, 1804. He was a resident of Canaan, Maine, and active in promoting its welfare and development. He married Lucinda Corson, by whom he had thirteen children, eight sons and five daughters, namely: Levi S., Alonzo C., Albion Dudley, William Henry, Frank A., Edward W., John W., George F., Lucinda S., Caroline L., Louisa O., Isabel A. and Elizabeth P. Four of the sons—Alonzo C., Albion Dudley, William Henry and Frank A.—served in the Civil war, and all returned home safe and well. William Henry was a captain and brevet major at the close of the war.

Levi S., eldest son of Levi and Lucinda (Corson) Barrett, was born December 14, 1830. He was a resident of Canaan, Maine, and was in the lumber business. He was an exemplary citizen in every respect, and faithfully performed all the duties allotted to him. He was united in marriage with Hannah Holmes, of Canaan, Maine, born August 4, 1833, and died January 11, 1888. Five children were born to them: Kate M., wife of Havilah Burritt Hinman; Alonzo D., Carrie L., Hattie, died in infancy, and Ensign H. Mr. Barrett is living at the present time (1907) in Gorham, New Hampshire.

FIFIELD The name Fifield is a contraction of "finefield," the place by which the first Fifield lived, first using the expression "finefield" to designate his place of residence, and later as his surname. The Fifields of this sketch are not shown by the records to be connected with the pioneers of Massachusetts from whom they are probably descended.

(I) John Fifield was born in Brentwood, New Hampshire, May 27, 1799. About 1840 he removed from Brentwood to Fayette, Maine, where for many years he was engaged in farming and carpentering. He died in February, 1882. He was a man of strong religious convictions and a member of the Baptist Church. He married, November 14, 1826, Mary Morrill, of Brentwood, who was born April 25, 1798, and died October 4, 1861. She was a descendant of Captain William and Mary (Gordon) Morrill, of Brentwood. (See Morrill, VII). Their children were: Sarah, John Morrill, Mary Ann, Hubbard, killed in Civil war. The only living child is Mary Ann Watson, of West Boxbury, Massachusetts.

(II) John Morrill, son of John and Mary (Morrill) Fifield, was born in Brentwood, May 6, 1830. He was educated in the public schools of Fayette, and at the Maine Wesleyan Seminary at Kents Hill, Maine. He engaged in trade at Mount Vernon, where he remained twelve years. In 1866 he went to Portland, where he was associated with different dry goods firms, including Locke, Meserve & Company, Deering, Milliken & Company, Locke, Twitchell & Company, and Twitchell, Chapman & Company, having an interest in some of these firms, and in others serving as a clerk or commercial traveler. For Albion, Little & Company he was collecting agent for four years. About 1887 when the store of Twitchell, Chapman & Company was burned, he removed to Conway, and there in company with F. W. Davis and H. B. Fifield purchased the store of Roscoe Flanders, and from that time till his death, October 7, 1896, he carried on business with them as partners, under the name of J. M. Fifield & Company. He married, December 14, 1854, Elizabeth A. Boardman, who was born in New Sharon, Maine, May 6, 1832, and who is now living in Conway. She is the only surviving child of Holmes Allen and Betsey T. (Titcomb) Boardman, of New Sharon. Five children were born of this union, three of whom died in infancy, and only two of whom are now living, Holmes B., who is mentioned below, and Horace P., who was born June 28, 1862. For a number of years he was a clerk in his father's store, following that employment up to the time of the death of his father. Afterward he was manager of the business, of which he was part owner. In 1904 he removed to Lynn, Massachusetts, where he is now in business as general merchant. He married Alice Ward Burnham, daughter of Albert W. and Ellen (Ward) Burnham, of Lowell, Massachusetts. They have two children: Dorothy B. and Donald Morrill.

(III) Holmes Boardman, eldest surviving child of John Morrill and Elizabeth A. (Boardman) Fifield, was born in Mount Vernon, Maine, December 22, 1855. He attended the common and high schools of Portland, and at the age of twenty entered Bowdoin College, from which he was graduated in 1879. During the six years following he was employed as a clerk in a wholesale dry goods house in Portland. In 1884 he went to Conway, New Hampshire, and there formed a partnership with Frank W. Davis under the firm name of Davis & Fifield, dealers in dry goods and men's clothing. This partnership continued thirteen years and then dissolved, each partner taking certain lines and continuing in business. Mr. Fifield was one of the firm of Fifield Brothers, grocers, till 1904, and since that time is of the firm of H. B. Fifield & Co. He was president of the Conway Water Company for several years, and is now one of its directors and was for several years vice president of the Conway Savings Bank. In politics he is a Republican. He has filled the office of moderator three years, was a member of the legislature in 1893, has been a member of the board of education for six years, and special justice of the police court since its establishment. He is a member of the Congregational Church at Conway and has been its clerk for twenty-three years. Fraternally he is a member of Mt. Washington Lodge, No. 87, Free and Accepted Masons, of North Conway, of which he is a past master; of Signet Royal Arch Chapter, of North Conway; of Swift River Lodge, No. 84, Independent Order of Odd Fellows, of Conway. He married, June 20, 1888, Helen M. Gibson, who was born in Paris, Maine, 1864, daughter of James M. and Martha (Eastman) Gibson. (See Gibson, VII). Mrs. Fifield is a member of Anna Stickney Chapter, Daughters of the American Revolution, of North Conway. The children born to Mr. and Mrs. Fifield are: Ernest G., Martha B., Lillian and Mildred.

JONES The name Jones is of Welsh origin, being in the possessive case, so to speak, and is derived from the christian name John. The Welsh distinguished themselves one from another by employing the Welsh preposition "ap," which literally rendered means "the son of," If a Welshman named John had a son named Thomas, the son was called, for distinction, "Thomas Ap Jon" or Thomas, the son of John, Later an "s' was added, also an "e" inserted, for the sake of euphony and the "h" dropt (Johns, Johnes, Jones). The great warrior and crusader, Sir Hugh Johnys, or Jones, derived his name in this way.

Jones, or Ap John, was the name of one of the princely tribes of the Cimbri. They ruled as independent princes when Wales was free. This was the name of one of fifteen nobles, or princely houses of Wales. Their possessions were in the north of Wales, chiefly in Denbigh. Here they lived for several generations, and in the time of Henry the Eighth were active in public life during the troubles that arose so thickly about the latter part of King Henry's reign. A part of the family went into England, others went to Ireland and in the history of the Jones family in Ireland we quote:

"The family of Joneses were able men in every department of public life, great statesmen, great prelates and victorious generals. There is that equal blending of the physical, mental and the moral, never found but in pure races of people." The transmission of physical conformation and facial expression of the Jones family has been an interesting study to the philosopher. In some families one can trace for centuries the same expression, features and color. Captain Jones, Royal Navy, M. P. for Londonderry, Rear Admiral Sir Tobias Jones, the Rev. Thomas J. Jones, of Armagh Diocese, have the same class of features, type of expression, etc.

(I) Lewis Jones, born 1600, and Ann his wife, came to Roxbury, Massachusetts, from England, about 1640, bringing with them two children. The late Amos Perry said they came from county Berkshire, England, in the ship, "Increase." Their names are on the records of John Eliot's church in Roxbury. Lewis lived in that part of Roxbury called "the Nookes, next Dorchester." In 1650 he moved his family to that part of Watertown called "the Farms," and now part of the town of Weston, where he had commercial transactions, bought and sold land and owned much real estate, some of which is still in the hands of his descendants. A monument has been erected by his descendants to his memory in Mount Auburn cemetery, Cambridge, Massachusetts. He made his will January 7, 1678, and died April 11, 1684. His wife died May 1, 1680. He brought from England a silver tankard, on which is engraved a coat-of-arms, which is now in possession of a descendant, Mrs. Octavius Newell, of Kenosha, Wisconsin. His children were: Lydia, Josiah, Phoebe and Shubael.

(II) Josiah, first son and second child of Lewis and Ann Jones, was born about 1640. He married Lydia, daughter of Nathaniel and Sufferance (How) Treadway, of Watertown, Massachusetts, October 2, 1667. He procured a tract of land near the center of the town of Weston, Massachusetts, which was then a part of Watertown. He was admitted freeman April 18, 1690. Bond's "History of Watertown" says: "About 1691-2 the town was divided into three military precincts. The third was the precinct of Lieutenant (Josiah) Jones's company of those who belonged to the Farmer's precinct, now Weston." He was later appointed captain of the militia. He was one of the original members and one of the first deacons of Weston Church, to which office he was elected January 4, 1709-10. He was selectman in 1685-87-90, 1702-09. The record of Captain Josiah's grandchildren and great-grandchildren contains numerous facts of interest. A good number of his descendants were graduates of New England colleges and some were benefactors. Josiah died October 3, 1714, aged seventy-four years. His widow died September 16, 1743, aged ninety-four years. His children were: Lydia, Josiah, Mary, Nathaniel, Samuel, James, Sarah, Anna, John and Isaac.

(III) Samuel, third son and fifth child of Josiah and Lydia (Treadway) Jones, was born July 9, 1677. He married Mary Woolson, daughter of Thomas and Sarah (Hyde) Woolson, of Weston, May 19, 1706. He settled on the east side of his father's farm. His will, dated January 14, 1717, was proved April 9, 1718. He died January 6, 1718. On his gravestone he is called "Ensign." His children were: Samuel, Moses and Mary.

(IV) Moses, second son and second child of Samuel and Mary (Woolson) Jones, was born in Weston, June 20, 1709. Married Hannah Bemis, July 20, 1737. He died July 21, 1755. His children were: Moses, Joseph, Solomon, Mary, Hannah.

(V) Solomon, third son and child of Moses and Hannah (Bemis) Jones, was born April 20, 1742. Married, March 14, 1764, Beulah Stratton, daughter of Jonathan and Dinah (Bemis) Stratton. He was a sergeant in the Revolutionary war, after which service he moved to Hillsboro, New Hampshire, where he died February 18, 1806. His widow died in Washington, New Hampshire, June 28, 1832. His children were: Moses, Lydia, Sally, Solomon, Joseph, Martha, ——— (died eight months old).

(VI) Moses (2), first child of Solomon and Beulah (Stratton) Jones, was born in Weston, June 20, 1765, and married (first), May 12, 1786, Hepzibah Dillaway. Directly after his marriage he moved to Hillsboro, New Hampshire, and after residing a short time on Bible Hill, settled in the same town, on the highlands, a mile and a half south of East Washington Village. The farm, though long since deserted, is still known as the "Tenney Place." In 1817 he removed to the east part of Washington. His wife died in Hillsboro, January, 1801, and he married (second), Catherine, daughter of Deacon William Graves, of Washington, New Hampshire, February 9, 1802. He died in Washington, May 7, 1840. Catherine, his wife, died January 21, 1865. His children were: (first wife) Moses, Charles,

Joseph C. Jones

Solomon E Jones

Solomon E. Jones

William, Isaac, Mary, Martha; (second wife) Solomon E., Simon W., Nathaniel G., Hiram, Catherine M., Amos B. and Eliza A. (Mention of Solomon E. follows in this article).

(VII) Charles, second son of Moses (2) and Hepzibah (Dillaway) Jones, was born in Hillsboro, New Hampshire, September 25, 1789. Married Abigail Seaverns. of Westford, Massachusetts., residing a short time after marriage in Roxbury, Massachusetts, but removed to Washington about the year 1812, and settled on the hill, two miles south of East Washington. He was the first settler on the farm, and was a respected and prominent citizen and often held town office. A short time before his death he removed to Hillsboro with his son, William F., with whom he resided, and died there December 12, 1872. His wife died in Hillsboro, October 4, 1878. His children were: Abigail S., Adaline B., Charles, Samuel. Martha, Catherine, William F., Henry D., Joannah, Mary D., Joseph C., Nancy A. Eliza N. and Moses G.

(VIII) Joseph Clark, fifth son and eleventh child of Charles and Abigail (Seaverns) Jones, was born in Washington, New Hampshire, May 25, 1825. Married Clara H. Dow, of Washington. January 28, 1847. She died in Washington, September 16, 1865. He married for his second wife, Mrs. Mary F. (Carr) Morrill, October 16, 1866. He resided many years in Washington, where he was an influential citizen. He served as selectman 1861-62-64, also as town clerk 1859-60, and represented the town in the legislature 1866. He was a captain in the state militia. He moved to Manchester, New Hampshire, and carried on the grocery business until his second marriage, when he removed to Claremont, New Hampshire, where he still resides, and has been engaged in the meat, milk and cattle business. He is a noted sportsman, and few are his equal with the gun and rod. His children were: (First wife) Clark C., born in Washington, December 28. 1847, died November 14, 1859. Mary E., born in Washington, August 4, 1852. Fred D., born in Washington, November 6, 1861, died April 29, 1863.

(IX) The only child of the second wife, Gertrude B., born in Claremont, New Hampshire, September 9, 1871, married, December 17, 1890, Charles H. Bartlett, son of Gustavus and Susan A. (Nichols) Bartlett, of Milford, New Hampshire. Was educated in public schools in Claremont, New England Conservatory of Music and Boston University. Upon her marriage she went from her native town to Manchester, New Hampshire, where her home was until 1895, when she removed to Boston, and has since resided there. She has taught music for many years, and her compositions have been well received by music publishers. She is a member of various organizations, among them the Manchester Musical Club, where she held the office of president; New Hampshire's Daughters' Club, in which she has held office, and is a member of the Portia Club of Boston, an organization composed of women lawyers of Massachusetts.

(VII) Solomon E., fifth son of Moses (2) Jones, and eldest child of his second wife, Catherine Graves, was born September 12, 1803, in Hillsboro, and removed to East Washington with his parents in youth. There he spent the remainder of his life. In early manhood he was a successful and popular teacher in the district schools of Washington and vicinity. For a short time he was engaged in farming, and purchased a store at East Washington of Cooledge, Graves & Company, which he conducted successfully. He was an influential citizen, and always took a deep interest in everything that pertained to the town of Washington, and was called to fill all the important offices of the town. He was the friend and promoter of all worthy causes. and was cordial with all whom he met, thus winning their respect and love. He died July 19, 1871, near the close of his sixty-eighth year. He was married June 9, 1831, to Harriet Louise Smith, of Sharon, Massachusetts, who survived him more than twenty years, dying early in January, 1892. Following is a brief account of their children: Harriett A., the eldest, died at the age of three years; Amos B., the second, graduated at Dartmouth College, was an officer in Berdan's famous regiment of sharp shooters during the Civil war, and has been engaged in various mining and railroad enterprises in the southern states of this country and in Mexico. He resided for a time in Duluth, Minnesota, in Seattle, Washington, and is at present in Havana, Cuba.

(VIII) Julia Ann, youngest child of Solomon E. and Harriet L. (Smith) Jones, was born January 3, 1841, in Washington, and graduated at New London Literary and Scientific Institution (now Colby Academy) in 1861, as valedictorian of her class. She was class historian two years later. For some time she was principal of the Rumford Grammar School in Concord, New Hampshire. She has been frequently invited to speak before women's clubs and teachers' associations, and has met with very flattering success in that line. She has traveled extensively, has resided in Washington. D. C.; in Brooklyn, New York; and Englewood, New Jersey. Since 1900 her home has been in the Borough of Manhattan, Greater New York. She was married, December 25, 1867, to General Samuel A. Duncan, a native of Meriden, New Hampshire, a distinguished and brilliant man, who died October 17, 1895. Their children were: Frederick S., Robert J., Mabel T., Alice B. and Ruth H. The first is a graduate of Harvard College and Columbia Law School, and is a practicing lawyer in New York. The second son died at the age of thirty-five years, and the eldest daughter in her twentieth year. The second daughter is the wife of McGregor Jenkins, who is connected with the management of the *Atlantic Monthly*. The youngest married Judge John Duff, of Boston, Massachusetts.

(Second Family.)

JONES Many branches of this family are scattered throughout the United States, while but few lines can be traced to the original American ancestor. The one herein treated is among the oldest, and has contributed many useful citizens to New England and the United States.

(I) Thomas Jones, of Gloucester, Massachusetts, was born about 1598, probably in England or Wales, and is found in Gloucester as early as 1642. when he owned a house near the burying place in that town. He was made a freeman in 1653, and died September 2, 1671, leaving an estate valued at £147, 15s. He went to New London, Connecticut, in 1651, and returned the same year. His wife Mary, daughter of Richard and Ursula North, survived him about ten years, and died February 4, 1681-82. Their children included Thomas, North and Ruth (twins), Samuel, Ephraim. Benjamin, Remember, Susanna and two other daughters whose names are not preserved.

(II) Thomas (2), eldest child of Thomas (1) and Mary (North) Jones, was born March 15, 1640, in Gloucester, and died August 6, 1718, in New London, Connecticut, where he was buried. He disappears from the records of Gloucester soon after attaining his majority, and probably removed at that time to New London. He lived at first near Alewife Cove, but moved to the north parish. He was among the original proprietors of Colchester, same colony. He was married, June 25, 1677, to Catherine, daughter of Thomas Gammon, of Newfoundland. They were the parents of a son Thomas and two daughters, and probably others about whom the records are silent.

(III) Thomas (3), son of Thomas (2) and Catherine (Gammon) Jones, was born probably in New London, Connecticut, and settled in Colchester, where he died October 27, 1729. He married, Mary Potter, and their children were: James, Jabez, Jonathan, Joshua, Rachel, Sarah, Susannah, Mary and Lucy.

(IV) Jabez, second son of Thomas (3) and Mary (Potter) Jones, was born in Colchester Connecticut, and undoubtedly passed his life in that town. He was married in 1730 to Anna Ransom, and they were the parents of the following children: Thomas, Jabez, Amos, Anna, Israel, Asa, Hazel, Jehiel, Ariel, Sarah and Abigail.

(V) Lieutenant Asa, fifth son of Jabez and Ann (Ransom) Jones, was born January 9, 1739, in Colchester, Connecticut, and was married April 19, 1761, to Sarah Treadway, who was born March 3, 1742, daughter of Josiah and Emma (Foot) Treadway. He removed to Claremont, New Hampshire, in 1768, being one of the pioneer settlers of that town, and died there June 19, 1810. After the Revolution, with his family he became affiliated with the Union Church at West Claremont, and his body was buried in the churchyard there, where five generations of his descendants also lie. The following is the inscription upon his tombstone: "Here lies Lieutenant Asa Jones, one of the first settlers of the town of Claremont, who died June 15, 1810, aged 71 years." Sarah (Treadway) Jones died at the home of her son Edward, in Richmond, Vermont, and was buried there. They were the parents of seventeen children, and thirteen of these followed his body to the grave. He built the house in which his descendants have lived, and which was kept in the family until very recently. It then passed into the hands of Captain George Long, and was destroyed by fire in September 1906. His farm lay on the banks of the Connecticut river. He was a soldier in both the Colonial service and the Revolutionary war. His children were: Asa, born July 18, 1762; Josiah, August 28, 1763; Sally, March 5, 1766; Jerusha, July 28, 1767; Jabez, November 10, 1768; Eunice, July 30, 1770; Lovice, November 13, 1771; Edward and Lucy, January 24, 1775; Thomas, December 25, 1778; Ansom, July 6, 1782; Ramson, July 23, 1784; Anne, May 3, 1786. Some of his sons were graduates of Dartmouth Colege, and one of these, Thomas, of Chelsea, Vermont, was a lawyer, a fine scholar and business man. The home stead passed by deed of gift to the eldest son May 4, 1787. In this deed the father is styled "gentleman" and the son, "yeoman."

(VI) Asa (2), eldest child of Asa (1) and Sarah (Treadway) Jones, was born July 18, 1762, in Colchester, Connecticut, and was six years of age when the family settled in Claremont. He received from his father's estate a tract of land on which now stands the Claremont Junction Station, of the Boston & Maine railroad. He was a fine business man, and added to his inheritance. He was married January 20, 1783, in Claremont, to Mary Pardee, daughter of Benjamin (2) and Hannah (Beecher) Pardee, of New Haven, Connecticut. The last named was a daughter of Samuel and Hannah (Farrington) Beecher, a relative of Rev. Lyman Beecher. They were the parents of eleven children: Worcester, born November 8, 1783; Zabina, June 20, 1785; Asa, February 22, 1787; Mary, October 18, 1788; William, February 11, 1791; Augustus, June 6, 1793; Fanny Beecher, April 28, 1795; Sally Rosetta, July 13, 1797; Nancy Malinda, September 17, 1799; Philander, August 13, 1801; Eliza Maria, March 9, 1804.

(VII) William, fourth son of Asa (2) and Mary (Pardee) Jones, was born February 11, 1791, in Claremont, New Hampshire, and lived on the estate inherited from his father, to which he added until it embraced about four hundred acres. He was active in securing the completion of the Sullivan railroad, whose station stands on his farm. In 1854 he built a large brick house on the side of the original homestead. While on a visit to his eldest daughter, Harriet P. Jones, he died in West Salisbury, Vermont, July 24, 1874, and his body was interred in the Union churchyard at West Claremont. He married (first), Harriet Patrick, who bore him two children, and was married (second), May 19, 1830, to Elisabeth Mary Mann, daughter of Stephen and Alice (Ainsworth) Mann. Stephen Mann came from Randolph, Massachusetts, and was one of the first settlers in Claremont. She was the mother of four children Harriet Patrick, born February 6, 1833; Lucien Eugene, May 26, 1834; Alice Ainsworth, January 9, 1836; Helen Elisabeth, August 29, 1838.

(VIII) Lucien E., only son of William and Elisabeth M. (Mann) Jones, was born May 26, 1834, in Claremont, New Hampshire, and remained on the parental homestead where he died January 3, 1891. He was married, May 26, 1869, to Ellen Jordan McLoughlin, widow of Francis Chase McLoughlin, and daughter of Charles P. Jordan, of East Bridgewater, Massachusetts. She survives and resides with her youngest son, on the homestead, where three generations have lived their entire lives.

(VIII) Helen Elisabeth, youngest child of William and Elisabeth M. (Mann) Jones, was born August 29, 1838, in Claremont, New Hampshire, and was married, August 9, 1865, to George Franklin Davis, of Windsor, Vermont. He was a son of Daniel Davis, who was born in Springfield, Vermont, a son of John and Elizabeth (Herrick) Davis, Chelmsford, Massachusetts. His mother, Alice Morgan, was born in Wethersfield, Vermont, a daughter of Colonel Samuel and Sybil (Huntington) Morgan, of Windham, Connecticut. The last named was a daughter of Eliphalet Huntington, who was born April 24, 1737, and died in Windham, Connecticut, June 15, 1799. Mr. Davis died in Windsor, Vermont, May 18, 1900. He was a very active business man all his life, and dropped dead at eight o'clock in the morning, while directing his men about some farm work. He was a breeder of fine stock, for which he found a ready market in Illinois and Missouri, at whose fairs he received numerous premiums. He spent the summers of 1869-70-71-72 in Kansas and Missouri, buying up large quantities of wool which he shipped to the Boston market. His first trip to the west was made at the age of sixteen years. In 1856-57 he resided in Springfield, Illinois, where his eldest child was born. After the death of his father he settled on the paternal acres in Windsor. At one time he had forty choice colts of his own breeding. He traveled much in New England and Canada, and was a noted story-teller. As he left his door for the last time, he turned back to relate a pleasing anecdote. Of his three children only one is living, namely:

(IX) William Jones Davis, born October 2,

1866, in Springfield, Illinois. He resides with his mother, on the estate of his father in Windsor, one of the old landmarks of that town. It includes five hundred acres lying on the west bank of the Connecticut river, and extending to Mount Ascutney.

(Third Family.)

JONES This name is very numerously represented in New Hampshire and has borne no inconsiderable part in the development of the state and its best interests. Its representatives have been modest and have made few claims to public attention, but the name has always carried with it respectability, faithfulness to duty and a firm standing in behalf of principle.

(I) Robert Jones is supposed to have been born about 1633. It is quite possible that he was a son of Thomas Jones, who was at Newbury in 1637, and Charlestown, Massachusetts, in 1650. Robert Jones was granted a "township" in Amesbury, Massachusetts, in 1666, and the next year received "children's land" for his son. He appears of record as a commoner and holder of a meeting house seat in 1667, and in the same year "Goodwife Jones" had a seat. He served under Captain Turner in King Philip's war, and participated in the Falls Fight in 1686. He signed a petition in 1630, and the records show himself and wife to have been living in 1686. He is referred to as Robert Jones Senior, in 1710. This is the last record of him, and his death does not appear. He was married about 1658 to Joanna Osgood, daughter of William and Elizabeth Osgood, pioneer residents of Salisbury, Massachusetts. She was born about 1638. Their children were: William, Robert, Elizabeth, Joseph, Mary, Hannah, Samuel and Jonathan.

(II) Joseph, third son and fourth child of Robert and Joanna (Osgood) Jones, was born October 7, 1664, in Salisbury, and resided in Amesbury. The inventory of his estate was made in 1689, indicating that he was at that time deceased. He was married before 1689 to Mary Gould, daughter of Nathan and Elizabeth Gould. of Amesbury. She was born June 24, 1661, and lived at some time in the service of George Carr, of Amesbury. She survived her husband, and was still living in 1714. Their children were: John, Damaris, Hannah and Mary.

(III) John, eldest child and only son of Joseph and Mary (Gould) Jones, resided in Amesbury. The record of his birth does not appear. He was married (first), April 27, 1706, in Amesbury, to Hannah "Hoege" of that town. His second wife was Susanna Fowler (intention of marriage published April 28, 1711, at Amesbury). daughter of Samuel and Hannah (Worthen) Fowler, granddaughter of Samuel Fowler, and great-granddaughter of Philip Fowler, of Ipswich, who was born before 1600, and died in 1678. She was born March 10, 1679, in Salisbury, and was still living in 1727. The will of Joseph Jones was made January 16, 1750, and proved June 25 following, which indicates the time of his death. His children were: Ebenezer (or Eleanor), Hannah, Abigail, Mary, Ann, Nathan, Lydia, Joseph, John, Susanna, Abner and Ezekiel. (Joseph and descendants receive mention in this article).

(IV) Nathan, eldest son and sixth child of John Jones and son of his second wife Susanna Fowler, was born, 1717, in Amesbury and settled in Kingston, New Hampshire. His wife's name was "Allas" and they were identified with the first church of Kingston.

(V) Jonathan, son of Nathan and Allas Jones, was born September 2, 1756. in Kingston, and settled in Danville, New Hampshire. His wife's name, as appears on the vital records of New Hampshire, was Nanney. He must have had two wives, as the records of South Hampton show his marriage, August 23, 1781, to Judith Jones, whose maiden name may or may not have been Jones. The records show the births of the following children: Jacob, Daniel, Jonathan, Ezekiel, and perhaps others.

(VI) Ezekiel, son of Jonathan and Nanney Jones, was born January 19, 1790, in Danville and died in Lakeport, 1874, aged eighty-four years. He settled first in Lakeport, and later was engaged in farming in Center Harbor. In politics he was a Republican, and in religious faith a Baptist. He married (first), Louise Timothy, and (second), Cynthia Clark, who was born in Moultonborough, July 1, 1817, and died in Lakeport, November 17, 1898, aged eighty-one years. By his second wife he had two children: Samuel Robinson and Eben Clark.

(VII) Samuel Robinson, elder of the two sons of Ezekiel and Cynthia (Clark) Jones, was born in Center Harbor, August 13, 1834, and died January 13, 1901. He attended the common schools, and then served as a locomotive fireman on the Boston, Concord & Montreal railroad, running principally between Concord and Woodsville, New Hampshire. Later he was promoted to engineer and ran an engine while he remained in the service. He then became a mechanic in the employ of the Concord & Montreal Railroad Company, and for twenty-seven years worked in their shops at Lakeport. Subsequently he engaged in the grocery business at Lakeport, where he did a profitable business. In 1879 he opened a branch store at Gilford, and carried on the two until 1898. He married Sarah Jane Durgin (deceased), who was born in Sanbornton, June 26, 1837, and they had one child, Herbert A., the subject of the next paragraph.

(VIII) Herbert Almon, son of Samuel R. and Sarah Jane (Durgin) Jones, was born in Lakeport, April 18, 1861, and attended the common schools of his native village and the Tilton Seminary, taking a commercial course at the latter institution. At the close of his school attendance he entered his father's store at Gilford, where he was employed as a clerk until 1898, when he bought out both his father's stores, and has since conducted them as sole owner. Mr. Jones is one of the leading merchants of his town, and has the confidence and respect of his townsmen. In politics he is a Republican. He was assistant postmaster nineteen years; trustee of the town library three terms, and town clerk since 1894. He married, June 24, 1883. Lizzie Emma Hunter, who was born in Gilford, September 11, 1861, daughter of Heman and Mary Jane (Folsom) Hunter. They have three children: Gardner Hunter, born in Gilford, June 3, 1888; Helen May, born July 27, 1890; and Carrie Maud, born October 10, 1897.

(IV) Joseph (2) second son and eighth child of John Jones, by his second wife, Susanna Fowler, was born 1722, in Amesbury, and settled in Kingston, New Hampshire, where he was married, January 11, 1744, to Abigail Flanders. Their children were: Philip, Richard, Johanna, Joseph and James.

(V) Richard, second son and child of Joseph (2) and Abigail (Flanders) Jones, was born February 19, 1750, in Kingston. He was a resident for many years in that part of Gilmanton, New Hampshire, which is now Belmont. He was married there, September 12, 1774, to Anna Weed, who bore him four children: James, Nicholas, Anna and Susan. After 1760 he removed to the wilderness of

Carroll county and settled in Wolfboro, where he cleared up land and established a home. He was a devout member of the Society of Friends, and was one of the four persons who formed a meeting of Friends in Gilmanton about the year 1780. He was an upright and modest man, and gave his attention to making a home for himself and family, paying no attention to political affairs. As a consequence very little is found of him in the records.

(VI) James, son of Richard and Anna (Weed) Jones, was born August 31, 1775, in Gilmanton, now Belmont, New Hampshire. He was faithful to the religious instruction of his parents and all his life walked honestly as a consistent member of the Society of Friends. In the same manner lived Nicholas, his brother, who appears to have shared with James the fortunes of life during his earlier years. James Jones was both a tiller of the soil, and a manufacturer of linseed oil at Jones Mills, Gilmanton, New Hampshire, and as a Friend probably took small interest in the affairs of the town in which he lived. James Jones married Ruth Hanson of Franconia, New Hampshire, and had four sons, Richard, Amos, James and William Jones.

(VII) Amos, second of the four sons of James and Ruth (Hanson) Jones, was born at Jones Mill, at Gilmanton, New Hampshire, May 18, 1816, and died there April 16, 1849. He too was a Friend, and married in that faith. In 1848 he moved with his father's family to Dover, New Hampshire, He married Hannah Bean Bassett of Wolfboro. She was born there March 18, 1816, and died March 13, 1889. Their children were John Gurney, Daniel Wheeler, Charles Amos, James Edward and George Washington Jones. The latter died in infancy.

(VIII) Charles Amos, third child and son of Amos and Hannah Bean (Bassett) Jones, was born in Gilmanton, New Hampshire, March 31, 1844, and was four years old when his father died. As a boy he attended the public schools at Gilmanton and Weare. He lived in the family of his grandparents in Gilmanton until old enough to begin work on his own account. When fourteen years old he went to Weare and found employment in the woolen mills. He was quick to learn, faithful in the performance of every duty given to him and in the course of a short time became well acquainted with the details of the work in the several departments of the factory. In one capacity and another Mr. Jones continued his connection with the mills in Weare more than twenty years, and during that time formed an excellent acquaintance with the people of the town and became interested in various local institutions. He is one of the charter members of Mt. William Lodge, Independent Order of Odd Fellows, and still is in good standing with that organization. For several years he served as member of the school board and in 1879 represented Weare in the lower house of the state legislature. In 1879 he was offered and accepted the position of superintendent of the Contoocook Mills at Hillsborough, New Hampshire, and soon afterward moved to that town. There, as in Weare, he has become identified with the best interests of the locality. He is a member of the Congregational Society of Hillsborough and has held the office of treasurer of that society more than twenty-five years.

On October 2, 1867, Mr. Jones married Anna Maria Sawyer of Weare, who was born May 3, 1847. She is a daughter of the late Allen Sawyer, born August, 1803, and died March 15, 1867, and Mary B. (Peaslee) Sawyer, born in Henniker, New Hampshire, December 26, 1819, and died February 26, 1882. The children of Charles Amos and Anna Maria (Sawyer) Jones are Helen Mabel, born September 16, 1878; Anna Alice, born April 7, 1871, and died June 7, 1871; and Chauncey Giles, a son by adoption, born December 7, 1875.

(Fourth Family.)

JONES This surname undoubtedly has been handed down from the Welsh of a period within the twelfth or thirteenth century, and while perhaps the name prevailed among that people for centuries, it eventually spread throughout England with the emigration of the seventeenth and eighteenth centuries found numerous representatives in America. The name itself is only one of the many derivations of the simple root John. In England there are known at least seventy-three distinct families of the surname Jones, each with its own coat-of-arms, and from these English and Welsh Joneses have sprung the later numerous families of that name in America, now more numerous beyond all question than in any other country of the earth. It cannot be said, therefore, that all the Joneses of America are descended from a common ancestor, or from one of the proverbial "three brothers." There are extant today at least half a dozen Jones family genealogies, each traced to the separate American ancestor of Welsh or English origin, and in no way related to each other except in name, while scores and possibly hundreds of other Jones families of no kin whatever to one another are scattered throughout the United States. Each of these has its own immigrant ancestor, and from each has sprung in later generations a numerous line of descendants until the Jones surname ranks second only to that of Smith in number of representatives.

In New England the surname Jones has been known for at least two and a quarter centuries, and represents probably a dozen families not related, and each traces descent from a distinct head, although in many instances the line of descent from the ancestor to the present generation of his representatives is broken by imperfect family and parish records and the wide separation of the branches of the parent tree during the period of colonization and settlement of regions remote from the seat of the ancestor. One of the notable Jones families of New England was that seated in Woburn, Massachusetts, during the first half of the eighteenth century, and whose descendants are now scattered throughout the land; but little is known of them or the family history except that they were settled in Wilmington about the time mentioned.

(I) Hugh Jones, the first of the family known in America, was born about 1635, and was located in Salem, Massachusetts, in 1650. He died there in 1688. A deposition on record shows that he came from Wincanton, a small parish in Somersetshire, England. He was apprenticed to Robert Gutch, with whom he came across the water at the age of fifteen years. After the expiration of his apprenticeship he was employed for some time by Thomas Gardner. About the time of his marriage he received from the town a homestead grant of three acres. This he sold to William Robinson, April 22, 1673. On April 13, of the following year he purchased from Thomas Gardner five acres in the "North Neck." He was a small farmer and is described in the records as a planter. It is evident that he had a hard struggle in life in rearing his large family, but he left a race of hardy descendants who have been noted as farmers and blacksmiths, conspicuous for their vigor and long lives. A large number of his descendants have been very active in the military service. The inventory of his estate was

Eben Jones.

made in 1688, and an additional inventory was filed in 1690. In 1692 Elizabeth Booth testified that the ghost of Hugh Jones appeared to her, and said Miss Elizabeth Proctor had killed him for a "poght of syder." About 1794 his widow and some of their children removed to the northern part of Woburn. On May 7th of that year, William Butters and Samuel Snow, Jr., gave bonds in the sum of one hundred and fifty pounds to indemnify the town of Woburn against the risk of supporting Mary, John, Sarah, Rachel and Hugh Jones. These men had married daughters of Hugh Jones, the elder, and were thus interested in behalf of the family. Hugh (1) Jones was married (first), June 26, 1660, to Hannah, daughter of John and Margaret Tompkins, of Salem. She was born February 20, 1641, and died May 10, 1672. He was married (second), December 31, 1672, to Mary, daughter of John and Martha (Tompkins) Foster, a cousin of his first wife. She was baptized March 29, 1650, and died in Woburn, May 29, 1717. There were eight children of the first wife, namely: Hannah (died young), Sarah (died young), Sarah (died young), Elizabeth, Mary, John, Deborah and Samuel. The children of the second wife were: Rebecca, Abigail, Hannah, Rachel, Sarah, Hugh and Lydia.

(II) Samuel, second son of Hugh Jones and youngest child of his first wife Hannah, was born April 30, 1672, in Salem, Massachusetts, and was twenty years of age when he removed with his family to Woburn. He resided there throughout his life, and died in 1753, aged over eighty years. As a prudent and foreseeing man, he had made his will October 18, 1733, and this was proved December 24, 1753. He was a successful farmer. He was married about 1695 to Abigail, daughter of Samuel and Sarah (Wilson) Snow. She was born April 4, 1677. Their children were: Samuel, Ebenezer, Jonathan, Abigail and Joshua. The second son was a captain of the colonial troops, and was killed in the French and Indian war in 1758.

(III) Lieutenant Jonathan, third son and child of Samuel and Abigail (Snow) Jones, was born July 26, 1702, in Woburn, and resided in the northern part of what is now Wilmington in 1730. He died there May 24, 1753. He was a farmer and a man of enterprise, and became an extensive land holder in Wilmington, and in Monson, New Hampshire. He served as a lieutenant in the militia. His will was made the day before his death. He was married August 7, 1721, in Woburn, to Elizabeth, daughter of William and Ruth (Richardson) Russell of Salem Village. She was a granddaughter of William Russell, of Salem, whose wife Elizabeth Nourse, was a daughter of Rebecca Nourse, a victim of the witchcraft delusion in 1692. Lieutenant Jonathan Jones's children were: Elizabeth (died young), Jonathan, William, Caleb, Martha, Mary (died young), Joshua, Josiah, Samuel (died young), James, David, Elizabeth, Samuel (died young), Mary, Samuel (died young), and Samuel. (Mention of Josiah and descendants appears in this article).

(IV) William, second son and third child of Jonathan and Elizabeth (Russell) Jones, was born August 23, 1724, in Woburn, Massachusetts, and was a very early resident of Hillsboro, New Hampshire. His name appears in the early records, and he is mentioned as a soldier of the Revolution, and probably came to Hillsboro before 1775. He was married March 25, 1745, to Rebecca Jenkins, probably of Woburn and they had four sons and five daughters.

(V) James, fourth son of William and Rebecca (Jenkins) Jones, was probably born in Woburn, but no record of his birth appears in either Woburn or Hillsboro. He died in the last mentioned town, July 18, 1839. For some time after his marriage he resided in Billerica, Massachusetts and came thence to Hillsboro, where he was engaged in farming. He was married in Hillsboro about 1778, to Anna Coolidge, who was born August 5, 1757, in Weston, Massachusetts, daughter of Nathaniel and Sarah (Parker) Coolidge. She survived her husband nearly four years, and died in Hillsboro, March 30, 1841, having borne him twelve children: Jonathan, born September 3, 1778, died March 5, 1810; Anna, February 18, 1780, March 18, 1829; James, December 9, 1782; Silas, March 6, 1784, October 6, 1832; Cooledge, February 4, 1786, February 9, 1856; Sarah, March 22, 1788, July 3, 1788; Nathaniel, May 3, 1789, August 19, 1867; Ebenezer, February 7, 1892, December 1, 1864; Parker, February 13, 1794, May 28, 1861; Solomon, born February 7, 1796, died August 23, 1842; Warren, born February 3, 1798, March 21, 1868; Silas P., June 7, 1801, November 3, 1844.

(VI) Ebenezer, eighth child and sixth son of James and Anna (Coolidge) Jones, was born in Billerica, Massachusetts, February 7, 1792, and before settling permanently in Hillsborough lived for several years in Unity, New Hampshire, where he was a farmer. Subsequently he returned to Hillsborough and bought the Nathaniel Johnson farm, where he lived until the time of his death, December 1, 1864. He married, October 6, 1816, Mary Turner Carr, daughter of Nathan and Elizabeth (Smith) Carr of Deering, New Hampshire. She was born in the town of Windham, New Hampshire, February 9, 1793, and died in Hillsborough, January, 1867. Ebenezer and Mary Turner Jones had nine children: Charlotte, born January 6, 1818; married Alonzo Tuttle of Hillsborough; died August 31, 1861. Nathan P., in Unity June 3, 1820; died August 4, 1820; Parker, in Unity July 31, 1821; married, July 14, 1859, Julia C. Andrews of Pawlet, Vermont; died at the Astor House, New York City, November 12, 1868. James, born in Unity November 17, 1823; died January 23, 1898. George, born in Unity February 16, 1826; married Mrs. Mary (Goodale) Smith of Hillsborough. Mary Elizabeth, born May 22, 1828; married David W. Grimes of Hillsborough. Harvey, born July 6, 1830; died July 1, 1900. Ebenezer, born October 24, 1832; married Malvina Shedd of Hillsborough. Sarah A., born March 29, 1836; married Colonel James F. Grimes of Hillsborough.

(VII) Ebenezer (2), ninth child and youngest son of Ebenezer (1) and Mary Turner (Carr) Jones, was born in the town of Hillsborough, New Hampshire, October 24, 1832, and died in that town September 12, 1891. He was a farmer by occupation and lived many years on the old home farm. He married, December 11, 1856, Malvina Shedd, who was born January 27, 1834, daughter of Levi and Jane (Hosley) Shedd. Mr. and Mrs. Jones had two children: James Harvey Jones, born November 25, 1860, and Parker Jones, born October 22, 1864. Parker Jones married Jennie Green of Lowell, Massachusetts, and is a farmer of Hillsborough.

(VIII) James Harvey, elder son and child of Ebenezer (2) and Malvina (Shedd) Jones, was born in the town of Hillsborough, November 25, 1860. As a boy he was given a good education in the public schools of the town, and at home was brought up to work on the farm. After marriage he started out for himself, and soon came to be recognized as one of the best farmers in the town; and Hillsborough for many years has been noted for the substantial character of its farming population. His lands are extensive, thoroughly cultivated and hence productive, well stocked, and provided with buildings which are an ornament to the county. His cattle at times as many as a hundred head, are sleek and show good keeping; and in addition to his general farming and dairying interests Mr. Jones deals considerably in live stock. Mr. Jones is counted among the most substantial farmers of Hillsborough, and while he takes a deep interest in the welfare of the town as a citizen and large taxpayer, he has no inclination for political office. He is a thoroughly reliable Republican, and a member of Valley Grange, Patrons of Husbandry, of Hillsborough. He married, December 14, 1887, Edith Luella Steele of Stoneham, Massachusetts. She was born April 20, 1864, daughter of John and Mary Ann (Wiley) Steele, both of Stoneham. Mr. Steele was born September 29, 1818, and his wife was born January 26, 1823. James Harvey and Edith Luella (Steele) Jones have five children: Clara L., born November 23, 1888; Jeanette E., born March 23, 1890; Edna S., born July 1, 1892; Eben P., born March 18, 1895; Arthur J., born September 1, 1901.

(IV) Josiah, fifth son and eighth child of Jonathan and Elizabeth (Russell) Jones, twin brother of Joshua, was born March 23, 1731, in Wilmington, Massachusetts, and died August 16, 1796, in Londonderry, New Hampshire. Records preserved by his descendants show that his wife was Rebecca Jenkins.

(V) Jonathan (2), son of Josiah and Rebecca (Jenkins) Jones, was born April 15, 1766, and died 1834. He was married, November 22, 1794, to Mehitable Goodwin, who was born November 22, 1772, in Londonderry, and died February 9, 1863, in Weare, New Hampshire. She was a daughter of David and Mehitable (Jackson) Goodwin, born respectively in 1744 and 1741, both dying in 1822. David Goodwin was a son of David Goodwin. Mehitable Jackson was born in Rowley, Massachusetts.

(VI) David, son of Jonathan (2) and Mehitable (Goodwin) Jones, was born October 9, 1804, in Weare, where he grew up, receiving a common school education. He became a farmer and lumber dealer, and was among the most active citizens of the town of Merrimack in his day. In 1839 he kept a hotel at Merrimack, and in 1845 and 1846 cleared by contract a large tract of land near Reed's Ferry, known as the Parker Lot. He also maintained lumber yards at Thornton Ferry, and was a very influential citizen of the town. He was a member of the Congregational Church at Merrimack, and served as selectman and representative of the town in the state legislature. He was married, March 11, 1830, to Dorothy Tewksbury, who was born January 28, 1808, in New Boston, and died July 24, 1836 in Merrimack. He was married (second), March 2, 1837, to Rosannah, sister of his first wife, who was born August 10, 1816. (See Tewksbury). His children are accounted for as follows: David Tewksbury was a resident of the town of Merrimack, where he died in 1893. Ames, the second, died in infancy. James Thornton is the subject of the succeeding paragraph. These are the children of the first wife. Daniel, the first child of Rosanna (Tewksbury) Jones, resides in Merrimack. Sarah Elizabeth is the widow of Henry W. McQuesten, residing in Merrimack. (See McQuesten). George Henry, died May 6, 1905. Rosannah is the wife of George W. Dow of Port Jervis, New York. Louise M., is the wife of Frank P. Jones of Merrimack, q. v.

(VII) David Tewksbury, eldest son of David and Dorothy (Tewksbury) Jones, was born March 20, 1831, in Merrimack, and died there October 16, 1893. His schooling began in the district school of the town, and ended at the age of nineteen years in Crosby's private school of Nashua. He was early accustomed to aid his father in his agricultural and lumbering operations, and continued with him and carried on the same line of business as his successor, being a large land holder. He was active in promoting the general welfare, especially of his native town, and enjoyed the respect and esteem of his townsmen. A Democrat in political principle, he was elected selectman and served with fidelity, thus justifying the support of his political opponents. Both he and his wife were faithful members of the Congregational Church. He was married June 28, 1855, to Lucretia Reed, who was then seventeen years old, and died in 1865. She was a daughter of Luther W. and Martha (Kittredge) Read. The last named was born January 16, 1817, a daughter of Eri and Lucretia (Woods) Kittredge, the former of whom was born October 27, 1794, in Reading, Massachusetts, and was married October 27, 1816, to Miss Woods.

(VIII) David Read, only son of David T. and Lucretia (Reed) Jones, was born in Merrimack, December 27, 1864. His studies in the public schools were supplemented with a commercial course at a business college in Manchester, which he completed at the age of eighteen years, and he shortly afterwards engaged in the grain trade at Merrimack, operating a grist-mill and transacting a profitable business for the succeeding eight years. He then turned his attention to manufacturing, purchasing in company with Henry W. McQuesten, a half interest in a water-power privilege at the old Thomas Parker stand, and for the past thirteen years has devoted his energies chiefly to the production of tables, the superior quality of which enables him to find a ready market for their disposal. In addition to his activities in behalf of the industrial interests of Merrimack, he is prominently identified with public affairs, having served as a town clerk for ten years, and in 1905 he represented his district with marked ability in the lower branch of the state legislature. Politically he supports the Democratic party. He is a member of the Independent Order of Odd Fellows, and formerly affiliated with the local grange, Patrons of Husbandry. In his religious belief he is a Congregationalist.

On December 4, 1884, Mr. Jones married Alice E. Burgess, of Foster, Rhode Island, born August 4, 1871; they have two children: Nellie E. and Bertha M. Jones.

(VII) James Thornton, third son and child of David and Dorothy (Tewksbury) Jones, was born July 4, 1836, at Thornton's Ferry, and grew up in the town of Merrimack, attending the common schools and Colby Academy, David Crosby's school at Merrimack, and also Barnstable high school. Young Jones worked his way through school by his own labors, and at nineteen began teaching. In April, 1860, he went to California, where he was engaged in teaching for more than fifteen years, and again returned to Merrimack, where he taught two winters in the district schools. He was appointed station agent at Merrimack, December 5, 1881, and was also a representative of the express company and postmaster. He held the last named position continuously for twenty-six years, but some time since resigned the position of station agent. Both he and his wife were members of the Baptist Church, their membership having been formed in Hudson, which organization they joined in its early day, and now are with the Crown Hill Church of Nashua. Mr. Jones is a member of Thornton Grange and of the Golden Cross, a benefit order. He has always been a steadfast supporter of Republican principles, but his only official position outside that of the government service has been that of justice of the peace, which he has held continuously for the last twelve years. He is a highly cultivated and intelligent gentleman. Long years of reading and study have made him a most pleasant and agreeable conversationalist. He was married, May 5, 1864, to Martha Frances Marsh, who was born April 20, 1836, in Hudson, New Hampshire, and died February 5, 1906, in Merrimack. She was a daughter of Deacon Enoch S. and Martha (Whittier) Marsh, natives respectively of Hudson and Londonderry. (See Marsh.) Mr. and Mrs. Jones had two sons born in California, namely, James Ernest and Leslie Egbert. The former is station agent for the Boston and Maine railroad at Tufts College, and the latter is traveling agent and manager of Smith Premier Typewriter Co., and resides at Bangor, Maine. Both have received liberal educations. A daughter, Grace Marsh, born in Merrimack, is the wife of Louis Hoffman, and resides with her parents at Merrimack. She is the mother of two children: Margaret Frances, born March 31, 1900, and Maurice Leslie, March 1, 1902.

(Fifth Family.)

JONES The origin of this family in New Hampshire, like many others of the first in what is now Rockingham county, is lost in uncertainty, partly through the destruction of early records upon the accession of Massachusetts authority in this region. It is not certain that this family is distinct from the Massachusetts family elsewhere treated in this work.

(I) William Jones was a resident of Cambridge, Massachusetts, in 1635, and sold out his lands there in 1638. He appears at Portsmouth in 1644, and was at Bloody Point (Dover) in 1644. He is not found in the records of that town after 1648.

(II) Stephen, supposed to have been a son of William Jones, subscribed to the oath of allegiance at Dover in 1665, and was an accepted inhabitant in 1666. He took the freeman's oath May 15, 1672, and was made ensign in 1691. In 1694 he was in command of a garrison at his house, and he was continuously representative at the general court from 1709 to 1715, inclusive. He was taxed at Oyster river from 1709 to 1715, inclusive. He was at Oyster River in 1675, and was among the petitioners for making that a separate town in 1669 and 1695. In 1665 he was paid twenty-five pounds for keeping a pauper woman and child, and in 1669 the town meeting made arrangements to compensate him for work already done in building a meeting house. In 1696 he was selectman. He was married, January 29, 1663, to Elizabeth Field. The Stephen Jones figuring later in the town must have been his son. (Joseph Jones, who is mentioned with descendants in this article, was probably a son of Stephen (1).

(III) Stephen (2), undoubtedly a son of Stephen (1) and Elizabeth (Field) Jones, was a selectman in 1724 in Dover, and captain in 1729. No record of his family can be found, except in the parentage of a son. He resided in that part of Dover which became the town of Durham, and was among the petitioners for its separation.

(IV) Major Stephen (3), son of Stephen (2) Jones, was born March 3, 1706, in Durham, and was a citizen of that town. He was married about 1762 to Susannah Millet, who was born March 22, 1740, a daughter of Thomas Millet, her mother being a Bunker. The children were: Stephen Millet, William, Susannah, Abigail and Thomas.

(V) William, second son and child of Stephen (3) and Susannah (Millet) Jones, was born May

23, 1766, in Durham, and settled in New Durham, New Hampshire, where he was accidentally killed while hauling logs. He married Love Smith about 1792, and their children were: John, Sally, Susannah, Stephen, Ebenezer, Lydia S. and Lewis.

(VI) Lewis, son of William and Love (Smith) Jones, was born in New Durham, 1812, and died February 14, 1887, aged seventy-three years. He moved to Alton while a young man, and was a farmer. In his old age, about 1869, he moved to Farmington, where he died eighteen years later. He married, 1834, Betsey Edgerly, who was born in 1809, and died 1897, aged 88, daughter of Jeremiah and Betsey (Layton) Edgerly. They had eight children: Lewis F., who is mentioned below; Lucy J., Fannie B., who married Charles Hanson; Sarah, wife of Almon Leavitt; Charles W., of Washington; Oscar E., of New Haven, Connecticut; Clara A., who married Frank Gilson, and a child which died young.

(VII) Lewis Freeman, eldest child of Lewis and Betsey (Edgerly) Jones, was born in New Durham, September 9, 1839. At eighteen years of age he began work at the shoemaker's trade, and continued in that industry until August 22, 1862, when he enlisted as a private in Company A, Twelfth New Hampshire Volunteer Infantry, from the town of Alton, and was mustered in August 30, 1862. He was on that part of the battlefield of Gettysburg called the Peach Orchard, July 2, 1863, and was severely wounded, losing his left arm, and was discharged on account of wounds November 9, 1863. After his discharge from the military service he peddled about fifteen years, was engineer in charge of a stationary engine three years and kept a saloon in Farmington two years. He is a member of Carlton Post, No. 24, Grand Army of the Republic, and was a delegate to the National Encampment at Indianapolis in 1906. He married (first), Augusta Taylor, daughter of Rev. Chase Taylor, of Abington, Massachusetts. They had three children born to them: Ada E., who married Orrin N. Blaisdell; Annie, who married Lewis Gould; and Frank J., who died young. He married (second), Georgia A. Lawrence, of Nashua. Three children were born of this marriage: Ethel Blanche, who married (first) John Driscoll, and had one child, Gladys Jones, and (second), Harry Wentworth; George F., who resides in Somersworth, a veteran of the Spanish-American war; and Alice Maud, wife of Leland J. Smith, of Rochester.

(III) Joseph Jones was undoubtedly a son of Stephen (1), born probably before 1680, and died before January 30, 1744, at which time the inventory of his estate was made. This amounted to four thousand four hundred and fifty-six pounds, four shillings and six pence. His estate was divided in 1746, the beneficiaries being his widow Ann, his sons Joseph, Benjamin, John, Anthony, Richard, and a daughter of a deceased son Samuel.

(IV) Benjamin, second son of Joseph and Ann Jones, was born soon after 1700, in Durham, and probably settled in Lee, New Hampshire. His wife, Hannah Chesley, was born in 1751, in Durham, and they were married about 1767-8. He settled in Canterbury about 1773-4, and this may have been a second marriage. His children were: Benjamin (died young), Rosa, Elizabeth, Daniel, Henry and Benjamin.

(V) Daniel, second son and fourth child of Benjamin and Hannah (Chesley) Jones, was born in

1776, in Canterbury, in which town he passed the most of his life, engaged in farming on Jones Hill. He died in 1832, in Dorchester, Massachusetts, whither he had removed but a short time before. He was married in Loudon, New Hampshire, October 4, 1803, by Rev. Jedediah Tucker, to Sophia, daughter of Henry and Janet (McCurdy) Parkinson, of Canterbury. (See Parkinson II). Their children were: Abigail, Lucinda, George S., a daughter who died in infancy, and Charles, the subject of the succeeding paragraph.

(VI) Charles, youngest child of Daniel and Sophia (Parkinson) Jones, was born on the homestead, in Canterbury, August 22, 1817, and died May 14, 1879. His father and his family moved to Dorchester in 1823. After staying there a year Charles made his home with James Peverley, of Canterbury, until he was sixteen years old, working on his farm and attending school. At sixteen Charles went to Quincy, Massachusetts, where he learned stone-cutting, and worked at that trade twelve years. He then bought what was known as the Brown farm in Canterbury, a very stony place with poor buildings. He improved the farm very much, reconstructed the buildings, and planted a large orchard. Until that time orchards in that vicinity had produced only natural fruit, but he grafted his trees, and raised a superior quality of apples. In politics he was a Democrat. He married, September 9, 1846, Sarah Pickard, who was born in Canterbury, May 24, 1826, and died July 18, 1886, aged sixty years. She was the daughter of Daniel and Susan (Harvey) Pickard. Their children were: Frank P., deceased; Emily J.; Ellen, deceased; Edea F., deceased; Paul H., Charles F., Seth W., and Mary S. Emily J. married Charles E. Morrill. Mary S. married John French.

(VII) Charles F., sixth child and third son of Charles and Sarah (Pickard) Jones, was born in Canterbury, September 4, 1858. After leaving the district school he attended Tilton Academy two terms. When about twenty he and his brother, Paul H., took charge of his father's farm and carried it on two years. He subsequently worked in West Acton and Hamilton, Massachusetts, about six months. In 1883 he bought his present place in the northern part of the town of Canterbury, known as the Foster farm, which he carried on until 1891, when he rented it, and went to Green Carbon county, Wyoming, where he had charge of a sheep ranch, until 1896, when he returned to his homestead, which he has since cultivated. He is engaged in dairying and stock raising, and has a large sugar grove. All the buildings on the farm above mentioned were destroyed by fire between one and two a. m., Friday, November 2, 1906, and Mr. Jones and family now reside on the old Brown farm, which his father purchased and of which mention is made in this sketch. He is an influential citizen, a liberal supporter of churches and schools, and has been chairman of the school board and was elected selectman in 1892, and served one year. He married, August 6, 1893, at Saratoga, Carbon county, Wyoming, Mary Emma Rubersdorf, who was born in Germany, a daughter of John Rubersdorf, of Germany. They have three children: John Paul, born August 18, 1894; Thomas Rubersdorf, born November 2, 1895; Charles Carroll, born June 21, 1897.

JONES The ancestry of Frank P. Jones, as far as known, begins with Joshua Jones, who was a blacksmith, residing at Salisbury Centre, New Hampshire. His wife was Betsey Waldron, and they were the parents of twelve children. Of these Isaac resides at Danbury, New Hampshire, William, the second, died at Nashua, this state. Ephraim, the third, is a citizen of Amherst, New Hampshire. Archibald, the fourth, receives further mention below. Hiram was killed by a sawmill accident in North Chelmsford, Massachusetts. Joshua was killed in Salisbury, New Hampshire, while a young man. Dalinda, married Schuyler C. Corey, and died in Craftsbury, Vermont. Betsey was the wife of James Coburn, and died in North Chelmsford. Others died in infancy.

Archibald, son of Joshua and Betsey (Waldron) Jones, was born January 29, 1821, in Salisbury, New Hampshire, and died March 3, 1901, in Merrimack, being over eighty years of age. He grew up and passed most of his life in the town of Salisbury. He was a shoemaker and butcher, and could turn his hand to many kinds of labor, and was active almost to the day of his death. His wife was a member of the Baptist Church in Salisbury, and later of the First Baptist Church of Concord. He was a member of the Methodist Church at Salisbury, and was a steadfast adherent of the Democratic party in political affairs. He was married in August, 1846, to Eunice Carr Roby, daughter of Ezekiel and Naomi (Carr) Roby, natives respectively of Warner and Antrim, New Hampshire. The children of Archibald and Eunice C. (Roby) Jones, are noted as follows: Alzira Ann is the widow of John Gordon Sanborn, of Sanbornton, a soldier of the Civil war who died in 1874. She resides in Concord. Frank Pierce is the subject of the following paragraph. Kate Maria is the wife of Daniel McQuesten, and resides in Litchfield, New Hampshire. Isaac Gerrish is a cabinet maker, employed and living in St. Johnsbury, Vermont. Bessie Miranda is the wife of Louis G. Bryant, residing in Manchester. George Archibald is also a resident of Manchester. Edwin Freeman resides in Merrimack, and Fannie Grace is the wife of Leonard J. Gordon, with home in Concord, this state.

Frank Pierce Jones, son of Archibald and Eunice (Roby) Jones, was born in Salisbury, New Hampshire, March 27, 1847, and educated in the common schools. At the age of seventeen he went to Concord, New Hampshire, and in the two following years learned the trade of cabinet maker. From Concord he removed to Merrimack where he now lives. He carried on the business incident to his trade until about 1895. He has been attentive to business, and has taken much interest in local public affairs and has filled public offices for many years. For thirteen years he was tax collector. He has always been a consistent member of the Republican party. In 1875 he joined the Independent Order of Odd Fellows, Mechanics Lodge, No. 13, of Manchester. He has been a member of Thornton Grange, No. 31, Patrons of Husbandry, for an equal length of time. He is a member of the Congregational Church at Merrimack. June 7, 1871, Frank P. Jones married Louise Jones, daughter of David and Rosannah (Tewksbury) Jones, born July 31, 1849. They have no children.

JONES This is one of the earliest Welsh names and is derived from John. By the addition of the possessive form it becomes Johns and in time Jones and is equivalent to John's son. This is one of the three great family names among English speaking people, and has numbered among its bearers many persons of distinction in the various walks of life.

(I) Joseph Jones was born March 4, 1774, in

Charles F. Jones

Truly Yours

A. G. Jones

Bow, and resided for many years in his native town. When well advanced in life he removed to Londonderry, where he died. He was a mason by trade but was most of his life a farmer. He suffered the loss of one of his legs through a fall from a load of hay and was thus largely handicapped in the struggle for existence. He reared a large family who grew up to be respectable citizens and he is said to have been a fine looking man. He was married, September 15, 1796, in Concord, to Sarah Clough, who died June 26, 1827, in Bow. His second wife was a widow, whose name was Wilkins, at the time of her marriage to him. He had eight children, of whom seven grew to maturity. The eldest, Shubael Tenney, lived and died at Amoskeag, New Hampshire. Philip receives extended mention in the succeeding paragraph. Seth Kendrick died at Concord. Ann was the wife of Dr. Daniel Flagg, who died at Albany, New York. Joseph died at Amoskeag. Walter Bryant lived and died at Hooksett. Sarah married a Griffin and died in Albany. All of the sons were masons by trade and earned by working at it sufficient to establish themselves in business and were prosperous.

(II) Philip, second son and child of Joseph Jones, was born April 3, 1802, in Bow, and died January 26, 1836, in Hooksett. Like all of his fathers' sons he became a mason and was an industrious and successful workman, and by saving his earnings was in time enabled to engage in business. He embarked in trade in Suncook, and subsequently established an extensive general store at Hooksett, and was a popular and prosperous merchant. He was a leading man in that town, and was elected to nearly every town office and also served as postmaster. He was married in Bow, to Sarah Mead Gates, daughter of Rev. Abraham and Judith (Tenney) Gates, of Bow (see Gates, XIV). They were the parents of two children: Abraham Gates, who is the subject of the succeeding paragraph, and Augusta A., who is the wife of Charles Haseltine, of Concord. She has one son, George K. Haseltine.

(III) Abraham Gates, only son of Philip and Sarah M. (Gates) Jones, was born in Bow, October 21, 1827. At the age of nine years he was left by the death of his father to the sole care of his mother. In 1839 she went on a visit to northern New York, leaving her son in the care of his legal guardian. Taking advantage of this opportunity to begin life for himself, the boy, now twelve years old, "ran away" and went to Concord, where he attended the town school the following year and the academy in the years 1841 and 1842. Anxious to engage in business he became a newsboy and followed that vocation during most of all of the years, 1843-44. On the 26th day of May, 1845, he entered the office of Isaac Hill & Sons, editors, publishers and proprietors of *Hill's New Hampshire Patriot*. At the end of twelve weeks he was enthusiastically discharged. August 18 following he was invited to return and did so. At the end of ten weeks he was uproariously discharged. At the end of twenty-three weeks he was with less excitement again discharged. He was again invited to return. He did so, staying with the firm till the two *Patriots* united, May 15, 1847, a period of forty-eight weeks. Each return was accompanied with a substantial increase of wages, and time lost was paid for in each case. Early in June, 1847, Mr. Jones went to Lowell, Massachusetts, and there, in the office of the *Vox Populi* he performed his first day's work as a full fledged journeyman printer. After a short period of employment he fancied his health needed attention and he spent the time to little purpose till he was tendered a situation in the office of the *Independent Democrat*, January 24, 1849. From that time until February 21, 1854, he was constantly employed in the various printing offices in Concord, New Hampshire. April 4, 1854, Mr. Jones, with Parsons B. Cogswell, a fellow craftsman, purchased the office of the firm of Tripp & Osgood, printers, and commenced business under the firm name of Jones & Cogswell, and continued until the fall of 1858. Mr. Jones then sold his interest to Mr Cogswell and entered into business with the firm of Fogg & Hadly, editors and publishers of the *Independent Democrat*, under the firm name of Fogg, Hadley and Company, having the general care and management of the typographical affairs of the office, and so continued until the *Democrat* entered what was called the Republican Press Association. During this time Mr. Jones was severally chosen ward clerk, selectman, moderator, councilman, alderman, superintendent of repairs of highways and bridges, overseer of the poor, treasurer, and finally in 1870 and 1871 was elected and re-elected mayor of Concord. In the meantime he sold his interest in printing, retiring from that vocation forever, by the advice of his physician, which was as follows: "Get out of office, out of printing offices, and out of doors." in 1860 Mr. Jones built a residence on Orchard street, and in 1871 purchased a small farm on Fruit street and entered into agricultural pursuits, which he still follows. He has always taken a whole-hearted interest in every enterprise he has undertaken. He has been an industrious and enthusiastic worker in private and in public life. His record attests his energy and ability and the confidence reposed in him by his fellow citizens. He is a Republican whose membership dates from the early days of the party. He is a prominent member of the Universalist church, and has filled various positions in that society. From his twenty-first birthday, October 21, 1849, he has personally had no use for a physician. Although he has never been a user of intoxicating liquors to excess, he has been, since October 31, 1860, a total abstainer from the use of strong drinks or tobacco in any form. He married, June 10, 1856, Helen Augusta Edmunds, born February 4, 1831, in East Weare, daughter of John and Diantha (Hovey) Edmunds, farmers. They have two children: Anna E. and Isabelle G. Anna Edmunds, born in Concord, May 14, 1863, married William Durant, of Concord, and they have one son, Anson Russell. Isabelle Gates was born in Concord, January 27, 1872, and married James H. Leighton, local manager for Swift & Company, packers, and resides at Nashua.

JONES The ancient and honorable family of Jones has many branches and many distinguished members, but the multitude bearing the name make kinship for more than three or four generations back a difficult matter to trace without more complete records than are generally found.

(I) Albert Jones was born June 5, 1813, and was a broom manufacturer nine years at North Hadley, Massachusetts, whence he moved to Springfield, same state, where he died January 12, 1850, in his thirty-seventh year. He married, at North Hadley, Massachusetts, Mary Ann Hibbard, who was born September 4, 1814, in that town, and died November 1, 1896, aged eighty-two years. Five children were born to them: William, Everett, Philo, George and Frank H. The three older sons enlisted in the

Union army, and served under Grant in the Civil war.

(II) Frank H., youngest child of Albert and Mary Ann (Hibbard) Jones, was born in Springfield, Massachusetts, February 1, 1846, and died July 11, 1895. He spent the greater part of his life as a traveling salesman. He settled in Rochester, New Hampshire, and resided there some years. The seven years preceding his death he was employed in the United States custom house in Boston. In politics he was a Republican. He married, December 27, 1870, Martha A. Dodge, who was born January 19, 1850, daughter of Jonathan and Sarah (Hanson) Dodge. Two children were born to them: Charles, who died young; and Albert Dodge, who is mentioned below.

(III) Albert Dodge, son of Frank H. and Martha A. (Dodge) Jones, was born in Rochester, June 28, 1875. He graduated from the high school of his native town in 1894, and the same year matriculated at Dartmouth College, where he was graduated with the class of 1898. The following seven years he read law in the office of Daniel Hall, Esq., and other lawyers, and was admitted to membership in the New Hampshire bar, June 22. 1905. Soon afterward he established himself in business at Rochester, where he has since been busy in building up a successful practice. He is a Republican in politics and liberal in religious ideas. He is a member of the Humane Lodge, No. 21, Free and Accepted Masons, of Rochester; the Royal Arch Chapter, Council of Royal and Select Masters; Commandery of Knights Templar; and Bektash Temple, Ancient Arabic Order of the Mystic Shrine of Concord. He married, September 21, 1898, Sarah Amanda Warren, daughter of Joseph and Adelaide (Elliott) Warren. They have one child, Warren Dodge, born October 16, 1899.

JONES Hon. Frank Jones, fifth son of Thomas and Mary (Priest) Jones, was born in Barrington, September 15, 1832, and died in Portsmouth, October 2, 1902. He spent his childhood and youth on his father's farm, which was one of the best in the township, and had been inherited by the father from his father. Frank was a sturdy, self-reliant boy, and even when but a youth took charge of affairs at home in the absence of his father and older brothers. At seventeen years of age he decided that there was no reward sufficient to keep him on the farm, and in spite of every inducement offered by his father for him to remain at home, the young man went to Portsmouth where his elder brother Hiram had a general hardware store, and entered into his employ. It was the custom in those days to send loads of goods into the country to be sold throughout the rural districts; and to be a successful salesman required more accomplishments than are now necessary to the sale of goods in stores where the customer goes when he wants to buy. The salesman had to be strong, hardy and full of pluck, to be out in all kinds of weather and travel over all sorts of roads; he had to be good natured, shrewd, alert, a good reader of human nature, and full of commercial enterprise. Into this business the young man entered, and the quality of his ability as a merchant, and the extent of his success as a salesman is attested by the fact that at the end of four years he had saved sufficient capital to buy an interest in his brother's business, so that at twenty he was one of the business men of Portsmouth. Not long afterward he became sole proprietor of the business, which he continued on an enlarged scale until 1861, when he disposed of it to his younger brother, True, who was an employe in the establishment. Meantime, in 1858, he bought an interest in the brewery established by the Englishman, John Swindels, in 1854. For a few years after Mr. Jones became interested in this establishment it was conducted under the firm name of Swindels & Company. Then Mr. Jones became sole proprietor, and inaugurated those improvements and reforms in the methods and processes of manufacture which resulted in brilliant success. The buildings of the little brewery of 1858 were replaced by larger ones from time to time, until nothing of the original was left, and new structures covering five acres of ground succeeded them, and the establishment became one of the largest in the country, furnished with all modern improvements and requiring one hundred men to operate it. The old idea that first class ale and porter could not be brewed in America was quickly disproved by Mr. Jones, and those products of quality equal to any brewed in England or Ireland were produced in this brewery. Great care was exercised as to the quality of the product, and nothing of an inferior grade was ever permitted to be sent out. In 1863 a large malt house was built, the present brewery was erected in 1871, and a second and still larger malt house was constructed in 1879, giving the brewery a producing capacity of two hundred and fifty thousand barrels, and a malting capacity of three hundred and seventy-five thousand bushels, annually. In 1875 Mr. Jones became the leading member of a company which purchased the wellknown South Boston Brewery of Henry Souther & Company, under the firm name of Jones, Johnson & Company, Honorable James W. Johnson, of Enfield, being a member of the firm. Changes in the personnel of the company, and the style of the firm occurred, and finally the title became Jones, Cook & Company, Mr. Jones retaining the position of senior partner. The production of this establishment was nearly equal in quanity and quality to that of the Portsmouth brewery.

The residence of Hon. Woodbury Langdon, judge of the supreme court of New Hampshire, and brother of Governor Langdon, was burned in the first great fire in Portsmouth in 1781. The house was rebuilt on the same spot in 1786, and in 1830 the house and lot were purchased by a joint stock company, and converted into a house of public entertainment. This house was enlarged and remodelled by Mr. Jones in 1870, and burned in 1884. The "Rockingham," for that was and is the name of the hotel, was rebuilt by Mr. Jones and opened to the public February 3, 1886, and had he done nothing else for the credit of Portsmouth than to erect this magnificent hotel, he would have earned the gratitude of every citizen. The structure is of brick and free stone, five stories high, with a frontage of upwards of one hundred and fifty feet, and has first class accommodations for about two hundred guests, with all up-to-date conveniences, and is sumptuously furnished throughout. Besides this great public house, Mr. Jones built the Wentworth Hotel, in Newcastle, which is acknowledged to be the leading seaside hotel in New England. These two most famous hostelries were built from plans of Mr. Jones's own designing, and erected and equipped under his own direction. Mr. Jones's great success in everything he undertook made him a man much sought for as a business associate, and in consequence he became closely identified with the leading banks, railroads and other great corporations. He was a director of the Lancaster Trust Company; the Wolfboro Loan and Banking Company, and the New Hampshire National Bank of

Frank Jones

Frank H. Jones

Portsmouth; president of the Portsmouth & Dover railroad; the Granite State Fire Insurance Company; the Portsmouth Fire Association, and the Portsmouth Shoe Company. For many years he devoted much of his time to the active duties of the presidency of the great Bostin & Maine railroad.

His prominence in business affairs and his interest in all that concerned the city of Portsmouth, led his nomination as the candidate of the Democratic party for the mayoralty of that town. He elected in 1868 and re-elected the following year. His administration was marked by progress and improvement without excessive taxation. He had no need of the salary of the office, and devoted it to public purposes. The first year's salary he gave as a trust fund, the interest of which was to be used annually for the purchase of books for the library of the high school. The salary of the second year he put in the hands of trustees on the condition that if $5,000 more could be raised in five years, he would then add another thousand dollars for the purpose of establishing a public library to be presented to the city. Subsequently he was a candidate for presidential elector, but the normal Republican majority could not be overcome, though he received vote nearly as large as that cast by the Republicans in the district. In 1875 he was the nominee of the Democracy for congressman, and though the district had been carried by the opposition at the previous election, he was elected by a plurality of three hundred and thirty-six votes. Two years later he was renominated, and the Republicans put in opposition to him a candidate who had won distinction both as a civilian and as a soldier, and had been elected three times to the same office in past years; yet Mr. Jones's popularity prevailed, and he was returned to congress by a plurality of forty votes. At the end of his second term in this office he refused to be a candidate again, since the demands of his business were such that they could no longer be neglected. He regarded this as his final withdrawal from politics; but in 1880, against his emphatic protest, and with a unanimity never before equalled in New Hampshire, he was nominated for governor; and though the defeat of his party was known to be certain as the national campaign proceded, he received a larger vote than any Democratic candidate had ever before received, and a greater number of votes than had ever been given to the candidate of any party in a state election. His services were marked by fidelity to the interests of the people, and in committee work he was particularly efficient, his knowledge of business and business methods making him especially strong in that field. His residence, about a mile from the Rockingham Hotel, is situated on property known as "The Farm," containing about one thousand acres, and is enclosed with hedges, charming grounds, conservatories, and other appendages, and is by courtesy called the "Public Garden of Portsmouth."

Phenomenally successful in his enterprises and busy with the cares and responsibilities of a multitude of business ventures, he seemed to enjoy his wealth and his work, and took pleasure in discharging his duties to his fellow citizens in both his public and private relations. "In all his successful business career," it has been written, "he never for one moment forgot his duties to his fellow men, nor the claims his native state and adopted city had upon him; he did all in his power to promote the welfare and obtain the good will of all men, and most strenuously labored for the health, wealth and prosperity of the city of Portsmouth and its neighborhood." His social and genial nature and innumerable acts of kindness and courtesy caused him to be held in the highest esteem by the people at large, regardless of party or condition.

Mr. Jones married, September 15, 1861, Martha S. (Leavitt) Jones, daughter of William B. and Louisa D. Leavitt, and widow of his brother, Hiram Jones, who died in July, 1859, leaving one child, Emma I. Jones, who became the wife of Colonel Charles A. Sinclair, of Portsmouth. Colonel Sinclair died in Brookline, Massachusetts, April 22, 1899. To Colonel and Mrs. Sinclair were born four daughters: Grace J., married Parker W. Whittemore; Martha S., married Sherburn M. Merrill; Mary Louise, married John C. Spring; Ellen Marie, unmarried.

JONES The Jones name is so numerous and contains so many different branches that it has been found impossible to trace the connection of this family.

(I) John Jones was born in Chichester, New Hampshire, in 1842. He married Martha L. Wales, who is now living in Concord.

(II) Dr. Edwin Emery, son of John and Martha L. (Wales) Jones, was born at Loudon, New Hampshire, January 4, 1870. He was educated at Pembroke Academy, spent one year at Dartmouth College, and was graduated from the Dartmouth Medical School in 1894. While a student he was distinguished in athletics, and played on the foot ball team, where he was captain in 1893. He practiced three years in Norwich, Vermont, also doing hospital work a year and a half at Hanover Hospital, and in 1898 came to Colebrook, New Hampshire, where he is permanently located. During the time he spent in Vermont he served as health officer. He was a member of the board of health in Colebrook for six years. He is a Mason, belonging to the Blue Lodge, Eastern Star, and to North Star Chapter, Eastern Star Council. He is a trustee of the Methodist Church, and was its treasurer until January 1, 1907. He is a Republican in politics. On July 3, 1894, he married Maude, daughter of Edwin P. and Diantha Northrop, of Suncook, New Hampshire. They have one son, Ralph Northrop, born at Concord, January 16, 1898.

FRENCH This ancient and respectable family established itself in America about the end of the first decade of colonization in Massachusetts, and has furnished many valued citizens. The name comes either from a French ancestor who settled in Britain and was called "the French," in reference to his nationality, or from his having lived in France.

(I) Edward French was born about 1590, in England, and died December 28, 1674, in Salisbury, Massachusetts. With his wife Ann and two or more sons he came to America about 1637, and received land in the first division at Salisbury, where he also bought land in 1642. He was a tailor by trade, and probably possessed means when he left England. He was a selectman in 1646-47-48, and his name appears on most of the early town lists as "commoner," taxpayer, etc. His will was made April 10, 1673, and proved two years and three days later. His widow, who was probably a sister of Richard Goodale (1), died March 9, 1683, in Salisbury. Edward French is listed among the settlers of Ipswich in 1637-38. His children were: Joseph, John, Samuel and Hannah, the second born before 1633. (Samuel and descendants receive notice in this article.)

(II) Joseph, eldest child of Edward and Ann

(Goodale) French, was born in England, and was reared to his father's trade. He and his wife Susannah were members of the Salisbury church in 1687. He was taxed in Salisbury as early as 1652, and received land there in 1654. His wife died February 16, 1688, and he survived her over twenty-two years, passing away June 6, 1710. Their children were: Joseph, Elizabeth, Simon, Ann, Edward (died an infant), Edward and John.

(III) Joseph (2), eldest child of Joseph (1) and Susannah French, was born March 16, 1654, and died December 14, 1683, in Salisbury, where he was probably a farmer. He subscribed to the oath of allegiance and fidelity in December, 1677. He was married June 13, 1678, to Sarah, eighth child of Roger Eastman (q. v.), who survived him and was married August 4, 1684, to Solomon Shepherd. Joseph French's children were: Joseph, Timothy and Simon.

(IV) Joseph (3), eldest son of Joseph (2) and Sarah (Eastman) French, was born March 26, 1679, in Salisbury, and was known as "junior" while he lived in that town. He appears in Salisbury records as a carpenter in 1728 and 1739, and as husbandman in South Hampton in 1747. He probably did not change his residence, at least, for a great distance, as the establishment of the province line in 1741 set many residents of Salisbury into New Hampshire, in what was organized as the town of South Hampton in 1742. He was married, December 20, 1699, to Abigail, daughter of Philip and Mary (Buswell) Brown, and granddaughter of Deacon Henry Brown of Salisbury. Mary was a daughter of Isaac and Susanna Buswell. Joseph (2) French died December 27, 1756. His children were: Sarah, Joseph, Ebenezer, Daniel, Abigail and Obadiah. (Daniel and descendants receive mention in this article.)

(V) Joseph (4), eldest son of Joseph (3) and Abigail (Brown) French, was born February 27, 1702, in Salisbury and remained in that town until after 1740, probably all his life. He was married in Salisbury, Massachusetts, February 22, 1731, to Ruth Knowles.

(VI) Simon, son of Joseph (4) and Ruth (Knowles) French, was born in Salisbury, October 27, 1740. In 1764 he came to New Hampshire, settling upon a farm in Candia, where he resided for the remainder of his life, which terminated August 3, 1823. He married for his first wife ——— Shackford, daughter of John Shackford, of Chester, and his second wife was Comfort Weeks Moore, widow of Dr. Moore. His children were: Ruth, who became the wife of Samuel Colby; Dolly, married Andrew Rankin; and John, who was the next in line of descent. All were of the first union.

(VII) John, youngest child and only son of Simon and ——— (Shackford) French, was born in Candia, March 25, 1770. He was an industrious and energetic farmer, residing for the greater part of his active life upon a farm in the immediate vicinity of the property now owned and occupied by his grandson, John P. French, and he was regarded as an eminently useful citizen, who fully merited the esteem and good will which was accorded him by his fellow-townsmen. His church affiliations were with the Congregationalists. He died in Candia, December 24, 1845. His wife was before marriage Comfort Moore, daughter of Dr. Moore, a native of Stratham, New Hampshire. She became the mother of five children, namely: Martha, Simon, Coffin Moore, Lucinda and Evelina.

(VIII) Deacon Coffin Moore, third child and youngest son of John and Comfort (Moore) French, was born in Candia, April 6, 1799. In early manhood he settled upon the farm which is now owned by his son, John P., and a considerable portion of his long and useful life was devoted to the service of the town in a civic capacity and also to teaching school. For a number of years he served with ability as a member of the board of selectmen, and he held other town offices. Politically he was in his latter years a Republican, having united with that party at its formation. He lived to be eighty-two years old, and his death, which occurred in 1881, was not only the cause of general regret, but was especially deplored by his fellow-members of the Congregational Church, which he had served as deacon for many years. In 1825 he married Dolly Pillsbury, daughter of Samuel and Mary (Currier) Pillsbury, of Sandown, or Hanover. In her younger days she was a school-teacher, and for many years prior to her death, which occurred in 1879, she was an earnest member of the Congregational Church. Deacon and Mrs. French were the parents of four children, namely: John Pillsbury, who will be again referred to; Mary Celinda, born May 6, 1832, married Rev. James H. Fitts; Samuel Franklin, born December 22, 1835, graduated from Dartmouth College and from the Andover Theological Seminary, married Martha J. Upton, of Andover, Massachusetts; and George Henry, born July 27, 1838, died October 2, 1906. The latter, who was also a graduate of Dartmouth and of the Andover Theological Seminary, married Fannie E. Kilburn, of Holden, Massachusetts, who bore him three children—Warren Kilburn, Irving Joseph and George Franklin.

(IX) John Pillsbury, eldest child of Deacon Coffin M. and Dolly (Pillsbury) French, was born in Candia, September 14, 1826. Having concluded his education with a course of advanced study at the Pembroke Academy, he turned his attention to agriculture, and for many years was associated with his father in carrying on the homestead farm, which he inherited at the latter's death. He also inherited the spirit of energy and thrift which predominated in the character of his progenitors, and has made excellent use of these essential qualities, keeping well abreast of the times in the line of improvements and taking advantage of every available means of preserving the fertility of his land. The major portion of his farm, which comprises one hundred and fifty acres, is divided into pasture and woodland, while the remainder is devoted to the usual products of that locality, and he keeps an average of ten head of cattle, six cows and three horses. Mr. French has not only adhered in his daily life to the traditions of his family, but has also preserved their allegiance to the cause of morality and religion. For more than thirty years he has been a deacon of the Congregational Church, and for a period has served as superintendent of the Sunday school. In politics he is a Republican. In 1861 he married Edith Knight, of Atkinson, New Hampshire, who died in 1863, and on February 20, 1872, he married for his second wife Mary E. Craig, daughter of Leonard and Betsey (Stone) Craig, of Leicester (or Auburn), Massachusetts. She is a graduate of Abbott Academy, class of 1859, and was formerly engaged in educational pursuits.

(V) Daniel, son of Joseph (3) and Abigail (Brown) French, born in Salisbury, August 21, 1708, died September 1, 1783, aged seventy-five. He married, May 28, 1730, Sarah Gould, born 1710, died January 25, 1773, aged sixty-three, daughter of Samuel Gould, born February 3, 1668, died 1725, and Sarah (Rowell) Gould, born March 1674, and granddaughter of Valentine Rowell (q. v.). The children of Daniel and Sarah (Gould) French were: Abigail, Sarah, Barzillai, Daniel, Gould, Elihu, Daniel, Sarah and Judith, the first five born in Salisbury, Massachusetts, the other four in South Hampton, New Hampshire.

(VI) Gould, third son and fifth child of Daniel and Sarah (Gould) French, born in Salisbury, Massachusetts, September 17, 1741, died May 12, 1823, in St. Albans, Maine, aged eighty-three, and was buried in Palmyra, with his son Dr. Benjamin's family. He resided in Epping, New Hampshire, where he was a farmer, living on a farm given him by his father. He served as a private in the revolution in Captain Joseph Chandler's company, of Colonel Isaac Wyman's regiment. He moved to Maine about 1802. He married, November 24, 1763, Dorothy (Dolly) Whittier, of Amesbury, Massachusetts, born November 30, 1745, died December 13, 1804, daughter of Joseph and Martha (Evins) Whittier. Their children were: Sally, John E., Daniel and Dorothy (twins), Benjamin, and Joseph (twins) Deborah and Martha.

(VII) Daniel, second son and third child of Gould and Dorothy (Whittier) French, born at Epping, February 22, 1769, died in Chester, October 15, 1840. He was a student at Exeter under Dr. Abbot two years, and also was under the tuition of Rev. Robert Gray, of Andover, some time. He studied law with Hon. William K. Atkinson, of Dover, was admitted to the bar in 1796, and immediately afterward proceeded to Deerfield Parade, where he practiced two years. He then went to Chester and succeeded Hon. Arthur Livermore, who was appointed judge of the superior court, December, 1799. He was appointed solicitor June, 1808; was admitted to practice in the United States court in 1809; and appointed attorney general, February, 1812, and resigned in 1815. He was appointed postmaster of Chester, April, 1807, and retained the place through all the changes of administration till 1839, when he resigned, and his son Henry F. succeeded him. Loammi Davidson, Edmund Flagg, Abner Emerson, Stephen Crooker, Jabez Crooker, B. B. French, Eben French, and Henry F. French were students at law in his office. "He was undoubtedly a lawyer of more than ordinary ability and attainments." He owned lands and was interested in cultivating them, but continued to practice his profession and to attend the courts with regularity until within a few years of his death. He married (first), September 15, 1799, Mercy Brown, died March 8, 1802, daughter of Benjamin and Prudence (Kelly) Brown, of Chester; (second), June 30, 1805, Betsey Van Mater Flagg, born February 12, 1778, died April 23, 1812; and (third), November 6, 1812, he married the sister of his late wife Sarah Wingate (Flagg) Bell, widow of Jonathan Bell, born May 31, 1782, died December 18, 1878, aged ninety-six. By these marriages he had eleven children. By the first wife there was one child, Benjamin B.; by the second four children: Arthur Livermore, Ann Caroline, Catherine J. and Sarah; and by the third wife, six; Henry F., Harriette Van Mater, Elizabeth Jane, Edmund Flagg, Arianna and Helen Augusta.

(VIII) Henry Flagg, eldest child of Daniel and Sarah W. (Flagg) French, born in Chester, New Hampshire, August 14, 1813, died in Concord, Massachusetts, November 29, 1885, was educated at the Pinkerton Academy, at Derry, and at Pembroke, and at Hingham, Massachusetts, where he went to study French. He studied law in his father's office in Chester, and at the Harvard Law School, and was admitted to the bar August 14, 1834. He practiced law with his father till the death of the latter, 1840, was at Portsmouth one year, then removed to Exeter, and held the office of county solicitor ten years from 1838; and that of bank commissioner four years from 1848; and practiced law in Exeter until appointed a justice of the court of common pleas, August 15, 1855, which office he held till August 1, 1859. He opened an office in Boston, September, 1859, and removed his family to Cambridge in 1860; was appointed assistant district attorney for Suffolk county, November 19, 1862, and held that office (at the same time practicing law) until June, 1865, when he was elected the first president if the Massachusetts Agricultural College. He removed to Amherst, where the college was established, September, 1865, having resigned his office in Boston. Being unable to organize the college according to his ideas of what such an institution should be, he resigned his position there October 17, 1866, and resumed the profession of law in Boston in the spring of 1867, where he practiced until 1876, when he was appointed second assistant secretary of the United States treasury, at Washington, which office he held till 1885, when he returned with impaired health to Concord, Massachusetts, where he remained till his decease, the following November. Charles H. Bell, in "The Bench and Bar of New Hampshire," says: "Judge French was a man of ability and sense, of great readiness, and superior professional attainments. His knowledge was always at his tongue's end. It was said of him that his opinion given at sight was as much to be relied upon as if he had taken days for consideration. He was prompt in all his business methods. While he occupied the bench he never left questions over to be decided in vacation, but had every transfer drawn out, submitted to counsel, and settled, before the term ended. His sense of humor was keen, and he uttered many a bright saying to enliven the tedium of long trials. He never lost his balance whatever happened. One one occasion, in a hearing before a jury, his opponent introduced a crushing piece of evidence. With perfect presence of mind Judge French turned to his associate counsel and in a whisper inquired, 'Had we better be surprised?' "

All his life long Judge French manifested his fondness for the cultivation of the soil, and he had an extensive reputation as an agriculturalist. In 1857 he went to Europe, where he travelled for a year on an agricultural mission, and communicated the results of his observations in addresses, letters to the *New England Farmer*, and in a very full treatise which he published on farm drainage. He had a great love for trees, and was active in ornamenting his native town with them. He set the elm trees in front of his father's office, and was a leader in setting other trees on Chester street, and active in ornamenting Exeter in a like manner. He was president of the Rockingham Agricultural Society from its organization in 1852 till he left the state. For many years he was a contributor to agricultural papers. Dartmouth conferred the honorary degree of Master of Arts upon him in 1852; and he was elected an honorary member of the Phi Beta Kappa Society, at Cambridge, July, 1861. He was a man of amiable disposition and even temper, and fulfilled his public and private duties with equal fidelity. He married (first), October 9, 1838, Anne Richardson, born in Chester, September 26, 1811, daughter of Chief Justice William Merchant and Betsey (Smith) Richardson. She died at Exeter, New Hampshire, August 28, 1856, and he married (second) Pamela M. Prentice, of Keene. The children of Henry F. and Anne French were: Harriette Van Mater, William M., Richardson, Sarah Flagg and Daniel Chester.

(IX) Harriette Van Mater, eldest child of Judge Henry F. and Anne (Richardson) French, was born September 29, 1839, and married July 9, 1864, Major Abijah Hollis, of Milton, Massachusetts (see Hollis, VII).

(II) Samuel, third son and child of Edward and Ann French, resided in Salisbury, where he signed petitions in 1658, and was a member of the church in 1677 and 1687. He died July 26, 1692, in Salisbury. Administration of his estate was established November 16 following. He was married (first), June 1, 1664, in Salisbury, to Abigail Brown, daughter of Henry and Abigail Brown, of Salisbury. She was born February 23, 1644, in Salisbury, and died January 11, 1680, in that town. Samuel French's second wife was named Esther, and she survived him. Six of his children were born of the first wife and three of the second, namely: Abigail, Hannah, Samuel, Henry, Joseph, Nathaniel, Johanna, John and Esther. (Nathaniel and descendants receive extended mention in this article.)

(III) Joseph, third son and fifth child of Samuel and Abigail (Brown) French, was born about 1676, in Salisbury, and resided in that town, where he was a cordwainer. His will was made March 20, 1745, and proven September 18, 1749. This goes to show that he was prudent, as his will was probably made some years before his death. His wife's name was Hannah as indicated by his will. Their children were: Abigail, Samuel, Nathaniel, Elizabeth and Joseph.

(IV) Samuel (2), eldest son and second child of Joseph and Hannah French, was born December 11, 1699, in Salisbury, and lived in that town until the establishment of the province line in 1741 threw his home into South Hampton, New Hampshire, where he continued to reside throughout his life. He had sons, Samuel, Henry, Benjamin and, probably, Simon, and a daughter, who married Moses Page. Benjamin settled in Gilmanton.

(V) Samuel (3) French, called Samuel, Jr., lived for a time in Salisbury, and was perhaps all his life in the same location. A part of that town was included in South Hampton, New Hampshire, by the establishment of the province line in 1741. The birth of his fifth child is found in the records of the South Hampton church, from which it would appear that he was a resident of South Hampton in 1753. His wife's name was Mary, and their children were: Reuben, Green, Henry, Samuel, Ezekiel, Ruth, Deborah, Hannah and Mary. (Mention of Ezekiel and descendants forms a part of this article.)

(VI) Samuel (4) French married Anna Sweat, June 24, 1771, by whom he had among other children: Samuel, born December 22, 1778; Reuben, born March 19, 1784; Anna, born July 26, 1788.

(VII) Samuel (5), son of Samuel (4) and Anna (Sweat) French, was born December 22, 1778. He married Susanna (Sukey) Tilton, of Loudon, March 21, 1804. Their children were: Eliza, born July 11, 1805; Clarissa, born November 10, 1806; Hiram, born August 8, 1808, married Lydia Bachelder, of Loudon, November 25, 1830; Olive, born June 30, 1810; Samuel, born November 9, 1812; Mary Ann, born December 26, 1814; Reuben Lowell, born April 19, 1818; and two others.

(VIII) Reuben Lowell, third son and seventh child of Samuel and Susanna (Tilton) French, was born in Loudon, April 9, 1818. He received his education in the public schools. At the age of eighteen he became a clerk in the country store of his brother Hiram in Gilmanton, but soon followed his brother to the Water street store in Pittsfield. Soon afterwards, in company with James Munroe Tenney, an early playmate, later well known as a brilliant and prominent merchant of Boston, he purchased the store of his brother Hiram and soon after became sole owner of the lucrative business, continuing therein nearly forty years. During this time he won the reputation of being an unostentatious and upright man, honest in all his dealings. His word was never broken nor his honor tarnished. In public affairs he proved himself an able and useful citizen, was prominently connected with banks, a leading trustee of Pittsfield Academy, and for many years its treasurer. He was the main mover and persistent promoter of the Suncook Valley railroad, the water works, and shoe manufactory. He was also the leading spirit in the laying out of the Floral Park Cemetery, and a large owner. Though aspiring to no political office, he was honored by his party to an election to the state senate. He was a warm and sincere advocate of temperance, good order and sobriety, and heartily identified himself with every movement looking to the best welfare and greater prosperity of the community and town.

In early manhood he publically confessed his faith in Christ and united with the Congregational Church in 1843. He continued a devout and active member through life. He was chosen to positions of responsibility in the church, was elected deacon in 1855, and for many years was superintendent of the Sunday school. He was also treasurer of the society. When his old church home was burned on the morning of February 14, 1876, he was the first one moving for its rebuilding, and generously gave one thousand dollars in aid. The old bell in the tower was a precious gift, and from its melted metal he had a new bell cast and donated it to the society. At his death, which occurred December 14, 1896, the village and town lost a true christian friend, and the family a loving father. As a mark of respect during the funeral services, in which Rev. Samuel Bell officiated, all places of business were closed. Special music was rendered by a local quartet, and his remains were laid at rest in Floral Park Cemetery.

Mr. French was married, August 15, 1844, to Mary Jane, daughter of Nathaniel and Eliza B. (Bickford) Nutter. She was born in Barnstead, August 16, 1827, and was the granddaughter of Deacon Ebenezer Nutter of Revolutionary fame, and one of the early settlers of Barnstead (see Nutter). Mrs. French and her elder sister Eliza who became later the wife of Andrew Bunker, of Concord, were in 1840 students in the old academy. After her marriage to Mr. French they lived in the house now owned by Charles S. French. Later the house was bought and remodelled, and became their home for over fifty years. It is now occupied by their daughter, the wife of Clarence Edwin Berry, grandson of the pioneer John Berry. The house was built for comfort, and is sufficiently elevated in the center of the village to command a beautiful and picturesque landscape.

Mrs. French united with the Congregational Church in 1840, during the pastorate of Rev. Jonathan Curtis, and as long as able, like her husband, was a faithful and active worker. For forty years she sang in the choir, was a faithful and successful teacher of a class of boys in the Sunday school, as those now living will testify, and an efficient director in the Ladies' Aid Society connected with the church. After the death of her husband she was an invalid, unable to leave her home or converse with her friends, but bore all with christian resignation and was ready when the summons came to go up higher! Her death occurred November 2, 1903.

Mrs. French was the mother of five daughters, namely: Laura Celestia, Helen Lowell, Mary Nutter, Susan Gates and Annie Eliza. The first became the wife of George B. Smith, of South Hadley, Massachusetts. She was well educated, the possessor of fine musical talents, and a popular school teacher. She died at Atlantic, Massachusetts, leaving one daughter, Catherine Smith, now the wife of Frank H. Hobbs, of Baye, New Jersey. The second and third died when small children. Susan Gates became the wife of Clarence E. Berry, of Pittsfield (see Berry). Annie Eliza, the youngest, was born February 24, 1867. Her preliminary studies were pursued in public schools of Pittsfield, and the academy under the instruction of Professor D. K. Foster. Afterwards she entered Abbot Academy at Andover, Massachusetts, for a two years' course, but was obliged to leave before its completion on account of ill health. After regaining her normal health she attended the School of Expression in Boston to prepare herself for a public reader and instructor in elocution, from which she graduated with much distinction. Her fine personal appearance won her many friends as a public reader. Among the places where she gave public readings before large and cultivated audiences were Tremont Temple, Steinert and Music Halls, Boston, and many of the principal cities of Massachusetts and New Hampshire. She taught elocution for several years in Boston and vicinity, and for one year at a prominent female college in Milwaukee, Wisconsin. She spent several months abroad in 1892. In early life she united with the Congregational Church, then under the pastorate of Rev. George E. Hill. She was a member of the orders of the Daughters of the Revolution, and Daughters of New Hampshire, and an active and potent factor in the promotion of both. She was also a member of the Abbott Club, devoting herself so closely to its interests as to cause failure of health. April 23, 1892, she was united in marriage to Captain George E. Mahoney, of Boston, at the parental home in Pittsfield. Her married life was short, and she died childless, October 26, 1897. The funeral services were conducted by Rev. Samuel Bell, of Deerfield, assisted by Rev. George E. Lovejoy, pastor of the church, a select quartet furnishing appropriate music.

(VI) Ezekiel, fifth son and child of Samuel (3) and Mary French, was born May 20, 1753. He married (first) Hannah, daughter of Dr. Nehemiah Ordway, of Amesbury, Massachusetts, and married (second) Sally Smith, of Loudon. He was a farmer. Their children were: Polly, Hannah, Sally, Eunice, Thomas and John.

(VII) John, son and sixth child of Ezekiel and Hannah (Ordway) French, married Lucy Tilton Prescott, who lived to be nearly ninety-four years old. He moved from Loudon to Gilmanton and became a representative citizen of the town, and a wealthy farmer, owning at the time of his death thirteen hundred acres. He was a member of the Congregational Church. His age was seventy-five years. His children were: Thomas H., Samuel Prescott, who graduated from Dartmouth College in 1841, and became a celebrated physician in Massachusetts; John O., who also became a physician and celebrated surgeon in the Civil war, married (first) Martha Peaslee, and (second) Martha Percival, of Massachusetts; Ann M., who married (first) Daniel Williams, of Gilmanton, (second) William Brackett, of Epsom, and (third) Nathaniel Clough, of Loudon; and Warren B., who now resides on the old homestead in Gilmanton.

(VIII) Thomas H., first child of Dr. John and Lucy Tilton (Prescott) French, was born in Gilmanton in 1815. He was a farmer and in political faith Whig, like his ancestors. He held a captain's commission in the state militia, and at the time of his death at the age of thirty-seven was about to be promoted. He married Sarah Ann, daughter of Richard Brown, of Loudon. Their children were: Merwin E., a farmer in Gilmanton and a soldier in the Civil war, who married Addie M. Gilman and had children (John H., Mabel and William A.); Albin H., Harland P. and Harriet Newell, the two last dying respectively at one and two years of age. Mr. French survived his wife by two months. Mrs. French was a member of the Congregational Church.

(IX) Albin H., second child of Thomas H. and Sarah Ann (Brown) French, was born in Gilmanton, March 27, 1849. He spent his early life with his grandfather, John French, on a farm in Gilmanton. He received his preliminary education in the district school of his native town. He attended Pembroke Academy, Northwood Seminary and Pittsfield Academy, finally returning to Gilmanton Academy, and fitting for college under Professor Edgar R. Avery, of Tilton Seminary, his tutor for one year. He then studied medicine as his one hundred and third student, under the instruction of Dr. Nahum Wight, who had previously instructed his two uncles, Samuel P. and John O. French. He afterwards entered the University of Vermont at the age of twenty-two, and also had access to the class rooms, taking advantage of the opportunity to study Latin and Greek. Graduating in 1875, he was in practice at Epsom till 1883, when he removed to Leominster, Massachusetts, where he had a drug business in connection with his practice until 1887, when he returned to Gilmanton, New Hampshire, on account of poor health, but soon left for a tour of hospital work in Boston and New York City, attending many clinics, reviewing in surgical lines. He has taken a post-graduate course in the Polyclinic in New York City, and at Long Island College Hospital, New York, in the meantime. He returned to Gilmanton in 1892, but after a few weeks' rest he located at Pittsfield village, where he has been in active practice for thirteen years. During the thirteen years of practice in Pittsfield, and the surrounding towns of Chichester, Epsom, Loudon and Gilmanton, he has only lost one day from his professional duties. He has ridden twenty-four days and nights without sleep in bed, and his work-day for thirty years has averaged seventeen hours. He keeps three horses, and his practice is an extensive one. He was a delegate to the National Medical Convention in New York City in 1880.

Aside from his large practice he owns, what is known now as a historic fact, the pioneer farm, as the following certificate shows, where the first white woman set foot on the soil of Gilmanton, and passed one night in town with no other woman nearer than Epsom.

The certificate taken from the proprietary history of Gilmanton, dated 1845 reads as follows:

"I, Hannah Mudgett, the wife of Benjamin hereby certify that I was born 9th of June 1739 was married to Benjamin Mudgett on the 21st of Dec. 1761—and arrived in Gilmanton on the evening of the 26th-7, Dec. the same year, where I have lived ever since. I moreover state that I was the first white woman who ever set foot in Gilmanton, was the first woman who ever came here to settle, and that I passed one night is town before any other woman arrived. This I now state in my 78th year.

her
"Hannah X Mudgett"
mark

"Nov. 3, 1817."

Her son Samuel was the first male child born in town.

Dr. French's farm comprises two hundred and forty acres, the finest and most picturesque of Gilmanton. He has spent thousands of dollars in improvements, and his buildings are of the best. His farm is in a high state of cultivation. Where the present fine buildings stand the first white male child was born. He is a member of the Grange, and New England Order of Protection. He married (first) Emogen F. Grant, of Gilmanton, August 23, 1873, who died at forty-one years of age, leaving one daughter, Ethel M., and (second) Lila M., daughter of Albert and Olive Jane (Towle) Thompson, of Chichester, September 19, 1892.

Like his ancestors, the Doctor is a Republican in politics. He is one of the representative citizens of the town and has served nine years on the Board of Education, three years as chairman. Mrs. French is a member of the Methodist Episcopal Church.

(X) Ethel M. French resides at home.

(III) Nathaniel, fourth son and sixth child of Samuel and Abigail (Brown) French, was born December 8, 1678, in Salisbury. He was a resident of Hampton in 1701, and later made his home in Kingston. He married Sary Judgkin (probably Judkins), and they were the parents of seven children, most of whom settled is points north of Kingston, in Rockingham and Belknap counties. They were: Samuel, Nathaniel, Sary (died young), Jonathan, Sary, Benjamin and Mary.

(IV) Nathaniel (2), second son and child of Nathaniel (1) and Sary (Judgkin) French, was born April 1, 1709, in Kingston, and continued to reside in that town. No record appears of his marriage, but his wife's name is given as Abigel. Their children were: Elizabeth, Abraham, Nathaniel, William, Secomb, Abigel, Mary and Marthay.

(V) William, third son and fourth child of Nathaniel (2) and Abigel French, was born May 23, 1738, in Kingston, and settled in Stratham, New Hampshire. His wife's name was Olive, but no record appears of her maiden name, or of their marriage.

(VI) Reuben, son of William and Olive French, was born December 1, 1765, in Stratham, and resided in Newmarket, New Hampshire. His wife Lydia, was born January 26, 1766, in Stratham. Their children were: Thomas, Lucy and Polly.

(VII) Thomas, eldest child of Reuben and Lydia French, was born July 17, 1786, in Newmarket, and died December 10, 1864, in Tuftonboro, New Hampshire, where he was an early resident. He married Elizabeth Foss, who was born May 22, 1790, and died August, 1834.

(VIII) James, son of Thomas and Elizabeth (Foss) French, was born July 29, 1811, in Tuftonborough. During his early life he was a country merchant in the town of his birth. In 1851 he moved to Moultonboro, and continued in business on a larger scale until 1869, when he retired, his son James succeeding him. He joined the Methodist Church in 1858, and was active in religious work, and a liberal contributor to the cause of religion. He was an aggressive advocate of Republican principles, an earnest anti-slavery man, and allied with temperance movements, and took the lead in keeping up party organization in his town and in educating the voters. The town was strongly Democratic for many years, therefore he was never chosen to hold any local office with the exception of that of postmaster of Moultonborough, in which capacity he served for many years. He married Eveline Ann Moulton, who was born March 30, 1814, and died October 18, 1899, daughter of Simon and Lydia (Miller) Moulton, the former born 1783, died 1867, and the latter born 1788, died 1860. Mr. French died November 4, 1886. Simon Moulton was a son of Nathan Smith and Mehitable (Perkins) Moulton, and Lydia (Miller) Moulton was the daughter of Edward Brown and Ann (Smith) Miller, the former named having been an officer in the revolutionary war. Moultonborough was named in honor of the ancestor of Eveline Ann (Moulton) French. James and Eveline had four children: James E.; Lydia E., who married Simeon Estes; George B.; and John Q. A., who died in childhood.

(IX) George Barstow, son of James and Eveline Ann (Moulton) French, was born at Tuftonborough, New Hampshire, November 27, 1846. He attended the common schools, New Hampshire Conference Seminary and Female College, Tilton, from which he graduated as valedictorian in 1868, and Dartmouth College, which he entered in 1868 and from which he graduated in 1872. He assisted materially in defraying the expenses of his law studies by teaching for three winters and in taking the census of three towns in the year 1870, performing all the field work on foot. He served as principal of Milford (New Hampshire) high school from September, 1872, to June 25, 1874. He pursued a course of study in law with Wadleigh & Wallace, Milford, New Hampshire, from September, 1874, to the summer of 1875; from October, 1875, to June, 1876, he studied with Nathan Morse, of Boston, Massachusetts, and attended lectures at Boston University Law School. He was admitted to the bar in Massachusetts in May, 1876, and to the New Hampshire bar in September of the same year. He began the practice of his profession at Nashua, New Hampshire, September 1, 1876, and has been actively engaged there ever since, a period of almost thirty years. His practice has been general and laborious; he argues his cases before juries and law courts, has been connected with many important cases, and has acted as counsel for some of the largest corporations of Nashua for many years.

Mr. French was president of the Nashua Trust Company for eleven years, and at the present time (1907) is director in the same. He was president for one term of the New Hampshire Bar Association; for a number of years was a member of the Board of Education of Nashua; was a member of the Constitutional Convention of 1889, and was appointed on the committee to revise the statutes, but declined to serve. He was formerly a member of the Methodist Episcopal Church, but is now a member of the Congregational (Orthodox) Church. He also holds membership in Rising Sun Lodge, Free and Accepted Masons, and the Holeb Club, of which he is president, which is devoted to fishing and hunting, having a club house and camp in Maine. Fishing and hunting are the recreations to which Mr. French turns when seeking rest and recuperation from business pursuits. He is a Republican in politics.

Mr. French married, at Milford, New Hamp-

C. H. French

[illegible] rendent as [illegible] about [illegible] years [illegible] daughter of [illegible] Veazey. [illegible] children [illegible] Thomas, [illegible] William, [illegible]

[illegible] son of [illegible] Braintree, [illegible] 1717. [illegible] 1718. [illegible]

[illegible] Massachusetts [illegible] New Hampshire, were [illegible] died [illegible] He married [illegible] died January 7, [illegible] of whom [illegible] Joseph, Abraham, Isaac, [illegible]

[illegible] child of [illegible] and [illegible] French [illegible] in Braintree, Massachusetts [illegible] removed as early as 1781 [illegible] New Hampshire, where he died [illegible] 1788, aged twenty-eight. He married Abi-

[illegible] removed to Boston, Massachusetts, [illegible] New Hampshire, where [illegible] 1884. He married [illegible] December [illegible] 1857, [illegible] A. Allcock, who died May [illegible] child, Charles H., whose sketch [illegible] (second), September 23, 1869, [illegible] died in 1902.

[illegible] child of William B. and [illegible] was born in Washington, New [illegible] He was [illegible] at [illegible] Academy [illegible] his [illegible] completing his [illegible] parents to Manchester, New Hampshire [illegible] was engaged with his father in the [illegible] business for some years. He then [illegible] where for the ensuing six years he [illegible] engaged in the same line of business. [illegible] he removed to Nashua, New Hampshire, [illegible] in the manufacture of furniture [illegible] Howard & Company. [illegible] completed three [illegible] and from that [illegible] (1907) [illegible] furniture [illegible] concern in [illegible] Mr. [illegible] into [illegible] manufacturing part of [illegible] Milford, where Mr. French built a [illegible] and in addition to this [illegible] wholesale house in Boston [illegible] of J. Woodbury Howard [illegible] and [illegible] Heald; the [illegible] the firm name of Howard, [illegible] 1893, when Mr. Howard [illegible] the firm name has been [illegible] French, who was a [illegible] looked after the [illegible] been built up almost [illegible] addition to this [illegible] entire business [illegible] and sales, and Mr. [illegible] Mr. French was a [illegible]

shire, December 24, 1879, Sarah French Burnham, a graduate of Milford high school and Wheaton Seminary. She is a daughter of Dexter S. and Harriet M. (Crosby) Burnham, who died December, 1892, and March, 1903, respectively. Dexter S. Burnham was a druggist and hardware merchant at Milford, a member of the Board of Education of Milford, for many years, president of the Milford Savings Bank for a number of years, and a leading member of the Orthodox Congregational Church. Harriet M. (Crosby) Burnham was a descendant of the Crosby family, of which Dr. Dixi Crosby and others were distinguished representatives. The children of George B. and Sarah F. (Burnham) French are: Ruth Hawthorne, born at Nashua, October 17, 1880, graduate of Nashua high school, 1898, Smith College, 1902. Robert Allan, born at Nashua, September 13, 1882, graduate of Nashua high school, 1901, Dartmouth College, 1905, now at Harvard Law School. Helen Burnham, born Nashua, September 5, 1884, graduate from Nashua high school, 1902, attended Andover Academy from 1902 to 1903; and Smith College from 1903 to 1904. George Moulton, born Nashua, May 2, 1888.

(Second Family.)

FRENCH Several families of this name are descended from very early settlers in Massachusetts. The founders of this sketch are frequently referred to as the Braintree Frenches. Many good citizens have sprung from them.

(I) John French was born in England about 1612, and emigrated to New England about 1635. He was admitted a freeman in 1639, and after living in Dorchester, Massachusetts, a short time he removed to Braintree, where he was a resident as early as 1640. He died August 6, 1692, aged about eighty years. He married (first) Grace ———, who died February 28, 1681, aged fifty-nine years. Married (second), July 8, 1683, Elinor, daughter of Rev. William Thompson, widow of William Veazey. She died April 23, 1711, aged eighty-five. His children, all by his first wife, were: John, Thomas, died young; Dependence, Temperance, William, Elizabeth, Thomas and Samuel.

(II) Thomas, seventh child and fourth son of John and Grace French, was born in Braintree, March 10, 1658, and died there September 22, 1717. His wife, Elizabeth, who died December 23, 1718, bore him children: Elizabeth, Thomas, Moses, Jonathan, Rachel, Samuel, Abijah, Ebenezer, Sarah and Seth. (Mention of Moses and descendants appears in this article.)

(III) Thomas (2), second child and eldest son of Thomas (1) and Elizabeth French, was born August 5, 1698. He married (first) Rebecca ———; (second), November 5, 1723, Mary Owen. By his first wife he had one child, and by the second eleven.

(IV) Elijah, second child of Thomas (2) and Mary (Owen) French, was born November 23, 1726. Before 1790 he removed from Massachusetts to Washington, New Hampshire, where he died January 15, 1800, aged seventy-three. He married, July 13, 1750, Mary Clark, who died January 7, 1812. They had nine children, several of whom settled in Washington, viz.: Joseph, Abraham, Isaac, Betsey and Seba.

(V) Joseph, third child of Elijah and Mary (Clark) French, was born in Braintree, Massachusetts, March 10, 1760. He removed as early as 1784 to Washington, New Hampshire, where he died May 2, 1788, aged twenty-eight. He married Abigail Farnsworth, who bore him two children: Charles and Betsey.

(VI) Captain Charles, the elder of the two children of Joseph and Abigail (Nabby) (Farnsworth) French, was born in Washington, New Hampshire, November 16, 1784. His father died when he was less than four years old, and from that time forward, during childhood and youth, he resided with his uncle, Deacon David Farnsworth, of Washington. In 1808 he purchased the farm which was ever afterwards his home. He was a man of sterling character and highly esteemed, was a captain in the state militia, and in later times was generally spoken of as "Captain French." He died April 15, 1880, at the great age of ninety-five years. Two months before his death he participated in the public celebration of the one hundredth birthday of his neighbor Deacon Samuel P. Bailey. He married, November 27, 1806, Hannah Clark, of Sharon, Vermont, who died February 22, 1873. They had thirteen children: Joseph, deceased; William B., died young; Sabrina, deceased; William B., deceased; Mary J., deceased; Emily D., died September, 1907; Elizabeth F., deceased; Catherine, deceased; David F., deceased; Sarah F., living in Dexter, Maine; Abigail W., deceased; Charles A., living at Hillsborough Bridge, New Hampshire, and Clark, deceased.

(VII) William Bigsby, fourth child and third son of Charles and Hannah (Clark) French, was born in Washington, New Hampshire, May 20, 1812. He was engaged in trade in his native town until 1864, when he removed to Boston, Massachusetts, and later to Manchester, New Hampshire, where he died August 16, 1884. He married (first), December 27, 1837, Aura A. Allcock, who died May 23, 1868, leaving one child, Charles H., whose sketch follows. He married (second), September 23, 1869, Jennie E. Forsaith, who died in 1902.

(VIII) Charles H., only child of William B. and Aura A. (Allcock) French, was born in Washington, New Hampshire, September 1, 1840. He was educated in the common schools and at Tubbs Academy in his native town, and after completing his studies there accompanied his parents to Manchester, New Hampshire, where he was engaged with his father in the flour and grain business for some years. He then went to Boston, where for the ensuing six years he was engaged in the same line of business. In 1876 he removed to Nashua, New Hampshire, and became a partner in the manufacture of furniture in the firm of Howard & Company. At the start they only employed three men, and from this small beginning built up the present enormous business, being now (1907) the largest furniture manufacturing concern in the east. After admitting Mr. David Heald into the firm they removed the manufacturing part of the business to Milford, where Mr. French built a new factory, and in addition to this opened a large store and wholesale house in Boston. The firm then consisted of J. Woodbury Howard, Charles H. French and David Heald; they conducted business under the firm name of Howard, French & Heald, till 1893, when Mr. Howard went out, and since 1893 the firm name has been French & Heald. Mr. French, who was a thrifty, energetic, hard-working man, looked after the manufacturing, which had been built up almost by his own efforts, and in addition to this acted as the general manager of the entire business, giving a part of his time to the store and sales, and Mr. Heald took charge of the factory. Mr. French was a man of quiet, home-loving proclivities, and was possessed of keen business acumen and personal probity. He was affiliated with no fraternal or social orders, but was a Universalist in religious belief.

Mr. French married, January 1, 1863, Mary Helen Howard, who was born in Washington, New Hampshire, daughter of Ezra P. and Mary (Perkins) Howard. She died August 30, 1869, leaving an only child, Mary Helen, born in Manchester, June 20, 1869, married, 1894, Dr. Claude Freleigh, of Nashua. Mr. French married (second), November 9, 1881, Mrs. Lorenza A. Wright, of Nashua, daughter of Joseph Starret Atherton, of Antrim, New Hampshire. Mr. French died at his home in Malden, Massachusetts, October 31, 1907, aged sixty-seven years and two months.

(III) Moses, second son of Thomas and Elizabeth French, was born and lived in Braintree.

(IV) Moses (2) French was the son of Moses (1). He married Esther Thayer. All were of Braintree.

(V) Rev. Jonathan, son of Moses (2) and Esther (Thayer) French, was born in Braintree in 1740. He was a man of education, and was a surgeon in the English army several years before his attention was turned to the ministry, while practicing among the sick soldiers at Castle William in Boston Harbor. While there he commenced his study preparatory for the ministry, and finished his course at Harvard College, and was installed pastor of the South Parish in Andover, Massachusetts, in 1773, which position he held till his death, July 28, 1809, nearly thirty-seven years. He had the reputation as standing high in the esteem of the clergy, and was a man of great influence for helping all good causes in his community. His wife was Abigail Richards, daughter of Dr. Benjamin and Sarah Thayer Richards, of Weymouth, a distinguished physician of that town. She was born in 1742, and died August 28, 1821. Her mother and her husband's mother were sisters, Sarah and Esther Thayer. This relationship makes Mrs. Dearborn a descendant in the seventh generation in two lines from John Alden and Priscilla Mullen, who came over in the Mayflower and landed on Plymouth Rock, December 21, 1620. This interesting genealogy is shown as follows: John Alden and Priscilla Mullen, his wife, had nine children. Their daughter Esther married John Bass. A daughter, Sarah Bass, married Ephraim Thayer; Ephraim and Sarah (Bass) Thayer had fourteen children. all of whom lived to grow up, marry and have families. One of the fourteen, Esther, married Moses French, and they had several children. one of whom was the Rev. Jonathan French, of Andover, as before stated. Another daughter married Dr. Richards, as above stated, so Mrs. Dearborn is one of the bluest of New England blue blood of the Pilgrim stock. John and Priscilla (Mullen) Alden's granddaughter was grandmother of Rev. Jonathan French (and his wife), of Andover, who were the grandparents of Sperry French, Mrs. Dearborn's father.

(VI) Rev. Jonathan (2) French, D. D., of North Hampton, was a son of Rev. Jonathan (1) and Abigail (Richards) French. He married Rebecca Mercy Farrar, of Lincoln, Massachusetts.

(VII) Professor Sperry French, son of Rev. Jonathan (2) and Rebecca M. (Farrar) French, was born in North Hampton, January 9, 1823. He was principal of the grammar school at Exeter fifty years, beginning when he was twenty years old, and retiring when he was three score and ten. Mr. French kept up with the advanced ideas and methods of education, down to the very last year of his teaching; he did not retire because he was superannuated in mental power or antiquated in his methods of instruction; he was equal to the best of them, but decided to retire and take life easy. He was a strict disciplinarian, but always kept on good terms with his pupils. He was a born teacher, and when the boys left his school it was not his fault if they were not capable of pursuing their studies in the schools for higher education.

BUCK Among the earliest names in New England this has borne an honorable part in the development of the states of Massachusetts and New Hampshire, as well as of other states in the Union, and is still borne untarnished by leading citizens of this state. While not so universally represented as some others, it has borne its full share in the spread of civilization.

(I) William Buck (sometimes written Bucke), was born in 1585, in England, and died in Cambridge, Massachusetts, December 24, 1658. He came to New England in the bark "Increase," in 1635, and was then fifty years old. He was accompanied by his son Roger, a young man of eighteen, and resided in the west field, Cambridge, northeasterly from the present Garden street, where was formerly a highway to the great swamp, now called Raymond street. He was a manufacturer of plows.

(II) Roger, son of William Buck, must have been born about 1617. He inherited the homestead and occupation of his father. Soon after 1685 he removed to Woburn, and there in 1688 acknowledged the sale of a part of his homestead to his son-in-law, Thomas Baverick. A condition of this sale was that if Baverick should sell the property, Roger's son, Ephraim Buck, should have the preference as purchaser. Roger Buck died at Woburn, November 10, 1693, at the age of seventy-six years. His wife's name was Susan, and their children were: Samuel, John, Ephraim, Mary, Ruth, Elizabeth, John and Lydia. Susan, mother of these children, died September 10, 1685, and this fact seems to have led to the removal of her husband to Woburn, where some of his children were already settled.

(III) Ephraim, third son and child of Roger and Susan Buck, was born July 26, 1646, in Cambridge, and resided in Woburn. He was taxed there in the meetinghouse rate in 1672. His death occurred between November 23, 1717, and March 20, 1721, the respective dates of signing and proving his will. He was married January 1, 1671, at Woburn, to Sarah, daughter of John Brooks, and their children were: Sarah, Ephraim, John (died young), John, Samuel, Eunice, Ebenezer and Mary. His descenants are numerous in Wilmington, Massachusetts.

(IV) Ebenezer, fifth son and seventh child of Ephraim and Sarah (Brooks) Buck, was born May 20, 1689, in Woburn, and probably resided in Wilmington, Massachusetts.

(V) Ebenezer (2), son of Ebenezer (1) Buck, is found on record as a resident of Framingham, Massachusetts, in 1768, and of Woburn in 1769. After 1770 he resided in Upton, Massachusetts, where he died August 7, 1827, then said to be eighty-seven years old. He was a soldier of the Revolution and his descriptive list would make it appear that he was born in 1742. His wife, Mary survived him thirteen years, and died August 18, 1840. Before 1770 he had three children born, namely: Ezra, Elijah and Amos. Ten children were born in Upton from 1772 to 1792, namely: Anna, Henry, Charles Gates, Mary, Ruth,

Wm. E. Buck

Susanna, Ebenezer, Moses, Mehitable and George Washington. Of these Ezra, Elijah and Charles Gates died young.

(VI) Amos, son of Ebenezer (2) and Mary Buck, was born November 16, 1769, in Westboro, Massachusetts, and was brought up from infancy in Upton. He resided for a time in Bradford, Massachusetts, and died at the home of his son Amos in Hampstead, New Hampshire, July 8, 1859, aged ninety years.

(VII) Amos (2), son of Amos (1) Buck, was born March 24, 1808, in Bradford, Massachusetts, and died at the home of his son, William E. Buck, in Manchester, New Hampshire, January 29, 1881. For forty-five years he was a prominent citizen of Hampstead, and was there commonly known as "Captain Buck" because of his official connection with the state militia during his early manhood. He was a man of marked native talent and much public spirit, whose counsel and leadership his townsmen often sought. He was a justice of the peace for many years; and being uncommonly well versed in a knowledge of law, he did considerable business as an attorney in writing deeds and wills, and in settling the estates of persons deceased. As counselor he generally affected settlements by compromise in instances among his townsmen who from time to time threatened one another with lawsuits, in cases of serious disagreement. Captain Buck was a stanch Republican; as a political leader he had a strong and loyal following, who conferred upon him their highest political honors. He was chosen moderator of fifteen town-meetings; a member of the board of selectmen seventeen times, chairman of said board fifteen times; and twice as the town's representative to the state legislature. Though not a churchman, Amos Buck was chiefly respected for the nobility and sympathetic nature of his character. He was modest, charitable, and trustworthy. Occasionally he was heard to repeat Pope's aphorism, "An honest man's the noblest work of God"; and it may be said that Mr. Buck's life was an exemplification of his belief in the truthfulness of the quotation. Amos Buck was married in Derry, December 1, 1836, to Mary Jane Ela, daughter of Deacon William Ela (see Ela IV). Immediately after their marriage they settled in Hampstead, where the remainder of their lives were spent. Mrs. Buck died in Hampstead, April 22, 1879. She was an intelligent and capable christian woman, loyal to her husband and devoted to her children. She was admitted to membership in the Hampstead Church August 7, 1851. They were the parents of three sons; William Ela, the eldest, receives mention in succeeding paragraphs. George Mitchell, the second, died in his ninth year. Amos Henry, the third, was near the close of his twenty-second year at the time of his death.

(VIII) William Ela Buck, at this writing, still survives, and resides in Manchester, New Hampshire, where he has made his home since April, 1869. He was born April 8, 1838, in Hampstead, New Hampshire. In childhood he there attended the central village school about twenty-five weeks a year, until he was thirteen years of age. After that he attended the same school one or two winter terms. It had a new teacher nearly every term, but no course of study; hence the work was disconnected, and progress slow. However, the young man had so improved his vacations by working in his father's shop that at the age of seventeen he had accumulated about six hundred dollars; this, together with scholarships won and what he earned during subsequent vacations, enabled him to pay his expenses one term at Chester Academy, two terms at Atkinson Academy, and three years at Phillips Exeter Academy, where at the age of twenty-one he found himself well fitted for entrance to Harvard University. Mr. Buck, at this time, also found himself without money and with health somewhat impaired and consequently deemed it wise to postpone entrance to Dartmouth College, where he had proposed to go, until he could refill his purse and improve his health. Accordingly in the fall (1859) he went to Bloomingdale, Illinois, and there taught his first school, in a country district, out on a wide prairie twenty-five miles west of Chicago. He returned home the following spring and temporarily re-entered the shop at Hampstead, where he could for a short time earn more money than elsewhere, intending to enter college in the fall. He was, however, soon asked to teach the village school at home; and he could not refuse, remembering the great satisfaction he derived from his first term's experience at teaching, being also aware that the conditions of his purse and health were not what they should be for entrance upon a four years' course at college. Further experience in teaching was so enjoyable to Mr. Buck, he concluded before the opening of another college year to make teaching his life work, and consequently gave up both the college course and his intention of studying law.

After teaching other schools in New Hampshire, at Danville and Pelham, Mr. Buck established a private high school at Penningtonville, Pennsylvania, in the spring of 1863. This school became highly prosperous, and he there had the satisfaction of fitting several pupils for college who afterwards became prominent in Pennsylvania life. Owing to the decease of his wife and the consequent removal of his infant son to Hampstead, New Hampshire, Mr. Buck sold his private school in the fall of 1867, and immediately became principal of the public high school at Cohasset, Massachusetts. He taught there about a year and a half, and the school committee publicly pronounced his service as "very satisfactory"; but in April, 1869, he had a call at a higher salary to the principalship of the "Intermediate" school in Manchester, New Hampshire. He at once accepted the call, but chiefly because of the better outlook there. In seven months Mr. Buck was promoted to the principalship of the Spring street grammar school, where he taught till the fall of 1874, when he was promoted to the principalship of a new school in the then new Ash street schoolhouse. He taught this school till April, 1877, when he was given a superior promotion by being chosen superintendent of public instruction for the city of Manchester, which position he held till July 1, 1900. He tendered his resignation, on account of poor health, May 4, 1900, and it was accepted subject to the retention of his services till the close of the spring term. This record shows that Mr. Buck was teacher eighteen years and superintendent twenty-three years, and that his work during all these forty-one years was highly efficient and satisfactory is amply evidenced by his repeated promotions as teacher and his long retention as superintendent. His merit was recognized by Dartmouth College when, in 1886, it conferred upon him the honorary degree of Master of Arts. Upon Mr. Buck's withdrawal from the superintendency, Manchester's corps of teachers publicly expressed kind personal regards, and high appreciation of his service, by presenting him with a beautiful and costly hall clock, to the purchase price of which testimonial every member of the corps made contribution. Mr. Buck made a feeling response, in which he expressed much satisfaction that there had ever been between them and himself mutual feelings of confidence and respect, and an official loyalty to one another that had largely contributed to the success of the schools.

In his earlier manhood Superintendent Buck belonged to several fraternal societies; but after twenty years of conscientious devotion to the growing interests of the schools under his care, he found his health so impaired that it was necessary for him to forego other responsibilities than those pertaining to his family and the schools under his supervision. The result was that outside associations were relinquished and thereby opportunity was afforded him successfully to continue his chosen life work for another score of years which terminated in 1900 by his resignation on account of physical disability, as before said.

December 29, 1864, William Ela Buck married Helen Meribah Putnam, only daughter of Mr. and Mrs. Henry Putnam, of Hampstead, New Hampshire. She was born there May 28, 1841; and died in Penningtonville, Pennsylvania, October 30, 1865. They had one child, William Putnam Buck, who was born at Penningtonville, October 2, 1865; and at this writing resides in Denver, Colorado.

July 16, 1872, William Ela Buck married Harriet Ann Mack, the elder daughter of Mr. and Mrs. Daniel Kendrick Mack, of Manchester, New Hampshire. She was born there October 27, 1848; and at this writing resides in Manchester. They have had six children, as follows: George Kendrick, born September 9, 1874, graduated from Williams College, 1896. Walter French, born January 3, 1876, graduated from New Hampshire State College, 1897. Burton Winthrop, born January 19, 1878, graduated from Dartmouth College. 1900. Arthur Ela, born January 28, 1880, graduated from Dartmouth College, 1901. Edward Morris, born November 4, 1882, died July 12, 1883. Helen Isabella, born October 29, 1883, graduated from Mount Holyoke College, 1905.

SAWTELLE

Probably few New England names have shown greater variation in the spelling and pronunciation than has this. Sartel, Sattell, Sautell, Sautle, Saretell, Sartwell, Sortwell, Sawtel are some of the peculiarities found in the ancient records. The most general form of usage in the first five generations was Sawtell, but in more recent times one letter has been added, giving the present form.

(I) Richard Sawtell, the ancestor of many families bearing the name in New England and elsewhere, was a native of England. He was a resident and a proprietor of Watertown, Massachusetts, previous to 1637. Subsequently he was one of the first settlers and a proprietor of Groton, Massachusetts, and was the clerk of the town during the first three years after its incorporation in 1662. He was active and prominent in Watertown and in Groton. He died August 2, 1694, and his wife Elizabeth survived him a little more than two months, dyng October 18, of the same year. Their children were: Obadiah, Elizabeth, Jonathan, Mary, Hannah, Zaccharia, Enoch, John, Ruth and Bethia.

(II) Obadiah, eldest child of Richard and Elizabeth Sawtell, resided in the town of Groton and is honorably mentioned in the records of the town. But few items of his family history are recorded. It is shown, however, that his wife's name was Hannah, and that he had children, Obadiah and Abigail.

(III) Obadiah (2), son of Obadiah (1) and Hannah Sawtelle, was born about 1650, in Groton, and lived in that town where he died March 20, 1740, as shown by his headstone. He married Hannah Lawrence, who was born March 24, 1761, a daughter of George and Elizabeth (Cripe) Lawrence. The births and baptizms of their six children are recorded in Groton, namely: Elnathan, Josiah, Hannah, Abigail, Obadiah and Hezekiah.

(IV) Hezekiah, youngest child of Obadiah (2) and Hannah (Lawrence) Sawtelle, was born March 2, 1703, and probably passed his entire life in Groton. His descendants are very numerous. He married Joanna Wilson and their eleven children were born between 1724 and 1747. He died March 11, 1779, and was survived more than several years by his widow, who died September 11, 1786.

(V) Ephraim, son of Hezekiah and Joanna (Wilson) Sawtelle, was born January 18, 1734, and was married December 22, 1757, to Abigail Stone, who was born December 2, 1736, daughter of Deacon James and Abigail (Farwell) Stone, of Groton. His children were: Abigail, Lucy, Josiah (died young) Molly, Eli, Josiah, Ephraim and Sarah.

(VI) Eli, second son and fifth child of Ephraim and Abigail (Stone) Sawtelle, was born November 26, 1765, in Groton, and settled in Brookline, New Hampshire, where he cleared up and developed a farm. He married Lydia Hunt, who was born April 20, 1769, in Tewkesbury, Massachusetts, daughter of John and Lydia (Thorndyke) Hunt. She was the youngest of the six children of her parents. Their children were: Mary, Lydia, Isaac, John, Eli, Eldad, Joseph, Ithamar, Abigail.

(VII) Joseph, fourth son of Eli and Lydia (Hunt) Sawtelle, was born at Brookline, New Hampshire, April 22, 1804. He was a farmer and surveyor. He was active in the affairs of the town, and was a man of substance and standing in the community. He held all the town offices, was selectman for many years, and represented Brookline in the legislature. He was a member of the Unitarian Church. He married Catherine, daughter of Eli Parker, of Brookline. They had three children; two died young. Joseph Sawtelle died at his home in Brookline, March 8, 1883.

(VIII) Ellen Catherine, daughter and only child to attain maturity of Joseph and Catherine (Parker) Sawtelle, was born in Brookline, New Hampshire, March 16, 1843. She was educated in the public schools of her native town and at McCollom Institute, Mont Vernon, New Hampshire, and at the normal school at Salem, Massachusetts. Miss Sawtelle has become one of the most distinguished educators who has ever gone forth from New Hampshire. In 1864 she entered the Hancock School of Boston, Massachusetts, with which she has been connected ever since. Few teachers can show a longer term of service. She became principal in 1904, and now conducts a school of sixty-two teachers and two thousand four hundred pupils.

LORD

Many of the Lords of New Hampshire trace their descent to Robert, the immigrant, who since he settled in New England before 1650, is entitled to be called a pioneer. Sterling worth and upright character have been attributes of the Lords as a family, and many of them have attained positions of prominence in manufactures, trade and the professions.

(I) Robert Lord. the immigrant, was born in England in 1603. and appears to have been the son of widow Catherine Lord, who was residing in Ipswich, Massachusetts, in 1637, and was a commoner in 1641. Robert Lord took the freeman's oath at Boston, March 3, 1636. His house lot on High street was granted to him February 19, 1637. In 1639 he had a houselot on High street, which property yet remains a possession of his descendants. He was one of Denison's subscribers in 1648; had a share in Plum Island, in 1664; and was a voter in town affairs in 1679. He was on a committee with Richard Saltonstall and others, empowered to grant houselots to settlers, in 1645. He was representative in 1638; selectman in 1661 and many years after; and was appointed "searcher of coin" for the town of Ipswich in 1654. He was long town clerk, and also clerk of the court till his decease. The latter office included the duties now performed by the clerk of probate and register of deeds. He served more than twenty years in the Indian wars and became so inured to camp life and exposure that he could never afterwards sleep upon a feather bed. He is said to have been below the medium stature, but of powerful mould and one of the most athletic, strong, and fearless men in the Colonial service. There is a tradition that the Indians themselves at one time, when confronted by Lord's rangers, proposed to decide the battle that was anticipated by an encounter between the champions of the two parties; to this the whites agreed, and Robert Lord walked to the front. The Indians selected the most powerful of their tribe, a perfect giant, full seven feet in stature. The two men were to meet at full run and take the "Indian hug" as they closed. The savages anticipated an easy victory. They came together like two infuriated bullocks with a tremendous shock, but in an instant the redskin lay stretched upon the earth, and the shouts of the Colonial scouts rang out in the forest. Not satisfied with a single experiment, they were required to rush and clinch again. In this encounter Lord took the "hip-lock" on his greasy antagonist and threw him with such force that a blood vessel was ruptured in the fall. The Indians took him up and carried him from the arena, fully acknowledging themselves defeated; they afterward reported that some whiteman's devil invested Lord with supernatural strength. He died August 12, 1683, in the eightieth year of his age. His will, dated June 28, was proved September 25, 1683. He married Mary Waite in 1630. In his will he mentions his wife, Mary, "with whom by God's good providence we have lived comfortably together in a married condition almost fifty-three years." He bequeaths her all his estate during her life. Their children were: Robert, Sarah, Nathaniel, Thomas, Samuel, Susannah, Abigail, Hannah, and one who married a Chendler.

(II) Robert (2), eldest son of Robert (1) and Mary (Waite) Lord, was born in 1631, and died November 11, 1696, aged sixty-five years. He had a share in Plum Island in 1664, was a voter in town affairs in 1679. and was one of twenty-four of "the young generation," who joined the church by taking the covenant, between January 18 and February 1, 1673. He was a selectman, and held other offices in the town of Ipswich, being marshal of the court as early as 1669, and holding that office ten years. He is usually designated Marshal Lord. He married Hannah Day, who survived him. Their sons were: Robert, John, Thomas, James, Joseph and Nathaniel.

(III) Thomas, third son of Robert (2) and Hannah (Day) Lord, married, May 24. 1686, Mary Brown. Their children were: Thomas, John, Jonadab, Mary and Robert.

(IV) John, second son and child of Thomas and Mary (Brown) Lord, settled in the town of Exeter, New Hampshire, and on October 31, 1712, married Abigail Gilman, who was born July 24, 1693, daughter of Moses and Anne Gilman, by whom he had sixteen children: Anne, John (died young), Mary, Abiel, Robert (died young), John (died young), Edmund, Abigail, John, Robert (died young), Elizabeth (died young), Jonathan, Eliphalet, Robert, Samuel and Elizabeth.

(V) Robert (3). ninth son and fourteenth child of John and Abigail (Gilman) Lord, was born in Exeter, April 8, 1733, and died in 1801. He was a farmer in Exeter and lived there in a garrison house during the Revolutionary war. Robert Lord is credited in the Revolutionary War Rolls of New Hampshire with service in Captain Peter Coffin's company of minute-men, mustered by Joseph Cilley, muster master at Portsmouth, November 24, 1775. He married a Miss Crane, of Sanbornton, and they had ten children: Hannah, John, Deborah, Abigail, Anna. Robert, Samuel, James, Nathaniel and Polly.

(VI) Robert (4), sixth child and second son of Robert (3) Lord, was born in Exeter, and removed to Ossipee, where he dwelt the remainder of his life. He married, September 30, 1789, Mary Davis, of Poplin, and they had: Robert and Abigail, and others.

(VII) Robert (5), third son of Robert (4) and Mary (Davis) Lord, was a farmer and resided in Ossipee. He married Nancy Goldsmith, and her line of descent is as follows:

(1) Richard Goldsmith, who was a grantee of land in Wenham. Massachusetts, June 23, 1644, was killed by lightning May 18, 1673. His wife's baptismal name was Mary.

(2) Zacheus, son of Richard and Mary Goldsmith, was born in 1662, and died October 30, 1747. He married Martha Hutton, of Wenham.

(3) Zacheus (2), son of Zacheus (1) and Martha (Hutton) Goldsmith, was born April 7, 1701. He removed from Wenham to Ipswich, and thence to Essex, Massachusetts. He married, December 14, 1724, Tabitha Dodge, who died October 8, 1726. He married (second) Mehitable Kimball.

(4) John, son of Zacheus (2) Goldsmith, was born in Wenham, February 23, 1736. He was a soldier in the Revolutionary war, and served in Captain Dodge's company, of Colonel Little's regiment. He married, in Ipswich, March 11, 1761, Martha Lamson, and in 1777 settled in Ossipee. New Hampshire.

(5) Benjamin, son of John and Martha (Lamson) Goldsmith, was born March 13, 1764, and died May 1, 1841. He married Abigail Rogers, and their daughter Nancy married Robert Lord, as above stated. Their children were: John R., Alvah, Mary R., Francis H., William H., Jesse and Vesta. (Francis H. is mentioned at length in this article).

(VIII) Alvah, second son and child of Robert (5) and Nancy (Goldsmith) Lord. was born in Ossipee. He was a farmer. In politics he was a Democrat, and in religious faith an Adventist. He married Betsey Moody, and they had two children: Edwin Francis and William Henry.

(IX) Edwin Francis, son of Alvah and Betsey (Moody) Lord, was born in Tamworth about 1852. He was a successful farmer. He voted the Democratic ticket, but had no taste for politics and preferred the independence of life he enjoyed as a farmer to all the official positions he might have been elected to. He was an Adventist in religion and a faithful worker in his church. He married,

1872, in Moultonboro, Julia A. Hodsdon, daughter of Eliza Hodsdon, of Moultonboro. Two children were born to them: Lester W. and Ralph S.

(X) Lester Winslow Lord, M. D., son of Edwin F. and Julia A. (Hodsdon) Lord, was born in Tamworth, October 2, 1874, and at an early age showed an aptitude for study and an ambition for knowledge. He entered the Nute high school at Milton at sixteen years of age, and two years later passed the examination required before entering Bowdoin College, but he did not enter college until 1894. After completing the freshman year in the literary course he became a student at the Baltimore Medical College, from which he graduated in 1897, having taken a four years' course in three years. He began practice in Tamworth, New Hampshire, in 1897, and remained there until 1899, except while absent studying dentistry at the American Dental College of Chicago, practicing medicine while there. At the outbreak of the war with Spain he was appointed assistant surgeon with the rank of first lieutenant. He spent the greater part of his term of service in the Philippines with General Funston's and General Otis' commands, in the Ninth Regiment of infantry, whose colonel was E. N. Liscum, later killed in the Chinese campaign, who was a warm personal friend of Dr. Lord. Dr. Lord took part in some of the campaigns of the war and was in that famous advance of the Ninth Infantry in pursuit of Aguinaldo. He participated in many running battles and skirmishes. notable among them being the engagement at Tarlac, Luzon. In 1899, when ordered to the Philippines, he went via the Suez canal and the Mediterranean sea, visiting various parts of Asia, Africa and Europe on the voyage. In 1902, while still in the service, he sailed from Manila, Philippine Islands, and visited Japan. At the close of his term of service he returned to the United States, and took a course in the Ohio Institute of Pharmacy, from which he graduated in 1903. He also took a course in advanced ophthalmology in Golden Cross College, Chicago, taking his diploma in 1905. In 1903 he resumed his professional practice, bought and rebuilt an old grocery store at West Ossipee and converted it into a drug store, adding a splendidly equipped operating room. and making surgery a specialty. The thoroughness and care which characterized his work while in the army rapidly built up his practice, and recently he has added a new and larger operating room which is as near perfect for the work for which it is designed as modern equipment can make it.

He is a member of Manila Lodge, No. 342, Free and Accepted Masons, of Manila, Philippine Islands; Passaconaway Lodge, No. 84, Independent Order of Odd Fellows, of Tamworth; Syracuse Lodge, No. 27, Knights of Pythias, of Sanbornville, and Charles N. Willey Commandery, No. 25, Uniform Rank, and is also captain and assistant surgeon of the First Brigade of the Uniform Rank, Knights of Pythias, and member of Dover Lodge, No. 184, Benevolent and Protective Order of Elks. Dr. Lord is a fellow of the American University Association, vice-president of the Association of Physicians and Surgeons of America, member of the Association of Military Surgeons of the United States, Carroll County and New Hampshire Medical societies, and New Hampshire Pharmaceutical Society. He is an active member of that exclusive military brotherhood, the Military Order of the Carabao, which claims as members Otis, Funston, Wheaton, Grant, Bell, Chaffee, of the regular army, and of the Regular Army and Navy Union. He married, in October, 1906, Rena A. Thompson, of Lawrence, Massachusetts, who was born in Lawrence, January 6, 1880, daughter of Joseph and Margaret (Kenyon) Thompson.

(VIII) Francis Hubbard, fourth child and third son of Robert, Jr., and Nancy (Goldsmith) Lord, was born in Ossipee, April 6, 1825. In his earlier life he was engaged in agriculture and was also a drover. Later he became a dealer in lumber and timber lands. He married, in 1887, Hannah Blaisdell, who was born in Tamworth, New Hampshire, 1835, daughter of Stetson and Sally (Emery) Blaisdell. (See Blaisdell. VIII). The children of this marriage are: Frank Stetson, Addie L. and Effie. Frank S. is the subject of the next paragraph. Addie L. was born in Ossipee, July 21, 1862, and was educated at Fryeburg, Maine. She married George F. McIndoe, and resides in Dorchester, Massachusetts. She is a member of the New Hampshire Daughters, and Daughters of the Revolution. Effie, who was born in Ossipee, September 22, 1873, was educated in Fryeburg, Maine, and Roxbury, Massachusetts, and is now a stenographer at the Boston Exchange.

(IX) Frank Stetson, only son of Francis H. and Hannah (Blaisdell) Lord, was born in Ossipee, April 18, 1858, and obtained his education in New Hampton, New Hampshire, Poughkeepsie, New York, and New York City. He taught school, and was a member of the school board of Ossipee for several years. He is a civil engineer and subsequently was employed in making various surveys and in engineering enterprises in the states of Maine, New Hampshire. Vermont, Massachusetts, New York, North Carolina and Florida. In 1883 he became a real estate dealer and lumber manufacturer, operating mills at Albany, West Albany, Bartlett, West Ossipee, and Tamworth, and doing a large and profitable business. In politics Mr. Lord is a Republican and for a time took an active part in politics, holding various town offices and serving as county commissioner for six years. In 1906 he was offered the nomination for another term, but declined it on account of the amount of his private business. He was elected to the state senate in 1906, and served at the following meeting of the general court on the most important committees. He is fraternal and a member of various orders. He is a member of Saco Valley Lodge, No. 21, Independent Order of Odd Fellows, and of Ossipee Valley Lodge, No. 74, Free and Accepted Masons; Columbia Royal Arch Chapter, No. 18, of Farmington; and St. Paul Commandery, Knights Templar, of Dover.

(Second Family.)

LORD The family under consideration in this article has been distinguished by men and women of brains, has included scholars and divines, and is still contributing much to the progress of the nation along uplifting lines. It is undoubtedly of English origin, but the place of birth of the first ancestor or the exact time of his coming to America has not been discovered. It has been conspicuous in New Hampshire and is still so.

(I) Nathan Lord is found of record in Kittery, Maine, as early as 1652, when he with others signed an agreement as follows: "We, whose names are underwritten, do acknowledge ourselves subject to the government of Massachusetts Bay in New England." There can be no doubt that he was English, as that locality was settled at that time exclusively by English people. Nathan Lord was a planter and appears to have dealt in real estate. Previous to 1662 he was located in a district called Sturgeon's Creek, where he received a grant of land. This location is now in the town of Elliott, once a part of ancient Kittery. After 1662 Nathan Lord seems to have owned a homestead at or near what is now called Mt. Pleasant,' in South Berwick. In 1676, with his son and namesake, he took possession of an estate of seventy-seven acres, on which was a house and barn, and this was held about five years in joint ownership, when the father transferred his right and title to his son. This was located in the district known as Oldfields in South Berwick. Upon this place a garrison was maintained during the Indian troubles, and was occupied as a residence as late as 1816. This was a unique and extensive edifice and had a door through which could be driven a yoke of oxen and cart. The door was surmounted by a carved figure head, representing the prow of a ship, while many wood carvings on its interior added to its adornment. Nathan Lord died in 1733, and in his will bequeathed to his minister a gold ring, and he also left twenty pounds for the purchase of communion plate. His estate was valued at one thousand eight hundred and seventy-six pounds, two shillings and two pence. He was twice married, but the name of his first wife does not appear. She was a daughter of Abraham Conley, who made Nathan Lord executor of his will and gave to him the latter's land at Sturgeon's Creek. He was married (second), November 22. 1678, to Martha Tozer, daughter of Richard and Judith (Smith) Tozer. She appears to have been the mother of his children, namely: Martha, Nathan, William, Richard, Judith, Samuel, Mary, John, Sarah, Anne and Abraham. (Mention of Samuel and descendants appears in this article).

(II) Nathan (2), eldest child of Nathan (1) and Martha (Everett) Lord, was born about 1657. and died in 1733. He was married November 22, 1678, to Martha, daughter of Richard and Judith (Smith) Tozier. Their children were: Martha, Nathan, William, Richard, Judith, Samuel, Mary, John, Sarah, Anne and Abraham.

(III) Abraham, youngest child of Nathan (2) and Martha (Tozier) Lord, was born October 29, 1699, in Kittery, and continued to reside through life in that town. His will was dated April 11, 1772, and was probated April 20, seven years later. He probably died about the close of the year 1778. He was married April 10, 1717, to Margaret, daughter of Nicholas and Abigail (Hodsdon) Gowen. She was born March 19, 1699, and died February 11, 1775. Their children were: Simeon, Benjamin Meads, Abraham, Jeremiah, David, Solomon, Elisha, Margaret and Sarah.

(IV) David, eighth son and child of Abraham and Margaret (Gowen) Lord, was baptized April 30, 1732, in Kittery, where he made his home through life. He was married December 6, 1759, to Phoebe, daughter of Dr. Edmond and Sarah (Bartlett) Coffin. She was born March 15, 1735, in Kittery, and died June 30, 1832. aged ninety-seven years. She survived her husband about twenty-five years; he died in 1807. Their children were: Shuah, Enoch, Humphrey, Susanna, Margaret, Edmond, Sarah and Mary.

(V) Mary (Polly), youngest child of David and Phoebe (Coffin) Lord, was baptized April 8, 1770, and became the wife of Maturin Abbott (see Abbott, VII).

(II) Captain Samuel, fourth son and sixth child of Nathan and Martha (Tozer) Lord, was born June 14, 1689, in what is now Berwick, Maine, and lived in that town, where he died about 1763. His will was dated February 23, 1761, and was

proven soon after. He was married October 19, 1710, to Martha Wentworth, who was born February 9, 1684, daughter of Catherine and Paul Wentworth, and granddaughter of Elder William Wentworth. (See Wentworth, XX). His children were: John. Nathan, Abraham, Samuel, Ebenezer and Mary.

(III) Abraham, third son of Captain Samuel and Martha (Wentworth) Lord, resided in Berwick, Maine, where he died in 1783. His will was dated May 12, of that year and proven June 10, following. He married Betsey Davis, and their children were: Tozer, Abraham, Daniel, Wentworth, James and Nathaniel.

(IV) Rev. Wentworth, fourth son of Abraham and Betsey (Davis) Lord, was born September 14, 1755. in Berwick, Maine, and became a Baptist clergyman. He was pastor in Ossipee, New Hampshire, and Parsonsfield, Maine. He was a sergeant of the Colonial forces in the siege of Boston, in 1775. He was married in February, 1777, to Patience Brackett, who was born August 6, 1754, and died February 8, 1841. He survived her four years, dying February 28, 1845. Their children were: Noah, Wentworth, Abraham. Hannah, Lydia, George, Patience, Margaret, Sally and Jemima.

(V) George, fourth son and sixth child of Rev. Wentworth and Patience (Brackett) Lord, was born November 22, 1793, and resided in Ossipee, New Hampshire, where he died July 1, 1863. He was a farmer and also the proprietor of a wool carding mill at Water Village. He married Patience Titcomb. George and Patience (Titcomb) Lord had Daniel, who resided in Dunkirk, New York. where he was in the hardware business. He was killed on a boat on the Ohio river. Abraham B., a dentist who practiced many years in Manchester, where he died in 1864. Also three daughters: Patience and Margaret, each of whom married a man named Haines, and Susan, who married a man named Brown. All these children are dead.

(VI) Calvin L., son of George and Patience (Titcomb) Lord, was born in Ossipee, 1822, and died November 9, 1861, aged thirty-nine years. He lived in Francestown, where for some years he was second hand in a cotton mill. About 1855 he engaged in farming for about two years, and then went into trade and occupied the Long store until nearly the time of his death. He married, November 10, 1847, Nancy A. Taylor, of Francestown, who was born May 17, 1826, and died in Francestown, December 17, 1873, aged forty-seven. She was the daughter of William Taylor, who was born December 9, 1797. He was an honest and respected farmer. He first lived in Lyndeboro, then in Francestown. Late in life he removed to Troy, where he died November 6, 1876. He married, December 30, 1821, Mary L. Balch, of Francestown. The children of Calvin and Nancy A. Lord were: George C., mentioned below, and Ida F., who was born in Francestown, December 11, 1851, and married, September 28, 1875, Edward Richardson, of Lyndeboro, now dead, and she now resides in Manchester.

(VII) George Calvin Lord, only son of Calvin and Nancy A. (Taylor) Lord, was born in Manchester, November 30, 1848, and was educated in the common schools and Academy at Francestown. He was a clerk in the store of Whipple & Atwood, three years, at New Boston, New Hampshire. He then came to Manchester and filled a like position in the store of Stearns & Palmer for five years. Then he went to East Wilton and was in the employ of

S. H. Dunbar for three years, at the end of which time he returned to Manchester and took charge of the meat department of Poore & Rowell two years. August 1, 1881, he bought out Woodbury Q. Sargent's grocery store, at the corner of Lowell and Maple streets, which he carried on profitably until May. 1906, when he sold out after a quarter of a century in business for himself. He has been successful and has a very comfortable fortune. He resides at No. 336 Myrtle street, where he has built a commodious house, and busies himself during the warm season in cultivating vegetables, fruits and flowers, of which he has an abundance.

He is a Republican in politics and has held the office of selectman four years. He attends the Franklin Street (Congregational) Church, of which Mrs. Lord is a member. He is a member of Pacific Lodge, No. 45, Ancient Free and Accepted Masons, of Francestown, and of Wilde Lodge, No. 45, and Mt. Washington Encampment, No. 16, of the Independent Order of Odd Fellows, of Manchester, and of Delta Lodge, No. 84, Royal Arcanum. He married, October 15, 1879, Addie S. Brown, of Greensboro, Vermont, who was born June 14, 1855, daughter of Timothy C. and Martha B. (Curtis) Brown.

LORD It is probable that the present family is descended from the Lords who have been prominent in the region of the Saco Valley, Maine, for several generations. Abraham Lord came from Ipswich, Massachusetts, to Kittery, Maine, as early as 1670, and was undoubtedly a relative of other Lords in that state. The family has been numerous and influential at Hiram, Kennebunkport and especially at Berwick, Maine, where a reunion of Lords is held every summer. It is from the Berwick branch that President Nathan Lord, of Dartmouth College, who held the office from 1828 to 1863, is descended, and it was at Berwick Academy that he fitted for college. On account of lack of records it has not been possible to connect the following line with those branches of the family, whose history has previously been written.

(I) John Lord, son of Andrew Lord, was born at Shapleigh, Maine, about the beginning of the nineteenth century. He was a merchant and hotelkeeper. He married Frances Hubbard, who bore him eight children: Hope, Andrew J., Fanny, John (2), whose sketch follows; Moses, Charles E., Love, Martha. Hope married John Calvin Marsh, of Acton, Maine. Andrew J. married Hannah Hall, and they had one child, Ida May. Fanny married Alonzo Templeton, of Louisville, Kentucky. Moses married ——— ———, from Clifton, New York, and they had four children: James, Margaret, Stella and Lloyd; the family now lives in Memphis, Tennessee. Charles E. married Vesta Earl, and they had four children: Harvey, Winifred, Frank and Elizabeth; the family lives in Acton, Maine. Love married Stephen Adams, of Newfield, Maine, and they had one child, Clement. Martha married Luther F. Lary, of Acton, Maine, and they had three children: Fanny, Daisy and Claudius.

(II) John (2), son of John (1) and Frances (Hubbard) Lord, was born in that part of Shapleigh now called Acton, Maine, in August, 1836. He attended school and helped on the farm till the age of nineteen, when he was left with the care of the homestead, and also of his mother. He managed the farm from 1856 till 1872, when he engaged in the express business, which he followed for two years. He then opened a store, which he conducted till 1884, meanwhile taking his son, William M. Lord, into partnership. After giving up his mercantile business in 1884, he returned to the farm. John (2) Lord was active in politics, and served his town many years as selectman, and also as collector for the Democratic party. He belongs to the Congregational Church, and also to the Independent Order of Odd Fellows. About 1856 John (2) Lord married Fidelia A. Sanborn, daughter of Veasie and Phoebe (Tibbetts) Sanborn, of Acton, Maine. They had four children: William M., whose sketch follows; Eva O., Exa L., and Andrew Jackson. John (2) Lord is still living at Acton, Maine.

(III) William Marshall, eldest child of John (2) and Fidelia A. (Sanborn) Lord, was born at Acton, Maine, April 10, 1857. He lived on the home place and attended school till the age of seventeen, when he went into business with his father under the name of John Lord. In 1884 he succeeded his father, and carried on the business till 1891, when he removed to Union, New Hampshire, where he bought out the store which he still conducts. In 1902 he formed what is known as the W. M. Lord Company and bought an excelsior mill, whose annual output of two thousand tons is marketed in New York and the west. The firm also does a big lumber business, cutting a million or more feet each year. Mr. Lord is a man of sound business judgment and pleasing personality, which is shown by the fact that in a town strongly Republican he was elected Democratic representative in 1900. He has also served as member of the school board. He is a Mason of the thirty-second degree, a member of Unity Chapter, Order of the Eastern Star, and treasurer of his Masonic lodge. On February 24, 1880, William Marshall Lord married Julia Rowell, daughter of Charles and Frances (Hemenway) Rowell, of Fairfield, Maine. There are no children.

HEARD Three centuries seem like a lifetime, but nearly that number of years have elapsed since the progenitor of this line, strong of body, brave of heart and devout in spirit, sought the wilderness of New England to worship God in his own way and founded an honored family.

(I) William Heard, of the Devonshire family of England, was probably the American ancestor of the Heard family of Massachusetts. He was among the emigrants who arrived at Plymouth, Massachusetts, on the ship "Ann" in August, 1623. In 1624 he was granted an acre of land in the north part of Plymouth.

(II) Zachariah Heard, born 1675, died December 27, 1761, is the next of the family of whom we have record. "In August, 1707, he was the owner of a homestead and clothier shop in Cambridge, on the Watertown road." About 1709 he moved to Wayland, where he was prominent in the affairs of the town and held many town offices. He married, 1707, Silence Brown, of Wayland, by whom he had a considerable number of children.

(III) Richard, fifth child of Zachariah and Silence (Brown) Heard, was born April 2, 1720, died May 16, 1792. He was captain of a company of troopers under George III, represented Sudbury in the first provincial congress which convened at Salem, October 7, 1774, and was sent by his townsmen in East Sudbury to represent them in the general court in the sessions of 1780-81-83. He married Sarah Fiske, of Wayland, by whom he raised a family.

(IV) David, son of Richard and Sarah (Fiske) Heard, was born June 2, 1758, died January 22, 1813.

He married (first), May 24, 1784, Eunice Baldwin, of Wayland, who died September 5, 1785, and (second), March 31, 1789, Sibyl Sherman, of Wayland, who died September 2, 1845.

(V) William, son of David and Sibyl (Sherman) Heard, was born in Wayland, September 19, 1795, died there March 30, 1869. "He was very prominent in the history of the town, and held every office in its government. He was coroner of Middlesex county for many years. He was a man of very strong will, unswerving honesty and untiring zeal in carrying out whatever he undertook. During the war he traveled a short time in the South, visited the soldiers in camp, with whom he had much sympathy and for whose interests he spent much time and labor." He was a Whig and Republican in politics, and in religion a Unitarian. He married, March 14, 1825, Susan Mann, of Oxford, New Hampshire, who died July 14, 1870. Their children: Samuel H. M., William A., Jared M. and Susan E.

(VI) Hon. William Andrew, second child and son of William and Susan (Mann) Heard, was born in Wayland, Massachusetts, August 25, 1827, died at Centre Sandwich, New Hampshire, April 15, 1901. He attended the common schools and Wayland Academy until he was fifteen years old, and then entered mercantile life as a clerk in the store of Timothy Varney, of Centre Sandwich, Carroll county, New Hampshire; this business he purchased when twenty-two years of age and continued in the same line of business until retiring in 1878, after nearly twenty-eight years of active service and successful merchandising. In August, 1862, Mr. Heard enlisted as a soldier in the Fourteenth Regiment, New Hampshire Volunteers, was commissioned quartermaster of the regiment at its organization and accompanied it to the scene of its operations in Virginia, then the center of military activity in the east. In November, 1862, he was made brigade quartermaster and discharged the duties of the position till failing health compelled him to resign in September of the following year. Mr. Heard's business ability was early recognized by those who knew him, and he was called upon to fill numerous public offices. He was clerk of Sandwich in 1859-61, representative in the New Hampshire legislature in 1873-74, treasurer of Sandwich Savings Bank from September, 1872, until January, 1887, was appointed clerk of the courts of Carroll county in August, 1874, and was re-appointed in August, 1876, holding the office until 1887. In January, 1887, he was appointed national bank examiner for the states of Maine and New Hampshire, and in order to devote his entire time to this office resigned all other official trusts. August 16, 1889, Mr. Heard was appointed bank commissioner of the state of New Hampshire, which office he filled until August, 1893, resigning to accept the receivership of the National Bank of the Commonwealth of Manchester, New Hampshire.

In his early life he was a Whig, but upon the dissolution of that party united with its successor, the Republican party, supporting Lincoln and the war measures, but sided with the Liberal Republicans in 1872 and voted for Greeley. Subsequently he adhered to the Democratic party. He was an active member of the Methodist Episcopal Church and one of its most liberal supporters. He was made a Mason at the organization of Red Mountain Lodge, of Sandwich, and filled its principal chairs. He was a prominent member of Moulton S. Webster Post, Grand Army of the Republic, and was also a member of the Massachusetts Commandery of the Military Order of the Loyal Legion of the United States. Mr. Heard started in life equipped with a sound mind in a sound body, making up what he lacked in book lore by fidelity and unflinching firmness of purpose in the pursuit of his chosen vocation in life. His personal character was above reproach, and his church relations exemplary. All these things contributed to make his life a success and render him a prominent and influential man in business, social and political circles.

He married, June 6, 1850, Anne Elizabeth, daughter of Hon. Moulton H. and Ann M. (Ambrose) Marston, of Sandwich, New Hampshire. Mrs. Heard died January 4, 1854, leaving one child, Edwin M., who resides in Sandwich, New Hampshire. Mr. Heard married (second), April 25, 1855, Emily Maria Marston, sister of his first wife, born April 17, 1833. Of this marriage there were two sons: William, who resides in Sandwich, New Hampshire, and Arthur Marston.

(VII) Arthur Marston, the younger son of William A. and Emily Maria (Marston) Heard, was born at Sandwich, New Hampshire, February 13, 1866. After receiving the usual training in the public schools he prepared for college at Tilton Seminary, from which he was graduated in 1884. He began his college course at Boston University, but after one year at that institution entered the sophomore class at Amherst College and was graduated in 1888. Soon after leaving college he went west, and for several years was in the employ of the First National Bank of Arkansas City, Kansas, where by rapid promotions he filled the various clerical positions of the institution. In the panic of 1893 he was appointed special national bank examiner and did acceptable work among the banks of southern Kansas and Oklahoma, but in the succeeding year he resigned to return to New Hampshire. In April, 1895, he was appointed national bank examiner, a position which he filled with credit to himself and satisfaction to the national officers. In December, 1895, he resigned this position and was elected cashier of the Merchants' National Bank of Manchester, New Hampshire. December 13, 1902, Mr. Heard was elected cashier of the Amoskeag National Bank to fill the vacancy caused by the death of John M. Chandler, brother of the late president, George Byron Chandler. On July 11, 1905, following the death of George Byron Chandler, he was elected president of the Amoskeag National Bank, making him the head of one of the largest and strongest banking institutions in New Hampshire. He is also president of the People's Gas Light Company, director and member of the finance committee of the New Hampshire Fire Insurance Company, and is also connected with various other corporations. He is a member of Red Mountain Lodge, Free and Accepted Masons, of Sandwich, New Hampshire; Trinity Commandery, Knights Templar, of Manchester, and intermediate Masonic bodies; Sons of American Revolution; Massachusetts Commandery, Loyal Legion of United States. He is an attendant at the services of the Franklin Street Congregational Church. He married, June 12, 1895, Ora B. Farrar, at Arkansas City, Kansas. Their children are: Marston, born December 2, 1897; Carlton Farrar, March 24, 1900.

(I) Tristam Hurd was born in Rochester, and died in Manchester, 1865, at seventy-five or seventy-six years of age. He settled in Manchester in 1842, and spent the remainder of his life there. He was a painter and was a long time in the employ of the Amoskeag Mills, and served in the War of 1812 in defence of Dover. He was married February 1, 1818, to Sarah Hurd, both being of Rochester.

(II) Charles W., only son and third child of Tristam and Lydia Hurd, was born in Durham, July 24, 1835, and died in Manchester, May 12, 1899. At the age of seven years he was brought to Manchester by his parents, and at seventeen made a voyage to China in a sailing vessel. After his return home he learned painting and frescoing, and was employed for many years in the paint works of the Manchester Mills, and was superintendent of the painting department of the Manchester Print Works to 1885. On the very day Fort Sumter was fired on, April 19, 1861, he enlisted in the First Regiment, New Hampshire Volunteer Infantry, was mustered in May 2, as sergeant, and mustered out August 9, 1861. He again enlisted August 19, 1861, as a private in Company G, Fourth New Hampshire Volunteer Infantry, was appointed first lieutenant September 20, 1861, commissioned September 18, 1861, as lieutenant, and served until March 20, 1862, when he resigned. April 28, 1863, he enlisted at Boston, Massachusetts, for one year as a landsman. He served on the United States ships "Ohio," "Princeton," and "Memphis," and was discharged July 26, 1864, as master at arms from the receiving ship at Philadelphia, Pennsylvania, his term of service having expired. He married Martha A. Farnham, born at Tilton, New Hampshire, daughter of Asa and Martha Farnham, of Tilton, who died November 6, 1899. They had three children: Viola, who died in infancy; Charles Asa, who died at the age of twenty-seven years; and William H., the subject of the next paragraph.

(III) William Hursey, youngest child of Charles and Martha A. (Farnham) Hurd, was born in Manchester, July 22, 1863. After attending the Manchester schools for a while he went, at the age of twelve years, as newsboy on the Concord Railroad, where he remained two years. He then learned the printer's trade, at which he worked several years in various places, first in the office of the *Manchester Union;* then on the *Chicago Inter-Ocean;* the *Savannah* (Georgia) *News; Jacksonville* (Florida) *Times;* and in Boston, Massachusetts. From 1883 to 1885 he was employed in a retail establishment in Boston. In the latter year he returned to Manchester, and in June bought a fine café which he carried on until 1902. In 1897 he bought the New City Hotel of Manchester, where he had a flourishing trade until 1905, when he retired from active business. He is an admirer of fine horses, and has owned several fast trotters. Mr. Hurd is an agreeable companion, an entertaining talker, and a self-made man. He is a life member of the Benevolent and Protective Order of Elks, of Lawrence, Massachusetts, and of the Order of Eagles, of Manchester. He was the first chairman of the board of trustees of Aerie No. 290, of Manchester. He is also a member of Amoskeag Veterans and the Calumet Club. He married, January 1, 1891, Alice B. Knowlton, daughter of James and Mary Frances (Marshall) Knowlton, of Sutton. They have spent winters in southern California, Cuba, Jamaica, Porto Rico, Florida and Bermuda.

HUTCHINS This name which usually indicates an English ancestry, is claimed in the present instance as the heritage of Scotch-Irish whom royal disfavor and local race hatred forced out of Ireland, where the family had existed for some time. Two brothers landed in Plymouth, Massachusetts, in 1630, went from there to Dover, New Hampshire, then to Londonderry.

(I) Ebenezer Hutchins, the earliest known member of the Hutchins family of this article, is said to have been of Scotch-Irish ancestry, and Londonderry is named as the place of his birth, which is stated to have been in 1776. He died in September, 1858. Before his marriage he went to live in Canterbury, and there, January 1, 1807, he was married by Rev. William Patrick to Abigail Brier, of that town, who was born in London, New Hampshire, 1787, and died in Concord, New Hampshire, 1851. Their children were: Nancy, Reuben, John, Sarah, Ebenezer, Hannah, Josiah, Jane.

(II) Ebenezer (2), son of Ebenezer (1) and Abigail (Brier) Hutchins, was born in Canterbury, August 3, 1822. He grew up on his father's farm, and at the age of twenty-one years went into the employ of the Boston, Concord & Montreal railroad, and was station agent at Canterbury about 1857, then yardmaster at Concord twenty years, and then lived on a farm in Canterbury three years. Since 1888 he has been tender at a railroad crossing in Laconia. He married, March 16, 1847, Citana McDaniel, who was born April 23, 1827. Her father, Jonathan McDaniel, was born in Northfield, and died March 31, 1858, aged fifty-three years. Charlotte Foss, his wife, was born in Northfield, and died there December 6, 1868, aged sixty-three years. Nehemiah McDaniel, father of Jonathan McDaniel, died in Londonderry in 1840. Five children were born to Ebenezer (2) and Citana McDaniel.

(III) George Eugene, son of Ebenezer (2) and Citana (McDaniel) Hutchins, was born in Concord, October 16, 1848. At thirteen years of age he took service with the Boston, Concord & Montreal Road as a section hand, and followed that vocation three years. At sixteen years of age he went to Concord, New Hampshire, and there worked a year in a tannery. From 1865 to 1869 he was a locomotive fireman for the Boston, Concord & Montreal road, and at the last given date became an engineer. He ran between Concord and Woodsville for some years, residing at Concord; then was removed to the Whitefield branch, where he served five years. For sixteen years he resided at Jefferson. In 1893 he was transferred to the Berlin branch, and has since ran between Berlin and Whitefield Junction, residing at Berlin since 1895. In political sentiment Mr. Hutchins is a Democrat. While in Jefferson he served on the board of education three years, 1888-1891. In 1903 he was elected to the lower house of the legislature, and served with credit. In 1904 he became a candidate for the office of mayor of Berlin on the Labor ticket, and was elected. Five months after election he succeeded in breaking up the corrupt ring that had governed the city, had an expert examine the city's books of records and accounts, who found a shortage of $17,000 in the accounts of the city clerk and treasurer. That individual was prosecuted, found guilty, and sent to the penitentiary. Such was the vigorous start made by George E. Hutchins in the mayor's office. His administration of affairs in this case and in general has been so satisfactory to all the better element of Berlin that he has been twice re-elected, and is now (1907) serving his third term. Mr. Hutchins is a thirty-second degree Mason; he is a member of White Mountain Lodge, No. 86, of Whitefield, of which he was a master in 1889; North Star Royal Arch Chapter, No. 16, North Star Commandery, No. 4 Knights Templar, of Lancaster; and Edward A. Raymond Consistory, Sublime Princes of the Royal Secret, of Nashua. He is also a member of St. John's Lodge, No. 58, Independent Order of Odd Fellows, of Whitefield, of which he was noble grand in 1879; and Mt. Lafayette Lodge, No. 572, of the

John C. Hutchins.

Brotherhood of Locomotive Engineers. He became a member of the Congregational Church in 1901, and is now a deacon of the church of that denomination at Berlin, and superintendent of its Sunday school. He married, in Woodsville, December 26, 1870, Helen Marr Chamberlain, daughter of Warren Kasson and Statira Frances (Edwards) Chamberlain. The following is a brief account of Mrs. Hutchins' ancestry:

(1) Richard Chamberlain was born in Oxford, Massachusetts, July 9, 1714. He ascended the Connecticut river from Hinsdale, New Hampshire, in a boat, taking seven of his fourteen children, and some most necessary articles, and settled in Newbury, Vermont, in June, 1762. He was in Captain Phinehas Stevens' company of sixty men at Charlestown, New Hampshire, during the siege of 1747; was also in Colonel Williams's regiment for the invasion of Canada, from March 13, to December 18, 1758, and was a minute-man in 1775. He died October 16, 1784. He married Abigail, daughter of Remembrance Wright, of Northampton, Massachusetts.

(2) Benjamin son of Richard and Abigail (Wright) Chamberlain, was born in Northfield, Massachusetts, December 15, 1747, and went to Newbury with his parents. He served a short time in the Revolutionary war. His wife was Widow Eaton.

(3) Benjamin (2), son of Benjamin (1) Chamberlain, was born in October, 1774, and died December 3, 1872. He married Sally, daughter of Thomas Kasson. She was born January 31, 1787, and died April 15, 1868.

(4) Warren K., son of Benjamin (2) and Sally (Kasson) Chamberlain, was born May 6, 1815, and was a farmer in Newbury. He died July 3, 1894. He married Statira Frances Edwards, who was born in Gilmanton, New Hampshire, 1827, daughter of David and Alciemena (Frisby) Edwards, of Maine. Their daughter, Helen Marr, born June 18, 1848, married George E. Hutchins, and they have had two children: Eben W., born in Concord, New Hampshire, 1872; and Frank Eugene, who died young.

(Second Family.)

HUTCHINS The immigrant ancestor of this family of Hutchins was one of those soldiers who came to put down the American rebels of 1776, and remained after they had won their independence to assist them in the work of building up a mighty nation.

(I) Parley Hutchins was born in Edinburgh, Scotland, and in 1774 came from there to America as a private in the British army to assist in keeping order in the colonies, then on the eve of open rebellion against the English government. He served throughout the Revolution which followed, and after the close of the war settled in Connecticut, where he became a farmer and resided until his death. He married and raised a family.

(II) Parley (2), son of Parley (1) Hutchins, was born in Connecticut, removed to Wolcott, Vermont, and settled there about the year 1816. He built a cabin on the Lamoille river, and began his life in the wilderness by clearing the timber off the land on which he settled, and putting it in a fair state of cultivation. He built a large and commodious tavern on the land he had cleared in 1830, which he conducted very successfully until his death, which occurred in July, 1858. He married, 1813, Polly Whitney, born in 1794, died April 18, 1878, and they were the parents of: Charles; Sidney; Lewis Smith, see forward; John Corbin and Mary.

(III) Lewis Smith, third son and child of Parley (2) and Polly (Whitney) Hutchins, was born in Wolcott, Vermont, August 6, 1825, and died in North Stratford, New Hampshire, April 8, 1895. He continued the hotel business commenced by his father, and in addition to this was engaged in farming. Before the construction of the Portland & Ogdensburg railroad, he was extensively engaged in teaming to St. Johnsbury, Montpelier and Burlington, Vermont. In politics he was one of the two Democrats of the town, and was a stanch supporter of the principles of the Democratic party. For a number of years he filled the office of selectman. He married, 1844, Marcia M. Aiken, born February 11, 1826, died April 13, 1878, daughter of Solomon and Mary (Warner) Aiken. Solomon Aiken was born in Hardwick, Massachusetts, July 15, 1758, and served two years in the army during the Revolutionary war. He then entered Dartmouth College, from which he was graduated in 1784. He was ordained pastor of the church in Duxbury, Massachusetts, June 4, 1788, and enlisted as chaplain in the United States army, June 11, 1812. He removed to Hardwick, Vermont, in 1818, was representative in 1821-2, and died in June, 1833. He married, October 12, 1788, Mary Warner, daughter of Captain Daniel Warner, and they were the parents of four sons and five daughters. Lewis Smith and Marcia M. (Aiken) Hutchins had children: Emma C.; Mary P.; Warner J.; Marcia M.; Frederick L.; Burt M.; Kate A.; John Corbin, see forward; and Frank D., mentioned with descendants in this article.

(IV) John Corbin, fourth son and eighth child of Lewis Smith (3) and Marcia M. (Aiken) Hutchins, was born in Wolcott, Lamoille county, Vermont, February 3, 1864. He attended the public schools of his native city until he was thirteen years of age, and then became a student at the academy at Hardwick, where he attended the spring and fall terms for four years, teaching the district schools in winter, and assisting his father in the cultivation and management of the home farm during the summer months. At the age of seventeen years he became the assistant principal of the academy, filling that position for a period of two years, and subsequently taking a post-graduate course in the same institution. He went to Northfield, Vermont, in 1883, where he lived during the winter, at the same time teaching in the high school at Gouldsville. In the spring of 1884 he removed to Stratford, New Hampshire, and during the year following his arrival in that town was employed as a clerk in the drug and jewelry store of W. C. Carpenter. The next year he filled the position of teacher of the higher grade in the grammar school of the town, and employed all his leisure time in the store of Mr. Carpenter, acquiring a further knowledge of the drug and jewelry business. Failing health compelled Mr. Carpenter to remove to California in 1886, and he disposed of his business to Mr. Hutchins, who had passed his examination before the New Hampshire Board of Pharmacy, April 25, of that year. In politics Mr. Hutchins is a Democrat, and as such has been elected to various offices, and in these as well as in a number of other ways has rendred his town and district good service. He was elected chairman of the board of selectmen in 1889, and re-elected to the same office in the two following years. Important matters came up for consideration during his term of office, and were disposed of in such a manner as to be of the greatest advantage to the town. During that time the Maine Central railroad was constructed and, with the New Hampshire railroad commissioners, Mr. Hutchins was one of the board to settle the amount of damage to lands occasioned by the carrying out of this work. The righteousness of the awards of the board was so apparent to all concerned that but one appeal was taken from its decisions, and then the judgment of the board was sustained. Mr. Hutchins was tax collector from 1896 to 1906, inclusive, with the exception of 1899 and 1900. He was elected to the legislature in 1898 by the largest plurality ever received by a candidate in the town. At the following sitting of the general court he was a member of the committee of appropriations and of that of national affairs. He was elected a member of the board of education in 1900, and with the assistance of others established a high school in North Stratford, which has taken a high position for excellency. He takes an active and prominent part in several secret societies, being a Mason and a Knight of Pythias of high degree. He became a member of Evening Star Lodge, No. 25, Free and Accepted Masons, of Colebrook, in 1886; later joined North Star Royal Arch Chapter, No. 16; North Star Commandery, Knights Templar, of Lancaster; Edward A. Raymond Consistory, Thirty-second degree, Sublime Princes of the Royal Secret of Nashua; and is a charter member of Stratford Lodge, No. 30, Knights of Pythias, instituted August 5, 1886, in which he has held every office. He became a member of the grand lodge at its session in Lancaster in 1893; the next year, at Manchester, he was elected grand outer guard, from which office he rose by regular gradation until at Woodsville, in October, 1900, he was elected grand chancellor of the state, in which office he served one year. He married, in West Stewartstown, October 24, 1889, Sadie H. Mayo, born June 6, 1866, daughter of Thomas Henry and Ellen (Rowell) Mayo (see Mayo, VII), and they have had children: Ralph Mayo, born August 20, 1890; Ruth Ward, born August 29, 1892; died January 10, 1896; Paul Aiken, born August 17, 1900.

(IV) Frank D., youngest child of Lewis S. and Marcia M. (Aiken) Hutchins, was born in Wolcott, June 8, 1864. He studied preliminarily in the public schools and was graduated from the Hardwick (Vermont) Academy in 1880. After teaching in the public schools for two years he abandoned educational pursuits, and going to Chicago was for a similar period employed in a wholesale hat and cap establishment. Returning to New England he secured a position as bookkeeper in the office of the American Express Company as a messenger with headquarters at Concord, and he continued in that capacity until 1894, when he was advanced to the position of local agent at Pittsfield, where he has ever since represented the company with ability and faithfulness. Progressive, energetic and keenly alive to the possibilities obtainable through the development of the business resources of the town, Mr. Hutchins has acquired wide-spread popularity, and he is ready on all occasions to contribute both his time and means in promoting any well-conceived movement calculated to be of benefit to the general welfare of the community. In politics he is a Democrat, and in addition to serving as chairman of the Pittsfield Democratic Club for seven years has been a member of the board of selectmen a number of years, was its chairman for four years, and in 1902-03 was representative to the legislature. In the capacity of chairman of the board of selectmen he was a leading spirit in public ceremonies conducted during Old Home week in 1902, on which occasion was dedicated the Public Library presented by Mr. and Mrs. Josiah Carpenter, of Manchester, and his acceptance of the gift in behalf of the town was both eloquent and appropriate. He is a member of Corinthian Lodge, Ancient Free and Accepted Masons, and of Norris Lodge, Knights of Pythias, both of Pittsfield; also of Rumford Lodge, Independent Order of Odd Fellows, and Tahanta Encampment, of Concord.

At Concord, April 17, 1894, Mr. Hutchins was united in marriage with Edna Whittier, of Calais, Maine, a representative of a highly reputable family of that state. They have one daughter, Madeline Edna, who was born January 27, 1895, and is now an apt scholar well advanced in her studies.

MAYO The Mayo family is one which has one distinction in many directions since its advent in this country. It came from England to America at a very early date, and has been identified with the learned professions and various lines of industry since that time, and has been continuously located in New England. It bore an active part in the development of Manchester, New Hampshire, and in the pioneer period of the northern section of the state.

(I) John Mayo, the first of this family of whom we have any definite record, was brought from Rawling, Kent county, England, by his parents in 1632. He was the first settled pastor of the Old North Church in Boston, Massachusetts, later made famous by Paul Revere, being installed November 9, 1655, and left his pastorate in 1672. He married Hannah Graves in 1654, and died in 1676.

(II) Thomas Mayo, born July 29, 1667, son of John and Hannah (Graves) Mayo, married (first), 1734, Elizabeth Farley; (second), 1749, Mary Heart; (third), 1763, Catherine Williams. He was the father of seventeen children.

(III) Thomas (2), son of Thomas Mayo, married Elizabeth Davis.

(IV) Thomas (3) Mayo, son of Thomas (2) and Elizabeth (Davis) Mayo, was born in Roxbury, and married Lucy Richards.

(V) Thomas (4), son of Thomas (3) and Lucy (Richards) Mayo, was born in Roxbury, Massachusetts. He was the proprietor of the old Mayo Tavern. He married August 29, 1791, Amy Davis, born September 3, 1771, and they had thirteen children.

(VI) Aaron Davis Mayo, son of Thomas (4) and Amy (Davis) Mayo, was born in Roxbury, Massachusetts, March 13, 1796, and died October 14, 1880. Like his father he was a hotel keeper in Roxbury, and also in Andover, Massachusetts. He married, April 24, 1820, Sarah Day, born December 13, 1794, died March 7, 1842, and they had children: Sarah Jane, born February 15, 1821; Matilda Elizabeth, born June 4, 1822; Thomas Henry, born June 28, 1824; Thomas Henry (second), see forward; Sarah Augusta, born January 8, 1828; Helen Louisa, born November 1, 1831.

(VII) Thomas Henry Mayo, second son and fourth child of Aaron Davis and Sarah (Day) Mayo, was born in Andover, Massachusetts, June 28, 1826. He was apprenticed to learn the trade of decorating and followed this occupation during the active years of his life. While still a young man he went to Manchester, New Hampshire, and from there to West Stewartstown, New Hampshire, where his entire married life was spent. During the civil war he enlisted in Company I, Fourth New Hampshire Volunteer Infantry. His political affiliations were with the Republican party, and his religion was that of the Adventists. He married, in Manchester, New Hampshire, May 30, 1853, (Rev. B. M. Tillotson officiating,) Ellen (Flanders) Rowell, born in Pittsburg, New Hampshire, February 16, 1834, died May 2, 1907, daughter of David and Elizabeth (Smith) Rowell, and they were the parents of children: 1. Ellen Louisa, died at the age of nine years. 2. Edward, was drowned at the age of eight years. 3. Sadie Helen, mentioned below. 4. Ella Amy, born March 26, 1868; married Garvin R. Magoon, of Derby Center, Vermont, and has children: Ethel Caroline; Ellen Colby and Mayo McKinley. 5. Edward Davis, who died at the age of two years. Thomas Henry Mayo departed this life August 29, 1907.

(VIII) Sadie Helen, second daughter of Thomas H. and Ellen F. (Rowell) Mayo, was born June 6, 1866, and is now the wife of John C. Hutchins of Stratford, New Hampshire. (See Hutchins, IV.)

COLBURN This is a name of a family quite numerous in Massachusetts and New Hampshire. The race is an energetic one, and its members inclined rather to active than sedentary employment. They are self-reliant and most of them accumulate above the average amount of substance. Many members of the family now spell the name Coburn.

(I) Edward Colburn, the pioneer in America, came from England to Massachusetts about 1635, and died February 17, 1700. He settled in Chelmsford, Massachusetts, and became the progenitor of a large family which has spread over the land. He had sons, John, Thomas, Robert, Daniel, Ezra and Joseph. (Ezra and descendants are mentioned in this article).

(II) Thomas, son of Edward Colburn, was born 1674, in Chelmsford, and resided in Dunstable. He was a soldier in the second expedition led by Captain John Lovell, and on account of this service he was a grantee of Kingstown, now Manchester. He died November 2, 1770, and his wife died September 7, 1739. Her name has not been preserved. Their children were: Elizabeth, Thomas, Hannah, Edward, Sarah, Bridget, Lois and Rachel.

(III) Thomas (2), eldest son and second child of Thomas (1) Colburn, was born April 28, 1702, in Dunstable, and was a farmer, living in the part of that town which is now Hudson. He and his son Thomas were killed by lightning August 30, 1765. His wife's name was Mary. After his death she married Colonel Samuel Moore, of Richfield, and removed to Hudson at the time of the marriage. The children of Thomas and Mary included sons Thomas, Isaac and Zaccheus. (Mention of Zaccheus and descendants appears in this article).

(IV) Thomas (3), eldest child of Thomas (2) and Mary Colburn, was born June 2, 1731, in Dracut, Massachusetts, and died before 1814. He was married in Salem, Massachusetts, in 1761, to Sarah Eaton, who was born in Reading, Massachusetts, a daughter of Silas and Jerusha (Gould) Eaton. Their children were: Thomas, Sally, Silas (died young), Silas, James (died young), Daniel, Deborah (died young), Deborah, James, Sybel and Jacob.

(V) Jacob, youngest child of Thomas (3) and Sarah (Eaton) Colburn, was born April 1, 1782, in Dracut, Massachusetts, and died in Hollis, New Hampshire, February 22, 1836, aged fifty-four. He was a major in the Massachusetts militia. He married Lydia Haseltine, of Dracut, who died May 26, 1841, aged fifty-nine years. Their children were: Thomas Jefferson, Sarah Jones, Charles Louis, Jacob, Peter and Mary. The last three died young.

(VI) Charles Louis, son of Major Jacob and Lydia (Haseltine) Coburn, was born in Dracut, Massachusetts, July 17, 1815, and died in Nashua, New Hampshire, December 28, 1892, aged seventy-seven. He started in life as a clerk in a shoe store in Lowell, where he was employed a year or two. He then learned to make shoes, and opened a shop in that city, where he employed several men. Subsequently he removed to Pepperell and carried on the same business with a force of fifteen or more men, finding this employment detrimental to his health he removed in 1841 to Nashua, where he bought a farm which finally came to include two hundred and fifty-six acres, two miles west of the city of Nashua. This land was well timbered, and he cut large quantities of lumber from it. He was a thrifty and prosperous man and before his death he owned besides his farm three houses and lots in Nashua, and other property. In 1871 he removed to Nashua, where he resided seven years, but later returned to the farm where he passed the last nine years of his life, and where his widow now resides. Until the dissolution of the Whig party he affiliated with it, and afterward with the Republican party. He filled the offices of alderman, selectman and road commissioner, holding the latter office six years.

He married in Hollis, April 2, 1839, Emeline Wright, who was born in Hollis, May 5, 1821, daughter of Miles Johnson and Betsey (Jewell) Wright, both of Hollis. Miles J. Wright was a blacksmith, and a farmer of ample means. He was born March 13, 1791, and died February 25, 1859, aged sixty-nine. He was a sergeant in a company of cavalry in the militia. His father, Lemuel Wright, son of Captain Joshua Wright, was born December 30, 1752, and died May 13, 1833, aged eighty-two. Lemuel Wright and three brothers were in the Revolution. He was in Colonel Joshua Wingate's Regiment in 1776-77, and was at the battle of White Plains and at Ticonderoga. He was fond of the military, and at one time had a great barbecue at his place at which a large number of militry guests were present, the principal gastronomic attraction being an ox roasted whole. He married Mary Godfrey Johnson, widow of Edward Johnson, of Woburn, Massachusetts, and daughter of Captain Godfrey, of Greenland, Massachusetts, who was killed and scalped by the Indians, when she was a young child. She died December 30, 1838, aged ninety-one.

Betsey Jewell, wife of Miles Wright, was the daughter of James Jewell, a soldier of the Revolution, who was paid off at the end of his term of service in Continental money. He received nine hundred dollars of this depreciated currency, all of which he gave for a cow. He died September 24, 1851, aged ninety-eight years, and five months. To Charles L. and Emeline (Wright) Coburn there were born four sons and one daughter: Charles J., Sarah E., George W., John H., Arthur J. Charles J., born January 16, 1840, married Mary Jane Woods of Nashua, July 2, 1865. She died October 1, 1890. He married (second), Ida Louise Casavant of Lynn, Massachusetts, January 3, 1900. Sarah Emeline, born March 8, 1842, married, July 24, 1862, Franklin Tyrrell. George William, July 7, 1844, married, July 27, 1871, Nancy Poore Kimball. John H., is mentioned below. Arthur Jefferson, December 23, 1850, married, October, 1872, Kate Manning; they had one child, Grace Emma, born May 8, 1874, died October 1, 1880.

(VII) John Henry, fourth child and third son

of Charles L. and Emeline (Wright) Coburn, was born in Nashua, July 8, 1850. He attended the district school near his home, the Nashua High School, and Crosby's Institute. He left the last named school at nineteen years of age, after having attended there two years. He then became the proprietor of two milk routes. His business required him to work at half past twelve in the morning and continue until half past seven in the morning, and to drive sixteen miles in the afternoon to collect milk for next day's delivery. The amount of milk delivered daily was six hundred quarts. He also dealt in hay and straw. After seven year's steady work at this business he found his health impaired, and he sold out and went to Lynn, where he was employed in a shoe shop three years. Two years of this time he had charge of the shoe burnishing department. After a short stay on Long Island, Boston Harbor, he removed to Concord, New Hampshire, where he was engaged in the livery business five years, 1882-87. He then went to Lynn, Massachusetts, where he took a contract to do the buffing, burnishing, inspection, boxing, etc., of all the shoes produced by one of the factories there. He was thus engaged four and one-half years, when his health again broke down, and he removed to Nashua where he was in the loan business with Franklin Tyrrell two years. In May, 1891, he removed to Concord, and has since resided at the old Lyman Walker place. He does a large trucking and hauling business, employing several double teams and from five to fifteen men. He also does grading and supplies mineral building material, including sand, stone, etc. He married, January 5, 1882, in Concord, Sarah Abby (Walker) Chandler, widow of Horace W. Chandler, and daughter of Lyman Abbott and Lucy Ann (Pratt) Walker, of Concord. She was born October 24, 1847, and died June 10, 1905. She married (first), Horace William Chandler, January 31, 1867, who was born June 4, 1846. He died 1877, leaving one daughter, Mabel Walker Chandler, born December 7, 1868, who lives with Mr. Coburn.

(II) Ezra, son of Edward Colburn married, 1681, Hannah, daughter of Samuel Varnum, of Ipswich, Massachusetts.

(III) Samuel, son of Ezra and Hannah (Varnum) Colburn, married, 1717, Mary Richardson.

(IV) Jonathan, son of Samuel and Mary (Richardson) Colburn, born in 1729, and died in 1803, married 1754, Mercy Hildreth, who died in 1807. They had nine children: Saul and Jonathan, twins; Mercy, Leah, Thaddeus, Abi, Sarah, Zachariah and Micah, the subject of the following paragraph.

(V) Micah, youngest child of Jonathan and Mercy (Hildreth) Colburn, born in 1774, was a farmer in Dracut, Massachusetts, where he died. He married Sybil Flint, born in Dracut.

(VI) Heman Flint, son of Micah and Sybil (Flint) Colburn, was born in Dracut, January 28, 1805, and died May 25, 1876, at Lawrence, Massachusetts. He was educated in the common schools, and on coming of age learned the trade of millwright, at which he worked for half a century. A few years before his death he moved to Lawrence, and dealt in wood and coal. In politics he was a Democrat and in religion a Congregationalist. He married Julia Ann Colburn, born in Dracut, October, 19, 1807, died May 28, 1845. She was a daughter of Gideon and Mary Colburn. Their children were: Dimond, Lydia A., Andrew Jackson, Amos, Lucy Jane, Charles Lewis, Maria Lewis, and William F.

(VII) Amos Lincoln, third son and fourth child of Heman and Julia Ann (Colburn) Colburn, was born in Dracut, June 11, 1832. After acquiring a common school education he engaged in business with his father as a millwright for three years. Subsequently he was a bridge builder in the employ of the Concord railroad, until the outbreak of the Rebellion. April 20, 1861, he enlisted as a private in Company I, First New Hampshire Regiment, and campaigned in Maryland and Virginia. He was at Williamsport and Martinsburg, Virginia, and under command of General Patterson in the attack on Winchester. August 9, 1861, he was mustered out of service in New Hampshire, as a corporal. He re-enlisted in the same month in Company I, Fourth New Hampshire Regiment, at Concord. Returning to the front via Washington, the regiment took ship at Fortress Monroe to join Sheridan's expedition to Hilton Head, South Carolina. From there after a few months the Fourth was sent to Florida, where it was stationed at various places the following year. He was made first sergeant at muster, and while at Hilton Head, May 17, 1862, was appointed second lieutenant. He was made first lieutenant, December 1, 1863, and declined a captain's commission November 9, 1864. Returning to Beaufort, South Carolina, he assisted in the siege of Charleston. From that place he accompanied his command to join General Butler in Virginia, and was promoted to first lieutenant and assigned to Company F. He was in the battle of Drury's Bluff, May 11, 1864, and was reported killed there. He was present at the siege of Petersburg, and was wounded twice in a mine explosion, June 30. On August 16, following he was seriously wounded at Deep Bottom by a minie ball entering above his right knee. The next three months he spent in Hampton hospital. While there he was promoted to captain, but did not serve, as he was very soon mustered out.

After returning to New Hampshire, Captain Colburn entered the employ of the Fairbanks Scale Company, as a salesman, and repair expert and was thus employed from 1866 to 1872. He then established a business for himself in Manchester, New Hampshire, repairing and setting up scales, at which he was an expert. In 1876 he opened a shop in the same line of business in Lawrence, Massachusetts, and later, in connection with his already extensive business, engaged in the sale of coal and wood. Two years later he sold out and engaged in the bundle wood business. Removing to Concord, New Hampshire, in 1897, he started the pioneer wood yard, which he operated until the fall of 1895, when ill health compelled him to give it up. Mr. Colburn has had wide experience in making mauls for driving piles and has shipped them to South America, Australia and various parts of the world. He was the first man to make a heel maul for use in shoe shops.

Mr. Colburn has always been a live member of the Grand Army of the Republic, since he joined Louis Bell Post, No. 3, of Manchester, about 1872. On removing to Massachusetts he transferred his membership to Needham Post, No. 39. When he removed to Concord he became a member of E. E. Sturtevant Post, No. 2. One day as he was visiting Blossom Hill cemetery, in Concord, he discovered a marker at a grave bearing his name, and on investigation he learned that the post had been decorating his grave for several years; therefore in sending in his card for admission to the post he enclosed a check for $25 for services for decorating his grave. Comrade Dan Newhall, commander at the time, said he was entitled to the money, as he did the work, so he kept the check as a joke. Captain

Colburn is now ruined in health, yet he never regrets that he fought for his country, and no one takes a greater pride in the Grand Army of the Republic than does this worthy, fearless, upright man, who is ever true to his country and the flag. He was married June 8, 1884, to Lydia Ann Dunne, born in Fort Covington, New York, and died February 16, 1888, aged thirty-five years. In 1897 Mr. Colburn married Lydia H. Caldwell, daughter of John and Eunice (Gilman) Osman, and widow of William Caldwell. She has a son by her first marriage, Harvey Maharg, of Chelsea, Massachusetts.

(IV) Zaccheus, youngest son of Thomas (2) and Mary Colburn, was born February 16, 1765, in Hudson, New Hampshire, and died October 10, 1851, aged eighty-six. He married in Hudson, April 29, 1785, Rachel Hills, who was born April 10, 1765. Both were descendants of pioneers of Nottingham West, now Hudson.

(V) Dr. Elijah, son of Zaccheus and Rachel (Hills) Colburn, was born in Hudson, September 8, 1795, and died in Nashua, January 13, 1881, aged eighty-six. After obtaining what education he could in the common schools he attended Harvard Medical College, from which he graduated with the degree of M. D. in 1823. He practiced a short time in Hudson, and soon after, 1823 or 1824, he removed to Nashua, where he was perhaps the first permanently located physician. There is no doubt that he was the first physician who traveled with a horse about Nashua and the then sparsely settled towns adjacent. The Nashua Manufacturing Company was at that time starting in business, and from it Dr. Colburn bought the land upon which he erected the house which was his home the remainder of his life. During his early years he had his office on the site of the present Odd Fellows' building, but in his later years it was in an addition which he made to his residence on Main street. Dr. Colburn was a sagacious man, and learned in the ways of his day and time, and as a physician he took a leading place in his profession. He was ambitious to excel, conscientious, a close student, and always industriously employed. Having toiled for his own education, he was deeply interested in schools and anxious to help those who were trying to become better informed. For many years he was one of the trustees of the Nashua Literary Institution, and a member of the school committee before Nashua became a city. He was one of the incorporators of the Nashua Gas Light Company, and one of its early presidents. He was an honorable man, and faithful to the teachings of the Unitarian Church, of which he was a member. He was a member of Rising Sun Lodge No. 39, Free and Accepted Masons, and in 1843 and 1844 he was its worshipful master.

He married, June 22, 1826, Sarah Belknap, of Framingham, Massachusetts, who was born October 16, 1806, and died in Nashua, daughter of Luther and Hepsibah (Brown) Belknap, of Sudbury, Massachusetts. Luther Belknap, a leading citizen in the region about Framingham, Massachusetts, was born November 7, 1789, and died February 16, 1855, aged sixty-six. He was a representative, justice of the peace, selectman twenty-two years, and town clerk seventeen years. Hepsibah Brown was born in Sudbury, Massachusetts, July 28, 1769, and died August 5, 1852, aged eighty-three. When a small child she was left an orphan and adopted by her uncle, Adam Howe, who was the proprietor of the tavern at Sudbury, made famous by Longfellow's poem, "Tales of a Wayside Inn." She was a member of her uncle's family until her marriage. The children of Dr. Elijah and Sarah (Belknap) Colburn were: Luther B., Edwin A., Sarah M., Belknap S. and Susan E.

(VI) Dr. Edwin A., second son and child of Dr. Elijah and Sarah (Belknap) Colburn, was born at Nashua, December 13, 1829, and died in Nashua, March 5, 1892, aged sixty-three. After acquiring his early education in the public schools of Nashua, he attended the Nashua Literary Institution of which Professor David Crosby was then and for many years afterward principal. He was also a student at Derry Academy. He studied medicine in the office of his father, and was carefully instructed by him. Following this he attended the Medical College at Woodstock, Vermont, two years. He subsequently matriculated at the New York Medical College, in New York City, from which he was graduated with the degree of M. D. in 1854. After his return to Manchester he was associated in practice with his father until the retirement of the latter, about 1861. Dr. Colburn was a quiet, modest and retiring man, whose greatest pleasure was in the company of those who gathered about his fireside. Public life had no attractions strong enough to allure him from the domestic circle when his professional labors permitted him times of leisure. The only office he ever held was that of city physician, and that in 1861. He never allowed himself to be a candidate for office. Most doctors are excellent judges of horses, and lovers of fine steeds. Dr. Colburn shared this regard for equine excellence, and owned and drove some of the best stock in the state. After the sale of the family estate he erected a fine dwelling on Concord street, where he intended to spend the evening of life in the enjoyment of domestic tranquility and indulge his love of animals. But he had occupied his new place but a short time when he was found with his skull factured under the feet of an unbroken colt, and lived but a few hours afterward. He had no affiliations with secret societies. He attended the Unitarian Church, but was not a member of any sect. His religion was more in action than profession. He married, June 26, 1861, Anna S. Dodge, of Antrim, who was born September 16, 1838, daughter of Alvah and Lydia (Elliot) Dodge (see Dodge, V), who survives him, and occupies the handsome home he provided for her. She attends the Unitarian Church, and is a member of Matthew Thornton Chapter, Daughters of the American Revolution, and the Benevolent Circle.

JENKINS This is one of the many forms of names indicating Johnson. It is derived from two ancient words, the second of which indicates small and the literal translation of the name would be "Little John." It has numerous representatives throughout the United States, and has been identified with the pioneer settlement of Maine and New Hampshire. The records show that Reginald Jenkins, who was perhaps a son of Reginald Jenkins who settled in Dorchester in 1630, was a resident of Kittery, Maine. He was among those who petitioned in 1652 to be placed under the jurisdiction of Massachusetts, and subsequent to that period removed to Dover. His wife's name was Ann and they had a daughter Philadelphia, who was married June 14, 1676, at Dover, to Matthew Estes.

(I) William Jenkins, who was probably a descendant of Reginald Jenkins, died at Dover, December 10, 1785. He was married at Hampton to Phoebe Hoag, who died at Dover, March 29, 1774. Their children were: Hannah, Elizabeth, Phoebe,

William, Joseph, John, Jonathan and James. By the (second) wife Ruth, William Jenkins, who was then residing at Lee, had Sarah, Phoebe, Hannah and Timothy. He and his family were Quakers, and like other poor Quakers of that time were much persecuted and of course had no ooportunity to take part in civil affairs. Hence the only record to be found of this family is in that made by the Dover monthly meeting of the Quakers.

(II) John, third son and sixth child of William and Phoebe (Hoag) Jenkins, was born September 30, 1752, in Lee, New Hampshire, and settled in Barnstead, where he purchased a tract of land near Suncook pond, and settled upon it. He finally became the owner of considerable land in Lee, where he died. His children were: John, Joseph, Lois, Hannah, Sally and William. John lived and died in Lee; Joseph is mentioned below; Lois married Sargent Hanson, and lived in Madbury; Hannah married Jacob Odell, of Durham; Sally married John M. Chesley, and lived in Barnstead; William was a manufacturer of starch, and lived in New York (further mention of him appears below).

(III) Joseph, second son and child of John Jenkins, was born February 15, 1794, in Lee, and removed to Barnstead when a young man. He was one of the most considerable landowners of the town, and was largely engaged in buying and selling timber lots. He served as selectman many years, and was a representative in the state legislature two years. He died in Barnstead, 1886, at the age of ninety-two years. He married (first) Nancy Walker, born in Portsmouth, died in Barnstead in 1833, aged forty; and he married (second), Lydia Merrill. The children by the first wife were: Louisa, William A., Joseph, John W., and Oran J.; and by the second wife: Charles F., Everett, Lewis C. and Louisa (twins), Calvin, Melvin, and Mary and Lyman H. (twins). (Oran J. and descendants are noticed in this article.)

(IV) William Albert, eldest son and second child of Joseph and Nancy (Walker) Jenkins, was born in Barnstead, January 10, 1822, and died July 21, 1890. He was educated in the common schools. In political sentiment he was first a Republican and in later life an Independent. In his young manhood he was a lieutenant in the state militia. He was a man whose sound judgment and good common sense were relied on by his fellow citizens, who elected him to the office of county treasurer, in which he served in 1873-74. He married Maria Garland Berry, daughter of Samuel G. and Mary (Chamberlain) Berry. She was born February 9, 1821, and died April 7, 1875. They were the parents of nine children: Samuel Franklin, Albert Thompson, Nancy Maria, William Gilmore, William Edgar, Solon Berry, La Forest, Clarence S. and Elizabeth Belle.

(V) Samuel Franklin, eldest child of William A. and Maria G. (Berry) Jenkins, was born in Barnstead, October 7, 1847. After completing his attendance at the common schools he went to Nebraska and took up a farm in that state, in the valley of the Platte river. After a residence of several years there he returned to his native town and bought and operated a saw mill. In 1888 he removed to Pittsfield, where he has been the local representative of the *Manchester Union* for fourteen years, and did considerable other newspaper work. He has filled the office of judge of the police court for fourteen years, and justice of the peace and member of the school board. He is independent in politics, and attends the Baptist Church. He married in Fremont, Nebraska, May 7, 1868, Martha Zelanda Eaton, daughter of Peter and Elizabeth (Cleayes) Eaton. Her father was a millwright and machinist. She received a common school and academic education. Their children are: Winifred Ella, born in Barnstead, January 7, 1879, graduated from the Pittsfield high school, and now teaches in the village schools; and Arthur Eugene, born in Barnstead, November 20, 1882, a graduate of the Pittsfield high school, who is now a salesman in a boot and shoe store in Pittsfield.

(IV) Oran Jerome, fifth child and fourth son of Joseph and Nancy (Walker) Jenkins, was born in Barnstead, October 2, 1829. He attended the common schools, and a short time at Pittsfield Academy. He was born and brought up on the farm, and has always followed that calling except for a few years when he was conducting a potato starch factory in Bombay, New York. In 1880 he settled permanently in Pittsfield. He has a farm and a comfortable home on Concord hill, which commands a pleasant view overlooking the village. He was brought up a Republican, and adheres to that faith. He attends the Baptist Church. He married, in Bombay, New York, December 27, 1856, Mary Adelaide Sweet, born in Bombay, New York, December 19, 1839. Her parents were Stephen C. and Mary Sweet. Mr. and Mrs. Jenkins have three children: Aston S., Wilber E. and Alvira L. Aston S. was born September 15, 1858, and has three children: Gertrude, Catherine, and Bessie May. Wilber E., born September 16, 1861, is a merchant in Amsterdam, New York. He married, in Amsterdam, Minnie Snyder, of that place, and they have one son, Volney G. Alvira L., born May 5, 1863, married George Salter and died in 1898, leaving two children, Grace and Mildred Alice.

(III) William, son of John and Abigail (Varney) Jenkins, by deed dated February 19, 1806, transferred land in Barnstead to his son John. His wife was Joanna Foss.

(IV) William, son of William Jenkins, was born January 4, 1799. He married Abra H. Hanscomb, daughter of John and Hannah (Foss) Hanscomb, who was born August 5, 1807. They had four children born to them: John Hanscomb; Frank, died in childhood; Mary Augusta, died in childhood; William Albert, died at age of eleven years. William Jenkins died May 13, 1882; his wife, December 25, 1890.

(V) John Hanscomb, son of William and Abra H. (Hanscomb) Jenkins, was born September 24, 1832, at Barnstead, New Hampshire. He was educated in the public schools at Barnstead, at Pittsfield Academy, a select school at North Barnstead, taught by Dr. Walker, at Pembroke and Gilmanton academies and the McGaw Institute where he was a student 1855-56. He began teaching school in the fall of 1853 and so continued for nearly twenty-five years, being engaged in six different towns in New Hampshire, also Maine and Massachusetts. He taught the grammar school in Newmarket three years, 1860-62. He was also assistant for a time in Pittsfield Academy and at the McGaw Institute. In political faith he has always been a staunch Democrat, casting his first vote in 1854. With the exception of two he has been honored with all the offices of the town. He owns a farm about three-quarters of a mile from Barnstead Centre, which he has cultivated in connection with his teaching. In his church affiliations he has been connected with the Congregational Society. He is a Free Mason, having been connected with the order for nearly fifty years; a member of Morning Star Lodge, No. 17, Wolfboro. He is also a member of the Grange, Patrons of Husbandry, and has been a member of Sons of Temperance. He was a member of the state and national societies of Sons of Temperance.

He married, December 16, 1858, Alvira R., daughter of Jacob and Emma (Richardson) Wilker. Her twin sister was married the same day occasioning a double wedding. His wife traces her lineage back to John White, who came to America in 1620. Their children are: 1. Mary Augusta, born at Newmarket, New Hampshire, September 15, 1861, married Llewellyn H. Emerson (his second wife), December 16, 1893, and has one son, Ray J. Emerson, born August 18, 1894. 2. Frank Albert, born January 22, 1864, died October 30, 1869. 3. William Augustus, married Margaret A. Foss, daughter of James L. and Eliza Foss, December 25, 1889; their children are: Clarice A., born August 4, 1890; Evelyn Agatha, December 22, 1892; Harvey Foss, February 1, 1894; Asahel Mayland, August 28, 1897. 4. Emma Abra, born March 7, 1868. 5. Grace Darling, born March 31, 1870, married Llewellyn H. Emerson, son of Charles F. and Emily J. (Hall) Emerson, December 25, 1888, and died May 12, 1892. 6. John J., born May 6, 1872, married Mary Edith Maxfield, daughter of Henry W. and Harriette L. (Mellen) Maxfield, April 25, 1898, and their children are: Earle Maxfield, born January 4, 1899; Grace Darling, January 19, 1900; Nina Harriette, December 30, 1900, died August 20, 1901; Harriette Neva, April 26, 1902. Mary Edith (Maxfield) Jenkins died October 9, 1903. 7. Warren Washington, born May 10, 1874, died June 24, 1879. 8. Joseph Mayland, born April 25, 1876, died June 24, 1879. 9. Mirie Abbie, born May 28, 1880, married Frederick P. Frame, son of Henry L. and Ellen M. (Alley) Frame, June 18, 1906. 10. Warren Mayland, born November 14, 1881, died March 19, 1882.

HANSON The surname Hanson is of very ancient origin, and was handed down by the Flemings to the English speaking people. The root of the name was Hans, which is the only one of the abbreviations of the original Johannes, and from the latter we derive the familiar Hansons, Hankins, Hankinsons, Hancocks and others.

The family has been traced through many centuries and generations in the Old World. For the purpose of this article we shall begin by numbering the American ancestor I. The generations which appear to be authentic in the Old World begin with I. Roger de Rastrich, living in 1251, time of Henry III, in Wapentake of Morley, Yorkshire, England; held lands in Rastrich, Skircoat, Clayton, Bradford, etc. II. Hugh de Rastrich, III. John de Rastrich, IV. John de Rastrich, V. Henry de Rastrich, VI. John de Rastrich, called "Henry's son," then Hanson. VII. John Hanson, VIII. John Hanson. IX. John Hanson, whose descendants founded the family in New Hampshire.

(I) Thomas Hanson had a grant of one hundred acres of land (II, 11mo. 1658) near Salmon Falls, in the province of New Hampshire. He came to Dover, New Hampshire, in 1639, and died 1666. He was admitted a freeman, May 4, 1661, and in 1664-65 lived at Cochecho, where he was taxed as Thomas, Sr., 1664-65. His name does not appear again on the list of taxables, but his widow was taxed in 1666 and 1672. "Old Widow Hanson," as the record reads, was killed June 28, 1689. The will of Thomas Hanson was admitted to probate June 27, 1666, and his wife Mary was named in that instrument as his executrix. He gave money to his two daughters, and divided his real estate and other property among his sons, Tobias and Thomas, and two others then under age, Isaac and Timothy. The children of Thomas and Mary Hanson were: Thomas born about 1643; Tobias; Isaac, taxed at Cochecho in 1672; Timothy, and the two daughters who are not named. (Tobias and descendants receive mention in this article.)

(II) Thomas (2), son of Thomas Hanson, of Dover, and Mary, his wife, was born about 1643, and was taxed at Cochecho from 1664 to 1667. He married and had children, but the name of his wife is not known. His children were: Thomas, born about 1680; John, Nathaniel, Nancy, Elizabeth, James and Abigail. (John and descendants are noticed at length in this article.) The will of this Thomas (2) was dated February 4, 1711, and mentions his wife as Mercy, also all of the children above noted except his son John.

(III) Thomas (3), son of Thomas and Mercy Hanson, was born about 1680, and married for his first wife Margaretta Maul; second, Hannah ——. His children were: Thomas, born 1702, married Patience Mason; Robert, married Lydia Varney; Timothy, married Keziah ————; Maul, married (first) Sarah Twombley, (second) Mary Canney, (third) Anne Austin; Jonathan; Sarah; Samuel, born July 19, 1717, married Sarah French; Solomon, born January 29, 1719, married Anna Varney; Abigail, born December 23, 1821; Ebenezer, born June 4, 1726, married (first) Anne Hodgdon, (second) Hannah ————, and was a member of the Society of Friends.

(IV) Solomon, born January 29, 1719, eighth child of Thomas and Margaretta (Maul) Hanson, married Anna, daughter of Ebenezer and Mary (Otis) Varney. Mary was born June 5, 1718, and both she and her husband were members of the Society of Friends. Solomon died December 13, 1780. Their children were: Zaccheus, born September 17, 1742, married Sarah Sawyer; Abijah, Jacob, married Phebe Perkins; Solomon, married Mary Chase; Otis, married Ruth Gove; Mercy, married Nathaniel Meader; Sarah, married Oliver Winslow and had eleven children; Judith, married James Torrey; Ann and Martha.

(V) Solomon (2), born in Dover (date unknown), the fourth child of Solomon and Anna (Varney) Hanson, was a tanner and farmer in Kensington, New Hampshire, but later in life removed to Pittsfield, New Hampshire. He married Mary Chase, of Kensington, and had three children: Annie, Abial, married Jonathan Chase, and Nathan.

(VI) Nathan Hanson was born in Pittsfield, New Hampshire, in 1784, and died in Weare in 1864. Like his father he was a farmer and tanner. He removed from Pittsfield to Weare in 1842, and from that time devoted his attention to farming alone. He bought and settled on what was known as the Stephen Dow farm, about one-half mine west of Weare Center, which was one of the best farms in the town and was brought to a high state of cultivation through his patient toil. He was a consistent man in all that he did, whether as a farmer or in the private walks of life. His life as a farmer was rewarded with substantial success, and he raised many fine cattle and grew fruits of superior quality. By inheritance and personal inclination he was a very pious man, and like his ancestors was a devout member of the Society of Friends. Nathan Hanson married (first) Lydia Allen, of Maine; (second) Sarah Austin, of Maine, died in

1836, aged thirty-five years; (third) Mary Paige, of Weare; she died in 1862. In all he had three children, one by his first wife and two by his second wife. They were Sabina, who became the wife of Daniel Paige, of Weare; Alvin, who was born February 18, 1826, and died single in 1848; and John W.

(VII) John Winslow Hanson, of Weare, New Hampshire, has been a prominent character in the industrial and business life and history of that town for a full half century, and now although virtually retired from active pursuits is still in close association with the best interests of the locality and of Hillsborough county. He has not achieved prominence in the sense that he has been conspicuous in either county or town politics, but in the ordinary business sense in that he has been an important factor in building up and maintaining manufacturing and business enterprises, and thereby furnishing employment to many working men and adding to the population of the town and the value of its property and promoting the welfare of all its people. A glance at the town records shows that whenever occasion has arisen in which public interests were concerned and public action became advisable, John W. Hanson was generally a member of the special committee appointed to investigate and determine upon the proper action to be taken.

Mr. Hanson is a native of Pittsfield, New Hampshire, and was born September 22, 1830. He was eleven years old when his parents moved from Pittsfield to Weare, and has lived in the latter town sixty-five years. He received his education in public schools, Pittsfield Academy, Cartland's school at Clinton Grove, and what is now Moses Brown School of Providence. Rhode Island. He worked on his father's farm until he reached the age of eighteen years, and from 1848 to 1857 engaged in the stove and tinware business at Weare Center, selling annually from five thousand to ten thousand dollars worth of merchandise. He moved to North Weare in December, 1857, and in partnership with Lindley M. Sawyer carried on a shoe business in the shops of Allen Sawyer until June, 1865, when he began the manufacture of shoes on his own account, a business he continued with gratifying success until 1891, when he retired. For many years he was the most extensive manufacturer in the town of Weare. He is a Republican in politics, and in 1897 was a member of the legislature and served on the committee on banks. Mr. Hanson was one of the incorporators of the Weare Mutual Fire Insurance Company in 1856. In 1886 Mr. Hanson, Charles A. Jones and L. M. Sawyer established a hosiery factory upon the site of the old Weare Woolen Mills, and Mr. Hanson was treasurer and manager, and so continued until the closing up of the business. Since retiring from active business Mr. Hanson has been solicited and served in the settling of a number of estates in Weare; his advice is frequently sought upon matters of this character, and he has devoted considerable time to these matters. He was a member of the Union League at the time of the Civil war, and has been a member of the Derryfield Club in Manchester.

Mr. Hanson married, November 17, 1852, Mary Jane Sawyer, who was born May 13, 1832, daughter of Allen and Anna (Osborne) Sawyer, of Weare (see Sawyer).

(III) John Hanson, second son of Thomas (2) Hanson, lived at Nock's Marsh. Quint's "Ancient Dover" states that, as he was a Quaker, he declined to leave the exposed place where he lived when the Indian troubles of 1724 began, and his home was marked for an attack by thirteen Indians and French Mohawks, who lay several days near it in ambush, waiting until Hanson and his men should be away. Then when he had gone to the week-day meeting of his church, August 27, 1724, and his two sons were at work at a distance, the Indians entered the house. Mrs. Hanson, a servant and four children, were in the house, of which one child the Indians immediately killed to terrify the others; two other children were at play in the orchard and would have escaped, but just as the Indians had finished rifling the house, the two came in sight and made such a noise that the Indians killed the youngest boy to stop an alarm. They then started for Canada with Mrs. Hanson (who had been confined but fourteen days prior), her babe, a boy of six years, and two daughters, one fourteen years old, the other sixteen, and the servant girl. All reached Canada, but the party was repeatedly subdivided during the journey. The first person who discovered the tragedy was Hanson's eldest daughter, on her return from meeting. Seeing the children dead, she uttered a shriek which was distinctly heard by her mother in the hands of the enemy, and by her brothers at work. Pursuit was instantly made, but the Indians avoided all paths and escaped undiscovered. After this disaster Hanson removed the remainder of his family to the house of his brother, "who," says Belknap, "though of the same religious persuasion yet had a number of lusty sons and always kept fire-arms in good order for the purpose of shooting game." Mr. Hanson, soon after the attack, went to Canada to ransom his family. The following item from the *News Letter* of 1725 is of interest in that connection:

"Newport, August 27th (1725). On Tuesday last, (Aug. 24) arrived here, Mr. John Handson, of Dover, Piscataqua, and about a Month's time from Canada, but last from New York, with his wife & three children and a Servant Woman; as also one Ebenezer Downs, having a wife & five children at Piscataqua; also one Miles Thompson, a Boy, who were all taken Captives about Twelve Months since, by the Enemy Indians, and carried to Canada, except the above said Handson; who at the same time lost Two of his Sons by the Indians; & now it hath cost him about £700 for their Ransom, including his other necessary charges. He likewise informs, That another of his children, a young woman of about Seventeen Years of Age was carried Captive at the same time with the rest of the family, with whom he convers'd for several Hours, but could not obtain her Ransom: for the Indians would not consent to part with her on any terms, so he was obliged to leave her."

Mr. Hanson reached home September 1, 1725, but he could not content himself while his daughter Sarah was in Canada; and about April 19, 1727, he started in company with a kinsman who with his wife was bound on a similarly sad errand to redeem children; but he was taken sick on the journey, and died about halfway between Albany and Canada—one account says Crown Point. The daughter married a Frenchman, and never returned. So far as records are obtained, John Hanson's family were as follows: He married 23 5mo. 1703, Elizabeth ———. Their children were: Hannah, Sarah, Elizabeth, John, Isaac, Daniel, Ebenezer, Caleb, and a daughter whose name is not given.

(IV) John (2), fourth child and eldest son of John (1) and Elizabeth Hanson, was born in Dover, 17 1 mo. 1712. He married (first) 27 12mo. 1735, Phebe, daughter of Nathaniel and Catherine

J. W. Hanson

clined to leave the exposed place where he lived when the Indian troubles of 1724 began, and his

ver, 17 1 mo. 1712. He married (first) 27 12mo. 1735, Phebe, daughter of Nathaniel and Catherine

J. W. Hanson

(Neale) Austin, who was born March 14, 1718. They were Quakers, or Friends. Their children were: Sarah, Patience, Phebe, John, and Catherine. He married (second) 21 4mo. 1750, Sarah, daughter of Thomas and Mary (Brackett) Tuttle, who was born 16 4mo. 1727, and died 12 11mo. 1804. He died 9 11mo, 1784. Their children were: James, Elizabeth, Mary and Isaac.

(V) John (3), fourth child and eldest son of John (2) and Phebe Austin, was born 17 11mo. 1746.

(VI) Samuel, son of John (3) Hanson, was a man of great strength and courage, and was nicknamed "Cat" Hanson from the circumstance of his having drawn from its den in the rocks a Canada lynx, colloquially referred to as a "cat," while holding its feet with his hands.

(VII) John (4), son of Samuel Hanson, married Elizabeth Emerson and resided in Unity, New Hampshire.

(VIII) Hezekiah Emerson, second son and second child of John (4) and Elizabeth (Emerson) Hanson, was born in Unity, New Hampshire, August 18, 1819, and died October 4, 1897. He was educated in the common schools, and possessed a natural aptitude for mathematics. He owned and cultivated a farm, and also operated a saw mill for many years at Croydon, New Hampshire. He was a lifelong Democrat, and was honored by his fellow townsmen with the office of selectman, and was chairman of the board of selectmen of Croydon for three years. He married, in Claremont, February 27, 1848, Cornelia Clark Taylor, who was born in Brockport, New York, February 10, 1817, and died in Goshen, New Hampshire, November 28, 1894, aged seventy-seven years. She was the daughter of Nathan and Hannah (Bixby) Taylor.

(IX) Frank Llewellyn, only son and only child of Hezekiah E. and Cornelia Clark (Taylor) Hanson, was born in Newport, New Hampshire, January 18, 1856. He grew up on his father's farm, and was educated in the common schools and in the high school of Newport, New Hampshire, and at Bryant & Stratton's Business College in Manchester. Until twenty-two years of age, such time as he was not in school he was employed in work on the farm or in saw mills in Croydon, and spool and bobbin shops in Lowell, Massachusetts. Subsequently he was employed five years as a clerk in the freight department of the New York & New England railroad at Boston, Massachusetts. Then returning to Croydon he was engaged in the lumber business with the firm of Hanson & Walker. From Croydon he removed to Goshen, and engaged in farming until 1906, when he bought a country store which he has since successfully conducted. Politically Mr. Hanson is a Democrat. He has served his fellow citizens faithfully in the following capacities: Town clerk of Croydon five years; town clerk of Goshen ten years, and now holds that office; delegate to the constitutional convention of 1902, and was for several years member of the library committee of the Olive G. Pettis Free Library of Goshen, and is now (1907) member of the legislature, having been elected in 1906.

Mr. Hanson married, in Boston, Massachusetts, March 11, 1883, Hannah Ann, widow of Albert J. Darrah, who was born in Vienna, Maine, April 18, 1852, daughter of Timothy Varney and Mercy Ann (McFarland) Wight, of Vienna, and granddaughter of Asa Wight, a soldier of the war of 1812. Mrs. Hanson has a son by her former marriage, Fred A. Darrah, who was born in Boston, Massachusetts, September 20, 1877. He was educated in the common schools, and is now a clerk at Goshen. He married October 22, 1904, Lena G. Cozzens, of Natick, Massachusetts, who died August 6, 1905.

(II) Tobias, second son of Thomas Hanson, of Dover, was killed by the Indians, and his wife captured May 10, 1693. They had children: Joseph, Benjamin, and Tobias, whose sketch follows.

(III) Tobias (2), son of Tobias (1) Hanson, was born in Dover, where he lived and died. He married (first) Lydia Canney; and (second) Ann Lord, of Berwick, Maine. The children by the first wife were: Benjamin and Elizabeth; by the second: Mercy, Tobias, Judith, Joseph, Nathaniel, Isaac, Samuel and Aaron.

(IV) Joseph, fourth child and second son of Tobias (2) and Ann (Lord) Hanson, was born January 15, 1705. He was a potter and lived in Dover until his death, September 5, 1758. He married (first), November 23, 1727, Rebecca Sheppard, who was born in 1708 and died April 19, 1736; (second), May 25, 1737, Sarah Scammon, who died September 2, 1738; (third), June 6, 1739, Susanna Burnham, who was born March 1, 1715, a daughter of Robert and Elizabeth Burnham. She died March 4, 1758. By the first wife there was one child, Ephraim; by the second, one child, Humphrey; by the third, two children, Rebecca and John B.

(V) Humphrey, only child of Joseph and Sarah (Scammon) Hanson, was born May 27, 1738, was baptized September 3, 1738, and died November 13, 1766. He married Joanna Watson, and they had four children: Dominicus, born March 19, 1760, not married; Sarah, December 22, 1762, married ——— Richardson; Joseph, December 18, 1764, married Charity Dame; Elizabeth, December 12, 1767, married ——— Gilman.

(VI) Joseph (2), son of Humphrey and Joanna (Watson) Hanson, was born on what is now Hanson street, Dover, December 18, 1764, and died at Rochester, New Hampshire, December 19, 1832. He married, March 4, 1798, Charity Dame, of Rochester, who was born September 1, 1755, and died February 3, 1833. They had: Humphrey, born January 3, 1799, died July 20, 1826; Mary Dame, April 23, 1800, died April 25, 1853; Hannah, May 23, 1802, died February 9, 1803; Joseph Scammon, July 27, 1803, died April 21, 1828; Meribah, February 4, 1805, died November 18, 1863; Johanna, March 10, 1807, died October 10, 1884; a child, November 18, 1808, died November 22, 1808; Hester Ann, January 20, 1810, died March 31, 1856; Dominicus, mentioned at length below. Asa P., of Newton, Iowa, was born April 20, 1817, married Rooxbe Kimball, and their children were: Henry A., born March 23, 1841; Emma, Ella, Mary and Belle, deceased.

Joseph Hanson came to Rochester from Dover, New Hampshire, when a young man, and immediately engaged in the general grocery and mercantile business, which he successfully followed until within a few years of his death. He was a man of excellent judgment, good common sense, shrewd, cautious, industrious and economical. He built in Rochester the first brick store ever erected in Strafford county, which they came to see from far and near. It was two story with pitch roof tinned and the door and window shutters were also tinned, there being no fire apparatus in those days in the village. This building stood opposite the present (1907) McDuffee block and where now stands Wentworth block. At a very early day he made a brick vault on his land behind his store for the deposit of his and other people's papers, etc., there being no bank in the village. He inaugurated many useful schemes which have had a tendency for good, and his name was held in grateful rememberance by those who knew him. He was justly considered one of the best business men of his day, and his ample fortune left to his family fully attests this estimate of him. Mrs. Hanson was a member of the Methodist Church, and he was an attendant and supporter of the various churches, though not a member of any, rather leaning towards Universalism.

(VII) Dominicus, third son of Joseph and Charity (Dame) Hanson, was born August 23, 1813, in same house in Rochester, New Hampshire, in which he died, June 1, 1907. He received the advantages of a common school education until he was some fifteen years of age, and this was supplemented by an academic education at Rochester Academy, Parsonfield Seminary, Maine, Hopkinton, New Hampshire, and Pembroke, New Hampshire. In 1830 he commenced the drug business as an apprentice to his brother-in-law, Dr. Joseph Smith, and served him two years and in 1832 bought Dr. Smith's interest and continued in the business until the fire of 1880 except some two or three years when away to school. As an evidence of the confidence reposed in Mr. Hanson as an honest and trustworthy gentleman we may mention that, at the time of the great Civil war, at the earnest solicitation of the business men of his native town, he issued script of the respective denomination of ten cents, twenty-five cents and fifty cents, to the amount of eight thousand dollars which read as follows:

"State of New Hampshire,
Rochester, Sept. 27, 1862.

For Value received I promise to pay on demand, in current Bank Bills in sums of one dollar and upward at my place of business.

Dominicus Hanson."

This scrip was issued when there was a scarcity of circulating money during the great Civil war and before the general government had issued any money. This scrip circulated throughout New England, and was never refused, all of which was promptly redeemed when the general government made its issue. Hence the name "Honest Dominicus," as he has been known by his friends for long years. Who ever saw the goodly village of Rochester in Norway Plains but has seen his prim, circular front, pressed brick, two-story apothecary store erected by him in about the year 1837 (on the site of an earlier one which was destroyed by fire) once the most stylish store in the whole state of New Hampshire. Its long remembered and excellent brick sidewalk in front, dating back to time immemorial before Rochester knew the luxury of brick sidewalks, its broad stone steps, always a delight to the innumerable patrons of this popular resort, who climbed them with assurance of safe foothold, and excellent reception beyond.

If Noah could by any means have been compelled to refit and rearrange the Ark and take in all that he considered necessary to stock a new world, he couldn't collect the six or eight million invaluable articles which are here gathered together from the four corners of the earth (or is coming next day) unless he had the nearly miraculous experience of our subject and to acquire such an experience would cost a frightful expenditure of both time and money.

The following description was written shortly before his death by one who knew him well: "Mr. Hanson was six feet in height, standing quite erect, moved with an elastic step quickly and lightly. His hair at death was white with the frost of nearly a century. He was of a marked nervous organization, his thin cut face bearing its certain evidence. Nothing about the face or general appearance especially marked him above many other men you may meet in the course of a day's ride in any portion of Yankee Land; by that sign you can judge the man. If ever wit or drollery overflowed in one person here it is. I know of no two faces in the country that so nearly resemble each other as that of 'Honest Dominicus' and the happy countenance of America's humorist, Mark Twain. The general impression left by the two faces is the same, the same mysterious gleam, sure token of the mental flash, occurs in each and the wit and humor of each is fully recognized among their friends. The parallel holds good still further, in neither case can the purpose or intent be solved. A matter of the lightest import may be treated with ponderous gravity befitting a funeral oration, and while either of the two are discussing with lengthened faces upon the topic the bystanders are convulsed with laughter. On the contrary many things which bewilder the brains of common people are heartily laughed at by them. Either of these worthies are a puzzle to their many friends, and like all human enigmas of course, they are idolized. But Mr. Hanson is a study. In him lives the gentle graces of geniality and cute Yankee, and the subtle and evanescent essence of fun. In him dwells a constant gleam of drollery always as welcome as sunshine in winter or flowers in May. The mirth which overflows in his happy moments is all the more welcome because of the uncertainty of the aim. It may be gentle invectives of society shams; perhaps a tinge of sarcasm wittily said lightens his efforts."

Mr. Hanson continued the business at the old stand until the fire of 1880 in which his store was badly damaged. He soon, however, repaired and added a story and then retired from the drug business in favor of our present esteemed pharmacist, R. DeWitt Burnham, who at once entered into business in the remodeled store and who has merited the large patronage he has received up to the present time (1907) and long may his star continue in the ascendency.

Mr. Hanson's residence erected by his father over one hundred years ago, the erection of which was celebrated by people from Middleton, Tamworth, Ossipee and nearby towns including the citizens of Rochester which were numerous, cordial and welcome, was celebrated in the good old way of those days in which the product of the West Indies and of France were much in evidence at the time of laying the ridge pole, after which verses composed for the occasion were read and the frame named and christened the "General Washington," a celebration in which all became most gloriously interested. The house then boasted of a fine balustrade around the roof which has since been removed. When the railroads were built through Rochester, he opened the thoroughfare known as Hanson's street through his garden, never receiving any recompense for opening the same, although promised, and has always constructed and maintained, at his own expense, (except sanding and breaking in the winter) spending many thousand of dollars in construction and keeping it in proper condition and paving it in the fall of 1901 at the expense of several thousand dollars with first class granite blocks from the well known and celebrated quarry of Charles A. Bailey, of Suncook, New Hampshire, of whom Mr. Hanson speaks in the highest terms of praise as a man of honor and integrity. Mr. Bailey furnished fifty-six thousand first-class granite

D. Harrison

Written at Age 94

blocks besides three first-class honey comb hammered crossings. No finer could have been found in any city in the United States, making twenty-seven cars, being twenty-four cars of blocks and three cars of crossings. The paving was also a first-class job and done by the well known and celebrated electric railroad builders and pavers, Soule Dillingham & Company, of Boston, the builders of the Rochester Electric Railroad.

In connection with the paving Mr. Hanson also had cast by the Rochester Foundry & Machine Company, new special sewer grates to conform to the paving bearing the street monogram in place of earlier grates which were also put in by Mr. Hanson a number of years ago. The people of Rochester have known for years that enchanting stretch of woodland on the bank of our beloved Cocheco (now almost in the center of our city) known as Hanson's Pines, which Mr. Hanson preserved from the axe of the woodman at a money loss in fires, etc., beside being most valuable building lots, if cleared, (there being one hundred and four lots) well knowing the exquisite pleasure their charming shades bestowed on a tired and weary world, besides being the trysting place of many moon-eyed lovers who have there discoursed to their ladies eyebrows for better of for worse.

Mr. Hanson married, September 19, 1839, Betsey S. Chase, daughter of Simon Chase, who conducted a mercantile business in Rochester. Two sons were born to them, Charles A. C., August 18, 1844, and George Washington, July 6, 1854, died January 6, 1856. It is to the elder son, Charles A. C., that the credit is due for the establishment of the Old Cemetery Conservation Fund—Perputa—for the perpetual care and improvement of the Old Cemetery. He bore the original expense of over three hundred dollars from his own pocket and raised a fund of about five thousand dollars which he turned over to the town for the purpose specified. While engaged in making the final arrangements for the completion of this work he was severely injured by an elevator and crippled for life.

Dominicus Hanson was an earnest supporter of General Jackson for president at the time of his candidacy for second term, although he was not old enough to vote. His first ballot was cast for Martin Van Buren. Before attaining his majority he was appointed postmaster by General Jackson in 1835 and continued to hold the office under the administrations of Van Buren and Harrison fourteen years in his store, making great improvements in the office and introduced the first boxes. Mr. Hanson instituted the first independent postoffice in Rochester, erecting a building on Hanson street in 1873 expressly for it, which he rented to the government at a nominal price (the postoffice up to this time had been located in stores). The postoffice remained in this building twenty-six years until 1899, when it was removed to its present location in Farrington Block, Hanson street, by our present enterprising and most worthy postmaster, Osman B. Warren, Esq., who newly equipped it, making it one of the finest offices in the state.

We find among Mr. Hanson's effects an old paper yellow with age which reads as follows:

"The State of New Hampshire,
To Dominicus Hanson: Gentleman;
Greeting.

We reposing especial trust and confidence in your Fidelity, courage and Good Conduct, Do. by these Presents constitute and appoint you, the said Dominicus Hanson PAY MASTER of the 39th Regiment of Militia in the State of New Hampshire with the Rank of Leutinant etc etc etc. signed His Excellency the Governor, Isaac Hill 24th day of August 1836."

He was a director of the Norway Plains Savings Bank for a number of years.

In religious views Mr. Hanson was a liberal, although specially interested in the Universalist faith. He was kindly disposed to all and gave liberally to all improvements and benefits for the pubilc good, believing in the fatherhood of God and the Brotherhood of man and a higher and better life for all.

HANSON There is no doubt whatever that the Hanson families of Barnstead, New Hampshire, who have lived in that town in one generation after another for more than one hundred and fifty years are direct descendants of Thomas Hanson, of Dover, New Hampshire, although there is no record by which to determine which of the sons of Thomas is in the line from the ancestor to Ebenezer, the progenitor of the Barnstead Hansons. But notwithstanding this it is safe to assume that the families are in direct relation, although the descent connot be distinctly established.

(V) Ebenezer Hanson, progenitor of the numerous family of that name in Barnstead and other towns of the state, was born April 12, 1759, and died May 26, 1826. He married, September 6, 1789, Abigail Caverno, born May 10, 1770, and died April 14, 1854. She was a daughter of John Caverno, of Barrington, New Hampshire, and granddaughter of Arthur Caverno, who immigrated to America about 1735 from the north of Ireland, and was of Scotch-Irish descent. Arthur Caverno was born about 1718, and married Fanny Potts, who was born in Ireland about 1720. Ebenezer and Abigail (Caverno) Hanson had thirteen children: Caverno, Paul, John, Sally, Polly, Ebenezer, Hannah, Judith, Nathaniel, Caleb, Abigail, Sarah and Jeremiah Hanson.

(VI) Nathaniel, ninth child and fifth son of Ebenezer and Abigail (Caverno) Hanson, was born May 11, 1807, and died October 5, 1891. He married, April 16, 1829, Margery Evans, who was born June 20, 1809, and died March 9, 1891. They had children: John, Caleb W., Levi H., Nathaniel L., Ebenezer, Lewis F., Joseph B., and George and Jennie B. Hanson. Margery Evans, wife of Nathaniel Hanson, and mother of Ebenezer Hanson of Barnstead, was a daughter of Edmund and Dorothy (Hardy) Evans, and Dorothy Hardy was a daughter of Theophilus Hardy and Mary (Sullivan) Hardy. Mary Sullivan was born in Berwick, Maine, in 1752, and died in Strafford, New Hampshire, in 1827. She was a sister of General John Sullivan, of Revolutionary fame, and a daughter of John Sullivan, of Berwick, Maine, who was born in Limerick, Ireland, June 17, 1690, and died in Berwick, June 20, 1785. He emigrated from Ireland to America about 1723 and settled at Berwick, where he was a farmer, conveyancer and school teacher until he was ninety years old. About 1735 he married Margery Brown, born in Cork, Ireland, in 1714, and died in Berwick, Maine. He married (second), at Fort Pownal, Maine, Abigail Bean, daughter of John Bean, who with others obtained a patent for the land on which the town of Sullivan, Maine, is built.

(VII) Ebenezer, fifth child and fifth son of Nathaniel and Margery (Evans) Hanson, was born in Barnstead, New Hampshire, March 22, 1841, and is numbered among the oldest and most prominent business men of that town. He was brought up on his father's farm and sent to the district school, and afterward was a student in the academies at Pittsfield, New Hampton and Gilmanton. After leaving school he learned the trade of shoemaking and followed it for some time. Later on he went to Boston and engaged in mercantile pursuits, and after having acquired an understanding of the business returned to New Hampshire and for some time carried on a general store at New Market. From that place he soon removed to South Barnstead, where for many years he has been proprietor of an extensive general mercantile establishment. For twenty-eight years previous to the Cleveland administration Mr. Hanson was postmaster at South Barnstead, and also for some time was a justice of the peace. Besides general merchandising he deals considerably in lumber and real estate, and takes a commendable interest in the welfare of the town and its people. He is a member and clerk of the Congregational Church of Barnstead and a member of its ministerial committee. On Thanksgiving day, December 7, 1865, at Pittsfield, New Hampshire, Mr. Hanson married Jennie M. Hodgdon, who was born April 1, 1841, daughter of Timothy E. and Mary E. (George) Hodgdon. Their children are: Anna, who married Rev. James C. Emerson, both dead; Alice E., who married Chapin Osgood and removed to Medford, Massachusetts; George, now living at home, and Carroll A., a druggist of Medford, Massachusetts.

JUNKINS The name Junkins which is probably a corruption of Jenkins, is ancient in those parts of Maine and New Hampshire which lie adjacent to each other. It is not improbable that all persons of this name in those parts are descendants from one pair of ancestors.

(I) James Junkins lived in York, Maine, and was born there probably. His wife Eleanor (Junkins) was born in June, 1771, and died February 18, 1849, aged seventy-eight years, eight months, at the home of her son in Wakefield.

(II) Rufus Junkins was born January 16, 1798, probably in Maine, and died April 17, 1854, aged fifty-six years, four months and one day, at Union, New Hampshire, where for years he followed blacksmithing. He married (first) Sally Hayes, who was born April 1, 1803, and died July 12, 1828. Two children were born of this union: James H. and Rufus A. He married (second) Temperance P. Adams, and they had seven children: Sallie, who married Charles Wentworth; Elizabeth, wife of Charles Nurte; Ellen, who married H. P. Gilman; Edwin, Priscilla, George W., and George E., both died young.

(III) James Hayes, eldest child of Rufus and Sally (Hayes) Junkins, was born in Union, February 3, 1823, and died December 11, 1896. He followed blacksmithing which he learned of his father, and was a competent and respected citizen. He was social and fraternal in disposition, and was for many years a member of the Order of Free and Accepted Masons. He married, October 23, 1853, Sallie A. Wentworth, who was born in Wakefield, May 27, 1829, and died May 20, 1903, daughter of Albra and Rhoda (Cook) Wentworth, of Wakefield. (See Wentworth, VI.) They had three children: Clarence E., the subject of the next paragraph; Rufus Albra, born March 30, 1858, for twenty-eight years past with the Simonds Manufacturing Company of Chicago, who married, June 24, 1882, Mary A. Stickney, of Ackworth, and has one child, Roger Wentworth; and Arthi E. Edna, April 1, 1864, who married Moses G. Chamberlain, of Milton.

(IV) Clarence Elmer, eldest child of James H. and Sally Aroline (Wentworth) Junkins, was born in Union, October 10, 1855. He attended the common schools until about sixteen years of age, and then apprenticed himself to Benjamin Edgerly, of Union, for whom he worked three years, learning the tinner's trade. He then worked at his trade in Dover a year. Following that he was in the employ of the Simonds Manufacturing Company of Fitchburg, Massachusetts, fifteen years. At the end of that time he settled in Rochester, New Hampshire, and bought a half interest in the stove, tinware and plumbing business of L. G. Cooper, the two forming the firm of Cooper & Junkins, and carrying on the business until January, 1904, when Mr. Junkins bought his partner's interest, and has since carried on the business alone. He is a respected member of Mt. Roulstone Lodge, No. 98, Independent Order of Odd Fellows of Fitchburg. He married, in New Sharon, Maine, September 19, 1888, Nellie P. Tucker, who was born in Waldoborough, Maine, January 17, 1858, daughter of Daniel S. and Mercy S. (Howes) Tucker.

JUNKINS Circumstances indicate that this branch of the Junkins family is descended from Robert Jenkins or Junkins, who was at Dover, New Hampshire, in 1657, and at York, Maine, in 1674, and after.

(I) David Junkins was born in February 21, 1776, and died in York, Maine, December 3, 1855, aged nearly eighty. He married, November 12, 1801, Abigail Junkins, who died in York, June 25, 1853. They had seven children: Nathan, David, James, Salome, Hosea, Abigail and James.

(II) David Junkins (2), second son and child of David (1) and Abigail (Junkins) Junkins, was born in York, Maine, December 9, 1804, and died in Portsmouth, New Hampshire, March 22, 1889, aged eighty-four. At the early age of seventeen he came to Portsmouth and was apprenticed to his uncle, Isaac Junkins, who was at that time foreman ship carpenter at the navy yard. After serving his time he went to work for Jacob Remick, who had a ship yard on the site now occupied by Call's lumber yard. The following year he went to Durham and worked on a ship built by Joseph Coe. In the year 1828 he commenced work for George Raynes, working on the brig "Planet," and in the following year he got out the timber for the ship "Joseph and Mary" built at Kittery by Thomas Cottle. In 1830 he returned to the employ of Mr. Raynes and worked for him until the suspension of work at that yard. Among the vessels built during his employment there were the ships: "Alexander," Nestor," "Harriet and Jesse," "Pontiff Rockingham, Portsmouth," Susanna Cumming," "Hindoo," "Isaac Newton," "John Cumming Henry," "Nicholas Biddle," "Charles Isaac Allenton," and "Witch of the Waves," beside numerous small craft. The apprentices were placed in his care for instruction, and he was by them familiarly called "Uncle David," a name he was known by until his decease. After the suspension of work at the Raynes yard he worked at the navy yard and for Tobey & Littlefield, William Fernald, Daniel Marcy and other well known ship builders. He was one of the oldest members of Piscataqua Lodge, No. 6, Independent Order of Odd Fellows, and also a member of the Associated Mechanics' and Manufacturers' Association.

He married in Portsmouth, February 9, 1832, Betsey Pearson, born in Newburyport, Massachusetts, December 31, 1810, and died June 30, 1901, in her ninety-first year. Her parents were Abner and Betsey (Woodwell) Pearson. Her grandfather (a pensioner of the Revolution) helped build the historic frigate "Constitution" at the Boston yard in 1797. Children of David and Betsey B. Junkins were: Mary E. W., born August 25, 1832; Mary Abbie, born June 17, 1834, died August 10, 1894; George James, born March 21, 1836, died June 9, 1836; Orren Clark, born July 24, 1837, died February, 17, 1892; James Augustus, born August 5, 1839, died October 15, 1870; Almira Dennett, born September 24, 1841, died March 13, 1862; George Pearson, born November 5, 1843; Emma Frances, born October 11, 1845; William Wallace, born December 5, 1847; Horace, born September 20, 1849, died September 29, 1850; Albert Rand, born September 7, 1852; David Edwin, born July 28, 1854; Ann Mary, born September 5, 1857, died November 23, 1857. (Albert R. and descendants receive mention in this article.)

(III) William Wallace Junkins, eighth child and fourth son of David and Betsey (Pearson) Junkins, was born in Portsmouth, December 5, 1847, and educated in the common schools of that city. He learned the joiner's trade of Nathan Tarlton, of Portsmouth, continuing with him about two and one-half years, and then went to Jamaica Plains, Massachusetts, and worked for Prindle & Heath, contractors and builders, for a year. He was afterward employed on Long Island, Boston Harbor, and Somerville, being employed at the latter place seventeen years. Then, after a stay of a year in Charlestown, he returned to Portsmouth and was in the employ of William A. Hodgdon seventeen years, and Anderson & Junkins two years. In politics Mr. Junkins is a Republican. He is a member of Carpenters' and Joiners' Union, No. 921, of Portsmouth, also of Howard Lodge, No. 22, of Charlestown, Massachusetts, Somerville Encampment, No. 48, and is past commander of Canton Senter, of Portsmouth; a member of the Golden Eagles, No. 4, Alpha Council of the Royal Arcanum of Portsmouth, and Union Rebekah Lodge, No. 3.

He married, June 26, 1895, at Portsmouth, Emma Florence Manent, born in Portsmouth, December 25, 1861, daughter of Charles and Eliza (Pitman) Manent. They have one child, Ruth L., born June 20, 1904, in Portsmouth.

(III) Albert Rand Junkins, eleventh child and seventh son of David and Betsey (Pearson) Junkins, was born in Portsmouth, September 7, 1852. After acquiring a common school education, he learned the carpenter's trade as an apprentice to Thomas J. Spinney, in whose employ he remained eight years. In July, 1877, Mr. Junkins and Albert C. Anderson formed a partnership under the firm name of Anderson & Junkins, contractors and builders, which continued through twenty-nine years of successful business, until the death of Mr. Anderson, July 3, 1906, and during that time they erected many well known buildings, among which are the residences of John Sise, H. Fisher Eldredge, Morris C. Foye, G. Ralph Laighton, Gustave Peyser, and many others, also Rockingham county jail.

Mr. Junkins is a Republican, and was for three years a member of the city council of Portsmouth, and was president of that body two years. He was also alderman two years. In March, 1907, he was elected chairman of the board of assessors for the term of six years. He is a prominent member of the Court Street Christian Church, of which he is warden, and for thirty years has been superintendent of its Sunday-school. For many years he has been a trustee of the Howard Benevolent Society. He has seen twenty years service as a member of the Portsmouth fire department, and is a past captain of the steamer Colonel Sise, No. 2. He is a member of the Mechanics' Fire Society, organized in 1812. In Masonic and Odd Fellow organizations Mr. Junkins is particularly prominent. He is a member of Piscataqua Lodge, No. 6, Independent Order of Odd Fellows; Strawberry Bank Encampment, No. 5; Canton Senter and Union Rebekah Lodge, No. 3, in all of which he has passed the chairs. He is a past grand patriarch of the Grand Encampment, and a past grand representative. He is a past master in all these lodges. He is a member of St. Johns Lodge, No. 1, Free and Accepted Masons; Washington Royal Arch Chapter, No. 3; Davenport Council, No. 5, Royal and Select Masters; DeWitt Clinton Commandery, Knights Templar, of Portsmouth; Edward A. Raymond consistory, thirty-second degree, of the Sublime Princes of the Royal Secret, of Nashua; is past district deputy grand master; officer of the Council of High Priesthood; grand conductor of the Grand Council of Royal and Select Masters; member of the Grand Commandery of New Hampshire; thrice potent master in the Ineffable Grand Lodge of Perfection; senior warden in the Grand Council of the Princes of Jerusalem; member of New Hampshire Rose Croix Chapter; and the Council of Deliberation of New Hampshire; also of Aleppo Temple of the Ancient Arabic Order of the Nobles of the Mystic Shrine (of Boston); and the New Hampshire Veterans' Masons' Association.

He married, October 13, 1875, Flora E. Anderson, born May 29, 1853, daughter of Andrew and Betsy J. Anderson, of Portsmouth.

The Junkins homestead at No. 12 Deer street, is one of the oldest houses in the city. A block of marble is inserted in the chimney bearing the date 1705. This house was built by John Newmarch, whose wife was a sister of Sir William Pepperrell.

LOUGEE

But little is known of the early history and character of this family. The emigrant coming to this country about 1685 was an inhabitant of the Isle of Jersey, England. The family, however, seems to have possessed a sterling military spirit and a noble patriotism which led certain of its members in the country's emergency to spring to arms and battle valiantly for its protection. Some of them certainly have been eminent for their high christian character and salutary influence. The name is probably of French origin, and is not widely spread in this country, though numerous in certain localities. More than the usual proportion of descendants had families of uncommon size.

(I) John Lougee was born 1700 in the Isle of Jersey and came to this country at the age of eighteen. In 1710 he served in a scouting party in pursuit of savages, under Captain Gilman. He was captured by the Indians, but made his escape. He was by trade a knitter, and he settled in Exeter, New Hampshire, where he died at the age of seventy-seven years. He married Mary Gilman, daughter of Moses Gilman, of Newmarket. They had eight children: John, Joseph, Moses, Edmund, Gilman (mention of Gilman and descendants forms part of this article), Shuah, Anna and Joanna.

(II) John (2), eldest child of John and Mary (Gilman) Lougee, was born in Exeter. He married (first) Molly Leavitt, by whom he had Sarah, John, Nehemiah, Jesse, Molly, Jonathan, Elsey and William; married (second) Susan Hull, by whom he had Henry, Shuah, Benjamin, Susan, Emerson and Sarah; married (third) Mrs. Judith Beal.

(III) Nehmiah, second son and third child of John and Molly (Leavitt) Lougee, was born in Exeter, and married Mary Marsh by whom he had seven children as follows: Nehemiah, Lucy, Nancy, Isaac, John, Dudley and Betsey.

(IV) John (3), third son and fifth child of Nehemiah and Mary (Marsh) Lougee, was born in Exeter, January 17, 1771. He was a soldier in the War of 1812, and was wounded. He learned the hatter's trade and wrought at it in his early days, but in later life became an invalid as the result of his wounds. He married, April 1, 1801, Betsey, daughter of Joseph Marsh. She was born in Gilmanton, October 23, 1781, and died July 14, 1867. Her father was born in Exeter, December, 1754. He was a soldier in the Revolution serving in Captain Philip Tilton's company, Colonel Enoch Poor's regiment, from May 26, 1775, two months and eleven days. He also enlisted in Captain John Nesmith's company raised for Canada, was mustered in July 11, 1776, and marched July 22. Later he enlisted in Captain Frye's company, Colonel Matthew Thornton's regiment, and was mustered in February, 1777. He afterwards resided in Exeter till 1788, when he removed to Gilmanton Iron Works, where he lived till his death, March 17, 1839. He was an honest and exemplary christian man. His children were: Betsey, who married John Lougee, Olive, who married a Thurston, Joseph, Caleb and Amos, born July 4, 1799, who lived the longest of any in the village. Like his father he followed the trade of blacksmith. Politically he was a staunch Republican, and represented his town in the legislature in 1854 and 1855. He united with the Congregational Church in 1838. The children of John and Betsey (Marsh) Lougee were: Leavitt, born in 1801; Olive, who married Timothy Barnard in the west; Eliza, who married Frank Martin, John; Joseph, born in 1808, died young; Charles, born in 1810, married Mary Ross; Hazen, who married a Packard; Jacob Moody, born in 1820, died when a young man; Merrill, born in 1825, who married Susan Wheeler, and Joseph, born in 1826, married Mary Ann Sargent.

(V) John (4), second son and fourth child of John and Betsey (Marsh) Lougee, was born October 10, 1806. He married, January 5, 1831, Rebecca Edgerly, daughter of David Edgerly. Their children were: George, who died young; Laura, who married Charles H. Thompson; Julia A., who married Horace Edgerly; George, who died young; Clara and Emma, both of whom died young.

(VI) Julia A., second daughter and third child of John and Rebecca (Edgerly) Lougee, was born in Gilmanton. She married Horace Edgerly, of Gilmanton, (see Edgerly, VII), by whom she had Albert Clark, born May 18, 1872, and Annie M., born May 4, 1874.

(II) Gilman, fifth son and child of John and Mary (Gilman) Lougee, if the order is correct, was born February 3, 1729, probably at Exeter, New Hampshire. In March, 1763, he moved to Gilmanton, this state, where he reared a family of fourteen children. Gilman Lougee married Susanna Mudgett, born March 5, 1737, and they had: Gilman, Samuel, John, Susanna, Jonathan, Susanna, Simeon, Anna, Betty, Levi, Joseph, Levi, Molly and Lydia. Gilman Lougee died June 28, 1811, and his wife died January 4, 1811. The three eldest sons settled in Parsonfield, Maine.

(III) Samuel, second son and child of Gilman and Susanna (Mudgett) Lougee, was born about 1760, perhaps in Exeter, New Hampshire. With his two brothers, Gilman and John, he moved to Parsonfield, Maine, in June, 1778, and built a log house at the foot of Mudgett's hill. Samuel Lougee was the first settler of East Parsonfield where he moved with his wife in 1780. He married Sarah Rand, and had three children, Taylor, whose sketch follows, Annie and Betsey.

(IV) Taylor, son of Gilman and Sarah (Rand) Lougee, was born at Parsonfield, Maine, January 3, 1784. For many years he was well known as a hotel proprietor there. In 1840 he removed to Effingham Falls, New Hampshire, where he died. Taylor Lougee was thrice married, and had two sons by each wife. He married (first) Hannah Watson, and they had four children: Sarah, Samuel, Thomas and Hannah. His second wife was Jerusha, daughter of Simeon Tibbetts, and their children were: Greenleaf, Sylvester T., whose sketch follows, Sophia Ann and Elizabeth. His third wife was Sabina Hayes, and the children were: Cyrus and Hayes.

(V) Sylvester Tibbetts, second son and child of Taylor Lougee and his second wife, Jerusha Tibbetts, was born at Parsonfield, Maine, July 11, 1819. After attending the public schools he learned the carpenter's trade, and later engaged in contracting and building. He moved to Effingham, New Hampshire, in early life, there made his permanent home and died January 6, 1892. He always took an active interest in Masonry. Sylvester Lougee married Ruhamah Burleigh, daughter of Winthrop Marston and Sarah (Gile) Burleigh, who was born in Effingham, this state, December 26, 1826, and died March 28, 1907. They had seven children: Edwin, born September 9, 1845, died July 17, 1897. He served on the police force of Boston twenty-three years; he was sunstruck while on duty and died the same day. He was a member of the Masonic fraternity. Hayes, born September 19, 1848, read law with the late Thomas J. Whipple, of Laconia, and has practiced his profession more than twenty years in Boston. He is a thirty-second degree Mason. Abbie S., born January 23, 1852, has served in the capacity of teacher for many years. Josiah B., born November 2, 1853, is a successful merchant in Canton, Connecticut. He is a prominent Knight Templar. George Woodworth, whose sketch follows. Frank T., born September 13, 1862, graduated from medical department of Dartmouth College, class of 1886, after which he immediately settled in Lynn, Massachusetts; he is connected with several hospitals, and is a fine surgeon. Mott R., born November 11, 1866, died of typhoid fever, August 18, 1881.

(VI) George Woodworth, sixth son and seventh and youngest child of Sylvester and Ruhamah (Burleigh) Lougee, was born in Effingham Falls, June 3, 1859. He was educated in the public schools of Chelsea, Massachusetts, and later at Parsonfield Seminary, Maine. About the age of nineteen he began the study of medicine. In 1880 he entered the medical school of Bowdoin College, from which he was graduated in 1883. Dr. Lougee at once began the practice of medicine at Freedom, New Hampshire, where he has achieved most gratifying success. Although having an extensive practice, he has found time to look after town affairs. He is a Democrat in politics, and has served as selectman four years, and as representative to the New Hampshire legislature in 1901. In 1906 he was nominated for state senator, but the region being strongly Republican, he failed of election by a small majority. He is a member of the Carroll County Medical Society, of which he has been president, and also belongs to the New Hampshire State Association and to the American Medical Association. He is a member of the Board of Health in Freedom, and has served on the school board for six years. He has always been an enthusiastic worker in the several secret societies to which he belongs. He is a member of Carroll Lodge, Ancient Free and Accepted Masons, Carroll Chapter at Wolfboro; Saint Paul Commandery, Dover, New Hampshire; and Prospect Lodge, Independent Order of Odd Fellows, of which he was the first noble grand, also Costello Tribe, Independent Order of Red Men, at Kezar Falls, and is a member of Calvin Topliff Chapter, Order of the Eastern Star.

On November 25, 1885, Dr. George Woodworth Lougee married Edith L. Merrow, daughter of Dr. A. D. and Jane (Topliff) Merrow, of Freedom, New Hampshire. Mrs. Merrow was a daughter of Dr. Calvin Topliff, of Freedom, the father of Dr. Albion P. Topliff, so it will be seen that the family has extensive medical connections. (See Topliff.) Dr. George W. and Edith L. (Merrow) Lougee have two children: Louise M., born September 16, 1893, and Hayes, December 6, 1896.

GIBSON From the immigrant, John Gibson, has sprung a progeny of worthy citizens of New England, among whom have been found tillers of the soil, professional men, patriotic and valiant soldiers who fought both red and white foes, sober God-fearing church members, and keen successful business men.

(I) John Gibson was born (probably in England) in 1601, and died in Cambridge, Massachusetts, in 1694, aged ninety-three years. The name of the ship, the year of his arrival, and the place of his first settlement are unknown. He was in Cambridge in 1634, and was made a freeman May 17, 1637 (U. S.) He first appears on Cambridge (formerly Newtown) records of August 4, 1634: "To John Gibson 6 Ackers," in the list of lots granted in Westend, that part of the town lying between Sparks, Wyeth and Garden streets, Harvard and Brattle Squares, and Charles river. His house was built before "10th October 1635." Family tradition says that Gibson planted linden trees, and if tradition and boundaries can be made to agree, perhaps "The old house by the lindens," corner of Brattle and Sparks streets, made familiar by Longfellow's poem, "The Open Window," may have stood on land once owned by John Gibson. He was probably a member of the church formed by Rev. Mr. Hooker on his arrival in 1633; and on the removal in 1635 and 1636 of the pastor and most of the families to Hartford, Connecticut, he became one of the succeeding society or First Church organized February 1, 1636, by Rev. Thomas Shepherd. In addition to his 'nyne acr" house lot in the Westend Goodman Gibson had other real estate in Cambridge, records of which appear in the usual quaint form in the record books of that place and time. He was a husbandman, not an artisan, and an old record shows that John Gibson agreed with the town May 8, 1637, to summer one hundred cows for £20. There is no evidence that he ever held any church office and of town offices only minor ones—appointed March 15, 1676, to view fences, and in 1678 to drive Westfield. He was a party to one law suit. In 1660 Winifred Holman was plaintiff against John Gibson, Sr., and his wife and others, as the result of the defendants having accused Mary Holman, daughter of Widow Winifred, of being a witch; and at the hearing "3 day of Aprill," several months after the accusation, the finding for John Gibson was "costs of Court, fifteen shillings, ten pence." In the time of the tyrant Andross, John Gibson and George Willow, whose respective ages were "about 87 and 86 yrs." as representatives of the settlers, petitioned James II for redress, stating that "our title is now questioned to our lands, by us quietly, possessed for near sixty years, and without which we cannot subsist." He married (first) Rebecca, who was buried December 1, 1661, in Roxbury burying ground and the burial recorded by Rev. John Eliot. He married (second), July 24, 1662, Joan, widow of Henry Prentice, of Cambridge, "planter." The children of John Gibson, all by the first wife, were: Rebecca, Mary, Martha, John and Samuel.

(II) John (2), of Cambridge, Massachusetts, fourth child of John (1) and Rebecca Gibson, was born at Cambridge about 1641, and died there October 15, 1679. He lived in his native town and doubtless on the homestead in the Westend, deeded him by his father November 30, 1668, "3 acres and ½ my house Cambridge." There is no record that he ever owned any other real estate. Although a minor at the time of the suit "Holman versus Gibson" in 1660, he was one of the defendants, and boylike must have been very vehement against the supposed witch, widow Winifred's daughter, as he was sentenced either to openly acknowledge in court that "he hath wronged and scondalously slandered Marye Holman, by speeches irregularly, rashly and suddenly spoken," or refusing to do this, to pay the plaintiff five pounds; of the two alternatives he wisely chose the former. He was a soldier in King Philip's war—a private on the list of Captain Thomas Prentice's troopers August 27, 1675, in the first, or Mt. Hope expedition, the company leaving Boston the preceding June 24, fighting at Swansea, June 28, skirmishing in July on Mt. Hope Necks near Mt. Hope or Pokanoket (Bristol, Rhode Island), the home of King Philip; private on list of Lieutenant Edward Oake's troopers March 24, 1676, scouting near Marlboro; private, on pay list of Captain Daniel Henchman's company of foot, September 23, 1676, impressed the preceding April 27, starting May 27 and reaching Hadley, June 14; possibly the John Gibson on the list of Captain Joshua Scottow's men at Black Point near Saco, Maine, September, 1677, the garrison being captured the following month by Mogg Megone, the celebrated Indian chief. Before and ever after his military service, he was a quiet farmer with nothing more to change the monotony of his life than fell to the lot of any other inhabitant of Cambridge at that time. He was admitted freeman about October 11, 1670. His name appears from time to time on the town records as the holder of some small office, the last and most important, the appointment in 1678 "to view fences in Westfield." He died of smallpox when only thirty-eight years of age. The inventory of his estate showed forty-seven pounds, sixteen shillings including his house and three acres of land; £16. In June following the court ordered: "Charlestown 15. 4. 1680 The Selectman of Cambridge ordered to dispose of ye children of Jno. Gibson & of such a pt of his estate as shall be necessary for ye putting them forth to service," etc.

In the proprietor's records of 1683, under division of lots "beyond the 8 Mile line," is given this allotment in the ninth squadron; "John Gibson's heirs Twenty accers Three Commons." He married "9.10.1668," (December 9, 1668), Rebecca Errington, who was born in Cambridge, baptized in the First Church, December 4, 1713, daughter of Abraham and Rebecca (Cutler) Errington. They had four children: Rebecca, Martha, Mary, and Timothy, whose sketch follows.

(III) Deacon Timothy (1), of Sudbury and Stow, Massachusetts, fourth child of John (2) and Rebecca (Errington) Gibson, was born in Cambridge, Massachusetts, about 1679, and died in Stow, July 14, 1757, and was buried in the Lower Village cemetery in the easterly part of Stow. He was brought up by Selectman Abraham Holman, of Cambridge, son of William and Winifred Holman, and after 1689 removed with him to Stow. He continued a member of the Holman household till into 1703, when he removed to the northwest of Sudbury, and settled north of Assabet river on a sixty acre farm deeded to him June 21, 1703, by Mr. Holman "for divers and sundry good and weighty reasons moving me thereunto but in special manner to shew My love unto and care of Timothy Gibson now living with me & hath done from a child." Timothy Gibson received a second deed November 29, 1708, to twenty acres from the same source, and again ten acres April 23, 1711. Abraham Holman also appointed Timothy Gibson executor of his will. He was also the grantee of forty acres, house and bar from Mrs. Sarah Holman, and had other property in Stow, about one hundred acres in all. He was a large landowner in Lunenburg. Between 1728 and 1731 he removed from Sudbury to Stow—perhaps by merely moving to another part of his home farm which lay on both sides of the town line. He was selectman of Stow 1734-35-36-39, and dissented to a grant of £60 for Rev. John Gardner, May 17, 1736. He was deacon of the First Church probably during the pastorate of Mr. Gardner. His "house and fifty acres in Stow on Ponicitcut Hill" passed from sire to son for nearly one hundred years, finally going to strangers in 1823. Deacon Timothy Gibson married (first) at Concord, Massachusetts, November 17, 1700, Rebecca Gates, of Stow, who was born in Marlboro, July 23, 1682, and died in Stow, January 21, 1754, in the seventy-third year of her age. She was the daughter of Stephen and Sarah (Woodward) Gates. He married (second), (published November 30, 1755) Mrs. Submit Taylor, of Sudbury, who died at Stow, January 29, 1759, "in the 75 yr of her age." Twelve children were born to him, all by the first wife: Abraham, Timothy, Rebecca, John, Sarah, Samuel, Stephen (died young), Errington, Stephen, Isaac, Mary and Reuben. (Mention of Errington and son Thaddeus appears in this article.)

(IV) Captain Timothy (2), of Sudbury, Groton and Stow, Massachusetts, and Henniker, New Hampshire, second child of Deacon Timothy and Rebecca (Gates) Gibson, was born in Stow, January 20, 1703, and died in Henniker, January 18, 1782, aged seventy-nine. He was very young when his parents moved from Stow to Sudbury, and in some inexplicable way his birth is entered on Sudbury copied records although not on the original; there is, however, no question that he was born in Stow. His boyhood and early manhood were spent in Sudbury and he never occupied house lot 33 in Lunenburg, Massachusetts, bought of Ephraim Sautle in 1723 by "Timothy Gibson for son Timothy," the father retaining it for another son. About the date of his marriage he removed to Groton, locating most likely on property which he purchased December 11, 1724, from two parties, one tract of thirty acres from S. Scripture for £35, the other of twenty-five acres from "eleven persons" for £30, both deeds describing him as "Timothy Gibson, Jr., of Sudbury, yeoman;" between December 23, 1729, and October 7, 1730, he made three other purchases in Groton. Whether he remained in the town any length of time after 1730 is not clear. In 1733 he was living in Stow as is shown from the sale made May 7, 1733, by "John Forster to Timothy Gibson, Jr., of Stow, yeoman, 134½ acres in Stow including cornet's pond, the south side of Elsabeth (Assabet) river, southerly of a great brushy hill," etc., "also all my right in the meeting house," and this property in the southeast of Stow, was his home for the next forty years. He bought other land in Stow, and also owned land in Lunenburg. He was prominent among the men of Stow—selectman 1734-35-36-39, constable 1745 and probably holder of some military office as he was always called Captain Gibson. He was also an active member of the First Church, joining his father May 17, 1736, in the negative vote for a £60 pound appropriation to Rev. John Gardner, and on January 27, 1755, buying the "northeast corner of pew ground," that is, the northeast corner pew in the old church. As eldest of the sons surviving Deacon Gibson in 1757, he was of great help to his stepmother, Mrs. Submit Gibson, who by her will left bequests to his wife and daughters, and made him her residuary legatee. Early in 1774, when over seventy years old, Captain Gibson removed to Henniker on the Contoocook river, a promising New Hampshire town incorporated November 10, 1768, his farm lying at the foot of Craney hill, south of the Contoocook. His patriotic and beneficial influence was felt in the neighborhood, and until his death he rendered service in the Revolutionary struggle, especially by pecuniary aid. He was among the fifty-one signers of the "Association test." He married, December 29, 1725, Persis Rice, who was born in Sudbury, January 10, 1707, and died in Henniker, March 22, 1781, daughter of Deacon Jonathan and Anne (Darby) Rice, of what is now Wayland. Their children were: Jonathan, Timothy (died young), Timothy, Persis, Lucy, Abel, John, Joseph and Jacob.

(V) Captain Timothy (3), of Stow, Massachusetts, Henniker, New Hampshire, and Brownfield, Maine, third child of Captain Timothy (2) and Persis (Rice) Gibson, was born in Stow, December 17, 1738, and died in Brownfield, January 16, 1814, aged seventy-six. Before reaching his majority he served in the French and Indian war. His record is: "Muster Roll, Capt. Abijah Hall's company, Col. Willard's regiment, in expedition to Crown Point, from May 9, 1759, to January 12, 1760. Timothy Gibson, sergeant, Stow—from May 2, to November 27—30 weeks." Perhaps this service as sergeant gave rise to his familiar appellation of "Captain Gibson." He resided under the paternal roof until his marriage. February 19, 1770, he bought for three hundred pounds, of John and Mary Gordon "35 acres in Stow, estate of our father Ebenezer Graves," ½ house and the Mill." September 1, 1733, he bought of Jonas Temple thirty acres of White's Pond between Stow and Marlboro. He probably removed from Stow to Henniker with his parents in 1774, and ran saw and grist mills on the Contoocook. During the quarter of a century he remained in New Hampshire he filled many offices of trust, both town and state. He was delegate to the Provincial congress convened at Exeter, May 17,

1775, and to the convention held at Concord, June 13, 1778, "to form the state government," was the first justice of the peace in Henniker by vote of March 21, 1776, was selectman 1766-68, town clerk 1776-77-78, representative 1776-77-94-96-97. He further showed his love of country by signing the "Association test" in 1776, and procuring men and money throughout the Revolutionary war. In 1798, four years prior to its incorporation, February 20, 1802, he settled in the north of Brownfield, Maine, on a tract of nine hundred acres of tillage and timber land, which he bought together with one hundred acres in the adjoining Freyburg, August 18, 1797, in consideration of $3,500. With Captain Gibson's removal to his new home he carried the reputation as "possessor of sound judgment and excellent executive ability, and as one of the ablest citizens of the state." He was buried in Burnt Meadow, Brook cemetery, the old East Brownfield cemetery. He was "published" February 20, 1773, and soon after married Margaret Whitman, who was born in Stow, January 14, 1755, and died in Brownfield, June 29, 1838, and buried beside her husband. She was the daughter of Zachariah and Elizabeth (Gates) Whitman, of Stow, and a descendant of John Whitman, the English pioneer of Weymouth, Massachusetts, in 1638. The children of this union were: Moratha, Jonathan, Daniel, Timothy, Zachariah, Henry G., Polly, Robert, Abel, Margaret Whitman, Jane and Samuel.

(VI) Lieutenant Robert, of Brownfield and Bangor, Maine, eighth child of Captain Timothy (3) and Margaret (Whitman) Gibson, was born in Henniker, New Hampshire, August 22, 1787, and died in Paris, Maine, March 12, 1866, aged seventy-nine years, and was buried in Brownfield Center cemetery. He served in the War of 1812, was third lieutenant of the Thirty-fourth United States Infantry commanded by Colonel J. D. Learned, April 30, 1813; was promoted second lieutenant March 7, 1814, and first lieutenant August 13, 1814, and discharged June 15, 1815. The official record states "On recruiting service at Portland from April 18 to October 1, 1813, and from March, 1814, until discharge." He is also on record as "belonging to Massachusetts" of which the Province of Maine was then a part, this record varying a little from his commission which states that he was an "ensign in the second regiment of infantry, Mass. Militia, resigned Nov. 30, 1814, and Dec. 27, 1814, was commissioned by President Madison, first lieutenant in the Thirty-fourth regular United States Infantry to date from Aug. 13, 1814." He married, February 12, 1815, Sarah Kast McHard Molineux, who was born in Fryeburg, Maine, December 15, 1857, daughter of Robert and Peggy McHard (Kast) Molineux, of Boston, Massachusetts, and Hopkinton, New Hampshire. They had five children: Sarah M., Robert M., Maria Emeline, James M., and George Lafayette.

(VII) James Molineux, fourth child of Lieutenant Robert and Sarah Kast McHard (Molineux) Gibson, was born in Brownfield, June 17, 1821, and died in Conway, New Hampshire, November, 1900, aged seventy-nine. For a time he was in trade in Fryeburg, Maine, and in 1859 moved to North Conway, New Hampshire. He went to the gold fields of the "Far West" about 1850, and mined and conducted a hotel in Carson City, Nevada. On his first trip to California Mr. Gibson went via the Isthmus and was detained there six months, before proceeding on his journey. His next trip he went by Cape Horn and his subsequent journeys were across the continent. Returning to Maine he farmed four years in Paris. He then went west again and returned, and in 1868, succeeded his father-in-law as landlord of the well known Washington House at North Conway, which he conducted until 1878. He returned to California a third time and still a fourth and spent several years in Butte county, at both Cohasset on a timber ranch and Pine Creek on a fruit farm. He married, October 18, 1854, Martha L. Eastman, who was born in North Conway, May 13, 1827, and died November 4, 1878, daughter of Major Daniel and Martha L. (Chadbourne) Eastman. They had seven children: James Lewis, George Kast, Charles Edgar, Robert, Daniel Eastman, Helen Maria and Anna Molineux. 1. James L., mentioned below. 2. George Kast, of Cohasset, was born in North Conway, August 11, 1858, married, September 24, 1885, Queen Broyles, of Cohasset. They have four children, born in Cohasset: James Franklin, Jessie Esther, Helen Luellen and Hazel Lewis. 3. Charles Edgar, a New York City manufacturer, was born in Fryeburg, September 3, 1859, married, May 29, 1894, Anna Sheehy, of Nova Scotia. 4. Robert, born in Fryeburg, September 30, 1860, and died December 14, 1861. 5. Daniel Eastman, of Melrose Massachusetts, was born in Fryeburg, August 13, 1862, married, July 2, 1896, Mrs. Florence (Preble) Grant, of Melrose. 6. Helen Maria, born in Paris, November 24, 1864, married, June 20, 1888, Holmes Boardman Fifield, of Conway Corner. (See Boardman). 7. Anna Molineux, born in Paris, December 1, 1867, is unmarried.

(VIII) James Lewis, eldest child of James Molineux and Martha Lewis (Eastman) Gibson, was born in Fryeburg, December 2, 1855. His education was obtained in the common schools at Fryeburg and Paris Hill Academies, and Portland Business College. At nineteen years of age he was made telegrapher and station agent of the Maine Central Railroad Company at North Conway, and held that position twenty-three years. He then started in business as a dealer in lumber and building material, which business he has since carried on with very satisfactory results. He is a director in the North Conway Loan and Banking Company. In politics he is a Republican, and active in party affairs. He was elected town clerk in 1877 and filled that position by successive elections for five years. He has also been town treasurer for seven years, treasurer of the school district, treasurer of the town library, town auditor a number of years, and justice of the police court since its institution in 1903, delegate to the constitutional convention in 1902, and member of the legislatures of 1905 and 1907. In Masonic circles he has also attained high rank. He is a member of Mt. Washington Lodge, No. 87, Free and Accepted Masons, of North Conway; Signet Royal Arch Chapter, No. 24, of North Conway; Portland Commandery, No. 2, Knight Templars, of Portland, New Hampshire Consistory, Ancient Accepted Scottish Rite, of Nashua; Kora Temple, Ancient Arabic Order of Nobles of the Mystic Shrine, of Lewiston, Maine, also a charter member of Highland Lodge, Knights of Pythias, of North Conway. He was made a Mason in 1876, elected to office of secretary at the first annual meeting, then to junior warden, then to worshipful master seven consecutive terms, and has held office continuously since. He has never missed a meeting, regular or special, during the ten years he served as master, junior warden and secretary.

James L. Gibson married, January 2, 1877, Addie W. Dow, who was born June 30, 1854, daughter of

Joseph and Mary Dow, of Wheelock, Vermont. They have two children: Fanny L. and Harvey Dow. Fannie L., graduate of Lasell Seminary, class of 1880, married in 1883, Ernest R. Woodbury, principal of Thornton Academy of Saco, Maine, formerly of Kimball Union Academy, Meriden, New Hampshire. Harvey Dow graduated from Bowdoin College in 1902. He entered the employ of the American Express Company, and was soon afterward made financial agent for the provinces, and is now assistant financial manager with jurisdiction over New England.

(IV) Arrington, sixth son and eight child of Deacon Timothy Gibson, was born in 1717, and did not remove with his father to Henniker.

(V) Thaddeus, son of Arrington Gibson, was born in or near Stowe, in 1757, and was a soldier in the revolution. He settled in that part of Warner, New Hampshire, known as Peabody Pasture Parade, but remained there only a short time. He lived for a time in Milford, and removed thence in 1783 to Henniker, and settled on the border of what was than an almost unbroken wilderness. Being strong, athletic and resolute he did much towards bringing that portion of the township under cultivation. He died February 23, 1834. The church record of Milford shows that he came to reside in that town January 10, 1772, accompanied by his wife Elizabeth, and two children. She died March 17, 1819, and he was married March 30, 1831, to Lydia Kent. His children were: Lewis, Polly and Nahum.

(VI) Polly, only daughter of Thaddeus and Elizabeth Gibson, was born in 1780, and became the wife of John Whitcomb (see Whitcomb III).

DEMERITT

This name is an unusual one in America, and seems to be confined to the neighborhood of Dover, Durham and Madbury, New Hampshire, and to settlers who have gone forth from those regions. Without doubt all of the family are descended from Elie or Ely de Merit, a Huguenot refugee, who came to this country from the Isle of Jersey, shortly after the revocation of the Edict of Nantes, and had a grant of land in the township of Dover, New Hampshire, April 11, 1694. He married as early as 1695, Hopestill or Hope ——, and died about 1747, leaving five children. His will seems to indicate that he had an estate in the Isle of Jersey, where the family had first taken refuge. The eldest son of the pioneer was Eli Demerit, born March 1, 1696, who lived both in Durham and Madbury, and received the grant of the township of Peeling, now Woodstock, this state, in 1763. His eldest son, Captain Samuel Demerit, served in the Colonial wars. The present line is undoubtedly derived from this stock, but the connecting links are lacking.

(I) Major John Demeritt was born in Madbury, New Hampshire, and carried powder to the American troops at Bunker Hill, afterward serving through the Revolution.

(II) Paul, son of Major John Demeritt, was born at Madbury, New Hampshire, and married Betsey Davis, of the neighboring town of Lee, by whom he had four children: The youngest, Mark, is mentioned below.

(III) Mark, youngest of the four children of Paul and Betsey (Davis) Demeritt, was born at Farmington, New Hampshire, June 6, 1792, and died November 3, 1876. In 1817 he married Abigail Leighton, who was born at Farmington in 1799. They had ten children: Four of whom are now living: Martha F., Joseph L., Lois S., and Emma B.

(IV) Emma B., youngest daughter of Mark and Abigail (Leighton) Demeritt, became the wife of Edward P. Hodsdon, now of St. Louis (See Hodsdon VIII).

FISHER

The possession of a family record extending several generations beyond the emigrant ancestor, shows that this family was one of intelligence and prominence. The record its members have made in New England shows that the Fishers have been an intelligent, active, brave and energetic family, holding leading positions in the localities where they lived. Their Revolutionary record shows the Fishers of that day to have been courageous men thoroughly imbued with the desire for civil liberty, just as the first "settlers" had been imbued with a desire for liberty to worship God as they chose. Their monuments are the records which as citizens they have left, and they made substantial improvements upon the property they have held, much of which they hewed out of the untrodden wilderness.

(I) Anthony Fisher lived in the latter part of Queen Elizabeth's reign, in the parish of Sylcham, county Suffolk, England, on the south bank of the Waveney river, which separates Suffolk from Norfolk, on a freehold estate called "Wignotte." His wife was Mary, daughter of William and Anne Fiske, of St. James, South Elsham, county Suffolk —an old Puritan family of that county, which had suffered during the religious persecutions of Queen Mary's reign. The parish record of Syleham contains several references to Anthony Fisher and his descendants which are annexed in the language of the records, namely: Anno Domini 1585, Joshua Fysher et Maria Fysher, Gemini baptisandi fuer 24th die Februarii ano Super dicto.

Anno Domini 1591. Antonius Fysher bapt. erat 23 Aprilis anno sup. dicto.

Anno Domini 1599. Cornelius Fysher the sonne of Anthonye Fisher was bap. the six daye of Augusti.

Anthony Fysher was buried the eleventh day of April, 1640.

Anno Domini 1621. Joshua Fysher, the sonne of Joshua Fysher, was baptized on the ii daye of Aprille.

Anno Dom. 1633. Amos Fysher and Anne Lord were married September 24.

Joshua Fysher and Anne Luson were married 7th February, 1638.

This Anthony Fisher, of Syleham, had four sons and two daughters as appear from the record: Cornelius, Joshua, Anthony, Amos, Marie Brigge and Martha Bucingham.

(II) Anthony (2), son of Anthony (1) Fisher, of Syleham, county Suffolk, England, was baptized there April 23, 1591. He came to New England with his first wife Mary and children, probably from Yarmouth, in the ship "Rose," arriving in Boston, June 26, 1637, and settled in Dedham. He subscribed to the Dedham Covenant, July 18, 1637. January 1, 1638, he was one of the committee "Chosen to continue the Fabricke of a Meetinghouse." On July 28, 1638, he was assigned his house lot: "Anthony Fisher twelve Acres more or lesse made vp good by an inlargmnt Runs in amongst the Rockes, & for Woode & timbr as it lyeth betweene Mr. John Allin through out towards the South & Thomas Wighte through out towards the North. And abutts vpon the Waest towards the Eeast & the Waest in the Rockes towards the Waest the limitts marked & doaled accordingly," and other parcels of land.

He bought a farm of one hundred and fifty acres, a house lot and other lands in Dedham, of the estate of Samuel Cooke, of Dublin, October 19, 1652.

Anthony's wife Mary joined the Dedham Church, March 27, 1642, but he was not "comfortably received into the church," "on account of his proud and haughty spirit" until March 14, 1645. He was made a freeman, May, 1645, was chosen selectman of Dedham "to act in town affaires" in 1646-47, county commissioner, September 3, 1660, a deputy to the general court, March 21, 1649, and was woodseve in 1653-54-55-57-58-61-62. He was chosen commissioner, March 5 1666, and selectman of Dorchester, December 5, 1664, December 4, 1665, and December 3, 1666. From a minute bearing date March 9, 1652, it is inferred that he gave the bulk of his property to his sons and they bound themselves to support their mother if she were left dependent. The inventory of his estate, showing only personal property in Dedham and Dorchester, was presented July 26, 1671. He died at Dorchester. "Mr. Anthony Fisher Departed out of this life in the 80th year of his age (April 18), 1671." "In Anthony Fisher we find an Englishman of strong, positive points of character, with liberal means for the times, of favorable consideration by his fellow-settlers as a citizen."

The time of the death of his wife Mary is uncertain; he married again "the 14th of (9 mo:) 1663," Isabell, widow of Edward Breck, of Dorchester (who had died November 2, 1662), "She being by her first marriage the widow of John Rigben, and probably the latter's second wife; Anthony "being at the time of the marriage about 72 years of age." His widow, "The Widow Fisher Departed this life the 22d (mo:4) called June, 1673." His children, all by the first wife and born in England, were: Anthony, Cornelius, Nathaniel, Daniel, Lydia and John.

(III) Anthony (3), eldest child of Anthony (2) Fisher of "Dorchester," came with his parents to New England and settled in Dedham, 1637: was a member of the Ancient and Honorable Artillery Company in 1644; made a freeman May 6, 1646, and joined the Dedham church July 20, 1645. He was chosen surveyor of Dedham, 1652 to 1654; in 1652 he settled the estate of Henry Brookes; February 3, 1652, Anthony was one of those appointed to capture wolves at ten shilling for each wolf killed, and May 5, 1662, Dorchester "voted whether Anthony Fisher shall have four ponds allowed out of the town rate for killing six wolves: the vote was affirmative."

Anthony Fisher, Jr., and Samuel Fisher were among the first to go to Wollomonopoag (Wrentham) in 1661, and to claim part of the six hundred acres for the encouragement of the plantation, Anthony being one of the committee of Dedham Proprietors who were assembled January 12, 1662 to look into the matter and reported "they have secured but ten men, and they cannot go with so small a company—'that they are not desirous to leave the world altogether,' as they put it, but will go if they can 'proceed in a safe way.'" Anthony located his improvements upon the easterly and southeasterly side of Whiting's Pond or the Great Pond, but their houses (his and those of others) were some distance from the pond, probably on what is now Franklin street and on South street. In 1688 there were but thirty-six taxpayers living in Wrentham. November 6, 1664, he was sent from Dedham to view the land "about 12 or 14 miles from Hadley," Pocomptuck, the land which Dedham took instead of that which it claimed at Natick, and in 1669 Anthony received one hundred and fifty acres there for his part in surveying the grant. November 8, 1669, he was one of those who went and treated with Philip Sagamore and bought the land at Wrentham.

Anthony's name first appears in the records as paying the town and county rate in 1648. Soon thereafter he rented land of Governor Stoughton, and on "ye 6th of ye 11th mo. 1651. (January 6, 1652) he paid his annual rent in 5 bushels of Indian Corne 0-15-0." Each year thereafter he came before the selectmen of Dedham and paid the rent due. He was assessed for ninety-five pounds, ten shillings, February 20, 1657. The history of Dorchester says Anthony, Jr., was selectman of Dorchester in 1664. We learn that Dorchester "paid Anthony Fisher £4. 10s. for printing the catechism," prepared by Rev. Richard Mather, the pastor. Anthony probably lived just previous to his death, on the land bought of Mr. Stoughton, situated near the Neponset river, but within the bounds of Dorchester. The inventory of his estate made April 7, 1670, includes "Houses and lands thereof belonging in Dedham," £40; lands purchased of Mr. Stoughton and other landed property the total being three hundred and fifty-nine pounds, five shillings, two pence.

Anthony Fisher married, in Dedham, September 7. 1647, Joanna, only daughter of Thomas and Joane Faxon, of Braintree. Anthony died February 13, 1670, and his wife died October 16, 1694. Their children were: Mehitable, Experience, Josiah, Abiah, Sarah, Deborah, Judith, and Eleazer.

(IV) Eleazer, youngest son of Anthony (3) and Joanna (Faxon) Fisher, was born in Dedham, September 18, 1669, and died there February 6, 1722. The size of the appraisement of his property at his death, six hundred and sixty-five pounds, indicates that he was a prosperous man of substance. He married, in Dedham, October 13, 1698, Mary, daughter of William and Mary (Lane) Avery, born in that town August 21, 1674, and died in Stoughton, March 25, 1749. Her father, William Avery, was baptized October 27, 1647, in the parish of Brekham, near Oakingham, a market town in county Berks, England, and was the son of the immigrant, Lieutenant William Avery, also a physican. The children of Eleazer and Mary were: Eleazer, William, Jemima, David, Ezra, Nathaniel, Mary, Ezekiel, Timothy, Stephen and Benjamin.

(V) David, third son of Eleazer and Mary (Avery) Fisher, was born in Dedham, June 21, 1705, and died July 30, 1779, aged seventy-four. He joined the South Parish Church (in Norwood) with his wife, November 7, 1736. His will shows him to have been the owner of valuable real estate and farm property. He married (first) at Walpole, February 16, 1732, Deborah Boyden, of that town, who died July 18, 1770, aged fifty-nine; he married (second) November 7, 1770, Elizabeth Talbot, of Stoughton, probably a daughter of Ebenezer and Elizabeth Talbot, of Stoughton, who was born there February 22, 1754. Elizabeth died July 2, 1802, aged seventy-six. The children all by the first wife, were: David, Thomas, Jacob, Deborah, Hannah, Nathan, Oliver, Abigail, Mary and Abner.

(VI) David (2), eldest child of David (1) and Deborah (Boyden) Fisher, was born in Dedham, January 22, 1733. He was a member of the South Parish Church, December 5, 1762, but soon became a member of the Rev. Philip Curtis' Church at Sharon; lived on Moose Hill in Sharon, then Stoughtonham. In the final settlement of his father's estate, February 15, 1781, the other heirs quitclaimed to David for seven hundred pounds all their right in the estate except that part set to the widow, Elizabeth, as her right of dower. David was lieutenant in Captain Savel's Company, Colonel Lemuel Robinson's regiment, which marched from Stoughtonham (now Sharon) on the 19th of April. He also served in Stephen Penniman's company, Robinson's regiment, and in Theophilus Wilder's company, Colonel Dike's regiment, from December, 1776, to March 1, 1777. He made his will March 19, 1812, probated September 1. 1812. His inventory showed property of the value of two thousand eight hundred and seventy-six dollars and sixty-two cents. He married, September 21, 1758, Abigail, daughter of Isaac and Mary (Whiting) Lewis, of Dedham, who was born there December 4, 1738. Their children were: David, Moses, Aaron, Ebenezer, Catherine, Rebecca. Mary and Mary (2).

(VII) David (3), eldest child of David (2) and Abigail (Lewis) Fisher, was born in Sharon, June 26, 1759, and died in Francestown, New Hampshire, November 8, 1829. "David Fisher, with other settlers from Dedham and Sharon, came here (Francestown, New Hampshire) about the year 1780, and cleared the farm known as the James Whitfield place, on the northeastern slope of Oak Hill. Here he reared a family of thirteen children. He was large and athletic, his 'common weight' when in the prime and vigor of life was 250 pounds. He was known in both Dedham and Francestown as 'King David.' He entered the Revolutionary Army when 16 years of age." "Fisher's sawmill was built by David Fisher about the year 1800. This mill stood about two miles north of the village toward Deering. Now owned by Samuel E. Bryant, who put up a new mill in the place of the old in 1890. The stream is called Fisher's brook." He married, November 20, 1781, Mehitable, daughter of Lieutenant Ebenezer and Mercy (Guild) Hewins, of Sharon. who was born there February 20, 1762, and died at Francestown, New Hampshire, May 4. 1849. Their children were: Mehitable, David, Ebenezer, Joel, Susanna, Increase, Enoch Hewins, Benjamin, Asa, Nancy, Levi, Mary and Thomas.

(VIII) Levi, eleventh child and seventh son of David (3) and Mehitable (Hewins) Fisher, was born in Francestown, March 14, 1803, and died at Merrimack, where he resided November 29, 1880. He was a farmer and stone mason. "The young days of Levi Fisher were spent on the farm of his father, receiving a common school education. He worked on the foundations of two factories of the Nashua Manufacturing Company, but after his marriage returned to his father's farm for a few years. Then with his wife and two children he moved to New London, New Hampshire, where he owned and operated a grist mill for several years. In the spring of 1842, he bought a farm in Merrimack, where he lived until his death. He was an active member of the Congregational Church for more than fifty years, a highly respected citizen. Politically he was a Democrat." He married, February 24, 1829, Fanny, daughter of Alexander and Eliza (Gage) Wilkins. of Merrimack, who was born in Merrimack, June 12, 1808, and died April 22, 1905. Their children were: Levi W., Sarah W., George W., Anna L. and Cynthia M.

(IX) Levi W. Fisher, eldest child of Levi and Fanny (Wilkins) Fisher, was born in Francestown, September 19, 1829. He was educated in the public schools, and at the age of twenty went to Canton, Massachusetts, where he was employed four years in a sash and blind factory. In 1855 he went to Lowell. Massachusetts, was employed at the same kind of work till 1860, and later at Springfield, Massachusetts, Burlington, Vermont, Potsdam, New York, and Lowell, Massachusetts, and in 1871 at Manchester, New Hampshire. In 1874 he returned to his home in Merrimack to take care of his parents and cultivate the home farm, and there resided until his death, January 25, 1907. The farm is five miles west of Reed's Ferry, near the Amherst line, and half a mile east of Boboosic Pond. He was a Democrat, and a member of the Congregational Church. He married (first) October 15, 1856, Lucy A. Freeman, of Potsdam, New York, born June 2, 1829, died January 26, 1875. Married (second), May 23, 1883, Frances E. Bowen, of Rutland. Vermont, daughter of Milo and Martha (Berry) Bowen, born September 1, 1851. The child of the first wife was Maria L., born January 28, 1857, married Frank B. McAfee, of Bedford. The children of the second wife are: Fanny W., born March 9, 1884. married John T. Graves, of Merrimack; Ella G., born March 3, 1886, unmarried, lives with mother. Edwin Milo, born September 20, 1889, at home.

(Second Family.)

FISHER The name of Fisher was a leading one among the Scotch-Irish colonists of the early settlements. The holders of this name have been noted for their indomitable energy, their bravery under misfortune, and many of them have made a notable record in the civic. religious and educational affairs of the various communities in which they lived.

(I) Deacon Samuel Fisher emigrated from the north of Ireland in 1740, in the nineteenth year of his age. The vessel in which he had embarked was scantily provisioned, and the voyage an unusually long one, and the passengers had come to the conclusion to sacrifice one of their number to preserve the lives of the remainder. This direful lot fell to Mr. Fisher. Before the sentence had been carried into execution a sail was sighted and their signals of distress being observed, they were rescued from their terrible position. Upon his arrival in this country Mr. Fisher was bound to labor for a certain length of time for a man in Roxbury, Massachusetts, to pay for his passage. Subsequently he found a home and employment in the family of Matthew Taylor of Londonderry, New Hampshire. Deacon Fisher was by trade a weaver, and although he turned his attention to farming he continued to make use of his loom to supply his family with all manner of cloth for household and personal needs. His personal appearance was tall and commanding, and he was of dignified bearing. From the town records it appears that he held many positions of trust and responsibility in public affairs. He was elected a ruling elder in the Presbyterian Church thirty years prior to his death, and faithfully performed all the duties pertaining to this office until compelled to resign by the infirmities of old age. This love for ecclesiastical office seems to have been bequeathed to his descendants, as about half of them in the second and third generations were deacons, and three grandsons were ministers of the Gospel. He married (first) Sarah Taylor, daughter of Matthew Taylor. He married (second) Janet Wilson. He married (third) Sarah Barber, who was of English descent. Among his seven children, was a son, Ebenezer.

(II) Ebenezer Fisher was the son of Deacon Samuel (1) and Sarah (Barber) Fisher. He was of a studious disposition, and in his youth had looked forward to a collegiate education, but as he was not of a sufficiently robust constitution to withstand the necessary confinement, he was obliged to give up this plan and settled upon a farm adjoining that of his father. For a number of years he continued to

Levi W. Fisher

teach school during the winter months, and he retained his interest in educational matters throughout his life, frequently holding the office of superintending committeeman. He was an influential citizen, and was active in the civic affairs of the town in which he resided. In his seventeenth year he removed with his family to Bedford, New Hampshire, and although in feeble health he kept in touch with all the important movements of the times. His death occurred during the winter of 1848-49, he being the last survivor of the large family of his father. He married (first) Polly Dean, and had six children. He married (second), in 1816, Jane Orr, daughter of George Orr, of Bedford, New Hampshire, and their children were: George Orr, born December 30, 1817, died August, 1845; Mary Jane, born August 10, 1820, married, February 5, 1850, Ebenezer Tolman Conant.

(III) Mary Jane, daughter of Ebenezer (2) and Jane (Orr) Fisher, was a very young child when deprived by death of her mother. She was reared by her aunt, Ann Orr, a noted teacher of Bedford and its vicinity for the long period of fifty years, and who was a woman of great strength of mind and character. Her influence was potent in molding the character and habits of the young girl, and this stern teaching enabled her to bear with fortitude the trials of her later life. Miss Fisher began teaching at an early age, and at the age of twenty-eight years went to Greensboro, Vermont, where she taught in the family of the Congregational minister, and later was for a short time a teacher in the public schools. She taught one term when she had reached the advanced age of sixty years. She was married February 5, 1850, to Ebenezer T. Conant, (see Conant, IX) who died in April, 1858. Being early left a widow, with eight children to support and a farm to manage, she faced her troubles with dauntless courage and took up her tasks heroically and cheerfully. She rose above circumstances, and was the home maker for her aged father-in-law, while her children were given a training whose influence was felt throughout their lives. She died at the home of her daughter in Hardwick, Vermont, in May, 1903.

NUTTER The Nutters were among the earliest settlers of New Hampshire, and have spread from its southeastern borders over the state and through the United States. "They have been husbandmen, sailors, fishermen; with notable examples in the trades and employments of southeastern New Hampshire. Of good judgment in woodcraft, as well as lands, and of lasting, enduring qualities as seamen, they have been thrifty. Contented in their abundance, unpretentious for affluence or station, they have constituted a numerous class of the sturdy citizens whese firmness, constancy and reliability have given character to New Hampshire men. One looks in vain for their names on college catalogues or state prison rolls, and they are seldom found in professional or official life. Their active pursuits have been in the open air, and their gray hairs have found rest in quiet graves."

(I) Hatevil Nutter was born 1603 in England, and came with wife, Annie, and son, Anthony, to Dover, New Hampshire, in 1633. He received several grants of land, and became a large holder of real estate. He was a ruling elder in the first church at Dover, and sometimes filled its pulpit. In April, 1669, he gave lands to his son Anthony, and February 13, 1670, gave land on Dover Neck to his son-in-law, John Winget. He filled various offices in church and state, and was highly respectable and possessed of a good share of this world's goods. His will was dated December 28, 1674, and was proved June 29 of the year following, which approximates the time of his death, at the age of seventy-one years. Four of his children are on record, namely: Anthony, Mary, Elizabeth and Abigail.

(II) Anthony, son of Hatevil and Annie Nutter, was born 1630, in England, and died February 19, 1686, of small pox. His wife, Sarah, was a daughter of Henry Langstaff. They lived for a time at Dover Neck, but moved to Welshman's cove, in what is now Newington, New Hampshire. Mr. Nutter was a prominent man in the colony and exercised a wide influence. He was admitted freeman in 1662, was "Corporall" in 1667, and "leftenant" in 1683, being thereafter known by that title. He was selectman, a member of the general court when under the jurisdiction of Massachusetts, and later of the general assembly of New Hampshire; and in 1681-82 a member of the provincial council. He had three sons, John, Hatevil and Henry, and one daughter, Sarah. (Mention of Hatevil and descendants appears in this article.)

(III) John, eldest son af Anthony and Sarah (Langstaff) Nutter, was born December 27, 1663, in Dover, New Hampshire. No record of his wife has been found but his children were: John, Matthias, James, Hatevil, Sarah, Thomas and Rosimond.

(IV) James (2), son of John Nutter, married Abigail Thurber, of Newington, where they resided. Their sons, James and Anthony, were baptized September 29, 1736, in Newington (the former receives further mention, with descendants, in this article).

(V) Anthony (2), son of James Nutter, born 1736, was married June 1, 1756, to Sarah Nutter, of Portsmouth, New Hampshire. They had sons, William and Anthony, baptized May 8, 1757.

(VI) William, son of Anthony (2) and Sarah Nutter, was born December 13, 1756, served in the United States navy during the Revolution, was married November 7, 1781, to Anna, daughter of John and Ann (Simes) Nutter, who was born March 6, 1760. He died February 15, 1811, and his wife survived him two and one-half years, passing away August 17, 1813, both in Barnstead, New Hampshire. Their children were: Dorothy, Anna S., Abigail and William. The second daughter became the wife of Samuel Perkins, and the third of Charles Foster. The son married Eleanor Peavey and all resided in Barnstead, New Hampshire.

(VII) Dorothy, the eldest child of William and Anna (Nutter) Nutter, became the wife of Nathaniel Nutter, of Barnstead, hereinafter mentioned (see Nutter, VI).

(III) Hatevil (2), second son of Anthony and Sarah (Langstaff) Nutter, was among the inhabitants of Bloody Point in 1713 who petitioned the general court that they, "By maintaining the minister, school and poor among themselves, may be exempted from all other charges, save only the province tax." This resulted in the establishment of the town of Newington, so named by Governor Dudley, May 12, 1714. By his first wife, whose name does not appear, Mr. Nutter had four children. He was married May 16, 1716, to Leah Furber, who survived him, and was the mother of five of his children. He died in 1745, and left to his widow in his will, dated November 12, 1745, all of his movables, including his "Negro Caesar." They were admitted to the church in 1630. His children were: Hatevil,

Anthony, Eleanor, Sarah, John, Elizabeth, Joshua, Abigail and Olive.

(IV) Hatevil (3), eldest child of Hatevil (2) Nutter, was a cordwainer (shoemaker), and lived in Newington. He was married in 1741 to Hannah Decker, and was admitted to the church in 1756. His children were: Sarah, Hannah, Joseph, Mary, John, Benjamin, Elizabeth, Hatevil and Lois.

(V) Benjamin, third son of Hatevil (3) and Hannah (Decker) Nutter, was born November 25, 1744, at Newington. He moved to Barnstead, New Hampshire, and the first deed of land in that town was to him, 1777. He was the first town clerk, 1775 to 1781, and was one of the committee of safety, April 12, 1776. He was for many years one of the selectmen of the town, and for several years the town meetings were held at his house. He married (first), in 1778, Mercy Tasker, by whom he had two children: John and Abigail; (second), in 1781, Mary Walker, by whom he had five children: Nathaniel, Lois, Hannah, Mary and James. He died at Barnstead in 1832.

(VI) Nathaniel, son of Benjamin and Mary (Walker) Nutter, was born at Barnstead, June 12, 1781, and was a farmer. He died at Barnstead, January 3, 1871. He married Dorothy Nutter, daughter of William and Anna Nutter (see William, VI, ante). Their children were: George Langdon, William, Nancy, John Simes and Nathaniel Simes.

(VII) George Langdon, eldest child of Nathaniel and Dorothy (Nutter) Nutter, was born in Barnstead, New Hampshire, November 10, 1806, and died at Concord, September 8, 1879. He married, May 13, 1830, Fanny Wilson Proctor, daughter of Thomas Proctor, born in Barnstead, April 16, 1812, died at Newton Centre, Massachusetts, January 4, 1900.

Robert Proctor settled at Concord, Massachusetts, where he was made a freeman in 1641. (2) James, his son, born at Chelmsford, Massachusetts, 1658, died there January 11, 1709. (3) James, born at Woburn, Massachusetts, April 2, 1696. (4) James, his son, was born at Woburn, June 18, 1722, and died May 3, 1812. (5) Thomas, his son, was born at Woburn, July 28, 1748, and died at Loudon, New Hampshire, June 1, 1830. (6) Thomas, his son, was born at Loudon, New Hampshire, June 12, 1781, and died at Barnstead, New Hampshire, June 25, 1856. He married three times. By his first wife, Martha (Drew) Proctor, he had eight children: John Drew, Thomas Kimball, Fanny Wilson, Joseph Drew, Jane Drew, Mary, Samuel B. and William. George Langdon and Fanny Wilson (Proctor) Nutter had five children: Thomas William, John Proctor, Annie Martha, Isabel Frances and Malvina Drew.

(VIII) John Proctor, son of George Langdon and Fanny Wilson (Proctor) Nutter, was born at Barnstead, New Hampshire, January 26, 1833, and was educated in the public schools of his native place and of Pittsfield and at Pittsfield Academy. He was a clerk in his father's store and later in the store of Reuben L. French until 1850. He was in the furniture business from the latter date until 1854, and from 1858 to 1865 was in the clothing business, all at Pittsfield. In 1867 and 1868 he was a clerk in the Traders' and Mechanics' Insurance Company at Lowell, Massachusetts. In 1869 he engaged in the hardware business at Pittsfield, continuing until 1876. July 25 of that year he was appointed by Governor Person C. Cheney, register of probate for Merrimack county. By a change in the constitution of New Hampshire this office became elective in 1878, since which time Mr. Nutter has been elected annually and biennially at each succeeding election for that office. His political affiliations have ever been with the Republican party, and he was elected representative in the New Hampshire legislature in 1873, from Pittsfield. He attends the South Congregational Church at Concord. He joined the Odd Fellows, and is now a member of Suncook Lodge, No. 10, Pittsfield, New Hampshire.

April 15, 1856, he married Elizabeth Hogan Berry, daughter of John and Marianna Berry, of Pittsfield, New Hampshire, born February 18, 1833, died at Concord, June 19, 1896 (see Berry, VI). She was educated in the public schools at Pittsfield and Pittsfield Academy, and Bradford Academy, Bradford, Massachusetts. The children of John P. and Elizabeth Hogan (Berry) Nutter are: Mary Fanny, born at Pittsfield, July 8, 1857, educated in the public schools, Pittsfield Academy, and the Concord high school, from which she graduated in the class of 1876. Charles Carroll, born at Pittsfield, August 22, 1859, died there November 20, 1869. William Albert, born at Pittsfield, January 20, 1862, was educated in the public schools of Pittsfield and the high school at Concord. He is chief clerk in the Concord postoffice, having been employed in that office continuously since 1880. Alice Berry, born at Concord, April 15, 1879, attended the schools and graduated from the high school of Concord in the class of 1897, and spent three years at Radcliffe College, Cambridge, Massachusetts.

(V) James (3), son of James (2) and Abigail (Thurber) Nutter, was born in Newington, and baptized there September 29, 1736. He married Esther Dame, and died in Newington. Children born to them were: Ebenezer, Nathaniel, Abigail, Jethro and Dorothy. The three sons moved to Barnstead and were among the early settlers of that town. (Mention of Nathaniel and descendants forms part of this article.)

(VI) Deacon Ebenezer, son of James (3) and Esther (Dame) Nutter, was born October 10, 1756, in Newington, and spent all of his adult life in Barnstead, New Hampshire, where he died April 17, 1843, in his eighty-sixth year. He married Temperance Colebath, of Portsmouth, and they removed from Newington to Barnstead on horseback, in 1783, bringing a babe in arms. There was no road, and they made their way by the aid of spotted trees. Their first habitation was a log cabin, four miles from any other human being; it was located on a pleasant site, commanding a view of the surrounding country. Mr. Nutter had served as a soldier in the Revolution under John Sullivan, and in his old age he drew a pension for that service. He was an upright and industrious man and was prosperous. For more than fifty years he was a deacon of the church in Barnstead. He had seven sons and four daughters. They included: George, Betsy, Dolly, John, Nathaniel and William. (The last named and descendants are mentioned farther in this article.) The estate is still in the hands of one of his descendants, Deacon Ebenezer Nutter, of Lynn, Massachusetts. The first death in the town of Barnstead was that of his elder daughter, who was nineteen years old. Before her death, she desired that her body be buried beneath a favorite birch tree on the farm. The trunk of this tree is still standing, and is now nine feet in circumference; it is the only one of original growth remaining on the homestead.

(VII) Nathaniel, son of Deacon Ebenezer and

Temperance (Colebath) Nutter, was born 1796, in Barnstead, and died January 13, 1875, in Pittsfield, in his seventy-ninth year. He was a carpenter and followed that occupation and erected many buildings in Boston and vicinity. The autumn of his life was passed in Pittsfield, where he owned and operated for a number of years a planing mill, and manufactured sashes, blinds and doors. In religion he was a Congregationalist, and in politics a Democrat. He represented Pittsfield in the legislature. His wife, Eliza B. (Rickford) Nutter, was born 1807, in Boston, Massachusetts, and died in Pittsfield, December 1, 1891, at the age of eighty-four years. Their children were: Ann Eliza, who became the wife of Andrew Bunker; Mary Jane, who married R. L. French, and resided in Pittsfield; Franklin C., who receives mention in the succeeding paragraph; and Horatio G., who died in 1902, in Winthrop, Massachusetts.

(VIII) Franklin C., eldest son and third child of Nathaniel and Eliza B. (Rickford) Nutter, was born September 10, 1833, in North Barnstead, and died April 23, 1896, in Pittsfield. He received his education in public schools, and learned the business of making sashes, doors and blinds in Concord, and subsequently carried on this business in connection with his father until the death of the latter. He assumed its control and carried it on for a number of years. After disposing of this he continued to work at his trade until his death, which occurred April 23, 1896. He was a member of the Congregational Church, in which his wife still retains membership. In politics he was a Republican. He was married January 1, 1855, to Susan E. Emerson, who was born June 27, 1837, in Hopkinton, New Hampshire, daughter of Jeremiah and Judith P. Emerson, and is still living and residing in Pittsfield. Their children were: Edward F., Deacon Matthew Harvey and Helen P. The last named died at the age of seven years.

(IX) Matthew Harvey, second son and child of Franklin C. and Susan E. (Emerson) Nutter, was born July 6, 1858, in Pittsfield. He was educated in the public schools and an academy of that town, and left school at the age of sixteen years to learn the trade of tinsmith. He subsequently entered the Concord high school and remained about two years, returning to Pittsfield at the end of that time. He resumed work at his trade, as a journeyman, and so continued until April 1, 1887. Since that date he has been engaged in business for himself in Pittsfield, and the business is now conducted under the name and style of Nutter & Foss, the junior partner being Mr. W. E. Foss. With the years, and the energy and industry of its founder, the business has grown and prospered. The firm carries a stock of stoves and kindred articles, besides general hardware, paints and oils, and deals in farming machinery. It makes a specialty of all kinds of sheet metal work and the installation of heating appliances. Mr. Nutter is one of the substantial and highly-respected citizens of Pittsfield, and exercises a strong influence upon its affairs. The trade of the firm is drawn from a large region of the country, and he is known for his upright principles and kind heart. Deacon Nutter has been chairman of the Pittsfield school board for the past three years. He has been a member of the Congregational Church for twenty-six years, and during all of that time except one year has been both deacon and church clerk. He has also served as superintendent of the Sunday school and warden of the church, and is a trustee of the Pittsfield Academy. He was married May 8, 1882, to Minerva Jane Merrill, daughter of Stephen B. and Luthera (Norcross) Merrill. She was born June 28, 1862, in Deerfield, New Hampshire, and they have the following children: Carl Nathaniel, born May 29, 1883, a graduate of the Pittsfield schools and of Brown University; Lewis Harvey, July 6, 1884, is now a student at Brown University; Helen Ruth, December 14, 1885, is attending Mt. Holyoke College; Mabel Frances, October 15, 1888, died in her ninth year; Lucy Hayes, February 5, 1893, Ralph Edward, September 29, 1894, and Franklin Harris, October 29, 1896, are at home with their parents.

(VII) William, son of Ebenezer and Temperance (Colbath) Nutter, was born in Barnstead, about 1795, and died in Concord, about 1854.

(VI) Nathaniel, son of James (3) and Esther (Dame) Nutter, married Dorothy Marshall, whose father a sea captain, died of yellow fever. Their children were: Abigail, Betsey (died in infancy), Nancy, Betsey, Alice, Eleanor, John M., Jethro, Hannah, Martha, Ann and Lucy.

(VII) Eleanor, daughter of Nathaniel and Dorothy (Marshall) Nutter, married, in 1819, her cousin, William Nutter, who was born about 1792 or '93. She was born in Barnstead in 1797, and died in 1879.

(VIII) William S., son of William and Eleanor (Nutter) Nutter, was born in Barnstead, New Hampshire, December 18, 1820, and died April 25, 1898. He was an influential farmer, who varied the monotony of agriculture in the colder season of the year by lumbering. His character and business qualifications commanded the respect and confidence of his fellowtownsmen, who called him to fill the office of selectman and lieutenant of militia under the old military system of the state. In politics he was a Democrat. He married, November 1, 1842, Mary E. Collins, who was born October 14, 1826, daughter of John H. and Phebe (Hanson) Collins, of Barnstead. She died January 1, 1892. Five children were born to them: John D., born March 30, 1848, now living in Barnstead. Charles C., born November 30, 1850, died July 16, 1904. James Albert, born September 21, 1852, died May 31, 1891. Frank S., born October 18, 1855. George W., born June 21, 1858.

(IX) George William Nutter, M. D., youngest child of William S. and Mary E. (Collins) Nutter, was born in Barnstead, June 21, 1858. He was educated in the common schools and at Pittsfield Academy, and read medicine for three years in the office of A. H. Crosby, of Concord. In 1882 he entered Dartmouth College, medical department, from which he graduated with the class of 1883. He opened an office and practiced in Manchester eight years, and then removed to Salmon Falls and purchased the store and stock of Ezra H. Wheeler, and has since devoted himself to trade rather than to the practice of medicine. Since he started in the drug business he has established a drug store at Somersworth and one at Concord, and now operates the three. In politics he is a Democrat, and he has been elected on that ticket to various offices. He was a representative from ward eight, Manchester, in the legislature in 1889; has been selectman of Rollinsford several times; was a delegate to the last constitutional convention, and now (1907) is tax collector of Rollinsford. In Masonry he has attained the thirty-second degree. He is also a member of Ridgeley Lodge, No. 74, Independent Order of Odd Fellows, of Manchester, and Dover Lodge, Benevolent Protective Order of Elks. He married (first), December 3, 1896, May Lord, who was born December 3, 1870, daughter of William E. and Josie (Alley) Lord, and who died February 10, 1900. March 25, 1903, Dr. Nutter married (second), Bertha A. Johnson, who was born October 7, 1878, daughter of Charles A. and Eva E. Johnson, of Bangor, Maine. They have one child, Ruth, born September 3, 1904.

(IX) Frank S., fourth son and child of William S. and Mary E. (Collins) Nutter, was born in Barnstead, October 18, 1855, and received his education in district schools. He was brought up on a farm, and when old enough to learn the trade of a shoemaker; his principal occupation in business life has been farming and shoemaking, and upon the death of his father he succeeded to the ownership of the old place, which now has been in the family fifty-two years. He is known among his fellow townsmen as an industrious and provident man, with a capacity for hard work and of sound judgment in business matters. For five years he held the office of supervisor, and for about the same length of time was selectman, and was representative in 1893 and 1894. In politics he is a Democrat. Mr. Nutter has been twice married. He married (first), in 1876, Sarah E. Caswell, of Stratford, New Hampshire. She was born in 1854, and died March 10, 1882, leaving two children. On October 10, 1886, Mr. Nutter married Ida Kimball, born August 12, 1861, daughter of James and Nancy (Locke) Kimball. James Kimball, born in 1825, died February 25, 1903, was a son of Jeremiah Kimball, born about 1799, died in 1876, and whose wife was Tomason (Hayes) Kimball, of Farmington, New Hampshire. Nancy Locke, who married James Kimball, was a daughter of Sampson B. and Esther (Nutter) Locke, his wife, and Esther (Nutter) Locke is a daughter of Jethro and Polly (Elliott) Nutter, granddaughter of James and Esther (Dame) Nutter. The children of Frank S. Nutter by first marriage are as follows:

(X) Forest L., son of Frank S. and Sarah E. (Caswell) Nutter, was born in Barnstead, July 19. 1879. He was educated at the Stafford public school and Coe's Academy at Northwood, New Hampshire, where he graduated. He has served three terms as tax collector of Rollinsford, New Hampshire. He married Margaret Sears, and has one child, Agnes W. Nutter. He resides at Salmon Falls, New Hampshire.

(X) Frank C., son of Frank S. and Sarah E. (Caswell) Nutter, born on the old homestead farm in Barnstead, June 28, 1881, educated in public school and graduated at Coe's Academy, Northwood, New Hampshire, then taught school for a few years, and afterwards devoted his time to agricultural pursuits. He is now serving his second term as town clerk of Barnstead. He married, December 10, 1904, Iva P. Berry, daughter of Stephen J. and Emma Berry, have one child, Sarah E., born November 18, 1905. They reside in Barnstead Centre, New Hampshire.

McCURDY This name. which was formerly spelled Mackirdy, originated in Lanarkshire, Scotland, and the Mackirdys where the ancient possessors of the Island of Bute, a prominent landmark on the western coast. During the exodus from Scotland to Ireland in the latter part of the seventeenth century, five brothers named Mackirdy, accompanied by their families, crossed the Irish sea and found a safe abiding place at Ballymony in the county of Antrim, where they could enjoy unmolested the benefits of religious freedom. In Ireland the spelling of the name was changed to McCurdy. At least one of these brothers, James, and perhaps more, assisted in defending the city of Londonderry during the siege of 1688. It is quite probable that the family now being considered is descended from the above-mentioned James, but the fact has not been, as yet, fully verified.

(I) Archibald McCurdy of Ballymony, who was born in Scotland about the year 1684. emigrated to America in 1737, bringing with him his second wife and several children. He settled in New Hampshire and resided there until his death, which occurred February 8, 1776. His first wife, whose maiden name does not appear in the records, bore him three sons, namely: Robert, Daniel and John, all of whom were pressed into the British navy after their arrival in New England, and Robert died of yellow fever in Jamaica. Daniel (born in 1715) died in Dunbarton of hemorrhage of the lungs March 28, 1791, and John will be again referred to in this article. Archibald's second wife, whose maiden name is also unknown, became the mother of several children, but two of whom lived to maturity, James and Sarah, and one died at sea during the passage from Ireland. Part of the descendants now spell the name Macurdy.

(II) Robert, eldest son of Archibald Macurdy, was a native of Ireland and died in Jamaica, while serving in the British navy.

(III) Matthew Scobey, son of Robert Macurdy, was born in Ireland, and died in America. He married a Miss Fulton, and they were the parents of seven children: Daniel. Robert, John, Matthew, Margaret, Elizabeth and Mary.

(IV) Daniel, eldest child of Matthew S. Macurdy, was born in Dunbarton, New Hampshire. 1798, and died in Boscawen in November, 1860, aged sixty-two years. He lived on his father's farm, and attended school until he was about twenty-one years of age. He then hired out on farms for several years and with his earnings bought a farm. This he sold in 1849, and in February, 1850, he bought another farm of about one hundred and fifty acres in Boscawen, now Webster, where he resided as long as he lived. He was an industrious worker, and preferred to attend to his own farm rather than engage in public business. He became a member of the Republican party at its formation. He married Betsy Cunningham Alexander, who was born in Dunbarton, daughter of David and Martha Alexander, of Dunbarton. Their eight children were: John, David A., Daniel L., Matthew, Oscar D., Martha Jane, Elizabeth, and Mary Ann.

(V) David A., second son and child of Daniel and Betsy C. (Alexander) Macurdy, was born in Dunbarton, June 23, 1832. He attended the district schools and the high school at Dunbarton Center until he was seventeen years old. In 1850 he moved with his parents to Boscawen, and the two years next following worked on his father's farm. In 1852 he married and went to live with his father-in-law, and assist him in his store at Courser Hill. Three years later the father-in-law, Mr. Fellows, died, and Mr. Macurdy took charge of the store and carried on the business until 1862. August 11 of that year Mr. Macurdy, with his brother Matthew, enlisted as a private in Company H, Fourteenth New Hampshire Volunteers, and in October was made orderly. During the following fall and winter the regiment was on duty in Washington and along the Potomac, picketing the river for forty miles and enduring great hardships. The summer of 1863 was passed doing guard duty from Harper's Ferry to Fortress Monroe, and in November of that year was

D. A. Macmurray

commissioned second lieutenant. In the spring of 1864 the regiment was ordered to the Department of the Gulf, and came near being shipwrecked on the voyage to New Orleans. After a short service on the Mississippi the regiment returned to the Potomac and joined Sheridan's corps on the Shenandoah on August 18, 1864. Lieutenant Macurdy was promoted to first lieutenant May 27, 1864, and transferred to Company B. He was present with his regiment at the battle of Berryville, September 19, This was a very hotly contested battle, and the loss to the Fourteenth was thirteen officers and one hundred and thirty privates, killed and wounded. Matthew Macurdy was instantly killed. Lieutenant Macurdy was wounded, and after the action was furloughed. After his wound had healed he rejoined his regiment, having been promoted to a captaincy November 22, 1864. January 1, 1865, he accompanied his regiment to Savannah, Georgia, where it remained until the close of the war, and was mustered out July 8, 1865. (In June, 1864, Captain Macurdy served on a board of survey at Carrollton, Louisiana, and in August of the same year was appointed quartermaster for a battalion of recruits for General Sherman's army in the Shenandoah valley. In March, 1865, he served on a court martial at Savannah, Georgia. In May, 1865, he was in command of Company B, Fourteenth New Hampshire Volunteers, and had in charge Jefferson Davis, Alexander Stevens, Captain Wirz, and others of the Confederate officers in Augusta, Georgia, after their capture.)

Returning to Boscawen, Captain Macurdy reopened his store, and was engaged in the trade until August, 1870, when he sold out all his property and removed to Concord, where he opened a grocery, flour and grain store. This he carried on until 1877, when he removed to Webster, built and stocked a store and started in business. The following March, store and stock were destroyed by fire, and Mr. Macurdy went to Minneapolis, Minnesota, where he filled a position in the freight department of the Chicago, Milwaukee & St. Paul railroad, until 1901. Returning to New England, he lived in Boston part of one year, and in 1903, removed to Webster, where he now lives retired. Captain Macurdy's conduct and capabilities have been such as to entitle him to the friendship of all those who know him, and his fellow citizens have honored him with the offices of selectman one term; town clerk, one term; representative, two terms, and moderator, four times. He is a Republican, and still maintains the principles for which he fought in the civil war. He is a member of Colonel Putnam Post No 5, Grand Army of the Republic; Minnehaha Lodge No. 165, Free and Accepted Masons, and White Mountain Lodge No. 3, Independent Order of Odd Fellows, of Concord. He married first, January, 1852, Salome Fellows, who was born August 25, 1827, and died January 2, 1901, aged seventy-four years, daughter of Hezekiah and Pamelia F. (Senter) Fellows, of Boscawen. Three children were born of this marriage: Hill B., Lucy E., and Senter G. He married second, September 17, 1902, Nancy Eastman Couch, who was born in Boscawen, February 12, 1835, daughter of Enoch and Nancy (Eastman) Couch. (See Couch IV.)

(II) John, youngest son of Archibald McCurdy by his first union, was born in Ballymony in 1718. He resided in Dunbarton and died there August 6, 1813. In 1765 he was chosen first constable and also tax collector, and for the years 1766 and 1770 he served as a selectman. In the French and Indian War he served as a lieutenant. He married Mary Scoby, who died September 20, 1809, and their children were: Martha, Archibald, James, Robert, Elizabeth, Matthew Scoby, Daniel, Mary and Peggy.

(III) Matthew Scoby, third son and fifth child of John and Mary (Scoby) McCurdy, was born in Dunbarton, November 23, 1766, and died March 23, 1850. In 1790 he was chosen deacon of the church in Dunbarton and was noted for his piety. No food was allowed to be cooked in his house on Sunday, and it is related that on one occasion, having lost his reckoning, he hauled a load of grist to the mill, but upon learning his mistake he returned home with his load, preferring to make an extra trip to the mill rather than leave it there on the Lord's day. He was quite prominent in public affairs and between the years 1791 and 1808 he served six terms as a selectman. He was the father of ten children, namely: Peggy, Daniel, Martha, John, James, Mary, Robert, Elizabeth, Mary Ann and Matthew.

(IV) Daniel, second child and eldest son of Matthew McCurdy, was born in Dunbarton, September 16, 1798, and died in what is now Webster, November 9, 1859. He married Betsey Alexander, who was born in Dunbarton, February 28, 1805, daughter of David and Martha (Cunningham) Alexander, the former of whom was born July 11, 1781, and died June 23, 1852, and the latter born March 15, 1779, died March 30, 1854. David and Martha (Cunningham) Alexander, who were married March 8, 1804, became the parents of seven children, two of whom died in infancy. Those who lived to maturity are: Betsey (previously mentioned); Nancy, born June 6, 1807, (became the wife of John Healy and died November 30, 1895); Mary, born October 24, 1808 (became the wife of Orren Morse); Harriet, born November 22, 1812, married Hugh Jameson and died February 17, 1901); and Maria born December 25, 1815 (married Joshua Vose). Daniel and Betsey (Alexander) McCurdy had a family of eight children, namely: John, born April 27, 1831, died January 8, 1871); Capt. David A., born June 23, 1832, (married Salome Fellows, who was born August 25, 1827, died January 2, 1891, and he is now residing in Webster, this state); Martha Jane, born February 2, 1834; Daniel L., born December 27, 1835, (died July 24, 1897); Elizabeth, born June 29, 1837, married Thomas Kilbourne, born February 26, 1835; Mary Ann, born December 24, 1838, who is again referred to in the succeeding paragraph; Matthew, born November 5, 1840, (died in Virginia September 19, 1864); and Oscar D., born in 1842, died January 31, 1843). The mother of these children died May 13, 1888. Capt. David A. McCurdy, previously referred to, is a veteran of the Civil war, was wounded and won promotion for his gallantry. His younger brother, Matthew, was killed in battle during that struggle. Both enlisted August 11, 1862, in the Fourteenth Regiment, New Hampshire Volunteers

(V) Mary Ann, sixth child and youngest daughter of Daniel and Betsey (Alexander) McCurdy, was educated in the select and high schools of Boscawen and Contoocook, New Hampshire. In 1859 she became the wife of Prescott C. Hall of Salem Depot, and went to reside in that town. (See Hall.) She is the mother of four sons, all of whom are living, namely: Clarence P., Arthur C., Clifton S. and Lester W. Mr. Hall died suddenly in June, 1906, having retired from active business pursuits some years previous, and he left a good estate, including valuable residential property in Boston.

McGREGOR The Scotch Highlanders of this name, who were the forefathers of all of the McGregors in America, have for centuries inhabited the wild, mountainous region bordering upon Loch Lomen, and their most famous chieftain, Rob Roy, or Red Rob, is the hero of one of Sir Walter Scott's most facinating tales. They were a haughty people, who, clinging tenaciously to the ancient traditions of their race, stoutly refused to abandon their independent life, and were among the last of the Gaelic tribes to cease their opposition to the sway of English, or as they termed it, Saxon civilization. Warlike and ready to avenge a wrong they followed to many a victory the standard of their chief, when summoned to the fray.

> "The moon's on the lake and the mist's on the brae;
> And the clan has an aim that is nameless by day;
> Then gather, gather, gather Gregarlach."

The great religious upheaval which swept over Scotland during the seventeenth century seems to have had little effect upon the highland clans. A few of them, however, joined the Covenanters, and among the latter were some of the McGregors, who, as might have been expected, were as firm and unbending in their christian zeal as the rugged crags which formed the battlements of their picturesque retreat. Such were the ancestors of the venerable centenarian of North Newport, whose long and interesting life forms the chief inspiration for this narrative.

(I) John McGregor came from Scotland prior to the beginning of the eighteenth century or shortly afterward, and settled in Enfield, Connecticut.

(II) Ebenezer, son of John McGregor resided in Enfield and reared a family.

(III) John, son of Ebenezer McGregor, was born in Enfield, June 29, 1736. He was a Revolutionary soldier. In 1787 he went to Newport, New Hampshire, locating on the Wylie farm (so called), and he resided in that town for the remainder of his life. He married Lucy Chapin, who died May 29, 1836. His children were: Joel, Asa B., John B., Elias, Lucy, Norman and Lois.

(IV) Joel, eldest child of John McGregor, was born in Enfield, November 22, 1760. April 17, 1777, he enlisted in a Connecticut regiment for service in the war for national independence, and was in the Continental army five years, during which time he spent eight months in the famous old sugar-house in New York city as a prisoner of war. In 1789 he settled upon the William Tilton farm in North Newport. The McGregors are noted for their longevity, as will be seen later, and Joel was no exception to the rule as he died in Newport in 1861, at the ripe old age of one hundred and one years. He married Martha Bellows, and reared seven children, namely: Gaius, born August 27, 1786, married Betsey Hoyt, and settled in Bethlehem, New Hampshire. Polly, July 15, 1788, married Silas Wakefield. Cyrus R., September 27, 1791. Laomy, in February, 1794, married Fanny White, and settled in Whitefield, New Hampshire. Martha, July 16, 1799, married for her first husband Willard Wakefield, and for her second husband Captain Nathaniel King, of Claremont, New Hampshire. James B., who will be again referred to. Ruby, in July, 1806, married John Barnard. All lived to an advanced age, one, Gaius, becoming a nonogenarian and dying at ninety-four years, while James B., who is still living, is now far beyond the century mark.

(V) James Bellows, fourth son and sixth child of Joel and Martha (Bellows) McGregor, was born on the William Tilton farm in North Newport, September 6, 1801. His education, which was begun in the district schools, was completed at the Newport Academy, and for a number of years afterward he was a successful school teacher both in his native town and in other places. One of his pupils was Mrs. Electa Kelley, of Newport, who recently died at the age of ninety-two years. She was the seventh child of Ephraim Fletcher. On attaining his majority he visited his brother in Lyman, New Hampshire, and being solicited to take charge of the school there he accepted and at times had one hundred and six pupils. In 1829 he purchased a general country store in Lunenburg, Vermont, where he remained until 1831, and he was subsequently for some years engaged in the manufacture of barrels at Waterville, Maine. While there he acquired a wide reputation as a singing master and afterward taught singing schools in New Hampshire and Vermont. In the early forties he owned and operated a sawmill, and while running a circular saw had the misfortune to lose some of his fingers. He next turned his attention to carpentering and contracting, and erected several buildings in Newport. He was at one time employed by Aaron Nettleton, Jr., as clerk at the old Nettleton store in Newport, which stood on the site of the present Lewis block, and he also held a similar position in Salisbury, Massachusetts, for some time. Early in the seventies he resided for a time in Albany, New York, but a fondness for the surroundings amid which the happiest years of his life have been spent eventually caused his return to North Newport, and he has ever since remained there. He acquired possession of the house he now occupies in May, 1842, and he not only set out all of the shade trees which adorn the property, but the fences too are the work of his hands.

On November 9, 1832, Mr. McGregor was united in marriage with Elizabeth J. Townsend, who was born February 6, 1806, and died August 25, 1869. She was a sister of Mrs. Amos Tuck. The only child of this union was James H. McGregor, who was born April 12, 1820, and for nearly fifty years was a well-known commercial traveler. He suffered severely from asthma, which eventually caused his death, January 10, 1906, at the home of his father. February 15, 1872, he married Emily Melendy, of Pomfret, Vermont, who was born in Hartland, Vermont, September 26, 1856. She died leaving one daughter, Alice, who is now residing with her grandfather in Newport. She was married November 21, 1906, to Orren J. Clement, a Carpenter of Newport.

A centenarian and an optimist may appear to the majority of readers as somewhat paradoxical, but in the case of James B. McGregor this assertion is absolutely true. To all appearances he seems to possess the strength and agility of a man of fifty years. He is still able to prepare fire wood, works in his garden, thereby obtaining a sufficient amount of physical exercise to preserve a normal circulation of his blood, and his mental faculties are equally active. He converses intelligently upon a varied line of subjects, including the many notable improvements in mechanic arts during the last century, and his memory is unusually accurate. He has a vivid recollection of the days when corn pone, baked on a smooth board in front of the fire, was the addition to fried salt pork, considered both healthy and sufficient food by the average New Hampshire farmer;

of the flint lock musket and the manner of kindling a fire prior to the introduction of Lucifer matches; and recently in speaking of the time when farmers found it necessary to raise flax for the purpose of clothing the family, he humorously remarked that these home-made garments fitted like a shirt on a bean-pole. When interviewed by the representative of the publishers of this work he cheerfully and without the slightest effort gave the desired information relative to his ancestors and the principal incidents of his own unusally long life, and at an opportune moment he tenderly embraced his granddaughter, at the same time paying her a truly beautiful tribute of love and devotion, concluding with the pathetic words: "This is all I have left to comfort me in my old age."

The fact that Mr. McGregor has now reached the age of one hundred and six years is not the only unique feature of his life, as he is considered the oldest living Free Mason in the country, having joined that order at Salisbury, Massachusetts, in 1825, and has therefore affiliated with it for eighty-one years. At the observation of the one hundredth anniversary of his birthday, which took place at his home in 1901, the ceremony was of a semi-Masonic character, the house being decorated with emblems symbolical of the order, and many of the participants being fellow-craftsmen. Provided for the occasion were two handsome birthday cakes, one by his neighbors and friends, and the other by his relatives, and each was inscribed: 1801-1901. One was surrounded by one hundred wax tapers which, when dinner was announced, were lighted and they burned out one by one during the progress of the repast, emblematical of each successive year in the life of the honored centenarian who, at the proper time, cut and distributed the cake among the guests. Past Worshipful Master Albert S. Wait, of Mount Vernon Lodge, No. 15, presented him with an easy chair in behalf of that body. Though the Rev. C. H. Fletcher his neighbors and friends presented him with a handsome house-coat, a pair of slippers, a silver match-box and a well-filled purse, while appropriating speeches were made and aptly responded to. During the past summer (1906) Mr. McGregor and his friend, Ezra T. Sibley, who is a nonegenarian, were tendered by Colonel Seth M. Richards an automobile ride in the latter's handsome touring car. They were carried through Northville, thence by a circuitous route back to the point of departure, and both enjoyed the trip immensely, Mr. McGregor remarking that he could stand the trip to Boston. This incident certainly served to link the far away past with its proverbial slow coach, and the present day with its speedy and luxuriant means of public and private conveyances.

PUTNEY For more than one hundred years a certain locality in the town of Dunbarton, New Hampshire, has been described as "the old Putney farm"; for more than a century and a half the children in the public schools have been taught how James Rogers and Joseph Putney made the first civilized white settlement within the limits of the town and the destruction of their buildings and property by the Indians, but a search of the various town records and an examination of the productions of earlier chroniclers of contemporary history fails to reveal more than meagre mention of the adventures of Joseph Putney and furnishes no account whatever of his family life and connections other than the fact that he had a son.

In early New Hampshire history Joseph Putney played an important part as a pioneer of Dunbarton, and proved himself worthy of a conspicuous place in the archives of the state as the founder of one of its best towns, a daring pioneer, fearless Indian fighter, and as the progenitor of a family whose descendants in all generations from his time have been men of action and solid worth. It is within reason to state that all persons in New Hampshire of the surname Putney and who have lived within that jurisdiction during the last century and a half are descendants of Joseph Putney, first of Londonderry and afterward of Dunbarton, and have reason to feel just pride in the deeds of their common ancestor.

Joseph Putney was of Scotch birth and ancestry, and is believed to have come to the colony of people of his own nationality at Londonderry, New Hampshire, within ten years after the settlement of that town was effected. He was not among the signers of the memorial addressed to Governor Shute, nor one of the proprietors to whom the grant was made, nor does his name appear at all in connection with the settlement and organization or subsequent history of that town; but there is abundant evidence of his having been there within a very short time after the town was settled, and that he joined with James Rogers, who was one of the proprietors of Londonderry, in venturing out into the then uninhabited regions of Dunbarton and making a settlement there somewhere about the year 1740.

The story of the adventures of James Rogers and Joseph Putney has been told by various writers of New Hampshire and Dunbarton history, and while in the main their accounts agree there are a few differences in respect to dates; but from information drawn from all reliable sources it appears most probable that Rogers and Putney left old Londonderry and went out to the region now known as Dunbarton sometime between the years 1735 and 1740, and that then their first object was to hunt for wild game. While on an expedition of this kind they discovered the "great meadow," which even then was covered with a heavy growth of natural grass, and naturally the thought was suggested that the locality was a most desirable one for a new settlement. They accordingly erected log houses, says the "History of Dunbarton," and removed their families from their former abodes in Londonderry to their new homes, at a time when Bow probably was without an inhabitant and Rumford (Concord) was the nearest settlement. In their isolated position they struggled on, clearing land, planting orchards and raising stock until 1746, when a body of hostile Indians appeared in the Merrimack valley to destroy unprotected settlements, plunder houses and carry away captives: but before an attack was made on the homes of these pioneers a messenger from the garrison at Rumford had warned them of their peril, and on that very night Rogers and Putney abandoned their property and with their families sought safety at the garrison. The next day Rogers and Putney went back after the cattle and found that they had been killed and all the buildings destroyed by fire. After that they remained with their families at the garrison until the Indians left the vicinity, and in 1749 returned to the place, rebuilt their houses and settled permanently near the great meadows. On one occasion, however, while Joseph Putney was at work on the intervale he was surprised by a party of Indians, but managed to escape capture, although one of his arms was broken by a musket ball fired by one of his pursuers.

(I) Joseph Putney, the Scotch immigrant, the pioneer of Dunbarton, was a man of courage and a man of peace, and after the troublous period was passed he resided for the remainder of his life at the place where his first settlement had been made, and died there at an advanced age. It is known that he had a family, but the number and names of his children are not now known. The house of his son Henry was the accustomed meeting place for the selection of a representative to the general assembly.

(II) Henry, son of Joseph Putney, the pioneer of Dunbarton, is believed to have come with his father and mother to Londonderry and afterward shared with them the vicissitudes of pioneer life. He became a man of consequence in the town and filled some town offices. Other than this little indeed is known of him, except that he married three times, namely: Mary Wells. Dolly Jewett and Deborah Austin. He died April 13, 1807, leaving children, and "his descendants have gone out into all the land." Two of Henry's sons were David and Daniel, and there is reason to believe that John was another of them, but this is not certain. (He receives mention in this article).

(III) David, son of Henry Putney, and grandson of Joseph Putney, was born in Dunbarton and spent his life in that town, on the farm where his grandfather settled and where his father also lived. David married and his wife's name was Rebecca. Their children were: Molly, born March 23, 1791; Rebecca Sawyer, July 10, 1793; Adna, July 10, 1796; Fanny, February 27, 1799; David, September 4, 1801; Fanny, September 22, 1805; Henry, June 11, 1807; Louisa, December 5, 1810.

(IV) David, son of David and Rebecca Putney, born in Dunbarton, September 4, 1801, died February, 1881. He was given a good common school education, and afterward taught several years in Bow and other towns in the vicinity of his home, but his chief business occupation was farming. He was a man of understanding and influence, served as selectman, representative to the state legislature, and was one of the most intense abolitionists in his town. Originally he was a Democrat and afterward a firm Republican. Mr. Putney married, 1827, Mary Brown, daughter of Jonathan Brown, of Bow, and of their fourteen children ten grew to maturity, viz.: John B.. of Granville, Vermont. Eliza A., wife of William Doherty, of Danvers, Massachusetts. George H. (now dead). Charles E., a graduate of Dartmouth, class of '70; a noted educator, for fifteen years principal of St. Johnsbury (Vermont) Academy, and now teaching at Burlington, Vermont. Albert B., a retired Boston merchant. Lucretia C., wife of Charles W. Brown, of Concord, New Hampshire. Walter of Bow, New Hampshire. representative and state senator. Freeman, superintendent of schools at Gloucester, Massachusetts. David N., a graduate of Dartmouth, class of '75, formerly principal of Leicester and Monson academies, Massachusetts. Milton K., of Revere, Massachusetts, for many years teacher and superintendent of schools.

(V) Freeman Putney, superintendent of public schools at Gloucester, Massachusetts, and a teacher and educator of wide experience, was born in the town of Bow. Merrimack county, New Hampshire, August 23, 1847. His elementary and secondary education was acquired in public schools and academies. and his higher education at Dartmouth College, where he finished the course and graduated with the degree of Bachelor of Arts in 1873. He worked his way through college and taught school to gain the means with which to pay his tuition and expense of maintenance. Having chosen the profession of teaching, Mr. Putney, after graduation, began his career at South Hadley, Massachusetts, in the high school in that town, and afterward taught in Revere, Massachusetts. His work up to the time of leaving Revere had extended over a period of fifteen years, and gave to him an excellent experience. In 1880 he went to Gloucester, Massachusetts, filled a pedagogue's chair there for eight years, and in 1888 was appointed superintendent of schools in that city. On June 17, 1876, Mr. Putney married Alice C. Knight, born February 4, 1858, daughter of Rev. Richard Knight, an Englishman by birth and a clergyman of the Congregational Church. Mr. and Mrs. Putney have three children: Freeman, Jr., born June 24, 1877, Brown University. 1899. Walter K., born May 6, 1879, educated at Brown University and the Massachusetts State Normal School at Salem, Massachusetts. Willis R., born October 31, 1893.

(III) John Putney, progenitor of the Hillsborough and Cheshire Putneys, was a descendant of Joseph Putney. and probably his grandson, for the period of his life was contemporary with that of those who are known to have been the sons of David and Daniel Putney, who were sons of Henry, as has been mentioned. Little is known, however, of this John other than that he had a son, John Tracy Putney.

(IV) John Tracy, son of John Putney, was born in 1780, and settled in Washington, New Hampshire, about 1830, where two of his sons afterward lived. His wife was Judith Ordway, daughter and third of nine children born to Eleazer and Susan (Dow) Ordway. who lived many years at West Deering and moved from there to Francestown about 1815, lived there about nine years and then returned to West Deering, where Susan died. Her husband died in Goffstown, New Hampshire. When John and Judith Putney went to Washington they settled on a farm on the southeast slope of Lovewell's mountain, at the place where John Vose is said to have made the first improvement, but later on removed to Bradford, New Hampshire, in which town both of them died.

(V) Andrew Jackson, son of John Tracy and Judith (Ordway) Putney, was born in Antrim, New Hampshire, December 15, 1830, and for about twenty years during the earlier part of his active business life was a farmer in the town of Bradford, New Hampshire. From there he moved to Hooksett, New Hampshire, and carried on lumbering operations for General Samuel Andrews, but after a little more than a year went to Melrose, Massachusetts, and for the next two years engaged in the manufacture of shoes. He then returned to New Hampshire and for the next ten years was connected with the Jones and Gage bobbin works, and afterward for something like a year and a half was half owner of that plant and its business; but soon disposing of his interest in the works he went to Hillsborough Bridge, carried on a farm and did other kinds of work until he was appointed overseer of the town poor farm. This position he held about six years, and during the following five years was connected with his son in the hotel business at Hillsborough Bridge. Now he is living comfortably on a small place in the town of Hillsborough. Mr. Putney married Julia Ann Jones. who was born at Brookline, Massachusetts, 1833, daughter of Nathaniel G. Jones, and by whom he has two sons: George H., born September, 1856, married Lizzie Duddleson, of Waltham, Massachusetts, and Charles Gordon, now of Keene. New Hampshire. Mrs. Andrew Jackson Putney died May 11, 1898.

(VI) Charles Gordon, younger of the two sons of Andrew Jackson and Julia Ann (Jones) Putney, was born in the town of Washington, New Hampshire, March 2, 1861, and was educated in public schools. After leaving school he worked with his father, and in the course of about three years found a position as clerk in the Valley Hotel in Hillsborough, and after some three years in that capacity he bought out Childs Bros., the former proprietors, and became himself the landlord. Here he made his real beginning as a practical hotel man and he made a success of the business from the outset. After five years' experience in Hillsborough he went to Boston and became cashier and clerk in the Quincy House. but at the end of six months took the management of the Hotel Eagle at Keene, New Hampshire, and after about seven years there succeeded to the proprietorship of that well-known hostelry, in partnership with J. W. Buckminster. Besides his work in connection with the hotel and its management Mr. Putney deals somewhat extensively in real estate, carries on lumbering operations and generally finds his time pretty well occupied with business affairs.

November 23, 1898, Mr. Putney married Maud Russell, born November 21, 1880, daughter of John J. Russell, born at Stoneham, Massachusetts, July 21, 1841, and Ella F. (Wood) Russell, born at Hartford, Vermont, October 18, 1849. Mr. and Mrs. Putney have two children: Russell G., born September 26, 1901; and Olande C., born August 26, 1904.

NETTLETON The Nettletons of the town of Newport and Sullivan county, New Hampshire, are all descendants of Jeremiah Nettleton, who made a settlement in the town of Newport in the year 1779, lived there about thirty-five years, and at his death left a large family of children from whom in later years has come a numerous line of descendants, and in each succeeding generation from the time of the settler there have been men of prominence in the civil, political and industrial history of the state.

(I) John Nettleton, of Kenilworth, England, is mentioned in history as the founder of this particular branch of the Nettleton family of New England, but of his antecedents contemporary genealogists give little information of value. It is known, however, that he lived about fifty miles west of the city of London, and that after his immigration to America was one of the early colonists of Connecticut. He married, and among his children was a son Joseph.

(II) Joseph, son of John the ancestor, married, February 18, 1712, Hannah Bushnell, and had a son Jeremiah.

(III) Jeremiah, son of Joseph and Hannah (Bushnell) Nettleton, and grandson of John the ancestor, was of Killingworth, Connecticut, which appears to have been the principal seat of the family in that state. The family name of his wife is not mentioned by any of the earlier chroniclers of Nettleton history, but it is known that he married and that one of his sons was Jeremiah Nettleton, progenitor of the family of that surname in New Hampshire.

(IV) Jeremiah Nettleton was a descendant of the fourth generation of John Nettleton, the ancestor, and was born in Connecticut, probably at Killingworth, October 17, 1738, and died in Newport, New Hampshire, in 1815. He settled in Newport in 1779, having come from Connecticut during that year with his wife and eight children, the eldest of whom was then less than seventeen years old. Jeremiah settled on what afterward became known as the Paul farm, and he owned Bald mountain and the land extending thence southward to the river. He married, at Killingworth, Connecticut. November 19, 1761, Love Buell, of whose ancestors a brief mention in this place is appropriate. She was a daughter of Daniel and Elizabeth (Post) Buell, granddaughter of Samuel and Judith Buell, great-granddaughter of Samuel and Deborah (Griswold) Buell, and great-great-granddaughter of William and Mary Buell. Jeremiah and Love (Buell) Nettleton had nine children, all of whom save the youngest were born in Connecticut. They were as follows: Mabel, born November 15, 1762, married Aaron Buell, Jr. Charity, July 27, 1764, married a Mr. Story and settled in Goshen, New Hampshire. Aaron, November 11, 1766, married Mehitable Dow. Jeremiah, Jr., September 11, 1768, married Lydia Ledoyt. Nathan, June 21, 1770, married Hannah Wheeler. Rachel, October 4. 1772, married Joshua Heath. Deborah, February 11, 1775, married Peter Stow. Joel, February 6, 1778, married Elizabeth Dow. Daniel, born in Newport, New Hampshire, December 1, 1780, married (first) Esther Peck, and (second) Rhoda Ryant.

(V) Joel, eighth child and fourth son of Jeremiah and Love (Buell) Nettleton, was born in Killingworth, Connecticut, February 6, 1778, and was about one year old when he was brought with his father's family to Newport. Having reached his majority he became a farmer in the northeast part of the town, but soon afterward purchased the old Newport House, which he enlarged and turned into one of the most famous taverns in that part of the state, while he himself was one of the most popular landlords in Sullivan county for many years; and in connection with his tavern he was proprietor of a line of stages. His wife, whom he married March 5. 1805, was Elizabeth Dow, daughter of Jeremiah Dow, and who with her brother Nathaniel and her sister Mehitable removed from Salem, New Hampshire, to Newport in 1792 and settled in the eastern part of the town. Mehitable Dow afterward married Aaron Nettleton, older brother of Joel Nettleton. Joel and Elizabeth (Dow) Nettleton had six children, viz.: Joel Parker, born August 21, 1806, succeeded his father as landlord of the Newport House, married Charlotte Lyon, and died in Connecticut. Mary Hendrick, April 9, 1810, married Cyrus Walker. Gilbert, March 24, 1812. Elizabeth, October 7, 1814, married Zepheniah Hutchinson, a noted singer, and settled in Illinois. Persis D., July 27, 1818, became the second wife of Cyrus Walker. Daniel. February 6, 1821.

(VI) Daniel Nettleton, youngest son and child of Joel and Elizabeth (Dow) Nettleton, was born in Newport, New Hampshire, February 6, 1821, and died in the same town October 1, 1875. His young life was spent at home with his parents, whom he helped with the work about the Newport House. but after he became of age he went to Wilmot, New Hampshire, and for twelve years carried on a tanning business. He was a capable and successful business man, and occupied a prominent place in the public affairs of that town. He was selectman in 1860-61-62, and representative of Wilmot in the general court in 1865-66, and after returning to Newport was selectman of that town in 1873-74. He also was actively identified with the state militia, in which at one time he held the rank and commission of colonel, hence the military title by which he was generally addressed—Colonel Nettleton. He was a man of decisive character and sound judgment, whether in official or personal business affairs, and his frank manners and generous disposition won for him many warm friends and made him one of the most popular men in Newport. In July, 1850, he married Ellen C. Wilmarth (see Wilmarth), eldest daughter of Jonathan M. and Lucy (Cheney) Wilmarth, and a descendant of some of the best families of New England. Two children were born of the marriage of Daniel and Ellen C. (Wilmarth) Nettleton, viz.: Lucy E., born May 27, 1851, and Fred. H., February 12. 1861, was graduated at Newport high school, Kimball Union Academy, Meriden, New Hampshire, and Dartmouth College, Hanover, New Hampshire.

(VII) Lucy E., daughter of Daniel and Ellen C. (Wilmarth) Nettleton, and a descendant of the seventh generation of John Nettleton, of Kenilworth, England, and Killingworth, Connecticut, was born in Newport, New Hampshire, May 27, 1851. She was educated at Colby Academy, New London, New Hampshire. She married Arthur C. Bradley, formerly of Vermont and now of Newport, New Hampshire.

FOLLANSBEE The history of this family begins with the early settlement of New England, and covers a wide range of this country. It is represented in New Hampshire in a worthy way by many descendants, as well as through all sections of the United States.

(I) Thomas Follansbee, sometimes spelled in the records Follinsby and Follansbury, was a resident of Portsmouth and Newbury. He is supposed to have been born about 1640. His first marriage was before 1672, his wife's Christian name being Mary. His second wife, Sarah, died in Newbury, November 6, 1683, and it appears that he was married (third), April 4, 1713, in Newbury, to Jane Moseman, of Boston. He was of Portsmouth from 1665 to 1671, and of Newbury in 1677 and subsequently. He was still living in 1713, and probably in 1726. His children were: Rebecca, Anne, Mary, Thomas, Francis and Hannah.

(II) Thomas (2), eldest son of Thomas (1) Follansbee, was born about 1670. He resided in Newbury, Massachusetts, where he was a housewright and an inn holder. His will was made July 30, 1753, and proved June 23, 1755, which indicates that he died in the early part of the latter year. He was probably survived by his second wife, Mary, whom he married after 1724. He was married (first), June 19, 1694, to Abigail Roafe, who was probably a daughter of John Bond, of Newbury, and widow of Ezra Roafe. Their children were: Mary, Thomas, Francis, and William.

(III) Thomas (3), eldest son and second child of Thomas (2) and Abigail (Bond) Follansbee, was born March 28, 1697, in Newbury, where he resided and was still living in 1753. He was married January 5, 1715, to Hannah March, who was living in 1726. She was a daughter of Captain Hugh and Sarah (Moody) March, and granddaughter of Hugh March, of Newbury, who came from England in the ship "Confidence" in 1638. The records of Newbury give only one child of this marriage, who is mentioned in the succeeding paragraph.

(IV) Thomas (4), son of Thomas (3) and Hannah (March) Follansbee, was born in 1730, and lived for a time in the town now Danville. He was married there April 19, 1770, to Martha Collins, and subsequently removed to the town of Weare, where he was a pioneer settler.

(V) Samuel, son of Thomas Follansbee, was born in Weare, New Hampshire, in 1760. The history of Weare shows him to have been one of the taxpayers there between 1788 and 1793, inclusive. The Follansbee name is numerous in Weare to this day, and a Samuel Follansbee was frequently mentioned there during the last generation.

(VI) Levi, son of Samuel Follansbee, was born in Salisbury, New Hampshire, February 19, 1794. He married Asenath Goodwin.

(VII) Lucian Augustus, son of Levi and Asenath (Goodwin) Follansbee, was born in Hill, New Hampshire, October 16, 1816. He was educated in the district schools of Hill. He was a successful carpenter and farmer. He became a colonel in the state militia. He was a Republican in politics, served in the legislature, and held all the town offices. He married Sarah Clark Sargent, daughter of Ephraim Kendall and Lydya Sargent, of Warner, New Hampshire. They had nine children, four of whom grew to maturity. They were: Ephraim K., born April 19, 1840; Augustus Damon, born May 11, 1842; Louisa, born September 26, 1844; and Sarah C., born February 3, 1845. Mrs. Sarah (Sargent) Follansbee died August 21, 1874, and her husband survived her eighteen years, dying April 16, 1892. Mrs. Sarah Clark (Sargent) Follansbee was of direct Revolutionary descent. Her father, Ephraim K. Sargent, born in 1791, at Deerfield, New Hampshire, was the son of Barnard Sargent. The name of Barnard Sargent appears on the roll of minute-men organized at Haverhill, Massachusetts, in 1773. He is described in that record as short of stature, light complexioned, curly haired, a minor. He was in the fight at Lexington and Concord, Massachusetts. He was a member of the Second Company, First Massachusetts Regiment, and took part at Bunker Hill. During the retreat from Bunker Hill, while Barnard Sargent was assisting a feeble soldier, a cannon ball struck the soldier, cutting him in two. Barnard Sargent was with Washington's army at Valley Forge, where he contracted smallpox. In 1779 there is a record that the government was owing him eighty-two pounds seven shillings, English money. In 1780 Barnard Sargent married Judith Hanaford, at Concord, New Hampshire. The muster rolls show that on March 8, 1781, Barnard Sargent, age twenty-seven, enlisted for three years from Deerfield, New Hampshire. The date of discharge is not given, but the records show that Sargent was owed sixty-five pounds ten shillings at that time. At the private's usual rate of pay, not to exceed two pounds a month, this would give him a service of three and a half years for the first enlistment, and two years and nine months the second time.

(VIII) Augustus Damon, second son of Lucian Augustus and Sarah (Sargent) Follansbee, was born in Hill, New Hampshire, May 11, 1842. He was educated in the district schools of Danville, New Hampshire. He came to Sutton about 1862, and bought a farm of two hundred and twenty-five acres, making a specialty of raising fine stock. He was a Republican in politics, and was chairman of the board of selectmen in 1894-95-96. He was road surveyor and supervisor. He was greatly interested in temperance, and belonged to several societies for promoting the cause. He attended the Advent

Church. He married Sarah M. Messer and they had four children. The eldest died young; the others were: Sarah G., Ada Matilda, born January 16, 1866, and Charles Reuben, born April 15, 1870.

(IX) Charles Reuben, son of Augustus and Sarah (Messer) Follansbee, was born in North Sutton, April 15, 1870. He was educated in the district schools of North Sutton and at New London Academy. In April, 1891, he was graduated from Bryant & Stratton's well-known business college at Manchester, New Hampshire. He first tried his hand at stonecutting; but not caring for that, he came back to Sutton in 1897, and went into the hotel business. The Follansbee is a large, convenient hotel, situated at the lower end of Keyser lake, and its popularity is widespread. He also owns two roomy cottages, and in the summer time the accommodations are not equal to the demand. He also manages a hundred acre farm and does considerable in the dairy line. He is a Republican, and active in politics. He was selectman in 1895-96-97-98. He was on the school board from 1894 to 1900. He was road agent for two years, and represented his town in the legislature of 1905. He is an Odd Fellow, and past noble grand of Heidelberg Lodge, No. 92, of New London. He attends the Universalist Church. He married Nellie Belle Pressey, daughter of John and Betsey R. Pressey, of Sutton, New Hampshire. They were married September 24, 1894, and have two children: Harold John, born August 26, 1895, and Winthrop, born October 27, 1896. Mrs. Follansbee is active in church work.

GUNNISON Sometime within the next half score of years after the planting of the colony at Plymouth in 1620, there came to New England five immigrant families who bore the surnames of Scammon, Frost, Bryar and Raynes, two having the same name. These are said to have been families of English birth and origin, and that with them came one of another nationality—a Swede, young, strong and of good appearance, whose name was Hugh Gunnison, founder of the first family of that name in New England.

It may be said, however, that early New England records are not quite clear in respect to the date of birth, the year of landing and the events of the early life of Hugh Gunnison, or in respect to the date of his first marriage, the family name of his first wife and the precise number of his children; but the best information drawn from all reliable sources, supplemented with well preserved family tradition, indicate that he was born about the year 1610, and came to New England probably in 1630; that the colonists of whose number he was one entered Piscataqua harbor before there was any habitation of man at Portsmouth and when there were only two small huts on Great Island (New Castle). His later movements, so far as the records searched tend to throw light on the matter, cannot be given with any safe degree of accuracy, but generally it may be said that he was first of Vintner, New Hampshire, then of Boston, and later of Kittery, Maine, where he died September 21, 1658.

(I) Hugh Gunnison was in Boston as early as 1634, and on May 25, 1636, with sixty-eight others subscribed to the test oath and was accepted as a freeman. In the distribution of lands to the freemen of Boston on January 9, 1637, there was allotted to "Brother Hugh Gunnison at the Mount for three heads," indicating that he then had a wife and one child, although "Records of Boston" says that Sarah Gunnison, daughter of Hugh Gunnison and Elizabeth his wife, was born December 14, 1637. From the same source it is learned that Elizabeth Gunnison, daughter of Hugh and Elizabeth Gunnison, was born February 25, 1640, and also that their third child, Deborah Gunnison, was born in August, 1642. It may be well to state in this connection that Sarah was not the first born of Hugh and Elizabeth Gunnison, but that their first child died in extreme infancy. Elizabeth, first wife of Hugh Gunnison, died November 25, 1646 (Records of Boston), and after her death he married Sarah Lynn, who bore him two sons, Joseph, born January 31, 1649, and Elihu, born February 12, 1650. In November, 1637, Hugh Gunnison was one of fifty-eight of "the best citizens of Boston" who were charged with complicity in the Hutchinson heresy, and for that offense were deprived of the privilege of bearing arms. He must have gone from Boston to Kittery, in Maine, before 1651, for in that year he was noticed by the grand jury of that town. In 1654 (date of May 3), he was representative of Wells to the general court.

(II) Elihu, sixth child and youngest son of Hugh Gunnison, was born in Boston, February 12, 1650, and died after March 29, 1729. He was a shipwright by business occupation and a man of considerable influence among the townsmen. In 1680 he joined with other inhabitants of York, Kittery and Wells in an address to Charles II, praying to be relieved of the Puritan government of Boston, and in the same year he was acting magistrate. His name does not appear in the public records of Kittery before the year 1693, when he was chosen selectman, in which capacity he continued to serve until 1710. On May 9, 1693, he was appointed with others to give instructions to the deputy of the representatives to the general court at Boston. From 1699 to 1726 he was moderator of the town. Elihu Gunnison married, first, November 10, 1674, at Dover, New Hampshire, Martha Trickee, who died before November 23, 1765. The christian name of his second wife was Elizabeth, but her family name is unknown. By his first wife Elihu Gunnison had four children, and two by his second wife. Mentioned in the order of birth these children were as follows: Elihu, born in Dover, New Hampshire; a child, born in Dover and afterward killed by the Indians; Priscilla, born at Kittery, and married Nicholas Weeks; Mary, married Joseph Weeks; Joseph; Elizabeth, married John Walker.

(III) Joseph, son of Elihu Gunnison and Elizabeth, his wife, was born October 14, 1690, and died September 8, 1748. He was by trade a shipwright, following the occupation of his father; and he was a pious man, upright in his daily walk, and exercised an influence for good in the community in which he lived. He was admitted to the church April 14, 1720, and was elected deacon April 2, 1731. On July 15, 1724, he was made clerk of the parish of Kittery. He married four times: First, Susanna Follett; second, Elizabeth Lewis; third, Margaret Wilson, and fourth, Susanna Ayers. His children, in the order of birth, were: Samuel, John, David, William, Christopher, Benjamin, Margaret, William (the second child so named), Elizabeth and Lydia.

(IV) Samuel, eldest son and child of Joseph Gunnison, of whom mention is made in the preceding paragraph, and of the fourth generation of the descendants of Hugh Gunnison and Sarah his wife, was born in Kittery, Maine, January 27, 1720-1, and to him is accorded the honor of having founded in New Hampshire that particular branch of the Gunnison family whose representatives in succeeding generations have been so prominently identified with the best interests and history of Sullivan county for nearly a century and a half of years. Samuel Gunnison was a carpenter in Kittery until 1749, when he removed to Halifax, Nova Scotia, where his wife and the second of their children died. He afterward returned to Kittery, lived several more years in that town, and in 1765 moved with his second wife and family to the town of Goshen, New Hampshire. He was one of the pioneers of the town and one of its foremost citizens until the time of his death, May 14, 1806. He married, first, February 6, 1745, Jane Fernald, who died January 20, 1750, and married, second, May 3, 1752, Alice Fernald, a sister of his first wife, and who died July 5, 1804. She was born February 21, 1725-26. The children of Samuel Gunnison were Susanna, who married Edmund Wilson; Joseph; Margaret, who married Joseph Chandler, of Goshen; Samuel; Ephraim, who died in infancy; Daniel; Ephraim and Nathaniel, twins, and Alice.

(V) Ephraim Gunnison, son of Samuel and Alice (Fernald) Gunnison, was born in Goshen, New Hampshire, July 16, 1766, and with his twin brother Nathaniel was the first of his surname to be born in that town. He was a farmer by occupation, a thorough, practical, hard-working farmer, and by his energy and thrift acquired a fair competency for his time. He lived to attain the full age of eighty-five years and for many years was a consistent member of the Methodist Episcopal Church. In politics he was a Democrat. Ephraim Gunnison died June, 1851. His wife, whom he married August 6, 1787, was Deborah Freeman, born January 24, 1764, died April, 1853. They had seven children: Eunice, who married Ebenezer Batchelder; Deborah, who married Abner Colby; Lucy, who married James Osgood; Lois, who married John Stephens; Vinal, who married Eliza Baker and had eight children; Ebenezer; and Margaret, who became the wife of David Hastings.

(VI) Vinal, fifth child and elder son of Ephraim and Deborah (Freeman) Gunnison, was born in Goshen, New Hampshire, March 31, 1798, and died 1858. Like his father he was a farmer, thrifty and provident, but in politics he affiliated with the Whig party, whereas his father always was a staunch Democrat. He was chosen to fill various town offices, among the more important of which was that of selectman and also overseer of the poor. His farm lands included six hundred acres and his farm was one of the best in the town. He married, December 27, 1821, Eliza Baker, of Goshen, who survived him fifteen years and died in 1873, at the age of seventy-two years. They had eight children: John (died young), Arvin Nye, Miriam Weston, Sarah Ann (now Mrs. Brickett, of Mendota, Illinois), Eliza B. (Mrs. Chandler, of Salem, Oregon), John Vinal (ex-high sheriff of Sullivan county), Amos B. (dead), and Horace B. (of Phillipsville, California). (John Vinal receives extended mention in this article).

(VII) Arvin, second son and child of Vinal and Eliza (Baker) Gunnison, was born June 1, 1824, in Goshen. When about nineteen years of age, he went south and taught school for some years in Georgia. Subsequently he settled in New Orleans, engaged in the manufacture of cotton gins. After the outbreak of the Civil war, he manufactured arms for the Confederate armies until New Orleans was captured. At the close of the war he bought a plantation of four hundred acres in Bolivar county, Mississippi, on which has since grown up the present town of Gunnison, named in honor of this family. He resided on this plantation until his death in March, 1882. He married, December 13, 1859, Sarah H. Putnam, who was born in Milford, New Hampshire, November 2, 1839. She is a daughter of Daniel and Elizabeth (Hale) Putnam, of Milford. Five children were born of this marriage: Samuel, Putnam, Arvin, William T., of whom later; John T., who conducts a typewriters' exchange in Philadelphia, Pennsylvania. The others are deceased.

(VIII) William Towne, fourth son and child of Arvin and Sarah H. (Putnam) Gunnison, was born in Greenville, Bolivar county, Mississippi, September 22, 1869. He prepared for college at Exeter Academy, and entered Dartmouth College in 1888, graduating with the class of 1892. Subsequently he entered Harvard Law School, and in 1895 received the degree of Bachelor of Law. Immediately afterward he opened an office in Rochester, New Hampshire, where he has since resided, and now has a large clientage and a good business. In politics he is a Republican. In 1903 he sat in the constitutional convention as representative of Rochester. In the year 1889 he married Grace M., daughter of William and Mary A. (Colby) Horney, of Rochester, New Hampshire. They have two children: Arvin, born March 18, 1900; John V., born November 18, 1902.

(VII) John Vinal, sixth in order of birth of the sons and daughters of Vinal and Eliza (Baker) Gunnison, is a native of Goshen, New Hampshire, born February 27, 1837, and is known throughout Sullivan county as a straightforward business man and a competent public official. He was brought up on his father's farm, the same old farm which his great-grandfather cleared and brought under cultivation almost one hundred and fifty years ago, and which he now owns, although for nearly twenty years he has lived in Newport and engaged in other pursuits than farming. As a boy Mr. Gunnison attended the public school in Goshen and afterward was given a good academic education in Meriden and New London, New Hampshire. After leaving school he returned home and engaged in lumbering, farming, dealing in stock and at one time operated a saw mill. In 1888 he took up his residence in Newport and carried on business operations in various directions. In 1892 he was elected high sheriff of Sullivan county, and was re-elected to that office from year to year until having reached the age limit, seventy, he was no longer eligible. For more than thirty years he has been a prominent figure in Sullivan county and New Hampshire state politics, and always on the Republican side. In 1872-73-74 he was county commissioner, and in 1885 represented his town in the general court. He holds membership in various subordinate Masonic bodies and is a Knight Templar.

On January 16, 1867, John Vinal Gunnison married Angie Carr, born in Hillsborough, New Hampshire, September 12, 1846, daughter of Robert and Claora (Goodale) Carr, and granddaughter of Robert Carr, who was an early settler in Hillsborough, and one of the foremost men of that town in his time. Four children have been born to Mr. and Mrs. Gunnison. Their eldest daughter, Belle G. Gunnison, born in Goshen, December 30, 1868, was educated in the schools of that town and Newport, and afterward for a time was a teacher. Later on she was appointed to a position in the Newport postoffice; she married, May 8, 1902, William H. Nourse. Their second child, Sadie H. Gunnison, was born in Goshen, June 9, 1870. She graduated from Newport High School, afterward taught school three years and then received an appointment as manager of the Newport telephone exchange. Their

JOHN V. GUNNISON.

third daughter, Claora A. Gunnison, was born in Goshen, December 20, 1873, and was educated in the public schools of that town and Newport and the Bradford Female Seminary at Bradford, Massachusetts. She also became a teacher in the public schools and later was made assistant in Newport high school. She married, June 28, 1898, Rev. Sheridan Watson Bell, a minister of the Methodist Episcopal Church, whose home was Xenia, Ohio. Their children are: Corinne Gunnison, Alice Virginia, Clara Elizabeth. Alice M., fourth child of John V. and Angie (Carr) Gunnison. was born in Goshen, April 11, 1877, and died May 30, 1895, while a student in Newport high school.

KITTREDGE The ancestor of the Kittredge family of this article was a pioneer settler of Billerica, Massachusetts, in 1660. The family was prolific, and now its members are found in nearly all parts of the United States. Many of the name, to the present time, have been physicians, some of them becoming prominent, and are particularly well known in New England.

(I) John Kittredge was a seaman (bone setter); was forced to leave England because of practicing his profession. which was contrary to law. He received a grant of five acres of land in the town of Billerica, Massachusetts, September 25, 1660. John Parker is called "his Master." His house lot was "Ten acres of land on ye south-east of bare hill." He had "also four acres of meadow all which is bounded with Shawshin road, east." In July, 1663, the town "granted more to him, that instead of tenne poles of land, which he should have had upon ye township (by willm pattin's house-lot) to set a shop upon that he now shall have it added to his house-lot upon the south of it." His first grant within that part of Billerica which was afterward Tewksbury, where his descendants were located, was in December, 1661, "sixty and four acres, lying on ye east side of ailwife brook, and upon ye south side ye highway as you go to globe hill." This home lot of John Kittredge was a mile south-east of the village, and the other grant, beyond Pattenville, near the Shawshin. He married, November 2, 1664, Mary Littlefield, who was born December 14, 1646, probably the daughter of Francis Littlefield, of Woburn. Ralph Hill calls her granddaughter in his will. The children of this marriage were: John, James. Daniel, Jonathan, and Benoni. John Kittredge died October 18, 1676, and his widow married John French.

(II) John (2), eldest child of John (1) Kittredge and Mary (Littlefield) Kittredge, was born in Billerica, January 24, 1666. The record states that "Doct. John Kittredge dyed" April 27, 1714. He married, August 3, 1685, Hannah French, born January 20, 1664, daughter of John and Hannah (Burridge) French, of Billerica. She died October 9, 1745, aged eight-one. Their children were: John, James, Hannah (died young), Jacob, Hannah, Joseph, Jonathan, William, Abigail, Jane, Marah, and Francis. Jonathan was killed by the Indians in Lovewell's fight at Pigwaket, in 1725.

(III) Francis, youngest child of John (2) and Hannah (French) Kittredge, was born in Billerica, October 27, 1706. His first wife Lydia died August 1, 1736; and he married, before 1740, Susanna Snow. She married, second, a Phelps, of Andover, and third, Thomas Kidder. The thirteen children of Francis Kittredge were: Francis, Josiah, Zephaniah, Lydia, Solomon, Reuben (died young), Jessoniah, Susanna (died young), Susannah, Rebecca, Reuben, Josiah, and Abial.

(IV) Solomon, fourth son and fifth child of Francis and Lydia Kittredge, was born in Billerica, Massachusetts, June 9, 1736; and died in Amherst, New Hampshire, August 24, 1792. About 1766, he removed to that part of Amherst, New Hampshire, now called Mont Vernon. He was a blacksmith, and a man of considerable prominence in the Northwest parish. He was selectman in 1777, and one of a committee of three to procure soldiers for the Continental army. He was an influential church member, and an independent thinker. He married, May 14, 1755, Tabitha Ingalls, of Andover, who died May 8, 1794, aged fifty-nine years. They had twelve children, and their grandchildren were very numerous. Their children were: Solomon, Zephaniah, Tabitha, Josiah, Phebe, Stephen, Lydia, Ingalls, Betsey, Peter, Asa, and Sally.

(V) Solomon (2), eldest child of Solomon (1) and Tabitha (Ingalls) Kittredge, was born in Billerica, Massachusetts, in 1755, and died in Mont Vernon, New Hampshire, October 22, 1845, aged ninety. He removed with his father to Amherst in 1766, and at the age of twenty enlisted in the Continental army. He was a member of Captain Crosby's company, of Colonel Reed's regiment, and was present at the battle of Bunker Hill; and in 1777 was a private in Captain Bradford's company of Colonel Moses Nichol's regiment at the battle of Bennington. He was taken prisoner by the British and Indians at the "Cedars" in Canada, May 19, 1776, and shamefully treated. His clothing was mostly taken from him, but he managed to escape and reached his home in a destitute condition, having neither hat, coat nor shoes. He was a patriotic citizen and a brave soldier. He married, first, in 1777, Anna Kittredge; he married, second, April 13, 1815, Betsey Holt. The children, all by the first wife, were: Solomon, Anna, Susan, Thomas, Josiah, Jeremiah, Harriet, Hezekiah, Zephaniah, Lucy and Betsy.

(VI) Deacon Josiah, fifth child and third son of Solomon (2) and Anna (Kittredge) Kittredge, was born in Mont Vernon, 1787, and died in Mont Vernon, 1836. He married first, December 27, 1812, Hannah Mace; he married second, Nancy Cochran. She died 1829, and he married, third, September 1, 1830, Relief Bachelder. He had nine children born to him: Hannah, Mary Ann, Franklin F., Ingalls, Elizabeth, Charles (died young), Charles A., Nancy, and Harriet.

(VII) Charles Alfred, eighth child and fourth son of Deacon Josiah and Nancy (Cochran) Kittredge, was born in Mont Vernon, August 24, 1829, and died in Nashua, December 31, 1898. His mother died when he was about six months old, and his father when he was six years old. Left an orphan, he was bound out to his uncle Fletcher, of Amherst. This uncle was a strict and stern man, and the boy found his lot an unhappy one. Winter nights he counted the stars through an opening in the roof of the room where he slept, and in the morning on waking he often found his bed covered with snow. At the age of fourteen he exercised his legal right to choose a guardian, and selected Captain Timothy Kittredge, of Mont Vernon, with whom he lived several years. He went to Lowell, Massachusetts, and worked for a baker, and on the outbreak of the great excitement over the discovery of gold in California he prepared to go there. In 1850 he went from New York to the Isthmus of Panama by steamer, crossed to the Pacific side on foot, and there took a boat for San Francisco. The ship ran short of water and was compelled to put into the Sandwich Islands for a supply. There Mr. Kittredge met his relative, Mrs. Stearns, daughter of Timothy Kittredge, who with her husband, were the first missionaries to the island. After arriving at San Francisco, Mr. Kittredge worked for a carpenter, and later was a cook in mining camps. In 1853 he returned and settled in Concord, New Hampshire, where he engaged in the grocery business with John Nichols. In 1864 he removed to Mont Vernon, where he carried on a meat and provision business until 1867, when he engaged in the same business at Milford. In 1872 he went to Nashua and engaged in the same business, carrying it on for sixteen years, and then retiring on account of ill health. He was a stanch Republican, and active in the councils of his party, both state and local. May 15, 1853, he was married, in the First Baptist Church of Lowell, Massachusetts, to Maria E. Chase, who was born in Lowell, 1829, daughter of John Chase, who was a captain in the War of 1812, and also in the Florida war. She died November, 1899. Four children were born of this union: Charles W. (died in infancy), Adelaide M., Frank E., and Frederick L., both further mentioned below.

(VIII) Dr. Frank Everett Kittredge, third child and second son of Charles A. and Maria E. (Chase) Kittredge, was born in Concord, New Hampshire, May 8, 1862, and was educated in the common schools of Nashua. In 1882 he matriculated at the University of Pennsylvania, where he was graduated from the medical department with the class of 1885. He at once began practice at Center Harbor, New Hampshire, where he remained until 1889, when he moved to Nashua, where he now has a large and successful business, and makes a specialty of treatment of diseases of the nose, throat, and ear. He is a member of the following named organizations: The American Medical Association; the New Hampshire and Nashua Medical societies, the New England Otological Society, and the New Hampshire Surgical Club. He was one of the early presidents of the Nashua Medical Society. In Masonry he has attained the thirty-second degree. He is also a member of Penachuck Lodge, No. 44, Independent Order of Odd Fellows. For many years he has been an attendant at the Congregational Church.

He married, in Nashua, December 21, 1887, Mary Lizzie Combs, who was born in Nashua, November 1, 1865, daughter of James B. and Mary Jane (Donovan) Combs, and granddaughter of David Combs, one of the earliest settlers of that part of Dunstable which later became Nashua, at one time being the owner of nearly all the land which constitutes what is now the south part of the city of Nashua. They have one child, Helen C., born November 10, 1898.

(VIII) Frederick Lincoln Kittredge, youngest son of Charles A. and Maria E. (Chase) Kittredge, was born in Mont Vernon, January 18, 1865. He accompanied his parents on their removal to Milford, and afterward to Nashua. His education was obtained in the public schools in Nashua, where he prepared for business life. In September, 1884, when nineteen years of age, he went to Denton, Texas, where he was employed two years in the First National Bank. Returning to New Hampshire, he remained a short time, and then went back to Texas and went into the mercantile business. After tarrying there a year he then settled in Rochester, New York, where he engaged in preparing and putting up medicine in cases for family use. This business he carried on successfully for three years. In December, 1904, he became a member of The Stationery Supply Company of Rochester, New York, dealers in papers and typewriter supplies, with which he has since been connected. He is an energetic and reliable business man, and a respected member of the Brick Presbyterian Church. He is a member of Valley Lodge, No. 109, Ancient Free and Accepted Masons; Hamilton Chapter, No. 62, Royal Arch Masons, and Monroe Commandery, Knights Templar, No. 12, of Rochester. He married, October 24, 1894, Marion Niven, born in Rochester, March 26, 1868, daughter of James M. and Mary (Robinson) Niven, of Rochester, New York. She is a member of the Brick Presbyterian Church, and Monroe Chapter, Order of the Eastern Star, in both of which organizations she takes an active part.

EVERETT

One of the families of New England who is distinguished for the quality of its members is that of the Everetts. A high moral tone and intellectual qualities above mediocrity have graced many of the names, and two scions of this ancient lineage—Edward Everett and Edward Everett Hale—rank among the first citizens of the Republic.

(I) Richard Everett, the immigrant ancestor of the family in America, came to New England as early as 1636, although no definite information has yet been obtained as to the time of his arrival, or from what part of England he came. From the fact that he was for several years in the employ of William Pynchon, that Pynchon himself was connected by marriage with the Everard family of county Essex, England, and that Richard was a very common baptismal name in the same Everard family, it is surmised that Richard Everett was born in county Essex. Tradition says that Richard Everett first settled in Watertown, Massachusetts, and the memorandum of the deed shows that Richard Evered, of Dedham, owned land in Cambridge. Hence, it is inferred that he may have resided near the dividing line between Cambridge and Watertown, and in changing that line, his residence may have been changed from one town to the other.

In the year 1636 he was with William Pynchon, who led a party of settlers and their families to the place called by the Indians, Agawam, near Springfield, Massachusetts. There he made his mark as one of the white witnesses to the Indian deed, conveying the land to William Pynchon, Henry Smith and John Burr, July 15, 1636. On August 18, 1636, he attended at Watertown the first recorded meeting of the new town, called by them "Contentment," but by the general court named Dedham. In early records his name was often spelled Euered. March 20, 1637, a town meeting at Springfield ordered John Searl and Richard Everett to lay out twenty-four acres of mowing marsh for Mr. Pynchon. The records of the two towns of Springfield and Dedham show that he frequently passed from one to the other, and that he was a person of much importance in each of them. The number of entries in the records concerning him is so large as to preclude any enumeration of them. After 1643 he resided continuously in Dedham. He and his wife were received into the church in Dedham, March 6, 1646. May 6 of the same year he was admitted freeman, and from that time on served as a town officer, and on town committees, frequently called upon to lay out lots and roads. The first tax found against him is for his "countrey rate," in 1648, when his house was valued at £4: 6: 10, being the fifty-seventh in point of value, out of eighty; and his tax was 3s., being the seventy-eight out of ninety persons assessed. In 1660 his tax was third in amount assessed, out of eighty-seven names. January 1, 1651, he was elected one of the three surveyors and constable. In 1652 and 1653 he was again constable. In 1655 he was again elected surveyor. January 1, 1661, he was elected selectman. In 1652 he served on a committee to lay out the way between Dedham and Braintree. In 1659 he was one of a committee of three to act with a similar committee from Dorchester to lay out the highway between Dedham and Dorchester, and he was also on a committee of eight to lay out two thousand acres granted by the town to the Indians at Natick. In 1664 he served on more land committees.

In June, 1660, he was granted land adjoining Neponset plain, and northward thereof, or if that is already divided, at a place called "the twenty-acre plain." In March the proprietors of Woolomonupake (Wrentham) drew their lots. He drew lot No. 8, containing eleven and one-half acres. At a division of land at Medfield he drew lot No. 70, which appears to have been in the present town of Norfolk. In 1669 the town bought from Philip Sagamore, all his rights in the lands within the town bounds, not yet purchased, for £17:8, and the eighty town proprietors were assessed this amount. Richard Everett's share was 6s 9½d. In 1667 he collected from the town 20s for killing two wolves. Richard Everett died July 3, 1682. He made his will May 12, 1680, and it was proved July 25, 1682. His inventory amounted to £277: 15: 11. He married (first), Mary, whose surname is unknown; (second), in Springfield, June 29, 1643, Mary Winch. She came to America from England at the age of fifteen, in the "Francis" of Ipswich, April, 1638, with the family of Rowland Stebbins. The children by the first wife were: John, Israel (died young), Mary, Samuel, Sarah (died young), and James; by the second wife: Sarah, Abigail, Israel, Ruth and Jedediah.

(II) Captain John, eldest child of Richard and Mary (Winch) Everett, was baptized the fifteenth day of the first month, 1646, in Dedham, Massachusetts, and died there June 17, 1715. His name appears first in the town records on the tax list of 1662. In 1668 and 1674 he received small grants of land. He is named on a committee to run the line between Dedham and Dorchester in 1682-85-86-91-94 and 97; and in 1684-85 on a committee to buy of Josias, sachem, a right of land south of Neponset river. In 1685 he and his brother Samuel paid 7s 8d for clearing the Indian title to their father's land. He was one of the committee to lay out highways in 1685-86: surveyor of highways in 1704 and 1705, and tithingman in 1700. He is first styled captain in 1693 in the town records of Dedham. During King William's war he was called into active service to command a company of men stationed in New Hampshire and Maine, to protect the inhabitants from the Indians. After the massacre at Oyster River (Dover), New Hampshire, in July, 1694, Captain John Everett had command of a company raised to assist in protecting the frontier from further attack by the Indians. He was stationed at Kittery, Maine. In the latter part of 1696 a petition was presented to the Massachusetts general court by Samuel Wheelwright and others, of Wells, Maine, requesting that Captain Everett and his soldiers, then stationed there, might help them rebuild their fort. This petition was granted. This probably closed his military service. His will was dated August 16, 1710, and proved July 7, 1715.

He married, in Dedham, May 13, 1662, Elizabeth Pepper, daughter of Robert and Elizabeth (Johnson) Pepper, of Roxbury. She was born May 25, 1645, and died April 1, 1714, at Dedham. Their children, recorded at Dedham, were: Elizabeth, Hannah, Bethia, John, William, Israel and Richard.

(III) Deacon John (2), fourth child and eldest son of Captain John (1) and Elizabeth (Pepper) Everett, was born in Dedham, June 9, 1676, and died there March 20, 1751, aged seventy-five. He was selectman 1724-32. His name appears on the valuation and assessment list in 1727-32-42; also in 1729 on a petition to the general court for a new parish in the south part of the town. This, the second parish of Dedham, was established in 1730, and John Everett was moderator of the first meeting. He was also appointed an assessor. June 20, 1736, he was dismissed from the First Church of Dedham to the Second Church, of which he was the first deacon. His will was dated January 1, 1750, and proved April 2, 1751. He married (first), January 3, 1700, Mary Browne, who died November 27, 1748, aged about seventy. He married (second), August 31, 1749, Mrs. Mary Bennett, of Wrentham. His children, all by the first wife, were: John, Joseph, Ebenezer, Eleazer (died young), Mercy, Eleazer, Edward, Hannah, Abigail and Mary.

(IV) Deacon Ebenezer, third son and child of Deacon John (2) and Mary (Browne) Everett, was born in Dedham, August 5, 1707, and died June 19, 1778, aged seventy-one. In 1731 Ebenezer Everett, of Dedham, bought lot No. 47 in Suncook, New Hampshire, for £55; in 1732, forty acres in Methuen, Massachusetts, for £160; in 1734, twelve acres in Methuen adjoining his previous purchase for £48. In 1738-39 he was called of Methuen, but in 1745-52 he was again called of Dedham, when he sold land in Methuen. He was dismissed from the First Church of Methuen, and his first wife, Joanna, from the First Church of Andover, to the Second Church of Dedham, March 22, 1741. He was chosen deacon of the Second Church, November 30, 1760, and was selectman 1760-64. His will, dated January 10, 1776, was proved July 18, 1778. He married March 9, 1734, at North Andover, Joanna Stevens, daughter of Ebenezer and Sarah (Sprague) Stevens. She was born in September, 1711, and died June 21, 1791, aged eighty. Their children were: Ebenezer, John, Asa, Andrew, Joanna, Phinehas, Aaron, Moses and Oliver.

(V) Phinehas, sixth child and fifth son of Deacon Ebenezer and Joanna (Stevens) Everett, was born in Dedham, September 1, 1745, and died at Montville, Maine, May 27, 1813, aged sixty-eight. He removed to Rutland, Massachusetts, and about 1805 to Montville, Maine. He died suddenly in his chair after supper. He married, June 6, 1770, Mary Clap, daughter of Seth and Mary* (Bullard) Clap, of Walpole. She was born January 28, 1742, and died in April, 1833, in the ninety-first year of her age. They had six children: Mary, Phinehas, Betsey, Ebenezer, Cynthia and Sarah.

(VI) Phinehas (2), second child and eldest son of Phinehas (1) and Mary (Clap) Everett, was born in Rutland, Massachusetts, April 22, 1776, and died in Bradford, New Hampshire, July 30, 1830, aged sixty-four. He was a farmer at Stockbridge, Vermont, and Bradford, New Hampshire. His will, dated July 29, 1830, was proved the following month. He married (first), Lydia Bullard, who was born in Oakham, Massachusetts, and died in Deering, New Hampshire; (second), Hannah Sawyer, who was born in Dracut, Massachusetts, February 10, 1773, and died September 27, 1860, aged eighty-seven. She was the daughter of Josiah and Lydia

Sawyer. The children of this union were: Alice Lydia, Lucius and Horace.

(VII) Lucius, second child of Phinehas (2) and Hannah Sawyer Everett, was born in Stockbridge, Vermont, April 16, 1804, and died at Dover, New Hampshire, April 14, 1878, aged seventy-four. He was a carriagemaker and removed to Dover, New Hampshire, and in partnership with John O. Janes carried on an extensive factory. After the death of Mr. James, he continued the business. He married, October 15, 1826, at Charlestown, Massachusetts, Judith Delano, daughter of Isaac and Elizabeth (White) Delano. She was born in Duxbury, Massachusetts, October 15, 1803. They had seven children: Charles Edward, Elizabeth Ann, Walter, Clarendon Adams, Helen Frances, Lucius Theodore and Mary Low. All the sons were in the war of the Rebellion.. Charles Edward enlisted in Company K, Eleventh New Hampshire Volunteer Infantry, in Dover, August 7, 1862; was mustered in September 5, 1862, as a private; appointed second lieutenant, December 24, 1862; first lieutenant, September 1, 1863; captain of Company D, May 15, 1865; mustered out June 4, 1865, as first lieutenant of Company K. He died in Dover, April 26, 1892. Walter was a colonel of a Massachusetts regiment. Clarendon A. is mentioned below. Lucius Theodore enlisted in Dover, August 7, 1862, and was mustered in September 2, 1862, as a corporal; appointed sergeant; was transferred to Company E, Seventh Regiment Invalid Corps, February 15, 1864; and was discharged June 29, 1865, at Washington, D. C.

(VIII) Clarendon Adams, fourth child and third son of Lucius and Judith (Delano) Everett, was born in Dover, New Hampshire, February 21, 1835, and died in Portsmouth, November 28, 1883. He engaged in the carriage business with his father in Dover, and in 1870 established himself in the same business in Portsmouth, continuing until his death. He enlisted at Dover, August 8, 1862, in Company K, Eleventh Regiment, New Hampshire Volunteer Infantry, was mustered in September 2, 1862, as first sergeant; and was discharged for disability March 5, 1863, at Newport News, Virginia. He enlisted at Dover, December 10, 1863, in Company A, Thirteenth Regiment Veteran Reserve Corps, was mustered in the same day, and was discharged November 17, 1865, at Boston, Massachusetts. He married, at Dover, Mary Josephine Clark, daughter of Joseph and Nancy Clark. She was born in Dover, February 9, 1841, and died at Dover, September, 1885. Their children were: Horace Delano, Theodore, Carrie Ordway and Edith. Of these, Horace D., born June 24, 1860, attended the public schools of Dover, Phillip's Academy, and Harvard University, but he did not remain to graduate from the latter. He married Sarah M. Bock, of Boston, Massachusetts, and they have one child, Margaret.

(IX) Theodore, second son and child of Clarendon A. and Mary J. (Clark) Everett, was born in Dover, New Hampshire, October 2, 1862. He received his primary education in the common schools, his higher education at Phillips Exeter Academy, and his medical education at Harvard University, where he graduated M. D. in 1888. Subsequently he spent a year at New York Medical College, and practiced medicine two years in Haverhill, Massachusetts. In 1891 he relinquished medicine and became a partner with his brother Horace D. in the Everett Press Company of Boston, since incorporated as the Everett Printing and Publishing Company of Boston, of which Horace D. Everett is president, and Theodore Everett treasurer. They employ over fifty persons, and do a thriving business. Dr. Everett resides in Arlington, Massachusetts, where he is a member of the First Congregational Church, and a member of its finance committee. He married, September 20, 1888, at New Hartford, Connecticut, Luna E. Vickery, who was born in Unity, Maine, December 10, 1861, daughter of John and Abigail W. (March) Vickery, of Bedford, Maine. They have two children: Caroline Vickery and Judith Delano.

EVANS This honored Welsh name has been borne by many citizens of New Hampshire, and many families not related upon this side of the Atlantic are found often in the same neighborhoods. The stock is good, and the state owes something of its high standing among commonwealths to the moral and intellectual vigor of those of this name.

(I) Henry Evans is believed to be the progenitor of the family herein traced, but little is found of record concerning him. He was probably an old man, coming with a son to America. He settled in that part of Malden, Massachusetts, which subsequently became a part of Reading.

(II) Nathaniel, son of Henry Evans, came with his father from Wales, and settled in Malden, Massachusetts. His was one of the ten families set off from Malden in 1729 and annexed to Reading, constituting the present village of Greenwood. He died in 1710. He was married before 1680, to Elizabeth, daughter of Samuel (1) Dunton. Tradition says: "her temper was less amiable than her looks," and the neighbors said: "Evans had spoiled his family for the sake of a pretty face." She survived him about thirty years, dying in 1740. They had a son, Nathaniel, and John Evans, who married Sarah Sweetser, in 1719, is supposed to have been also their son.

(III) Nathaniel (2), son of Nathaniel (1) and Elizabeth (Dunton) Evans, was born 1680, and succeeded his father on the original homestead, where he died in 1750. He was married in 1704 to Abigail Townsend, who died in the same year as himself. Their first four children are recorded in Malden, and all in Reading, namely: Abigail, Sarah, Andrew, Elizabeth (died young), David, Elizabeth, Jonathan and Mary.

(IV) Jonathan, seventh child and third son of Nathaniel (2) and Abigail (Townsend) Evans, was born 1722, in Malden, and reared in Reading, though on the same farm. He lived on a farm at the southerly end of Smith's Pond, his residence being near the present Boston & Maine railroad bridge. The track crosses the site of the cellar. He lived to the age of seventy-five years, dying 1797. He was married in 1744 to Eunice, daughter of David and Martha Green. It is said of her: "This woman had more dignity of manners, and was more reserved and discreet in conversation than her husband." Their children were: Jonathan, Thomas, Jonas, Amos, Samuel, Eunice, Timothy, Sarah, Lois and Abigail.

(V) Jonathan (2), eldest child of Jonathan (1) and Eunice (Green) Evans, was born 1746, in Reading, and settled in Winchendon, Massachusetts. He enlisted in 1776 as a Revolutionary soldier, and was in the service at Ticonderoga in that year. He was at Cambridge in garrison in 1777.

(VI) Daniel, son of Jonathan Evans, was born in Massachusetts, in 1776. He and his wife were among the earlier settlers of Shelburne, New Hampshire, where they made their permanent home.

Daniel Evans married Phila Clemons, daughter of Benjamin Clemons, who was in the New Hampshire Continental line, and received a government pension during his later years. They had eleven children, but their names are not recorded. Daniel Evans died at Shelburne, New Hampshire, November 29, 1846, and his widow survived him thirty years, dying at Shelburne, April 8, 1876, aged ninety-eight years, four months and twenty-five days.

(VII) Otis, son of Daniel and Phila (Clemons) Evans, was born at Shelburne, New Hampshire March 12, 1811. He was a farmer, born and bred to that vocation, intelligent, prosperous and well informed, and passed all his life on the land where he was born and died. On May 29, 1834, Otis Evans married Martha Pinkham, daughter of Daniel and Esther (Chesley) Pinkham, who was born at Jackson, New Hampshire, January 15, 1815. Her father's name is imperishably associated with the White Mountains. Daniel Pinkham was born in Madbury, New Hampshire, in 1776, and died in Lancaster, New Hampshire, June 25, 1855. He was a farmer and blacksmith and a licensed Free Baptist preacher, laboring chiefly in Bartlett, Jackson, Randolph, Jefferson and Lancaster. Between 1824 and 1834 he built the state road from Adams, now Jackson, to Durand, now Randolph, receiving therefore by special act of the legislature the lands now known as Pinkham's Grant, near the easterly base of Mount Washington, and also other state lands. To Otis and Martha (Pinkham) Evans were born three children: Daniel P., December 6, 1835, who died April 30, 1889; William W., September 17, 1837, who died November 29, 1861; and Alfred R., whose sketch follows. Otis Evans died in Shelburne, October 13, 1886, and his wife died there August 7, 1885.

(VIII) Alfred Randall, youngest of the three sons of Otis and Martha (Pinkham) Evans, was born at Shelburne, New Hampshire, March 21, 1849. He was educated in the common schools of his town, the academy at Lancaster, New Hampshire, the Nichols Latin School at Lewiston, Maine, and was graduated from Dartmouth College, class of 1872. He read law in Gorham, New Hampshire, was admitted to the Coos county bar in the spring of 1875, and has been in active practice at Gorham since that time. In 1889 he was admitted to practice before the United States circuit court. On January 1, 1895, he was appointed by the governor and council judge of probate for Coos county, which position he still holds. Judge Evans is an ardent Republican, and represented Shelburne in the state legislature in 1874-75-78. In 1902 he received the nomination from both political parties, and also received every ballot cast for delegate from Gorham to the state constitutional convention. In January, 1807, Judge Evans was appointed quartermaster-general upon the staff of Governor Charles M. Floyd. He was served his town as chairman of the board of selectmen, superintendent of schools, library trustee, is president of the Gorham board of trade, and has served it in various other capacities. Upon the organization of the Berlin National Bank at Berlin, New Hampshire, in 1891, he was chosen president, and held the position for ten years, declining further election. He is now the president of the Gorham Savings Bank at Gorham. Judge Evans is the president of the Berlin-Gorham Bar Association, is an honorary member of the New Hampshire Veterans' Association, belongs to the New Hampshire Club of Boston, and is a Mason of the thirty-second degree, serving for thirty-three years as secretary of Gorham Lodge, No. 73, Ancient Free and Accepted Masons. He attends the Congregational Church. On June 1, 1880, Alfred R. Evans married Dora J. Briggs.

(Second Family.)

EVANS Evan is the Welsh equivalent of John, therefore Evans is the Welsh Johns, or Johnson. The Evanses of the present day in America are the progeny of various ancestors who came to this country from the British Isles at different times.

(I) David Evans, the progenitor of the Evans family of this article, was of Charlestown, Massachusetts, but whether he was the immigrant ancestor of the family cannot now be determined. He married, September 22, 1729, Abigail Walker, born in Woburn, August 21, 1703, daughter of Timothy Walker of Woburn, and probably a cousin of Rev. Timothy Walker, the first minister of Penacook, later Rumford, now Concord, New Hampshire. David and Abigail lived for a time in Woburn, where one or both of their sons were born; and in 1731 removed to Penacook. Further records of David are wanting. He probably lived and died in Penacook. His two sons were David and John.

(II) David (2), eldest son of David (1) and Abigail (Walker) Evans, was born in Woburn, Massachusetts, before 1731, and grew up in Penacook, New Hampshire, where he was taken by his parents when an infant. His name is frequently mentioned in the histories of Concord. He and his brother John were members of that famous organization known as "Roger's Rangers," in which John held the rank of sergeant. They participated in that expedition sent by General Amherst against St. Francis Indians, and were among the few survivors of the terrible homeward march through the wilderness where the greater part of their number perished from starvation and exposures to the frosts of winter. At the time of the settlement of Pigwacket, now Fryeburg, Maine, 1763, David was unmarried and lived with his brother John. It is said that about two years after the first settlement, reckoning from the autumn of 1762, when some of the men came through to Pigwacket and made preparations to receive their families in the spring of 1863, David Evans and Nathaniel Merrill, another young bachelor, went away and brought back wives with them. In one of the diaries of Rev. Timothy Walker, of Penacook is the entry: "Aug. 27, 1764, matrimonio Junxi (joined in marriage) David Evans and Catherine Walker." David died in Fryeburg, March 21, 1810, aged about eighty years. Catherine died November 15, 1798. Their children were: Sarah, David, Elizabeth, Timothy and Ruth.

(III) Timothy, fourth child and second son of David and Catherine (Walker) Evans, was born in Pigwacket, July 30, 1772, and moved to Sweden, Maine, in 1812. He married Polly, daughter of Joshua Gamage of Fryeburg, and they had eight children: Peter, Polly, James, Abigail, Sarah Ann, Caroline, David and Eliza.

(IV) James, third child and second son of Timothy and Polly (Gamage) Evans, was born in Fryeburg, June 20, 1805, and died in Sweden, March 24, 1870. He was seven years old when his father removed with his family to Sweden. He married Caroline E. Eastman, of North Conway, New Hampshire, daughter of Abiathar and Susan (Durgin) Eastman, by whom he had eight children: Charles, John H., Susan R., Samuel E., Cavlin E., George Meserve, Susan Isabel and Mary Arabell (twins).

(V) John Henry, second son and child of James and Caroline E. (Eastman) Evans, was born in Sweden, April 16, 1834, and died October 2, 1889, in Sweden. He settled in Sweden and was a farmer and blacksmith. He married, October 23, 1859, Lydia C. Tucker, who was born in Portland, Maine, April 2, 1837, daughter of Captain Lemuel and Statira Tucker, of Portland, Maine. They had ten children: Ida I., died in infancy; Henry J., Mary Ellen; Carrie G., died in infancy; Albert Tucker, died at two and one-half years; Frank Webster, John Conkey, Charles Maurice, Walter Eastman and Eva Belle.

(VI) Frank Webster Evans, M. D., sixth child and third son of John H. and Lydia C. (Tucker) Evans, was born in Sweden, Maine, August 20, 1868. He attended the common schools and the academy at Bridgton, Maine, and then took a course of lectures in the Maine Medical College, from which he went to Dartmouth College, and there received the degree of Doctor of Medicine, November 23, 1897. Soon after graduation he settled in Coos, in the town of Stratford, New Hampshire, where he has since resided, and by care, skill and strict attention to business, has gained the confidence and esteem of the citizens of that region and now has a flourishing practice. He is secretary and treasurer of the Coos Medical Society, and a member of the New Hampshire Medical Society, and the American Medical Association. He is a Mason of the thirty-second degree, and a member of the following named Masonic bodies: Evening Star Lodge, No. 37, of Colebrook; North Star Royal Arch Chapter, No. 16; Evening Star Council, No. 13, Royal and Select Masters; North Star Commandery, Knights Templar, of Lancaster; Edward A. Raymond Consistory, Sublime Princes of the Royal Secret, of Nashua; and Mt. Sinai Temple, Ancient Arabic Order of the Mystic Shrine, of Montpelier, Vermont. Also of Cumberland Lodge, No. 30, Independent Order of Odd Fellows, of Bridgton, Maine, and Strafford Lodge, No. 30, Knights of Pythias, of Strafford.

He married, at Strafford, June 12, 1901, Olive L. Beecher, who was born in Barnet, Vermont, August 10, 1879, daughter of Victor and Amanda (Mulliken) Beecher. She was a successful school teacher and musical instructor before her marriage, and for eight years was organist of the Baptist Church of Strafford. They have one child, Beatrice L., born September 27, 1905.

EVANS This is the name of an extensive family connection or clan of Celtic or ancient British blood, in Wales. Through intermarriages with Saxon and Norman families, their descendants have become essentially English. Many of the name emigrated to this country, and their descendants are found in nearly every state in the Union. In the early days the Welsh had no surnames, but used the patronymic with the conjunction "ap"; thus: Evan, a son of John, would be called "Evan-ap-John": and Thomas, the son of Evan, would be called "Thomas-ap-Evan." When in the time of Queen Elizabeth the British Parliament enacted a law requiring every citizen of the realm to take a surname, it was very common for Welshmen to assume their fathers' names, dropping the use of the "ap." In time this came to be called Evans, and so it has remained.

(I) Elijah Evans' home is supposed to have been near St. Albans or Burlington, Vermont. He kept his own counsel, was quiet and reticent about his own affairs, and it is not known that any of his acquaintances in later life knew where his parents lived, or where he spent his years of young manhood. Some time in middle life he settled in the town of Wilmington, Essex county, New York, where he married Abigail Lawrence. By her he had eight children: George, Sophronia, Oliver, Rhoda Ann, Lucius, William, Henry, and Mary.

(II) Henry, seventh child and fifth son of Elijah and Abigail (Lawrence) Evans, was born in Wilmington, New York, September 2, 1834. He attended the common schools until sixteen years of age, and then obtained employment in a chair factory where he worked about eighteen months. At eighteen years of age he went to Somersworth, New Hampshire, where he followed house painting for nine years, and established a furniture business. He then sold his interests and went to Berlin, Wisconsin, where he remained a year. He then removed to South Berwick, Maine, where he carried on the painting and furniture business for nine years more. In 1876 he settled in Rochester, New Hampshire, and engaged in the furniture trade, and has since done a large and lucrative business. About 1900 he took his son William into partnership, and since that time they have done business under the firm names of the Evans Furniture Company. In 1905 Mr. Evans established a hardware business in the Dodge Block, which is conducted under the style of Henry Evans & Company. Mr. Evans is a man of strict integrity and sound business principles, and his success in life comes to him as the reward of well directed energy and industry joined with a proper regard and attention to his rights and duties. He is a member of Libanus Lodge, No. 49, Free and Accepted Masons, of Somersworth. He is a Republican in politics. He married, first, Isabel E. Blodgett, daughter of Wilder and Eliza J. (Ellinwood) Blodgett. She died 1901. He married, second, Annie E., widow of George Willey. Three children were born of the first wife: William W., married Emma Ellis, of Rochester; Lillian J., and George H. William W. is with his father in the furniture business; Lillian J. married James B. Young, of Rochester; George H. is a printer in Lynn, Massachusetts.

NIMS This old French name was transplanted to New England at an early date because of the persecution of the Hugenots in France. Their descendants may feel the same pride which is cherished by the offsprings of the Puritans, as in both cases the immigrants left their native land and all their possessions for religion's sake. The French immigrants proved just as earnest and patriotic citizens of the colonies as did their English brothers, and the descendants of this family have been among the most worthy American citizens.

(I) Godfroi De Nismes (Godfrey Nims), a French Huguenot, first appeared in North Hampton, Massachusetts, September 4, 1667. There as a boy he was arrested for stealing fruit. He participated in Turner's fight with the Indians, May 18, 1676, and was also a soldier in King Philip's war. He was married (first) in North Hampton, November 6, 1677, to Mrs. Mary (Miller) Williams, daughter of William Miller and widow of Zebediah Williams. He removed to Deerfield, Massachusetts, and there his first wife died April 27, 1688. He was married (second), June 27, 1692, to Mehitable (Smead) Hull, the widow of Jeremiah Hull and daughter of William Smead. The house of Godfrey Nims was burned by the Indians on February 29, 1794, and three of his children were slain or burned with the house. His wife was carried away captive by the

Indians and killed on the way to Canada. He had eleven children in all.

(II) Ebenezer Nims was captured at the destruction of Deerfield, February 29, 1704, as was also his future wife, Sarah Hoyt. She was born May 6, 1686, in Deerfield, and died there January 11, 1761. She was a daughter of David and Sarah (Wilson) Hoyt. While in Canada, Ebenezer Nims was adopted by a squaw. An Indian chief desired to marry Miss Hoyt, but she refused and was married, while still a captive, to Ebenezer, in Canada, where their first child was born. After great difficulty Mr. Nims and his wife were redeemed by Stoddard and Williams, in 1814, after having been captives ten years, and they returned to Deerfield, where he lived on his father's farm for many years. He was born March 14, 1687, in Deerfield, and died there in 1762.

(III) David Nims was married June 20, 1742, to Abigail Hawkes, daughter of Eleazer and Abigail (Wells) Hawkes. She was born October 17, 1719, in Deerfield, and died July 13, 1799, in Sullivan, New Hampshire. David Nims went to Keene with the earliest settlers in 1740, and in that year was granted ten acres of uplands in Keene for the hazarding of his life and estate by living there in order to bring forward the settling of the place. Later he was granted one hundred four acres in that part of the town which is now Roxbury, and this has continued in the possession and occupancy of his descendants down to the present time. He was chosen by the proprietors of Keene as their scribe as early as July 25, 1737, and he was also chosen as the town clerk and treasurer of Keene at the first town meeting, May 2, 1753. He held the office almost continually until 1776. A quaint portrait of him was made by the artist, Jeremiah Stiles, as he used to look upon the street, which portrait now hangs in the city hall at Keene. One of his descendants, the late Colonel F. C. Nims, has placed an elegant monument over his grave in the Washington street Cemetery. He was the father of ten children.

(IV) David (2) Nims was married January 1, 1768, to Jemima Carter, who was born September 14, 1747, in Lancaster, Massachusetts, and died in Roxbury, New Hampshire, January 29, 1832. She was the daughter of Samuel and Jemima (Houghton) Carter. David Nims lived in Roxbury, on the farm originally granted to his father, already mentioned. He had a family of ten children.

(V) Roswell Nims was married January 1, 1810, to Sarah Wilson, who was born April 16, 1789, in Sullivan, New Hampshire, and died October 24, in Keene. Thomas Wilson was the first English settler in Dublin, New Hampshire. Roswell Nims was a prosperous farmer, spending his early life in Sullivan, and his last days were passed on the Beech Hill Farm. He was the father of twelve children.

(VI) Chester Nims was born February 20, 1817, in Keene, and died in that town April 26, 1872. He succeeded his father on the old Beech Hill Farm, and was a successful farmer and prominent in public affairs. He was a man of broad ideas, inflexible integrity, and good administrative ability. He was repeatedly chosen by the town to fill important municipal offices. He served ten years upon the board of selectmen, several years as its chairman. His term of service covered the anxious years of the Civil war. During that period, he was most efficient in procuring enlistments and attending to the wants and needs of wives, widows, and children of the soldiers. His sound judgment of values and the care which he exercised in supervising appropriations and expenditures were highly appreciated throughout his official career.

April 4, 1842, he married Cynthia Maria Wilder, who was born March 16, 1820, in North Leominster, Massachusetts, and died August 11, 1881, in Keene. Their children were: 1. Emily W., born May 23, 1845, married Henry W. Nims, of Keene, has one child, William Chester. 2. Frank W., born September 14, 1848, married Jennie I. Munroe, has two living children: James Alexander and Gladys. 3. Charles R., born July 25, 1851, died May 3, 1855. 4. Mary Elizabeth, born September 23, 1853. 5. George Adams, born November 6, 1855, died April 23, 1906. 6. William Frost, born September 17, 1857, died November 25, 1903. 7. Louis A., see forward. 8. Frederick C., born February 4, 1866, married Harriet Parker, no children.

(VII) Louis Arthur Nims was born October 24, 1862, in Keene. He was educated in the schools of Keene, and fitted himself for an active business life rather than for a profession. He inherited from his father a natural aptitude for business, being a man of sound judgment with respect to values, and a careful calculator in buying and selling. He established a market in Keene, in connection with his brother Fred C., in 1891, and has built up a highly prosperous trade. He has been careful to maintain the highest standards, not only with respect to the quality of the goods which he sells, but also as respects the character and quality of his help and his general methods of doing business. In this way, he has won the respect and good will of the community, which has implicit confidence in him and in his business methods. About two years ago, in 1905, in conjunction with his brother Fred. C., he succeeded to the livery business of his deceased brother, George A., near the Cheshire House, in Keene. Louis attends to the business of the market and Fred. C. manages the stable. Louis has one son in the Worcester (Massachusetts) Polytechnic Institute. He has a handsome residence upon Park avenue, provided with every comfort, where he dispenses a kind and liberal hospitality. He has been much interested in the fire department of Keene, of which he has been eighteen years a member, and has been its chief for two years. He has added greatly to its efficiency and brought it to a high degree of perfection. He is a useful man in many ways and much esteemed by his fellow townsmen. He belongs to several social orders, including the Patrons of Husbandry, the Benevolent and Protective Order of Elks, and the Odd Fellows. He is also a member of the Unitarian Club of Keene. He was married October 14, 1885, in Keene, to Martha A. Cutler, who was born in that town July 14, 1865, daughter of Charles H. and Eliza (Burnham) Cutler. Mr. and Mrs. Nims are the parents of three sons: Stewart A., born April 2, 1887; Robert C., born March 29, 1890, died February 13, 1906; and Oscar B., born February 15, 1892.

POND This good old English name appeared in New England at an early date, and its bearers are now numerous in both eastern and western states. Many of them have won distinction, and all have been reputable citizens.

(I) Robert Pond and his wife Mary were early arrivals at Dorchester, Massachusetts. They had sons Daniel and Robert. The latter settled in

Milton. Mary survived her husband and was married a second time to Edward Shepard, of Cambridge.

(II) Daniel, son of Robert and Mary Pond, settled in Dedham, Massachusetts, about 1652, and on March 30 of that year he purchased land of Nathaniel Fuller. He also owned land in that part of Dedham which was set off as the town of Wrentham in 1661. He died February 4, 1697-98. In 1651 he married Abigail Shepard, daughter of Edward Shepard (previously referred to), by the latter's first union. She died July 5, 1661, and on September 18 of the same year Daniel married for his second wife Ann Edwards, who survived him. The children of his first union were: Abigail, born at Dedham, Massachusetts, May 9, 1652, married March 26, 1678, John Day. Daniel, died March 4, 1661-62. John. Ephraim, baptized July 6, 1656. Rachael, baptized September 5, 1658. Hannah, born July 27, 1660. Those of his second union were: Daniel, born February 17, 1663. Robert, born August 5, 1667. William, born September 20, 1669, probably the William Pond who died in Dedham, November 16, 1723. No record of marriage. Caleb, born December 13, 1672. Joshua, born March 11, 1674, died February 24, 1676. Jabez, born January 6, 1677. Sarah, born May 10, 1679, married, June 14, 1698, Eleazer Holbrook, of Sherborn.

(III) Robert, fifth son and eighth child of Daniel Pond, was born in Dedham, August 5, 1667. He resided in Wrentham, where he followed the occupation of a house carpenter, and he became the owner of considerable real estate. In certain records of deeds he is called captain. His death occurred July 31, 1750, and on August 22 following his son Baruch was appointed executor of his will, which disposed of property valued in the inventory of one hundred and eighty-four pounds. The date of his marriage with Joanna Lawrence, his first wife, does not appear in the records of either Dedham or Wrentham. On January 16, 1728-29, he married for his second wife Abigail Fisher, and his third wife, whom he married November 17, 1747, was Mrs. Sarah Shuttleworth, a widow. His children were: Anne, Sarah, three Roberts, each of whom died young; Ezra, Ichabod, Baruch and Eunice, all of whom were of his first union.

(IV) Ichabod, fifth son and seventh child of Robert and Joanna (Lawrence) Pond, was born in Wrentham, May 31, 1699. In January, 1722, he received by conveyance from his father the latter's estate on Mine Brook, Wrentham, consisting of a valuable farm and a new house, together with the cattle, farm implements and all personal property therein contained. He married (first), May 30, 1721, Milcah Farrington, who was the mother of all his children; (second), May 25, 1747, Deborah Thurston; and (third), September 28, 1762, Mehitable, widow of John Aldis. Her death, which occurred February 26, 1785, was speedily followed by that of her husband, who died in Franklin, May 2, of the same year, leaving no will. He was the father of twelve children: Mercy, born June 11, 1723; Elisha, March 25, 1725; Ichabod, December 3, 1726; Nathan, October 27, 1728; Meletiah, September 12, 1730; Benjamin, March 21, 1732; Esther, March 14, 1734; Eunice, March 1, 1736; Lois, September 17, 1737, married, January 6, 1757, Henry Daniel; Jonathan, October 19, 1740; Eli, February 16, 1743; Amos, June 2, 1745.

(V) Jonathan, sixth son and tenth child of Ichabod and Milcah (Farrington) Pond, was born in Wrentham, October 19, 17·0. He settled in Keene, New Hampshire, where on May 12, 1766, he purchased of Daniel Kingsbury two lots of land, and is supposed to have resided there for the remainder of his life. He was married October 6, 1763, to Thankful Thomson, of Bellingham, Massachusetts, who died at Keene, September, 1820, aged seventy-seven years. She was the mother of seven children, all of whom were probably born in Keene, and their names were: Matilda, Phineas, Thankful, Fransena, Rhoda, Philester and Pamelia.

(VI) Philester, second son and sixth child of Jonathan and Thankful (Thomson) Pond, was baptized in Keene, September 17, 1780. The greater part of his life was spent upon a farm in Keene, but he resided a few years in Orange and he died in Walpole, New Hampshire. He married Rhoda Howard, daughter of Nathan Howard, of Surry, this state, and her death occurred in that town. Their children were: Luman, Thankful, Jonathan, Amos, Henry, Theodocia, Pamelia, William and Mary E.

(VII) Henry, fourth son and fifth child of Philester and Rhoda (Howard) Pond, was born at Keene, in September, 1818. He was first apprenticed to a blacksmith, but not liking that calling he tried the printer's trade in the office of the *Keene Sentinel*, with which he was also dissatisfied, and he finally learned the hatter's trade. Establishing himself in the hat manufacturing business at Winchester, New Hampshire, he remained there a few years. Upon returning to Keene he purchased the Anderson Hat Manufactory where he had learned his trade, and he subsequently acquired large interests in that line of trade, having branch stores in Burlington, St. Albans, Brattleboro, and Rutland, Vermont; in Claremont, New Hampshire, and Greenfield, Massachusetts. He also engaged quite extensively in the manufacture of brick at Keene, and was a successful as well as an able business man. About 1864 he sold the Anderson business on account of failing health and went abroad. Among the changes made in Keene in the decade ending 1860 was that of the Cheshire House, purchased and remodelled by Mr. Pond, who added the south wing with stores on the ground floor and a hall above, forty by seventy-six feet, seventeen feet high, also large stables in the rear. In 1862 Mr. Pond served as representative to the state legislature. He was always interested in the welfare of his town, and no one was more active in promoting its business prosperity than he, attempting more than his health would permit of, and his death occurred in Roxbury, Massachusetts, January, 1866, at the age of forty-eight years. Beaver Brook Lodge, No. 36, Independent Order of Odd Fellows, was instituted at the town hall in Keene, March 17, 1851. "Henry Pond and nine other candidates were at this time initiated into the mysteries of the order." After the initiation the lodge was fully organized for the work of the order, and Henry Pond was appointed left supporter noble grand. About July 14, 1852, the lodge moved into a new hall that Mr. Pond had fitted up in the brick block at the head of Central Square, he having purchased it and added fourteen feet to the west end thereof. This hall was occupied by the lodge until 1883. Mr. Pond was also a member of the Masonic fraternity. In April, 1842, he married Amelia N. Wilson, daughter of Oliver and Nancy Wilson. She died shortly afterwards and he married her sister Harriet, who survived him. Of his second union there were two sons, Charles H., born January 1, 1844, died August 18 of the same year, and Herbert. Mrs. Harriet

Herbert Pond.

[illegible] and was married a second time to a Mr. Briggs, of Keene. She died March 2, 1895, aged sixty-six years, eight months and twenty-eight days.

(VIII) Herbert, second son and child of Henry and Harriet (Wilson) Pond, was born in Keene, August 7, 1848. He was educated at Miss Julia [illegible] private school, the public schools of Keene, including the high school, Powers' private school, [illegible] and Bryant and Stratton's Business College, New York City. Since attaining his majority [illegible] devoted his energies to the care of [illegible] interests in Keene, and he has given [illegible] improving real estate and the [illegible] buildings. Politically he acts [illegible] party. He attends the First Congregational [illegible] of which his wife is a member. [illegible] 1897, he married Mrs. Mertie E[illegible], who was born in Harrisville, [illegible] daughter of Sewall Abijah and [illegible] Seaver, the latter of whom was born [illegible] in this state, October 9, 1838.

[illegible] Seaver came from England in [illegible] and John" in 1633-34, and settled [illegible] Massachusetts. He had a numerous [illegible] sons, Nicholas, dropped the a [illegible] possibly others may have done the [illegible] William settled in Kingston and [illegible] now standing and used for a summer [illegible]. The Seaver genealogy is very [illegible] out the lines of only three of the [illegible] original Robert Seaver and those [illegible] Robert Seaver had four sons and three [illegible] one daughter died in infancy. One line [illegible] as been able to be traced it is as follows: R[illegible], Nathaniel 2, John 3, Nathaniel 4, Abijah 5, [illegible] 6, and Benjamin 7, born in 1795, who [illegible] in the capacity of mayor of Boston. The [illegible] from which those of the name in this sketch [illegible] their ancestry, was Robert 1, Nathaniel 2, [illegible], Nathaniel 4, Abijah 5, Benjamin 6, William [illegible] G. F. 7, William 8, Sewall A. 9, Mertie [illegible] (Seaver) Pond. William Seaver, first of the above mentioned, lived in R[illegible], Massachusetts, and owned considerable property for those [illegible] Seaver street, so called, being a part of the Seaver estate. He married, December 14, 1795, Lucy Heath, and their children were: [illegible], born October 2, 1797, married [illegible] Franklin, New Hampshire, and [illegible] born December 31, 1798 [illegible] born October 4, 1800 [illegible] born January 9, 1802 [illegible] Heath, born [illegible] 4, 1807 [illegible] William Seaver, Jr., son of William and Lucy (Heath) Seaver, of Roxbury, Massachusetts, came to what was then called Nelson, [illegible] now Harrisville, [illegible] He purchased a large farm which [illegible] of the best in the town, and which [illegible] of his [illegible] He married [illegible] Susan Gurler, [illegible] New Hampshire, daughter of Thomas Gurler and [illegible] The Gurlers [illegible] earliest settlers [illegible] section, coming from [illegible] Massachusetts, to Nelson, now Harrisville [illegible] adjoining farms as early as [illegible]. Afterward the Gurlers removed to Keene, New Hampshire. Children of William and Susan (Gurler) Seaver: George W., born in Nelson, November 2, 1823. Lucy Ann, born in Nelson, May [illegible] born in Nelson, [illegible] William W., born in Nelson, July 13, 1831 [illegible] Abijah, born in Nelson, November 12, 1833, died at Harrisville, New Hampshire, June, 1875; Edward [illegible], born in Nelson, May 3, 1840, died unmarried at Harrisville, New Hampshire; Albert Andrew, born in Nelson, May 17, 1841, died in Harrisville, New Hampshire.

PINKHAM. Among other things tradition tells us that the ancestor of the Pinkhams of this article came from the Isle of Wight, but there is no historical evidence to support it. However Richard Pinkham early and his descendants to the ninth and tenth generation are inhabitants of New Hampshire. Staunch dispositions have been characteristics of the members of the race.

(I) Richard Pinkham, the settler, was at Dover as early as 1640, for on October 22, 1640, the inhabitants of Dover established or renewed a formal government, and the name of Richard Pinkham is attached to the document they then prepared. Quint's History of Dover, [illegible] by John Scales, speaking of him in 1852, [illegible] "The spot where he early dwelt is said to [illegible] the same on which stood the Pinkham garrison [illegible] Richard afterwards made his habitation [illegible] precise situation of this is easily pointed out [illegible] as it continued to be the dwelling [illegible] side fell down seven and twenty ye[illegible] event rendered it necessary for the [illegible] which they did as soon as possible [illegible] new house about five rods from the old one." [illegible] was on Dover Neck, and there [illegible] and died. His character must have been [illegible] he would not have been placed in the [illegible] position he was. The town records of Dover [illegible] under date of "27 of the 9mo, 1648:" It [illegible] day [illegible] at a publique Towne meeting [illegible] Richard Pinkham shall beat the drum on the Lord's day to give notice [illegible] the time of meeting, [illegible] the meeting-house for the which he shall be allowed six bushels of Indian corn for his pay this yeare, and to be free from rates." Richard Pinkham's name is on the list of those of Dover Neck and [illegible] who were assessed the "Provision Rate" in [illegible] was [illegible] the list of those [illegible] Oyster River, but [illegible] of [illegible] Richard Pinkham [illegible] twenty acres, which [illegible] the west side of Back river [illegible] Richard Pinkham granted [illegible] his house, lands [illegible] cattle, [illegible] in a deed [illegible] Richard [illegible]

[illegible]

married Rose Otis, daughter of Richard Otis, of

Pond was married a second time to a Mr. Briggs, of Keene. She died March 2, 1895, aged sixty-six years, eight months and twenty-eight days.

(VIII) Herbert, second son and child of Henry and Harriet (Wilson) Pond, was born in Keene, August 7, 1848. He was educated at Miss Julia Hall's private school, the public schools of Keene, including the high school, Powers' private school, Boston, and Bryant and Stratton's Business College, New York City. Since attaining his majority he has devoted his energies to the care of his financial interests in Keene, and he has given considerable attention to improving real estate and the erection of buildings. Politically he acts with the Republican party. He attends the First Congregational Church, of which his wife is a member. September 22, 1897, he married Mrs. Mertie Eliza Tyler, nee Seaver, who was born in Harrisville, February 18, 1868, daughter of Sewall Abijah and Maria Lucy (Derby) Seaver, the latter of whom was born in Dublin, this state, October 9, 1838.

Robert Seaver came from England in the ship "Mary and John" in 1633-34, and settled in Roxbury, Massachusetts. He had a numerous family. One of the sons, Nicholas, dropped the a from the name, and possibly others may have done the same. His son William settled in Kingston and built the house now standing and used for a summer home, in 1760. The Seaver genealogy is very imperfect. It follows out the lines of only three of the sons of the original Robert Seaver and those not in full. Robert Seaver had four sons and three daughters; one daughter died in infancy. One line as near as it has been able to be traced it is as follows: Robert 1., Nathaniel 2., John 3., Nathaniel 4., Abijah 5., Benjamin 6., and Benjamin 7., born in 1795, who served in the capacity of mayor of Boston. The line from which those of the name in this sketch trace their ancestry, was Robert 1., Nathaniel 2., John 3., Nathaniel 4., Abijah 5., Benjamin 6., William G. G. F. 7., William 8., Sewall A. 9., Mertie E. 10. (Seaver) Pond. William Seaver, first of the name above mentioned, lived in Roxbury, Massachusetts, and owned considerable property for those days, Seaver street, so called, being a part of the old Seaver estate. He married, December 14, 1795-96, Lucy Heath, and their children were: Elizabeth C., born October 2, 1797, married a Hayward, of Dublin, New Hampshire, and died April 2, 1835. William, born December 31, 1798, died March 23, 1867. Abijah, born October 4, 1800, died May 5, 1823. A son born January 9, 1803, died January 24, 1803. Lucy. Heath, born August 4, 1805, died August 14, 1805. William Seaver, Jr., son of William and Lucy (Heath) Seaver, of Roxbury, Massachusetts, came to what was then called Nelson, New Hampshire, now Harrisville, when quite a young man. He purchased a large farm which was considered one of the best in the town, and which now belongs to one of his grandsons. He married, July 15, 1823, Susan Gurler, of Keene, New Hampshire, daughter of Thomas Gurler and ——— Farwell. The Gurlers and Farwells were among the earliest settlers of that section, coming from Marblehead, Massachusetts, to Nelson, now Harrisville, and taking up adjoining farms as early as 1772. Afterward the Gurlers removed to Keene, New Hampshire. Children of William and Susan (Gurler) Seaver: George W., born in Nelson, November 2, 1823; Lucy Ann, born in Nelson, May 1, 1825; Charles C., born in Nelson, August 26, 1826; William W., born in Nelson, July 15, 1831; Sewall Abijah, born in Nelson, November 12, 1833, died at Harrisville, New Hampshire, June, 1875; Edward Lorin, born in Nelson, May 3, 1836, died unmarried at Harrisville, New Hampshire; Albert Andrew, born in Nelson, May 17, 1841, died at Harrisville, New Hampshire.

PINKHAM Among other things tradition tells us that the ancestor of the Pinkhams of this article came from the Isle of Wight, but there is no historical evidence to support it. However, Richard Pinkham early and his descendants to the ninth and tenth generation are inhabitants of New Hampshire. Staunch dispositions have been characteristics of the members of the race.

(I) Richard Pinkham, the settler, was at Dover as early as 1640, for on October 22, 1640, the inhabitants of Dover established or renewed a formal government, and the name of Richard Pinkham is attached to the document they then prepared. Quint's History of Dover, edited by John Scales, speaking of him in 1852; says: "The spot where he early dwelt is said to be the same on which stood the Pinkham garrison, which Richard afterwards made his habitation. The precise situation of this is easily pointed out, insomuch as it continued to be the dwelling house until one side fell down seven and twenty years ago; that event rendered it necessary for the family to remove, which they did as soon as possible, into a new house about five rods from the old one." This fortress was on Dover Neck, and there Richard lived and died. His character must have been good, else he would not have been placed in the public position he was. The town records of Dover show under date of "27 of the 9mo., 1648:" It is this day ordered at a publique Towne meeting that Richard Pinkham shall beat the drum on the Lord's day to give notice for the time of meeting and to sweepe the meeting-house for the which he shall be allowed six bushels of Indyan corn for his pay this yeare, and to bee free from rates." Richard Pinkham's name is on the list of those of Dover Neck and Cocheco who were assessed the "Provision Rate" in 1675. His name was also on the list of those similarly taxed at Oyster River, but opposite his name and the names of some others the word "nothing" was entered, showing he was not required to pay the rate there. Richard Pinkhom was granted lot 24, containing twenty acres, within the division of land on the west side of Back river, in 1642. June 12, 1671, Richard Pincom granted to John Pincom (his son) his house, lands, meadow, orchard, household goods, cattle, etc., for which John agrees to support his father "in a christian Way" and give him every year four pounds. June 22 following, Richard granted John his three and one-half acre lot with orchard, for twelve pounds. After this he is heard no more. So far as known he left three children: Richard, John and Thomas.

(II) John, son of Richard Pinkham, was born about 1644, and died August 27, 1724, aged about eighty. He was first taxed on Dover Neck in 1665. "He first assumed the care of his father, legally, and took possession of the homestead in 1671, just before the time it became necessary to build garrisons and carry guns to meeting. He was a man of good ability, acquired property and distributed it as follows: To his eldest son Richard, land at Cohoes, June 19, 1714; to his son Otis, land March 16, 1722; to his son Amos, July 4, 1715, certain lands on condition that he pay to each of his sisters five pounds. This land and conditions were transferred to his brother Otis, August 8, 1720. He married Rose Otis, daughter of Richard Otis, of

Cocheco, who was a prominent man and an officer of the colony whose name appears often on the records of his time. Rose Otis was one of the inhabitants of the Otis garrison which was captured by the Indians; and after the peace of Casco, January 9, 1699, she (with others of her family) was returned, and later married John Pinkham. They had at least nine children: Richard, Thomas, Amos, Otis, Solomon, James, Rose, Elizabeth and Sarah.

(III) Otis, fourth son of John and Rose (Otis) Pinkham, inherited the old homestead and resided there until the time of his death about 1763. The inventory of his estate was returned November 30, 1764, by his widow. He married "22 9mo. 1721," Abigail Tibbetts, who was born "12 6mo. 1701," daughter of Ephraim and Rose (Austin) Tibbetts. Their children were: Samuel, Ann, Rose, Paul, and John, whose sketch follows.

(IV) John (2), youngest child of Otis and Abigail (Tibbetts) Pinkham, was born August 29, 1739, and died August 14, 1815, aged seventy-six. He inherited from his father the homestead, garrison and all. He married Phebe Tibbetts, who was born in Rochester, April 5, 1744, and died January 24, 1823, aged seventy-nine. Their children were: Elizabeth, Otis, Edmund, Elijah, Joseph and Benjamin (twins), Enoch, Sarah, Nicholas, Abigail, Phebe, John and Samuel.

(V) Joseph, fifth child and fourth son of John (2) and Phebe (Tibbetts) Pinkham, and twin of Benjamin, was born January 18, 1772, and lived in Tuftonborough, where he died April 18, 1842, aged seventy. He married Sally Young, of Dover, who was born May 2, 1775, and died September 5, 1868, aged ninety-three. They had children: William, Martha, Enoch, Hannah, Mary (died young), Richard, John, Mary, Charles, Lewis, Hollis, David and George Washington.

(VI) John (3), seventh child and fourth son of Joseph and Sally (Young) Pinkham, was born in Wolfborough, January, 1804, and died in Newmarket, August 3, 1832, aged twenty-eight. He married Mrs. Betsey (Smith) Doe, who was born May 22, 1790, and died August 31, 1866, aged seventy-six. Their children were: Ann Elizabeth, Joseph, Hollis Hamden and Lydia Miranda.

(VII) Hollis Hamden, third child and second son of John (3) and Betsey (Smith) (Doe) Pinkham, was born in Newmarket, September 22, 1829, and died March 9, 1897. He was educated in the common schools of Newmarket, and learned the carpenter's trade, and later the tailor's trade with his brother Joseph. Finally he went into the retailing of shoes, and followed that occupation until his death. Originally a Jacksonian Democrat, he kept pace with the progress of the world, and at the outbreak of the Rebellion became a Republican and adhered to that faith as long as he lived. He married, October 9, 1854, at Casco, Maine, Abbie Meserve Pinkham, who was born in Dover, September 29, 1833, daughter of William and Martha (Hill) Pinkham. She died April 5, 1901. Their children were: Frank Herbert and Ernest Percy, both of whom receive further mention below.

(VIII) Frank Herbert, eldest son and child of Hollis H. and Abbie M. (Pinkham) Pinkham, was born in Casco, Maine, October 9, 1854, and educated in the common schools of Newmarket and at Tilton Seminary, Tilton, New Hampshire. He learned the printer's trade, and in 1875 founded the *Newmarket Advertiser*, Newmarket, New Hampshire, which he has since successfully edited and published. He is senior partner in the firm of Pinkham & Neal, proprietors of a restaurant and lunch room at Newmarket. In politics he is a Republican. He has filled the office of town treasurer eight terms, and is now (1907) serving his eleventh year as treasurer of the school district. He is a member of numerous fraternal and social organizations. He is a member of Rising Star Lodge, No. 47, Free and Accepted Masons, of Newmarket, of which he is a past master, and is now serving as secretary; Pioneer Lodge, No. 1, Knights of Pythias, of Newmarket; Lamprey River Grange, No. 240, Patrons of Husbandry; is a member of Pocasset Tribe, Improved Order of Red Men; past warden and past supreme representative of the New England Order of Protection, with membership in Piscataqua Lodge, No. 72; member of North Star Lodge, No. 259, Knights of Honor, of Dover; and the Pascatoquack Club of Newmarket. He married, April 22, 1875, at Lake Village, now Laconia, New Hampshire, Marion L. Ritchie, who was born March 13, 1854, daughter of William K. and Adelaide (Kent) Ritchie, of Everett, Massachusetts. They have two children: Bessie Mae, born March 30, 1880; and Ada Marion, May 23, 1884. Bessie M. is the wife of Clarence H. Neal, and Ada M. is the wife of Amede Magnon, both of Newmarket.

(VIII) Ernest Percy, second son of Hollis H. and Abbie M. (Pinkham) Pinkham, was born in Newmarket, February 9, 1862. He learned the printer's trade in the *Advertiser* office in Newmarket, and later was foreman of the *Cape Elizabeth Sentinel*, at what is now South Portland, Maine. From January, 1884, to January, 1889, he was a clerk in the shoe store of the late John L. Boardman in Newmarket. On the latter date he bought his employer's stock in trade, and has since conducted a successful and constantly increasing trade. In December, 1892, he bought out the fire insurance business of the late Timothy Murray, and since that time has also conducted an insurance business. His political faith is Republican, and he has been elected to various offices by his party. He was town clerk in 1903-04; representative in the general court, 1898-99; selectman, 1902-03; has been secretary of the school board since March, 1904; and was elected town treasurer on the Citizen's ticket in 1906. He is socially and fraternally connected with many orders whose object is the enhancement of the happiness of mankind. He is a member of Swamoscott Lodge, No. 8, Independent Order of Odd Fellows, of Newmarket, of which he was elected noble grand in 1889, and of which since July, 1890, he has continuously been secretary; member of Star of Hope Rebekah Lodge, No. 19; a member of Rising Star Lodge, No. 47, Free and Accepted Masons; a charter member of Lamprey River Grange, No. 240, Patrons of Husbandry, of which he was the first secretary, and of which he was master in 1902-03. June 11, 1903, he joined Pioneer Lodge, No. 1, Knights of Pythias, in which he served two terms as chancellor commander, and in which he is now keeper of the records and seals; member of Pascatquack Club, a social club of Newmarket. He married, in Saco, Maine, November 10, 1886, Estella Merrow Ham, who was born in North Shapleigh, Maine, March 31, 1868, daughter of Norris S. and Mary A. (Milliken) Ham, of Saco, Maine. They have two children: Beatrice, born in Saco Maine, June 15, 1891; and Helen, in Newmarket, New Hampshire, December 21, 1895.

PARMENTER French Huguenots of this name fled to England in 1520 to escape massacre. The name is variously written Parmenter, Parmiter and Parmeter. John

Parmenter, who came from England to Massachusetts, is said to be the ancestor of all the Parmenters in New England.

John Parmenter, Sr., with his son John, was among the first settlers and proprietors of Sudbury, and took the freeman's oath May 13, 1640. He was selectman in 1641, and he (or his son) was on a committee of inspection into the moral condition of families, etc., February 28, 1665, and selectman in 1660, and deacon. In 1654 he was agent at Sudbury for Herbert Pelham, Esq., and Captain William; also for Thomas Walgrave, Esq. He removed from Sudbury to Roxbury, where in 1670 he sold to Thomas Rice, of Marlboro, several parcels of land in Sudbury. He died May 1, 1671, aged eighty-three. He married (first) in England, Bridget ———, who died April 6, 1660; (second) in Roxbury, August 9, 1660, Annis Dane, widow of John Dane.

John (2), only child of John (1) Parmenter, mentioned in Massachusetts records, was born in England, and came to Massachusetts with his parents. He was among the first proprietors of Sudbury, and took the freeman's oath, May 10, 1643. He bought a house lot in Sudbury in 1642, and in 1649 sold his house and other property in Sudbury. He or his father was one of Major Willard's troopers at Dedham in 1654, and the "mayor's man." In 1665 he was allowed to keep a house of entertainment at Sudbury. He died at Sudbury, April 12, 1666, and his will was proved the same year. His wife Amy died in 1681. Their children were: John, Joseph, George, Mary, Benjamin and Lydia.

(I) Martin Parmenter, was a native of Connecticut, and settled in Pittsfield, Vermont, where the remainder of his life was spent.

(II) Martin (2), son of Martin (1) Parmenter, was born in Pittsfield, February 19, 1816, and died October 14, 1863. He was educated in the common schools, and devoted his whole life to agricultural pursuits. He attended the Methodist Church, and voted the Republican ticket after the organization of that party. He was married March 3, 1846, to Louise Holt, who was born in Pittsfield, Vermont, February 11, 1816. She was the daughter of Erastus Holt, who removed from Connecticut to Vermont, where he afterwards resided. Six children were born of this union: Alonzo, Sevilla, James F., George R., Ada and Charles H. Alonzo was a member of the Fourteenth Vermont Volunteers in the war of the Rebellion, and died of disease at Pensacola, Florida. Sevilla married Thomas Smith, of Brookfield, Vermont. James F. is a retail grocer in Brookfield, Vermont. George R. resides in Concord, New Hampshire. Ada died at the age of nineteen years. Charles H. is the subject of the next paragraph.

(III) Charles Harris, youngest child of Martin (2) and Louis (Holt) Parmenter, was born in Warren, Vermont, February 20, 1857. After passing the common schools he attended the academies at St. Johnsbury and Pittsfield, each one year. Then returning to the farm, he has ever since followed agricultural employment. He resided in Pittsfield until 1905, when he removed to Henniker, New Hampshire, where he owns the old Wadsworth farms which embrace between six hundred and seven hundred acres of land. He also owns land in Deering, New Hampshire. Mr. Parmenter's farming is on a large scale; he cuts from seventy-five to one hundred tons of hay, and keeps about forty head of cattle, mostly cows, and does a large dairy business. He is a Republican, and attends the Congregational Church. He married, in Stockbridge, Vermont, September 16, 1880, Harriet E. Martin, who was born in Hancock, Vermont, December 3, 1859, daughter of Thomas B. and Frances E. (Richardson) Martin, of Hancock, Vermont. Their children are: George, who was educated at the Henniker high school; Chester, died at the age of six months; Wilber, a graduate of the Henniker high school, class of 1903; Alba, Clarence, Leon, Electa and Florence.

NICHOLS For many generations the Nichols family has resided in New England, exemplifying that type of citizenship which leads in national growth and progress, energetic, intellectual, guided by high ideals. Several of the name through different generations have offered their services to their country in time of peril, prominent among these having been General Moses Nichols, whose career as a soldier was well worthy of emulation and reflected great credit on his ancestors.

(I) Richard Nichols, the pioneer ancestor, was a freeman of Ipswich in 1638. He removed from that town to Reading, locating in the westerly part of the south parish, where his death occurred September 22, 1674. His wife, Annis Nichols, survived him for many years, passing away in 1692. Their children were: Mary, Thomas, James, John, Richard, Hannah.

(II) Thomas, eldest son of Richard and Annis Nichols, was a prominent citizen of Reading, serving in the capacity of representative and deacon. He was a member of Captain Davenport's company in King Philip's war, and in reward for the service was a grantee of Narragansett No. 2, now Westminster, Massachusetts. He married in 1680, Rebecca Eaton, born 1665, daughter of John and Elizabeth (Kendall) Eaton. Their children were: Thomas, Rebecca, Ebenezer, Judith, Abigail, Elizabeth, Timothy, Daniel. Thomas Nichols, father of these children, died in 1737.

(III) Timothy, third son of Thomas and Rebecca (Eaton) Nichols, born May 16, 1702, married, October 7, 1725, Hannah Perkins, and their children were: Hepsibah, Hannah, Timothy, Thomas, Sarah, Moses, Lucy. Timothy Nichols and his wife resided several years in Reading, removing to Amherst prior to the year 1770.

(IV) General Moses, fourth son of Timothy and Hannah (Perkins) Nichols, was born in Reading, June 28, 1740. Upon attaining young manhood he chose the profession of medicine and practiced the same most successfully in Amherst, New Hampshire. He served as colonel of the geographical regiment, which included a large part of Hillsborough county; in 1777 commanded a regiment at Bennington; in 1780 commanded a regiment at West Point, and near the close of the war was commissioned a brigadier-general. In civil affairs he was the recipient of local honors, serving as representative, councillor, and magistrate for many years. He married Hannah ———, and their children were: Hannah, Moses, Joseph, Elizabeth, Eaton, Perkins, Polly, Pearson, Charity. General Nichols died in Amherst, New Hampshire, May 23, 1790, after a useful and well-spent life. His widow died June 17, 1802.

(V) Elizabeth Nichols, second daughter of General Moses and Hannah Nichols, born January 8, 1768.

MAJOR The name Major is not common in New England, and the greater number of the Major family is probably descended from the ancestor mentioned below.

(I) Captain ———— Major was a native of England, and for many years was a seafarer and commanded a merchant vessel. He brought his family to Derryfield, New Hampshire, where they resided. He was drowned at sea.

(II) John, son of Captain Major, was born in that part of old Derryfield now included within the limits of Manchester. He was a farmer, an upright citizen, a good neighbor, and a man of strict integrity, and from his well known probity was often familiarly spoken of by his friends as "honest John." He married, January 28, 1802, Mary Cheney, and they had children: Maria, married Samuel Morison and had two children: Elizabeth T., married (first) Jesse Mellen and (second) Wilder M. Gates; Ann. Eliza, married ———— Melvin, children: Elizabeth, George, James, Maria, William. John, married Mary McIntire, one child, Josephine. John Major married (second) Martha Cheney.

(III) Thomas P., child of John and Martha (Cheney) Major, was born in Derry, April 25, 1822, and died in Derry, 1899, aged seventy-seven years. He had but little opportunity to acquire an education, but was always a careful reader and a well-informed person. From the age of ten to twenty-one he worked on a farm near the home of his parents. Afterward he learned the trade of tanner and currier, at which he worked four years, when ill health compelled him to give it up and from that time he was a farmer. In 1878 he removed to Derry and was one of the first to build in that locality. In politics he was a Republican, and for three years he served as selectman of Derry, and also served some years as highway surveyor. He was fond of the fellowship and belonged to various fraternities. He was a Mason, an Odd Fellow, a Knight of Pythias, a member of the United Order of Pilgrim Fathers, the Order of the Eastern Star and the Daughters of Rebekah. He married, September 24, 1845, Rachel E., daughter of Deacon Daniel W. Hayes, of Farmington. She died in 1882, leaving no children. He married (second), December 18, 1884, Harriet N. McGregor, daughter of James and Mary (Plummer) Nevins (see Nevins, IV), and widow of W. K. McGregor, of Derry.

OLIVER The name of Oliver is numerous and notable among the seventeenth century immigrants to Boston and its neighborhood. The original ancestor appears to have been Elder Thomas Oliver, who came to Boston from Lewes, Sussex, England, in 1632, with his wife and eight children. He was a chirurgeon, as it was then called, and was the ruling elder of the Old South Church, Boston. Peter left four sons, of whom the youngest, Daniel, married Elizabeth, sister of Governor Jonathan Belcher. Their son Andrew was lieutenant governor of the Province, and another son, Peter, became chief justice of the supreme court of Massachusetts. In 1828 no less than twenty-five Olivers had been graduated from Harvard College, most of them descendants of Elder Thomas. The Oliver coat of arms is an arm extended, holding a hand couped at the wrist and dropping blood. The crest is a dove with an olive branch in its mouth, whence the name is doubtless derived. As the present line came directly from England after the Revolution, it cannot be nearly related to the early immigrants, but probably all are descended from a common ancestral stock.

(I) Dr. William Oliver was born in England in 1766, and settled in Boston. He afterwards moved to Acworth, New Hampshire, and finally to Oliver's Corner, Province of Quebec, Canada. He married Elizabeth Kinston, who was born November 10, 1751, and they had several children: Esther, William, Ebenezer, Polly, George and John.

(II) Captain William (2), son of Dr. William (1) and Elizabeth (Kinston) Oliver, was born July 20, 1793, at Acworth, New Hampshire. He was a farmer and lived at Oliver's Corner, town of Magog, Province of Quebec. He served as a lieutenant in the war of 1812, and while in the army learned to make boots and shoes. He was a man of great industry, hewing his farm out of the forest and often sitting up till twelve o'clock at night to do shoemaking. Captain Oliver acquired his title from an office in a local militia company. He was a Conservative in his political affiliations, and attended the Congregational Church. Captain William (2) married Polly Remick, born in Dunbarton, New Hampshire, August 19, 1798, and there were three children: Edward B., whose sketch follows, Marion B. and William W. Captain Oliver died March 12, 1881, and his wife died August 16, 1848.

(III) Edward Bernard, eldest child of Captain William (2) and Polly (Remick) Oliver, was born May 22, 1818, at Hatley, Province of Quebec, Canada. He was a carpenter by trade, and his home was always at Oliver's Corner. He was a member of the Congregational Church at Fitch Bay, Province of Quebec, of which society he was deacon for many years. On February 14, 1839, Edward B. Oliver married Mary Q. Foss, who was born at Stanstead, Province of Quebec. They had six children: Aza, James B., Ida M., Marian B., Adams P., and William W., whose sketch follows. Deacon Edward B. died at Oliver's Corner, on September 1, 1896, and his wife died August 29, 1886.

(IV) William Wallace, fourth son and sixth and youngest child of Deacon Edward B. and Mary Q. (Foss) Oliver, was born March 7, 1858, at Oliver's Corner, Magog, Province of Quebec, Canada. He was educated in the schools of his native place and at Magog Academy in the town of Magog. At the age of twenty-one he went to Fitch Bay, Canada, where he clerked for T. B. and H. M. Rider, remaining there one year. The succeeding year he went to Sherbrooke, Canada, where he worked as clerk for W. W. Beckett in the wholesale and retail hardware business. The next two years he spent in Newport, Vermont, where he worked for H. S. Root, dealer in hardware and furnishings. In January, 1883, Mr. Oliver moved to Lisbon, New Hampshire, which has become his permanent home. He entered the employ of Oakes & Bennett, dealers in general merchandise, and after serving as clerk for six years in 1889 he formed a partnership with Carlos M. Cogswell. Their business was extensive and lucrative, and extended over the surrounding country. This partnership was dissolved in 1901, and Mr. Oliver engaged in the grain and feed business in the firm known as Oliver & Gates. In 1906 he sold his interest in this business, that he might devote more time to the care of the Lisbon Light and Power Company, of which company he has been, for several years, manager and treasurer. He is also president of the Lisbon Building Association. He is Republican in party affiliations, but is too busy to give much time to politics. He is much interested in Masonic societies, and has taken high rank therein. On September 5, 1881, he was admitted to Memphremagog Lodge, Ancient Free and Accepted Masons, of Newport, Vermont, and on October 25, 1886, was admitted to Kane Lodge, Lisbon. He was elected senior warden in 1894, and worshipful master in 1896, serving two

THOMAS P. MAJOR.

years. In 1883 he was made Royal Arch Mason in Cleveland Chapter, Newport, Vermont, and demitted to Franklin Chapter, Lisbon, in 1887. He held the office of master of third veil in 1887, principal sojourner in 1889, high priest in 1890-01-02, and secretary in 1893. He was elected thrice illustrious master for the years 1903 and 1904, receiving the orders in St. Gerard Commandery, No. 9, of Littleton. In 1895 he was appointed grand steward, which office he still holds. In 1888-89, he was appointed Grand Royal Arch captain and representative to the Grand Chapter of Colorado from the Grand Chapter of New Hampshire, a position which he still holds. He was elected E. Grand Captain of the Host in 1900 and 1901, R. E. Grand Scribe in 1902, R. E. Grand King in 1903, R. E. Deputy Grand High Priest in 1904 and 1905 and M. E. Grand High priest of the state of New Hampshire in 1906. Mr. Oliver is a member of North Star Lodge of Perfection, at Lancaster, and master of ceremonies in that body. He is perfect master of Littleton Chapter, Rose Croix, at Littleton, and a member of Edward A. Raymond Consistory at Nashua. On September 15, 1887, William Wallace Oliver married Alice M. Boynton, daughter of Dr. Charles Hart and Mary Huse (Cummings) Boynton, of Lisbon. (See Boynton, XXX). There were three children of this marriage: Mary B., born June 7, 1890, at Lisbon. Charles Edward, February 11, 1895, who died February 8, 1898. Alice Louise, April 2, 1899, at Lisbon. Both Mr. and Mrs. Oliver are members of the Congregational Church at Lisbon.

PUCHALA Rev. John B. Puchala, son of Charles Puchala, deceased, was born in Silesia, Prussia, July 18, 1874. His education has been chiefly acquired in the colleges of Prussia, but he completed his studies in philosophy and theology in the University of Louvain, in Belgium, which institution has a world-wide reputation. He was there ordained to the priesthood. He came to America, arriving here October 2, 1900, and his first clerical labors were in the cathedral under Bishop Bradley. He was appointed to take charge of St. Hedwig's Church, Manchester, New Hampshire, in 1902. This is situated on the site of the first Christian church in the city, and is of the Polish Catholic denomination. Rev. Puchala is a man of great energy and force of character, and places all his best powers in the service of his congregation, which numbers about two thousand. Since his advent in the parish he has introduced many much-needed reforms and improvements, among them being a brick school building which is now finished, and which is in charge of the Felician Sisters, whose mother institution is near Buffalo, New York. Ths building has four classrooms, and will accommodate two hundred children. It consists of two stories and a basement. It has metal ceilings and all modern improvements, and is located on Union street, below Hanover. There are five classrooms on the first and second floors, with modern furnishings. At the time that the church was acquired by its present congregation it was a plain building without a tower. On the first Sunday in August, 1902, the first mass was intoned in the edifice and the building dedicated to the service of the Polish Catholic Church. Many improvements have been made both in the exterior and interior of the building, and it now has a seating capacity of six hundred, including the gallery. The statues, which have been placed wherever they were appropriate, are of the very finest. It is further ornamented with a coat-of-arms, elaborately carried out in colors, which bears the inscription "God Save Poland." Altogether, the improvements which have been made in the church edifice since the advent of Rev. Puchala amount to upward of five thousand dollars. The Polish residents of Manchester are highly pleased with their church and school, as is attested by the liberal support they afford to them.

ODELL The surname Odell is frequently met in the eastern states, but its representatives in New Hampshire are not numerous. William Odell was of Concord, Massachusetts, in 1639, and had a son James, born there in that year. John Odell was in Fairfield, Connecticut, in 1668.

(I) Thomas Odell, of Stratham, New Hampshire, was the earliest known ancestor of the families of that name in Sanbornton and town adjoining.

(II) Thomas (2), son of Thomas (1) Odell, of Stratham, settled in Nottingham, New Hampshire, married and had children.

(III) Joseph, son of Thomas (2) Odell, of Nottingham, was born in that town November 1, 1772, and died in Sanbornton, December 29, 1825. About 1802 he moved with his family to Sanbornton and settled on a farm on the Roxbury road. He was a deacon of the First Bay Baptist Church. His wife, whom he married March 10, 1797, was Nancy Ford, born March 5, 1775, ('77) died March 9, 1852. Their children: David, born December 27, 1797, died October 25, 1831. Jacob, April 2, 1799, died June 9, 1862. Joseph, December 18, 1800, married (first) Elizabeth Pierce; (second) Sarah, widow of Alvah Graves. Samuel Gerrish, June 11, 1803, died Spetember 19, 1803. William, September 4, 1804. Ebenezer Ford, August 17, 1808. Ira Pottle (twin), January 5, 1813. Zina (twin), January 5, 1813, died June 25, 1813.

(IV) Jacob, second child and son of Joseph and Nancy (Ford) Odell, was born in Nottingham, New Hampshire, and was about five years old when his parents went from that town to Sanbornton. He was an excellent singer and acquired considerable fame as a singing master, having taught about one hundred different schools of vocal music. In connection with this vocation he also was a farmer. On January 17, 1827, he married Elmira Aiken, born in Francestown, New Hampshire, December 17, 1804, daughter of John Aiken. Their children: Laura Jane, born September 30, 1828, married Chase Rollins. Nancy Maria, April 1, 1830, died September 4, 1888; married, May 17, 1853, Stephen Coffran Robinson (see Robinson, III), and had one child: Frank Orrin Robinson, born January 31, 1854, died April 23, 1893. Joseph Franklin, November 3, 1831, died July 25, 1856. William Moore, March 27, 1835, married Mary E. Hunkins. John Henry, February 21, 1838, married Nancy Abbie Tuttle. George Delevan Terry, September 5, 1840, married Frances Tucker. Orrin Fuller, November 22, 1844, died November 4, 1846. Jacob Hermon, February 4, 1846, married Lucy Tay.

ARNOLD The family of Arnold is of great antiquity, having its origin among ancient princes of Wales, according to pedigree recorded in the College of Arms. They trace from Ynir, King of Gwentland, who flourished about the middle of the twelfth century, and who was paternally descended from Ynir, the second son of Cadwaladr, King of

Britons, which Cadwaladr built Abergaveny in the county of Monmouth and its castle, which was afterwards rebuilt by Hamlet, ap Hamlet, ap Sir Druce, of Balladon in France, and portions of the wall still remain. (II) Calwalader the Great. (III) Idwallo. (IV) Roderick Moelwynoc. (V) Conan Dyndocthwy. (VI) Eisylht, Queen of Wales. (VII) Roderick Mawr the Great. (VIII) Morgan Mawr. (IX) Owen, King of Glanmorgan. (X) Ithel Dhu. (XI) Gwrgant, King of Glenmorgan. (XII) Jestyn. (XIII) Ynir. This Ynir, King of Gwentland, by his wife Nesta, daughter of Jestyn, son of Gargan, King of Glamorgan, had a son.

(XIV) Meirie, who succeeded his father as King of Gwentland, and he left by his wife Eleanor, daughter of Onired, son of Jerworth, of the house of Trevor, a son

(XV) Ynir Vichan, who was also King of Gwentland, and who married Gladise, daughter of Rhys Goch, son of Maenerch, Lord of Astroydir, Brecknockshire, by whom he had a son

(XVI) Caradoc, Lord of Gwent, whose wife was Nesta, daughter and heir of Sir Rydereck le Gros, Knight, by whom he had a son

(XVII) Dyfnwell, Lord of Gwent, who married Joyes, daughter of Hamlet, son of Sir Druce, Duke of Belladon, in France. Her brother Hamlet rebuilt the castle of Abergaveny, as before mentioned. Their son

(XVIII) Systal, Lord of Upper Gwent, married Anwest, daughter and heir of Sir Peter Russell, Knight, Lord of Kentchurch in the county of Hereford, and by her had a son

(XIX) Arthur, married Jane, daughter of Lein, son of Moreidhec Harrion, Lord of Cantisblyn. Their son

(XX) Meirie, married Anwest, daughter of Cradock, son of Einon, son of Golproyn, by whom he had a son

(XXI) Gwillim, married Jane, daughter and coheir of Iver, son of Assylet, Lord of Lyho Talybout, and had a son

(XXII) Arnholt, married Janet, daughter of Philip Fleming, Esq., and had a son

(XXIII) Arnholt, married Sybil, daughter of Madoc, son of Einon, son Thomas, by whom he had a son.

(XXIV) Roger Arnold, of Llamthony, in Monmouthshire, the first of the family who adopted a surname. He married Joan, daughter of Sir Thomas Gamage, Knight, Lord of Coytey or Coity, and had two sons. Joan (Gamage) Arnold traces her ancestry through Sir William Gamage, Gilbert de Gamage, Sarah de Tuberville, married William de Gamage Lady Wenthian Talbot married Sir Payne de Tuberville. Lady Sarah de Beauchamp married Richard VI, Baron of Talbot. William VI, Baron de Beauchamp. Lady Isabelle de Maudwit married William V, Earl D. Maudwit. Lady Alice de Newbury married William VI, Earl de Maudwit. Waleram IV, Earl Warwick. Lady Gunreda Warren married Roger de Belmont. William Gunreda Warren II. William, Earl of Warren, married ——— Gunreda. William de Martel. Nicholas de Barcharville de Clare. Baldrick Tewtonicus. Vigerius. Charles, Duke of Loraine. Louis IV, King of France. Edgar A. married Chales III, of France. Edward the Elder. Alfred the Great. King Ethelwolf. Matilda married William the Conqueror. Adelis married Baldwing. Robert the Wise. Huch Capet. Huch the Great. Robert the Strong. Arnolph II. Baldwin III. Baldwin II married Alph Alfritha, daughter of Alfred the Great. Arnolph the Great married Alice, great-great-great-granddaughter of Charlemagne. Baldwin I Married Judith. Charles the Bald, grandson of Charlemagne.

(XXV) Thomas Arnold, married Agnes Wainstead, who bore him a son

(XXVI) Richard Arnold, married Emmace Young, who bore him a son

(XXVII) Richard Arnold, married ———, who bore him a son

(XXVIII) Thomas Arnold, married twice and by second wife had a son

(XXIX) Thomas Arnold, married Phebe Parkhurst, who bore him a son

(XXX) Eleazer Arnold, married Eleanor Smith, who bore him a son

(XXXI) Joseph Arnold, married Mercy Stafford, who bore him a son

(XXXII) Samuel Arnold, married Elizabeth ———, who bore him a daughter

(XXXIII) Elizabeth Arnold, married Christopher Brown, and her brother, Israel Arnold, married Deborah Olney.

(XXXIV) Nabby Brown, married her cousin, Israel Arnold II, son of Israel Arnold I.

(XXXV) Charlotte Brown Arnold, married William Bibby, and their daughter, Maude Bell Bibby, who is a member of the Daughters of the Crown, and has her coat of arms, became the wife of Samuel De Wolf Lewis, of Newport, New Hampshire (see Lewis, IV).

JACOBS The progenitor of the Jacobs family of Hingham, Massachusetts, was Nicholas Jacobs, who came from Hingham, England, and from the Jacobses of Hingham have descended a great number of the name who are now scattered to all parts of the United States.

Nicholas Jacobs was one of the very early planters who settled in "Bare Cove," Hingham, Massachusetts, prior to the arrival of Rev. Peter Hobart and his company in 1635. According to Cushing's manuscript, "Nicholas Jacobs with his wife and two children and their 'cosen' Thomas Lincoln, weaver, came from old Hingham and settled in this Hingham, 1633." In September, 1635, he had a grant of a house lot containing three acres. Other lands were also granted to him at different dates for planting purposes. He was made freeman in 1636; was selectman in 1637; deputy to the general court, 1648-49, and often engaged upon the business of the town. He died June 5, 1657. He made his will May 18, 1657, which was proved July 25 following. His estate was appraised at three hundred ninety-three pounds eight shillings six pence. The christian name of his wife was Mary. She survived him and married (second), March 10, 1659, John Beal, widower. The children of Nicholas and Mary were: John, Elizabeth, Mary, Sarah, Hannah, Josiah, Deborah and Joseph.

Justine, a descendant of Nicholas Jacobs, the immigrant, resided in Rhode Island, and died in Windsor, in that state December 9, 18—. He took part in the revolution, and assisted in the capture of a British vessel, and as his share of the prize money distributed to the captors he received one hundred and twenty thousand dollars. He married, October 11, 1811, Polly Sargent, who was born in Windsor, Vermont, October 2, 1793, and died in May, 1880, daughter of Moses and Sarah (Cram) Sargent, of Weare. (See Sargent, VI.) They had four children: Fernando C., Justine, Emily and Mary C.

Fernando C., oldest son and child of Justine and Polly (Sargent) Jacobs, was born in Warren,

H. F. JACOBS.

Vermont, January 16, 1813, and died in Stewartstown, New Hampshire, August 11, 1899, aged seventy-six. When a lad he went with his uncle, Moses Sargent, to Troy, New York, and lived with him for several years, and then returned to Vermont and learned the tanner's trade at New Haven. In 1835 he went to Albany, New York, and worked at his trade there and in Troy two years. He then resided and was employed three years in Colebrook, New Hampshire, and two years in Stanstead, province of Quebec, Canada, and then removed to Canaan, Vermont, where he enlarged his business, erected a tannery, and carried on tanning and the manufacture of shoes and harness for sixteen years. He was successful in business and accumulated property, and with his savings he established a resort for tourists and hunters in the wild and delightful region of the Upper Connecticut, where sportsmen found rare game and fish, and the tourist pure air and lovely scenery. In 1860 he built the Connecticut Lake House, on the shore of Connecticut Lake, in the town of Pittsburg, Coos county, which formed the terminus of a carriage drive of twenty-five miles from Colebrook, and became headquarters for sportsmen and lumbermen. There he remained eleven years, and then removed to Lancaster, where he spent the two following years farming; then three years as proprietor of the Brunswick Springs House; and the next three years in the grocery trade in Colebrook. In 1880 he located at Stewartstown Hollow, where he formed a partnership with Lucius Parkhurst under the firm name of Parkhurst & Jacobs, and conducted a general merchandise store until he retired from active business.

Mr. Jacobs was an intelligent and well-informed man, and as active in public affairs as he was in his private business. In politics he was first a Whig and then a Republican. From 1850 to 1860 he was master in chancery in Essex county, Vermont, and from 1857 to 1860 notary public in the same county. He was postmaster at Canaan four years; deputy sheriff four years; lister, and holder of other offices. During the civil war he was a deputy provost marshal; he represented Pittsburg in the legislature in 1865-66; was collector and selectman some years; was postmaster at Stewartstown six years; justice of the peace in Pittsburg from 1861 to 1871, and of Stewartstown from the time of his becoming a citizen of that town until his death. In his later life he was as agile and vigorous as a younger man, and retained his activity and strength until a short time before his death.

He married (first), September 7, 1845, Julia A. Cooper, who was born in Canaan, Vermont, October 21, 1821, and died in Canaan September 20, 1867, daughter of Judge Jesse and Sarah (Putnam) Cooper, of Canaan, Vermont, the latter a granddaughter of General Israel Putnam, of revolutionary fame. Of this union were born five children: Alma P., Sarah C., Henry F., Charles J. and Julia Anna. Alma P. married Captain H. S. Hilliard, of Lancaster; Sarah C. married Dr. David O. Rowell, of Coos; Henry F. is the subject of the next paragraph; Charles J. was superintendent of the Baldwin bobbin mill at West Manchester, and died in 1896; Julia Anna resides at Fall river. F. C. Jacobs married (second), in Danvers, Massachusetts, Caroline Putnam. For his third wife he married —— Barnett.

Henry Fitz Jacobs, eldest son and third child, of Fernando C. and Julia A. (Cooper) Jacobs, was born in Canaan, Vermont, September 24, 1850, and was educated in the common schools. At the age of fourteen years he entered the employ of C. D. Cobb, of Boston, and F. E. Downer, where he was employed three years as a clerk. In 1872 he settled in Colebrook, where he has since resided. From 1872 to 1892 he was engaged in the livery business. Since 1895 he has been a broker and speculator in real estate. In connection with this he was for twelve years interested in a carriage manufactory and in dealing in grain, and was extensively engaged in farming, having charge of several large farms. He is also active in the production of wood pulp. It was through his instrumentality that fine concrete sidewalks were laid in Colebrook, and it is to his efforts that the village is indebted for the posession of two stone watering troughs. The streets were macadamized, so far as they have been done, while he held the office of superintendent of streets. It was through his endeavors that the streets were lighted, he having purchased the first street-lamp ever set in the village. He is an authority on fast horses, has fitted and sold dozens under the mark of 2:30, including Clifford, 2:13, and now owns a horse with a record of 2:05¼.. He has been successful in business, and is a director in the Colebrook National Bank. In politics he is a Republican, and for eight years he was deputy sheriff, and for more than twenty years he has been justice of the peace. He is a member of Excelsior Lodge, No. 73, Independent Order of Odd Fellows, of which he is a past grand; and also a member of Colebrook Grange, No. 223, Patrons of Husbandry. He married, March 20, 1878, at Colebrook, Florence G. Carlton, who was born in Colebrook, February 5, 1859, daughter of Calvin C. and Sarah (Watkins) Carlton, of Colebrook. Two children have been born of this marriage: Fernando C., deceased, and Ida A., who is a graduate of Tilton Seminary and resides with her parents.

Mr. Jacobs is a cousin of Henry Dennison, who is the legal adviser of the Mikado of Japan, and whose sketch appears elsewhere in this work.

LAW

(I) James Law, son of Thomas and Abbie (Pike) Law, was born in Brookline, Massachusetts. He was educated in the common schools of Brookline. His trade was that of a wool scourer; later he was a teamster in Lowell. In politics he was a Democrat. He attended the Universalist Church. He married Rebecca Jane Holt. They had three children: John Kittredge, George A., who is a conductor on the Concord & Portsmouth railroad; and Emily.

(II) John, eldest of the three children of James and Rebecca Jane (Holt) Law, was born in Franklin, New Hampshire, August 12, 1836. He was educated in the public schools of Lowell, Massachusetts. After completing his education he went to work in a cotton mill there. Later he was in the employ of the old Boston & Lowell railroad for a number of years. In 1859 he came to New Hampshire, and was in the shoe manufacturing business until 1862, when on August 12 he enlisted in the Eleventh New Hampshire Regiment, Company B, under Colonel Walter Harriman. In a short time he was promoted to sergeant, and was in line for higher promotion when he was wounded at Fredericksburg. He hoped to be able to enter the service again, but could not; so he was discharged on January 19, 1864. Mr. Law prides himself on his patriotism. He enlisted for the war just before his first son was born.

After his discharge he came back to New Hampshire and resumed the shoe business. In the late sixties he went to work for the Howard & Quimby Company, of Boston, installing woolen machinery.

He was with them about four years, and covered both the United States and Canada. He then went to Norfolk, Massachusetts, and was superintendent of the carding and sewing department of the Elliot Felting Company. This company afterwards established a leather board factory at Webster, New Hampshire, and he was made resident superintendent of the branch; but later the company changed hands and he discontinued his work with them. Mr. Law is a fine machinist, understanding all about mill machinery, and he has refused many excellent positions. In 1876 he came to New London and bought a two hundred and fifty acre farm. He has carried on general farming, and was one of the first to take summer boarders. His farm was considered one of the best in the county, and has recently been sold to a man from Cleveland, Ohio. Mr. Law now lives on another adjoining it. In politics he is a Republican. He has been moderator for forty-five years in succession. He has been constable many times and chief of police, and is now holding those offices. He has served on the board of selectmen five terms, and for two terms was chairman. He has been justice of the peace several years. In 1899 he represented the town in the state legislature, and was sergeant-at-arms of the house of representatives. He holds that commission still. He was sergeant-at-arms of the constitutional convention in 1902.

Mr. Law is an Odd Fellow. He was made a Mason in Lafayette Lodge of Manchester. He is past master of King Solomon's Lodge of New London, and a member of the council, chapter, Knights Templar and Ancient Arabic Order Nobles of the Mystic Shrine. He is a member of the Grand Army of the Republic, and was a delegate to the last encampment at Denver, Colorado. He was a delegate to the national convention, at Louisville, but did not go. He attends the Episcopal Church.

John Kittredge Law married Mehitabel L., daughter of Ahijah and Maria Ring, of Deerfield, New Hampshire, in October, 1858. They have two children: John Walter Harriman, born September 9, 1862, and Fred Albert, born March 4, 1868. John W. H. Law married Myra Andrews, of Warner, New Hampshire, and they have one child, John W. John W. H. Law is a rural mail carrier in New London. Fred A. married Caroline G. Currier, daughter of Herman and Susan Currier, of New London; they have one child, Nina Ruth. Fred A. Law is a mechanical engineer, and is at present at Hartford, Connecticut, in the automobile business. He was for nine years with the Columbia Company. He is an inventor, and has perfected many machines.

GOWING Gowing is a name not numerous either in America or England. It may possibly be related to the Irish Gowan, through the first American ancestor is said to have come from Scotland. In this country the name is especially associated with Lynnfield, Massachusetts, where the family was prominent for generations. Daniel Gowing is a name constantly recurring in the history of that town, though the family is now practically extinct there. During Revolutionary times there was a noted tavern kept in Lynnfield by Joseph Gowing, and the building is still standing and occupied. In England the name appears among the directors of the East India Company in 1805.

(I) Robert Gowing, the immigrant ancestor of the family, was probably a native of Scotland and was born in 1618. He came to Massachusetts in 1634, being then but sixteen years of age, and resided in Dedham, Wenham and Lynn. He was made a freeman in 1644, in Dedham, having previously been in Watertown, and lived in Wenham from 1640 to 1660. After this his home was in what is now Lynnfield. He was married October 3, 1644, to Elizabeth Brock, and died June 7, 1698.

(II) John, son of Robert and Elizabeth (Brock) Gowing, was born December 9, 1645, (Savage says November 13) in Dedham, and lived through his adult life in Lynn, where he died May 28, 1720. No record of his marriage is found, but his wife's name appears as Joanna, and their children, born from 1683 to 1704, were: Annis, John, Daniel, Thomas, Elizabeth, Samuel, Joanna, Lois and Timothy.

(III) Samuel, fourth son and sixth child of John and Joanna Gowing, was born March 10, 1696, in Lynn, and lived in that part of the town which is now Lynnfield, where he died September 3, 1733. He was undoubtedly a cultivator of the soil. He was married about the beginning of 1730 (intention published December 21, 1729) to Patience Bancroft, who was born July 14, 1708, daughter of Ebenezar and Abigail Bancroft.

(IV) James, son of Samuel and Patience (Bancroft) Gowing, was born January 18, 1736, in Lynnfield. He was an early settler in Jaffrey, New Hampshire, removing thence from Lynn in 1777. He settled on lot sixteen, in range two of that town on land which is not now occupied. He was a man of considerable prominence in Jaffery, holding the offices of moderator, selectman and tythingman, and was respected and esteemed. His death occurred very suddenly on June 6, 1805, when he fell and expired immediately in the road near his house. He was married, January 10, 1760, to Lydia Wellman, who was born May 7, 1735, daughter of Jonathan and Esther Wellman, said to be of Welsh descent, and died January 4, 1826. They were the parents of twelve children: Lydia, Samuel, James, Benjamin, William, Azeal, Levi, Rosanna, Simeon, Thirza, Joseph and Esther.

(V) James (2), second son and third child of James (1) and Lydia (Wellman) Gowing, was born April 16, 1763, in Lynnfield, and settled in Dublin, New Hampshire. He was twice married. His first wife was Abigail, eldest of the seven children of Moses and Elizabeth Greenwood, of Dublin. She was born April 27, 1774. They had twelve children: Anna, Elmira, Moses Greenwood (who is mentioned below), Almerin, Harriet, Lyman, Betsey, James, Jonathan, Abigail G., James and Harriet. Several of these children died in infancy. Mrs. Abigail (Greenwood) Gowing died January 10, 1817, and James Gowing married Mrs. Lucy Wilder for his second wife. They had one child, James R.

(VI) Moses Greenwood, eldest son and third child of James (2) and Abigail (Greenwood) Gowing, was born June 27, 1797, at Dublin, New Hampshire. He was a farmer and lived on the ancestral homestead. He married Lucy, daughter of Samuel Derby, of Dublin. They had three children: Maria B., Lucy, who died in infancy; and Calvin Clark, whose sketch follows. Moses G. Gowing died September 11, 1860; his wife died October 13, 1884.

(VII) Calvin Clark, only son and youngest child of Moses Greenwood and Lucy (Derby) Gowing, was born August 14, 1831, at Dublin, New Hampshire. He attended the public schools of his native town, and carried on farming. He was a Republican in politics, and an attendant of the Unitarian Church. He lived on the old Gowing homestead till March 12, 1868, when he removed to Walpole, New Hampshire, and bought the farm of twenty-two acres where his daughter now lives. This place is located half a mile south of the town on the river road. Calvin C. Gowing married Elmira M., daughter of Dr. Asa and Elmira (Sanderson) Heald, of Dublin. Calvin C. Gowing died August 25, 1883, at Walpole. His wife died January 27, 1867.

(VIII) Clara, daughter of Calvin C. and Elmira M. (Heald) Gowing, was born March 28, 1864, at Dublin, New Hampshire. She lives on the place bought by her father in Walpole. Her house contains many ancestral relics, among them the old knapsack, bayonet and canteen belonging to her great-grandfather, Moses Greenwood, which date from Revolutionary days.

FARRINGTON (I) Henry G. Farrington, son of Captain Philip Farrington, was born in Fryeburg, Maine, and was a carpenter and contractor. In 1845 he removed to Manchester, New Hampshire, where he lived the remainder of his life, carrying on the same business. He was a member of the Unitarian Church, and was active in its interest. He married Sarah Charles, daughter of Major James Charles. She died in 1846. Three children were born of this marriage.

(II) Henry Arthur Farrington, son of Henry and Sarah (Charles) Farrington, was born in Fryeburg, Maine. He was educated in the common schools, and learned the trade of carpenter under the supervision of his father, and later qualified for teaching, but did not enter that profession. From 1855 to 1862 he was clerk in the Amoskeag mills. In the latter year he entered the employ of Kidder & Chandler, merchants. The following year he was appointed enrolling officer in Manchester, and performed the duties of that office for the town. He was appointed clerk in the United States Treasury, Washington, D. C., which he declined. Returning to the mill, he was appointed overseer of the finishing department, which position he filled until 1906, when he was appointed superintendent of the finishing department. By steady work and careful use of his earnings, Mr. Farrington has been able from the first to save money which he has judiciously invested, at one time was junior partner in the firm of Temple & Farrington, the leading stationers of Manchester, and is also treasurer of the Hygienic Finger Tip Company. He has been active in politics for years, and as a Republican has served in the common council and board of aldermen of Manchester. He has been elected to the board of selectmen where he served two years, was a member of the constitutional convention in 1902, and represented ward 4 in the legislature in 1899. He is a member of the Unitarian Church, of which he has been a director. He became identified with Odd Fellowship by joining Mechanics Lodge, No. 13, at Manchester, May 11, 1858. Withdrawing from that lodge he became a charter member of Wildey Lodge, No. 45, in 1866, and was its first noble grand. He was admitted to the Grand Lodge in 1867, and passed the chairs in that body, being grand master in 1878. The two following years he was grand representative, and again served as such in 1893 to fill a vacancy. He was a charter member of Wonolancet Encampment, and past chief patriarch, and was first commandant of Grand Canton Ridgeley. In 1866 he was appointed colonel of the military branch, and as such commanded the New Hampshire contingent in the parade at the session of the Sovereign Grand Lodge in September, in Boston. He was made brigadier-general of the Second Brigade in December, 1866, and for the next five years served as such at many brilliant functions. June 4, 1891, he declined further honors. He has been treasurer of the Odd Fellows Home for twenty-four years, and is still serving in that capacity. In 1907 the annual report of the treasurer shows the following financial condition of the home: Cash assets, $38,771.51; real estate, $100,000.00. He is a member of the Derryfield Club.

He married, December 25, 1857, L. Augusta Adams, born in Vermont, daughter of Stephen Adams, of Vermont. They have had three children: Grace W., Arlie A. and Georgia.

FOOTE There are several representatives of this family among the early American immigrants, Nathaniel Foote, of Wethersfield, Connecticut, was born in England, about 1593, and was one of the pioneers of that New England settlement, where he died in 1644. He left a numerous progeny, and a large number of the name in this country trace their ancestry to him. This branch of the family has a coat of arms bestowed by King James, and there is a pretty legend connected therewith. The symbol consists of a shield divided by a chevron, and having quarterings of clover leaves. The crest is an oak tree, and the motto, "Loyalty and truth." It is said that during one of the wars between the English and the Scotch, King James was in danger of his life, and was rescued by an officer named Foote, and conveyed to a wood nearby where he was concealed in a hollow oak tree; and that the arms and motto were bestowed in recognition of this deed. The following line is probably descended from the Massachusetts Footes, though all may have had a common English ancestry, if it could be traced sufficiently far. The early links are lacking, but the unusual name of Pasco would seem to indicate that the present branch is derived from Pasco Foote, who had land granted him in Salem, Massachusetts, in 1637. He probably did not actually settle there till some years later, perhaps in 1653, in which year all of his eight children were baptized on the same day, February 6. Among these children was Theophilus, who also lived in Salem. By his first wife he had three children, the youngest of whom was named Pasco (2).

(I) Deacon William Lowell Foote, son of Chellis and Sarah (Lowell) Foote, and grandson of Pasco Foote, was born at South Berwick, Maine, near the close of the sixteenth century. He was a woolen manufacturer. He was a deacon of the First Baptist Church for many years. He married Mary Plummer Wood, daughter of Daniel and Miriam (Bodwell) Wood, of Lebanon, New Hampshire, and granddaughter of Major Daniel Wood. They had six children: Daniel W., William Lowell (2), whose sketch follows, Hannah M., Sarah and Susan E.

(II) William Lowell (2), second son and child of Deacon William L. and Mary P. (Wood) Foote, was born June 26, 1827, at Rollingsford, New Hampshire. He attended the common schools at South Berwick, Maine, until 1845, when at the age of eighteen he became associated with his father in a woolen mill, owned by the latter. Mr. Foote remained in this business till 1857, when the mill was sold. He afterwards became bleacher in the beetling department, in which he continued for about thirty years, or until 1889, when he retired from active work. He attended the Baptist Church, and was a Republican in politics. He was prominent in Odd Fellowship, and was past grand of Washington Lodge, No. 4, Independent Order of Odd Fellows, at Somersworth, New Hampshire.

On August 10, 1848, William Lowell Foote married Elizabeth Ann Meserve, born July 27, 1825, daughter of Colonel John and Sally (Hayes) Meserve, and granddaughter of Jonathan Meserve, of South Berwick, Maine. The Meserves are an ancient New England family, and the name has been traced to a Norman-French source. Colonel John Meserve, born April 14, 1785, was colonel of New Hampshire volunteers in the War of 1812 and saw service on the northern frontier under General Hull. His wife, Sally (Hayes) Meserve, was born March 13, 1785. William L. and Elizabeth A. (Meserve) Foote had six children: Julia Anna, born at South Berwick, Maine, October 27, 1849; Ellen Jane, May 3, 1851; Louis William, September 21, 1852; George Henry, July 11, 1857, at Somersworth; Adelbert, April 25, 1859, at Somersworth; and Arthur Lowell, whose sketch follows. William Lowell Foote died December 28, 1906, at Greenland, New Hampshire, and his wife, Elizabeth Ann, died November 24, 1892, at Somersworth, New Hampshire.

(III) Arthur Lowell, fourth son and sixth and youngest child of William (2) Lowell and Elizabeth Ann (Meserve) Foote, was born in Lewiston, Maine, December 25, 1863. In his second year he moved with his people to Somersworth, New Hampshire, where he attended various schools till June 27, 1883, on which day he was graduated from the high school. The following Monday he began the study of law with Beecham & Pierce, of Somersworth. After the dissolution of the firm he continued to read law with George E. Beecham, the former senior partner, till March 11, 1887, when he was admitted to the bar of New Hampshire. During the year 1886 he had formed a partnership with George E. Beecham to carry on the insurance business, with his office in Sanbornville, and after Mr. Foote's admission to the bar, the partnership was extended to cover the practice of law, with offices at Somersworth and Sanbornville. Soon after this time Arthur E. Wiggin was taken into the firm, which was then known as Beecham, Foote & Wiggin, and an office was opened at Farmington, and they attained considerable prominence in the practice of general law. In 1892 Mr. Beecham died and the dissolution of the partnership followed. Mr. Foote continued at Sanbornville, where he is established in practice alone, and has built up a well deserved reputation as a lawyer. He was county solicitor in 1896-97. December 19, 1899, he was admitted as an attorney and counsellor to the circuit court of the United States. He is a Republican in politics. He is a member of the Theosophical Society of New York City. Mr. Foote is much interested in fraternal organizations, and is past master of Libanus Lodge, No. 49, Ancient Free and Accepted Masons, of Somersworth; past great sachem of the great council of New Hampshire, Improved Order of Red Men, and four times elected great representative to the great council of the United States. He belongs to Dover Lodge, No. 184, Benevolent and Protective Order of Elks, by which he has several times been elected to deliver the memorial address. On June 1st 1888, Arthur Lowell Foote married Carrie Bell Sanborn, daughter of Charles and Elizabeth Sanborn, of Somersworth, New Hampshire, and they have one child, Lowell Sanborn, born June 2, 1891.

LOVELL The Lovells in America are of English origin, and there was a long line of this name in England, but the Peerage is now extinct. Lord Francis Lovell was Lord Chamberlin to Richard III and took part in the battle of Bosworth when King Richard was killed. The first Lord mentioned was Lord John who was Knight of the Garter during the reign of Henry IV. The family of Lovell has a large representation throughout this country, and many of its members have occupied important positions of trust and honor.

(I) Alexander Lovell was the first of the line concerning whom there is authentic information in America. He was in Medfield, Massachusetts, as early as 1645, and was one of its citizens when the town was burned by the Indians. The date of his death does not appear, but his will was dated August 15, 1707. He married, October 30, 1658, Lydia, daughter of Benjamin and Hannah Albie, probably of Medfield.

(II) Nathaniel, son of Alexander and Hannah (Albie) Lovell, was born in Medfield, and died March 16, 1731, probably in Medway, Massachusetts, as he finally became a resident of that town. He married (first) Abigail Davis, and (second) Elizabeth ———.

(III) Michael, spelled by himself Mical, was the son of Nathaniel and Abigail (Davis) Lovell, and was born March 13, 1705, in Medway. He married Mary ———. The family resided for several years in Medway and later removed to Worcester, Massachusetts. There were nine children by this marriage, the first three were born in Medway and the others in Worcester. About 1754 six brothers of this family—Michael, Ebenezer, Oliver, Timothy, John and Elijah—came from Worcester to Rockingham, Vermont, being among its earliest settlers. That they were men possessing considerable property and business ability is evident from the fact that in a few years they owned practically all of the town of Rockingham. When the war of the Revolution broke out, three of the brothers remained adherents to the British Crown, and hence were termed Tories, while the others took the part of the Colonists.

(IV) Michael (2), eldest son of Mical and Mary Lovell, was born July 5, 1728, in Medway, Massachusetts, and died in Rockingham, Vermont, in 1786. He was a zealous patriot and was captain of a company in the war of the Revolution. He married Hannah, but no record of her surname appears. From all accounts she was a very efficient and brave woman. During the absence of her husband she managed the two or three farms they owned and it is said she often mounted her horse and carried important messages to commanding officers, and the hospitality of their home was always offered to both officers and privates during the progress of the war. After the death of her husband Mrs. Lovell removed with her children from Rockingham to Cavendish, Vermont, where her remains lie buried in a small cemetery in which there are only thirteen graves, the stone bearing only the inscription, now legible, of "Hannah, relict of Captain Michael Lovell." Their five children were—Enos, who was the second child born in Rockingham, date about 1760. Michael. Randall, born in 1766, and there were two daughters—Elizabeth and Mary. Oscar Lovell Shafter, who was for many years chief justice of the state of California, and James McMillen Shafter, who was also a judge on the bench in California, and General William Rufus Shafter were direct descendants of Enos Lovell.

(V) Michael (3), son of Captain Michael and Hannah Lovell, was born December 29 1764, in Rockingham, Vermont. He removed to Claremont, New Hampshire, in 1820, and purchased a valuable farm on which he passed the remainder of his life and where he died April 29, 1860. He married Sally Kimball, about the year 1791; she died January 11, 1838. Their nine children were: Darexa, Elvira,

JOHN W. DICKEY.

Sally, Polly, Sophie, Seymour, Martha, Porter Kimball, and Maria Retsey. This family of children fully sustained the reputation of their ancestors for superior intelligence and executive ability. The son who had the most public career was Porter Kimball Lovell. He was a graduate of Bowdoin College and also studied in Paris and became a physician. He went to Hayti with Dr. James Hall, who was once a resident of Claremont and later made governor of Liberia. On their arrival there the yellow fever was raging and Dr. Lovell soon became famous by reason of his successful treatment of this disease. He was surgeon general in the army of the Revolution of Hayti in 1842-44, and died there November 19, 1846, at the age of thirty-seven years. The eldest son, Seymour Lovell, also studied medicine and died January 2, 1844, while attending medical lectures at the College of Physicians and Surgeons in New York City. Maria Retsey, youngest child of Michael (3) and Polly (Kimball) Lovell, was born April 8, 1813, and married Herman Allen Wightman in 1834. She died in Claremont, May 1, 1894. Their five children were—Frances M., Nellie S., Martha L., Mary J. and Caroline E.

(VI) Mary J. Wightman, born January 19, 1843, married, February 22, 1882, Osmon B. Way, M. D., of Claremont. (See Way).

DICKEY Several families of this name settled in New Hampshire, all Scotch, and no doubt all of one stock. There were three James Dickeys in the Revolutionary army from this state; one from Londonderry, one from Raby (Brookline), and one from Antrim. In those several branches we find the names of William, John, Adam and Samuel, and soon, over and over, so as to render it difficult to keep them distinct.

(I) William Dickey and his wife Elizabeth were the immigrant ancestors of many of those who settled in Londonderry. The exact date of their landing on these shores cannot be ascertained. It must have been prior to 1730, and may have been as early as 1725. They came from the north of Ireland, bringing with them their three children—Samuel, Elias and Elizabeth—and located on one of the best and most attractive farms in the westerly part of Londonderry, near a small stream known as "Todds Brook." William Dickey died October 9, 1743, aged sixty, and Elizabeth, his wife, died October 21, 1748, aged seventy. Each of their graves is marked by a respectable slab in the old "hill graveyard" in Londonderry.

(II) Jonathan Dickey was born in Manchester, New Hampshire, and died about 1833. He is believed to be descended from ancestors who lived in Londonderry. He was a farmer, and resided about three-fourths of a mile south of Massabesic Lake. He married Sarah Webster, who died at the age of eighty-seven years. They were the parents of five children: John Webster, see forward; Rebecca Perham, deceased; Lydia, deceased; Mary Stark, deceased; Joshua, deceased.

(III) John Webster, eldest son of Jonathan and Sarah (Webster) Dickey, was born in Manchester, January 16, 1823, died June 22, 1901, aged seventy-eight. He was reared on a farm, educated in the public schools, and worked on his grandfather's farm from the age of ten years, when he lost his father by death, until he was twenty-one years old. He then went to California and there remained for one year. After his return he was employed by the railroad company for a short period of time, and in 1852 entered the employ of the Amoskeag Manufacturing Company of Manchester, where he served forty-five years about its yards, fifteen years of which time he was yardmaster. He was very attentive to the duties of his position, and was promoted to the place he last occupied as a reward for his efficiency and long service. At the time of the Civil war he was a patriotic citizen, and fought for the preservation of the Union. He enlisted as a private in the First New Hampshire Volunteer Light Battery, August 20, 1861, and was mustered into the service of the United States on September 26, 1861. He was later mustered out, and February 22, 1863, he re-enlisted and was mustered in December 26, 1863; he was later appointed company quartermaster-sergeant, and served till the close of the war; he was finally mustered out June 9, 1865. He participated in the battles of Rappahannock Station, Gainsville, Second Bull Run, Antietam, Fredericksburg, Chancellorsville, Gettysburg, Wilderness, Cold River, Pennsylvania, Spottsylvania, North Anna, Sheldon's Cross Roads, Cold Harbor, Petersburg and Deep Bottom. He was inclined toward the Congregational religion, and attended the Hanover Street Congregational Church, of which Mrs. Dickey and his daughter are members. His services as a citizen merited the confidence of the public, and he was elected councilman and alderman of the city of Manchester, and filled those offices with credit. He was a member of Washington Lodge, No. 61, Free and Accepted Masons, in which he took the entered apprentice degree, March 13, 1873. He joined Mt. Horeb Royal Arch Chapter, No. 11, in June, 1877, and later Adoniram Council, No. 3, Royal and Select Masons, Trinity Commandery, Knights Templar, all of Manchester, also the Consistory of Nashua. He was a member of Mechanics Lodge, Independent Order of Odd Fellows, and of the Sons of Temperance. In political sentiment he was a Republican.

Mr. Dickey married, in Manchester, March 22, 1855, Mary M. Clark, born August 27, 1828, at Landaff, New Hampshire, daughter of Simeon and Mehitable (Clement) Clark. Simeon Clark was born at Landaff, October 21, 1803, died December 31, 1879, aged seventy-six. He married (first) Mehitable Clement, born at Landaff, 1803, died January 2, 1840. She was the mother of five children, two of whom are now (1907) living, namely: Mrs. Dickey, and Mrs. Joseph Abbott, of Rumney. Simeon Clark married (second), in 1859, Mary Ann Brown, of Rumney, who died in 1900. Two children were born to John W. and Mary M. (Clark) Dickey: Jessie F., wife of Robert R. Chase, who is an insurance agent, and who served as state senator in 1907; and Mary B., widow of Arthur H. Cate, late of Manchester, who died in 1898.

OTTERSON In old days, in Scotland, this name was spelled "Oughterson," and gradual changes have brought it to its present form, though it still has some variations in use among the American bearers. Soon after the beginning of the seventeenth century many thrifty and industrious people of Scotland were induced to settle in northern Ireland, where lands were cheap. About a century later their descendants made an extensive emigration to America, and New Hampshire is now indebted to these immigrants for many of her best citizens. While the hardy Scotch in Ireland refused to mix with their neighbors, they kept up commuunication with their relatives and compatriots at home, and thus preserved in remarkable degree the traditions, customs and habits of thought of their ancestry, and they have often been characterized as "More Scotch than the Scotch." Certain it is that they and their posterity have been noted for their industry, intelligence and independence, their thrift and piety, and have always been well settled in their principles, opinions and habits. The bitter struggles for supremacy between the Catholic and Protestant factions in England, which culminated in the siege of Londonderry, Ireland, in 1688-89, gave them untold hardships and much loss of life, and settled still more firmly their tenacity of religious faith. Naturally their attention was turned to this country, where religious freedom was guaranteed to all, and a large immigration followed. In 1718 a considerable company came from the vicinity of Londonderry, Ireland, and wintered in Massachusetts and Maine, settling in the following spring in Londonderry, New Hampshire, where a strong colony was built up, whose influence is still strongly felt by the state in many ways.

(I) Among those who founded the town of Londonderry was James Otterson, of whom little can now be learned. His will, made in 1760, is on record in that town, and names his wife, Agnes, and sons—James, George and John, and the two children of his son, William, who was then deceased. This is probably the James Otterson whose age is given among centenarians of Chester as one hundred and three years at death.

(II) William, son of James and Agnes Otterson, was born in Ireland, and married Jean Sample. He is found of record in that part of ancient Chester which is now Hooksett, May 25, 1757, when he purchased lot No. 128, fifth division, of Robert Boyes, though he is known to have previously lived in what was then Chester. His brother, Andrew Otterson, was also an early resident of this region, and like him, enlisted in the French and Indian war, after which he disappeared from this vicinity. At the close of that struggle William Otterson was in northern New York, and set out with his companions to cross Lake Champlain, on the way home. A number were embarked in an unseaworthy canoe, and all save one of its occupants were drowned, including Mr. Otterson. This occurred early in 1760, so that he enjoyed little of the benefit of his Hooksett land. However, his widow and two children continued to reside upon it, and all reached great age. The daughter, Mary, died November 22, 1845, aged eighty-six years. She never married, and was noted as a nurse, and familiarly and gratefully known as "Old Aunt Molly" throughout a wide district.

(III) James, only son of William and Jean (Sample) Otterson, was born August 19, 1757, somewhere in Chester, probably on the Hooksett estate of his father. As a boy he lived in Pembroke, where he learned the trade of cooper, which occupied him until his marriage, when he settled on the paternal homestead and continued farming during the remainder of his life. He died December 22, 1846, in his ninetieth year. Though not a member of any religious body he was a strict and moral man, respected by all. It is related that he would not permit any of his boys to take fish from the pond adjoining his farm after they had secured all that could be advantageously used by the family. In politics he was a Whig, and always took a keen and intelligent interest in the progress of his country, as well as of the community in which he lived. In his day his home was still in Chester, remote from the center of the town, and he mingled little in public affairs. A good citizen, he lived a long and useful life, and enjoyed in old age the fruits of his industry and thrift. His wife, Martha (Chase) Otterson, of Sutton, New Hampshire, died in 1845, aged eighty years. She was a daughter of Abner Chase, of Concord. The fate of their children is indicated as follows: William was a farmer and mill operator in Hooksett, where he died at the age of eighty-two. James died in Hooksett. Elizabeth married Nicholas Dolloff, of Epsom, and resided in Hooksett. Isaac and John A. were twins; the latter died in Clinton, Massachusetts, at the age of sixty-five years. Mary became the wife of John Young, of Deerfield, and died in Methuen, Massachusetts. Jotham Dutton was several times mayor of Nashua, and died in that city. Martin Luther died at the age of twenty-one. Three others died in infancy.

(IV) Isaac Chase, third son and fourth child of James and Martha (Chase) Otterson, was born September 11, 1797, on the old Hooksett homestead, where he grew up, receiving his education in the local district school. When a young man he was joint owner with Hiram Brown of a quarry below Hooksett, from which was taken stone now in Fanueil Hall, Boston. He also engaged in lumbering on the Merrimack river, and tilled the old farm. He passed away February 15, 1874, in his seventy-seventh year. With his wife he attended the Congregational Church, and he was universally respected as an upright man and good citizen. He was several years a member of the board of selectmen, being chairman part of the time, and served as tax collector over twenty years. Although the town had a Democratic strength of two to one in political contests, he was an outspoken Whig and later a Republican, but was held in such high regard as a man and citizen that his election was ever sure when a candidate for town office. He was married February 25, 1824, to Margaret Head, of Hooksett, youngest child of Nathaniel and Annie (Knox) Head, of that town (see Head, IV). She was born December 10, 1796, and died December 30, 1866. The location of her children is noted as follows: Martha Ann is now the widow of Jesse Gault, of Hooksett, and resides in Manchester. (See Gault, V). Nathaniel H. lived and died in Hooksett. Nancy H. married Hiram N. Ash, and lived and died in Lyman, New Hampshire. Martin L. and Mary were twins; the former is a farmer, residing on the original homestead, and the latter died at the age of nineteen years. Sarah Fernald was many years a teacher and died unmarried in Hooksett. John died in infancy, and a second John died when eleven years old. William and Henry reside in Hooksett.

MOSES The name of John Moses appears in the records of three New England communities prior to 1640—in Plymouth, Massachusetts, in Windsor-Simsbury, Connecticut, and in Portsmouth, New Hampshire. The southern members of this group were doubtless father and son, the progenitor, John Moses, of Plymouth, shipwright, having emigrated in 1632, with the tools of his trade, which yet remain in the family. This John was a good workman, no doubt. At any rate, he deemed the laborer worthy of his hire, and in 1641 is found "in the quarter court held at Boston," suing Thomas Keyser and John Guy, "of Lynne," for some twenty pounds alleged to be due on a piazza which he had built for them.

John Moses, of Plymouth, was of Welsh stock, and of no traceable connection with John Moses, of Portsmouth. The latter was of Scotch extraction, and came to New England in 1639, indentured to seven years' apprenticeship. At the expiration of his service, in 1646, he received from George Cleeves and Richard Tucker, proprietors, a deed of release from apprenticeship and conveying, under the feudal plan by which all of the Gorges lands were to be granted, a tract of one hundred acres of land on Sagamore creek. In 1660 these acres were increased to one hundred and eighty-three by a distribution of lands to "all such as were reported inhabitants and free comyuers unto the year 1657."

In 1679 one-half of the "plantation farm or tenement," as the instrument runs, was set off to Aaron, John Moses' son, and it is noteworthy that the original farm has for more than two hundred and sixty-one years remained in the possession of the first grantee's direct descendants and until recent years has been held as well in the Moses name. The farm lies on the south bank of Sagamore creek, in Portsmouth, within sight of Sagamore bridge, yet entirely secluded. On the crest of its slope stands the homestead, the third structure erected on the original foundation, and built about the middle of the eighteenth century by one Nadab Moses, a great-great-grandson of the first of his name in New Hampshire. Near the house stands an old well, dug no doubt by the first settler, and shading the low roof is a quaint oak which as a sapling was probably a companion of the pioneer's days. Within the house are treasured the documentary links which bind the present occupants to the soil chosen by their ancestor, all the wills and deeds and the original certificate of the first survey of the farm being personal.

John Moses was not a great figure in his time, but he bore a respectable part in the affairs of the infant colony. From some source he secured the title of sergeant; presumably he was sent over as a soldier by Sir Ferdinand Gorges, and in the church records he is set down as having been allotted a prominent seat in the first meeting house, under the veritable drippings of the sanctuary, indeed, having the first of the three seats "under the pulpit." To his son "Aron Moses," was assigned a seat "in the mens gallery fronting the pulpit." In 1658 the name of John Moses is found leading a subscription for the support of the minister, his contribution being one pound.

He was twice married, but of his first wife no trace is found. His second spouse was Ann Jones, widow, who appears in the early records (1661) as executrix of her first husband's estate. To John Moses his first wife bore one child, Aaron, who succeeded to his father's lands and made written agreement with his father to pay five pounds to his sister Sarah upon her marriage, doubtless as her portion. She was the child of the second marriage.

(II) The date of Aaron Moses' birth is not to be found. He married, in 1677, Ruth or Mary, daughter of Henry Sherburne, and he died in June, 1713. He was a man of some note, holding several offices of importance in the community. He was a lieutenant in Captain Tobias Langdon's company, and as such was summoned by Governor Usher to sit on a court martial which convened at New Castle. September 29, 1696. His was a family suited to a growing colony, numbering four sons and an equal number of daughters: James, Joseph, Josiah, Mark, Martha, Hannah, Abigail and Sarah. (Mention of Mark and descendants forms part of this article).

(III) Of the four sons of Aaron Moses, the eldest, James, clung closest to the old home. There he was born, lived and died, purchasing from his brothers and sisters all their interest in the property. He worked as a farmer and a cordwainer, married, joined the church, and begat seven children. His brother, Joseph, became a house-carpenter and was a quaint character in early Portsmouth, one of the first of the "odd sticks" which have adorned so many family stories there and won undying literary fame from the loving fun of Thomas Bailey Aldrich. The third son, Josiah, followed a tanner's trade, and was in 1736 a constable. November 12, 1719, he married a wife of whom no more is known than that her name was Abigail Nelson and that she bore him two sons, George and Daniel. The youngest son of Aaron was Mark, farmer and cordwainer, who married Martha Williams, October 29, 1794, and had seven children. He moved from Portsmouth to Epsom and from there sent forth descendants who now make up the chief portion of the Moses family in central New Hampshire, and of whom more hereafter.

(IV) The eldest son of Josiah Moses was George, who was baptized at Portsmouth, July 5, 1722, when as was the custom then he was probably but a few days old. He, too, was a cordwainer, and is so set down in a deed which shows him to have been joint owner with his father and mother of two small lots of land on Islington street, in Portsmouth, which were mortgaged and redeemed, one of them finally falling to the sole and unencumbered ownership of George. He married and in October, 1754, with his wife, Frances, is found conveying the title to the Islington street property. In the deed he is described as of Scarborough, York county, Massachusetts, whither he had removed earlier in the same year, and this deed was the severance of all his material ties with New Hampshire. In Scarborough he settled upon a farm in Scotlow's Hill, a prominent headland used as a landmark in early surveys and by mariners, and became the progenitor of the sturdy branch of the Moses family in Maine, whose members have had no inconspicuous share in the work of carrying forward the name and fame of the Pine Tree State. His children were numerous, eight living to marry and rear families for themselves.

(V) Of these the eldest was George, who was born in Portsmouth, and baptized there March 22, 1747. As a lad he went with his father to Scarborough and there, August 27, 1772, he married Anna Harmon. He served as a private in the Revolutionary war, having two enlistments and tours of service. July 18, 1775, he enlisted in Captain Knight's company and served in the defence of Falmouth. He enlisted again in 1779, in Captain Benjamin Larrabee's company, in Colonel Mitchell's regiment, marching in July of that year on the Penobscot expedition, which returned two months later, and he was discharged September 12, 1779. To him were born seven children, of whom two sons, William and John, came to manhood.

(VI) William Moses was the eldest of the second George's family. He was born December 29, 1772, and died September 29, 1829. He lived as a young man at Scarborough and at Buxton, in Maine, and in 1822 removed to Eaton, in Carroll county, New Hampshire. January 31, 1796, at Scarborough, he had married Anne Milliken, who gave him nine children, all of whom were born in Maine and with one exception lived to an extreme age, most of them evidently deeming it to die disgraced at less than eighty.

(VII) William's oldest child was Cyrus, who was born at Scarborough, September 2, 1796. He was a farmer and also followed his father in the trades of tanner and shoemaker. As such he labored at Eaton, where his father died, and where he is recorded as administrator of the estate. He married, March 20, 1819, Eunice Underwood, from a family founded, according to tradition, by English refugees from a family of consequence in the mother country, who fled from British jurisdiction during the early days of the Revolution because of irreconcilable differences with the government as to policies relating to the revolting colonies. They lived at Eaton and at Freedom, in New Hampshire, and at Parsonsfield, Saco, and Standish, in Maine. At Standish he became possessed of an extensive farm, where he and his wife both ended their days, and where their youngest child now lives. Their family numbered six sons and three daughters.

(VIII) The sixth child and fourth son of Cyrus and Eunice Moses was Thomas Gannett Moses, who was born in Eaton, New Hampshire, March 7, 1829. His grandfather died a few months later than this date, and his father removed to Maine not long afterward. His boyhood was spent upon the farm, with limited opportunity for education until the family took residence in Saco, where young Thomas made good use of the advantages of the academy there and is remembered by his fellows as a diligent and brilliant student, quick to assimilate knowledge and securing far more from the limited sources of the old-time academy than most of his mates. He worked for a time at his father's trade of shoemaker and was also for a short period a carpenter. But as a young man he went into trade and remained in mercantile pursuits until about his thirtieth year, when he embraced religion, and such were his intellectual gifts that it was at once predicted of him that he would become a preacher.

Setting himself to prepare for the ministry, he turned again to his books with new zeal and purpose and placed himself, as was the custom of the time, under the tuition of the clergyman of the community for instruction in theology. In December, 1862, he was licensed to preach by the York and Cumberland Christian Conference, and from that time till now has been borne on the rolls of the ministry of the Christian Convention, a sect once numerous in New England, but now chiefly influential in the Middle West, where their churches and colleges are leaders in religious and intellectual life. The repute of the young licentiate had spread through the counties in Maine where his conference had jurisdiction and more than one pulpit was ready to receive him. He was formally ordained, June 15, 1863, at Kittery, Maine, where he had his first pastorate, which lasted till 1866, when he was called from the extreme west to the extreme east of Maine, and became pastor of the Christian Church at Lubec, in Washington county. Here he remained for six years, relinquishing his charge to accept the pastorate of the North Church at Eastport, Maine. Here he entered upon a most fruitful pastorate of nearly twelve years' duration, during which his parish became enlarged in numbers, with material additions to its ecclesiastic plant, while the congregations who flocked to hear the preacher were limited only by the size of the church edifice.

In 1883 Mr. Moses accepted a call to the pastorate of the Christian Church at Franklin, New Hampshire, and remained there for more than ten years. During all this time he served as secretary to the New England Christian Convention, in which are affiliated all the denominational activities of the Christian connection in the territory designated by its name, and his zeal and efficiency in that position of executive responsibility so impressed his colleagues that, after repeated urgings, he resigned his pastorate to become New England missionary for his church, the funds of the denomination having so increased during his incumbency of the secretary's office that it had become possible to establish a permanent salaried field agent.

His resignation was regretfully accepted by his Franklin congregation, and Mr. Moses took up his new duties. He found a peculiar situation confronting him. His church had once held a place of commanding influence in the religious life of many a New England community and in many such places, during its time of potency, the Christian Church had erected a fine church structure and had often provided itself with a parsonage. The sect had arisen as a means to express religious liberty in respect to written creeds, and in many places had done a noble work in freeing the elders ecclesiastical orders from intolerant restraint. With the more general religious freedom, not only in thought but in action, which has characterized the last quarter century, the Christian Church necessarily found itself brought into wide competition with other beliefs and in many places its spacious meeting-houses sheltered a beggarly congregation, in point of numbers. As New England missionary Mr. Moses deemed it better denominational policy and wiser religious strategy to reclaim these decadent parishes than to attempt to start new ones, while the economic point of view was plain in the attempt to save to the church in their efficiency the parochial plants which a former generation had provided. To this task, unique as it then was among church activities, Mr. Moses gave himself ardently, and took up his residence at Skowhegan, Maine, where conditions presented themselves in such wise as to sum up the extreme of the problem he had set himself to solve.

For more than two years he remained in this field, seeking to build up a parish to receive and maintain once more a permanent pastor. But more than thirty years in the active work of some of the largest parishes which his denomination could offer, together with prolonged labor in the evangelical field, had drained the preacher's powers lower than he thought, and it became necessary for him to seek a less exacting field of activity. Accordingly, he accepted a call to the pulpit of the Christian Church at York, Maine, and from 1895 to 1900 ministered to that people most acceptably. In the latter year the parish to which he had given the strength of his younger manhood sought once more his guidance. Family ties also drew him back to the former field and he took up a vacant pastorate at Westport, which lasted until 1904, when his retirement from the active ministry became imperative through failing strength.

He now lives in retirement at Eastport, Maine, the guide, counselor and friend of the community, to whom his fruitful years are filled with the odor of blessing. His has been a rich and fruitful life. Blessed with rare natural powers, Mr. Moses has had remarkable success as a preacher and an evangelist, and many are those whom he has led to a better life. The evening of his life is quiet and content, and the leveling shadows of his sunset years are illumined and cheered by the affectionate solicitude of his children and those amid whom his life has been spent in blessing.

He married, December 1, 1850, Ruth Sprague Smith, at Standish, Maine. She died in 1878, and he married, June 6, 1880, Florence Della Higgins, at Westport, Maine. A daughter and five sons were born to him by his first wife: Luella Adelaide, Frank Elbridge, Charles Thomas, William Herbert, John Winfield, George Higgins. By his second wife he had one son, Cyrus Arthur, who died in infancy. The other children are all living, except Luella Adelaide, who married Andrew T. Capen, and died in Palatka, Florida, in January, 1892.

(IX) George Higgins, youngest child of Thomas

T. S. Moses.

William

William H Moses

Gannett and Ruth (Sprague) Moses, was born at Lubec, Washington county, Maine, February 9, 1869. When his father took a new pastorate in Franklin, New Hampshire, the boy entered the public schools at that place, and graduated from Franklin high school in the class of 1885. Two years at the Phillips Exeter Academy followed, and in 1887 he graduated with high rank as a scholar. In the fall of the same year he entered the sophomore class in Dartmouth College without conditions, and received the degree of Bachelor of Arts in 1890, being elected class day orator by his associates. In 1893 he was made Master of Arts. In 1889 he was appointed private secretary to David H. Goodell, governor of New Hampshire, and served in that capacity during the term of the legislature of that year, which was the last summer session of the general court. In 1890, upon graduation, he became manager of the *New Hampshire Republican,* and also served as private secretary to the chairman of the Republican state committee during the campaign of 1890. In the fall of the latter year he joined the staff of the *Concord Evening Monitor* and *Independent Statesman,* and was soon promoted to the position of news editor, and in 1892 to managing editor, which place he still holds. In 1898, upon the organization of the Monitor and Statesman Company, he became its president. In that same year he helped to organize the Rumford Printing Company, and was elected its treasurer. In 1893, when the law was passed establishing a forestry commission, he was appointed a member of the board and was made its secretary, serving by successive appointments until January, 1907, when he resigned. In 1905, during the session of the Russo-Japanese peace conference at Portsmouth, he acted as secretary to the governor of New Hampshire, who was the official host of the plenipotentiaries. In 1902 he was elected member of the board of education for Union school district, and was again elected in 1906, being still a member of the board. A glance at what is above written will show that George H. Moses is in the front rank of New Hampshire men who do things. While yet a boy his native ability and integrity attracted attention and won him friends who helped him to positions where he could be useful and receive proper compensation for his services. Leaving college equipped to fill a place in the newspaper field, he had no difficulty in finding employment and efficient work brought rapid promotion, so that today, while still a young man, he is ranked among the foremost leaders in journalism in New Hampshire.

His official life has shown that a pleasing personality and a faithful discharge of the duties of office are recognized by an approving public. As a citizen Mr. Moses has always supported with tongue and pen those measures which benefited his fellow citizens. His labors so far enumerated would prove his life to have been a busy one; but he has done much literary work not yet mentioned. In addition to his newspaper writing he has contributed frequently to magazines and other columns, and is the author of "John Stark," published in 1891, and "New Hampshire Men," published in 1893. In 1894 he had editorial supervision of the *Granite Monthly,* and wrote one sketch for each issue of the magazine; during this period the publication had its largest success. Nor is this the limit of his activity. He has been a frequent speaker on forestry and other topics at farmers' institutes, grange meetings, and meetings of scientific associations, including the American Forestry Association and the American Association for the Advancement of Science, numerous clubs, boards of trade, etc. He has also been a contributor to the arguments of the stump and before legislative committees. He belongs to no secret orders except the Grange and college fraternities. He attends the South Congregational Church.

George Higgins Moses married, October 3, 1893, at Franklin, New Hampshire, Florence Abby Gordon, who was born May 11, 1870, daughter of Hiram S. and Elberta C. (Martin) Gordon. They have one child, Gordon, born October 5, 1900.

(III) Mark, fourth son of Aaron and Ruth or Mary Moses, was probably born in Portsmouth. He was a cordwainer and also a farmer, and resided first in Portsmouth, later in Greenland, and settled in Epsom, New Hampshire, about the year 1760. His residence was about a half mile northeast of the present railroad station. He was married (first), October 29, 1724, to Martha Williams, and their children recorded at Portsmouth in the church and family records were: Elizabeth, Samuel, Aaron, William, Sylvanus and James. (The last named and descendants are noticed in this article). The seventh child, Jennie, was baptized in the Epsom Congregational Church, December 18, 1763, at which time she was probably an adult as the record shows that she owned the covenant in the church at that time. He married (second) Jane Wallace.

(IV) Aaron, second son and child of Mark and Martha (Williams) Moses, was born in 1742, probably in Greenland, and died March 20, 1816, in Greenland. He was married about 1765 to Dorothy Sanborn, who died at Gilmanton, New Hampshire, June, 1820, aged seventy-five. Their children were: William, George, Abrathor, Aaron, and probably a daughter Susan.

(V) Abrathor, third son of Aaron and Dorothy (Sanborn) Moses, had sons John, William, and Sanborn, and a daughter Olive.

(VI) William, son of Abrathor Moses, was born in 1808, and for many years had a transportation line between Kensington and Boston, between which points he hauled a great deal of merchandise. He married Abigail Darling, born October 5, 1806. They had children: Stephen T., Thaddeus S., Lydia Almira and Robert T. He died February 14, 1875, at the age of sixty-seven years. His wife died December 14, 1861, aged fifty-five years.

(VII) Thaddeus S., son of William and Abigail Darling (Keniston) Moses, was born at Campton, New Hampshire, January 28, 1835, and was educated in the common schools of Plymouth and the academy at Laconia. When a young man he learned the trade of tinsmith at Plymouth. In 1860 he removed to Meredith, where he bought out a business which he carried on for forty years. He was a prosperous citizen, had the confidence of his fellow townsmen, and in politics was a Democrat. He was one of the selectmen, was town treasurer for ten years, was representative from Meredith one term, in 1888 was elected state senator from his district, was a delegate to the constitutional convention, and a member of the building committee which had charge of the construction of the court house of Belknap county. In his religious faith he was a Baptist, and for many years he was a deacon in the church at Meredith. Mr. Moses married, February 22, 1862, Emily S. Currier, daughter of Aaron and Anna (Hoag) Currier, who was born November 26, 1840. Of this marriage there were four children: William H., Geneva A., now wife of Dr. Hawkins, of Meredith; Chester S., of New York City; and Mina M., wife of Frank H. Shumway, of Somerville, Massachusetts. Thaddeus S. Moses died January 13, 1902.

(VIII) William Hammond, eldest son of Thaddeus S. and Emily S. (Currier) Moses, was born September 3, 1863, in Meredith. He was educated in the common schools of Meredith and Tilton Seminary, graduating from the latter institution in 1886. He learned the business of his father while young, and at the age of twenty-three went into partnership with him. This relation lasted from 1886 to 1890, when he came to Tilton, and began to learn the art and mystery of cloth making in the Tilton Mills. After the death of Mr. J. J. Pillsbury, in 1895, Mr. Moses was elected treasurer of the Tilton Mills, and in 1901 was elected president of the company. Both these offices he now holds. He is also president and treasurer of the Tilton Electric Company, treasurer of the Tilton & Northfield Aqueduct Company, and director in each of them, and in the Concord & Montreal railroad and Manchester National Bank. He is a trustee of the Tilton Seminary, of the Iowa Savings Bank and of the Park Cemetery Association. He is a member of Doric Lodge, No. 78, Ancient Free and Accepted Masons, and of the Winnepesaukee Yacht Club. He is a member of the Democratic state committee. Mr. Moses is one of the leading citizens of Tilton, and well known throughout the state as a manufacturer and financier. William H. Moses married, June 11, 1890, Mabel T. Pillsbury, daughter of Alpha J. and Eliza S. (Tucker) Pillsbury, of Tilton, born August 27, 1870 (see Pillsbury, VIII). They have two children, Hazel Pillsbury, born October 2, 1893, and Margery, May 22, 1897.

(IV) Sylvanus, fourth son and fifth child of Mark and second child of his second wife, Jane (Wallace) Moses, was born August 25, 1754, probably in Greenland, and died in January, 1832, in Epsom, New Hampshire. He was a soldier of the Revolution, serving nine months under Captain Emery at White Plains. After his discharge he settled on a farm in Sagamore. He was married August 22, 1776, to Miriam Young, of Danville, New Hampshire, and their children were: Sarah, John, Joseph, David, Miriam, Joshua, Elijah and Polly. On May 6, 1820, he and his wife deeded the farm, valued at two thousand dollars, to John B. Girard, in consideration of support in old age. The wife survived her husband eight years, and died in 1840.

(V) David, third son and fourth child of Sylvanus and Miriam (Young) Moses, was reared in Epsom, and subsequently resided in Concord, Chichester, and Stewartstown, New Hampshire. A deed on record shows that he sold one hundred and ten acres in the northeast corner of Concord, February 14, 1823. The inventory of his estate in Chichester was made October 20, 1828, showing a value of fifteen hundred and ninety-seven dollars and ninety-four cents. He married Mehitable Rand, of Epsom, and the vital records of the state show the birth of three sons: Willard, John and Charles.

(VI) John, second son of David and Mehitable (Rand) Moses, was born July 12, 1817, in Concord, and died October 8, 1894, in Colebrook, New Hampshire. He was reared on a farm, and was very fond of hunting, being especially expert in the capture of foxes. On attaining manhood he settled in Colebrook, where he engaged in agriculture. He was married in 1841, to Fanny Munn, daughter of Deacon James Munn, of Hereford, province of Quebec. Their children are accounted for as follows: 1. Charles Ezra receives extended mention in the following paragraph. 2. Emma died in 1900; married (first) Ezra Howard, and (second) Obadiah Call. 3. Flora became the wife of Herbert Penny. 4. Eliza is the widow of Berkley Keazer, and lives in Beecher Falls. 5. Lubian E. is a citizen of Warren, this state. 6. Willard E. lives in Lancaster, New Hampshire. Fanny (Munn) Moses died March, 1896.

(VII) Charles Ezra, eldest child of John and Fanny (Munn) Moses, was born March 26, 1845, in Hereford, province of Quebec. On leaving home he was employed for two years in making brick, and subsequently worked three years as a carpenter. He began the study of medicine, but abandoned it as uncongenial. He was much employed as a teacher, spending two years thus in Colbrook Academy, and nine years in other towns in the vicinity. For a period of fourteen years he kept the Willard House at North Stratford, and then traded the hotel for a large farm in Lunenburg, Vermont, on which he settled. He made a specialty of dairying, and kept seventy-five head of cattle. In the spring of 1907 he leased the farm and moved to Lancaster to reside. While a resident of Lunenburg he served two years as selectman and five years as lister (assessor). He is a Republican in political principle, and is popular with his contemporaries. He was one of the reorganizers and is now vice-president of the Coos and Essex Agricultural Society, is a member of the Independent Order of Odd Fellows and Knights of Pythias, and is engaged in spreading the spirit of fraternity among men. Mr. Moses was married December 24, 1871, at Columbia, New Hampshire, to Amanda Melissa Frizzell, daughter of Amasa Frizzell, of South Canaan, Vermont. The children of this union are: Frank E., who is again referred to in the succeeding paragraph; Mertrude G., who is now the wife of Frederick C. Cleaveland, of Lancaster; and Lester Ezra, who is now (1907) a student at Dartmouth College.

(VIII) Frank Elmon, eldest son and child of Charles E. and Amanda M. (Frizzell) Moses, was born in Colebrook, January 14, 1873. From the Lewiston (Maine) grammar school, which he attended three years, he entered the Portland Business College, remaining there one year, and in 1890 took a position in Wilson's drug store at Groveton. He shortly afterwards entered the employ of C. T. McNally as a bookkeeper; was still later employed in the same capacity at the Berlin (New Hampshire) National Bank, and returning to Groveton resumed his connection with the drug business. He next became associated with his father in the dry goods business in Groveton, but after continuing in trade some eighteen months he sold his interest in 1897, and accepting the position of bookkeeper in the office of the Odell Manufacturing Company at Groveton, paper manufacturers, he has ever since remained in their employ. Here he has worked his way upward to a position of responsibility and trust, being at the present time chief accountant and assistant to general manager George B. Bearce. In politics Mr. Moses is a Republican. He is a member of the Masonic Order, belonging to the North Star Lodge, North Star Chapter and North Star Commandery, of Lancaster, is officially identified with the Knights of Pythias, having occupied all of the important chairs in the local lodge and being at the present time district deputy grand chancellor; and also affiliates with the Independent Order of Foresters. On October 12, 1895, he was united in marriage with Bertha Blanche Hayes, daughter of William Hayes, of Northumberland. Mr. and Mrs. Moses have had two sons: Vernard E., born November 24, 1899, died November 18, 1906; and Kenneth L., born May 5, 1901. Mrs. Moses is active in religious and musical circles, is an accomplished instrumentalist and officiates at the organ in both of the Groveton churches.

Frank I. Smith

(IV) James, fifth son and sixth child of Mark and Martha (Williams) Moses, was born in Greenland, February 27, 1758, and died August 17, 1819. He was a farmer and settled on the home place in Epsom. He married, March 9, 1780, Elizabeth Sherburne, of Northwood, and they had six children: Mark, James, Jane, Betsey S., Mary and Sarah.

(V) Mark, eldest child of James and Elizabeth (Sherburne) Moses, was born January 19, 1781, and died March 11, 1811. He married, June 19, 1802, Betsey Cate, and they had three children: Joseph J., Dearborn B. and Mark S.

(VI) Dearborn B., second son and child of Mark and Betsey (Cate) Moses, was born in Epsom, August 3, 1805, and died August 23, 1881, aged seventy-six years. He married, February 13, 1839, Sally H. Locke, and they had one child: Sarah L.

(VII) Sarah Locke, only child of Dearborn B. and Sally H. (Locke) Moses, was born in Epsom, November 25, 1841, and married, June 19, 1869, James H. Tripp (see Tripp, IV).

SMITH The early immigrants to New England were mostly artisans and many of them men of little learning. That they were possessed of strong characters is evidenced in a thousand ways to the student of history. While the pen was an awkward instrument to many of them, they were industrious and conquered the wilderness, establishing the foundation of the civilization which we enjoy. Among the most useful men in the colonies were the Smiths who made all the nails used in the construction of buildings and nearly every implement of every sort employed in the rude life of the pioneers. A century previous the country people in England had taken surnames, and it fell out that many who were smiths by occupation took the word for a patronymic. In the midst of these, where christian names were oft repeated, it has been difficult to trace a line of descent in many cases.

(I) John Smith and his wife Isabella resided in Watertown, Massachusetts, and subsequently in Lexington, same colony. Here John died July 12, 1639, at the age of sixty years. His wife survived him three months, dying October 12 of the same year, at the same age. It is deemed probable by authorities on genealogy, that John and Thomas of Lexington and, perhaps, Francis and Daniel were sons of John and Isabella Smith.

(II) Thomas Smith came to America in 1635, and was admitted freeman May 17, 1637. He probably resided in Lexington, and died March 10, 1693, aged ninety-two years. He married Mary, daughter of William Knapp, and their children were: James, John (died young), Thomas, John, Joseph, Mary, Ephraim, Jonathan and Sarah.

(III) Thomas (2) Smith, third son and child of Thomas (1) and Mary (Knapp) Smith, was born August 26, 1640, and died in Lexington, Massachusetts, December 25, 1727, at the age of eighty-eight years. He and his wife were admitted to the church in Lexington, June, 1701, by a letter of dismission from Weymouth, from which it is apparent that he had previously resided in Weymouth. He was taxed in Lexington in 1693, and honorable mention of him appears in the records there in 1700. In placing the seats of citizens in the meetinghouse we find that he and John Stone, "were Plast in ye fore seatt of ye body of seats." He married, in 1663, Mary Hosmer, daughter of James Hosmer, of Concord. She died October 1, 1719, aged sixty-four. His children, the first three born in Concord, were: Thomas, James, John, Samuel, Joseph and Benjamin.

(IV) Benjamin Smith, youngest son of Thomas (2) and Mary (Hosmer) Smith, was born September 24, 1689, in Lexington, Massachusetts, and was for a long time a popular citizen of that town. He held numerous offices and was for twelve years a member of the board of selectmen. Five of his children died in childhood or infancy. He married, July 9, 1713, Martha Comee, who died November 19, 1749. He married (second), May 3, 1750, Mistress Esther Green. He died December 9, 1779, in his ninety-first year. Of his children, all born of the first wife, only the eldest and the youngest survived. They were: Benjamin, Daniel, Ezekiel, Martha, Thomas (died young), Solomon and Thomas.

(V) Benjamin (2) Smith, eldest child of Benjamin (1) and Martha (Comee) Smith, was born July 20, 1714, in Lexington, and passed his life in that town. He married, November 17, 1734, Anna Parker, who survived him and died, his widow, June 10, 1768, in Waltham, Massachusetts. Their children were: Solomon, Benjamin, Anna, Martha, Esther, David and Thomas.

(VI) Benjamin (3) Smith, second son and child of Benjamin (2) and Anna (Parker) Smith, was born March 11, 1741, in Lexington, and was a resident of that town through life. He married Mary Lee, and they were admitted to the church in Lexington, June 24, 1768. Their children were: Anna, Benjamin and David.

(VII) David Smith, youngest child of Benjamin (3) and Mary (Lee) Smith, was born September 29, 1776, in Lexington, and settled in Ashby, Massachusetts. The History of Lexington says that he married a Foster, if so, she did not long survive. He married, in Ashby, May 7, 1807, Rachel Whitney, born April 10, 1783, a daughter of Ephraim and Sarah (Burgess) Whitney, of Stow and Ashburnham. Ephraim Whitney died in Ashby, November 17, 1784, and eight years later his home estate was annexed to Ashby.

(VIII) Ira Smith, son of David and Rachel (Whitney) Smith, was born probably in Ashby, Massachusetts, October 24, 1813, and was a farmer. After residing for some years in New Ipswich, New Hampshire, he removed to Milford, and died October 3, 1887, aged seventy-four. He was a member of the Methodist Episcopal Church, and in politics a Republican. He married, December 6, 1843, Hannah P., daughter of Francis B. and Susan (Preston) Maxwell, who was born in Boston, Massachusetts, November 13, 1822, still living in Milford. They had two children, born in New Ipswich, New Hampshire: Frank Ira and Charles Henry. Frank Ira is mentioned below. Charles Henry was born December 26, 1848, is a janitor and resides in Weymouth, Massachusetts. He married, September 3, 1868, Jennie, daughter of Joseph and Mary Tilson, of New Ipswich.

(IX) Frank Ira Smith, son of Ira and Hannah P. (Maxwell) Smith, was born in New Ipswich, New Hampshire, April 9, 1846. He was educated in the Appleton School at New Ipswich, where he fitted for college. He then taught school three years in Mason, New Hampshire, and two terms as assistant in the high school at Ashby, Massachusetts. In 1871 he began a veterinary course under Dr. Day, of Charlestown, Massachusetts, which he completed three years later, and began practicing at Milford, New Hampshire, in 1872. He removed from there in 1880 to Rochester, where he has since resided. He is a Republican, and for many years has taken an active part in politics. He was elected to the legislature from Rochester, ward five, in 1898, and was deputy sheriff of Strafford county continuously from 1895 till 1906. In the latter year he became a candidate for high sheriff and received the largest number of votes ever cast for a candidate in the county. He is a member of Custos Morum Lodge. No. 42, Independent Order of Odd Fellows, of Milford, New Hampshire, which he joined in 1869. He is also a member of Rochester Grange, No. 86, of the Patrons of Husbandry, and also of Knights of the Golden Eagle.

Mr. Smith married (first), in Amherst, New Hampshire, November 26, 1869, Esther M. Fuller. Married (second), November 24, 1884, at Barnstead, New Hampshire, Martha J. Emerson, born in Barnstead, New Hampshire, October 1, 1848, daughter of Timothy and Sarah (Foster) Emerson, of Barnstead. Three children were born of the first marriage: Esther, Frank W. and Mary E.; the latter is the wife of Charles Malley, of Boston.

(Second Family.)

SMITH There are numerous branches of the various Smith families of New England scattered about New Hampshire, and it is said that seven or eight distinct branches were represented among the early settlers of Sanbornton alone. The family was very early at Hampton and has contributed much to the development of many sections of the state.

(I) Robert Smith was born about 1611, and was among the first at Exeter. New Hampshire, being a signer of the Combination in 1639. He settled in Hampton as early as 1657, and died there August 30, 1706. He was by trade a tailor, but probably engaged chiefly in husbandry in that pioneer period. His wife Susanna was killed by lightning June 12, 1680, and he lived a widower for more than twenty-six years. No record of the births of his children were made, and they may not appear herein in their chronological order. They included: John, Merribah, Asahel, Jonathan and Joseph.

(II) Jonathan, son of Robert and Susanna Smith, was a brick maker and settled in Exeter. He was married January 25, 1670, to Mehitabel Holdred. Their children were: Israel, Jacob, Ithiel, Abigail, Joseph, Leah and Mehitabel.

(III) Joseph, fourth son and fifth child of Jonathan and Mehitabel (Holdred) Smith, was born probably about 1682, in Exeter, and was one of the grantees of Stratham, being the fifteenth to sign his name on the petition for the incorporation of that town, 1748. Four years subsequently, on the division of lands, he drew lots numbers forty-four and eighteen, and the latter subsequently fell to his son Elisha.

Joseph Smith evidently was a man of some consequence in the early history of Sanbornton, and some of his sons after him also became prominently identified with local affairs. Those of them who are said to have been conspicuous in this respect were Joseph, junior, and Elisha Smith. (Elisha and descendants receive mention in this article).

(IV) Joseph (2) Smith, son of Joseph (1), went from Stratham to Sanbornton, and in the allotment of lots drew numbers seventy-one and sixty, and built his house on the former. It is not certain whether he or his eldest son Joseph served during the Revolution, but one of them was there, the weight of opinion according the honor to his son, who is said to have come to the town in advance of his father. Joseph the elder in early life served his time as a ship carpenter in Newburyport, and built the first dam at the "threshing mill," where he sacrificed his own life, July 4, 1795, while rescuing a boy from drowning. One of the stories regarding this event is that he drowned himself, but the stronger belief always has been that while walking on the dam with the rescued child in his arms he fell and struck his head on an exposed pin (treenail) and fractured his skull. Near the same brook his wife had died of apoplexy, June 29, 1790. Henry Smith, son of Joseph, always said that he was the middle one of a family of fifteen children, seven being older and seven younger than himself, but the christian names of all of this Joseph Smith's children cannot be given. Those whose names are known were: Joseph, William, Henry, Solomon, Stephen. Hannah, Michael, Enoch and Samuel.

(V) Joseph, son of Joseph last mentioned, settled on his father's lot, and between him and his parent lies the honor of being in the first band of revolutionary soldiers from the town of Sanbornton. His first wife was Mary Sleeper, an excellent woman, but who was lame, eccentric and given to the exercise of her native gifts in preaching. She died April 21, 1801, (or December 11, 1811). and on February 16, 1812, Joseph married Sarah (Sally) Robinson. All of his children were by his first wife, and were Robert, Cephas, Joseph and Margaret.

(VI) Cephas Smith was born in Sanbornton, New Hampshire, in 1791, and died February 26, 1850. When a young man he removed to Moultonborough, New Hampshire, but afterward returned to Sanbornton and lived on or near his father's place. He was an extensive farmer, having about seven hundred acres, a part of which was well timbered, and in clearing the land he carried on an extensive lumber business. He was a man of good business capacity and as his enterprises were generally successful he accumulated a comfortable fortune. He married twice. The name of his first wife is unknown, but she bore him children. His second wife, whom he married, September 24, 1824, was Mrs. Sally (Morrison) Calley, widow of William Calley and daughter of Thomas W. and Betsey (Cass) Morrison. (See Morrison. IV). In Runnel's "History of Sanbornton" the children of Cephas Smith are given as Mary Jane, born April 25, 1821; Lavina, born April 26, 1823; Priscilla M. (by his second wife), born April 13, 1826. The Smith family record gives the names of the children of Cephas as Rufus, Eliza, Lovina, Sarah, Lydia, Priscilla D. and Catherine. The latter record is undoubtedly nearer correct, although the order of birth of the children may not be preserved.

(VII) Rufus, son of Cephas, was born in Sanbornton, New Hampshire, 1819, and was twelve years old when his father removed with his family to Moultonborough, in Carroll county, New Hampshire. When seventeen years old he went with his uncle to Boston, with the intention of remaining in that city, but afterward he determined to go to sea, and made a voyage to the Grand Banks of Newfoundland. Returning home he engaged in lumbering with his father, and also established a freight boat line from Alton bay, the termination of the Cochecho road at that time, to Centre harbor, Meredith village and Lake village (Lakeport). The boat used by Mr. Smith in this pioneer transportation enterprise was a unique affair, built after the fashion of a scow, of light draught in the water, but of good carrying capacity, and was propelled by horse power. He operated the boat and also continued lumbering until 1864, and then removed with his family to Lakeport and engaged in mechanical pursuits and work for the Cole Manufacturing Company until he retired from active business. Mr. Smith died in Lakeport March 13, 1902. He married Nancy Parker Lovejoy, who was born in Meredith, New Hampshire, June 17, 1817, daughter of Caleb Lovejoy of Meredith. They had two children: Lucy Jane, born in Moultonborough, 1843; unmarried, and now lives on the old homestead in Lakeport. George Henry, a business man of Lakeport, New Hampshire.

(VIII) George Henry, only son of Rufus and Nancy Parker (Lovejoy) Smith, was born in Moultonborough, New Hampshire, June 18, 1847, and came to Lakeport with his parents in 1864. He was educated in the common schools of Moultonborough and Wolfborough Academy, and after leaving school was employed for the next ten years as machinist in the works of the Cole Manufacturing Company. During the last three years of this time he was kept on the road engaged setting up mill machinery. In 1874 Mr. Smith began merchandizing at Lakeport in company with Horace Bugbee, under the firm name of Bugbee & Smith. This partnership relation was continued about two and one-half years, when Mr. Smith succeeded to his partner's interest and has since been sole proprietor of the business. He is a Republican in politics, and served one year as town clerk of Gilford and for three years was a member of the Republican State committee. He has been an Odd Fellow ever since he attained his majority; he was brought up under the influence of the Free Will Baptist Church. Mr. Smith has been married twice. He married (first), December 20, 1876, Eliza Edith Gardner, who died September 22, 1885. He married (second), January 23, 1889, Carrie Alice Bryant. She was born January 12, 1858, daughter of Wyatt and Hannah (Chick) Bryant of Tamworth, New Hampshire. Mr. Smith has one son, born of his first marriage: Harry Lincoln Smith, born February 12, 1879, in Lakeport. He is by profession a civil engineer and now employed as assistant foreman in the car department of the Boston and Maine Railroad Company at Lakeport. He is a member of the city council of Laconia, and has held an office of some kind since he became of age.

(IV) Elisha, second son of Joseph (1) Smith, was born in Stratham, New Hampshire, in 1723 (possibly 1733) and died March 12, 1811. He married Lydia Norris, of Stratham, and soon afterward settled in Epping, where most of his children were born. Besides the land which came from his father, he acquired other considerable tracts, and at one time owned a solid body of nearly seven hundred acres extending through from his home lot to the Meredith line. He frequently walked from Epping to work at clearing his lands, and at one time while traveling with a willow cane divided it into four parts and stuck them in the earth near the log house which he was building; and from one of the pieces came the big willow tree near his homestead until about 1880. In the winter of 1775-76 Mr. Smith moved his family to his new home in Sanbornton, and in the following summer was one of those who signed the association test act. He was a man of integrity and enterprise, and exercised much influence throughout the town. He built a saw mill on Black Cat brook, and gave one hundred acres of land to each of his six sons. His wife Lydia died November 12, 1819. Their children were: Mercy, Lydia, Molly, Benjamin, Mehitable, Zebulon, Elisha, Josiah, Nathaniel, Joseph, Abigail and two others whose names are unknown.

(V) Zebulon Smith was born April 1, 1767, and was a farmer, receiving his portion of his father's estate. He married (first), Betsey Hoyt, who died February 2, 1801; married (second), Elizabeth Sanborn, who died April 5, 1824; and married (third), Mrs. Mary (Polly) Rosebrook of Sandwich, New Hampshire, and daughter of Captain Chase, of Conway. She died October 2, 1847, and Zebulon died February 13, 1848. His children were: Stuart, Zebulon, Hezekiah, Nancy, Josiah, Elisha, David, Samuel, Betsey H. and Barnard.

(VI) David Smith, sixth son and seventh child of Zebulon Smith, was born in Sanbornton, July 8, 1805, and died March 1, 1883. After his marriage he was for five years a saw mill employe in Littleton and Bristol, and in 1841 settled in the northeast part of Sanbornton, on land bought and cleared by his father. On August 23, 1834, he married Olive Knowlton, who was born in Northfield, New Hampshire, October 12, 1804, and died May 30, 1880. Their children: Ruth Knowlton, born March 30, 1836; married, February 27, 1862, Joseph Noah Sanborn (see Sanborn, VII). Lizzie Sanborn, born December 29, 1839; married Stephen M. Woodman. Olive Jane, born August 3, 1847; died December 18, 1863.

(Third Family.)

SMITH The family herein traced was very early located in New Hampshire, but the lack of records in the early days of Rockingham county makes it extremely difficult to trace a continuous line.

(I) Nicholas Smith, who was probably a brother of other Smiths in the vicinity, was located at Exeter as early as 1658. His children are on record in Exeter, namely: Nathaniel, Nicholas, Anna and Theophilus.

(II) Theophilus, youngest child of Nicholas Smith, was born February 14, 1667, in Exeter, and further account of him does not appear.

(III) Theophilus (2) Smith was probably a son of Theophilus (1), of Exeter. He resided in Stratham, and is referred to in the records as "Esquire." This occurs in connection with the birth of his son, and concerning him there is no further record.

(IV) Theophilus (3), only son of Theophilus (2) Smith, Esq., was born May 15, 1741, in Stratham. He was a signer of the association test in that town at the opening of the Revolution, and appears as a member of various committees, such as those appointed to engage a minister and to make repairs on the meetinghouse. His wife, Sarah, was born January 28, 1742, at Exeter, the fourth daughter of Dr. Josiah Gilman. Their children were as follows: Sarah (died young), Theophilus, Josiah Coffin, John, Mary, Abigail, Samuel (died young), Sarah, Samuel, William, Elizabeth (died young), and Elizabeth.

(V) Josiah Coffin, second son and third child of Theophilus (3) and Sarah (Gilman) Smith, was born July 15, 1764, in Stratham, and resided in Exeter and owned an extensive tract of land along the river, where the present High street in Exeter is. His homestead was on or near the line of the present street. Josiah C. Smith and Annie Leavitt were married in Exeter, July 11, 1789, by Isaac Mansfield, clergyman. Their children were: George, Josiah G., Emma, Eliza, Charles Coffin and Sarah Ann. George was a lumberman, surveyor and justice of the peace. He married Sarah Smith, of Massachusetts, and had Ann Maria, George, and Georgiana, who died young. Josiah Gilman, born December 28, 1792, died January 2, 1877. He was a merchant and carriage maker. He married (first), Mehitable Sheafe Burleigh, and had Frances Rodgers (died young), and Elizabeth Frances. He married (second), Frances Ann Eastman, and had Charles Gilman and Harriet G. Emma married Robert Shute, merchant, of Exeter, and had Emeline, Joseph M. (twins), Elizabeth and Isaac. Eliza married Henry Shute, merchant, of Exeter, and had George, Henry A. (died young), Sarah (died young), and Eliza (died young). Charles Coffin is the subject of the next paragraph. Sarah Ann married Joseph Boardman and had no children.

(VI) Charles Coffin, fifth child and third son of Josiah C. and Annie (Leavitt) Smith, was born in Exeter, January 26, 1807, and died there, July 24, 1863. He was educated in the public schools, and then learned carriage-making, including carriage painting, and later engaged in the same business on his own account, and continued in that line all his life. He was a successful manufacturer and a good citizen. In politics he was a Republican. For many years he was a faithful and honored member of the Baptist Church. He married, in Pittsfield, November 20, 1834, Mary W. Berry, who was born in Pittsfield, August 18, 1812, and died in Exeter, August 12, 1868. Her parents were Thomas and Annie B. (Shaw) Berry. Four children were born to this union: Mariana B., Caroline, Helen G. and Charles J. Mariana B. was born May 31, 1836, and died September 13, 1896. She married, April 18, 1860, Rev. C. H. Cole, and had two children, Arthur, studying medicine in Baltimore, and Howard, of Lynn. Caroline, born November 17, 1837, died February 11. 1894. For several years she was a teacher at Selma, Alabama; Vicksburg, Mississippi and New Orleans, Louisiana. Helen Gilman, born September 2, 1847, was educated at Exeter high school. Her residence is in Exeter. She married, September 30, 1907, Andrew M. Moulton, of Hampstead, New Hampshire. Charles Josiah was born September 11, 1848, and died January 17, 1893. He was educated in the common schools, and at the age of seventeen began to learn the machinist's trade, at which he worked twenty-eight years, and became an expert in the making and erection of stationary steam engines, boilers, etc., at which he continued the remainder of his life. He was successful in business and was one of the promoters of the Co-operative Bank of Exeter. In politics he affiliated with the Republicans, and was elected by that party to the legislature in 1891. He was a member of Sagamore Lodge, Independent Order of Odd Fellows.

(Fourth Family.)

SMITH This is universally known as the most numerously represented name in American annals, although it is likely to lose its supremacy because of the large surplus of Scandinavians bearing the name of Johnson. It is probably no exaggeration to say that those bearing the name of Smith have participated in the development and civilization of this country in full proportion to their numbers, and many have occupied conspicuous positions in New Hampshire as well as in other states.

(I) The immigrant ancestor of the line herein traced was Henry Smith, who came from England in 1637, accompanied by his wife Elizabeth and two sons. He settled in Dedham, Massachusetts, and the burning of his house was an event noted in the town records. In 1651 he removed to Medfield, Massachusetts, where he was active in town affairs and was a selectman thirteen years. He died in 1687, having survived his wife, who died in 1670, about seventeen years. Their sons were: John, Seth, Daniel, Samuel and Joseph.

(II) Samuel, fourth son and child of Henry and Elizabeth Smith, was born in 1641, in Dedham, Massachusetts, and inherited the homestead in Medfield on which he lived, and where he died in 1691. He was married December 22, 1669, to Elizabeth Turner, who was born 1647, daughter of John and Deborah Turner, of Medfield. She was the mother of Elizabeth and Samuel. In the Indian attack upon Medfield in 1676, she was killed while carrying her son Samuel to a place of safety. At the same time the child was thrown to the ground and left for dead, when found he had crept to the side of his dead mother. The father was married (second), February 22, 1677, to Sarah (Clark) Bowers, who was born 1651, a daughter of Joseph Clark, and at the time of this marriage she was the widow of John Bowers, who was killed by the Indians on the same day that Samuel Smith's first wife was killed. He died 1691, and was survived about thirteen years by his widow, who died May 20, 1704. The children of the second marriage were: Sarah, Henry, Daniel, Nathaniel, Abigail, Mary and Prudence.

(III) Henry (2), eldest son and second child of Samuel Smith and his second wife, Sarah Clark, was born December 16, 1680, in Medfield, and passed his life in that town, dying April 14, 1743. He was a selectman and held other offices in the town. He was married February 20, 1703, to Deborah Pratt, who was born 1684, daughter of John and Rebecca (Colburn) Pratt. She died August 5, 1706, and he was married (second), March 4, 1708, to Mary Adams. She was born August 4, 1681, daughter of Jonathan and Mary (Ellis) Adams, and died February 23, 1725. Henry Smith was married (third) September 1, 1730, to Ruth Barber, who was born March 5, 1696, daughter of Zachariah and Abigail (Ellis) Barber. His children were: Daniel, Mary, Henry, Jonathan, Sarah, Benoni, Ruth, Moses and Asa.

(IV) Henry (3), son of Henry (2) and Mary (Adams) Smith, was born April 24, 1711, in Medfield, and removed from that town to Walpole, Massachusetts, where he probably died. He was married in 1730 to Abigail Clark, who was born 1711, daughter of Captain Joseph and Abigail (Smith) Clark. She died February 13, 1747, but no record of his death appears. Their children were: Seth, Abigail, Samuel, Henry, Hannah, Maria, Amos, Sarah and Azuba.

(V) Henry (4), third son and fourth child of Henry (3) and Abigail (Clark) Smith, was born January 28, 1736, probably in Walpole and lived in that town. He was a soldier of the Revolution. He was married, February 5, 1761, to Barsheba Blake, and their children were: Royal, Eunice, Enos, Mary and Lydia.

(VI) Enos, second son and third child of Henry (4) and Barsheba (Blake) Smith, was born October 16, 1771, in Walpole, Massachusetts. In the record of his birth the name was written Eneas, but all other records show it as Enos. He lived many years in Medfield and late in life removed to Walpole, where he died in 1861. He was married in Medfield, March 31, 1797, to Amy Plimpton, who was born April 30, 1774, in Medfield, daughter of Silas and Esther (Clark) Plimpton. Their children were: Esther, Royal, Amy, Olive, Arnold, Edwin and Katherine.

(VII) Edwin, youngest son and sixth child of Enos and Amy (Plimpton) Smith, was born July

Edwin W. Smith

E. E. SMITH.

17, 1807, in Medfield, and became a machinist. He was employed several years by the manufacture corporations of Manchester, New Hampshire. In 1847 he removed to Milford where he was successful in business. He died May 31, 1882. He was a Universalist in religious faith and a thinking man. While employed in Manchester, he lived a portion of the time in Goffstown. He was married, May 20, 1830, to Sybil Wallace, who was born September 2, 1809, in Townsend, Massachusetts, daughter of Benjamin and Rebecca (Whitney) Wallace. She was a descendant of John Wallace, of Stowe and Townsend, Massachusetts (which see) through his son Jonathan, who was the father of Benjamin. There were five children in this family: Edwin W., whose sketch follows. Sarah M., Henry P., Nancy C. and Joseph W., the last four are dead.

(VIII) Edwin Wallace, son of Edwin and Sybil (Wallace) Smith, was born at Goffstown, New Hampshire, July 28, 1831. He was educated in the common schools, afterwards engaging in the machinist's trade at Milford, New Hampshire. In 1893 he moved to Brookline, New Hampshire, and bought a farm of ninety-six acres, which he has brought to a high state of cultivation. He is a member of the Independent Order of Odd Fellows. On October 25, 1853, Edwin W. Smith married Eunice Augusta Hobart daughter of David and Eunice (Wright) Hobart, of Hollis, New Hampshire. They have one son, Edwin E., born July 13, 1856.

(Fifth Family.)

SMITH

(I) Hugh Smith and his wife Mary were residing in Rowley, Massachusetts, as early as the year 1654. In all probability they were not among the Rev. Ezekiel Rogers' company which originally settled the town in 1638, but arrived there at a later date. The records indicate that they were the parents of seven children: John, Samuel, Edward (born in 1654), and four daughters, whose names do not appear.

(II) John Smith, who was of Rowley in 1659 was, as near as can be ascertained from the records, the John previously mentioned as the son of Hugh and Mary. The maiden name of his wife was Faith Parrot and he was the father of John and Jonathan (twins), born at Rowley in 1669; and probably of Benjamin.

(III) Benjamin Smith, probably the youngest son of John and Faith (Parrot) Smith, married Martha Kilborn and had Moses, born in 1711; Benjamin, the date of whose birth will be recorded presently; Jacob, born in 1720; Joseph, in 1724; and four daughters.

(IV) Benjamin (2), second son of Benjamin (1) and Martha (Kilborn) Smith, was born in Rowley in 1719. His wife was before marriage Elizabeth Creasey, and his children were: Isaac, the next in line of descent; Benjamin, born in 1756; Joseph, born in 1765; and four daughters, whose names are not given.

(V) Isaac Smith eldest son of Benjamin and Elizabeth (Creasey) Smith, was born in Rowley in 1743. He married Elizabeth Hibbert and had ten children, namely: Isaac, who will be again referred to; James, born in 1768; Benjamin, born in 1771; Moses, born in 1773; David, born in 1776; George, born in 1779; Edward, born in 1784; Thomas (called Lorane), born in 1787; Amos, born in 1790; and a daughter.

(VI) Isaac (2), eldest child of Isaac (1) and Elizabeth (Hibbert) Smith, was born in Rowley, June 25, 1766. He acquired a good education and for many years was engaged in teaching school. For intervals he resided in Ipswich, Massachusetts, Canterbury, Concord, Loudon and Hopkinton, New Hampshire, and while in Loudon he owned and operated a saw and grist mill. At one time he was postmaster at Ipswich, held town offices and was a deacon of the Baptist Church. His death occurred in Hopkinton, December 23, 1857, in his ninety-second year. On December 6, 1789, he married Abigail Coggswell, daughter of Dr. Nathan Coggswell of Rowley, and had a family of thirteen children namely: Elizabeth, born September 2, 1790; Nabby, May 24, 1792; Charles, who is referred to in the succeeding paragraph; John born March 19, 1795; Abigail, born October 21, 1796; Sarah, born June 30, 1798; Isaac, born March 14, 1800; Hannah C., born September 10, 1801; David Francis, born March 15, 1804; Nathaniel, born March 4, 1806 (died young); Louisa, born August 4, 1808; Nathaniel C., born March 26, 1809; and Edmund Emery, born February 9, 1811. The mother of these children died January 7, 1838.

(VII) Charles, third child and eldest son of Deacon Isaac and Abigail (Coggswell) Smith, was born in Rowley March 11, 1794. When a young man he was with his father at Loudon where he operated a saw mill for a time, and in 1824 he removed to a farm in Candia. The rest of his active life was spent in tilling the soil, and his death occurred in Candia in 1873. Politically he was a Democrat. In his religious belief he was a Baptist. He married Louise Batchelder, who died in 1863, daughter of Abraham Batchelder, of Loudon. They had children: Charles, Louisa, Emeline, Edmund Emery, see forward; Alvah A., Abbie C. and Clara R.

(VIII) Edmund Emery, second son and fourth child of Charles and Louise (Batchelder) Smith, was born in Candia, August 20, 1830. His early education was obtained in the public schools, and after completing his education at the Pembroke Academy, he taught school, and for a time resided at Dedham and South Reading (now Wakefield), then in West Boylston. He then returned to the homestead in Candia, and assisted in the cultivation and management of the farm during his father's declining years. Having succeeded to the property upon the death of his father, he was energetically engaged in its cultivation with very profitable results. He was also engaged in the lumber business for a number of years. In politics he is a Republican, and has served as a member of the board of selectmen for two years. He is a member of the Congregational Church. Mr. Smith married (first), 1857, Mary Fitts, of Candia, daughter of Abraham and Mary (Emerson) Fitts, and granddaughter of Abraham Fitts, who was born in Salisbury in 1736, and later settled in Candia. They had children: 1. George F., a farmer and jeweller in Auburn, where he has filled the office of tax collector for a period of fourteen years. He married (first), Mary A. Fitts, and had one child: Howard E., married (second), Carrie E. Simpson. 2. Mary A., married George Currier, of Deny, and had children: Helen Florence and Mabel Henriette. Edmund Emery Smith married (second) Sarah A. Patten, of Auburn, and had children: 1. Henry C., born March 10, 1866, died January 11, 1893. He was an expert machinist. He married Mary E. Johnston, of Manchester, and they had one son, born March 10, 1893. 2. Charles S., born November 6, 1875. He was educated in the public and high schools of his native town, and spent one year in Pembroke

Academy. He resided at the home of his parents until he had attained his majority, then obtained a position in the Mirror office, Manchester, New Hampshire. At the expiration of two years he went to Boston, Massachusetts, and secured employment with the *Colonial Press*, of which C. H. Symonds is the proprietor. Mr. Smith is now engaged as a cylinder pressman. He is a member of Berkley Temple Church, the Gymnasium and Glee clubs of the Young Men's Christian Association, and of the De Soto Lodge, Knights of Pythias.

(Sixth Family.)

SMITH One of the numerous families of this name in New Hampshire came through Dunstable, originally Massachusetts, and has now numerous branches in various parts of the state. They seem to have been people of strong character, both physically and mentally, and still evince the sturdy nature of their forebears.

(I) The name of Abraham Smith appears early in the records of Cambridge, Massachusetts, the occasion being a fine of sixpence for permitting his heifer to trespass in the planting field November 4, 1646.

(II) John Smith, who is presumed to have been a son of Abraham, in the absence of any records, was married at Cambridge, June 8, 1676, to Sarah Prentice. Their children, born in that town, were: Sarah (died young), John, Sarah and Joseph. There were probably other children, but they are not recorded.

(III) Samuel Smith, born about 1690, was probably a son of John and Sarah (Prentice) Smith. He resided in Menotomy, and had by his wife, Sarah, the following children: Sarah, Susannah, Anna, Pelatiah, Samuel, Michael, Joseph, Benjamin, Robert (died young), Thomas, Robert and Daniel.

(IV) Deacon Benjamin, fifth son and eighth child of Samuel and Sarah Smith, was born January 13, 1736, in Menotomy, and was a pioneer of Dunstable, Massachusetts, where he was held in high regard, as a member of the church and active in the development of a frontier community. He died in March, 1821, at the age of eighty-five years. He was married, October 6, 1762, to Joanna Lund, of Dunstable.

(V) Benjamin (2), son of Benjamin (1) and Joanna (Lund) Smith, was born June 2, 1765, in Dunstable, and was, like his father, a pioneer in frontier development. He spent a short time before his majority in Boscawen, but soon pushed on into newer regions. In 1785, according to the "History of Coos county," Benjamin and Caleb Smith came from Boscawen to Stark, New Hampshire. They were probably brothers, and both were strong, sinewy men, well fitted to hew a way out of the wilderness. Benjamin Smith built the first house in Stark, which was situated on a hillside in what is now the center of the town, near the Ammonsuc river. As illustrating his strength it may be mentioned that the sheriff once came to arrest him for a small debt. The officer took hold of Smith, and they started home, but the latter kept up such a rapid gait, leaping five foot fences and clearing away everything that came in his way, that the sheriff, completely exhausted, gave up his game and never renewed the attempt at capture. The tax list of Stark for the year 1809 rates Benjamin Smith at one poll, one horse, one colt, two oxen, one cow, five young cattle, three acres pasture, five mowing, two arable. He was a farmer all his life, held various town offices, and attended the Methodist Church. About 1786 Benjamin Smith married Hannah Smith, possibly the daughter of Caleb, and they had seven children: Sally, born April 1, 1787; Nancy, born June 6, 1789; Benjamin, born March 2, 1792; Nathan, born August 27, 1794; Hannah, born January 18, 1798. No records are preserved of the birth of the others, but their names are given as Jeremiah E. and Lucinda.

(VI) Jeremiah E., son of Benjamin (2) and Hannah (Smith) Smith, was born at Stark, New Hampshire, probably about 1800. He was a farmer all his life, and was a prominent and useful citizen of his native town. He was a Democrat, but took small part in politics. He was a member of the Methodist Church, and was strong in his religious faith. On January 29, 1827, Jeremiah E. Smith married Olive Cole, daughter of Clifford Cole, a member of a prominent family in Stark. There were four children: Jane E., Louisa M., one died in infancy, George W. R. M., whose sketch follows, is the only one of these children now living. Jeremiah E. Smith died in 1885, and his wife died January 5, 1865.

(VII) George Washington Rowell Michael, son of Jeremiah E. and Olive (Cole) Smith, was born at Stark, New Hampshire, November 30, 1841. He was educated in the district schools of his native town, and did farming in early life. For several years he conducted a store in Stark, and afterwards became a member of the Percy Lumber Company, of which he has been manager since 1880. The officers of this company, whose business is the leading industry of the region, are: President, John C. Littlefield, Manchester, New Hampshire; secretary, James F. Baldwin, of Manchester; treasurer and general manager, Luther C. Baldwin, Providence, Rhode Island. Mr. Smith is also a member of the firm of Baldwin & Smith, manufacturers of bobbins. The product is manufactured at Percy, New Hampshire, and finished at Auburn, Maine; and the firm employs from one hundred and fifty to two hundred men at Percy and about forty at Auburn during the winter. They have also a plant at West Bethel, where they give employment to a large number of men. In 1889 Mr. Smith, in partnership with Henry R. Girard, bought out the Lumber Company's store at Percy. Mr. Smith is considerably interested in farming, and cuts about four hundred tons of hay on the company's land and his own. The Percy Company owns about seven thousand acres of timber land, and they also buy stumpage. In politics Mr. Smith is independent, but he has never sought office. He was selectman for a number of years, and was representative in 1881, and has held minor local offices. He attends the Methodist Episcopal Church, and has been a member of the finance committee since he was eighteen years of age. He belongs to the Knights of Pythias and to the Odd Fellows. Mr. Smith is a vigorous man, apparently just in the prime of middle life, and enjoys the respect of the community to a marked degree. He has never used tobacco, liquor, beer or cards, and has never attended dances. For thirty-seven years he has had control of men in mills and lumber camps, the number varying anywhere from thirty-five to two hundred and fifty, and he has helped many a worthy young man under his charge to rise in the business. On May 7, 1863, Mr. Smith married Mary Jane, daughter of Edmond and Hannah (Leavitt) Cole, of Stark. There are no children.

(Seventh Family.)

SMITH The Smith family, of which Joseph Brodie Smith, of Manchester, New Hampshire, is a representative, is of English descent, and is traced as follows:

(I) Silas Smith, born and married in England, came to America with the Plymouth Company and settled at Taunton, Massachusetts.

(II) Silas Smith, (2), son of Silas Smith (1), married Hannah, daughter of Daniel Gazine, who came over with the London Company. Their children were: Isaac, Elijah, Silas, Cornelius, Elkanah, Bial, Samuel, Hannah, died in Oneida county, New York; Rachel and Sally.

(III) Samuel Smith, seventh son and child of Silas (2) and Hannah (Gazine) Smith, served in the Continental army duiing the Revolution. He married Abigail, daughter of John Wright, and died at Henderson, New York, April 17, 1827. Their children were: Amasa, died at the age of one and a half years; Daniel, Mary, Abigail, Sylvester, Lydia, Polly, Samuel, Jr., Sally, Mercy, Anna and Amasa (2). Of these children Abigail married Rev. Elisha P. Sangworthy, of Balston Springs, New York; Sylvester married Nancy Kniffin, of Rutland, New York, March 19, 1806; Lydia married ——— Skellinger; Polly married Dr. William Priest; Sally married Samuel Mills; Mercy married Henry Millard; Anna married Jonathan Ruff; Amasa (2) married Sally Sykes of Watertown, New York.

(IV) Daniel Smith, born in Spencertown, Columbia county, New York, February 26, 1775. He was educated in the common schools, was a farmer by occupation, and in 1802 came to Ellisburg, Jefferson county, and spent the summer there clearing lands. In the fall of that year he went to Schuyler, Herkimer county, where he married, and in December, 1803, with his wife and infant daughter came to Rutland, Jefferson county, and purchased a farm near Burr's Mills. Two years later he moved to Hounsfield, same county, purchased some land and erected a saw mill, the place being known for some time as Smith's Mills, later Camp's Mills. From Hounsfield he returned to Rutland, purchased another farm, built a frame house, where he lived until 1818, when he purchased and removed to a large farm in Rodman, where he spent the remainder of his life, and which is still owned by his descendants. He was a lieutenant in the war of 1812-14 and distinguished himself by his bravery at the battle of Sackett's Harbor, when their house was practically a hospital for sick soldiers. Daniel Smith married Susan Holmes, of Keene, Cheshire county, New Hampshire, who for sometime previous to her marriage lived with her aunt, Mrs. Lucy (Holmes) Wheeler, wife of John Wheeler, of Keene, New Hampshire. Their children were: Abigail, born November 6, 1803, died March 14, 1854; Laura, born January 30, 1805, died 1891; infant son, born August 1, 1806, died same day; Nancy M., born September 1, 1807, died February 1, 1887; Almira H., born May 2, 1809, died December 25, 1896; Daniel, born February 26, 1811, died December 19, 1813; William P., born February 7, 1813, died January 5, 1899; Daniel, Jr., born March 19, 1815, died August 2, 1896; infant daughter, born April 19, 1817, died April 19, 1817; Susan H., born May 6, 1818; Lucy Ann, born September 15, 1819, died March, 1900; Eveline M., born May 2, 1821, died March 13, 1906; Emeline L., born September 10, 1823; Mary M., born May 5, 1825, died August 14, 1845; Nelson Slater, born July 11, 1827; Martha Jane, born June 19, 1829, died October 12, 1867. Daniel Smith, Sr., died March 11, 1854. His wife, Susan (Holmes) Smith, died August 5, 1864.

Thomas Holmes, father of Susan (Holmes) Smith, was born in Woodstock, Connecticut, 1756, died in Wethersfield, Connecticut. The following items were copied from "Record of Connecticut men in War of Revolution," State House Library, Boston, Massachusetts: Thomas Holmes enlisted May 15, 1775, discharged December 17, 1775. Ninth Company, Second Connecticut Regiment, Colonel Spencer, Captain John Chester, of Wethersfield. This regiment was raised on first call for troops by State in April, 1775, marching by companies to the camps about Boston; it took part at Roxbury and served during the siege till expiration of term of service. Detachments of officers and men were in the battle of Bunker Hill and with Arnold's Quebec expedition, September to December, 1775. His name appears in list of Knowlton's Rangers, 1776, Connecticut, by Lieutenant-Colonel Knowlton. He was detached from Wyllys Connecticut regiment, and was taken prisoner at surrender of Fort Washington, New York, November 16, 1776. Thomas Holmes, of Wethersfield, sergeant in Captain Whiting's company, Colonel Webb's regiment, enlisted March 1, 1777 for the war. Colonel Webb's regiment was one of sixteen infantry regiments raised at large for Continental Line of 1777, and served in Parson's brigade under Putnam the following summer and fall. In October crossed to west side of Hudson and served under Governor Clinton, of New York, for a time. In summer of 1778 was attached to Varnum's brigade and went to Rhode Island, commended in battle there August 29, 1778. Wintered in Rhode Island, 1778-9. In the fall of 1779 marched to winter quarters at Morristown, New Jersey. Assigned to Stark's brigade at battle of Springfield, New Jersey, June 23, 1780, and during summer served with main army on the Hudson. Thomas Holmes was sergeant in Captain Riley's company, Wethersfield, third regiment, Connecticut Line, 1781-83. Recorded as paid from January 1, 1781, to December 31, 1781. Sergeant Thomas Holmes is reported as a Revolutionary pensioner on list of Connecticut pensioners in 1818. His name is among pensioners dated 1832 and recorded as residing in Hartford, Connecticut. His name appears on list of pensioners as returned in census of 1840. Residence, Wethersfield, Connecticut, aged 84. His name appears on list of applicants for pension on file in county clerk's office, Hartford, Connecticut. Residence Wethersfield.

Thomas Holmes married Tamar Harris, and their children were: Sally, married Eldad Granger; Lucy, married John Wheeler; John, Mary, Rachel, Joseph, Lydia, married Ashael Cleveland, in Buffalo, about 1814; Abigail, married Jonathan Slater, Champlain, New York; Susan, married Daniel Smith, aforementioned.

(V) William Priest Smith, born February 7, 1813, at Hounsfield, New York, died January 5, 1899. He was educated at Rodman, New York. He was at one time colonel of the old time Thirty-sixth regiment, New York state militia, which was composed of men from Jefferson and Lewis counties. After his marriage he removed to St. Lawrence county, engaging in the business of manufacturing lumber, and became the owner of valuable farming and timber land. He served as justice of the peace and supervisor, being chairman of the board of supervisors. Later in life he was for three successive terms elected associate judge of the county court. In politics he was a Republican from the very organization of that party, and by his voice, efforts and vote contributed to its success. William P. Smith married, July 9, 1843, Sarah Porter Hungerford, born April 18, 1823, who traces her ancestry to Sir Thomas Hungerford, who in 1369 purchased from Lord Burghersh, Farley Castle, county of Somerset, England, which castle for more than three hundred years continued to be the principal seat of his descendants, down to 1686. Sir Thomas was steward for John of Ghent, Duke of Lancaster, son of King Edward III, and in the thirty-first year of that King's reign was elected speaker of the English house of commons, being reputed to be the first person chosen to that high office. He died December 3, 1398. His son, Sir Walter, afterwards Lord Hungerford, K. G., was the first to adopt the crest of a garb, or wheat-sheaf, between two sickles erect, with the motto "Et Dieu Mon Appuy" (God is my support). This has since been the crest of the Hungerford family.

John Hungerford, a lineal descendant of the above named, resided at Southington, Connecticut, where he died December 24, 1787. He served with distinction in the Colonial wars, holding the ranks of ensign, lieutenant and captain. He took an active part in the siege of Crown Point, on Lake Champlain. His son Amasa served in the Revolutionary army, participating in the battle of Bennington, where he served as colonel. His son, Amasa, Jr., was the father of Sarah (Hungerford) Smith, was enrolled as one of the "Minute Men" in the war of 1812. He resided in Henderson, Jefferson county, and was a prosperous farmer and widely known. At one time he was interested in ship-building at Stoney Point, on Lake Ontario. He died December 18, 1859, aged seventy-nine years.

Mr. and Mrs. William P. Smith were attendants at the Baptist Church. They had eleven children, as follows: Lois Elizabeth, married William G. Brown. She died December 10, 1882. Amasa Daniel, chemist and druggist, Manchester, New Hampshire, married Josephine L. Jones, September 18, 1883. Annie Eliza, died February 26, 1873. Frances Sally, died January 12, 1899. George William, attorney and counselor at law, Keeseville, New York, married Harriet P. Wells, May 19, 1887. Jay Hungerford, Ph. C., manufacturing chemist, president of the J. Hungerford Smith Company, Rochester, New York; he married, May 17, 1882, Jean Dawson. Mary Louise, died March 27, 1857. Jennie Venila, of Manchester, New Hampshire, married Edgar Ellsworth Castor, May 9, 1894. Joseph Brodie, see forward. Frank Robbins, manufacturing chemist, Toronto, Ontario, married Ada Margaret Perkins, May 6, 1903. May Lillian, of Manchester, New Hampshire.

(VI) Joseph Brodie Smith was born at Richville, St. Lawrence county, New York, April 6, 1861, being the ninth child of the marriage of William P. and Sarah (Hungerford) Smith. He was educated in the Union Free School of his native village, and subsequently took a course in higher mathematics to fit himself to become an expert electrician. Early in life he became deeply interested in electrical science, and in 1878 constructed a telegraph line between two small villages in New York state. In 1880 he removed to Manchester, New Hampshire, where he has since resided. At first he engaged in the drug business with his eldest brother, Amasa D. Smith. He made himself a thorough master of the business, and passed the state examinations, requisite to become a registered pharmacist in both New Hampshire and New York. During all his career in the drug business, Mr. Smith never for an instant lost his interest in the subject of electricity and still continued his studies, and so laid the foundation of a knowledge of the subject by which he has become a recognized authority in applied electricity. In 1885, finding the field of electrical work more alluring than the mortar and pestle, he retired from the drug business and began to do electrical contracting of all kinds, and was appointed superintendent of the municipal fire alarm telegraph service, a position which he held for about two years.

Mr. Smith has had a hand in the develoment of most of the electrical business in and around Manchester, excepting only telephones and telegraph. The Manchester Electric Light Company was the pioneer in the business of furnishing electric lights and power, but it was not left alone in the field for any great length of time. The Ben Franklin Electric Light Company was organized as a rival, and Mr. Smith was its first superintendent, and when the consolidation of the two companies was effected, he became superintendent of the Manchester company. This company was afterwards sold out to the Manchester Traction, Light and Power Company, which, by owning all the stock of the Manchester Street Railway, the Manchester and Nashua Street Railway, Manchester and Derry Street Railway, and all the electric light and Power companies in the neighborhood, and possessing valuable water power on the Merrimack and Piscataquog rivers, has acquired control of the electrical situation in Manchester and vicinity. Mr. Smith was superintendent of the Manchester Electric Light Company until 1896, when he resigned and took a trip of several months to Europe. On his return he was chosen general manager of the same company, and in 1901, when the Manchester Traction, Light and Power Company acquired control, he was elected a director and general manager, and in 1905 he was chosen vice president and has since occupied those positions with credit to himself and to the satisfaction of the stockholders and the public with whom he deals. He is assistant treasurer and general manager of the Manchester Street Railway, also general manager of the Manchester and Nashua Street Railway, and the Manchester and Derry Street Railway, and is treasurer of the Brodie Electrical Company of Manchester, which is engaged in the manufacture of electrical specialties, of which Mr. Smith is the inventor. He is financially interested in several lighting companies and street railways in other parts of the country. He is an associate member of the American Institute of Electrical Engineers.

However, Mr. Smith's labors are not limited to the electrical business. He has other interests in Manchester. He is a trustee of the Manchester Savings Bank, one of the largest savings institutions of the state, and vice president of the Manchester Garment Company. He assists in every movement for the welfare of the city. He is one of the foremost workers in the Manchester Institute of Arts and Sciences. In politics he is a staunch Republican, but has never sought or held an elective office. Socially he is a member and director of the Derryfield Club, a leading social club of New Hampshire. In Odd Fellowship he is a charter member of Ridgely Lodge and a member of Wonolancet Encampment, and of Canton Ridgely. But it is in the work of the ancient and honorable fraternity of Free Masonry that Mr. Smith has found his chief diversion from his daily duties. He is a member of Washington Lodge, Mount Horeb Royal Arch Chapter, Adoniram Council, and Trinity Commandery of Knights Templar, all of Manchester. He is a past master of Adoniram Council, and a past grand master of the Grand Council of New Hampshire. In the bodies working the Ancient and Accepted Scottish Rite, he has received signal honors. He is a member of the bodies at

J. Brodie Smith

J. Brodie Smith

Nashua, New Hampshire, and received the degrees up to and including the thirty-second. In 1905, at Indianapolis, Indiana, he was given the last degree of the Scottish Rite, the thirty-third, a privilege and an honor which comes to but few Masons. He is a trustee of the Masonic Home, which is located in this city.

Mr. Smith is unmarried, but maintains a comfortable home, where his aged mother and sisters reside with him.

(Eighth Family.)

SMITH A large number of Smiths were among the emigrants from Old England to New England in Colonial days. The line of descent from Samuel Smith of unknown antecedents but probably a native of England, are traced in this sketch.

(I) Samuel Smith, of Haverhill, Massachusetts, is first mentioned in the records of that town under date of November 30, 1683, when he married Abigail Emerson. She lived to the age of more than one hundred and two years, and is believed to have moved in her old age to Hudson, New Hampshire, where it is believed she died.

(II) Samuel (2) Smith, son of Samuel (1) and Abigail (Emerson) Smith, was born May 1, 1696. He settled in Hudson and married Hannah Page, daughter of Abraham and Judith (Worthen) Page, who had settled in Hudson in 1710. (Their son, Page Smith, and descendants receive mention in this article.)

(III) John Smith, who was probably a son of Samuel (2) Smith, resided in Nottingham West, now Hudson. No further record of him is obtainable.

(IV) Samuel (3), son of John Smith, was born in Nottingham West, and was married in Pelham, October 18, 1857, to Agnes Grimes, of that town. They had two sons, Samuel and Alexander.

(V) Alexander, second son of Samuel (3) and Agnes (Grimes) Smith, was born August 24, 1793, in Nottingham West. He was a blacksmith by occupation and lived in Londonderry, where he died in 1859. He was a Presbyterian and a Democrat. He married, February 19, 1822, Sarah Melvin of Peterboro. She died 1888. Their seven children were: Reuben A., Sarah A., Daniel D., Clarissa N., Mary J., Charles S. and Walter A.

(VI) Reuben A., eldest child of Alexander and Sarah (Melvin) Smith, was born in Londonderry, March 8, 1823, and died in Auburn, February 16, 1903. He learned the shoemaker's trade, and after working at that for a short period removed to Weare, where he bought and cultivated a farm. In politics he was a Republican, and in church affiliations a Universalist. He married, October, 1848, Laura J. Jones, of Bradford, who was well educated and was for a time a teacher. She was a member of the Universalist Church. Two children were born of this union: Story A., whose sketch follows, and Etta L., who married Henry C. Jones, of York Beach, Maine.

(III) Page, the eleventh child of Samuel (2) and Hannah (Page) Smith, was born February 28, 1750. Family record says he marched with a company to Cambridge at the time of the Lexington alarm. The revolutionary rolls of New Hampshire give his name as on the pay roll of a number of men under the command of Captain James Ford, who marched from Nottingham West for Ticonderoga, when he served a short time as a private, beginning June 30, 1777. He was a deacon in the Congregational Church of Pelham, and held town offices. He married Lydia, daughter of John and Lydia (Marsh) Haseltine. She was noted for her wonderful ability as an arithmatician, solving mentally and very quickly difficult problems. Several of her sons inherited this ability, though much less in degree. She had a knowledge of medicinal herbs, and was often called upon to give relief to her neighbors when they were ill.

(IV) Alvan, son of Page and Lydia (Haseltine) Smith, was born January 30, 1793. He was a typical country school master of the olden time, being eagerly sought after to serve as master of schools where the young men in attendance were particularly unruly. It is said that he invariably enforced a rigid discipline, and was never successfully defied by any pupil, however muscular or accustomed to overawe his teacher. He was selectman of Hudson many years, and filled the office of superintendent of schools for several years. He married Patty Robinson, born in Hudson, October 25, 1800, and died December 15, 1825, aged twenty-five years. She was descended from several of the old Scotch-Irish families which settled in Londonderry, New Hampshire, in 1719, notable among them being the Andersons and Davidsons. Her parents were David and Martha (Anderson) Robinson.

(V) David Onslow, only child of Alvan and Patty (Robinson) Smith, was born November 12, 1823, at Hudson, and died February 15, 1906, aged eighty-two. He studied at Nashua Literary Institute and Pinkerton Academy of Derry, New Hampshire. For several years he taught public and private schools in his own and neighboring towns with great success. In 1850 he graduated from Harvard Medical School. There he was a favorite pupil of Dr. Oliver Wendell Holmes, then a professor in that institution, and graduated with honor, winning the prize offered to the student passing the best examination in surgery. After graduation he settled in Hudson, where he soon had a large practice. For nearly twenty years he was superintendent of the public schools in Hudson, one of the graded schools being named in his honor. In early manhood he held the office of captain in the state militia. In politics he was a Republican, and was a member of the constitutional convention of 1889. Greatly interested in music, he taught singing schools in several towns, and for a number of years served as conductor of a chorus recruited from a half dozen surrounding towns. He also composed considerable music of merit. He was a member of the Hudson Baptist Church, to which he presented a fine pipe organ, and with his wife and brother-in-law a large vestry.

He married, August 30, 1855, Mary Hannah Greeley, born October 30, 1832, and died in Hudson, December 27, 1867, aged thirty-five years, daughter of Reuben and Joanna Colby (Merrill) Greely, of Hudson. Reuben Greeley, sixth in line from Andrew Grele, the emigrant, was a very prominent man in his town and county, filling many offices with great credit to himself. He was a lifelong resident of Hudson, in which town Joseph Grele, son of the emigrant, settled in his old age. Joanna was the daughter of Rev. Daniel Merrill, a Baptist clergyman of considerable note, who when a mere youth enlisted for a term of three years in the Continental army, and was present at the surrender of Cornwallis. Subsequently he graduated from Dartmouth College. He was the author of several pamphlets and books on religious subjects, and several of his sermons have been printed. While pastor at Sedgwick, Maine, he represented his district in the Massachusetts general court at Boston, and later, when Maine had became a state, he served as a member of the governor's council. The founding of Waterville College, now known as Colby College, was largely the result of his persistent efforts. The children of David and Mary Smith are: Minnie Eugenie, Martha Robinson, Herbert L. and Henry O. Minnie Eugenie was born June 5, 1856, educated at Salem Normal School, Salem, Massachusetts, and married William H. Bruce, druggist of Groton, Massachusetts. Martha Robinson, born July 21, 1859, was educated at the Nashua Literary Institute, and the New England Conservatory of Music. Sketches of Herbert L. and Henry O. follow. One son, Edmund Greeley, died in early youth.

(VI) Herbert Llewellyn, third child and eldest son of David O. and Mary H. (Greeley) Smith, was born in Hudson, January 9, 1862. He completed his preparatory course in 1878 by graduating from the Nashua high school, and went from there to Dartmouth College, from which he graduated with the class of 1882. He afterward entered Harvard Medical School, where he received the degree of M. D. in 1887. During his years of student life he assisted in the payment of his expenses by teaching the village school at Hanover, 1882-83, and by teaching English and shorthand writing in the Boston evening high school, 1883-87. In 1886-87 he was house surgeon in the Boston City Hospital; assistant superintendent of that institution in 1887-89; and acting superintendent a portion of that time. Entering the practice of medicine in Boston, in 1889, he was professor of surgery in the Boston Dental College from 1889 to 1896; surgeon to out patients and assistant surgeon in the Boston City Hospital from 1890 to 1896. He studied in London, Paris, and Vienna, in 1891-92; was secretary of the Suffolk District Medical Society from 1891 to 1896; secretary of the Boston Medical Association from 1892 to 1896; professor of clinical surgery in Tufts Medical School in 1895-96, and made special study of fractures of the elbow joint and devised a method of treatment which has since been used extensively in hospital practice and recommended by authorities. While at the hospital he invented apparatus and instruments now in general use.

In 1896, after an attack of pneumonia, his health failed and he was obliged to give up work for a year, and remained during that time at the old home in Hudson. He opened an office in 1897 in Nashua, and has since then been engaged in practice there, where he has taken high rank in both medical and surgical circles. He has been a member of the Massachusetts Medical Society, the New Hampshire Medical Society, the American Medical Association, the New Hampshire Surgical Club, and the Nashua Medical Association. He is a member of the staff of the Nashua Emergency Hospital. In addition to attending to the numerous and exacting demands of a large practice, he has prepared and published various medical papers, including those on original operations for fractures of the elbow joint and cleft palate.

Dr. Smith is a Republican in politics, but has never held political office. For several years he was hospital steward of the First Regiment, Massachusetts Volunteer Militia. He is a member of the Baptist Church, a director in the Nashua Young Men's Christian Association; a trustee of the Young Women's Christian Association, and a director of the Protestant Orphanage. His connections with secret societies include the two greatest fraternal orders, the Masons and the Odd Fellows. He is a member of Hudson Lodge, No. 94, Independent Order of Odd Fellows; Nashoonon Encampment, and Canton A, of Nashua. He is a member of the Ancient York Lodge, No. 89, Ancient Free and Accepted Masons; Meridian Royal Arch Chapter, No. 9; Israel Hunt Council, No. 8; St. George Commandery, Knights Templar; Edward A. Raymond Consistory, thirty-second degree, of Nashua, also Bektash Temple, Ancient Arabic Order Nobles of the Mystic Shrine.

Dr. Herbert L. Smith married, in Charlestown, Massachusetts, September 24, 1890, Charlotte S. DeWolfe, born in Charlestown, Massachusetts, April 22, 1867, daughter of Lewis E. and Louisa (Graves) DeWolfe, of Charlestown, both of whom were natives of Nova Scotia. The father was for many years a prominent tailor in Charlestown. He was a musician of note, leading choruses and choirs in various churches. Miss DeWolfe graduated from Charlestown high school, the Boston girls' high school, and the Boston Normal school. She has always been prominent in musical circles as a pianist and a vocalist. The children of this union have been four: Theodora Lottchen, born in Vienna, Austria, January 18, 1892, and died in Charlestown, February 18, 1899. Although but seven years old at the time of her death, she gave evidence of much musical ability, as might have been expected from the family history of both parents. David Onslow, born in Boston, November 22, 1894. From infancy he lived with his parental grandfather until the death of the latter. Llewellyn DeWolfe, born in Nashua, April 18, 1898. Marion Louise, born in Nashua, February 3, 1900.

(VI) Henry Onslow, second son and fourth child of David O. and Mary H. (Greeley) Smith, was born in Hudson, New Hampshire, December 18, 1864. After graduating from the Nashua high school in 1882, he studied at Dartmouth College two years. He then matriculated at Bellevue Hospital Medical College, New York, from which he was graduated in 1887. He was assistant physician in Kings County Hospital, New York, from April, 1887, to May, 1888. At the latter date he returned to Hudson, where he has since practiced his profession with success. He is a member of the New Hampshire Medical Society, and the American Medical Association. His political affiliations are with the Republican party. He has been a member of the Hudson School board for six years; health officer and chairman of the board of health over fifteen years; and trustee and treasurer of the Greeley Public Library since it was established. He is a member of the First Baptist Church of Hudson, and for many years was its clerk and treasurer, also a director of the Nashua Protestant Orphanage Association. He is a member of Hudson Lodge, No. 94, Independent Order of Odd Fellows, Nashoonon Encampment, and Canton A., of Nashua.

Dr. Smith married, September 4, 1889, Marcia A. Deering, born June 3, 1867, daughter of Isaac N. and Almira (Guptill) Deering, of Waterboro, Maine. She graduated from Westbrook Seminary, Portland, in 1886, and taught school from that time till her marriage. Isaac N. Deering, of the seventh generation from George Deering, the emigrant, lived on the large ancestral farm and carried on an extensive lumbering and ice business. He served in nearly all the town offices, also as representative in the legislature, and sheriff of York county. Dr. and Mrs. Smith have one child, Deering Greeley Smith, born June 5, 1896.

(Ninth Family.)

SMITH In the year 1718 a considerable number of "Inhabitants of ye North of Ireland" presented a memorial to the governing authorities of the province of New Hampshire in which was expressed "a sincere and hearty inclina-

H. W. Smith, M.D.

tion to Transport ourselves to that very excellent and renowned Plantation upon our obtaining from his Excellency suitable incouragement" to that end. Among the more than three hundred names which were signed to the memorial were seven who bore the name of Smith, and two whose family name was Ker; yet among those who came to occupy the lands set off to them in pursuance of the memorial there were none of either of the names mentioned.

The colony at Londonderry was planted in the year 1719 by immigrants from the north of Ireland, and contemporaneous with that event one Thomas Smith, who also was born in the north of Ireland, came to America and first appeared in New Hampshire history as one of the grantees of the town of Chester; not, however, as one of the original proprietors, but as successor to the property rights of Richard Swain, and was admitted as a grantee by the committee of the proprietors. Among the first settlers of Chester were others of the name of Smith, but whether of the same family as Thomas history gives us no account. There was one John Smith, who is vaguely mentioned as a brother of Thomas but the statement finds no corroboration. Another name prominently mentioned in early Chester history is that of John Ker (otherwise Karr and Carr), whose sister Thomas Smith married and founded a family which in each succeeding generation from his time have been men of achievement, prominently identified with the civil and political history of the state.

(I) Lieutenant Thomas Smith was born in the north of Ireland, and is known to have been in the town of Chester as early as the year 1720 and while there is no present means to determine whether he was of the family of Smiths whose members joined in the memorial to the provincial governor, it is fair to assume that, such was the case and that he came to this country from the north of Ireland with the first colony of Scotch and English immigrants who planted the settlement at Londonderry, New Hampshire. Tradition says that Thomas Smith first settled in Hampton, and from there soon went to Chester, but there is nothing to support this supposition and his name is not found in any of the records of that town. From what is disclosed by town records and the chronicles of earlier writers it is evident that Thomas Smith was possessed of a resolute and determined character and great physical as well as moral courage, and it is clear that he was a man of considerable influence among the settlers. He was constable in 1724, lot-layer from 1725 to 1727, selectman in 1728 and fence viewer in 1729. He was a member of the military company formed in the town in 1731 and was chosen lieutenant in 1732, hence the title by which he was afterward known. In 1724 he and John Karr, his brother-in-law, were captured by a band of prowling Indians. At the time Karr was about eighteen years old, and with Smith was engaged in making a brush fence to secure the latter's cow from the savages, when they were surprised at the report of a gun and a bullet passing between them, just touching Smith. The Indians then sprang upon the whites and in the struggle that followed Smith endeavored to use the butt of his musket on the head of the leader, the notorious Joe English, but missed his aim and was captured, and the unfortunate two, closely guarded, were started off in the direction of Canada. At night they were securely bound and carefully watched, but during the course of the second night Smith managed to free himself without discovery by his captors, then released Karr and both made their way back to the settlement on the night of the third day after they were taken.

About 1734 or '35 Thomas Smith sold his lands in Chester and went to New Boston before the grant of that town had been made. He settled in the northeast part of the town, on what is now known as "the plain" where he built a cabin and cleared a small piece of land by girdling the trees and burning over the ground. For nearly two years he was the solitary inhabitant of that region, and was the pioneer of the town. Near his house the proprietors afterward built sixty dwellings, a grist and saw mill and a meeting house; but this was not done until the pioneer had lived several years in the town. Here, as before in Chester, he was once the object of an Indian attack, but managed to escape without harm. He then left the town for a time and on coming back brought his family with him. A few years afterward he procured from the proprietors, either by purchase or settlement, a large tract of land in the northwest part of the town, near the great meadows, which remained in the possession of his descendants until about twenty years ago.

Thomas Smith built the first frame house in New Boston and was a man of substance and influence, although he appears not to have taken much part in public affairs. Of his family life little is known except that he married a sister of John Karr and had several sons, who like himself, were upright men, thrifty and prosperous, qualities which have characterized their descendants in all later generations. Among his children were his sons: Samuel, James (who is said to have perished with cold on the road from his father's house to Parker's in Goffstown), Reuben (who was a soldier of the Revolution and afterward settled in Maine) and John.

(II) John Smith, better known in New Boston town history as Deacon John Smith, came with his father from Chester. His first wife was a daughter of William McNiel, whose home in New Boston was about a mile from the house of Thomas Smith. By his first wife Deacon John Smith had five children: Martha, Sarah, Janey, Mary and John. His second wife was Ann Brown, of Francestown, who bore him fourteen children: Janey, Thomas, Elizabeth, William, David, Susanna, Ann, Samuel, Martha, Reuben, Elizabeth, Robert, James D. and in infant child who died unnamed.

(III) David, son of Deacon John and Ann (Brown) Smith, married Eleanor Giddings, and had thirteen children.

(IV) Ammi, son of David and Eleanor (Giddings) Smith, was born in the town of Acworth, Sullivan county, New Hampshire, in the month of August, 1800. He early became connected with the lumber industry, and operated a saw mill at Hillsborough for some years, conducting a profitable business. About 1833 he went to Saxton's River, Vermont, and engaged in the manufacture of woolen goods, which he continued for fourteen years with marked success. In 1847 he moved to Hillsborough, retired from business, and died December 24, 1887. Mr. Smith was married, in 1826, to Lydia F. Butler, daughter of Dr. Elijah and Lydia (Fifield) Butler, of Weare; she was born in Weare, New Hampshire, August 29, 1802, and died at Hillsborough in April, 1865. Eight children were born to Mr. and Mrs. Smith: Eliza Ann, Frank Pierce, John Butler, Cynthia Jane, Lydia Ellen, and three who died in early childhood. Eliza Ann married Frederick W. Gould, of Hillsborough.

(V) John Butler, son of Ammi and Lydia (Butler) Smith, was born at Saxton's River, Vermont,

April 12, 1838, and was nine years old when his father returned to New Hampshire and took up his residence at Hillsborough Bridge. He was educated in the public schools of Hillsborough and Francestown Academy, in the latter taking a college preparatory course, but a short time before graduation left the academy and went to work in a general store in New Boston; at that time he was seventeen years of age. When he attained his majority he engaged in business for himself. For a time he was in the dry goods jobbing trade in Boston, afterward carried on a tinware business at Saxton's River, Vermont, his old home and birthplace, and still later was a druggist in the city of Manchester, New Hampshire. Neither of these undertakings were particularly profitable from a financial standpoint, nor were they carried on at pecuniary loss, but taken together furnished an excellent business experience and training and gave the young man an opportunity to measure his own capacity for future enterprises and therefore were years well spent in his early business career. In 1864, being then a little more than twenty-five years old, Mr. Smith began the manufacture of knit goods at Washington, New Hampshire. At the end of a year he moved the works to Weare and after another year to Hillsborough, where he found a better location both for manufacture and shipping, and where he established his equipment in a mill built by him for that purpose. The business was started in a small way, for his means were not large, and from the outset of his career his cardinal business principle was to operate and live within the extent of his own capital and not hazard an end which could not be reasonably well calculated from the beginning. This quality in the man never has been called timidity, for no man who knows John Butler Smith and has watched his reasonable success in private business life, or his public career, will assume to charge him with lack of courage in any respect. For more than thirty years he has been known as a prudent man of affairs, with an excellent capacity for measuring ultimate results, whether in the transaction of private concerns or the still more uncertain operations of state politics.

In Hillsborough he stands today at the head of one of the greatest industries in the county outside the cities of Nashua and Manchester, and whatever success has attended his efforts has been the result of his own foresight and judgment. In 1882 his manufacturing interests were incorporated under the name of Contoocook Mills Company, and since that time he has been its president and active managing officer. The company under normal conditions employs about two hundred and fifty hands and has principal distributing centers for its product in New York City and Boston. Besides his manufacturing and mercantile investments he is owner of considerable real property in various parts of New Hampshire and in the city of Boston, and president of the Hillsborough Guaranty Savings Bank; and notwithstanding the constant demands upon his time in connection with personal affairs he has found time to take a loyal citizen's interest in local and general politics, and for more than twenty years has been an influential factor in the councils of the Republican party in New Hampshire. In 1884 he was an alternate delegate from this state to the national Republican convention at Chicago, and in the fall of that year was a presidential elector on his party ticket. From 1887 to 1889 he was a member of the governor's council, and in 1890 was chairman of the state Republican central committee. In 1888 he was a candidate for nomination in the state convention for the governorship of New Hampshire, but was defeated, and in 1890 declined to contest for nomination because of the candidacy of his warm personal and political friend, Hiram A. Tuttle. However, in 1892 he again entered the list for gubernatorial honors, received unanimous nomination by acclamation in the convention, and was elected at the polls in November of that year by a splendid plurality. He served two years, 1893-95, as chief executive of the state and in that high office carried himself honorably and to the entire satisfaction of the people without distinction of party. In his domestic and home life in Hillsborough Mr. Smith finds perfect contentment. He is a consistent member of the Congregational Church of that town, a liberal supporter of the church and its dependencies, and a generous donor to all worthy charities and to whatever tends to the best interests of the town and the welfare of its people.

He has been twice married. On November 1, 1883, he married Emma Lavender, of Boston. She was born in Lansingburg, Rensselaer county, New York, February 20, 1858, and is a descendant of the ancient Lavender family of Kent county, England; a woman of education, refinement and high social connections. She enjoys the acquaintance of a wide circle of friends in New Hampshire and Massachusetts, especially in Hillsborough and the cities of Manchester and Boston. In Hillsborough, where she has lived a comparatively short time, she is known and admired for her ever agreeable manners, dignified christian character and unselfish devotion to home and family, the church and the benevolent work of its auxiliary societies; her benevolences are bestowed liberally and wholly without display. The Smith residence on School street in Hillsborough is one of the finest in the state, a seat of comfort and refined hospitality. Three children have been born to Mr. and Mrs. Smith. Their first child, Butler Lavender Smith, was born in Hillsborough, March 4, 1886, and died in St. Augustine, Florida, April 6, 1888. Their second child, Archibald Lavender Smith, was born in Hillsborough, February 1, 1889, and their third child, Norman Smith, was born in Hillsborough, May 8, 1892. These sons have been brought up under the careful training of their mother, and having passed beyond the scope of the Hillsborough schools are students in a college preparatory school in Boston, near the winter home of their parents in that city.

George Edward Gould, son of Eliza Ann, sister of John B. Smith, was born in the month of November, 1852. He is the treasurer of the Contoocook Mills Company, a man of wide experience in the woolen goods business, and he has been associated with Mr. Smith for a period of forty years, having risen step by step, until he attained the responsible position he now fills. He married Addie Ellsworth, of Hillsborough, and they have one child, Mary, wife of George H. Chandler, treasurer of the Amoskeag Savings Bank, of Manchester.

SMITH Family tradition has it that the line of Smith of this article is of Scotch-Irish descent. The family has been established in southeast New Hampshire for a century and a half, as its records show.

(I) John Smith, the earliest ancestor now known, resided in West Nottingham.

(II) Samuel, son of John Smith, was born in Nottingham and had two sons: Samuel and Alexander, the latter named the subject of the next paragraph.

J. C. Smith

(III) Alexander, son of Samuel Smith, was born in Nottingham, August 24, 1793, was a blacksmith and died in Londonderry in 1859. He was a Presbyterian and a Democrat. He married, February 19, 1822, Sarah Melvin, of Peterboro, who died 1888. Their seven children were: Reuben A., Sarah A., Daniel D., Clarissa N., Mary J., Charles S. and Walter A.

(IV) Reuben A., eldest child of Alexander and Sarah (Melvin) Smith, was born in Londonderry, March 8, 1823, and died in Auburn, February 16, 1903. He learned the shoemaker's trade, and after working at that for a short period of time removed to Weare, where he bought and cultivated a farm. In politics he was a Republican, and in church affiliations a Universalist. He married, October, 1848, Laura J. Jones, of Bradford. She was well educated and was for a time a teacher. She was a member of the Universalist Church. Two children were born of this union: Story A., whose sketch follows, and Etta L., who married Henry C. Jones, of York Beach, Maine.

(V) Story Alonzo, son of Reuben A. and Laura J. (Jones) Smith, was born in Stoneham, Massachusetts, June 1, 1851. He was educated in the common schools, at Derry Academy and in Manchester high school, and worked in Weare and Goffstown. In 1892 he settled in Auburn and owned and conducted a hotel on the east shore of Lake Massabesic, where he furnished entertainment for summer guests. He is a Republican, and holds to the religious faith of the Universalists. He has been a Mason twenty years. He married, in 1895, Elvira Severance, daughter of William and Eliza (Ricker) Severance, of Auburn. They have three children: Severance A., born July 17, 1896; Henry G., September 3, 1898; and John Story, March 13, 1903.

SMITH This is one of the names which it is extremely difficult to trace because of the large number bearing it and the confusion arising from repetitions of the same Christian name. This is to be regretted as those bearing the name have borne their share in the development of civilization and all that makes for human progress. Its bearers are still contributing their share to the moral and material development of their respective communities.

(I) The first of this family now known positively was John Smith, of Beverly, Massachusetts. It is probable that he was a son of Thomas and Abigail (Baker) Smith of that town, but no proof can be found to establish such a fact. The first record of him is found in the publishment of his intention of marriage to Abigail Baker, February 24, 1788. It is apparent from this that the date of his marriage given in the history of Salisbury, New Hampshire is incorrect. He had three children baptized in Beverly as follows: John Baker, July 10, 1791; Robert, October 2, 1792, and Sally, November 24, 1793. In February, 1794, Mr. Smith removed with his family to Bradford, New Hampshire, and remained three years, removing in February, 1797, to Unity. He continued to reside in that town nearly forty years and removed, in 1836, to Salisbury, New Hampshire, where the balance of his life was passed. His wife, Abigail Baker, was a daughter of Jonathan and Mary (Conant) Baker. (See Baker, second family, IV).

(II) Colonel John Baker Smith, eldest son and child of John and Abigail (Baker) Smith, was born December 2, 1789, in Beverly, Massachusetts, and died in Salisbury, New Hampshire, January 3, 1859, aged seventy. He was brought by his parents to New Hampshire when five years old. He lived in Bradford and Unity until March, 1828, when he removed with his family to Salisbury to take care of his mother's brother, Benjamin Baker, after whose death he bought out the tavern stand of John Shepherd, which he kept at various times for a long period of years. During one of his occupations the house became extensively known as "Smith's Temperance House," as at that time it was an unusual thing to keep a public house and not sell liquor. In 1832 he served as deputy sheriff, and continued as such for a number of years. His title of "colonel" was due to his appointment to the command of the Sixteenth New Hampshire Militia, previous to his removal to Salisbury. Early in life he became a cattle drover for the market at Danvers, Massachusetts. He married, July 4, 1813, Hannah Huntoon, who was born in Unity in 1793, and died May 1, 1880, aged eighty-seven. She was the daughter of John and Susannah (Chase) Huntoon. John Huntoon served at Ticonderoga and was a captain in the Revolution. He was born at Kingston, January 4, 1753, and died in Salisbury, at the age of eighty-five. He was the son of Charles, son of John, son of Philip, the common ancestor. The children of John B. and Hannah (Huntoon) Smith were: John C. and Nancy M.

(III) Colonel John Cyrus Smith, only son of Colonel John Baker and Hannah (Huntoon) Smith, was born in Unity, August 13, 1815, and died in Salisbury in October, 1900, aged eighty-five years. In 1828, when thirteen years old, he was brought to Salisbury by his parents on their removal to that town. He received a good common school education and began life for himself as a dealer in cattle, which business he had learned well from his association with his father. He sold his stock, which he drove on foot, principally in the Massachusetts markets. For some years he was associated with Jonathan Arey in the wheelwright and blacksmith business, and for a time freighted goods over the road to Boston, Massachusetts, and that vicinity. He afterwards purchased the hotel property of his Uncle Nathan, which, with several intermissions, he conducted for twenty-one years. While owning the hotel he purchased the farm where he afterward resided. He was quite extensively engaged in farming in which he was successful. As a business man he was thorough and systematic in all his undertakings. On the completion of the Northern railroad to Franklin, superseding the stage route, he took the first contract, in 1846-47, to carry the United States mail, receiving it at Boscawen, making daily trips and bringing it to what is known locally as South road. This route he sold out in 1859 when the post office was established at West Salisbury.

He commanded the Franklin Rifle Company, was appointed adjutant of the Twenty-first Regiment, passed up through the line of promotion, and was made colonel of the regiment in 1848. Report says: "He made a very efficient officer, a strict disciplinarian, and was familiar with all military movements." Under Sheriff P. Gale he served as deputy in 1854, receiving a similar appointment under William H. Rixford. He was appointed justice of the quorum, July 11, 1856, and of the state, June 10, 1879, and in that capacity (outside of the profession) did more business than any man in town after the time of Dr. Joseph Bartlett, Sr. In the settlement of estates he did a great deal. A sound and eminent judge of Merrimack county said of him: "He was the best administrator and caused the least trouble of any one I knew." He was the acknowledged leader of the Democratic party in town affairs for many years, but gave up that place some time before his death. He held at times all the town offices, and no person living in his time was so well informed on the town's affairs as he. He married, May 26, 1841, Clara Johnson, who was born in Concord, December 3, 1817, and died October 1, 1903. She was the daughter of Reuben and Judith H. (Chandler) Johnson, of Penacook. The children of this marriage were: George F., Clara J., May Ella, John R., Cornelia M., Hannah Elizabeth and Cyrus H. George F. was a soldier in the Civil war and served in the Sixteenth New Hampshire Regiment. He went to Minneapolis, Minnesota, in 1864, and became a leading hardware merchant. Clara J. married Samuel C. Forsaith, and lived in Manchester. May Ella married Henry Burleigh and resides in Franklin. John R. is mentioned at length below. Cornelia M. is single. Hannah E. married Arthur T. Burleigh, of Franklin. Cyrus H. died in Minneapolis.

(IV) John Reuben Smith, fourth child and second son of John C. and Clara (Johnson) Smith, was born in Salisbury, New Hampshire, April 21, 1850. He attended the common schools in Salisbury and Pembroke until he was eighteen years old and then took a brief course in a business college. At twenty-one years of age he went to Minneapolis, Minnesota, where he was employed as a clerk in the store of his brother, George F. Later Mr. Smith and William H. H. Day formed the co-partnership of Smith & Day, and engaged in the hardware business in Minneapolis. This firm was in business seven years and then Mr. Smith became a commercial traveler for Strong, Hackett & Company, of St. Paul, dealers in hardware, and covered the state of Minnesota. In 1882 Mr. Smith bought a hardware store in Bismarck, Dakota, which he kept until 1883, when he sold out and went to Chicago, Illinois, and took the road for Markley, Alling & Company, hardware dealers, for whom he traveled two years in Minnesota and Dakota. The following two years he worked the same territory for the Simmons Hardware Company of St. Louis, Missouri, the largest hardware company in the world. The two years next following he sold hardware for Jenney, Semple & Company, of Minneapolis, in Dakota, Montana, Washington and Oregon. Returning to New Hampshire in 1892 he found employment with John B. Varick & Company, of Manchester, for whom he sold hardware in New Hampshire and Vermont six months. He then sold goods over New Hampshire, Vermont, and Massachusetts for S. A. Felton, Son & Company, brush manufacturers in New Hampshire, Vermont and Massachusetts. In 1893 he became bookkeeper for the S. C. Forsaith Manufacturing Company. At the end of a year Mr. Smith took the position of superintendent of the lumber department and managed the affairs of this department for the company between four and five years. This box shop was purchased by D. B. Varney, who employed Mr. Smith to manage this, which he did for three years. Mr. Varney died, and Mr. Smith was retained to conduct the business for his wife for another year. In 1902 the Smith Box and Lumber Company was formed with James G. Fellows, president; Bert J. Fellows, treasurer; and J. R. Smith, general manager. The business is located in Manchester and has flourished under Mr. Smith's energetic and efficient management. Nine million feet of lumber, enough to load one thousand cars, is made into packing cases and boxes annually. The number of persons employed by the factory is seventy-five and nine horses. Mr. Smith is a man of extensive and varied experience, of fine executive ability and an untiring worker. Equipped as he is for business, he has made the company of which he is a member a success from the beginning. He married (first), in Minneapolis, Minnesota, November 25, 1875, Lenora B. Day, by whom he had two children, John R., and Rena A., who now resides in Minneapolis. The son is now a first lieutenant in the United States service in the Ninth United States Infantry in the the Philippines. He married (second), in Manchester, New Hampshire, September 18, 1897, Florence Hodge, widow of David A. Hodge, of Manchester. By her first marriage she had one child, David Albert, who has assumed the name of Smith. Mr. Smith is a Democrat in politics. He owns one of the finest homes in Manchester, at No. 274 Prospect street, where he keeps a stable of fine horses.

SMITH In the history of the world the Smith has been a pioneer of civilization in every country. in every clime, and in every age. He forged the swords and plowshares and made the coats of mail and war chariots of all the nations of antiquity. His value as a member of the community has never been denied. Among our Anglo-Saxon ancestors the smith was a member of his lord's council, and at feasts sat in the place of honor, at the lord's right hand. The name Smith, anciently spelled Smythe, is derived from "smite," and signifies "striker," or "one who beats," referring to the use of the hammer. It was one of the first occupative surnames adopted by an English speaking people when they stepped out of the twilight of the middle ages into the light of modern civilization. As there were unrelated smiths at their forges who became ancestors of Smith families, so there are many families of Smith in no way related to each other. The surname has been borne by many distinguished men both in England and America, from early times to the present, and it now seems to be as suggestive of energy, industry and excellence, as it was a thousand years ago.

(I) Joseph Smith, a soldier in the Revolutionary war, joined the Continental army at Saratoga in 1777, and served as adjutant in Lieutenant-Colonel Welch's battalion, under Brigadier-General Whipple. After that war he resided in Plaistow, nearly opposite to the residence of George Donecuer. He married a Miss Sawyer, and had a son Timothy, and by a second marriage James and Isaac, and perhaps others. The family were known as "store-keepers." The sons moved to Hampstead about 1824.

(II) Isaac, son of Adjutant Joseph Smith, and his wife Mary, was born at Plaistow, May 31, 1793, and died June 11, 1869, aged seventy-six years. He was a merchant in Hampstead for many years, was successful in business, and a leading citizen in the town. He was always interested in the political, financial, educational and religious affairs of the community in which he dwelt. Was town clerk from 1825 to 1832; supervising member of the school committee 1842-44, 1849-51, and selectman in 1844, 1846 and 1847. In 1849 he was chairman of the committee of arrangements to celebrate the one hundredth anniversary of the incorporation of the town of Hampstead. For some years he had the only store at Hampstead, and was the postmaster. An authority says that "Major Isaac Smith was one of the prosperous merchants of the town." He was a liberal and cheerful supporter of the Congregational Church. He was married July 1, 1822, to Mary Clarke, daughter of Nathaniel and Abigail

Clarke (see Clarke, III), born in Plaistow, January 21, 1800, by Rev. John Kelly, of Hampstead. Three children were born to them: Mary Clarke, at Hampton, September 16, 1823, married James Brickett, September 6, 1853, and died August 19, 1875; Isaac William, born May 18, 1825; and Nathaniel Clarke, born in Hampstead, December 4, 1827, died December 11, 1901. Mary Clarke Smith died June 6, 1833. Mr. Smith was married (second), October 23, 1834, to Sarah Clement, of Salisbury, by Rev. Benjamin F. Foster, of that place. They had two children: Rufus Clement, born in Hampton, June 19, 1836; and Joseph, born March 12, 1839, died in childhood. Sarah Clement Smith died May 2, 1866, and her husband married (third), March 20, 1867, Mrs. Abigail Clarke, of Lowell, Massachusetts, who died August 27, 1879.

(III) Isaac William, second child of Isaac and Mary (Clarke) Smith, was born in Hampstead, May 18, 1825, and died at Manchester, New Hampshire, November 28, 1898. His early years were passed in his native village and in attendance of brief periods at the academies in Salisbury, Derry and Sanbornton. He entered Phillips Academy, Andover, Massachusetts, at the age of fifteen years, and having completed his preparatory course there in 1842, entered Dartmouth College in the fall of the same year. He graduated in 1846, and spent some months in teaching. In 1847 he commenced the study of law in the office of William Smith, of Lowell, Massachusetts. After spending nearly a year there he removed to Manchester, New Hampshire, and completed his studies in the office of Hon. Daniel Clark, who was later a member of the United States senate and United States district judge for the district of New Hampshire. He was admitted to the bar July 9, 1850, and at once began the practice of his profession. In 1851 he formed a partnership with Herman Foster, which existed until the latter part of the following year. In December, 1856, he became a partner with Mr. Clark, with whom he had studied. This relationship lasted five years. In 1851 and 1852 Mr. Smith was president of the common council, city solicitor in 1854-55 and mayor in 1869. He also served two years as a member of the school committee. In 1855 he received the appointment of judge of the police court of Manchester, which position he filled until 1857, when he resigned to enable him to give his entire attention to the practice of law. In 1859 he was elected to represent his ward in the state legislature, and was re-elected the following year, and in the latter part was chairman of the judiciary committee of the house of representatives. He was elected to the state senate in 1862 and 1863, and was chairman of the judiciary committee of that body. He was appointed in 1863 by President Lincoln to be assessor for the second revenue district of New Hampshire, and held this office until 1870. He was appointed associate justice of the supreme judicial court of New Hampshire, February 10, 1874, by Governor Straw. In August of that year the court was reorganized and he was appointed by Governor Weston associate justice of the new court, and held the office until the court was again reorganized, in August, 1876. He then resumed the practice of law, which he continued until 1877, when he was appointed by Governor Prescott associate justice of the supreme court to fill a vacancy upon that bench, and occupied the position until he retired by reason of having reached the age limit prescribed by the constitution, May 18, 1895. After a service of twenty years upon the supreme bench he again entered upon the practice of his profession, with a degree of vigor belonging to a much younger man. As a lawyer, Judge Smith in his practice was characterized by a clear judgment, unsparing industry and unbending integrity. Upon the bench his ability as a lawyer, his conscientious and thorough examination of every case upon which he was called to express an opinion, and the judicial poise and impartiality which he always maintained, secured for his decisions the highest degree of confidence and respect. Judge Smith was one of the trustees of the Manchester City Library from September, 1872, and a trustee of the Manchester Savings Bank from 1841. He was also a member of the bank committee upon investments. He was an old-time stockholder of the Manchester Athenaeum upon which the City Library was founded, and a short time before his death was elected vice-president of the Athenaeum, the organization of which is always kept up. He was president of the Dartmouth Alumni Association in 1881-83, and of the Phi Beta Kappa Society in 1882-84. In college he was one of the charter members of the Dartmouth Chapter of the Alpha Delta Phi Society. In 1880 he delivered before the Alumni Association a eulogy upon the life and character of the Hon. William H. Bartlett, late associate justice of the supreme court of New Hampshire. In March, 1885, he was elected one of the trustees of the college, and held that position until his death, at that time being clerk of the trustees. He received the degree of Doctor of Laws from the college in 1889. He had been a member of the New Hampshire Historical Society since 1861. As early as 1849 he delivered an address which was subsequently published, at the centennial celebration of the incorporation of his native town. His taste for historical investigation gave a special zest and value to a visit which he made in the summer of 1878 to several scenes of historic interest in the old world. In 1889 he was a delegate from Manchester to the New Hampshire constitutional convention. Politically Judge Smith was a strong Republican from the organization of the party, and was very active in politics until he went upon the bench. He was an earnest advocate of the principles of the party during the Civil war and in reconstruction times. In 1856 he was a delegate to the national convention which nominated Fremont and Dayton as Republican candidates for president and vice-president. Religiously, by education and conviction, his sympathies were with the Orthodox Congregationalists. He early identified himself with the Franklin Street Church, with which he was connected for over forty years, and assumed his full share of the burdens and responsibilities, being called at different times to fill the offices of president, treasurer and director in it. In 1870 he became a member of the church in full communion. Judge Smith was a Knight Templar, and although not active in the order while upon the bench, took an interest after that time. He died very suddenly and unexpectedly of heart disease, while at work in his office, November 28, 1898.

Judge Smith married, August 16, 1854, Amanda W., daughter of Hon. Hiram Brown, the first mayor of Manchester. They had eight children: Mary A., wife of Vincent C. Ferguson, of Roswell, New Mexico; William I. Clarke, of Wayne, Pennsylvania; Arthur Whitney, deceased, March 5, 1886; Julia B., wife of Walter B. Cowan, of Sidmouth, England; Edward C., of Manchester, New Hampshire; Daniel C., of Lawrence, Massachusetts; Jennie P., wife of Dr. James F. Bottfield, of Newton, Massachusetts; Grace L., of Manchester, New Hampshire.

(IV) Edward Clark, son of Isaac William and Amanda W. (Brown) Smith, was born in Manchester, October 24, 1864. He attended the public schools of his native city, and graduated from the high school in 1884. He then entered the drug business as a clerk in the store of Park H. Kelly, where he remained two years, and then filled a like position with John B. Hall for about three years. In 1890 he opened a drug store on his own account at the corner of Elm and Orange streets, where he was in business until 1897. He subsequently bought a half interest in John B. Hall's drug store, which he now owns. He has taken an active part in politics from early manhood, and in 1897 was elected city clerk. He was annually re-elected in 1898 and 1899, and bi-ennially in 1901, 1903, 1905 and 1907. In the year 1903 the Uncanoonuc Inclined Railroad and Development Company was organized for the purpose of constructing a railroad to the summit of Uncanoonuc Mountain, and improving real estate in the vicinity, and Mr. Smith was elected president and treasurer of the company, which position he still holds. He was president of the Young Men's Republican Club, one of the most active and influential clubs in Manchester, for eight years. He is a member of Washington Lodge, No. 61, Ancient Free and Accepted Masons; past chancellor commander of Golden Rule Lodge, No. 45, Knights of Pythias, and chairman of the joint board of trustees. He is also a member of Passaconnaway Lodge, No. 5, Improved Order of Red Men, and of the Derryfield Club. In religion he is a Congregationalist, and is a member of the society of the Franklin Street Church. Mr. Smith is one of Manchester's most energetic, industrious and trustworthy citizens, and a successful business man. He married, April 14, 1891, Anna M. Spencer, daughter of John and Charlotte Spencer, of Manchester.

SMITH It has not been possible to connect this line with those of the Smiths whose history has previously been written. The present family can be traced as far as the Revolution only.

(I) Abijah Smith, of Ashford, Connecticut, was a Revolutionary soldier, but the dates of his birth and death are not known. He served sixteen days at the time of the Lexington alarm, and also served in Captain Knowlton's company of Ashford from May 6 to December 10, 1775.

(II) Abijah (2), son of Abijah (1) Smith, was born probably in Ashford, Connecticut. On August 28, 1783, he married Judith Whiton, and they had seven children: Martha, Stephen, Judith, Polly, Abijah, Elijah W. and Howard. Abijah (2) Smith died in Randolph, Vermont.

(III) Elijah Whiton, third son and sixth child of Abijah (2) and Judith (Whiton) Smith, was born in Randolph, Vermont. He was a farmer and lived all his life in Randolph. He belonged to the local militia, and was captain of the Light Artillery Company of his town. Captain Smith married (first), a Miss Arnold, whose christian name is unknown. She died, leaving six children: Avery, Eleazer, Caroline, Ellen, Ann and Abby. Captain Smith married for his second wife Mrs. Dolly Higgins Stevens a native of Randolph. There were four children by the second marriage: Harriet, Delia, Edgar W. whose sketch follows; and Prentiss C. Captain Elijah W. Smith died in 1850 at Randolph, Vermont, and his widow survived him more than forty years, dying in May or June, 1894, at Randolph.

(IV) Edgar William, third child and eldest son of Captain Elijah Whiton Smith and his second wife, Mrs. Dolly Higgins Stevens, was born at Randolph, Vermont, July 3, 1845. He was educated in the schools of his native town and at New Hampton Institute, New Hampton, New Hampshire. He afterwards taught school in Fairview, New Jersey, for several years, and then returned to East Randolph, where he taught a select school for a time. He began the study of law in the office of Philander Perrin and N. L. Boyden, of Randolph, and continued his study in the office of former Governor George W. Hendee, at Morrisville, Vermont, and later in the office of Judge Abel Underwood, of Wells River, Vermont. He was admitted to the Vermont bar on January 1, 1872. Mr. Smith then took up his residence at Wells River, and began the practice of law by himself, occupying the same office as Judge Underwood. After the death of the latter he took the entire office where he has maintained a large practice down to the present time. In 1884 he admitted Scott Sloane as partner, and a few years later they opened an office across the river at Woodsville, New Hampshire. This partnership continued till May 1, 1899, when Mr. Sloane retired and Mr. Edgar W. Smith received his son, Raymond U., as partner. On August 17, 1869, Edgar William Smith married Emma M. Gates, who was born January 11, 1849, at Morrisville, Vermont. They had three sons: Percy G., Raymond U., whose sketch follows; and Llewellyn, who died in infancy. Mr. and Mrs. Smith attend the Congregational Church, and live at Wells River, Vermont.

(V) Raymond Underwood, second son and child of Edgar William and Emma M. (Gates) Smith, was born September 11, 1875, at Wells River, Vermont. He was educated in the schools of his native town, and was graduated from Norwich University at Northfield, Vermont, in 1894. He then studied law with his father in the offices at Wells River and Woodsville, and was admitted to the Vermont bar in 1897, and to the New Hampshire bar in 1900. He went into the office of Smith & Sloane, in whose employ he remained till 1899, when his father dissolved partnership with Mr. Sloane, and the son became a member of the firm, which is now known as Smith & Smith, with offices at Wells River and Woodsville. Raymond U. Smith is a Republican in politics, and is much interested in fraternal organizations. He belongs to Pulaski Lodge, Ancient Free and Accepted Masons of Wells River; Mount Lebanon Chapter of Bradford, Vermont; Omega Council of Plymouth, New Hampshire; to Palestine Commandery, Knights Templar, of St. Johnsbury, Vermont; and Mount Sinai Temple, Mystic Shrine, of Montpelier, Vermont. He is a member of Moosehillock Lodge, Independent Order of Odd Fellows, of Woodsville, New Hampshire. Mr. Smith belongs to the Bar Associations, both of New Hampshire and Vermont, and is a member of the Vermont Fish and Game League. He is unmarried.

SMITH (I) Samuel Smith was born 1766, perhaps in Peterboro, and died October 6, 1840, aged seventy-four. He married Hannah Mills, who died September 15, 1847, aged eighty-two. Their children were: Hannah, who died September 1, 1795, aged eleven months; Leonard, March 24, 1814, aged fifteen years; Hannah, February 21, 1849, aged fifty-two years; George, a physician, who died in Georgia; and Elisha, whose sketch follows.

(II) Elisha, son of Samuel and Hannah (Mills)

Smith, was born in Alstead, January 25, 1787, and died in Keene, March 27, 1835, aged forty-eight He was a farmer in Alstead until a short time before his death, when he moved to Keene. He married, December 13, 1821, Betsey Warren, who was born in Alstead, February 21, 1794, daughter of Levi and Molly (Abbot) Warren. Levi Warren was a native of Nelson, New Hampshire, and was a farmer in Alstead. His death was the result of accident; he drank poison by mistake. His wife Molly. was born June 18, 1773, daughter of Joseph (2) and Mary (Barker) Abbot. (See Abbot, IV). Their children were: Mary M. (Polly); Betsey, died young; and Emily Elizabeth (Betsey). After the death of Mr. Smith his widow married, March 4, 1840, Colonel David Low, a prosperous merchant of Hancock. He was a man of influence in religious, political and military circles.

(III) Mary M., eldest of the daughters of Elisha and Betsey (Warren) Smith, was born May 19, 1825. She married Dr. Charles Wells, of Manchester. He died childless, and left his wife an ample fortune which she enjoyed until her death. They resided in Manchester, where he built a large and handsome house surrounded with spacious and well kept grounds. Mrs. Wells was a very charitable lady, and furnished and afterward kept up an operating room in Elliott hospital. Manchester. She died July 3, 1898, aged seventy-three years.

(III) Emily E., younger daughter of Elisha and Betsey (Warren) Smith, was born in East Alstead, November 12, 1826, and was seven years old when her father died. After the marriage of her mother to Colonel Low, she lived at his home. For many years she resided with her sister, Mrs. Wells, and became heir to the large property she left. She now resides in the Wells mansion on Elm street, and has a large circle of friends. She has a tender regard for the poor and distressed, and is well known for her deeds of charity. She maintains the operating room and other benefactions of her sister.

SMITH

(I) Ezra Smith was a native of Winchendon, Massachusetts, born September 13, 1778, and one of the early settlers of Langdon, New Hampshire, where he cleared a good farm and spent the remaining years of his life. He is mentioned by biographers as a man of great physical strength and wonderful power of endurance, and he also was a man of more than ordinary mental capacity, a leader among the townsmen, an ardent Whig, hence a loyal supporter of Madison's administration in the second war with Great Britain and fully capable of maintaining his ground against the clamors of the Federalistic element of the community. He died July 14, 1864, having attained the unusual age of eighty-six years. His wife, Hannah Henry, was born in Vermont, August 10, 1779, and died in Langdon, New Hampshire. June 25, 1850, having borne her husband five children, as follows: Nancy, Orrin and Alden, twins, Franklin, and a daughter that died aged about six years.

(II) Orrin, son of Ezra and Hannah (Henry) Smith, was born in the town of Langdon, New Hampshire, November 11, 1807, and was a twin. Like his father, he too was a farmer and lived at home with his parents until several years after attaining his majority. In 1862 he removed to Peterborough in Hillsborough county, and bought the farm of one hundred and sixty acres on which he afterward lived and on which he died August 6, 1886. In politics he followed the paternal example and was a Whig and later a Republican, his father having died before the latter party came into existence. Mr. Smith married, June 9, 1836, Marinda Partridge, daughter of Sylvester Partridge, of Alstead, New Hampshire, and she, like her husband, was a twin. She was born in Alstead, October 25, 1814, and died in Peterborough, December 19, 1889. Orrin and Marinda Smith had seven children: Ezra Murray, born in Langdon, January 25, 1838. Irving Henry, born February 2, 1840, received a good common school education and was engaged in mercantile pursuits in Peterborough previous to the late Civil war; married Clara L. Gray. Hattie Marinda, born July 6, 1842, married Alden B. Tarbell. Albert Orrin, born May 1, 1845, married Josie L. Hovey. Silas M., born February 21, 1847. married Marinda K. Parker, and has one son. Emma Rosanna, born December 5, 1850, now lives in Peterborough. Alden Emmons; born April 25, 1853, married Aldana Andrews.

(III) Ezra Murray, eldest son and child of Orrin and Marinda (Partridge) Smith, was born in the town of Langdon, New Hampshire, January 25, 1838, and received his early education in public schools and Cold River Union Academy, in the latter preparing for college. For a time he taught school in the towns of Henniker, Marlow and Francestown, and also studied law at Charlestown with Judge Cushing and at Peterborough with Dearborn & Scott, and having grounded himself in elementary law he became a student in the law department of the old University of Albany (now Albany Law School—the law department of Union University). He completed the prescribed course of that still famous institution and was graduated February, 1861. Having been admitted to practice in the courts of New Hampshire Mr. Smith located at Peterborough and succeeded Mr. Dearborn as member of the firm of Dearborn & Scott. His partnership relation with Mr. Scott continued three years, and from the time he entered the firm had been active in the professional life; he is a member of the Hillsborough county bar. In the course of a few years he built up an extensive and lucrative general practice, and from the outset of his career has been regarded as one of the safest lawyers and counselors at the bar in his county—a county always famous for the strength of its bar. Like all of the younger and more enterprising lawyers of his time Mr. Smith took an active part in public and political affairs, and while he never was ambitious for political honors he frequently was appointed or elected to positions of a political character. For forty years he has been a justice of the peace, besides which he served as selectman twenty-two years, and is now (1907) a member of the school board ten years, and justice of the police court four years. He represented his town in the legislature in 1841, 1871-72, 1901 and again in 1903, and was a member of the constitutional convention of 1876. He is an Odd Fellow, member of Peterborough Grange and of the Congregational Church.

He married, October 4, 1866, Mary S. Fairbanks, daughter of Moses and Abigail (Hadley) Fairbanks. She was born in Dublin, New Hampshire, February 13, 1845. Their children are: Etta Marinda born December 2, 1870. Harlan Beecher, born March 9, 1874, died November 21, 1892. Orrin Fairbanks, born June 28, 1886, a graduate of Cushman Academy.

SMITH

(I) Joseph Smith, of Loudon, New Hampshire, was engaged in farming there at the beginning of the nineteenth century. He married Abigail Morrill, of Orange, this state.

(II) Micajah M., son of Joseph and Abigail (Morrill) Smith, was a native of Loudon. The greater part of his life was spent in Orange, where he followed argiculture industriously during the active period of his life. He married Abigail Cole, daughter of Thomas Cole, of Orange, and had a family of eight children: Olive, Ann, Thomas, Joseph, Jason, Elijah, Samuel and Micajah.

(III) Elijah, fourth son and sixth child of Micajah M. and Abigail (Cole) Smith, was born in Orange, February 11, 1832. Reared to agricultural pursuits he has devoted much of his time and energy to that calling, but has availed himself of eligible opportunities in other directions, including the surveying of land and the buying and selling of real estate. About the year 1863 he settled in Canaan and has ever since resided there. Politically he is a Democrat and was formerly quite active in local civic affairs, serving as sheriff for some time and representing his district for one term in the lower house of the state legislature. He is a Master Mason and a member of Summit Lodge, No. 98, of Canaan. On April 11, 1857, he married Eliza Davis, who was born in Canaan, October 8, 1837, and died there October 29, 1863. For his second wife he married Isabella L. Goss, born September 8, 1842. The children of his first union are: Alden E. and Carey. Those of his second marriage are: Cora B. and Henry R.

(IV) Carey, second son and child of Elijah and Eliza (Davis) Smith, was born in Orange, March 12, 1861. His preliminary studies were pursued in the public schools of Canaan, where he went to reside when two years old, and completed his education at the New Hampshire Conference Seminary, Tilton, from which he was graduated in 1881. Shortly after leaving the seminary he engaged in the grocery business at Canaan, and followed it continuously and with prosperous results for over twenty-five years, or until 1907, when he sold his mercantile establishment to his brother. For the past twenty years he has conducted a profitable lumber business, and still retains it in connection with the undertaking business which he has carried on since 1900. He is also engaged in farming on what was formerly the Canaan fair ground. In politics he acts with the Democratic party, and served as postmaster during each of President Cleveland's administrations. He is an advanced Mason, belonging to Summit Lodge, of Canaan, St. Andrews Chapter, (Royal Arch) of Lebanon, and Sullivan Commandery (Knights Templar), of Claremont. He is also a member of Mount Cardigan Lodge, Knights of Pythias, and India River Grange, Patrons of Husbandry, both of Canaan.

September 13, 1891, Mr. Smith was united in marriage with Lizzie Idella Barney, daughter of Charles and Harriet (Wells) Barney, of Canaan. Mr. and Mrs. Smith have one son, Ned Barney, who was born February 16, 1893, and is now attending the Canaan high school.

SMITH (I) James W. Smith, born in Ipswich, was educated in the district schools of his native town, and afterward worked at farm labor. After his marriage he lived in Hillsborough and engaged in the grocery business. He was a Republican, and a regular attendant of the Congregational Church. He died in Manchester, Vermont, of yellow fever. He married Louisa Bennett.

(II) Daniel Bennett, oldest son and second child of James W. and Louisa (Bennett) Smith, was born in Hillsboro. He received a common school education, became a musician, and was a noted performer on the violin. He was one of the first daguerreotype artists, and had a studio in Hillsboro for many years. He married, 1842, Mary H. Goodell, born in Hillsboro, New Hampshire, daughter of Levi and Mary Howlet Goodell. She was a member of the Methodist Episcopal Church. The children of this union were: Orlena C., and Daniel Bennett. After the death of Mr. Smith his widow married, in 1853, George Jones, a farmer of Hillsboro, and died in 1897, leaving children: Levi G., and Mary Elizabeth, who died at the age of twenty-two.

(III) Daniel Bennett, eldest son and second child of Daniel B. and Mary H. (Goodell) Smith, was born in Hillsboro April 10, 1848. After obtaining a common school education he worked on the farm for his stepfather until 1873. He then went to Ispwich and spent two years in the same employment, and then (1885) bought the farm his widow occupies, on the road from Concord to Hopkinton, where are fifty acres of land and a large set of buildings. He was engaged in stock-raising. He voted the Republican ticket, and took an active part in politics. He was a councilman three years, an alderman two years, and member of the house of representatives 1891-93. He was a past grand of Valley Lodge, Independent Order of Odd Fellows, of Hillsboro Bridge, New Hampshire, and a member of the Methodist Church. He was an enterprising, popular and well known citizen. Mr. Smith married, May 23, 1867, at Nashua, New Hampshire, Mary E. Small, born in Hillsboro, July 9, 1838, daughter of John and Mary Daforth Small, of Antrim, New Hampshire. Mr. Smith died July 1, 1907.

SMITH It has not been possible to trace the connection of this branch of the family with those whose history has previously been writtten.

(I) John Smith married Hannah Burnham. Their children were: Daniel Lowe, whose sketch follows; George W., Ziba and John B.

(II) Daniel Lowe, eldest child of John and Hannah (Burnham) Smith, was born January 17, 1804, at Essex, Massachusetts, and moved to Enfield, New Hampshire, when a child. He had very little opportunity for schooling, but became a man of substance and standing in the community. He was a farmer by occupation, and an official of the Methodist Church all his life. He was a Democrat in politics, served on the board of selectmen several terms and represented the town of Enfield during two sessions of the state legislature. On March 30, 1830, Daniel Lowe Smith married Mary Flanders, daughter of Moses and Ann Flanders, of Enfield. She died July 8, 1841, leaving two children: Ann C., born November 18, 1837; and Mary F., born June 27, 1841. The eldest child died in infancy. On June 2, 1843, Mr. Smith married his second wife, Mrs. Sophronia Eastman Richardson, daughter of James and Polly (French) Eastman, of Enfield. (See Eastman VII). Two children were born of this marriage: Wilbur Fisk, whose sketch follows, and Moses F. E. Mrs. Sophronia (Eastman) Smith died May 10, 1871; and Daniel Lowe Smith died April 16, 1882.

(III) Wilbur Fisk, older of the two sons of Daniel Lowe Smith and his second wife, Sophronia (Eastman) Smith, was born at Enfield, New Hampshire, September 27, 1844. He was educated in the common schools of his native town, and at the Seminary at Newbury, Vermont. He has followed farming most of his life. He is a Democrat in politics, and was selectman of Enfield for six years, also supervisor of the check list and a member of the school board. In 1890 he moved to Lebanon, New Hampshire, and was commissioner of Grafton county in 1891-92, and register of deeds for the county in 1894. He was elected town clerk of Lebanon, New Hampshire, March, 1907, being the first Democrat to be elected to that office for fifty years in this town, which is an eloquent index of his popularity and standing in the community. He has been on the official board of the Methodist Church for thirty-five years, and is a Mason of the thirty-second degree. On March 7, 1866, Wilbur Fisk Smith married Maria A. Sargent, daughter of Winthrop and Louise (Smith) Sargent, of Claremont, New Hampshire. She was born April 10, 1845, and died May 27, 1902, leaving three sons: Daniel Leon, Wilfred Olen and Harold Elmo. Daniel Leon Smith was born September 13, 1867, and was graduated from Dartmouth College in 1891 and from Harvard Law School in 1894, and is now an attorney in Boston. He married, April 4, 1895, Virginia Scott, daughter of Jesse Yeates, M. C., from North Carolina. Three children were born to them, the first dying at eleven months old; Louise Orme, born November 14, 1904; Virginia Yeates, March 13, 1907. The mother of these children died March 20, 1907. Wilfred Olen Smith was born April 25, 1869, and is now a clerk in the office of the Amoskeag Corporation at Manchester, New Hampshire. He married Lottie Louise Bishop, of Littleton, New Hampshire, June, 1893. They have one daughter, Marie Antoinette, born January 24, 1904. Harold Elmo Smith was born May 2, 1882, graduated from Dartmouth in 1903, and is now assistant examiner in the United States patent office, Washington, D. C.

SMITH The representatives of the great Smith family below mentioned are of Vermont extraction, and their more remote forefathers probably migrated from the state of Massachusetts before the Revolutionary war. Various members of this family have long resided in Thetford, Vermont.

(I) Frederick P. Smith was born in Tunbridge, Vermont, son of Thurston and Betsey Smith. He married Hannah M. George, daughter of Samuel and Hannah George, of East Randolph, Vermont. He was at one time a resident of Manchester, New Hampshire. He was a skillful mechanic and an inventive genius, and to him we owe the invention of the hill-side plow, which he manufactured at La-Porte, Indiana, for some years. Later he resided in Northfield, Vermont, where he died in 1882, aged seventy-one years.

(II) Captain George H., son of Frederick P. Smith, was born in Thetford, Orange county, Vermont, in 1834, and settled in Farmington, New Hampshire, when a young man. He responded to his country's call early in the Civil war, and the following is an epitome of his war record. While residing at Nashua, New Hampshire, he enlisted, August 24, 1861, and was mustered in Company I, Third Regiment, New Hampshire Volunteer Infantry, as a wagoner; and was discharged May 15, 1862, at Hilton Head, South Carolina. January 3, 1864, he enlisted in Company C, Thirteenth Regiment New Hampshire Volunteer Infantry, and was mustered in the same day as a private; discharged April, 1864, to accept promotion. Appointed second lieutenant of Company E, First Regiment New Hampshire Volunteer Cavalry, March 18, 1864; mustered in July 8, 1864; appointed first lieutenant Company F, August 11, 1864. Captain of Company M, June 10, 1865, not mustered; mustered out July 15, 1865, as first lieutenant of Company F. He learned the business of shoemaking, and after some years as a hand was promoted to foreman of the finishing room of the Nute Shoe Factory at Farmington. After filling that place some twenty-five years, he was foreman for Furbush and Brown, shoe manufacturers of Grafton, Massachusetts, until age and ill health compelled him to resign the place. He died at the house of his daughter, Marion M. Hoyt, at Manchester, in 1898. He married, in 1854, Marion H. Brown, who was born in Wilmot, New Hampshire, September 29, 1835, died in 1903, daughter of Joseph and Betsey Brown, of Wilmot. They had twelve children: 1. Frank J. 2. Adelaide O., wife of Dr. P. B. Foss, now deceased. 3. Fred P., member of firm of Kent & Smith, of Lynn, Massachusetts. 4. Alice C., wife of Eugene Williams, of Brockton, Massachusetts. 5. Marion Myrtella, born in 1863, died in 1902, was wife of Harry M. Hoyt, of Manchester. 6. Henry, resides in North Grafton. 7. Lizzie, born in 1870, wife of E. Perley Elliot, of Manchester, New Hampshire; died in 1904; at the time of her death was a member of the Bostonian Opera Company. 8. Eva May, died in 1875, aged two years and six months. 9. Joseph P., lives in Grafton, Massachusetts. 10. Thaddeus, an electrical designer in Springfield, Massachusetts. 11. Roscoe, resides in Lynn, Massachusetts. 12. Bessie, wife of Henry Bushard, druggist, Grafton, Massachusetts,

(III) Frank J., eldest child of Captain George H. and Marion H. (Brown) Smith, was born in Wilmot, New Hampshire, September 28, 1855. He was educated in the public schools of Farmington, and when about twenty years old became a bookkeeper for Nute & Sons, shoe manufacturers, of Farmington, and filled that position eleven years, and then took a place in the finishing department with his father and has ever since been employed in that department. In politics he is a Republican. He was elected selectman in 1901 and has been re-elected every year since except 1906, and has been chairman of the board during the time of his incumbency since 1902. He is a member of Harmony Lodge, No. 11, Knights of Pythias, of Farmington, of which he is a past chancellor; member and past master of Henry Wilson Grange, No. 205, Patrons of Husbandry, of Farmington; master of the Eastern New Hampshire Pomona Grange in 1906 and 1907. He married, in Farmington, 1882, Ada Lund, who was born in Warren, New Hampshire, in 1854, daughter of Abram Cookson.

SCHMIDT The principal subject of this sketch is one of the great multitude of foreign-born citizens who have in recent years come as poor men to New England and by a proper use of their time and energies, built up good business and comfortable homes for themselves.

(I) Reinhold (1) Schmidt resided in Coppus, Germany, where he spent most of his life as a potter.

(II) Reinhold (2), son of Reinhold (1) Schmidt, was born in Forst, Germany, where he also died. He was a woolen weaver by trade. He married Pauline Haermsdorf, and they had four children: Albert, Reinhold, Annie and Frederick.

(III) Reinhold (3), second son and child of

Reinhold (2) Schmidt, was born at Forst, Germany, December 5, 1861, and received a common school education. He learned the carpenter's trade, at which he worked until he left Germany. In 1882 he sailed from Forst on the steamship "Ethiopia," and landed in New York. Soon after he settled in Manchester, New Hampshire, where he worked seven years in the Amoskeag mills as a weaver, after which he resumed the carpenter's trade, at which he has since been employed. After working for wages for several different employers, he started out as a contractor and builder in 1901, and now has a successful business.

He married, in Manchester, Augusta Connor, who was born June 5, 1863, daughter of Frank Connor, of Manchester, New Hampshire. They have two children: Oscar, born May 4, 1887, and Reinhold, June 21, 1889, both natives of Manchester.

JACKSON This name is undoubtedly of Scotch origin and was brought to this country from northern Ireland, which was so largely settled by Scotch immigrants near the close of the seventeenth century.

(I) The first of whom definite knowledge has been brought to America was Robert Jackson, who was born about 1766, in county Antrim, Ireland, and died at Milford, Ireland, about 1863. He was a farmer and held a farm under a lease of the Earl of Leitrim and continued on the same until his death, when he was succeeded by his son and namesake. His wife was Mary (Martin) Jackson, and their children were: William, James, Margaret and Robert.

(II) William, eldest child of Robert and Mary (Martin) Jackson, was born February 3, 1807, in Milford, Ireland, and died March 17, 1897, in Littleton, New Hampshire, aged ninety years. He left his native land in 1831, sailing from Londonderry, and landed at Quebec, Canada. After staying a little over a year at that place he removed to Walcott, Province of Quebec, where he was engaged in farming one year. In 1835 he moved to Barnet, Vermont, where he learned the trade of finishing in a woolen factory. He remained there until 1840, and then removed to Littleton, New Hampshire, where he passed most of his subsequent life. He was boss finisher employed by the Littleton Woolen Manufacturing Company, and continued under the same management for a period of thirty-five years, excepting two years when the mills were closed. At the end of this time he retired from the mills and amused himself by the cultivation of a small farm near the village until his death. He was a Presbyterian in religious faith, and supported the Democratic party in political matters. He was married December 7, 1837, to Prusia, daughter of Joseph Morrell. She was born January 8, 1816, in Danville, Vermont, and died in Littleton, November 17, 1880. Their children were: James, Robert, Andrew, William, Mary Jane, Julia O., Laura P., Henry Oliver and Alice E. The eldest daughter married Henry H. Metcalf, of Littleton, and now resides in Concord, New Hampshire. The second daughter is the wife of William Burns Hurd, a farmer residing in Littleton. Alice E. married Elmer E. Day.

(III) James Robert, eldest child of William and Prusia (Morrell) Jackson, was born October 5, 1838, in Barnet, Vermont, and was educated in the common schools of Littleton and select schools taught by Colonel Emery, Samuel B. Page, Warren McIntire. He entered the law office of H. & G. A. Bingham, as a student. He went out with the Fifth Regiment of the Volunteer Infantry as company's clerk of Company C band of that regiment. Having completed his law studies, he was admitted to the bar at Lancaster in the July law term of the supreme court in 1867, and continued in practice two years thereafter with his preceptors. He then engaged in practice independently and so continued until 1873, when he turned his attention to matters outside the practice of the law. Proceeding to Dover, New Hampshire, he engaged as associate editor with his brother-in-law, Henry H. Metcalf, on the *State Press* and this arrangement continued five years, until 1878. He has written continuously for various newspapers and prepared a historic sketch of the town of Littleton for the *Grafton County Gazeteer*. He also compiled the history of Littleton published by the town, and was a contributor and an editor to the *Littleton Sentinel* published in 1884. His writings are largely upon political and historical subjects. Mr. Jackson is an earnest Democrat in politics, and served as secretary of the Democratic state committee from 1888 to 1893. He was moderator of his town in 1873-74-75, was clerk of the house of representatives in 1871 and secretary of the constitutional convention of 1889. From 1894 to 1897 he was United States consul at Sherbrook, Canada. He represented the Concord railroad before legislative committees from 1881 to 1885, and the Boston & Maine railroad from 1887 to 1893. Since April, 1864, he has served as justice of the peace and holds the oldest commission for that office in Littleton. He was superintendent of the school committee in 1866-67-68, and was a member of the first board of education after the establishment of the Union School District in 1867, and continued five years in this capacity. He was a trustee of the Public Library during the first five years after its organization, at the end of which time he resigned. He was a member of the committee on town history from the appointment of that committee until the completion of the work. He was married July 16, 1879, to Lydia Ann, daughter of George K. Drew, of Durham, New Hampshire. She was born December 30, 1854, in New Market. Seven children have been born to them, namely: Robert, Andrew, Harry Bingham, William Mitchell, Elizabeth, Katharine Florence and Rachel Pierce. The eldest son is a graduate of Dartmouth College and is now practicing law with ex-Judge James W. Remick, of Concord. The second is also a Dartmouth graduate and is now a submaster of the Nashua high school. The third and fourth are students of Dartmouth.

JACKSON "Surnames from 'John' are as multifarious as is possible in the case of a monosyllable, ingenuity in the contraction thereof being thus manifestly limited." "John" was early corrupted to Jack, and from Jack we have the patronymic Jackson.

(I) Thomas Jackson was born in Lancaster county, England. Subsequently he emigrated to America, and later removed to Nova Scotia. He married Sarah R. Parmenter, and among their children was a son, James T.

(II) James T., third child of Thomas and Sarah R. (Parmenter) Jackson, was born in Medford, Nova Scotia, and his death occurred at the age of eighty-nine years. He was a ship builder by trade. In 1869 he removed to Boston, Massachusetts, but after a short residence there returned to Nova Scotia. He married, in Windsor, Nova Scotia, Sarah R. Smith, born in Windsor, daughter of William Smith, of Windsor, Nova Scotia, and a descendant of

James Smith, of Oldtown, Maine. Five children were born of this union: Mary E., Myra A., Lilla, Edith L. and George Frederick.

(III) George Frederick, fifth child and only son of James T. and Sarah R. (Smith) Jackson, was born at Canning, Nova Scotia, February 14, 1864. When he was a child his parents removed to Boston, Massachusetts, and his education was acquired in the Rice, Dwight and Lowell public schools. At the close of his school days he entered a dry goods establishment in Boston, Massachusetts, where he was employed three years. He next obtained a position as traveling salesman for a fancy goods and importing house, and was on the road for more than four years. He began the study of law in the office of Captain B. Atherton, and continued the same for a period of two years. From the law office he went to Boston University Law School, and after taking the entire three years' course in two years was graduated with the class of 1894, with the degree of Bachelor of Laws. The July following he passed his examinations for admission to the bar of New Hampshire, standing at the head of a class of thirteen. He immediately formed a partnership with Edward H. Wason, under the firm name of Wason & Jackson, which was continued until July, 1900. In politics he was a stalwart Republican, and as such was elected city solicitor of Nashua, and continued in that office by successive elections for four years. In business he is a studious, careful and successful lawyer; in social life an agreeable companion and trustworthy friend. He is a thirty-second degree Mason, and is a member of the following divisions of the Masonic Order: John Hancock Lodge, Mt. Vernon Royal Arch Chapter, Roxbury Council of Royal and Select Masters, Joseph Warren Commandery, Knights Templar, and Massachusetts Consistory, all of Boston. He is a member of Pennichuck Lodge, No. 44, Independent Order of Odd Fellows, Phi Delta Phi fraternity, Sigma Alpha Epsilon college fraternity, Roxbury City Guards, of which he was a member five years, Company D, First Regiment, Massachusetts Volunteer Militia, and for seven years was a member of the Ancient and Honorable Artillery Company of Boston.

JACKSON This patronymic is obviously one of those directly derived from a christian name. Jackson, like Johnson, originally meant the son of John. The name is numerous among the early settlers, and it reached the climax of its distinction in Andrew Jackson, one of the most brilliant and daring presidents. The following family is not connected with the Jackson family of Madison, New Hampshire, which is descended from Dr. James Jackson. He had a son James who married Abigail Merrill, of Conway, and they had seventeen children. Three of their sons, Thomas, Daniel and William, became ordained ministers, and their descendants are numerous in the central part of the state.

(I) Aaron Jackson, the original American ancestor of this family, came from England to South America during the eighteenth century, going thence to Salem, Massachusetts, and finally settling in Stark, New Hampshire. Little is known about him except that he fought in the Revolutionary war, and married a woman named Cole, who lived in Stark. This town was originally incorporated as "Piercy" in 1795, and the petition of incorporation is signed by four Coles, Jonathan, Nathan, Clafford and Edmund. The signature of Aaron Jackson follows, the only one of

that name, and if the ancestor of this line was in Stark at that time it must be he. In that case he was a man of prominence among the early settlers, being chosen on the first board of selectmen, March 3, 1795, and again in 1799, 1800-04-06. In 1809 he was taxed for one horse, two oxen, four cows, two acres of pasture, one arable, two mowing land. The name of Aaron Jackson (2) appears on the board of selectmen in 1817-18-19. He had sons: Aaron, Moses and Jonas Isaac.

(II) Moses, son of Aaron and Sarah (Cole) Jackson, was born at Stark, New Hampshire, May 1, 1800. He was a farmer and stood well in the community, being honored with all the town offices. He was selectman in 1826-42-43-44-50-51-60. Moses Jackson married Lucy Furbush, probably of Stark. Moses Jackson died in 1887.

(III) Hiram, son of Moses and Lucy (Furbush) Jackson, was born at Stark, New Hampshire, April 27, 1825. He was a farmer and also managed a saw mill, though during the latter part of his life he devoted himself entirely to farming. He joined the Congregational Church early in life, but in later years remained at home with his invalid wife. Hiram Jackson married Lucy Rich, daughter of Enoch Chaney and Sarah (Rowell) Rich, of Stark, New Hampshire. They had two children: Dexter M., who died in 1891, and Albert Henry, whose sketch follows. Moses Jackson died at Stark, April 7, 1906.

(IV) Albert Henry, second son and child of Hiram and Lucy (Rich) Jackson, was born at Stark, New Hampshire, November 16, 1859. He was educated in the common schools and worked on the farm till he was eighteen years of age. He has been in the mill business since then, and is now mill engineer for the Percy Lumber Company. He is a member of the Methodist Church, and belongs to the Grange, the Knights of Pythias, and the Odd Fellows. In 1882 Albert Henry Jackson married Clementine L. Rich, daughter of Daniel Rich. She died in 1895, leaving no children.

GOSS The absence of complete records precludes the writing of a connected history of the very early generations of the Goss family in New Hampshire. Richard Goss was of New Hampshire as early as 1689. Richard Goss, a twin brother of Robert, of Greenland, had twenty acres of common land granted him in Rye in 1701. Robert Goss was of Portsmouth in 1693, and was probably the same Robert who settled at Greenland, near Green Bay. From these pioneers have sprung generations of descendants, energetic and successful, moral and patriotic.

(I) Jonathan, son of Richard Goss, married, May 22, 1735, Salome Locke. They had five children: Richard, Salome, Jonathan, Joseph and Elizabeth.

(II) Jonathan (2), third child of Jonathan (1) and Salome (Locke) Goss, was born in 1743. He served in the Revolution in Captain Parson's company, and later sailed in the privateer "Portsmouth," under command of Samuel Seavey, and was captured and taken to England, where he died of smallpox in Dartmoor prison. He married, February 16, 1769, Elizabeth Brown, by whom he had two sons, Joseph and Jonathan.

(III) Jonathan (3), son of Jonathan (2) and Elizabeth (Brown) Goss, was a farmer. He was in the War of 1812, and served in Captain Berry's company of Light Infantry. He died August 29,

1851. He married Patty Davison, who died May 21, 1843. Their children were: Sarah Blake, William Davison.

(IV) Sarah Blake, eldest child of Jonathan (3) and Patty (Davison) Goss, was born September 13, 1797, and married, November 24, 1825, Captain Daniel Lord. (See under Batchelder, IX).

GOSS The origin of the Goss family in America dates from the early Puritan settlement in Massachusetts. John Goss came from England, probably with Winthrop in 1630, and became a freeman in Watertown, Massachusetts, May 18, 1631, and died February 16, 1644, one of the first settlers in Watertown. He married Sarah ——, and had seven children. Philip Goss, who may have been a son of John and Sarah Goss, of Watertown, resided at "Muddy River," or Roxbury. He married Hannah Hopkins, and had Philip, Hannah, Mary, and probably others. Philip Goss died at Lancaster, Massachusetts, and administration on his estate was granted May 26, 1698. The authentic history of this branch of the Goss family begins with Philip, whose sketch follows. It is quite probable that he was Philip (3).

(I) Philip Goss, born in Lancaster, Massachusetts, in 1720, moved to Winchester, New Hampshire, where he was a leading man, and was one of the signers of the articles of agreement at the reorganization of the church in 1764, his colleague on the part of the people being Josiah Willard, and the other party to the agreement was the pastor, Rev. Micah Lawrence. He married, intention published April 16, 1748, Hannah Ball, of Bolton, Massachusetts, who was born in 1727, and had: John, Hannah, Philip, Abel, Levi, Mercy, Sarah, David, Nathaniel and Samuel.

(II) Abel, fourth child and third son of Philip and Hannah (Ball) Goss, was born in Winchester, New Hampshire, March 31, 1763. He lived a few years in Hartford, Vermont, and moved March 1, 1793, to Waterford, Vermont, near the Connecticut river, a part of the town not then much settled, where he lived, active in labor and usefulness, until his death, May 29, 1825, aged sixty-two years. He married, May 3, 1787, Irene Sprague, who was born February 16, 1763, and died October 5, 1853, in the ninety-first year of her age, retaining her faculties to the last, and leaving to surviving friends that "memory of the just which is blessed." The children born of this union were Mehitable, Otis, Milo, Zenas, Richard, Irene, Abel, Charles 1. and Zebina.

(III) Richard, fifth child and fourth son of Abel and Irene (Sprague) Goss, was born March 29, 1794, and was the first white child born in that part of the town of Waterford. Most of his life was spent in that town and in Littleton, New Hampshire. He married (first), June, 1817, Betsey Buck, of Waterford, who died in Littleton, November 22, 1850. He married (second), Mrs. Eliza (Wells) Luce, of Barnet; she died in August, 1880. The children, all by the first marriage, were: Azro Ashley, Richard O., Horace S., Levi, Silas Buck, Lyman B., Abel Brown, Reuben C., George W., Charles, Betsy Jane and Laura Ann. He died in Kansas, February 12, 1883, while on a visit to his son George W. The remains were brought to Waterford for interment.

(IV) Abel Brown, seventh son and child of Richard and Betsey (Buck) Goss, was born in Waterford, Vermont, October 24, 1828, and died there August 24, 1896, aged sixty-eight years. He lived on the farm at his father's until he was twelve years of age, when he went to live with Elisha Brown, of the same town, and there remained until reaching his majority. He then learned shoemaking in Milford, Massachusetts, where he worked ten years. After spending a year in Webster City, Iowa, and other parts of the west, he settled in Waterford, where he passed the remainder of his life. He was a deacon in the Congregational Church, and held town offices. He married, October 1, 1856, Lucy Stoddard Ross, who was born in Waterford, Vermont, February 21, 1837, daughter of Royal and Eliza Mason Ross, and sister of Jonathan Ross, of St. Johnsbury, Vermont, who was chief justice of the supreme court of that state from 1890 to 1900. She died January 5, 1894. The children of this union were Herbert Irvin, Harlan Page, Eliza Mason, Edward Raymond, Ethel Abby, and Mary Lucy. Herbert is mentioned below. Harlan is a farmer in Waterford, Vermont. Eliza is editor of the *Berlin Reporter*, in Berlin, New Hampshire. Edward is a farmer and merchant in Waterford, Vermont. Ethel died at Waterford, June 22, 1892. Mary married Miner B. Carpenter, and resides at Concord, Vermont.

(V) Herbert Irving, eldest son of Abel B. and Lucy Stoddard (Ross) Goss, was born in Waterford, Caledonia county, Vermont, December 4, 1857. He attended the country district school, and later the St. Johnsbury Academy, from which he graduated in 1880. After teaching two terms of school he studied law in the office of Bates & Macy, at St. Johnsbury, Vermont, where he was admitted to the bar in June, 1883. Following this a year was spent in Minnesota, mostly in Minneapolis; but in 1884 he located in Lancaster, New Hampshire, forming a partnership with the late Hon. Jacob Benton, which continued two years. He then removed to Gorham, where for a year he was in partnership with the late General A. S. Twitchell. In November, 1888, he settled in Berlin, where he has since resided. In 1891 he formed a partnership with Daniel J. Daley, which contiuued till January 1, 1903. When Mr. Goss went to Berlin it was a village of about twenty-five hundred inhabitants. His residence in Minneapolis had opened his eyes to the increased value which must accrue to lands as the development of the place progressed, and though without means of his own, he with others promoted several important land transactions. The stock of one corporation, which at one time owned a large part of the residential portion of the city of Berlin, is now his exclusive property; only the less accessible lands are now left, however. In 1892, he with others, organized the Berlin Aqueduct Company. Later it was reorganized as the Berlin Water Company, the stock then being held by Mr. Goss and Mr. Daley, who sold the property some five years ago. This company supplies the city of Berlin with water for domestic and fire purposes. For twelve years Mr. Goss has been a director in the People's Building and Loan Association, and for several years he was a director in the Berlin Savings Bank and Trust Company. In 1902 he with others built the Berlin Street Railway, a road which connects the two villages of Berlin Mills and Berlin Falls, and extends to Gorham, having a total length of seven and one-half miles. He has been a director in this road ever since its organization. In 1894 he was elected county solicitor for Coos county, being on the first Republican county ticket ever elected in Coos. He was renominated and reelected in 1896 and 1898. In 1903 he was elected to the legislature, and was given a place on the judiciary committe, one of the most important committees in the house. As a lawyer he has achieved a good measure of success. He has a clear analytical mind, which readily grasps the salient points in a controversy, and makes the best use of them when they are developed. His legal opinions are well considered; and as an advocate he is earnest and forceful. His various business enterprises have given him a wider experience in commercial matters than falls to the lot of most lawyers. Having a taste for literature, he wrote "T. Thorndyke," a novel, the plot of which is laid in northern New Hampshire. This story at once became widely popular. One hundred and fifty copies were sold in Berlin, New Hampsire, alone within a week from the date of its issue. In his religious belief he is liberal, but he attends the Episcopal church. Mr. Goss is a member of the Sabatis Lodge, No. 95, Free and Accepted Masons, of Berlin.

He married, October 8, 1886, Agnes Rooney, who was born in Leeds, Province of Quebec, May 29, 1870, the daughter of James Rooney and Elizabeth Shepherd Rooney. Both her parents were natives of Ireland. They have five children: Ethel Elizabeth, born February 16, 1888; Irvin James, born October 6, 1889; Herbert Abel, born December 26, 1891; Philip Henry, born October 10, 1895; John Arthur, born February 21, 1899.

(I) Nathan Goss with his son Joseph belonged to the Stratham militia. The Revolutionary records of New Hampshire on the return of Captain Joseph Parsons' company, on Great-Island, November 5, 1775, gave Nathan Goss as second lieutenant. The name of Nathan Goss is on the pay roll of Captain John Dearborn's company, Colonel Jonathan Moulton's regiment of militia, which marched from Hampton, New Hampshire, and joined the army under General Gates near Saratoga, October, 1777. His date of entry into the service was September 30; date of discharge October 10; time of service four months, five days; allowance for travel to Saratoga at three pence a mile out, and two pence home; distance two hundred and fifteen miles; and allowance four pounds, nine shillings, seven pence. Nathan Goss was selectman of Rye in 1775 and 1781. "December 9, 1775, it was voted that Nathan Goss should represent the parish in the General Assembly." "May 16, 1775, it was voted Nathan Goss should go to Exeter to Congress." Late in life he removed to Epsom. He married Deborah Wiggin, by whom he had sons Joseph and Samuel, and probably other children.

(II) Samuel, son of Nathan and Deborah (Wiggin) Goss, was born in 1756. The name of Samuel Goss, corporal, is twentieth on the roll of those of Captain Mark Wiggin's company, Colonel Long's regiment, who receipted for pay received at Portsmouth, January 14, 1777. In another roll he is described as one of those of that company "who are fit to march to Ticonderoga, being for one month's advance pay from 7th January to 7th February, 1777." He is said to have served three years in the Revolution. He was a hardy, robust, energetic man, and after the Revolution he removed from Greenland to Epsom, and there bought of his brother Joseph a tract of land since known as the Goss homestead, and there he died at the age of seventy-five years. He married, in 1779, Abigail Lucas, of Pembroke, who was born in 1759. Their children were: Daniel, Nathan, Susan Jane, Deborah, Samuel, and Jonathan, whose sketch follows.

(III) Jonathan, youngest child of Samuel and Abigail (Lucas) Goss, was born in Epsom, July 16, 1793, was by occupation a blacksmith and farmer, and was also a soldier in the war of 1812. Like his father he was rugged of frame and strong of constitution, and well qualified to act a part in the frontier settlement where he was born. He was a man of untiring energy and indomitable courage, and successful in life. That characteristic that is said to be pre-eminent in the New Englander was his in a marked degree—he was of an ingenius and inventive turn of mind, and very fond of mechanical employment. He originated many mechanical devices, some of which are in use and unsurpassed at the present day. He possessed wonderful muscular power, and performed many extraordinary feats of strength which are remembered by some of the older inhabitants of the community. His son remembered that on one occasion when the father was more than fifty years of age he lifted with one hand a forty gallon cask of cider. He realized his own want of education, recognized the value of liberal literary instruction, and gave his children all the advantages that his circumstances in life afforded. He married, September, 1816, Sally Yeaton, who was born July 30, 1793, and they were the parents of seven children: Noah, William, Hannah Y., Nancy L., Sally, Mary C. and Andrew J.

(IV) William, second son and child of Jonathan and Sally (Yeaton) Goss, was born in Epsom, July 13, 1820. He obtained his education in the public schools, assisted his father on the farm and in the shop, and remained at the paternal homestead until he was twenty-five years of age. After his marriage he settled on a farm adjoining that of his father, and remained there till March, 1855, when he sold that farm and purchased the place where he subsequently resided, close to the railroad station, in Epsom. There he gave his attention to stock raising, and by prudence, industry and skill, achieved success not only in raising stock but also in dealing in real estate. Convinced of the possibility of making use of the natural advantages and creating a village about him, Mr. Goss began to erect houses and form the nucleus of a village, since called in his honor, Gossville. He purchased the house in which his father was born, and also the one in which he was born, moved them over to his settlement, refitted them, and made them into residences which are still in use. He also built many houses, so that the greater number of residences in the village are the fruit of his labor. The old Baptist church building he moved into the village and converted into a store. In this way he constantly and assiduously labored to build up a prosperous village about his abode. The erection of a new church at Gossville was principally due to the energy, perseverance and personal influence of Mr. Goss. When others lost courage and hope, he took the lead in the matter and carried it forward and saw it successfully and satisfactorily terminated. In manufacturing Mr. Goss took a leading part, and was a prime mover and promoter of the building of a shoe factory in which he owned a controlling interest, which employs sixty hands or more, managed by his son, Nathan J. Goss, who is agent for the business.

Mr. Goss was by inheritance a Democrat, and throughout his life always cleaved to the faith of his father in the democracy of Jefferson and Jackson. He was honored by his townsmen with the office of selectman, which he filled one term, and that of representative to which he was twice elected. He was a member of the Baptist Society. In all the relations of life Mr. Goss was a true man, in whom his fellow citizens recognized high integrity and sterling worth. Mr. Goss married (first), June 2, 1846, Maryetta, daughter of William and Esther

(Fowler) Abbott, of Pembroke. She died May 3, 1873. He married (second), December 23, 1873, S. Rebecca Randall, widow of ——— Crockett. By the first marriage there were four children: John Abbott, whose sketch follows. Elizabeth J., born September 2, 1849, married Alfred Porter Bickford, of Epsom. Noah William, born July 12, 1861, grain merchant and grocer at Pittsfield; married Clara Jackson. Nathan Jonathan, born September 13, 1863, married Ida Marden, children: Ethel and Nathan, Jr.

(V) John Abbott, eldest child of William and Maryetta (Abbott) Goss, was born in Epsom, August 26, 1847, and died in Pittsfield, February 3, 1903, aged fifty-six years.. He was educated in the common schools and Pittsfield Academy. At the age of fourteen he became an apprentice to learn blacksmithing, which paved the way to carriage manufacturing, for which he had a decided taste, and in which he was interested througout his entire career. He became a resident of Pittsfield in 1876, entering upon the duties of cashier of the Pittsfield National Bank, succeeding Josiah Carpenter. When it was proposed to move the bank to Dover, Mr. Goss exerted himself with great zeal for its retention in Pittsfield, and was successful in the undertaking, the bank being reorganized under the direction of a new set of stockholders. and put upon a sound financial basis, Mr. Goss remaining cashier. In 1884 he founded the Farmers' Savings Bank, which he called the pride of his life, of which he became treasurer, which office he held until his death. Although professionally devoted to his duties and responsibilities imposed upon him by three banks, his enterprising mind took a wider range, and through his efforts public conveniences were added to the village. He was active in the organization of the Aqueduct Company, was interested in the formation of the Pittsfield Gas Company, and served as treasurer of both companies from the time of their incorporation until his demise. Realizing the value of an institution for higher education in the village, he was a prime mover and active in erecting the buildings of the present Pittsfield Academy. He made his presence felt in the affairs of the town, acting as its treasurer for ten years, and also as treasurer of the school fund for the same period. In these positions his services were efficient, and he never failed to promote the interests of the town whenever it was possible. In politics he shared the faith of his ancestors. He was elected representative to the state legislature in 1892, and while there was further honored by being one of the representatives of the state of New Hampshire to the World's Columbian Exposition, at Chicago, in 1893. He was an esteemed Odd Fellow and Mason, a member of Corinthian Lodge, No. 82, Free and Accepted Masons, and Suncook Lodge, No. 10, Independent Order of Odd Fellows, fiftieth of Pittsfield, and a valued member of the Amoskeag Veterans of Manchester. His life was a busy one, as every enterprise of magnitude in his village or town claimed his attention or assistance in some way. His fellow citizens reposed great confidence in him, as he never undertook the management of an enterprise in which he did not succeed. He married, June 15, 1869, Electa Ann Carpenter, born August 2, 1847, daughter of Charles H. and Joanna (Maxfield) Carpenter, of Chichester (See Carpenter, XVII), and they became the parents of three children: Charles Carpenter, mentioned hereafter. Clara Helen, who married Herbert B. Fischer, of Boston, assistant cashier of the Pittsfield National Bank. She died September 22, 1906, leaving one son, Robert Hathaway. William Abbott, a graduate of Holderness School for Boys at Plymouth, now a student in Harvard University. Mrs. Goss was educated in the public schools and at a select boarding school in Concord, from which she graduated. After the death of her husband she took his place as cashier in the bank, and has ever since filled the position with great credit to herself and satisfaction to patrons. She is a lady of culture and unusual executive ability, and is one of the leaders of Pittsfield in social, financial and educational matters.

(VI) Charles Carpenter, eldest son of John A. and Electa A. (Carpenter) Goss, was born February 9, 1871, in that part of Epsom known as "Gossville." In 1876 he was taken by his parents to Pittsfield, where his father was to serve as cashier of the Pittsfield National Bank, of which his maternal grandfather, Charles H. Carpenter, was and still is president. He attended the public schools of Pittsfield and Phillips Exeter Academy, and went from the latter institution to Dartmouth College, where he took the degree of B. S. in 1893. He had literally grown up in the banking business, having been actually employed in the National and Savings Banks from boyhood with intervals in his school life. After graduating from Dartmouth, he was employed in the Shawmut National Bank of Boston. From there he was called home by the last illness of his father to take his place in the Pittsfield banks. During his stay in Pittsfield he was town treasurer and prominent in the business and social life of the town. In 1900 he organized the Merchants' National Bank of Dover with Charles H. Carpenter, president, John A. Goss, vice-president, and Charles C. Goss, cashier. Mr. Goss removed to Dover, and has since managed that institution and the Merchants' Savings Bank of Dover, which he organized in April, 1901, of which he is treasurer. He is active in other financial enterprises, is treasurer of Strafford county, and a director in the Pittsfield National Bank. He is a young man of energy and sterling integrity, and in seeking his own interests he does so only by the fairest means. He is an attendant of the Congregational Church. He is a Master Mason of Moses Paul Lodge, No. 96, Dover; and a member of Olive Branch Lodge, Knights of Pythias, of Dover. He also holds membership in the various social clubs of the town. He is descended from a long line of Revolutionary and Colonial forebears, and through his mother belongs to one of the wealthiest and most influential families of New Hampshire. He married, June 26, 1895, Winifred Lane, who was born in Pittsfield, April 30, 1875, the only living child of Charles H. and Lorena A. (Perkins) Lane. (See Lane, VII). She was educated in the Pittsfield public schools and the Kimball Union Academy, Meriden, New Hampshire, graduating from the latter with the class of 1894. In 1892 she became a member of the Congregational Church, the church of her fathers—one of her ancestors. Jonathan Perkins, having been a deacon and clerk of that church for forty years. He was her maternal great-great-grandfather. Since removing to Dover she has engaged in Sunday school, church and club work. Probably her deepest interest lies in patriotic work, being a member of New Hampshire Society of Colonial Dames, and in that line peculiar to the Daughters of the American Revolution. She is widely known both for her ability and for her gracious manner and pleasing address. She is regent of Margery Sullivan Chapter, Dover, secretary of the state organization, and one of the managers and corresponding secretary of the Children's Home. One son has been born to Mr. and Mrs. Charles C. Goss, Charles Lane, February 24, 1903.

GOSS In the early colonial records this name is written with a double "f" instead of a double "s." John Goss, his wife Sarah and several children, arrived at Boston with Governor Winthrop in 1630, and settled at Watertown, Massachusetts. John was made a freeman in 1631, and died in 1644. His wife married for her second husband Robert Nichols. John and Sarah Goss were the original American ancestors of nearly all who bear the name in Massachusetts and New Hampshire, as the Goss family of Maine is descended for the most part from an immigrant who came from England more than a hundred years later. Philip Goss, a descendant of John, was born in Lancaster, Massachusetts, in 1720, and in 1764 settled in Winchester, New Hampshire, where he died April 17, 1804.

(I) Joshua Goss, the place and date of whose birth is not at hand, resided in Canaan. There is some slight evidence that he was a son of Thomas Goss, the founder of the Maine family just referred to who came from England in 1756, but a record of this line of the Gosses now in hand is wanting. The christian name of Joshua's wife was Hannah, and his children were Richard, Reuben, John, Levi, Orville, Daniel, Abbie, Sarah and Roxanna.

(II) Colonel Reuben, second son and child of Joshua and Hannah Goss, was a lifelong resident of Canaan. He was married, February 25, 1841, to Susan B. Lathrop, who was born April 30, 1818, and died in 1866. In connection with farming Colonel Goss operated a mill on the Mascoma river, and he commanded one of the regiments of the state militia. His wife Susan bore him five children: Isabella L., wife of Elijah Smith, of Canaan; Harris J., who is referred to in the succeeding paragraph; Calista S., deceased; Wallace R., and Bernice E.

(III) Harris J., second child and eldest son of Reuben and Susan B. (Lathrop) Goss, was born in Canaan, January 7, 1845. He was educated in the Canaan common schools, and assisted in carrying on the homestead farm until enlisting for service in the Civil war as a private in Company F, Eighteenth Regiment, New Hampshire Volunteers. At the siege of Petersburg he was a veritable target for the enemy, receiving no less than five wounds within the short space of twenty minutes, and he was sent to the Chestnut Hill Hospital, Philadelphia, where he remained until the close of the war. Upon his return from the army he resumed farming in his native town, and is still engaged in that honorable calling. In addition to tilling the soil he has bought and sold real estate, and dealt quite extensively in lumber and firewood. He is one of the leading supporters of the Democratic party in Canaan, and prominently identified with local public affairs, having served as a selectman for several terms, has held all of the other important town offices, and in 1891 was representative to the state legislature. He is a member of Mount Cardigan Lodge, No. 31, Knights of Pythias, Canaan, and a comrade of the local post of the Grand Army of the Republic.

On January 8, 1870, Mr. Goss was united in marriage with Lizzie B. Norris, daughter of Benjamin and Zaphira (Ross) Norris, of Dorchester, this state. Of this union there are two children: Ben A., and Ruby I. The latter is the wife of John P. Currier, of Canaan.

Joseph Towle, son of Samuel and Susan (Towle) Goss, was born in Epsom, April 8, 1820, and died in Hooksett, October 24, 1876. His youth was spent on his father's farm and at study in the common schools. While still a boy he worked some time in the mills at Lowell, Massachusetts, and then settled in Hooksett when about eighteen years of age. After attending Pembroke Academy some time he became a clerk in the store of his brother-in-law, George W. Converse, at Hooksett. In 1845 he purchased the stock of goods and continued the business as sole proprietor until he sold out in 1872. In business he was a successful and leading merchant, and much esteemed and respected in the community. As a Republican he was elected to the principal offices of the town, and to a seat in the legislature. He was an attendant of the Congregational Church, and a member of the Independent Order of Odd Fellows, of Suncook. He married, July 22, 1845, Lydia Stearns, who survived him and afterward married Rev. Moses Patten (see Patten). There was one child of this marriage, Susan Frances Goss, who married John W. Odlin, of Elizabeth, New Jersey.

SHEPARD The town records of Rowley, Massachusetts, make frequent mention of the Shepards—from "30 of Appril, 1666," when "Mr. Samuel Shepard and Mrs. Dorothy Flint were joyned in marriage," down to 1730. This Samuel Shepard, who was a minister, was probably the ancestor of the Ebenezer Shepard, born in 1741, who married Mrs. Jane McCordy, of Dedham, Massachusetts, in 1762.

(I) Ebenezer Shepard was the founder of the Shepard family in New London, New Hampshire, a family which for six generations has maintained an honored and influential place in the town. Ebenezer won his title of lieutenant in the Revolutionary war. He was recorded as a private on the Lexington alarm roll of Captain Aaron Fuller's company, which marched April 19, 1775, from Dedham First parish. He was commissioned second lieutenant of the First Suffolk Regiment January 26, 1779, and promoted to first lieutenant the next year, September 12, 1780. According to the records of the First church (Congregational) of Dedham, "July 8, 1764, Ebenezer Shepard and Jane his wife took covenant;" and their nine children, born between 1763 and 1780, received infant baptism into that same church. Some time prior to 1790, Lieutenant Shepard and his son-in-law, David Smith, removed with their families from Dedham to New London, New Hampshire, and settled in the Low Plain district. We find in Elder Seamans' list of baptisms that Ebenezer Shepard was baptized at New London, June 23, 1790, while the names of his wife, his children and his grandchildren follow at short intervals. Men of the energy and standing of Lieutenant Shepard soon make themselves felt in a community. In 1794 he was chosen tithingman, and David Smith, highway surveyor. Ebenezer was a joiner by trade, but according to the records, he was a large holder of real estate as well. In December, 1794, Ebenezer was moderator of a meeting called to vote for a representative to Congress.

Ebenezer Shepard died April 12, 1811, aged seventy years. His wife Jane died March 30 1819, aged eighty years. Their nine children, all born in Dedham, Massachusetts, were Catherine, who married David Smith; Elizabeth, who married James How Messer; Ebenezer, who married Sally Burpee; Jesse, who married Hannah Paige, of

Dunbarton; Hannah, who married Samuel Peaslee, of Sutton, New Hampshire; Mary, who married Jonathan Greeley, of Warner; Sally, who married Jonathan Hunting; Mindwell, who married William Stead; and John, who married Caty Ward. Of these nine children, all of whom married and made creditable records for themselves, the first four with Mary, the sixth, settled in New London, New Hampshire. Hannah and Sally lived in Sutton, a near-by town, while the two youngest went to New York. Mindwell (Mrs. William Stead) lived at Albany, and John became a capitalist in New York City. His son ,William Stead Shepard, became a capitalist like his father, but lived in Albany.

(II) Ebenezer, Jr., eldest son and third child of Lieutenant Ebenezer and Jane (McCordy) Shepard. was born in Dedham, Massachusetts, in 1767. Instead of coming to New London with his father, he appears to have gone to Vermont, for he was "of Brookfield," that state, when he married, January 8, 1793, Sally, daughter of Lieutenant Thomas and Joanna (Foster) Burpee, who was born at Rowley, Massachusetts, February 26, 1775. They came to New London in the eighteenth century, because there is record that on June 12, 1800. Ebenezer moved his house from its original location to a place across the road, now owned by Alvin F. Messer. At this moving, James, the eight-year-old son of Elder Seamans, "had his leg crushed in a frightful manner." In 1803 Ebenezer, Jr.. moved again, exchanging the Messer place for wild land on Low Plain where is now the present homestead of James E. Shepard. One of the grandchildren remembers hearing Mrs. Sally (Burpee) Shepard tell that they moved earlier that spring than they otherwise should, because they wanted to set their goose. Ebenezer, Jr., was a man of untiring industry and great physical vigor, and was more than ordinarily successful as a farmer and trader. He died at Wilmot, New Hampshire, December 7. 1849. His wife survived him less than five months, dying April 25, 1850. They had eleven children. Mary, married Otis Everett. Abigail, married Manning Seamans. Daniel Woodbury, married Jane Hamilton Robinson. Amial, married Elizabeth Connor. Samuel, married Phebe Hoskins. Jeremiah Burpee, married (first), Mary Everett, and, after her death. Lavinia Austin. George married Mrs. Abigail (Hill) Chadwick. Sylvester Foster married Catherine Barrett. James G. married Mary A. Cogswell. Benjamin Franklin served in the Civil war, and died unmarried.

(III) Samuel, third son and fifth child of Ebenezer, Jr., and Sally (Burpee) Shepard, was born December 9, 1802, at New London, New Hampshire. He married Phebe, daughter of Eli Haskins, of Grafton, New Hampshire. They went to live in Grafton, going by spotted trees a mile into the forest, and making a clearing in the dense woods. They lived there five years, and then moved to Danbury, New Hampshire. They returned to New London in 1834, and there Samuel lived till his death, May 19, 1861. His wife survived him less than a month, dying June 12, 1861. They had ten children. William Haskins, the eldest, was twice married; first to Emeline C. Todd; and second. to Frances Maria Frisbie, daughter of Doctor E. Willard Frisbie, of Phelps, New York. Lucina Hill married Adna Sylvester Fowler and lived in New London. Sarah Burpee married William Slade and finally moved to Merrimack, Wisconsin. Rhoda Emily married James Greeley Trayne and also lived in Merrimack, Wisconsin. Samuel George married Malvina Abbie Mussey and also migrated to Merrimack, Wisconsin. Martha Albina, the sixth child, graduated from Ripon College, Wisconsin, in 1872, and became a prominent teacher in several states and later a missionary among the Sioux Indians. Sylvester Foster married Helen Comstock and lived in Janesville, Minnesota. Abigail Seamans married Jacob H. Todd. She lived in New London, as did her brother, James Eli, who married Lucia Nelson. Franklin Pierce, the tenth and youngest child, lived but a year, dying October 12, 1845.

(IV) James Eli, fourth son and ninth child of Samuel and Phebe (Haskins) Shepard, was born at New London, March 13, 1842. He inherited the vigorous qualities and untiring industry of his ancestors. He is widely known as a dealer in peat stock and timber, and he is a large owner of real estate. His home farm, The Sheepfold, is one of the finest in New London. Mr. Shepard has been very active in Grange work. He was one of the founders of the New London Grange, and its first master. He has been prominent in the county and state granges and was especially successful as president of the State Grange Fair Association. He is a Mason, also a member of Heidelberg Lodge, Independent Order of Odd Fellows, has held various town offices, was delegate to the constitutional convention in 1889, and has received several Democratic state nominations. He is one of New London's most public-spirited citizens, and since 1891 has been a trustee of Colby Academy. James E. Shepard married November 9, 1863, Lucia, daughter of Mark and Lucia (Fifield) Nelson, of New London. Mrs. Shepard has been of great assistance to her husband, and to her has been due in a large measure the successes that have come to him. They have six children. Charles Everett married Maude Hersey and lives in New London. Lucy Nelson married Wilfred E. Burpee, and lives in Manchester, New Hampshire. She is a graduate of Colby Academy, New London, and of the Emerson School of Oratory in Boston. She was a successful teacher previous to her marriage. Frank Sylvester married Stella Hersey and lives in New London. Mary Ellen was graduated from Colby Academy in 1891, and from Smith College in 1897.. On September 21, 1897, she married Reverend Clarence E. Clough, of Wilmot Flat, New Hampshire. He was a Colby Academy classmate of his wife's and also a graduate of Yale University, 1895. After completing his course at the Divinity School of Chicago University he was called to the pastorate of the First Baptist Church of Bloomington, Indiana, where they now live. Mark Nelson, the fifth child, studied at Colby Academy, and is his father's valued assistant at home. Emma Trayne graduated from Colby Academy in 1897, and lives with her parents.

(V) Charles Everett. eldest son and child of James Eli and Lucia (Nelson) Shepard, was born in New London, New Hampshire, November 10, 1864. He inherits to a marked degree the business aptitude that has characterized the Shepard family for so many generations. He was educated at Colby Academy. His first occupation was that of a butcher, and he worked over a large section of country. About 1890 he became associated with Amos H. Whipple in the management of the Potter Place stage line and attended livery stables. In 1900 he bought a half interest in the stage and livery business of A. J. Gould, of which in November, 1905, he became sole proprietor. Mr. Shepard now owns seventy horses, and the stable is the largest

Chas. E. Shepard

in that section. In summer time he also runs a stable at Lake Sunapee. He has become a well known contractor, and deals in hay, grain, wood and carriages. He employs thirty men, and is extensively engaged in lumbering. He has just completed two sets of buildings for Hon. E. W. Converse, of Newton, Massachusetts; also buildings for B. H. Campbell, of Elizabeth, New Jersey, and for W. H. Halsey of Jersey City and and for Abraham Lisner of Washington, District of Columbia. His best piece of work is William Van's house at George's Mills on Lake Sunapee. He has just completed a new drug store at New London. In politics he is a Democrat and has held minor town offices. He is an Odd Fellow, belonging to Heidelberg Lodge, No. 92, and has been through all the chairs. He attends the Baptist Church. On January 3, 1889, he married Maude Hersey, daughter of Andrew Mellen and Amanda (Jewett) Hersey of Ashland, New Hampshire. She was born October 22, 1868. They have five children: Robert Hersey, born April 29, 1890; James Eli, born January 2, 1893; Marion, born September 23, 1896; and twin sons, Mailand C. and Morris Everett, born April 29, 1894. Mrs. Shepard is active in church work and has been secretary and president of the Ladies' Aid Society. Her vivacious disposition makes her a social favorite and draws many people to the hospitable Shepard home.

McCRILLIS This name is of Scotch origin. Between the years of 1719 and 1742 four immigrants of the name of McCrillis, William, Daniel, John and Henry, probably brothers, came to New England from the north of Ireland. William located first in Gilmanton, New Hampshire, but subsequently went to Coleraine, Massachusetts, accompanied by John. Daniel settled in Lebanon, Maine, and Henry established himself in Nottingham, New Hampshire. They were descended from Scotch Covenanters and were therefore zealous Presbyterians. It is claimed that they were the first to cultivate potatoes in the Granite state, and they also applied themselves diligently to the use of the spinning wheel. The branch of the family now being considered is the posterity of Henry.

(I) Henry McCrillis, whom it is believed came to this country in 1742, settled in Nottingham and became an industrious farmer. The name of his wife does not appear in the record at hand, and the names of his children, with the single exception of his son John, are also wanting.

(II) John, son of Henry McCrillis, married Margaret Harvey, and was the father of William, John, David, James and Henry.

(III) William, eldest son of John and Margaret (Harvey) McCrillis, resided in Deerfield, New Hampshire. His children were: John, Reuben, Andrew, Moses, William, Hannah, Mary, Margaret and James.

(IV) John, eldest son and child of William McCrillis, resided in Salisbury, Massachusetts. He reared three children, namely: Nathaniel D., John B. and Andrew.

(V) John Belcher, son of John McCrillis, was born in Salisbury, Massachusetts, September 18, 1815, and died in Manchester, New Hampshire, November 27, 1885. He married, February 18, 1841, Mary Shorer Kilgore, who was born in Mercer, Maine, August 15, 1817, and died September 8, 1884. Three children were born to them: John Almon, Mary Lizzie and Gertrude. John A. is mentioned below; Mary Lizzie is the wife of John Foster. (See Foster, VIII). Gertrude died an infant, October 15, 1857. In 1848 Mr. McCrillis established the carriage manufacturing and lumber business, which he continued till his death. He employed many skilled workers, and the products of the concern of which he was the directing head were noted the country over for thoroughness of construction and beauty of finish. No higher tribute to his memory can be paid than the following extract from the *Manchester Mirror* and *American*, of the date of November 30, 1885:

"Said a leading citizen and prominent business man, in the presence of a group of friends, Friday night, (the night of his death) 'John B. McCrillis was the most honorable man that I ever had business dealings with, he was honest in every sense of the word.'"

He was prominent in many ways among his fellowmen, untiring in application to the details of his business. He loved truth and honor and hated sham and deception. He was a Universalist. He was conspicuous for his uprightness and morality, his devotion to his family, his church and his friends, and in all the goings and comings of his long and busy life he was faithful, brave and true. He was unpretending and unassuming, but outspoken in his loyal adherence to his convictions, a sterling representative of a generation that has now disappeared.

Gone but still we hear their footsteps,
Their virtues yet remain;
And sometime in the great beyond,
They may come to us again.

(VI) John Almon, eldest child of John B. and Mary Shorer (Kilgore) McCrillis, was born in Haverhill, Massachusetts, September 11, 1845, and was brought to Manchester, New Hampshire, when a child of three years. He was educated in the public schools, and graduated from the Manchester high school. He then learned carriage making with his father, and after the death of the latter successfully continued the business. He is a Republican in politics, has taken a prominent part in local affairs, and has filled the office of alderman two years, and that of common councilman four years, and was president of the latter body. He is a member of Washington Lodge, No. 61, Free and Accepted Masons, and of Wildey Lodge, No. 45, Independent Order of Odd Fellows, of Manchester. He married, in Newton, Massachushetts, October 9, 1872, Mary Pierson, who was born in St. Albans, Vermont, daughter of Ambrose and Mary (White) Pierson. They have two children: Belle, born March 12, 1877, married Edgar E. Farmer, and has one daughter, Alice, born August 16, 1905. John Donald was born December 11, 1881.

McCOY This name is variously spelled McKay, McKey, McKie, McKee, by different families, but all are descended from Scotch forebears and are of the same stock.

(I) Nathan McCoy was born in Goffstown, and died in Thornton, April 10, 1863. He lived in Plymouth from 1851 to 1855, and removed to Thornton, where he owned a considerable amount of real estate, including timber lands. He was a surveyor, and ran many lines in that region and had charge of the construction of a highway over a rough and mountainous country from Thornton to Waterville. He married, September 3, 1811, Batheba Sargent, died April 2, 1880. Their children were:

ing land, logging on the Merrimack river, upon whose bank his home was situated, also was part owner of a saw mill on the Litchfield brook. John Watt married Susanna, who died August, 1826, aged seventy-three years. Their children were: Susanna, married William Fling. Jennie, married Moses Garvin. Margaret, married Jacob Garvin. Rachel, married Isaac Darrah. John, never married. Daniel, married (first) Polly Darrah; married (second) Lucy B. Flanders.

(III) Daniel, son of John Watt, was born April 4, 1785, probably near Goffs Falls, Manchester; this was formerly known as Derryfield. He lived here until 1834, when he bought a farm in Londonderry. He was a man who possessed Scotch shrewdness in a great measure, and like the other members of his family, both before and after him, was a man of business, respected and consulted by friends upon all matters of importance. He followed for some years his father's occupation of logging on the Merrimac river, also going as far as Canada to engage in the work. While living in Manchester he was identified in many ways with the early growth of the city and the founding of its institutions, especially the forming of the First Congregational Church and the Manchester National Bank. He married Polly Darrah, of Bedford, New Hampshire, and they were the parents of one child, Horace Perkins Watts. She died September 27, 1850, and he afterwards married Mrs. Lucy Baldwin Flanders, February 6, 1855. He died August 23, 1858.

(IV) Horace P., only child of Daniel and Polly (Darrah) Watts, was born on the old Watts farm, just below Goff's Falls, Manchester, November 12, 1819, and died in Manchester, August 14, 1890, aged seventy years. He was given the advantages of the schools in the vicinity, and afterward attended the Pinkerton Academy of Derry. He spent the first half of his life in Londonderry, where he owned a farm which he successfully cultivated. He served one term in the lower house of the legislature from Londonderry, and was also a member of the board of commissioners of Rockingham county. About the year 1865 he sold his farm and removed to Manchester, where he engaged in the grain business on Elm street, with A. F. Hall, under the firm name of Hall, Watts & Company. The firm's mill was located on the Piscataquog water privilege. Some years after the formation of the partnership Mr. Hall retired, and Mr. Watts took as his partner, W. F. Holmes. The business, as conducted by them, was very profitable and extensive, being the largest of its kind in the state, and at the time of the loss of the mill by fire in 1875, it was grinding about seventy-five thousand bushels of wheat and the same amount of corn each year. After the destruction of the mills the water privilege and land connected therewith were sold.

During the entere period of his residence in Manchester, Mr. Watts plainly saw the grand possibilities of the city's future, and made judicious investments in real estate, which appreciated handsomely in his lifetime, and have since continued to do so. He was elected director of the Manchester National Bank after the death of his father, who was a charter member and director of that institution. He was a close friend and business associate of its president, Hon. Nathan Parker. He was for some time previous to 1880 a director of the Nashua and Lowell railroad, now absorbed by the Boston & Maine system, and he had large investments in the securities of that and other railroad corporations. Soon after the destruction of the Piscataquog mill, Mr. Holmes, his son-in-law, went west and Mr. Watts became interested with him there in financial enterprises. He became president of the Security Loan and Trust Company of Castleton, Dakota, and he was also one of the active managers of the First National Bank of the same place. He made many visits in the last twelve years of his life to Dakota in the interests of his business there.

Mr. Watts took a lively interest in the organization of the board of trade. He was one of the first to join, and was made a member of the finance committee, on new enterprises, and on the conference committee with the city government in regard to the statistical work of the board. His last public appearance previous to going west the last time was at a meeting of the board in which he made a sturdy address. He saw the value of the shoe factory enterprises, and subscribed liberally to its stock. He was a valuable member in the executive work of the board, and his removal by death was the first which the membership sustained. Politically he was a Republican, but never an aspirant for political honors. The only public service (politically) which he rendered in Manchester was a membership of one year in the board of assessors, but he was always looked upon as one of the strong men of the community, and possessed the confidence of the people of Manchester in full measure. He was a man of excellent judgment and thorough reliabilitiy. He was honest and safe, unassuming, industrious and successful. His private life was without a blemish, and he was a good neighbor and devoted husband and father. A truthful history of his long and active life would contain nothing which his best friends would wish to have omitted.

Perhaps one of the most conspicuous services which he rendered the city of Manchester was in connection with the building of the elegant and commodious house of worship of the First Congregational Society. When it was proposed to make some changes in the old structure he opposed it, and was the first person to propose the erection of a new edifice, and contributed five thousand dollars for that purpose. When his pastor remarked to him with regard to the amount of his donation, that he was very liberal, Mr. Watts replied "Why no, that is only a matter of business. We must have society, and we cannot have good society without the church." He gave his personal attention as one of the building committee to the work of erection, and had the satisfaction of seeing the project, largely through his energy and determined will, become a financial and architectural success. He had long been a member of the church, and for a decade until the year before his death he was president of its ecclesiastical society. In the charitable work of Manchester, Mr. Watts was much interested. The Elliott Hospital, the Children's Home, the City Mission, and the Woman's Aid Home were objects of his solicitude and liberal contributions.

Mr. Watts married at Londonderry, March 28, 1842, Maria Boyd, who was born August 19, 1819, daughter of Captain William and Martha (Dickey) Boyd, of Londonderry. She died March 28, 1895. They were the parents of four children: Martha B., Daniel M., who died in infancy; Mary Alice, Annie E., Martha B. married, May 31, 1864, William F. Holmes, who was later a partner of her father in business. She died February 21, 1877. Annie E. married, December 10, 1885, Rosecrans W. Pillsbury, of Londonderry (see Pillsbury, V).

H. P. Watts

... Pillsbury, of Londonderry (see Pillsbury, V).

H. P. Watts

Mary Alice received her early education in the public schools of her native place, and the Abbott Academy of Andover, Massachusetts. Subsquently to leaving school she spent a year in travel in Europe where she had exceptional opportunities for observation and self culture, which she thoroughly improved. From her youth she has been fully imbued with the noble spirit that prompted her father to do so much for his church, and for the charitable institutions of the city, and the Woman's Aid Home, the Elliott Hospital, the City Mission and Children's Home have been frequent recipients of her bounty. For nine years she has been a trustee of the Elliott Hospital, and for a portion of that time the principal work of the committee was transacted by her in a manner that manifested her experience in business matters and her executive ability. So zealous and attentive was she to the discharge of her duties in this position, that her health gave way, and she was for some time unable to give the hospital or any of her extensive business interests any of her attention. She is a member of the First Congregational Church, and an unfailing helper in its manifold works of philanthropy and charity. She is a woman of noble character and charming personality, and resides on the paternal homestead, where, with the society of her many friends, the entertainment afforded by a well selected library and the labor incident to the care of her property and the duties entailed by her connection with the institutions above mentioned, she leads a busy and a useful life.

MASSEY The name Massey and its similar forms—Massie, Maas and Masse—is thought to be one of those patronymics taken directly from the earth's topography, like Hill, Peake, Craig, Stone, Littlefield, and many others. The name of Massey is better known in England than in America. Readers will recall Gerald Massey, the poet, also Mrs. Gertrude Massey, painter of children and dogs to the royal family. Massey is also the family name of the Baron Clarina. Among Amercans bearing the name are Dr. George B. Massey, a noted physician of Philadelphia; Chief Justice W. A. Massey, of Nevada; and Professor Wilbur Fisk Massey, professor of horticulture and botany in North Carolina. The first American ancestor of this family is not known. Thomas Massey migrated to Pennsylvania before 1687, and lived in Marple, that state. Samuel Massey and his family came from Cork, Ireland, to Philadelphia, in 1711. They were members of the Society of Friends. Owing to the absence of printed records, it has been impossible to trace the remote ancestry of the present line.

(I) Jonas Dennis Massey lived in Marblehead, Massachusetts. He served in the revolution both on land and sea. He was a private in Captain William Harper's company from March 1, 1776, to January 1, 1777. This company was in the artillery service. He was seaman on the brigantine "Massachusetts" from March 7 to August 31, 1777. He evidently possessed the sturdy and patriotic qualities characteristic of the men of his sea-faring port. He died at Marblehead in the year 1818.

(II) Information about this generation is lacking.

(III) Stephen Decatur, grandson of Jonas Dennis Massey, was born at Marblehead, Massachusetts, in the year 1815. He was in the drug business at Marlborough, Massachusetts, about three years, and afterwards went to Boston and engaged in the shoe business as manufacturer and broker. He continued in the shoe business about forty years, and during the latter part of his life also dealt quite extensively in real estate. In politics he was originally a Whig, and afterwards became a Democrat He married Lucretia Derby Smith, daughter of Andrew Smith, of Salem, Massachusetts. They had three children: Horace A., whose sketch follows; Stephen Decatur (2), and Dudley A. Stephen Decatur Massey died at Danvers, Massachusetts, about 1872-74.

(IV) Horace Andrew, eldest of the three sons of Stephen Decatur and Lucretia D. (Smith) Massey, was born in Boston, Massachusetts, June 17, 1840. He was educated in the common schools of Boston and Chelsea, Massachusetts. In early life he was employed as a clerk by the Union Mutual Fire Insurance Company of Boston. At the outbreak of the civil war he enlisted in Company B, First Massachusetts Infantry, and served at Washington, D. C., and at Budd's Ferry, Maryland, about one year. He was afterwards appointed pay clerk in the United States navy, and served on the gunboat "Anacosti," and later on the ship "Seminole" and on the "Pawtuxent." About 1886 he left the naval service at New York, and came to Portsmouth, New Hampshire. For a few years after that Mr. Massey was engaged in the hotel business in the White Mountains, but he is now on the retired list. Mr. Massey belongs to the Sons of the Revolution, and is prominent in the Masonic fraternity, being a member of Saint John's Lodge, Washington Chapter, Davenport Council, De Witt Clinton Commandery, and has attained the thirty-second degree, Ancient Accepted Scottish Rite. Horace Andrew Massey married Isabelle Stearns Jones, daughter of Nathan Jones, and niece of Frank Jones, of Portsmouth, New Hampshire. They have three children: Charlotte L., Horace Andrew (2), and Frank Jones.

COLLINS This family has contributed pioneers and valuable citizens to New Hampshire, and is now amiably represented in many sections of the United States by men in the learned professions, in business circles, and all the various activities of modern life. Since it was first planted in Massachusetts many marvelous changes have occurred in the methods of conducting business, and men's ideas and controlling influences have been greatly modified. It is easy to conceive that, when the patriarch of the family settled in Salisbury, Massachusetts, the luxuries enjoyed by the people there were few and their methods of progress were extremely primitive as compared with those of to-day.

(I) Benjamin Collins, who was possibly a brother of Robert Collins, is found of record in Salisbury, Massachusetts, November 5, 1668, when he was married to Martha Eaton, daughter of John and Martha (Sowlandson) Eaton, and granddaughter of John Eaton, the pioneer of Salisbury and Haverhill. She was born August 12, 1648, in Salisbury. Benjamin Collins was a householder of Salisbury in 1677, and died there December 10, 1683. The inventory of his estate was made January 3, following, and administration was had on March 25. His widow was married November 4, 1686, in Salisbury, to Philip, son of Stephen Flanders. Benjamin Collins' children were: Mary, John, Samuel, Anna, Benjamin and Ephraim.

(II) Samuel, second son and third child of Benjamin and Martha (Eaton) Collins, was born January 18, 1676, in Salisbury, residing in that town. He was a soldier in the campaign against the Indians at Wells, Maine, in 1696, and at Haverhill in 1697-98. He was married in Salisbury, March 16, 1699, to Sarah White. Their children were: Benjamin, Joseph, John (died young), Merriam, John and Hannah.

(III) Joseph, second son and child of Samuel and Sarah (White) Collins, was born June 27, 1702, in Salisbury, and passed his life in that town. He was married to Hannah Sargent, the publication of their intentions being made in Amesbury, July 13, 1723.

(IV) Deacon John, son of Joseph and Hannah (Sargent) Collins, was born February 14, 1740. (Recorded in Amesbury.) He died September 11, 1844, in Salisbury, New Hampshire. He settled first in Kingston, this state, and removed thence, previous to 1768, to Salisbury, locating south of the south rangeway. He soon became an extensive owner of lands, and was a prominent citizen of the town, identified with the conduct of public affairs. He was the first deacon of the Congregational Church, and his life was free from reproach. He was married, October 1, 1761, to Ruth Challis, of Amesbury, Massachusetts. She was born June 10, 1741, in Amesbury, and died July 5, 1832, in Salisbury. Their children were: Winthrop, Charles, John, Carteret, Joseph, Enoch, Enos, Sarah, Annie and Seth C.

(V) Seth C., youngest child of Deacon John and Ruth (Challis) Collins, was born February 15, 1785, in Salisbury, and died January 25, 1847, in Springfield, New Hampshire. He cleared up a farm in that town, and was an industrious and useful citizen. He was married, October 11, 1807, to Marion Sawyer.

(VI) Samuel, son of Seth C. and Marion (Sawyer) Collins, was born in Springfield, 1815. He settled in Bakersfield, Vermont, where he followed agriculture in connection with the lumber business, and he participated quite actively in local public affairs, holding some of the important town offices. His latter years were spent in Johnson, same state, and he died in 1902, at the ripe old age of eighty-seven years. He married Harriet K. Stone, and those of his children now living are: Chellis Oliver, who will be again referred to; Leonard, who is a resident of Johnson, and Mary, who became the wife of George Butler.

(VII) Chellis Oliver, son of Samuel and Harriet K. (Stone) Collins, was born in Bakersfield, September 22, 1845. He was educated in the public schools, and began the activities of life as a cooper. He subsequently entered mercantile business as a clerk, and still later took a similar position in a hotel at Bakersfield. For nearly forty years he devoted his time and energies exclusively to the textile industry. Entering the employ of the Androscoggin Cotton Mills Corporation at Lewiston, Maine, in 1869, as "second hand" in the weaving department, he worked his way forward to the position of overseer. He resided in Lewiston some eighteen years. In 1887 he accepted the position of overseer of the dressing department in the mills of the Nashua Manufacturing Company at Nashua, and was employed in that responsible capacity until his death, which occurred January 17, 1907. Mr. Collins was far advanced in the Masonic Order, having attained the thirty-second degree, and was a member of the various bodies from the Blue Lodge to the consistory. He occupied all of the important chairs in Knights of Pythias Lodge at Lewiston, and was a member of the Grand Lodge of Maine. In his religious belief he was a Baptist. He married Lizzie N. Cheney, daughter of John and Katherine (Morse) Cheney, of Island Pond, Vermont. Mr. and Mrs. Collins have one son, Ernest, principal of the high school at Athol, Massachusetts; and one daughter, Mrs. Leda M. Buttrick, of Nashua.

COLLINS The Collins family of this article has been represented in the United States about one hundred years, and its members have been patriotic citizens of the republic where they came to enjoy liberty and have contributed money and shed blood to sustain it.

(I) Patrick Collins was born in Cork, Ireland, in 1810, and when but two months old was brought to America by his parents, who settled in Maine. He worked on a farm while a lad, and at the age of sixteen enlisted in the United States army, and served through two five-year enlistments. After leaving the military service he went into trade at Houlton, Maine, and was actively engaged in business until his death in 1857. He married Margaret Staples, who bore him children: 1. Thomas A., lived in Wisconsin. 2. William A., lived in Wisconsin. 3. Winfield S., was lieutenant of Company E, First Maine Cavalry, and was killed at Boydton Road, October 27, 1864; he had four horses killed under him during the war. 4. Samuel Abbott, see forward. 5. Henry C., who lived at Ft. Fairfield, Maine. 6. Dora, widow of Edwin Davis, of Cambridge, Massachusetts.

(II) Samuel Abbott Collins, son of Patrick and Margaret (Staples) Collins, was born in Houlton, Maine, December 12, 1845. He was educated in the public schools and by private tutors. At the age of eighteen, August, 1864, he enlisted in Company K of the Twentieth Maine Volunteer Infantry, and served until July, 1865. He was in seven general engagements. At the battle of Hatcher's Run he was wounded in two places by an exploding shell, which tore his chest, but he did not leave his company and remained on the field. The day before the battle of Five Forks he was one of a detail of skirmishers which was recalled. Knowing that a battle was imminent, he and two others attempted to join their regiment, which they succeeded in doing, but too late to be marked present on the company roll. He fell into rank, however, and participated in the battle and received three wounds. He was shot below the knee of the right leg, through the right kneecap, and through the left leg below the knee. His right leg was amputated above the knee the next day. The report of his absence with the skirmishers never was corrected, and he never was given credit in the war records for that engagement. After the war he worked at harness making in Houlton until 1869, when he moved to Gorham, New Hampshire. He carried on his trade there ten years, and in 1879 removed to Milan, where he continued in business the following ten years and where he now resides. During these years he also carried on farming, and lumbering to some extent. Since 1887 he has been retired. He is a Republican and still votes as he shot in the war. He was town treasurer of Milan ten years (1882-92), and chairman of its board of selectmen in Milan, 1892-1901, and was again elected chairman of that body in 1907. He represented Milan in the general court in 1904-05, and was a member of the convention which nominated Charles M. Floyd for governor in 1906. He is a member of Willis Post, Grand Army of the Republic, of Gorham, and of Androscoggin Lodge, No. 76, Independent Order of Odd Fellows, of which he was secretary ten years. He has been an industrious citizen, has always taken an active interest in public affairs, and for years has been one of the most prominent men in his town in politics and public life.

He married, November, 1868, Louise A. Hillman, born in New Brunswick, daughter of John T. Hillman.

COLLINS Lewis Peter Collins, one of the most highly valued citizens of Manchester, New Hampshire, prominent in financial and industrial circles, owes his present condition and prosperity to his indomitable spirit and unaided efforts.

Peter Collins, father of Lewis Peter Collins, was a native of England and emigrated to this country, where he engaged in farming. He married Sarah Sallaway and had nine children.

Lewis Peter, son of Peter and Sarah (Sallaway) Collins, was born in New Brunswick, June 15, 1851. He was but three years of age when his father died, and was educated in the common schools of the district. He was apprenticed to the carpenter's trade, and learned that of woodworking at the age of sixteen years. He went to Lawrence, Massachusetts, in 1879, and entered the employ of the Briggson, Allen Company, manufacturers of sashes, doors, blinds, etc., remained with them for thirty-three years, and in that time passed through all the grades of this kind of work, from the rank of plain carpenter to that of superintendent, and is now interested in this company in Lawrence, Massachusetts. He removed to Manchester in 1903, and since that time has been superintendent of the Derryfield Board and Lumber Company of that city. He has many additional business interests, being a director of the Lawrence National Bank, and trustee of the Brooklyn Savings Bank. While a resident of Lawrence, Massachusetts, he was a member of the common council, of the board of aldermen, board of trade, and the mayor of the city in 1891-92. He is a member of the Baptist Church, and connected with the following organizations: Calumet Club, Free and Accepted Masons, Mayors' Club of Massachusetts, New England Water Works Association. He is a man of sterling qualities and is highly esteemed by his fellow citizens. He married Lavinia E. Hanze, daughter of Daniel Hanze, of Belfast, Maine, and has one child: Frederick Lewis, a resident of the city of New York, who is connected with the *Review of Reviews.*

GAY In ancient times, before surnames were fashionable, men were sometimes distinguished from one another by reference to their temperament, and in old records men are designated as the lively, the blithe, or the gay; and probably the ancestor of this family took his surname from his disposition to be gay.

(I) John Gay came to America from England about 1630, and first settled at Watertown, Massachusetts. He was one of the grantees of lands in the Great Dividends and in Beaver Brook plow lands, receiving altogether forty acres. He was made a freeman May 6, 1635, and was subsequently one of the founders of the plantation of Dedham. He was one of the original proprietors of the town, his name appearing on the petition for incorporation September 6, 1636. He was a selectman of Dedham in 1654, and died in that town March 4, 1688. His wife Joanna died August 14, 1691. It is a matter of family tradition that she was the widow Balewicke when she married John Gay. His will appears in the Suffolk records, being dated December 18, 1686, and was proved December 17, 1689. His wife and son John were the executors, and his estate was valued at ninety-one pounds, five shillings, eight pence. His children were: Samuel, Hezekiah, Nathaniel, Joanna, Eliezer, Abiel, Judith, John, Jonathan, Hannah and Elizabeth. (Mention of Nathaniel and descendants forms a part of this article.)

(II) Samuel, eldest child of John and Joanna Gay, was born March 10, 1639, in Dedham, and always resided in that town. By his father's will he received the lands situated near Medfield line granted to the father by the town. He was selectman in 1698, and died April 15, 1718. He was married, November 23, 1661, to Mary, daughter of Edward Bridge, of Roxbury, Massachusetts. Their sons were: Samuel, Edward, John, Hezekiah and Timothy.

(III) John (2), third son of Samuel and Mary (Bridge) Gay, was born June 25, 1668, in Dedham, where he resided all his life and was a selectman in 1721. He was married, May 24, 1692, to Mary Fisher, who died May 18, 1748. She was survived more than ten years by her husband, who died June 17, 1758. Their children were: Mary, Mercy, John, Samuel, Margaret, Eliphalet and Ebenezer.

(IV) Eliphalet, third son and sixth child of John (2) and Mary (Fisher) Gay, was born September 24, 1706, in Dedham, Massachusetts, and lived a few years in Newton, Massachusetts, where his two eldest children were born. He was married in Newton, April 20, 1732, to Dorothy Hall, daughter of Andrew and Susanna (Capen) Hall, and passed the latter years of his life in Dedham. His children were: Ephraim, Susanna, Lydia, Mehitabel, Ebenezer, Eliphalet and Hepsibah.

(V) Ephraim, eldest child of Eliphalet and Dorothy (Hall) Gay, was born September 13, 1734, in Newton, Massachusetts, and lived for some time in Attleboro, that state, where ten of his children were born. Soon after 1780 he removed to New London, New Hampshire, where he died March, 1817, at the age of eighty-three years. He was married September 29, 1758, in Dedham, to Lois Fisher who was born March 3, 1736, in Walpole, Massachusetts, daughter of William and Elizabeth Fisher. Their children were: Eliphalet, William, Fisher, Ephraim, Seth, David, Asa, Stephen, Lois, Lydia and Eunice.

(VI) Fisher, third son and child of Ephraim and Lois (Fisher) Gay, was born in 1767, and died September 11, 1853. When he was twenty-one years old his mother made him a "freedom suit" from a bed blanket, probably spun and woven by her own hands. It was colored with hemlock bark, and the buttons were disks cut out of sole leather. With this suit for Sunday wear he started out in life for himself. He went from Springfield to Keene, New Hampshire, performing the journey on foot. After working a year at the tanner's trade he went to Hillsboro, where he was given an acre of land near the brook that flows not far from the present Gay homestead. There he built a house, using the upper portion for a residence and the lower story for a shop, where he made shoes. This building is still standing. After a time his brother David assisted him in his work, and for years they had a very busy place, tanning leather and making shoes, the shoes being sent to the Boston market. Fisher Gay married Mehitable Kimball, daughter of Benjamin and Hannah (Parker) Kimball (see Kimball, VI), and they had five children: Gardner, Mehitable, Benjamin, Betsey and Langdon.

(VII) Benjamin Holton, third child and second son of Fisher and Mehitable (Kimball) Gay, was born in Hillsboro, June 24, 1807, and died January 9, 1880, aged seventy-three. He was a tanner, and for many years carried on the trade he had learned from his father. He finally gave up this occupation and settled on the farm which is still in the possession of the family, and now known as "Maplewood Farm." It is situated about two and a half miles from Hillsborough Bridge, near what is known as the "Centre," and now embraces about one hundred and sixty acres of land, although a considerable amount of outlying pasture and woodland is owned in connection with it. He married, September 23, 1834, Ann Duncan Stow, born December 12, 1811, who died February 27, 1896. Their children were: William E., Charles C., Robert D., Margaret Ann, and Ellen Maria.

(VIII) William Edwin, eldest child of Benjamin H. and Ann D. (Stow) Gay, was born July 18, 1835, and resided all his life on the farm where he was born, except two years which he spent as a clerk in Boston. He gave to the cultivation and improvement of his farm the energy and devotion of a tireless, purposeful life, seeking the best results through the application of the most approved methods, dairying and fruit culture being his leading specialties for many years. He kept from twenty to thirty cows, largely Jerseys, and produced for a time upwards of four thousasd pounds of butter per annum, which commanded the highest market price, on account of its superior quality. Some two or three years previous to his decease he changed from butter to milk production, finding his market in a milk route at Hillsborough Bridge. Upon making this change he gradually disposed of his Jerseys, substituting Ayrshires in their place, as the most desirable cows for milk alone. Of fruit in the culture of which he took special delight, he raised all kinds in abundance, and numerous varities. Apples, pears, plums, peaches, apricots and grapes were grown in profusion, over thirty varieties of grapes being included among his bearing vines. His peaches were of special excellence, and in one season he sold upwards of one hundred dollars worth of them alone. He exercised great care not only in the cultivation but in the harvesting, storing, and marketing of his fruits, and was particularly successful in preserving apples in perfect condition for the late winter and spring markets. The annual hay crop on this farm amounts to some seventy-five tons, and this has been supplemented with corn, of which several hundred bushels have been raised annually. Potatoes are raised in considerable quantities, and were at one time quite a specialty. In some years from fifty to sixty head of cattle and horses have been kept on the farm, the latter kind of stock usually including some good animals, which is the case at the present time. The location and surroundings of "Maplewood" are most attractive for summer boarders, and for more than forty years a number of these have been accommodated there. So popular had the place become as a home for those seeking the genuine comforts of country life during the heated term, that in 1892 a separate house, with rooms for the accommodation of thirty or forty people, was erected near the farm house, and has been filled every succeeding season.

Mr. Gay was a Republican in politics, taking much interest in public affairs, but never seeking office, though he was three years a member of the board of selectmen. In religion he was a Methodist, and the family are connected with the Methodist society at the Centre. Mr. Gay was a charter member of Valley Grange, of Hillsborough, taking a deep interest in the welfare of the organization from the first, holding many of its offices, including that of lecturer, to which he gave his best efforts for several years, and manifesting his devotion to the principles of the order in all fitting ways up to the time of his death. He was a man of strong moral convictions, careful, methodical, and unusually energetic and a model farmer. Perhaps no man in the entire history of the town did more for agriculture than he. William E. Gay married, in Hillsborough, March 17, 1861, Mary J. Blanchard, born in Washington, October 27, 1836, daughter of Elijah and Mary (Friend) Blanchard, of Washington. Six children were born to them: 1. Nellie M., born June 18, 1862, married, November 26, 1881, Charles Morgan, a farmer of Hillsborough, residing near "Maplewood Farm," and has seven children: Frank H., Mary, Marieta A., Annabel, Edith M. and Helen (twins), and Walter E. 2. Frank D., born July 27, 1865, married, May 21, 1896, Mabel Wyman. He remained on the homestead farm until his marriage, and then removed to the "Bridge" village, where he is engaged in the milk business and is also deputy sheriff. 3. Walter E., mentioned below. 4. Julia M., born December 3, 1868, a graduate of Colby Academy, who continued her studies in special lines in Boston and Chicago universities for two years, is now superintendent of schools at the village of Dundee, Illinois. .. Lisabel. born March 1, 1877, a graduate of the Dundee school, and the Plymouth State Normal School, and is a teacher at Rock Springs, Wyoming. 6. Ethel A., born April 6, 1880, at home.

(IX) Walter Ellis, third child and second son of William E. and Mary J. (Blanchard) Gay, was born on the ancestral homestead, February 9, 1867. He was educated in the common schools of Hillsborough. For ten years he was engaged in business in Manchester with his uncle, Robert D. Gay, in the upholstering business, but returned home upon his father's decease and his brother's removal, and has since that time managed the farm. In addition to that he deals extensively in live stock, and during the warm season has the comfort of a throng of boarders to look after. He is an energetic man of progress and influence in his town, and shows by his actions that he has an object in life. He is a Republican in politics, and attends the Methodist Church. He is a member of the Ridgely Lodge, No. 74, Independent Order of Odd Fellows, of Manchester. He married, October 5, 1903, Wilhelmina Pundt, born in Dundee, Illinois, December 25, 1875, daughter of John and Mary (Matz) Pundt, of Carpentersville, Illinois.

(II) Nathaniel, third son and child of John and Joanna (Baldewicke) Gay, was born in Dedham, January 11, 1643. From his father he received a gift of a tract of land lying near the present town of Medfield, and another in Pocumtock "alies Derefield in Hamshier." He was made a freeman May 23, 1677, served as a selectman in 1704 and other years, and died February 20, 1712. He married Lydia, daughter of Major Eleazer Lusher, a prominent town official and representative to the general court. Major Lusher appears to have been as popular as he was prominent, and for many years after his death the people of Dedham were in the habit, whenever his name was mentioned, of repeating the following couplet:

"When Lusher was in office, all things went well.
But how they go since it shames us to tell."

Lydia died August 6, 1744, aged ninety-two years

George W. Gay

having had a family of ten children, namely: Benjamin and Nathaniel, both of whom died young; Mary, Lydia, Nathaniel, Lusher, Joanna, Benjamin, Abigail and Ebenezer. The will of Nathaniel Gay was made February 16, 1712, and probated March 20, same year. His property was inventoried at two hundred and twenty-seven pounds, nineteen shillings, six pence, and after naming as executors, his wife and his sons Nathaniel and Lusher, he made the following provision, viz.: "Whereas I have been att considerable expense in bringing up my son Ebenezer Gay" (referred to in the opening paragraph of this article), "fitt for, and in placing him att Harvard College, where he now remains, I do appoint that ye charge of his further continuing there until the taking of his first degree shall be payd and discharged out of my estate, which shall be reckoned and accounted with him as his full share of my estate."

(III) Lusher, fourth son and sixth child of Nathaniel and Lydia (Lusher) Gay, was born in Dedham, September 21, 1685. His portion of his father's estate consisted of a farm located in that part of Dedham known as the Clapboard Trees, and he occupied that property until his death, which occurred October 18, 1769. In 1746 he was a member of the board of selectmen. His wife was before marriage Mary Ellis, daughter of Joseph and Mary (Graves) Ellis, and she died October 7, 1780, aged ninety years. They were the parents of nine children, namely: Lusher, Ebenezer, Richard, Jabez, Ichabod, Mary, Lydia, Joseph and Bunker. Bunker Gay was graduated from Harvard College in 1760.

(IV) Lusher (2), eldest son and child of Lusher (1) and Mary (Ellis) Gay, was born in Dedham, December 15, 1716. In 1738 he received from his father the title to a tract of land with buildings and fruit trees thereon in Thompson Parish, Killingly, Connecticut, whither he removed the following year, and in 1747 he was chosen a deacon of the church in Thompson. His death occurred in Killingly, February 19, 1803. On April 11, 1739, he married Mary Colburn, daughter of Joseph and Mehitabel (Whiting) Colburn, of Dedham. She died in Thompson, June 13, 1746, and on June 22, 1748, he married for his second wife Hannah Cady, daughter of David and Hannah (Whitmore) Cady. She died October 21, 1810. His children were: Lusher, Lydia, Mary, Calvin, Ebenezer, David (died young), Joseph (also died young), David, Joseph, Theodore, Sophia, Martin and Hannah, all of whom were born in Thompson (Killingly).

(V) Lusher (3), eldest son and child of Lusher (2) and Mary (Colburn) Gay, was born in Killingly March 21, 1740. April 30, 1761, he married Judith Green, daughter of Henry and Judith (Guile or Guild) Green. He died April 18, 1778, and his widow subsequently became the wife of David Wilson, of Dedham. Lusher Gay was the father of seven children, namely: Willard, Lemuel, Mary, Sally, Colburn, Hannah and Nabby.

(VI) Colburn, third son and fifth child of Lusher and Judith (Green) Gay, was born in March, 1770. He resided in Dedham, Massachusetts, until about 1815, when he moved to New Hampshire, and died in Surry, October 26, 1824. He was twice married—first to Sarah Ellis, who died in 1803, and his second wife, whom he married in 1810, was Mrs. Lucy Brackett (nee Walker), of Stoughton, Massachusetts. His children were: Willard (who died young), Phineas Ellis, Willard, Sally, Hiram, John and Annie.

(VII) Willard, third son and child of Colburn and Lucy (Walker-Brackett) Gay, was born in Dedham, February 11, 1811. He settled upon a farm in Swanzey, New Hampshire, and resided there for the remainder of his life, which terminated in 1882. His first wife, whom he married April 14, 1841, was Fanny Wright, daughter of Caleb Wright of Keene. She died March 30, 1842, leaving one son, Dr. George Washington Gay, who will be again referred to. On March 30, 1843, he married for his second wife Emily H. Farwell, daughter of Samuel Farwell, of Nelson, New Hampshire. She became the mother of six children, namely: Ella Harriet, born February 4, 1844, became the wife of Z. G. Taft; Phineas Ellis, born May 14, 1846, married Lizzie Hill; Mary Anna, born November 23, 1847; Reo A., born March 24, 1851, died December 1, same year; Emma W., born May 10, 1855, died December 18, that year; and the latter's twin sister, Carrie Louise, who died February 18, 1861.

(VIII) George Washington Gay, M. D., only child of Willard and Fanny (Wright) Gay, was born in Swanzey January 14, 1842. His early education was acquired in the public schools and at Powers Institute, Bernardston, Massachusetts. His professional studies were pursued under the direction of Dr. Twitchell, of Keene, and at the Harvard Medical School, from which he was graduated in 1868, and he immediately began the practice of his profession in Boston, giving his attention almost exclusively to surgery. His professional advancement was rapid, and the thoroughly able and conscientious manner in which he handled a number of serious cases during the early days of his career resulted in the creation of a very large private practice, and this, together with his public hospital work, has gained for him an honorable position among Amercan surgeons of the highest rank. Dr. Gay's professional appointments have been somewhat limited owing to his unusually extensive private practice, but those which he has considered a duty to accept have been highly important. From 1872 to 1899 he held the post of visiting surgeon to the Boston City Hospital, when he was appointed senior surgeon, which position he still holds. In 1888 he was appointed instructor in clinical surgery at the Harvard Medical School, in which capacity he continued to serve until 1900, when he became lecturer on surgery and still retains that position. He is president of the Massachusetts Medical Society (1906-08), a member of the American and the British Medical Associations, and of the American Surgical Association, and also affiliates with other professional bodies and with the Masonic order. His contributions to the literature of his profession, which have appeared from time to time in the standard medical journals, cover a varied line of subjects relative to surgery, and perhaps the latest and most opportune are those upon Appendicitis, in the diagnosis and treatment of which he stands high among the surgeons of this country.

On November 25, 1868, Dr. Gay married Mary E. Hutchinson, daughter of B. F. Hutchinson, of Milford, New Hampshire, and she died February 22, 1873. His present wife, whom he married in 1875, was Grace Greenleaf, daughter of J. H. Hathorne, of Boston.

GUAY The family of Guay comes into New Hampshire from the Province of Quebec, Canada, where the family has been seated for many years, although it had its origin in France. Through the several generations of the family life in the Province of Quebec the Guays, like nearly all others of the same nationality, came to be known as French-Canadians, but unlike most of them the Guays have occupied a higher station in the social and civil history of the province and the name is known in the professions, trades and in the church, having representatives in each.

(I) Thomas Guay was a Farmer of Point Levis in the county of Levis, Province of Quebec, Canada. His lands were extensive and he was thrifty, provident and much respected in the community in which he lived. His wife before her marriage was Julia Poire, a woman of French ancestry and Canadian birth, and she bore her husband five sons and three daughters.

(II) Thomas, son of Thomas and Julia (Poire) Guay, was born at Point Levis, Province of Quebec, and lived there until he had passed middle age, and then removed to Laconia, New Hampshire. He married Sarah Nolan, daughter of John Nolan, of St. Agathe, Canada, who was born in Cork, Ireland, and came to Quebec when he was a young man. On her father's side Sarah was of Irish birth, while through her mother she was of English and Scotch descent. Thomas and Sarah (Nolan) Guay had a large family of thirteen children, several of whom died in extreme infancy. Thomas J., now a contracting builder in Laconia, senior member of the firm of Guay & Wallace. John Michael, mentioned below. Alfred (1) and Alfred (2), both of whom died very young. Emma, who died at the age of nineteen. Catherine, wife of I. J. Malouin, of Laconia. Alfred L., a foreman carpenter, living in Laconia. Joseph T., a painter, living in Laconia. Albert T., a painter, living in Laconia. Four other children whose span of life was very short.

(III) John Michael, second child and second son of Thomas and Sarah (Nolan) Guay, was born at St. Agathe, Province of Quebec, Canada, September 28, 1861, and was eighteen years old when his father left that place and came to Laconia, New Hampshire. At St. Agathe he was given a good education in public schools and also in an institution of a grade equal to that of the normal schools in this state, and after the removal of the family to Laconia he learned the trade of general and decorative painting, and followed it, steadily for a time and afterward in the intervals of service under the municipal government of Laconia, for since 1889 he has been more or less closely identified with the department of police of that town and subsequent city, and now is head of the department. In 1889 Mr. Guay was appointed town patrolman, and in 1891 became chief of police and served in that capacity until 1893, when the charter of the incorporated city of Laconia was granted and an organization was effected under it. He then returned to his trade in the car shops, and in 1896 was appointed postman under the free mail delivery service inaugurated in Laconia during that year. He was mail carrier about five and a half years, then returned to the car shops, worked there between four and five years, and November 4, 1905, was appointed city marshal by the board of police commissioners of Laconia. This office he still holds, and it is said by business men and others who represent large property interests that the high standing of the police department of the city is largely due to the capable and efficient superintendence of its present marshal. Mr. Guay is a Democrat—there is no question about that—but he never has been offensive in his partisanship and has many warm political supporters in the opposite party. In 1902 he was the Democratic candidate for the office of sheriff of Belknap county, which is a reliable Republican jurisdiction so far as majority is concerned, but Mr. Guay fell short of election by only eighty-five votes. He was a member of the city council of Laconia from March to November, 1905, and retired from that office to enter upon his duties as city marshal, as has been mentioned.

July 8, 1888, John Michael Guay married Mary Murphy, daughter of Jeremiah and Mary Murphy, of Erving, Massachusetts. Two children have been born of this marriage: Irene Bernadette, born in Laconia, January 20, 1891, and John Augustus, born in Laconia, March 10, 1894.

KINGSFORD This family name, which is borne by only a small number of persons in this country, is derived from the name of the English town whence came the bearer of the name.

(I) Charles C. Kingsford was born in Lakeville, Massachusetts. He married Sarah Ashley and they had three children: Arthur, Charles and John, whose sketch follows:

(II) John C., youngest son of Charles C. and Sarah (Ashley) Kingsford, was born in Lakeville, May 4, 1845. He attended the common schools of Lakeville, and also two years at Taunton high school. After farming a short time in Middleboro, then in Taunton, Massachusetts, he went to Providence, Rhode Island. After conducting a gentleman's furnishing store for a short time, he became a clerk in the post office at Riverside, a suburb of Providence, and has ever since been in that employ and resided in Providence. In politics he is a staunch Republican. For a time he was captain in the United Train of Artillery of the Rhode Island state militia. He is a member of the Riverside Congregational Church, and has been superintendent of its Sunday school. He is a past master of St. Andrew's Lodge, No. 21, Free and Accepted Masons, of East Providence. He married Arabella F. Thatcher, who was born in Providence, daughter of Nelson Wood and Deborah (Pratt) Thatcher. Their children are: Howard Nelson, Gertrude Ashley, Arthur Henry, Gorham, Frank W., Carlton Lynwood, and Winthrop Cox. Howard C. is mentionel below. Gertrude A., married William E. Atkinson and lives at Riverside, Rhode Island. Arthur Henry resides in Providence. Frank Wentworth is in the automobile business in Detroit, Michigan. Carlton L. attends the East Providence high school. Winthrop Cox is in school.

(III) Howard Nelson, eldest child of John C. and Arabella F. (Thatcher) Kingsford, was born in Providence, Rhode Island, September 24, 1871, and attended the common and high schools in East Providence. He entered Dartmouth College in 1893, and graduated with the class of 1897, and subsequently took a post-graduate course at Harvard. He was made instructor in pathology and bacteriology in Dartmouth College. In 1901 he became professor in these sciences, and the following year was appointed bacteriologist for the state of New Hampshire, having charge of the state laboratories in Concord and Hanover. He is also medical director for Dartmouth College. In politics he is a Republican. He is a member of St. Andrew's Lodge, No. 21, Free and Accepted Masons, of East Providence, Rhode Island; St. Andrew's Royal Arch Chapter, No. 1, of Lebanon; Washington Council, No. 10, Royal and Select Masters, of Lebanon; Sullivan Commandery, Knights Templar, of Claremont; Edward A. Raymond Consistory, Sublime Princes of the Royal Secret, thirty-second degree, Nashua; and Bektash Temple, Ancient Arabic Order of the Mystic Shrine of Concord. He married, July 16, 1898, Mabel P. Clark, who was born October 21, 1869, in Pawtucket, daughter of Charles R. and Sarah P. (Reney) Clark, of Pawtucket, Rhode Island.

MACKENZIE The clan Mackenzie, one of the ancient tribes of Scotland, has an honorable record, and has produced many men of prominence in peace and in war. Among the former are Sir Alexander Mackenzie, the Arctic explorer, for whom the Mackenzie river was named; George, author of "Writers of the Scots Nation"; and Henry, who was the author of "The Man of Feeling."

(I) Alexander Mackenzie, a native of Scotland, was probably a fisherman.

(II) Colin, son of Alexander Mackenzie, was born in Scotland, in 1844, and after receiving a common school education fitted himself for the position of electrician. In 1866 he came to America, landing on Cape Breton Island, and finally settling at Ellsworth, Maine, where he now resides. For years past he has been an employe of the Western Union Telegraph Company. He is a member of the Independent Presbyterian Church, and in political faith is a Democrat. He is a valued member of the Masonic order, in which he has attained the thirty-second degree. He married Elizabeth Corbett, who was born in St. John's, New Brunswick, daughter of Alexander Corbett, the father being a native of Scotland. They have seven children: Daniel, an electrician, resides in Boston; Colin, conducts a hotel in Ellsworth; Nicholas B., is mentioned below; Annie Louise, Maud Eva, Minnie Elizabeth and Jessie May.

(III) Dr. Nicholas Bradford, third son and child of Colin and Elizabeth (Corbett) Mackenzie, was born in Ellsworth, Maine, August 14, 1876. His literary education was obtained in the common schools. He entered the medical department of Dartmouth College, from which he graduated in the class of 1891. After graduation he was a physician in the City Hospital of Boston three months, at the Massachusetts General Hospital three months, and then at the Children's Hospital, four months, in which time he became excellently prepared for general practice, in which he engaged soon after at Tremont, Maine. He remained there only four months, and in May, 1902, removed to Salisbury, New Hampshire, where he has since been successfully engaged in the practice of his profession. He married Addie, daughter of Julius K. Trask, of Salisbury, who came to the latter town from Stockholm, New York.

PLACE Enoch Place was in Dorchester, Massachusetts, in 1657. He was born in 1631, and died in 1695. He married in Dorchester, November 5, 1657, Sarah ———, who died in 1695, after him. In 1663 Enoch Place was in King's Town, Rhode Island, and with others of Narragansett desired to be under the protection of Connecticut. In 1664, May 5, he was ordered released from prison on giving bonds for one hundred pounds "to appear and speak further to matter concerning Timothy Mather, whom he accused of speaking words of a very dishonorable nature against his majesty." In 1671, May 19, Enoch Place took the oath of allegiance to Rhode Island; in 1687 was taxed ten shillings four pence, and in 1688 was a grand juror. Under the date of 1693 Daniel Gould writes in his journal: "I went over the water in a canoe with old Place to Canonicut." In his will, proved September 11, 1695, Enoch Place calls himself sixty-four years old. His property, besides lands, inventoried at seventeen pounds nineteen shillings, and comprised a cow, heifer, two yearlings, calf, four sheep, two or three lambs, pewter, iron, etc. This appears to be the earliest mention of the family name Place in New England colonial history, and it is supposed that all the other Places in the several states in that region have descended from Enoch and Sarah, of Dorchester and King's Town. Their children were Enoch, Peter, Thomas, Joseph and Sarah, all of whom married and had families.

The first of the name mentioned in the early history of New Hampshire is in the Newington Church records: 1716, John Place married Eunice Row of Newington; 1719, Ebenezer Place married Jane Pevey; 1727, Samuel Place married Mary Row; 1727, James Place married Mary Walker; 1745, Abraham Place married Mary Rawlins; 1751, Joseph Place married Alice Dam. It may be assumed that the more recent generations of the Places in New Hampshire are descendants of those of the same name found in the church records, and it also is fair to assume that they of Newington were in some manner associated in kinship with the Places of Dorchester and King's Town, but from any record now in existence it is difficult to trace descent from any of these heads to Jacob Place of Alton, New Hampshire, and his descendants, several of whom are still living in that town.

(I) Jacob Place was born in Alton, New Hampshire, October 25, 1794, and died there. The farm on which he settled after marriage was cleared by him, and now is owned and occupied by one of his grandsons, having been in the family more than three quarters of a century. On July 26, 1812, Jacob Place married Hannah Clough, daughter of Perley and Sally (Smith) Clough. Jacob and Hannah (Clough) Place had nine children: Sally Pinkham, Smith Clough, Harriet Jewell, Stephen Smith, Luther Brown, Perley Clough, Nancy Olive, Hannah Elizabeth and Jacob Cogswell Place.

(II) Smith Clough, second child and eldest son of Jacob and Hannah (Clough) Place, was born 1816, and died March 5, 1890. He was about forty-five years old when he enlisted for service in the civil war with the Eighth New Hampshire Volunteer Infantry. He was a farmer by occupation, and was much respected in the town of Alton. He married, 1839, Nancy J. Dicey, died in 1888. Their children were: George E., Mary, William, Fanny, Josiah S., Washington N. G., Armetta, Ernest L., and Jesse Franklin Place.

(II) Luther Brown, fifth child and third son of Jacob and Hannah (Clough) Place, was born in Alton, New Hampshire, 1825, and although beyond the eightieth milestone of life's journey is one of the best preserved men of his town, and even at the present day reads well without the aid of glasses. He was baptized by a minister of the Advent Church, but was not brought up under the influence of that denomination. His occupation has been that of millwright and farmer, chiefly the latter, and his endeavors in life have been rewarded with success. He has seen generations one after another of the old families come and go, and is regarded as one of the best authorities on Alton history now living. Mr. Place married, 1850, Emeline M. Glidden, who was born in Alton, 1833, and died there, 1892. Their children are: Clara R., James Buchanan, Cora E., and Charles L. Place.

(III) Jesse Franklin Place, son and youngest

child of Smith Clough and Nancy J. (Dicey) Place, was born in Alton, New Hampshire, 1861, and has spent his entire life in that town. He was educated in the town school, and when old enough learned the trade of millwright, which has been his main occupation in business life to the present time. He moved to his present farm in 1882, and has so improved it that it is regarded as one of the most attractive home farms in Alton. It is pleasantly situated on the shore of Crystal Lake, with Mt. Belknap and other noted heights in plain view from his house. Mr. Place married, June 7, 1884, Grace W. Page, who was born in Gilmanton, New Hampshire, daughter of Asa and Eliza (Edgerly) Page, of Gilmanton. Their children are: Franklin S., Mildred and Josephine S. Place.

(III) James Buchanan, second child and elder son of Luther Brown and Emeline M. (Glidden) Place, was born on the homestead farm in Alton, March 2, 1857. He was educated in the Alton public school and in the academy at Wolfborough, New Hampshire, and after leaving school he taught one year; but his chief occupation has been farming and shoemaking, and in connection with the farm he and his father own and operate a saw mill at Place's pond. He is a member of Highland Lodge, No. 93, Independent Order of Odd Fellows, of Gilmanton Iron Works, and of Merry Meeting Grange, Patrons of Husbandry, of Alton. In February, 1890, Mr. Place married Miss Amy E. Stephens, of Bangor, Maine. Their children are: Walter R., Hazel Olive and Faith Emeline Place.

NELSON The name of Nelson is of Scandinavian origin, and was derived from Nilsson, meaning son of Nils. It is not only to be found in Scotland and Ireland, but is to be met with in nearly every county in England, especially in those along the seaboard, which in ancient times were exposed to the ravages of the piratical Norsemen in their Vikings.

(I) The Nelsons of Maine, New Hampshire and the northern counties of Massachusetts are the posterity of Thomas Nelson, who was one of the company of colonists which immigrated with the Rev. Ezekiel Rogers from Rowley, Yorkshire, England, in 1638, and settled the town of Rowley, Massachusetts. This company was composed of twenty families, the majority of whom were weavers, and they were the first to manufacture woollen cloth in New England. Thomas Nelson appears to have been one of the wealthiest as well as one of the most able among the Rowley settlers, and acquired prominence both in business and official life. He was made a freeman in 1639, was chosen deputy to the general court in 1640, and in the following year became chairman of a committee formulated to make a general survey of the town, lay out and register houselots and transact other business in relation to land grants. In 1644 he was appointed to solemnize marriages. His death occurred in England in 1648, while on a visit to the mother country for the purpose of transacting some important business, and an item in the records states that he prudently made his will prior to his departure from Rowley. The name of his first wife, whom he married in England, does not appear in any record on this side of the ocean. His second marriage took place about the year 1642, in Massachusetts, to "Joane" Dummer, daughter of Thomas Dummer, of Badgeley, England, and a niece of Richard Dummer, one of the original settlers of Newbury. Of this first union there were two sons: Philip, who will be again referred to; and Thomas, who was born in England in 1635, and married Ann Lambert. The children of his second marriage were: Mercy, born in Rowley, December 26, 1643; Samuel, born in Rowley about 1646, died in England prior to 1676; and Mary, who was also born in Rowley, and of whom there is no further mention.

(II) Captain Philip, eldest child of Thomas Nelson and the latter's first wife, was born in England, about the year 1633, and came to New England in early boyhood. He was a student at Harvard College during the days of its infancy, graduating in 1654, and he attained eminence in both civic and military life, serving as a justice of the peace and as captain of a company which was attached to the command of Sir William Phipps on an expedition against the French in Nova Scotia. His death occurred August 19, 1691. He was twice married, first, June 24, 1657, to Sarah Jewett, daughter of Joseph Jewett, who died prior to December 17, 1665, which was the date of her burial; second, November 1, 1666, to Elizabeth Lowell, who was born February 16, 1646, daughter of John Lowell of Newbury, and she died December 14, 1731. The children of his first marriage were Philip and Mary. His second wife bore him ten children, namely: John, Jeremiah (died in infancy), Elizabeth, Sarah, Jeremiah, Martha, Ruth, Joseph, Jemima and Lucy.

(III) Joseph, fourth son and eighth child of Captain Philip and Elizabeth (Lowell) Nelson, was born November 28, 1682. He resided in Rowley, and his death occurred February 8, 1743-44. For his first wife he married Hannah Brocklebank, daughter of Samuel Brocklebank, and she died June 5, 1732, in her forty-eighth year. His second wife, whom he married in Ipswich, September 5, 1732, was Mrs. Elizabeth Jewett, widow of Jeremiah Jewett. She died May 24, 1761, aged eighty-one years. His children were: Jeremiah, Joseph, Moses, Mary, Samuel (died young), another Samuel, David, Francis, Jonathan, Philip and John, all of whom were of his first union.

(IV) Jonathan, eighth son and ninth child of Joseph and Hannah (Brocklebank) Nelson, was born in Rowley, July 27, 1723. He served as a soldier in the French war, and afterward settled as a pioneer in Perrystown, New Hampshire, where he assisted in constructing the first highways, and it is said that with other early settlers there he hewed the logs for the first meeting house in Mill Village. He resided on what was known as the mill lot, and occupied it for a number of years, or until his removal to Sutton, New Hampshire, whither he was soon followed (or perhaps accompanied) by his two sons, Asa and Philip, from whom have descended a numerous posterity. He had been a deacon of the church in Rowley, and forever afterward preserved his allegiance to the church, not alone contenting himself with merely professing piety, but labored incessantly for the propagation of religious work. In manner he was kind and pleasant, and in personal appearance he was tall, slender and remarkably erect even in old age. He died in 1801. December 24, 1752, he married Hannah Cheney, of Haverhill, Massachusetts, who died July 14, 1802, and it is quite probable that she was his second wife, as a record found in Rowley states that Jonathan Nelson, on March 10, 1743 or 1744, filed his intention to marry Mary Peasley, or Pearse, but no further knowledge relative to this marriage is obtainable. His wife Hannah bore him three children: Betsey, born March 11, 1753; Asa, born April 3, 1754; and Philip, who is the next in line of descent. All were natives of Rowley.

(V) Philip (2), youngest child of Jonathan and Hannah (Cheney) Nelson, was born in Rowley, June 3, 1756. At the commencement of the war for national independence he espoused the cause of patriotism, and after his discharge from the continental service he resumed the implements of peace, settling upon a farm on Nelson's Hill in the western part of Sutton, where he resided for the rest of his life. In addition to general farming he transacted quite an extensive cattle business, and he also had other outside interests of considerable importance. He died September 4, 1841. His first wife, whom he married October 24, 1778, was Hannah Quimby, who was born in Sutton, October 18, 1758, and died April 16, 1831. March 28, 1834, he married for his second wife Elizabeth Goodwin. He was the father of six children: Moses, Jonathan, Judith, Hannah, Philip and William.

(VI) Philip (3), third son and fifth child of Philip (2) and Hannah (Quimby) Nelson, was born in Sutton, December 22, 1790. He was a butcher and carried on business for some years in Amoskeag. He was married, October 17, 1813, to Mary Teel, who was born in Goffstown, August 4, 1793, daughter of Aaron and Rebecca (Tweed) Teel. She became the mother of eight children, namely: Milton, Judith, Mary T. (died young), John A. T., William, Mary, Susan and Celinda.

(VII) John A. T., second son and fourth child of Philip and Mary (Teel) Nelson, was born in Woburn, Massachusetts, 1826. He learned the butchering business, which he followed for a short time, and then became a drover, residing about four years in Franklin and moving from that place to Hill Village. Removing to Pennacook he carried on the clothing business there some nine years, and was engaged in the same line of trade for about two years in Manchester. In 1873 he purchased a farm in Candia, and cultivated it successfully for the succeeding twenty years, or until his death, which occurred in 1893. Politically he acted with the Republican party. In his religious belief he was a Congregationalist. His fraternal affiliations were with the Masonic Order. He married Deborah Norton, daughter of Moses Norton of Cabot, Vermont. The children of this union are: Mary E., Flora I., John B., Allan H., William S., Selinda and Jennie W.

(VIII) Allan H., second son and fourth child of John A. T. and Deborah (Norton) Nelson, was born in Franklin, March 14, 1858. After concluding his attendance at the Pennacook high school he was employed as a store clerk in Manchester for a time. and in 1878 he went to reside in Candia. He has followed agriculture to some extent and was for a number of years connected with the shoe manufacturing industry. In 1900 he was appointed deputy sheriff of Rockingham county, and is still serving in that capacity. In politics he is a Republican and holds the office of supervisor. He attends the Congregational Church. He is a Master Mason, belonging to Rockingham Lodge, and also affiliates with the Independent Order of Odd Fellows. In 1878 Mr. Nelson married for his first wife Clara Rowe, a well-known school teacher, daughter of Freeman and Angeline (Dow) Rowe of Candia. She died July 3, 1883, leaving one child, Philip Allan. His second wife, whom he married February 7, 1892, was Carrie B. Rowe, daughter of Charles H. and Jennie (Worthen) Rowe, of Candia. She was educated at the Pembroke Academy and also taught school The children of this union are: John H., born August 1, 1892; and Clara B., born January 19, 1896. Mr. Nelson's second wife died May 19, 1905.

(IX) Philip Allan, son of Allan H. and Clara (Rowe) Nelson, was born June 26, 1883. He was three years with the John B. Varick Hardware Company, of Manchester, and is now in New Mexico, with the Lake Valley Mining Company. He married, August 19, 1907, Effie Lucy, of Manchester.

NELSON This name is of Scotch origin, and in its primitive form meant "the son of Neil." The present branch came directly from Scotland, and its early members played an important part in the settlement of Ryegate, Vermont. So far as can be traced there is no connection between this line and the one descended from Thomas Nelson, whose history has previously been written.

(I) William Nelson, or Neilson (the name is spelt both ways in Scotland, even by members of the same family), was born in 1742, in Scotland. In the year 1774 he migrated from the parish of Erskine, in Renfrewshire, to this country, bringing with him his wife and three children—William, Robert and Mary. The story of the exodus is interesting. In the winter of 1773 a company was formed by a number of farmers near Glasgow, in Scotland, for the purpose of buying a large tract of land in America. David Allen and James Whitelaw were sent on to explore, and after a search of five months they bought outright the south half of the township of Ryegate, Vermont, which township contained twenty-three thousand acres. The owner was Rev. John Witherspoon, D. D., president of Princeton College, and later a signer of the Declaration of Independence, to whom the land had been chartered by New Hampshire. In 1774 ten Scotchmen (William Nelson, John Waddle, James Nelson, half brother to William; Thomas McKeith, Patrick Lang, David Reid, Robert Gammel, Robert Tweadale, and Andrew and James Smith) came over to settle the wilderness, four of whom, William Nelson, David Reid, Robert Gammel and Robert Tweadale, brought their families with them. Nelson seems to have been one of the bravest men of the party. The first year they were in great danger from the Indians, and had to move to Newbury, Vermont. Before leaving, Nelson filled a large Scotch chest with a variety of articles, and buried it for safety's sake. The party stayed at Newbury for a while, but were obliged to return or starve because of their crops that had been planted at Ryegate. Nelson came back first and lived alone in a hut for some time, sleeping with his gun by his side, saying "It is better to die by the sword than famine." In 1776, when the town of Ryegate was organized, Nelson was appointed constable, and soon after was made selectman. In 1793 Nelson and two others were appointed managers of the company, taking the deeds from General Whitelaw, who could no longer act as agent, having been appointed surveyor general of Vermont. Besides carrying on his farm in Ryegate, William Nelson built a saw and grist mill on the Connecticut, at Canoe, later called Dodge's Falls, being the first to dam the river at that point. He accumulated large tracts of good farm land in Ryegate and Monroe, New Hampshire (or West Lyman, as it was then called), turning over to his sons William and Robert all the land bordering on the Connecticut river from Barnet bridge to the Littleton line. William Nelson's wife, whom he married in 1765, was Jean

Stewart, born in Erskine in 1737, but not much is known about her. It is said that she was short and thickset, and very industrious, and would work very late evenings, while she would banter her husband because he did not do the same. "Ould Willie," as he was called, would retort that she ought to work more than he because she was the oldest. She was born five years before him, and died six year sooner than he did. She died September 15, 1825, aged eighty-eight years. He died January 23, 1831, and is buried at Ryegate Corner beside his wife and daughter Mary. Their children were as follows: 1. William, born in Erskine, Renfrewshire, Scotland, in 1767, died September 29, 1830, in Monroe, New Hampshire, aged sixty-three years; he married Hannah Moore, of Bow, New Hampshire, about 1791-92; they had nine children, six sons and three daughters; she died in 1828; second marriage, Hannah Nelson, of Ryegate. 2. Robert, born in Inchinan (Ancient Killian) parish, Renfrewshire, Scotland, in April, 1770, and died in Monroe, New Hampshire, March 20, 1848, aged seventy-eight, minus one month; he was married in Ryegate, December 26, 1793, to Agnes Gray, of Ryegate, who was born April 9, 1778, and died June 18, 1850, by Rev. David Goodwillie, of Barnet; they had fourteen children, nine daughters and five sons. 3. Mary, born March or April, 1772, in Erskine parish, Scotland, died in Ryegate, October 6, 1825, aged fifty-three years; she was married to Hugh Gardner, February 9, 1781, by Josiah Page, Esq.; they had twelve children, nine daughters and three sons. Her daughter Isabel married Edward Miller, who came from Erskine and settled in Ryegate, and to their son Edward we are indebted for practically all of the data extant relating to the Nelson family. The genealogical matter collected by Mr. Miller is in the hands of William S. Nelson. 4. John, born about February 5, 1776, in Ryegate, being the second boy born in Ryegate; he died September 5, 1854, aged seventy-eight years and seven months; he married Jane Duncan, of Barnet, about March 11, 1814, and Polly Ann Finley, of Acworth, New Hampshire, about 1819. Eight children, five daughters and three sons. A eulogy of John Nelson by Rev. James McArthur was published in the *Vermont Quarterly* for October, 1862. 5. James, born in June, 1778, died June 23, 1840, aged sixty-two years; he married Agnes Gibson, December 28, 1808; he married (second), Jean Rohan, widow of Andrew Buchanan, June, 1839; they had ten children, six sons and four daughters. He was a man of affairs, and represented the town of Ryegate in the legislature five successive terms. The oldest son, Dr. William Nelson, was an eminent physician in Cambridge, New York. 6. Thomas, born in Ryegate, April 4, 1780, died November 30, 1860, aged eighty years and seven months; he was married September 28, 1804, by Rev. David Southerland, to Mary Allen, of Ryegate; they had twelve children, eight daughters and four sons. 7. Jenett, born about 1782, in Ryegate, died about 1794. 8. Isabel, born in Ryegate in 1785, died in Groton, March 14, 1831, in her forty-sixth year; she married Peter McLaughlin, of Groton, about June 16, 1809; they had seven children, six daughters and one son. Summary of grandchildren: Twenty-eight sons, and forty-four daughters; total, seventy-two. Ten died in infancy or childhood, viz: Robert had three, Mary three, James one, Thomas two, Isabel one.

(II) William (2), eldest son of William (1) and Jean (Stewart) Nelson, was born in 1767, in Erskine, Scotland, and came to this country with his parents in 1774. He and his brother Robert lived in Ryegate, Vermont, until men grown, when they moved across the river to Monroe, New Hampshire, upon the lands given them by their father, as referred to. William (2) Nelson married (first) Hannah Moore, of Bow, New Hampshire, about 1791. She died January 3, 1828, aged fifty-six years. He married (second), 1829, Hannah Nelson, of Ryegate. She was the widow of Henry Buchanan, and died May 7, 1839, aged fifty-nine years. William (2) died in Monroe, New Hampshire, September 19, 1830, aged sixty-three years. His children are as follows: 1. William (3), was born in Monroe in 1792, and died November 9, 1840, aged forty-eigth years. He married Lima Hibbard, of Bath, New Hampshire, who died about 1854. They had no children. 2. Elsie, born 1794, died August 3, 1818, aged twenty-four. 3. Hannah, born 1799, died February 15, 1833, aged thirty-four. She married Michael M. Stevens of Monroe, New Hampshire, who died April 11, 1851, aged fifty-one. There were four children, three boys and one girl. 4. John, born October 16, 1801, died February 15, 1865. He married Harriet Kelsea, of Derby, Vermont. They had seven children. 5. Richard Moore, born in 1806, died in Monroe, November 19, 1849. He married Margaret Ferguson, of Monroe, who died at Monticello, Illinois, 1878. They had three children, all girls. 6. Robert Stewart, born in 1808, died at Hillsborough, Illinois, aged about fifty. He married Eliza Kelsea, of Derby, Vermont, sister to Harriet, mentioned above. They had three children, two boys and one girl. 7. Benjamin, born August 9, 1812, married Emily, daughter of James Moore, of Monroe, April 18, 1836. They had nine children, seven sons and three daughters. He went to Illinois, and died about 1884. 8. Mary Gardner (Maria), born January 10, 1815, married Eben W. Blake, of Brighton, Maine, January 13, 1836. He died October 25, 1874, aged sixty-five. They had five children, one son and four daughters. She died in Littleton, New Hampshire, March 15, 1885. 9. Rev. Horatio, born September 11, 1818, in Monroe, New Hampshire. In 1836 he married Angeline, daughter of James Moore, born April 21, 1818, in Monroe, who died June 18, 1877. They had eight children. He died in Illinois about 1888.

John, son of William (2) and Mary (Moore) Nelson, was born at Monroe, New Hampshire, October 16, 1801, and died February 15, 1865. January 15, 1823, he was married at Derby, Vermont, to Harriet Kelsea, of that place, by John Stewart, Esq. She was born in Albany, Vermont, August 8, 1803, and was the daughter of Daniel Kelsea and and Mary Mansfield Kelsea, who was born in Londonderry, New Hampshire, and son of Hugo Kelso, one of the Scotch Irish immigrants from Londonderry, Ireland. Both John Nelson and his wife died at Monroe, where they spent nearly all their lives. Their children were as follows: 1. William Curtis, born in Monroe, New Hampshire, March 2, 1824, and died January 1, 1865. He married Percis Paddleford, a daughter of Seth Paddleford, about 1850. They had one son and one daughter. 2. George, born July 23, 1826, died August 4, 1826. 3. Eliza Ann, born November 30, 1830, died November 10, 1848. 4. John Milton, born June 5, 1833, married Sarah Wilson, of Jacksonville, Illinois, in 1856. She died in Jacksonville in 1871. They had no children. He married (second), about 1880, Mary ——, and she had one child, James Milton. John Milton died in Grinnell, Iowa, April 17, 1882. 5. Edwin, born September 1, 1836, married Phebe J. Gibson, of Lyman, New Hampshire, August 26, 1860. 6. Almon, born July 7, 1840, died November 17, 1841. 7. Henry

W. S. Wilson.

Clinton, born September 21, 1844, married, March 29, 1866, Mary Moulton, who was born in Bath, New Hampshire, March 11, 1846. They have one son, and live on the John Nelson farm in Monroe.

Edwin, fifth child of John and Harriet (Kelsea) Nelson, was born at Monroe, September 1, 1836, and lives in Lyman, New Hampshire. He is a farmer and lived in the adjoining town of Monroe until 1872. when he moved to Lyman, his present home. He married (first), August 26, 1860, Phebe Jane Gibson, daughter of Samuel and Mercy (Hoskins) Gibson, of Lyman, who was born February 23, 1842, and died January 1, 1877. They had four children: 1. William Stewart, whose sketch follows. 2. Albert John, born in Monroe, April 19, 1865, died there September 10, 1868. 3. Frank Kelsea, born in Monroe, January 21, 1870, lives in Lisbon. 4. George Edwin, born in Monroe, January 14, 1872, died in Lyman, September 23, 1872. Edwin Nelson married (second), Anna Hadley, in 1879; no children. He married (third), Irena Scales, in 1888; one child, Marian Belle.

William Stewart, oldest son of Edwin and Phebe Jane (Gibson) Nelson, was born June 6, 1861, in Monroe, New Hampshire. He received a few months schooling in Monroe and Lyman, and when quite young went to work in a peg factory in Lisbon Village. He began work as a "chore boy" at seventeen cents a day of eleven hours, but believing then as now that anything worth doing at all was worth doing well, he did whatever was before him the best he possibly could, and he says that whatever small success he had had in business since is wholly due to that idea. Very soon a better position was given him, and continuing in this way he learned all parts of the very complicated business of making pegs, and in 1884 became superintendent of the factory. In December, 1887, he went to Los Angeles, California, for the benefit of his wife's health, and while there was manager of circulation on the *Los Angeles Times* for the east side. He returned to Lisbon in June 1890, and found the peg business which had been carried on in a desultory manner for some years entirely dead. One factory with liabilities of more than $100,000 was in the hands of the sheriff, and the other had lost its market because of the poor quality of the goods manufactured, and it was freely said by those most interested that no more pegs would be made, as there was no money in the business at the prevailing export prices. After several interviews Mr. Nelson convinced Ovid D. Moore and Fred J. Moore that a peg factory under common sense management would at the least pay its own bills, and December 1, 1890, they began business in what was known as the old mill under the firm name of the Moore Peg Company. Although pegs had been made in this mill for a number of years, it had never really been fitted up as a peg factory; it was simply an experiment in the machinery line, and anyone who has had experience with the mechanical failures of other people will appreciate the situation of the new firm. Mr. Nelson had entire charge of the mechanical part of the business, and he overhauled the machinery as thoroughly as was possible in the time at his disposal, and proceeded to make a sample lot of pegs to be used in securing a market. At this time split wood pegs for boots and shoes had ceased to be of any commercial account in this country, and the European market, being controlled by a few large firms was limited. The sample lot was submitted to the largest peg dealer in Europe, and he was so well pleased with the quality of the goods that he at once agreed to take the whole production of the factory. The business was a success from the start, in spite of the experimental machinery, and was continued in the old building until 1896, when it was decided to erect a new factory on practical lines. In this year Mr. Nelson made a journey to Europe in the interest of the business, and upon his return completed plans of machinery and buildings for an entire new plant, which was erected at the east end of Main street, Lisbon, in 1897. As has been said, Mr. Nelson believes in doing things well, and as economy is of first importance in making goods for export, the main idea with him in building the new factory was that it should be a machine that would turn out the largest possible quantity of good pegs at the smallest possible cost. His success may be judged from the fact that although the new factory was equipped with the same number of machines as the old one, the production of pegs was one-fourth larger, and the amount of fuel used for both heat and power was less than was used in the old factory for heat alone. As to machinery it is enough to say that all of the peg machines now running in the United States are patterned after those designed by Mr. Nelson in 1896. Upon the death of Ovid D. Moore, in 1902, Mr. Nelson bought the interest of the estate and Fred J. Moore in the business, and has continued by himself in the manufacture of shoe pegs until the present time, under the original firm name of the Moore Peg Company, and has the distinction of being the only man in this country who manufactures and exports shoe pegs. He employs no agents, but takes his timber from the forests and delivers the finished product in Germany, France, Denmark, Russia, Turkey, Italy, Austria, Hungary, Mexico and South America, himself. Mr. Nelson is a Republican in politics, is not (as he says) a "joiner," but he has a library that a reader would like to see. July 3, 1886, Mr. Nelson married Genevieve Moore, daughter of Ovid D. and Harriet I. (Howland) Moore, a lady of fine literary mind, who was born in Bristol, New Hampshire, November 10, 1856, and died in Lisbon, May 11, 1894. (See Moore, V).

It is of interest to note that Mr. Nelson and his first wife both descended from John Moore, (Moor, or Muir, as the name was originally), one of the Scotch Irish company who settled in Londonderry, New Hampshire, in 1722. The line on his side runs back as follows: William S. Nelson, Phebe J. Gibson, Samuel Gibson, Mary Moore, John Moore, Elder William Moore, John Moore; and on his wife's side, Genevieve Moore, Ovid D. Moore, Joseph Moore, Captain Robert Moore, Colonel Robert Moore, John Moore. Mr. Nelson married (second), November 11, 1903, Eva Dennett, who died January 21, 1905.

FURBER The family of this name was early in the Dover settlement, and all the Furbers of that region may be descended from one immigrant ancestor.

(I) William Furber was born in London, England, in 1614, and died in Dover, New Hampshire, in 1692. He shipped from Bristol, England, in the ship "Angel Gabriel," and was wrecked in a storm off Pemaquid, Maine, in the great storm of August, 1635. He was later a citizen of Dover, one of the witnesses of the true deed of independence to Wheelwright. 1638, a representative in 1648, and in 1683 one of the two hundred and fifty citizens of Dover, Portsmouth, Exeter, and Hampton, who sent King Charles II a remonstrance against the oppressive administration of Governor Cranfield. William Furber married Elizabeth ———, and they had six children: William, Jethro, Moses,

Elizabeth, Susanna and Bridget. Two or more generations must have passed away before the records show a definite account of the Furbers again.

(IV) Captain Joshua Furber was born in Newington, May 24, 1744. He removed to Northwood in 1767, and died there April 27, 1827. He was a member of Captain Enoch Payne's company, of Lieutenant Colonel Senter's regiment, enlisted September 4, 1777, mustered in September 20, 1777, and discharged January 7, 1778, serving in the Rhode Island campaign. He was also a private in Captain Edward Hilton's company, Colonel Joshua Wingate's regiment, New Hampshire Volunteers in the expedition to Rhode Island in 1778, serving from August 6 to August 28. In after years he was known as "Captain of the Parish." The Revolutionary Records show that he was one of the selectmen of Northwood in 1781. He manufactured potash on a considerable scale, by filtering and evaporating the lye of wood ashes. He also made what is commercially known as pearlash from potash, by calcenation. His principal market for it was in Newburyport, Massachusetts. Captain Furber married Betsey Page, and they had eleven children: Moses, Catherine, John, Nancy, Betsy, Thomas and Josephine (twins), Mary, William, David and Samuel.

(V) David Furber, tenth child and sixth son of Captain Joshua and Betsey Page, was born in Northwood, September 12, 1787, and died December 31, 1858. He was engaged in farming and saw milling. About 1814 he built the house at Furber's Corner, which is still in possession of a member of the family. He married Sally Haley, of Epping. Their children were: Samuel H., mentioned below; William H., twin brother of Samuel; Franklin, Methodist clergyman; and Martha, who married Samuel F. Leavitt, of Northwood.

(VI) Samuel H., eldest child of David and Sally (Haley) Furber, was born in Northwood, August 1, 1814, and died 1899, aged eighty-five. He always lived on the old homestead, to the ownership of which he succeeded after the death of his father. He married Mary Leavitt, who was born 1814, daughter of Rev. Dudley Leavitt, of Northwood. Seven children were born of this marriage: Frank, born in 1842, died in 1906; Mary, born in 1844, died in 1861; William M., born in 1846, is cashier of the Craft Shoe Manufacturing Company of Manchester; Sarah E., born in 1847, is the wife of George W. Hill, of Concord; Dudley L., mentioned below; Rev. Harrison W., pastor of the Baptist Church at Pittsfield, was born in 1850, and died in May, 1898; Carrie F., born May, 1852, married Frank M. Knowles, of Concord.

(VII) Dudley L., fifth child and third son of Samuel H. and Mary (Leavitt) Furber, was born in Northwood, August 18, 1848. At an early age he left the homestead and went into the employ of Pillsbury Brothers, manufacturers of shoes, at Northwood, and was afterward employed in the same business in Lynn, Massachusetts, and New York City. In 1872 he took charge of a department in the establishment of John F. Cloutman, and was employed there thirteen years. He then began the manufacture of shoes on his own account at Northwood, and carried on that business eight years. In 1893 he established himself in Dover, where he has since been successfully engaged in the manufacture of ladies' and gentlemen's special shoes. In politics Mr. Furber is a Democrat, and as such represented Farmington in the legislature in 1883. He is now a member of the board of water commissioners of Dover. He has been a member of the Masonic order since 1872, having taken the first three degrees in Tucker Lodge, in North Bennington, Vermont. He is now a member of Moses Paul Lodge No. 96, of Dover, and also of the Knights of Pythias. He married, 1874, Cora C. Carlton, of Farmington, who was born in Farmington, daughter of Captain Ralph and Amanda (Pearl) Carleton.

MUDGETT The first of this name mentioned in the Colonial Records is Thomas Mudget, of Salisbury, Massachusetts, who married (perhaps for his second wife), October 8, 1665, Sarah Morrell, eldest daughter of Abraham (1). Their children were Mary and Temperance. Another Thomas of Salisbury was perhaps a son of this Thomas. The family is one comparatively limited in number. None were in the Revolution from Massachusetts; and only four from New Hampshire.

(I) Elisha Mudgett, a native of Massachusetts, settled in Sandwich, New Hampshire, and engaged in farming.

(II) Samuel, son of Elisha Mudgett, was born in Sandwich, New Hampshire, in 1805. He was educated in the common schools, and in early life learned the dyer's trade, and was employed in mills in Lowell and Lawrence, Massachusetts, and became an expert in his business. In 1885 he bought a farm of one hundred acres in Meredith, where he lived the remainder of his life. He was a deacon in the Free Will Baptist Church, and was a highly respected and influential man. In politics he was a Democrat, and was elected by his fellow townsmen as road surveyor, justice of the peace, and selectman. He married Sarah Eaton, who was born in Alton. Her parents were Josiah and Hannah Eaton. The children of Samuel and Sarah M. (Eaton) Mudgett, were: Rhoda, Hannah, Horatio, and George M., whose sketch next follows.

(III) George M., youngest child of Samuel and Sarah M. (Eaton) Mudgett, was born in Sandwich, February 3, 1846. He was educated in the public schools of Lawrence, and at Comas Business College in Boston. After the settlement of the family in Sandwich, Mr. Mudgett worked on the farm until November, 1862, when he enlisted in Company B, Fourth Regiment Volunteer Infantry. He was under command of General Banks, and saw service at Port Hudson, Louisiana, where he was under fire forty days. After leaving the army he was engaged in shoe manufacturing in Danvers and Haverhill, Massachusetts. In 1869 he went to Colorado, and was engaged in mining in the vicinity of Denver, being superintendent of a mine and proficient as an assayer. His father being advanced in years and in feeble health, Mr. Mudgett returned to New Hampshire, and took charge of the farm until his father's death, and has since resided there. He is still interested in mining, and owns a one-half interest in the Uncle Ned Mine, in Novia Scotia. He is a member of the American Mechanics in which order he has held minor offices, and is also a member of the Knights of Pythias, in which he has filled the office of Sir Knight. He married Cora D. Dodge. They have one child, Charles.

BOSTON Family tradition states that the immigrant ancestor came from England to American and settled in or near Wells, Maine, in the eighteenth century. Another version of the early history of the family is that the immigrant came from Scotland. Deficient records preclude the possibility of a complete early record of the race. Hannah Boston was a member of Rev. Mr. Emery's church in Wells. His pastorate of twenty years began in 1701. Major John Storer enlisted a company of men in Wells to be a part of Sir William Pepperell's force in the expedition which captured Louisburg, the stronghold of France in America, in 1744. Gershom Boston, Joseph Boston. Shebuleth Boston and Thomas Boston were of this company. Shebuel and Thomas Boston were left in Louisburg, but probably returned after their companions.

(I) Joseph Boston, according to family tradition, was born in England, and settled in Wells, Maine, in the eighteenth century; it is more probable that he was born in Wells. He followed the sea and was drowned. He married an Indian girl named Newell, and they had one or more children.

(II) Oliver F. Boston, son of Joseph and ——— (Newell) Boston, was born in Wells, in 1808, and died in 1894. He was a shipbuilder. For many years he was an active member of the Baptist Church. He married Dorcas Moody. Their children were: Lydia, who married Sylvester Grant; Catherine, who married Ransom Crook; Margaret, who married Seth Rowe; Oliver F., who settled at Barrington, New Hampshire; Stephen, mentioned below; Fannie, who married Harrison Foss; Agatha; and Hannah, wife of George Marble.

(III) Stephen A., fifth child and second son of Oliver F. Dorcas (Moody) Boston, was born in South Berwick, Maine, May 17, 1841. He was engaged in saw milling until 1893, when he removed to Bennington, New Hampshire, and bought a farm and has since been engaged in agriculture. He married Hannah Giles, who was born in Dover, daughter of Daniel Giles. Twelve children have been born to them: Frank H., of Rochester; Ida, deceased; Charles Henry, of Haverhill, Massachusetts; Millie B., wife of Herbert Trafton; Stephen A., deceased; Oliver, deceased; Stephen A., mentioned below; Harry E., of Exeter; George Wilber, of Dover; Dorcas; Almira; and one who died in infancy.

(IV) Stephen A. (2), seventh child and fifth son of Stephen A. (1) and Hannah (Giles) Boston, was born in South Berwick, Maine, February 19, 1872. He was educated in the public schools and at the academy at Somersworth, New Hampshire. At eighteen years of age he went to Boston and learned the trade of painter and decorator, residing there seven years. He then entered the employ of the American Painting and Decorating Company as foreman, and filled that place two years. While with that company he had charge of the work on the Mt Washington Hotel, and on several other important structures. In 1903 Mr. Boston started in business for himself in Dover, and later admitted his brother, George W., to a partnership, the firm assuming the style of Boston Brothers. They have been successful in business. One of their latest pieces of work was the painting and decorating of the Wentworth Hospital..

Mr. Boston married (first), 1895, Mamie Richardson. He married (second), 1900, Alvina Marston, of Exeter; (third), 1904, Julia Vatcher, who was born in Dover, England, March 12, 1885. By his first wife there was one child, Alfred Noah, born July 3, 1896; by the second wife one child, Nellie E., born January 22, 1901.

WESLEY George Wesley was born in the city of New York, December 25, 1849, and was a son of Benjamin Wesley, who went south with his family when George was an infant, and remained there until after the end of the late Civil war.

About the time of the close of the war, George Wesley, then a young man, returned to the north and went to the state of Maine, where he took up his residence at South Berwick, and for several years afterward was an employee and foreman in the Salmon Falls cotton mills. In 1869, while living in that town, he married Katherine McGraw, by whom he had eight children. In 1878 Mr. Wesley moved with his family to Dover, New Hampshire, and for a time was employed as a watchman, and he also engaged in various other occupations, for he always was a man of modest means, a wage earner, but industrious, frugal and of good habits. Of his eight children four died young and one after marriage. The children of George and Katherine (McGraw) Wesley are as follows: Susie, married, and is now dead; Charles Henry, died at the age of six years; John H., now of Dover; Katherine, died in childhood; Sarah, died in infancy; George B., died at the age of eight years; and Maggie, wife of Hubert Millen.

John H. Wesley, present representative of ward five of Dover in the New Hampshire legislature, is third in the order of seniority, and eldest surviving son of George W. and Katherine (McGraw) Wesley. He was born at South Berwick, Maine, October 16, 1873, and was five years old when his parents moved from that town to Dover. He was educated in public schools and Franklin Academy, and after leaving school at once turned his attention to business pursuits. For the last twelve or more years he has been popularly identified with the management of various theatrical and amusement enterprises, and during the last three or four years has gained special prominence as one of the leaders of the Democratic party in Dover, and also has come to be recognized as an active figure in the councils of that party in Strafford county. His democracy is of the true Jeffersonian order, and his courageous advocacy of party principles and his unyielding loyalty to the cause of the workingman has won for him a warm place in the hearts of the people of his county, and rewarded his aspirations for public office with unvarying success. He has served several times in both branches of the municipal government, and left the board of aldermen in 1903 to occupy a seat in the lower house of the state legislature. He is still a member of that body by successive re-elections, and on the floor of the house has ably championed the principles he has stood for before his constituents; and it was he who introduced the bill amending section fourteen of chapter one hundred and eighty of the public statutes regulating the hours of labor of women and minors. In 1904 he was elected a member of the board of education of Dover, to serve for two years, and received the unanimous vote of the council and board of aldermen, which joint body comprised five Democratic members and twenty from the opposite political party. In 1906 he organized what is known locally as the John W. Wesley Hand Tub Association, a social organization for advancing the interests of its members. He is chairman of the executive committee of ward five of Dover, ward clerk, member of the board of selectmen and member of Portsmouth Aerie of the Fraternal Order or Eagles.

HAWKINS The name Hawkins is one of the most common among the earliest settlers in Massachusetts. Among the heads of the families of this name in New England before 1650 are: Abraham, of Charlestown, 1642; Anthony, of Windsor, before 1644; George, of Boston, 1644; James, of Boston, 1635; John, of Boston, 1630; Richard, of Boston. 1637; Robert, of Charlestown, 1635, and many others. The number of persons of this name in New England in the early Colonial times suggests that the Hawkins family must have been mainly composed of Puritans.

(I) Amos A. Hawkins resided in Grafton, Massachusetts, where he was employed in the cotton mills as a ring spinner. He died July 12, 1879, aged fifty-nine. He married Angeline Davis, who was born in Patchogue, Rhode Island, and died in Warren, Rhode Island, February 29, 1904, aged eighty-two. Six children were born to this union: Fannie C., Garophelia, Eliza Ann, Jessie, Franklin A., and William H. Fannie C. is single and resides in Warren, Rhode Island. Garophelia (now deceased), married Thomas Foshay, of Grafton Center. Eliza Ann married Truman P. Fenton and lives in Warren, Rhode Island. Jessie married John Wilson, and resides in Taunton, Massachusetts. Franklin A. is mentioned below. William H. resides in Providence, Rhode Island, where he is an overseer of ring spinning in the Nantic mills.

(II) Franklin A., eldest son and fifth child of Amos A. and Angeline (Davis) Hawkins, was born in Grafton, Massachusetts, July 23, 1860. He acquired his education in the schools of Grafton, and at the age of eighteen became a spinner in the cotton factories of Grafton. In 1889 he removed to Lawrence, where he remained until 1899, as overseer of the spinning department of the Atlantic cotton mills. In 1899 he removed to Manchester, New Hampshire, where he became overseer of the ring frames, which position he still holds. He has charge of one hundred and twenty employes who operate twenty-five thousand spindles. It is a fact that hardly needs to be mentioned that men who hold responsible positions in the employ of great corporations like the Amoskeag are men of ample qualifications and always to be relied on. Mr. Hawkins is a man of that character. His record is an honorable one. Mr. Hawkins and his wife and daughters are members of Congregational Church. He is a Republican but has nothing to do with politics. He married, February 18, 1879, at Grafton, Massachusetts, Eliza J. McHenry, born May 7, 1858, daughter of Joseph and Elizabeth (Barr) McHenry, of Grafton, Massachusetts. Both her parents were born in Scotland. The children of Mr. and Mrs. Hawkins are: Elizabeth A., born March 31, 1881; Mildred I., August 26, 1883; Harry F., April 17, 1886, assistant overseer of ring spinning in the Amoskeag mills; Joseph A., July 4, 1888, died January 28, 1893; Sadie E., August 10, 1890; Florence M., November 9, 1892; Hazel J., November 28, 1896.

RÖDELSPERGER This family, though German in both name and nationality, is descended from Huguenot ancestors who were driven out from France at the time of the Huguenot expulsion.

(I) Sebastian Rödelsperger, was born in Henbach, in 1771, and died September, 1840, aged sixty-eight years. He was a farmer and had a farm of one hundred acres which in most parts of Europe is considered a considerable estate. He had three children: Sebastian, Mary and Johann, the subject of the following paragraph.

(II) Johann, second son and third child of Sebastian Rödelsperger, was born in Henbach, Germany, in 1817, and died in Giessen, 1890, aged seventy-three years. He was educated at Freiburg, Germany, and devoted his life to teaching, continuing until he was sixty-eight years old. He was a thoroughly competent man and according to the German custom spent most of his life in teaching at one place, Lollar, where he taught forty years. He attended the Presbyterian Church. He married, at Gruenberg, in 1849, Elizabeth Buck, of Gruenberg, who was born at Gruenberg, 1819, and died August, 1872, aged fifty-three. They had three children: Emma, Herman and Sophia.

(III) Herman, second child and only son of Johann and Elizabeth (Buck) Rödelsperger, was born in Giessen, Herren, April 19, 1853. After completing the course of study in the high school of Giessen, from which he graduated in 1870, he kept books for a large cigar manufacturing establishment for a time. In 1873 he came to the United States, landing at New York from the steamship "Deutschland," April 19, 1873. He engaged in the sale of sewing machines for several years in different states. In 1876 he entered a village school in Hanover, New Hampshire, where he studied one term to acquire a knowledge of the English language. In 1879 he removed to Manchester, New Hampshire, where he was the representative of the Davis Sewing Machine Company for a year. The following year he became a teacher in the Manchester German School, where he taught until 1889, the last years of the time being principal of the school. He then formed a partnership with Reinhardt Hecker, under the firm name of Rödelsperger & Hecker, grocers, and carried on that business until 1890. Since 1890 Mr. Rödelsperger has conducted a concert hall in West Manchester. He is also engaged in the real estate and insurance business, and is agent for the sale of steamship tickets. He is a justice of the peace and a notary public. Mr. Rödelsperger is one of the most active and energetic among the German population of Manchester, and takes a sincere interest in promoting their welfare. He has been president of the German school board for three years past. He is president of the Turner Society and is a member of every German society in the city, in all of which he is or has been an officer. In politics he is an independent.

He was a member of the New Hampshire legislature of 1907 and now is a member of the committee on education. He married, October 10, 1887, in Manchester, Anna Winkler, who was born in Liebenstein, Austria. 1865, daughter of Johann and Elizabeth Winkler, of Liebenstein. They have six children: Emma, Bertha, Minnie, Maria, Agnes and Anna.

COIT This family is of Welsh origin and its American branch was established in Connecticut. Some of its representatives have acquired distinction as preachers, and a large number of them have been closely identified with religious work.

(I) John Coit, the immigrant, who was probably of Glamorganshire, Wales, arrived in New England between the years 1630 and 1638, going first to Salem, Massachusetts, where land was granted him the latter year, and in 1644 he removed to Gloucester. He was made a freeman in 1647; was a selectman in Gloucester in 1648, and the name of his son John appears in the records of that town at the same period. With other Gloucester residents he went in 1640 to New London, Connecticut, where he acquired land on the water front and there he

F. A. Hawkins

followed his trade, that of a ship-carpenter. The "History of New London" states that he died there August 29, 1659. He was married in Wales to Mary Gammers, or Jemmers, and she died January 2, 1676, aged eighty years. His son John, previously mentioned, remained in Gloucester. His will, made in August, 1659, provides for his son Joseph, his daughters Mary and Martha, and mentions two sons and two daughters as being "absent from him." One of these was John, and as the names of the other three do not appear in the records of Gloucester or New London, it is quite probable that they remained on the other side of the ocean.

(II) Deacon Joseph, son of John and Mary (Jemmers) Coit, was probably born in Salem, and followed the trade of a ship-carpenter in New London. In company with his brother-in-law, Hugh Mould, he engaged in building vessels, and among those launched by them were the "New London," 1666, and the "John and Hester," 1681. The "New London" made a voyage to Europe in 1689. and on her return she brought as a part of her cargo two large brass church bells with wheels, one of which was the first church bell ever used in eastern Connecticut. In 1645 Joseph Coit was elected constable, and in 1683 was appointed one of a committee to procure a minister. July 15, 1667, he married Martha Harris, of Wethersfield, daughter of Willliam and Edith Harris. He and his wife were admitted to the church at New London, April 3, 1681, and the records mention him as a deacon in 1683. He died March 27, 1704, and his wife died July 14, 1710. His estate, which was inventoried at three hundred and twelve pounds, seventeen shillings and four pence, was divided between his widow, his son John, who received a double portion; his son Joseph; the heirs of William, a deceased son; and Solomon. His other children, not mentioned in his will, were Daniel and Samuel.

(III) Rev. Joseph, second child and son of Deacon Joseph and Martha (Harris) Coit, was born in New London, April 4, 1673. He took his bachelor's degree at Harvard College in 1797, and was made a Master of Arts at the first commencement at Yale College in 1702. He was first called to the church in Norwich, Connecticut, but shortly afterward (1698) went to Plainfield, same state, where he continued to preach until 1748, in which year he was dismissed at his own request. His death occurred in Plainfield, July 1, 1750, at the age of seventy-seven years. His estate included one male and two female negro servants. September 18, 1705, he married Experience Wheeler, daughter of Isaac Wheeler, of Stonington. She died January 8, 1759, aged seventy-nine years. His children were: Elizabeth, Samuel, Joseph, Martha, Isaac, Abigail. Mary, William, Experience and Daniel.

(IV) Colonel Samuel, second child and eldest son of Rev. Joseph and Experience (Wheeler) Coit, was born at Plainfield in 1708. He settled in what was then known as the North Society of Preston, now the town of Griswold, Connecticut, and his descendants have been designated the "Preston Coits." He derived his military title from his long and honorable connection with the Connecticut militia, and in 1758 he commanded a regiment raised in Norwich and vicinity for the defense of the colonies against the threatened French and Indian invasion. This regiment served as garrison at Fort Edward for several months. For the years 1761, '65, '71, '72 and '73 he represented Preston in the general assembly; was judge of the county court. and also of a maritime court during the Revolutionary war; was in 1774 chosen moderator of a town meeting which took action relative to the "Boston Port Bill;" and was a member of the Preston committee on correspondence. In 1761 he was selected by the proprietors of Amherst, Nova Scotia, to serve upon a committee formulated for the purpose of forwarding the interests of that enterprise. Colonel Coit died in Preston, October 4, 1792. March 30, 1730, he married Sarah Spaulding, daughter of Benjamin Spaulding, of Plainfield; she died July 11, 1776, aged sixty-five years. His second wife, whom he married March 22, 1779, was Mrs. Jemima Hall. In 1742 he joined the church in Preston, to which his first wife had been admitted in 1733. His children, all of his first union, were: Benjamin, Samuel, William, Oliver, Wheeler, John, Sarah, Joseph, Isaac and Olive.

(V) William, third child and son of Colonel Samuel and Sarah (Spaulding) Coit, was born February 13, 1735. He became a sea captain and a merchant in Norwich, where he established his residence, and in 1761 he advertised for horses suitable for shipment. In 1771 he was one of the managers of a lottery. the proceeds of which were used for the construction of a bridge over the Shertucket river, and in 1778 was interested with Whitelaw and Savage in developing what is now Waterville, Vermont. He was one of an association to take action against illicit trade in 1782. In 1800 the firm of Coit, Lanman & Huntington was established and their ship, the "Three Friends," brought merchandise direct from Liverpool to Norwich. His honorable career as merchant closed November 16, 1821, and his remains were interred in the old cemetery at Norwich. His first wife, whom he married March 21, 1735, was Sarah Lathrop, who was born October 2, 1735, daughter of Ebenezer Lathrop, of Norwich. and she died February 21, 1780. On October 15, of the latter year he married for his second wife Mrs. Elizabeth Coit, widow of Joseph Coit, of Hartford. Her death occurred August 29, 1803. His children were: Abigail, William, Elisha, Sarah, Lydia, Daniel, Levi, Eliza and Lucy, all of whom were of his first union.

(VI) Levi, fourth son and seventh child of William and Sarah (Lathrop) Coit, was born in Norwich. April 24, 1770. When a young man he engaged in mercantile pursuits in New York City, and for many years was a member of the firm of Coit & Woolsey, which was one of the prominent mercantile houses of the metropolis during the early years of the last century. In his latter years he was a stock broker in Wall street. He lived to be nearly eighty years old, and died in New York City, January 6, 1850. He was married, February 5, 1794, to Lydia Howland, who was born October 3, 1773, daughter of Joseph Howland. She survived her husband but a short time, dying January 8, 1851. She was the mother of seven children, namely: Caroline. born November 11, 1794, died April 13, 1797; Edward William, born August 17, 1796, died February 27, 1798; Cornelia Ann, born September 1, 1798, died October 25, 1818; Henry A., born August 20, 1800, married Sarah Borland; Joseph H., who will be again referred to; Harriet Frances, born August 15. 1805, married Daniel W. Coit, and Thomas Thornby, born October 17, 1807, died December 30, 1809.

(VII) Joseph Howland, fifth son and third child of Levi and Lydia (Howland) Coit, was born in New York City, November 3, 1802. Late in life he decided to enter the Protestant Episcopal ministry, and was ordained a deacon by Bishop Griswold. He died in 1866. November 2, 1825, he married Harriet Jane Hand, of Abington. Vermont. The children of this union are: Henry Augustus, born January 10, 1830, now a clergyman of the Protestant Episcopal Church; Joseph Howland and James Milnor (twins), born September 11, 1831, the latter died April 3, 1833; William Noble, born December 24, 1834; Edward Woolsey, born July 26, 1837, became a merchant in Philadelphia; Levi, born June 9, 1840, sometime United States consul at Valentia, Spain; Harriet Jane, born September 26, 1842; and James Milnor, born January 31, 1844. The latter acquired a responsible position in the service of the Lake Shore and Michigan Southern railway.

ALEXANDER This surname is very common in Scotland, and the Alexanders of this sketch are without doubt descended from Scotch ancestors, who settled in Ireland in the time of the exodus of the Scotch from Argyle to that island.

(I) Randall or Randyl Alexander, with two brothers, James and John, came from the North of Ireland, and were among the first sixteen settlers of ancient Nutfield (now Londonderry), New Hampshire, Randall being one of the six grantees of the town. His farm has always been kept in the Alexander name, and the house he built on his farm, about 1720, is still in good condition, having been kept up by its successive owners. The children of Randall were: Robert, born November 14, 1720; Mary, March 5, 1722; Isabel, February 15, 1723; David, April 9, 1728; John, April 22, 1730; Randall; James; William; and Samuel, the subject of the next paragraph.

(II) Samuel, ninth and youngest child of Randall Alexander, was born in 1737, in Nutfield and died in Bow, June 25, 1835, at the age of about ninety-eight years. He moved to Bow previous to or early in 1767, and resided there the remainder of his life. He married Mary Boynton, of Londonderry, and their children included: Enoch, William, Mary and Patty.

(III) William, second son and child of Samuel and Mary (Boynton) Alexander, was born June 28, 1767, in Bow and died at Tunbridge, Vermont, December 9, 1847, in his eighty-first year. He moved to Tunbridge about 1789, and there cleared up land and was a successful farmer. He was married, February 28, 1788, in Dunbarton, to Polly Putney, who was born April 22, 1770, in that town, and died at Tunbridge, Vermont, May 4, 1860, having survived her husband more than twelve years. Their children were: David, William, Daniel, Samuel, Sally, Dorothy, Polly and Rhoda.

(IV) William (2) Alexander, second son of William (1) and Polly (Putney) Alexander, was born December 10, 1790, in Tunbridge, Vermont, and died in East Andover, New Hampshire, October 15, 1877, in his eighty-seventh year. He was a successful farmer in Tunbridge, Vermont, until the Civil war, when he retired and subsequently resided in Concord and Andover with his children. He was married September 16, 1813, at Strafford, Vermont, to Abigail Moore, who died August 30, 1814, leaving a daughter, Abigail Moore Alexander. Mr. Alexander was married (second), to Edna Putney, of Dunbarton who died in East Andover, New Hampshire July 16, 1875. Their only child William H., is the subject of the following paragraph. Mr. Alexander's daughter, Abigail M., became the wife of Henry Putney, and resided in East Andover, New Hampshire.

(V) William Henry, only son of William and Edna (Putney) Alexander, was born in Tunbridge, Vermont, November 24, 1836. He obtained his education in the common schools of New Hampshire and at several academies of note in that state. At the age of seventeen he took employment in a general store in Manchester, where he performed the duties of a clerk for two years. He next worked two or three years as a clerk in the freight office of the Concord railroad, and was then transferred to Concord, where he filled a position in the office of Joseph Gilmore, afterward governor of New Hampshire, then superintendent of the line. In 1861 he was appointed station agent of the Concord & Portsmouth railroad, at Portsmouth, which place he filled until 1865. From the latter date he was conductor of a passenger train on the Concord railroad, first between Concord and Portsmouth, and later between Concord and Boston, until 1882. He was then appointed purchasing agent for the road and filled that position until July, 1895, when he retired from the railroad service, after being continuously employed forty-two years by one company. Soon after quitting the railway service he was made manager of the Beecher Falls Furniture Company, at Beecher Falls, Vermont, which position he is now filling (1907).

Mr. Alexander comes of ancient and honorable lineage, and like many others of the stock is a companionable gentleman, a good business man and an upright and highly respected citizen. He is a member of Eureka Lodge, No. 70, Ancient Free and Accepted Masons; of Trinity Royal Arch Chapter, No. 2; of Horace Chase Council No. 4; and of Mount Horeb Commandery, Knights Templar. He married, August 30, 1878, at East Concord, Leodore E. Eastman, daughter of Samuel and Mary (Brown) Eastman (see Eastman VI), born in Hartford, Connecticut, August 11, 1847. They have two children: Harry L., teller in the Mechanicks' National Bank of Concord, and Mary E., who is a well known artist.

ALEXANDER (I) Anson Alexander, born in Massachusetts in 1803, resided in Littleton from 1847 to 1863. He was a farmer, a citizen of good repute, and was a member of the board of selectmen in 1850. He married Lucy Crouch, born in Massachusetts in 1799, daughter of John and Lucy (Willard) Crouch.

(II) Wesley Alexander was born in Swanzey, New Hampshire, January 29, 1823, and died in Penacook, New Hampshire, June 25, 1900. He resided in Littleton from 1847 to 1863, and was a scythe manufacturer by trade. He took an active part in public affairs. Originally a Whig, he became one of the original promoters of the Republican movement in his state. For more than thirty years he used his influence successfully in securing the predominance of these parties in Littleton. He was a man of integrity and good judgment, and was placed in affairs of importance by his fellow citizens. He was selectman in 1855, representative in 1858, and was also justice of the peace. He married, July 4, 1848, Sarah B. Bray, who was born May 5, 1820, and died in Lancaster January 18, 1890. The children of this marriage, all born in Littleton, were: Clara A., Edward B., Anson Colby, Fred B. and Mabel.

(III) Dr. Anson Colby Alexander, second son and third child of Wesley and Sarah B. (Bray) Alexander, was born in Littleton, October 10, 1855. He acquired his early education in the public schools, and at the New Hampton and New London academies. He began the study of medicine at Lancaster, in the offices of Drs. Daniel Lee Jones and Charles W. Rowell, and afterward matriculated in the Philadelphia School of Anatomy and Surgery, from which he graduated in 1879. The following year he received his diploma from the Hahnemann Medical College, homoeopathic, of the same city. He also graduated from the Penn Hospital. He was the only student from the New England states in many years who won the gold medal at the Hahnemann College, for superior scholarship in every department. In the spring of 1881 he began the practice of his profession at Penacook, New Hampshire, succeeding Dr. S. M. Emery, deceased, and occupying the Dr. Emery residence. His ability and success as a physician soon attracted a large practice in the village, and from the surrounding towns. In 1890 the demands of his business required more room and better accommodations, and he purchased the Mechanics' block, and fitted up a commodious set of offices in that building, and there he has remained to the present date. His bent of mind has always been toward independent and original investigation of causes and cure of disease, and to the burdens of his regular practice he has added other labors none the less onerous—the study of specific remedies for disease. Success in a much greater than the usual degree has crowned his efforts, and he has discovered a specific inhalent for catarrhal troubles, which is now manufactured by a corporation organized for its production. He has also discovered a new treatment for cancer which has recently attracted the attention of the public and likewise the profession. His practice in this specialty brought so large a number of patients for treatment that it became necessary to secure a permanent hospital for their use. In 1898 a corporation was formed which built the Alexander Sanatorium. This is a commodious, comfortable and well ventilated building, located on the Boscawen side of the Contoocook river, fitted with rooms for about thirty-five patients. An associate physician resides at the sanatorium, and this enables Dr. Alexander to devote a portion of his time to general practice. The doctor's successful treatment for cancer has led to the establishment of offices in Boston, where he is associated with Dr. Frank O. Webber. The business has grown rapidly, and the remedy is now given to the medical profession at large, and physicians in all parts of the world are now making successful use of it.

Dr. Alexander's energetic and successful use of his knowledge and skill as a physician have brought joy to many a one who sorrowed as one whose troubles could never be alleviated except by death. His successful practice and general business ability have brought him into prominence with his fellow citizens, and he is a stockholder in various organizations, has filled official positions, and is prominent in social circles. He is a member of the N. E. Gynecological and Surgical Society, of Boston, a trustee of the New Hampshire Savings Bank of Concord, and a stockholder in other organizations. He is a Republican in politics has been an active member of the school board on the Boscawen side of the river, and has served the citizens of his town as a representative in the New Hampshire legislature. He was one of the organizers of the Union Club of Penacook, and is a past president of that organization. He is a Mason of high degree, being a past master of Horace Chase Lodge, No. 72; a member of Trinity Chapter, No. 2, Royal Arch Masons; and of Mount Horeb Commandery, Knights Templar, of Concord. He is also a past grand of Dustin Island Lodge, Independent Order of Odd Fellows, as well as a member of the Knights of Pythias. He has much natural talent for music, and delights to indulge in musical exercises. He is a strong tenor singer, a violinist, and an excellent conductor of chorus singing. He is a member of the First Baptist Church, and conducts the music for all the Sunday school concerts at Easter and Christmas. He married, June 22, 1882, Fannie Goodwin, born in North Attleboro, Massachusetts. They have two children, Marion and Harold Wesley.

BABBITT The Babbitt family of this article was founded in New Hampshire soon after the Revolutionary war.

(I) Asa Babbitt was a native of England, from whence he came to America, settling in Hanover, New Hampshire, where he conducted a farm for many years, and where his death occurred. He was a man of sound judgment and exemplary habits. His wife Ruth (Harriman) Babbitt, survived him several years. Their children were: Montgomery, John, Isaac, Olive and Harmie.

(II) John, second son of Asa Babbitt, was born in Hanover, New Hampshire, April 24, 1797, died January 19, 1879, aged eighty-two years. He resided in Enfield many years, and subsequently removed to West Andover, where he resided until his death, a period of about five years. He was a successful teacher in his earlier years, and later was a farmer. His good judgment and natural capabilities made him a popular citizen, and he was elected to office by the Whigs, and later the Republicans, and was a member of the school committee and representative to the general court. He married, February 6, 1823, Salome Marden, born in Lancaster, January 26, 1805, and died November 16, 1869, in her sixty-fifth year. She was the daughter of John and Fannie (Massure) Marden, of Lancaster. Ten children were born of this marriage: 1. Alonzo, deceased. 2. Mary Ann, deceased. 3. Elvira, deceased. 4. Martha, deceased. 5. Orpha Ann, deceased; she married Stephen Place, and two children were born to them: Eva, deceased, and Ida, married Dr. Charles S. Dewey, who died January 20, 1887; Mrs. Dewey resides in Lebanon, New Hampshire. 6. Hannah, deceased. 7. Carlos Caldwell, see forward. 8. Franklin, twin of Carlos Caldwell, died December 8, 1903. 9. George Milton, an optician, resides in Syracuse, New York. 10. Melissa B., married Augustus A. Heath, of Enfield, who died December 14, 1901; she resided in Lebanon, New Hampshire, up to her death, March 16, 1907.

(III) Carlos Caldwell, seventh child and second son of John and Salome (Marden) Babbitt, was born in Hanover, New Hampshire, June 6, 1834. He received his education in the common schools of Enfield. At the age of twenty he engaged in the optical business. He located first in Lisbon, New Hampshire, remaining until 1876, when he came to Manchester, locating at 721 Beech street, where he still resides. He is one of the oldest opticians in New England, and during his fifty years' connection with the trade has had in his employ a large number of young men who, as a result of his training, have become successful business men and are now occupying prominent positions in both professional and business circles. He was made a Master Mason in Kane Lodge, No. 64, Free and Accepted Masons, of Lisbon, in 1866, and was made a Royal Arch Mason by Franklin Chapter, No. 5, of Lisbon. On his removal to Manchester, in 1876, he was demitted from these and then joined Washington Lodge, No. 61, Mt. Horeb Royal Arch Chapter, No. 11, and Adoniram Council, No. 3, and

Trinity Commandery, Knights Templar. In political faith he is a Republican. He and his wife are members of St. Paul's Methodist Episcopal Church, of which he is a trustee.

He married, June 10, 1857, Martha J. Holton, born in Landaff, December 14, 1835, daughter of Jehiel W. and Hannah S. (Eaton) Holton, and granddaughter, on the paternal side, of Bela and Patty (Olcott) Holton, and on the maternal side of Eben and Ruth (Hutchins) Eaton. Jehiel W. Holton was a merchant in Landaff with his brother, Elias O. Holton, for a number of years; later he retired and died at the home of his son-in-law, Carlos C. Babbitt. He was born August 15, 1799, died July 11, 1884. His wife also died at the home of Mr. Babbitt, April 10, 1880, aged seventy years. Mrs. Babbitt was their only child. For a few years prior to her marriage she was a successful teacher in the public schools of Lisbon. Carlos C. and Martha J. (Holton) Babbitt were the parents of one child, Charles Holton, see forward.

(IV) Dr. Charles Holton, only child of Carlos C. and Martha J. (Holton) Babbitt, was born May 25, 1869. He was prepared for college in the common schools and by a private tutor, and was a student at Harvard University one year. He then spent three years in the study of medicine in Boston, after which he entered the medical department of the University of the South at Sewanee, Tennessee from which he graduated, receiving the degree of Doctor of Medicine. He at once engaged in the profession of optician and oculist in which he has attained much success. The optical business of The Babbitt Company, Opticians (the name under which his optical business is carried on) is undoubtedly the largest in the state, exclusive of the manufacturing plant at Tilton. His residence and main office is in Nashua, with branches in Lowell, Manchester and other cities. He is a member of St. Paul's Methodist Episcopal Church Manchester. He is a Mason, holding membership in Washington Lodge, No. 51; Mt. Horeb Royal Arch Chapter, No. 11, Adoniram Council, No. 3, Trinity Commandery, Knights Templar, all of Manchester; also the various Scottish Rite Masonic bodies, including the New Hampshire Consistory thirty-second degree of Nashua; and Bektash Temple, Mystic Shrine of Concord, New Hampshire.

Dr. Babbitt married, May 25, 1903, Ada E. Bumpus, daughter of Abel M. and Eliza V. (Gordon) Bumpus, of Nashua. She was educated in the common schools of Vienna, Maine, attending until twelve years of age, when she removed to Nashua, New Hampshire, where she attended the public schools, graduating from the high and later from the training school for teachers. She began at once teaching in the schools of Nashua and continued until her marriage, a period of eight years. She is a member of the Pilgrim Congregational Church, and of the Nashaway Woman's Club.

HUSSEY This name seems to be fairly well authenticated as an ancient one, among the first in New England. John Hussey of Dorking, in the county of Surrey, England, was married December 5, 1593, to Mary Wood, or Woodin. Circumstances indicate that they were people of good standing. He died in England, and the records show that he had children, John (died young), Christopher and one or more daughters. Among the grantees of Hampton, New Hampshire, were "Christo" Hussey and a widow, Mary Hussey, the latter presumed to have been the widow of John Hussey of Dorking. It is believed that Christopher was the son of Mary Hussey. They resided on opposite sides of the meeting house green in Hampton, the five-acre house lot of the widow being about the present site of the town house. She died June 16, 1660. Ten years previously seats in the meeting house were assigned to "ould mistris husse and her dafter husse." No record of such daughter appears, and it is presumed that this record refers to the wife or daughter of Mary Hussey's son.

(I) Christopher Hussey, captain and deacon, probably son of John and Mary Hussey of Dorking, was born in 1595-6. The son of John of Dorking was baptized February 18, 1599. He was probably among the parishoners of Rev. Stephen Bachiler, and went to Holland with others to avoid religious persecution. It was only upon his promise to emigrate to America that Rev. Bachiler consented to give his daughter to Hussey. The marriage took place in England, either before or after the exodus to Holland. Christopher Hussey and his wife Theodate sailed in the "William and Francis" from Southampton sometime in May, 1730, and arrived at Charlestown, Massachusetts, about July 23. They took up their home in Saugus (Lynn), and were joined two years later by Rev. Bachiler and others. (See Batchelder). Christopher Hussey was later a prominent man in Newbury, Massachusetts. It is presumable that widow Mary Hussey accompanied her son on his voyage to America, but she may have come later with other Puritans. As before related, Christopher Hussey was a grantee of Hampton, with Bachelor and many others. He was the first deacon of the church, and otherwise an influential man, a captain in the militia, town clerk, selectman and representative. When New Hampshire was made a royal province he was one of the commissioners named in the charter. In 1650 he sold all his property in the present Hampton, and soon moved to the "Falls Side" (Hampton Falls). He was one of the purchasers of Nantucket in 1659, and subsequently commanded an ocean vessel. It is supposed that the record of death (October 20, 1649) refers to his wife Theodate, but is may have been their daughter, as her death appears on the record at the same date. The wife was dead December 9, 1658, on which day Christopher Hussey was married to Ann, widow of Jeffrey Mingay. She died June 24, 1680, and was survived nearly six years by her husband, who passed away March 6, 1686, being about ninety years old. His children were: Stephen, Joseph, John, Mary, Theodate and Huldah. John was the second white child born in Lynn, and the first baptized in America by Rev. Stephen Bachilor.

(II) Stephen, eldest child of Christopher and Theodate (Bachiler) Hussey, was born about 1632, and settled in Nantucket, Massachusetts, where he died April 2, 1718. He was married in Nantucket, October 8, 1676, to Martha Bunker, who was born November 11, 1656, and died September 21, 1744, a daughter of George and Jane (Godfrey) Bunker and granddaughter of William Bunker. Before his marriage Stephen Hussey lived at Barbadoes, and was possessed of considerable property when he settled in Nantucket. He was a member of the Society of Friends, and was representative to the general court at one time. His children were: Puella, Abigail, Sylvanus, Bachelor, Daniel, Mary, George and Theodate.

(III) Bachelor, second son of Stephen and Martha (Bunker) Hussey, was born February 18, 1685, in Nantucket, where he lived many years, settling later in Biddeford, Maine. He was probably engaged in the coasting or West India trade. He was married,

C. H. Babbitt

October 11, 1704, to Abigail Halle, the record appearing in Hampton, with the births of four children, namely: Christopher, Mary, Jedidah (daughter) and John. Others were born to them in Nantucket or Biddeford.

(IV) Stephen, son of Bachelor and Abigail (Hall) Hussey, was born about 1715, and died May 8, 1770, in Berwick. He married Eunice Baxter, who died April 9, 1769. Their children were: Daniel, Batchelor, William, Margaret, Deborah, Hepzibah, Phebe, Stephen, Ruth, Paul, Miriam and Walter, the last three born in Berwick, all the others in Biddeford.

(V) Batchelor, second son of Stephen and Eunice (Baxter) Hussey, was born June 1, 1745, in Biddeford, and resided in Berwick, where he died February 15, 1794. He was married in Berwick, December 12, 1767, to Sarah Hanson, daughter of Isaac and Sarah Hanson of that town. Their children were: Sylvanus, Isaac, Peter, James, Huldah, Batchelor, Daniel and Stephen.

(V) Isaac, second son of Batchelor and Sarah (Hanson) Hussey, was born February 12, 1772, in Berwick, and resided some years in Sanford, Maine, whence he removed to Acton, Maine, where he died aged seventy-eight years. His entire life was devoted to farming. He married Lydia Merrill, by whom he had eight children: Daniel, who died in the Civil war; Mary Ann; Eliza, who married Sewell Cowell; Amanda, who married James Caswell; Asa A., who lives in South Boston; Isaac, who is mentioned below; Eunice, wife of William S. Knox of Lawrence, Massachusetts; and Charles, who is of South Boston.

(VI) Isaac (2), sixth child and third son of Isaac (1) and Lydia (Merrill) Hussey, was born in Sanford, Maine, 1841. He accompanied his parents in their removal to Acton, and has ever since resided there where he is engaged in farming. For some years he was overseer of the Acton town farm. He married Harriet Miller, who was born April 18, 1842, daughter of Woodman and Nancy Miller of Acton, and died August 9, 1907. They have seven children: Orrin N., mentioned below; Cora B., who married Charles E. Ross, of Eastport, Maine; Annie, who married (first), Fred Chisholm, and (second), Granville Varney; Amanda, who married Charles I. Smith; Nettie May, wife of Charles Furbush, of Somersworth, New Hampshire; Nina, who married Gardner G. Lord of Acton, Maine; and Hattie.

(VII) Orrin Newton, eldest child of Isaac (2) and Harriet (Miller) Hussey, was born in Acton, February 22, 1866. He was educated in the common schools of Acton and North Shapleigh. After leaving school he worked in the factories of Burleigh and Usher, learned the art of shoe cutting, worked in different factories as inspector of uppers, and finally had charge of a cutting room in Lynn, Massachusetts. In September, 1899, he bought the store fixtures of Levi Pinkham, of Farmington, New Hampshire, and put in a new stock of shoes, and has since carried on a successful business. He is financially sound, and is one of the trustees of the Farmington Savings Bank. He is a staunch Republican, has been treasurer of the precinct for some years; was secretary of the Strafford County Republican Convention in the fall of 1906, and the same year was nominated for the legislature for Farmington, and at the election following received the largest vote of any candidate for office in Farmington in that year. He served in the legislative session of 1907 and was a member of the Committee on Banks. He is a member and junior warden of Fraternal Lodge, No. 71, Free and Accepted Masons, of Farmington; of Olive Branch Lodge, No. 28, Independent Order of Odd Fellows, and also the Encampment, both of South Berwick, Maine. He is prelate of Harmony Lodge, No. 11, Knights of Pythias, of Farmington, and is a member and warden of the Free Baptist Church of Farmington. He married, February 10, 1893, at Lyman, Maine, Lucy A. Goodwin, of that place, daughter of Jacob and Rhoda (Smith) Goodwin.

(Second Family.)

HUSSEY Captain Joseph Hussey, a brother of Christopher, was of Hampton, which he represented in the legislature in 1672. Robert Hussey was taxed in Dover in 1659. Other settlers of this name were in New England at an early date. Some of the above named were of kin, but the records fail to show what if any relation any of them bore to Richard Hussey, the first known ancestor of the following line.

(I) Richard Hussey, with his wife Jane, settled in Dover, New Hampshire, about 1690. June 20, 1696, he sells for a consideration of fifty pounds to Leonard Weeks, of Portsmouth, his interest in thirty acres of upland adjoining the Great Bay in Dover. He is called in the deed "a weaver." February 25, 1710, he sells to Benjamin Weymouth for thirteen pounds a tract of land situated at a garrison called Sligoe (now Somersworth), containing thirty acres, bounded by land of said Weymouth, by land of Joseph Roberts, and southward by the lot called Cowell's. He had a grant of land in the Great Bay below the present city of Dover. He died previous to August 21, 1733, at which time his son Richard was appointed administrator of Jane Hussey's estate. The children of Richard and Jane Hussey were: Richard, Job, Robert, Mary, Joseph, Elizabeth, Eleanor, Abigail, Jane, William, Margaret and Benjamin.

(II) William, tenth child and fifth son of Richard and Jane Hussey, was born March 24, 1711. He was a "Friend," and in a deed is called "a taylor," but in his will he describes himself as "a husbandman." He died January 22, 1778. His will dated "27th of 7th Month of 1777," was probated the second Wednesday of February, 1778. He mentions his wife, Hannah, sons Paul, William, Timothy, and Stephen, and daughters Mercy Hussey, Mary Fry and Abigail Varney. He married, near 1730, Hannah Robinson, who was born November 21, 1707, and died April 20, 1793, daughter of Timothy and Mary (Roberts) Robinson. Mary Robinson was the daughter of John and Abigail (Nutter) Roberts, and Abigail Nutter was the daughter of Hatevil and Anne Nutter. (See Nutter).

(III) Paul, son of William and Hannah (Robinson) Hussey, was born in 1730, and died November 22, 1796. He married as early as 1760, Mary, daughter of Joseph and Peniel (Bean) Hall. Joseph Hall and Peniel Bean were married in Dover, December 19, 1731. He was the son of Ralph and Mary (Chesley) Hall. Ralph Hall and Mary Chesley were married in Dover, May 26, 1701. Mary (Hall) Hussey died in 1813. The children of Paul Hussey were: Huldah, Daniel, Elijah and Micajah.

(IV) Daniel, eldest son and second child of Paul and Mary (Hall) Hussey, was born September 22, 1750. He married Margaret Garland, of Lebanon, Maine, who was born September 3, 1768. Their children were: Ezekiel, Hannah, Mary, Jonathan, David, Huldah, Olive, Elijah, Paul and Joan or Johanna. Ezekiel, born 1787, married, December 7, 1815, Mercy Horn, of Rochester, and they had: Jane, Daniel and Oliver P. Jonathan, born April 20, 1793, married (first), November 1, 1819, Polly Hayes, who was born August 23, 1787, and died January 15, 1849; (second) August 29, 1849, Joan Flagg. He died January 25, 1863. His children were: Mary, Charles, Elijah M., Rosina and Jonathan Jackson. Huldah, born April 25, 1797, married, March 21, 1824, Benjamin E. Page, of Rochester, and died August 20, 1879. Olive, born November 5, 1799, married, March 27, 1831, Benjamin, son of William and Alice Coleman Furber. She died at Somersworth, October 4, 1871. Elijah, born April 28, 1801, married a Miss Moore, and had Charles, Luther, Augustina and Elvira.

(V) Paul, ninth child and fifth son of Daniel and Margaret (Garland) Hussey, was born in Rochester, May 2, 1803, and died October 28, 1871. He was a farmer and resided in Rochester. He married, March 5, 1828, Nancy Colbath, who was born November 6, 1800, and died February 9, 1872. Their children were: Joanna, George Dame, Hannah, Daniel, Martha Frances, Paul Freeman, Louis McDuffee, Walter Scott and Charles Burney. Joanna was born December 17, 1828, and died October, 1876. George Dame, born May 14, 1831, married, March 8, 1859, Mary Jane Foss, who was born September 6, 1839, and died September 18, 1886. They had eight children: Clara, Laura Frances, Mabel Eldorado, George, Charles Lincoln, Annie Mary, Albert Warren and Frank. Hannah, born April 30, 1832, married, November 15, 1848, George Allison, of Grutland, Yorkshire, England. Daniel, born May 23, 1833 married, April 22, 1855, Mary Frances Evans, of Rochester, born March 23, 1833. They had two children: Edward H. and Frank Evans. Martha Frances, born January 20, 1835, married, February 12, 1862, Joseph Warren Colbath, of Exeter. She died December 10, 1906. Paul Freeman, born in Rochester, April 6, 1836, married, January 1, 1878, Mary Elizabeth Kimball. He died December 1, 1893, leaving one child, Freeman Garfield. Louis McDuffee is mentioned below. Walter Scott, born April 6, 1840, married (first), January 23, 1864, Emily Pinkham, who died May 13, 1891; and (second), November 27, 1893, Addie F. Morrill, born April 19, 1869. They had three children: Cora Edith, Maud E., and Walter Lewis. Charles Burney, born November 19, 1844, was a member of Company H, Ninth Regiment, New Hampshire Volunteer Infantry, was wounded and taken prisoner at the battle of Spottsylvania Court house and died in a Confederate prison at Richmond, Virginia, May 31, 1864.

(VI) Captain Louis McDuffee, seventh child and fourth son of Paul and Nancy (Colbath) Hussey, was born in Rochester, November 6, 1837. He enlisted in Company B, First Regiment, New Hampshire Volunteer Infantry, at the beginning of the Civil war, being the second soldier enlisted from the town of Rochester. He was mustered in May 2, 1861, and served until August 9, 1861, when he was mustered out. He re-enlisted in Company A, Fourth Regiment, New Hampshire Volunteers, and was made sergeant. He was mustered in September 18, 1861, re-enlisted January 1, 1864, and was mustered out August 23, 1865. Battles engaged in were: Pocataligc, Morris Island, Seige of Wayne, Seige of Sumter, Bermuda Hundred, Drury's Bluff, Cold Harbor, Hatcher's Run, Seige of Petersburg. "The Mine," New Market Heights, Fort Fisher. He was promoted to first lieutenant of Company A, November 9, 1864, and captain of Company C, Fourth Regiment, February 17, 1865 He was employed in the shoe factories of Rochester from the time of his return from the army until he retired. He was the first marshall of Rochester after it became a city, and served in that important office one year. He is a member of Humane Lodge, Free and Accepted Masons; Temple Chapter, Royal Arch Mason. He married, October 22, 1896, Harriet E. Dame, who was born in Rochester, 1843, and died January 4, 1902. She was a daughter of Levi and Olive (Garland) Dame, of Rochester.

(I) John Hussey lived and died in Lebanon, Maine. He married Joyce Clark, by whom he had seven children: John, Richard, Reuben, Stephen, Eliza, Mary and Lottie.

(II) Richard, second son of John and Joyce (Clark) Hussey, was born February 16, 1783, and died February 1, 1868, aged eighty-five years. He was a farmer in Acton, Maine, and died in that town. He married Alice Thompson, who was born January 30, 1792, in Shapleigh, Maine, and died January 9, 1861. Seven children were born of this union: John, Miles, Harriet, Joyce, Miriam, Ann M. and Alexander T.

(III) John, eldest child of Richard and Alice (Thompson) Hussey, was born in Acton, May 18, 1810, and died September 30, 1892. When a young man he removed to Somersworth, New Hampshire, learned the carpenter's trade, and was a lifelong carpenter and builder. He married Mary Locke, who was born August 31, 1812, and died March 31, 1901, daughter of Simon and Oliver (Chadbourne) Locke, of Barrington, New Hampshire. Nine children were born to them: Olive, Howard E., Mary E., John S., Ann M., Harriet, Charles M., Freeman F. and Etta G. Olive was born in 1836, and died at the age of twenty-one. Howard E., resided in Somersworth. Mary E., married Gilman C. Robinson, and resided in South Exeter, Maine. John lived in Somersworth. Ann M. married Perkins F. Mott. Harriet G., died in infancy. Charles M., of Somersworth. Freeman is mentioned below. Etta G., married Charles Hodgdon, and lives in Somersworth.

(IV) Freeman Alexander, eighth child and fourth son of John and Mary (Locke) Hussey, was born in Somersworth, January 23, 1852. When about nineteen years old he began to learn the baker's trade with James A. Locke, with whom he remained until May 1879, and then bought out his employer and carried on the business until 1902, when he retired. This was one of the largest and best equipped bakeries in Strafford county, and employed four or five men the greater part of the time. Having a thorough practical knowledge of the business, Mr. Hussey carried it on with success and made money which he invested in other paying enterprises. He has been a director in the Somersworth National Bank, and a trustee in the Somersworth Savings Bank for some years. His political faith is staunchly Republican. and his party has placed him in various offices, the duties of which he has acceptably discharged. In 1887 and 1888 he was a member of the board of selectmen. After the incorporation of the city he was elected alderman and served three terms as a member from Ward Three. In 1900 he was elected representative to the general court, and served at the following session. He is a member of Libanus Lodge, No. 49, Free and Accepted Masons; Edwards Royal Arch Chapter, No. 21; and St. Paul Commandery, Knights Templar; also of Washington Lodge, No. 4, Independent Order of Odd Fellows, of which he is a past grand; and of Great Falls Encampment, No. 15. He and Mrs. Hussey are members of the Free Baptist Church, in which he is a chief warden.

He married, October 23, 1878, Celia A. E. Fall, of Somersworth, who was born July 17, 1855, daughter of Noah L. and Amanda (James) Fall. Three children have been born to them: Leona E., born May 5, 1880, married, May 25, 1903, Jordan S. Savithes, of Lowell, Massachusetts, and has one child, Edith Dorothea, born June 17, 1904; Edith Amanda, born July 17, 1882; Kirke Herbert, born March 28, 1884, died young.

HUSSEY The Husseys of the following sketch are probably of the descendants of John Hussey, of Dorking, England, and of his son, Christopher Hussey, deacon and captain, who is supposed to have landed in Charlestown, Massachusetts, July 23, 1630.

(I) Micajah Hussey was a resident of Farmington in the latter part of the eighteenth century. He married Olive Hanson.

(II) Silas Hussey, son of Micajah Hussey, was born in Farmington, in 1795, and died in 1869 in Rochester, where his entire life had been spent in tilling the soil successfully. He married Lucy Varney, and their children were: Maria, Stephen, George, John, Silas, Sarah E., Daniel and James, twins; Hannah A., James, Oliver W.

(III) Silas (2), fifth child of Silas (1) and Lucy (Varney) Hussey, was born in Rochester, New Hampshire, January 24, 1828. He grew up on his father's farm, and was educated in the common schools. When a young man he went to Rockport, Massachusetts, and learned the art of cutting granite. In 1849 he heard of Marshall's discovery of gold in Sutton's Millrace in California, and at once decided to go to the newly discovered Eldorado. So he made his way by the Cape Horn route to the land of gold, starting November, 1849, and reaching San Francisco, May, 1850 after spending one hundred and seventy-seven days on the route. He at once went to the mines at Middle Fork, American river, and there until 1853 was working at placer mining. In 1863 he returned to California via the Isthmus route, and was fifteen months engaged in contracting on the Central Pacific railroad. In these four years he made more money than he could have made in New Hampshire, but saved only enough to amount to fair wages. Soon after his return to Rochester he engaged in mercantile business for a short time, and then returned to the granite business and contracting which he has followed most of his life. Previous to 1895 he had put in the foundations for the principal business blocks in Rochester. In 1881 he built a twin arch bridge across the Cocheco, in the main street of Rochester, and in 1883 erected the monument to the soldiers of the Civil war in the park of that place. For the first of these contracts he received $13,800, and for the other $2,500. In 1869 he represented Rochester in the legislature, being elected on the Republican ticket. He has also served as police judge and deputy sheriff. For some years he was chairman of the town and county Deocratic committee and a member of the state Democratic committee. For forty-six years justice of the peace, and for ten years state justice. Since 1896 he has been independent in policies. He married April 18, 1854, Rosanna A. Hussey, who was born in Rochester, daughter of Jonathan and Mary (Hayes) Hussey. Seven children were born to them: Mary, 1856, died 1866. Lucy, 1858, died young. Frank, mentioned below. George, 1862, died young. Grace, died young. Angie, 1870, married Edward Leighton, and died in 1891. Mabel, 1871, married A. L. Marshall, of Newport, Rhode Island.

(IV) Frank, only living son of Silas (2) and Rosanna A. (Hussey) Hussey, was born in Rochester, in 1860, and educated in the common schools of that town. For some years he was engaged by his father as overseer in his business. In 1894 he entered the employ of the Swift Packing Company, and in 1897 was made manager of that company's business at Rochester, and still holds the place. In politics he is an independent. During the year of 1898 and 1899 he was a member of the Rochester police force. In 1906 he was elected to a seat in the common council on the Republican ticket. He is a member of Dover Lodge, Benevolent Protective Order of Elks, and of the Ancient Order of United Workmen, of Rochester. He married (first), Luella Wellman; one child was born of this union, Mildred, born 1881, now the wife of Frank Gleason, of Haverhill, Massachusetts. He was married (second), October 16, 1892, Teresa Burger, who was born in Roxbury, Massachusetts, 1864, daughter of Anton and Elizabeth (Bowen) Burger, of Roxbury. They had two children: Ruth, born 1895, and Silas F., born 1899.

(I) Burleigh Hussey was born, lived and died in Dover, where he was a farmer. He married a Miss Watson, and they had five children: Charles Paul, Hoag, Burleigh, John and George.

(II) Charles Paul, eldest son of Burleeigh Hussey, was born in Dover, November 14, 1830, and died in Rochester, August 13, 1894. About 1848 he settled in Rochester, where he was foreman in the woolen mills for some years. He was also foreman in a shoe factory in Haverhill for some time. In 1878 he bought a farm of Silas Hussey, of Rochester, and lived upon it till his death. In politics he was a Republican. He was a member of Montolina Lodge, No. 18, Independent Order of Odd Fellows. He married, 1848, Caroline Watson, who was born September 16, 1828. They had five children: Burleigh, Charles P., Carrie, Minnie, and Jay D., whose sketch next follows.

(III) Jay Dow, youngest child and third son of Charles P. and Caroline (Watson) Hussey, was born in Rochester, August 15, 1868. He graduated from the Rochester high school in the class of 1884, and then entered the employ of the Boston & Maine Railroad Company as a telegraph operator at Rochester. After a year service in that capacity he was sent to Portsmouth, where he was cashier in the freight department of the road for eight years. From that time till the present he has been ticket agent of the union depot of this road at Rochester. In politics he is a Republican. In 1897-98-99, he was a member of the city council of Rochester. He has been active in this party, and has been a delegate to three state conventions and chairman of his ward committee for a number of years. He was the first chief telegrapher of the Order of Railway Telegraphers in Council No. 65, and a member of the Boston & Maine Agents Association, Council No. 8 of the Boston & Maine Relief Association, the Order of United American Mechanics of Portsmouth, and Lodge No. 184, Benevolent Protective Order of Elks, of Dover. He married, January 4, 1887, Maud Cushman, who was born September 15, 1872, daughter of Zebediah and Augusta L. (Herrick) Cushman, of Kennebunk, Maine. They have two children: Maud Frances and Minnie Caroline.

WASON In the tide of immigration that set into the colony of New Hampshire from Ireland about two centuries ago, came the ancestor of the Wasons. Like the great majority of settlers from that island, the immigrant

Wason came to the wilderness of a new country to bear the hardships and privations and enjoy the freedom and advantages of a land in a state of almost primitive nature. He proved his good qualities as a pioneer, was an enterprising and respected citizen, and became the ancestor of men who today are among the leading citizens of the state.

(I) James Wason, a native of the parish of Ballymena, county Antrim, Ireland, was born in 1711. When a young man he removed to Portsmouth, New Hampshire, and subsequently to Nottingham, now Hudson, where he lived until his death, August 22, 1799, aged eighty-eight. He married at Portsmouth, New Hampshire, November 30, 1736, Hannah Caldwell, also a native of Ballymena. She died April 6, 1786, at the age of eighty years.

(II) Lieutenant Thomas, son of James and Hannah (Caldwell) Wason, born in Hudson, December 26, 1748, died November 18, 1832. He married at Londonderry, December 1, 1772, Mary Boyd, born May 27, 1749, died October 20, 1832, daughter of Robert Boyd, of Londonderry. She was a granddaughter of Robert Boyd, Sr., who with his wife, whose maiden name was Morrison, emigrated from Ireland to New England about the year 1720 and settled in Londonderry.

(III) Robert, son of Lieutenant Thomas and Mary (Boyd) Wason, was born in Nottingham West, now Hudson, June 14, 1781. He went to New Boston, April, 1803, to live with Robert Boyd, his uncle, who settled on lot No. 30, near Joe English hill, "being advanced in years." Robert Wason inherited his uncle's farm and resided upon it for the remainder of his life. He took an active part in public affairs and served in various offices. He united with the Presbyterian Church in 1815, and a few years afterwards was elected elder, which office he held until his death. Deacon Wason was a man of great energy, and entered with zeal upon every enterprise adopted to benefit the church or the community, so that he was a "doer of the word" as well as a hearer, and his death, August 7, 1844, aged sixty-three, was greatly lamented and the loss of his influence seriously felt. He was married, December 2, 1808, by Rev. Mr. Bruce, to Nancy, daughter of John Batchelder, of Mount Vernon. She was born October 13, 1789, died July 28, 1863, aged seventy-four, having survived her husband nineteen years. She was a faithful mother, and a woman of many christian virtues. Children of Robert and Nancy Wason were: 1. Elbridge, see forward. 2. Louisa. 3. Hiram W., born December 18, 1814, graduated at Amherst, 1838, and later from Andover Theological Seminary, and then settled at Vevay, Indiana. 4. Nancy. 5. Mary. 6. Robert Boyd, see forward. 7. Adeline. 8. Caroline. 9. George Austin, see forward

(IV) Elbridge, eldest son of Deacon Robert and Nancy (Batchelder) Wason, was born in New Boston, September 26, 1809, reared in that village and educated in New Boston and at Pinkerton Academy, Derry, New Hampshire. He came to Boston, Massachusetts, March 5, 1832, and entered the employ of Pierce & Gardner, where he remained in the position of clerk until September 1, 1837, when he formed a partnership with Henry Pierce, which continued uninterruptedly until his death, August 19, 1887, a period of fifty years. He was one of the oldest and best known business men of Boston, upright and honorable in all his dealings, respected by all who knew him. He was a member of the Masons, in which organization he held office at different times. He married (first), April 24, 1851, Mary Stickney, born June 30, 1809, died August 15, 1863. Married (second), May 17, 1865, Mary Isabella Chase, born March 30, 1835, daughter of the Hon. Leonard Chase, of Milford, New Hampshire. Two children were born of this marriage: Mary Isabella, born January 11, 1867, married, June 4, 1890, Jesse S. Wiley, of Brookline, Massachusetts. Leonard Chase, born August 5, 1868, married, October 8, 1896, Harriet C. Willis, of Boston.

(IV) Robert Boyd, sixth child and third son of Robert and Nancy (Batchelder) Wason, was born in New Boston, New Hampshire, July 13, 1820. He was educated in the common schools and fitted for college in the New Ipswich and Pembroke academies, and taught school two winter terms, 1840 and 1841, in Amherst and Merrimack, New Hampshire. In June, 1841, he went to Boston and entered the employ of Wason, Pierce & Company, wholesale grocers and West India importers, a firm of which his brother, Elbridge Wason, one of the partners, had organized in September, 1837. After a term of service of about seven years as an employe, Robert B. Wason was admitted as a member of the firm, which on the death of Mr. Pierce became Wason & Company. The business has been prosperous, and now Mr. Wason, at the age of eighty-seven, after sixty-six years of mercantile life, fifty-nine of which he has been an active member of the firm, finds himself senior member of the concern, and in the enjoyment of good health, vigorous and vivacious for one of his age, and still able to look after business affairs with an alertness not possessed by many of his juniors by a quarter of a century. He is a Republican, and a member of the General Theological Library for many years.

(IV) George Austin Wason, youngest of the nine children of Deacon Robert and Nancy (Batchelder) Wason, was born in New Boston, September 17, 1831. His education was obtained in the common schools. He inherited the ancestral estate which now contains four hundred and seventy-five acres, and devoted his life to the pursuit of agriculture. He was engaged in general farming, but made a specialty of raising thoroughbred Devon cattle, in which he attained gratifying success. He lived on the farm until 1885, when he removed to Nashua and resided there until his death, June 21, 1906, aged seventy-one. He kept the farm and managed it until 1903. He was a member of that class of New England farmers who have elevated agriculture to the dignity of a science. His interest in this industry was a more than ordinary depth, and his efforts for the improvement of stock resulted in much gain not only for himself but to farmers all over New England. He was a member of all the leading agricultural societies of his vicinity and of the state. He became interested in the grange during the early years of the organization in this state, and was a charter member of Joe English Grange of New Boston, and served for years as its master. For four years he was master of the state grange, and at the time of his death was the oldest living past master of that institution. To his work the present standing of the order in this state is due to a considerable extent. He filled the office of president of the Hillsborough Agricultural Society, and president of the Piscataqua Valley Fair Association. For over twenty years he was trustee of the New Hampshire College of Agriculture and Mechanic Arts at Hanover and Durham, and served as president of the board for over seven years, being forced to resign owing to ill health in 1904. He was the first Republican moderator in the town of New Boston, in which town he maintained his legal residence and voted up to the time of his death.

Robert Bagnell

Wason cam
bear the har
dom and ad
primitive na
pioneer, was
and became
among the l
(I) Jam
Ballymena, c
When a youn
Hampshire,
Hudson, whe
1799, aged ei
New Hampsh
well, also a n
1786, at the a
(II) Lie
Hannah (Cal
cember 26, 17
ried at Londo
born May 27,
of Robert Boy
daughter of R
whose maiden
Ireland to New
tled in Londo
(III) Robe
Mary (Boyd)
now Hudson, J
ton, April, 1803
who settled on
"being advance
his uncle's far
mainder of his
public affairs an
with the Presb
years afterward
held until his de
great energy, a
enterprise adopt
community, so th
well as a hearer,
sixty-three, was
his influence seri
cember 2, 1808, b
ter of John Batc
born October 13
enty-four, havin
years. She was
many christian
Nancy Wason
Louisa. 3. Hira
uated at Amh
Theological Se
diana. 4. Nan
ward. 7. Ad
see forward
(IV) Elbri
Nancy (Bat
Boston, Sept
and educate
Academy, D
ton, Massac
employ of
in the positi
he formed
continued
19, 1887, a
the oldest
upright an
by all wh
Masons, ir
ferent tim
Mary Stickney, born

Robert Boyd Wason

Few men were better known than he throughout the county and state. He was county commissioner of Hillsborough county six years, was representative from New Boston in 1883-95, and state senator in 1891-93. He was instrumental in securing the charter of the New Boston railroad, and was its first president, serving until his death. He was a man of upright character, honest in all his dealings, prompt to keep his word, kind and sympathetic by nature, a member of the best class of manhood this or any other state may produce. His interest in public affairs was such that he was many times placed by his fellow citizens in positions of trust and honor, and always sustained with credit the duties they entailed, hiwever great their magnitude. George A. Wason married, September 17, 1863, Clara Louisa Hills, born in New Boston, October 15, 1843, daughter of Sidney and Louisa (Trull) Hills. Three children were born to them: Edward Hills, see forward; George B. and Robert S., of Boston.

(V) Edward Hills, eldest son of George A. and Clara Louisa (Hills) Wason, was born in New Boston, September 2, 1865. He acquired his education in the public schools, at Francestown Academy, and at the New Hampshire College of Agriculture and Mechanic Arts, from which he was graduated with the degree of Bachelor of Science in the class of 1886. He subsequently read law in the office of George B. French, of Nashua, and while reading his course taught as principal several terms in the Main street evening school. He attended lectures at the Boston University School of Law, from which he graduated in the class of 1890, with the degree of Bachelor of Laws. In March of the same year he was admitted to the New Hampshire bar, and at once opened an office in Nashua and began a successful practice. Later he became associated professionally with George F. Jackman under the firm name of Wason & Jackman.

Mr. Wason has shown a decided aptitude for politics ever since he attained his majority, and has already filled various offices in the city of Nashua and in the state. In 1887 he was elected sergeant at arms of the New Hampshire senate, and in 1889 was re-elected to the same position. In 1891 he was chosen assistant clerk of the senate and returned to the same position in 1893. Two years later he was elected clerk of the same body, a high testimonial of his fidelity and ability as a public officer. In 1891 he was elected a member of the Nashua board of education, and in January, 1895, in recognition of his services, his associates elected him president of that body. In 1894 he was elected city solicitor, and re-elected the following year; in 1897 he was elected to the common council, and served as president of that body two years; in 1898 was member of the legislature; in 1902 member of constitutional convention; in September, 1902, was elected county solicitor, and in 1904 was re-nominated and re-elected. In 1906 he was elected president of the Citizens' Institution for Savings, and trustee of the New Hampshire College of Agriculture and Mechanic Arts. He is an admirer of horses, and for some years has been treasurer of the Nashua Driving Park Association. Mr. Wason is a leading citizen and business man of Nashua, and has made an enviable record in the discharge of the duties of the various positions he has filled. He is a member of Rising Sun Lodge, Ancient Free and Accepted Masons, of which he is a past master; Meridian Sun Royal Chapter; Israel Hunt Council; Saint George Commandery; Knights Templar; Edward A. Raymond Consistory; Aleppo Temple of Boston; Nashua Lodge, Knights of Pythias; Nashua Lodge, Benevolent and Protective Order of Elks, of which he was elected exalted ruler in 1903.

(V) George Butler, son of George A. and Clara L. Wason, was born in New Boston, April 20, 1869. After graduating from the Nashua high school, he went to Boston, 1889, and entered the employ of the firm of Wason & Company, of which his uncle, Robert B. Wason, is a senior member. After serving five years as a clerk, he became a member of the company in 1894. He is vice president of the Boston Wholesale Grocers' Association, a director of the new England Wholesale Grocers' Association, from 1903 to 1906 was a director of the Boston Chamber of Commerce, is president of the Liberty Trust Company, of Boston, and member of Mount Olivet Lodge of Free Masons. In politics he affiliates with the Republicans. He married, April 20, 1895, Lillian Maude Fletcher, born in 1869, daughter of Joseph and Bertha Fletcher, of South Orange, New Jersey. Their children are: George Fletcher and Richard Austin.

(V) Robert S., son of George A. and Clara L. Wason, was born in New Boston, December 10, 1871. He attended the Nashua high school, Berkley School of Boston, and Massachusetts Institute of Technology, graduating from the latter institution June 9, 1906. He began his business career as clerk in the firm of Wason & Company, and continued in that capacity until admitted to membership in 1898, the firm then consisting of Robert Boyd Wason, his uncle, George Butler Wason, his brother, and himself. Mr. Wason is a Republican in politics, member of various college fraternities, and was president of National convention of Sigma Alpha Epsilon Fraternity held at Washington, D. C., 1895. He married, January 28, 1903, Estelle Sperling, daughter of Ellis Joseph, of New York City.

DURRELL This family is descended from ancestors who were pioneers in the settlement of New Hampshire.

(I) Colonel Nicholas Durrell was born in Gilmanton, in 1800, and died there in 1841. He married Sophronia Pulsipher. Their children were: Mary Ann, who married John G. Sawyer; Exalia, who married Abram Tilton; Caroline; Emeline, who married Hiram Allen; John S., who married Mary A. Kelley, and Aaron.

(II) John S., fifth child and the elder of two sons of Colonel Nicholas and Sophronia (Pulsipher) Durrell, was born in Gilmanton, and died in 1859. He married Mary A. Kelley. They were the parents of six children: Edwin N., born October 14, 1841, died, 1901, married Julia Snell; Ellen, born, 1844, is not married; George A., married Addie Woodman, and they have two children—Carl and Harry; Emma E., married Charles H. Classen; John F., married Emma Phillips, and they have four children—Stella H., Josephine, Pauline and Leslie; Amelia, married Fred S. Phillips, and has two sons—Leon and Burton D.; Edwin N., married Julia Snell; two children were born to them—Mamie Josephine and Virgil T., both of whom died young.

CLOW This family of which two generations have been born in America, is descended from an ancestor who resided in a county of England from which many early New

England settlers came when religious troubles forced them to the colonies. As in the case of their predecessors, their industry has brought its reward.

(I) William Clow was the son of Cady Clow, a hosiery maker in Leicestershire, England, and born in the same county in 1834, and died in Lakeport, New Hampshire, in 1900. At the age of eighteen he left England and came to America, landing at New York. From there he went to Portsmouth, New Hampshire, where he was employed in the manufacture of hosiery for eighteen years. The following twenty-three years he was in the same business in Manchester, whence he went to Lakeport, where the last twenty-five years of his life were passed. He was an Episcopalian, and a Republican. He married Harriet Cartledge, who was born in Derbyshire, England, in 1835. They were the parents of seven children: Thomas, Sarah, Emma, Harry, Maria, Frank and Alice.

(II) Frank William, sixth child and third son of William and Harriet (Cartledge) Clow, was born in Portsmouth, December 4, 1866. He was educated in the common schools, attending the high school in Manchester. He worked with his father in the hosiery factory, and in time was promoted. In 1892 he became a retail dealer in coal, wood and ice in Lakeport, in which business he has since been successfully engaged. He is a Republican in politics, and of liberal views in religion. He is a past grand of Chocorua Lodge, No. 57, Independent Order of Odd Fellows, of Lakeport. He married Rose Girard, who was born in Quebec, Canada, December 8, 1870. They have six children: Harriet, born May 31, 1891; William Frank, January 24, 1893; Daisy Rose, February 21, 1896; Guy Leland, February 22, 1899; Blanche Ellen, March 15, 1901; and James Girard, October 22, 1904.

GALLAGHER The name O'Gallchobhair, anglicized Galchor and Gallagher, is from the Irish "gall," signifying a foreigner; and "chobhair," help. O'Gallchobhair, son of Gallchobhair, flourished in the year 950 A. D., and was the descendant of Anmire (Latinized Anmireus) who was the 138th monarch of Ireland, and brother of Fergus, who is No. 91, of the O'Donnell pedigree.

(I) Manasseh Gallagher was born in the North of Ireland about 1800, and in 1830 came to America and settled in Stanstead, Province of Quebec, Canada, and later resided at Linden and Derbyshire, Vermont. He married Mary Sweeney and they were the parents of ten children, four of whom are now living. Margaret married James L. Mead, of Linden, Vermont; Sarah, married John Donald, of Northfield, Vermont; Daniel, resides in Boise, Idaho; Stephen F. is mentioned below.

(II) Stephen Frank, son of Manasseh and Mary (Sweeney) Gallagher, was born in Derbyline, Vermont, November 27, 1864. He was educated in the common schools. He engaged in the hotel business at Linden, and afterward went to Derbyline, where he continued the business some years longer. He afterward carried on a boot and shoe store and a grocery store, and was express agent at White River Junction. There he learned telegraphy, and in 1883 went to Fabyans, where he was telegraph operator. Later he performed similar service at Groveton and Laconia. In 1893 he returned to Fabyans, where he has since been station master and ticket agent for the Boston & Maine and Maine Central railroads. In politics he is a Democrat. In 1900 he was elected town clerk and town treasurer of Carroll, and re-elected in 1902. He was also elected representative in 1902, his majority being a single vote. He is a member of North Star Lodge, No. 8, Free and Accepted Masons, of North Star Royal Arch Chapter, of Lancaster; and St. Gerard Commandery, Knights Templar, of Littleton. He is also a member of the Independent Order of Odd Fellows. He married Helen Splaine. They had one child, a daughter, who died young.

PULVER The family of Pulver removed from Holland to Nieuw Nederlandt, now New York state, and settled on the east bank of the Hudson river, in what is now Columbia county, as early as 1636, at which time and later the Dutch government was making grants of land in consideration of certain improvements and the settlement of a certain number of families in a given time, to certain persons of means called Patroons.

(I) Nathan Pulver, son of Henry and Mary Pulver, was born in Luzerne county, New York, in 1844. He was a man of means and had a mercantile establishment at Luzerne, and also dealt extensively in lumber. He held various town offices and was a member of the legislature. He married, February 22, 1869, at Luzerne, Estella Dubois, who was born in Hadley, New York, 1851, daughter of Cornelius Dubois. Seven children were born of this union.

(II) Willis, eldest son of Nathan and Estella (Dubois) Pulver, was born at Luzerne, New York, June 24, 1871, and attended the public schools and Glens Falls Academy until 1894, when he entered the University of Maryland, from which he was graduated in 1898. He then took a special course at Yale University. He began the study of law in 1895, and was admitted to practice in 1897. The following four years he practiced in Michigan. In 1904 he removed to Nashua, New Hampshire, and was engaged in the practice of law with gratifying success until March, 1906, when he located in Salem, New Hampshire, and opened a law office at Salem Depot, where he is now in business. He is secretary of the Board of Trade, president of and general manager of the Salem Light, Heat & Power Company, and tax collector.

Mr. Pulver is descended from a line of worthy ancestors from whom he inherits sturdy qualities which made them men among men. His energy and companionable qualities have made him successful in business. He is a member of Lodge No. 456, Ancient Free and Accepted Masons, of Glens Falls, New York; Royal Arch Chapter No. 56, of the same place; Gebal Council, Royal and Select Masters, of Urichville, Ohio, and Washington Commandery, Knights Templar, of Saratoga Springs, New York. He is a charter member of Bektash Temple, Ancient Arabic Order of the Mystic Shrine, of Concord. He married, June 6, 1902, at Massilon, Ohio, Jennie Remington, who was born at Fenton, Michigan, 1878, daughter of James P. and Elizabeth Remington, of Fenton, Michigan. She died May 4, 1905.

HARVEY Since the landing of the early ancestors of the families of this name in America, the Harveys have been regarded as a race who attended to their affairs with fidelity, made the best of their opportunities, and never lamented what could not be bettered.

(I) Warren Harvey, son of Gilman and ——— (Perry) Harvey, was born in Manchester in 1837, and died there in 1904. He was educated in the public schools and soon after quitting them obtained a position in a bank in Manchester. Afterward he engaged in teaching, at which he proved successful. He was made superintendent of streets, and held that office and carried on teaching for a number of years. He engaged in the business of contracting and building granite work, and while in that employment, which he carried on until 1894, he put in the foundations and other stone work of a large number of the principal buildings in the city of Manchester. He was a Republican in politics, and was a representative in the New Hampshire legislature. He was a member of the Improved Order of Red Men, the Benevolent and Protective Order of Elks, and a thirty-second degree Mason, having membership in the following divisions of that body: Washington Lodge; Horeb Royal Arch Chapter, No. 11; Adoniram Council No. 3, Royal and Select Masters; Trinity Commandery, Knights Templar, and Edward A. Raymond Consistory. He married (first), Josephine Dustin, who was born, 1843, in Manchester, and died 1881. (Second), to Mary Chevill, who was born in Runney, New Hampshire. The children of this union are: Harry W., who is mentioned below; Anna, born November 30, 1873; Florence, born April 18, 1876, who married George Currier, and Burnham, born May 4, 1887.

(II) Harry Weston, eldest child of Warren and Mary (Chevill) Harvey, was born in Manchester, July 18, 1870. After passing through the schools of Manchester he spent five years as the local representative of several insurance companies. The two following years he was engaged in the retail shoe trade, and then joined his father in the granite contracting business. Since the retirement of his father he has carried on the industry alone. Mr. Harvey is an energetic and successful business man. In politics he is a Republican. His tendencies have a social turn, and he is a member of the following societies and orders: The Amoskeag Veterans, the Benevolent and Protective Order of Elks, the Improved Order of Red Men, and the Patrons of Husbandry. He married, October 14, 1891, in Manchester, Emma Tozier, who died in 1900.

MCKEEN or MCKEAN The now numerous family of this name which is descended from Scotch-Irish ancestors who were pioneers in New Hampshire and Pennsylvania, has had many representatives who distinguished themselves in war and in peace. Patriotism and executive ability have been and still are marked traits of the McKeens.

(I) James McKeen, as the name is written in the old records, undoubtedly a descendant of Scotch immigrants who settled in the north of Ireland about 1612, was probably born in Ireland, and resided at Ballymoney in the county of Antrim. He was devotedly attached to his people, a zealous Protestant, and one of that band who made the defence of Londonderry one of the most remarkable events in the history of the British Isles. He had three sons: James, John, and William. James was one of the grantees and a leading man in the settlement of Londonderry, New Hampshire; John is the subject of the next paragraph; William settled in Pennsylvania and was the progenitor of a large family. Among his grandsons was Thomas McKean, a signer of the Declaration of Independence, and for nine years governor of Pennsylvania.

(II) John, the second son of James McKeen, was born in Ireland, and prepared to come to America with his elder brother James, but died a short time previous to the embarkation. His widow Janet, with her three sons, James, Robert, and Samuel, and her infant daughter Mary, accompanied James and his family to America in 1718, and settled in Londonderry, where she had a lot assigned to her She afterward married Captain John Barnett, who was one of the early settlers of the town.

(III) Samuel, third son and child of John and Janet McKeen, was born in Ireland and came to America with his widowed mother when but a lad. After marriage he settled in Amherst. By his wife Agnes he had a family of ten children, six sons: Hugh, John, Robert, James, Samuel, William; and four daughters: Mary, Martha, Agnes, and Jane. Several of his sons were in the prime of life for military service in the time of the old French war, and took an active part in it. Hugh was killed by the Indians in that war. John was taken at the capture of Fort William Henry, his flesh stuck full of pitch-pine skewers, and he was burned at the stake. Robert was a "captain of renown," settled at Cherry Valley, New York, and was killed by the Indians in the battle of Wyoming, Pennsylvania. He was the grandfather of United States Senator Samuel McKeen, of Pennsylvania. James settled in Amherst; Samuel lived in New Hampshire, and afterward moved to Maine, and finally died with his sons in Acworth; William is the subject of the next paragraph.

(IV) William, sixth son of Samuel and Agnes McKean, was one of the first settlers in Deering. In 1776 he was the fifth subscriber to the Association Test in Deering, a sufficient proof of his loyalty to the American cause. The name of Robert McKeen appears on the roll of officers of Deering; first in 1782 as selectman, and often afterwards; also as representative. He married Ann Graham (or Grimes), a sister of Francis Grimes, one of the earlier settlers of Deering. They had six sons and five daughters: John, David, Robert, William, Moses, Samuel, Rose, Mary, Betsey, Jane, and Agnes.

(V) Robert, third son of William and Ann (Graham) McKean, was born in Deering, where he resided, and was engaged in agriculture. He married Sally Barnes, of Deering. They were the parents of three children: Leonard, Elbridge, and Adaline.

(VI) Leonard, eldest child of William and Sally (Barnes) McKean, was born in Deering, and died in Manchester, aged sixty-nine years. He was for many years a merchant in Deering. He removed to Manchester, where he spent the remainder of his life. In politics he was a Democrat and held town offices. In 1852 he was town clerk; selectman in 1853, 1855 and 1856, and representative in 1855 and 1856. He married Angeline Dickey.

(VII) Robert Edgar, son of Leonard and Angeline Dickey, was born in Deering, December 16, 1862, and was educated in the public schools and at Bryant & Stratton's Business College in Manchester. In March, 1875, he started in business in Manchester as a clothier and merchant tailor. From 1882 to 1888 he was junior partner in the firm of Williams & McKean, but subsequently bought his partner's interest, and since then has been sole proprietor of the business. Williams & McKean were the first tenants in the Opera House Block. In 1891 Mr. McKean moved to Elm Street, where he has since been located. In the thirty-two years he has been in business he has "never had a fire nor a failure." He is a Democrat in politics, and has for many years taken an active part in the affairs of his party. He has served as moderator of Ward Eight, and in 1899 and 1907 was representative in the legislature. He is a member of Washington Lodge, Free and Accepted Masons. Mechanics Lodge, Independent Order of Odd Fellows, and the Derryfield Club. He married, July 4, 1883, Ada Colby, who was born in Deering, February 24, 1859, daughter of Eben M. and Ella (Gove) Colby, of Deering. They have four sons: Arthur G., George R., and Clarence T. (twins), and Robert L.

MALONEY Descended from sturdy Irish ancestry. the efficient superintendent of the Manchester Street Railway has developed unusual executive ability during the past five years, and as he is yet on the right side of forty, it may be safely conjectured that he will achieve a still higher reputation in his chosen field of usefulness.

D. J. Maloney, an industrious Irish farmer, left Ireland at the age of about thirty years, in 1855, to seek his fortune in the United States, which was then as now the Mecca of all his liberty-loving countrymen. After residing in Exeter, New Hampshire, a short time he went to Rutland, Massachusetts, and engaged in farming. He subsequently removed to Worcester and is still residing in that city. He married Catherine Laula, whose birth took place in the same locality as that of her husband.

William Edward, son of D. J. and Catherine (Laula) Maloney, was born in Rutland. July 17, 1872. During his early childhood his parents went to reside in Worcester, and he was educated in the public schools of that city. After the completion of his studies he entered the employ of the Holyoke Machine Company, but two years later returned to Worcester and accepted a clerkship in the office of the Worcester Street Railway Company. He was shortly afterwards advanced to the responsible position of cashier, and still later was placed in charge of the transportation department of the Consolidated Company, serving in that capacity with ability for a number of years. In 1901 he was called to the superintendency of the Manchester Street Railway, which he accepted, and commencing his duties in November of that year he immediately set in motion a series of practical ideas, based upon his personal experience, which proved exceedingly beneficial to the road. The line, which comprises thirty-seven and one-half miles of track running directly through the business section of the city, is continually undergoing changes for the better both in regard to its service and the character of its equipment, and the high standard of excellence which has been attained under the present superintendent, is certain to be maintained as long as he chooses to direct its operation. He takes an earnest interest in all matters relative to the welfare and development of the city. In his religious faith he is a Roman Catholic, and he is a member of St. Joseph's Parish. Mr. Maloney married Miss Mary E. Schofield, and has one daughter. Helen.

BURLINGAME This family is one of limited numbers, and although of ancient English origin is not found among the early colonists of New England. The distinguished diplomatic service of Anson Burlingame forty years ago made the name familiar to the civilized world.

(I) William A. Burlingame was father of:

(II) Andrew Jackson Burlingame, born in Buxton, Maine, 1833, and died in Berlin, 1874. In 1859 he settled in Berlin, and carried on a prosperous lumber business for a number of years, retiring some time before his death. In politics he was a Democrat. He married Matilda W. Wilson, daughter of William A. Wilson.

(III) William Wilson, son of Andrew J. and Matilda W. (Wilson) Burlingame, was born in Berlin, December 17, 1870. He was educated in the common schools, the Berlin high school, and at Burdette Business College in Boston. After leaving the high school he ran a level for a line of lumber railroad for a year. He has since been profitably engaged in the insurance business in Berlin. In politics he is a Democrat, and was city clerk four terms, 1898-1902, and has been a member of the board of trustees of the public library for a number of years. He is a member of the Independent Order of Odd Fellows, and Knights of Pythias, and is treasurer of both local lodges.

QUINN In the last sixty years the Irish have assisted very materially in the devolopment of this country by contributing their labor in constructing and operating railroads and factories, and erecting many public and private buildings. The Quinn family of this article have made a good record in these lines of employment.

(I) Michael, son of Thomas Quinn, was born in county Cork, Ireland, April 1, 1832, and died in Keene, New Hampshire, August 15. 1890. In 1852 he came to America, and for a time was employed at farm work, but soon went into the employ of the Cheshire County Railroad Company, and after working on the section went into the shops of that company (now the Boston & Maine) and worked at the trade of springmaker for thirty years. He relinquished that occupation about two years before his death He married in Keene, Mary Joyce They had five children: Margaret, deceased: John T., who is mentioned below; James, deceased; and Mary and Bridget, who lived in Keene.

(II) John Timothy, second child of Michael and Mary (Joyce) Quinn, was born in Keene, November 27. 1863. He learned the springmaker's trade, and worked in the shops at the Chesire road, and then engaged in the plumbing business, being employed seven years in Keene, three years in New York City, and at Northfield and Bellows Falls, Vermont, about a year each. In 1895 he took the position of superintendent of the plumbing and heating department of the Berlin Mills Company, which he has since filled to the satisfaction of that company He married Catherine E. Dolan, of Boston, Massachusetts. They have two children: John Michael and James Morris.

CADY This ancient and honorable cognomen was borne by early settlers in Massachusetts. The Cadys of this article are thought to have sprung from Nicholas Cady, of Watertown, Massachusetts, who married Judith, the daughter of William Knapp. Sr., and afterwards moved to Groton. Their children were: John, Judith, James, Nicholas (died young), Daniel, Ezekiel, Nicholas, and Joseph.

(I) Elisha Cady resided in Stowe, Lamoille county, Vermont, where he married Elizabeth ——

(II) Oral, son of Elisha and Elizabeth Cady, was born in Stowe, December 22, 1822, and died in Morrisville 1898. At nineteen years of age he started in business at Cady's Falls, and followed merchandising for years. He finally became a manufacturer of starch and of lumber, a contractor and a speculator in general produce. In political circles he was prominent. He was a member of the general court in 1868, high sheriff of Lamoille county for a number of years, and trial justice thirty years. He was not a member of any church, but worshipped with the Universalists. He married Ellen L. Smith, daughter of Daniel Smith, of Vermont. They had two children: Elisha H., and Plenny, who married T. Spalding, of Morristown.

(III) Elisha Healy, only son of Oral and Ellen L. (Smith) Cady, was born in Morristown, Vermont. April 30, 1865. He attended the public schools, and then became a clerk in a drug store in Morristown. In 1887 he went to Gorham, New Hampshire, and was in the employ of Fred W. Noyes as a clerk for three years, then in the grocery trade for himself in Morristown, until 1894. He next re-entered the employ of Mr. Noyes at Gorham, and there spent the following nine years, then two years in the employ of Bennett Brothers, druggists; and in December, 1905, he was made treasurer of the Gorham Savings Bank, and has since filled that position. In politics he is a Democrat, and is now serving as a member of the board of selectmen. He is a member of the Universalist Church, of which he is a trustee. He married Estie S. Hayes, daughter of Oran Hayes, of Stowell, Vermont. She died February, 1907. Three children were born of this union: Bessie, who married H. A. Hall, of Nashua; Harold Oral, who is in the Berlin National Bank; and Agnes E.

MERRIAM This name was originally spelled Meryham, Merryham, Meriham, and Mirriam. *Ham* means home or house, and the word in its literal signification meant *merry house*, or *happy house*, in modern phrase. The family is an ancient one, for there is record that in the year 1295-6 Laurence de Meryham paid taxes to Edward I at Isenhurst in Sussex. In the sixteenth century there was a manor of Meriham in Pembrokshire, the southwest corner of Wales. It is somewhat singular that the name, though fairly numerous in America, is now practically extinct in England.

(I) William Merriam, the first fully authenticated ancestor of this family, was a resident of the county of Kent, England, during the latter part of the sixteenth century. He was a clothier, which meant in those days that he made cloth and handled the manufactured goods. The business required more than ordinary intelligence, and was usually very profitable. His wife's name was Sara, and eight children are recorded, though the order of their births is not known: Susan, Margaret, a daughter, who married Thomas Howe; Joseph, whose sketch follows; George, born about 1603; Joane; Sara and Robert, born about 1613. The will of William Merriam of Harlow in Kent. was proved November 27, 1635.

(II) Joseph, son of William and Sara Merriam, and the eldest as mentioned in the father's will, was probably born in the county of Kent about the year 1600. Like his father he was a clothier or cloth maker and merchant, and there is reason to suppose that he was possessed of considerable property when he set out for the new world. He settled in Concord, Massachusetts, in June, 1638, and soon after was admitted to the church, and was made a freeman of the Colony of Massachusetts Bay. Joseph Merriam married in England, about the year 1623, Sara, daughter of John and (probably) Frances (Jefferie) Goldstone of the county of Kent. They had seven children, all of them born in England except the youngest, who was a posthumous child, born at Concord, Massachusetts, six months after the death of his father. The children were: William, Sarah, Joseph, mentioned below; Thomas, Elizabeth, Hannah and John. Joseph Merriam died at Concord, Massachusetts, January 1, 1640-1, after a residence of less than three years in America. His widow afterwards married Lieutenant Joseph Wheeler, and died March 12, 1670-1.

(III) Joseph (2), son of Joseph (1) and Sara (Goldstone) Merriam, was born in England about the year 1629. He migrated with his people to Concord, Massachusetts, but removed when adult to Cambridge, living in the part called "The Farms," which afterwards became the parish and town of Lexington. He was admitted to the church, and was made a freeman, May 22, 1650. He accumulated something of an estate and, like his father, died in early middle life. Joseph Merriam married at Concord, July 12. 1653, Sarah, daughter of Deacon Gregory Stone. There were nine children: Sarah, Lydia, Joseph, Elizabeth, John, Mary, Robert, Ruth and Thomas, the subject of the succeeding paragraph. Joseph (2) Merriam died April 20, 1677, and his grave-stone is the oldest now standing in the ancient "Hill Burying Ground" at Concord, Massachusetts. His widow died April 5, 1704.

(IV) Thomas, fourth son and ninth and youngest child of Joseph (2) and Sarah (Stone) Merriam, was born at Concord, Massachusetts, about 1672. He removed to Cambridge Farms (Lexington), and was one of the original members of the church there. In 1698 his wife was dismissed from the church at Concord to join the one at Lexington, and on March 6 of that year Thomas Merriam, his brother Robert, and others were permitted to "build a seat for their wives on the within back side of the meeting-house, from Goodwife Reed's seat to the woman's stayers" (stairs). Thomas Merriam was selectman from 1718 to 1725, and a constable in 1716. On December 23, 1696, Thomas Merriam married Mary Harwood of Concord, Massachusetts, and there were seven children: Mary, Thomas, Lydia, Nathaniel, Simon, David and Isaac, whose sketch follows. Thomas Merriam died August 16, 1738, aged sixty-six, and his widow died September 29, 1756, aged eighty-one.

(V) Isaac, fifth son and seventh and youngest child of Thomas and Mary (Harwood) Merriam, was born at Lexington. Massachusetts, July 5, 1714. He lived in the neighboring town of Bedford, and owned a tract of land in Townsend among other properties. On September 1, 1736, Isaac Merriam married Sarah Davis, and there were three children: Isaac (2), Sarah and Eleazer. Isaac Merriam died April 19, 1741, at the early age of twenty-seven, and his widow on September 10, 1746, married Nathaniel Ball of Concord, Massachusetts. She died at Groton, New Hampshire, May 25. 1799, in her eighty-ninth year.

(VII) Isaac (2), eldest child and only son of Isaac (1) and Sarah (Davis) Merriam, was born at Concord, Massachusetts, September 2, 1736. He was a felt-maker and hatter; but on December 4, 1771, he sold his land and shop in Concord and removed to Ashburnham, where he was prominent in town affairs, serving as selectman and in other capacities. In 1790 he was living in Concord again, and in 1793 removed to Groton, New Hampshire. and in his old age to Brandon, Vermont, where he died. Isaac (2) Merriam was twice married. His first wife was Eleanor Munroe of Lexington, Massachusetts, whom he wedded April 10, 1759. She died at Concord, July 19, 1768, leaving four children: David, Isaac (3), Jonathan and Benjamin. On December 2, 1768, Isaac (2) Merriam married his second wife Rebecca, daughter of Gershom Davis, of Acton, Massachusetts. She died at Brandon, Vermont, April 20, 1812, leaving two children: Joshua and Jonas Davis. Isaac (2) Merriam died at Brandon, Vermont, December 1, 1825, at the age of eighty-nine, being the first of his family to attain great length of years.

(VII) Isaac (3), second son and child of Isaac (2) and his first wife, Sarah (Davis) Merriam, was born at Concord, Massachusetts, January 29, 1762. He lived in Ashburnham, Massachusetts, in early life, removing thence to Northumberland, New Hampshire, and finally to Jackson, New York, where he died. He was a hatter and a soldier in the Revolution. In 1789 he married Betsey Waite, daughter of William Waite, who was born April 8, 1765. They had eight children: David, Isaac, Betsey, William, Jonas, whose sketch follows; Benjamin, Joseph Waite, and Sarah. The third son, William, was born March 21, 1796, and died July 5, 1814. at the battle of Chippewa. Isaac (3) Merriam died at Jackson, New York, February 1, 1853, at the advanced age of ninety-one years.

(VIII) Jonas, fourth son and fifth child of Isaac (3) and Betsey (Waite) Merriam, was born at Northumberland, New Hampshire, May 23, 1798. He lived at Stratford, New Hampshire, and was a farmer all his life. He attended the Methodist Church, and held all the town offices. His first wife and the mother of his children was Mrs. Lucinda B. (Gramsby) Day, daughter of George Gramsby. She was born August 27. 1811, and died August 25, 1866, leaving three children: Harvey Rice, Edward Benjamin and Charles Henry, whose sketch follows. Harvey Rice, the eldest son, was born July 6, 1841, enlisted in the Fourth Iowa Cavalry during the Civil war, and was killed at the battle of Red River, Louisiana. In 1868 Jonas Merriam married his second wife, Mrs. Ann Maria (Bond) Wilson, who died in May, 1883. There were no children by the second marriage. Jonas Merriam died at Stratford, January 25, 1889, in his ninetieth year, almost equalling his father and exceeding his grandfather in length of days.

(IX) Charles Henry, youngest of the three sons of Jonas and Lucinda (Gramsby) (Day) Merriam, was born at Stratford, New Hampshire. May 1, 1850, and now lives on the same farm where he first saw the light. He was educated in the common schools, and began farming at an early age. He has about hundred and twenty acres under cultivation. On October 24. 1872, Charles Henry Merriam married Emma A. Gardner, daughter of Ezekiel and —— Gardner of Stratford, who was born September 29, 1853. There are four children: Marion Eames, born March 12, 1874, married John Carl Burbank. December 28, 1904, and lives in Brunswick, Vermont; Thomas Oakley, born November 22, 1878. married Agnes St. John on November 24, 1903, and is a farmer at Stratford: Carrie Belle, born December 1, 1882, lives at home, and Henry Albert, born December 31, 1886, is employed by the Telephone Company at Stratford.

HARRINGTON Patrick Harrington, who lately passed away in Manchester, was among the industrious and successful business men of that city. He was a native of Mitchelstown, Ireland, born in 1838, a son of Daniel and Margaret (Carey) Harrington. When the son was about two years of age the parents started for Quebec. The father died in Liverpool before they had embarked, and was buried there. The mother with her children proceeded on the voyage, and very soon found their way from Quebec to Manchester, New Hampshire. Here the son was educated in the public and parochial schools, and at the age of fourteen years set out to maintain himself by taking employment in the print works. He was subsequently employed in Aretus Blood's locomotive works as a watchman, and subsequently drove a team about the city. Having saved his wages, after a time he became proprietor of a team, and continued as a teaming contractor until 1890. His earnings were invested in real estate which soon came to be valuable, and through the improvements which he made made him a comparatively wealthy man. He first purchased property at 43 Lake Avenue, and engaged in the bottling business, to which he subsequently added wholesale trade in liquors. In 1895 he bought property at 17 Lake Avenue, and the next year built a large brick building in which are thirty-two tenements, and on the ground floor continued his business there until his death, which occurred June 26. 1905, at the age of sixty-seven years. He was one of the originators of the Portsmouth Brewing Company at Manchester, of which he continued to be a director during his life, and was also a stockholder in various local interests. Having been reared in the Roman Catholic Church, he allied himself with the Cathedral Parish of Manchester, to which he gave faithful and liberal support. In political affairs he had acted with the Democratic party until its national platform was dominated by the free silver idea, after which he abandoned it. He served at one time as a member of the common council of Manchester, but as a rule declined to accept any official station. He was married to Margaret Carey, who was born in Limerick, Ireland, daughter of James and Ann Carey, and came when three years old to America with her parents, who lived in Manchester. James Carey was for many years engaged in teaming for the Amoskeag Mills, and subsequently engaged in the wood business in Manchester, and has been many years deceased. Five of the six children of Mr. and Mrs. Harrington are now living. The eldest. James P., died in 1900. William F., the second, is the subject of the succeeding paragraph. Ellen is the wife of Patrick H. Sullivan, residing in Manchester. Lawrence J., the fourth, is engaged in continuing the business of his father in conjunction with his elder brother. Annie F. (Mrs. Thomas Collins) resides in Boston. Mary C., the youngest, resides with her widowed mother in Manchester.

William Francis Harrington, eldest surviving son of Patrick and Margaret (Carey) Harrington, was born September 11, 1871, in Manchester, and was educated in the public schools of the city. graduating from the high school in 1891, in his twentieth year. He was early accustomed to assist his father in the conduct of his business, and became bookkeeper of the establishment and was later employed in the same capacity by the Portsmouth Brewing Company, of which he is now the treasurer. Upon the death of his father he became the active manager of the business established by the latter, which still occupies the major portion of his time. He is a director of the Merchants' National Bank, and in some other interests of the city, having succeeded his father in these latter positions. He is identified with numerous social organizations and fraternal bodies of the city, being affiliated with the Benevolent Protective Order of Elks, Knights of Pythias, Knights of Columbus, Amoskeag Veterans, and the Derryfield Club. He is a member of the Cathedral Parish of the Roman Catholic Church in Manchester, and gives his political allegiance to the Republican party. Mr. Harrington is an active and successful business man, having extensive real estate interests to care for in connection with the business inherited from his father. He is genial, affable and intelligent, and a pleasant person to meet in either a business or a social way.

TASKER One of the earliest settlers of this name in New Hampshire was William Tasker (or Tasket), who was of Dover from 1675 to 1689. Samuel Tasker, probably his son, was of Dover, and was mortally wounded by the Indians in June, 1704. The subjects of the following sketches are probably descended from William Tasker, the settler.

(I) Moses S. Tasker was born in Strafford, New Hampshire, and died in 1894. When a young man he located at Centre Ossipee and by diligence, economy and good management, became one of the prosperous farmers of Carroll county. He married Salome Nichols, a daughter of James and ——— Nichols. Her father was a soldier in the was of 1812. Six children were born to them: Amanda (died young), Doxan (died young); Amanda, the second of that name, married Frank Heath; Lydia, married Frank Foss; one child died young, unnamed; George F. is the subject of the next paragraph.

(II) George F., only son and youngest child of Moses S. and Salome (Nichols) Tasker, was born in Moultonville, December 9, 1866, and was educated in the common schools. He grew up on his father's farm and followed farming, and then went into the butcher business until 1907, having a successful trade. He then sold out and has again turned his attention to that ancient and independent employment—the cultivation of the earth. He is a member of Ossipee Tribe, No. 19, Improved Order of Red Men.

ATKINSON The immigrant ancestor of the Atkinsons of this sketch was one of that vast army of ambitious citizens who leave their early homes in Europe to make their homes in America, and find here in the newer parts of the country the success that circumstances denied in the crowded centers of a thickly populated country.

(I) Thomas Atkinson was born in England. He settled in Melbourne, Province of Quebec, Canada, where he was a brick and stone mason. In the latter part of his life he was a contractor at Compton, where he died in 1865. He married Melissa Nott, daughter of George Nott, of New Hampshire. Three children were born of this marriage: Louisa Ann, Christopher George, and Thomas C., whose sketch follows. All live in Coos.

(II) Thomas C., youngest child of Thomas and Melissa (Nott) Atkinson, was born in Melbourne, April 13, 1846. He was educated in the common schools and began to work at lumbering. In 1859 he went to Orono, Maine, where he was employed for twenty years. In the fall of 1879 he removed to Coos, in the town of Strafford, New Hampshire, and became the proprietor of a hotel, which he conducted for some time, and then took the Mill Hotel. He carried that on until 1898, and then built the Hotel Atkinson, which he has ever since managed, doing a prosperous business. In 1904 he was elected selectman, and in 1906 was elected to the lower house of the legislature; and received in each case at the end of his term the approbation of his fellow citizens for the manner in which he had discharged his duties. He has a decided liking for fraternal organizations, and is a member of several of them. He is a member of the Masonic fraternity—lodge, chapter and commandery; the Independent Order of Odd Fellows; Knights of Pythias and Knights of Honor. He married (first), Louise Stafford, who was born at Oldtown, Maine. He married (second), Annie Hartwell. The children of this marriage are: Harold Hartwell and Frances Georgiana.

LODGE This surname is probably derived from the place of abode of its first possessor. Only three generations of the Lodges of this article have resided in America.

(I) Berington Lodge, a native of England, came to America and settled in Kingsley, Province of Quebec, Canada, where he lived on a farm.

(II) George Henry, son of Berington Lodge, was born in Kingsley, Province of Quebec, April 30, 1831. He was a lifelong and prosperous farmer, owning a place of three hundred acres. He married Sarah Jane Burbank, who was born in Slatington, Province of Quebec, December 9, 1833. Their children, all born in Slatington, were: William, born February 23, 1858, married Frances Willows; Clara, October 24, 1860, married Clarence Matthews; Hollis H., December 9, 1861; Etta Sarah, May 13, 1862, married Wallace Stevens, and resides in Manchester; Thomas Elson, November 24, 1863; and Ernest Linsey, the subject of the next paragraph.

(III) Ernest Linsey, sixth and youngest child of George H. and Sarah Jane (Burbank) Lodge, was born in Slatington, Province of Quebec, January 22, 1866, and educated in the common schools. He worked at agricultural pursuits and in the slate factory until about twenty-one years of age, and then went to Bangor, Pennsylvania. He afterward settled in Manchester, New Hampshire. He worked at carpentry for a time, and later took small contracts on his own account for a few years. Since 1894 he has been successfully engaged as a carpenter and builder, and has erected a large number of buildings in Manchester, principally dwellings. Mr. Lodge is a member of the Congregational Church, and in politics is a Republican. He married Etta M. Willie, who was born in Nicolet Falls, Province of Quebec, May 9, 1863, daughter of Norris M. and Mehilla Willie. They are the parents of Alberta Maud, Beatrice, Harold, James, Primrose, and George Frederick. Primrose, born June 3, 1868, married W. J. Moyles, and lives in Manchester. George Frederick, born January 3, 1870, married Ida Moyles, and lives in Slatington. They have three children: Hildah, Edith and Elvira.

WIER From the land of O'Connell and Goldsmith have come many of the families of Canada; and from Canada many of the descendants of those families have found their way to the United States, and are today among those whose labors are increasing the wealth of the nation. Of these are the Wiers of this article.

(I) Alexander Wier was born in Cork, Ireland,

and came to America with his parents at the age of seven, and settled near Sherbrooke, Province of Quebec, Canada. He grew up on a farm, and when of age owned one himself, and carried on a lumbering business, that country at that time bearing a large amount of first class timber. He got a good deal of ship timber, including mostly masts, knees, etc. He was successful as a business man, and accumulated what was there and then considered a handsome property.

(II) Joseph Alexander, son of Alexander Wier, died in California. He learned the carpenter's trade, at which he worked in Sherbrooke, and then removed to Auburn, Maine, where he resided and followed his calling until about 1879. In that year he went to California and engaged in trade which he carried on until his death. He married in St. Francis, Canada, Amelia Barney. Of this marriage were born two children: William C. and Ada Barney.

(III) William C. Wier was born in Auburn, Maine. March 26, 1872. He was educated in the common schools and worked on a farm and in a mill in Sherbrooke until he was sixteen years old. In 1888 he went to Stewartstown, New Hampshire, where he has since resided and has followed lumbering. He is a very enterprising man and a good citizen. He owns and operates a steam saw mill and does a thriving business. He is a member of the Knights of Pythias, Independent Order of Foresters, and Improved Order of Red Men: in each of which he has passed the chairs. He and his wife Lillian have one child, Harry.

CASSIDY Irish history teaches that the Three Collas, the sons of Eochy Dubhlen, who was the son of Carbry Liffechar, the 117th monarch of Ireland, conquered Ulster in the fourth century and there founded for themselves and their posterity the Kingdom of Orgiall, sometimes called Oriel and Uriel. From the Three Collas descended many noble families of Ulster, Connaught, Meath, and Scotland. One of the principal families of the chiefs and tribes of the race is that of the Cassidys, whose ancestor was Muireadach, or Colla de Chrioch (or Facrioch), meaning "Colla of the Two Countries." (Ireland and Alba).

(I) Patrick Cassidy was born in the northern part of Ireland. In 1849 he removed to America and settled in Methuen, Massachusetts, where he was engaged in agricultural pursuits. He died there in October, 1877. He was an industrious citizen, and he and his family were consistent members of the Catholic Church. He married in Methuen, Elizabeth Boyd, who died in Methuen, in January, 1878. The children of this union were: Peter, who married (first), Bridget Colbert: and (second) Rosanna Henry: Mary, now the wife of Joseph Martin, of Everett, Massachusetts: Jane who married J. F. Merrill of Methuen: John, whose sketch is found below; and a child which died young.

(II) John Francis, fourth child and second son of Patrick and Elizabeth (Boyd) Cassidy, was born in Methuen, 1851, and was educated in the public and parochial schools. When a young man he worked in the shoe factories in Methuen, Haverhill and Marlborough, and in Manchester, New Hampshire. In 1871 he was appointed to a place on the police force of Manchester, where he has since served continuously and faithfully. His efficiency has been noted by his superiors, and since May 11, 1891, he has been deputy chief of the department. In politics he is a Republican. He was married, March 30, 1875, to Clara E. Colby, daughter of Emerson and Mary (Greeley) Colby, of Londonderry, the latter being a first cousin of the late distinguished Horace Greeley. Mrs. Cassidy was born in Londonderry, and died in Manchester, February 9, 1906. The children of this union are: Florence E., born April 4, 1876, who died September 14, 1878; John W., born May 2, 1879, now a clerk in the employ of the Boston & Maine railroad at Concord, New Hampshire.

O'DOWD Fiachra Ealg, one of the Princes of Hy-Fiachra in Connaught, brother of Eocha Breoc, was the ancestor of O'Dubhda, a name which has been anglicized Doody, Dowd, Dowde, O'Dowd and Dowda. All those bearing these names are theoretically, if not literally descended from the one ancestor.

(I) James O'Dowd was born in Ireland, where he was a farmer. He removed to England, and for some years worked in the cotton mills. He migrated from England to Quebec in Canada, and from there moved to the United States. He was a Democrat in politics, and a Catholic in religious faith. He married, in Ireland, Mary Moran, a native of the same county, by whom he had nine children. She died in 1898. Their children were: John H., James, Patrick, Michael, Matthew, Thomas and three others who died young.

(II) John H., eldest child of James and Mary (Moran) O'Dowd, was born in Ireland, June 17, 1833. He was educated in private schools, and accompanied his parents to England, where he worked in the mills, and then removed to Canada, where for twenty years he was engaged in farming. In 1856 he settled in Manchester, New Hampshire, and for twenty-five years was employed in the Manchester boiler house. He removed to Portsmouth in 1864, and afterward was engaged in farming for twenty-five years. In political sentiment he was a Democrat, and in religious faith a Roman Catholic. He married (first) in January, 1858, Mary Carr, who was born in Ireland, and died May 8, 1870, the daughter of Thomas and Bridget (McCarty) Carr, natives of Ireland. He married (second) Bridget Dodd, who was born in Ireland, and came to America. The children by the first wife were: John T., James L., Michael Matthew, Frank, Catherine M., and Mary A. Those by the second wife were: Charles W., Andrew and Mary A.

(III) John Thomas, eldest child of John H. and Mary (Carr) O'Dowd, was educated in the public schools. He worked in the print works, and later learned the painter's trade. In 1878 he became a member of a ball club. He went to Manchester and worked as a painter one year, and worked the following year in the Manchester Mills. January 1, 1881, he became a member of the Manchester Fire Department, and was a driver of a hose wagon for five years and nine months following. In April, 1888 he enrolled as a member of the Manchester police force and for two years walked a night beat, and the two years following was a day officer. In 1896 he was appointed inspector and sergeant, and has since served as such. Sergeant O'Dowd has distinguished himself in the Manchester public service as an efficient and reliable officer. He is a Republican and a Catholic. He is a member of the Ancient Order of United Workmen, the Golden Cross, and treasurer of the Fraternal Order of Eagles, fraternal insurance organizations. He married, in Manchester, November 21, 1883, Minnie F. McDonough, daughter of

Lemuel F. Liscom

John and Mary (Willis) McDonough. Their children are: Francis G., Alice M. and Richard M.

STEELE The Steeles of this sketch are of good old Scotch stock, like the immigrants who peopled portions of New Hampshire, and the southern colonies two hundred years ago.

(I) Matthew Steele was born in the north of Scotland, and came to America and settled in Peacham, Vermont, where he bought a large farm upon which he lived until his death. He married Lillian Calderwood, who died in Peacham. Their children were: Anna, Agnes, Robert, Alexander, Charles, Isabella, John, George, and [illegible].

(II) Charles David, fifth [illegible] third son of Matthew and Lillian (Calderwood) Steele, was born July 18, 18[illegible], in Peacham, Vermont. He attended the schools of his native town until he was fourteen years old, and then went to Woodsville, New Hampshire, where he apprenticed himself to a butcher, and learned the trade. Subsequently he bought out his employer and [illegible] the business until 18[illegible], when he removed to Manchester, and opened a grocery store and [illegible] market on Chestnut street, which he has since successfully carried on. He is a member of St. Paul's Methodist Episcopal Church, and in politics is a Republican. He is a member of the Ancient Order of United Workmen. He married [illegible] who was born in Woodsville. They have three children, all born at Manchester: [illegible], Howard and [illegible].

LISCOM Hon. Lemuel [illegible] Liscom, fifth child and third son of Lemuel (2) and Emerancy ([illegible]) Liscom, was born February 17, 1841, on his father's farm, at the [illegible] part of Hinsdale, New Hampshire.

He attended the town schools and then completed his studies at Kimball Union Academy, Meriden, New Hampshire. August [illegible], 1862, he enlisted in Company A, Fourteenth New Hampshire Volunteer Infantry, and belonged at different times to the [illegible], Sixth and Nineteenth Army Corps. He [illegible] much of the time on duty at the [illegible], along the [illegible] and at Harper's Ferry, [illegible] then transferred to the Department of the [illegible] and was on the Red River expedition and [illegible] the Mississippi. He was also at the [illegible] at the battle of [illegible] and the second battle of Malvern Hill. In August, 186[illegible], [illegible] was transferred to the Shenandoah Valley [illegible] Sheridan, and served in eight engagements. [illegible] was transferred to Savannah, Georgia, where he [illegible] to Battery B, Heavy Artillery, in the [illegible] of Savannah, Georgia. He was one of the [illegible] present at the capture of President Jefferson [illegible] a body of infantry having [illegible] from the east and cavalry from the west, [illegible] pursuit and capture. He assisted [illegible] President Davis through Augusta to the [illegible]. He was discharged at Savannah, [illegible] July [illegible], 1865, retiring from the service with [illegible] sergeant. He was confined to the hospital [illegible] during his term of service.

Mr. Liscom returned north after the expiration of [illegible] of enlistment, and located in Boston, Massachusetts, securing employment in the shops of the National Bridge and Iron Company, for which business he had partially fitted by the course in engineering taken at the academy. [illegible] in the engineering department, and in the office of the company, and secured a thorough mastery of the [illegible] business. He became superintendent of [illegible], and in that capacity had charge of [illegible] of the train sheds of the old Boston and Lowell railroad, and of the Boston and Providence railroad in Boston, Massachusetts. He was also employed by the Keystone Bridge Company, Edgemore Iron Works, and by others. [illegible] the first iron bridge on the Vermont Central railroad at [illegible] River, and erected the first three iron cantilever bridges constructed in this country, on the European and North American railroad, in New Brunswick. He also had charge of the construction of many fine bridges and buildings, including the [illegible] work of the Boston post-office, and of the Art Museum in Boston, and did much other work of that character during his twenty-five years of service, acting as his own engineer.

Mr. Liscom was receiving a salary of twenty-five hundred dollars a year and had flattering prospects of advancement, but in 1880, his father being well along in years, he resigned his position and returned to the old homestead in Hinsdale. Previous to this time he had bought up tracts of timber as opportunity offered, and had quite extensive lumber interests. He engaged in farming, and finally bought out his father's property and started a saw mill. At present he owns about four hundred and fifty acres of forest, partly pine, and in 190[illegible] [illegible] and sawed the lumber on one hundred and fifty acres. For years he has made a specialty of raising hay and tobacco, selling about eleven tons of the latter product each year. He has devoted much time and effort to his tobacco crops, taking pride in obtaining a good quality of leaf, not only on his own farm but throughout the tobacco growing districts in the Connecticut Valley around Hinsdale. A few years ago he cleared up about twenty acres of an upper level pasture and planted it [illegible] tobacco, [illegible] at immense [illegible].

Mr. Liscom is a Republican in politics, and for years has taken an active interest in [illegible]. In 1891-92 he represented his town in the legislature, and was clerk of the committee on roads, bridges and canals. In 1893-94 he was returned to the general court, and served as chairman of the public [illegible] committee. He was also a member of [illegible] State Library. While a [illegible] he [illegible] the first Farmers' [illegible] Committee ever [illegible] the state, its [illegible] give [illegible] influence to the agricultural [illegible]. He was one of the first [illegible] the Agricultural [illegible] to [illegible] secure [illegible] Thompson [illegible] and he has always been a warm [illegible] of the [illegible] [illegible] Hinsdale [illegible] Vermont [illegible] his influence [illegible] secure its [illegible] [illegible] introduced a [illegible] the [illegible] court. [illegible] District in [illegible] to the senate by [illegible] candidate [illegible] [illegible] and [illegible] for governor [illegible] chairman [illegible] on the committees on revision of laws, [illegible] affairs, and roads, bridges and canals. Here he

John and Mary (Willis) McDonough. Their children are: Francis G., Alice M. and Richard M.

STEELE The Steeles of this sketch are of good old, honest Scotch stock, like the immigrants who peopled portions of New Hampshire, and the southern colonies two hundred years ago.

(I) Matthew Steele was born in the north of Scotland, and came to America and settled in Peacham, Vermont, where he bought a large farm upon which he lived until his death. He married Lillian Calderwood, who died in Peacham. Their children were: Anna, Agnes, Robert, Alexander, Charles, Isabella, John, George, and Mary.

(II) Charles David, fifth child and third son of Matthew and Lillian (Calderwood) Steele, was born July 18, 1872, in Peacham, Vermont. He attended the schools of his native town until he was fourteen years old, and then went to Woodville, New Hampshire, where he apprenticed himself to a butcher, and learned the trade. Subsequently he bought out his employer and conducted the business until 1894, when he removed to Manchester and opened a grocery store and meat market on Chestnut street, which he has since successfully carried on. He is a member of St. Paul's Methodist Episcopal Church, and in politics is a Republican. He is a member of the Ancient Order of United Workmen. He married Millie May Pennock, who was born in Woodsville. They have three children, all born at Manchester: Harold, Howard and Nigera.

LISCOM Hon. Lemuel Franklin Liscom, fifth child and third son of Lemuel (2) and Emerancy (Horton) Liscom, was born February 17, 1841, on his father's farm, at the north part of Hinsdale, New Hampshire.

He attended the town schools and then completed his studies at Kimball Union Academy, Meriden, New Hampshire. August 11, 1862, he enlisted in Company A, Fourteenth New Hampshire Volunteer Infantry, and belonged at different times to the Third, Sixth and Nineteenth Army Corps. He was much of the time on duty at the national capitol, along the Potomac, and at Harper's Ferry; was then transferred to the Department of the Gulf, and was on the Red River expedition, and up the Mississippi. He was also at the siege of Petersburg, at the battle of Deep Bottom, and the second battle of Malvern Hill. In August, 1863, he was transferred to the Shenandoah Valley, under Sheridan, and served in eight engagements. Later he was transferred to Savannah, Georgia, where he belonged to Battery B, Heavy Artillery, in the defenses of Savannah, Georgia. He was one of the soldiers present at the capture of President Jefferson Davis, a body of infantry having been sent from the east and cavalry from the west, to make the pursuit and capture. He assisted in transfering President Davis through Augusta to the gunboats. He was discharged at Savannah, Georgia, July 8, 1865, retiring from the service with rank of orderly sergeant. He was confined to the hospital but five days during his term of service.

Mr. Liscom returned north after the expiration of his term of enlistment, and located in Boston, Massachusetts, securing employment in the shops of the National Bridge and Iron Company, for which business he had partially fitted by the course in engineering taken at the academy. He worked in the engineering department, and in the office of the company, and secured a thorough mastery of the details of the business. He became superintendent of construction, and in that capacity had charge of the building of the train sheds of the old Boston and Lowell railroad, and of the Boston and Providence railroad in Boston, Massachusetts. He was also employed by the Keystone Bridge Company, Edgemore Iron Works, and by others. He put in the first iron bridge on the Vermont Central road, at Dog River; and erected the first three iron cantilever bridges constructed in this country, on the European and North American railroad, in New Brunswick. He also had charge of the construction of many fine bridges and buildings, including the iron work of the Boston postoffice, and of the Art Museum in Boston, and did much other work of that character during his twenty-five years of service, acting as his own engineer.

Mr. Liscom was receiving a salary of twenty-five hundred dollars a year and had flattering prospects of advancement; but in 1880, his father being well along in years, he resigned his position and returned to the old homestead in Hinsdale. Previous to this time he had bought up tracts of timber as opportunity occurred, and had quite extensive lumber interests. He engaged in farming, and finally bought out his father's property and started a saw mill. At present he owns about four hundred and fifty acres of forest, partly pine, and in 1906 cut and sawed the lumber on one hundred and fifty acres. For years he has made a specialty of raising hay and tobacco, selling about eleven tons of the latter product each year. He has devoted much time and effort to his tobacco crops, taking pride in obtaining a good quality of leaf, not only on his own farm but throughout the tobacco growing districts in the Connecticut Valley around Hinsdale. A few years ago he cleared up about twenty acres of an upper level pasture and planted it all to tobacco, building an immense barn.

Mr. Liscom is a Republican in politics, and for years has taken an active interest in public measures. In 1891-92 he represented his town in the legislature, and was clerk of the committee on roads, bridges and canals. In 1893-94 he was returned to the general court, and served as chairman of the public improvement committee. He was also a member of the committee on State Library. While in the legislature he formed the first Farmers' Legislative Council ever organized in the state, its object being to give weight and influence to the agricultural element. He was one of the first to advocate moving the Agricultural College to Durham, in order to secure the Benjamin Thompson school fund and he has always been a warm friend and supporter of the college in the matter of securing appropriations and other advantages. He also introduced a bill providing for an electric road from Hinsdale to Brattleboro, Vermont, and used all his influence to secure its passage. It was defeated, however, through the influence of the railroad; but on being introduced a second time both parties agreed to leave the discussion of the question to the supreme court.

In 1896 Mr. Liscom was nominated for senator in the 14th District by acclamation, and was elected to the senate by the largest majority ever given a candidate in that district, his vote being two thousand and fifteen to his Democratic opponent's six hundred and eighteen, a vote far exceeding that cast for governor. During this term of service he was chairman of the committee on claims; also served on the committees on revision of laws, military affairs, and roads, bridges and canals. Here he introduced a bill to give the Connecticut River Power Company a franchise to build a water system across the river between Brattleboro, Vermont, and Hinsdale, New Hampshire, for generating electricity and other power.

With a strong affection for the old place, Senator Liscom still resides on the old homestead of his father. The old mansion he occupies is one of the show-places of the town, and was erected in 1759 by Squire Jones. It was, in the early days of its magnificence, the residence of Governor Hunt; later of his daughter, Mrs. Anna Marsh, who founded the Brattleboro Retreat for Insane, at Brattleboro, Vermont. This old mansion is a square, hip-roofed, two-story building, constructed after the fashion of the better class of colonial residences, and is older than the American Revolution. The main part of the building remains as originally built, but during her residence Mrs. Marsh added a wing, which was fitted up as a drawing room in a manner to excite the admiration of the neighborhood; it had an arched ceiling, and its furnishings were costly and elegant; and here she was accustomed to entertain parties from Brattleboro and vicinity. The garden was laid out in elaborate design to suit her esthetic fancy. The house is well preserved, and the original clapboards riven out of pine logs and shaved by hand, still cover it; the nails used in the construction of the house were hand-made.

People whose memories extend back for seventy or eighty years or more, can recollect when the great deer park belonging to the estate was one of the chief show-places of the town, the great resort for pleasure drives. It was a noble range of woodland, with magnificent trees, greenest grass, a brook winding through the glades, and all kept in neatest trim. This estate formerly belonged to Colonel Hinsdale, one of the founders of the town and its foremost man, who in 1742 built Fort Hinsdale (the old cellar hole of which is now indicated by a depression about twenty rods back from the old mansion in an orchard) on top of the first terrace back of from the Connecticut river, a site overlooking a long stretch of the river and surrounding country. It was one of the town's main defenses against the Indians. Colonel Hinsdale also erected the grist-mill (now the saw-mill) still standing on the place.

Senator Liscom has one of the largest farms in town, some two hundred and fifty acres, much of it timber growth. Small crops of corn, potatoes and other farm products are raised, besides hay and tobacco, the staple crops. Farming and lumbering, together with dealing in ashes and other fertilizers, have constituted his business, but he now feels that the time has come when advancing years demand a husbanding of strength and vigor, and so is planning to reduce farm labor to a minimum and take life a little easier. He still continues, however, to give the best of his strength and talent to the interests of his fellow citizens. He was active in securing the erection of the new iron bridge, three hundred and twenty feet single span, over the Connecticut river opposite Brattleboro, Vermont, and was its Inspecting Engineer; he drew the specifications for super and substructure. In the New Hampshire legislature of 1907, in the interest of the town of Hinsdale, county and state, he, with others, secured five amendments to the charter of the Connecticut River Power Company to construct a dam across the Connecticut river between Hinsdale, New Hampshire, and Vernon, Vermont, which dam is now under construction, and is rated as one of New England's greatest water powers.

Senator Liscom is not a member of any church, but sees good in all, and is a generous supporter of local religious and educational institutions, and is a staunch temperance man. He is a member of Golden Rule Lodge, No. 77, Ancient Free and Accepted Masons, of Hinsdale; also of Royal Arch Chapter, No. 4, of Keene, New Hampshire; Saint John's Council, No. 7, Royal and Select Masters, of Keene; and Hugh de Payne's Commandery, Knights Templar, of Keene; also of Sheridan Post, No. 14, Grand Army of the Republic; Tribe, No. 27, Improved Order of Red Men, of Hinsdale; and of Wantastiquet Grange, Patrons of Husbandry, Hinsdale.

Senator Liscom married, in Truthville, New York, February 21, 1872, Dollie Amelia Mason; she was born in Fort Ann, New York, December 7, 1848, to Orrin T. and Sarah Ann (Otis) Mason, giving her a good old colonial and patriotic ancestry. Mrs. Liscom was of most lovable disposition and noble character. She had great artistic ability, and continued her art studies and painting during her married life. By her death, from pneumonia, March 2, 1896, Senator Liscom suffered an irreparable loss. Two daughters were born to them—Flora Dollie, January 22, 1875; and Mary Edith, October 31, 1878. Flora D. married Charles Victor Stearns, and they reside in Somerville, Massachusetts; they have one son, Charles Liscom, born May 8, 1905. Mary E. married Burton P. Holman, and lives in West Nutley, New Jersey.

The study of family history, if useful for no other purpose, is of value in yielding data that will give a clearer insight into the settlement and development of this great land, and show how its history has been made. As indicative of the various streams of settlers whose immigration and subsequent development have made New Hampshire what it is, Senator Liscom's connection with representatives of the old pioneer families of New England might well be cited. His paternal ancestor, from whom the family originated in this country, was Philip Liscom, who represented an ancient English family of the Celtic-British stock. He first appears in Milton, Massachusetts, in 1700, and married, December 24, 1701, Charity Jordan, daughter of John Jordan, of Milton, likewise of English ancestry. In 1708 Philip Liscom removed to the old Ponkapoag Indian Reservation in Dorchester territory, south of the Blue Hills, and it was here that he and his descendants lived for almost ninety years. This section is now the Ponkapoag District of Canton, Massachusetts, but in those days it was the South Precinct of Old Stoughton, which was set apart from Dorchester, 1728. Philip Liscom bought a large farm of some seventy-five acres, part of the old Fenno Farm which had recently been purchased from the Indian chiefs. He was a prominent man; constable in 1718; traded considerably in tracts of land; and when he died, June 27, 1743, his estate was inventoried at two thousand one hundren and forty-five pounds, about eleven thousand dollars.

Philip (2) was born February 15, 1704, in Old Stoughton; died there October 24, 1772. He was a farmer and land trader, and served in the Crown Point expedition of the French and Indian war, 1755-58. He married, December 8, 1724, Desire Sylvester, of Scituate, fourth in line from Richard Sylvester, the emigrant ancestor, probably of French stock, settled in England in the time of the Conqueror. Desire's mother was a Stetson, descended from Cornet Robert Stetson, prominent in Old Plymouth Colony.

Philip Liscom (3) was born June 23, 1731, in Stoughton; died there February 8, 1774. He was a farmer, and later kept a tavern in Stoughton. He served in the Crown Point expedition of the French and Indian war, 1755. He was a member of one of the singing societies which flourished in Stoughton at that time, later becoming merged into the Stoughton Musical Society (still existing) one of the oldest societies in the country. He married, November 16, 1752, Miriam Belcher, daughter of Samuel and Mary (Puffer) Belcher. She was a descendant of Jeremy Belcher, a proprietor of Ipswich, Massachusetts, who came in the "Susan and Ellen" from Wiltshire, England, 1635. The line spread into Lynn and later to Stoughton. The Belcher line intermarried with other old pioneer families, Holbrooks of Roxbury; and Farnsworths of Dorchester from the old family of Lancashire, England.

Lemuel (1), son of Philip (3), born April 8, 1767, was the youngest of the five children. Miriam (1) born August 25, 1753, married July 1, 1772, Joseph Wright, of old Dedham stock, who later settled in Hinsdale, New Hampshire. Samuel (2) born September 14, 1755, was later a resident of Attleboro, Massachusetts, and a soldier from there on the Lexington Alarm; married September 25, 1776, Deborah Read. In 1803 he removed to and settled in Halifax, Vermont, where his descendants lived until about 1870, when they removed west. Hannah (3) born May 3, 1757, married December 9, 1773, Jeremiah Fisher, also of old Dedham, Massachusetts, stock, who likewise later settled in Hinsdale, New Hampshire. Eunice (4) born April 29, 1765; married September 29, 1785, Benjamin Tower, of the old Scituate family, who likewise later settled in Hinsdale, New Hampshire. Lemuel 1st (5) probably removed to Hinsdale with his relatives about 1790. Here he married, September 26, 1796, Submit, daughter of John Barrett, of Hinsdale, who was probably a descendant of the Benjamin Barrett families of Old Deerfield, Massachusetts, who represented an ancient Norman family settled in England at the time of the Conquest. John Barrett was an early settler in Hinsdale, and held town office. Lemuel 1st was a farmer and breeder of horses, also ran a flatboat on the Connecticut river before the days of railroads. When a lad of nine years he assisted in carrying supplies to Dorchester Heights for the use of the Continental army while besieging Boston. He was an early settler in that part of Hinsdale, New Hampshire, which is now Vernon, Vermont. Subsequently he bought a farm on the Chestnut Hill road where he lived for a time; then resided on the Brattleboro road, and finally settled in the locality known as Slab City. His farms were small and remote from market; he was troubled by Indians, and he had all the unpleasant experiences of a pioneer. He died July 7, 1836, and his wife died October 25, 1839. Both are buried in the old Dummer burying ground at North Hinsdale. Mrs. Liscom was a fine Christian woman, and brought up her family to be honorable and respected men and women. They had a family of nine children. Mary (1) born January 4, 1798; married, December 23, 1823, Henry Reed, a resident of Brattleboro, Vermont. Lemuel (2). Gratia (3) born July 20, 1801; married January 29, 1837, Williard Arms of Brattleboro, Vermont. Philip (4) born June 24, 1803; married May 1, 1824, Philena Bascom. He had a large farm in West Brattleboro, Vermont, still held by his son John. John (5) born January 6, 1806; married September 13, 1837, Eliza Amidon of Boston, Massachusetts. He resided in Boston for a time, but returned to Brattleboro, where he died. A daughter, Mrs. Lizzie Ranney, resides in Cambridge, Massachusetts, and a son, George, lives in West Brattleboro. Levi (6) born June 6, 1808; married September 6, 1832, Mary Odiorne Akerman of Portsmouth, New Hampshire. He removed to Boston, and engaged in the pianoforte business. He has descendants residing in Dedham, Massachusetts. Sophronia (7) born August 24, 1810; married March 31, 1834, Enos Crosby, of Brattleboro. Charles (8) born September 24, 1813; married June 1, 1842, Elizabeth Sartwell. He was in the coal business, but went to California in '49 and settled in Arcata, where he has numerous descendants. Samuel (9) born February 19, 1816; died in Boston, November 1, 1835.

Lemuel 2nd (2) was born October 9, 1799, in that part of Hinsdale which later became the town of Vernon, Vermont. At an early age he went to Boston, Massachusetts, and entered the employ of Lyman & Ralston, coal dealers, at the North End, the first firm in that city to deal in hard coal. Some years later Mr. Liscom started in the same business for himself, being the second anthracite coal dealer in the city. His coal was brought from the Lehigh mines in Pennsylvania. The Boston people were skeptical about the combustibility and heat-producing qualities of anthracite coal and many believed it to be nothing but stone. One person to whom Mr. Liscom sold some coal, not understanding how to burn it, had the coal man arrested for selling worthless stone for fuel; but Mr. Liscom was able to show the utility of the fuel and the honesty of the transaction, and was found not guilty and discharged from custody. He subsequently found it convenient even in summer to keep a hard coal fire burning in his fire-place to convince skeptics of its utility as fuel. He shipped the first cargo of coal to Lowell, Massachusetts. After eight successful years Mr. Liscom had accumulated a small fortune, and returning to Hinsdale, married. He went back to Boston, staying only a year on account of his wife's delicate health. He finally settled in North Hinsdale on the old Marsh Place (earlier mentioned), which he bought upon settling in Hinsdale, and for which he took a deed October 10, 1835. He engaged in farming and lumbering, and was among the first to take up the raising of tobacco in the valley; he raised large and profitable crops on the lower meadows. He was at first a Whig in politics, later a Republican; he took an active part in town affairs, serving as selectman for several terms; was also justice of the peace. In religious faith he was a Baptist, and took a prominent part in the affairs of his church. He was a teacher of vocal music. He died July 5, 1886.

Mr. Liscom's marriage to Emerancy Horton, of Hinsdale, took place September 20, 1831. Mrs. Liscom was a daughter of Hezikiah and Sally (Burnham) Horton, of Scotch and English descent, and of kin to Lord Burnham at one time a member of parliament.

The Hortons and Burnhams were old settlers and lived up the valley behind the Mine Mountain Range. Hezikiah Horton's father was Stafford Horton, who died February 7, 1813, and his wife, Eunice (Martin) Horton, died February 8, 1813, one day later; both were buried at one funeral in the North Church burying ground. This Eunice (Martin) Horton was the woman who, when a child of seven years, rode horseback with her mother through the primeval forests by trail to the raising of the first frame house in Hinsdale, known as the Marsh Place.

The Hortons were an ancient family in England, of Roman origin.

Walter Le Ventre came to England at the Conquest (1066) in the train of his cousin-german, Earl Warren, and at the survey (1080) was made lord of the Saxon villages of Burnham, and of other manors. From these manors he took the name "de Burnham." It was probably never used as a surname until after the Conquest (when surnames came into fashion) changing later to just "Burnham." In Saxon days it was probably just a place-name, so commonly found in England to-day.

From the best information obtainable at the present day, it appears that the three brothers—John, Thomas and Robert, sons of Robert and his wife, Mary (Andrews) Burnham, of Norwich, Norfolk county, England—came to America early in 1635; that they came in the ship "Angel Gabriel," in charge of their maternal uncle, Captain Andrews, the master of said ship; that they were wrecked on the coast of Maine; that with the freight thrown overboard to relieve the vessel at the time of the disaster was a chest (containing valuables) belonging to the three boys; that the boys came to Chebacco (Ipswich) in the colony of Massachusetts Bay, with their uncle, Captain Andrews, who, having lost his ship, settled there, the boys remaining with him. John and Thomas Burnham served (boys as they were) in the Pequot expedition, 1636-37.

(I) Thomas (1) Burnham was selectman in 1647, and on town committees; in 1664 was made sergeant of Ipswich county; in 1665 made ensign; 1683 appointed lieutenant; deputy to the general court 1683-84-85. In 1667 "Thomas Burnham is granted the privilege of erecting a sawmill on the Chebacco river, near the falls"; in 1657 "a road or way to be laid out through Thomas Burnham's land, across the swamp"; in 1678 "Ensign Thomas Burnham of Ipswich has right of commonage according to law." He owned much real estate in Ipswich and also in Chebacco. His houses and farms were divided between his sons Thomas and James. He was born in England 1623; married 1645, Mary, daughter of John Tuttle; died June, 1694.

(II) James (4), third son of Thomas (1) Burnham, born 1650; resident of Chebacco, Massachusetts; married; died June 30, 1729.

(III) Thomas, son of James (4) Burnham; married September 30, 1703, Margaret Boarman.

(IV) Offin, born in Ipswich, Massachusetts, July 10, 1712. "Descended from Robert and his wife, Mary (Andrews) Burnham, of Ipswich, Norfolk county, England, an old Norman family."

(V) Deacon William Burnham, son of Offin, was born November 21, 1759; married Sarah Thomas June 5, 1780. He died October 11, 1818.

(VI) Sally Burnham, daughter of Deacon William and Sally (Thomas) Burnham, was born September 8, 1789; married November 17, 1806, Hezikiah Horton; she died November 27, 1839.

Emerancy Horton, daughter of Hezikiah and Sally (Burnham) Horton, was born October 19, 1807; married Lemuel (2nd) Liscom, September 20, 1831.

Sally Thomas, wife of Deacon William Burnham, was a daughter of Nathan Thomas, of Chesterfield, New Hampshire, and Hephziba Farr. Nathan Thomas was from Hardwick, Massachusetts, and a descendant of Evan Thomas, who emigrated from Wales to Newton, Massachusetts, 1640; of ancient Welsh family.

William Thomas, Sr., of Newton, son of Evan, was born in 1656. Died December 1697.

William Thomas, Jr., was born August 31, 1687; settled in Hardwick, Massachusetts, some time previous to 1732; he is considered by good authority as one of the earliest, if not the very earliest, white inhabitant of Hardwick, Massachusetts.

Nathan Thomas, son of William Thomas, Jr., was born November 12, 1745; married, 1741, Hephziba Farr. He died June 27, 1790.

Sally, daughter of Nathan and Hephziba (Farr) Thomas, born March 18, 1760; married Deacon William Burnham, June 5, 1780; died March 28, 1842.

Sally Burnham, daughter of Deacon William and Sally (Thomas) Burnham (as above stated) was born September 8, 1789; married Hezikiah Horton, November 17, 1806; died November 27, 1839.

Emerancy Horton, daughter of Hezikiah and Sally (Burnham) Horton (as above stated), was born October 19, 1807; married Lemuel (2nd) Liscom, September 20, 1831; she died November 11, 1887. Mrs. Liscom was a devout Christian character, a woman of sterling worth.

To Mr. and Mrs. Liscom were born ten children. Sarah (1) born March 12, 1834; married Pardon D. Smith, December 12, 1854; lives in Hinsdale, New Hampshire. Charles Horton (2) born January 2, 1836; was a coal and real estate dealer at Clinton, Iowa. He enlisted in the Twenty-sixth Iowa Volunteer Infantry, and died at Helena, Arkansas, February 24, 1863, of wounds received at the battle of Vicksburg. Samuel Elliot (3) born May 24, 1837; enlisted from Hinsdale in Company A, Fourteenth New Hampshire Volunteer Infantry; participated in eight battles and was seriously wounded in the head and leg at Opequan Creek. He was transferred to Company C, Twenty-first Regiment Veteran Reserve Corps, January 24, 1865, and was discharged July 10, 1865, at Trenton, New Jersey; married Maria Thomas. Julia Elizabeth (4) born September 28, 1838; married Allan Cox, Esq., and resides in Conneaut, Ohio. Lemuel Franklin (5) born February 17, 1841; married Dollie Amelia Mason, February 21, 1872; resides in Hinsdale, New Hampshire. Emerancy Ann (6) born May 28, 1842; was drowned April 14, 1844. Lucy Rebecca and Lucius Gray, twins, (7 and 8), born August 28, 1843. Lucy Rebecca married Julius Mason, May 13, 1869; lived in Granville, New York, also in New York City and in Brattleboro, Vermont. Died in Brattleboro, December 8, 1907. Lucius Gray married Susie Clark; lives in Port Huron, Michigan. Is superintendent of the Maccabees Temple in that city. Henry Cabot (9) born May 4, 1846; married Keziah Dickerman Putnam December 20, 1870; resides in Brattleboro, Vermont; dealer in lumber and real estate. Emma Isabella (10) born May 18, 1850; married Scott A. Thrower; resides in Gardner, Massachusetts.

BARRON The Barron family, long resident in Massachusetts, sent pioneers into the towns of Bradford and Hartford, Vermont, where they were citizens of prominence. From the Vermont ancestry have descended the Barrons of this sketch, men of much prominence in New Hampshire.

(I) Abel Barron secured a good education, and for a time taught school. Subsequently he bought and cultivated a farm, but still taught in the winter seasons for some years. He was an industrious man and a good manager, accumulated a large property and became one of the leading citizens in the locality where he lived. He married and was the father of four sons: Clinton, Asa T., Oscar F., Orlando, drowned when young; and one daughter, Amanda.

(II) Asa Taylor Barron, son of Abel Barron, was born at Quechee, in the town of Hartford, Vermont, December 16, 1814, and died in August, 1887. He engaged in commercial business, having several stores in Hartford. In 1868, perceiving the necessity for a good hotel to accommodate travelers, he built the Junction House at White River Junction, in partnership with his brother, Oscar F., the firm being known as A. T. & O. F. Barron, and conducting the hotel under that style until Oscar F. died in 1879. This business was conducted for two years by Asa T. alone, when he was taken ill and took into partnership Mr. C. H. Merrill and O. G. Barron, the firm being Barron, Merrill & Barron. This continued till 1886, when the property was leased to O. G. Barron and Mr. Merrill and Asa T. Barron retired, living retired till his death in 1887. The properties were conducted a few years by O. G. Barron and Mr. Merrill. Later Mr. William A. Barron became associated with O. G. Barron, and Mr. Merrill, the firm being Barron, Merrill & Barron, which continued till 1899, when the partnership was turned into a corporation, and this corporation has operated the properties up to the present time. The ownership was the estate of Asa T. Barron and this was settled in 1896 by the organization of the Barron Hotel Company. This is at present the holding company and leases its properties to the Barron, Merrill & Barron Company, which company in addition to this leases and operates the Fabyan House and the Summit House for the Boston & Maine railroad. Mr. Barron soon discovered that he was peculiarly qualified to be a hotel keeper and began to look about for a new location. This he found at Twin Mountain, Coos county, New Hampshire, where he bought a cottage which he rebuilt and converted into a commodious and attractive hostilery for tourists and other travelers. The demand for accommodations grew as the reputation of the hotel spread, the wealth of the country increased, and the number of guests multiplied, and it was enlarged until now it has a capacity to house and feed two hundred guests. Improved facilities for getting to Mount Washington were required and Mr. Barron was quick to see that, and bought the stage line to that mecca of many modern pilgrims, and put on first class service and made it a popular and profitable line. From this time on, knowing his ability and responding to or forestalling demands for first class hotel accommodations, Mr. Barron and those interested with him built or leased various hotels at popular resorts. In 1871 he bought the Crawford House to which he built additions, then erected a new house which now accommodates three hundred and fifty guests. In the early eighties he leased the Fabyan Hotel from the Concord & Montreal railroad, and at the same time he also leased the Summit House on Mt. Washington. These hotels now accommodate comfortably three hundred and fifty and one hundred and fifty persons respectively. Asa T. Barron was a man of splendid judgment, quick perception, unusual executive ability, and unsurpassed as a popular and successful hotel keeper.

He married (first) Clarissa Demmon. There were born of this marriage three children: Mary B., married W. C. Bradley, of Lyndon Center, Vermont. Abel, who resides at White River Junction, Vermont. Oscar G., who is the subject of a succeeding paragraph. He married (second) Lydia Maria Andros, who was born in Derby, Vermont, 1833, daughter of Major William Andros, a custom house officer of Derby Line, Vermont. Three children were born of this union: Josie L., married Frederick E. Thompson, of Boston. William A., who is mentioned below. Harry B., manager of the Twin Mountain House.

(III) Oscar G., second son and third child of Asa T. and Clarissa (Demmon) Barron, was born in Quechee, in Hartford, Vermont, October 17, 1851, and was educated in the common schools of Quechee, Springfield, White River Junction, Williston, Fairfax and Poultney, Vermont. When he was but a lad his father began has career as a hotel keeper, and with every feature of the business the boy soon became familiar, and at an early age showed his ability to manage a hostelry with skill and success. He began to act as an independent manager in 1868, when he took charge of the Twin Mountain House. Since then he has managed the United States senate restaurant at Washington, D. C., (being appointed to that position by Vice-President Wheeler in 1877, and retaining the management five years); the Putnam House, Palatka, Florida; the Eastman Hotel, Hot Springs, Arkansas; the Raymond and Whitcomb Grand, Barron's Suburban Hotel and the Harvard Hotel, Chicago; the Twin Mountain House, the Fabyan House, and the Mt. Pleasant House, in the White Mountains; the Senter House, Center Harbor, New Hampshire; and the Quincy House, Boston. From an early age he was financially interested in the business of hotel keeping with his father, and contributed largely by his skillful management to the success of their various enterprises. The Barron Hotel Company was organized and O. G. Barron was made its president. For many years he has had personal supervison of the Fabyan House during the tourist season. Mr. Barron has devoted his life to one occupation, and in the pursuit of that vocation has made a success in which he has few equals and still fewer superiors. He is widely known and deservedly popular. Besides attending to the great interests under his care he has devoted much time to public affairs. In politics he is a Republican. He has served the town of Carroll as selectman for twenty-five years, and in 1888-90-95-96, as representative in the legislature. By appointment of Governor Sawyer he was made aide-de-camp with the rank of colonel and served as such during the governor's term of office. He was made postmaster at Twin Mountain in 1872 and held the office until 1892. He has been a member of the Ancient and Honorable Artillery Company of Boston. He is a member of White Mountain Lodge, No. 86, of Whitefield; North Star Royal Arch Chapter, of Lancaster; St. Gerard Commandery, Knights Temple, of Littleton; Edward A. Raymond Consistory, Sublime Princes of the Royal Secret, of Nashua, in which he took the thirty-second degree; and Aleppo Temple, Ancient Arabic Order of the Nobles of the Mystic Shrine, of Boston.

He married, at Montpelier, Vermont, May 16, 1872, Jennie Lane, who was born in Montpelier, Vermont, daughter of Dennis Lane. They have one daughter, Maude Lane.

(III) William Andros, second child of Asa T. and Lydia Maria (Andros) Barron, was born at White River Junction, Vermont, April 18, 1868. He was educated in the common schools, and at the high schools of Newburyport, Massachusetts, from which he graduated in 1884, and Phillips Exeter Academy, from which he graduated in 1887. Like his older brothers he has grown up in the hotel business, and was familiar with every detail of it. Immediately after leaving school he began his course as a hotel manager, and has since attended solely to the one business continuously. He has been manager of hotels as follows: Summit House at Mount Washington, three summers; Twin Mountain House, eight summers; Hotel Belleview at Belclair, Florida, four years; The Ericson, Commonwealth avenue, Boston, two years; and associated in management of The Crawford House at White Mountains, New Hampshire; proprietor and manager of Westminster Hotel, Boston, six years. He is treasurer of the Barron Hotel Company; the number of persons employed by the Barron Hotel Company is about five hundred, and the number of guests their hotels will accommodate is eleven hundred. The Barrons of Vermont are as much born to successful hotel keeping as are the Lelands of New York, and William A. Barron's success shows him to be a worthy member of the family. In politics he is a Republican. His interest in public affairs is never lukewarm, and although not an office seeker he has filled public offices. He was the representative from the town of Carroll in the general court in 1896, an aide-de-camp with the rank of colonel on Governor Ramsdell's staff, and commissary general with the rank of brigadier-general on Governor Batchelder's staff. In religious faith he is an Episcopalian. He is a highly esteemed member of White Mountain Lodge, No. 86, Free and Accepted Masons, of Whitefield; North Star Royal Arch Chapter, of Lancaster; St. Gerard Commandery, Knights Templar, of Littleton; and Edward A. Raymond Consistory, Sublime Princes of the Royal Secret, of Nashua.

He married, at Newburyport, Massachusetts, October 16, 1890, Mary Lawrence Todd, who was born May 15, 1869, daughter of T. Gillis Todd, of Newburyport, Massachusetts. They have one son, William A., Jr., who is in Middlesex School, at Concord, Massachusetts.

DUNBAR Dunbar as a surname was taken first from the seaport of that name in the county of Haddington, near Edinburgh, Scotland. William Dunbar, born in 1460, was one of the most distinguished of the early poets of Scotland.

(I) Caleb Dunbar, the son of Dustin Dunbar, a native of Scotland, was born in Grantham, New Hampshire, 1808, and died in Manchester, aged seventy-seven. He was a carriage maker, and manufactured carriages at Newport for a number of years. About 1850 he removed to Manchester, where he continued the business until about three or four years before his death. He was a man of integrity, and a constant attendant of the Baptist Church. He married Elizabeth Young, who was born April 14, 1810, and died aged seventy-seven. She was the daughter of William Young, of Pawtucket, Rhode Island. They had ten children: Augusta, married a Cunningham; Charles D; Eveline, married Alanson P. Marshall; George H.; William E.; Frances; Sidney A.; Eugene B.; and Edward and Eugene, who died young. Four of these now live in Manchester; Charles D., George H., William E. and Eugene B., are subjects of the next paragraph

(II) Dr. Eugene Buchanan Dunbar, eighth child and fifth son of Caleb and Elizabeth (Young) Dunbar, was born in Manchester, September 5, 1857. He attended the public schools of Manchester, from which he graduated in 1875. He read medicine in the office of Dr. George Hoyt one year, and then pursued his studies in the office of Dr. Flanders until he finished his course. He graduated in medicine at Dartmouth with the class of 1887, and returned to Manchester, where he has since had a successful practice in general medicine. He is a member of the American Medical Association, the New Hampshire Medical Association, and the Hillsborough County Medical Society. He is much interested in the efficiency and progress of the public schools, and has been a member of the school board for eight years. He is a member of the Improved Order of Red Men; the New England Order of Protection; and the Ancient Order of United Workmen, for the last two of which he is medical examiner. He is also a member of the Derryfield Grange. He married (first) Lizzie Blodgett, died 1895. She was the daughter of William C. and Susan (Lord) Blodgett, of Manchester. He married (second) Rose Milton, who was born in Warner, and was the daughter of Daniel and Hannah (Danforth) Milton. She died 1900, and he married (third) Edith E. Little, who was born in Newport, Vermont, daughter of Charles and Mary M. Little. Two children were born of the first wife; Clarence E. and Victor Y. The former graduated from the Manchester high school in 1904, and is now a member of the class of 1909 of Dartmouth College, where he matriculated in 1905.

DUNBAR This family in Pennsylvania is probably descended from progenitors who settled there at the time of the exodus of Scotch to that state before the American Revolution.

(I) John Dunbar was a resident of Centreville, Crawford county, Pennsylvania, and engaged in farming. He married Margaret Hilliard, and they were the parents of six children: Elisha, William, John, Enos, Maria and Sarah.

(II) Elisha, son of John and Margaret (Hilliard) Dunbar, was born in Centreville, Pennsylvania, 1843, and died at Mountain Home, Pennsylvania, 1900. He was a farmer and blacksmith for some years, but finally gave up agriculture to devote all his time to manufactures. He moved to Doylestown and engaged in the manufacture of rake handles, and carried on that industry for several years, until an opportunity offered to engage in the manufacture of pegs. He was in the latter business some time and made it a paying investment. He was a good business man; in politics a Democrat, and popular with his townsmen, who elected him to the principal town offices in Doylestown. In religious belief he was a Lutheran. He was fraternal, and was a member of the Masonic and Odd Fellows organizations. He married Harriet Hester, who was born in Richmond, Pennsylvania, daughter of Henry Hester. Three children were born of this union: Luther A., Annie and Laura.

(III) Luther Albertus, eldest child of Elisha and Harriet (Hester) Dunbar, was born in Centreville, Pennsylvania, December 7, 1861. He was educated in the public schools, and then went into business with his father. After a short time he preferred to go west, and in 1880 took the position of timekeeper for a contractor who was constructing the railroad between Point St. Ignace and Marquette, Michigan. In 1884 the Kearsarge Peg Company having dealings with the elder Dunbar, made arrangements to have the son take charge of their plant in Bartlett. He took the place the same

Eugene B. Dunbar M. D.

year, and has ever since been the company's superintendent. He takes an interest in public affairs, and has filled several public positions. He was moderator for a period of six years some time previous to 1907, when he was re-elected to that place. He has been a member of the school board, and a trustee of the Bartlett Public Library. In politics he is unfettered by party ties, and acts independently and upon his own judgment. For some years he has been president of the Congregational Society of Bartlett. He is a member of Mt. Washington Lodge, No. 87, Free and Accepted Masons, of North Conway; Signet Royal Arch Chapter, of Littleton, New Hampshire; St. Gerard Commandery, Knights Templar; and Mt. Sinai Temple, Ancient Arabic Order of the Mystic Shrine, of Montpelier, Vermont. He married, at Canadensis, Pennsylvania, June 28, 1892, Grace Lewis, daughter of Laban and Margaret (Sutherland) Lewis. They have two children: Leon and Kenneth.

PAUL The name of Paul is one of the most ancient in this country. In the early records the name is sometimes spelled with two "l's"; but the single "l" seems the older form. William Paul is usually considered the first American ancestor, but there are other Pauls in other states, apparently unrelated, who are contemporaneous with William. William Paul, born in Scotland in 1624, left Gravesend, England, for the Bermuda Islands on the ship "True Love de London," and settled at Dighton, since a part of Taunton, Massachusetts, in 1637. He was one of the pioneers of Taunton, where he was a large landowner; he was also a weaver and a mariner. He married Mary, daughter of John Richmond, and they had six children. He died at Taunton, November 9, 1704, aged eighty years; his widow died in 1715. The Pauls of Vermont are descended from this ancestry. Another early Paul was Joseph, who died at Abington, Pennsylvania, in 1717. He was a member of the Society of Friends, owned hundreds of acres about Abington, and was a member of the Assembly of the colony. There is nothing to show that he was kin to William, and he probably came direct from England in the seventeenth century. The state of Connecticut numbers two other Pauls among her early settlers. Benjamin Paul was at New Haven in 1639, and Daniel at New Haven in 1643; they may have been brothers. It is probable that Daniel Paul, whose descent follows, may have been derived from the Connecticut Benjamin, or Daniel, but direct proof is lacking.

(I) Daniel Paul came from Woodstock, Connecticut, in 1798, and bought the farm at Newport, New Hampshire, afterwards owned by his grandson, Doddridge Paul. He married Lovisa Answorth, of Woodstock, and they had ten children: Charlotte, born February 3, 1784, married Azor Perry, and went west. Lovisa, October 7, 1785, married John Ryder, of Croydon. Luke, see forward. Loren, December 25, 1788, married Susan Walton. Alexis, November 30, 1790, married Andrew Perry, of Vermont. Doddridge, September 19, 1794, married Roxana Whiting. Ira, January 25, 1799, died in 1875. Daniel, May 31, 1801. Andrew, September 21, 1803, married Clarissa Lamb, went to New York. Alvah, July 14, 1805, became a physician at Royalton, Ohio, married Nancy Bigelow, of Middletown, Vermont.

(II) Luke, eldest son and third child of Daniel and Lovisa (Answorth) Paul, was born June 28, 1787, at Croydon, New Hampshire. He was educated in the district schools. He taught school in the winters and farmed in the summers. He cleared his farm out of the wilderness, and was enterprising and prosperous. He married Sarah Cooper, daughter of Samuel Cooper, of Croydon, and they settled on the old Gibson farm at Baltimore Hill. They had one child, Azor. Luke Paul and his wife are buried in Croydon.

(III) Azor, son of Luke and Sarah (Cooper) Paul, was born April 12, 1812, in Croydon, New Hampshire. He was educated in the district schools and became a successful farmer. He moved from Croydon to the eastern part of Newport. His first home was where Reed's saw mill is now located. After a time he moved back to Croydon, where he remained two and one-half years, and then purchased the old homestead. Later he moved on the direct road to Newport, where he continued farming and lived there till his death. Azor Paul was twice married. His first wife was Roena, daughter of Stephen and Lovina (Wakefield) Reed, of Newport. They had two children: Roena, born in 1840, married Thomas C. Rider. Eugene A., born February 17, 1847, married, December 12, 1876, Jennie H. Hurd; they had one child, Eugene Ralph, born January 9, 1878. Mrs. Roena (Reed) Paul died in October, 1843, and Azor Paul married her sister, Rosella Reed. There were four children by the second marriage who lived to man and womanhood: George E., born August 17, 1845, married Susan Cole. Sidney, who died at the age of nine years. Anna R., June 15, 1855. Fred. A., March 23, 1859. McClellan, December 26, 1864. Azor Paul died in January, 1890, and his wife, Mrs. Rosella (Reed) Paul, died in August, 1892. Both are buried in the Maple Street cemetery at Newport. The ancestry of the wives of Azor Paul is interesting. They were the granddaughters of Peter Wakefield (see Wakefild, V).

(IV) George E., eldest son and child of Azor and Rosella (Reed) Paul, was born August 17, 1845, at Newport, New Hampshire. He was educated in the public schools and remained on the home farm till the age of twenty-one. The farm where he lives now is on the main road to Newport, Sunapee, Newbury and Bradford. It is the site where John Trask, Senior, and Zachariah Batchelder first lived while they were clearing their farms. Mr. Paul has worked early and late, removing the stones from his land, and to-day it is one of the most productive farms in Sullivan county. There are two hundred and sixty acres, well drained. Mr. Paul is considered one of the most substantial farmers in this part of the state. Since he first owned the place he has put up a complete set of new buildings, which present an attractive appearance from the roadside. He takes great pride in keeping things in good shape, and his buildings are painted annually. The farm itself yields a handsome profit, the maple sugar alone furnishing a good revenue, as hundreds of gallons of superior syrup are made every spring. Mr. Paul winters from thirty to thirty-five head of cattle in his modern barns, besides keeping four horses. He milks twenty cows on an average, and ships the product direct to Boston. His hay crop amounts to seventy-five tons or more. George E. Paul was married to Susan Cole, daughter of Benjamin and Lucy (Hatch) Cole, of Plainfield, New Hampshire. They have two children: Sidney E., born June 8, 1875, married Lenore Philbrick, daughter of Elwin and Ella (Sargent) Philbrick, of Springfield, New Hampshire; they were married December, 1905. George Merton, born November 19, 1877, married M. Alice Young, daughter of Wilbur and Margaret

(Pyke) Young. They were married October, 1897, and have one son, Stanley, born July 26, 1903. They live on the home place, and Mr. Paul is station agent at Sunapee on the Boston & Maine railroad.

(II) Daniel Paul, Jr., eighth child and fifth son of Daniel and Lovisa (Answorth) Paul, was born in Newport, New Hampshire, May 31, 1801, and died on the old home farm in that town. He married, November 30, 1828, Experience C. Whipple, born November 22, 1808, daughter of David Whipple of Croyden, New Hampshire. Three children were born of this marriage: Laban, born January 5, 1832, died in 1859; Epaphras, born December 17, 1833, married Mary George of Sunapee and settled at Croydon; and Doddridge, of Newport.

(III) Doddridge, youngest of the three sons of Daniel and Experience (Whipple) Paul, was born in Newport, New Hampshire, October 12, 1835, and lived nearly sixty years on the old farm where his grandfather settled before 1800. Doddridge Paul has not been content with merely maintaining the paternal acres, and added to his lands in that vicinity until at one time he owned six hundred acres. Some parts of these lands were afterward sold, and in 1894 he removed with his family to his present farm in East Unity. He is known as one of the most thrifty, successful and well-to-do farmers of the town of Newport, and now owns and with the assistance of his son carries on about five hundred acres of farm lands. Mr. Paul never has been active in either town or county politics, having no ambition for public office, and in both politics and religion he holds to liberal views. He is an active man, holds his years well, a close observer of men and affairs and a careful reader of the events of the day.

He married, March 20, 1864, Rosetta Rogers, of Goshen, New Hampshire. She was born June 15, 1843, and died at East Unity, November, 1905. Six children were born of this marriage, viz.: Daniel, born December 14, 1864; Lovisa A., born July 17, 1866, married Elmer Dodge, of Newport; Jennie L., born December 16, 1871, married Frank Putnam, of Claremont, New Hampshire; James R., born January 17, 1874, died in 1851; Isabel H., born July 5, 1877, married Ralph Johnson; John L., now living at home.

MORRISON George H. Morrison, proprietor of the Morrison Hospital, Whitefield, New Hampshire, was born in Jefferson, New Hampshire, December 7, 1854, a son of Calvin and Elmira (Jordan) Morrison. Calvin Morrison being a man of limited means, depending solely upon his labor for the support of his family, and his wife dying in 1861, leaving him with three small children, he was unable to give his son the educational advantages which are so essential to a successful career, and accordingly at a very early age George H. was obliged to maintain himself by manual labor.

George H. Morrison was first employed on farms and in saw mills, but being an ambitious lad, desirous of acquiring an education and studying a profession, he made good use of every opportunity, and prior to attaining the age of twenty-one was thoroughly versed in rudimentary knowledge. He studied medicine with Dr. Charles E. Rowell, of Lancaster, and saved sufficient capital to defray his expenses through college. In 1877 he entered Boston University, where he remained two years, and then went to Philadelphia and in 1881 graduated from the Hahnemann Medical College. He immediately began the practice of his profession at North Strafford, New Hampshire, and the following year (1882) came to Whitefield and succeeded to the practice of Dr. C. S. Snell. He conducted a general practice successfully until 1902, when he took up general surgery as a specialty. In 1886-87-88-89 he pursued post-graduate courses at the Post-Graduate and Polyclinic Hospital, New York City, and each year since then has spent some time visiting the hospitals in the large cities of the country. The summer of 1900 he spent in visiting the more important hospitals of Europe, and in this way kept abreast with the advanced and more modern methods of surgery and medicine. In the winter of 1901 an epidemic of small pox broke out in Whitefield, and Dr. Morrison gave up his large practice and took charge of the cases, treating them successfully, not losing a single case, and the fees paid him by the county commissioners he used to beautify the public common of Whitefield. There being no hospital in northern New Hampshire and the need being great, in 1902 Dr. Morrison established a private hospital at his residence, but his quarters soon became inadequate, and the following year he erected his present commodious building. Dr. Morrison is a member of the Coos County Medical Association, New Hampshire Medical Society, American Medical Association, Ancient Free and Accepted Masons, Royal Arch Masons, Knights Templar, Independent Order of Odd Fellows, Knights of Pythias. Politically he is a Republican.

Dr. Morrison organized the Board of Health in Whitefield, and has acted in the capacity of chairman of the same for more than two decades. He, with a partner, established the electric light plant and owned and managed it for twelve years, disposing of it in the fall of 1907. He has taken stock in all companies conducting business in his adopted city, and was one of the organizers and has since been a director of the Whitefield Bank and Trust Company. He has always been a leader in all enterprises that would prove of benefit to the town and community. He presented to the town the clock which adorns the cupola of the town hall. Dr. Morrison was married in 1878 to Carry F. Snow, of Columbia, New Hampshire, daughter of Dr. Lewis and Jannett (Hobert) Snow.

The Morrison Hospital, completed and opened to the public March 20, 1903, has a picturesque situation at the edge of the village, on a commanding rise known as "The Highlands," a location which not only furnishes a magnificent view of White Mountain scenery, but which is at the same time eminently healthful on account of its dry sandy soil, and invigorating on account of its pure balmy air and abundant sunshine. The handsome building has more the appearance of a fine mountain hotel or of a large private house than of a hospital. It is one hundred and six feet long, is admirably located in ample grounds, embracing about one acre of well laid lawns decorated with flowers and shrubbery. The building was originally designed for a surgical institution, but now all cases are admitted except contagious. This is the largest and probably the only private hospital in the state that is self-sustaining, and being located in the heart of the White Mountains, where many tourists come, their patients are from all sections of the country. Each floor has five pleasant and cosy private rooms, while there are also two wards, each containing eight beds, on each floor. One of the private rooms is reserved for Catholic patients, and has been furnished by the local church. Throughout the hospital the greatest care has been taken with the steam heating and the ventilation, and every

G. H. Harrison

MORRISON H[illegible]

MORRISON HOSPITAL.

John C Littlefield

tent in 1643, and it is quite probable that he built : first dwelling house in that town, also the first w and grist mills. He was a grand juryman 1645, took the oath of allegiance in 1653, and his ll, which was dated December 11, 1661, was proted on December 24 of that year. His wife, whose ristian name was Annis (or Annas), was born in ngland about the year 1600. She became the other of eight children: Francis, Anthony, Eliza-:th, John, Thomas, Mary, Hannah and Francis (2). rancis (1), who was born in 1619, mysteriously isappeared from his home in England when about x or seven years old, and his parents, supposing im to be dead, named their youngest son in memory f their lamented first-born. He subsequently came ɔ America and was reunited with his family. He ıarried and was the father of one daughter.

(II) Ensign Francis, youngest son and child of Edmund and Annis Littlefield, was born in England about the year 1631. He was a carpenter in Wells, and is sometimes mentioned in the records ıs Francis the Younger. His will, which was witıessed by his brother Francis, was made February 5, 1674, and probated April 6, 1675. His widow, whose christian name was Meribah, was living in 1677. His children were: Joseph, Nathan, Jonathan, Job, David, Mary, Joanna, Tabitha and Hannah.

(III) David, fifth son of Francis and Meribah Littlefield, was born in Wells, about 1653. He was baptized an adult in July, 1707. He resided in Wells, and there reared his family. His children were: David, Eleanor, Nathan, Mary, Jeremiah, Meribah, Tabitha and Ithamar.

(IV) Ithamar, son of David Littlefield, was born in Wells, 1670.

(V) Ithamar (2), son of Ithamar (1) Littlefield, was born July 20, 1727. His intentions to marry Margaret Williams was published April 10, 1745. He was a resident of Kennebunk, Maine, and a prosperous farmer.

(VI) Obadiah, son of Ithamar (2) and Margaret (Williams) Littlefield, was born in Kennebunk, 1747. He married Lydia Perkins, of Kennebunk, Maine.

(VII) Joshua, son of Obadiah Littlefield, was born in Kennebunk, April 6, 1810, died April 6, 1887. He was reared to farm life, but abandoned it for the sea, which he followed for several years in the merchant service, and visited all parts of the civilized world. Deciding at length to remain on shore, he entered the lumber business in Sanford, Maine, shipping lumber from there to Boston, and followed that occupation for several years. He was for some time in charge of a brick yard in Sanford, Maine, and later at Cambridge, Massachusetts. He subsequently served as sheriff of York county, and also as captain in the state militia, Third Regiment, Third Brigade, First Division, and his son still has his commission, dated July 9, 1839. August 20, 1846, he was appointed sergeant of Company C. First Regiment of Volunteers, raised in the state of Maine for the prosecution of the war between the United States and the Republic of Mexico. He married Mary Clough, born May 10, 1811, died April 21, 1900, daughter of Samuel Clough, of Alfred, Maine. Of the seven children of this union but one is now living, John C., who is mentioned at length in the succeeding paragraph. Emery P., a brother of John C., who resided in Manchester, died February 27, 1907. He left a widow and two children, William E. and Andrew G.

(VIII) John Clough, son of Joshua and Mary (Clough) Littlefield, was born in Sanford, July 15,

precaution has been used to secure the prevention of dust, and to leave no breeding or even harboring place for microbes of any kind. Throughout the building the floors are of hardwood, finished in wax; the walls are all in hard finish, done in oil, and ceilings handsomely frescoed. The electrical room contains the electrical appliances, consisting of several small Faradic batteries, one large fifty-cell galvanic battery, and one ten-plate Morton-Wimshurst static generator, with which is a complete outfit for X-ray work, including the special German tubes for the treatment of all forms of cancers. On the north side of the building is located the well lighted operating room. Beside the complete outfit of surgical instruments, glass topped iron tables and stands, this room contains one dressing sterilizer for dressings and instruments, also one water sterilizer having two fifteen-gallon tanks with filtering device attached which filters the water before it enters the tanks. Other rooms namely, the recovery room, sun parlor and sitting room for nurses, are modern in their appointments, and compare favorably with similar institutions in the larger cities. The hospital is at the disposal of any reputable physician who may wish to bring patients for either operation or treatment, the operating room, which is fitted up with the most modern apparatus, being always available with trained assistants, and patients cared for afterwards as he may direct. The hospital business has more than quadrupled in the past five years.

In connection with the hospital Dr. Morrison has a Training School for Nurses, which, like the hospital, has proved a success from the start. They have a Nurses' Home near the hospital, and furnish trained nurses for the towns in northern New Hampshire and Vermont. A three years' course of training is required before graduating. This includes a thorough course of instruction in medical, surgical, gynecological and maternity nursing. Three months is required in the diet kitchen, where special instruction is given in the cooking and preparation of foods for the sick. Nurses are not sent out on private cases until they have been in the hospital at least six months, and no diploma is granted to a nurse who has not spent at least twenty-four months' actual work in the hospital. The training school is now under the superintendency of Miss Mae S. Intire, who is a graduate of the school. This school took an active part in securing the bill for the registration of nurses which passed the legislature in 1906. The staff of the hospital comprises some of the most eminent physicians and surgeons in this part of the country, namely: G. H. Morrison, M. D., R. E. Wilder, M. D., H. M. Wiggin, M. D., G. W. McGregor, M. D., L. C. Aldrich, M. D., J. C. Breithing, M. D., C. A. Cramton, M. D., and W. C. Leonard, instructor in pharmacy.

LITTLEFIELD

This family has been prominently identified with southwestern Maine from the early settlement of that section to the present time, and not a few of its representatives have acquired distinction in other states of the Union. It is of English origin.

(I) Edmund Littlefield, of Tichfield, England, emigrated about the year 1637, accompanied by his son Anthony, and the remainder of the family came in the "Bevis" in 1638. He went from Boston to Exeter, New Hampshire, and thence to Wells, Maine, where he was granted land under the Gorges Patent in 1643, and it is quite probable that he built the first dwelling house in that town, also the first saw and grist mills. He was a grand juryman in 1645, took the oath of allegiance in 1653, and his will, which was dated December 11, 1661, was probated on December 24 of that year. His wife, whose christian name was Annis (or Annas), was born in England about the year 1600. She became the mother of eight children: Francis, Anthony, Elizabeth, John, Thomas, Mary, Hannah and Francis (2). Francis (1), who was born in 1619, mysteriously disappeared from his home in England when about six or seven years old, and his parents, supposing him to be dead, named their youngest son in memory of their lamented first-born. He subsequently came to America and was reunited with his family. He married and was the father of one daughter.

(II) Ensign Francis, youngest son and child of Edmund and Annis Littlefield, was born in England about the year 1631. He was a carpenter in Wells, and is sometimes mentioned in the records as Francis the Younger. His will, which was witnessed by his brother Francis, was made February 5, 1674, and probated April 6, 1675. His widow, whose christian name was Meribah, was living in 1677. His children were: Joseph, Nathan, Jonathan, Job, David, Mary, Joanna, Tabitha and Hannah.

(III) David, fifth son of Francis and Meribah Littlefield, was born in Wells, about 1653. He was baptized an adult in July, 1707. He resided in Wells, and there reared his family. His children were: David, Eleanor, Nathan, Mary, Jeremiah, Meribah, Tabitha and Ithamar.

(IV) Ithamar, son of David Littlefield, was born in Wells, 1670.

(V) Ithamar (2), son of Ithamar (1) Littlefield, was born July 20, 1727. His intentions to marry Margaret Williams was published April 10, 1745. He was a resident of Kennebunk, Maine, and a prosperous farmer.

(VI) Obadiah, son of Ithamar (2) and Margaret (Williams) Littlefield, was born in Kennebunk, 1747. He married Lydia Perkins, of Kennebunk, Maine.

(VII) Joshua, son of Obadiah Littlefield, was born in Kennebunk, April 6, 1810, died April 6, 1887. He was reared to farm life, but abandoned it for the sea, which he followed for several years in the merchant service, and visited all parts of the civilized world. Deciding at length to remain on shore, he entered the lumber business in Sanford, Maine, shipping lumber from there to Boston, and followed that occupation for several years. He was for some time in charge of a brick yard in Sanford, Maine, and later at Cambridge, Massachusetts. He subsequently served as sheriff of York county, and also as captain in the state militia, Third Regiment, Third Brigade, First Division, and his son still has his commission, dated July 9, 1839. August 20, 1846, he was appointed sergeant of Company C, First Regiment of Volunteers, raised in the state of Maine for the prosecution of the war between the United States and the Republic of Mexico. He married Mary Clough, born May 10, 1811, died April 21, 1900, daughter of Samuel Clough, of Alfred, Maine. Of the seven children of this union but one is now living, John C., who is mentioned at length in the succeeding paragraph. Emery P., a brother of John C., who resided in Manchester, died February 27, 1907. He left a widow and two children, William E. and Andrew G.

(VIII) John Clough, son of Joshua and Mary (Clough) Littlefield, was born in Sanford, July 15,

1841. After concluding his attendance at the public schools he became an operative in a textile mill, and going to Manchester, April 5, 1858, was employed there in the same calling for one year. For the ensuing seven years he followed the trade of millwright. He then became connected with the James Baldwin Bobbin and Shuttle Company, had charge of the shuttle department, was one of the directors, and succeeded the late Mr. Baldwin as president. Some time since this enterprise, which constitutes one of the most important industries in Manchester, was consolidated with other large concerns of a similar character, and is now known as the James Baldwin Division of the U. S. Bobbin and Shuttle Company (see Baldwin family). Mr. Littlefield is one of the proprietors in the Percy Lumber Company, having extensive works at Percy, New Hampshire, and at Auburn, Maine, and is president of the company. He is also president of the Ranno Saddlery Company of Manchester, manufacturers of all kinds of saddlery and harnesses. In politics he is a Republican. Although not being a political aspirant, he consented to and served with ability in the city council in ward 8, and was a delegate to the constitutional convention in 1902. Mr. Littlefield and his family are members of the First Baptist Church. He was many years a director of the Young Men's Christian Association of Manchester.

Mr. Littlefield married, July 12, 1864, Mary E. Baldwin, daughter of the late James and Mary (Butrick) Baldwin, the former of whom was the founder of the Baldwin Company previously referred to (see Baldwin). Mr. and Mrs. Littlefield have one daughter, Minnie E. After her graduation from the high school, where she was the valedictorian of her class, she entered the Emerson School of Oratory of Boston, from which she was graduated with high honors and received the degree of O. B., and since then has been a successful teacher of elocution.

LITTLEFIELD This name is of the class known as local, and was adopted as a surname by a person who lived at or by a little field. The Littlefields are numerous in New England, and many of them have been prominent citizens.

(I) Erastus Joseph Littlefield was born probably in Frankfort, Maine, in 1808, and died in 1863. He spent his first years on a farm. When a young man he worked some years in the saw mills at Vesey, Maine. From there he removed to Monroe, Maine, where he was engaged in farming. In 1855 he removed to Bangor, where he carried on a small farm, and also conducted teaming in the city. He died there in 1862. He married Elizabeth B. Washburn, of Hebron, Maine, who was born in 1823, and died in 1897, aged seventy-four. They had six children: Horace, George H., Chauncey B., Van Rensselaer, Eva L. and Addie L.

(II) Chauncey Bonny, third child and second son of Erastus J. and Elizabeth B. (Washburn) Littlefield, was born in Monroe, Maine, February 9, 1846, and was educated in the common schools of Bangor, and at East Corinth Academy. At the age of sixteen he went to Boston, Massachusetts, and became a clerk, first in the wholesale and retail drug house of S. M. Colcord & Company, where he remained until 1865, and then with Joseph T. Brown & Company, where he remained until 1869. On the opening of the Massachusetts College of Pharmacy, Mr. Littlefield entered on a course of study there under Professor George F. Babcock, Professor George F. H. Markoe, and others. Here he attended two years. In 1869 he removed to Manchester, New Hampshire, where he has since resided, and opened a drug store, carrying on business under the name of C. B. Littlefield until 1892, when the Littlefield Drug Company was incorporated, of which Mr. Littlefield was made president. From 1870 to 1907 Mr. Littlefield was engaged in the manufacture of a meritorious proprietary medicine, which was a profitable industry. Mr. Littlefield has been engaged in the real estate business since 1902. From the time of his coming to Manchester until the present, Mr. Littlefield has been successful, liberal and cheerful, and his business generally prosperous. He has been popular and respected. He has taken some interest in politics. In 1877, while absent on business in Canada, he was nominated without his knowledge as a candidate for the common council, and duly elected. In 1886 he was elected representative to the legislature from Ward two. In 1871 he was made an Odd Fellow in Hillsboro Lodge, No. 2, and afterward joined Mt. Washington Encampment, No. 16. At the formation of the Calumet Club, Mr. Littlefield was a charter member.

He married (first), in Manchester, 1872, Fannie E. Porter, daughter of Benjamin F. and Eliza A. (Buffun) Porter; she died in 1901. He married (second), in 1902, Laura A. Campbell, a native of Manchester, daughter of Henry R. and Adeline (Dickey) Campbell. They attend the Methodist Church.

TOWLE From one couple of this name comes a large progeny of Towles in southeastern New Hampshire and Maine, who are people of good standing. The early Towles were patriotic, and many of them fought for liberty in the Revolution. The early generations were strong and hardy, and noted for longevity. Vitality and vigor characterize their descendants.

(I) Philip Towle, seaman, is supposed to have been of Irish descent. April 15, 1664, he bought a dwelling and outhouses and a house lot containing seven and one-half acres, and about seventy acres of outlying lands and some shares in common lands in Hampton. Part or all of this land is still owned by his descendants. He married at the age of forty-one years, November 19, 1657, Isabella, daughter of Francis and Isabella (Bland) Austin, of Colchester, England, and Hampton, New Hampshire, and granddaughter of John and Joanna Bland, of Edgartown, England. She was born about 1633, and was the eldest of three daughters. She was once the victim of persecution for witchcraft. She and Rachel Fuller were accused in the summer of 1680. Rachel confessed and accused Isabel. Both were committed to prison, where they remained until the sitting of the Hampton court, September 7, when the case was heard, and later released on bail of £100 each, and discharged the next year. Isabella was then the mother of eight children, from two years old upward. Philip and family lived in what is now the heart of the village of Hampton. Fve of their sons—Joseph, Philip, Benjamin, Francis and Caleb—served in King Williams war, 1689-1698. Their children were: Philip, Caleb (died young), Joshua, Mary, Joseph, Benjamin, Francis, John and Caleb.

(II) Sergeant Joseph, fourth son and fifth child of Philip and Isabella (Austin) Towle, born May 4, 1669, died September 2, 1757, probably lived a little north of the village of Hampton. He served in King William's war, and was selectman in 1723-29-33. He married (first), December 14, 1693, Mehitabel Hobbs, born February 28, 1673, daughter of John and Sarah (Colcord) Hobbs; and (second),

March 4, 1731, Sarah, daughter of Morris Hobbs. The children, all by the first wife, were: John, Joseph, James, Mary, Jonathan, Mehitabel and Amos. (Mention of Jonathan and descendants appears in this article).

(III) James, third son of Joseph and Mehitabel (Hobbs) Towle, was born in 1698. He was selectman of Hampton, and with his sons is known to have been connected with church, for we know their children were baptized. In 1725 he married Keziah Perkins. He died April 14, 1756, leaving seven children: Mary, Mehitabel, Anna, Huldah, Abraham Perkins, James and Jonathan, the sons being respectively sixteen, thirteen and nine years of age. The two elder daughters had previously married, but of the other two we have no record but their baptism. Jonathan afterwards named his first two daughters after them.

(IV) Jonathan, son of James and Keziah (Perkins) Towle, was born in 1747. He was an honest, genial man, industrious and thrifty, a progressive farmer giving unusual attention to the raising of fruit and potatoes. He removed from Hampton to Pittsfield in 1780, and began cutting down the forest on a lot about a mile west of Wild Goose pond, bought of Samuel Marston, of Deerfield, for four hundred pounds of continental currency. This lot was No. 15 of the first range of the second division, then of Chichester. In 1786 he bought of Stephen Cross lot No. 14, west, for nine pounds. It contained fifty acres and extended to Barnstead line. Fifty acres more were subsequently added. He was one of eight owners of a sawmill at the outlet of the pond. At the outbreak of the Revolution in 1775, when the alarm following the battle of Lexington reached Hampton, it is said that Jonathan and his brother Abraham were in the field plowing. They immediately ran for their guns and started with the Hampton company for Boston, leaving the oxen for the women to unyoke. At Ipswich, Massachusetts, they were met with an order to return, probably for coast defence.

Jonathan was without doubt in the battle of Bunker Hill. He served in Captain Moses Leavitt's company, Colonel Abraham Drake's regiment, sent to reinforce the northern Continental army at Stillwater, New York, from September 8 to December 16, 1777. He was credited two pounds and two shillings for travel home from Windsor, Vermont, two pounds and eleven shillings and four pounds four shilling for wages. He was probably present at the time of Burgoyne's surrender. His brother, Abraham P., was paid one pound and sixteen shillings "toward hiring to go to Peekskill for the first time." The three brothers with thirteen other Towles signed the Association Test in 1776. Thirty-two names of Toweles are recorded in the New Hampshire Revolutionary Rolls. The tradition is that Jonathan went to Pittsfield the year after the Dark Day, which would have been in 1781. The log house built the year before on a little knoll some twenty rods south of where he afterwards built, is now marked by a large mound of stones. While living in Hampton, Jonathan and his wife were members of the Congregational Church, uniting October 16, 1774. In Pittsfield he became a pioneer Free Baptist. The family were of strong constitution, equal to the hardships they were called to endure, and attained remarkable longevity. Jonathan married Miriam Marston, of Hampton, in 1773, and died in 1822. His wife was born in 1749 and died in 1835. Their children were Molly, Huldah, Jonathan, Daniel, James, Sally, Abraham Perkins and Nancy.

(V) James (2), son of Jonathan and Mirian (Marston) Towle, was born in 1781. He settled on the old homestead. He was short and of medium height, but very strong, in which he took great pride. One of his feats, which cost him his life, was the carrying of four bushels of salt up stairs, which resulted in an immediate attack of spinal difficulty making him helpless. After thirteen months of suffering he died, June 13, 1813. This was a severe blow to his father, who was depending upon him for care in his old age. He married, January 13, 1806, cousin Polly, daughter of Robey and Hannah (Drake) Marston, of Deerfield. She was born March 22, 1779, and died September 24, 1854. Their children were Robey Marston and Samuel.

(VI) Samuel, son of James and Polly (Marston) Towle, was born October 19, 1811. He lived on the home place in Pittsfield.' He married Betsey, daughter of Thomas and Hannah (Meserve) Snell, of Barnstead, New Hampshire, December 8, 1835. She was born January 26, 1815, and died January 19, 1902. Their children were: Angeline Alvina, Alvin Freeman and Louisa Hannah. The last named died in her sixth year.

(VII) Angeline Alvina, daughter of Samuel and Betsey (Snell) Towle, was born May 27, 1838. She married, July 3, 1869, Charles Carroll Rogers, son of Jacob and Hannah (Kelley) Rogers of Pittsfield. Mr. Rogers moved with his parents to Pittsfield when a small boy. His father kept hotel at Pittsfield Corner. Mr. Rogers was raised and educated in Pittsfield, and continued to live there after his marriage. His business was that of a hardware merchant, which he continued till 1883, when he sold out and took up a small farm on Berry Hill, where his widow now resides. He served as selectman five years, and also as road agent. He was not a member of any church, but was reared in the Episcopal Church. By a former marriage he had two children, Abbie E. and George Edward, both of whom are dead. He had no children by his second marriage. His widow is a woman of great prudence, energy and strength of character, and is respected by all who know her.

(VII) Alvin Freeman, son of Samuel and Betsey (Snell) Towle, was born February 8, 1842, and now resides in Northwood, moving there after the death of his wife. He married, February 21, 1865, Francena Floyd, daughter of George and Sarah (Goodwin) Stockman of Pittsfield. She was born February 21, 1848, and died April 8, 1881. Their children are: Herbert Clarence, born July 31, 1867; Hattie Belle, born October 30, 1870, and Arthur Daniel, born April 27, 1876. They lived in Pittsfield until 1881. The family are noted for their intellectual tastes, and have one of the best libraries in the vicinity. Louisa Hannah was born September 16, 1844, and died February 17, 1850.

(III) Jonathan fourth son and fifth child of Joseph and Mehetabel (Hobbs) Towle, born April 5, 1703, died April 23, 1791. He married, December 12, 1728, Anna Norton, born March 20, 1708, daughter of Bonus Norton, of Hampton Falls, and probably settled in Rye. They had children: Jonathan, Levi, Joseph, Samuel, James, Anna, and Nathan.

(IV) Jonathan (2), eldest child of Jonathan (1) and Anna (Norton) Towle, born July 4, 1729, died in Epsom. He married Elizabeth Jenness, born April 4, 1734, a native of Rye, and they had children: Hannah, Simeon and Levi.

(V) Hannah, eldest child and only daughter of Jonathan and Elizabeth (Jenness) Towle, married William Yeaton, of Rye. They removed to Epsom, and settled near the Suncook river (see Yeaton, II).

(V) Simeon, eldest son and second child of Jonathan and Elizabeth (Jenness) Towle, married Elizabeth Marden, of Rye, and settled in Epsom. and they had two sons, Simeon (2), and Benjamin, next mentioned.

(VI) Benjamin Marden, second son of Simeon (1) and Elizabeth (Marden) Towle, was born in Epsom, and there married Hannah Sanborn.

(VII) Lemuel B., son of Benjamin and Hannah (Sanborn) Towle, died September 30, 1895, was a farmer and prominent citizen of Chichester, having his residence near Chichester station, on the Suncook Valley railroad. He married Mary Ann Prescott. died January, 1904. Both were members of the Congregational Church. Their children were: Mary Elizabeth, died in infancy, Charles, resides in Epsom, Frank C. is the subject of the next paragraph; George C. is in Alaska.

(VIII) Frank Clifton, second son and third child of Lemuel B. and Mary Ann (Prescott) Towle, was born May 30, 1847, in Epsom, where he grew up on his father's farm. He attended the common schools and Pittsfield Academy, and when eighteen years old took a place in the store of his uncle, Joseph Towle Goss, in Hooksett. Later he became station agent for the Boston & Maine railroad, and purchased the store in which he had been employed. He carried on the store for many years, and also acted as chief assistant to the late Jesse Gault, who was a large brick manufacturer of Hooksett. Mr. Towle was an active and successful business man, and left a comfortable fortune. He was a Republican, and a political leader in his town. He represented Hooksett in the lower house of the legislature, and was afterward a member of the senate. Naturally social, he was a valuable member of the Masonic order, in which he attained the thirty-second degree, being a member of Hooksett Lodge, Trinity Royal Arch Chapter, No. 2; Horace Chase Council; Mount Horeb Commandery, Knights Templar; Horace Chase Council No. 4, Concord; and Edward A. Raymond Consistory, Nashua. He was also a member of Friendship Lodge, Independent Order of Odd Fellows, of Hooksett, and for many years an honored member of the Congregational Church. He married, October 19, 1870, Myra Clement Gault, daughter of Jesse (2) Gault, of Hooksett (see Gault, V). She was born April 7, 1847, and now resides with her widowed mother in Manchester. They were the parents of two children: Annie is a teacher in Tilton Seminary; Helen Augusta is the wife of Adam D. Smith, of Danvers, Massachusetts.

TOWLE There is little doubt that the present branch is descended from Philip Towle, the patriarch of the Towles in this country, who came to Hampton, New Hampshire, as early as 1657. He reared a numerous family, some of them lived in Hampton for generations, while others spread over the surrounding country. Some of the female descendants in the fifth generation married and settled in Epsom, and others doubtless migrated there. As it has been impossible to determine the parentage of Colonel Isaac Towle from the record of vital statistics or otherwise, the present branch must begin with him.

(I) Colonel Isaac Towle was born in Epsom, New Hampshire, October 17, 1794. A little before 1840 he moved to Sutton, New Hampshire, where he was a farmer and an exemplary and useful citizen. At some time of his life he was a colonel in the militia. In 1818 he married Rebecca, daughter of Jonathan and Alice Locke, of Epsom, who was born in 1798. They were the parents of sixteen children: James, born October 28, 1820, died in November of that year; James M., Henry, Horace E., Rodney, died young; Charles, died young; Almira J., George, died young; Charles A., whose sketch follows; Mary Ann, died young; Mary Ann, Albert, Ellen M., Elizabeth, George and William Perry, who was born October 28, 1843, and died in the army, July 13, 1863. Colonel Isaac Towle died at Sutton, January 14, 1884, aged eighty-nine years, and his wife died at Sutton, March 31, 1879, aged eighty-one years.

(II) Charles Augustus, eighth son and ninth child of Colonel Isaac and Rebecca (Locke) Towle, was born at Canaan, New Hampshire, June 14, 1833. On December 1, 1854, he married Maria Scates, daughter of Oliver and Sally (Leighton) Scates. (See Scates, III). They had three children: Charles Frank, born March 29, 1856, who now lives in New York; Willis A., born August 31, 1861, who died January 18, 1864; and Fred Scates, whose sketch follows. Charles A. Towle died August 18, 1870, at the early age of thirty-seven years.

(III) Dr. Fred Scates, third son and child of Charles Augustus and Maria (Scates)) Towle, was born at Boston, Massachusetts, December 28, 1863. He was educated in the Boston public schools, and was graduated from the Medical College of Columbia University in the class of 1893. He took a post-graduate course in the hospitals of New York, and practiced one year in Boston. In 1894 he took up his permanent abode in Portsmouth, New Hampshire, where he has since continued in general practice. During his residence there he has been city physician and chairman of the Board of Health. He is surgeon of the Boston & Maine railroad, surgeon of the Cottage Hospital of Portsmouth, and in 1897-1899, was on the staff of Governor George A. Ramsdell, as surgeon general. Dr. Towle is a man of genial nature, and his very entrance to a sick room brings cheer to the patient. As a surgeon he stands at the head of his profession, and is well known throughout the state, being frequently called in council with the leading physicians. Dr. Towle is a member of the New Hampshire Surgical Club, the American Medical Association, and the following societies: Portsmouth Medical, Strafford County Medical, Rockingham County Medical, and New Hampshire Medical. He belongs to the Masonic order in all its branches, and has attained to the thirty-second degree. He is a member of the various bodies in the Independent Order of Odd Fellows, and also of the Knights of Pythias. Dr. Towle is not only one of the substantial citizens and leading physicians of Rockingham county, but is well liked as a man. He is president of the Wallack Social Club of Portsmouth, and is a member of the Sons of the American Revolution. In 1885 Dr. Towle married Martha Horne Perry, daughter of Alfred Perry of Boston. They have one son, Charles Augustus, born in Boston, 1886. He was educated in the public schools of Portsmouth and at a military academy in New York, and possesses a mechanical turn of mind.

SCATES The name of Scates is most unusual in this country, and seems to be confined to the eastern part of New Hampshire, reaching from Dover upward to Lake Winnepesaukee. It may possibly be related to the old Dutch Skaats, first represented in this country by Dominie Gideon Schaats, who came from Holland in 1652, and for forty-two years was pastor of the Old Dutch Church at Albany, New York. The earliest reference to Scates that has been found is in the records of Milton, New Hampshire, originally a part of Rochester. In 1772 or 1773 one Benjamin Scates settled on Plummer's Ridge in what is now Milton. Probably he was related to the following line.

(I) Dodonah Scates had two brothers, Ithiel and Benjamin; possibly the latter may have been the one who settled at Plummer's Ridge. Dodonah Scates married Mrs. Lydia (Hansen) Manning, and they have five children: Jack, Abigail, Oliver, mentioned below, Zimery and Maria. All of these lived to marry and raise families.

(II) Oliver, second son and third child of Dodonah and Lydia (Hanson) Manning, was born at Milton, New Hampshire, April 21, 1800. In 1819 he married Sally Leighton, daughter of Ephraim Leighton, of Ossipee, New Hampshire, who was born April 16, 1801. They had eight children. Dodonah, Sally, Clark Swett. Maria, mentioned below; Sally Alice. Annie Elizabeth and John. Of this large family all of them lived to grow up and marry, the only survivors in 1907 are Maria, whose sketch follows, and John, who was born April 28, 1841. Oliver Scates met with an accidental death.

(III) Maria, second daughter and fourth child of Oliver and Sally (Leighton) Scates, on December 1, 1854, married Charles Augustus Towle. (See Towle, II).

TOPPING Ancestors bearing this patronymic came from England in the year 1620, and settled upon the southern shores of the eastern end of Long Island, where a number of their descendants still reside upon the original tracts settled by them. The family furnished several soldiers to the cause of the Revolution, and took an active in the early affairs of this country. From them a numerous lineage has sprung. most of whom always remained in the state of New York, only a few representatives going into other states. The original settlers bearing the family name consisted of two brothers, John and Thomas. Among the descendants of John was the subject of the following paragraph.

(I) John Topping died at Harpersville, New York, leaving three children: Elizabeth, Katherine and Henry S., the subject of the next paragraph.

(II) Henry S., son of John Topping, conducted a large painting and decorating business for years in Waverly, New York. He served three years in the Union army in the Civil war, being a member of the cavalry arm of the service, and being badly wounded once in action. In politics he was always a Republican, and in religion a Methodist. He was a member of the Grand Army Post at Waverly, up to the time of his death in 1897 He married, in 1863. Lydia A. DeForest, who still resides at Waverly, New York. She is a daughter of Charles and Jeanette (Hedges) DeForest, of North Barton, New York, whose ancestors settled in Connecticut previous to the war of the Revolution, and whose great-grandfather was one of the pioneers to leave a legacy to Yale College, and the "DeForest prize," one of the most sought at the college today, is the result of this legacy. Their children are Charles A., now deceased; Mildred E., who married Ellis Crandall, a jeweler at Owego, New York, and William H., the subject of the next paragraph.

(III) William Harold oldest son of Henry S. and Lydia A. (DeForest) Topping, was born in Waverly, November 26, 1865. He attended the public schools of his native city. He learned the printer's trade in the office of the Waverly *Advocate* and Waverly *Free Press*, and later drifted into journalism. After an experience of years at his trade and profession in Waverly, New York City, and Spencer, New York, he went to Hillsborough, New Hampshire, in 1889, with the Hillsborough *Messenger*. With the birth of the New Hampshire *Daily Republican*, Mr. Topping became connected with its staff, and was its legislative and special state corespondent. Later Mr. Topping was connected with the Manchester *Union*. In 1893 he removed to Manchester and became a member of the city staff of the Manchester *Daily Mirror*, and rose to the position of city editor. which he filled for some time. In 1899-1901 he was assistant clerk of the house of representatives of the state legislature, but resigned in 1901, owing to the fact that he had been elected in 1900 clerk of the committee on invalid pensions of the national house of representatives, which position he held during the Fifty-sixth, Fifty-seventh, Fifty-eighth, Fifty-ninth and Sixtieth Congresses. In 1907 he was appointed by Governor Floyd and council as executive commissioner for New Hampshire at the Jamestown Exposition. Mr. Topping was married, in May, 1896, to Etta Louise Bartlett, daughter of Ezra and Mehitable E. Bartlett, of Manchester, a former business man and one of the pioneer residents of the city. In politics Mr. Topping has always been a staunch Republican.

BROWN This name has been variously represented in New England from the earliest colonization of the country; and in Westminster, Massachusetts, the early seat of the family of this article they were so numerous, the branches so various, the records so fragmentary and heterogeneous, that it has been found impossible not only to trace any of the family to its original progenitor, but also to connect the different families with each other to any great extent.

(I) Nicholas Browne, son of Edward Browne, of Inkburrow, Worcestershire, England, settled first at Lynn, Massachusetts, and early removed from there to Reading, where he appears to have owned two places. He was a man of comfortable means as appears from the fact of his sending his son John, in 1660. to England, to look after certain property to which he had become heir. He died in 1673. His wife's name was Elizabeth. and their children were: John, Edward, Joseph, Corneilus, Josiah, and perhaps Elizabeth.

(II) Jonathan Brown was no doubt a descendant of Nicholas Browne, and resided in Westminster. He married Mehitable Hay. Her father, James Hay, was an original proprietor of No. 2 drawing in the first division of lands, lot No. 106, near Wachusettville.

(III) Jonathan (2), son of Jonathan (1) and Mehitable Brown, probably located on the lot No. 106, mentioned above, occupying a house built some years before by Benjamin Gould. He was first taxed in 1764. and in 1769 a public school was kept in his house. January 3, 1771, he purchased of Joseph Lynde, of Charlestown, lot No. 105, lying directly south of the Hay lot, which was long known as the Brown estate, more recently owned by Asaph Carter and his son Edward R. On his way from Reading to Westminster, Mr. Brown seems to have sojourned awhile in Leominster, where he married Huldah Hawkes. He died March 14, 1820, aged eighty. She died January 1, 1818, aged seventy-five. Their children were: Jonathan,

Benjamin, Joseph (died young), Huldah, Sally, Joseph, and John.

(IV) Jonathan (3), eldest son and child of Jonathan (2) and Huldah (Hawkes) Brown, was born in Reading, August 30, 1765, and died in Gardner, July 24, 1840, aged seventy-five. He removed to and resided in Gardner on a farm in the east part of that town where his grandson Charles, lately lived. He married Beulah Jackson, daughter of Elisha and Beulah (Taylor) Jackson. She died November 24, 1839, aged sixty-seven. Their children were: Jonathan, John. Charles (died young), Elisha, Charles, Sally (died young), Sally, Benjamin B., Lucy and Nancy.

(V) Charles, fifth son and child of Jonathan and Beulah (Jackson) Brown, was born in Gardner, Massachusetts, March 12, 1800, died in Boston, October 16, 1863, aged sixty-three. When twenty years of age he settled in Boston, where he was for many years successfully engaged in the retail grocery business. In politics he was an old line Whig, and took part in the public affairs of the city. He was a member of the common council in 1844-45, and in 1847 was an alderman from the sixth ward. He married Susan Morehead, of Gloucester, who was born there, and died in Boston, aged seventy-three. Five children were born to them: 1. Susan, married O. H. Underhill. 2. Abbie, married R. G. Davis. 3. Mary E, married Edward J. Brown. 4. Sarah J., married Charles F. Dunck-lee. 5. Charles S., mentioned below.

(VI) Charles Severance, youngest child of Charles and Susan (Morehead) Brown, was born in Boston, November 18, 1844. He was educated in the common schools of that city and at Chauncey Hall. In 1872 he engaged in the carriage service, and has given it his unremitting attention ever since that time; he is the oldest man in that line in town, and his business has steadily grown from the beginning. He has a summer home in New Ipswich, New Hampshire, where he passes the summer months. In politics he is an Independent. He is a member of the Free and Accepted Masons of New Ispwich, New Hampshire, and the Algonquin Club of Boston. He married (first) 1867, Frances Partridge, born in Boston, died in New Ipswich, 1889, daughter of Adrian and Abbie (Harding) Partridge. Two children were the issue: 1. Albert, married Grace Thayer, in Hartford, Connecticut; engaged in electrical business there. 2. Susan. Married (second), 1891, Ruth Miller, born in Salem, daughter of Ephraim Miller, of Salem, Massachusetts, and granddaughter of General James Miller. One child was the issue: Philip.

HAMILTON

Samuel King Hamilton, of Wakefield, Massachusetts, is the youngest of six sons of Benjamin Ricker Hamilton and Sarah Carle, and a grandson of James Hamilton and John Carle, both farmers and respected men of Waterborough, Maine. Mr. Carle served in the Revolutionary war, and was the first settler of the little hamlet known as Waterborough Centre. The village was formerly called Carle's Corner, having taken its name from his son. Peter Carle, who built the first house, kept the first store and tavern at that place.

Mr. Hamilton was named in honor of Samuel King, who married his cousin, and who was mayor of the city of Calais, Maine, and for many years one of the leading lumber manufacturers on the St. Croix river, and who afterwards removed to St. John, New Brunswick, where, in connection with his sons, he had one of the most extensive lumber interests on the St. John river.

The Hamilton family for centuries has been one of the most distinguished in Scotland and England, and closely related to royalty in both countries. Mr. Hamilton's earliest ancestor in America was David Hamilton, who lived in the township of Hamilton, near Glasgow, Scotland, and who was taken prisoner by Cromwell at the battle of Worcester, on September 3, A. D., 1651, and who was transported to this country by him in the ship "John and Sara," which sailed from Gravesend, near London, on the 8th day of November of that year, and arrived at Charlestown, Massachusetts, prior to May, A. D. 1652. There he was sold into servitude to work out his liberty. He was probably held in this service for from five to ten years. After the expiration of this term he went to Dover, New Hampshire, and soon settled in what is now the town of Rollinsford, on the westerly bank of the Salmon Falls river, at a place then called Newichawannok, and which he purchased in 1669, and where he lived until the time of his death in 1691, being slain by the Indians. On July 14, A. D. 1662, he married, at Biddeford, Maine, Annah Jaxson (Anna Jackson) daughter of Richard Jackson, who was a neighbor of David Hamilton in Scotland, and who was taken prisoner at the same battle and transported to this country in the same ship and also sold into servitude, at the expiration of which he settled on the west bank of the Saco river.

Samuel King Hamilton is of the sixth generation in a direct line from David, and was born at Waterborough, Maine, July 27, A. D. 1837. His early life was spent upon his father's farm. The rudimentary education which he obtained at the district school was supplemented by a single term at Limerick Academy, then a famous institution of learning; six months' private tuition under M. D. L. Lane, of Hollis, Maine, who was just then beginning the practice of law, and who afterwards became prominent in politics and was appointed consul to Vera Cruz by President Lincoln and later was appointed judge of the superior court of the county of Cumberland, a position which he held at the time of his death; and a part of one year at the high school in Saco, Maine, under the instruction of William Hobson, a graduate of Bowdoin College, who at the breaking out of the Civil war entered the army and served his country with conspicuous ability and bravery, returning with the rank of colonel and brevet brigadier-general.

In February, 1856, Mr. Hamilton began teaching his first school at the district now called East Waterborough, then the "Ford District," and from that time to August of the same years he was engaged there and in his home district. In the autumn of that year he entered the Chandler Scientific Department of Dartmouth College, of which the late Professor John S. Woodman was the head, from which he graduated in 1859. During the winter season of his course in that school he taught school in Waterborough and in Wells, Maine. In August, 1859, with a view to the legal profession, he entered the office of Hon. Ira T. Drew, at Alfred, Maine, where he remained several years, pursuing his legal studies and teaching a portion of the time in Wells, Alfred, and South Reading (now Wakefield), Massachusetts. In 1860 he was principal of Alfred Academy, a position in which he had been preceded by such men as Hon. Bion Bradbury, Hon. John M. Goodwin, Professor Charles Cumston,

Hon. Hampden Fairfield and Hon. Amos L. Allen.

In June, 1862, after an examination by Hon. E E. Bourne, Hon. Increase S. Kimball and Hon. Edwin R. Wiggin, and upon their recommendation, he was admitted to the bar at Alfred before Hon. Charles W. Walton, who was then holding his first term as a judge of the supreme judicial court. On the day of his admission he was offered a co-partnership with Mr. Drew, which was quickly and gladly accepted, for it opened the way at once for a young and penniless lawyer to earn his livelihood. This co-partnership continued until April, 1867, when Mr. Hamilton removed to Biddeford, and a co-partnership was entered into between himself and B. F. Hamilton, who descended from the same ancestor in a different line, and who was born in the same town and studied law in the same office and was admitted to the bar in 1860. During the continuance of the co-partnership of Drew & Hamilton the firm had the largest docket in the county, and were engaged in substantially every important case arising in that jurisdiction. While at Biddeford, Mr. Hamilton built up a substantial law business which was left to his partner on his removal to Wakefield.

While living in his native town Mr. Hamilton served two years upon the school committee. He served two years on the board of aldermen in the city of Biddeford, and in 1872, with Hon. Ferguson Haines, represented that city in the Maine legislature. In these positions he established a reputation as a safe legislator and a ready and able debator.

In December, 1872, he left Biddeford and his native state and removed to Wakefield, and formed a co-partnership with Chester W. Eaton, a college classmate, and opened law offices in Wakefield and Boston. This co-partnership continued to 1879, when it was dissolved by mutual consent, Mr. Hamilton retaining the Boston offices and Mr. Eaton those in Wakefield. Soon after beginning practice in Boston he acquired considerable business which has been continually increasing, and for a number of years has almost constantly engaged in the trial of cases in the court or in hearing those which have been referred to him by the court, and his practice has extended into every state in New England and into New York. In 1899 Mr. Theodore Eaton, son of his former partner, became associated with him in practice, and this co-partnership continues to the present time (1908).

Soon after his settlement in Wakefield, Mr. Hamilton became prominent in town affairs, and has served twelve years upon the school board, nine of which he was chairman, and was instrumental in effecting a complete re-organization of the school system. His efforts in this work were appreciated by the people of the town, who recognized it in a conspicuous manner by a vote in town meeting that the new brick school house then being erected be called in his honor the "Hamilton School Building." He was also chairman of the board of selectmen six years, chairman of the board of trustees of the Beebe Town Library, counsel for the town for over twenty years, and moderator in nearly all the town meetings for even a longer period. He had charge of the litigation which resulted in the town acquiring the plant of the Citizens' Gas Light Company, which was the first and the leading case of the kind in the commonwealth.

He was an alternate delegate to the national Democratic convention in 1868, a delegate to the national convention which nominated General Hancock in 1880, and William J. Bryan in 1896. He, however, did not support the last named. He has presided over many Democratic conventions, and was candidate for district attorney for the northern district of Masachusetts in 1887, and in 1890 was a candidate of the Democratic party for congress from the Seventh congressional district, and in 1892 a candidate for presidential elector in the same district. In 1893 he purchased and became president of the Wakefield Water Company, which he controlled for ten years. He was one of the originators of the Pine Tree State Club, of Boston, which he served as treasurer for the first eleven years of its existence, and afterwards as president. He became a member of the Bar Association of the city of Boston shortly after it was organized, and upon the organization of the Bar Association of the County of Middlesex in 1898, he became its president, a position which he now holds.

In 1874 Mr. Hamilton became connected with the Congregational Church in Wakefield, of which he has been ever since an active member. He was chairman of the committee which erected the beautiful stone edifice connected with the church, and aided materially by his efforts and money in paying the debt thereby contracted. He presided and made an address at the centennial celebration of the church in 1876, and when the town in connection with Reading celebrated its two hundred and fiftieth anniversary he presided at the proceedings on Settlers' Day and delivered an address. In every capacity he has exhibited the highest qualities of a progressive, patriotic and public spirited citizen, and is universally respected and esteemed.

February 13, 1867, Mr. Hamilton was married to Miss Annie E. Davis, eldest daughter of the late Joseph B. and Harriet N. (Dam) Davis of Newfield, Maine. They have lived a simple and beautiful life, devoted to each other, and their home has been the abode of happiness and good cheer and from it has emanated much kindly and charitable work.

HEAD This is among the earliest names of New Hampshire, being first found at Portsmouth. It is said to be of Welsh origin, but that is tradition, which research proves to be extremely unreliable. At any rate it has conferred honor upon the state of New Hampshire and has been honored in the annals of the state, having furnished one of the governors of the commonwealth and many useful and honorable citizens in many walks of life.

(I) Arthur Head, first in New Hampshire, is first of record December 25, 1671, when he took a deed of land and houses of Christian Goss at Portsmouth. On November 5, 1690, "Arthur Head of ye Great Island, in ye Town of Portsmouth, in ye Province of New Hampshire, Fisherman," deeded a warehouse and land to Thomas Paine. He died prior to September, 1711. His wife Sarah died probably, no later than 1718. Their children were: James, Ann and Grace.

(II) James, son of Arthur and Sarah Head, was born in 1683, in Newcastle, then part of Portsmouth, and was married February 13, 1709, to Sarah Atwood. After her death he married her sister, Elizabeth. They were daughters of Captain Philip Atwood, of Bradford, Massachusetts. James Head was an extensive landholder, as evidenced by numerous transfers on the records, and resided in Bradford, Massachusetts. Before the death of their mother, September 8, 1711, Mr. Head and his two sisters deeded to Captain Atwood the paternal homestead. He received by deed from Captain Atwood, February 27, 1715, sixty acres of land in

Bradford, and on May 6, three years later, seventy acres adjoining. On June 13, 1718, he deeded to John Pecker, of Haverhill, Massachusetts, one-sixth of a tract of one hundred and eight acres, and November 5 of the same year deeded one acre to John Ringe. He died September 16, 1743, at his home in Bradford. His first wife was born April 13, 1689, and died before August, 1717. The second was born May 19, 1700. His children were: Sarah, Elizabeth, Mary, John, Ruth and James. The first wife was the mother of the first three. She joined the church January 3, 1716, and the children were baptized August 6, of the same year.

(III) Major James (2), youngest child of James (1) and Elizabeth (Atwood) Head, was born November 16, 1727, in Bradford, and resided in that town until about 1770, when he removed to Pembroke, New Hampshire. His farm was east of Pembroke street, on an elevation above the cemetery. He gave his life for his country in the Revolutionary war, dying from wounds received in the battle of Bennington, August 31, 1777. His will was dated three days previously, at Camp Bennington, and he was buried there, before the completion of his fiftieth year. He was married December 14, 1748, to Mrs. Sarah Thurston, a widow, who bore him the following children: Bettee, Sarah, Nathaniel, Richard, James, Mary and Hannah. The mother died August 28, 1784, and was buried in the cemetery on Pembroke street. (James (3) and descendants are mentioned at length in this article).

(IV) Captain Nathaniel, eldest son and third child of James (2) and Sarah Head, was born March 6, 1754, in Bradford, Massachusetts, and was sixteen years old when his parents moved to Pembroke. In 1783 he settled in that part of Chester which is now Hooksett, and built a house that is still standing, soon after his location here. His first home was in a log house, soon succeeded by a frame house, which must have been a pretentious one in its day. It now stands only a short distance from its original location, which is at the summit of the hill on the road from Hooksett village to Suncook, at its junction with the "back road," only a few steps from the fine mansion built later by Governor Head, his grandson. He was an industrious and prosperous farmer, and a captain in the Revolutionary army. His wife, Anna Knox, daughter of John Knox, granddaughter of Timothy Knox, whose ancestors settled in Lancaster, Massachusetts, bore him the following children: Samuel, Richard, Mary, John (died at the age of four years), Nathaniel, Nancy, John, Betsey and Margaret.

There is an interesting tradition concerning the marriage of Captain Nathaniel Head (IV). His intended bride was the daughter of one of the Scotch-Irish settlers of the region, and his father objected to her on account of nationality. One day, while father and son were plowing together, the former asked the latter if he intended to marry "that Irish girl" On receiving a prompt and firm affirmative answer, he said: "Then you shall receive none of my property." The son immediately dropped the ox goad, with the remark, "I can care for myself," and abandoned his father's home before the day was done. Shortly after he settled in Hooksett, as above related, and became in time a prosperous farmer and business man by his own exertions. He received one dollar from his father's estate, simply to prevent breaking the will, but was successful and became one of the most wealthy of the name.

(V) Colonel John, fifth son and seventh child of Captain Nathaniel and Anna (Knox) Head, was born May 30, 1791, on the homestead in what is now Hooksett, where he died August 7, 1835. He was associated with his father in the management of the farm and sawmill, and by purchase from other heirs became owner himself. He was an industrious and efficient business man, as well as farmer, and held an honored position in the community. An active and useful member of the local militia, he rose to the position of lieutenant-colonel in the seventh regiment. He was married July 16, 1822, to Anna Brown, of Chester, daughter of Captain William Brown. She was born February 26, 1799, and died April 3, 1849. She was a woman of much energy and executive ability, and proved a valuable aid to her husband in the management of a large estate. Both were members of the Congregational Church of Pembroke. Their children are accounted for as follows: Hannah Ann, married Colonel Josiah Stevens, of Concord, and resided in Manchester; she died June 28, 1896, in Pembroke. Sally Brown became the wife of Hall Burgin Emery, of Pembroke, and died September 1, 1868. Natt and William Brown were twins, the latter dying at the age of one year and four months; the former is the subject of a sketch in this article. John A. resided at Fort Atkinson, Wisconsin, and Boone, Iowa, and now has his home in Rockford, Illinois. William F. is mentioned at length hereinafter.

(VI) Hon. Natt, third child and eldest son of John and Anna (Brown) Head, was born in Hooksett, Vermont, May 20, 1828, and died November 12, 1883, at his home in that town. After concluding his studies at the Pembroke Academy he became actively concerned in the management of the homestead farm, and he also identified himself with the lumbering business established by the grandfather. In 1852 his brother, William F. Head, became associated with him in business in Hooksett, which then included in addition to the lumber trade the manufacture of brick and some twenty years later the brothers became members of the Head & Dowst Company, of Manchester, which engaged extensively in the contracting and building business. These enterprises became prominent industrial features in the above towns, employing a large number of men, and not only supplied the material but also participated in most of the important building operations of that locality for many years.

Although widely and favorably known, throughout the Granite state as an able and successful business man, Natt Head derived his prominence more particularly from his conspicuous public services, both civic and military, and he rose to the highest honors within the gift of the commonwealth. Prior to his majority he was appointed drum major of the Eleventh Regiment, Third Brigade, First Division, New Hampshire Volunteer Militia, in which capacity he served for a period of four years; was drum major and chief bugler of the famous Horse Guards during the existence of the corps; and in 1864 was appointed by Governor Gilmore adjutant, inspector and quartermaster-general. For a number of years he served as deputy sheriff; was for two years, 1861-62, a member of the lower branch of the state legislature, and as a candidate for the state senate in 1874 he was elected in a moral sense but owing to a controversy over the spelling of his name, instituted by his Democratic opponent, many of the votes cast for him were thrown out and he was thereby defeated. Some votes were cast cast for Nathaniel, others for Natt. He was, however, elected to the senate by a large majority the following year. In 1878 he was the Republican candidate for governor and was elected to that office for a term of two years, being the first chief executive of the state under the Biennial law, which went into effect at that time, and his administration was characterized by the same ability and superior judgment for which he had been previously noted during his private business career.

Governor Head's retirement from the public service was followed by a long lingering illness, and his death occurred November 12, 1883, and as might be expected the passing away of such an able and high-minded public official was universally deplored throughout the state. In spite of the fact that both his business interests and public services were practically confined to his own state, he acquired without any seeming effort on his part what might be considered a national reputation, and he had the distinction of numbering among his warm personal friends Generals Grant, Sherman and Sheridan, who frequently invited him to accompany them on their various trips to different parts of the country. Aside from his business affairs in Hooksett he was connected officially with several important enterprises of a semi-public character, having been president of the China Savings Bank of Suncook, a director of the First National Bank, of Manchester, and of the New Hampshire Fire Insurance Company, a trustee of the Merrimack River Savings Bank, Manchester, and of the Suncook Valley Railway Company. He was a charter member of Jewell Lodge, Free and Accepted Masons, and of Howard Lodge, Independent Order of Odd Fellows, both of Suncook, affiliated with the Knights of Pythias of the same town; vice-president of the New Hampshire Historical Society; a member of the Amoskeag Veterans, of Manchester; and an honorary member of the Ancient and Honorable Artillery of Boston; and of the Lancers of that city.

While Governor Head made an enviable record as chief executive and in every official capacity undertaken, he was universally popular as a man and his service as adjutant-general was probably of greater value to posterity and the military branch of the public service than all his other works. When he was appointed to this position in 1864, he found that there was not a complete record of any of the organizations that went into service from New Hampshire in the Civil war, or of the general military concerns of the state for the previous thirty-eight years. When he entered upon his office as adjutant-general, the state had already sent twenty-six thousand men to the front, but not one complete muster roll had been made of a single organization. At his own expense, trusting to the legislature for ultimate reimbursement, he immediately employed clerks and set about completing the records. After several rebuffs that would have discouraged one less persistent, General Head secured permission to copy from the National archives, and in his reports for 1865 and 1866 a complete record was given, including the military annals of the state from 1823 to 1861. The four volumes comprising these reports contain the military history of every man, officer or private, who went from New Hampshire to the defense of his country's integrity between 1861 and 1864. They include brief accounts of all the regiments and battalions, with their movements, battles and other data, with biographical notices of all officers who died in the service, whether from wounds or disease contracted in the line of duty. General Head had inherited from worthy martial sires a love of everything pertaining to military matters, and he gave six of the best years of his life chiefly to this preservation of invaluable records. His interest and labors did not end with his official term or with the completion of the records, but he was ever ready and anxious to do anything possible for the soldier or his widow and family. He was much interested in the work of the Grand Army of the Republic and never tired of doing what he could for the honor and glory of the man who served his country in the place of danger. He conceived the idea, in 1867, of issuing the "soldier certificate" to the honorably discharged soldiers of the state and to the families of those who died in the service, and this was carried out as he planned and wished. That his unselfish labors were appreciated at the time is shown by the following extract from an address of Governor Smyth to the legislature: "In the difficult adjustment of our military affairs, you will agree with me in a warm approval of the energy and efficiency of the adjutant-general, whose work has been, in all cases, well performed. When it has been my grateful duty to extend a welcoming hand in behalf of the people of this state to our brave returning soldiers, he has forwarded my purpose with unflagging interest and zeal. You will not forget that around his department all the memories of the contest now cluster. The long roll of honor is there. There are gathered the blood-stained battle flags, and there will always be found those associations which should inspire us with love of country and an appreciation of those who gave their lives and shed their blood for the blessings which God bestowed when he gave us the victory."

Governor Head was active in so many ways for the general welfare of his state that he might be said to have been always in the public service, though not ever in official station. He gave much effort to the advancement of agricultural interests, and originated the plan of holding farmers' conventions, the first of which was held at Manchester in 1868. He was a leading member and served as president of the State Agricultural Society, and was president of the New England Agricultural Society. He also served as master of Hooksett Grange, Patrons of Husbandry. In Free Masonry he attained the thirty-second degree, including all those of the "Scottish rite" and the "rite of Memphis." He was identified with the Knights of Pythias and Knights of Honor bodies of Manchester. He passed through the encampment work in the Independent Order of Odd Fellows, and was a loved and honored member of all bodies. While his high positions in the affairs of state commanded due respect, yet he was held in still higher esteem because of his warm heart and manly qualities. His character is well summed up in the following extract from an obituary notice in the Manchester *Mirror*: "Other men may have been greater and stronger than he; may have lived longer and accomplished more; have died and been respectfully buried. Their death has been counted a loss to the state, to the professions in which they were leaders; but it caused no deep grief among those who were not bound to them by family ties. They are remembered as governors, senators, millionaires, not as men, and when once their places are filled and their estates distributed they have been well-nigh forgotten. The hold they had was upon the brain, not upon the heart. It was not so with Natt Head. People who knew him loved him while he lived and mourn for him because he is dead." Another said of him: "He never did anything by halves, and that cause which attracted his support received the benefit of his able and untiring efforts. As a public officer, he could say with Othello, 'I have done the State some service, and they know it.' No man in New Hampshire knew so many people personally and few, if any, had so strong a hold upon the popular good will. His word needed no writing to make it good." * * * "Wherever he went, among all classes of people, without effort and seemingly without purpose, he won the hearty and lasting friendship of all with whom he came in contact. He had a warm heart and a face always beaming with good humor, and was ever courteous, genial and generous."

Natt Head was married, November 19, 1863, to Abbie M. Sanford, daughter of Stephen R. and Maria (Fisher) Sanford, of Lowell, Massachusetts. Maria Fisher was a descendant of John Webster, fifth governor of Connecticut. Three children were born to Governor and Mrs. Head, namely: Annie Sanford, June 23, 1865; Lewis Fisher, February 18, 1868; and Alice Perley, December 20, 1870. The second died at the age of four years, and the youngest near the close of her ninth year. Mrs. Head and her surviving daughter have resided for several years in Brookline, Massachusetts.

(VI) William Fernald sixth child and youngest son of John and Anna (Brown) Head, was born in Hooksett, September 25, 1832. He completed his education at the Pembroke Academy, and prior to inaugurating his business career devoted his time exclusively to agricultural pursuits at the homestead farm. In 1852 he became associated with his brother Natt in the lumber business and also in the manufacture of brick and for the succeeding thirty years the Head Brothers conducted an extensive business enterprise in Hooksett, producing large quantities of building material which greatly facilitated the development of the industrial resources in that locality. Brotherly ties between them were unusually strong, their attachment to each other being particularly emphasized by the implicit confidence which characterized their business relations, and the company possessions were regarded by them as common property, thus doing away entirely with the formality of individual expense accounts. William F. Head also managed the homestead farm containing two hundred and fifty acres of fertile land which is devoted almost exclusively to the cultivation of hay, and the average production amounts to two hundred and fifty tons annually. In 1871 was organized the Head & Dowst Company, contractors and builders, of which Mr. William F. Head became vice-president.

In politics Mr. Head was a Republican, and while his activity in civic affairs was not at any time during his active life as extensive as that of his brother Natt, he nevertheless rendered valuable public services both to his town and state, having served upon the board of selectmen for the years 1859-60, and in 1869-70 was a member of the New Hampshire house of representatives. He was a delegate to the constitutional convention of 1876. Well versed in monetary affairs and a man of marked ability, he was a director of the Suncook Valley Railway Company, a trustee of the Merrimack River Savings Bank, and of the First National Bank of Manchester, New Hampshire, and a trustee of the New England Agricultural Society. For many years he was prominent in the Masonic fraternity, belonging to Eureka Lodge, Free and Accepted Masons, of Suncook, and a member of Trinity Commandery, Knights Templar, of Manchester.

(IV) James (3), third son and fifth child of Major James (2) and Sarah Head, was born October 16, 1759, in Pembroke, and resided on the paternal homestead in that town until 1805, when he removed to Conway, New Hampshire. His wife's christian name was Sally, but her family name is not of record. Their children, born in Pembroke, were: James, Benjamin, Asa, Nathaniel, Sally, Moses, Richard, Nancy, Robert and John.

(V) James (4), eldest child of James (3) and Sally Head, was born January 27, 1779, in Pembroke, and removed with his father to the northern part of the state. He was a farmer by occupation and possessed one hundred acres of land. He was a member of the Free Will Baptist Church, was a Democrat in politics and was much respected as a man and citizen. He married, Jemima Brown, of Albany, New Hampshire, and had children: John, Asa, Sampson, Deering, Joseph, Lindy and Kingman Freeman. Of these Joseph was noted for his great strength.

(VI) Kingman Freeman, son of James and Jemima (Brown) Head, was born in Hooksett, New Hampshire, and was a small child when his father removed to Conway. He was educated in the common schools of Madison, New Hampshire, and on attaining man's estate took the management of his father's farm, on which he continued to reside until old age compelled his retirement from active labor. He died at the age of seventy-five years in Lakeport. He was a member of the Free Will Baptist Church, and like his father sustained the Democratic party in political contests. He was married, September 21, 1828, in Conway, by Rev. B. S. Manson, to Almira Davis, daughter of Israel Davis, who was born in Madison, New Hampshire. She lived to the age of eighty years. Their children were: Eden, George, Charles, Elizabeth, Israel Davis and Thomas. All except one of these died in infancy.

(VII) Israel Davis, only surviving child of Kingman Freeman and Almira (Davis) Head, was born December 29, 1843, in Madison, New Hampshire, and grew up in that town, receiving his education in its common schools. He was early accustomed to the industrious habits of farm life, and on leaving school took employment for two years in a hotel at Conway. Later he was employed as a stage coach driver in summer, between Glenhouse and Crawford Notch. He is now the oldest professional stage driver living in the state. For eight years he operated a freight team in the winter between Jackson and Portland, a distance of sixty miles. Having decided to settle down to farm life, he purchased the present homestead of eighty acres, lying in the town of Laconia, New Hampshire. He subsequently purchased an adjoining farm which he uses for a pasture for his herds. Mr. Head has been industrious and prudent in the care of his earnings and the proceeds of his farm, and is now the owner of a valuable block in the city of Laconia, besides other real estate in that place. He is much interested in cattle raising and is an excellent judge of the qualities of live stock. He keeps a herd of thirty-six cattle and is the operator of one of the largest milk routes in the city. He is a thinking man and is interested in many of the movements for the uplifting of humanity. He is independent in his religious associations, and is a Democrat in political principle. He is a member of the Independent Order of Odd Fellows and of the Patrons of Husbandry, and has filled all of the principal chairs in the local Grange. He was married in 1872, to Sarah Jane Gray, who was born June, 1843, in Jackson, New Hampshire, daughter of John and Miranda (Gannet) Gray. She died at Conway, 1899, leaving one child, Albert Watson Head. He was born, 1873, in Lakeport. He married Abbie Young and they have no children.

FOSS The name of Foss appears to have been of Dutch or German origin and was originally Vos, a word signifying fox. It is probable that the first that took the name was so nicknamed because of his shrewdness or cunning, or because he used the fox as a sign at his place of business. The name was early implanted in New England and is still most numerously represented, especially in New Hampshire.

(I) John Foss, the ancestor of those bearing the name, is said by tradition to have arrived at Boston on a British war vessel on which he was employed as a calker. While the vessel was lying in Boston harbor, he deserted by jumping overboard and swimming ashore. He soon settled in Dover, New Hampshire, where he first appears of record May 14, 1661, when he witnessed a deed. His first wife was Mary Chadburn. His second wife, Elizabeth, presumably the widow of John Locke and daughter of William and Jane Berry, was appointed administratrix of his estate January 8, 1699. He received a deed of land in Rye in 1668. His children were: John, Humphrey, William, Hannah, Joshua, Hinckson, Mary, Benjamin, Thomas, Jemima, Elizabeth and Samuel. (Joshua and descendants receive extended mention in this article).

(II) John (2), son of John (1) Foss, probably married Abigail, daughter of John Berry, as he refers to Berry in a deed as his father-in-law. In 1710, being feeble, though not aged, he disposed of most of his property, deeding land to his son John in Greenland, to sons Joshua and Zachariah lands in Rye. He was in Newcastle in 1696, was selectman there in 1698, and paid a minister's rate there of one pound and fourteen shillings in 1701. His children, of whom six settled in Barrington, were: Isaac, Zachariah, John, Samuel, Nathan, Hinkson, Ichabod, Abigail, Joshua and Priscilla.

(III) John (3) Foss, third son of John (2) Foss, was married March 11, 1745, to Tabitha Sargent, daughter of Ensign Jacob and Judith (Harvey) Sargent. He removed from Greenland to Chester, and settled on lot 105 in the "Addition" on Great Hill, where he died November 14, 1745. His wife was granted letters of administration thirteen days later. She became the second wife of Hezekiah Underhill, whom she survived, and died August 24, 1803. The inventory of John (3) Foss' estate was made June 6, 1746, and amounted to seven hundred, eighty-nine pounds and nine shillings. He left only one child.

(IV) David, only child of John (3) and Tabitha (Sargent) Foss, was born October 12, 1744, in Chester, and settled near his birthplace, on lot 107, where he died December 8, 1786. He was married in 1767, to Anne Richardson, and their children were: Elizabeth, Hannah, John, Anna, Tabitha, Abigail, Jonathan, Joseph, Daniel and Lucretia.

(V) Joseph, third son and eighth child of David and Anne (Richardson) Foss, was born October 30, 1782, in Chester, and resided for some years in Stratham, New Hampshire. He remained there until past middle life and then moved to Tuftonboro, where he was an early settler. He married a Clark, and they were the parents of five children: Joseph, mentioned below; Dolly, who married James Doe; Ann, who married Thomas French; John and Jerry. John had five children: Sarah, Jacob Clark, Frank, Charles and Albert. Jacob Clark was the only one who left children. He had one son Fred, who married and has four children: Walter Clark, aged thirty; Nora Marion, aged eighteen; Willard Roy, aged eight, and Clyde Bernard, aged three years.

(VI) Joseph (2), eldest child of Joseph (1) Foss, was born in Stratham, and when a young man went to Tuftonboro, where he followed farming till his death. He died in 1852, at the age of forty years. He married Nancy Sargent, and they had children: Thomas, Andrew, Isaac, Minnie, Nancy, James, Alice and Joseph.

(VII) Isaac, third child of Joseph (2) and Nancy (Sargent) Foss, was born in Tuftonboro, in 1839, and died there May 18, 1887. He was a farmer and carpenter. He married, in 1861, Amanda D. Ham, daughter of Samuel and Sarah (Tibbetts) Ham. They had six children: Albert L., John A., Eugene C., Annie M., Alice G., and Minnie. Albert L., born May 3, 1862, a real estate broker in New York City; John A., March 19, 1864, a butcher in Stanford, Connecticut; Eugene C., mentioned below; Annie M., October 1, 1869, married Virgil P. Hersey; Alice G., January, 1871, wife of Marvin L. Blaisdell; Minnie, December 25, 1874, died December 10, 1905.

(VIII) Eugene Clark, third son and child of Isaac and Amanda D. (Ham) Foss, was born in Tuftonboro, February 18, 1866. At twelve years of age he went to work on his father's farm for himself, and at nineteen he became a clerk for F. W. Emery & Company, for whom he worked five years, and he worked twenty years in one other store for Emery and J. B. Moon & Co. In July, 1905, he established himself in the hardware business in partnership with Henry Evans, the firm taking the style name of Henry Evans & Company, and has since that time been successfully engaged in that line. He is a member of Tribe No. 9, Improved Order of Red Men. He married, June 6, 1891, in Rochester, Laura Frances Clark, born September 26, 1861, daughter of Jacob Clark, of Rochester. They have had two children born to them: Erving E., born March 20, 1895, died March 17, 1899, and Bernice E., born May 20, 1901.

(II) Joshua, fourth son and child of John (1) Foss, settled in Barrington, where he died at the age of ninety-nine years and six months. He married Sarah Wallis and their children were: Thomas, Nathaniel, John, Job, Wallis, Jane, Hannah, Mark and George. (Mark and George and descendants receive mention in this article).

(III) Job, fourth son and child of Joshua and Sarah (Wallis) Foss, married, November 1, 1750, Sarah Lang. A tame Indian stayed at his house one night, and the board to which he was tied caught fire and came near burning a child and the house. His children were: Sarah, Hannah, John, Dorothy, Job, Joshua, Mary, Ebenezer and Comfort.

(IV) John, third child and eldest son of Job and Sarah (Lang) Foss, was baptized June, 1757, and died January 1, 1819. He was a Revolutionary soldier, and his name is found on the roll of Captain Joseph Parson's company, mustered in at Portsmouth, November 22, 1775, which proceeded to Cambridge "and served until the evacuation of Boston," as an endorsement attests.

He married, March 6, 1783, Sarah Tucker. Their children were: Job, Robinson, Betsey, Olive, Sarah, Richard, Anna Partridge.

(V) Job (2), eldest child of John and Sarah (Tucker) Foss, was born in 1785. He married,

March 22, 1809, Patty Berry, and they had six children: Olly, Elizabeth W., Alexander, Sally, Oliver and Jeremiah.

(VI) Elizabeth W., second child of Job and Patty (Berry) Foss, was born in May, 1811, and married Thomas Green. (See Green I, second family).

(III) Mark, sixth son and eighth child of Joshua and Sarah (Wallis) Foss, resided in the town of Rye, where he was born and was married November 28, 1745, to Amy Thompson. He removed to Strafford, and his last residence was on Strafford Ridge. His children were: Nathaniel, Mark, Abigail, John, George, Joshua and Timothy (John and descendants receive mention in this article).

(IV) Nathaniel, eldest child of Mark and Amy (Thompson) Foss, was born 1747, in that part of Barrington, which is now Strafford, New Hampshire. He settled in the present town of Strafford, on a road known as Pig Lane, which leads from Strafford Ridge to Bow Pond Road. He purchased a strip of land between the two roads, one rod wide, for a way to his mill. He built the first gristmill below Bow Pond, anld here he lived and died and was buried. He was a Revolutionary soldier, and served as an ensign in Captain Robert Pike's company, Colonel Senter's regiment, enlisting June 26, 1779, and served six months and twelve days. He was also a sergeant in Captain Parson's company from September 19, 1781, to October 3 of the same year. His grave is annuallly decorated by his patriotic descendants. He married Mary Jenness, of Rye, who was born in 1750, a daughter of Captain Nathaniel and Hannah (Dow) Jenness, and their children were: Elisha, John, Richard, Jonathan, Sarah and Nathaniel.

(V) Richard, third son and child of Nathaniel and Mary (Jenness) Foss, was born April 4, 1783, in Strafford, which was then a part of Barrington. He continued to reside in that town, and died January 13, 1824. He married Mary Tuttle, who was born November 15, 1784, and survived him more than thirty years, dying September 7, 1855. Their children were: Richard, Nathaniel, Lydia, Mahala, Daniel, Dennis, Eliza, Esther and Sarah.

(VI) Dennis, fourth son and sixth child of Richard and Mary (Tuttle) Foss, was born January 5, 1819, in Strafford, and removed to Dover in 1874. He resided for many years at Bow Pond, in Strafford, and owned a sawmill and engaged in the manufacture of lumber. He also operated a gristmill and was a merchant. Removing to Dover, as above noted, he engaged extensively in the manufacture of doors, sash and blinds and other similar lumber products, and achieved notable success. He died in Dover, December 24, 1899, near the close of his eighty-first year. He was married, December 16, 1845, to Hannah Peary, born August 21, 1832, in Barrington, and died in Dover, April 28, 1904. Their children were: Alonzo Melvin, Sarah Ellen (who died in infancy) and Laura Emma. The latter married (first) Walter Leighton Woodman, and resided at Bow Pond, later at Dover. She is now the wife of James S. Burton, of Manchester, New Hampshire.

(VII) Alonzo Melvin, only son of Dennis and Hannah (Peary) Foss, was born July 23, 1847, in Strafford. He received his education in the public schools of his native town, passing through the high school. After leaving school he was employed two years in a grocery store at Strafford by Hon. John W. Jewell, after which he was partner in a general store for seven years with his father, and removed with the latter to Dover in 1874, and aided in founding the present manufacturing business. He was early associated with his father in the management of the manufacturing business and has succeeded to its charge. He has been active in developing the best interests of Dover, and is at present among the leading citizens of that city. The manufacturing business established by himself and father has grown to large dimensions. It now occupies a three-story mill, covering ground surface 100x85 feet, and is fitted with the most modern and improved machinery for its purposes. Among the specialties of the plant is the production or large packing boxes for the cloth mills of Dover, and a general line of similar goods for the trade. At first they engaged solely in the manufacture of boxes, together with a general grain business, and later added the production of doors, sash and blinds.

Mr. Foss has taken an active part in the social and political affairs of the city and served several years as a member of its school committee. In 1893 he was electd mayor by a large majority and in the two succeeding years was re-elected by increased majorities. He is intimately acquainted with the needs and resources of the city, and is qualified to aid in every worthy movement for its development and welfare. He is a man of progressive ideas and of the most upright moral standard, and his business success has been achieved through the best methods, and his character is thoroughly established. He has passed through the various degrees of Free Masonry, being a past master of Strafford Lodge of that order, past high priest of Belknap Chapter, Royal Arch Masons, past deputy master of Orphan Council, past eminent commander of St. Paul's Commandery, Knights Templar, and member of Bektash temple, Ancient Arabic Order Nobles of the Mystic Shrine. In 1906 he was appointed grand standard bearer of the grand commandery of the Knights Templar of the state. In 1905, Mr. Foss received the thirty-third and highest degree in Free Masonary in the Supreme Council Northern Jurisdiction, Ancient Accepted Scottish Rite. He is a member of the Ancient and Honorable Artillery Company of Boston, and is also a past exalted ruler of Dover Lodge, Benevolent Protective Order of Elks. On January 1, 1905, he was appointed a member of Governor McLane's staff with the rank of colonel. His services and associations above mentioned indicate clearly his political affiliation with the Republican party.

He was married, October 12, 1868, to Clara Salome, daughter of Frank and Alice Jane Foss, of Barrington, New Hampshire, whose ancestry follows hereinafter. The children of this union were two in number, the second of whom Minna Nutter, died in infancy. Ina G., the first, was born November 8, 1869, and was married November 8, 1891, on her twenty-second birthday, to E. Frank Boomer, of Dover. They have three children: Minna Gertrude, Marjory Ramsdell and Evelyn. Mrs. Foss is a member of the Daughters of the American Revolution.

(III) George, youngest child of Joshua and Sarah (Wallis) Foss, was born 1721, in Rye, and died 1807, at the age of eighty-six years. He was married April 3, 1746, to Mary Marden, who was born September 30, 1726, daughter of James and Abigail (Webster) Marden. He was a Revolutionary soldier and resided in Barrington, one mile from the present Strafford line. His children were: Judith, Rachel, John, Abigail, George, William, Richard, James, Mary, Samuel and Nathan.

(IV) Nathan, youngest child of George and Mary (Marden) Foss, was born August 13, 1766.

Eli H Fox

in Barrington, and resided in Strafford. He was married March 7, 1790, to Alice Babb, who was born June 6, 1769, and died May 20, 1859, almost ninety years of age. Their children were: Polly, Sarah, James Babb, George B., Eliza, Nathan, Richard and Harriett.

(V) George Babb, second son and fourth child of Nathan and Alice (Babb) Foss, was born August 16, 1798, in Strafford, and died August 18, 1869. He was married April 17, 1818, to Sally Drew, who was born May 10, 1798, and died January 4, 1881, in her eightieth year. Their children were: Stephen Drew, Lydia Drew, Nathan, Richard, Alice Jane, and Sarah Ann.

(VI) Alice Jane, second daughter and fifth child of George B. and Sally (Drew) Foss, was born December 10, 1830, in Barrington, and was married March 14, 1850, to David Franklin Foss. He was a son of Ephraim and Lucinda (Herson) Foss, and was born October 26, 1826. Their children were: Clara Salome, Clayton, Sarah and Susan.

(VII) Clara Salome, eldest child of David F. and Alice Jane (Foss) Foss, was born May 30, 1851, in Barrington, and was married to Alonzo Melvin Foss, as above noted.

(IV) John, son of Mark and Amy (Thompson) Foss, was born May 6, 1757, in Strafford, and was a farmer residing on Strafford Ridge. He married Sarah Blake, who died December 17, 1822, and both are buried in the burying ground in the rear of Strafford Academy. John Foss was a soldier of the Revolution, enlisting July 10, 1781, in Captain Joshua Woodman's company and was mustered out the September following. His children were: Sarah, Betsy, Jonathan, James, Priscilla, Abigail, John B.

(V) Jonathan, eldest son of John (2), was born at Strafford Ridge, March 22, 1790. He there owned a farm which he exchanged in 1817 for one of twenty-seven acres in Centre Barnstead, owned by Colonel W. Lyford. This alleged farm was covered with timber which he cleared off, and the village of Centre Barnstead now occupies the site. When Jonathan Foss took possession of this land there was upon it a small house, a shed, and a one-horse gristmill. Here he lived and continued to engage in agriculture until his death in 1876, at the age of eighty-six years. His marriage occurred in Strafford, the wife's name being Margaret Bean. She died in the course of a year, and he married (second), in Barnstead, widow (Alice) Ham, a daughter of Nathaniel and Dolly (Marshall) Nutter. She was a native of Newington, New Hampshire. Their children were as follows: Eli H., James L., Jonathan, Nancy, Margaret, Dorothy, Mary Ann and John. Eli H., is mentioned at length below; James L. lives in Barnstead and married Eliza Blake; Nancy married Nathan Aiken; Margaret married Samuel G. Shackford; Dorothy married Levi C. Scruton; Mary Ann married Jeremiah Hackett.

(VI) Eli Ham, eldest child of Jonathan and Alice (Nutter) Foss, was born in Center Barnstead, July 16, 1819. His education consisted of attendance at the common schools of four weeks each year, the full length of term then taught. Shortly before he was twenty-one he went to learn the blacksmith trade with a Scotchman named John Hendrick, of Pittsfield, for twelve dollars per month. After a time he went to Boston and worked as helper, receiving sixteen dollars per month for swinging the heavy sledge. After three years of this employment he returned to the home farm to assist his father, and soon resumed his work at the anvil at Centre Barnstead, completing the days of his apprenticeship with Asa Garland. In 1846 he built a shop opposite where he now resides, which burned, a year later. He rebuilt and for nearly fifty years carried on his trade there. In 1852 he started from Boston for the then newly discovered gold fields of California. He sailed on the ship "Mary Merrill," carrying one hundred and sixty passengers, touching at Rio Janeiro and Buenos Ayres for water, rounding the Horn, making a stop at Valparaiso for another supply of water and reaching San Francisco in one day less than six months from the date of leaving Boston. Going to the placer mines, he worked at mining for some time, but preferring to work at his trade, he went to Redwood where he received one hundred dollars per month as a smith. He remained in California five years and returned to New Hampshire via Panama route in 1857. Resuming his trade at Barnstead he labored at it until 1864, when he enlisted in Company C, Eighteenth New Hampshire Volunteer Infantry, and participated in the battles of that year and the one following, around Petersburg, Virginia. At the close of the war he again returned to his forge, and followed his vocation until he retired from active life. From the date of the formation of the Republican party he has been a Republican, and was elected by that party to the office of town treasurer, which he held six years. Mr. Foss was born with a strong liking for adventure and travel, and has been an active participant of two of the great events of the world's history—the early mining in California, and the war between the states. He was always rated high as a mechanic and was not excelled by any other smith in this region. He has always stood well as a citizen and made an excellent record as the custodian of the people's money. For forty years he has been a member of Fraternal Lodge, No. 91, Free and Accepted Masons, and is now the only survivor of those who lived in Barnstead in pioneer days. Arrived at the age of eighty-seven years, he has never yet used spectacles. He married, August 23, 1844, Mary Ann Furber, born March 12, 1818, daughter of Edmund and Deborah (Walker) Furber, of Alton, both members of pioneer families of Centre Barnstead. Edmund Furber was a well known business man and a leader in church work. He lived to be ninety-five years old, dying in the year 1894. Mrs. Foss died October 25, 1888, aged seventy years. The children of Eli H. and Mary Ann (Furber) Foss were: Oscar, Mary Ann, Nellie D., and Estie. Oscar is mentioned at length below; Mary Ann married John F. Chesley, and has two children: Harry O., a physician, and Nellie D. married Reuben G. York; Estie married Emory L. Tuttle, and has one child, Lloyd Foss, of Lynn, Massachusetts.

(VII) Oscar, eldest son and child of Eli H. and Mary A. (Furber) Foss, was born in Barnstead, November 17, 1845. He obtained his education in the public schools, and at Pittsfield Academy, attending the latter institution in the winter season and spending the remainder of the year in his father's blacksmith shop, learning the trade. At the age of twenty-one he bought a half interest in a saw mill business with Nathaniel Blaisdell. At the end of the year he became sole owner of the business, which he has since greatly enlarged and sold. Mr. Foss has not only manufacturd a great deal of lumber, but he has bought numerous lots of standing timber and by means of portable mills has prepared the lumber for market in various large cities. His first purchase was in Northwood, and since that time the business has been greatly enlarged and he now owns and operates a few mills in various districts. He had five mills operating in 1895-6-7-8, and millions of feet of standing timber and large quantities of cord wood and lumber. He began business with a capital consisting of a good reputation, good business capacity, and a little money. His success in business soon enabled him to command all the financial assistance required from others and his success has been continuous and satisfactory. He has been a promoter of business enterprises and a leading business man in his town for years. He was one of the chief promoters of the Barnstead shoe shop, of which he was owner. He was one of the prime movers in getting the railroad and telephone lines to Barnstead. As an individual he has done much to promote the growth of business enterprises in the town, and is always chosen to head the delegation to induce desirable business to locate there. He is a stalwart Republican and through his influence many changes have been wrought in the politics of Barnstead. When he became a voter, the vote of the town showed ninety-nine Republicans to three hundred Democrats. In 1896 the Republicans for the first time had a majority of the votes. He was elected town treasurer in 1892 and served one year, and in 1896 was elected supervisor and has filled that office two years. In 1898 he was elected county commissioner, having the largest vote of the board of Belknap county, and was re-elected in 1900 for two years. In 1906 he was elected representative. He married, November 5, 1871, Sarah Ursula Young, born December 3, 1851, a daughter of Oliver H. P. and Emily J. (Tuttle) Young, and granddaughter of Jonathan Young, one of the early settlers of Barnstead. Oliver Young, born on Beauty Hill, learned the carpenter's trade and followed that vocation for years. After a time he removed to Barnstead Centre. He was a member of Company B, Twelfth New Hampshire Volunteers, and served three years in the Civil war. He held the office of justice of the peace for thirty years in his later life, and while an incumbent of that office wrote many conveyances, mortgages and other legal instruments, besides attending to the duties of justice.

TRULAND This name was originally spelled Trolin and the family is originally from Ireland, where they were engaged in the linen industry. The name was changed to Truland when John and James came to America.

(I) Philip Truland was born in county Derry, Ireland, in the seventeenth century. He spent his life in his native land, passing away about the year 1827-28. His wife, Elizabeth (Murray) Truland, came to the United States, 1840, and located in Lowell, Vermont, where she spent the remainder of her life, dying at the advanced age of one hundred and five years. The children of Philip and Elizabeth Truland who came to the United States were: John, James, Thomas, Daniel, William, Eliza and Mary. They all located in Lowell, Vermont, and spent a large portion of their lives there. John subsequently moved to Illinois and died there; James, Thomas and Mary died at Lowell; Daniel died at Lancaster, New Hampshire, 1904; Eliza died at Freeport, Illinois, about 1895. Elizabeth (Murray) Truland, the mother of these children, was born in county Derry, Ireland, on the first Sunday of June, 1780, and died in Lowell, Vermont, 1885.

(II) William Truland was born in county Derry, Ireland, June 25, 1822. He came to the United States in 1840, with his mother. In his native land he was engaged in the linen industry, and during life in the United States followed the occupation of woolen operative in Lowell, Vermont, and Littleton, New Hampshire. He married, at Waterville, Vermont, 1848, Mary McGourty, born in county Leitrim, Ireland, April, 1827, and seven children were born of this marriage: Frank W., Louis Joseph, Eliza Jane, James, John, Mary and one who died in infancy. Frank W. and Louis J. have been interested in the job printing business at Laconia for over thirty-five years. William Truland (father) died at Littleton, New Hampshire, August 17, 1870.

(III) Louis Joseph, second son of William and Mary (McGourty) Truland, was born in Lowell, Vermont, October 4, 1853. He was educated in the common schools of Littleton, New Hampshire. For six years he worked in the card room of the woolen mills of Littleton, and in 1876 he began to learn the printing business in the office of the *Littleton Republic*, where he was employed three years. Since then he has been employed on the *Laconia Democrat* four years, *Lancaster Gazette* and the *Lake Village Times*. It is now thirty-five years since he settled in Laconia, and during this long period he has taken an active interest in its affairs. In political faith he is a Democrat, and has taken an active part in local politics, serving for four years (1902-06) as a member of the city council. He is a member of the Knights of Pythias, has passed the chairs and represented his lodge in the grand body of the state. He is also a member of the Order of United Pilgrim Fathers.

Mr. Truland married, in Laconia, New Hampshire, October 4, 1888, Sarah Frances Glidden, born in Gilford, New Hampshire, daughter of Daniel and Mary (Bennett) Glidden, of Gilford, New Hampshire.

JAMESON The Jamesons referred to in this sketch are descended from the same stock as the Scotch-Irish who settled Londonderry, New Hampshire, nearly two hundred years ago.

(I) William John Jameson, a descendant of Scotch ancestors, was born in the north of Ireland and died in Compton, Province of Quebec, Canada. He settled at Compton about the year 1830, where he cleared away the forest, and spent the remainder of his life in farming operations. He married Nancy P. Armstrong, and they had children: Thomas, James, Samuel, Shaw, Robert George, of whom later; Joseph, Mary, Sarah Ann and Nancy.

(II) Robert George, fifth son and child of William John and Nancy P. (Armstrong) Jameson, was born in Compton, Province of Quebec, Canada, June 20, 1833, and died in Colebrook, New Hampshire, December 17, 1905. He was but eight years of age when his father died, while his mother lived to the ripe old age of ninety years. His educational advantages were very limited, being confined to attendance at the common school during the three months of the winter. At the time of the death of his father he left his home and sought occupation wherever he could find any, being employed in various lines until he had attained the age of seventeen years. He was then apprenticed to learn the blacksmith's trade, in Barnston, Province of Quebec, and at the conclusion of a three years' apprenticeship went to Concord, New Hampshire, where he entered the employ of the Abbott Downing Company, carriage builders. He remained with them for one year and then went to St. Johnsbury, Vermont, later to Plattsburg, New York, from thence to Milford, New Hampshire, and in 1853 to West Stewartstown, New Hampshire, where he was associated in business as a blacksmith for one year with Davis Graham. He removed to Colebrook, New Hampshire, in 1860, establishing himself in the blacksmithing business with Sumner Cummings, and in 1865 removed to Lancaster, New Hampshire, and carried on the same line of business there for a time. His next place of residence was Bristol, New Hampshire, from whence he went to Franklin in the same state, and in the spring of 1871 returned to Colebrook, where he spent the remainder of his days. He was engaged in the blacksmithing business until 1904, making a period of forty years. In addition to this, in June, 1889, he purchased the general merchandise store of E. H. Williams, in conjunction with his son, Charles H., and the business was carried on under the firm name of C. H. Jameson & Company until they sold out to A. S. Franch in 1897 and established a flour, grain and feed business, under the firm name of R. G. and C. H. Jameson, in which Mr. Jameson was actively engaged until he retired from all business interests January 1, 1905. During the last year of his life he resided with his son, Charles H. He became interested in the oil wells of Bothwell, Ontario, in 1856, and invested considerable money in this industry, which was finally lost by unlucky operations. In politics he was a stalwart Republican, and cast his first vote for John C. Fremont in 1856. He was prominent in town politics, and at various times filled all the public offices of the township. He was a member of Excelsior Lodge, No. 73, Independent Order of Odd Fellows. He was respected and honored throughout the community for his many, upright principles, and possessed the confidence of all who knew him. He married first), April 25, 1858, Melvina M. Dirth, born in Canaan, Vermont, April 25, 1841, daughter of Parker and Alvira (Morrell) Dirth, and they had children: Hattie E., died at the age of four years; Frederick, died at two years of age; Albert G., succeeded to the blacksmith business of his father in Colebrook, New Hampshire; Charles H., see forward; Edward died at the age of nine years; Samuel, died in infancy. Mrs. Jameson died June 25, 1890, and Mr. Jameson married (second), November, 1891, Angina L. Keazer, who is still living.

(III) Charles Herbert, third son and fourth child of Robert George and Melvina M. (Dirth) Jameson, was born in Franklin, New Hampshire, January 1, 1870. He was educated in the public schools of Colebrook and the Colebrook Academy, and upon the completion of his education accepted a clerkship in a mercantile business until he became associated with his father, in 1889. The business was carried on under the joint management until the retirement of his father, since which time Mr. Jameson has been the sole manager of the business, in which undertaking he has been very successful. His trade extends over a radius of from twenty to thirty miles, and includes the lumber district of the mountains, which he supplies with grain and feed, doing a wholesale and retail business in this branch. Politically he affiliates with the Republican party. He is a member of Evening Star Lodge, No. 37, Ancient Free and Accepted Masons, having joined the order in 1892; North Star Chapter, No. 11, Royal Arch Masons; Evening Star Council, No. 13, Royal and Select Masters; North Star Commandery, Knights Templar; Mount Sinai Temple, Ancient Arabic Order of the Mystic Shrine; and of a number of other fraternal organizations. He married, October 17, 1893, Catherine M. Fuller, born in Canaan, Vermont, September 11, 1870, daughter of Luther and Fannie (Carleton) Fuller, of Vermont. Mrs. Jameson received an excellent education in the common schools of Colebrook and the Colebrook Academy, and for some years prior to her marriage taught school. Mr. and Mrs. Jameson are the parents of children: Pauline F., Marion M., Leila E., and Ruth F.

CAVANAUGH The Cavanaugh Brothers, who are in all probability the best known horse dealers in New England, having extensive sale stables in Manchester, New Hampshire, Boston and Taunton, Massachusetts, are descended from sturdy Irish ancestry and are typical Irish-Americans, possessing the energy, thrift and progressive tendencies characteristic of these useful citizens.

(I) Thomas Cavanaugh, the father, emigrated from Ireland when a young man and settled in Norton, Massachusetts. He was a natural mechanic and his ingenuity, together with a familiarity with all kinds of tools, enabled him to make himself useful in almost every calling of a mechanical nature. He was a man of untiring industry, and that commendable quality was inherited by his children. His death occurred in East Taunton (Taunton), Massachusetts, 1864. He married Ellen Collins, who survived her husband many years, and when the entire care of the family devolved upon her she accepted the task courageously and accomplished it with credit. She died in 1900. Thomas and Ellen (Collins) Cavanaugh were the parents of five children, among whom were Michael A., Margaret, married Angelo Smith; James F., and Thomas F.

(II) James F., son of Thomas and Ellen (Collins) Cavanaugh, began the activities of life at the age of thirteen years, when he became an operative in a nail factory, and he remained there some four years. He was employed in a blacksmith shop for a similar length of time, and then engaged in the hacking business. In 1882 he joined his brothers in the buying and selling of horses, organizing the firm of Cavanaugh Brothers and opening sale stables at about the same time in Manchester and Boston. Some five years later they inaugurated a branch establishment in Taunton. For the past sixteen years they have occupied their present quarters in Manchester, a three-story building with stall accommodations for over one hundred horses, and their Boston stable is equally capacious. Some idea of the character and magnitude of their business may be obtained from the fact that upwards of five thousand equines pass through their hands annually, a considerable portion of which come from the western states, where four representatives are engaged in securing saleable horses for eastern shipment. These animals are distributed among the three repositories previously mentioned, where they are sold on commission at private sale and also at their regular weekly auction sales held at each establishment. Their sales are attended by buyers from all parts of New England, and as the Cavanaugh Brothers have acquired a reputation for dealing solely in sound, reliable horses they have become the most extensive as well as the best known equine distributors in their particular field of operation. In addition to the above-mentioned enterprise the firm conducts quite an extensive contracting business in the line of excavating, grading and exterior decoration, and one of its most notable achievements in that direction may be seen at the New Hampshire Breeders' Club, Salem, this state. The firm employs in its stables an average of forty men, and in its contract work a much larger force is necessary.

Having attained prosperity mainly through his own exertions, James F. Cavanaugh is justly entitled to an honorable place among the self-made men of Manchester, where his various commendable qualities are perhaps best known and appreciated, and one of his chief purposes in life is to preserve untarnished his own personal reputation, as well as that of the firm he represents. Politically he is a Republican. In his religious belief he is a Roman Catholic and worships at St. Joseph's Cathedral. He is a member of the Elks and Knights of Columbus. Mr. Cavanaugh married Annie Cronin, of Manchester, and his children are: Thomas F. (died in 1905), Michael Angelo, James Harrison, Aloysius, John Carl, Harold and Paul.

GRAY The family of which this sketch gives some account, has dwelt under three governments, and for more than one hundred years its members have been doing pioneer work in the new country along the border.

(I) Nathaniel Gray was born about 1715, in Canada, where his parents had settled probably after migrating from the United States. His wife's maiden name was Miles. They had seven children.

(II) Miles Gray, son of Nathaniel and Marietta (Miles) Gray, was born in Holland, Orleans county, Vermont, about 1819, and died October 27, 1864. He was a lifelong farmer, attended the Methodist Episcopal Church and was a Republican in politics. He married, in 1840, Marion Blake, who was born in Derby, Vermont, 1821. Eight children were born of this marriage: Charles, Nathaniel, John, Laben, Milo, Harris, Miles W. and William H. John and Laben served throughout the Civil war, enlisting as drummers at the ages of sixteen and seventeen respectively. The second wife of Miles Gray was Sophia Kimball, by whom he had three children: Morrill, Nellie and Marietta. Nellie is the wife of Frank Gray, of Holland, Vermont, and Marietta died in childhood.

(III) Miles W., seventh child of Miles and Marion (Blake) Gray, was born in Lunenburg, Vermont, August 11, 1853. His mother died when he was three years old and at the age of eleven he lost his father. He grew up in Vermont, working on a farm and attending school during the winters until he was sixteen years old. In 1869 he went to Stewartstown, New Hampshire, where for six years he was employed by Chester H. Noyes. He then removed to Columbia, where he purchased a farm of one hundred acres which he afterwards sold. Later he bought the old Gilman farm, several other farms in different parts of the county and also one in Vermont. His home farm comprises two hundred and fifty acres of productive land and has a good set of buildings furnished with all modern improvements. He has supplied the horses and helpers for the livery at the Profile House, from fifty to fifty-five horses being used in a season. This line of business he has followed for eight years. He has been engaged in agriculture all his life and in connection with this has taken an interest in lumbering. He was one of the organizers of the East Columbia Cheese Company. He is successful in his vocation and a man of influence in the locality where he lives. He has served several terms as selectman, was a member of the legislature, session of 1897, and is now (1907) serving his second term as county commissioner. While in the legislature he served on the committee of education. He is a charter member of Colebrook Lodge, No. 38, Knights of Pythias of Colebrook.

He married, in Columbia, New Hampshire, October 29, 1880, Harriet L. Tilton, who was born in Lunenburg, Vermont, 1857, daughter of Gordon and Susan (Townsend) Tilton, of Lunenburg, Vermont, and one child has been born to thim, Merle A., who died at the age of fourteen years. They have an adopted son, Edward H., born in 1896.

COWAN This is a very ancient American family, coming probably originally from Scotland, and is found very early in Newton, Scituate, Brookfield, and other towns of Massachusetts. It has been impossible, however, to trace the connection of the line herein given to the original American ancestor.

(I) Zechariah Cowan was born May 19, 1770, in Lyman, New Hampshire, and lived in that town. He was the father of thirteen children.

(II) Charles, fourth child of Zechariah Cowan, was born November 19, 1796, in Lyman, and was well known as Elder Cowan, a Methodist minister, faithful in the service of his Master. He was educated in the public schools, and received license to preach the Gospel at Danville, Vermont, February 7, 1827. He was admitted on trial to the New England Conference the next year, and was ordained deacon by Bishop Hedding, at Barre, Vermont, June 27, 1830. On August 12, 1832, he was ordained Elder by Bishop Roberts, of Lyndon, Vermont. He was given the following appointments which he filled with satisfaction to the several parishes: Stratford, New Hampshire, 1828-9; Bethlehem and Whitefield, New Hampshire, 1830; Lancaster, 1831; Newbury, Vermont, 1832; Bradford and Fairlee, Vermont, 1833; Northfield, Vermont, 1834-5; Barnard, Vermont, 1836-7; Windsor, 1838-9; and Canaan, 1840. He was superannuate from 1841 to 1844, and was appointed for the year 1844-5 to a pastorate at Lisbon, New Hampshire, but was at Littleton the next year, and again pastor at Bethlehem and Whitefield in 1848. The next year his charge included Whitefield and Dalton, and in 1850, Dalton and Monroe, going the succeeding year to Lyman, New Hampshire. He was superannuated at the latter place from 1852 to 1858, and was pastor at Lisbon, 1858-60. He resided in the latter place from 1860 to 1869 and died there May 3, of the last named year. In 1846-7 he represented the town of Lisbon in the New Hampshire legislature. He was married, May 8, 1816, to Clarissa C. Bassett, who was born in November, 1800, a daughter of Lemuel and Polly Bassett, of Vershire, Vermont. She survived him nearly eight years, dying February 27, 1877, in Lyman, New Hampshire.

(III) Silas, eldest child of Rev. Charles and Clarissa (Bassett) Cowan, was born about December, 1817, in Lyman, New Hampshire, and died at Guild, New Hampshire, October 18, 1896, nearly seventy-nine years old. He was married, January 6, 1841, in Lyman, to Mialma, daughter of John and Pamelia (Eastman) Young. She was born in March, 1821, and died November 25, 1896, surviving her husband one month and one week.

(IV) Arthur, son of Silas and Mialma (Young) Cowan, was born June 11, 1842, and was married July 4, 1861, in Bath, New Hampshire, to Jennie Atwood, who was born May 29, 1847, and died April 23, 1896. They were the parents of three children: 1. Ardell Atwood, born in Manchester, New Hampshire, October 23, 1863, married D. J. Daley, at Lan-

Miles W. Gray

caster, 1886, new a resident of Berlin, New Hampshire. 2. Lizzie Loomis, mentioned below. 3. Florence Hall, born at Lancaster, April 12, 1882.

(V) Lizzie L., daughter of Arthur and Jennie (Atwood) Cowan, was born January 15, 1872, in Lisbon, and was married, January 15, 1890, to Albert F. Whittemore, of Colebrook. (See Whittemore, IX).

KERINS John Kerins, deceased. for many years a well known and highly respected citizen of Manchester, New Hampshire, was a native of county Kerry, Ireland, born 1836, and died in Manchester, New Hampshire, May 14, 1895, aged fifty-nine years.

In early manhood John Kerins emigrated to the United States, settling in Manchester. New Hampshire, where he resided when the great Civil war broke out. Being a man of patriotic spirit and devoted to the interests of his adopted country, he enlisted in the Tenth New Hampshire Regiment, and later re-enlisted in the regular army for a period of three years, the principal battles in which he participated having been the Wilderness, Fredericksburg, and Cold Harbor, being wounded in the latter battle and receiving therefor a pension from the United States government. Mr. Kerins was a member and active worker of St. Joseph's Cathedral parish.

John Kerins was married in the basement of St. Anne's Catholic Church by the Rev. Father William McDonald, the pioneer priest of that church, to Ellen Callity, who bore him the following named children: 1. Johanna, wife of Frank Emery, of Manchester, New Hampshire. 2. Mary Ann. wife of Henry Martin, of West Manchester, New Hampshire; two children: Margaret and Esther Martin. 3. Anne, died June 11, 1904, aged forty years. 4. Patrick, died in infancy. 5. Annie, died 1904, aged thirty-five years. 6. Timothy J., married Margaret Sullivan, and resides at No. 289 Lowell street, Manchester; he looks after his mother's property. 7. John, married Margaret Hall, one child, Ellen; the family reside in Manchester. 8. Margaret E., died in the sixth year of her age. The mother of these children is the eldest child of Michael and Johanna (Flynn) Callity. She came to Manchester when it was mostly a wilderness, and grew up with the city, witnessing its wonderful growth along different lines, especially that of religion, having seen all the churches, schools, convents and other Catholic institutions open and prosper. She attended mass when Father McDonald held services in a hall, prior to the erection of his church. She is one of the oldest Catholic women in the city of Manchester. She has been an indefatigable worker throughout the active years of her life, prudent and saving, and therefore acquired quite a competency for her declining years. Although at the present time (1907) she is over eighty years of age, she is very active and energetic and attends to her property, which is located in some of the best sections of the city, including that on Pine and Pearl streets.

Mrs. Johanna (Flynn) Callity, deceased, who was the wife of Michael Callity, and mother of Mrs. John Kerins, was born and educated in Ireland, and there married, the issue of this union being twelve children, all of whom were born in Ireland with the exception of Dr. James E. Callity, the youngest. Of these children the following attained years of maturity: Ellen, widow of John Kerins; Johanna McKenna, of Bakersville, New Hampshire; Timothy; Mary Sullivan; Julia, wife of Asa Smith; James E., mentioned below. In 1854-55 Mrs. Callity migrated from county Kerry, Ireland, to the United States, settling in Manchester, New Hampshire, accompanied by her children, who were of great help to her. Mrs. Callity was a woman of extensive ability, and at her death, at the age of seventy-three, she left her children an estate valued at thirty-five thousand dollars. Her first location in the city of Manchester was on Washington street, from whence she removed to Hanover street, which was then a row of wooden buildings, and is now a business block, and later removed to No. 268 Lowell street, where her death occurred. She was one of the charter members of St. Anne's Catholic Church was a close personal friend of Rev. Father McDonald, its pastor, and her devotion to the church and its work was most marked. She attended mass in a hall for a number of years before the church was erected, and during her residence in Manchester witnessed the great transfomation which took place in the business circles as well as in religious. She was of a genial, kindly nature, loved and respected by all who came in contact with her, and her life work should serve as an example and inspiration. As a Christian she was true to her God and church, living and dying a devout and practical Roman Catholic; as a wife and mother she performed her duties and obligations in an exemplary manner, and as a neighbor and friend she has left a tribute to her memory by her good acts and deeds and her liberality to the poor.

Dr. James E. Callity was educated in parochial schools, graduating in the class of 1870, and then entered Holy Cross College, at Worcester, Massachusetts, graduating in the class of 1876, his preceptor having been Dr. George Crosby, and the present president of that college was a classmate of Dr. Callity. In 1877, during the summer session, he pursued his studies in Dartmouth College, and in the class of 1879 graduated from Bellevue College, New York City; later in the same year he pursued post-graduate studies. In 1880 he opened an office in Manchester, his native city, and has since been engaged in active practice, a period of twenty-seven years. He held the position of city and county physician for thirteen years, resigning to accept a position on the United States pension board under President Harrison for four years. He is a member of the staff of Sacred Heart Hospital, and acted in the capacity of charity physician for twenty-five years, serving in the Charity Square Hospital, St. Patrick's Orphanage, Old Ladies' Home and Infant Asylum. He was the first physician to examine the order of Forestry in New Hampshire, and from the Granite State Court all the other courts have sprung. He is a member of the order of Foresters. He married Isabel Post, of New York.

MORRISON This is one of the old New England families, although it is not counted among the Puritan pioneers. It is not, however, to be confounded with the Scotch-Irish families of which there were several in southern New Hampshire and which have contributed many valuable citizens to the state. The line herein traced is probably of Scotch origin, but was planted in this country before the immigration of the hardy pioneers of Londonderry, New Hampshire, who were of undoubted Scotch blood.

(I) Daniel Morrison, first of whom we have record in this line, was living in Newbury, Massachusetts, before 1690. He subsequently removed to Rowley, Massachusetts, where he died between November 3, 1736, and May 10, 1737, the dates respectively of making and proving his will. His first wife Hannah (Griffin) Morrison, was the mother of five of his children, and died in Newbury, October 9, 1700. He was married (second), in 1707 (intention published March 27), to Mary Folsom, of Exeter, who was the mother of four of his children, all of whom died in infancy. She died February 14, 1711, and he married (third), in 1712 (published November 8), Abigail Kimball. She was born June 12, 1669, daughter of John and Mary (Jordon) Kimball, of Amesbury, Massachusetts, and was living in 1727. His will mentions a wife Mary, but no record of a fourth marriage has been found. He had ten children, all born in Newbury, namely: Mary, Daniel, John, Hannah, Ebenezer, two pairs of twins that died at birth, and Abigail.

(II) John, second son and third child of Daniel and Hannah (Griffin) Morrison, was born March 28, 1673, in Newbury, Massachusetts, and settled in Haverhill, East Parish, same colony, where he died at the close of 1769 or early in 1770. His will is on file at Salem, dated August 18, 1769, and was probated February 27, 1770. This will mentions his wife Lydia and ten children. His name is found upon tax lists and petitions and other affairs relating to Haverhill. He was probably a farmer. He was married in Haverhill, January 8, 1718, to Lydia Robinson, who was born in Exeter about 1700, daughter of John and Mehitabel Robinson, and granddaughter of Jonathan and Elizabeth Robinson. She was a sister of the John Robinson who married Elizabeth Folsom. The order of birth of their children is not known. They were: Bradbury, John, David, Daniel, Samuel, Ebenezer, Hannah, Abigail, Lydia and Jeremiah.

(III) David (2), third son of John and Lydia (Robinson) Morrison, was born 1732 or 1733, in Haverhill, Massachusetts. He resided for a time in Amesbury, Massachusetts, whence he removed to Epping, New Hampshire, about 1762. He returned to Amesbury and from there to Canterbury, New Hampshire, where he is first found on record in 1764 as being taxed fifteen shillings and six pence. He was tithingman in the Northfield parish of that town as late as 1782, and removed to Sanbornton about 1784, locating on Salmon brook at the place still known as Morrison's Mill. His property was lot number sixty-five in the first division and he was employed in tending grist mills. He was married (first), about 1753, to Keziah Whittle, daughter of Thomas and Molly (Cole) Whittle. Her father was born on the Isle of Wight and first settled in this country at Amesbury, Massachusetts. She was a noted singer and her descendants have inherited from her a talent in that direction. Two of her older daughter were much distinguished for musical ability. She died July 5, 1800, in Sanbornton, and Mr. Morrison married (second), Hulda Page, of East Andover. He died April 6, 1827, aged ninety-four years. His children were: Anna, Molly, David (died young), Lydia, David, Bradbury, John, Thomas W. and Keziah.

(IV) Thomas Whittle, fifth son and eighth child of David and Keziah (Whittle) Morrison, was born in Sanbornton, New Hampshire, and settled on Salmon brook just west of Turkey bridge in that town, where he died October 2, 1838. He was married, November 12, 1795, to Betsey Cass, daughter of Moses and Sarah (Wring) Cass, of Sanbornton. She was born May 26, 1777. Their children were: Sally, Bradbury, Thomas Whittle, Samuel, Nancy, David, Miriam P., Hannah, James Simonds and Lydia. The eldest daughter married (first), William Calley, and (second), Cephas Smith. (See Smith, IV).

(V) Thomas Whittle (2), second son and third child of Thomas Whittle (1) and Betsy (Cass) Morrison, was born September 12, 1800, in Sanbornton, and engaged in farming in New Hampton and Franklin, and a large portion of his life was spent in Weare. From Weare he removed to New Hampton, where he purchased a farm on the Tilton road. About 1874 he sold this farm and removed to Franklin, New Hampshire, where he purchased a dwelling and there spent the autumn of his life. He died in May, 1884, and his wife died in October, 1882. He was married in May, 1825, to Dorothy Gordon, of New Hampton, who was born March 23, 1798, in Brentwood, New Hampshire. Their children were: Ira Edwin, Charles Ewell, and Albert Palmer.

(VI) Albert Palmer, youngest child of Thomas W. and Dorothy (Gordon) Morrison, was born in New Hampton, February 6, 1833, and died January 2, 1873, aged forty years. He obtained his schooling in the common schools and at New Hampton Academy, and at the age of fifteen went to Boston where he entered the employ of a Mr. English and worked in a meat market. In 1858 he engaged in the same business on his own account at Boston, and carried it on four years. Subsequently he leased the Blackstone Hotel, Hanover street, Boston, and later opened the Mystic Hotel and park at Medford, Massachusetts. This he conducted until 1871. He married (first), September, 1856, Sarah C. Gage, who was born in Franklin, New Hampshire, daughter of Jacob Gage, of Franklin. She died July 30, 1863, leaving one child, Thomas Albert, who was born June 7, 1858, and now resides in Somerville, Massachusetts. Thomas Albert Morrison married, May 10, 1884, at Wauseon, Ohio, Cora Jane Newcomer, of Wauseon, Ohio. He married (second), in Boston, November 21, 1866, Esther F. Dimond, who was born April 24, 1832, daughter of Samuel and Susan (Dimond) Dimond, of Concord, New Hampshire. (See Dimond, V). Seventeen years after the death of her husband, Mrs. Morrison removed from Boston to Salisbury, New Hampshire, and has since resided on the one hundred acre farm in Salisbury village, formerly owned by her father.

(Second Family.)

MORISON Among the excellent and exemplary Scotch who came to Londonderry and settled in the early part of the eighteenth century was the ancestor of this family. His progeny has borne no mean part in the development of civilization in the New World.

(I) John Morison, tradition states, was born in county of Aberdeen, Scotland, in 1628; emigrated to America between 1720 and 1723; and died in Londonderry, New Hampshire, February 16, 1736, at the reputed age of one hundred and eight years. There is scarcely a doubt that he was born in Scotland and emigrated to Ireland some time before the siege of Londonderry. He certainly lived in Ireland, and had a family in 1688, and resided in or near the city of Londonderry during the war of James the Second for the throne of England. He and his family were at Londonderry during the celebrated siege and defence of that city, and they were among the number who were driven beneath the walls, and subsequently admitted within the city, remaining there until the city was relieved. He did not come to America in the first immigration of 1718, but continued to live in Ireland till about 1720, when he removed to America, with a young family by his last wife, Jane Steele. On December 25, 1723, his sons, James and John, who had preceded him to New Hampshire, deeded him a piece of land in Londonderry, in that portion of the present town of Derry now known as the "Dock." His children were: James, John, Halbert, Martha, Samuel Hannah, Mary and Joseph. All but the youngest were born in Ireland.

(II) Joseph, youngest child of John and Jane (Steele) Morison, was born on the passage of the family to America about 1720, and died in Londonderry, February 17, 1806, aged about eighty-six. He was of age and conveyed lands in 1841. He was a carpenter and farmer. In 1769 he was one of the undertakers for building the new church in Londonderry, (now Derry) East Village. He settled near the Windham line not far from the Londonderry turnpike, on a farm at that time within the limits of Windham, and his name appears on the tax lists of that town for several years. There he lived and died. He married Mary Holmes, of Londonderry, and they had eight children: Joseph, Abraham, Ann, Jane, John, Mary, Hannah and Jonathan.

(III) Mary, sixth child and third daughter of Joseph and Mary (Holmes) Morison, was born May 8, 1751, and died in Londonderry, March 31, 1836, aged eighty-five. She married, December 22, 1779, John Anderson, of Londonderry, who was born May 9, 1754, and died January 8, 1827. He was a farmer and resided in Londonderry. Their children were: Joseph, James and Nancy (twins), Mary, Jane and Betsey.

(IV) Mary Anderson, fourth child and second daughter of John and Mary (Morison) Anderson, was born in Londonderry, December 20, 1786, and died February 21, 1832. She married Captain Abel Plummer, of Rowley, Massachusetts. He was a farmer, and after 1776 resided in Londonderry, where he died November 3, 1841. Their children were: Mary, Nancy, John A., William, Susan, Elmira and Sarah.

(V) Mary Plummer, eldest child of Captain Abel and Mary (Anderson) Plummer, was born in Londonderry, August 23, 1809, and died March 9, 1873, aged seventy-five years. She married, October 25, 1830, Deacon James Nevins (See Nevins, V), of Londonderry, farmer.

TIBBETTS This is the usual spelling of the name in present use, though a part of the family employ the form, Tebbets, Tibbets or Tibbits. It is among the earliest in New Hampshire, and has been continuously associated with the development of the state in worthy ways. From southeastern New Hampshire it has spread to all parts of the United States and is found in connection with pioneer settlements in many localities.

(I) Henry Tibbetts, the ancestor of nearly all of the name in America, was born in England about the year 1596, and embarked from London, July 13, 1635, in the ship "James," bound for New England. He was accompanied by his wife, Elizabeth, born in the same year as himself, and sons, Jeremiah, born 1631, and Samuel, 1633. He was a shoemaker by trade, and soon settled in Dover, New Hampshire, where he had a grant of three and one-half acres of land for a house lot, at Dover Neck. At different times he had other grants, including one of twenty acres situated on the west side of Back river (now called the Bellamy river) and another of one hundred acres adjoining the Newichawanock river in what is now Rollinsford, then Dover. He held several minor offices in the town, was a hard-working, industrious farmer and, for some years, was the only shoemaker in the place. He died in 1676, at the age of eighty years, having survived his wife, Elizabeth, several years. They had several children born after their arrival in America.

(II) Jeremiah, eldest child of Henry and Elizabeth Tibbetts, born 1631, in England, died in the summer of 1677. His will was dated May 5, and proved October 31, of that year. His widow, Mary, survived him and married a Mr. Loomis. He lived at Dover, where he was a farmer and for several years kept the jail or prison of the colony. He had several grants from the town, one embracing one hundred acres of land in what is now Rollinsford and another of three and one-half acres at Dover Neck for a house lot, on which he built his residence. He inherited the greater part of his father's lands, including the one hundred acres tract in Rollinsford. He married Mary, daughter of Thomas Canney, a neighbor who lived but a short distance from the Tibbetts home. She died at Dover, July 2, 1706. They had eight sons and four daughters, namely: Jeremiah, mentioned in next paragraph. Mary, born April 15, 1658, married Ichabod Rawlins. Thomas, February 24, 1659, married (first) Judith Dame, (second) Elizabeth ——, (third) Sarah ——. Hannah, born February 25, 1661, married Nathaniel Perkins. Joseph, born August 7, 1663, married (first) Elizabeth ——, (second) Catherine Mason. Samuel, born 1666, married (first) Dorothy Tuttle, (second) Rebecca Willy, (third) Rachel ——. Benjamin, born about 1668. Ephraim, born about 1669, married Rose Austin. Martha, born about 1671. Elizabeth, born about 1672, married John Bickford. Nathaniel, born about 1674, married Elizabeth ——. Henry, born about 1676, married (first) Widow Joyce Otis, (second) Mary Akerman. (Mention of Thomas and Ephraim and their descendants forms part of this article.)

(III) Jeremiah (2), eldest child of Jeremiah (1) and Mary (Canney) Tibbetts, was born June 5, 1656, and died some time after June 27, 1735, and before December 17, 1743. He lived at Dover, New Hampshire, and was a farmer. He married Mary, daughter of Ralph and Elizabeth Twombly, and they were the parents of a large family of children.

(IV) John, son of Jeremiah (2) and Mary (Twombly) Tibbetts, was born about 1685. He was alive in 1743, and died before May 2, 1756. He resided in Dover, and followed the trade of carpenter. He married (first) Sarah, daughter of John and Sarah Meader, of Dover. She died and he married (second) Tamsen (Meserve) Ham, widow of Joseph Ham. He had three children by the first marriage and one by the second.

(V) John (2), eldest child of John (1) and Sarah (Meader) Tibbetts, was born November 14, 1711, the date of his death is unknown. He spent his life in Dover. He married Tamson, daughter of Ephraim Ricker, of the same place.

(VI) Ichabod, son of John (2) and Tamson (Ricker) Tibbetts, was born about 1745, but the date of his death is not known. He resided in Dover, and married Hannah, daughter of Jeremiah and Lydia Tibbetts, of Barrington, New Hampshire. She was born February 10, 1754, and died in 1831. They had twelve children.

(VII) John (3), son of Ichabod and Hannah

(Tibbetts) Tibbetts, was born July 5, 1784, and died in 1821. He resided in Dover, New Hampshire, and was a farmer. He married Deborah Ham, of Barrington, New Hampshire, who died February 8, 1858. They had four children.

(VIII) Samuel Ham, eldest child of John (3) and Deborah (Ham) Tibbetts, was born February 11, 1807, and died September 23, 1858. He resided at Dover, and married, December 7, 1826, Belinda, daughter of Joseph and Mary (Hayes) Cross, of Rochester, New Hampshire. She was born April 23, 1808, and died October 29, 1846. He had six children.

(IX) John Winslow, second child of Samuel Ham and Belinda (Cross) Tibbetts, was born January 5, 1831, in Dover, New Hampshire. He attended the common schools, and at the age of eighteen years apprenticed himself to the carpenter trade, and for two years worked for Woodbury S. Manes, a prominent builder of that day. In 1850 he settled in Rochester, where he became a master carpenter and worked at his trade a part of the time until about 1890, being also employed a large part of that time in lumbering, at which he did a quite extensive business. In 1862 he engaged in the livery business as a member of the firm of Tibbetts & Hays, which existed until 1880. In 1879 he erected the Glendon House at East Rochester, and has since been its proprietor, making the enterprise a success from the start, and never selling a drop of liquor. He has a warm interest in the affairs of the town, and has been a director in the Loan and Banking Company of Rochester for ten years past. In early manhood he was a Whig, and cast his first presidential ballot for General Scott in 1852. When the Republican party rose to power he joined its ranks and has ever since been one of its faithful supporters. He was selectman for two years immediately preceding the incorporation of Rochester as a city, and councilman the two following years. In 1873 and 1875 he was a representative in the state legislature. He is a Mason, and a member of Humane Lodge, No. 21, of Rochester; Temple Royal Arch Chapter, No. 20, and Orphan Council, No. 7, Royal and Select Masters. He is also a member of Cocheco Lodge, No. 39, Independent Order of Odd Fellows, of East Rochester, which he helped to organize, and of Norway Plains Encampment, No. 39, same order.

He married (first), in May, 1854, Charlotte F. Chamberlain, who died January 1, 1857, daughter of Amos Chamberlain, of Lebanon. He married (second), December, 1857, Clara W. Blaisdell, who was born in Lebanon, Maine, and died in Rochester, April 20, 1896, daughter of Jonathan and Sally Blaisdell. Two children were born of this union: Cora B., born July 12, 1858, married Joseph O. Hayes; and Avie E., born October 13, 1864, died January 14, 1890.

(III) Thomas, second son of Jeremiah (1) and Mary (Canney) Tebbets, was born February 24, 1659, and resided at Dover Neck, a few rods below the site of the old church on the hill, on the westerly side of the highway. For many years he was town clerk of Dover, and to him we are indebted for the collecting and preservation of nearly all of the vital records of early Dover. At the breaking out of King William's war he entered the Colonial army and was promoted from time to time until he became captain. He was also in the service during Queen Anne's war. He was an extensive land owner in Dover and vicinity. He married Judith, daughter of Deacon John Dame, who had formerly resided on the same farm. Captain Tebbets had eight children. As will be seen, this branch uses a different spelling from the others.

(IV) Moses, seventh child of Captain Thomas and Judith (Dame) Tebbets, was born January 27, 1701. The date of his death is not known, but he was living in 1748. He was a farmer and shoemaker and removed to that part of Dover which is now Rollinsford. He married, March 18, 1725, Mary, daughter of John and Grizzel Keay, of Berwick, Maine. She was baptized April 25, 1703, and died May 10, 1788, aged eighty-eight years. They had four children.

(V) Ebenezer, third child of Moses and Grizzel (Keay) Tebbets, was born in July, 1738, and died June 22, 1798, aged fifty-nine years and eleven months. He removed to Berwick, Maine, where he purchased a large farm. He married Sarah Larey, who died February 18, 1823, aged eighty-three years. They were the parents of five children.

(VI) James, youngest child of Ebenezer and Sarah (Larey) Tebbets, was born May 23, 1781, and resided in Berwick, Maine. He was a farmer and owned one of the best farms in that town, where he died April 20, 1861. He married Elizabeth, daughter of Jeremiah and Anna (Pray) Emery, of Shapleigh, Maine. She was born July 20, 1789, and died July 19, 1863. They had eight children.

(VII) Ebenezer Armstrong, seventh child of James and Elizabeth (Emery) Tebbets, was born August 1, 1824, at Berwick, Maine, and died in December, 1898. He removed to Somersworth, New Hampshire, in 1842, and was a prominent citizen and successful merchant of that place for fifty-six years. He married, September 2, 1852, Jane Amanda, daughter of Captain Daniel and Lydia (Towne) Nason, of Kennebunk, Maine. She died September, 1897. They had five children. He adopted the use of the letter "i" in the first syllable of his name.

(VIII) William Sewall, eldest child of Ebenezer Armstrong and Jane Amanda (Nason) Tibbets, was born March 2, 1854, in Somersworth, and attended the public schools of that place. He graduated from the Phillips Exeter Academy in 1872. From the date of his graduation until 1881, he was a clerk of the hardware firm of Tibbets and Brother, at Somersworth. In 1881 he was taken in as a partner by his father under the firm name of E. A. Tibbets & Son. In 1897 he was offered the position of cashier of the Great Falls National Bank, but not liking national bank work he declined. In 1898 he was elected treasurer of the Somersworth Savings Bank, which office he has continuously held until the present time (1907). The bank has increased in size and strength during his incumency, and is today rated as one of the very cleanest and safest savings banks in this state, not only in respect to its investments and securities but also its simple yet carefully guarded methods of doing the business and the bookkeeping of the institution. In 1905 he was elected president of the First National Bank of Somersworth. He married, December 23, 1883, Carrie Russell Perkins, of Somersworth. She was born there February 26, 1864. They are the parents of three children, namely: Albert Perkins, born November 14, 1884; Jane Nason, December 16, 1888; William Armstrong, December 3, 1891.

(III) Ephraim, sixth son of Jeremiah (1) and Mary (Canney) Tibbetts, was born about 1669. It is not known when he died, but he was living as late as 1751. He resided at Dover Neck, and was by trade a blacksmith. He belonged to the Society

+ George Albert Guertin,
Bishop of Manchester.

[illegible] friends. He married Rose, daughter of Thomas [illegible] Ayson, of Dover. She was born April [illegible] 1678, and died in 1755, aged seventy-seven years. [illegible] were the parents of eleven children.

(IV) Aaron, seventh child of Ephraim and [illegible] (Austin) Tibbetts, was born February 25, [illegible]. He was a [illegible], and resided at Dover for [illegible] years, then moved to Rochester, New Hampshire, living on what is called the Walnut Grove [illegible]. He married Phoebe Richardson, of Kittery, [illegible], and they had a family of [illegible] children.

(V) Stephen, eldest child of Aaron and Phoebe (Richardson) Tibbetts, was born about 1727, [illegible] died in Buxton, Maine, [illegible]. He resided in [illegible] Maine, for many years, finally removing [illegible] that state. He was [illegible], also a hard-working, industrious farmer. His wife's name was [illegible], her surname is supposed to have been Haynes. [illegible] date of her death is not known. They had [illegible] children.

(VI) Ephraim (2), son of Stephen and Alice [illegible] Tibbetts, was born September [illegible], 1753, and died October 21, 1818. He was a farmer, and settled in [illegible], Maine. He married (first) Eunice Tibbetts, of Rochester, New Hampshire, by whom he [illegible] one child. She died and he married (second) [illegible] second cousin, [illegible] Tibbetts, of Rochester, [illegible] January 9, 1762, daughter of Elijah, who was a [illegible] of Ephraim Tibbetts. She died July 31, 1851. [illegible] were the parents of [illegible] children.

(VII) George, son of Ephraim and Esther [illegible] Tibbetts, was born March 12, 1795, and [illegible] July 20, 1873. He resided at Lebanon, Maine, where he followed the occupation of farmer. He [illegible] six feet in height and weighed two hundred [illegible] five pounds, and was at one time the strongest [illegible] in town. He married, July 21, 1811, Mary [illegible], of Lebanon, who died April 13, 1888. They [illegible] a family of nine children.

(VIII) Orland [illegible], son of George and Mary (Foss) Tibbetts, was born October [illegible], 1823, and died March [illegible], 1870. He resided in Lebanon, Maine, his farm being about a half mile north of [illegible]'s Corner, and was a hard-working farmer. [illegible] married, November [illegible], Lydia Ann, daughter of Benjamin and [illegible] Place (Richardson) [illegible], of Rochester, New Hampshire. She died February 10, 1872. They were the parents of two children.

(IX) Charles W[illegible], eldest child of Orland [illegible] and Lydia [illegible] Tibbetts, was born July 8, 1846, in Lebanon, Maine, and was reared on his father's farm at that place. He was educated in the public schools of that town, and afterward took an advanced course of study at the [illegible] Lebanon Academy. He began teaching school [illegible] fall of 1868, and taught during the winter [illegible] for three years, reading law when not teaching, at the office of [illegible] Emery, Esquire, in [illegible]. In the fall of 1871 he removed to Somersworth, New Hampshire, where his law studies were [illegible] at the [illegible] of [illegible] J. Copeland, [illegible]. In the fall of 1872 he was admitted to [illegible] practice of law and settled in Farmington, New Hampshire, where he was engaged in [illegible] for five years. In January, 1870, he removed to Dover, New Hampshire, where he [illegible] resided, and has engaged in farming and [illegible] estate on his own account, [illegible]. In 1887 he became [illegible]. He was [illegible] corporation and other [illegible] New [illegible] Genealogical Society, [illegible] has been the financial agent [illegible] of

[illegible]

[illegible] far back as [illegible] France, [illegible] Louis [illegible] Montreal [illegible] daughter of [illegible] of Paris [illegible] the Guertin [illegible]

(I) On[illegible] was married [illegible] de Champ[illegible]. They settled [illegible] Hyacinthe, and [illegible] union.

(II) George [illegible] was born at [illegible] ship at St. Hy[illegible]. He married [illegible] Lefebvre, of S[illegible] 1864 he came to [illegible] himself in ba[illegible] New Hampshire [illegible] habits a con[illegible] born of that [illegible] namely: Ro[illegible] Josin, who [illegible] wife of A[illegible] married to [illegible] New Hamp[illegible] keen [illegible] institution [illegible] and [illegible] board [illegible] in 1902

(II[illegible] Hamp[illegible] Guertin [illegible] February [illegible] the [illegible] encourag[illegible] to [illegible] classical [illegible] lege, [illegible] Josin [illegible] He to[illegible]

[illegible] city. [illegible] he had [illegible] would [illegible] such beginning [illegible] eloquent w[illegible]

[illegible],
of Manchester

of Friends. He married Rose, daughter of Thomas and Anne Austin, of Dover. She was born April 3, 1678, and died in 1755, aged seventy-seven years. They were the parents of eleven children.

(IV) Aaron, seventh child of Ephraim and Rose (Austin) Tibbetts, was born February 26, 1701. He was a Friend, and resided at Dover for many years, then removed to Rochester, New Hampshire, living on what is called the Walnut Grove road. He married Penelope Richardson, of Kittery, Maine, and they had a family of five children.

(V) Stephen, eldest child of Aaron and Penelope (Richardson) Tibbetts, was born about 1727, and died in Buxton, Maine, in 1816. He resided in Berwick, Maine, for many years, finally removing to Buxton, that state. He was a Friend, also a hard-working, industrious farmer. His wife's name was Alice, her surname is supposed to have been Haynes. The date of her death is not known. They had eight children.

(VI) Ephraim (2), son of Stephen and Alice Tibbetts, was born September, 1754, and died October 21, 1836. He was a farmer, and settled in Lebanon, Maine. He married (first) Eunice Tibbetts, of Rochester, New Hampshire, by whom he had one child. She died and he married (second) his second cousin, Esther Tibbetts, of Rochester, born January 9, 1762, daughter of Elijah, who was a son of Ephraim Tibbetts. She died July 31, 1851. They were the parents of nine children.

(VII) George, son of Ephraim and Esther (Tibbetts) Tibbetts, was born March 12, 1795, and died July 20, 1873. He resided at Lebanon, Maine, where he followed the occupation of farmer. He stood six feet in height and weighed two hundred and five pounds, and was at one time the strongest man in town. He married, July 21, 1821, Mary Foss, of Lebanon, who died April 13, 1888. They had a family of nine children.

(VIII) Orland Harriman, son of George and Mary (Foss) Tibbetts, was born October 19, 1823, and died March 22, 1870. He resided in Lebanon, Maine, his farm being about a half-mile north of Blaisdell's Corner, and was a hard working farmer. He married, November 28, 1844, Lydia Ann, daughter of Benjamin and Abigail Place (Richardson) Clark, of Rochester, New Hampshire. She died February 10, 1872. They were the parents of two children.

(IX) Charles Wesley, eldest child of Orland Harriman and Lydia Ann (Clark) Tibbetts, was born July 5, 1846, in Lebanon, Maine, and was reared on his father's farm at that place. He was educated in the public schools of that town, and afterward took an advanced course of study at the West Lebanon Academy. He began teaching school in the fall of 1868, and taught during the winter season for three years, reading law when not teaching at the office of William Emery, Esquire, in Lebanon. In the fall of 1871 he removed to Somersworth, New Hampshire, where his law studies were continued at the office of William J. Copeland, Esquire. In the fall of 1873 he was admitted to the practice of law, and soon settled in Farmington, New Hampshire, where he was engaged in his profession for five years. In January, 1879, he removed to Dover, New Hampshire, where he has since resided, and has engaged in buying and selling real estate on his own account, especially beach property. In 1887 he became deeply interested in genealogical research. He was chiefly instrumental in the incorporation and organization of the New Hampshire Genealogical Society, 1903, and since that time has been the financial agent and librarian of that society. He also edits and publishes for that society a magazine, called the "New Hampshire Genealogical Record." He married, June 4, 1870, Hannah Chandler, daughter of Oliver and Dorcas R. (Blaisdell) Shapleigh, of Lebanon. She was born September 27, 1849. They have two children, namely: Laona Lydia, born August 28, 1871, at Somersworth, New Hampshire, and Rosa Dorcas, March 21, 1873, at Chelsea, Massachusetts.

GUERTIN This name, of remote French origin, was borne by one of the pioneers of lower Canada, and is traced as far back as 1635 to one Louis Guertin, of Daumeray, France, married to Georgette LeDuc, whose son Louis emigrated to Canada, and was married at Montreal, January 26, 1659, to Elisabeth LeCamus, daughter of Dr. Pierre LeCamus and Jeanne Charles, of Paris. This Louis Guertin was the founder of the Guertin family in America.

(I) One of the descendants, Toussaint Guertin, was married to Adelaide Dupont, at St. Antoine de Chambly, of which place both were natives. They settled on a farm at St. Jude, county of St. Hyacinthe, and eleven children were born of that union.

(II) George Guertin, son of Toussaint Guertin, was born at St. Jude, and served an apprenticeship at St. Hyacinthe at the trade of harness maker. He married Louise Lefebvre, daughter of Francois Lefebvre, of St. Hugues, Province of Quebec. In 1864 he came to the United States, and establishing himself in business as a harness maker in Nashua, New Hampshire, he acquired through his industrious habits a comfortable prosperity. Ten children were born of that marriage, four of whom are living, namely: Rev. George Albert, of whom later. John, who receives mention in this article. Alida, wife of A. M. Richards, of Nashua. Augustine, married to Adelard Labrecque, resides in Manchester, New Hampshire. George Guertin was a man of keen intelligence, took a deep interest in Republican institutions, became a naturalized American citizen, and served with marked ability on the Nashua board of aldermen. His death occurred in that city in 1902.

(III) Bishop George Albert Guertin, of New Hampshire, son of George and Louise (Lefebvre) Guertin, was born in Nashua, New Hampshire, February 17, 1869. He acquired his early education in the public and parochial schools of Nashua, after which he went to Sherbrooke, Province of Quebec, entering St. Charles College as a student, and here took the full commercial course and a part of the classical course. Then going to St. Hyacinthe College, at St. Hyacinthe, Province of Quebec, he completed his classical studies. He then entered St. John's Seminary at Brighton, Massachusetts, where he took his theological course.

Bishop Guertin was ordained to the holy priesthood by the Rt. Rev. Denis M. Bradley, December 17, 1892, in St. Louis de Gonzague Church in Nashua, New Hampshire, being the first in that parish to be ordained in the church of his native city. This event was looked forward to with so much interest by the people who had long admired the young student, that on that memorable day the edifice was filled to its utmost capacity. On several solemn occasions he was called upon to preach the word of God in the temple, where as a boy he had worshipped. On such occasions the church would be thronged with the congregation who took such legitimate pride in this Nashua boy, and whose eloquent words they were so eager to hear. With great interest they followed his career, feeling confident that this gifted priest was destined to do some great work in the vineyard of the Lord.

His initial assignment was that of assistant to the Rev. J. A. Chevalier, P. R., of St. Augustine's Church, Manchester, in which capacity he served four years and three months. The zeal displayed by the newly-ordained priest in the discharge of his duties, his fervor for the things of God, his ready sympathy for every sorrow, soon won him the affection of the whole community. It was not long before his talent as a preacher was recognized by the worshippers at St. Augustine. But the first opportunity afforded the public of Manchester to hear the young speaker was at the celebration of the semi-centennial of the Queen city, where in an eloquent address to the school children assembled on the Straw grounds he gave proofs of his great ability as an orator. It was with heartfelt sorrow that the people of St. Augustine's parish heard of Father Guertin's assignment to the Sacred Heart Church at Lebanon, New Hampshire, of which the Rev. Martin Egan was then pastor. Here he remained three years and seven months, endearing himself to the members of his church, among whom he labored unceasingly.

It was during Father Guertin's stay at Lebanon that Bishop Bradley first conceived the plan of having missions preached throughout the state, to which non-Catholics would be invited. His choice fell on the curate of Lebanon as the one best fitted to conduct these missions. But Bishop Bradley was forced to give up this cherished plan by a vacancy which occurred in East Manchester, and thither was Father Guertin sent October 7, 1900, to take charge of St. Anthony's parish, which had been founded in 1899 by the Rev. D. C. Ling. At the time Father Guertin was appointed pastor, a debt had been incurred by the erection of a chapel, which was not yet finished. It soon became apparent that it was too small for the fast growing parish, and Father Guertin, realizing this, bought land and moved the church. An addition was built and the building completed. He then opened a school in the basement, which accommodates two hundred and fifty children, under the supervision of four sisters of the Holy Cross and two lay teachers. A parsonage was built on the land adjoining the church, into which he moved, three houses were purchased, one used as a home for the Sisters, and the other two are rented and net a good income to the parish. Notwithstanding all these expenses the debt was reduced to eleven thousand dollars, and the property owned by the church is valued at forty-five thousand dollars.

Although the labors of Father Guertin were both arduous and incessant, he always preserved a cheerful spirit, being confident of his future reward, and he not only endeared himself to the Catholic population, but is also held in the highest estimation by his neighbors and fellow-citizens irrespective of creed or nationality. He is especially noted for his bountiful hospitality and attractive social qualities, and his ability as a christian worker is of inestimable value to the general community.

The first news that the Sacred Congregation of the Propaganda had recommended Father Guertin to the Holy Father, Pope Pius X, as third bishop of Manchester, was received through the Associated Press. A dispatch from Rome to that effect was published December 17, 1906, just fourteen years to a day after his ordination to the priesthood. The Papal Brief was received from Rome by Mgr. Falconio, Apostolic delegate at Washington, who delivered it to Bishop Guertin February 7, and on February 12 the bishop-elect took charge of the diocese of Manchester.

There was great rejoicing among the French-Canadians all over the country, when the glad news was confirmed, that one of their own had been elevated to the dignity of Prince of the Church, he being the first French-Canadian in the United States to be so honored. But it was a joy tinged with sorrow for the little flock at St. Anthony's parish when they realized that the close ties uniting pastor and people would be severed. On March 10 the bishop-elect bade farewell to his beloved people of St. Anthony's. From all the parishes of Manchester as well as from the neighboring town, people flocked to the little chapel in East Manchester, all anxious to be present at this touching scene between pastor and faithful. An incident worthy of note was the presence of Bishop-elect Guertin at St. Louis de Gonzague Church, Nashua, New Hampshire, a few days before his consecration. On that evening of March 15th, the episcopal ring, episcopal robes, and a purse were presented him as a testimonial from the people of his native city. Those fortunate enough to gain admission to the crowded church will never forget the young bishop's eloquent words as they welled up from his heart to the lips in grateful tribute to the aged pastor, the Rev. J. B. H. V. Milette, who had been his spiritual adviser, to the father and mother who were no more, to the relatives and friends who came to do him honor.

The Rt. Rev. George Albert Guertin was consecrated third bishop of the diocese of Manchester on Tuesday morning, March 19, 1907, at St. Joseph's Cathedral, by the Most Rev. Diomede Falconio, archbishop of Larisa and apostolic delegate. The day for this august event was happily chosen, being on the Roman Catholic calendar, that of St. Joseph, the patron saint of the cathedral, and the Catholic Church in the United States. The ceremony was witnessed by an assemblage that filled the cathedral, and included the state and city officials, leading men of the city, representatives of the various parishes of the diocese and of the various orders having a chaplain. Clergy from all parts of New England and Canadian provinces, archbishops and bishops, monsignori and vicars-general, pastors and curates, filled the sanctuary and the portion of the church set apart for them. Representatives of the various religious orders of the state and the city, and from all New England were there as delegates from their respective houses. The great ecclesiastical ceremony, one of the most impressive in the ritual of the Catholic Church in this country, was attended with all the solemn splendor befitting the occasion. The highest dignitaries of the church in New England and Canada wearing their robes of purple, significant of their special rank, added splendor to the occasion. Perhaps the most striking figure among the clergy was the Most Rev. John J. Williams, archbishop of Boston, and dean of the New England hierarchy, who has officiated at the consecration of every bishop of the Manchester diocese. Archbishop Williams, despite his advanced age, having passed more than four score, is still active in the performance of his duties. The Most Rev. L. N. Begin, archbishop of Quebec, the Most Rev. Paul Bruchesi, archbishop of Montreal, and the Right Rev. J. S. H. Brunault, bishop of Nicolet, were among the high dignitaries of the church from Canada to honor the occasion with their presence. From the New England states were present the Most Rev. William H. O'Connell, co-

adjutor archbishop of Boston, Massachusetts, the Right Rev. Matthew Harkins, bishop of Providence, Rhode Island, the Right Rev. Michael Tierney, bishop of Hartford, Connecticut, and the Right Rev. Thomas D. Beaven, bishop of Springfield, Massachusetts, and the Right Rev. Louis S. Walsh, bishop of Portland, Maine.

Bishop Guertin is possessed of those qualities which make and retain friendships among both priests and layman, whether Catholic or Protestant, and the rejoicing of the French-Canadians over his elevation to the position he so ably fills was generally shared by the citizens wherever he is known. His kindness of heart, his keen intelligence and his capacity as a leader are at once impressed upon those who meet him, and his genial manners, coupled with the dignity of bearing fitting his position, form a most happy combination that endears him at once to the visitor. Though he has but just begun the duties of a position which it is to be hoped he may long fill, until further promoted in his holy work, he readily proceeds with his labors, without hesitancy or error, and is destined to wield a great influence in his church and among the evangelizing influences of the Nation.

GUERTIN (III) Jean Baptiste A. Guertin, son of George and Louise (Lefebvre) Guertin, was born in Nashua, September 6, 1874 (see preceding article). He began his education in the public schools, which he subsequently left to enter a parochial school and after the conclusion of his studies he took a position as clerk in a grocery store. He later found employment in one of the Nashua mills, but soon relinquished that occupation in order to resume mercantile business as clerk in a furniture store, where he remained some three years, and at the expiration of that time he once more became a mill operative. After the death of his father, which occurred in 1902, he succeeded to the harness making business hitherto carried on by the elder Guertin, and is now well established in that line of trade. Mr. Guertin is a member of the Catholic Order of Foresters, the St. Jean de Baptiste Society, the League of the Sacred Heart, the Canado-American Association of Manchester, and of St. Aloysius Church. He married, July 25, 1898, Angeline Burque, daughter of Alphonse and Louise (Dutilly) Burque, and has had a family of five children, to of whom, Alphonse and George, are no longer living. The survivors are Anthony, Octave and Victor.

SCAMMON The Scammon family is of English origin. The first of the name of whom there is any record was Captain Edmund Scammon who commanded a war vessel under Admiral Rainsborough in the English naval expedition of 1637. The English branch of the family is represented at the present time by several families writing themselves Scaman, that live at or near Horncastle in Lincolnshire, where they are land holders. An ancient place in Yorkshire bears the name Scammonden and was doubtless the home of some of the family.

(I) The first American ancestor of the Scammon family appears to be Richard Scammon, who came to Boston and moved thence to Portsmouth and was living there about 1640. From Portsmouth there radiated five brothers and sisters: Richard, Anne, John, Elizabeth and Humphrey. Anne Scammon married, about 1650, Major Richard Waldron, of Dover, and died February 7, 1685. Her husband was the noted Major Waldron, who was killed by the Indians, June 27, 1689. John Scammon lived at Kittery, Maine, and had one daughter, Elizabeth, who married an Atkins. Elizabeth Scammon married (first), about 1649, Peter Sidgett, a merchant of Salem, Massachusetts; (second) Hon. John Saffin, judge of the superior court of Massachusetts; she died November, 1687. Humphrey Scammon, born 1640, married Elizabeth Jordan; settled at Saco, Maine, and died January 1, 1727. Among his descendants were Colonel James Scammon, of Saco, who commanded a regiment in the Revolution, and Hon. John F. Scammon, of Saco, member of congress, 1845-47.

(II) Richard (2), son of Richard (1) Scammon, was born probably in England and migrated to America with his father. He lived at Portsmouth for a time, then at Dover, being taxed there in 1662. He married, about 1661, Prudence Waldron, only daughter of William Waldron, of Dover. William Waldron was the eldest brother of Major Waldron, and was baptized at Alcester, Warwickshire, England, October 18, 1601, and came to Dover about 1635. In 1641 he was one of four magistrates appointed by Massachusetts. Was twice deputy to the general court and was recorder of court, also recorder of Maine. He was drowned while attempting to cross the river at Kennebunk, Maine, September, 1646. Waldron purchased shares in the Shrewsbury Patent, 1642, which were a part of his estate at the time of his death. The tract covered by this patent was located on the east bank of the Swamscot, extending from Wheelwrights creek to Moores creek and three miles inland, and covered the southern part of the present town of Stratham. Richard (2) Scammon acquired title to the remainder of this tract and settled on it 1665. The papers relating to his title were recorded June 11, 1666. His business after acquiring Shrewsbury Patent was farming and lumbering. The dam that marks the site of his mill is still pointed out on Thompson's brook. He took the oath of allegiance at Exeter in 1677, and was in garrison there during the Indian troubles. In some of the early records he is spoken of as living at Exeter but no part of his land was within the limits of that town. Exeter, however, was the nearest organized settlement and he was taxed there, held office there and was accorded all the privileges of an actual resident. In religion he was an Episcopalian and joined Edward Hilton and Francis Champernoune in efforts to secure protection for that faith. He was one of the defendants in the historc contest over the Mason claims and suffered loss from the consequent confusion of land titles. His business affairs were well handled, however, and he appears in the Exeter tax list of 1684 as one of the two largest taxpayers. He conveyed his land and property to his children by deed in 1691.

The children of Richard (2) and Prudence (Waldron) Scammon were: Richard, born about 1662. Thomas, born about 1663. William, whose sketch follows. Jane, born July 21, 1667. Prudence, born August 29, 1669. Elizabeth, born April 22, 1671. Mary, born May 31, 1673. The date of the death of Richard (2) Scammon is uncertain, but was previous to December, 1697. His widow survived some years but died before March, 1721, as on the third of that month her son William deeds land to his sister, Jane Deane, according as he says, to the desire and request of his honored mother, Prudence, late of Stratham.

(III) William, third son of Richard (2) and Prudence (Waldron) Scammon, was born February 29, 1664, probably at Dover. He received the home place at Stratham from his father. He was in the service against the Indians in 1696, and was selectman at Exeter in 1699 and 1700. When Stratham was chartered in 1716 he was one of the first board of assessors, and was one of the committee ordered to "take care to build a meeting house with all convenient speed." When the meeting house was "seated," after the custom of the time, he was seated on "ye first chief seat." He served as selectman in 1717-18-19. He was a large farmer and kept slaves. He married, January 4, 1721, Rachel, daughter of James and Elizabeth Thurber, of Rehoboth, Massachusetts. Her people were of the Rhode Island Baptists in religion, and Baptist historians credit her with having been the first Baptist in New Hampshire, and with having been instrumental in laying the foundation of several churches of that faith. The children of William and Rachel (Thurber) Scammon were: Richard (3), whose sketch follows, and Samuel, twins, born November 17, 1722. James, born November 10, 1725. Elizabeth, born August 13, 1728. Barnabas, born April 27, 1733. Of these children only Richard left descendants. William Scammon died September 28, 1743. His widow died September 25, 1761.

(IV) Richard (3), eldest son of William and Rachel (Thurber) Scammon, was born at Stratham, November 17, 1722, and inherited the home place. He was a farmer and old tax lists still extant give him as the town's largest taxpayer. At the beginning of the Revolution he was a member of the committee of safety, but is said to have disapproved of independence and to have become a Tory, though his oldest son was a Revolutionary soldier. In the latter part of his life Richard (3) became a shipowner and was interested in the West India shipping trade. He married, September, 1753, Elizabeth, daughter of Lieutenant Samuel and Mehitable (Pickering) Weeks, of Greenland, where Elizabeth was baptized in 1732.

Their children were: Rachel, born October 12, 1754, married Walter Neal, of Newmarket. William, born March 31, 1756, married Sarah Robinson. Elizabeth, born 1757, died in infancy. Samuel, born 1759, died in infancy. Mary, born September 24, 1760, married Edward Burleigh. Richard, born May 31, 1762. Samuel, born 1764, died in West Indies, mate on a vessel belonging to his father, 1789. Elizabeth, born May 9, 1768, married Kinsley Lyford, of Exeter. James, whose sketch follows. Hezekiah, born March 26, 1773, married Leah Stockbridge, and lived in Stratham. Jonathan, born 1775, died in infancy. Of these children Richard and James have descendants of the name living.

Richard married Elizabeth Chase and was the father of Hon. Eliakim Scammon, of East Pittston, Maine, who was a member of the Maine state senate. His son, Jonathan Young Scammon, born July 27, 1812, graduated at Waterville College, 1831, went to Chicago, 1835, and became eminent as a lawyer and banker. He was the head of the law firm of Scammon, McCagg & Fuller. He established the Marine Bank and was its president, and later was president of the Merchants' National Bank. He was a projector and director of the Chicago & Galena railroad, the first railroad built in northern Illinois. He was active in developing the Chicago school system and one of the city schools was named the Scammon. In 1872 he founded the Inter Ocean newspaper. His public benefactions included the founding of Hahneman Hospital, the building of a church for the Swedenborgian Society and he gave an observatory to the Chicago Astronomical Society. He was a devoted friend of Abraham Lincoln, whose son, Robert T. Lincoln, studied law in the office of Scammon, McCagg & Fuller. Mr. Scammon died March 17, 1890. E. Parker Scammon, son of Eliakim, graduated from West Point, 1837. Served in the war with Mexico. Later was president of St. Mary's Polytechnic Institute, Cincinnati. At the beginning of the Civil war was commissioned colonel of the Twenty-third Ohio Volunteers, was promoted brigadier-general for meritorious service at South Mountain, and served through the war. Was afterward in the consular service. Died at New York, 1894. Charles Melville, son of Eliakim, was appointed captain in the United States revenue marine service, 1862, serving on the Pacific coast. He is the author of an exhaustive work on "Marine Mammals," published 1874, that is a recognized authority on its subject. Captain Scammon is now on the retired list and is living at Fruitvale, California.

(V) James Scammon, son of Richard (3) and Elizabeth (Weeks) Scammon, was born April 26, 1771, at the home place in Stratham, and spent his entire life there. His principal business was farming, though he dealt considerably in real estate. He was a strong Democrat but was never in practical politics. He served as school committeeman and selectman. He reared four sons and two daughters, and gave each of the sons a farm and the daughters an equivalent. His wife was Lydia Parker, daughter of Stephen and Susannah (Wiggin) Wiggin, whom he married April, 1796. Their children were: John, whose sketch follows. Lydia, born February 9, 1800, married Benjamin Barker, of Exeter. Ira James, June 11, 1803, married Ann Lyford. Stephen, January 25, 1805, married Maria Gordon. Richard, whose sketch follows. Elizabeth Susan, born May 10, 1812, married Michael Dalton, of North Hampton. James Scammon died April 6, 1859, aged eighty-eight. His wife died October 15, 1840, aged sixty-three.

(VI) John, eldest child of James and Lydia P. (Wiggin) Scammon, was born at the old homestead in Stratham, August 22, 1797. He was educated in the common school of his native town, at Hampton Academy and at a private school at South Newmarket. He was a most industrious student and kept at his books so late that his landlady objected to supplying so many candles. After leaving school, teaching seemed his natural vocation, and he followed it many years with marked success. His fine presence and imposing size—he weighed about two hundred and sixty pounds in the prime of life—commanded instant respect, and his services were sought in difficult districts. Although the care of his farm was his nominal occupation through life, most of his time was spent in other duties. He was a fine mathematician and an accomplished surveyor, and was much called on for work of that sort. When about sixteen he saw service in the War of 1812, becoming ensign of a company which was stationed at one of the forts in Portsmouth Harbor. After that war he was made a captain in the militia, and was a popular and efficient officer. In town affairs he bore a lifelong and prominent part, being unusually well equipped for conducting all branches of that business. In politics he was an unswerving Democrat, but all classes recognized his intelligent judgment and natural leadership. He served as moderator for eighteen years, 1834-38, 1840-49, inclusive, also in 1851-52 and 1857; he was on the school committee in 1844-47-49; he was selectman in 1824-25-26 and chairman of the board for fourteen years—1834-38, 1841-47, inclusive, also in 1849 and 1850. He

John Scammon.

served as representative in 1835-36-37, serving on the judiciary committee. Although not formally trained in the law, few men in the profession had a more extensive and accurate knowledge of the subject than himself. His qualifications in this matter were so well understood that in 1853 he was made justice of the court of common pleas. Judge Scammon discharged his duties on the bench with credit to himself and satisfaction to the public, serving until the constitution of the courts was changed. He was one of those men who seem born to be a leader in the community, and he was probably the most influential man in Stratham during his day. In religion he was a Baptist, and was one of the committee having charge of the new Christian (Baptist) Chapel about 1840.

On October 31, 1824, Captain (afterwards Judge) John Scammon married Mary G. Barker, daughter of Noah and Deborah (Gilman) Barker, of Exeter. Mary Barker was the eldest child of her father and his second wife, and was born September 17, 1801. The four children of Judge John and Mary (Barker) Scammon were: Lydia Parker, born November 20, 1825. John James, whose sketch follows. Susan Deborah, November 16, 1837. Mary Ellen, October 11, 1839. Judge John Scammon died suddenly March 19, 1863, at the age of sixty-six. His widow, Mrs. Mary (Barker) Scammon, died May 7, 1894, aged ninety-three years.

(VII) John James, only son and second child of Judge John and Mary G. (Barker) Scammon, was born November 22, 1828, on the paternal homestead in Stratham, New Hampshire. He attended the schools of his native town, and subsequently studied at Exeter and Hampton academies. Like his father and others of the family, he taught school for a time; but afterward engaged in the meat and provision business. For a while he was a member of the firm of Mace & Scammon, at Exeter; but he finally gave his entire attention to farming. He owned about one hundred and seventy-five acres of excellent tillage land, situated two miles from the village of Exeter; and his substantial buildings and well kept fields bore witness to his thrift and prosperity. He was a man of great industry and continued in active work till the close of life. Like all his ancestors, Mr. Scammon was a Democrat of the old school; and he was often elected to local office, though not of the prevailing political party. He served as selectman, was deputy sheriff for eight years, and was connected with the school department for fifteen years. In religious belief he was a Congregationalist. On February 9, 1860, John James Scammon married Rachel S. Jewell, daughter of David and Rachel (Leavitt) Jewell, who was born at Exeter, January 11, 1836. Mrs. Rachel (Jewell) Scammon belongs to one of the oldest New England families, and is a great-granddaughter of Captain Daniel Jewell, who served in the Revolution (see Jewell, VII). To John J. and Rachel (Jewell) Scammon were born two sons: Frank H., born June 15, 1861; and John, whose sketch follows. Frank H. Scammon became a provision dealer in Exeter. He married Josephine Pickering of the neighboring town of Greenland; and they had three children: Helen R., Alice J. and Edwin H. Frank H. Scammon, the father of this family, died August 28, 1906, at the early age of forty-five years. His father, John James Scammon, died at Stratham, December 4, 1904, at the age of seventy-six.

(VIII) John, second son and child of John James and Rachel (Jewell) Scammon, was born at Stratham, September 30, 1865. He was educated at the Exeter high school and at Phillips Exeter Academy, and studied law with General Gilman Marston and Marston & Eastman of Exeter, and also took a course at the Law School of Boston University. For a time he abandoned the profession, and was employed in mercantile pursuits and by the Boston & Maine railroad. In 1896, while still in the service of the railroad, he resumed the study of law at night and during his unemployed time, and was admitted to the New Hampshire bar in 1898. He entered the office of Eastman & Young at Exeter, one of the prominent law firms of the state; and soon after the appointment of John E. Young, the junior partner, to the superior bench, Mr. Scammon became a member of the firm of Eastman, Scammon & Gardner, which association exists at the present time. Mr. Scammon is a director in the Hampton Water Works Company, the Union Publishing Company of Manchester, New Hampshire, and is interested in other business enterprises. The Scammon family has produced many distinguished lawyers and financiers, notably the late J. Young Scammon, of Chicago, and James Scammon, of Kansas City; and John Scammon, of Exeter, bids fair to sustain the reputation of the family in New Hampshire.

Politically Mr. Scammon departed from the traditions of his forefathers and became a Republican, and he has already achieved leadership in that party. He was a member of the New Hampshire legislature in 1903 and 1905, serving on the judiciary and other important committees. In 1907 he was chosen to the New Hampshire senate, and elected president of that body, an office which is likely to pave the way to future political honors. In religious matters he is affiliated with the Congregationalists, and in fraternal organizations he belongs to the Improved Order of Red Men, and is a Mason of the thirty-second degree.

On November 27, 1890, John Scammon married Mary G. Dixcy, daughter of Richard H. and Sarah J. Dixcy, of Lynn, Massachusetts, and great-great-granddaughter of General John Glover, a brigadier-general under General Washington, a member of the court that tried Andre, and in whose memory a bronze statue stands in Commonwealth avenue, Boston, Massachusetts. There are five children of this marriage: Oscar Jewell, born at Lynn, March 27, 1892; John James, born at Lynn, June 22, 1893; Marianna, born at Stratham, New Hampshire, March 17, 1895; Henry Glover, born at Newfields, New Hampshire, May 16, 1897; and George Albert, born at Exeter, August 20, 1899.

(VI) Richard (4), son of James and Lydia P. (Wiggin) Scammon, was born at the old homestead in Stratham, October 24, 1809. He was educated at Hampton Academy and taught school for a time at Portsmouth, but farming was his principal business, which he followed with much success, winning an unexcelled reputation for industry, good judgment and integrity. Was a Democrat, and served many years as chairman of the selectmen, though his party was then a hopeless minority in the town. Was trustee of several estates. Member of First Christian Church of Stratham and its principal supporter. He married, February 9, 1842, Abigail Batchelder, daughter of Edward C. and Nancy (Philbrick) Batchelder, of North Hampton. She was born February 14, 1813. Their children were: Hezekiah, born January 31, 1843. James, born June 10, 1844. Sarah Caroline, born December 16, 1848. Richard Montgomery, whose sketch follows. Hezekiah Scammon was educated at New London and Phillips Exeter academies, was a school teacher, farmer at Exeter, and active in Masonry and the Grange. Lecturer of New Hampshire State Grange, 1896. Died December 29, 1903. Married Mary E. Jewell, of Stratham, January 9, 1867, and had two sons: Everett, born May 5, 1868, educated at Phillips Exeter Academy and at Bryant & Strattons Business College; married, January 21, 1896, Gertrude Elizabeth Clapp, of Medford, Massachusetts, and is now in the insurance business in New York. James, born January 29, 1873, is in telephone service. James Scammon fitted for college at Phillips Exeter, graduated at Brown University, 1868; Albany Law School, 1870; was senior member of the firm of Scammon, Mead & Stubenrauch, lawyers of Kansas City. He "was a recognized leader and one of the best trial lawyers in the Missouri bar." Was general solicitor of the Kansas City and Eastern railroad; president of the Franklin Savings Bank, and president of the Kansas City Humane Society. He was a noted collector of rare books, and left a library of over seven thousand volumes. Died at Kansas City, May 30, 1900. His wife was Laura Everingham, whom he married March 4, 1876, and had one son, Richard Everingham, born July 9, 1883, graduated Lawrence University, Kansas, 1905, recently appointed an instructor at Harvard. Sarah C. Scammon graduated from Robinson Female Seminary, 1872, now lives at Exeter. Richard (4) Scammon, the father of this family, died February 21, 1878. His wife died September 6, 1873.

(VII) Richard Montgomery, son of Richard and Abigail (Batchelder) Scammon, was born December 6, 1859. He was educated at Exeter high school and Cornell University, and resides on the homestead at Stratham, where he has one of the largest and best farms in a town noted for agricultural excellence, and which has been in possession of his family since 1642. Politically he is a Democrat. He served as town treasurer, 1881; superintendent of schools, 1883-84; moderator, 1884 to 1894; member of legislature, 1885-86; state senator, 1891-92. Enlisted in the New Hampshire National Guard, 1882, and served in the different grades up to lieutenant-colonel of the First Regiment, holding the last commission from 1886 to 1892. Company E of his regiment adopted the name "Scammon Rifles." He has been trustee of the New Hampshire State College, at Durham, since 1899. Was appointed on the board of bank commissioners by Governor Bachelder, March, 1904; was appointed chairman of the board by Governor McLane, April, 1905, and re-appointed December 1, 1906. Has served two years as vice-president of the National Association of Supervisors of State Banks. He is an interested student of New Hampshire history and has been an occasional contributor to historical and other magizines. He married, January 7, 1897, Annie Prentice, daughter of George A. and Isabel Prentice (Tucker) Wiggin, of Stratham. She was born August 7, 1872, and graduated from Mt. Holyoke College, 1892.

GOULD This name has passed through various forms of spelling, such as Goold, Goolde, Gold, Golde and Gould, which latter is generally used at the present day. The name can be traced with accuracy in England to the middle of the fifteenth century.

(I) Thomas Goold was born about the year 1455 at Bovington, Parish of Hemel Hempstead, Hertfordshire, and died there in 1520. His will was proved September 28, of the latter year, and his widow Johan was co-executrix. His children were: Thomas, Richard, John, Alice, William, Henry and Joan.

(II) Richard, second son of Thomas and Johan Goold, was born in Bovington about 1479, and died at Stoke Manderville, Bucks, in 1531.

(III) Thomas Goolde, son of Richard Goold, was born in 1500.

(IV) Richard Gold, son of Thomas Goolde, was born a Stoke Manderville, about 1530. He married Jane Weeden, a widow.

(V) Richard Golde, son of Richard and Jane Gold, was born about 1553, and died in 1604. (Mention of his son, John, and descendants appears in this article.)

(VI) Zaccheus Gould, son of Richard Golde, was born about 1589 and resided in Hemel Hempstead, Herts, later going to Great Minenden, Bucks, where he was assessed in 1629. In 1638 he emigrated to New England, locating first at Weymouth, Massachusetts, whence he removed to Lynn, and finally to Topsfield, where he died in 1668. The christian name of his wife was Phebe and she died September 20, 1663. Their children were: Phebe, Mary, Martha, Priscilla and John.

(VII) Captain John, only son of Zaccheus and Phebe Gould, was born at Hemel Hempstead, June 10, 1635, and came with his parents to New England. He served in King Philip's war, was an ensign in the militia in 1679, a lieutenant in 1684, and captain in 1693. Between the years 1663 and 1702 he was chosen fifteen times as selectman in Topsfield, and was also representative to the general court. His death occurred in Topsfield, January 26, 1709-10. October 12, 1660, he married Sarah Baker, born at Ipswich, March 9, 1641, died January 20, 1708-09, daughter of John Baker, of Norwich, England, who arrived at Boston in 1637, in the "Rose of Yarmouth," with three children and four servants. She became the mother of eight children: John, Sarah, Thomas, Samuel, Zaccheus, Priscilla, Joseph and Mary.

(VIII) John, eldest son and child of Captain John and Sarah (Baker) Gould, was born at Topsfield, December 1, 1662. He was a weaver by trade and seems to have acquired both business and political prominence. He died November 5, 1724. November 10, 1684, he married Phebe French, who was born May 8, 1667, died April 25, 1718, daughter of John French. The ten children of this union were: Phebe, John, Mary, Nathaniel, Sarah, Hannah, Daniel, David, Solomon and Lydia.

(IX) John, son of John and Phebe (French) Gould, was born August 25, 1687. He resided in Boxford, Massachusetts, and his will, which was made December 30, 1756, was probated July 20, 1762. February 2, 1708-09, he married for his first wife Hannah Curtis, who died April 25, 1712, and he was married a second time, June 23, 1715, to Phebe Towne. The children of his first union were: Martha, Mary, John and Hannah (twins), Anna and Elizabeth. Those of his second marriage were: Phebe, Keziah, John, Richard, Stephen, Abner, Ruth, Jacob, Esther and Amos.

(X) Stephen, third son and fifth child of John and Phebe (Towne) Gould, was born in Boxford, July 6, 1724. He settled in Hillsboro, New Hampshire, and died in 1798. He was married, January 18, 1748, to Hannah Perkins, of Topsfield, born May 4, 1724, and died in 1811. Their children were: Hannah, Elijah, Stephen, Abner, Eunice, Jacob, Sarah and John.

(XI) Stephen, second son and third child of Stephen and Hannah (Perkins) Gould, was born

Richard M. Scammon

February 6, 1754. With his brother Elijah he enlisted in Captain William Perley's Boxford company of Colonel Frye's regiment, in 1775, for service in the Revolutionary war; was later in Captain Archaelus Towne's company of Colonel Bridge's New Hampshire regiment; and in 1777 was detailed to do guard duty at General Burgoyne's surrender. He died in September, 1825. November 30, 1779, he married Lydia, Fuller, born May 13, 1758, died May 16, 1817, daughter of Timothy and Sarah (Smith) Fuller. Their children were: Elijah, Stephen, Lydia, Abner, Timothy, Thaddeus and Jonathan.

(XII) Elijah, eldest son and child of Stephen and Lydia (Fuller) Gould, was born in Boxford, May 15, 1780, and died June 13, 1863. He went from Hillsboro to Antrim, New Hampshire. He first married April 30, 1805, Hannah Bradford, of Hillsboro, who died April 24, 1814. His second wife, whom he married September 18, 1823, was Mrs. Hannah Chapman, nee Spaulding, widow of Stephen Chapman, of Windsor, New Hampshire. She was born in Francistown, October 21, 1794, daughter of Henry and Joanna (Russell) Spaulding, and a descendant in the seventh generation of Edward Spalding, who emigrated to Virginia in 1619, and subsequently removed to Braintree, Massachusetts (see Spalding, I, II, III, IV, V). Henry Spalding (VI) was born in Merrimack, November 3 or 23, 1760, and died May 31, 1857. He married Joanna Russell, who was born June 21, 1766, and died November 1, 1853. Their children were: Achsah, Henry, Samuel (died young), Hannah, Elizabeth, Lucinda, Mary, Leonard, Edward Page, Samuel and Levi. Hannah Spalding was bereft of her first husband and two children, all of whom died the same year, and was again married, to Elijah Gould, as previously mentioned. She died September 15, 1878. The children of Elijah Gould's first union were: Franklin, David and Nancy. Those by his second marriage were: Hannah Louisa, Elijah Fuller, Louisa, Leonard Page, Luther, Adalbert and Emily.

(XIII) Leonard Page, second son and fourth child of Elijah and Hannah Gould, was born in Antrim, April 15, 1829. In early life he engaged in the commission business in Hillsboro, and later carried on business in the same line, in Lowell, Massachusetts. From the last named city he went to New London, New Hampshire, where he purchased a farm of one hundred and twenty-five acres, and in addition to agriculture he conducted an extensive produce business. In politics he acted with the Republican party, and served with ability as a selectman in New London for six years. His religious affiliations were with the Baptists. He married Sarah E. Coolridge, who was born September 7, 1833, daughter of John Coolridge, of Hillsboro. She became the mother of six children: George P., born January 7, 1858, is now a contractor in Minneapolis, Minnesota. Scott Reed, born October 18, 1860, deceased. Arthur J., who will be again referred to. Elmer A., born April 14, 18—, is now residing in Dallas, Texas. Hattie Mabelle, born April 22, 1870. Frank, born October 18, 1875, is now in the ice business in Lynn, Massachusetts. Leonard Page Gould died January 23, 1900.

(XIV) Arthur John Gould, third son and child of Leonard P. and Sarah E. (Coolridge) Gould, was born at Hillsboro Bridge, March 14, 1863. After concluding his attendance at the public schools of New London, he learned the meat business, which he followed for some time, and then went to Minneapolis and engaged in the ice business. Returning to New London in 1890 he became associated with C. F. Shephard in the stage and livery business under the firm name of Shephard and Gould, and conducted the largest stable in New Hampshire. Selling his interest in the business to his partner in 1905, he turned his attention to the real estate business and at the present time has several houses in process of construction. His business ability and progressive tendencies are proving exceedingly beneficial to the town, and his success in his new field of operation is already assured. He participates quite actively in civic affairs, having served as deputy-sheriff for the past three years, and at the present time he is chairman of the board of selectmen. In politics he is a Republican. While residing in Minneapolis he was chosen noble grand of the lodge of Odd Fellows, with which he was affiliated, and he is now a member of Heidelburg Lodge in New London. He is also a member of New London Grange, Patrons of Husbandry, and has held some of the offices in that body. In his religious belief he is a Baptist. Mr. Gould married Emma Train Shephard, June 24, 1890, daughter of James Eli Shephard, of New London. He has one son, Marshall C., born May 8, 1902.

(VI) John, son of Richard Golde, had wife, Judith, who survived him. In her will, dated 1650, she refers to her son, Nathan, "Now in New England."

(VII) Nathan, son of John and Judith Gould, was born in England, in 1616. He received lands in Amesbury in 1657 and 1667. His will, dated December 12, 1692, was proved September 27, 1693. He was married in England and the name of his wife was Elizabeth. She survived him. Their children were: Mary, Elizabeth, Samuel, Joseph and Hannah. His descendants have been numerous in New Hampshire and Vermont.

(VIII) Samuel, third child and eldest son of Nathan and Elizabeth Gould, was born in Amesbury, Massachusetts, February 3, 1668. He was a snowshoe man in 1708, and died in 1826. He married, April 6, 1693, Sarah Rowell, who was born in Amesbury, March 3, 1674, daughter of Philip and Sarah (Morrill) Rowell. They had ten children: Damaris, Nathan, Samuel, Joseph, Judith, Hannah, Elizabeth, Elihu, Sarah and Philip.

(IX) Joseph, third son and fourth child of Samuel and Sarah (Rowell) Gould, was born in Amesbury, July 1, 1700. He was one of the proprietors of Hopkinton, New Hampshire, but never lived in that town. In 1773 he removed from Amesbury, Massachusetts, to South Hampton, New Hampshire, where he died in 1752. He married, June 2, 1726, Abigail Hoyt, who was born in Amesbury, May 13, 1705, daughter of Robert and Martha (Stevens) Hoyt. His widow, Abigail, married (second), in 1757, Thomas Pike. The children of Joseph and Abigail were: Stevens, Joseph, Christopher, Gideon, Moses, Elias, John, Ebenezer, Martha and Abigail. Of these Moses, Christopher and Gideon settled in Hopkinton; John in Dunbarton, and Elias in Henniker. All were soldiers of the Revolution. (Mention of Gideon and descendants forms part of this article.)

(X) Moses, fifth son and child of Joseph and Abigail (Hoyt) Gould, was born in Newbury, Massachusetts, April 2, 1735, and died in Hopkinton, New Hampshire, October 26, 1815. After the death of their father, Christopher, Gideon and Moses with their widowed mother removed to Hopkinton, New Hampshire. Christopher settled on Gould's Hill and Moses nearby. Not long after the settlement Moses and Christopher exchanged farms, Moses moving to the farm on the hill which has been owned and occupied by his descendants since that time. The house built by Christopher about 1760 is still in use. Moses Gould married, November 25, 1773, Joanna Chase, born 1751, widow of Jonathan Chase, and daughter of Captain Francis Davis, a pioneer settler of Warner, New Hampshire (see Davis,V), in 1775. She survived her husband and lived with the Shakers at Canterbury from 1818 until her death, June 8, 1839, at the age of eighty-eight years. They had four children: Moses, Jothan, Stephen and Enoch.

(XI) Captain Moses (2), eldest child of Moses (1) and Joanna (Davis) (Chase) Gould, was born in Hopkinton, October 12, 1779, and died November 10, 1854. Moving to the hill with his parents when four years old, he spent the remainder of his life on the homestead, carrying on general farming and lumbering, his especial pride being the miles of stone wall built on his farm by his own efforts. He was a prosperous and enterprising farmer. In his younger days he trained in a company of the state militia and for several years served as captain. It is said that he with his neighbors used to send annually to Medford, Massachusetts, for a barrel of rum to do their haying on, the division of the spirits being an event of note, and all getting more or less "happy." Moses married Hannah, daughter of Daniel and Abigail (Chase) Currier, of Warner. She died November 29, 1861. They were the parents of five children: Joanna, born 1809, died January 19, 1878; she married Ambrose Chase. Abigail, died November 15, 1873, aged fifty-two years. Hannah, died at the age of twenty. Charles and Martha, twins; Martha married Franklin Frost.

(XII) Captain Charles, the fourth child and only son of Moses (2) and Hannah (Currier) Gould, was born on the old homestead, in Hopkinton, March 8, 1823, and died May 19, 1899. After completing his studies in the district school he attended the Hopkinton Academy, and for a period of forty years was engaged in the winter season as a teacher in the district schools, working his farm the remainder of the year. For a time he held a captain's commission in the Fortieth New Hampshire State Militia, in which his father had previously been an officer. For many years he served as one of the board of superintending school committee, in 1849-50-56-65-72 and 1873; was one of the selectmen in 1859, and held other positions of honor and trust given him by his townsmen. He married, in Hopkinton, November 4, 1847, Ruth Hill, who was born April 18, 1824, and died February 5, 1899. She was the daughter of Thomas and Ruth (Flood) Hill, of this town. Thomas Hill, with his father, Moses Hill, owned the waterpower at the place formerly called Hill's Bridge, now Contoocook. Both father and son served in the Revolutionary army, and Thomas afterward received a pension from the government. The children of Charles and Ruth were: Moses, died young; Moses Clarence, Louis Augustine, Charles Henry, Mary Adelaide, Clara Ida, Robert Truman, Helen Arvilla, George Herman and Herbert Julian. Moses, born November 17, 1848, died February, 1849. Moses Clarence, a dentist in Brooklyn, New York, born November 6, 1849, married, June, 1872, Charlotte I. Pearsall, of Trumansburg, New York, and they have three children: Charles P., married, June 23, 1900, Florence Catherine Pennock, of Syracuse, New York; one child, Theodore Pennock Gould, born August 6, 1901. Warren P., born February 7, 1879. Ethel Ruth, born November 24, 1890. Louis Augustine, born April 26, 1852, physician at Interlaken, New York, married Hannah B. Jones, of Ovid, New York. They have one son, Lewis Arthur, born July 5, 1887. Charles Henry, born May 29, 1854, stone contractor, Cambridge, Massachusetts, married December 14, 1887, Sarah Green, of Lowell, Massachusetts. They had two children: George Henry, died young, and Elizabeth Antoinette, born July 4, 1894. Mary Adelaide, born April 10, 1856, died in June of the same year. Clara Ida, born July 6, 1857, married, March 30, 1887, Otto L. Bullard, farmer, Bellingham, Massachusetts. They had one child, Walter Gould, born July 4, 1888. Robert Truman is mentioned below. Helen Arvilla, born March 30, 1863, married, December 25, 1886, George A. Newton, farmer, Henniker. She died Aug. 26, 1897, leaving three sons: George Robert, born April 11, 1899; Henry Arthur, August 18, 1890; and Charles Parker, August 25, 1893. George Herman was born and died in 1865. Herbert Julian, born January 8, 1870, is an overseer in the stone quarrying business. He married, November, 1905, and resides at Stonington, Maine.

(XIII) Robert Truman, fifth son and seventh child of Charles and Ruth (Hill) Gould, was born on the ancestral homestead, May 23, 1861. After completing the course of study in the district school, he attended Contoocook Academy, completing his studies at the age of twenty. He then returned to the farm which has always been his home. It is now a place of two hundred acres, fertile and well tilled, and here he devotes his time to the raising of fruit and hay and dairying. He is a Democrat in political sentiment, and a member of the Patrons of Husbandry. Being a member of an ancient and honorable family, and possessing the instincts and breeding of a gentleman, his position in business circles and social life is a secure and pleasant one, but he cares little for place or political honors, and derives his greatest pleasure from the society of his own household and the cultivation of his acres. He married, April 5, 1895, Mary Morgan Currier, who was born December 24, 1861, daughter of John F. and Nellie (Putney) Currier, of Hopkinton. She is of the fifth generation from John Currier, a pioneer settler of Hopkinton, who came from Amesbury, Massachusetts, bringing his family and goods by ox team. They have one child, Jessamine, born May 12, 1900.

(X) Gideon, son of Joseph and Abigail (Hoyt) Gould, was born about 1741, in Newbury, Massachusetts, and passed his entire adult life in Hopkinton, whither he removed with his widowed mother as a boy. He was a successful farmer, and left a family which has been honorably connected with the history of New Hampshire. He died in Hopkinton, March 1, 1821, aged seventy-nine years. His wife, Hannah, died December 3, 1843, aged ninety-seven years.

(XI) Nathan, son of Gideon and Hannah Gould. was born February 21, 1767, in Hopkinton, and on attaining manhood removed to Newport, New Hampshire, where he cleared up a farm and was an active and successful agriculturalist of his day. He married Elizabeth, daughter of Richard and Elizabeth (Heath) Goodwin, of Hampstead, New Hampshire. Richard Goodwin was born 1746, in Amesbury, Massachusetts, a son of Daniel and Hannah (Colby) Goodwin, of Amesbury. He was married, December 19, 1765, to Elizabeth Heath, and they were admitted to the church there September 27, 1767. Later they removed to Dunbarton, and in 1780 to Newport, where he died in 1821. Their children were: Betsey, Moses, Benjamin, Hannah and Polly. Nathan Gould and wife were the parents of: Alvira, Gideon,

Silva, Carlos, Moses Milton. Betsey, Zarilla, Nathan and Nancy. The original settlement of Nathan Gould was in the northwestern portion of the town of Newport, some four miles or more distant from the village of that name on the road from Northville to Cornish Flat. It is now called "Fruit Farm" and is occupied by Albert J., one of his descendants.

(XII) Gideon (2), eldest son and second child of Nathan and Elizabeth (Betsy) (Goodwin) Gould, was born March 3, 1796, on the Gould homestead, in Newport, and died there August 6, 1877. He spent his entire life on the homestead farm. He was a Democrat in political views, and a member of the Baptist Church. He was a progressive citizen of the town but never an aspirant for office. He was married to Sally Ward, of Croydon.

(XIII) Alfred J., the only living child of Gideon (2) and Sally (Ward) Gould, was born January 18, 1840, on the Gould homestead where he has always resided. He was educated in the district schools and Newport Academy. With a natural inclination for the occupation of his ancestors, he continued to reside upon the home farm and succeeded to the ownership of it upon his father's decease. He has devoted himself to agriculture, and by thorough cultivation has maintained the increased productiveness of the family home. This originally embraced one hundred and fifty acres, but has been added to until it includes some four hundred acres, both father and son adding to the estate each in his time. Nearly seventy-five acres are kept in meadow and tillage, and the annual hay crop averages about seventy-five tons. The farm has always been devoted to mixed vegetation and has had a reputation for the excellence of its dairy products during the last half century. It has been known particularly of late for the fine quality and large variety of its fruits. The breeding of dairy cows has been a feature in the original management of the farm, and it sustains from thirty to forty head of cattle, four horses and fifty sheep most of the time. The maple groves on this farm are well known, and the maple sugar which is sent to Boston and the superior syrup of which over four hundred gallons is produced are above the average standard. Nearly a ton of pork is produced annually for the market. Mr. Gould has a taste for fruit culture, and the soil of his estate being particularly adapted to the growth of the apple tree he has taken pains to graft upon his stock the best variety and has also set many so that he now has on his farm over one thousand grafted apple trees, and his market product runs up to eight hundred barrels. He is considered an authority and is frequently consulted by the surrounding farmers in matters pertaining to fruit culture. Mr. Gould endeavors to keep abreast of the times and is a member of the Sullivan County Grange, No. 8, of Newport. He is also a member of Sugar River Lodge, No. 55, Independent Order of Odd Fellows of the same place. He is liberal in religious views, and is a substantial Republican in political principle. He has served four years as selectman of the town, and was representative in the legislature in 1889. He is president and one of the trustees of the Newport Savings Bank and a director of the First National Bank of Newport, and has long been regarded as one of the most prosperous and successful farmers of the town.

He was married (first), December 17, 1861, to Sarah J. Ayers, of Cornish, who was born August 6, 1840, and died at the age of twenty-four years. She left one son Gideon Elmer, who died August 10, 1870, aged five years. Mr. Gould was married (second), in Lempster, February 3, 1866, to Orpha Elmira Honey. She was born September 16, 1847, daughter of Alpheus and Susan (Carr) Honey, and died April 18, 1902. She was the mother of children: Gideon, Alfred, Warren, Olin and Mary Alice. The last named graduated at the Newport high school in 1905. Both the sons died young. Mr. Gould was married (third), May 4, 1905, in Newport, to Ida M. Parker. She was born April 11, 1876, at East Mountain, Newport, daughter of Dexter and Maria (Hutchinson) Parker. (See further ancestry of Honey family for Revolutionary History).

TILTON The family of Tilton is undoubtedly Saxon. The town of Tilton in Leicestershire was in existence prior to the time of William the Conqueror, and in "Domesday Book" are mentioned the town and family. We are told that certain members of the family made honorable records in the Crusades (Sir John Tilton, Knight), and tradition says the lives of both Edward I and Edward III, were saved by Tiltons, and that on Bosworth Field seven of the family held positions under Henry in his fight against the third Richard, and several of them lost their lives that day. Many of the families in America use the Digby coat-of-arms. There is some doubt of their right to use it, though the Digby family of England were Tiltons, dropping the Digby De Tilton early in the seventeenth century, using the name of Digby simply.

(I) The earliest ancestor in this country was William Tilton, who came here between 1630 and 1640, accompanied by his brother John. Tradition has it that they were both younger sons of some one of the Digby family and kept the name of Tilton. From this tradition comes the claim of certain of them to the right to use the Digby coat-of-arms. Certain it is that both William and John were men of education. The two brothers settled in Lynn, Massachusetts, probably when they first arrived, and William seems to have been much the older; in fact some have claimed that John was his son, but it is more probable that he was his brother. About 1642 John's wife had serious trouble with the church by denying that infant baptism was an ordinance of God, and was fined by the church after much trouble. This resulted in part of the congregation who sympathized with her withdrawing, and all moving to Gravesend, Long Island. The books of the town government of Gravesend kept by John Tilton are still in existence, and show a fine penmanship and ability. From this family, some of whom later removed to Monmouth county, New Jersey, originate the Tiltons of New Jersey, Delaware and Maryland, many of whom have received honorable mention in the history of the country. Washington's first surgeon, General James Tilton, was of the Delaware family. Their descendants are found today in Florida and many western states.

William Tilton seems to have brought one son, Peter, with him. Some writers think he was by a former wife, as he was quite a little older than the other children. It is quite possible that all the older children may not have come with him here, though we have no records to show. Peter married several years after his arrival, and moved to Windsor, Connecticut, and later to Hadley, Massachusetts, where he seems to have been a very prominent man, was deacon of the church, town recorder, representative to general court, associate county judge, assistant of the colony, and had great influence in the state and church. It is said that because he gave shelter to the regicides Gough and Whalley in defiance of Parliament's order, a warrant for his arrest was issued by Charles II, which is said to be yet in existence. Certain it is that he never was taken before Parliament and tried, for he died July 11, 1696, leaving no male issue. William Tilton was freeman in Lynn, and seems to have been elderly at the time. He was engaged in the settlement of estates, was allowed his own seal by the court, and seems to have been a professional man. In 1649 he was excused from military duty by reason of infirmities of age. He died in Lynn in 1653, leaving his wife Susanna as executress of his will, which was probated by her in May of the same year. There were three sons (no record of any daughters): Samuel, Abraham and Daniel (mention of the last named and descendants appears in this work). The widow married the same year Roger Shaw, who held a position under the crown, and moved to Hampton, New Hampshire, taking with her Samuel and Daniel. (See Shaw). She died November 28, 1654. Samuel married, December 17, 1662, at Hampton, New Hampshire, Hannah Moulton, and removed to Martha's Vineyard, and they were the ancestors of the Tiltons at the Vinyard.

(II) Abraham, fourth son of William and Susanna Tilton, resided for a time at Hampton, where he was married January 25, 1665, to Mary Cram. Subsequently he removed to Hamilton, Massachusetts, and was the ancestor of most of the name in that state. No record of his children is found.

(III) In February, 1733, there were seven Tiltons at Hampton Falls, Massachusetts, viz: Jethro, Jonathan, Joseph 1st, Joseph 2nd, Josiah, Samuel and "Shurbun."

(IV) "Nathaniel Tilton was probably a son of Samuel, but very few reliable data respecting himself, his birth, his ancestry, or his immediate family have yet come to light," though his name is so prominent in the early history of the first church in the town of Sanbornton. He first settled between 1768 and 1771 on lot No. 65, 2nd Division (south end), nearly a mile above the bridge (now Colby's); was the second to put his name to the original "Church Covenant," November 13, 1771, and was chosen the second deacon, "Jan'y ye 2d, 1772." He served the old church more than thirty-nine years, and May 8, 1811, at the request of Deacon Tilton, it was "voted to excuse him from performing the services of a deacon." He was very strict in keeping the Sabbath and to prevent its desecration by his grandchildren used to tell them Bible stories. He married Abigail Gilman, a relative (cousin) of Governor John Taylor Gilman, who died in this town, October 14, 1803. He died February 11, 1814. There were seven children of this marriage, but the dates of their births are not known. Their names were as follows: Jacob, Abigail, Susannah, two daughters who joined the Shakers, names unknown, Jeremiah, and Peter Gilman.

(V) Jeremiah, son of Nathaniel and Abigail (Gilman) Tilton, was born in Stratham, or Newmarket, New Hampshire, in 1762, and was brought to Sanbornton by his parents when a child. At the age of sixteen he enlisted in the Revolutionary war and served six months as a teamster, his widow afterwards drawing a pension as a consequence. He built the original hotel at the Bridge (now Tilton), and occupied the same, on the site of the present Dexter House. He also carried on, in company with Benjamin Smith, a grist mill and factory, or triphammer shop, where they manufactured iron implements. He was a colonel in the state militia, a justice of the peace, and in all respects was a leader in founding the village that now bears his name. He married, February 21, 1786, Mehitable Hayes, born 1767, daughter of William Hayes (a revolutionary soldier, who died at Ticonderoga) and his wife Mary Plimner. He died April 10, 1822, and his widow January 19, 1842. Their children were: John, born July 16, 1787; Samuel, August 20, 1789; Sally, 1791, died January 31, 1818; Jeremiah, Jr., born September 10, 1793; James P., November 4, 1796; Abigail, 1798, died October 29, 1819; Mahala, born August, 1800, died June 12, 1820; Mary P., born December 13, 1802, died October 5, 1875; Alexander H., born December 24, 1804; Mehitable, August 26, 1807, died November 12, 1844; and Sophronia, born 1810, died March 12, 1845.

(VI) Samuel, son of Jeremiah and Mehitable (Hayes) Tilton, was born in Sanbornton, August 20, 1789, and began life as a blacksmith in his father's triphammer shop. He subsequently occupied the hotel at the Corner, to which he added another story. He always lived at the Bridge village, which owed much of its prosperity to him. He was a man of great energy and acumen, and was a "leading spirit" (with Colonel Charles Lane) in the town at large for many years. He served as representative in the New Hampshire legislature five times, 1826-29, and 1835. He was justice of the peace and sheriff of Belknap county. In 1848 he was chosen one of the presidential electors from his state, and subsequently filled the office of United States marshal under President Pierce, and in 1852 was a delegate to the Democratic convention at Baltimore. It has been said of him "As a friend, he was honest, firm and unwavering, and no falsehood or pretense whatever had the least influence in detaching him from those in whom he confided. The records of the schools, seminary and houses of religious worship in his native village, will all bear witness that no man among us gave more freely or abundantly than he did toward their establishment. Always conservative and patriotic in his feelings, a strong friend of the Union, and a most decided and outspoken opponent of all kinds of radicalism." He married, (first), January 31, 1815, Myra, daughter of Samuel Ames, of Canterbury, born September 28, 1792, and died March 7, 1857; reported as a lady of uncommon excellence. He married (second), March 16, 1858, Mrs. Elizabeth (Cushman) Haven, of Portsmouth, born January 17, 1817. He died November 12, 1861. The children of Samuel and Myra (Ames) Tilton were: Alfred Edwin, born November 11, 1815, died March 30, 1877. Sarah, born October 23, 1819. De Witt Clinton, born February 20, 1823, died October 22, 1824. Caroline Augusta, born October 2, 1825, died October 16, 1826. Charles Elliott, born September 14, 1827, died September 28, 1901.

(VII) Charles Elliott, youngest child of Samuel and Myra (Ames) Tilton, was born in the village of Tilton, September 14, 1827. He received his primary education in the common schools, and at the age of fifteen entered Sanbornton Academy, then under the charge of Professor Dyer H. Sanborn. Later he attended three years at Norwich University, a military school. When the war with Mexico arose, General Ransom, president of the university, was commissioned to raise a regiment, and induced nearly every student to enlist. Young Tilton was offered the command of a company, but declined through the influence of his father. Soon afterward he went to New York City, where his elder brother, Alfred Edwin, was engaged in business. He next sailed as the representative of his brother to the West Indies and South America, visiting the islands and prospecting the Orinoco and Amazon. He also journeyed overland to Caracas and LaGuayra, thence to Marcaibo, St. Martin, Carthagena and Chagres. Hearing of the discovery of gold in California, he at once proceeded to San Francisco via Panama and engaged in merchandising. In 1850 he went to Oregon, and the following year became a partner with W. S. Ladd for general mercantile pursuits, and this partnership continued till 1859. Mr. Tilton was interested in establishing a line of vessels to run between Oregon and China. One of these ships, the "C. E. Tilton," made the quickest passage from New York to Oregon on record to that time. She was afterward sold to the Japanese government and by it converted into a man-or-war, and was finally sunk in an encounter with the United States ship "Powhattan." In 1859 the banking house of Ladd & Tilton, of Portland, was organized, in which Mr. Tilton remained a partner till 1880. He was also interested in many other enterprises on the coast and in the interior states. He took a lively interest in the navigation of those two great waterways, the Columbia and Willamette rivers. He was one of the five who controlled what subsequently developed into the Oregon Railway and Navigation Company, with a capital of $24,000,000. He also had an interest in the firm of Ladd & Bush, bankers, Salem, in the First National Bank of Portland, and in the First National Bank of Walla Walla, Washington Territory. The business of transportation across the plains also received much of his attention. He sent great trains of merchandise from San Bernardino, California, to Utah, and from St. Joseph, Missouri, to Colorado, and from there to Montana, giving his personal attention to them all, when the country they traversed was still almost in a state of nature and full of Indians more or less hostile. Trains were often attacked in those days, and sometimes captured and destroyed by the savages. Foreseeing the advantage of investments in the western country Mr. Tilton made purchases of land in all the territories, which proved advantageous. He also engaged in many other enterprises connected with the development of the western slope, which with few exceptions turned out profitably. Mr. Tilton resided in Tilton after the year 1879, and became a large owner of the stock of the Concord & Montreal Railroad Company, in which he was a director. He built a magnificent residence in 1861, on an eminence overlooking the valley of the Winnepesaukee river from the north, which when built was said to be one of the finest in New England, the drawing room being unequalled in its appointments in New England. It is twenty-eight by thirty-eight feet in area and twenty-two feet high, finely finished in mahogany, and elegantly furnished and decorated, the carpets, rugs, drapery and furniture, mirrors and chandeliers having been manufactured for the room.

Mr. Tilton's love for his native town and its citizens was manifested in the form of many gifts to the public. Chief of these in the point of utility was the town hall, containing a market and town office, a store and a postoffice, all commodiously arranged, no expense being spared which would add to its convenience, the hall proper being completely furnished, even to a piano. They return a handsome rental. He also enlarged the island in the river and adorned it with a pagoda and statuary, fitting it as a place for the public to rest and recreate. He created the park on Main street, which is an ornament to the city. The first concrete pavement in Tilton was laid in front of his block and donated to public use by him. In 1882 he placed an iron bridge from Main street to Park Island at a cost of $1,800, and previously gave $500 toward an iron bridge between Tilton and Northfield. His donations to churches have been generous, and toward the remodeling of one he contributed more than $3,000. The fountain and statue in the middle of Main street, the fountain and statue at the depot, and the beautiful bronze statue of "Squantum, Chief, 1620," just east of the depot, were all given by him. It has been said that up to 1881 Mr. Tilton's gifts for the pleasure and benefit of his townsmen amounted to $40,000. The handsome railroad station and convenient grounds are also due to Mr. Tilton's influence. On the summit of the steep hill rising from the south bank of the Winnepesaukee river, in full view of his residence on the opposite side, and commanding an extensive view of the surrounding country is Mr. Tilton's most costly monument, a granite arch fifty-five high, an exact copy of the arch of Titus, in Rome, and a sarcophagus which Mr. Tilton intended should contain his body after his death. In the keystone of the arch is this inscription: "Memorial Arch of Tilton, 1882;" and upon the sarcophagus are the words: "Tilton, 1883." This monument, which cost $50,000, is one of the most imposing and enduring in New England. It has been said of Mr. Tilton: "While he was not responsible for all the improvements the town of Tilton possesses, yet without his public spirit there would not have been the bridges crossing the Winnepesaukee, the islands, a recreation place, roads that would be an example for many a large city, a handsome library building and a well selected library, a park complete in every detail, and railway accommodation that make the town accessible. All these things that mark the town are but a small portion of what he did for the state. There is the State Farm and a Soldiers' Home, for which Mr. Tilton was responsible."

He was peculiarly successful in business, but had no taste for politics, and never held a public office. His strict integrity and honesty were as proverbial as his public-spirited generosity. In his intercourse with his neighbors and acquaintances he was cordial and pleasant. In many matters he was very democratic, and it was no unusual thing for him to invite one of his laborers to a seat in his carriage and give him a ride. His friendship was as decided and marked as was his business capacity and generosity. His friends had no cause to complain of his loyalty. He is said to have once exhibited a note for $150,000, which a friend had made to him, but which was then rendered worthless by the insolvency of the maker. But Mr. Tilton only smiled and said: "Bill was a good fellow." The debtor's good fellowship outweighed his debt.

Mr. Tilton married (first), January 11, 1856, his cousin, Louisa P. Tilton, born April 30, 1827, daughter of Jeremiah, Jr., and Nancy (Carter) Tilton. She was a cultivated and excellent woman, but for years her health was feeble. She died unexpectedly, August 15, 1877. Three children were born of this marriage: Myra Ames, February 18, 1858. Alfred Edwin, June 15, 1861. William Ladd, January 9, 1865, died July 2, 1865. Mr. Tilton married (second) December 29, 1881, Geneveive Eastman, of Littleton, daughter of J. Frank Eastman, by whom he had one son; Charles E., born May 4, 1887, now a student in Harvard College.

(VIII) Alfred Edwin, eldest son of Charles E. and Louisa P. (Tilton) Tilton, was born in Tilton, June 15, 1861, and educated at the Tilton Seminary. At sixteen years of age he went to work in a printing office, and soon afterward became a fireman on the Concord railroad between Concord and Nashua, filling this place thirteen years. He then had a similar position on the Boston, Concord & Montreal road for one summer, on what was known as the White Mountain train. In 1887 he was promoted to engineer, working in the yards at Lakeport a short time, and then was made the first engineer on the Belmont road, filling this place three years. In 1893 he quit railroad business and took a trip south with his wife, visiting points of interest in the southern states and in the Bermudas. Returning to his home he rebuilt the old Piper residence, which he has since occupied. In politics he is a Democrat. He is a member of Doric Lodge, No. 78, Ancient Free and Accepted Masons, of Tilton, and of St. Omar Chapter, Royal Arch Masons, of Franklin. He is also a member of Peabody Chapter, No. 35, Eastern Star. He is not engaged in business other than taking care of his real estate. He married, June 25, 1890, Ella Augusta Freese, daughter of William W. and Carrie G. (Cooke) Freese. Mrs. Tilton's parents were natives of Moultonborough. She was educated in the schools of Concord, graduating from the high school, and from Deane Academy in Franklin, Massachusetts, and from the normal school at Plymouth, New Hampshire. Afterward she taught several years, three years of the time being in the graded schools of her native town. She is a member of Peabody Chapter of the Eastern Star.

(II) Daniel, youngest son of William and Susanna Tilton, was born 1646, in Lynn, Massachusetts, and settled in New Hampshire. Hampton being in need of a blacksmith, he learned the trade and was given by the town a tract of land, four acres, on the Falls Hill, in the center of what is now the town of Hampton, about 1665. He married, December 23, 1669, Mehetable Sanborn, a daughter of William and Mary Sanborn, and from this union originate very nearly all the Tiltons of New Hampshire and many of Maine and Vermont. Daniel Tilton was a strong man in town matters and government. As his family grew large he settled on land between Hampton and Exeter, building a block house which protected his family and other settlers from Indian attacks. History says that, having a large family of stalwart sons, they always successfully defended themselves when necessary to do so. He was known as Ensign in early history, and represented Hampton in general court from 1690 to 1713, during some of which time he served as speaker. Fnally, being very infirm, he asked and was excused by the court from further duty. He died February 10, 1716, in Hampton. His sons settled in Hampton and adjoining towns. Their descendants, moving to towns further out, spreading through New Hampshire to Vermont and Maine, were among the earliest settlers. We find them in the great west and on the Pacific coast, always among the pioneers, and many of them making honorable records in the new sections. The family has had many professional men, clergymen and doctors (but very few lawyers), and many military men who were distinguished in their services in all the colonial wars and the later wars of the republic. Daniel Tilton's children were: Abigail, Mary (died young), Samuel, Joseph, Mary, Daniel, David, Jethro, Mehetable, Hannah and Josiah.

(III) Captain Joseph, second son of Daniel and Mehetable (Sanborn) Tilton, born March 19, 1677, resided in Hampton, where he was a farmer, and died October 24, 1777, in Kensington. He was a prominent citizen, captain of colonial troops, first town clerk of Hampton Falls, representative to the general court and many years a selectman. He was an original proprietor of Chester, and many years proprietors' clerk. He married (first), December 26, 1698, Margaret, daughter of Samuel Sherburne; she died July 1, 1717, aged thirty-nine years, and he married (second), December 5, 1717, Mrs. Elizabeth Shaw, daughter of Timothy Hilliard; she died April 19, 1724, aged forty-five years, and he married (third), June 17, 1725, Mrs. Elizabeth Hilliard, daughter of Joseph Chase. She lived to be eighty years old, dying August 14, 1765. His children were, by first wife: Sherburne, John, Mary, Sarah, Jonathan, Joseph, by second wife: Daniel and Timothy (twins, Daniel died young), Joanna and Margaret.

(IV) Timothy, second son of Joseph and Elizabeth (Hilliard) Tilton, was born October 4, 1718, in Hampton Falls, and settled about 1770 in Loudon, New Hampshire, where he died December 1, 1785. The first town meeting in Loudon was held in his house, and he took a prominent part in town affairs during the Revolution. He was married, December 25, 1746, to Martha Boynton, of Kingston, who was born, 1726, and died November 25, 1822. They had a family of four sons and two daughters, namely: Joseph, Joanna, William, Nathan, Elizabeth, (probably John), and David. His eldest son, Colonel Joseph, was a prominent man in Loudon, whence he removed to Danville, Vermont. There the youngest son, David, joined him. William, the second, succeeded his father on the Loudon homestead.

(V) Nathan, third son of Timothy and Martha (Boynton) Tilton, was born February 3, 1757, in East Kingston, and established himself in Loudon as a farmer and miller. He died there December 28, 1814, near the close of his fifty-eighth year. He was married October 19, 1780, to Susanna Gail, who was born March 8, 1761, in Exeter, and died March 8, 1840, in Gilmanton. His children were: Betsey, Timothy, Susanna, Daniel, Nathan, Stephen, Newell, David, Joseph and Olive.

(VI) Stephen, fourth son of Nathan Tilton, was born September 29, 1793, in Loudon, and died December 17, 1867. After a few years residence in Northfield he removed to Meredith and thence in 1845 to Manchester, New Hampshire. In 1858 he moved to California, where several of his children had preceded him. He was married, January 10, 1816, to Julia Batchelder, who was born March 31, 1799, in Northfield, and died March 23, 1881. Both died, and are buried in San Mateo, California. Many of their descendants are living in California today. Their children were: Joseph Sullivan, Olive, Susan, Stephen S., Julia M., John Q. A., Sarah J., Mary C. (died young), Mary C., Henrietta, Georgietta, Georgiana and Charles H.

(VII) Joseph Sullivan, eldest child of Stephen and Julia (Batchelder) Tilton, was born June 13, 1818, in Northfield, New Hampshire, and was only two years old when his parents moved to Meredith. He grew to manhood in Meredith, and shortly afterward settled in Dorchester, New Hampshire, whence he moved to Manchester, New Hampshire, about 1848. In 1852 he, with two of his brothers, moved to California, where his family joined him a year later. He came back with his family to New Hampshire in 1857, and was one of the pioneers in the manufacture of hosiery in Laconia. He was a leading citizen of that city until his death. He

was active in raising the Twelfth Regiment, New Hampshire Volunteers, for the Civil war, and served as an officer in the same, commanding the Laconia company at Fredericksburg and Chancellorsville. He was permanently disabled by a wound in the last named battle, and died October 6, 1879. He was married in 1841, in Dorchester, to Betsey Ham, who was born June 20, 1820, in Strafford, New Hampshire, and died March 25, 1907. Their children were: Nancy A., George H., Emma Susan and Frank Sullivan.

(VIII) George Henry, elder son of Joseph S. and Betsey (Ham) Tilton, was born May 13, 1845, in Dorchester, and lived with his parents until the outbreak of the Civil war. He joined the Fourth Regiment New Hampshire Volunteers, September 14, 1861, and served three years. After his return to civil life he was trained by his father in his business, and became a partner in 1870. He has continued the business since his father's death, and has mills in the South, beside those at Tilton and Laconia, in which latter place he resides. He has represented his city in the legislature, and is an esteemed and respected citizen. He was married (first), June 19, 1866, to Marietta Randlett, who was born August 12, 1844, in Gilmanton, and died August 15, 1874. Mr. Tilton was married (second), April 11, 1883, to Calista E. Brown, of Meredith, who was born November 11, 1862, and died October 9, 1901. He married (third), September 20, 1902, his cousin, Julia Caroline Green, of San Mateo, California, who was born March 30, 1862, in San Bruno, same state.

(IX) Elmer Stephen, only son of George Henry and Marietta (Randlett) Tilton, was born October 11, 1869, in Laconia, New Hampshire, and was educated in the public schools of that city. After graduating from school he took a place with his father, learning the business, in which he has been for a long time a partner. He has represented his city several times in the house of representatives, and his district in the state senate. He is an active member of the Masonic fraternity, and a very well known man of his native state. He was married, January 26, 1892, to Lillian Gertrude Harrington, who was born August 21, 1868, in Laconia. Their children are: Charles Henry, born February 7, 1893; Elmer Harrington, September 14, 1895; and Kenneth Joseph, June 15, 1900, all in Laconia.

(V) John, possibly a son of Timothy and Elizabeth Tilton, was born about 1702, and died in 1784, in Kensington, aged eighty-two years. He was married, December 23, 1779, to Molly Cram, and their children on record in the archives of New Hampshire were: Nehemiah, John Sherburn, Betsey and Eunice.

(VI) Nehemiah, eldest son of John and Molly (Cram) Tilton, was born July 9, 1782, and resided in Barnstead, New Hampshire. He was married, September 10, 1804, to Hannah Philbrick, and they had thirteen children, namely: Molly (died young), John, Ruth, Daniel (died young), Daniel, Molly, Betsey, Benjamin, David, Lovicy, Eunice, Margaret and Hannah Cram. The youngest, who is the only survivor of the family, became the wife of David L. Green (see Green VII).

HODSDON This is the earlier form of a name which is now more generally written Hodgdon, though some of the Maine families in York county, where the line is quite numerous, prefer the early English spelling of Hodsdon. The branch in Barnstead, this state, spell the patronymic Hodgdon. Members of this family were pioneer settlers in Massachusetts and New Hampshire. The Hodgdons (Hodsdons) in early and recent times have earned a reputation for industry, loyalty and obedience to the law, which reflects credit on them as a race.

The Hodsdon English coat of arms is of quite unusual design. It has a field, *argent*, crossed by a wavy band, *gules*, between two horse-shoes, *azure*; crest, a man's head couped at the shoulders, vested *argent*, on the head of a cap, *or*. The motto is "Animo et fide."

(I) Nicholas Hodgdon was one of the immigrant settlers of Hingham, Massachusetts, where he was made a freeman March 9, 1636, and was granted a house lot the same year, in the center of the town, and later two meadows were granted him. About 1650, in company with others, he purchased a large tract of land at Cambridge Hill, now Newton. October 15, 1656, he received a grant of land from the town of Kittery, Maine, and soon removed to that place. December 13, 1669, he received another grant of land from the town of Kittery, both of the grants being bounded by or situated near Birchlea Point brook. He also purchased several other lots in the vicinity of the same brook. The farm occupied by him in the latter part of his life was purchased in 1674 of John Wincoll, and is situated on the east side of the Piscataqua river, and is bounded on the south by Thompson brook, which divides the town of Elliott and South Berwick, Maine. His farm descended to heirs of Nicholas regularly until 1828.

Nicholas Hodgdon married, about 1639, Esther Wines, who died in Hingham, Massachusetts, November 29, 1647. He married (second), Elizabeth, widow of John Needham. She was living in 1686. The children of the first wife, baptized in Hingham, were: Esther, Mehitable, Jeremiah, Israel and Elizabeth. The children of the second wife were: Benoni, Sarah, Timothy, John, Joseph and Lucy. (Benoni and descendants receive mention in this article).

(II) Jeremiah, eldest son and third child of Nicholas and Esther (Wines) Hodgdon, was baptized in Hingham, September 6, 1643. He removed with his father to Newton and Kittery. He settled in Portsmouth, and afterward resided in Newcastle, New Hampshire, where he died in 1716. He married, about 1666, Ann Thwaits, daughter of Alexander and Anne Thwaits, of Portsmouth. Alexander Thwaits came to America from London in the ship "Hopewell." The children of this marriage were: Alexander, John, Elizabeth, Nathaniel and Rebecca. After the death of her husband Anne Hodgdon lived in Boston, where she joined the Brattle Street Church. (An account of John and his descendants is found farther along in this narrative).

(III) Alexander, eldest child of Jeremiah and Ann (Thwaits) Hidgdon, was a soldier in the old fort of William and Mary, at Newcastle, 1708. He was taxed in Portsmouth in 1713, and in Greenland 1714. He bought an extensive tract of land near Welchman's Cove, in Newington, where he subsequently lived. He married, as early as 1716, Jane Shackford.

(IV) John, son of Alexander and Jane (Shackford) Hodgdon, was born in 1708, and resided in Newington. He married, January 30, 1729, Mary Decker, born in 1711, daughter of John and Sarah Decker, of Newington. Their eleven children, all born there, were: Jane, John (died young), Mary,

Phineas, Temperance, Charles, John, Hannah, Benjamin, Sarah and Joseph.

(V) Charles, third son and sixth child of John and Mary (Decker) Hodgdon, was born in Newington, in 1740, and baptized October 18, 1741. When a young man he resided in Portsmouth for a time, and some of his children were born there. In 1768 he settled in Barnstead, locating on the old Province road, and erected the first two-story dwelling house in that town. He was prominent in both political and religious affairs, serving as a selectman and representative to the legislature, acted as a justice of the peace, and was a deacon in the church for many years. His death occurred in Barnstead, March 23, 1817. While living in Newington, on December 12, 1765, Charles Hodgdon married Mrs. Hannah Dennett, widow of Charles Dennett, of Portsmouth, New Hampshire, and daughter of Hatevil and Hannah Nutter, of Newington. She was born in 1743, and died November 19, 1790, aged fifty-one years. After her death he married Abigail Thyng, of Brentwood, New Hampshire, who died March 29, 1830, aged eighty-three years. His children, all born in Portsmouth, by his first wife, were: Elizabeth, Benjamin, Olive, Nancy and Charles.

(VI) Benjamin, second child and older son of Charles and Hannah (Nutter) (Dennett) Hodgdon, was born in Portsmouth, June 28, 1768, and died June 6, 1849. The greater part of his life was spent in Barnstead, where he was a hotel keeper and trader, and one of the foremost public men in all that region. He held many public offices, both town and county, was justice of the peace and quorum, deputy sheriff, town clerk from 1787 to 1800, and representative to the general assembly in 1810-11. His famous old hostelry on the Province road was known far and wide as the Hodgdon House, while "the genial manners and warm hospitality of himself and his most estimable wife gained for them a large share of the public patronage. They continued in this business until the infirmities of age obliged them to seek a more quiet life." In September, 1797, Mr. Hodgdon married Polly, daughter of Timothy and Mary Emerson. She was born in Durham, New Hampshire, June 11, 1777, and died July 15, 1858. Their children included Hannah, Abigail, Timothy E., Mary and Alexander. (Mention of the last and descendants will be found in this article).

(VII) Timothy E., third child and elder son of Benjamin and Polly (Emerson) Hodgdon, was born in the town of Barnstead, New Hampshire, April 23, 1808, and died there October 1, 1864. During the early part of his business life he was a merchant in Barnstead, but in 1849 he was drawn to the Pacific coast by the "gold fever" so prevalent throughout the country, and spent some time in the promising gold fields of California; but unlike the great majority of the many thousands who were similarly attacked, Mr. Hodgdon accumulated a fortune and returned home a wealthy man. On September 28, 1830, he married Elizabeth Mary George, daughter of Rev. Enos George. (See George VI). She was born September 29, 1808, and died April, 1886. Their children: Mary, George, Hannah, Charles A., Julia A., Lyman, Sophia, Jennie M., Lizzie, Enoch George, Benjamin and Emerson. (Lyman and Enoch George receive mention in this narrative).

(VIII) Charles A., third child and eldest son of Timothy E. and Elizabeth Mary (George) Hodgdon, was born in Barnstead, August 4, 1833, and received his early education in the town schools. He was brought up to farm work, but in 1854, when he attained his majority, he went to California by way of the Isthmus of Panama, and worked in the "diggings" until 1865, when he returned to old Barnstead and began farming on "Beauty Hill." For about four years he drove stage from Barnstead to Rochester, New Hampshire. Mr. Hodgdon was married twice. His first wife was Addie, daughter of William and Charlotte (Langley) Pierce. She bore her husband one son, who died in infancy. His second wife was Mary Ann Nutter, widow of Samuel D. Nutter, and daughter of Greenleaf and Fanny (Langley) Allen, a descendant of Governor Samuel Allen, who in 1692 was a merchant in London, England. He purchased the Mason claim to the province of New Hampshire, and in September, 1698, came to America and asserted his authority over that jurisdiction. In 1703 he entered upon the duties of his gubernatorial office.

(VIII) Lyman, fifth child and second son of Timothy E. and Elizabeth Mary (George) Hodgdon, was born in Barnstead, June 30, 1837. When twelve years of age he went with his father to California, returning in 1865 after a prosperous sojourn in that "land of gold." In 1866 he married and bought out an established meat market in Dover, which he operated for some time. Selling his Dover business he went to St. Louis, Missouri, where in company with John Hayes, of Dover, he ran a large restaurant which he later sold out to Mr. Hayes. The next two years he was in business in Province, Rhode Island, then returned to Dover, where he again conducted a meat market. In 1883 he went to the Isthmus of Panama and there conducted a hotel and eating house for the English and American canal employes. Here he contracted the fever peculiar to that locality and died May 30, 1886. In his religious belief he was a Universalist. He married, April 4, 1866, Harriet Delaney, born September 4, 1847, daughter of John Delaney, of Dover, and reared one child.

(IX) Harry E., only child of Lyman and Harriet (Delaney) Hodgdon, was born in Dover, January 15, 1867. He attended the public schools until fourteen years old, when he entered the office of the *Morning Star* as an apprentice and learned the printer's trade. He was subsequently for a short time employed in a shoe factory, but finding that occupation uncongenial he resumed his former calling, and in 1897 established himself in the book and job printing business at Dover, which he has ever since conducted with gratifying success. He affiliates with Moses Paul Lodge, Free and Accepted Masons, the Knights of Pythias Lodge, No. 184, Benevolent and Protective Order of Elks, and Major Waldron Council, No. 989, Royal Arcanum. He is a member of the Universalist Church. Mr. Hodgdon married Edith J. Johnson, daughter of George B. and Angie P. Johnson, of Farmington, New Hampshire. Mr. and Mrs. Hodgdon have one daughter, Eileen J. born August 5, 1892.

(VIII) Enoch George, third son of Timothy E. and Elizabeth M. (George) Hodgdon, was born in Barnstead, March 4, 1839. He prepared for college in the public schools of Portsmouth, whither his father had moved, and at the Phillips Andover Academy, and entered the freshman class at Dartmouth College in March, 1858. During the winter vacations of his college course in common with the majority of his classmates he taught school in various places, and in the autumn of 1859 was the principal of the Guildhall (Vermont) Academy. At the outbreak of the Civil war he contemplated entering the Union army immediately after graduation, and with that purpose in view pursued a course of military instruction under the late General Alonzo Jackman, the professor of military science in Norwich University. Soon after his graduation he was appointed by Governor Berry, of New Hampshire, a recruiting officer at Portsmouth and Newmarket, with the assurance that a commission would be the reward for his services; although he had enlisted a sufficient number of recruits for the Fifth New Hampshire Volunteers to have received a subaltern's appointment his name was not among those to whom commissions were issued. He then commenced the study of law with the Hon. John S. H. Frink, at Portsmouth, which he continued until May, 1862, when he was solicited to assist in raising a company of the Ninth New Hampshire Volunteers at Portsmouth; this was soon accomplished, but that regiment being already filled upon the arrival at the rendezvous, it was assigned to the Tenth Regiment, and ordered to Garrison Fort Constitution until the completion of the latter organization. Mr. Hodgdon was appointed first lieutenant, his commission bearing date August 20, 1862. In September the Tenth was attached to the First Brigade, Third Division, Ninth Corps of the Army of the Potomac. After the battle of Fredericksburg the, Ninth Corps was sent to Newport News, Virginia. While there Lieutenant Hodgdon was attacked with pleuritic fever, and upon the advice of the attending surgeons resigned, February 13, 1863. Returning to New Hampshire, for several months his life was in jeopardy from the effects of the disease contracted in the service. Partially recovering, he was appointed, January 2, 1864, by President Lincoln, second lieutenant in the Veteran Reserve Corps, and assigned to staff duty in the Department of the Tennessee, organizing colored troops. He participated in the operations in northern Georgia and around Atlanta in the summer of 1864. Early in September of that year he was transferred to the Department of the Missouri, and became aide-de-camp upon the staff of Brevet Major-General Thomas Ewing, Jr., and as such took part in the campaign which resulted in driving out of Missouri the Confederate forces under General Sterling Price. He was promoted to the rank of captain, November 4, 1864; was recommended for a colonelcy of colored troops by the board of examiners at St. Louis in January, 1865, and was appointed January 24, 1865, lieutenant-colonel of the One Hundred and Thirteeth United States Infantry, but declined the appointment. He acted as judge advocate of the general court martial and military commission at St. Louis from January until May, 1865, when he was ordered to Gallop's Island, Boston harbor, to assist in mustering out of the United States service the Massachusetts Volunteers. March 29, 1866, he resigned his military commission, resumed the study of law, and was admitted to the bar of New Hampshire, October, 1866; he entered practice at Portsmouth, and at once attained a prominent position at the Rockingham bar and a lucrative practice. In politics he was a Democrat, and his party honored him in many ways. He was appointed solicitor for the years 1874-75-76, and was representative in the New Hampshire legislature 1875-76-1887-89, and mayor of the city of Portsmouth from August, 1887, to August, 1889. In all these positions he served his party faithfully and zealously, and in the house of representatives he acquired a reputation as a deep and logical thinker and a keen and invasive debater. He allied himself with the Grand Army of the Republic when that organization was first started, and always took a great interest in its affairs. In that order he filled many positions of honor and trust, having served as commander of Post 1 of Portsmouth in 1880, adjutant general of the department of New Hampshire for the year 1885, member of the National Encampment at Portland, Maine, June, 1885, judge advocate in 1886-87, junior vice-commander in 1889-90. In secret societies he was also prominent, having been elected, October, 1885, by the New Hampshire Grand Lodge of Knights of Honor, grand dictator of New Hampshire, and was also a leader in the Order United American Mechanics.

Always a great reader, Mr. Hodgdon turned his attention to local history and genealogy about 1880, and soon became fascinated with these subjects, giving all his leisure time to their study. As a result he attained high rank among the genealogists of the country, and was commissioned to write the genealogy and history of the Shannon family in America, to which work he devoted the spare moments of a busy career, and succeeded in producing one of the most succinct and readable family histories ever compiled in this country, "a monument of patient research and intelligent and faithful study." He also compiled histories of the Vaughn, Ambrose, and Ayres families of New England. As a local historian he was well known, and his work of editing "Adams s Annals" for the Portsmouth *Journal* and his copious notes and annotations in relation to the same aroused much interest during their publication. The greater part of his work in the historical field was published in the *Journal*, and by his death it lost a valuable and faithful correspondent—one whose contributions needed no verifications, and whose facts were never questioned.

He married, December 19, 1867, Mary Emma Webster, who died March 21, 1877, only daughter of Roswell W. and Sarah B. Webster, of Portsmouth. Of this marriage were born four children: Bertha, Mabel, Georgie Alice and Edith, the two last named dying in infancy. Bertha, born August 21, 1868, received her education in the public schools of Portsmouth and at Wellesley College, graduating from the high school in 1887, and from Wellesley in 1891. She rendered valuable aid to her father in his literary labors, and also designed and drew the plans of the spacious and handsome home her father built in Portsmouth. She married Cyril E. Jackson, a stock broker, of Portsmouth, who was born in Portland, Maine, 1868, son of Cyril E. and Mary (Weyman) Jackson, of Portland. Mabel, born September 12, 1872, graduated from the Portsmouth high school in the class of 1890. She married, June, 1898, Fred Hatch, and resides in Portsmouth. They have one daughter, Helen Mabel, born 1905.

(VII) Alexander, son of Benjamin and Polly (Emerson) Hodgdon, was born in Barnstead, New Hampshire, April 8, 1811, and died in Greenland, May 3, 18—. He was a farmer and stone mason, and lived nearly all his life in Greenland. He was a respected citizen, and filled the offices of school committee and selectman. He married Sarah Abby Walker, daughter of Captain William S. Walker. The children of this union were: Elizabeth, Sulden, Olive, Louise, Alexander, Charles, Sarah, William A., Ephraim, Helen, Anna, Manning and Ellsworth.

(VIII) William Augustus, eighth child and fourth son of Alexander and Sarah A. (Walker) Hodgdon, was born in Portsmouth, December 9, 1848. He received his education in the common schools of Portsmouth, and at Greenland Academy, and subsequently began to learn the carpenter's trade with Moses Yeaton, and completed his apprenticeship in New York City. In 1874 he returned to Portsmouth, and formed a partnership with Yeaton

& Son. In 1880 he began contracting and building on his own account, and has since been successfully engaged in that employment. He has given considerable attention to public questions and has filled various offices. He has been councilman, president of the council and alderman of Portsmouth, representative in the state legislature, and for fifteen years past a trustee of the public library of Portsmouth, and is also ex-president of the Mechanics' Fire Association, and of the Mercantile Library Association. He is popular in fraternal societies and clubs, and is a member of numerous organizations. He is pastmaster of St. Andrews Lodge, Free and Accepted Masons; Royal Arch Chapter; Commandery, Knights Templar; member of Piscataquog Lodge, Indenendent Order of Odd Fellows; past president of the Sons of the American Revolution; member of the Warrick and Country Clubs; and the Pepperell Society. He married (first), April 20, 1874, Clara A. Yeaton, who was born in Portsmouth, and died April 16, 1885, daughter of —— Yeaton, of Portsmouth; and (second), September 23, 1892, Clara I. Randall, daughter of —— Randall, of Portsmouth. One child, Ethel, was born of the first marriage.

(III) John, second son and child of Jeremiah and Anne (Thwaits) Hodgdon, was born in Newington or Portsmouth, and died probably in 1736. He married Mary Hoyt, and they had children: Jeremiah and John.

(IV) John (2), second son and child of John (1) and Mary (Hoyt) Hodgdon, was born in Newington in 1708, and died about 1793. He was married January 30, 1729, to Mary Decker, daughter of John and Sarah Decker, of Newington. Their eleven children were: Jane, John (died young), Mary, Phineas, Temperance, Charles, John, Hannah, Benjamin, Sarah and Joseph.

(V) Benjamin, ninth child of John (2) and Mary (Decker) Hodgdon, was born in Newington, May 20, 1750, and died March 1, 1823, aged seventy-three. In January, 1776, he signed the Association Test, which was posted for three Sundays before the meeting house door at Newington. November 5, 1775, he joined Captain Nicholas Rawlins company at Kittery Point. His name appears in the muster and pay roll of Colonel Evans' and Colonel Badger's regiments, and also among the names of privates of Captain Stephen Hodgdon's company, and on the roll of Colonel Abraham Drake's regiment, which was formed out of the regiment commanded by General Whipple, and sent to reinforce the Northern Continental army at Stillwater, September 8, 1777. He married Rosamond Coleman. Their children were: Lydia, Ephraim, Benjamin, Alexander, Sally and Temperance.

(VI) Ephraim, eldest son and second child of Benjamin (1) and Rosamond (Coleman) Hodgdon, was born in Newington, March 10, 1779, and died in Portsmouth, May 18, 1848, aged sixty-nine. He was a farm laborer. He lived in Newington about three years after he married, and then removed to Barnstead, where he resided about ten years, and then removed to Portsmouth. He married Abigail Thomas, and they were the parents of ten children: Mary, Benjamin, Sarah, Louisa, Alexander, Selden C., Obadiah M., John, Abigail P. and Ephraim.

(VII) Benjamin (2), eldest son and second child of Ephraim and Abigail (Thomas) Hodgdon, was born in Newington, May 20, 1805, and died in Portsmouth, September 8, 1894, aged eighty-nine. In early life he performed farm labor for hire. In 1835 he removed to Portsmouth, where he bought the farm now occupied by his son Charles. He married, April 22, 1832, Hannah Foster Frye, who was born in Portsmouth, February 16, 1810, daughter of Isaac and Rachel (Foster) Frye, of Portsmouth. She died May 13, 1886, aged seventy-six years. Their children were: Augustus L., Hannah E., Lydia F., Benjamin F., Henry C., Mary A. and Charles E., whose sketch follows.

(VIII) Charles Edward, youngest child of Benjamin (2) and Hannah Foster (Frye) Hodgdon, was born in Portsmouth, October 27, 1848. He was educated in one of the district schools of Portsmouth. He was employed on his father's farm until he was nineteen years of age, and then engaged in the ice business, which he has since successfully carried on in connection with farming. In political faith he is a Republican, and has taken an active interest in public questions. He was councilman in in 1877-78, alderman in 1895-96, and is now a member of the Portsmouth board of education. In Masonry he has attained the thirty-second degree, and is a member of the following divisions of that order: St. Johns Lodge, No. 1; Ineffable Grand Lodge of Perfection; Grand Council Prince of Jerusalem; New Hampshire Chapter of Rose Croix; and New Hampshire Consistory of the Sublime Princes of the Royal Secret. In Odd Fellowship he is a member of Osgood Lodge, No. 48; Strawberry Bank Encampment, No. 5; Canton Senter, No. 12; Patriarchs Militant; and Union Rebekah Lodge No. 3. He is also a member of the Massachusetts Society Sons of the American Revolution; of Ranger Section No. 17, of the Naval League of the United States; is president of the Paul Jones Club, S. A. R.; member of Strawberry Bank Grange, No. 251, Patrons of Husbandry; East Rockingham Pomona Grange, No. 11, and of the State Grange. He married (first), January 24, 1876, Martha J. Locke, who was born in Rye, New Hampshire, January 24, 1855, daughter of James and Hannah Locke, of Rye. She died December 23, 1879, and he married (second), November 30, 1882, Lillie Lewis Robertson, born in Northfield, New Hampshire, October 11, 1856, daughter of James Lewis and Elizabeth Susan (Carter) Robertson. (See Robertson, V). The children by the second wife are: Cora Elouise, born April 16, 1884; Mildred, November 12, 1887; Winifred, November 11, 1891; and Augusta, who was born August 5, 1894, and died September 24, 1894. The family are all members of the Middle Street Baptist Church, Portsmouth, New Hampshire. Cora E. married, in 1904, Albert Forrest Witham, and their children are: Edward Forrest, born January 16, 1905, and Pearl Elouise, September 15, 1906.

(II) Benoni, third son and sixth child of Nicholas Hodsdon, the youngest child of his first wife, Esther Wines, was baptized at Hingham, Massachusetts, December 5, 1647, after the death of his mother, which occurred November 29, 1647. He moved with his father to Boston, and later to Kittery, Maine. He made his own home first at Quamphegon, now Salmon Falls, New Hampshire; the Indians made a raid on the settlement, October 16, 1675, burned his house, and killed several of the family. His father gave him the homestead at Birchan Point, South Berwick, on October 22, 1678. Benoni Hodsdon was a prominent citizen of the part of Kittery which is now Berwick, Maine, and was selectman in 1692 and 1694, and representative in 1718. He was influential and energetic in church work, and was one of the committee to locate the meeting house in 1701. The name of Benoni Hodsdon's wife was Abigail, daughter of Thomas Curtis, of Scituate, Massachusetts, and York, Maine.

CHARLES E. HODGDON, MRS. CHARLES E. HODGDON,
MILDRED, CORA E., WINIFRED.

Their eight children were: Joseph, Samuel, Thomas, whose sketch follows; Hannah, Abigail, John, Esther and Elizabeth. Benoni Hodsdon died in 1718.

(III) Thomas, third son and child of Benoni and Abigail (Curtis) Hodsdon, was born at Kittery, Maine, probably between 1680 and 1690. On December 1, 1709, he married Mary, daughter of Nathan (2) and Martha (Tozier) Lord, and they had four children: Anna and John, twins, Thomas, whose sketch follows, and Mary, born in 1717. Thomas Hodsdon died early in the year 1717, probably not much past thirty years of age, and his widow afterward married Daniel (2) Emery.

(IV) Thomas (2), second son and third child of Thomas and Mary (Lord) Hodsdon, was born at Berwick, Maine, in 1715. He married Mary ——, and they had eight children: Thomas (3), whose sketch follows; Sarah, Eunice, Amy, Mary, Daniel, Jeremiah and Benjamin. Their home was at South Berwick, Maine. The will of Thomas (2) Hodsdon was dated June 3, 1774, and probated January 7, 1794, indicating that he lived to be nearly eighty years of age.

(V) Elder Thomas (3), eldest child of Thomas (2) and Mary Hodsdon, was baptized at Berwick, Maine, June 10, 1739. He served twice as a captain in the Revolutionary war. October 30, 1763, he married Margaret Goodwin, daughter of James and Margaret (Wallingford) Goodwin, who was baptized February 17, 1741-42. Elder Thomas Hodsdon's will was dated April 16, 1816, and probated at Berwick, Maine, in June, 1818. He bequeathed to his two sons, Ebenezer and Ichabod, each two hundred acres of land in Ossipee, New Hampshire. His children were: *Mary, Thomas, Sarah, Ebenezer, Ichabod, David, Elizabeth, James, Margaret, Olive and Peggy. (Ebenezer, David and descendants receive further mention in this article).

(VI) Thomas (4) Hodgdon, of Jeremy Island, undoubtedly eldest son of Elder Thomas (3) and Margaret (Goodwin) Hodsdon of Berwick, was one of the appraisers of the estate of Robert Wiley, Boothbay, Maine, on April 18, 1772. He was captain of the Ninth (Second Edgecombe) Company of the Third Lincoln County Regiment of Massachusetts Militia. It must be remembered that Maine at that time was a part of Massachusetts. Lincoln, Edgecomb, Boothbay and Westport were adjoining towns in Lincoln county. Colonel William Jones was in command of the Lincoln County Regiment, and Captain Hodgdon's name is given among the list of officers commissioned May 8, 1778. On October 24, 1777, a council warrant for four pounds sterling was drawn in favor of Colonel William Jones for the use of said Thomas Hodgdon for services rendered in retaking a mast ship. Captain Thomas Hodgdon had four sons: Thomas, Joseph, Benjamin and John. The first three served in the Revolution. Thomas Hodgdon, Jr., was an officer, and his commission precedes that of his father. Thomas, Jr., was a captain in the Tenth (Fifth Berwick) Company, Second York County Regiment of Massachusetts Militia; he was reported commissioned April 29, 1776. His company served at Peekskill, New York, for eight months. The home of Captain Thomas Hodgdon, Jr., was the house now occupied as the Berwick (Maine) town farm.

(VII) John Hodgdon, son of Captain Thomas Hodgdon, married Debra Dunton, and they had Timothy and other children.

(VIII) Timothy Hodgdon, son of John and Debra (Dunton) Hodgdon, was born at Westport, Maine. He married Frances Tibbetts, and they had Zina H. and seven other children.

(IX) Zina H. Hodgdon, son of Timothy and Frances (Tibbetts) Hodgdon, was born at North Boothbay, Maine. He married Rinda Reed, and they had Laura B. and five other children. They lived at Westport, Maine. He was a farmer and merchant, representative, selectman, and member of North Boothbay Free Baptist Church.

(X) Laura B., daughter of Zina H. and Rinda (Reed) Hodgdon, was born at Westport, Maine, June 11, 1850. She married Dr. Roscoe G. Blanchard, of Dover New Hampshire. (See Blanchard).

(VI) Ebenezer, second son and fourth child of Elder Thomas (3) and Margaret (Goodwin) Hodsdon, was baptized at Berwick, Maine, August 10, 1771, and was an early settler at Ossipee, New Hampshire. On January 16, 1797. Ebenezer Hodsdon married his cousin, Sally Wentworth, daughter of Lieutenant Timothy and Amy (Hodsdon) Wentworth of Berwick, Maine. She was born March 20, 1778, and died May 28, 1847. Her father, lieutenant Timothy Wentworth, served in the Revolution, and lived on the old homestead in Berwick, which had belonged to his grandfather, Timothy. He died there November 29, 1842, at the age of ninety-five. Ebenezer and Sally (Wentworth) Hodsdon had ten children: Belinda, married (first), Rev. Henry Smith, of Ossipee, New Hampshire, (second), Rev. Sydney Turner, of Bingham, Maine, both Congregational clergymen. Wentworth, died unmarried at the age of twenty-three. Olive, married Deacon Jonathan Ambrose, of Ossipee. Thomas, married twice and died in Sebec, Maine. Sally, married (first) Andrew Folsom, of Ossipee, and (second), John Burley, of Sandwich. Belinda, married Hollis Burleigh, of Ossipee. Amy Wentworth, married Calvin Sanborn, of Wakefield, New Hampshire. Ebenezer, whose sketch follows. Lucinda, married Nahum Perkins, of Great Falls, New Hampshire. Harriet Newell, married Hiram O. Tuttle, and lived in Sturgis, Michigan. Ebenezer (1) Hodsdon died at Ossipee, New Hampshire, July 12, 1840.

(VII) Ebenezer (2), third son and eighth child of Ebenezer (1) and Sally (Wentworth) Hodsdon, was born at Ossipee, New Hampshire, March 8, 1811. On March 16, 1834, he married Catherine, daughter of Lieutenant George, and Sarah (Gile) Tuttle, who was born at Effingham, New Hampshire, January 6, 1813. Ebenezer (2) and Catherine (Tuttle) Hodsdon had three children, all born in Ossipee: John W., January 4, 1835, enlisted in the Thirteenth New Hampshire Volunteers, in August, 1862, and served until June, 1865. He now lives in Ossipee. Edward P., whose sketch follows. Sarah E., December 7, 1843, married, January 13, 1867, Alphonzo Augustus Spear, of Buxton, Maine. Ebenezer (2) Hodsdon died at Ossipee, February 19, 1895.

(VIII) Edward Payson, second son and child of Ebenezer (2) and Catherine (Tuttle) Hodsdon, was born at Ossipee, New Hampshire, September 24, 1837. He was a man highly educated for those days and possessed unusual ability. In early life he taught for several years, in the public schools, and later was the successful principal of the acadamy at Wakefield, New Hampshire. He is a Republican in politics, and was elected railroad commissioner in 1873, serving for three years. He went to Dover, New Hampshire, to live, and in 1874 and 1875 was elected mayor of that city. He is now living in St. Louis, where he is engaged in the manufacture of rubber goods and belting. On January 28, 1862, Edward Payson Hodsdon married Emma B. Demeritt, youngest child of Mark and Abagail (Leighton) Demeritt, of Farmington, New Hampshire, who was born September 27, 1840. (See Demeritt III). They have one child, Ervin Wilbur, whose sketch follows.

(IX) Ervin Wilbur, only child of Edward Payson and Emma B. (Demeritt) Hodsdon, was born April 8, 1863, at Ossipee, New Hampshire. He was educated in the public schools of Ossipee and Dover and at Phillips Academy, Exeter, New Hampshire. In 1879, at the age of sixteen years, he went to St. Louis, Missouri, and attended Washington University, being graduated from the Missouri Medical College, in the class of 1884. He at once began practice in the City Hospital of St. Louis, where he remained two years, and then returned to Dover, New Hampshire, where he engaged in his profession. Removing to Sandwich, this state, he established himself as a physician, and also opened a drug store, which successful combination he continued till 1896, when he removed to Ossipee, where he now lives. Dr. Hodsdon conducts a drug store there, and also holds the office of postmaster, to which he was appointed in 1897. His large practice and other duties leave him little time for recreation or social affairs, but he is prominent in many secret societies. He belongs to Ossipee Valley Lodge, Ancient Free and Accepted Masons, of which he is past master; also to Ossipee Tribe, Improved Order of Red Men, and is past great sachem of that order for New Hampshire. He is a member and past master of the local Grange, and of the Ancient Order of United Workmen. Dr. Hodsdon is a Republican in politics, and attends the Methodist Church.

(VI) David, fourth son and sixth child of Elder Thomas (3) and Margaret (Goodwin) Hodsdon, was baptized in 1774, in Berwick, and some of his children settled near his brothers in Ossipee, New Hampshire. He was married, February 16, 1804, to Jane Fogg, daughter of Joseph and Mercy (Littlefield) Fogg, of Kittery (see Fogg, IV). She was born May 10, 1776, in Kittery, and died April 10, 1847.

(VII) Joseph, son of David and Jane (Fogg) Hodsdon, was born at Berwick, Maine, July 14, 1816, where after attending the common schools he served an apprenticeship at the tanner's trade. He subsequently conducted a large business in tanning and currying for several years. In 1839 he removed to Ossipee, New Hampshire, where he bought what is now known as the Hodsdon homestead. Tearing down the cottage that was on the property, he built the large house which the family still occupies. Joseph Hodsdon was a Republican in politics, and represented his town for two terms in the legislature, 1855 to 1857. He was colonel of the state militia and a Master Mason. He was an active member of the Congregational Church, and held the office of deacon for thirty-three years and superintendent of the Sunday school for forty years. On September 23, 1839, Deacon Joseph Hodsdon married Dorcas, daughter of John and Esther Gowell, of Berwick, Maine. There were seven children: Arthuria Isabella, born December 17, 1841; Arthur Lycurgus, whose sketch follows; Orlando Carlos, twin of Arthur Lycurgus, October 13, 1844; Abbie Etta, July 25, 1847; Lydia Ann, June 15, 1849; Sarah Climena, April 7, 1854; and Ida May, November 4, 1856. Orlando C. Hodsdon, the second twin, died January 18, 1863. Deacon Joseph Hodsdon died at Ossipee, April 15, 1897, in his eighty-first year.

(VIII) Arthur Lycurgus, eldest son and second child of Deacon Joseph and Dorcas (Gowell) Hodsdon, was born at Ossipee, New Hampshire, October 13, 1844. After attending the common schools of his native town and the academies at Effingham, New Hampshire, and Fryeburg, Maine, at the age of twenty-one he entered into business with his father and also became interested in lumbering. In 1881 he gave up the tannery and devoted his entire attention to the lumbering business. In 1887 he was elected president of the Pine River Lumber Company, and two years later bought out this company and organized it as the A. L. Hodsdon Lumber Company, with himself as president and agent. In politics a Republican, he served for twelve years as member of the state committee, and for many years as chairman of the town committee, and as a member of the New Hampshire senate for the term 1890-91. He is a member of Ossipee Valley Lodge, Ancient Free and Accepted Masons, also of the Odd Fellows and Knights of Pythias, and attends the Congregational Church. On September 4, 1870, Arthur Lycurgus Hodsdon married Charlotte M. Grant, daughter of Nathaniel and Charlotte S. Grant. They have three children: Walter Grant, born August 9, 1871; Herbert Arthur, November 18, 1873, and Mary Ellen, November 2, 1878. Walter G. was educated at the academy in Fryeburg, Maine, and the medical school of Boston University, where he was graduated in 1900. He is now a successful practitioner in Rutland, Vermont. Dr. Hodsdon married Anna Harris, of Honeoye Falls, New York, and they have two children: Reginald Grant and Madeline Harris. Herbert Arthur was educated in the academy in Fryeburg, Maine, and went to Rochester, this state, as proprietor of a general merchandise store. He married Lucy W. Charles, and became interested in the store owned by her father. They have four children: Helen Charles, Charlotte Whitman, Arthur Norman and Grant William. Mary Ellen attended the Nute high school at Milton, New Hampshire, and Lasell Seminary, at Auburndale, Massachusetts. She was graduated from the Emerson School of Oratory in Boston, in 1902, being president of her class. In 1907 she married Dr. Charles E. Rich, and they now live in Lynn, Massachusetts.

TURNER The Turner family is an ancient one of Norman-French origin, and appears in England at the time of the Conquest, when "Le sire de Tourneur" accompanied King William on his expedition. There are various coats-of-arms, belonging to the thirty-five different branches of the family in England. In most of these the mill rind or iron in which the center of the mill-stone is set appears as a distinguishing feature. This would seem to suggest that the name is derived from the turning of a revolving wheel, indicating that the early Turners might have been millwrights or millers. Several families of the name are among the early immigrants to New England. The first and perhaps the most important American ancestor of the name was Humphrey Turner, who arrived with his family at Plymouth, Massachusetts, in 1628. He had a house lot assigned him the next year, and built a cabin in which he probably lived till 1633. Soon after he moved to Scituate, Massachusetts, where he lived till his death, nearly forty years later. He had a tannery at Scituate as early as 1636, and seems to have been a man of prominence in that town. His wife was Lydia Gamer, and there were eight children living at the time of their father's death in 1673. It is quite probable that the following line is descended from Humphrey, of Scituate; but the Turner genealogies are not owned by any of the libraries of Concord; hence the writer is unable to trace the early antecedents of this branch.

That the family has been a numerous and powerful one in New England is shown by the fact that two villages, one in Massachusetts and the other in Maine, have been named for them. Turner's Falls, in the Connecticut valley, near Greenfield and Deerfield, Massachusetts, was named for Captain William Turner, who gained a victory there during King Philip's war, and was killed the next day, March 19, 1676. Previous to his death the region had been known as Great Falls. The town of Turner, north of Auburn and Lewiston, Maine, was names for Rev. Charles Turner, a descendant of Humphrey, who was born at Scituate, Massachusetts, in 1732, graduated from Harvard in 1752, and for several years was a preacher at Duxborough, Massachusetts. He afterwards moved to Maine, where he became influential in affairs, both of church and state, and left descendants who have attained distinction. The Turners of Newport, Rhode Island, who for so many generations have furnished officers to the army and navy of the United States, as well as consuls to foreign ports, are descended from Captain William Turner, who gave the name to Turner's Falls in Massachusetts. The line whose history follows has lived for five generations in Bethlehem, New Hampshire, and in view of the standing which it has in that town and the number of successful men which it has sent out into the world, may justly be considered the foremost family of that region.

(I) Samuel Turner and his wife Mary lived in Bernardston, Massachusetts, and little has come down to us of his early life. He was a soldier in the French and English war in Canada, in His Majesty's service (George II), and was discharged from the army at Fort Halifax, April 28, 1761, in the early reign of George III. By trade he was a brick maker. Samuel Turner and his wife Mary had eight children, among them James Turner, who commenced a settlement in Bethlehem in 1789. Samuel and his wife came to Bethlehem and spent their last days with their son James.

(II) James, son of Samuel Turner, was born in 1762. He lived at Bernardston, Massachusetts, (not Barnardston, Maine,) as Simeon Bolles's "History of Bethlehem" incorrectly states, and at the age of twenty-eight walked up the Connecticut river with a pack on his back. When near the present town of Hanover he met at the cross roads a young woman on horseback. They must have been attracted to each other at first sight, for she offered to carry his pack on her horse. They journeyed together till they reached her home, a modest cottage, where she offered him lodging for the night. The fair rider proved to be a young widow named Parker, with two children, and from this chance meeting developed a romance which culminated in marriage two or three years later. The guest departed the next morning and wended his toilsome way to what is now the town of Bethlehem, where he was the third settler. He worked on his land during the summers, returning to Massachusetts to spend the winters. After he had partially subdued the wilderness he went to Hanover to claim his bride. According to tradition she was a woman of more than ordinary ability and attractiveness. She was a skillful horsewoman, and possessed such medical judgment and knowledge of herbs that she became noted as a doctor and nurse for miles around. There was no physician in the region for many years, and Mrs. Turner's services were in demand. She would respond to calls at any hour of the night, without charges, and putting medicine into her saddle-bags would fearlessly ride long distances to minister to the ailing. The roads in those days were hardly more than trails, and journeys were frequently made by ox-team. It is said that Mrs. Turner and her husband went three times by this transportation to visit her friends in Hanover, which would be something like sixty miles from Bethlehem, and on one of these journeys she carried her six-weeks' old baby in her arms. The early settlers had to work hard for everything that they had. In those days there was no place nearer than Bath, twenty-five miles distant, where one could get corn ground. One day in early spring James Turner started on this errand, but as he was coming back the ice thawed suddenly and he encountered a freshet on the roaring Ammonoosuc. The usual place of crossing was near what is now Littleton, but the flood rendered this impassible, and Turner stayed two or three nights at a cabin, accompanied by a settler named Mann, the only habitation any where about. He worked three days before he could find a tree long enough to reach across the river. He succeeded in getting home by this rude bridge, but he had to leave his team till the waters subsided. In those days there was no regular pasturage, and cows were turned loose in the woods. Mr. Turner and a man named Oakes one day lost their two cows and were obliged to hunt for a week and a half before they found them, which was in a place called McGregory Hollow, near the Ammonoosuc. Mrs. Turner's skill was needed upon their return, and she succeeded in restoring the neglected animals to their former milk-giving conditions. Bears were plentiful in the neighborhood, and were caught in figure-4 traps. At one time the bear had remained too long in the trap, and Mr. Turner thought he would throw some of the meat to the hogs. This caused a riot in the pen, and the frightened animals fled in all directions, escaping through the logs to the woods. It was some time before they were recaptured, and Mr. Turner never again offended the sensibilities of his porcine charges in this manner. James Turner was a man of ability and accumulated considerable property, although he met with some pecuniary discouragement. After he had cleared his land and started a good farm, it was found that he did not possess a clear title; and not liking to leave a place on which he had spent so much labor, he paid for it a second time. Another way in which he lost money was by building a portion of the turnpike road between Portland, Maine, and the White Mountains. A company was formed to promote this scheme, which would afford the dwellers of the upper part of New Hampshire and Vermont a means of getting to market. Beside his own labor Mr. Turner paid two hundred dollars for help, no small sum in those days, and he never received a cent in return, as the company failed completely. James Turner and his wife had three children, among them: Timothy Parker, whose sketch follows. James Turner died in Bethlehem in 1835, aged seventy-three years.

(III) Timothy, son of James and Mercy (Parker) Turner, was born at Bethlehem, New Hampshire, in 1795. He became a man of prominence, served as town clerk for many years, was captain of the militia, justice of the peace and representative to the legislature. He was a man of dignified appearance, and of the old Puritan type. On February 3, 1818, Timothy Parker Turner married Priscilla

Bullock, and they had nine children, three of whom died young. The five sons had remarkable records. James N., the eldest, is mentioned in the next paragraph. Charles S. left home at the age of twenty-one and began railroad life at Norwich, Connecticut. He first served as station agent, and then became general agent of a railroad and steamboat company at Worcester. After fifteen years in this position he became superintendent of the Worcester & Nashua railroad, where he remained sixteen years. He was then made president of the consolidated Worcester, Nashua & Rochester railroads, and after four years of service retired from active business. The three younger Turners became apprentices in their elder brother's office. Timothy N. became a conductor on the Norwich line, and had charge of the steamboat train, which he managed for more than thirty years. William H. died January 31, 1890, but his railroad advancement had been rapid, including among other positions that of superintendent of the Portland & Rochester railroad at the time of his death, that of superintendent of the New York end of the New York, New Haven & Hartford railroad. His grave at Worcester, Massachusetts, is marked by an imposing monument of New Hampshire granite to which all the employes of the road, from the president to the water boys, claimed the privilege of contributing. Hiram N., the youngest of the Turner boys, began as general passenger and freight agent of the Worcester & Nashua railroad, and while in this office he published the first maps of the White Mountains, showing the different routes to the various summer resorts. He was subsequently made general traffic manager of the Boston & Lowell railroad, going with that road to the Boston & Maine, and from there to St. Johnsbury, Vermont, to become general manager and director of the Fairbanks Scale factories. He is a director in the Concord and Montreal railroad. Timothy P. Turner died February 16, 1872, and his wife died April 29, 1862.

(IV) James Nathaniel, eldest son of Timothy P. and Priscilla Turner, was born at Bethlehem, New Hampshire, April 18, 1824. He lives on the farm, halfway between the village and the maplewood, which has been occupied by five generations of Turners. It was originally deeded to Mr. Turner's grandfather James by the state committee in 1789. It descended to the father, Timothy P., and is now occupied by James N., his son, George Huffman, and his son's children. There are two hundred and fifty acres in all, and the farm proper is a beautiful one, containing seventy-five acres, entirely cleared of stone and under a high state of cultivation. In connection with this farm James N. Turner and his son George conduct a summer hotel, the Turner House, which accommodates about seventy-five guests, and has an enviable reputation among the best family resorts of this region. The same guests come there year after year. Among the many attractions is an unfailing supply of the purest and coldest water which supplies a wayside trough where all travelers stop. James N. Turner is a Republican in politics, and attends the Congregational Church. On December 20, 1857, James N. Turner married Mary Ann Hall, and they have three children.

(V) George Huffman, son of James Nathaniel and Mary Ann (Hall) Turner, was born in Bethlehem, New Hampshire, July 29, 1859. He was educated in the common schools and at the Littleton Academy in the neighboring town. He is associated with his father in the management of the farm and the hotel, and is also manager of the Bethlehem Electric Light Company, which supplies Bethlehem and Whitefield. He is one of the most trusted citizens of the town, and settles a good many estates. In politics he is a strong Republican, has been town treasurer and has served several times as selectman, beginning in 1887, and was representative to the legislature during 1907. He was treasurer of Grafton county for four years, has been county commissioner since 1897, and for the last eight years has been chairman of the board. He is an active member of the Congregational Church, and belongs to the Masonic fraternity, being a member of Burns Lodge, Littleton, and of Franklin Chapter, of Lisbon. On June 17, 1881, George Huffman Turner married Susan Rogers White, daughter of George Clinton White and Sarah Jane Huzzey, his wife, of Boston, Massachusetts. They have four children: Mary Elizabeth, born September 9, 1882, married Walter S. Noyes, of Littleton, New Hampshire; Helen Esther, born May 8, 1885; James Albert, born December 15, 1888; and Gertrude White, born November 8, 1891.

HILL This name was formerly spelled Hilles, and that form is still used by a large number of the descendants bearing the name. It has been traced to a somewhat remote period in England, having been found nearly two hundred years before the Puritan emigration. It has been borne by numerous prominent citizens of the American colonies and of the United States, and is still among the most widely distributed names known in the history of the country.

(I) The first of whom we have distinct information in the line herein traced was George Hilles, who resided in the parish of Great Burstead, Billericay, Essex county, England. Neither his birthplace nor his parentage has yet been discovered. The parish register of Great Burstead between 1579 and 1596 is still missing, and this prevents the discovery of name and parentage of his wife. The earliest known record of George Hilles is in relation to his marriage: "George Hilles, linen draper, and Mary Symonds of Billericay, County Essex, widow of William Symonds, late of the same, tanner; general licences of the Bishop of London, thirteenth of October, 1596."

(II) The records of Burstead gives the following: "1602, March, Joseph Hilles, sonne of George, was baptized the third day." He was married July 22, 1634, to Rose Clarke, in Great Burstead, and there his elder children were born. Not later than March, 1632, all the family moved to Malden, also of Essex, where three of his children were born. In 1638 he was the "undertaker" of the voyage of the ship "Susan and Ellen," which arrived in Boston, July 17, of that year. He first settled in Charlestown, upon the Charles and Mystic rivers. The family dwelling was near the market-place, but in a few years he became a resident of the north side on the Mystic river, and established his home on "Mystic Side," on a farm of considerable size. When this was set off in a separate town it became known as Malden, which name was probably given by him in memory of his former dwelling place in England. He was a man of much influence in the community, and served as selectman in 1644 and 1646, and was representative in the general court. He was re-elected in the following year and was chosen speaker of the house of deputies. During his residence in Mystic and Malden he was captain of the train band. At his death he willed his "buffe coate" to his son Samuel, and his backsword to his stepson Henry Lund. He was the first deputy of Malden, which had no other representative until 1664. He moved to Newbury, on the Merrimack river, and was succeeded in this office by his son-in-law, John Wade. In 1645 Joseph Hilles was the first named on a committee "to set the loss of the settlers of the Nashaway plantacon." Three years later he was the first of a committee of four "to change the location of the highway between Winnesemit and Reading." In 1650 he was the second of a committee to change the government, and was chairman to draw up instructions for blocks, to a gathering, where "commissioners of all the colonies shall meete." In 1635 he was one of a committee to consider whether the colonies by their articles of agreement were empowered to engage the colonies in "warre." In 1654 he was appointed with others to frame a reply to the Holden government, which had demanded an explanation of certain acts of the colonies. He was three times on a committee to audit the treasury accounts, and in 1648 was leading member of the committee which reported to the general court the first codification of the loss of the colony. He was the actual compiler of the law, prepared the copy for the press, and supervised the printing. Besides a money compensation he was granted by the colony for his work, five hundred acres of land on the Nashaway river, and the remission of his taxes in his old age.

His first wife, Rose Clarke, died March 24, 1650, in Malden, and he was married, June 24, 1651, to Hannah Smith, widow of Edward Mellows, of Charlestown, who died about 1655. In January, 1656, he married (third) Helen (Elline or Eleanor), daughter of Hugh Atkinson, of Kendall, Westmoreland, England. She died between January 8, 1861, and November 10, 1662. On March 8, 1665, he was married in Newbury, to Ann, the widow of Henry Lunt, of that town, and until his death resided in her dwelling in Newbury. He died February 5, 1688, at Newbury, having been deprived of his sight by blindness for about eight years. The children of his first wife were: Mary, Elizabeth, Joseph, James, Rebecca, Stephen, Sarah, Gershom and Mehitable. The first four were born in England. The children of Joseph and Hannah were: Samuel, Nathaniel and Hannah. The children of Joseph and Helen (Atkinson) Hilles were: Deborah and Abigail.

(III) Samuel, eleventh child of Joseph Hilles, and the eldest of his second wife, Hannah (Smith) Mellows, was born in July, 1652, in Malden, and died in Newbury, Massachusetts, August 18, 1732. He was sergeant in King Philip's war, and was at the battle of Bloody Brook and Narragansett, in 1675. He was married in Newbury, Massachusetts, May 20, 1679, to Abigail Wheeler, who died April 13, 1742. She was the daughter of David and Sarah (Wise) Wheeler, of Newbury, David being the son of John Wheeler, who was born at Salisbury, Wilkeshire, England, in 1625, and came to New England in the ship "Confidence," in 1638. He was married, May 11, 1650, to Mary, daughter of Samuel Wise. Their children were: Samuel, Joseph, Nathaniel, Benjamin, Abigail (died young), Henry, William, Josiah, John, Abigail, James and Hannah (twins), Daniel and Smith. (Mention of Daniel and descendants follows in this article.)

(IV) Henry, fifth son and sixth child of Samuel and Abigail (Wheeler) Hilles, was born April 23, 1688, in Newbury, and died August 20, 1757, in Hudson, New Hampshire. He received from his father, before his death, a deed of lands and meadow on the east side of the Merrimac river, in Dunstable, that portion which is now the town of Hudson. This was a part of the land granted by the colony to Joseph Hilles, the grandfather of Henry. On October 16, 1721, Henry Hilles bought of John Usher fifteen acres of land in Dunstable, where he was then living, and on the twentieth of the same month he sold his land in Essex county, Massachusetts, to his brother John. In the record of his third marriage at Newbury he is described as of Nottingham, which is the same locality as Hudson. It is probable that he removed to New Hampshire immediately after receiving his father's deed, which is dated August 22, 1721. He was married (intention published May 23, 1715, in Newbury), to Hannah, daughter of Henry and Bethiah (Emery) Bodwell, of Haverhill. She was born September, 1696, in Methuen, Massachusetts, which was formerly a part of Haverhill. Henry Hill's second wife was named Abigail, but no date of the marriage or of her birth and parentage has been found. He married (third) at Newbury, November 11, 1736, Dorcas Thornton. There were probably no children of the third marriage. Those of the first were: Ezekiel, and Henry and of the second, Ebenezer and Jonathan.

(V) Lieutenant Ezekiel, eldest child of Henry and Hannah (Bodwell) Hill, was born April 11, 1718, in Newbury, Massachusetts, and died in Hudson, New Hampshire, May 14, 1790. His wife Hannah was born in 1719, and died September 27, 1816, in Hudson. Their children were: Mehitable, Thomas and Esther.

(VI) Thomas, only son and second child of Lieutenant Ezekiel and Hannah Hill, was born March 30, 1751, in Hudson, and died in that town May 21, 1833. His wife Ruth died there August 25, 1826. Their children were: Amos, Isaac, Thomas, Hannah, Sally and Ruth.

(VII) Isaac, second son and child of Thomas and Ruth Hill, was born October 15, 1782, in Hudson, and resided in Arlington, Massachusetts. He died in 1881.

(VIII) Isaac (2), son of Isaac (1) and Lucinda (Cutter) Hill, was born October 13, 1829, in Arlington, Massachusetts. He was educated in Dracut, Massachusetts, and engaged there in farming. He was an attendant of the Congregational Church, and a Republican in politics. He was married, 1854, to Eliza Ann Peabody, daughter of Nathaniel Peabody, of Dracut (see Peabody, V). They had eight children: Frank A., John P., Fred Roland, Martha E., Orton, Grant, Sarah, and Emma.

(IX) John P., second son and child of Isaac (2) and Eliza A. (Peabody) Hill, was born September 15, 1856, in Dracut, Massachusetts, and was educated in the public schools of that town. He carried on the old farm there, of one hundred and fifty acres, for about fifteen years, when he engaged in the wholesale manufacturing of lumber, and in 1895 he removed to Warner, New Hampshire, and engaged in the lumber business there in which he has been successful, and is numbered among the representative citizens of the town, popular, and respected by his fellows. He has served the town four years as selectman, and is a leading member and treasurer of the Grange. He attends and supports the Baptist Church, and is an ardent Republican in politics. He is affiliated with Centreville Lodge, No. 215, Independent Order of Odd Fellows, of Lowell, Massachusetts, and of the Welcome Rebekah Lodge of Warner, and is past master of Haris Lodge, Ancient Free and Accepted Masons, of Warner. He was married, October 15, 1895, to Hannah Burbank, daughter of David S. and Amanda Augusta Burbank, of Warner. They have four children: Florence, Orton F., Edna Amanda and Alice Burbank. His wife died April 25, 1903, and June 28, 1906, he married Kate S. Hardy, of Warner, a daughter of Charles E. and Sarah A. (Clough) Hardy.

(IV) Captain Daniel, tenth son and twelfth of the fourteen children of Samuel and Abigail (Wheeler) Hills, was born at Newbury, Massachusetts, December 8, 1700. He was of the Colonial army that captured Louisburg in 1745. From March, 1748, to September, 1749, with the rank of captain, he was in command of a detached company in the unsettled district of Maine. He was connected with the artillery train under command of Colonel Richard Gridley from February 18, 1756, till his death in October of that year. For a short time, about 1730, he was living in a township that is now a part of Hudson, New Hampshire. In December, 1724 (published December 5), Daniel Hills married Elizabeth Biggs, daughter of John and Ruth (Wheeler) Biggs, who was born at Gloucester, Massachusetts, June 28, 1707. They had three children: Ruth, born February 5, 1726; Abigail, May 10, 1728; and Daniel (2), whose sketch follows. Captain Daniel Hills died October 28, 1756, on the second expedition to Crown Point.

(V) Captain Daniel (2), only son and third and youngest child of Captain Daniel (1) and Elizabeth (Biggs) Hills, was born in that part of Newbury, Massachusetts, which is now a part of Hudson, New Hampshire. From 1758 to 1786 he was assessed as a citizen of Haverhill, Massachusetts. In November, 1789, fifty acres of land in Northfield were deeded to him as a cordwainer in Concord, New Hampshire. In January, 1791, a lot of one hundred acres in the same township was conveyed to him as a resident of Haverhill, and in this conveyance he is styled gentleman. Like his father in the Colonial wars, he held a commission as captain in the Revolution, and he drilled the Haverhill company that marched upon the Lexington alarm. In the history of Haverhill, Massachusetts, among the list of those who gave clothing for the soldiers of the Revolution, appears the name of Captain Daniel (2) Hills, who contributed nine pairs of "Shuss." On May 10, 1757, at Newbury, Captain Daniel (2) Hills married Hannah Emery, daughter of David and Abigail (Chase) Emery, who was born in Newbury, in February, 1739. They had six children: Daniel, whose sketch follows; Abigail, born March 7, 1760, married Amos Clement; David, June 4, 1761, died at Northfield, March 9, 1820; Timothy, whose sketch follows; Hannah, July 17, 1768, died at Sanbornton, New Hampshire, July 24, 1826; John, June 15, 1770, died at Northfield, January 20, 1825. All of these children were born at Haverhill, Massachusetts. Captain Daniel (2) Hills died at Northfield, New Hampshire, some time after January 16, 1810.

(VI) Daniel (3), eldest child of Captain Daniel (2) and Hannah (Emery) Hills, was born at Haverhill, Massachusetts, May 12, 1758. He was in the Revolutionary army during the siege of Boston, and served six weeks in Roxbury in a company commanded by Captain Elton. On or before his marriage he moved to Northfield, New Hampshire, where he was town clerk for many years. Daniel Hills married Hannah Young, and they had five children, all born in Northfield: Betsey, whose sketch follows; Susan, married (first) Benjamin Darling, (second) ——— Favor, (third) Samuel Leanard, had six children and died at Troy, Indiana, August 10, 1855; Hannah, married Richard Blanchard, of Northfield; Sally, married Sherborn Locke, who moved to Schenectady, New York, with his family; Daniel, married Abi B. Ambler, and lived in Attleboro, Massachusetts. Daniel Hills died about 1815, at Northfield, New Hampshire, and his estate was administered on May 17, of that year.

(VII) Betsey, eldest child of Daniel (3) and Hannah (Young) Hills, was born at Northfield, New Hampshire, June 10, 1793. On May 27, 1814, she was married to John Cilley, who was born at Northfield, March 21, 1793. They removed to Columbia, Coos county, this state, where their six children were born: Mary A., Sarah J., Susan, Hannah, Lydia and John. Mary Ann Cilley married her second cousin, Barker Lanham Hill, of Northfield and Campton (see Hill, VII). Sarah J. Cilley married Jacob Sanborn, and died at Franklin, this state, March 18, 1884, aged forty-seven. Susan died unmarried, December 5, 1886, aged fifty-eight. Hannah and Lydia died in early childhood. John Cilley married Maria Hibbard, and lives at Colebrook, New Hampshire.

(VI) Coloniel Timothy Hill, third son and fourth child of Captain Daniel (2) and Hannah (Emery) Hills, was born at Haverhill, Massachusetts, January 27, 1764. Like his father and grandfather he saw extended service in behalf of his country. He was commissioned colonel of the First New Hampshire Regiment, July 4, 1812, and took part in the three years' war with England. Either before or at the time of his marriage, which took place about 1793, he migrated to Northfield, New Hampshire, where he was one of the first settlers. Colonel Timothy Hill married Elizabeth Lapham, born in Haverhill, Massachusetts, September 18, 1771, and they had five children, all born in Northfield, New Hampshire: King L., born January 22, 1794, married Sally Gillman, settled in Sheffield, Vermont, had twelve children, and died December 22, 1868; Harriet, born September 13, 1797, married Lowell Land, of Sanbornton, New Hampshire, had eight children, and died at the early age of thirty-three, June 4, 1830; Warren L., born September 28, 1801, married Betsey Tucker, had seven children, and died at Northfield, March 23, 1887; Betsey, born October 1, 1803, married Furber A. Goodwin, had seven children; lived at Sheffield, Vermont, and died at forty-three years of age, April 18, 1846; Barker L., whose sketch follows. Colonel Timothy Hill died April 22, 1850, at the age of eighty-six, and his wife died August 17, 1845, aged seventy-four.

(VII) Barker Lapham, third son and fifth and youngest child of Colonel Timothy and Elizabeth (Lapham) Hill, was born at Northfield, New Hampshire, September 20, 1805. He lived in his native town till the age of twenty-seven, when he removed to Campton, this state, where for sixty years he was a successful farmer and useful citizen. He was a Whig in politics, later joining the Republican party, and he held the position of highway surveyor and other minor town offices. On January 7, 1835, Barker Lapham Hill married his cousin, Mary Ann Cilley, daughter of John and Betsey (Hills) Cilley, who was born at Columbia, Coos county, New Hampshire, September 16, 1815 (see Hill, VII). They had two children: Elizabeth L., born at Campton, February 10, 1837, married Abel Mitchell, of Bridgewater, New Hampshire; and Daniel C., whose sketch follows. Barker L. Hill died at Campton, January 21, 1895, aged eighty-eight, and his wife died at Campton, February 13, 1888, aged seventy-one.

(VIII) Daniel Cilley, younger child and only

Daniel C. Hill,

son of Barker Lapham and Mary A. (Cilley) Hill, was born at Campton, New Hampshire, November 28, 1844. He was educated in the schools of Campton, Plymouth Academy and Tilton Seminary. For the next five years after finishing his studies he taught school in Campton, Thornton, Bridgewater, Hebron and Holderness. He served six years on the school board of his native town. Mr. Hill continued to live on the old Hill homestead at Campton till May, 1895, when he moved to Ashland village, where he has since made his home. On January 17, 1902, he was elected president of the Ashland Savings Bank, and was also made trustee. During that year he engaged in the fire insurance business with Willis F. Hardy, which partnership continues until the present time. Mr. Hill is a Republican in politics, and attends the Methodist Episcopal Church. He was selectman of Ashland in 1902-03-04-08, and tax collector of his town during 1904-05. He is not married.

(Second Family.)

HILL (I) Abraham Hill, the first American ancestor of this branch of the family, was born in 1615, and was an inhabitant of Charlestown, Massachusetts, in 1636. He kept a mill for John Coitmore, and was the owner of five lots of land in Charlestown and the neighborhood. He was admitted to the church in 1639, and his wife, Sarah Long, daughter of Robert Long, born in England in 1617, was admitted to the church in 1644. Abraham and Sarah (Long) Hill were married in 1639, and had eight children: Ruth, baptized in 1640, married William Augur; Isaac, 1641; Abraham, 1643; Zachary, whose sketch follows; Sarah, 1647; Sarah, born and died in 1649; Mary, 1652; Jacob, March, 1656-57. Abraham Hill died February 13, 1669-70, and the inventory of his estate amounted to six hundred and thirty-three pounds.

(II) Zachary, third son and fourth child of Abraham and Sarah (Long) Hill, was born in Charlestown, Massachusetts, probably about 1645, though the record of his baptism is not given, as in the case of his brothers and sisters. On September 24, 1667, Zachary Hill married Deborah Norton, daughter of Captain Francis and Mary Norton, of Charlestown, and they had three children: Zachary, born November 10, 1668; Abraham, born about 1670; and Benjamin, who died intestate about 1698. Zachary Hill probably died at the age of twenty-seven, as the inventory of his estate was taken June 12, 1672. The estate was valued at eighty-six pounds, and that same year the widow sold a house, probably the homestead, to W. Stilson. Mrs. Deborah Hill afterwards married Matthew Griffin, and died in 1698.

(III) Abraham (2), second son and child of Zachary and Deborah (Norton) Hill, was born about 1670, probably at Charlestown, Massachusetts, though he lived afterwards at Cambridge. Abraham Hill married Sarah Cooper, daughter of Timothy Cooper, of Groton, Massachusetts, and they had three children: Abraham, who died February 11, 1723-24, in his thirtieth year; Deborah, born February 25, 1696-97; and Zachariah, whose sketch follows. Abraham Hill (2) died March 9, 1746, at Cambridge, aged seventy-five, and his widow died March 30, 1762, at Cambridge, in her eightieth year.

(IV) Zachariah, second son and youngest of the three children of Abraham (2) and Sarah (Cooper) Hill, was baptized April 2, 1707 or 1708. He lived at Cambridge, Massachusetts, where he was probably born. On February 10, 1731-32, he married Rebecca Cutter, daughter of Deacon John and Lydia Cutter, and they had eleven children, some of whose names are not recorded. They were Sarah, born 1732, married William Adams; Abraham, whose sketch follows; Zachariah, born in 1737; Samuel, born 1741; Rebecca, who married John Cutter (3); Susanna, married Thomas Francis; Deborah, born in 1756, married Nehemiah Cutter. Zachariah Hill died March 10 or 11, 1768, aged sixty years. On December 11, 1770, his widow married Samuel Carter, and died February 1, 1797.

(V) Abraham (3), eldest son and second child of Zachariah and Rebecca (Cutter) Hill, was born in 1734 at Menotomy, now Arlington, Massachusetts. He was one of the minute men at Concord and Lexington, and also fought at Bunker Hill. It is said that he and his next brother Zachariah had also served in the French and Indian wars. Abraham (3) Hill has a record of five enlistments during the Revolution, and his longest term of service at one time was nine months, July 27, 1779, to April 27, 1780. His service was mostly in the Thirty-seventh Regiment of Foot, commanded by Captain Benjamin Locke, and known as the "Menotomy Boys." Abraham (3) Hill married, February 16, 1757, Susanna Wellington, daughter of Thomas Wellington, of Cambridge, and they had at least seven children, of whom the names of the fourth, fifth and seventh only have been preserved: Thomas; Isaac, whose sketch follows; and Sarah, born in 1769, who married Thomas Rand. Abraham (3) Hill died December 16, 1812, at Menotomy, now Arlington, Massachusetts.

(VI) Isaac, fifth child of Abraham (3) and Susanna (Wellington) Hill, was born at Menotomy, now Arlington, Massachusetts, in 1766. At the age of nine years he took part in the battle of Bunker Hill. With his brother Thomas, who was but eleven at the time, the boy Isaac drove a heavy rack, loaded probably with hay, which was used to fill the redoubts, and they were fired upon by cannon. Such childish heroism recalls Kipling's tale, "The Drums of the Fore and Aft," which had been thought to be almost without a parallel. The early life of Isaac Hill was one continued struggle. His father returned at the close of the revolution to take charge of a large family, who were nearly destitute, owing to the circumstances of the times, and the depreciation of his wages caused complete financial ruin.

Isaac Hill married, in 1787, Hannah Russell, daughter of Walter and Hannah (Adams) Russell, who was born in that part of Menotomy, now Charlestown, Massachusetts. She was a descendant of William Russell, the English emigrant, who came to Cambridge, Massachusetts, in 1645. Her father, Walter Russell, commanded a company of Alarmists at Lexington, and did great service in harassing the enemy. Walter Russell died March 5, 1783, aged forty-five years. Isaac and Hannah (Russell) Hill had nine children, four boys and five girls, and the mother of this family was but fifteen when she was married. The children were: Governor Isaac, whose sketch follows; Walter Russell, born February 22, 1790; Hannah Russell, born October 31, 1792, married George E. Cushing; Sultina, born June 2, 1795, married Reuben Townsend; Susan Wellington, born October 3, 1797, married Charles Hastings; Mary Adams, born July 10, 1800, married, August 26, 1820, Jacob Bailey Moore, a prominent publisher and historian of Concord, New Hampshire, and postmaster of San Francisco from 1849 to 1852; George Washington, born Jan. 4, 1804, lived at Montpelier where he was editor of the *Vermont Patriot;* Horatio, born March 19, 1807, was in the publishing business early in life, and afterwards moved to Chicago; Rebecca Russell, born July 3, 1810, married John R. Reding, member of congress from Massachusetts, 1841-45. Mrs. Reding died January 28, 1844, and the house adjourned to enable the members to attend her funeral, the first time such a mark of respect had been paid to a woman. Isaac Hill's health had become impaired, and the management of affairs fell upon his wife, who contrived to save enough out of their ruined fortunes to purchase a farm at Ashburnham, Massachusetts, where the whole family moved in the spring of 1798. In 1819 the farm was sold and the family removed to the central village, where Isaac Hill died December 23, 1843, aged seventy-seven; his wife died March 1, 1847, aged seventy-five.

(VII) Governor Isaac (2), eldest child of Isaac (1) and Hannah (Russell) Hill, was born at the home of his maternal grandfather at Menotomy, now Arlington, Massachusetts, April 6, 1788. His early educational opportunities were exceedingly limited, even for those times. Being the oldest of a large family, who were practically deprived of a father's support, he was his mother's chief assistant, and was early inured to constant labor. Although of weak constitution he did hard work on the farm at Ashburnham, Massachusetts, where the family moved when he was ten years of age. He had such limited schooling as the place afforded, and was an inveterate reader of everything that came in his way. Before the age of eight he had read the Bible entirely through in course, and even a few tattered leaves of Baxter's "Call to the Unconverted" were devoured with eagerness. Ashburnham at that time was twelve miles from the nearest post-town, but some of the inhabitants had formed a sort of club for the purpose of taking a small weekly paper, then published in Leominster. It was this sheet that probably determined Mr. Hill's subsequent career. Meanwhile he extracted all the information that he could from the neighboring district schools, sometimes walking four or five miles during the storms of winter in the daily pursuit of knowledge. He was a good speaker, even at the age of seven, and a ready debater. His thirst for knowledge led him to look upon the printer's trade as the ideal occupation, and at the age of fourteen the longed-for opportunity came. Joseph Cushing had just established the *Amherst Cabinet* at Amherst, New Hampshire, and was in need of an apprentice. Hearing good accounts of young Hill, he went to see him, and was somewhat surprised to find the future governor in ragged working clothes, laboring on the farm. But Mr. Cushing was sensible enough to see the bright mind and sterling qualities that lay beneath the unprepossessing exterior, and a bargain was soon concluded. On December 3, 1802, Isaac (2) Hill as an apprentice began his residence in the state of which he was subsequently to become the most influential citizen of his time. Mr. Hill remained in the office of the *Amherst Cabinet* for seven years, thoroughly mastering the details of the printing and newspaper business, ever faithful to the interests of his employer, and educating himself by hard study after his day's work was over. During his stay in Amherst he became a member of the Young Men's Debating Club, and the record of this society in his elegant and clerky handwriting are still preserved. On April 5, 1809, the day before he was twenty-one, he set out for Concord, which was to be his future home. About the same time his employer, Mr. Cushing, removed to Baltimore, Maryland, where he conducted a printing and book-selling establishment for many years. Six months before young Hill went to Concord, William Hoit had started a struggling sheet called the *American Patriot*. Prominent members of the Republican (Democratic) party advised Mr. Hill to purchase the newspaper and become the editor and publisher. Two weeks later, April 18, 1809, he issued the first number of the *New Hampshire Patriot*. My Hill's incisive style and able utterances soon attracted attention, and the paper, in spite of the bitter opposition, began to increase in circulation, till in a few short years it exceeded that of any other in the state, and the influence of the young editor had become unbounded. This result was not accomplished without a desperate struggle with rival sheets, some of which poured out vials of abuse, which would not be tolerated in these days. As illustrating the style of calumny that influenced the public mind, one opponent thought he had made a strong point by getting some astute antiquary to discover that Mr. Hill was a lineal descendant on both sides of the first witches who were hung in Salem! The personal power that Mr. Hill afterwards exercised and that keeps his name a household word in the state, even to this day, might well be attributed to something more than human.

Governor Hill edited the *Patriot* for twenty years, and during that time was twice chosen clerk of the state senate, once representative from Concord, and was four times elected to the state senate, 1820, 1821, 1822 and 1827. In 1829, soon after Jackson became president, he appointed Mr. Hill to the office of second comptroller of the Treasury Department, and he assumed his duties at Washington on March 21 of that year. The strong friendship between these notable men dates from this time, and was destined to continue unbroken till death. Mr. Hill held the office till April, 1830, and performed its duties in an eminently satisfactory manner, but the Senate, owing to the bitter personal animosities of the day, refused to confirm the appointment, and the future governor was forced to retire. He returned to his own state where his popularity was unbounded, and two months later the New Hampshire legislature triumphantly elected him to the United States senate, where he took his seat March 4, 1831. He remained there five years, and was one of Jackson's most intimate advisers, but in 1836, having been elected governor of the state by the unprecedented majority of nearly nine thousand votes, he resigned his seat to become chief executive of New Hampshire. He was re-elected governor in 1837 and 1838, and during all this time he was the popular idol, and had a personal following which has probably never been equalled in the state before or since. In 1840 Governor Hill was appointed by President Van Buren to the office of sub-treasurer at Boston, which place he held till March, 1841, when he was removed by the incoming administration. From that time till his death, ten years later, he was without public office; but in 1840, in connection with his two oldest sons, he established *Hill's New Hampshire Patriot*, which they published till 1847, when it was united with the original *Patriot*, which had been under different management. Governor Hill also edited and published the *Farmer's Monthly Visitor* for about ten years, and during the last fifteen years of his life he was extensively engaged in agriculture on his own account.

On February 2, 1814, Isaac (2) Hill married Susanna Ayer, eldest daughter and sixth child of Richard and Susanna (Sargent) Ayer, members of prominent Concord families. Mrs. Hill was a woman of strong character, marked personality and a notable housekeeper. She was born February 24, 1789, and lived till June 17, 1880, dying at her home on School street, in Concord, at the age of ninety-one years, three months and twenty-four days. Mr. and Mrs. Hill were active in establishing the Episcopal Church in Concord, of which they were ever after interested and influential supporters. Isaac (2) and Susanna (Ayer) Hill had four children: William Pickering, born October 19, 1819; John McClary, November 5, 1821; Georgiana Toscan, October 1, 1824, died September 12, 1825; and Isaac Andrew, September 16, 1827.

William P. Hill graduated from Dartmouth College in 1839, was for several years editor and proprietor of the Portsmouth (New Hampshire) *Gazette*, and was afterwards associated with his father and brother on the *New Hampshire Patriot*. He subsequently held a position in the Boston custom house, and died, February 17, 1901, at the home of his eldest daughter, Mrs. Robert Williams, at Denver, Colorado. On October 26, 1843, William P. Hill married Clara Ann West, daughter of John and Nancy (Montgomery) West and a sister of the wife of Senator Edward H. Rollins. The children of William P. and Clara (West) Hill were: Isaac William, born March 19, 1846, died December 22, 1903; Anna Montgomery, April 27, 1851; Susan Ayer, August 7, 1854; Ellen Russell, October 19, 1857, died in infancy; and Clara Turner, July 23, 1860, died June 26, 1872. Anna Montgomery Hill married Robert R. Williams, of Denver, Colorado, February 14, 1880. Their children were: Clara Turner Williams, born July 28, 1882, at Concord, New Hampshire, died at Denver, Colorado, February 15, 1889; and Edward Rollins Williams, born at Pitkin, Colorado, November 30, 1884. Susan Ayer Hill married, in April, 1882, Honorable James O. Lyford, at the present time naval officer of the port of Boston. Their children were: Agnes McLean Lyford, born April 6, 1884, at Concord, died at Denver, Colorado, January 21, 1891; Katharine Batchelder Lyford, born at Concord, November 11, 1888, died at Denver, February 1, 1903; and Richard Taylor Lyford, born January 6, 1896.

John McClary, second son of Governor Isaac (2) and Susannah (Ayer) Hill, was educated at the academy at South Berwick, Maine. He was for many years connected with the New Hampshire *Patriot*, served as treasurer of the Concord Gas Company for a long period, was Democratic candidate for governor in 1884, and died March 4, 1900. He was one of the most prominent and respected citizens of Concord, and a gentleman of the old school. John M. Hill married (first) Elizabeth Lord Chase, whose youth was spent in South Berwick, Maine. They were married November 15, 1843, and there were two children: Howard Fremont born July 21, 1846; and Robert Waterston, June 20, 1852, died January 15, 1854. Reverend Howard Fremont Hill, Ph. D., D. D., a clergyman of the Episcopal Church, was graduated from Dartmouth College in 1867, and is now living in Concord. Dr. Howard F. Hill married, October 17, 1870, Laura Sophia Tebbetts, daughter of Dr. Hiram B. and Laura S. (Watson) Tebbetts, who was born in Carroll parish, Louisiana, October 17, 1847. Their children were: John McClary Hill, born October 30, 1871, died December 4, 1872; Maria Dix Hill, December 11, 1873; and Grace Watson Hill, June 21, 1876. Maria D. Hill was married, February 11, 1907, to John Archibald Campbell, an electrical engineer, and they are now living in Rio de Janeiro, Brazil. Grace W. Hill was married, November 28, 1899, to Zolieth Sparrow Freeman, vice-president of the Merchants' National Bank, New York City. Mr. and Mrs. Freeman have two daughters: Laura, born February 9, 1901; and Mary, December 5, 1902.

Governor Isaac (2) Hill died in his sixty-third year at Washington, D. C., March 22, 1851, after an illness of five weeks, and is buried in the family lot at Blossom Hill cemetery, Concord, New Hampshire.

(VIII) Isaac Andrew, third son and fourth and youngest child of Governor Isaac and Susanna (Ayer) Hill, was born at Concord, New Hampshire, September 16, 1827, and died there February 28, 1903. He was educated in the public schools of his native town, in the Concord Literary Institution and at Phillips Andover Academy. During vacations he learned the printer's trade in his father's office where *The New Hampshire Patriot* was published. After leaving school he went to Boston, and was in the employ of Sayles, Merriam & Brewer, wholesale commission merchants, where he remained about five years. During this period Mr. Hill dwelt in the same house with John A. Andrew, afterward the distinguished war governor of Massachusetts, with whom he formed a pleasant friendship. Returning to Concord in 1849 he entered the *Patriot* office, where he remained till 1856. In that year he was appointed register of probate for Merrimack county, which office he held for eighteen years, or until 1874, when a change in politics caused a turn-over in appointive positions. In 1876 he was appointed deputy collector of internal revenue, which place he held till 1883. During the remainder of his life he was an active promoter of various enterprises connected with the upbuilding of Concord. The Board of Trade and the building which bears its name were the outgrowth of his foresight and energy. The incorporation of the Merrimack County Savings Bank, of which he was a trustee and the first depositor, the extension of Pleasant street, and the projection of the "New History of Concord" are some of the enterprises which should be credited to his public spirit and active endeavor. More petitions of a civic nature, looking toward the betterment of Concord, were presented to the city government through his instrumentality than came from any other source.

In politics Mr. Hill departed from the traditions of his family and became a strong Republican, though he did not care to hold office. In church associations he always kept to the faith in which he had been reared, although his religious sympathies were broad and inclusive. When an infant he was baptized in Saint Andrew's Church, Hopkinton, there being no Episcopal Church in Concord at the time. His parents helped to found Saint Paul's Church at the capital, and his constant services and best efforts during his mature years were given to the development of that parish. Mr. Hill not only did things himself, but he incited others to do them, and some of the most valuable gifts that Saint Paul's Church has received in recent years, may be traced to his suggestion. He was a member of Blazing Star Lodge, Ancient Free and Accepted Masons. Mr. Hill was an ardent lover of nature, and in his early life was skilled with the rod and gun, but he was no hunter merely. It was the out-door life and the poetry of the woods that appealed to him.

On October 5, 1858, Isaac Andrew Hill married Sarah Anne Sanderson, second daughter and child of Charles and Hannah Amanda (Stevens) Sanderson, who was born at Pittsfield, New Hampshire, September 19, 1839. She was educated at Pittsfield Academy and graduated from the high school at Lowell, Massachusetts, in 1857. She taught school a year in Concord, giving up the occupation upon her marriage at the early age of nineteen. Mrs. Hill was a member of the Congregational Church in Pittsfield during youth, but became a communicant of St. Paul's Church (Episcopal) in Concord soon after her marriage. She has been active in the parish work of that church, and has been especially interested in the Orphans' Home at Millville, serving at one time as chairman of the Building Committee and also as one of the committee appointed by Bishop Niles to decide on admissions to the home. Mrs. Hill was one of the directresses of the Concord Female Charitable Society from 1883 to 1886. A member of the Concord Woman's Club, she served as chairman of the committee on science from 1899 to 1902; and from 1901 to 1904 she was president of the Wild Flower Club.

Mr. and Mrs. Hill have had six children: Walter Bertram, born March 23, 1860; Josiah French, July 25, 1863; Charles Sanderson, July 4, 1867; Isaac, September 3, 1869; Andrew, April 8, and died August 8, 1872; Lawrence, February 3, 1878. Walter B. Hill studied civil engineering, and followed the profession for several years. In 1888 he went to Colorado and in 1892 to Montana, where he became superintendent of irrigation for the Crow Reservation. He is now government inspector of irrigation in all the Indian reservations. Josiah F. Hill was graduated from the Concord high school in 1880, and from Dartmouth College in 1884. He began railroad life in the auditing department of the Union Pacific at Omaha, advancing to assistant to the vice-president; then went to Washington D. C., where he was assistant to the vice-president of the Southern railway; finally becoming secretary of that railway in New York City. In 1900 he removed to Boston to become statistican of the firm of Lee Higginson and Company, bankers, with whom he has since remained. On December 28, 1887, he married Blanche Theodora Ford, of Concord, and they have two children: Gerald Ford, born December 29, 1892, and Blanche Theodora, February 21, 1903. Charles Sanderson Hill was appointed to the Naval Academy at Annapolis in 1883, and remained there over three years. At the beginning of the Spanish war he volunteered for service in the United States Marine Corps, and was appointed second lieutenant. He was assigned to immediate duty at Annapolis, and was placed in charge of the Spanish officers, who had been taken prisoners. He was subsequently appointed first lieutenant and went immediately to the Philippines, where he was stationed three and one-half years. He was made a captain in 1900, and is now in Cuba. Isaac Hill was educated in the public schools of his native city, and is now cashier of the National State Capital Bank at Concord, having been in the employ of that institution since 1887. He is a member of the Wonolancet Club, the Canoe Club, the Sons of the American Revolution, also of Blazing Star Lodge, Ancient Free and Accepted Masons. Lawrence Richardson Hill was graduated from the Concord high school in 1898, from Dartmouth College in 1902, and from Harvard Medical School in 1907. He is now assistant surgeon in the Massachusetts Soldiers' Home at Chelsea, Massachusetts.

(Third Family.)

HILL An examination of the records relative to the early history of the Hills in America discloses the fact that there were several immigrants of this name who arrived from England prior to 1650, namely: John Hill, of Dorchester, Massachusetts; John Hill, of Dover, New Hampshire, who was accompanied by at least one brother and perhaps more; and Peter Hill, of Saco, Maine. There are some slight indications that Dr. Gardner C. Hill, of Keene, is a descendant of Peter Hill, through the latter's son Roger, although conclusive evidence to that effect is lacking.

(I) Peter Hill probably settled near the mouth of the Saco river prior to 1648, in which year he joined the assembly in Liconia or Ligonia. He was accompanied from England by his son Roger, and both took the freeman's oath in 1653. Peter was one of the dissatisfied planters of York county who petitioned to have that territory admitted to the colony of Massachusetts. He died in 1667. The maiden name of his wife and the christian name of his other children (if there were others) are wanting.

(II) Roger, son of Peter Hill, was identified with his father in the settlement of Saco, and served as constable in 1661. It is supposed that he, with others, went to Salem, Massachusetts, in 1678, in order to escape Indian hostilities, but he returned to Saco later, and his death occurred there in 1696. In 1658 he married Sarah Cross, of Wells, Maine, and was the father of John, Samuel, Joseph, Benjamin, who died young; Ebenezer, Sarah, Hannah and Mercy. His son Samuel, who commanded a packet, engaged in transporting supplies from Boston to the ports eastward during the Indian wars, was, with his wife, captured by the French and Indians about the year 1701, and taken to Canada, where both were held as prisoners for a number of years. Ebenezer was betrayed by supposed friendly savages into captivity, but eventually secured his freedom, and died at Saco in 1745, aged seventy-nine years. John Hill, son of Roger, was commissioned an ensign in King William's war and rose to the rank of captain. The latter's brother Joseph resided in Wells and died there in 1743. He married Sarah Bowles, daughter of Joseph Bowles, of Wells (see Bowles), and a sister of Mary, wife of Major Charles Frost, of Kittery. Roger Hill's daughter Sarah married (first) Pendleton Fletcher, a prominent resident of Saco, who died a prisoner in Canada, and she married for her second husband William Priest. Her sister Hannah married Lieutenant Joseph Stover, at one time commander of the garrison at Wells, and was the ancestor of men of distinction, including Hon. Joseph Stover, Commodore Stover, United States navy, and Professor D. H. Stover, of Boston. Mercy Hill married Daniel Littlefield, and was the ancestor of many of that name in Wells and Kennebunk, Maine (see Littlefield). It is impossible to determine with accuracy the two succeeding generations in this line of descent. Information forwarded to the writer from Keene states that Roger Hill, great-grandfather of Dr. Hill, was born (perhaps) in 1750, but fails to mention his birthplace. There is, however, sufficient evidence to prove that his birth must have taken place several years prior to that date. It is reasonable to suppose that this Roger was a descendant of Peter in the fifth generation. Roger is known to have resided in Winchester, New Hampshire, but as the history of that town is yet to be written, no further information relative to him or his family is obtainable in the Boston genealogical collections.

(VI) Jonathan Hill, son of Roger Hill, was a native of Winchester, and when a young man removed from that town to Swanzey. At the break-

Gardner C. Hill

ing out of the American Revolution he enlisted in the Continental army and participated in the battle of Bunker Hill. He afterward returned to Winchester and resided there for the remainder of his life. He married Rusella Combs, of Winchester, and his children were: George, born in 1777; Reuben, the date of whose birth is not given; Joseph, born in October, 1781; Sally, born April 2, 1787, married Seth Leonard; Barney, whose birth date is also wanting; Jonathan, born October 14, 1792; David, born February 14, 1794; Caleb, who will be again referred to; Elisha, born April 12, 1800; Betsey, who became the wife of John Sanderson: Massa, who married George Darling; and Mary, who married Seth Pomroy, of Swanzey.

(VII) Caleb Hill, seventh son and eighth child of Jonathan and Rusella (Combs) Hill, was born in 1798. For a period of forty years he cultivated a farm in Winchester with prosperous results, and he died in that town at the age of fifty-eight years. He married Polly Howard, of Winchester, who bore him eight children, namely: Maria, Mary Sophia, Gardner C., Jonathan, Elmina D., Maria H. (died young), Elvira L. and Laura A.

(VIII) Gardner Caleb Hill, M. D., third of the children of Caleb and Polly (Howard) Hill, was born in Winchester, March 20, 1829. From the public schools of his native town he went to the Mount Caesar Seminary, Swanzey, and thence to the Seminary in Saxton's River, Vermont, where he was graduated in 1853. He subsequently taught school in Swanzey, Keene and Winchester. His preliminary professional preparations were pursued under the preceptorship of Dr. D. L. Comings, of West Swanzey, and he took his degree at the Castleton (Vermont) Medical College in 1856. These studies were augmented with a course at the Harvard Medical School. The first nine years of his professional career were spent in Warwick, Massachusetts, and during the whole of that period he served as a member of the board of education. From 1867 to the present time (1906) he has practiced medicine in Keene, and has attained a high reputation as a skillful and reliable physician. For seven years he served as city physician, and held the post of county physician for nearly that length of time; is a member of the board of United States penson examiners; of the staff of the Elliott City Hospital, and is medical examiner for the Aetna Life Insurance Company. For the past thirty-one years he has served upon the board of education of Keene, has also served as county treasurer two years, county commissioner three years, and in the city council three years. Aside from his professional and political services, which have proved exceedingly beneficial to the community, he devotes considerable time to other fields of usefulness, and as president of the Keene Savings Bank his integrity and sound judgment in financial matters are heartily appreciated. Dr. Hill affiliates with the New Hampshire State and Cheshire County Medical societies, and the Connecticut Valley Medical Association and the American Medical Association.

For his first wife he married, in 1856, Frances R. Howard, of Walpole, New Hampshire, who died early in 1864. A year later he married Caroline R. Hutchins, of Keene, daughter of Benjamin Hutchins. He has an adopted son, William H. Hill.

(Fourth Family.)

HILL Among the earliest New Hampshire names this has baffled genealogists in the effort to trace direct descent to persons now living in the state. Its bearers were evidently much more intent upon conquering the wilderness, preparing farms and providing for themselves and their families than they were in recording their achievements. That they bore their share in the struggle with the savage foe in the forbidding wilderness there can be no doubt. In the days when the ancestors of this family were making their way in New Hampshire every man was compelled to fight the savage foe as well as to labor industriously and unceasingly to clear the forest and make a home for himself and his posterity.

(I) John Hill, no doubt of English birth, was in Dover, New Hampshire, as early as 1649, for we find him on the list of those taxed in that year. It is probable that he was the same John Hill who was married in Boston, January 16, 1656, to Elizabeth Strong, for John Hill, whose wife was Elizabeth, received a grant of land at Oyster River (now Durham) in 1656 and three subsequent grants. He was a grand juryman from Dover in 1668 and 1671, and in 1683 he was defendant in one of the many suits brought by John Mason, which proves that he was a land owner. Evidently he was annoyed by the suits for about this time he was summoned to court at Great Island for saying "he did not judge that neither the king nor Mason had anything to do here." He was taxed in Dover as late as 1684. In 1659 he gave a deposition, saying he was about thirty-five years of age, from which it would seem that he was born about 1624. He had sons: Joseph, Samuel, John and Benjamin. (Mention of John and descendants appears in this article.)

(II) Samuel, son of John Hill, resided in what was then Massachusetts and what are now Maine and New Hampshire. He purchased land and moved to Kittery prior to 1696. A deed on record shows that he was residing there at that time with his family. His name appears in other records and on various petitions. He was once summoned in answer to a claim of the proprietors of the province in a plea of trespass with his father. He owned estates in Portsmouth which then included a large district, and some of his sons were settled in what is now New Hampshire on these lands. On February 9, 1695, he purchased an estate at Strawberry Bank of Samuel Cutts. His will was executed August 28, 1713, at which time he was in Portsmouth but called himself of Kittery. His will was probated in 1723, which approximately indicates the time of his death. He was married, October 28, 1680, to Elizabeth Williams, who was probably a daughter of William and Mary Williams, as all these parties joined in a deed of land at Oyster River in 1696. His wife survived him and administered his estate. His children were: John, Elizabeth, Mary, Hannah, Abigail, Samuel, Sarah, Benjamin and Joseph.

(III) Samuel (2), second son and sixth child of Samuel (1) and Elizabeth (Williams) Hill, was born December 13, 1696, probably in Kittery. He resided in that part of that town which in 1810 was incorporated as Elliot, and was an original member of the Congregational Church which was organized there in 1721. He subsequently settled upon a part of the ancestral estate which is in what is now Durham, New Hampshire, but little record of his movements can be found. He was married, November 22, 1716, to Mary, daughter of John and Elizabeth (Haley) Nelson, of Newington. His children were: Elizabeth, Samuel, Benjamin, Nelson, Joseph, George, Catherine, Temperance, Mary and John.

(IV) Samuel (3), eldest son and second child

of Samuel (2) and Mary (Nelson) Hill, was born December 12, 1719, probably in Kittery, and grew up in Durham, at Oyster river. He became a large landholder there, and left a good estate. Among his sons were Samuel and Benjamin. (Mention of the latter and descendants appears in this article.)

(V) Samuel (4), son of Samuel (3) Hill, of Durham, was the owner of a large estate in Durham, as evidenced by the number of land transfers on record. He married Hannah Longley, of Durham, and settled in Loudon, New Hampshire, before 1782. Their children were: Levi, Samuel, Parvis, Hannah, Thomas and Sarah.

(VI) Levi, eldest son of Samuel (4) and Hannah (Longley) Hill, was born May 5, 1782, in Loudon, where he passed his life, engaged in agriculture. He was married, September 12, 1802, in Canterbury, by Rev. Winthrop Young, to Lydia Wiggin, of Canterbury, and they were the parents of four sons and one daughter. Langdon, Joseph and Franklin resided in Springfield, New Hampshire. Susan was the wife of Rev. Timothy Coe, an Advent clergyman, of Haverhill, Massachusetts. Mention of the other son follows.

(VII) Cyrus, third son of Levi and Lydia (Wiggin) Hill, was born in 1815, in Loudon, and spent most of his life in Concord. In early life he learned the hatter's trade, and this he followed industriously and successfully. On account of impaired health he paid a visit to Minnesota, and thereafter made annual trips to that state to look after his business interests there. He became owner, in partnership with a Mr. White, of Claremont, New Hampshire, of a stage line, and also dealt extensively in ginseng root, making his headquarters at Faribault. He did a large business for many years in this herb, which found a ready sale in China, and realized a handsome profit from it. This illustrates his readiness to perceive and grasp an opportunity. Mr. Hill continued his residence in Concord until his death, which occurred April 10, 1875, and built the Cyrus Hill Building, which was completed in 1869. He was a staunch Democrat of the old school, was a member of St. Paul's Episcopal parish, and of the Independent Order of Odd Fellows, in which he filled the chairs of honor. He was a major of militia, and represented ward four of Concord in the state legislature. He was married, November 26, 1838, to Nancy L. Walker, a daughter of William Walker, of Concord (see Walker). They had ten children, of whom four are now living. Mention of William W. follows. Charles C. resides in Concord. Frank Pierce has charge of the Carnegie libraries in Brooklyn, New York. Mary W. is the widow of Hon. Fletcher Ladd, of Lancaster, New Hampshire.

(VIII) William Walker, son of Cyrus and Nancy L. (Walker) Hill, was born December 13, 1844, in Concord, and his home has ever been in that city. His education was supplied by its public schools and Pembroke and New London academies. In early life he was a clerk for his father, and became a partner in the business of the latter in 1869, which was discontinued soon after the death of the senior partner. In 1877 Mr. W. W. Hill was appointed a postal clerk in the railway mail service, and continued in that capacity for a period of eight years, resigning in March, 1885. In the following summer he was proprietor of the Winslow House, a summer hotel at Kearsarge, this state, and next year kept the Hotel Champlain at Maquam, Vermont. In January, 1887, following the death of his father-in-law, he became associated in the management of the Quincy House in Boston, one of the finest hotels in New England, and so continued three years. Mr. Hill is among the most steadfast supporters of Republican principles, and he has taken active part in public affairs in his home city and state. He served as ward clerk, and was appointed commissioner of deeds for Merrimack county, which position he filled creditably. Under Governor Sawyer he was appointed as liquor commissioner of the state, but did not serve, and he is ever ready to bear the part of a good citizen. Of social and genial nature, he enjoys the esteem of a large number of acquaintances. He was married, October 15, 1873, at Enfield Centre, New Hampshire, to Ella H. Johnson, daughter of James Willis Johnson (see Johnson). They had two daughters, Blanche and Gretchen, both of whom died in childhood.

(V) Benjamin (2), son of Samuel Hill, of Durham, was born probably about the year 1745, and it was he who left his home town and planted a branch of the family in Northwood, New Hampshire, having moved to that town from Epping, New Hampshire. He married Elizabeth Dudley, daughter of Nicholas and Elizabeth (Gordon) Dudley, of Brentwood, New Hampshire. She died about 1810 or 1811, having borne her husband ten children. Sarah, who married Colonel Samuel Sherborn. Nicholas Dudley, a soldier of the Revolution, and was with his father when he died at Ticonderoga, September 17, 1776. Jonathan, born in Epping, married Abigail Tilton. Elizabeth, married Nathaniel Dearborn, of Epping. Benjamin, married Lydia Bunker, of Barnstead. Samuel, married Judith Carr, of Epping. Deborah, married John Prescott, of Epsom. Trueworthy, married (first) a Miss Drew, and (second) Mrs. Chapman, and (third) a Miss Mathes. Noah, married Nancy Furber. Abigail, married a Miss Rowe, of Allenstown.

(VI) Samuel, third son and sixth child of Benjamin and Elizabeth (Dudley) Hill, was born in 1768, and died December 22, 1854. His wife, Judith (Carr) Hill, was born in 1771, and died November 4, 1864. They had twelve children, nine sons and three daughters, viz.: Chase C., born 1792, died November 28, 1868; married Comfort Palmer, of Deerfield, New Hampshire. Dudley C., born 1795, married (first) Judith Bartlett, (second) Mrs. Elizabeth Blake. Samuel, born 1797, died 1875; married Sally Edgerly, of Acton, Maine. Mary, born 1799, died at Worcester, Massachusetts; married (first) Daniel Hoitt, of Northwood, and (second) John Oakes. Joseph, born March 11, 1801, married, March 21, 1821, Matilda Danielson, born at Northwood, April 1, 1805, died March 6, 1868. Charlotte, born 1803, married Aaron Boody, of Barrington. John C., born March 26, 1805. Edson, born September 13, 1807, married Olive J. Durgin, of Northwood. Eliza, born 1809, died in infancy. Mark P., born 1812, married Mary Davis, of Boston. Charles C., born 1814, married Elizabeth Smith. Oliver N., born 1816, died 1855; married Elizabeth Bent, of Boston.

(VII) John C., seventh child of Samuel and Judith (Carr) Hill, was born in Northwood, New Hampshire, March 26, 1805, and died in that town, August 28, 1890. During early manhood he became a blacksmith and worked some time at that trade, but his chief occupation in life was farming. His wife was Rebecca J. Bartlett, daughter of Philip Bartlett. She was born in Northwood, June 30, 1807, and died in that town January 9, 1894. John C. Hill and his wife enjoyed worthy companionship for many years, lived a quiet home life together and attended regularly at the Baptist Church. Their

ROSCOE HILL.

family was not large, and comprised three children, one son and two daughters: Ivory B., see forward. Lauretta C., born April 21, 1838, married, May 20, 1868, Charles M. Perry, of Barrington, New Hampshire. Emily A., born May 4, 1845, married, May 1, 1865, Frank H. Bennett.

(VIII) Ivory B., only son and eldest child of John C. and Rebecca J. (Bartlett) Hill, was born in Northwood, New Hampshire, November 17, 1833, died April 21, 1906. For many years he had been a prominent man in that town, and for more than twenty-five years engaged in the lumber business and otherwise had been identified with its best interests. In religious preference he followed the instruction of his parents and was a Baptist, and in politics by birth and inclination a strong Democrat. On December 31, 1854, Mr. Hill married Eliza Fogg, who was born in Northwood, October 22, 1835. Their four children are: Roscoe Eugene P., born in Northwood, December 3, 1858, married Grace Babb and lives in Pittsfield, New Hampshire; Clarence I., born in Northwood, July 22, 1860, and lives in that town; Alice, born in Northwood, December 26, 1861, married Rev. W. F. Ineson, and lives in Littleton, New Hampshire; and Roscoe, born in Northwood, October 9, 1856.

(IX) Roscoe, oldest son of Ivory B. and Eliza (Fogg) Hill, was born in the town of Northwood, New Hampshire, October 9, 1856, and obtained his earlier education in public schools and Coe's Northwood Academy. Having determined to enter the medical profession, he took a course of preparatory studies and then matriculated at Bellevue Hospital Medical College in New York City (now the medical department of New York University), graduating with the degree of M. D. in 1882. He began his professional career at Norfolk, Connecticut, remained there two years, then practiced two years at Lynn, Massachusetts, and in 1887 located permanently at Epsom, New Hampshire. For twenty years Dr. Hill has engaged in active practice in the eastern part of Merrimack county and the northern part of Rockingham county, and is well known in medical circles in that part of the state. He has a good practice, and an excellent standing with men of his profession and in their organizations. He has passed all the chairs of Evergreen Lodge, Independent Order of Odd Fellows, member of Epsom Grange, No. 102, Patrons of Husbandry, member of the Baptist Church, and in politics is a Democrat. Dr. Hill married, October 29, 1884, Flora J. Holt, who was born in Pembroke, New Hampshire, August 22, 1857, daughter of Thomas R. and Esther M. (Parker) Holt, both natives of Pembroke.

(II) John (2), son of John (1) and Elizabeth (Strong) Hill, was born 1661, probably in Dover. The time is fixed by a deposition made by him, saying he was eighteen years of age, in 1679. He settled in Squamscot Patent, then in Exeter and near the present line of Greenland. He was styled "of Portsmouth" in 1716. When Stratham was incorporated it was ordered that the new town include Squamscot Patent, "except the farms of John Hill, Thomas Letherly, Enoch Bartlett and Michael Hicks, which shall belong to the parish of Greenland." In 1710 John Hill, "formerly of Strawberry Bank, now of the parish of Greenland," sold land in Portsmouth and Greenland. In the deeds his occupation is said to be a mason. His estate was in probate in 1781. No record of his marriage has been found. His sons were: Joshua, Joseph, John, and Benjamin. (The last named and descendants receive mention in this article).

(III) Joshua, probably eldest son of John (2) Hill, was the administrator of his father's estate. His petition was signed by Joseph, John and Benjamin, sons of the deceased. He lived in Stratham, where he was a farmer, and died soon after 1776. The name of his wife was Rachel. She survived him a dozen or more years, dying September 7, 1784, in Stratham. The only children found on record were Jane and Joseph. The former was born in 1731, and married in 1756, Jacob Rundlett, and lived in Stratham.

(IV) Joseph, son of Joshua and Rachel Hill, was born May 17, 1743, in Stratham, and resided in that town. He signed the association test there in 1776, and was a soldier in the Revolution. His wife's name was Molly, and they had eleven children born between 1765 and 1785, namely: Reuben, Joshua, Jonathan, Rachel, Molly, James, Polly, Lydia, Nancy, Betty and David.

(V) Joshua, son of Joseph and Molly Hill, was born November 27, 1766, in Stratham, where he lived and was engaged in farming. He died September 7, 1830, aged sixty-seven years. He married Lucy Chase, daughter of Moses and Anna (Rollins) Chase, of Stratham. She died July 8, 1834, aged seventy years.

(VI) Chase, son of Joshua and Lucy (Chase) Hill, was born at Stratham, May 20, 1795. He married Nancy Moore, of Stratham, born October 6, 1793, died December 14, 1881, aged eighty-eight years. Chase Hill died May 23, 1873, aged seventy-eight. He served at Portsmouth in the war of 1812, and was always known in later years as Colonel Hill. He was engaged in the leather business. He removed with his family to Concord, and resided there until the time of his death. The children of Chase and Nancy (Moore) Hill were: Elizabeth, Sarah, Thomas P., James R., Frances A., Hannah M. and Henry C.

(VII) James Riggs, fourth child and second son of Chase and Nancy (Moore) Hill, was born in Stratham, December 17, 1821, and came with his parents to Concord in 1836. Soon afterward he entered the employ of Abbott & Downing, and later served an apprenticeship with Greeley & Morrill, harness makers. In 1842 Oliver Greeley and J. R. Hill formed a partnership as Greely & Hill, and went into the harness manufacturing business. It was not long until Mr. Hill became sole proprietor of the business, which he continued until 1865, when the firm of James R. Hill & Company was formed to succeed him. This change was necessitated by Mr. Hill becoming interested in various other enterprises in the city, so that he was unable to devote all his time as formerly to the harness business. The partners in the company were J. R. Hill, George H. Emery and Josiah E. Dwight. They manufactured what was known as the "Concord harness," which became famous for its excellence throughout the civilized world. The quality of the harness was due to Mr. Hill's supervision of the business, in which he spent a large share of his time daily, until the end of his life. The events following the discovery of gold in California created a great demand for harness there in 1849, and in that year he made the first shipment of harness from any eastern point to that region. Four years later he made a shipment to Chile, South America. The profits of the harness business were very large, and were invested by Mr. Hill in real estate and in the erection of buildings. He built large blocks that were first-class structures, and an ornament to the city. In this he excelled any other person in Concord,

He built the State, the Columbian and the Centennial blocks, and many smaller structures. In 1866 he purchased the Phenix Hotel property, and at his death he possessed more real estate in Concord than any other person who has ever lived in the city. For some years before his death Mr. Hill was proprietor of the Phenix Hotel, which became widely and favorably known under his management. Mr. Hill was without doubt one of the most successful business men of the state of New Hampshire. His success arose from his knowledge of details and his steady and untiring application to doing things, well coupled with a prudence and economy that permitted no waste. His ability to decide promptly and act with courage and vigor were also prominent elements in his character, and which contributed to his success.

Mr. Hill was a Democrat, and a staunch supporter of the principles of Jefferson and Jackson, but he never placed party above principle, and never sought office, always preferring to work for the upbuilding of his home town in other ways, rather than fill the offices within the gift of its people. When convinced he could be most useful in a public position, he did not refuse its responsibilities, however. He was a member of the board of water works commissioners at the time of his death. He was a member of the Masonic Order. He was an attendant of the Congregational Church until the early sixties, and thenceforward until his death worshipped in the St. Paul's Church, Protestant Episcopal.

Mr. Hill was twice married. His first wife was Priscilla Chapman, by whom he had two daughters—Lucy Ann, married Josiah E. Dwight, of Massachusetts, who was a partner with Mr. Hill; and Elizabeth, married Henry J. Eaton, of Manchester, New Hampshire. In 1854 Mr. Hill married Sophia L. Pickering, who survived him. She was born in Barnstead, and was a descendant in the seventh generation from John Pickering, who settled in Portsmouth, New Hampshire, in 1633. She was one of the nine children of Joseph and Mary (Lyford) Pickering, and was born September 12, 1828, and died October 2, 1889 (see Pickering, VII). The line of her ancestors is as follows: John (1); Thomas (2); James (3); John (4); Stephen (5); Jacob (6); Joseph (7). Her children were: Edson J., born October 19, 1857; Solon P., born March 25, 1859, died July, 1886; Joseph C., born January 27, 1865, died August 19, 1891; Cora F., born February 15, 1867. The last is the wife of John I. Monroe, of Brookline, Massachusetts, and has three children.

Mr. Hill was thrown from a carriage in Main street, Concord, September 2, 1884, and received injuries from which he suffered until November 10, when he died.

(VIII) Edson James, son of James R. and Sophia (Pickering) Hill, was born in Concord, October 19, 1857, and was educated at St. Paul's school. He concluded his education at the age of seventeen, and from 1874 to 1884 he was employed as bookkeeper for J. R. Hill & Co. From 1880 he had charge of the Phenix Hotel, and the letting of his father's buildings and collection of rents on the various pieces of property. On the death of his father, Mr. Hill assumed charge of his various business interests, most of which is retained—the harness business being the only one disposed of. From 1884 to 1889 Mr. Hill was landlord of the Phenix Hotel, one of the leading hostelries of the state for half a century. In 1889 the Eagle and Phenix Hotel Company was organized with S. C. Eastman as president; Edson J. Hill, treasurer; and Oliver J. Pelren, manager, which positions they have since continuously held. Mr. Hill is president and treasurer of the Hill Associates; president of the Home Realty Company, and trustee of the Union Guaranty Savings Bank. He is also one of the board of water commissioners of Concord, and trustee of the public library. In politics he is a Democrat, and in 1899, 1903, 1905 and 1907 was elected as such to the assembly of the state of New Hampshire. The first and second terms he served on the committee on banks, and the third term as a member of the ways and means and banking committees. He is a member of St. Paul's Church, of which he is a vestryman, and is also a trustee of the Protestant Episcopal Church in New Hampshire. Mr. Hill is a Knight Templar in Masonry, a member of the Union Club, of Boston, and of the Beaver Meadow Golf Club. He has the keen foresight and aptitude for business that characterized his father.

September 23, 1885, Mr. Hill was married to Cora Hubbell, a daughter of Wesley B. and Mary (McLean) Hubbell, of Zanesville, Ohio. He resides in the house in which he was born, the one erected by his father in 1855, and occupied by him until his death.

HILL It is probable that the following line is descended from John Hill, of Dover, New Hampshire, but the connecting links have been lost, owing to the imperfection of the early records. It is likely that Joseph Hill, mentioned below, was a son of (V) Joshua Hill, of Stratham.

(I) William Holbrook, son of Joseph Hill, was born in Epping, New Hampshire, in 1815. When a boy he moved to the neighboring town of Deerfield, where he made his permanent home. He had a farm and general business at Deerfield Parade, and was a man well known and somewhat influential in the community. In politics he was a Whig, afterwards joined the Republican party, and though his town was Democratic half a century ago, he served as selectman in 1852 and 1853, and also as representative. He and his family attended the Free Will Baptist Church. William H. Hill married for his first wife Sarah Durgin, of Northwood, New Hampshire, and they had nine children: George, Frank, Jacob, Sawyer, Martin, Martha, Samuel, John M. and Charles. By the second marriage there were four children: Caroline, Daniel, Nellie, and one who died in infancy. William H. Hill, the father, died in November, 1897, at the age of eighty-two. His first wife, Mrs. Sarah (Durgin) Hill, died in 1863, when all her older sons were in the Union army in the south.

(II) John Moody, seventh son and eighth and youngest child of William Holbrook and Sarah (Durgin) Hill, was born at Deerfield, New Hampshire, October 8, 1852. He was educated in the schools of that town, and worked on his father's farm and in the business until the age of twenty. In 1872 he went to Haverhill, Massachusetts, and engaged in the shoe business, with which he has been connected ever since. He worked at first for the firm of Ordway & Clark, and later became superintendent for the firm of Griffin Brothers. Mr. Hill afterwards owned a contract shop for hand work, and later, when several firms were consolidated, became superintendent for the Griffin-George Shoe Company. In October, 1895, Mr. Hill was seriously injured by a carriage accident. He spent many months in the Massachusetts General Hospital, and for four or five years was a complete invalid. This necessitated his giving up active work, and he now spends his summers on the Deerfield farm, and in winters goes to Haverhill, where he still keeps up a connection with the shoe factory. In politics Mr. Hill has never been especially interested, but has always kept his voting place in Deerfield. He is much interested in fraternal organizations, especially in the Independent Order of Red Men, in which he has held all the offices. He also belongs to the Odd Fellows and to the Order of United American Mechanics. He is very fond of outdoor life, and is an enthusiastic sportsman and hunter. On July 3, 1873, John Moody Hill married Mary Adelaide Ladd, daughter of John F. and Mary (Rollins) Ladd, who was born at Deerfield, New Hampshire, June 20, 1854. (See Ladd, VIII). Mrs. Hill is a member of the Free Will Baptist Church in Deerfield, and belongs to the Daughters of Rebekah and Daughters of Pocahontas. John M. and Mary (Ladd) Hill have two children: George Vernon, whose sketch follows; and Loleta Estelle, born January 7, 1882. The daughter was educated in the schools of Bradford, and for some years was a pupil at Mrs. Gage's private school in that town. In September, 1904, Loleta E. Hill was married to Charles A. Piper, and they now live in Haverhill, Massachusetts.

(III) George Vernon, only son and elder child of John Moody and Mary (Ladd) Hill, was born at Deerfield, New Hampshire, November 3, 1875. In 1880 his people moved to Bradford, Massachusetts, and he was educated in the schools of that town, graduating from the high school in 1894. From September, 1891, to February, 1892, he studied at Phillips Academy in Andover, because the college preparatory course was for a time cut out of the Bradford high school, but upon its resumption he returned to his place there. He entered Dartmouth College in the class of 1898, but left college to take part in the Spanish war. While at Dartmouth he ranked well in his studies, winning the usual scholarships, and was a contributor to the *Dartmouth Literary Monthly*. On April 28, 1898, he enlisted as a private in the Eighth Massachusetts United States Volunteers, under Captain William C. Dow and Colonel William A. Pew. This was the only volunteer regiment in the country that saw a full year's service. In that year, Mr. Hill filled every non-commissioned office in the regiment, and was on special duty almost all the time. The regiment was at Chickamauga, Georgia, from May 5, to August 28; then at Lexington, Kentucky, till November 10; at Americus, Georgia, till December 20; and in Cuba the remaining four months. Mr. Hill was at first regimental clerk in the adjutant's office, then in the adjutant's office at division headquarters; and afterward sergeant in the brigade quartermaster's department. He was clerk of the field officer's court from July to April. During the last months he was detailed to detached service for the purpose of taking a census of Matanzas, Pueblo Nuevo and Versailles, all in Cuba. His regiment was engaged in clearing out guerillas from the province of Matanzas, a place which the bandits especially infested, because it is accessible both to the mountains and the fertile regions where the best plantations are cultivated. While in Cuba, Mr. Hill sent weekly letters to the *Boston Globe*.

Immediately upon his return to the states, Mr. Hill entered upon newspaper work, in which he has been engaged for the past eight years. He became connected with the Haverhill (Massachusetts) *Gazette* on May 1, 1899, and September 1 of that year he came to this state as one of the city reporters for the *Manchester Union* a paper with which he has been associated ever since. During the constitutional convention and legislature of 1902-1903 at Concord, he occupied the city editor's chair in the *Concord Monitor* office. Since then he has been the Concord correspondent of the *Manchester Union*, with his residence in the capital city. Mr. Hill's excellent and effective work is shown by the fact that the Concord circulation of the *Union* has more than doubled in that time, a substantial advertising business has been built up and that this increase has not only been established but maintained. Besides his regular work on the *Union*, he has written many special articles for Boston and New York papers and magazines. Notwithstanding Mr. Hill's successful journalistic experience he intends to make the law his profession. He began his studies in Haverhill a number of years ago with William H. Moody, since attorney general, and now one of the associate justices of the supreme court of the United States. Mr. Hill has prosecuted his studies at intervals, chiefly in the midnight hours, and was admitted to practice December 19, 1907. In politics Mr. Hill is a staunch Republican. On May 8, 1894, at the age of eighteen, he joined the First Congregational Church at Bradford, Massachusetts, founded in 1682. Like his father, Mr. George V. Hill is an enthusiastic sportsman, and he has fished and hunted along the Atlantic coast from Nova Scotia to northern Virginia. Most of his school vacations were spent in camping and tramping. He is also an enthusiastic devotee of golf. Mr. Hill belongs to many clubs, the Wonolancet, the Beaver Meadow and the Gun Club of Concord; and the Merrimack County Fish and Game League, besides social organizations in Haverhill and Manchester. In 1904 he was the moving factor in organizing Camp General J. N. Patterson, United Spanish-American War Veterans.

On November 14, 1906, George Vernon Hill was united in marriage to Mary Genevieve Gannon, daughter of Michael George and Sarah (Larkin) Gannon, who was born at Concord, New Hampshire, May 30, 1877.

HILL The family of whom this sketch treats have for generations been stout and sturdy laborers, members of which came to this country more than a century ago and by their industry and skill in the various fields of labor have become useful, respected and prominent citizens.

(I) Samuel Hill was born in Birmingham, England, where he was engaged in coal mining. In his young manhood he removed to South Wales, where he was employed in the extensive collieries near Swansea, and was also largely engaged in the building of canal boats.

(II) Samuel (2), son of Samuel (1) Hill, mentioned above, was born at Clydash, South Wales, May 28, 1810, and died in that town, February 25, 1895. He followed the occupation of his father in the coal mines, was the owner of a colliery, and a barge builder. He was a very upright man and held in high respect by all who knew him. For sixty years he held the office of deacon in the Congregational Church in Clydash. He married Emma Nichols, of the Mundels, of Wales, who was born September 5, 1816, and died in 1902, daughter of Henry and Emma Nichols. They had nine children.

(III) George William, sixth child of Samuel (2) and Emma (Nichols) Hill, was born in Swansea, South Wales, July 20, 1850. He attended the public schools until he was fourteen years of age and then apprenticed himself to learn the trade of carpentering. He emigrated to the United States in 1870, and after residing in various places, located in Nashua, New Hampshire, in 1872. He entered the employ of the White Mountain Freezer Company in 1887, and is still engaged with that company, having risen to the rank of foreman in the lumber department. He is an active member of the Christian Brethren denomination and highly respected in the community. He is also a member of Rising Sun Lodge, No. 39, Ancient Free and Accepted Masons; and Pennichuck Lodge, No. 39, Independent Order of Odd Fellows. He married in Wilmot, New Hampshire, October 20, 1879, Hattie Fisk, born in Sutton, New Hampshire, January 12, 1858, daughter of Levi F. and Susan Fisk. Levi F. Fisk was a farmer in Orange, and his parents were among the first settlers in Vermont, where they were also farmers. His mother, Susan (Rogers) Fisk, born in Vermont, was killed by the Indians while gathering berries. Mr. and Mrs. Hill have one child: Stanley F., born at Clydash, South Wales, March 2, 1885. He is now a junior in the New Hampshire College of Agriculture and Mechanical Arts, and is exceedingly proficient in music.

HILL One branch of the Hill family is traced to William Hill, a blacksmith, who was born March 4, 1788, and died in Grafton, this state, January 3, 1867. He was married, November 12, 1812, to Rebecca Hoskins, who was born March 28, 1791. and died, October 17, 1863. Brief mention of their children follows: Charles P., the eldest, died in infancy. Lucina P. married Stephen George, and lived and died in Grafton. William H. was a blacksmith, and resided long in Manchester, where his life ended. Varnum H. was also for many years a citizen of Manchester. Eli F. died at the age of twenty-six years. John M. died in Manchester, in 1897. Moses C. died at four years of age. Samuel D. at one year. Bushrod W. is the subject of the succeeding paragraph. The fourth died in infancy.

Bushrod Washington Hill, for many years one of the most substantial citizens in Manchester, was born June 26, 1832, in Grafton, New Hampshire, where he resided until nearly grown to manhood. His education was supplied by the country school of his native town, and previous to 1850 he went to Manchester and joined his older brother, who was then engaged in the express business which was established between Boston and Manchester via Lawrence. The younger brother soon became a partner in the business, and in 1882 became its sole owner. By his industry and faithful attention to the wants of customers he built up a very extensive and profitable business, and in 1894 this was sold to the American Express Company. Mr. Hill was an exceedingly careful and prudent manager, and made safe investments in real estate, and at the time of his death was the owner of a large farm on Mammoth road, near Derryfield Park. He was president of the Hillsborough County Savings Bank, and a director of the Merchants' National Bank, also the New Hampshire Fire Insurance Company, having been identified with the latter from a time shortly after its organization. He was a trustee of the Valley cemetery, and occupied a prominent position in the business circles of the city. His success in the management of his own affairs caused him to be frequently consulted in financial matters, and he was a trusted investor of money. Mr. Hill passed away at his home in Manchester, March 3, 1904, and his departure was mourned by a large circle of business associates and appreciative friends. He was a member of the Old Residents' Association, and was active in the Masonic order, affiliating with Washington Lodge, Mount Horeb Chapter, and Trinity Commandery, Knights Templar, of Manchester, being the oldest member in point of service of the latter body at the time of his death. In 1902 he represented the fourth ward of Manchester in the state legislature, and was a member of the last constitutional convention. He was a staunch supporter of Republican principles, and ever had the welfare of the community and his country at heart. He was a regular attendant and liberal supporter of the Hanover Street Congregational Church. Mr. Hill was married (first), to Ann Sweat Appleton, who was born January 31, 1828, in Nashua, a daughter of Thomas Appleton. His second wife was Helen M. Peaslee. His family includes two children: John Frank Hill, who now resides on the paternal farm in Manchester, and Sarah Louise, wife of James Howard Campbell, of Manchester. At the present time nine of his grandchildren are living.

BARNEY The ancestor of this family came to Massachusetts for the same purpose as nearly every other person did who settled in New England at that time—the opportunity to worship God according to the dictates of his own conscience.

Edward Barney, of Bradenham, county of Bucks, England, in his will dated 1643 makes a bequest to his son Jacob "if he be living at time of my death and come over to England."

(I) Jacob, the emigrant ancestor of the family, is said to have been a son of Edward Barney. He was born in England, 1601, landed in Salem, 1634, was made a freeman May 14, 1634, and died in Salem, April 28, 1673, aged seventy-two years. His wife, whose name was Elizabeth, survived him. A well-known writer says of Jacob: "An intelligent merchant, often selectman and deputy to the general court, 1635-38-47-53-65. and served on the first grand jury that ever sat in this country. The loss of such men as Mr. Barney is not easily supplied." His children were: Jacob, Sarah, Hannah and John. The last named died young.

(II) Jacob, eldest child of Jacob and Elizabeth Barney, and the only son surviving childhood, was born in England, died in Rehoboth, Massachusetts, February 12, 1692. He was a Baptist minister and founded churches in Charlestown and Swansea, Massachusetts. He married (first), in Salem, August 18, 1657, Hannah Johnson, who died June 5, 1659. He married (second), April 26, 1660, Ann Witt, who died in Rehoboth, March 17, 1701. His children were: Josiah, Hannah, Sarah, John, Abigail, Jacob, Ruth, Dorcas, Joseph, Israel, Jonathan, Samuel and Hannah.

(III) Joseph, ninth child and fourth son of Jacob Barney, was born in Salem, March 9, 1673. He lived in Swansea and later in Rehoboth, where he died February 5, 1731. He was a lieutenant in the army. He married in 1692, Constance Davis, born in Haverhill, March 9, 1674, daughter of James and Elizabeth Davis.

(IV) John, son of Joseph and Constance (Davis) Barney, was born April 2, 1703, in Rehoboth, and was married (intentions published March 8, 1729) to Hannah Clark.

(V) Aaron, son of John and Hannah (Clark) Barney, was born in Rehoboth, April 12, 1734. He purchased three thousand acres of land in Grafton, New Hampshire, on a part of which he settled in

T. B. W. Hill

Hial Barney

(Smith) Barney. was born in Grafton, January

and successful one, and he has conferred credit

April, 1773, and said part has ever since been known as Barney Hill. He gave each of his sons a farm. He married Susannah Carpenter, who bore him children: Jabez, John, Hannah, Aaron, Otis, Kezia and Susannah. The death of Mr. Barney occurred in Grafton, 1817, aged eighty-three years. (Mention of John and descendants forms part of this article.)

(VI) Jabez, eldest son of Aaron and Susannah (Carpenter) Barney, was probably born in Rehoboth or Swansey, Massachusetts, and accompanied his parents to Grafton in 1774. He married a woman of the same family name, perhaps a distant relative, and had a family of eight children, whose names are not at hand.

(VII) John, son of Jabez Barney, was a native of Grafton, and resided there his entire life. He married Nancy Martin, of that town, and was the father of Alfred, Horace, Eleazer, Jessie, Mary, and three others whose names do not appear in the records consulted.

(VIII) Eleazer, son of John and Nancy (Martin) Barney, was born in Grafton, March, 1819, and died there in 1884. He was a merchant in Danbury for a time, but returned to Grafton where he was in trade for a number of years, and removing to Canaan he carried on a general mercantile business there, selling out to his sons, after which he devoted his time to other interests. He was quite active in public affairs, representing his district in the legislature two terms, and with the majority of the old Whig element he joined the Republican party at its formation. In his religious belief he was a Baptist. In 1835 he married Emeline A. Durrell, of Grafton, and they were the parents of three children: Albert E., Arthur J. and Bertha E. The mother of these children died February 14, 1906.

(IX) Albert Eleazer, eldest child of Eleazer and Emeline A. (Durrell) Barney, was born in Grafton, September 8, 1843. He began his education in the Grafton public schools, continued it at the Kimball Union Academy, in Meriden, and completed it at the Union Academy in Canaan. Prior to former schooling mentioned, he took a course at Eastman's Business College at Poughkeepsie, New York. Entering his father's store as a clerk, he was admitted to partnership under the firm name of E. Barney & Son, who transacted a thriving business in Canaan. The retirement of the elder Barney was followed by the admission to partnership of the latter's youngest son, Arthur J., and the firm name became known as Barney Brothers. Shortly after its establishment the new concern began in a small way to manufacture pants, shirts and overalls, and this side speculation proved so successful that they increased their facilities, employing at the present time some fifty operatives and turning out a large amount of work annually. Albert E. Barney was chosen representative to the legislature for the years 1877-78, was also chosen town clerk, serving one year in that capacity, and in politics he is a Republican.

He married Abbie A. Hutchinson, born October 26, 1846, daughter of Richard Hutchinson, of Canaan. Mr. and Mrs. Barney have two children: Ernest A., born July 11, 1869, and John E., born March 14, 1876.

(VI) John, second son of Aaron and Susannah (Carpenter) Barney, was born in Rehoboth, Massachusetts, March 4, 1769, died October 3, 1840. He married Annie Smith, who bore him children: John, Jedediah, Amanda, Cyrus, Annie, Aarad, Amy, Rival and Nelson.

(VII) Jedediah, second child of John and Annie (Smith) Barney, was born in Grafton, January 17, 1798, and died there November 4, 1869. He resided on the farm formerly owned by his grandfather and later by his father, and was a leading citizen, holding various town offices, including representative to the legislature in 1848-49. He was also one of the foremost members of the Methodist Church. He married (first), February 13, 1824, Melancy Williams, daughter of Samuel Williams, and they had one child, Mark F., who died at the age of eighty-two years. Mrs. Barney died in her thirtieth year. Mr. Barney married (second), February 3, 1831, Eunice Blackman, born July 4, 1807, a native of Gilmanton, daughter of Adam Blackman, of northeastern Massachusetts. She died February 19, 1862, at the age of fifty-four years. She was an active member of the Methodist Church. They were the parents of eight children: Eliza, Harriet, Hial, Cyrell, Albert E., Charles B., La Fayette T., Jacob and Ellen F., all of whom are deceased but Hial and La Fayette T. (Jacob and descendants receive mention in this article.)

(VIII) Hial, eldest son and third child of Jedediah and Eunice (Blackman) Barney, was born March 26, 1836, in Grafton. He was educated in the common schools of that town and an academy in Thetford, Vermont. After leaving school he went to Brookline, New Hampshire, and was there engaged in agricultural pursuits for a time. Going to Bridgewater, Massachusetts, he learned the trade of butcher, and was subsequently located at Wareham, Massachusetts, where he carried on a profitable wholesale and retail business in meats. He bought and sold many cattle, and was interested in other business enterprises. He purchased a house and lot in Wareham, and made his permanent home there for twenty-nine years. He was a trustee of the Wareham Savings Bank, and took an active part in public affairs, being twice elected selectman and serving five years, also serving for a similar period of time as assessor and overseer of the poor. During the prevalence of tuberculosis among cattle, he was appointed deputy state inspector and held that office many years, resigning it upon his removal to Manchester, New Hampshire. He was also a member of the committee for the suppression of crime.

In September, 1862, he enlisted in Company K, Third Massachusetts Volunteer Infantry, and took part with his command in battles, namely: Kingston, White Hall, Gouldsboro, Newbern and Batchelders Creek, North Carolina, and in a number of skirmishes in the siege of Little Washington, North Carolina. He was discharged at Lakeville, Massachusetts, June 26, 1863. He was lieutenant in the New Hampshire state militia before the Civil war. In 1895 Mr. Barney removed to Manchester, New Hampshire, where he built a handsome residence on Pine street, and where he now lives in comfortable retirement. He is an attendant of the Universalist Church of Manchester, and has been president of the association seven years.

He was a member of William T. Sherman Post, No. 208, Grand Army of the Republic, of Wareham, Massachusetts, of which he was commander, and is now affiliated with Louis Bell Post, of Manchester. He was made a Mason in Wareham, and is a member of Social Harmony Lodge of that town. Since living in Manchester he has become a member of the Manchester Institute of Arts and Sciences and the Board of Trade. Throughout his life Mr. Barney has consistently adhered to the Democratic party in politics. His career has been a most active and successful one, and he has conferred credit upon the state of his nativity and his parentage. By unremitting industry and prudent investments he has accumulated the competence which now enables him to enjoy life. His life work has embraced more than a selfish accumulation of gain, and he has devoted time and money for the enhancement of the moral and social advantages of the public.

Mr. Barney married, February 19, 1868, Jane Cole, of Grafton, New Hampshire, daughter of Richard and Sylvia (Dwinnell) Cole. She died February 9, 1900.

(VIII) Jacob, youngest son of Jedediah Barney, was born in Grafton, and resided in Orange. He married Lois Walker, of Grafton, and reared five children: Jacob, James, Aaron, Charles and Ahira.

(IX) Major Aaron, third son and child of Jacob and Lois (Walker) Barney, was born in Orange, June 21, 1810. He was a prosperous farmer and a leading resident of Orange, serving as a member of the board of selectmen, was representative to the legislature for the years 1846 and 1853, and acted as a justice of the peace. Originally a Whig, he became actively identified with the Know-Nothing movement during the latter days of the anti-slavery agitation, and was subsequently an earnest supporter of the Republican party. In the state militia he ranked as major, and he evinced a profound interest in the welfare of that organization. Mr. Barney died March 24, 1882. He married Sarah Ann Chase, of Canaan, who died January 8, 1891. She bore him two children, Charles O. and Addie S.

(X) Charles Oscar, eldest child and only son of Major Aaron and Sarah Ann (Chase) Barney, was born in Orange, July 21, 1844. Having pursued the primary branches of study in the common schools at Grafton, he completed his education at the Canaan Union Academy, graduating in 1866, and in the following year he founded the *Canaan Reporter*, and espoused journalism as a permanent profession. He has ever since devoted his time and energy to the interest of this offspring of his enterprise, which has now passed its fortieth year of usefulness, and the successful career of the *Reporter* is due wholly to his ability and sagacious management. It is worthy of note that although frequently encumbered with important outside affairs, including public business, he never allows his managerial and editorial duties to be superseded by other interests, and from the first issue of the *Reporter* to the present time he has been away from the office but five publication days. Politically Mr. Barney is a Republican, and in addition to serving upon the board of supervisors for the past six years, he represented his town in the lower house of the legislature in 1901. He was mainly instrumental in promoting and organizing the Crystal Lake Water Company, drafted the bill constituting its charter which he guided to a final enactment by the legislature, and he is now one of the directors and clerk of that corporation. For twenty-seven consecutive years he was a director and secretary of the Mascoma Fair Association; was for many years master of the local Grange; and has occupied all of the important chairs in Mount Cardigan Lodge, No. 31, Knights of Pythias, including that of grand chancellor. In his religious faith he is a Methodist.

On July 21, 1874, Mr. Barney was united in marriage with Miss Mary Wilmarth, of Enfield, this state, who died February 4, 1887. She became the mother of five children: Lester O., Addie S., Edward A., Alice (deceased), and Ralph T. Edward A. Barney, born July 22, 1881, is a graduate of the Canaan high school, is now private secretary to the Hon. Frank D. Currier, a member of congress from this state, and has served as clerk of the house committee on patents since 1905. Ralph T. Barney, youngest son of Charles O. Barney, was born July 8, 1885, is also a graduate of the Canaan high school, and is now assisting his father in the office of the *Reporter*.

BARNEY Jacob Barney, who was made a freeman in Salem, Massachusetts, in 1634, was representative in 1635-38-47-53, and died in 1673, aged seventy-two. From him descended the Sudbury family of Barneys from whom the members of this family have probably sprung.

(I) George Darwin Barney, son of Nelson Barney, was born in the town of Shoreham, Vermont, June 16, 1852, and died at Island Pond, 1889. He was a farmer and lumberman for some years. For ten years before his death he conducted a hotel at Island Pond. He married Emma McNamara, daughter of Michael McNamara. Her father was a soldier in the war with Mexico, and was in General Scott's army at the capture of the City of Mexico. Two children were born of this union: Elmer J. E. and Catherine. She married Peter McCrystal, and resides in Berlin, New Hampshire.

(II) Elmer Joseph Barney, M. D., only son of George D. and Emma (McNamara) Barney, was born in Shoreham, Vermont, June 16, 1873. He attended the common schools of Island Pond, and then learned the printer's trade. In 1895 he removed to Berlin, New Hampshire where he started a job printing office with one Andros. Later he engaged in the printing business under the name of the Barney Reporter Press, and published the *Berlin Reporter*, of Berlin, a newspaper which is still published there. He was engaged in the printing business eight years and brought out the first city director of Berlin. He entered the University of Vermont as a student in the medical department and graduated with the degree of M. D. in 1905. He immediately returned to Berlin and opened an office and began the practice of his profession in which he has met with gratifying success, especially in obstetrics. He is both a musician and a poet, is leader of the Berlin orchestra, and plays the violin and trombone. He is a member of the Grand Council of the Alpha Kappa Kappa medical fraternity of the University of Vermont, and was editor-in-chief of its magazine, *The Centaur*. He is a member of the Coos Medican County Society, the New Hampshire Medical Association, and the American Medical Association. He is a member of Sabatis Lodge, No. 95, Free and Accepted Masons; the Knights of Pythias; Berlin Lodge. Benevolent Protective Order of Elks, and the Order of Eagles, of which he is president and examining physician. He married, June 20, 1899, Helen Maud Clark, who was born in Berlin, daughter of Thomas Clark. Mrs. Barney is a pianist, has a fine voice, and sings in the Congregational Church choir. She is very much interested in the kindergarten school established by President William W. Brown, of the Berlin Mills Company, of which she is a teacher. Dr. and Mrs. Barney have one child, George.

GAULT This name is of Scottish origin and originally, as found in the New England records, had various spellings, such as Gott, Gaat and Galt. It has been borne by many excellent citizens of New Hampshire and of other states, and has been especially conspicuous in railroad operations in the west, as well as in the various walks of life in New England.

(I) Samuel Gault was a native of Scotland, and married there Elsie Carlton, who is said to have been a native of Wales. They had three children born in Scotland, and two after they removed thence to Londonderry in the northern part of Ireland, whence they came to the United States in 1721, locating first in Massachusetts. In 1737 Mr. Gault settled in what is now the town of Hooksett, then part of Chester. The records show that he purchased of Joseph Hubbard, of Concord, lot No. 24, in the Suncook tract, the deed bearing date, May 25, 1736, in which his name is spelt "Gott," and his place of residence is given as Westford, Massachusetts. In the next year he settled on lot No. 25, and it is presumed that he purchased this at that time and was the owner of both. This property he deeded to his son, Mathew, January 29, 1789. His children were: Patrick, Mathew, Andrew, Samuel and Jane.

(II) Andrew, third son and child of Samuel and Elsie (Carlton) Gault, married Mary Ayer, of Londonderry. After her death he married a second time and the Christian name only of his second wife is known, namely, Gracy, as shown in his will. He resided in Pembroke, and died at the age of eighty-three years. His children were: Mathew, Elsie, Betsey, Samuel, Margaret, William and Molly.

(III) Mathew, eldest child of Andrew and Mary (Ayer) Gault, was born 1754, in Pembroke. He was a man of remarkable physique, and served as a soldier under General Stark in the Revolutionary war. He could out-run any man in the regiment and could also overcome any of them in a wrestling match. It is said that General Stark remarked: "If I had a regiment of men like Mathew Gault and Jimmy Moore, I could storm Hell." He with a brother Samuel was also in the Canadian expedition. For several years after the Revolution he resided in the town of Protectworth (now Springfield), but returned to what is now Hooksett and bought of the other heirs the family homestead. He married (first) Elizabeth Buntin, who was born in 1762 in Allenstown, daughter of Captain Andrew Buntin, who was killed at the battle of White Plains. His second wife was Mary MacConnell Emery. His children were: Andrew, Polly, Jane, Jesse, Betsey, Sally, Elsie, Mathew and William.

(IV) Jesse, second son and fourth child of Mathew and Elizabeth (Buntin) Gault, was born October 22, 1790, in Chester, and died September 25, 1855, on the homestead in Hooksett, which was his father's. He was a successful teacher and farmer, and was the first school committeeman under the old system in Hooksett. He was a great student and well-known teacher. He was married November 14, 1816, to Dolly, daughter of Josiah Clement. She was born April 21, 1794, in Pembroke, and died November 30, 1873, at her home in Hooksett. Their children were: Mathew, who was drowned at an early age. Elmira, the wife of Harlan P. Gerrish, of Boscawen. Jesse. Martha H., who died in her twenty-fifth year unmarried.

(IV) Mathew, third son and eighth child of Mathew and Elizabeth (Buntin) Gault, was born May 27, 1802, in Chester (now Hooksett) on the family homestead, and died there February 10, 1873. He was a farmer and was among the early brick manufacturers of Hooksett, being successful as a business man and respected in the community. He was one of the early members of Lafayette Lodge, Free and Accepted Masons, of Bedford, which was subsequently removed to Manchester. He was a Universalist in religious faith, and a Democrat in politics. For many years he served as first selectman of Hooksett, and was its representative in the legislature at the time of President Andrew Jackson's visit to Manchester. He was married in 1825 to Dolly Doe Cochran, daughter of Nehemiah Cochran. The following is a brief account of their children: James, eldest, was a forty-niner in the pursuit of gold in California, and died at Glen Ellyn, Illinois, in August, 1905. William also went to California in 1850, remained fourteen years, and was subsequently a railroad man in the west, dying at Sterling, Illinois, at the age of about forty-five years. John Cochran was a railroad man for many years and died in Chicago, Illinois, in 1894. Mary Elizabeth died at the age of three years. George died at the age of one month. Sylvanus Buntin is now a resident of St. Paul, Minnesota. Mathew Harvey died at twenty-two years of age. Norris Cochran receives extended mention below. Hiram Sargent died in infancy. Thomas Benton was a railroad man and died in Chicago. Anne Elizabeth married Daniel McCurdy, of Pembroke, and died at Fond du Lac, Wisconsin, in 1869. Sally Sargent is the widow of Charles Henry, residing in Fond du Lac.

(V) Norris Cochran, eighth child of Mathew and Dolly D. (Cochran) Gault, was born May 11, 1838, on the family homestead in Hooksett, which is now his property and where he makes his home. He grew up there, being educated in the local schools and in the Pembroke Gymnasium. He is a farmer and an extensive manufacturer of brick. He is a member of Friendship Lodge, Independent Order of Odd Fellows, of Hooksett, and of Jewell Lodge, Free and Accepted Masons, of Suncook. He was formerly connected with the Amoskeag Veterans and captain of a company. This is a prominent independent military organization, and he commanded a company at Philadelphia during the Centennial there (1876). He is a Universalist, and follows the political inclinations of his sires, giving allegiance to the Democratic party. He has filled most of the offices of the town, including selectman and representative in the state legislature. He was married December 2, 1857, to Annie Hunkins Mitchell, who was born October 8, 1841, daughter of Nathaniel and Sally Sanborn (Leavitt) Mitchell. (See Mitchell ——). She was the mother of four children. The eldest of these, Emma Cochran, was born August 20, 1858, and married in 1884, Anson S. Paine. She resides in Rochester, New Hampshire, having a son, Ralph G. Paine. Clara Gertrude, the second, born October 16, 1860, was married in 1881 to Robert W. Skelton, and resides in Milwaukee, Wisconsin. They had three children, Norris Gault, who died May 11, 1883; Kathryn and Robert Hewittson. Matthew, third child and eldest son of Norris C. Gault, was born August 18, 1867, and is a civil engineer at Worcester, Massachusetts, being chief of the city sewer department. He graduated from Dartmouth College in 1890. He was married in December, 1896, to Grace A. Stetson, of Worcester, and has two children, Warren Stetson and Helen Norris. John, see forward.

(VI) John, youngest child of Norris C. and Annie H. (Mitchell) Gault, was born February 28, 1872, on the family homestead in Hooksett, where he grew up. He attended the local public schools, the Pembroke Academy and graduated from Dartmouth College in the class of 1895. During his school years he engaged in teaching, and taught two winter terms at Alstead, New Hampshire. His first school was in a district lying jointly in the towns of Concord, Epsom and Pembroke. He became principal of the Haven school in Portsmouth, which he resigned December 1, 1896, to take charge of the Webster street school in Manchester, and here he is still engaged. He is the author of a text book for schools on the "Constitution of New Hampshire," which was prepared in co-operation with Fred L. V. Spaulding, who was then principal of the Lincoln street school. Mr. Gault is a member of Jewell Lodge, Free and Accepted Masons, and of Hiram Chapter. Royal Arch Masons, of Suncook, and of Damon Lodge, Knights of Pythias, of Portsmouth. He attends the Methodist Church, and is independent in politics with Democratic tendencies. In 1903 he purchased a handsome dwelling on Pine street, Manchester, which he occupies with his family. Of broad mind and genial and kindly nature, he forms and retains friendships. and is recognized as a good citizen. He was married August 27, 1902, to Sallie Head, daughter of William F. Head, of Hooksett (see Head IV).

(V) Hon. Jesse (2), second son of Jesse and Dolly (Clement) Gault, was born in Hooksett, New Hampshire, September 20, 1823. and died May 8, 1888, and grew up on his father's farm. He obtained his education in the public school and Pembroke Academy. At the age of sixteen he began teaching in his own district, where he taught the winter school four consecutive years, working on the farm in summer. Later he was a teacher in Suncook and Hooksett Village. He remained at his home until twenty-two years of age and then went to Baltimore, Maryland, where he became a bookkeeper and surveyor for Abbott & Jones, ship lumber merchants. He was very successful in his work there but the climate impaired his health and he was compelled to give up his situation. Returning to his home in the north he regained his health, and acceding to the requests of his parents remained in Hooksett. In 1843 he opened a brick yard of modest size in Hooksett and here he resided till his death. This he developed until its annual output was six million bricks, affording employment to sixty-five men. The burning of so many bricks required a large amount of fuel, to supply which Mr. Gault bought about three thousand acres of woodland. That portion of the wood that was fit for lumber went to market and the remainder was used in the kilns. Mr. Gault also engaged in extensive farming operations and owned several farms. His home farm produced seventy-five tons of hay annually and large crops of other kinds. In 1880 he built one of the most expensive residences in that section of the country, situated on the old Concord and Haverhill (Mass.) stage road. In politics Mr. Gault was a Whig and was active in politics at an early age, interested in school matters and a member of the board many years. After filling various local positions, he was elected chairman of the board of selectmen and filled that position for many years. In 1851 he overcame a Democratic majority of more than two to one and was chosen delegates from Hooksett to the constitutional convention, being the youngest member of the body. In 1857 he was elected to the New Hampshire house of representatives from his native town, and re-elected the following year. In 1867 he was elected a railroad commissioner for a term of three years, and during the last year was chairman of the board. He was selected as a delegate to the Republican National convention, in 1876, and was for years a member of the Republican state committee. He was elected in 1885 to the state senate from the Londonderry district, and was chairman of the committee on claims, and a member of the committees on claims, on revision of statutes, and on asylums for the insane, respectively.

Mr. Gault was a member of the Ancient Free and Accepted Masons of Hooksett. Though not a church member he was a constant attendant at the Congregational Church of Hooksett, and was one of its prompt and liberal supporters. Industry, energy, perseverance and a pleasant disposition were the characteristics which made Mr. Gault's life successful and eventually made him a large property owner, a stockholder and a director in railway corporations. His executive abilities were of the highest order. His judgment was so good that his opinions upon important matters, both public and private, were often sought. His character was upright, his life, public and private, spotless and pure, and his fidelity to his friends a thing they could ever rely upon. His home was always a place of generous hospitality and attracted many visitors. In personal appearance he was commanding, his features handsome and pleasing.

He married, April 23, 1846, Martha Ann Otterson, daughter of Isaac and Margaret (Head) Otterson (see Otterson V), born January 29, 1825. They were the parents of five children. two sons and three daughters. Four of these died in youth, one, the eldest, reaching the age of sixteen. The only surviving child is: Myra C., who married Frank C. Towle, who died 1885. He was a native of Epsom and assisted Mr. Gault, who conducted the business after his death. Mr. Gault died May 8, 1888. They have two daughters: Annie Gault Towle, who has been a teacher at Tilton, New Hampshire, Academy, and Mrs. Adam D. Smith. Mr. Smith is supervisor of the Hospital for the Insane at Danvers, Massachusetts. They have one child, Helen Gault.

SPENCER

The ancestry of this name is traced through centuries in England and extends to the ninth generation in this country. The name is of Norman origin, and relates to an occupation, known generally now as steward. The ancient family of this name was seated long in Stotford, Bedfordshire, England, and was founded in the time of William the Conqueror. In ancient times the kitchen was called the spence, and one who was designated as de (of) spence or spencer came in time to have this as a surname. It need not be observed that one in this position, who was a dispenser, was of trustworthy character. The plain virtues of the Puritan fathers of New England are still preserved as characteristics of the family in New Hampshire.

(I) Michael Spencer and his wife Elizabeth, residing in Stotfold, had four sons and two daughters, namely: Richard, Thomas, John, Gerard, Catherine and one whose name has not been preserved.

(II) Gerard (or Jarrard), fourth son of Michael and Elizabeth Spencer, was baptized May 20, 1576, at Stotfold, and died before March 17, 1645. He and his wife, Alice, were parents of four sons and a daughter, namely: William, Gerard, Michael, Thomas and Elizabeth. All of the sons except Michael came to this country about 1631.

(III) William, son of Gerard and Alice Spencer, was baptized October 11, 1601, at Stotfold. He was at Cambridge (then Newtown), Massachusetts. in 1631-32, and was a member of the first general court of the colony at Boston, and of most of the subsequent ones until his removal from Massachusetts. He was a lieutenant of the first military company and one of the founders of the "Ancient and Honorable Artillery," still in existence. Removing to Hartford with the founders of the Connecticut river colony, he was one of the committee of three to revise the laws of that body in 1639, being at

Jesse Gantt

that time a representative in the general court. He was also a selectman in that year, and died next year. His wedding occurred somewhere about 1633, and his wife, Agnes, is supposed to have been a daughter of Rev. Mr. Wakeman. After his death she married William Edwards, another pioneer settler of Hartford. William Spencer's children were: Samuel, Sarah and Elizabeth.

(IV) Samuel, only son of William and Agnes Spencer, died about 1716, surviving his wife Sarah, who passed away April 24, 1706. Their children were: Samuel, Sarah, Hannah, Elizabeth, Rachel, Mary, Abigail and Agnes.

(V) Samuel (2), only son of Samuel (1) and Sarah Spencer, lived first at Hartford and later in Colchester, spending his last days in Bolton, all in Connecticut, and died March 26, 1748, in the eightieth year of his age. He married Hepzibah Church, daughter of Deacon Edward Church, of Hatfield, Massachusetts, the latter a son of Richard Church, one of the first settlers at Hartford. She died September 13, 1745, and was buried at Bolton, where the bones of her husband also lie. They were the parents of seven sons and two daughters. It is probable that the next-named was one of these.

(VI) Asa Spencer came from East Haddam to Campton, New Hampshire, in 1770, and was one of the first settlers in that town. He enlisted as a soldier in the Revolution, February 10, 1776. and died March 7, 1778, while in the service. He was married in East Haddam, before 1764, to Deborah Patterson. Their children were: Huldah, Statira, Amasa, Deborah, Hannah, Asa and Israel.

(VII) Israel Spencer, youngest son of Asa and Deborah (Patterson) Spencer, was born in Campton, December 29, 1775, and died June 9, 1852. The active period of his life was devoted to farming. He was a member of the Congregational Church. He was married, October 13, 1803, in Campton, to Molly Tupper, daughter of Nathaniel and Hannah (Choat) Tupper, of that town. She became the mother of ten children: Nathaniel, Henry, Hannah, Mary, George, Gardner, Jerusha, Statiria. Eliza and Walter. Eliza married Kimball, and is now (1907) residing in Manchester.

(VIII) George Spencer, third son and fifth child of Israel and Molly (Tupper) Spencer, was born in Campton, December 31, 1812. He followed general farming in his native town until 1841, when he removed to Manchester and engaged in the grocery business, which he carried on successfully up to his death, December 10, 1861. Possessing a melodious voice and a good knowledge of music, he taught singing school in Manchester for a period of time, and was considered a very proficient instructor. He married, April 21, 1831, Mrs. Sarah Johnson (*nee* Bartlett), who was born in Campton, June 13, 1792, daughter of Thomas Bartlett, of Campton, granddaughter of Thomas Bartlett, of Newburyport, Massachusetts, and widow of William Johnson. She died in Manchester, July 24, 1876. Of this union there were two sons: Milton Ward. (see forward), and Thomas Bartlett (the latter is the subject of a sketch in this article).

(IX) Milton Ward Spencer, eldest son of George and Sarah Spencer, was born in Campton January 19, 1832. He studied preliminarily in the Manchester public schools, and concluded his education at Kendall's Academy, Piscataqua. When a young man he entered the grocery business in Manchester, and resided there until April, 1867, when he removed to Bedford, where he engaged in farming and lumbering. He purchased and carried on the McFerson Farm (so called), which he devoted chiefly to the dairying industry, and he improved that property by the erection of new buildings. In addition to farming and lumbering he dealt in real estate to some extent, and at the time of his death, which occurred February 3, 1889, he was regarded as one of the most prosperous residents of Bedford. As a Republican, he was several times chosen a member of the board of selectmen, and he also held other town offices including school committeeman, in which capacity he served for a number of years. His church affiliations were with the Presbyterians. He married, November 1, 1855, Theresa Amanda Stevens, born in Montville, Maine, 1833, daughter of Thaddeus H. and Eleanor (Atkinson) Stevens, and granddaughter of Major Thomas Atkinson, of Montville, an officer in the Revolutionary war. She became the mother of four children: 1. Oscar M., born September 22, 1856, died August 4, 1858. 2. Sarah Bartlett, October 16, 1858, married Rollin H. Allen, see forward. 3. George Orville March 24, 1864, a prominent farmer and lumberman of Bedford, is identified with Narragansett Grange, Patrons of Husbandry, and has served with marked ability as a selectman for several terms. 4. Gardner Ward, May 1, 1866, died in Los Angeles, California, December 11, 1904. He resided in Boston prior to removing to Los Angeles. He married Harriet H. Gilbert of Dedham, Massachusetts, who bore him three children: Helen Ward, born in Dedham, November 4, 1895; Miriam Dunbar, in Boston, July 13, 1897; Elise Hathaway, in Boston, August 22, 1899. His widow and children reside in Los Angeles, California.

Rollin H. Allen, aforementioned as the husband of Sarah Bartlett Spencer, traced his ancestry to Samuel Allen, who came from Scrooby, England, 1620, and whose children were: Samuel, Joseph, James, Sarah, Mary, Abigail. The next in line of descent was (2) Samuel, whose children were: Samuel, Essiel, Mehitable, Sarah, Bethiel, Nathaniel, Ebenezer, Josiah, Elisha, Nehemiah. The next in line of descent was (3) Josiah, whose children were: Micah, Josiah, Mary, Esther, Sarah, Nathan, Betty, William. The next in line of descent was (4) Micah, whose children were: Mary, Micah, Joseph, Daniel. The next in line of descent was (5) Micah, whose children were: Micah (died young), Catherine, Micah, Mary, Elisha, Nancy, Fanny, Oliver Otis, Chloe. The next in line of descent was (6) Micah, whose children were: Samuel B., Annie, Fanny, Eunice, Micah, Samuel Parker, Stephen Gans; Micah Allen, father of these children, resided in Mansfield, Massachusetts, followed farming as an occupation, and died there at the age of eighty-nine years. The next in line of descent was (7) Stephen Gans, born March 28, 1816, died October 5, 1878, aged sixty-two years. He was engaged in the iron business in Boston, but finally abandoned this and engaged in the real estate business, continuing the same until his demise. He married Sarah E. French, born in Bedford, February 11, 1826, died in Boston, March 25, 1889, daughter of Ebenezer C. French, a representative of an old pioneer family. Four children were the issue of this marriage, three of whom attained years of maturity, among whom was Rollin H.

(8) Rollin H. Allen was born on Mt. Vernon street, Boston, Massachusetts, February 26, 1863. He was reared in Boston and attended the schools of that city and Somerville, completing his studies in the high school of Boston. He accepted a position as clerk in a woolen business, but remained only a short time, resigning in order to engage in the real estate business with his father, whom he

succeeded in business, and has continued the same successfully up to the present time (1907). He is a charter member of Oakley Country Club at Waltham, Massachusetts, and the Country Club at Manchester, New Hampshire. He is a Republican in politics. He married, October 31, 1878, Sarah Bartlett Spencer (see Spencer family), who bore him two children: 1. Herbert Spencer, born in Boston, Massachusetts, April 19, 1881, educated at Hopkins private school, Harvard College and Harvard Law School, and is now practicing his profession in the city of Boston. He is a member of the University Club and a number of others. 2. Ruth, born in Boston, Massachusetts, November 1, 1885, educated in the private school of Mrs. Mays, received a private musical education, and completed her education in a school for young ladies conducted by Mrs. Hess in Paris, France.

(IX) Thomas Bartlett, younger son of George and Sarah (Bartlett) Spencer, was born October 2, 1834, in Campton. He was a sutler during the Civil war and was engaged in the grocery business at Manchester for several years. After living four or five years in Bedford, he returned to Manchester, where he died January 13, 1895. He was married February 19, 1855, to Thankful D. Combs, of Manchester (a cousin of Commodore Nutt), and they were the parents of two daughters, Ida Jane and Etta Maria.

(X) Ida Jane, elder daughter of Thomas B. and Thankful D. (Combs) Spencer, was born December 5. 1861, in Manchester, and was married July 17, 1883, to James Barnard (see Barnard, VI).

ALLEN This is one of the names most frequently met in the United States, and is represented by many distinct families. Several immigrants brought it to these shores among the earliest in New England. The family traced below has numerous representatives throughout the United States, and they are usually found among the useful and desirable citizens.

(I) George Allen, born in England about 1568, under the reign of Queen Elizabeth, came to America with his family in 1635, and settled in Saugus (Lynn), Massachusetts. He had ten children, some of whom had proceeded to this country and settled in the vicinity of Boston. In 1637 George Allen joined with Edmund Freeman and others in the purchase of the township of Sandwich. When this town was incorporated Mr. Allen was chosen deputy—the first officer in the town—and served in that capacity for several years. He was a conscientious Puritan, and a member of the Baptist Church. After the purchase of Sandwich several of his sons moved to that town with their families. George Allen died in Sandwich, May 2, 1648, aged eighty years. In his will he named five sons: Matthew, Henry, Samuel, George and William; and also made provision for his "five last children," without naming them. From the fact that settlers of the name came from Braintree, Essex, England, about the same time, it is inferred that he came from the same locality. In 1632 Samuel and Matthew Allen and their brother, Thomas Allyn (as he spelled it), came from Braintree and located at Cambridge, whence all of them subsequently moved to Connecticut.

(II) Samuel, third son and child of George Allen, was born in England in 1605, came to Boston in 1628, and on July 6, 1635, was made a freeman at Braintree. He received a grant of land in 1638, and in 1648 purchased a farm of John Webb, of Boston, the bounds of which are still traceable on three sides. He married (first), Anne ——, who died September 29, 1641, and (second), Margaret French, widow of Edward Lamb, who survived him. The children by the first wife were: Samuel, married Sarah Partridge; Mary, married Nathaniel Greenwood, of Boston; Sarah, married Lieutenant Josiah Standish, son of Miles Standish; and James. The children of the second wife were: Abigail, married John Carey, of Bridgewater, and Joseph, whose sketch follows.

(III) Joseph (1), second child and only son of Samuel and Margaret (French) Allen, was born in Braintree, May 15, 1650, died March 20, 1727. He became a member of the church in Braintree in 1711, and at the same time was made deacon. He married (first), January 30, 1670, Rebecca, daughter of John and Abigail Leader, born April 10. 1652, died April 23, 1702; (second), Lydia Holbrook, widow of Samuel, of Weymouth, died May 21, 1745. The children of the first wife were: Joseph, Abigail, Samuel and Benjamin; and of the second wife: Rebecca, John and Mary.

(IV) Joseph (2), son of Joseph (1) and Rebecca (Leader) Allen, born in Braintree, January 30, 1672. died April 16, 1727, married, August 14, 1701, Abigail Savil, daughter of Samuel and Hannah (Adams) Savil, born February 14, 1678, buried January 16, 1746. Their children were: Joseph, Abijah, Abigail, James, Bathsheba, Josiah, Elizabeth, Mehitable and Micah.

(V) Abijah (1), second son and child of Joseph (2) and Abigail (Savil) Allen. born August 22, 1704, married, June 3, 1725, Joanna Balter, and they had: Abijah, Abigail, Jacob and Thomas (twins), Joanna, Elizabeth, Josiah and Joseph.

(VI) Abijah (2), eldest child of Abijah (1) and Joanna (Balter) Allen, was born December 28. 1725, died November 10, 1795, married, July 11, 1749, Ruth Penniman, born November 11, 1730, died November 14, 1802, daughter of William and Ruth (Thayer) Penniman. Their children were: Ruth, Jacob. Abigail, Joanna and Lemuel.

(VII) Jacob, eldest son and second child of Abijah (2) and Ruth (Thayer) Allen, born December 23, 1754, died October 23, 1821, married, March 27, 1777, Hepsibah Vinton, born September 20, 1758, died June 23, 1886, daughter of John and Hepsibah (French) Vinton, and had by her: Abigail, Jacob, died young; Jacob, Abijah, died young; John and Abijah, the subject of the next paragraph.

(VIII) Abijah (3), youngest child of Jacob and Hepsibah (Vinton) Allen, born April 21, 1787. died March 17, 1824, married, December 21, 1809, Sarah Allen, born January 2, 1781, died July 5, 1861, daughter of William and Deborah (Clark) Allen. and they had six children: Deborah Clark, Hepsibah Vinton, John Brooks, Sarah Thompson, Abigail Paster and Abijah.

(IX) Deborah Clark, eldest child of Abijah (3) and Sarah (Allen) Allen, born September 15, 1810, became the wife of Thomas (4) Hollis (see Hollis, VI).

ALLEN Owing to the lack of records it has not been feasible to trace this family through many generations; hence it is impossible to tell whether it is related to the Allens whose history has previously been written.

(I) Ira B. Allen was born in Chelsea, Vermont, in 1816, the famous cold year when there was a frost every month and no corn ripened. His schooling was very limited, being confined to the opportunities afforded by the districts of his native town; but he was a great reader and had a faculty for retaining what he saw in books; and in due time, through his own efforts, he became a well informed man. About 1835 he began driving a stage for a Mr. Morton between Chelsea, Vermont, and Hanover, New Hampshire. This brought him into contact with the outer world and with educated people. He carried mail as well as passengers, and for seven years continued on this route. In 1844 he purchased an interest in the line from Montpelier, Vermont, to Hanover, and was identified with staging interests until the railroad succeeded the coach. In 1846 he moved to Hanover, and in company with his brother Samuel conducted a livery business till about 1850. Ira B. Allen opened the street bearing his name from School to Main streets in Hanover. From Hanover he went to Chili, South America, where he established a stage route, remaining three years. Returning to Hanover he re-purchased his old livery business and continued to live there till his death. He acquired a handsome property, and was one of the popular men of the college town. He was a great favorite with the college students, and always had a good story to tell. His varied experiences and sense of humor had supplied him with a fund of anecdotes. He was universally esteemed by his fellowmen, both in Hanover and in his native village of Chelsea. He lived to see the country grow from woodlands to modern farming communities, and he helped to make the change. Ira B. Allen married Harriet E. Avery. She died July, 1848. They had one son, George H., whose sketch follows. He then married Jane Carpenter, who died 1889. They had one son Frank C., who died in infancy. Ira B. Allen died May, 1890, and at his death Hanover lost one of its most substantial citizens, and the family a loving father.

(II) George H., only son of Ira B. and Harriet E. (Avery) Allen, was born August 12, 1848, at Hanover, New Hampshire. He was educated in the public schools of Hanover and under private tutors. He was graduated from the Chandler scientific department of Dartmouth College in 1867. He chose the profession of civil engineering. His first work after leaving college was with the United States government survey on the shore line of Lake Superior. The route lay along the northern shore from Pigeon river ninety miles. He then surveyed from Derby Line, Vermont, to Sherbrooke, Quebec, for the Massawippi Valley railroad. Mr. Allen then came to Manchester, New Hampshire, which city he has made his permanent home. He was first employed by James A. Weston, at one time governor of the state. After a time he purchased Mr. Weston's office business, and started a private engineering establishment of his own. He did all the surveying and engineering work for Manchester prior to the constituting of the office of city engineer. Mr. Allen afterwards went to Boston, and had charge of the grade department of the Roxbury branch of the city surveyor's office. After staying there five years he came back to Manchester and re-purchased his old office, which he conducted for two years. From 1881 to 1885, inclusive, he held the office of city engineer for Manchester. In his private engineering office he has had under his charge numbers of students, who are now holding responsible positions in different parts of the country. He has been preceptor for most of the engineers who have been employed by the city government. Having had a thorough training and having seen considerable of the country, he has a wide knowledge of surveying and engineering. He has assisted in laying out the greater part of the suburbs of Manchester, and is now carrying on a private office at No. 924 Elm street. He does all kinds of surveying and engineering, and his work extends from north of the White Mountains into Massachusetts territory. Mr. Allen is a Republican in politics, and is at present (1907) treasurer of ward four, Manchester.

In Masonic circles he is a member of Washington Lodge, Ancient Free and Accepted Masons, Mt. Horeb Royal Arch Chapter, Adorinam Council, and Trinity Commandery, Knights Templar, of Manchester. Past high priest of Mt. Horeb, Royal Arch Chapter, and past thrice illustrious master of Adoniram Council. He still owns the old Allen farm in Hanover. He is a member of the Good Samaritan Lodge, Independent Order of Odd Fellows, and the Golden Rule Lodge, Daughters of Rebecca, and was formerly a member of the Grange in Hanover. On December 15, 1872, George H. Allen married Ella A. Simons, daughter of Alfred G. and Mary Elizabeth (Davis) Simons. (See Simons Family). Mrs. Allen was born in Warner, New Hampshire, December 15, 1850, and was educated in the schools of that place. Mr. and Mrs. Allen never had any children, but it is a source of pleasure to this couple to place on record the life of a boy named Israel Aubey, who was taken at the age of eight into the home of Ira B. Allen, and there reared as a son. When the senior Mr. Allen died, this charge was given to George H. Allen and his wife. Israel Aubey was born December 28, 1875. His preliminary education was obtained at the public schools in Hanover. He was graduated with honors from the Manchester high school in the class of 1893. He took a post-graduate course in 1894, and was graduated from the scientific department of Dartmouth College in 1898. He then entered the office of Mr. George H. Allen and remained under his instruction for a time. His first position was with the Boston Elevated Railroad. He began as a rodman, and was promoted step by step to inspector of steel work. Having been a competent man he was given charge of inspection by that great corporation. Later he was engaged as inspector of a great steel construction in New York City. His present position is in the engineering department of the Massachusetts water and sewer commission. Israel Aubey married, September 4, 1904, M. Jennie Rines, a native of Massachusetts. They reside in Framingham, Massachusetts.

SIMONS Symonds, which seems to have been the earliest form of this name, later written Simonds and Simons, is frequently found among the immigrants of the seventeenth century.

(I) John Simons was born at Lebanon, New Hampshire, August 1, 1789. He married Mary Dennison Taylor, of Woodstock, Vermont, who was born August 15, 1796. They had six children: Mary A., whose sketch follows; Alfred F., Rachel B., John D., Hiram D. and John T.

(II) Alfred G., eldest son and second child of John and Mary D. (Taylor) Simons, was born at Lebanon, New Hampshire, April 5, 1825. In 1849 he married Mary Elizabeth Davis. They had one child, Ella A., born in Warner, New Hampshire, December 15, 1850. She married George H. Allen. (See Allen, II above).

ALLEN George Washington Allen was born January 27, 1863, in Sheffield, Vermont. He was educated in the common schools and at the Lyndonville Institute. When about twenty-three years of age he came to Laconia, New Hampshire, and worked in the shoe shop for a few months. He then spent four years with E. J. Dinsmore, learning the trade of harness making. About 1891 he moved to Lakeport, New Hampshire, and went into the harness-making business for himself, in which he still continues. His business is in Lakeport, but his home is in Laconia. In politics he is a Republican. He is a member of the Masonic blue lodge, and of Chocorne Lodge, Independent Order of Odd Fellows. He is president of the Building Association of Laconia, and belongs to the New England Order of Protection. He is a member of the Lowell Free Baptist Church. He married Emma Bennett, who was born in Gilford, New Hampshire.

TORR-GREENFIELD Tor or Torr as the name is now spelled, is a Celtic word and signifies a tower-like rock. In Devonshire, England, are found the names Yes Tor, Fur Tor, Hare Tor, Lynx Tor, and other tors. The first man named Torr probably took his name from his residence near a tor, and was designated Arthur attetor, or Geoffrey atto tor, or otherwise, as his baptismal name required.

(I) Vincent Torr, a native of England, came to America previous to 1733, and settled in Dover on a farm still owned by his descendants. He was a trained soldier in Dover in 1740. (New Hampshire State Papers). He died February 24, 1774. He married Lois Pinkham, who was born March 2, 1721. Their children were: Mary, Andrew, Eunice, Simon, Vincent and Lois.

(II) Simon Torr, fourth child and second son of Vincent and Lois (Pinkham) Torr, was born November 5, 1749, and died March 14, 1821.. He settled in Rochester in 1775, on the farm still owned by his great-grandsons. A part of the house then built is yet standing, and the same old clock which he brought from England is still in use there. Simon Torr was a private in Captain Caleb Hodgdon's Company at Seavey's Island, at Portsmouth Harbor, Nov. 5, 1775. (Revolutionary Rolls, volume 1, page 236). Simon Torr was Sergeant-Major of Col. John Waldron's Regiment, in 1776. (Revolutionary Rolls, Volume 1, page 476). Colonel John Waldron's regiment was stationed at Temple farm, in Brigadier-General John Sullivan's Brigade in the Continental army, March 6, 1776. No roll of the men has been found. After being drilled at Seavey's Island, in November, 1775, the company in which was Simon Torr, probably went to Winter Hill, Boston, and they were "six weeks men." Afterwards Waldron's regiment was raised out of these various "six weeks men-companies" to remain until April 1, 1776, and Simon Torr became the sergeant-major of this regiment. He married Sarah Ham, and had four daughters and three sons: Betsey, Mary, Abigail, Sarah, John, Simon and Jonathan. (Mention of Simon and descendants forms part of this article).

(III) John (Torr) Greenfield, fifth child and eldest son of Simon and Sarah (Ham) Torr, was born October 5, 1787, on the old Torr farm in Rochester, and died January 13, 1863. He was reared a tanner, shoemaker, and farmer, and very early showed signs of great foresight. About 1812 or 1813 he commenced trading in Rochester, and for nearly or quite fifty years was one of the most successful business men in town. He was full of energy, and possessing a sound judgment was always able to make good investments. Soon after he engaged in mercantile business in Rochester, his brother, Jonathan Torr, opened a store in the same place, and the goods consigned to the two brothers (being marked "J. Torr") were so often delivered to the wrong Torr, that John Torr had his name changed to John Greenfield. At his death in 1863 Mr. Greenfield left an ample fortune and an unsullied reputation. He married Phebe Wentworth, who was born November 22, 1798, daughter of Stephen and Sallie (Cottle) Wentworth. She was of the sixth generation from Elder William Wentworth, "the settler." Four children were born of this marriage: Charles, Sarah E. (see Wallace, II), Ella G. and George. (The last named and descendants are noticed in this article).

(IV) Charles, eldest child of John and Phebe (Wentworth) Greenfield, was born in Rochester, February 18, 1826, and died December 19, 1898. He attended school until fourteen years of age, and then began farming which was his principal employment in life. After the death of his father, in 1863, he received his portion of the estate to which he made constant addition until he owned several hundred acres of land in Rochester. Though nominally a farmer, he made much money in other ways than farming. He was a director of the Rochester National Bank, president and trustee of the Norway Plains Savings Bank, and a stockholder in various railroad and manufacturing enterprises, and at his death was one of the wealthy men of the town. He was a man of quick perception, clear judgment, and sound reason, and seldom if ever made a financial mistake. He was a man of sterling integrity, and in farming and financial circles was a leading citizen, intelligent, prudent and highly esteemed. In politics he was a Whig until that party passed away, and afterwards a Republican. He married, July 5, 1846, Aroline B. Downs, of Rochester, who was born May 17, 1826, and still lives in Rochester, daughter of Gershom and Sally P. (Richardson) Downs. Their children were: Millie A., John, Ella S., Sarah E., Hattie A., Frank, and a son who died in infancy.

(V) Millie A., daughter of Charles Greenfield, born June 27, 1847, married, June 27, 1872, Horace L. Worcester, of Lebanon, Maine. She is prominent in social circles and a member of the leading social organizations. In 1901 she was an honorary member of the board of women managers of the Pan-American Exposition at Buffalo, where she performed efficient service. In 1906 she organized Mary Torr Chapter, Daughters of the American Revolution, of which she was the first regent. This chapter was named for Mary, the wife of Judge Thompson, of Durham, daughter of the immigrant, Vincent Torr. She was born September 1, 1740, and died November 14, 1807. Mrs. Worcester is a past department president of the Woman's Relief Corps of New Hampshire. She is a member of James Farrington Chapter, No. 7, of the order of the Eastern Star, of Rochester, of which she was the first secretary, and afterward assistant matron and matron. She was the first president of the Rochester Woman's Club, and was historian and one of the managers of Margery Sullivan Chapter, Daughters of the American Revolution of Dover. John Greenfield is mentioned below. Ella S. was born November 23, 1851, and married, November 23, 1875, Justin M. Levitt, of Buxton, Maine. Sarah E., was born April 1, 1854, and married, June 16, 1885, George W. Young, of Lowell, Massachusetts. Hattie A. was born July 18, 1856, and married, June 8, 1904, Capt. Harry L. Wentworth, of Boston, Massachusetts. Frank, born February 13, 1859, resides in Rochester. He married, September 3, 1902, Cora A. Fogg, of Rochester.

(V) John, second child and eldest son of Charles and Aroline B. (Downs) Greenfield, was born in Rochester, March 28, 1849. After attending the

rles Greenfield

wi
m
H
bı
H
c
b
I

n
G
n

a

ea
w
Aft
the
unt
ser-
arah
Bet-
on-
ms
nd
as
d

brother, Jo...
place, and the goods consig...
(being marked "J. Torr") were so often ...

o.
D
Jol.
born
1875,
E., w
1885.
Hattie
8, 1904,
achusett
Rocheste
A. Fogg.
(V) Jo
and Aroline
Rochester, March 28, 1849. After attending the

Charles Greenfield

common schools and preparing for college in Phillips-Exeter Academy, he entered Dartmouth College in 1868, but ill health compelled him to give up his studies. He began to give his attention to farming in early life, and has always been interested in that calling. In politics he is a staunch Republican, and has been the recipient of many honors at the hands of his party, which he has always faithfully served. In 1876 he was elected member of the board of selectmen, and was re-elected four times. He has also served the town as tax collector, and as chief engineer of the fire department. In 1879 he was elected high sheriff of Strafford county, being the first man ever elected to that office. He was twice re-elected. He was a member of the city council seven years, and was postmaster of Rochester during Harrison's administration. He was one of the prime movers in organizing and starting the Rochester Water Works, was its first superintendent and served in that capacity for three years. He is a trustee of the Norway Plains Savings Bank, and has often served as administrator of estates. Like his father (Charles Greenfield) he is a man of the strictest integrity, his word being considered as good as his bond. He married Mary A. Smith, of Rochester, September 22, 1890.

(IV) George, fourth child and second son of John and Phebe (Wentworth) Greenfield, was born in Rochester, March 22, 1837, and died September 10, 1871. He followed the sea for a few years, when a young man, and then returning to Rochester, devoted the remainder of his life to farming. He married, in 1863, Mary Frances Parshley, daughter of Stephen and Jane (Fogg) Parshley. They had five children: Henry, George E., Herbert E., Emma J. and Mary E.

(V) George E., second son and child of George and Mary Frances (Parshley) Greenfield, was born in Rochester, May 3, 1866, and was educated in the common schools. For some years he was employed by the Boston & Maine Railroad Company in its construction department. In 1896 Mr. Greenfield and J. A. Morrill bought the wood and coal business of Samuel Stringer, which under the firm name of Morrill & Greenfield, they carried on for nine years. Mr. Greenfield then bought his partner's interest and has since conducted the business alone. He is a member of Humane Lodge, No. 21, Free and Accepted Masons; Temple Royal Arch Chapter, No. 20; Orient Council, Royal and Select Masters; and Palestine Commandery, Knights Templar; Bektash Temple, Ancient Arabic Order Nobles of the Mystic Shrine. He is a Republican He married, in Rochester, December 31, 1884, Delia A. Morrill, who was born in Rochester, August, 1865, daughter of Jedediah A. and Lucy A. (Tibbetts) Morrill. They have two children: Lucie May, born May 24, 1891; and Sarah Ella, born February 13, 1893. Members, with their mother, of the Congregational Church.

(III) Simon (2), sixth child and second son of Simon (1) and Sarah (Ham) Torr, was born on the home farm at Rochester, October 5, 1789, and died there February 17, 1858. He was a farmer and a tanner, politically a Whig, and was an adherant of the Congregational Church. He married Betsey P. Davis, who was born September 18, 1794, married, May 22, 1821, and died November 26, 1854. The children of Simon and Betsey P. (Davis) Torr were: Charles, born April 2, 1822, died May 21, 1838. Simon A., born July 28, 1825, died December 6, 1834. John F., see later on. Sarah E., born August 28, 1836, married Lewis Hanson, and died without issue.

(IV) John F., third son and child of Simon (2) and Betsey P. (Davis) Torr, was born on the homestead farm, April 28, 1829. He was a farmer all his life, died June 16, 1889. He was a Republican, and a member of the Congregational Church. He married, March 17, 1868, Mary C. Downs, born January 14, 1840, died February 1, 1904. Their children were: Charles C., born September 29, 1869. He was educated in the public schools, and is a farmer living on the Torr farm owned by him and his brother, George H. He is a member of the Independent Order of Odd Fellows, councilman of Rochester, and unmarried. Simon A., born December 13, 1871, died April 4, 1897.

(V) George H., youngest son and child of John F. and Mary C. (Downs) Torr, was born on the homestead, March 20, 1876. He grew up on the farm, and attended the public school and also took a course in the Dover Business College. He has always been a farmer, but now resides in Rochester. He is a member of Humane Lodge, Free and Accepted Masons, and a Republican. He married, October 5, 1904, Lillian M. Gerrish (see Gerrish, III) and they have a son,

(VI) Franklin G., born July 19, 1905.

FOGG The State of New Hampshire is largely indebted for its development—industrial, social and moral—to those bearing this name, who were among the first in the colony and are still numerous in many sections of the state.

(I) The first of the name in this country was Samuel Fogg, who was among the early settlers of Hampton, one of the first settlements in New Hampshire. He was a native of England, and received grants of land in Hampton at a very early period, which cannot now be exactly determined. In the second review of old grants made in 1658 he is found to have previously received separate grants of land aggregating eight and three-fourths acres, and it is presumed that he was among the original proprietors. He purchased the home of Christopher Hussey, who was one of the original proprietors, and who removed to what is now Hampton Falls upon selling his estate to Mr. Fogg. In 1669 the latter drew lot 60, comprising one hundred acres, which indicates that he was the owner of two or more shares in the common rights. This farm has never been conveyed by deed, and is still in the possession of his descendants, having passed successively from father to son. He was married (first), December 12, 1652, to Ann, daughter of Richard Shaw (see Shaw). She was the sixth child of her parents, and died December 9, 1663. Mr. Fogg was married (second), December 28, 1665, to Mary, daughter of Richard Page (see Page). She was born about 1644, and died March 8, 1700. Mr. Fogg died April 16, 1672. Five of his children were born of his first wife and three of the second, namely: Samuel, Joseph, John, Daniel, Henry, Seth, James and Ann. (Mention of Seth and descendants appears in this article).

(II) Daniel, son of Samuel and Anne (Shaw) Fogg, was born April 16, 1660, in Hampton, and settled first in Scarborough, Maine, whence he removed to Portsmouth, New Hampshire, in 1690. About 1700 he settled in that part of Kittery which is now Elliot, Maine. He died June 9, 1755. He was married about 1684 to Hannah, daughter of John Libby, of Scarborough. She died between 1730 and 1735. Their children were: Hannah, Captain Daniel, Mary, Rebecca, Samuel, Sarah, John, Joseph, Seth and James.

(III) James, youngest child of Daniel and Hannah (Libby) Fogg, was born March 17, 1704, in

Kittery, and lived on the paternal homestead, engaged in farming. He was married, October 23, 1728, to Elizabeth, daughter of Deacon James and Mary Fernald. She was born September 8, 1706, and died in 1766. He died September 24, 1787. Their children were: James, Mary, Elizabeth, Anne, Hannah, Eunice, Joseph, Abigail, John and Daniel.

(IV) Joseph, second son and seventh child of James and Elizabeth (Fernald) Fogg, was born February 12, 1745, in Kittery, and died in Berwick, September 30, 1807, in his sixty-third year. He was married in 1771 to Mercy Littlefield, of Wells, who survived him. Their children were: Joseph, Daniel, Jane, James and Isaac.

(V) Jane, only daughter and third child of Joseph and Mercy (Littlefield) Fogg, was born May 10, 1776, in Kittery, and became the wife of David Hodsdon of Berwick (see Hodsdon, VI).

(II) Seth, fifth son of Samuel Fogg, and eldest child of his second wife, Mary (Page) Fogg, was born November 28, 1666, and died September 6, 1755. He married Sarah, daughter of Benjamin Shaw, who was born 1641. He married (second), May 25, 1663, Esther Richardson, and resided on the homestead of his father in Hampton. His second wife died May 16, 1736, aged ninety-one years. His children were: Benoni, Hannah, Seth, Sarah, Esther, Samuel, Simon, Abner, Abigail, Daniel, Jeremiah and Ebenezer.

(III) Samuel, third son and sixth child of Seth Fogg, was born February 13, 1700, and resided in Hampton until 1735, when he was dismissed from the church there to the church at Eexter, New Hampshire. His wife's name was Mary, and their children were: Samuel, Steven, Mary, Josiah, Ephraim, David, Theodate, Phineas and Hulda.

(IV) Phineas, sixth child and eighth son of Samuel and Mary Fogg, was born July 11, 1738, in Exeter, and resided in Epping, New Hampshire, where he was a farmer. He married his cousin, Lydia Fogg, daughter of Simon Fogg, of Seabrook. She was born August 9, 1745, and died April 27, 1820. Their children were: Samuel, Simon, Nathan, Asahel, Mesach, Noah, Newell, Dearborn, Levi and David. (The last named and descendants receive mention in this article).

(V) Nathan, third son and child of Phineas and Lydia Fogg, was born December 31, 1768, in Epping, New Hampshire, where he passed his life. He was married about 1798 to Mercy Yuran, who was born July 21, 1773, and died December 14, 1863, aged over ninety years. He died March 20, 1867, in his ninety-ninth year. Following is an account of their children: Sally, born in 1800, married a McQuillis, and died in Rockland, Maine; David was a farmer in Center Harbor, New Hampshire, where he died; Nancy, born 1804, married a Pierce, and died in Sharon, Vermont; George died in Meredith; Mary became the wife of Henry Wilson, and died in Manchester, about 1898; Lydia died at the age of twenty-two years, unmarried; Arthur engaged in hotel keeping in the west, where he died. Sewall is the subject of the succeeding sketch.

(VI) Sewall Leavitt, youngest child of Nathan and Mercy (Yuran) Fogg, was born September 10, 1815, in Center Harbor, this state, and died May 9, 1892, at his home in Manchester. He grew up on the paternal farm in Center Harbor, receiving a limited education in the local district school. On account of ill health he was compelled to leave school at the age of seventeen, and on attaining his majority he went to Concord, where he was employed in a hotel kept by Gustavus Walker, who receives mention elsewhere in this work. Subsequently he went to Boston, where he was employed for some time as a coachman by a wealthy family named Wells. Thence he went to Methuen, Massachusetts, where he engaged in the dry goods business in partnership with his brother-in-law, Henry Wilson. Besides operating a store they sent out wagons through the country, and enjoyed an extensive trade. From Methuen he went to Manchester, in this state, and was for several years proprietor of the City Hotel. Subsequently he engaged in the livery business on the Bridge street, and later on Hanover street, on the site now occupied by the Opera House, being a partner of the late Eben James. Upon the expiration of their lease and preparation for the construction of the Opera House he retired from active business. He was early in life a member of the Freewill Baptist Church, and in his later years was an attendant of the First Congregational Church of Manchester. Upon the organization of the Republican party he became one of its supporters, but did not mingle extensively in politics. His public services consisted chiefly of two years as representative in the legislature from Manchester. He married (first), Sarah A. McGuire, who was born in 1821, and died February 12, 1844. He married (second), Susan Evans, who was born April 23, 1816, and died December 14, 1869. He was married (third), October 5, 1871, to Mariah A. Gove, who was born July 24, 1839, in Lynn, Massachusetts, daughter of Ira Gove (see Gove, VII). There was one child of the first marriage, Laroz, and one of the second, Charles H., both of whom died in infancy. Of the third marriage, there was a son Edward N., born May 6, 1856, and died August 8, 1891, in Manchester.

(V) David, youngest child of Phineas and Lydia (Fogg) Fogg, was born June 5, 1789, in Epping, New Hampshire, and died at Lebanon, same state.

(VI) Caleb Pierce, son of David Fogg, was a native of Epping, and resided in Epping and Franklin, Vermont. He removed from the latter point to Sturbridge, Province of Quebec, and from there to Magog, in the same province. He was a farmer by occupation, and a regular attendant of the Methodist Church. In political principle he was a Republican. He died in Manchester New Hampshire, at the age of about sixty-six years. He was married at Franklin, Vermont, to Lavina Cook, who was born there and died at Stanstead, Quebec. They were the parents of three children: Willis Pierce, Ann Elizabeth and Henry H. The last named was a farmer, and died at Etna, Minnesota. The daughter married Hollis P. Foss, of Montgomery, Vermont.

(VII) Willis Pierce, eldest child of Caleb Pierce and Lavina (Cook) Fogg, was born May 31, 1831, in Franklin, Vermont, and received his education in the public schools of Canada and of Manchester, New Hampshire. When fourteen years of age he left his home in Canada and went to Manchester, this state, where he was employed by his uncle, Willis P. Fogg, who conducted a hardware store. During this period he attended school a part of the time, and also subsequently after taking employment in the mills. He was gifted with abundance of Yankee ingenuity, and rapidly worked his way up after entering the mills, until he became superintendent of spinning, dressing, fulling, warping and twisting. His connection with the Amoskeag Mills continued for about forty years, and it was with reluctance that his employers gave up his services. Being apt in the use of tools, he did some building, and erected a beautiful home for himself in the city of Manchester. His skill in adapting himself to the needs of his employers is indicated by the fact that he was second hand in the spinning room of the Amoskeag Mills when only sixteen years old. Mr. Fogg is still vigorous and active for one of his years, and devotes considerable time to carpenter work and similar occupations. He is a Methodist in religious faith, and an ardent supporter of the Republican principles in governmental affairs. For many years he served as one of the selectmen of Manchester. He married (first), Sarah Ann Fletcher, a native of Franklin, Vermont, who died at the end of a year after their marriage, leaving a daughter, Minnie S., who is now the widow of Edward Bumstead, and resides in Boston, Massachusetts. He married (second), Frances A. Haff, a native of Peru, New York, who has been for many years deceased. There were two children of this second marriage, Ernest Willis and Mabel. The latter died in girlhood.

(VIII) Ernest Willis, only son of Willis Pierce and Frances A. (Haff) Fogg, was born and died in Manchester, New Hampshire. He married May Robinson, of that city, who survives him, together with their son, Willis Pierce Fogg.

(VI) Stephen and Sally Fogg are the first known of this line.

(VII) Chase Fogg, son of Stephen and Sally Fogg, resided in Meredith, New Hampshire. His wife's name was Sally.

(VIII) William Tailor Fogg, son of Chase and Sally Fogg, was born April 30, 1830, in Meredith and died in Manchester April 30, 1900. He grew up in his native town and attended the district schools and was subsequently a student at New Hampton Literary Institution. At the age of about twenty years he went to Manchester and there learned the trade of butcher, which he followed most of his life. Within a few years he engaged in business for himself and for many years he operated a wagon, supplying meat to customers in and about Manchester. At the age of thirty-five years he became a member of the city police force and so continued for eight years. For a long time he was a member of the Baptist Church and was also a member of Hillsboro Lodge, Independent Order of Odd Fellows of Manchester. In politics he was a Republican. He was married May, 1877, to Etta M. Wilson, who was born September, 1855, in Manchester, daughter of Freeman Wilson, a substantial resident of that city. They were the parents of two daughters: Bertha May and Grace Belle. The latter was for some years a teacher and is now the wife of Robert F. Means, of Everett, Massachusetts. The younger has received a business training and is now employed in an office in Manchester.

WILSON Freeman Wilson, who was born October 22, 1815, in Edgecomb, Maine, was for many years a well known citizen of Manchester, New Hampshire, where he died in the fall of 1870. He belonged to the Scotch strain which has infused so much of life blood into the development of New Hampshire. His mother lived to the age of more than one hundred years. Very early in life he went to Boston and engaged in the leather business for some time, and was subsequently on the police force of that city. About 1855 he went to Salem, New Hampshire, and purchased a farm. Not long thereafter he removed to Manchester and purchased land between Hall and Wilson streets, lying on both sides of Central. The growth of the city soon brought this land into demand for city lots and the great appreciation in its value gave to Mr. Wilson an important financial position in the city. When he first arrived in the city he began butchering and selling meat and this continued until his death. He was a regular attendant of the Baptist Church, of which his wife was a member and was a steadfast Republican in political principles. He married Mary Leavitt, who was born in Meredith, New Hampshire, and they were the parents of six children, three of whom died in infancy. Of the survivors, the eldest, Eugene Freeman, died in Manchester, in August, 1899, at the age of fifty-four years. The second, Etta, is the widow of William T. Fogg as above mentioned. Nellie, the third, is Mrs. Charles F. Fifield, of Manchester.

DUDLEY (I) William Dudley, born at Richmond, formerly Sheen, in Surrey, England, came to Guilford, Connecticut, from the town of Guilford, some thirty miles southeast of London, in the county of Surrey. He died at Guilford, March 16, 1684. He was married, August 24, 1636, to Miss Jane Lutman, by Rev. Henry Whitfield, Rector at Ockley in Surrey, England, according to parish register of Ockley. He and his wife came over to America and settled in Guilford, Connecticut, in 1639. They came with Rev. Henry Whitfield, as part of the Eaton and Hopkins expedition to Connecticut. This company sailed from London May 20, 1639. Mr. Dudley was a member of Whitfield's church and parish, and readily joined with his clerical friend in the emigration. When arrived with his young wife at Guilford, they established their home on what is now Fair street. There were distinguished men in the company with whom Mr. Dudley came to America, some of whom were Samuel Disborough, who returned to England, became Lord Keeper of the Great Seal in Scotland, a famous M. P., etc.; Mr. John Hoadley, who returned and became an eminent clergyman; Thomas Jordan, who returned and became an eminent lawyer of Westminster Hall; Mr. William Leete, who was Governor of Connecticut. Mr. Dudley was a representative to the general court for Guilford, and held other offices. Mr. Dudley was a farmer, as appears by his will and inventory. He made his mark on his will, but that does not prove that he could not write, as he might have been palsied or lame in his hand, or too ill to write. His wife, Jane, died May 1, 1674, at Guilford. Their children were: William, Joseph, Ruth, Deborah and another child whose name is not known.

(II) Deacon William (2), eldest child of William (1) and Jane (Lutman) Dudley, was born at sea, June 8, 1639, and died May 1701, at Saybrook, Connecticut. He was called a cordwainer by trade, and was admitted freeman at Guilford in 1670, and that year he removed to Saybrook, where he was a deacon of the church, and a representative to the general court many years, and commissioner several years. The town records say: "February 7, 1676, there were given to Deacon William Dudley, by the town of Saybrook, thirty-two and one-half rods of up-land as a plot to build his house on at what is now called Old Saybrook, and other pieces of land in that part of the town." The probate court at New London, Connecticut, April 14, 1719, appointed Mrs. Mary Dudley, widow of Deacon William Dudley, administratrix on his estate. Will of Deacon William Dudley: Oldest son William to have a double portion, and to have the homestead after the decease of his wife. Date of his will, September 2, 1700, proved May 29, 1701. His son William he enjoins to pay his mother, testator's widow, twenty shillings a year, and "if my son Daniel live to enter upon building a house for himself, then my will is that my son William do pay to my son Daniel five pounds in Lawful money of New England." He married, November 4, 1661, Mary Stow, who was living in 1702. Their children were: Mary, William, Abigail, Joseph (died young), Deborah, Samuel, Joseph, Sarah, Elizabeth, Daniel and Mehetabel.

(III) Daniel, fifth son of Deacon William and Mary (Stow) Dudley, was born 1688, in Saybrook, and was a freeman there in 1704. He married, September 2, 1714, Deborah Buell, of Killingsworth, Connecticut (marriage recorded at Saybrook). They were the parents of the following children: Lucia, Daniel, Deborah and Lucy.

(IV) Daniel (2), eldest son of Daniel (1) and Deborah (Buell) Dudley, was born July 29, 1719, at Saybrook, Connecticut, and died in Newport, New Hampshire, February 1, 1811, aged ninety-two years. He removed to Newport in 1772. He married, November 5, 1741, Susanna Chatfield, of Killingsworth, she died August 6, 1791, aged sixty-seven. Their children were: Susanna, Josiah, Deborah (died young), Chloe, Daniel, John, Elias, Anne and Ezra.

(V) Josiah, eldest son of Daniel (2) and Susanna (Chatfield) Dudley, was born December 27, 1745, in Saybrook, Connecticut, and moved to Newport, New Hampshire, in 1772, with his father. He lived nearly a hundred years, says his granddaughter, Mrs. Henry P. Carruthers, daughter of Clarissa (Dudley) Eaton. He married Elizabeth Denison of Saybrook, and they were the parents of the following children: Josiah, George, Jeremiah, Betsey, Clarissa, Anna and Minerva.

(VI) Jeremiah, third son of Josiah and Elizabeth (Denison) Dudley, was a farmer in Newport, New Hampshire. He married, February 4, 1790, at Andover, Mary Robards of Salisbury, Massachusetts, and they had the following children: Betsey, Calvin, Sophia, Fisher, Harvey, Willard and Denison.

(VII) Willard, fourth son of Jeremiah and Mary (Robards) Dudley, was born in Sutton, Massachusetts, February 22, 1800, and died in Calais, Vermont, October 17, 1866. He married Polly Edwards, who was born in Montpelier, April 10, 1802, and died at the same place April 12, 1880.

(VIII) D. Willard, son of Willard and Polly (Edwards) Dudley, was born January 26, 1832, at Montpelier. He married Helen Frances Hammond, who was born May 10, 1832, at Windsor, Vermont, and died September 6, 1892, at Montpelier.

(IX) Fanny Hammond, daughter of D. Willard and Helen Frances (Hammond) Dudley, was born September 22, 1854, at Calais, Vermont, and married Frank B. Emery (See Emery, IX).

FULLER The date upon which the ancestor of the family of Fuller came to Massachusetts Bay Colony is *prima facie* evidence of the fact that he was a Puritan who sought religious freedom in the woods of New England. The original Fuller was doubtless one whose occupation was fulling cloth.

(I) John Fuller, immigrant ancestor of a numerous family, was one of the early settlers of Cambridge, Massachusetts, where he died in 1698, aged eighty-seven. He was a farmer and a maltster, and lived on the south side of the Charles river in what is now Newton, where he became an extensive land owner and a prominent townsman. By his wife Elizabeth he had John, Jonathan, Joseph, Joshua, Jeremiah, Elizabeth and Isaac.

(II) John (2), eldest son of John (1) and Elizabeth Fuller, was born June 6, 1645, and died January 21, 1721, aged seventy-six. He lived in Newton. He married (first), June 30, 1682, Abigail Boylston; and (second), October 14, 1714, Margaret Hicks, who was born in Cambridge, July 3, 1668, daughter of Zachariah and Elizabeth (Sill) Hicks. The children of John and Abigail were: Sarah, John, Abigail, James, Hannah, Isaac, Jonathan, and Caleb.

(III) Isaac, sixth child and third son of John (2) and Abigail (Boylston) Fuller, was born November 22, 1695, in Newton, where he always resided. He married, July 19, 1721, Abigail Park. Their children were: John, Abigail, Samuel, Priscilla, and Richard.

(IV) Abigail, second son and child of Isaac and Abigail (Park) Fuller, was born June 1, 1723, and resided in Newton, where he died March 2, 1798, aged seventy-five. He married, January 16, 1755, Lydia Richardson, who was born about 1727, daughter of David and Remember (Ward) Richardson, of Newton, and great-granddaughter of Samuel Richardson and William Ward. Eight or more children were born of this marriage: Sybel, Rhoda, Lemuel, Esther, Elijah, Ezekiel, Amasa, and Isaac.

(V) Isaac, (probably) the eighth and youngest child of Abijah and Lydia (Richardson) Fuller, was born in Newtown about 1773, and died in 1819, aged forty-six. He lived a few years in Holden, Massachusetts, and in 1797 or 1798 removed to Marlborough, New Hampshire, and lived in that part of that town which was afterward included in Troy. He was a farmer and a carpenter. In the winter of 1819, while returning to his home from the village of Troy, in a severe snow storm, within sight of his house, he perished from cold while thus storm bound. He married, August 7, 1797, Patty Howe, who was born in Holden, Massachusetts, May 25, 1779, daughter of Jonathan and Dorothy (Smith) Howe. She died August 16, 1836, aged fifty-seven. Their children were: Amasa, Lucretia, Patty, Nancy, Dorothy, Stillman, Lydia, Isaac, Harriet and Eliza. Amasa was born in Holden, the others in Marlboro and Troy.

(VI) Amasa, oldest child of Isaac and Patty (Howe) Fuller, was born December 7, 1797, and died July 18, 1879, aged eighty-two. He grew to manhood in Troy. After learning the carpenter's trade he became a quite prominent builder in Troy and vicinity, and also cleared a farm. He acquired considerable property in Troy, and at the age of sixty years he improved a water power at Marlboro Depot, where he erected a saw and grist mill. He had also been engaged in the manufacture of wooden ware in Marlboro for some time, when, in 1865, he sold his factory to his son Levi. Late in life he removed to Swanzey, where he purchased a small farm. He died at Swanzey about fourteen years later. He married Anna Bemis, who was born in Marlborough, July 5, 1801, and died June 19, 1826; he married (second), January 11, 1827, Hannah Jackson, who was born in Wallingford, Vermont, November 5, 1803, a relative of the esteemed Rev. William Jackson, D. D., a graduate of Dartmouth College in 1790, pastor at Rupert, Vermont, whose son, Rev. Samuel Jackson, D. D., was secretary of the Massachusetts Board of Education, and whose daughter Henrietta (Jackson) Hamlin, was the efficient missionary at Constantinople. Hannah (Jackson) Fuller died April 5, 1845, aged forty-two. He married (third), October 2, 1845, Mary (Knight) Hager, who was born

Levi A. Fuller

February 14. 1802. He married (fourth), 1857, Lovey Kidder, who was born October 6, 1813. The children of the first wife are all dead. By the second wife there were eight children: Elvira, Amasa, Levi A., Erwin J. and four children who died in infancy.

(VII) Levi Aldrich, third son and sixth child of Amasa and Hannah (Jackson) Fuller, was born in Troy, May 4, 1836. His education was obtained in the schools of Troy and Marlboro, after leaving which he was employed for some time in his father's factory. At the age of twenty he went to Fitzwilliam, where he manufactured clothespins for a number of years. In 1865 he purchased his father's business at Marlboro, which he has since successfully carried on for forty years. He manufactures lumber, chair stock, pail handles, bale woods, etc. Aside from his home manufacturing business he owns about 1,200 acres of timber land, and employs from ten to twenty men, he has for the past ten years been engaged, in company with Chester L. Lane, in buying timber lands and cutting the timber into lumber with portable steam mills set up on the various lots. They own together more than 1,200 acres at the present time.

For many years Mr. Fuller has been prominent in public affairs in his town and county. He has settled a great many estates, and has been guardian in a large number of cases. In politics he is a Republican, and as such has served many years in official life. For more than thirty years he has been a justice of the peace. In 1869 he was made a member of the board of selectmen, serving four years in succession, one year as chairman, and has served at intervals five or six years, and has been chairman two or three times since. He was in the legislature of 1873 and 1874 and was a member of the constitutional convention of 1876. He served four years on the board of commissioners for Cheshire county, two years as chairman, and in 1903 and 1904 was a senator from the Thirteenth district. While senator he was chairman of the committee on towns and parishes, and a member of the committees on revision of laws, agriculture, claims, and soldiers' homes. For a number of years he has been a member of the board of education. He is a member of Marlborough Grange, No. 115, Patrons of Husbandry, and of Cheshire County Pomona Grange, No. 6. In 1869 he united with the Congregational Church of his town and in 1874 became one of its deacons, in which capacity he has ever since served. It may be truly said that there is no one in the community who takes a deeper interest in the welfare of his fellow citizens than Senator Fuller, or discharges more faithfully the tasks imposed upon him. He married (first), February 22, 1860, Elvira L. Bemis, of Troy, who was born June 4, 1839, adopted daughter of Joseph Bemis, of Ashburn. She died November 15, 1865, and he married (second), October 30, 1866, Emily L. Adams, daughter of Dr. William Adams, of Swanzey. The children of the first wife were: Cora A., died in infancy; and Elmer A., a resident of Danvers, Massachusetts, married Hattie C. L. Wilson, of Sullivan, New Hampshire, and has one son, Julian. The children by the second wife are: Ida E., Walter T., Arthur L., and Cora A. Ida E. is now the wife of Fred Farrar, of Troy, a well known merchant. Walter T. is a clerk for the Holbrook Grocery Company, Woodsville. He married Charlotte B. Farrar, of Troy. Arthur L. is a graduate from the mechanical engineering department, of the New Hampshire

College of Agriculture, a graduate of Cornell, class of 1905, and is now engaged in business in Boston. Cora A. is a graduate of the Keene high school, and a student in Boston Kindergarten.

BELL As long as the history of New Hampshire exists Londonderry will be regarded as a spot in the wilderness of its Colonial period in which immigrants of Irish nativity, but as Scotch in all their sentiments and feelings, likes and dislikes, as if they had been reared in Argyleshire, where their forefathers for centuries had their homes and lived their lives, settled and laid the foundations of a community whose members have sustained characters of the highest type. From those immigrants whom toil had made strong and persecution and privations had made virtuous and brave has sprung a progeny, who in the several professions and in the various walks of public and private life have sustained characters of distinguished excellence, and filled some of the highest offices—literary, military, civil, and sacred—in the country. Of the descendants of those pioneer settlers some have held seats in the American congress, some have presided in our higher seminaries of learning, some have filled places in the state council and senate, some have signalized themselves by military achievements, some have sustained the chief magistracy of the commonwealth, and some have been distinguished as ministers of the Gospel. Among all the families of this remarkable colony none has been more distinguished than the family of John Bell, which supplied to New Hampshire its ninth, thirteenth, and forty-first governors.

(I) John Bell, the immigrant ancestor of the distinguished family of this name in New Hampshire, was born in the vicinity of Coleraine, probably in the parish of Ballymony, in county Antrim, Ireland, in 1678, and died in Londonderry, July 8, 1743, aged sixty-four years. He was not of the first company of immigrants who settled Londonderry in April, 1716, but must have arrived there in 1720, as the first mention of his name upon the records is in the grant of his homestead, a lot of sixty acres, in Aiken's Range, upon which he spent the remainder of his life, and where his son John always lived. This record bears the date of 1720. Other lands were allotted to him in 1722, and afterwards to the amount of three hundred acres. After commencing a clearing upon a part of his lot and building a cabin there, he returned in 1722 to Ireland for his wife and two surviving daughters, two of his children having died in infancy. He held a respectable position among his townsmen, and for several years held various offices in the town. He married, in Ireland, Elizabeth Todd, a daughter of John and Rachel (Nelson) Todd, and sister of Colonel Andrew Todd. She was a person of much decision and energy of character, and survived until August 30, 1771, when she died, aged eighty-two years. Their children, four of whom were born in Londonderry, were: Samuel, Letitia, Naomi, Elizabeth, Mary and John. The daughters all married men of the name of Duncan.

(II) Hon. John (2), youngest child of John (1) and Elizabeth (Todd) Bell, was born in Londonderry, August 15, 1730. In early life he had the advantages of education afforded by the common schools in a community where almost every adult person could read and write, and where ignorance was regarded as a disgrace. He was not a scholar, but a thinking man, who was through life a diligent reader, especially of the Bible, the familiar handbook of that day and age. He lived on his farm in much the same manner as his neighbors did, until the breaking out of the Revolution. When that struggle began he was forty-five years old and had a family of eight children, "circumstances which must have prevented him taking a very active part, if he had desired it, in the military movements of the day." But he had arrived at the time of life when he possessed large experience in every day affairs and good judgment, and was still young enough to be active. In the spring of 1775 he was elected town clerk, and a member of the committee of safety of the town. In the fall of the same year he was elected a member of the Provincial congress, which met at Exeter, December 21, 1775, and which early in 1776 resolved itself into a house of representatives, and put in operation the independent government of New Hampshire, under the temporary constitution. In the autumn of 1776 he was re-elected and attended the seven sessions of the legislature which were held in 1776 and 1777, and was again a member from December, 1780, to 1781. In 1776 he was appointed a muster master of a part of the New Hampshire troops, and in 1780 was appointed colonel of the Eighth regiment of the militia. From the beginning to the end of the war he was a firm and decided patriot, and enjoyed the confidence of the more prominent men in the state government, who relied on his sound judgment and steady support of the cause. In 1786, under the new constitution, he was elected a senator and held the office by successive elections until June, 1790, and in 1791 he was elected to fill a vacancy and served at the winter session. He was one of the committee which effected a compromise of the Masonian proprietary clause, a subject which in its time was the cause of much strife between the Masonian grantees and settlers who claimed to hold under other grants, and before the adoption of the constitution of 1792 he was a special justice of the court of common pleas. He held during many years the office of moderator, selectman, or town clerk, and discharged the duties of those offices with unquestioned integrity and good judgment. He was a magistrate from an early period after the Declaration of Independence until disqualified by age. He was early a member of the church, and sustained the office of elder from 1783 until his infirmities required him to withdraw. He was justly esteemed a pious, devout, and sincere Christian, and a steady and consistent supporter through a long life of all the institutions of religion. At the age of seventy he determined to close his connection with the business of others, and ceased to act in the capacity of magistrate, and of administrator and guardian, in which through the esteem and confidence of his townsmen he had been extensively engaged. He found occupation as long as his physical ability continued in the cultivation of his farm, had all that was necessary for the satisfaction of his wants and never strove to acquire more. He lived in an age when the man of money was not placed above the man of honor and integrity, and he would have frowned on the strenuous struggle for wealth that marks the present day. He was a man of large frame, six feet one inch in height, had a powerful voice, and great personal strength and activity, having been for twenty years the champion in the wrestling ring, a favorite musement at public meetings at that day. He had naturally a good constitution, which with his temperate habits secured to him, with the exception of a single attack of rheumatic character in middle life, almost uninterrupted health till the close of his ninety-fifth year. He died November 30, 1825, aged ninety-five years, three months and fifteen days.

He married, December 21, 1758, Mary Ann Gilmore, a daughter of James and Jean (Baptiste) Gilmore, and a granddaughter of Robert and Mary (Kennedy) Gilmore, who were early settlers of Londonderry. She was thought to possess much personal beauty in early life, was a woman of great prudence and good sense, and of a kind and affectionate temperament. She died April 21, 1822, aged eighty-five years. He had twelve children, three of whom died early. The other nine were: James (died young), Ebenezer (died young), Jonathan, John, Samuel, Elizabeth, Susannah, Mary and Mary Ann. (Samuel and descendants receive mention in this article).

(III) Governor John (3), thirteenth governor of New Hampshire, fourth son and child of John (2) and Mary Ann (Gilmore) Bell, and younger brother of Samuel Bell, ninth governor of New Hampshire, was born in Londonderry, July 20, 1765, and died in Chester, March 22, 1836, in the seventy-first year of his age. His early scholastic training was received in Londonderry. On attaining his majority, being of an enterprising disposition, he became a merchant dealing in the products of Canada. His business required him to make repeated journeys to Montreal over the rough roads and trails of Northern New Hampshire and lower Canada, which in those days ran through almost continuous forests, broken occasionally by the farm of a settler or by a small village. These journeys were no holiday excursions, but toilsome and not without danger. About the beginning of the nineteenth century he established himself at Chester, where he resided during the remainder of his life. He was fortunate in the acquisition of property, retiring from business some years before his decease, and left at his death a handsome estate. He inherited those valuable qualities for which the Scotch-Irish settlers of New Hampshire were eminently distinguished. He was a born trader, was a close buyer and a swift seller, and could make money and make it honestly. His ability, probity and sound judgment, combined with a pleasing personality, rapidly won the confidence and respect of his fellow citizens and placed him in public office where the able discharge of his duties was rewarded by promotions to higher and more responsible positions until finally he was made chief magistrate of the state. In 1799-1800 he represented the town of Londonderry in the legislature. In 1803 he was elected senator for the Third district and served one term, and at the end of his term retired to private life. In 1817 he was elected a member of the executive council, and was annually re-elected for five successive years. In 1823 he was appointed sheriff of Rockingham county, and held that office until 1828. In the latter year he was elected governor as a supporter of John Quincy Adams and served one term. "In the discharge of these various public duties he uniformly exhibited the same traits of sagacity, diligence, justice and conscientiousness which achieved success for him in his business enterprises."

He married, December 25, 1803, Persis Thorn, third child and eldest daughter of Isaac and Persis (Sargent) Thorn, of Londonderry. She was descended on the paternal side from William Thorn, of Windham, New Hampshire, and on the maternal side from Rev. Nathaniel P. Sargent, of Methuen, Massachusetts. She was a woman of strong mind and character. She survived her husband a quarter of a century, dying in November, 1862, at the age of eighty-four years, beloved and deeply lamented. The ten children of this union were:

Mary Anne Persis, Eliza Thorne, John, Susan Jane, Harriette Adelia, Jane Gibson, Caroline, Christopher Sargent, James Isaac and Charles Henry.

(IV) Mary Anne Persis Bell, eldest child of Governor John (3) and Persis (Thorn) Bell, and sister of Governor Charles Henry Bell, was born September 2, 1804. She married Rev. Nathaniel Bouton, D. D., of Concord, where she died February 15, 1839. (See Bouton, VI).

(III) Hon. Samuel Bell, LL. D., youngest son of John (2) and Mary Ann (Gilmore) Bell, was born in Londonderry, February 9, 1770. At the age of eighteen he began the study of Latin, was subsequently a pupil at the New Ipswich Academy under the celebrated John Hubbard, and entering Dartmouth College as a sophomore was graduated in 1793. He immediately began the study of law under the preceptorship of Judge Samuel Dana, of Amherst, and after his admission to the bar in 1796 he began the practice of his profession in Francestown, but in 1806 located in Amherst and some five years later removed to Chester, where he resided for the rest of his life. Although Mr. Bell's legal ability was of a character well calculated to insure the speedy accumulation of wealth had he chosen to apply himself strictly to his profession, it can be truthfully said that he sacrificed his financial prospects to the service of the state and nation, devoting the most vigorous period of his life to public affairs, and receiving the substantial support of a numerous constituency which saw the wisdom of electing him to office as long as his health would permit. Beginning his political career in 1804 as a member of the legislature from Francestown, he was speaker of the house for the years 1805 and 1806, and declined the office of attorney-general in order to enter the state senate, of which he was president in 1807 and '08. In 1813 he was a member of the executive council; was in 1816 appointed an associate justice of the New Hampshire superior court, serving in that capacity for three years until elected governor in 1819, and he was three times reelected to that office. In 1823 he relinquished the gubernatorial chair to enter the United States senate, in which body he served with marked ability for two full terms, or a period of twelve years, and in 1835 he retired permanently from both public and professional life. The succeeding fifteen years were spent in the peaceful seclusion in his home in Chester, and his death occurred December 23, 1850. The fact that Governor Bell was neither a popularity seeker nor a political manager is conclusive evidence that his retention in high office for so many years was due solely to his superior ability and invulnerable integrity. Possessed of an unusually well developed mental capacity which was carefully cultured and perfectly disciplined, he was therefore a profound student of the law, a wise counsellor, an exceptionally able jurist and a thoroughly equipped statesman, entirely void of intrigue and conscientiously attentive to public business. In reference to his record as a jurist a contemporary states that "his published judicial opinions in the early volumes of the State Reports, bear testimony to his habits of thorough and careful research, his complete understanding of the rules and reasons of the law, and his clear, logical habits of investigation and statement." Bowdoin conferred upon him the honorary degree of Doctor of Laws in 1821. Governor Bell married for his first wife Mehitable Bowen Dana, daughter of Judge Dana of Amherst, previously referred to. The children of this union were: Samuel Dana, LL. D.; John (died 1830); Mary Ann; James; Luther V., M. D., LL. D.; and another child whose name is not at hand. July 4, 1828, he married, for his second wife, Lucy Smith, daughter of Jonathan Smith, of Amherst, and she bore him four children: George, John, Charles and Louis. Four of his sons, Samuel D., James, George and Louis, became lawyers of ability.

(IV) Hon. James Bell, third son and fourth child of Hon. Samuel and Mehitable B. (Dana) Bell, was born in Francestown, November 13, 1804. He pursued his preparatory course at Phillips Academy, Andover, Massachusetts, and was graduated from Bowdoin College in 1822. His legal studies, began in the office of his brother, Samuel Dana Bell, were completed at the Litchfield, Connecticut Law School in 1825, and he was admitted to the bar the same year. From the latter year until 1831 he practiced in Gilmanton, this state, from whence he removed to Exeter and became associated in practice with his former student, Hon. Amos Tuck, afterward a member of congress from New Hampshire. For many years this firm conducted a large and exceedingly profitable law business, being detained in most of the important litigations in Rockingham and Stafford counties during its existence, and Mr. Bell was almost constantly occupied in arguing before the court and jury. Severing his association with Mr. Tuck in 1847 he became counsel and legal agent of the Winnepesaukee Land and Water Power Company, and removing to Gilford, now Laconia, he entered with spirit upon the preliminary and most difficult part of the undertaking, that of securing the land and rights of flowage around Winnepesaukee Lake for a reservoir to supply the necessary water-power for the great manufacturing establishments on the Merrimac river. The remainder of his life was devoted exclusively to this work, and he died in Gilford, May 26, 1857. Mr. Bell was never an aspirant for political honors, but like his father was forced into civic affairs simply because he was superabundantly qualified to hold public office, and he performed his official duties with the same degree of ability and earnestness as that which characterized his distinguished predecessor. In 1846 he represented Exeter in the lower house of the state legislature, was a delegate from Gilford to the state constitutional convention in 1850, was twice a candidate for governor, and in 1855 was chosen United States senator, serving through the thirty-fourth congress and in the extra session of 1857. It has been said of him that no lawyer in the state was capable of rendering a wiser or more weighty opinion on a naked question of law than was he, and his understanding of the principles, intent and purposes of laws was both varied and profound. In his manner he was modest and unobtrusive, his professional deportment was a model for excellence and his life was stainless. In 1831 Mr. Bell married Judith A. Upham, daughter of Nathaniel and Judith (Cogswell) Upham, of Rochester, New Hampshire, a sister of Hon. Nathaniel Gookin, LL. D., once a justice of the New Hampshire superior court, and a grand-daughter of Lieutenant-Colonel Thomas Cogswell of Haverhill, Massachusetts, who served as an officer in the battle of Bunker Hill. She became the mother of five children: Mary A. Bell, wife of Nathaniel G. White, who was president of the Boston & Maine railroad, Eliza U. Bell, Lucy Bell, James Dana Bell, Charles Upham Bell.

(V) Hon. Charles Upham Bell, A. M., LL. D., son of Hon. James and Judith A. (Upham) Bell, was born in Exeter, February 26, 1843. He completed the regular preparatory course at Phillips Exeter Academy, and after studying an extra year at that institution he entered Bowdoin College, taking his bachelor's degree in 1863 and receiving that of Master of Arts in course (1866). At commencement he pronounced the English oration and was chosen a member in the Psi Upsilon and the Phi Beta Kappa societies. He was a law student in the office of his cousin, the late Charles H. Bell, LL. D., of Exeter, author of "Bench and Bar of New Hampshire," and having completed his legal preparations at the Harvard Law School was admitted to the Rockingham county bar at Exeter in February, 1866. Inaugurating his practice in Exeter he was associated at intervals with his cousins, Charles H. and John J. Bell. but in 1871 he removed from his native state and located in Lawrence, Massachusetts. Forming a law partnership with his brother-in-law, Nathaniel Gilman White, the firm of White and Bell conducted a successful general law business until 1878, when Mr. Bell withdrew and entered into partnership with Edgar J. Sherman, under the firm name of Sherman and Bell. In 1887 Mr. Sherman was appointed a justice of the Massachusetts superior court, and Mr. Bell continued in practice alone for the succeeding ten years or until 1897, in which year the firm of Bell and Eaton was established. The latter partnership was, however, of short duration, as on September 16, 1898, he was selected by Governor Wolcott to succeed as associate justice of the superior court the Hon. John W. Hammond, who had been recently elevated to the supreme bench. Although his practice was not confined exclusively to any one branch of the law, he nevertheless specialized to a considerable extent in real estate and probate matters, in which he became exceedingly well versed, and for many years he was universally recognized as one of the foremost members of the Essex county bar.

In politics Judge Bell is a Republican, and in matters relative to civic affairs he has emulated the sound political doctrine advocated and scrupulously followed by his father and grandfather, namely, that it is the duty of every intelligent citizen to render his share of public service solely for the benefit of the community, and not for pecuniary reward. He was a member of the Lawrence common council for two years and president of that body for one year served as city solicitor for six years, and was one of the presidential electors in 1888, casting his official ballot for Benjamin Harrison. In 1896 he was appointed one of the commissioners to revise and codify the laws of Massachusetts, serving in that capacity until called to the judiciary of that commonwealth. For three years he rendered valuable service to the Republican party organization as a member of the state central committee, and was twice the party's candidate for mayor of Lawrence. He has also accepted and conscientiously fulfilled various duties of a semi-public nature. In 1888 he was summoned to the board of overseers of Bowdoin College, is a trustee of the Brewster Free Academy at Wolfboro, New Hampshire, and of the Essex Savings Bank, Lawrence, has long performed similar duties for the White Fund and by virtue of the latter is a life trustee of the Lawrence Public Library. Judge Bell is a veteran of the Civil war, having served one hundred days in Company C, Forty-second Regiment Massachusetts Volunteer Infantry, and is a past commander of Needham Post, No. 139, Grand Army of the Republic. He is also a member of the Sons of the American Revolution, Society of Colonial Wars, and the Society of the Cincinnati, having served upon the standing committee. His religious affiliations are with the Trinity Congregational Church, Lawrence, and for many years he has served as one of its deacons. He has contributed some valuable additions to the literature of his profession, the most notable of which is a "Digest of Massachusetts Reports." His alma mater made him a Doctor of Laws in 1901.

On November 21, 1872, Judge Bell married for his first wife Helen Maria Pitman, daughter of Joseph P. and Charlotte A. (Parker) Pitman, of Laconia, New Hampshire. She died March 26, 1882, leaving four children: Alice Lyon, Mary White, Joseph Pitman, and Helen Pitman Bell. He was again married April 10, 1883, to Elizabeth Woodbury Pitman, a sister of his first wife. Judge Bell resides in Andover, Massachusetts.

CROSS There can be little doubt that this line of the name is an offshoot of the large family founded in Essex county, Massachusetts, which has furnished many of the leading citizens of New Hampshire. (See page 1197). It is probable that the first named below was from Methuen, Massachusetts, though no record can be found to establish the fact. The first found in the vital records of this state is Simeon Cross.

(I) Simeon Cross was a resident of Bridgewater, New Hampshire, with his wife Abigail. No record of their marriage appears in New Hampshire, but their children are recorded in Bridgewater, namely: George, Abigail, Simeon, Lydia, Abijah and Judith.

(II) Simeon (2), second son and third child of Simeon (1) and Abigail Cross, was born August 7, 1784, in Bridgewater, and was a pioneer settler of Stewartstown, this state. He cleared up lands and engaged in agriculture until his death.

(III) Simeon (3), son of Simeon (2) and —— Cross, was born at Stewartstown, New Hampshire, in 1827. In early life he went to Lowell, Massachusetts, and worked in the mills for a few years, and then came back to his native town and settled upon the farm where his son now lives. He was a Republican in politics, and served as selectman of the town. He was a constant attendant at the Methodist Episcopal Church, and though not a member, contributed liberally to its support. He married Susan, daughter of French and Polly (Piper) Hall. There were nine children: Ella, married George Hicks, and is now deceased; Loren, died in 1892; Mary, married A. L. Davis, and lives in Errol, New Hampshire; Frank H., of Berlin, New Hampshire; John, whose sketch follows; Stephen, of Berlin, New Hampshire; an infant; Hattie, married A. M. Newell, of West Milan, New Hampshire; and Annie, lives in Ohio. Simeon (3) Cross died in 1884.

(IV) John, third son and fifth child of Simeon (3) and Susan (Hall) Cross, was born on the farm where he now lives, at Colebrook, New Hampshire, on December 19, 1866. He was educated in the district schools of his native town, and began to farm early in life. He has about one hundred and fifty acres under cultivation. He is a Republican in politics, and represented his town in the legislature of 1904. He served as selectman of Colebrook in 1902 and 1903. He belongs to the Grange and to the Knights of Pythias, and was formerly captain in the Uniform Rank of the latter organization. He is not married, and he and his mother constitute the family on the old homestead.

HUNT This old New England family is not so numerously represented in New Hampshire as many others, but its representatives are usually men of highest character, and reflect credit upon the family as well as upon this and the communities in which they reside.

(I) Edward Hunt, of Amesbury, Massachusetts, must have been born as early as 1655 or sooner, and was the ancestor of the Amesbury branch of the family. He may have been a son of Edward Hunt, who was at Cambridge in 1635, and is possibly identified with the Edward Hunt who sold land in Duxbury in 1665. He subscribed to the oath of allegiance in Amesbury, 1667, and was a member of the Train Band in 1680. He died December 23, 1727, in Amesbury, and the administration of his estate was granted to his son Nathaniel, in 1729. His widow, Ann Hunt, was then living. He married, February 19, 1675, Ann Weed, born July 26, 1657, daughter of John and Deborah (Winsley) Weed, of Amesbury. John Weed was born about 1627, and was among the early planters of Amesbury. He was a lieutenant of the militia, and a leading citizen of the town. His wife, Deborah (Winsley) Weed, was a daughter of Samuel and Elizabeth Winsley. Samuel Winsley was a planter of Salisbury, and was one of the twelve who obtained a grant to begin a plantation at what is now Amesbury, in 1638. The children of Edward and Ann (Weed) Hunt included two daughters who died in infancy, besides Mary, John, Ephraim, Hannah, Samuel, Nathaniel and Thomas.

(II) Nathaniel, fourth son and eighth child of Edward and Ann (Weed) Hunt, was born September 27, 1693, in Amesbury. He died between 1724 and 1728, the dates, respectively, of the making and proving of his will. His estate included seventeen acres of land and was valued at fifty-seven pounds, three shillings and eight pence. He married, May 17, 1721, Hannah Tubury, daughter of Henry (2) and Hannah Tubury, and granddaughter of Henry Tubury, a weaver of Newbury and Amesbury. She was born August 26, 1697. Their children were: Philip, Moses, Nathaniel, Zacheus, Henry, Eliakim, Ann, Hannah, Judith, Mary, David and Sylvanus.

(III) Henry, fifth son and child of Nathaniel and Hannah (Tubury) Hunt, resided in Kingston, New Hampshire, where he died in 1794. The records of Kingston show that on February 24, 1730, he was paid the sum of sixteen pounds and five shillings for "Keping scool." He married Hannah Eastman, daughter of Roger and Rachel Eastman (see Eastman, IV), and they were the parents of children: Eliakim, Henry, Abner, Moses, Rachel, Hannah, Elizabeth, Judith, Miriam, Ann, Stephen and Eliphalet.

(IV) Henry (2), second son and child of Henry and Hannah (Eastman) Hunt, was born August 29, 1749, in Kingston, and resided in Gilmanton, New Hampshire, where he operated iron works. He married, December 27, 1777, Rhoda French, and their children were: John, Oliver, Henry, Rhoda, Nancy and Lois.

(V) Oliver, second son and child of Henry and Rhoda (French) Hunt, was born June 8, 1782, at Gilmanton Iron Works, and died in Manchester, November 24, 1857. He took up his residence in Alton, where he had a farm and blacksmith shop, and later removed to a farm in Manchester Center. Like his father he was a blacksmith and worker in iron, and was a most industrious man. He married, in 1803, Anna Gilman, born July 3, 1780, at Gilmanton Iron Works, a daughter of Dudley Gilman, and granddaughter of Stephen and Rebecca (Coffin) Gilman, and thus the Hunt family became allied with two of the principal families of Gilmanton. The children of this marriage were: Gilman, Dudley, died in Manchester, at the age of forty-two years. Jonathan Titcomb Parker, see forward. Olive A., M. D., an early woman physician of New Hampshire; she graduated in 1866-67, engaged in active practice in Manchester many years, and still actively engaged in the practice of her profession. Oliver Coffin, died in Manchester at the age of twenty-six years. These children were all born at Gilmanton Iron Works.

(VI) Jonathan Titcomb Parker, second son and child of Oliver and Anna (Gilman) Hunt, was born April 7, 1809, in Gilmanton, New Hampshire, and died February 23, 1865, in his fifty-sixth year, in Manchester. During his short life he accomplished much. He was a man of great ambition and industry, and early in life went to Lowell, where he became a mason contractor and built the Booth mills. Upon the organization of the Amoskeag Manufacturing Company he was induced to come to Manchester, then a small village, 1837-38, and was among the leaders in building up the present city. He built the mills of the Amoskeag Manufacturing Company, of Stark Corporation and the Print Works, and was continuously employed in that line of work until his retirement, in 1851-52, on account of failing health. He organized the Manchester Gaslight Company, built the entire plant, and became its agent and manager, in which capacity he continued until his death. He was a director of the Amoskeag Manufacturing Company, and was interested in various industries, including the scale factory and the iron foundry. He was one of the committee, in 1842, which built the town house of Manchester, on the present site of the City Hall, and after its destruction by fire he built the City Hall. For a time he engaged in the construction of the Manchester & Lawrence railroad, and after its completion was its superintendent until its operation was thoroughly organized. He was a director of the Manchester Bank from the time of its organization until its re-organization as a national bank in 1865, about the time of his death.

Mr. Hunt was an attendant of the Universalist Church, and constructed its house of worship. He was a member of Hillsborough Lodge and Mt. Wonolancet Encampment of the Independent Order of Odd Fellows, and was identified with Lafayette Lodge, Mt. Horeb Royal Arch Chapter, and Trinity Commandery, Knights Templar, of the Masonic Order. In early life he was an enthusiastic supporter of the Free Soil movement, and upon the organization of the Republican party was a leader in its affairs, and so continued until his death. At the first election carried by that party, in 1858, he was elected representative to the state legislature, re-elected in 1859, and shortly after that he served three years as a railroad commissioner of the state. He was at different time chief engineer of the fire department, and held that office in 1859, during the celebrated muster.

Mr. Hunt married, September 27, 1835, Irene Drew, born June 28, 1813, at Alton, New Hampshire, daughter of Nathan Drew, of Alton, whose wife was an Elliott. She survived her husband thirty-four years, dying February 25, 1899, in Manchester. Their children were: Irene Augusta, married Dr. Thomas Wheat, of Manchester. Nathan Parker, see forward. Annette, married William E. Drew, of Manchester. Oliver. Gilman, deceased. Abbie Maria, deceased, married Frank D. Everett.

(VII) Nathan Parker, eldest son and second child of Jonathan T. P. and Irene (Drew) Hunt, was born July 5, 1844, in Manchester, where his life has been spent. He has been active in developing all the best interests of the city, in whose founding his father took a prominent part. He was graduated from the high school of Manchester, and from Dartmouth College in the class of 1866. He took up the study of law with Samuel N. Bell, Esq., of Manchester, and was admitted to the bar in May, 1869. Immediately thereafter he began the practice of his profession, sharing the office of his preceptor, Mr. Bell, which office he still occupies. His time was given to general practice until the demands of various interests prevented further activity in that direction. In 1876 he was appointed judge of the police courts by Governor Cheney and served until 1895, when he resigned. He was city solicitor twp years, treasurer of Hillsborough county for three years, served upon the school committee many years, and in 1876, when the Democratic party lost control of the state government, he was elected representative from his ward, which was one of the Democratic strongholds of the city.

In 1879 he was made a director of the Merchants' National Bank at Manchester, and upon the death of Governor Weston, in 1895, he succeeded him as president of the bank. As one of the organizers of the Hillsborough County Savings Bank, he was made its treasurer, and has so continued to the present time. For many years he served as vice-president of the New Hampshire Fire Insurance Company, a most prosperous and worthy Manchester enterprise, and upon his election as treasurer of that company, to succeed the late George Byron Chandler, in August, 1905, he resigned the vice-presidency. He served as trustee of the City Library from September, 1873, until his resignation in May, 1906, and was treasurer of the board from 1879 until his resignation. He was one of the executors of the estate of Mrs. Mary G. Gale, and assisted in the organization of the Gale Home, one of the leading benevolent institutions of Manchester, of which he has been president down to the present time. He was one of the organizers of the Masonic Home at Manchester, and is now treasurer of that institution. For the past ten years he has been trustee of the State Industrial School, and is now president of the board. He has been a member of Wildy Lodge, Independent Order of Odd Fellows, since 1866, and one of the charter members of Mt. Washington Encampment, having passed through all the chairs of both orders. He has passed all the chairs of the Council, Chapter and Commandery, and is a member of the Consistory up to and including the thirty-third degree. He was for twenty-five years a member of the committee on jurisprudence, trials and appeals of the Grand Lodge. He is an active member of the Masonic Order as is indicated by his connection with the Masonic Home, and his connection with the official bodies of the school and city libraries indicates his interest in education and the general welfare of the community.

Mr. Hunt married, November 22, 1870, Elizabeth S. Bisbee., born in Derby, Vermont, 1844 daughter of David and Sarah (Albie) Bisbee. They are the parents of three children: Samuel Parker, who was an electrical engineer in Boston on the Old Colony railroad up to April, 1907, and since then has been assistant general manager of the Manchester Machine, Light & Power Company. Sara, married Albert L. Clough, one child, Elizabeth Louise Clough. Agnes, an instructor in Smith College.

HUNT

The Hunt family is a numerous and prosperous one in the United States. The ancestry of this line cannot now be discovered, though diligent search has been made.

(I) John Hunt, son of Levi Hunt, was born in Lisbon, New Hampshire, in 1821. He was a farmer and lived in Carroll, New Hampshire, from 1855 till 1894, when he moved to Whitefield. He was a Democrat in politics, and was selectman of the town in 1858-59-60-62-70, and represented Carroll in the legislature of 1874-75. He attended the Baptist Church, and was a respected citizen. John Hunt married Mary Ann, daughter of Samuel and Sabrina Ash, of Lisbon. They had ten children: An unnamed infant. Sabina, deceased. George H., deceased. Henry J., now living at Whitefield. Mary E., who married Hal E. Jenness. Samuel D., whose sketch follows. Ida E. John W. Mildred J., deceased. Augusta. John Hunt died at Carroll, New Hampshire, 1899, and his wife died March, 1891.

(II) Samuel Delbert, third son and sixth child of John and Mary Ann (Ash) Hunt, was born at Bethlehem, New Hampshire, August 24, 1852. He was educated in the common schools, and has farmed since then. His father moved to Carroll when he was three years old, and the son remained there till 1899, when he bought his present place in Whitefield. He is a Democrat in politics, and served as selectman in Carroll for four years, and is now (1907) holding his second term as selectman in Whitefield. He attends the Baptist Church. On August 2, 1877, Samuel Delbert Hunt married Alice M., daughter of Hosea and Annette Whitcomb, of Bethlehem. They had one child, Minnie, born 1878, and died at five months old.

DOWD

The families of Dowd or O'Dowd, Doody, and so on, as the name was variously anglicized, are of one stock, and descended from the princes and chiefs of Connaught. Many of them have been soldiers. The ancient Dowds were unusually tall, and all the O'Dowds even to the present day are so.

(I) Oliver Dowd was born in county Kerry, Ireland and there spent his life. He married Mary Sullivan.

(II) John, son of Oliver and Mary (Sullivan) Dowd, was born in county Kerry, in 1821, and died in Lewiston, Maine, in 1871, aged fifty years. He was a farmer and came to America after the "great famine" in Ireland in 1847-48. He was engaged in railroad work in New Haven, Connecticut, for a time, and went from there to Banger, Maine. Before the Civil war he assisted in the construction of Fort Knox at Bucksport, Maine. He was afterward in a wholesale grain firm in Bangor, Maine, He married Margaret Hannifin. Their children were: Thomas, Mary, Oliver, John, James, Patrick, Daniel, John H. and Cornelius.

(III) John (2), eighth child and seventh son of John and Margaret (Hannifin) Dowd, was educated in the common schools of Bangor and Lewiston. At an early age he entered the employ of the Lincoln Cotton Mills at Lewiston, Maine, where he worked four years. He then went to Bangor, where he spent three years learning marble cutting. From Bangor he went to Boston where he was employed in the same business by Enoch Wentworth, and later by Henry Murray. August 6, 1883, he entered the employ of John S. Treat, the proprietor of the oldest marble and granite cutting business in New England, where he remained four years. In 1887 he formed a partnership with Lowell Jenness, and they established themselves at Portsmouth in the business at which years of experience had made them proficient. Four years later Mr. Dowd bought his partner's interest in the business of which he has since been sole proprietor. Mr. Dowd has managed his affairs successfully and prospered. He has been active in public affairs and has been elected to positions of trust and honor. He served as assessor of taxes, as representative in the legislature, and as water commissioner of the city of Portsmouth. He married, January, 1886, Lena M. Hutchins, who was born in Portsmouth, daughter of George W. Hutchins. They have four children: Oliver H., Anna M., John F. and Lawrence.

DALEY (I) John Daley was born in county Cork, Ireland, in the year 1839. His only educational opportunities were a few days of schooling in the old country. He came to America about 1858. He worked on a farm in Lowell, Massachusetts, and for six years lived in the town of Tewksbury. He then went to Australia, where he remained for two years and where he worked at farming. When he returned to this country he settled in Londonderry, New Hampshire, where he hired a farm for three years. He then bought the Titcomb farm where he lived till his death. When he started in for himself he had twenty dollalrs in money, a cook stove worth five dollars, a hand-cart worth three dollars, and furniture to the value of five dollars more. He lived to be a respected citizen in the old town of Londonderry, where he held the office of road surveyor, and also served on the school committee. In politics he was a Republican. He belonged to the Roman Catholic Church. He married Julia Royah, daughter of Daniel Royah, and they had three children: James P., born December 18, 1866. John W., mentioned below. Daniel J., born August 3, 1874. Daniel was educated in the schools of Nashua, New Hampshire, at Pembroke Academy, and at the Boston Law School. He married Josephine C. Burke, of Manchester, New Hampshire. He was a lawyer in Manchester six years, and had a fine office in the Kennard, the best building in the city at the time it was burned. Daniel Daley died March 5, 1905. John Daley died March 31, 1901, at Londonderry. His wife is still living.

(II) John William, second son and child of John and Julia (Royah) Daley, was born on Candlemas Day, February 2, 1868, at Londonderry. He was educated in the district schools of Windham, New Hampshire, and worked on the home farm till he was twenty-nine years of age. He then came to Manchester and hired some land of the Mercy Home, and raised market vegetables for three years. On December 30, 1900, he moved across the river to Bedford and bought the John E. Underhill farm of twenty-five acres. His occupation is market gardening. He is a charter member of General Stark Grange, and has held office. He is a Republican in politics, and belongs to the Roman Catholic Church.

THORNE In the early records this name appears interchangeably Thorn, or Thorne. The latter seems to be the preferred modern spelling. Several of the family are found among the earliest American immigrants, especially in Virginia. February 16, 1623, Henry Thorne was living in the household of "Ensign Isack Chaplaine, Chaplaine's Choise, Charles Cittie, Virginia." Thomas Thorne, aged thirteen, embarked in the "Safety" for that colony, and Henry Thorne arrived in the "James" in 1622. The ancestor of the New England Thornes is probably Peter, who at the age of twenty sailed from England in the "Elizabeth" of London, April 10, 1635, and settled either in Lynn or Salem, Massachusetts. John Thorne, probably the son of Peter, with his brother, Israel Thorne, was in King Philip's war in 1665. Ten years later, August 21, 1675, he was enrolled at Rehoboth, Massachusetts, under Captain Daniel Henchman, in another expedition against King Philip. It is thought that Samuel, mentioned in the next paragraph, may have been a son of John. As it has been impossible fully to authenticate these early ancestors the line begins with a later generation.

(I) John, son of Samuel and Abigail (Barbour) Thorn, was born in Boston, February 10, 1697. His mother was the daughter of Captain George Barbour, a Puritan of distinction who came to this country in 1635 and was one of the first settlers of Dedham and Medfield, besides being the chief military officer of his district and a member of the colonial government. John Thorn moved to Kingston, New Hampshire, where his will was proved November 12, 1790, showing that he lived to the advanced age of ninety-three. In this will he mentions his wife Elizabeth, his daughter Elizabeth, three children of his daughter, Jemima Loveren, his son Jacob, who was executor, and his son John, to whom was given but five shillings, "he having received his part of my estate in his lifetime." Abraham, the youngest child, born January 31, 1757, was not mentioned in the will, and perhaps was not living at the time.

(II) John (2), son of John (1) and Elizabeth Thorn, always known as the "Old Quartermaster Thorn" from the office he held in the French and Indian wars, came up from Kingston, New Hampshire, in 1765, and settled on what was afterwards known as "Thorn Hill," in Sanbornton, this state. When at Kingston he served in Captain Marston's company, Colonel John Goffe's regiment, in the expedition against Crown Point, being enrolled September 30, 1762. The name of his wife is unknown. There were seven children: Phinehas, John (3), Mercy, Henry, Abram, Mary and Jeremiah. In his later years Quartermaster Thorn went to live with his son, Dr. John, at Sullivan, Maine, but he returned to Sanbornton, where he died in September, 1807. If his wife survived him, she was probably the Widow Thorn who died in Sanbornton, August 16, 1812. Quartermaster Thorn's eldest daughter Mercy married Samuel C. Dudley, of Sanbornton, and lived to be nearly one hundred years old.

(III) Phinehas, eldest son and child of John (2) Thorn, was born in Kingston in 1762, and moved with his parents to Sanbornton. He was a noted teacher in his day, and in his later years was known as "Schoolmaster Thorn." He had many men of mark in adult life among his pupils, and it is said that he taught Daniel Webster in his youthful days. Phinehas Thorn married Miriam Lovejoy, daughter of Chandler and Miriam Lovejoy, who was born July 25, 1767. Their children were: Sarah, Chandler, Harriet, Myra and Calvin, whose sketch follows. Sarah, born March 22, 1797, married Henry Lovejoy, and died in Tremont, Illinois, in January, 1867. Chandler, born January 28, 1800, went to Canada, where he died November 3, 1888. Harriet married Royal Gibson, a native of Canterbury, New Hampshire, on August 17, 1825, removing with him to Lind, Waupaca county, Wisconsin. Myra, born May 23, 1807, married Benjamin Pitts, August 31, 1840, and died in Waterboro, Maine, April 18, 1867. Some of this family are remarkable for their longevity. Schoolmaster Phinehas Thorn died in Sanbornton, April 29, 1853, aged ninety-one. His wife died in 1844, aged seventy-seven. The granite monument in Tilton Highlands cemetery to their memory was erected by their grandson, John C. Thorne, of Concord, in 1896.

(IV) Calvin, second son and fifth and youngest child of Phinehas and Miriam (Lovejoy) Thorn, was born November 24, 1811, at Sanbornton, New Hampshire. His education was gained in the public schools and at the academies in Hopkinton and

Franklin, New Hampshire. When a young man he taught several terms of district school in Bow and Salisbury, also at Millville and Horse Hill, in Concord. In 1834 he began the manufacture of shoes for Richardson and Company, and in 1835 he formed a partnership with Joel Frazier for the manufacture and sale of shoes at Concord. This establishment, which Mr. Thorn conducted independently after 1844 and which he left to his son, is the oldest store in Concord remaining in one name, and in 1910 will celebrate three-quarters of a century of honorable existence, a record which probably cannot be equalled in the state. Mr. Thorn was a member of the First Congregational (Old North) Church in Concord for fifty-one years. He was a Republican in politics, but had no ambition for political honors. On August 31, 1836, Calvin Thorn married Cynthia Morgan, third daughter and child of Jeremiah and Nabby (Johnson) Morgan, who was born at Pembroke, New Hampshire. December 9, 1804. (See Morgan Genealogy, Second Family. IV). There were two children: John Calvin, whose sketch follows, and Charles Henry, born November 30, 1848. Mrs. Thorn was a member of the First Congregational Church for fifty-four years, and a woman of saintly life and character. Calvin Thorn died of paralysis at his home in Concord, August 12, 1884, in his seventy-third year. Mrs. Thorn outlived her husband eight years, dying December 22, 1892, at the age of eighty-eight years.

(V) John Calvin, elder son and child of Calvin and Cynthia (Morgan) Thorn, was born November 6, 1842, at Concord, New Hampshire. He was educated in the public and private schools of his native town, including the high school, and was graduated from Kimball Union Academy at Meriden in 1864. He then entered into the shoe business with his father, in which he has been continuously engaged ever since, with the exception of a short interval which he passed in business in the city of Chicago and was a witness of the great fire of 1871. Although Mr. Thorne has had a long and prosperous business career he has also had wide outside interests, and has rendered large public service, particularly along religious and historical lines. He is a Republican in politics, and was a member of the common council in 1877 and 1878, serving as president during the latter year. He was alderman in 1883-4-5-6. He is a member of the Council of Associated Charities. and vice-president of the Concord Commercial Club. He is one of the oldest trustees in point of service of the New Hampshire Savings Bank, serving since 1880, and he was a member of the Board of Education for five years from 1883 to 1888. He joined the First Congregational Church in 1875, and has been its treasurer for nearly thirty years, beginning in 1879. He was librarian and superintendent of the Sunday school for several years, and was made deacon of the church in 1891. He has been a director of the Young Men's Christian Association of Concord, is chairman of the directors of the New Hampshire Bible Society, and was treasurer of the Ministers' and Widows' Charitable Fund of Congregational Churches of New Hampshire from 1880 to 1896, receiving the fund of $10,000 from former treasurer and passing it over to his successor, amounting to upwards of $45,000. Mr. Thorne became a member of the New Hampshire Historical Society in 1885, and has been most active in promoting its interests. He has served for years on the standing committee, and has had much to do with arranging the field days and other meetings. and it was through his efforts that the valuable Sabine Library of four thousand volumes belonging to the estate of Lorenzo Sabine. of West Roxbury, Massachusetts, was secured for the society. Mr. Thorne was chairman of the committee which purchased additional land for the use of the society, and he secured the gift of five thousand dollars from the Pearson Fund for the erection of a new building, also a like sum from Sherman Bouton, of Chicago, eldest son of Rev. Nathaniel Bouton, D. D., the historian of Concord. Mr. Thorne has compiled the (1907) History and Manual of the First Congregational Church in connection with the pastor, which is one of the most complete ever issued and has published several historical pamphlets, including an address delivered at the one hundredth and fiftieth anniversary of the First Congregational Church of Concord, and monographs (with many illustrations) on Rev. Enoch Coffin, the first preacher in Penacook, now Concord. and on Rev. Israel Evans, a chaplain during the entire period of the Revolution and the second settled minister of the first Congregational Church at Concord. Mr. Thorne also secured a portrait of Mr. Evans and a bronze tablet for this church, a work that involved much labor and research, as the clergyman left no descendants. The original, from which the portrait was reproduced, was a miniature on ivory painted by Kosciusko. Besides these separate publications Mr. Thorne has written many foreign letters for the Concord *Daily Monitor,* and has contributed important articles, both historical and descriptive to the *Granite Monthly.* Mr. Thorne has been an extensive traveler, visiting New Orleans in 1889, Florida in 1894. Mexico in 1902, and making comprehensive European tours in 1891 and 1906. Perhaps the culmination of Mr. Thorne's historical service has come in his connection with the Society of Colonial Wars in New Hampshire. He joined this society in 1895, was its secretary for several years, deputy governor from 1901 to 1903, and governor from June, 1903, to June, 1906. During his term as governor three important and interesting field days were held. The first one was at Newcastle, June 17, 1903, and was made the occasion of placing a bronze tablet upon Fort William and Mary in commemoration of the first victory of the American revolution, December 15, 1774. The second was at Charlestown. and was held August 30, 1904, the hundred and fiftieth anniversary of the Indian Raid when Mrs. Johnson and her companions were carried into captivity. A bronze tablet, set in a large boulder, on the main street of the village, was dedicated at this anniversary. In 1906 the society held a field day at Exeter, where they were entertained at the club houses of the Colonial Dames and the Society of the Cincinnati. The society always makes a point of observing June 17, the anniversary of the capture of Louisburg, and on one of these occasions they renewed the tablet on the tomb of Captain William Vaughan at the Point of Graves, Portsmouth, one of the heroes of 1745. Mr. Thorne is a gentleman of polished and courtly manners, a ready speaker with a fund of quiet humor, and an agreeable companion.

On July 8. 1873, John Calvin Thorne married Mary Gordon Nichols, daughter of Nathaniel Gordon and Lucia (Lovejoy) Nichols, of Tremont. Illinois, and great-granddaughter of Phinehas Thorne III. (See Nichols Genealogy, Second Family. III). Mrs. Thorne was born April 8, 1852, at Elm Grove. Illinois, and was educated at the State Normal University at Bloomington. Since her coming to Concord she has taken a prominent part in the religious, philanthropic and social life of the city. She is one of the active workers in the First Congregational Church, which she joined at the time of her marriage. Mrs. Thorne's outside interests have in no way interfered with her domestic duties, and her attractive home at the North End is the scene of generous hospitality and refined entertainment.

Although Mr. and Mrs. Thorne are without children of their own, they are seldom without young companionship. They brought up Waldo Thorne Worcester, a relative and a young man of fine promise, who was born at Chelsea, Massachusetts, November 2, 1872, the son of Hiram C. and Susan J. (Pitts) Worcester. He was graduated from the Concord high school in 1890, and was the first pupil to receive the first prize for original declamation at the annual prize speaking. He was subsequently graduated from the Emerson College of Oratory in Boston, and then engaged in the shoe business at Concord with Mr. Thorne. On June 29, 1899, he married Mabel Cooper Snow, of Hyde Park, Massachusetts, and they had two children: Dorothy and Thorne. Mr. Worcester's untimely death was caused by a canoe accident at Goff's Falls, near Manchester, on October 21, 1903, and was a loss widely felt beyond his immediate family. In 1906 Mr. and Mrs. Thorne invited Elsie A. Chandler, daughter of Henry and Elizabeth (Ferguson) Chandler, a descendant of one of the old Concord families to become an inmate of their home. She was born March 18, 1887, and is now being educated at Saint Mary's (Episcopal) School at Concord.

(Second Family).

NICHOLS The Nichols name is numerous among the seventeenth century settlers of this country. Most of the early immigrants settled in Connecticut or the neighborhood of Boston. This family does not appear to be related to the one whose history has previously been traced. (See page 1857 for First Family).

(I) John, son of Samuel and Susanna Nichols, was born in Washington, New Hampshire, October 11, 1797. In childhood he moved with his widowed mother to Claremont, where he spent his youth. In 1836 he migrated to Illinois and settled near Tremont, where he bought a farm, removing in 1854 to Logan county and buying a much larger tract of land. He was a Republican in politics, and united with the Methodist Church early in life. Mr. Nichols accumulated a competency and gave liberally to the church and to philanthropic undertakings. Possessing an energetic temperament, a cheerful disposition, and an inventive mind, he had a large circle of friends. On March 14, 1824, John Nichols married Mary Gordon, daughter of Nathaniel and Millicent (Rand) Gordon, who was born at East Washington, New Hampshire, December 9, 1801. They had eight children: George P., Nathaniel Gordon, mentioned below; Frances E., married M. D. Tenney, and lives in Chandler, Oklahoma; Harriet A., married M. R. Fuller, and lives in Blue Rapids, Kansas; Mary Gordon, died young; Sarah B. married William Jones, and lives in Delavan, Illinois; and Edwin F., who lives in Delavan. John Nichols passed his later years in quiet home enjoyments, in reading and caring for his invalid wife to whom he was united for nearly fifty years. He died suddenly of paralysis on April 25, 1871, at Logan county, Illinois, and his wife died in October, 1875, at Tremont, Illinois.

(II) Nathaniel Gordon, second son and child of John and Mary (Gordon) Nichols, was born at Boston, Massachusetts, September 17, 1826. At the age of ten he moved with his parents to Tremont, Illinois, which became his permanent home. He owns many hundred acres of rich prairie lands, and is one of the wealthy farmers of the state. Mr. Nichols attends the Congregational Church, and is a Democrat in his political affiliations, although he enjoyed the personal friendship of Lincoln. On January 29, 1850, Nathaniel Gordon Nichols married Lucia Jane Lovejoy, of Concord, New Hampshire. She was the daughter of Henry and Sarah (Thorne) Lovejoy, and was born May 30, 1828. Her maternal grandparents were Phinehas and Miriam (Lovejoy) Thorne. (See Thorne Genealogy III.) They had four children: Mary Gordon, who is mentioned in the next paragraph; Charles, Alfred Henry, and Emily Prentiss. Charles Nichols was born February 2, 1854, and married (first), Georgine Morse, of Tremont, Illinois; and (second), Mrs. Annie Wilson, of Green Valley, Illinois. He died on August 31, 1899. Alfred Henry Nichols was born July 26, 1860, and married Helen Stone Hayward, of Morton, Illinois. Emily P. Nichols, born June 29, 1863, married Samuel Addison Calhoun, on August 31, 1899, and lives in Oklahoma City. Mrs. Nathaniel Gordon Nichols died January 2, 1884.

(III) Mary Gordon, eldest child of Nathaniel Gordon and Lucia Jane (Lovejoy) Nichols, was born in Elm Grove, Illinois, April 8, 1852. On July 8, 1873, she married John Calvin Thorne, of Concord, New Hampshire. (See Thorne Genealogy V).

MORGAN The following line does not appear to be descended from Miles Morgan, of Springfield, Massachusetts, who is considered the earliest American ancestor. (See page 55).

(I) Luther Morgan, the founder of this branch, is said to have come directly from Wales, the ancestral home of all the Morgans. He lived in various towns in Southern New Hampshire, first at Kingston, afterward at Kensington, Exeter and Suncook, all prior to 1750. He married Abigail ——, and they had four children: Nathaniel, who lived at Canaan; Abigail, who married Samuel Smith, of Suncook; Rachel, who married John Fellows of Kensington; and Jeremiah, whose sketch follows. Luther Morgan died December 10, 1768, and his widow died March 30, 1785.

(II) Jeremiah, second son and youngest child of Luther and Abigail Morgan, was born August 18, 1741. On January 12, 1764, he married Elizabeth, daughter of Deacon David and Elizabeth (Chandler) Lovejoy, of Pembroke, New Hampshire, who was born January 10, 1742. They had six children, all born in Pembroke: Elizabeth, married Joseph Mann, of Pembroke; David, married Lois Ladd; William, married Betsy Russ, of Bow; Priscilla, married John Johnson, of Bow; Jeremiah (2), who is mentioned below; Sally, married Enoch Holt, of Allenstown. Jeremiah (2) Morgan died July 21, 1819, and his wife died April 11, 1815.

(III) Jeremiah (2), third son and fifth child of Jeremiah (1) and Elizabeth (Lovejoy) Morgan, was born August 12, 1776, in Pembroke, New Hampshire. On October 8, 1799, he married Abigail Johnson, who was born January 11, 1770. They had five children: Mary, married Dr. Moses T. Willard, of Concord, who was mayor in 1859-60; Melinda, married Jeremiah Gates, of Bow; Cynthia, who is mentioned below; Nathaniel, married Nancy Head Cochran; Eleanor Johnson, married John A.

Gault, of Concord. Jeremiah (2) Morgan died April 12, 1839. His widow survived him twenty years, dying March 3, 1859, at the age of eighty-nine.

(IV) Cynthia, third daughter and child of Jeremiah (2) and Abigail (Johnson) Morgan, was born December 9, 1804, at Pembroke, New Hampshire, and married Calvin Thorne, of Concord. (See Thorne, IV.)

HOPKINS The first one in the line now herein treated, of whom any definite knowledge is at present accessible, was Riley Hopkins, who married Jane Welch, and resided in Washington, Vermont.

John, son of Riley and Jane (Welch) Hopkins, was born 1854, in Washington, Vermont, and died March 29, 1903, at Potter Place, in the town of Andover, New Hampshire. He was a man of considerable enterprise and executive ability, and erected at Potter Place a very handsome hotel, which is the pride of his town, and known as the "Hotel Potter." It is very largely patronized by summer vacationists, and enables the temporary sojourner in the town of Andover to secure comfortable service at any time throughout the year. He was married, June 23, 1874, to Jennie Philbrick, who was born December 9, 1855, daughter of Eben Hadley and Jane Philbrick. Her father, Eben Hadley, died March 21, 1872, and her mother exactly two years later, March 21, 1874. These were the parents of three children: Jennie, Charles E. and Linnie C., the latter now deceased. Charles E. married Nellie Dunham, and is the father of one daughter, Jessie. Mrs. Hopkins has been manager of the Hotel Potter for the past nine years, and is still conducting that popular hostelry with marked success. She is a regular attendant of the Baptist Church, and enjoys the respect of the people of Andover and vicinity. She is the mother of two children: Gertrude M., the first, born May 19, 1875, is the wife of George T. Blackwood, and has one daughter Evelyn, born July 6, 1902. Harley, the second, born May 5, 1880, married Grace M. Adams, and has a son John, born June 20, 1907.

PINKERTON ACADEMY Pinkerton Academy has good claim to be called the cradle of Scotch culture in this country. It was the outgrowth of a classical high school that had been maintained among the Scotch people of Londonderry, New Hampshire, by voluntary contribution from as early as 1793. It was to continue the benefits of this school to the community that Major John Pinkerton, in 1814, at the suggestion of his pastor, Rev. E. L. Parker, gave $12,000 to make it the institution that has since borne his name. His brother, Elder James Pinkerton, afterwards added $3,000 to the sum. By way of showing their appreciation of the gift of the Pinkertons, the people of the town contributed the funds for the building in which until 1887 the school was housed. The land for the site was given by William Choate and Peter Paterson.

The intention of the founders was a school after the Scotch pattern, that should be within the means of the poorest and "promote piety and virtue, and educate Youth in the Sciences, Languages, and Liberal Arts." It is to be remembered that the colonists of Londonderry were Scotchmen, though from the north of Ireland, Londonderry being as much a bit of Scotland twice removed as the Plymouth of Protestant England. Love of learning is one of the chief characteristics of the Scotch race; no people are less troubled with fear of educating the common above his station. Some time it will be perceived that the Scotch, more than the English, sowed the seed with us of faith in general education, and gave us our particular type of free schools. The Pinkerton brothers stamped the new institution with their ideas, but those ideas were quite as much national as personal, and concurred in by the folk about them without dissenting thought.

It remained for a third Pinkerton, son of Elder James Pinkerton, to broaden the scope of the school to meet modern requirements and so greatly extend its influence. Dying in 1881, after a life of good works, John Morrison Pinkerton left a large estate, the income from which was to accumulate until a sufficient sum had been derived to meet the cost of erecting a new and improved school building, and thereafter be expended for the purchase of a library and the general support of the school. To make room for the new building, which was opened in 1887, the original wooden structure was removed to a site not far distant, where it still has its important use. The academy was increased in size and strength, otherwise the will of John Morrison Pinkerton left it as he found it. "Alumnus of Yale and lawyer in Boston," he was of one mind with the "old-time merchants of Londonderry," his father and uncle, as to the kind of training best fitted to make useful citizenship. He was careful to do nothing, as the dominant giver, to divert the academy from its original purpose, making provision that, with the larger institution made possible by his bequest, there should be no departure from the spirit of piety and zeal for the public welfare, in which it had its beginning.

In 1906, bronze tablets, the work of the sculptor, Daniel Chester French, (and as to the phrasing and arrangement of the inscriptions) of President Charles E. Eliot, of Harvard University were placed in the outer vestibule of the main building to commemorate the lives and special service of the three men who gave to Derry (as that part of Londonderry where the school stands is now known) one of the leading secondary schools of the state.

As with many similar schools in the century it has passed through, the academy's greatest praise is that it has served so well as a stepping-stone in the rise of the country boy. It has been its privilege to help to preferment in life many of the kind of young people that like to help themselves. Provision has been made in a very moderate tuition for such as these, and this liberality has not been without its reward. Only such charges have been made as have been thought requisite by the trustees as an evidence of sincere purpose on the part of the pupil. The rate, eight dollars a year to begin with, has never exceeded twenty-one dollars, the present rate. Always far from restricted in usefulness to the work of a college-preparatory school, the academy has, nevertheless, paid yearly tribute of its best scholars from the first to the institutions above it. At one time in the middle of the last century, when graduates of all schools were less numerous than today, seven graduates of Pinkerton were enrolled as tutors at Dartmouth. It was remarked by Horace Greeley at the celebration in 1869 of the one hundred and fiftieth anniversary of the settlement of Londonderry, that at that time the descendants of the Scotch colonists in this country furnished one-sixth of the teachers for the education of the west. Many of these went directly to

IN MEMORY OF
MAJOR JOHN PINKERTON
1735 —— 1816
AND ELDER JAMES PINKERTON
1747 —— 1829
OLD-TIME COUNTRY MERCHANTS
OF LONDONDERRY
WHOSE FAR-SIGHTED BENEFICENCE
IN 1814
MADE THIS INSTITUTION POSSIBLE

IN MEMORY OF
JOHN MORRISON PINKERTON
1818 —— 1881
A NATIVE OF LONDONDERRY
ALUMNUS OF YALE AND LAWYER IN BOSTON
WHOSE GENEROUS BEQUEST IN 1881
STRENGTHENED THE GOOD WORK BEGUN HERE
BY HIS UNCLE AND FATHER

PINKERTON ACADEMY

J. M. Pinkerton.

[illegible] from the older Pinkerton Aca[illegible] a few indirectly by way of the [illegible] only boys at the first it seen[illegible] local but the female department [illegible] in 1821 and not resumed until [illegible] time the girls have formed a [illegible] student body, and have earned [illegible] of the honors and prizes. Its [illegible] comprehensive curriculum of st[illegible] the requirements of colleges and sc[illegible] been provided, and the alumni [illegible] ward to the higher institutions [illegible] mony to the intelligent, broad [illegible] tal and moral training the academ[illegible] their subsequent careers.

The charter members of the [illegible] had an important part in [illegible] the school, were, Rev. W[illegible] setten, Jr., John Burnham, [illegible] Pinkerton, Rev. Edwar[illegible] rter, Alan[illegible] Tucker, Rob[illegible] ssive members of the board [illegible] as they occurred, have b[illegible] Edwards, D. D., James [illegible] D. D., Rev. Dan[illegible] M. D. William M. [illegible] John H. Church, D. D., W[illegible] Adams, Thornton Betton, [illegible] D., Rev. Jonathan Clem[illegible] Brainerd, Samuel [illegible] John M[illegible] A. M., Rev. [illegible] Ebenezer G. Parsons, [illegible] Pinkerton, Rev. W[illegible] Barker, D. D., Rev. [illegible] Fisher, D. D., [illegible] David [illegible] Benjamin F. [illegible] Rev. Charles T[illegible] P. Prescott, W[illegible] G. Mear[illegible] Newell, Edward S[illegible] M. D., [illegible] George [illegible] Putnam, [illegible] N. [illegible] Bartlett, [illegible] Merriam [illegible]

Of these the following have [illegible] Jones Pinkerton, from [illegible] Porter, from 1816, Rev. Daniel [illegible] William M. Richardson, from [illegible] H. Church, from 1828, Rev. [illegible] from 1840, John Porter, from 1850 [illegible] from 1858, John M. Pinkerton [illegible] Rev. Ebenezer G. Parsons, from 1881 [illegible] P. Newell, from 1900.

[illegible] following have served as secretary: [illegible] from [illegible] James [illegible] from 1824; [illegible] from 1841; Rev. [illegible] B. Day [illegible] Rev. Joshua W. Wellman, from 18[illegible] Ebenezer G. Parsons, from 18[illegible] Rev. [illegible] from 18[illegible] Rev. [illegible] John C. Chase, from 1901.

[illegible] following have served as tr[illegible] from 1814; William Ch[illegible] Anderson, from 1856; [illegible] 1888.

[illegible] ing are names of the [illegible] of the school: Samuel [illegible] Adams, Abel F. Hildreth, A. [illegible] Elihu T. Rowe, M[illegible] W. Ray, A. M., [illegible] John V. Stanton, A. M., [illegible] Lyman W. Hazen, A. M. [illegible] George T. Tuttle, A[illegible] A. M., Edmund R. [illegible] gham, A. M. The [illegible] most noted term of administration was that of [illegible]

the field from the older Pinkerton Academy, but not a few indirectly by way of the colleges. Receiving only boys at the first, it soon became co-educational. but the female department was discontinued in 1821 and not resumed until 1853. Since that time the girls have formed a good half of the student body, and have carried off their full portion of the honors and prizes. In recent years the more comprehensive curriculum of study demanded by the requirements of colleges and scientific schools has been provided, and the alumni who have gone forward to the higher institutions bear gratifying testimony to the intelligent, broad and effective mental and moral training the academy gave them for their subsequent careers.

The charter members of the board of trustees, who had an important part in shaping the destinies of the school, were, Rev. William Morrison, John Pinkerton, Jr., John Burnham, Isaac Thom, Elder James Pinkerton, Rev. Edward L. Parker, John Porter, Alanson Tucker, Robert Bartley, M. D. Successive members of the board chosen to fill vacancies as they occurred, have been as follows: Rev. Justin Edwards, D. D., James Thom, Rev. Asa McFarland, D. D., Rev. Daniel Dana, D. D., George Farrar, M. D., William M. Richardson, LL. D., Rev. John H. Church. D. D., William Choate, Samuel Adams, Thornton Beeton, Rev. Pliny B. Day, D. D., Rev. Jonathan Clement, D. D., Rev. Timothy G. Brainerd, Samuel H. Taylor, LL. D., John M. Pinkerton, A. M., Rev. Joshua W. Wellman, D. D., Rev. Ebeneezer G. Parsons, William Anderson, David H. Pinkerton, Rev. William House, Rev. Leonard S. Barker, D. D., Rev. James T. McCollom, D. D., Rev. Caleb E. Fisher, D. D., Rev. David Bremmer, Rev. Benjamin F. Parsons, Rev. Robert W. Haskins, Rev. Charles Tenney, Rev. Charles Packard, Nathan B. Prescott, William G. Means. Rev. John P. Newell, Edward Spalding, M. D., LL. D., Hon. John W. Noyes, George L. Clarke, John C. Chase, Rev. Hiram B. Putnam, Frank N. Parsons, LL. D., Greenleaf K. Bartlett, Perley L. Horne, A. M., Rev. Charles L. Merriam. Hon. Charles W. Abbott.

Of these the following have served as president: Elder James Pinkerton, from 1814; Rev. Edward L. Parker, from 1819; Rev. Daniel Dana, from 1822; Hon. William M. Richardson, from 1826; Rev. John H. Church, from 1838; Rev. Edward L. Parker, from 1841; John Porter, from 1850; Samuel H. Taylor, from 1858; John M. Pinkerton, from 1871; Rev. Ebeneezer G. Parsons, from 1881; Rev. John P. Newell, from 1900.

The following have served as secretary: John Porter, from 1814; James Thom, from 1824; Samuel Adams, from 1831; Rev. Pliny B. Day. from 1838; Rev. Joshua W. Wellman, from 1850; Rev. Ebeneezer G. Parsons, from 1854; Rev. Benjamin F. Parsons, from 1872; Rev. Hiram B. Putnam, from 1896; John C. Chase, from 1901.

The following have served as treasurer: John Porter, from 1814; William Choate, from 1842; William Anderson, from 1856; Frederick J. Shepard, from 1888.

Following are names of the successive principles of the school: Samuel Burnham, Weston Bela Adams, Abel F. Hildreth, A. M., Caleb Emery., Rev. Elihu T. Rowe, Marshall Henshaw, A. M., John W. Ray, A. M., Henry L. Boltwood, A. M.. John Y. Stanton, A. M., John P. Newell, A. M., Marshman W. Hazen, A. M., Rev. Ebeneezer G. Parsons, George T. Tuttle, A. M., Homer P. Lewis. A. M., Edmund R. Angel, A. M., George W. Bingham, A. M. The longest and perhaps the most noted term of administration was that of Mr. Hildreth, which extended from 1819 to 1846, and gave the academy a wide reputation for its general thorough instruction and as a fitting school for college. The standard then established has been fully maintained up to the present time.

In 1866 was celebrated the semi-centennial anniversary of the school, and much was made of the occasion, many distinguished alumni being present and taking part in the exercises. At that time the school had begun to feel cramped by want of means, and the voices of several of the speakers were raised in an appeal for help. The response was to come shortly in the shape of the munificent gift of John M. Pinkerton, which opened a future to the school such as its founders did not dream of. Since then its responsibilities, both to those destined to college and to those not, increased as they have been by the growth of the town of Derry, have not been increased beyond its ability to meet them fully. An idea of the growth of the school may be gained from the statement that the attendance, including the preparatory department abolished in 1901, rarely exceeded one hundred before that date, while in 1907 it had reached one hundred and thirty-five. Mr. Burnham, the first principal. managed the school with one assistant; in 1907 Mr. Bingham has ten.

Nearing the end of its first century of existence, it can safely be said that the academy has well performed its expected work, and fully met the anticipations of its founders and later benefactors.

WRIGHT (I) David Wright, who was born in Ashford, Connecticut, in July, 1759, and died in Hanover, New Hampshire, in 1852. was a soldier of the Revolution and served at various times from 1775 until 1781. He enlisted first in 1775 as a private in a company of riflemen from Hanover, New Hampshire, and under command of Lieutenant James Parr was in service at Great Island in November of that year; enlisted at Hanover, August 16, 1776, in Captain David Woodward's company of rangers for the state of New Hampshire, and was credited with forty-six days service; March 17, 1777, was mustered as private in Captain House's company of Colonel Cilley's regiment, and in September, 1777, was private in Colonel Jonathan Chase's regiment of militia which marched from Cornish, New Hampshire, to Saratoga. New York, and joined General Gates's army in opposing and overwhelming the British under General Burgoyne at Stillwater; service one month and three days. April, 1778, he was mustered with other men from Hanover for that town's quota in Colonel Jonathan Chase's regiment of the Continental army, and is described as then being twenty years old and five feet seven inches tall. February 17, 1779, he enlisted and was mustered, in April, for three years' service as private in Colonel Chase's regiment in the Continental army, and in the next year was reported as a private and sergeant of the fourth company of Colonel Cilley's regiment of the Continental army; and in 1781 he was reported as sergeant in the same company and regiment.

David Wright, of Hanover, married, September 16, 1783, Lydia Tenney. She was born October 23, 1761, and died at Hanover, New Hampshire, April 27, 1832, daughter of John and Olive (Armstrong) Tenny. David and Lydia had in all nine children, three of whom were born at one time. Their first child, name unknown, was born June 24, 1784, and died June 25, 1785. Their second child, Wealthy, was born July 31, 1785, died April 8, 1864, married

Asher Ladd and settled in Painesville, New York. Their next children were triplets, born March 10, 1788, and died two on March 11, 1788, and the third March 25, 1788. Their sixth child, Anna, was born May 20, 1790, and died May 1, 1875; married, September 11, 1811, Henry Hilton Chandler (see Chandler, VII), of Hanover, New Hampshire. Their seventh child, Hannah, was born February 4, 1792, and died December 10, 1795. Their eighth child, David Jr., was born January 17, 1794, and died in Hanover; married, 1815, Irene Ladd, born March 21, 1793. Their ninth child, Caleb, was born January 14, 1798, and died July 11, 1802.

CLARK The same causes which led to the settlement of the Pilgrims at Plymouth, Massachusetts, led to the settlement of the Scotch-Irish at Londonderry, New Hampshire. The settlers in each case fled not so much from the civil government as from the hierarchy and the laws which enforced conformity to the church establishment, or at least compelled them to aid in supporting a minister of the established religion; and, in the case of the Scotch-Irish, a tenth part of all their increase was rigorously exacted for this purpose. They also held their lands and tenements by lease from the crown only, and not as proprietors of the soil. Their inextinguishable love of liberty, both civil and religious, would not permit them to remain in Ireland so situated; and knowing that they were leaving that country for one much its inferior in an agricultural sense, to make their homes in a wilderness whose solitude was broken only by the cries of wild beasts and blood thirsty savages, they chose to make the change rather than to live as they had been compelled to live.

Among those early settlers of Londonderry were the Clarks, honorable men and women from whom have descended many worthy citizens who have lived or are now living in all parts of the Union.

(I) Robert Clark, of the Scotch colony in Ireland, came to Londonderry, New Hampshire, about the year 1725, and settled on the height of land northwest of Beaver Pond. His example and his labors were of great service in promoting the interests of the colonists. He died in 1775. He married Letitia Cochran, daughter of John Cochran, of Londonderry, Ireland. She died in 1783. They had eight children, as follows: William, John, Samuel, Miriam, Jane, Letitia, Agnes and Elizabeth.

(II) William Clark, eldest son of Robert and Letitia (Cochran) Clark, was born in Londonderry. In 1766 he settled in New Boston, where his grandson, George W. Clark, lived one hundred years later. "He was the only justice of the peace in New Boston, and received his commission from the British government; he did not sympathize at first with the patriots of the Revolution, and made enemies thereby. But he was a man with whom his fellow-citizens could not afford to be long angry. As a surveyor of land he had no equal in the town; as an intelligent justice his services were of great value. He was a just man, and sought to promote peace and save the town and private parties from litigation; he was employed in the service of the town for a long session of years in almost every capacity, and had the unbounded confidence of the people." From 1766 to 1776 inclusive he was town clerk; and in 1766-67 he was one of the selectmen. He was a member of the Presbyterian Church, and lived and died as a Christian, and left a name that will not soon be forgotten. He died March 9, 1808, aged seventy-three. He married, February 2, 1764, Anne Wallace, who was born in Londonderry, in 1736, and died in New Boston, June 12, 1792, aged fifty-five. She was the daughter of John Wallace, who came from county Antrim, Ireland, to Londonderry, in 1719 or 1720, and married Annie Barnett on May 18, 1721, being the first couple married in Londonderry. The children of William and Anne were: Robert, John, Ninian, Rebecca, Anne and Letitia.

(III) John Clark, second son and child of William and Anne (Wallace) Clark, was born in New Boston, September 3, 1768, and died in Francestown, February 12, 1831, aged sixty-three. He settled in the northerly portion of Hancock about the year 1792, on forest land which had been purchased for him by his father. "He took to his forest life an earnest nature and a resolute spirit, with more than the ordinary culture of that day. In the winter he taught in the district schools of the vicinity, and having a good knowledge of music he often taught a singing school. He was also a practical surveyor, and had many calls for that kind of work. His political sympathies were with the Federal party, consequently he was not called upon to fill any important civil office; however, as a justice of the peace he was widely and favorably known. He early connected himself with the Congregational Church, and was a consistent Christian and a liberal supporter of religious institutions. In 1824 he sold his farm, and two years later removed to Francestown, where he spent the remainder of his life." He married, October 17, 1793, Rebecca Wallace, of Londonderry. She was an intelligent Christian woman, a true yoke-fellow and helper to her husband, whom she survived a quarter of a century. After his decease she, with her daughter, established a home in Amherst, where she died in 1855, at the age of eighty-three, leaving a fragrant memory. Their children were: Annie Wallace, Samuel Wallace, William, Gilman, Rebecca, John, Lydia Gordon, Letitia Rebecca, and Mary Abigail.

(IV) Rev. Samuel Wallace Clark, second child and eldest son of John and Rebecca (Wallace) Clark, was born in Hancock, December 15, 1795, and died in Greenland, August 17, 1847, aged fifty-two. He fitted for college at the academies at Hancock and New Ipswich, graduating from Dartmouth College in 1823 and from Andover Theological Seminary in 1827. He was ordained pastor of the Congregational Church in Greenland, to fill that office until his death, after a useful and happy pastorate of eighteen years. He married (first), October 13, 1829, his cousin, Frances (Moor) Clark, who was born in Hancock, 1832, daughter of Deacon Robert and Annie (Wallace) Clark, and granddaughter of William and Ann (Wallace) Clark, of this sketch. He married (second), Rebecca Elizabeth Howe, of Templeton, Massachusetts, a descendant in the sixth generation from John Alden and Priscilla Mullins. One child, Frances M. W., was born of the first marriage, and three of the second: John Howe, Lucy Barron, and William Wallace, the latter dying at the age of twenty months. Lucy Barron resided with her mother in Amherst.

(V) John Howe Clark, eldest child and only son of Rev. Samuel W. and Rebecca E. (Howe) Clark, was born in Greenland, April 16, 1837. After preparing at Kimball Academy, Plainfield, he entered Dartmouth College, from which he was graduated in 1857 with the degree of Bachelor of Arts. Immediately afterward he entered the medical department of Harvard College, from which he received the degree of Doctor of Medicine in 1862.

October 19, 1861, he was appointed assistant surgeon in the United States navy, and joined the United States gunboat "Scioto," of the West Gulf Blockading Squadron, under Admiral Farragut, in May, 1862. He served on this vessel on the Mississippi river and off the Texas coast until she was sunk in a collision with the United States steamship "Antona," below Forts Jackson and St. Philip, in May, 1863. While on the "Scioto" he ascended the Mississippi as far as Milliken's Bend, where General Grant cut his famous canal in the siege of Vicksburg. He accompanied Farragut's fleet in its run past Vicksburg, and was in several minor engagements on the lower Mississippi and off Galveston, Texas. After the sinking of the "Scioto" he was assistant surgeon in the temporary naval hospital at New Orleans, which was located in a hotel which had been appropriated for that purpose. While there sixty cases of yellow fever were admitted. Among them twenty deaths occurred, in most of which cases necropsy was performed, which afforded valuable experience to the doctor who has since had occasion to treat the disease. In June, 1864, he left New Orleans and reported at Portsmouth, New Hampshire, where he remained until the following May and then joined the United States ship "Mohongo," which soon after reported on the Pacific station, touching on the voyage thither at St. Thomas, Barbadoes, Natal, Bahia, Rio de Janeiro, Montevideo, and passing through the Straits of Magellan. While at Valparaiso he witnessed the bombardment of that city by the Spanish fleet. In, 1866, during the attempt of Maximilian, supported by the French, to make himself emperor of Mexico, the "Mohongo" visited the Bay of Acapulco, the bay and city of that name being held by the French land and naval forces. A forced loan was about to be exacted of all foreigners in Acapulco, but the presence of the "Mohongo" prevented it. After almost three years' service on the waters of the Pacific, the cruise terminated at Mare Island Navy Yard, in May, 1867, and Dr. Clark was assigned to duty on board the receiving ship "Vandalia," at the Portsmouth Navy Yard, where he was stationed until 1870.

May 14, 1867, he received his commission as surgeon. In 1870 and the two following years he served on the United States steamer "Alaska," on the Asiatic station, going and returning by way of Cape of Good Hope, touching at Cape Town, South Africa, the Comoro Islands and Singapore, on the Straits of Malacca. While in China he visited Hong Kong, Foochow, Ningpo, Shanghai, Chinkiang, Kinkiang, Hankow, Cheafoo, and Newchang. In Japan he visit Yokohama, Tokio, or Yesso, Nagasaki, Kobe, Osaka and Yokaska. At Osaka he witnessed the opening of the mint for coining the first Japanese gold and silver currency, and at Yokaska he saw the opening of the first dry dock of Japan, a basin cut in the solid rock. In 1871 the "Alaska" and three other United States war vessels paid a visit to Korea, the "hermit nation," where a fruitless attempt was made to open that country to the commerce of white nations.

Having returned to the United States in 1873, Dr. Clark spent the years 1874 and 1875 chiefly as senior assistant medical officer in the naval hospital at Chelsea, Massachusetts, and the three subsequent years on the United States ship "New Hampshire," at Port Royal, South Carolina, where that vessel went to prepare the way for the establishment of a naval station which has since been begun there.. From 1878 to 1883 he was attached to the receiving ship "Wabash," at the Boston Navy Yard. Twice during that time he was temporaarily detached to serve as a member of the naval examining board sitting at Philadelphia for the examination of candidates for the position of assistant and past assistant surgeons in the navy.

In 1884 and 1885 he was fleet surgeon of the Pacific Squadron, attached to the flagship "Hartford," cruising between Valparaiso, Chile, and San Francisco, making one visit during that time to Honolulu, in the island of Hawaii. June 8, 1887, he was made medical inspector. In 1886 and 1887 he was on special duty in Portsmouth, New Hampshire, and in 1888 and 1889 was again a member of the naval medical examining board. In 1890 he went in the United States steamer "Baltimore" to Stockholm, Sweden, with the remains of the Swedish inventor, John Ericsson, the designer and builder of the "Monitor," which vanquished the rebel ironclad "Merrimac" and revolutionized modern naval warfare. Marked civilities were extended to the ship's officers by the Swedish King, and his court, and medals commemorative of the occasion were presented to the officers and crew. After accomplishing the primary object of her cruise the "Baltimore" visited Copenhagen, Gibraltar, Spezia, Nice and Toulon. While at Toulon the "Baltimore" was ordered to Valparaiso, Chile, to watch the progress of a revolution and protect American interests there. While in Valparaiso the capture of the city by revolutionists was witnessed by the people of the "Baltimore." In 1892 Dr. Clark returned to the United States with the "Baltimore," and from May, 1892, to May, 1895, he was president of the naval board of medical examiners; and from the later date to May, 1898, he was in charge of the naval hospital at Chelsea, Massachusetts. During the service there aseptic operating, chemical, bacteriological and microscopic rooms were installed and steam disinfector introduced. From the date last mentioned to April, 1899, he was a member of the naval retiring board at Washington, District of Columbia. April 16, 1899, having attained the age limit of the United States navy, Dr. Clark was placed on the retired list, and since that time has resided at Amherst, New Hampshire.

After a period of thirty-seven years of service in the United States navy, Dr. Clark is still in the enjoyment of the mental and physical vigor that usually characterize men who number fewer years than he does. His life has been spent in the service of a great free country whose institutions it is a satisfaction to him to have assisted in maintaining when the integrity of the nation was threatened, and in perpetuating since it entered upon the unparalelled period of prosperity it has enjoyed since the suppression of the Rebellion.

FERNALD This family, which is numerous in New England and represented by individuals in all the states of the Union, enjoys the peculiar distinction of being descended from one of the earliest pioneers, who was the first physician to settle in New Hampshire. This name has been locally known in Merrimac county for more than one hundred fifty years, and today stands among the most trusted in this region The family has produced many members who have filled positions of trust and bore reputations for integrity and fidelity in all matters committed to them.

(I) Dr. Reginald (or Renald) Fernald came from England in Captain John Mason's company, and settled in Portsmouth, New Hampshire, about 1630, and was the first physician to settle in the state. He held the offices of register of deeds and probate, town clerk at Portsmouth, and was a lawyer and commissioner. He died in 1856. His children were: Thomas, Elizabeth, Mary, Sarah, John, Samuel, and William. (Mention of John and William and descendants follows in this article).

(II) Thomas, eldest child of Reginald Fernald, was born about 1633, in Portsmouth. In 1645 he leased from the agent of Sir Fernando Gorges, Puddington's Islands, and it seems that he subsequently purchased at least one of them, for he deeded this to his brother William in 1671, "for the fulfilling of the last Will of our Dere father Renald Firnald." The inventory of his property was returned August 25, 1697, from which it would appear that he was then deceased. The larger of his two islands, afterwards known as Seavey's Island, was divided by his widow, November 20, 1702, among the surviving children. Only her Christian name is preserved, viz: Temperance. Their children were: John, Ann, Patience, Thomas. Mary, Samuel, Joanna, Sarah, Hercules, and Elizabeth.

(III) Hercules, fourth son and ninth child of Thomas and Temperance Fernald, was born about 1680, and was a shipwright, residing in or near Portsmouth. He married Sarah, daughter of Hon. John and Elizabeth (Fryer) Hincks, of Newcastle. He died before 1731, and his widow was still living in 1746. Their children were: John, Jane, and Sarah.

(IV) Jane, elder daughter and second child of Hercules and Sarah (Hincks) Fernald, was born about 1720, and became the first wife of Samuel Gunnison, of Kittery. (See Gunnison, IV).

(II) John, second son of Dr. Reginald Fernald, married Mary Spinney. Their children were: John, James, Thomas, and others.

(III) Thomas, son of John Fernald, married Mary Thompson, November 28, 1700. Their children were: William, Lydia, Hannah, Mary, Margery, Thomas and Abram.

(IV) Thomas (2), son of Thomas (1) and Mary (Thompson) Fernald. born March 3, 1717, married (first), Mary Scroggins, December 30, 1738. They had one child, Benjamin. Thomas Fernald married (second), Sarah Fernald, prior to May, 1747. She was the daughter of Hercules Fernald, who was a son of Thomas Fernald and wife Temperance, the latter Thomas being a son of Dr. Reginald Fernald. The children of Thomas and Sarah Fernald were: Mary, Archelaus, Dimond, Renald, and Robert. Thomas Fernald married Grace Remich and their children were: Hannah, Nancy, and Sarah.

(V) Dimond, son of Thomas and Sarah Fernald, born April 2, 1750, in Loudon, New Hampshire, married Margery (or Margaret) Fernald, born in Kittery, Maine, June 20, 1758. He was a farmer and his life was passed in his native town. Their children were: Sarah, Polly, Nabby, Thomas, David. Robert, Josiah, Comfort, Rachel, Eunice, Susan, John, Dimond, Chase and Charlotte. (Mention of Josiah and descendants forms part of this article).

(VI) Thomas, eldest son and fourth child of Dimond and Margaret Fernald, was born May 27, 1783, in Loudon, and died July 19, 1862, in Loudon, where he was a farmer. He married Polly Blanchard, who was born October 28, 1786, and died September 26, 1870, in Loudon. Their children were: Seth, John, Nancy, Ruth Y., Harriet N. and Adelia C.

(VII) Adelia C., youngest child of Thomas and Polly (Blanchard) Fernald, was born March 21, 1828, in Loudon, and died October 2, 1906, in Canterbury. She became the wife of Thompson Beck, of Canterbury. (See Beck, VI).

(VI) Josiah, seventh child of Dimond and Margaret (Fernald) Fernald, was born December 20, 1788, in the town of Loudon. He married, July 9, 1816, Sophia Eastman, daughter of Jacob and Abigail (Kimball) Eastman, born July 7, 1799. Her father was a soldier in the Revolution (see Eastman). Mr. Fernald died in Exeter, Maine, May 27, 1863, and his wife died in the same town April 21, 1885. Their children were thirteen in number, as follows: Josiah, Sophia E., Robert, John, Mary Jane, Emily E., Lucy E., Jacob E., Persis C., Lucretia E., Charlotte M., Amanda F. and Benjamin F. Josiah Fernald learned the trade of morocco dresser, and followed it for some time, but later was a farmer. He lived first in East Concord, but in 1636-7 moved to Exeter, Maine, and spent the remainder of his days there. Several of the younger children were born in that town. Robert Fernald, one of the sons, was the father of Merrick C. Fernald, Ph. D., Professor Emeritus, University of Maine, at Orono, a scholar and a gentleman of the old school. Josiah was a soldier in the war of 1812, and his wife drew a pension on that account after his death. His service was rendered at Portsmouth, where he spent some months on guard duty. He was a Whig, and later a Republican, and a member of the Masonic fraternity.

(VII) Josiah (2), eldest son of Josiah (1) and Sophia (Eastman) Fernald, was born at Concord, January 17, 1817. He married, August 31, 1843, at Concord, Mary Esther Austin, daughter of Abel and Sally (Morse) Austin, born at Canterbury, New Hampshire, October 13, 1815, died at East Concord, January 24, 1901. Their children were: Sophia, Frank Eugene, George A., Ella M. and Josiah E. Josiah Fernald attended school as opportunity offered until he was seventeen years old. He worked at farming until he was twenty, and then thoroughly learned the business of tanning and currying. For fifteen years he was in the employ of Robinson & Upsham and their successors, at Concord. He afterward moved to Loudon, where he was in the employ of Joseph Wiggins, tanner, for about seventeen years. For two years he had a farm at Loudon. He moved to Pittsfield in 1872 to educate his younger children, and remained there five years. In 1877 he moved to East Concord and bought property on Penacook street, near the summit of the hill, and next to the old Eastman property. Mr. Fernald was a Whig until the formation of the Republican party, when he joined it. He never missed voting at a presidential election after he cast his first vote in 1840, and thus cast seventeen ballots. He passed away at his home in East Concord, March 29, 1906. Prior to his death he was the only living charter member of the Old Fort Engine Company, which was organized in 1841.

(VIII) Sophia and Ella Fernald are unmarried, and were the housekeepers for their aged father, whose life and home were made happy by them.

(VIII) Frank E. Fernald married Emma L. Tucker, November 26, 1870. He is connected with the wholesale tea house of Carter, Macy & Company, for which he is the buyer, and makes annual trips to Japan to oversee the curing and packing of the tea for his firm. He resides in Chicago, Illinois.

(VIII) George A. Fernald, born in East Concord, February 13, 1850, is engaged in a very successful banking business in Boston.

(VIII) Josiah Eastman, son of Josiah and Mary Esther (Austin) Fernald, was born at Loudon, June 16, 1856. He married, December 8, 1880, Anna White, daughter of Curtis and Hannah (Buntin) White, of Bow, descendants of an early family of that town (see White, IV). Their children are: Edith, Mary, Ruth and Josiah White. Mr. Fernald was educated in the public schools at Loudon, and at Pittsfield Academy, spending four years in the last named institution. While at Loudon he was employed part of the time as clerk in a store. At Pittsfield he was engaged in surveying, and also in mercantile employment, as he had time from his studies. Just before graduating he was offered a position in the National State Capital Bank in Concord, which he accepted, and at once entered upon the duties of clerk and messenger (1875). In 1882 he became cashier of that institution and filled that position until he was elected president in 1905. He has been vice-president of the Loan and Savings Bank of Concord since the death of Mr. Lewis Downing, Jr., in 1901; treasurer of the Capital Fire Insurance Company of Concord since its organization, and is also president of the Concord Axle Company of Penacook. Mr. Fernald is comparatively a young man, yet his natural ability and fidelity to the trusts confided to him have placed him in positions the mere mention or whose names do not convey a full idea of their responsbility. A fuller understanding is gained from knowing that the assets of the National State Capital Bank are over a million and a quarter dollars, and the assets of the Loan and Trust Savings Bank are nearly three and a quarter million of dollars, the combined capital of the two institutions being nearly four and a half millions of dollars. Mr. Fernald has been treasurer of the Commercial Club of Concord since its organization in 1889. In politics he is a Republican. He is an Odd Fellow, and a member of White Mountain Lodge. In religious faith he is a Baptist, and has been a member of the First Baptist Church of Concord since 1878. In his summer vacations Mr. Fernald ranges from the Atlantic coast to the Rocky Mountains, where he recuperates his energies for the next year's labors. In 1900 he visited Agonquit, Maine, and while there rescued three women from drowning, for which he was presented with a silver medal by the Humane Society of Massachusetts.

(II) William, youngest child of Reginald Fernald, was born March 5, 1646, in Portsmouth, and resided for many years in what is now Kittery, on the site of the United States Navy Yard. This was known at the time of his purchase in 1671, as "Lay Claim" island. This he purchased from his brother Thomas, and while residing there he is said to have built a vessel of one hundred and forty-eight tons for Isaac Boyd. He was selectman in 1674, 1692 and 1696. On the 10th of February in the last named year he was commissioned lieutenant of militia by Sir Edmund Andross, and in the town records of 1695 he was called Captain, probably a local title in colonial militia. During his last years he lived on his farm near Spruce Creek, where he died July 5, 1728. He was married, November 16, 1671, to Elizabeth, daughter of Tobias and Elizabeth (Sherburne) Langdon, of Portsmouth. She survived him nearly twelve years, dying May 11, 1740. Their children were: Elizabeth, William, Tobias (died young), Margaret, Temperance, William, Joseph, Sarah, Lydia, Benjamin, Nathaniel, Ebenezer, and Tobias. (The last named and descendants receive further mention in this article).

(III) Ebenezer, seventh son and twelfth child of William and Elizabeth (Langdon) Fernald, was born October 7, 1699, in Kittery and passed his life in his native town, where he died January 29, 1787. He was married, December 22, 1724, to Patience, daughter of Jonathan and Sarah (Downing) Mendum. She was born in Kittery about 1700, and died January 5, 1775, aged seventy-four years. Their children were: Alice, Sarah, Joanna, Ebenezer, Jonathan, Olive, Dorothy, Elizabeth, Simeon, Miriam, Patience, and Joshua Downing.

(IV) Alice, eldest child of Ebenezer and Patience (Mendum) Fernald, was born January 21, 1726, in Kittery, and died July 5, 1804, in her native town. She was married, May 3, 1752, to Samuel Gunnison, being his second wife. (See Gunnison, IV).

(III) Tobias, youngest child of William and Elizabeth (Langdon) Fernald, was born December 3, 1702, probably in Portsmouth, and died May 11, 1761. He was probably a mariner, and is recorded with the title of captain. He was married, December 22, 1724, to Mary, daughter of Jonathan and Sarah (Downing) Mendum. She died October 16, 1767. Their children were: Dennis, Mary, Miriam, Robert (died young), Robert, Tobias and Eleazer.

(IV) Eleazer, youngest child of Captain Tobias and Mary (Mendum) Fernald, was born September 23, 1746, locality not certainly known, and was a farmer. He passed his last days at Ossipee, New Hampshire, where he died in 1823. He was married, January 31, 1771, to Margery, eldest daughter of Nathaniel and Margery (Frost) Staples, of Cape Elizabeth. She was born November 18, 1747, baptized May 10, 1751, and died in 1826, at Ossipee. Their children were: Tobias, Nathaniel, Mary, Elliott, Margery and Joanna.

(V) Tobias (2), eldest child of Eleazer and Margery (Staples) Fernald, was born November 8, 1771, in Kittery, and lived for a time in North Berwick, Maine. He removed to Ossipee, New Hampshire, about 1795, making the journey on horseback from Kittery by means of a trail through the forest, marked by blazed trees. He died July 3, 1849. He was married, August 2, 1792, to Sally Pray, of Lebanon, Maine, and their children were: Joanna, Dorothy, Joseph, Mark, Charles, Nathaniel, John Yeaton, Abigail and Samuel Pray.

(VI) John Yeaton, fifth son and seventh child of Tobias (2) and Sally (Pray) Fernald, was born December 2, 1803, in Kittery, Maine. He married Sally Trickey, daughter of Jabez or Joseph and Mary (Wentworth) Ricker. She was born at Waterboro, Maine, September 12, 1806. In 1794 Jabez or Joseph Ricker purchased the Poland Springs property in Maine. The estate is still in the hands of the Ricker family who have made the waters of the springs known throughout the world, and incidentally have built the finest hotel and summer resort on the New England coast. Jabez or Joseph Ricker's wife, Mary Wentworth, was a great-granddaughter of William Wentworth, the immigrant ancestor of all the Wentworths. John Y. and Sally Trickey (Ricker) Fernald had children, among them Harriet N., mentioned below. John Y. Fernald died at Ossipee, New Hampshire, August 7, 1877, and his wife died there October, 1868.

(VII) Harriet N., daughter of John Y. and Sally Trickey (Ricker) Fernald, was born at Ossipee, New Hampshire, May 19, 1841. On April 15, 1858, she was married to Jacob Abbott, of Ossipee. (See Abbott, III).

HEVEY The name of Hevey is one which has been identified with the history and progress of France in various directions for a number of generations. One of the ancestors of the subject of this sketch, whose baptism took place in 1696, was the first child to be baptized in the city of Quebec.

Ignace Hevey was a very young child when he lost his father by death, and he was the youngest of a large family. He followed agricultural pursuits throughout his life, and died at the age of fifty-five years. He married Josephte Guilbert, who survived her husband and died at the advanced age of ninety-one years. She was the daughter of Jean Baptiste and ——— Guilbert, both natives of Canada. The Guilbert family is one of the very old ones of France, one of its representatives having been a general in the French army as early as the fourteenth century. Mr. and Mrs. Hevey had twelve sons and three daughters, of whom seven lived to attain maturity. Of these there at present (1907) three living: Rev. Pierre Hevey, see forward; one daughter living in Canada at the age of eighty-nine years, and another, at the age of eighty-seven years.

Right Reverend Pierre Hevey, youngest child of Ignace and Josephte (Guilbert) Hevey, was born at St. Barnabé, Province of Quebec, October 31, 1831. This parish adjoins that of St. Hyacinthe. He was the only one of his generation in the family to adopt a professional career. His preparatory education was acquired in the parochial schools of his native town, and he then became a student at St. Jude's Academy, from there passing on to Chambly College and St. Hyacinthe College. In the latter institution he made a special study of theology, and was ordained priest in the seminary chapel, July 12, 1857, by Archbishop Tache, one of the most eminent prelates of his time. After his ordination, Rev. Pierre Hevey remained at the residence of the bishop for about two and one-half years; from 1859 until 1866 was stationed at St. Jean Baptiste, Province of Quebec; and five years at Gregoire, Iberville, till 1871; and went to Lewiston, Maine, in October, 1871. His successors in this latter charge were the Dominican Fathers. After leaving Lewiston he rested for a time, and then assumed charge of St. Mary's Parish, West Manchester, New Hampshire. He soon found that the majority of his communicants, consisting of eighteen hundred souls, resided in Manchester proper. St. Mary's parish was organized in 1880. Bishop Healy having commissioned Rev. D. J. Halde to take this matter in hand. The latter secured land and erected a church, and in 1882 was succeeded by Rev. Pierre Hevey. At that time the church building was a frame structure near the present fine edifice, and in 1883 Rev. Father Hevey purchased a large tract of land on Wayne street, and later converted the dwelling bought by Father Halde into a rectory. The original chapel, together with the additions which had been made by Rev. Father Hevey, was destroyed by fire, October 16, 1890. After that event the services were conducted in St. Mary's Hall until a new church building should have been erected. This was commenced in 1898, and it was ready for occupancy in December, 1900. Rev. Father Hevey erected a building in 1885 which served the double purpose of convent and school for girls, and placed it in charge of a branch of the Order of Grey Nuns, whose home institution is in St. Hyacinthe, Province of Quebec. In the same year an orphanage was opened in the building. The following year he built a school for boys on Wayne street, which he placed in charge of a branch of the Order of Marist Brothers, in 1890. There are at the present time (1907) five hundred and forty pupils in this school. Shortly after he brought the Sisters of Presentation to Manchester, and established a parochial school for girls. About the same time he was successful in building the Hospital of Notre Dame de Lourdes, which is a hospital for the aged and an asylum for orphans, and placed this under the control of the Grey Nuns. This has since been enlarged by the addition of a brick structure in which three classrooms have been reserved for boys. A kindergarten established at an earlier period is still retained in the old building. The hospital occupies five hundred feet on Notre Dame avenue, and the entire square between Wayne and Putnam streets. The boys' school is three hundred by one hundred feet in size. The boys were transferred to the St. Peter's Orphanage in 1901, and the total number of orphans in the building at the present time is two hundred and seventy-five. Altogether the orphans attending the school number fifteen hundred pupils. Rev. Father Hevey also erected a large brick residence as a home for the eleven brothers in charge of the school. The hospital takes rank with the best in New England, and the operating room, which is of solid glass wherever practicable, is circular in shape externally, and immediately attracts the notice of every stranger who passes the building. It is fitted with every modern improvement and device which may tend to the safe outcome of the many operations performed within its walls. Its staff of surgeons is considered among the best in the state. Rev. Father Hevey has been untiring in his efforts in behalf of the parish in his charge, and is greatly beloved by all. Although advanced in years, he is as active in mind and body as many men greatly his juniors in point of years. No detail concerning the welfare of his parish seems to him too trivial to be investigated, and if it seems to contain any elements of benefit to his beloved people, it is given his personal attention.

The church is centrally located, overlooking the city of Manchester, and is one of the finest in the city. The height of the spire to the top of the cross is two hundred and twenty-three feet. The ground dimensions are one hundred by ninety-nine feet, and the basement, which is of Concord granite, was completed in 1892. This was used for divine services until the body of the church was completed. The interior furnishings are of oak, the altars being of onyx, and the sanctuary stalls of carved oak. The floor of the sanctuary is of German cement. A large pipe organ is operated by electricity, and in the right transept there is an echo organ which is operated by the organist seated at the large organ. In the echo organ gallery there is also space for the choir of one hundred boys. The opposite gallery is reserved for the Sisters, sixty in number. There is a statue of St. Joseph, made in Belgium, which is considered a very fine work of art. The church is well lighted by electricity, and is fitted with all improvements which tend to the comfort of the worshippers. The vestry has also German cement floors, and the woodwork is of oak. It is spacious and well ventilated, and the ceilings are high. The entire ground space covered by the church, vestry, etc., is two hundred and fifty feet on Notre Dame avenue, and more than three hundred on Wayne street. Besides

Rev. Father Hevey, there are four assistant priests. The number of communicants has increased to such an extent that it is now the largest parish in the diocese, having fourteen hundred families, and renting one thousand six hundred and eighty-six pews. Rev. Father Hevey purchased a set of chimes in Montreal, in 1906, these having been imported directly from France, and they are rung by means of electricity. The total weight of these bells is thirteen thousand nine hundred and ninety-five pounds, and their music can be heard all over the city. They are considered to have the finest tone of any in the state, and their cost was six thousand dollars.

Rev. Father Hevey received the honorary title of Prothonotary Apostolic from Rome June 20, 1890. Bearing this title, he has the right to wear the mitre while celebrating mass, and he always does this on the most important holy days of the year, such as Easter, Christmas, and the fete day of his patron saint, Saint Peter.

TENNEY Among the names identified with the Puritan immigration to America, with the development of civilization on this continent, and with the early settlement of New Hampshire, this has borne an honorable part. It has given to us learned and able ministers of the gospel, profound judges, enterprising business men and good citizens in large number. In the present generation it is represented at Claremont by Judge Edward J. Tenney, one of the selfmade men of New Hampshire. The little village of Rowley, in Yorkshire. England, now a hamlet of very small importance, in the early part of the seventeenth century, sheltered a man destined to exercise a large influence in the settlement of Massachusetts, namely: Rev. Ezekiel Rogers. He could not perform acts required of him by his sovereign, which his conscience told him were sacrilegious, and he gathered about him a band of souls equally conscientious, and set out for America in the autumn of 1638. They arrived at Salem, Massachusetts, in December, and began a settlement in the spring of 1639, at what is now Rowley, at first called Rogers' Plantation. In September of that year the general court formally bestowed upon it its present name.

(I) In Rev. Rogers' company were Thomas Tenney and his wife Ann. He was then about twenty-four years old, according to a statement made by him in 1680, when he gave his age as about sixty-six years. His wife is supposed to have been a sister of Deacon Thomas Mighill, of the same company. She was buried September 26, 1657, and Mr. Tenney was married February 24, 1658, to Elizabeth, widow of Francis Parrat, also among the early settlers of Rowley. In the survey of 1643. Mr. Tenney had a house lot of one and one-half acres, and the records show that he was possessed of several parcels of land. His house lot has been occupied by a store since 1701, and his house was torn down in 1838. He was active in the affairs of the settlement in many ways, serving as ensign, marshal, warner of town meetings. overseer of the plains, selectman, viewer of fences, highways and chimneys, constable and tithing man, filling some of these offices repeatedly. In 1667 he was appointed to see that the Sabbath was duly observed, and in 1680 was inspector of ten families. The early church records cannot be found, but later ones show him to have been a member in 1669. As freemen were limited to church members, it is apparent that he was in good standing in church among the first, else he could not have served as a civil officer. His last days were passed in Bradford, Massachusetts, where he deeded over seventy acres of land to his son John, June 15, 1694, in consideration of support during his old age. He died February 20. 1700, and was buried in the old cemetery. His children were: John, Hannah, Mercy, Thomas, James and Daniel

(II) Daniel, youngest child of Thomas Tenney and Ann, his first wife, was born July 16, 1653, in Rowley, and lived in Bradford and Byfield parish of Rowley. His farm was on the northwest side of Simons brook, and remained in possession of his descendants until the beginning of the present century. The records show the sale of his land in Rowley and the deeding of his estate in 1715 to his son Daniel, with próviso that the latter support the father and his wife during the remainder of their lives. He was a soldier in the Indian wars under Major Richard Waldron, of Dover, New Hampshire. the payroll, dated March 24, 1676, showing him entitled to compensation of one pound nineteen shillings four pence. He died in his ninety-fifth year, and was survived a short time by his widow who passed away September 5, 1749, aged over eighty years. Mr. Tenney was married (first), July 21, 1680, to Elizabeth, daughter of Lieutenant Samuel and Julia (Swan) Stickney. She was born May 9, 1661, in Rowley, and died there April 28, 1694. Mr. Tenney married (second), Mary Hardy, and (third). June 5, 1712, Elizabeth Woodman, daughter of Joshua and Elizabeth Stevens. The children of the first wife were: Thomas, Daniel, Sarah (died young), and Daniel and Sarah, twins. The second wife was the mother of: John, William, Richard, Ebenezer and Mary.

(III) William (1), fifth son and seventh child of Daniel Tenney, was born October 23, 1698, in Rowley, and resided in that town and in Newbury. After purchasing small parcels of land for thirteen and fifteen pounds respectively, he took deed September 6, 1726. of thirty acres in Rowley, for which the consideration was two hundred and fifty pounds. In one of these deeds he is styled "cordwainer." He died September 29, 1784, being then almost eighty-six years of age. He was published as intending marriage in Newbury, September 3, 1720, to Mehetable Pearson, daughter of Benjamin and Hannah (Thurston) Pearson. No record of their marriage was made, though she is known to have been his wife. She was born May 18, 1695, in Newbury, and died March 1, 1749. Their children were: Mehetabel, William, Oliver. Jane, Ruth, Eunice, Hannah, Benjamin, Richard and Mary.

(IV) William (2), eldest son and second child of William (1) and Mehetable (Pearson) Tenney, was born July 19, 1723, in Rowley. He removed from that town to Hollis, New Hampshire, in 1746, and was sealer of leather there in 1748 and selectman in 1769-70. He died there March 22, 1783, in his sixtieth year. He was married November 7, 1745, to Ann Jewett, daughter of Deacon Daniel and Elizabeth (Hopkinson) Jewett. She was born July 19, 1723 in Rowley, and survived her husband until July 1, 1794, near the close of her eighty-first year. Their children were: Benjamin, Martha, William and Ann.

(V) Benjamin, eldest child of William (2) and Ann (Jewett) Tenney, was born November 8, 1746, in Hollis. this state, and settled after 1775 in Temple, New Hampshire. He was among those who started for Cambridge on the alarm of April 19,

1775, but of course was unable to reach the scene of action in time to participate. He engaged in 1776, under Captain Adams and Lieutenant Colonel Bradford, to go to the re-enforcement of General Gates at Ticonderoga, and was discharged November 16, 1776. He again enlisted, June 29, 1777, as a private in Captain Gershom's company, under Lieutenant Colonel Thomas Heald, and marched to join the Continental army at Ticonderoga. He was discharged from this service July 12, 1777. He died September 2, 1790, in Temple, and his widow married Darius Hudson, of that town. He was married January 28, 1772, in Andover, Massachusetts, to Ruth Blanchard, his cousin, daughter of Samuel and Ruth (Tenney) Blanchard, of Andover. Their children were: Ruth, Benjamin (died three years old), Samuel (died at one), William, Lucy, Benjamin, Amos, David, Solomon and John. Ruth Blanchard was born August 18, 1751, and died April 13, 1831, in Antrim, New Hampshire.

(VI) Amos, sixth son and eighth child of Benjamin and Ruth (Blanchard) Tenney, was born February 19, 1785, in Temple, and became a merchant in Greenwich, Massachusetts. There is record of his purchase October 20, 1826, of a parcel of land in Greenwich. He was married in Pepperell, Massachusetts, September 1, 1807, to Lucy Read, of Westford, that state, who was born September 22, 1785, and died February 16, 1857, in Claremont, at the home of her son. Amos Tenney died May 17, 1839, at Claremont. Their children were: Amos Jewett, Benjamin Blanchard, Lucy Abigail and Emeline Eliza.

(VII) Amos Jewett, eldest child of Amos and Lucy (Read) Tenney, was born July 31, 1808, in Jaffrey, New Hampshire, and became an active factor in the business development of Claremont. He was reared in Greenwich, Massachusetts, was a farmer, shoemaker and merchant. In April, 1837, he removed to Claremont and engaged in mercantile business. He became interested in the Claremont Carriage Company, which got into financial difficulties. With one other director, Mr. Tenney assumed the responsibility of the concern, and after a hard struggle paid one hundred cents for each dollar of its liabilities. In the settlement he came into possession of the water power and a grist mill, and he continued to deal in real estate with success. His untimely death cut short a career calculated to benefit his town in many ways. He passed away August 3, 1855, being four days over forty-seven years of age. He was married in Greenwich, Massachusetts, May 28, 1832, to Persis Sexton Pomeroy, daughter of Joshua and Persis (Sexton) Pomeroy of that place, formerly of Somers, Connecticut. She was born, 1810, at Greenwich, and died July 28, 1843, at Claremont. Mr. Tenney married (second), Elizabeth Richards. His children were: Charles Amos, a graduate of Dartmouth College and a brilliant scholar; Edward Jewett and George Pomeroy. The first resided in Claremont, and died there in 1856. The third served three years as a soldier in the Civil war, as a member of the Second New Hampshire Regiment, and died in Washington D. C., in 1892, while an employe of the surgeon general's department.

(VIII) Edward Jewett Tenney, second son of Amos J. and Persis (Pomeroy) Tenney, was born December 11, 1836, in Greenwich, Massachusetts. The following April he moved with his parents to Claremont, New Hampshire, where he passed the remainder of his life, and died January 15, 1906. After receiving the schooling customary in those days for a boy not contemplating a college course, he entered a general merchandise store in Claremont where he remained, a most efficient clerk, until the death of his father in 1855. Soon after this Mr. Tenney engaged in the grocery trade with Edwin W. Tolles. He later sold his interest in this business and became a partner of J. W. Dane under the firm name of J. W. Dane & Company manufacturers of cigars and wholesalers of tobacco. A branch was established in Concord, of which Mr. Tenney had charge for a year or more, and contemplated removing to that city, but on the outbreak of the war the business was seriously interfered with, and was closed out about 1865. He then became a partner of Russell Farwell, of Claremont, bearing the firm name of Farwell & Tenney, manufacturers of shoes. In 1871 Mr. Tenney bought his partner's interest, selling it again to Mr. Augustus Barrett, which firm, under the name of Barrett & Tenney continued until 1881, when the latter partner sold out his interests to Mr. Barrett's son. Mr. Tenney then retired from active business, but his time became fully occupied in the discharge of duties he was asked to assume. He was twice a member of the legislature, and served in the important position of railroad commissioner of his state for three terms. From 1887 to 1889 he was deputy internal revenue collector for western New Hampshire, and eastern Vermont. He also during these years served his town in various public offices, and was one of the chief movers in many local enterprises. In 1890, associating himself with the leading citizen of his town, he became treasurer and director of the Claremont Building Association which accomplished the building of the Claremont Hotel Block, giving the town one of the best hotels in the state. Mr. Tenney was the treasurer and one of the directors of the Claremont Electric Light Company from its inception until it was absolved into the Claremont Street Railway Company. In the organization of the Sullivan County Park Association, he was one of its active members and for many years an executive officer. In 1891 Mr. Tenney was appointed judge of probate for Sullivan county, and held that office at the time of his death. He was also identified with the banking interests of his town, and it was through his efforts that the People's National Bank of Claremont was organized in 1892, an institution that he saw grow to be one of the strongest banks in the state, and one in which, as one of its leading directors he took great pride. Judge Tenney was a man strong mentally, and with a keen analytical mind he possessed excellent judgment and was held in the highest esteem by his fellow citizens. Although he was not educated for a lawyer, he was rated the best probate judge the county ever had. He was for many years a strong force in the councils of the Republican party in both town and state, and was considered an able, resourceful and reliable member of his party. He was a demitted Mason and an attendant of the Episcopal Church. Edward J. Tenney married, in 1859, Frances M. Hall, daughter of Stephen and Charlotte (Green) Hall, both natives of Concord, where for many generations their families were prosperous farmers and neighbors on lands now owned by St. Paul's school. Mrs. Tenney, a most estimable woman, is still living (1907) in the delightful old family home in Claremont. Two children were born of this union: Edward Hall, the eldest, died at Claremont at the age of twenty-six years. He was a promising young man and gave every evidence of a brilliant business career. George Amos, the second son, was born in Claremont, February 11, 1864. He is cashier of the People's National Bank of Claremont, and is one of the prominent business men of his town. In North Adams, Massachusetts, May 21, 1890, Mr. Tenney married Sarah Estelle Ballou, a descendant of the famous Hosea Ballou. They have two children: Edward Ballou, born May 4, 1891; and George Pomeroy, November 17, 1899.

BLACK Among the earliest epithets to distinguish men from each other were those which referred to personal characteristics and peculiarities. Those that referred to complexion were very common, and five or six centuries ago, when our ancestors in Britain were assuming surnames, many made use of those descriptive epithets as surnames. Those of White and Read (Red) and Black were among the oldest and most common of such names.

(I) Neil Black, son of Daniel Black, was born in 1832, and was employed in iron works as a forger. In 1895 he removed to Nashua, New Hampshire, where he was employed until 1896, when he retired from industrial labor. He married Ann Leonard. Four children were born of this union: Neil, Daniel, John, James S. and Dennis.

(II) Dr. James Stainsland, fourth son and child of Neil and Ann (Leonard) Black, was born in Pembroke, Maine, December 21, 1875. He obtained his literary education in the common schools, and at the New Hampshire College of Agriculture and Mechanical Arts, and then entered Dartmouth Medical School, from which he graduated in 1900. For a year and a half next following his graduation he was a member of the medical staff of Deer Island Hospital, Boston Harbor. From there he went to the Massachusetts General Hospital and for six months was on the staff, having charge of the department of contagious diseases. Later he settled in Nashua, New Hampshire, where he opened an office and has since been engaged in a successful and steadily growing general medical practice. He is a member of the Hillsborough County and the Nashua Medical societies.

MOODY The earliest known instance of this name in England is that of Reginald Moody (spelled Mody), living in Norfolk county, in the reign of Edward I, A. D., 1272. In Oxfordshire and Wiltshire the name anciently appears both as Modi and Mody, but in Somerset and Hampshire counties it was invariably spelled Moody. It is suggested that the name may have been derived from the Anglo-Saxon Mod (force), or from the ancient city Modessa, in Italy. In America the Moody family has been prominent from very early times in Essex county, Massachusetts, its chief seat being at Newbury. William Moody, the progenitor of the name in New England, came, according to the best records that can be obtained, from Wales, in 1633. He wintered in Ipswich, in 1634-5, and removed to Newbury with the first settlers of that place in 1635, where he resided until his death, October 25, 1673. Mr. Moody was made freeman on his arrival in Newbury, and received a grant of ninety-two acres of land. He is said to have been a saddler by trade, and also skillful as a farrier. It is also stated on good authority that he was a blacksmith and had the reputation of being the first smith to shoe oxen. It appears evident that he was interested in whatever furthered educational interests, and a large number of his immediate descendants entered the learned profession and were distinguished for their superior intelligence quite in advance of the age in which they lived. Nearly forty persons of the name were graduated from the New England colleges previous to 1847. William Moody was a man of note, both in the ecclesiastical and civil affairs of his town. No date of his marriage is given. The christian name of his wife was Sarah. She died in Newbury, January 13, 1673. Their children were: Samuel, Joshua and Caleb.

Joshua Moody, the second son of William and Sarah Moody, was born in England, in 1633, shortly before his father came to America. He received the rudiments of his education in Newbury, and graduated at Harvard College, class of 1655. He studied Divinity, and commenced his ministerial labors in Portsmouth, New Hampshire, early in the year 1658, founding the First Congregational society in that town. In consequence of dissensions arising later, which amounted to persecution, he removed to Boston in 1684 and became the assistant pastor of the First Church. On the death of President Rogers of Harvard College, July 2, 1684, Mr. Moody was elected his successor, but declined the honor. After many urgent requests from his former parishioners, he returned to Portsmouth in 1692, where he passed the remainder of his days and died July 4, 1697. Rev. Josiah Moody is said to have been remarkable for his decision of character, his firmness under great trials, and particularly for his decided opposition to the delusion which in the time of the Salem witchcraft in 1692 had so largely deceived the population of Massachusetts. Mr. Moody was twice married. It is probable that his first wife was a daughter of Edward Collins, of Cambridge. His second wife was Ann Jacobs, of Ipswich, who survived him. The names of three daughters are given, but we have no evidence that he had more than one son, namely, Samuel, who was probably born in Portsmouth. No date of his birth appears, but he was a graduate of Harvard College in 1689, and was for several years a preacher in Newcastle, and later at the Isles of Shoals. He finally laid aside his calling as clergyman and assumed that of a military commander. He took command of a body of men in an expedition against the Indians, and frequently adjusted matters of dispute. Samuel Moody eventually located in Portsmouth, and was considered one of the foremost settlers in building up that colony. He married, in 1695, Esther, daughter of Nathaniel Green, of Boston, by whom he had two sons, Joshua and Samuel, and one daughter Mary.

(I) Elias Moody, it is claimed, was descended from William the emigrant through the lines of (II) Joshua and (III) Samuel, recorded above, but the scanty records obtainable do not indicate which one of Samuel's sons was his ancestor. He was born in Unity, New Hampshire, in 1771, and died in Newport, August 24, 1856. It is stated that his father's name was Daniel, and it appears reasonable that he is identical with Daniel Moody whose name is recorded among the signers of a petition to divide the town of Unity and address to the legislature in 1791. There is little room to doubt that Daniel Moody (of Unity) was a native of one of the southeasterly towns of New Hampshire, not far removed from Portsmouth, where Rev. Joshua Moody labored so long. Elias Moody was a farmer, a Democrat in politics, and his religious affiliations were with the Baptists. He married Polly Critchet, of Unity. Their six children were: Jonathan, Mary, Mathew Harvey, Nathan, Josiah and Melindy. Mathew Harvey Moody is said to have been a man of more than ordinary ability. He received little education until his marriage to Olive Dunham, a noted school teacher of her time. He became the pupil of his wife, and turned the opportunity thus afforded him in good account. In addition to his trade of shoemaking Mr. Moody farmed on a large scale, and carried on an extensive cattle business. He was a justice of the peace for thirty years, performing creditably the duties incident to the office, and having the confidence and good will of the community in which he lived. One of his sons, Andrew J. Moody, was in the government detective service from 1854 to 1885, when illness compelled him to resign his office. He has been a justice of the peace for forty years, and is a resident of Amherst, New Hampshire.

(II) Jonathan, eldest son of Elias and Polly (Critchet) Moody, was born in Unity in 1801. He removed in early manhood to Claremont, where he died in 1883. He was by trade a shoemaker, using pegs of his own manufacture, and had in his employ a force of several men. He is said to have been a famous tenor drummer, and was in request at all military trainings. He was a man of unique personality, and strict business integrity. Mr Moody married (first), Emily Walker. She died September 8, 1836, aged twenty-eight years. Their children were: Susan Addie, John Walker, Emily Maria and Leonard Otis Tracy. He married (second), Mary Chase, who was born in Claremont, in 1813, and died in her native town in 1890. She is said to have been a very superior woman. The children by this marriage were: Mary Elizabeth, James Chase, William Henry Harrison, Eli Tolman, George Washington, Clara Belle and Ada Frances.

(III) William Henry Harrison, third child and second son of Jonathan and Mary (Chase) Moody, was born May 10, 1842, in Claremont. His school advantages were limited to a few years in the district schools of that day. When about fourteen years of age he entered a shoe factory in Claremont, and continued in its employ four years. In 1861 he enlisted in Troop L, New England Cavalry, served a few months and was honorably discharged. In the fall of 1862, Mr. Moody engaged as traveling salesman for a large shoe jobbing firm, and sold goods all over the country. His extraordinary business ability was soon recognized, and in 1867 he was admitted as a partner in a concern under the firm name of McGibbons, Moody & Radin, of Boston. In 1873 he became a partner in the firm of Crain, Moody and Rising, and they established a shoe manufactory at Amoskeag, New Hampshire, employing one hundred hands, and making shoes for the Western and Southern trade. In a few years the business having outgrown its quarters, the firm removed to Nashua and continued there about seven years, when the shoe manufacturing firm of Moody, Estabrook & Anderson was organized. They built at Nashua a three-story brick factory large enough to accommodate from nine hundred to one thousand hands, and to turn out over eight thousand pairs of shoes of various styles per day, it being at the time the largest manufactory of its class of goods in the country, and having an office and warehouse in Boston. Mr. Moody became a director in the National Shoe and Leather Bank of that city. In 1895 after amassing a snug fortune, he retired from business and returned to his native town, where he erected a commodious set of buildings surrounded by beautiful and extensive grounds. He has always been a great admirer of horseflesh, and his stables for many years contained a fine lot of thoroughbreds.

The family maintains a summer home in Claremont, but usually spends the winter in a more favorable climate. Mr. Moody takes a vital interest in whatever pertains to the advancement and welfare of his town, and has been a wise and generous benefactor. He is the owner of Hotel Claremont, a handsome and well appointed structure. In politics he is a conservative Republican, hence, does not believe in sacrificing principle to party affiliation. While considered liberal in religion, he has a firm belief in the overruling power of God. October 25, 1866, in Bowdoinham, Maine, Mr. Moody married Mary, daughter of Levi P. and Lovana (Orr) Maynard. She was born September 6, 1841, in Fairfield, Maine, and was educated in the academy of that town. She is a woman of superior attainments, and in the words of her husband, she has been "a sustaining power for good" during the years of their wedded life. Two children died in infancy.

LOMBARD The first known ancestor of this family is found in the records of Springfield, Massachusetts, but there seems to be no record of his arrival in New England. Bernard and Thomas Lombard, Lumbard or Lombart, of Tenterden, county of Kent, England, were in Scituate, Massachusetts, as early as 1637, but whether or not they were related to the Lombards of Colebrook, now under consideration, cannot be ascertained.

(I) John Lombard went to Springfield in 1646, and received in all five grants of land there between the years 1651 and 1664. He served as fence-viewer in 1655 and again in 1667. He died May 15, 1672. He was married September 1, 1647, in New Haven, to Joanna Pritchard and was the father of John (who died young), David and Nathaniel.

(II) David, son of John and Joanna (Pritchard) Lombard, was paid the sum of ten shillings for killing a wolf in 1679. He served as surveyor in 1696, and as tithingman in 1698-99, and being chosen constable in 1707-08, he hired Samuel Warner to perform the duties of that office. His death occurred August 17, 1716. The maiden name of his wife is not known. His children were: Mary, Margaret, Abigail, John, David, Ebenezer, Joseph, and two other children who died in infancy.

(III) John, son of David Lombard, was born in Springfield, in 1685, and settled in Brimfield, Massachusetts.

(IV) Joseph, son of John Lombard, resided in Brimfield and may have been a native of that town

(V) Joseph (2), son of Joseph (1) Lombard, was a lifelong resident of Brimfield and followed general farming.

(VI) Joseph (3), son of the preceding Joseph, was born in Brimfield. He married Mary Faulkner and had at least eight children.

(VII) Lyman Lombard, M. D., eighth child of Joseph and Mary (Faulkner) Lombard, was born in Brimfield, March 15, 1788. His boyhood and youth were spent in attending school and assisting his father in carrying on the homestead farm, where he acquired a robust constitution and a splendid physique. A natural capacity for learning enabled him to make good use of the slender advantages for obtaining an education, and preferring professional life to that of a farmer he took up the study of medicine under the direction of Dr. Keyes, of Brimfield. His studies were interrupted by the War of 1812-15, in which he served for a period of nine months, and having concluded his professional preparations in 1815 he selected the upper Connecticut valley as a promising field for operation, inaugurating his professional career in Columbia, New

Hampshire. In the autumn of 1818 he removed to Colebrook, where he purchased the residence and succeeded to the practice of Dr. Thomas Flanders, a pioneer medical practitioner in that locality, and here he enthusiastically accepted his increased professional duties, which at that time as well as for many years afterwards were attended with hardships unknown to the country physician of the present day. During the early days of his practice he traveled on horseback, but later rode in a gig, and his circuit extended north to the Canada line, south to Northumberland and Guildhall and east to Errold and Dummer. He practiced both medicine and surgery, was equally skillful in each, and for nearly half a century withstood the constant exposure to the severe winter weather and the oppressive heat of the summer season, his almost invulnerable constitution seemingly defying the frequent storms and searching winds of the vigorous northern New England climate. He was not only faithful to his patients but labored diligently to elevate the standard of his profession and in various other ways made himself a useful and indispensable member of society. In addition to his professional popularity, his amiable disposition, genial manner and keen sense of humor made him a general favorite, and his large, well-proportioned frame and commanding presence gave him an air of dignity which was perfectly in keeping with his position.

Dr. Lombard was a member of the county, state and other medical bodies, and for a number of years served as surgeon of the Twenty-fourth Regiment, New Hampshire Volunteer Militia. Politically he was a Democrat, and for the years 1851-52 represented his district in the state legislature. In 1823 he was made a Mason in Evening Star Lodge, of which he was secretary for many years, was one of the petitioners for the restoration of its charter in 1859 and was chosen worshipful master. In his religious belief he was a Universalist. Dartmouth College conferred upon him the honorary degree of Doctor of Medicine in 1860. His death occurred in Colebrook, October 21, 1867, after a short illness. On December 21, 1820, he married Betsey Loomis, a native of Hebron, Connecticut, daughter of Joseph and Anna (Bissell) Loomis. She became the mother of six children, namely Anna Smith, who became the wife of Hazen Bedel and is no longer living; Mary F., who died February 26, 1871; Isabel A., who became the wife of Corydon Farr and died April 2, 1900; Emma E., who became the wife of S. S. Merrill and died in March, 1872; Erasmus Darwin, who died July 8, 1857; and Joseph E., who is the only survivor. Mrs. Betsey Lombard died March 22, 1872. She was a woman of superior intelligence and kept a diary which covered a period of fifty years.

(VIII) Joseph Erastus, youngest son and child of Dr. Lyman and Betsey (Loomis) Lombard, was born in Colebrook, December 28, 1837. He began his education in the public schools of his native town, continued it in those of Thetford, Vermont, and North Bridgton, Maine, and concluded his studies with a course at the Colebrook Academy. He began the activities of life as a farmer, continued in that occupation for a number of years, but relinquished agriculture for the real estate business and has for a long time given his attention almost exclusively to buying and selling land, being one of the most extensive dealers in the state. In politics he acts with the Democratic party, was a member of the board of selectmen for a number of years, has held other town offices and represented Colebrook in the lower house of the states legislature for the years 1867 and 1871. He is now the senior member of Eastern Star Lodge, Ancient Free and Accepted Masons, having been admitted to that body in 1861, is a member of North Star Chapter, Royal Arch Masons of Lancaster, and also belongs to the Knights of Pythias. His religious affiliations are with the Congregationalists.

Mr. Lombard was married February 7, 1863, to Ellen L. Merrill, a native of Woodstock, New Hampshire, daughter of Hon. Sherburne R. Merrill, and a descendant of Nathaniel Merrill, who settled at Newbury, Massachusetts, in 1634 (which see). Mr. and Mrs. Lombard have two sons, Darwin and Lyman, who are now engaged in mercantile business at Colebrook under the firm name of Lombard Brothers. Darwin married Rosa Capen, a native of Vermont, and they have had three children: Ruth, who died in infancy; Ellen, born in 1894; and Isabel, born in 1900, died in 1901. Lyman married Angie Marshall, daughter of George Fayette Marshall, of Colebrook. Their children are: Merrill Erastus, born in 1894; and Marshall Lyman, born in 1898.

MARBLE — The names of Marble, Marable and Marvel are probably derived from the same source, but which of them was the original cannot be definitely determined. The family is of English origin and includes among its representatives the inventor of calico-printing. The posterity of William of Charlestown, Joseph of Andover, Gershom of Hingham, Nicholas of Gloucester, John of Boston and Samuel of Salem, who settled there early in the colonial period, constitutes the various branches of the family in America. Samuel married Rebecca Andrews and his son Freegrace became one of the original settlers in Sutton, Worcester county, Massachusetts. The maiden name of his wife was Mary L. Sibley, and she bore him three sons: Samuel, Malachi and Enoch. John Marble, eldest son of Enoch, was born in Sutton in 1751, and participated in the battle of Bunker Hill. In 1794 he went to Dixfield, Oxford county, Maine, as a pioneer. Loammi Marble, mentioned in the succeeding paragraph, belonged to the Dixfield branch of the family.

(I) Loammi Marble, a descendant of Freegrace of Sutton, Massachusetts, a native of Worcester (date of birth not at hand) went from there to Dixfield, Maine, where he engaged in farming, and resided in that town for the rest of his life. He married Harriet Barnard and reared a family.

(II) Barnard L., son of Loammi and Harriet (Barnard) Marble, was born in Dixfield in 1821. His early life was spent at the homestead but becoming tired of the monotony of farm life he sought a more congenial occupation and finally became proprietor of a hotel in Maine, which he conduceed successfully for a number of years. He was a pro-slavery Democrat and a man of pronounced opinions, entertaining at his home the famous secessionist leader, Jefferson Davis, during the latter's visit to Maine, and although practically surrounded by abolitionists he displayed the courage of his convictions by openly sympathizing with the Confederate cause during the rebellion. He served as postmaster and his death occurred in Dixfield in 1802. He married Lucy Trask Abbott, who became the mother of five children.

(III) Henry Marble, M. D., son of Barnard L. and Lucy T. (Abbott) Marble, was born in Dixfield September 5, 1848. His early education was completed at the Norwich (Vermont) University, and his professional preparations were concluded at the Maine Medical School, from which he was graduated in 1870, being twenty-one years old and the youngest member of his class. Locating in Auburn, Maine, he practiced medicine there for ten years or until failing health caused him to seek an occupation wherein he would be less exposed to the inclemency of the weather, and he accordingly established himself in the drug business at Gorham, New Hampshire. At the expiration of three years, with renewed health made possible by the invigorating atmosphere of that locality, he resumed the practice of his profession in Gorham and has ever since continued it with gratifying success. Dr. Marble is not only an able medical practitioner, but is a progressive citizen as well, and evinces a profound interest in all matters relative to the welfare and progress of the community. While residing in Auburn he represented that city in the Maine legislature and, as a member of that body in 1879, the year in which occurred the famous political movement known as the "state steal," he was largely instrumental in bringing to an amicable settlement a contest which threatened to produce serious results. Since settling in Gorham he has served on the board of United States pension examiners for twelve years; was chairman of the board of education for nine years and for the past ten years has rendered excellent service upon the board of health. He is a member of the Maine State and the Androscoggin County Medical societies; the New Hampshire State and the Coos County Medical societies, and is well advanced in the Masonic Order, belonging to the Blue Lodge in Dixfield, the Royal Arch Chapter in Berlin, the council of Royal and Select Masters in Lewiston, and the commandery of Knights Templar in that city. In his religious belief he is a Universalist.

Dr. Marble married Mercy Littlefield, daughter of Thomas Littlefield, who at one time held the office of sheriff of Androscoggin county and was elected the first mayor of Auburn. Dr. and Mrs. Marble have two children: Thomas L., who is now practicing law in Berlin, this state; and Laura K., now the wife of Walter Weston.

BUSWELL This family is among the early Massachusetts stock and has numerous representatives scattered throughout the United States. In course of time, like many other American names, it has undergone many modifications in spelling. In sections of New Hampshire are many who spell the name Busiel, in other sections it is spelled Buzzell, but the major portion of the tribe probably maintain the original spelling, as given at the head of this article. They have all been noted for their sturdy character, their industry, intelligence and moral worth.

(I) Isaac Buswell was a weaver of Salisbury, Massachusetts, born about 1592, without doubt, in England. He was made a freeman of Salisbury in 1640 and received land in the first division in that year and is again mentioned as townsman in 1650. His death, July 8, 1683, is found in the Salisbury records. His will was dated April 9, 1680, and was proven September 25, 1638. The christian name of his wife was Margaret. She died September 29, 1642, in Salisbury, and about 1614, he married Susannah (surname unknown). She died March 27, 1677 in Salisbury. The first wife was the mother of three children and the second, two, namely: William, Phoebe, Samuel, Mary and Isaac.

(II) Samuel, second son and third child of Isaac and Margaret Buswell, was born about 1628, probably in England. He was a resident of Salisbury in 1662, and probably as late as 1669, and appears to have resided for a short time in Andover. At the time of his death, he resided in Bradford, Massachusetts. He was a planter or husbandman and according to Savage, may have lived in Marblehead for a short time, in 1667. His death occurred previous to July 27, 1704, when his will was proven. In that instrument, mention is made of his wife, Sarah, and her brother, Solomon Keyes of Chelmsford and John Boynton of Bradford, who were overseers of his estate. He was married, in July, 1656, to Sarah Keyes, who probably survived him. Their children were: Isaac, John, Samuel, William, Robert, James, Mary and Joseph.

(III) Isaac (2), eldest child of Samuel and Sarah (Keyes) Buswell, was born August 6, 1657, in Salisbury, and was a weaver in that town. He was made a freeman in 1690 and died July 16, 1709. His estate was administered in August, following his death, and was divided in 1718. He was married about 1690 to Anna Ordway, who was admitted a member of the Salisbury Church, October 25, 1719. She was married February 21, 1723, to William Baker, of Ipswich. The children of Isaac and Anna (Ordway) Buswell, were: Isaac, Daniel, William, John, Samuel, James and Hannah.

(IV) Isaac (3), eldest child of Isaac (2) and Anna (Ordway) Buswell, was born January 5, 1692, in Salisbury and continued to reside in that town for many years. He was a weaver by occupation and was noted for the beautiful patterns of table linen and coverlets which he produced, being handsome both in color and design. He died in 1778, in Salisbury. His children were: Jonathan, James, Benjamin, Moses and Betty. The first removed to Wells, Maine, the second to Hopkinton, New Hampshire and the fourth to Sunapee, same state. The third son continued to reside in Salisbury. The daughter became the wife of Captain Pike of Salisbury, who distinguished himself at the battle of Bunker Hill. Another daughter, whose name is not known, married a Sawyer of Haverhill.

(V) Benjamin, third son of Isaac (3) Buswell, resided on the paternal homestead in Salisbury. He was a carpenter and cabinet maker and some excellent specimens of his work are preserved by his descendants. Among these, is a desk which he constructed previous to 1775, now in the town of Hopkinton, New Hampshire. He was among the Minute Men of the Revolution and served at Bunker Hill. He died in August, 1776. He had six children: Hannah, Elizabeth, Mary, Sally, Benjamin and Elizabeth.

(VI) Benjamin (2), fifth child and only son of Benjamin (1) Buswell, was born August 25, 1766, in Salisbury, and soon after attaining his majority, about 1787, he removed to Concord, New Hampshire. For sometime, he was employed at West Concord by Lieutenant Ezekiel Carter and subsequently bought a large tract of land in Hopkinton which he cleared and on which he built a house. He was a very industrious and energetic man and this building with the chimney was constructed by himself without the aid of any skilled mechanic. He was a very successful farmer and a prominent representative citizen of Hopkinton. He made a special study of horses and was a skilled veterinary and also practiced the healing art much among his neighbors of the human family. He died June 1, 1851, much lamented by his neighbors and contemporaries. He married Joanna, daughter of Ezekiel Carter, (see Carter, IV, second family) and they moved to their new home on Christmas day, 1790. For more than sixty years he resided in that house. They were the parents of twelve children, including the following: John, Carter, Samuel Smith, Andrew, Moses, Jane, Katherine, Rhuey, Elenor, Elizabeth and Judith. All the sons settled in the vicinity of their native home. The first daughter above named, married Marshall Richardson and lived on Beech Hill, in Hopkinton. Katherine became the wife of Edwin Terry, and lived on Horse Hill. Elenor was the wife of Eli Lamprey, of West Concord and Judith married Nathan Davis, of Davisville in the town of Warner. The other daughters died unmarried. The list above given, is not supposed to be in the order of birth.

(VII) Samuel Smith, son of Benjamin (2) and Joanna (Carter) Buswell, was born on the western border of the town of Concord and passed his life there, engaged largely in farming. He was also something of a carpenter and engaged much in the practice of medicine. He was an officer of the militia and was a man of affairs, generally. During his last years, he was a member of the Episcopal Church. In politics, he was a Democrat. He was married in 1854, to Deborah Elder, who was born in East Machias. Maine, daughter of Charles and Mary Esther (Lowry) Elder. She survived him, and now resides with her youngest daughter in Concord. Their children are accounted for as follows: Lorin Webster resides in Newbury, Vermont, where he is engaged in the lumbering business; Mary Esther, resides in Hopkinton near her native spot; Josephine is the wife of Abraham Burgois, of Peterboro; Emma is the wife of Erbon Hall, of Bow. Frank is in San Francisco, California; Rhuey fills a desirable business position in Boston; Maud Davis, is the wife of Leon F. Shallis, residing in Concord.

DOWST A master workman, a master builder and a master of himself, a friend of all honest men and women, and a doer of things "strictly on the square;" in fact, an exemplar of Masonry in its highest aspects—these were the main traits in the massive character of the late Frank Dowst, which made him one of the foremost, as well as most beloved men in the Granite state. He possessed the character of granite—substantial and massive, yet showing a warmth and richness of coloring as its most marked outward characteristics.

Mr. Dowst was a native of Allenstown, New Hampshire, born on the 3rd of April, 1850, and was a son of Henry and Hannah Dowst, pioneers of the town and splendid types of New Englanders. The farm on which he was born has been in the possession of the family for a period of one hundred and fifteen years, and his father. now eighty-seven years of age, with his sister, Nettie L. Dowst, still reside on the historic homestead. Frank attended the Allentown schools until he was seventeen years of age, when he entered the employ of Mead & Mason, of Concord, a prominent firm of builders and contractors. During his connection of three years with them he not only became a thorough carpenter, but a useful factor in the carrying out of the various contracts prosecuted by the firm. For nearly a year he was identified with the erection of the Soldiers' Home at Togus, Maine. At the conclusion of his service with Mead & Mason he returned home and completed his education at the Pembroke Academy, and in July, 1871, soon after attaining his majority, formed a partnership with the late Governor Natt Head, of Hooksett, under the firm name of Head & Dowst, and began the business in Manchester which he finally brought to such fine proportions. The partnership with Governor Head continued until the death of the latter in 1883, when his brother, William F. Head, became active in the firm. In 1891 the Head & Dowst Company was incorporated, with Frank Dowst, president, William F. Head, vice-president, and John Dowst, treasurer. Another brother, Henry Dowst, was a director.

The first building erected by this firm, which became the New Hampshire leaders in the building and contracting lines. was the Pickering House, of Manchester, completed in the fall of 1871. Among other prominent structures which are the product of the company's able and honest work may be mentioned the Daniel Connor block, Opera House block, the Government building, the Elliot silk mill, McElwain Shoe Company's buildings, the Varney, Straw, Wilson and High schools, and the passenger stations at Manchester and Concord.

The deceased was the dominant force in this extensive business, and as a man of exceptional executive ability was also able to successfully control other large interests. He was president of the People's Gas Light Company, and president and director of the Elliott Manufacturing Company. Despite his widely extended interests of a business nature, he also found time for social affairs, and was a director and former vice-president of the Derryfield Club. Naturally, his temperament drew him forcibly to Masonry, and many years ago he joined Blazing Star Lodge, Ancient Free and Accepted Masons, of Concord, but when he became a resident of Manchester he was transferred to Lafayette Lodge. He was a Thirty-second degree Mason, being a member of Trinity Commandery, Knight Templars, Edward Raymond Consistory of Nashua, and the Mystic Shrine of Boston. In politics. he was a Democrat, but never held other than minor local offices. He was too outspoken and uncompromisingly honest to be a successful politician.

In 1872 the deceased was united in marriage with Miss Martha Tallant, the ceremony occurring at Pembroke in 1872. The wife and their only child, a daughter, died a number of years ago. The survivors are the father and a sister, already mentioned; the two brothers noted as partners in the Head & Dowst Company, as well as a third brother, George, of Allenstown; and the elder sister, Mrs. A. L. Ricker, of Short Falls.

Frank Dowst passed away on the 27th of November, 1905, his death following a stroke of paralysis, which was the result of an accident sustained by him several months before. He was a powerful and healthy man both physically and mentally, and therefore possessed in a marked degree the spirit of cheerfulness and hopefulness. He was not only complete master of his calling, but. as stated by one of his intimates, "he was incapable of trickery, deceit. sharp practice or meanness of any kind, and he abominated all who tried to succeed by crookedness. He was the most modest and democratic of men. He never sought an office. He never desired prominence outside of his business. He was generous to a fault. He was public-spirited, and he was the most loyal and profuse of friends and the most delightful of associates. He did a great deal to make Manchester what she is, and for what he did for those who were fortunate enough to be intimately connected with him, there is no measure. Yesterday there was but one Frank Dowst. There is none now."

(For ancestry, see page 257.)

MORSE (II) Benjamin, fifth son of Anthony and Mary Morse, was born March 4, 1640, in Newbury, and resided in that town where he was living in 1707, together with his wife. He was made a freeman in 1673, and subscribed to the oath of fidelity and allegiance in 1668, and again in 1678. Both he and his wife were members of the Newbury Church in 1674. He was married, August 27, 1667, to Ruth Sawyer, and their children were: Benjamin, Ruth, Joseph, William, Sarah (died young), Philip, Sarah, Ann, Esther, Hannah, Mary and Samuel.

(III) Benjamin (2), eldest child of Benjamin (1) and Ruth (Sawyer) Morse, was born August 24, 1668, in Newbury, and was a weaver by occupation, residing in that town where he died October 25, 1743. His will which was made on February 4, of the previous year, was probated November 7, following his death. He was married, January 28, 1692, in Newbury, to Susanna, daughter of Abel and Priscilla (Chase) Merrill, a granddaughter of Aquilla (2) Chase, and of Nathaniel (1) Merrill. (See Merrill and Chase.) She was born November 14, 1673, in Newbury, and was the mother of the following children: Abel, Ruth, Priscilla, Judith, Stephen, Mary, Hannah, Susanna and Benjamin.

(IV) Abel, eldest child of Benjamin (2) and Susanna (Merrill) Morse, was born October 5, 1692, in Newbury, and settled in Chester, New Hampshire, before 1742. He purchased several lots of land there, and also mills, and was a most active and influential citizen. He was the first representative admitted into the General Association in 1748. In 1746 he had the title of Captain. He was married (first), June 3, 1714, in Bradford, Massachusetts, to Grace Parker. The name of his second wife has not been preserved. His children were: Parker, Abel, Nathan, Josiah, Stephen, Rebecca, Eleanor, Oliver, Abraham and Susanna. The eldest was a graduate of Harvard, and became a practicing physician. The third resided in Moultonborough, New Hampshire.

(V) Josiah, fourth son of Abel and Grace (Parker) Morse, was born in 1721, and resided in Chester, where he married Mary, daughter of Joseph Chase. their children were: Mary, Josiah, Anna, Parker, Joseph, Amos, and perhaps others. (Amos and descendants receive mention in this article).

(VI) Joseph, third son of Josiah and Mary (Chase) Morse, was born May 12, 1753, in Chester, and there made his home. He married Mary Randall, and they were the parents of nine children: Molly, Rachel, Hannah, Lucy, Joseph, Oliver, Levi, Walter and Edmund.

(VII) Joseph (2), fifth child of Joseph (1) and Mary (Randall) Morse, was born March 20, 1784, in Chester, and died there October 22, 1862. He married Phebe D. West, and their children were: Lavina, Mary, Lucy, Jane, Edmund Hill, Nason Hovey, Joseph West, Emily, Amos Foster, Harriet Foster (died young), Nathan Spalding and Harriet Elizabeth.

(VIII) Nathan Spalding, tenth child of Joseph (2) and Phebe D. (West) Morse, was born March 30, 1830, and resided in Chester, where he died October 23, 1902. He was educated in the public schools of his native town and at Pembroke Academy, and was an auctioneer and dealer in real estate, in connection with farming. He served for many years as moderator of town meetings, and was a very active and popular citizen. His activities extended far outside of his home town, and he was widely known and esteemed. He was a ready speaker, noted for witty sayings, and commanded attention wherever he went. He was married, May 19, 1853, to Caroline E. Webster, of Derry. (See Webster, VIII). Their children were: Roger Spalding, Lawrence Lee, Morris Webster and Annie Lucy. The eldest died at the age of twenty-one years. The second resided in Derry, where he died in his fiftieth year. The third is a graduate of Pinkerton Academy and Dartmouth College, and of the Hartford Theological Seminary. At the latter institution he received the Wells' Fellowship, and studied two years at Leipsig, Germany. He has filled several pastorates in California, Nebraska and Washington, and is now located at Ilwaco, in the last named state. The daughter was educated at Pinkerton Academy and at Mount Holyoke, Massachusetts, and is now the wife of Charles A. Sprague, of Haverhill, Massachusetts.

(VI) Amos, son of Abel and Sarah (Chase) Morse, was born August 7, 1758, in Chester, where he resided. He married Hannah Blaisdell, of that town.

(VII) Josiah, son of Amos and Hannah (Blaisdell) More, was born March 3, 1786, in Chester, and passed his life in that town, where he married Lydia Shannon.

(VIII) Josiah D., son of Josiah and Lydia (Shannon) Morse, was born September 28, 1823, in Chester, where he made his home. He was married, December 31, 1843, to Emeline Robie, of that town, who was born September 22, 1822. Following is a brief account of their children: Clara Augusta, the eldest became the wife of William Thompson, of Derry, and left no issue; Lavator Onville was born in 1847, in Chester, and resided in Maine, leaving no issue; Oscar Eugene married Abbie A. Sanborn, of Chester, and had children: Herbert Oscar, Lilla A., Blanche Augusta, and Lena M.; Irvin Dearborn died when eleven years old; Jennie Eveline married John P. Green, of Chester, and had daughters, Gertrude, Jennie and Mildred Emeline; Sarah Elizabeth became the wife of Brock Dearborn, of Belmont, New Hampshire, and died in 1906. She had two sons, William Clark and Clarence Brock.

(IX) William Tappan, youngest child of Josiah D. and Emeline (Robie) Morse, was born in Chester August 14, 1857. He was educated in the public schools of that town, and graduated from Chester academy in 1880. He taught school in Belmont and served as clerk in a general store in Chester till 1889, when he moved from Chester to Derry to assume the duties of editor of *The Derry News*, of which newspaper he had been agent and correspondent for several years. He is still occupying the position of editor of that paper and is also doing other work in journalism. He is a member of the Echo Lodge of Odd Fellows, and chairman of its board of trustees. He is master of Derry Grange, clerk of the town school district, of the fire precinct, and of the Baptist Church. He is also interested in the Board of Trade, being a director, and is always interested in the general welfare of the town.

(Previous Generations on Pages 478-9).

CILLEY (III) Benoni Selley, son of Richard Sealy, was born in Hampton Falls. and afterward resided in Salisbury and Seabrook, where he was a farmer. He married (first), August 28, 1703, Elenor Getchell, who died June 28, 1736; (second), October 9, 1739, Rachel

Tappan, of Kensington, New Hampshire. His children by his first wife were: Mehitable, Elizabeth. Thomas, Martha, Samuel, Benjamin, Eleanor, Sarah and Dorcas. By the second wife he had Mary and Abigail.

(IV) Samuel Selley, fifth child and second son of Benoni and Elenor (Getchell) Selley, was born April 19, 1711. He married Martha ———, and they had six children: Benjamin, Thomas, Jonathan, Mehitable, Elinor and Mary.

(V) Benjamin Cilley, eldest child of Samuel and Martha Selley, was born in 1744, and died in Weare, in 1811 or 1812. He married, May 19, 1771, Elizabeth Edmonds, of Salisbury, Massachusetts, who was born in 1731. Their children, born in Weare, were: Polly, July 31, 1772; Betsey, July 17, 1773; Sally, August 6, 1774; Benjamin, 1775; Jonathan, 1776; and Jerry D., 1778.

(VI) Benjamin (2), fourth child and eldest son of Benjamin (1) and Elizabeth (Edmonds) Cilley, was born September 4, 1775, in Weare. He was twice married. His first wife was a Miss Bean. He had five sons: Stephen, Moses, Madison, Benjamin. Ezra.

(VII) Benjamin (3), fourth son of Benjamin (2) Cilley, was born in Newbury, where he followed farming throughout the active years of his life, dying at the age of thirty. He married Caroline Peasley, who bore him one child, Ezra.

(VIII) Ezra, only child of Benjamin (3) and Caroline (Peasley) Cilley, was born September 12, 1835, died September 24, 1905, aged seventy. He was a prosperous farmer, and was much in public life. For seventeen years he was chairman of the board of selectmen, and was twice representative of the general court. In politics he was a Democrat, but in 1871 was the unanimous choice of both parties for representative. He was an attendant of the Universalist Church. He was a noble grand of the Independent Order of Odd Fellows, and later was a deputy grand master of the order. He married Laura L. Morse, daughter of Captain Joseph Morse. They had four children: Joseph E. (died young). Wesley E., engaged in the census department in Washington. District of Columbia. He married Mary Bly, of Newbury, New Hampshire, and they have two children: Alice B. and Jay W. Carrie B., died in infancy. Alman Benjamin, see forward.

(IX) Almon Benjamin, third son and fourth child of Ezra and Laura L. (Morse) Cilley, was born in Newbury, New Hampshire, May 7, 1865. He was a farmer boy, and acquired his early education in the public schools. He was employed as a clerk by his brother, Wesley E., in a country store; was stitcher in a shoe factory; clerk in the United States railway mail service. In 1896 he became a solicitor in Boston for the United States Casualty Company of New York. He rose by unremitting industry to the position of general agent for the company in Boston, and held that position six years. He then resigned and in 1906 went to England, where he was successful in inducing the Norwich and London Accident Insurance Assocation of Norwich, England, to enter the United States for business, and secured for himself the appointment of manager for the United States. with the chief American office in Boston. His success in the insurance business from the start has been exceptional, but it is all due to the energy and good judgment which he has given to the work. He is an untiring worker, and his judgment of men, in the selection of agents and other assistants, is conceded to be rarely equalled in this country, and he knows how to secure the most work out of the men around him. His methods are clean, and he has the faculty of infusing into his agents much of the energy which animates him. He is a member in high standing in the following named divisions of the Masonic Order: St. Peter's Lodge, No. 31, Free and Accepted Masons, of Bradford, New Hampshire (now senior warden of this lodge); St. Paul's Royal Arch Chapter, of Boston, (now master of the third veil in this chapter); Boston Council, Royal and Select Masters; De Molay Commandery, No. 7, Knights Templar; Massachusetts Consistory, Sublime Princes of the Royal Secret, of the thirty-second degree; Aleppo Temple, of the Ancient Arabic Order Nobles of the Mystic Shrine, of Boston. He is also a member of Massassecum Lodge, Independent Order of Odd Fellows, of Bradford, New Hampshire, of which he is past noble grand, New Hampshire Club of Boston, and Boston City Club.

Mr. Cilley married, January 7, 1888, Bertha J. Cressy, who was born in Bradford, New Hampshire, daughter of Mason Cressy, of Bradford. They have one child, Arnold Benjamin, born July 9, 1907. at Boston, Massachusetts.

(Preceding Generations on Pages 593-4.)

CHENEY

(III) Joseph, third son of Daniel and Sarah (Bayley) Cheney, baptized in Newbury, April 9, 1682, married (first), Sarah, daughter of Noah and Theodocia (Jackson) Wiswall. She died June 27, 1718, and he married (second), October 12, 1721, Abigail, daughter of James and Margaret (Atherton) Trowbridge, and widow of James Greenwood. The town made Joseph Cheney a subordinate officer in 1714, constable and collector in 1723, and selectman in 1741. In 1744 he was chosen member of a committee "to fill up vaquent Room in the Meeting-house" so as to "give men their Dignity in their setting, in proportion to what they pay to the Minister's Rate." He died May 2, 1749. His children were: Sarah, Judith, Hannah, Joseph and James.

(IV) James, youngest son and child of Joseph and Sarah (Wiswall) Cheney, was born in Newton, May 1, 1716. Married (first), January 10, 1740, Sybil, daughter of Ebenezer and Lydia Littlefield, born November 1, 1714, and died May 19, 1743. He married (second), May 31, 1745, Elizabeth Toser. He lived first in Newton. where he filled several town offices and about 1760 removed to Dedham. His will, made January 29, 1766, was admitted to probate March 7 following. His children were: Sarah, Lydia, Jonathan, Sybil, James, Elizabeth, Esther, John, Olive, Joseph, Abigail and Hannah.

(V) Joseph. tenth child of James and Sybil (Littlefield) Cheney, was born in 1761, and died at the home of his son, Rev. Martin Cheney, of Olneyville, Rhode Island. in 1834. He enlisted in Captain Battle's company of Colonel McIntosh's regiment, December 11, 1776, and served nineteen days at Castle Island. His home was in the fourth parish of Dedham, afterward incorporated as Dover, Massachusetts. May 5, 1778, an order was granted to James and Joseph Cheney and Nathaniel Mellen for one hundred and fifty days guarding Burgoyne's troops, twenty-eight pounds each. His name was on the United States pension roll in Hillsborough county, New Hampshire, in 1819, and in that for Norfolk county, Massachusetts, April 12, 1833, having a pension of $37.98 per annum. Joseph Cheney married, March 23, 1782, Susannah Wadsworth, and had four children: Joseph, Martin, Polly and Lucy.

(VI) Lucy, daughter and youngest child of

Joseph and Susannah (Wadsworth) Cheney, was born in Dover, Massachusette. November 9, 1800, and died March 21, 1851. She married, December 29, 1825, Jonathan Munroe Wilmarth (see Wilmarth) and had eight children.

(Preceding Generations on Page 616.)

BLAISDELL (III) Jonathan, eighth child and fifth son of Henry and Mary (Hodsdon) Blaisdell, was born in Amesbury, October 11, 1676, and was a blacksmith by occupation. He succeeded to his father's homestead, located in that part of Salisbury which in 1668 was incorporated as the town of Amesbury. He taught school and served in various town offices, and was a man of prominence in the community. He was dead before November 28. 1748, as administration on his estate was granted at that time. His real estate was divided in 1750. He married Hannah Jameson, and they had: Mary, Daniel, Anne, Elijah, Jonathan, David, Enoch, Samuel, Hannah, Elizabeth and Henry.

(IV) Jonathan (2), fifth child and third son of Jonathan (1) and Hannah (Jameson) Blaisdell, was born in Amesbury, August 15, 1709. He removed to Kingston, New Hampshire, in 1731, and purchased nineteen acres of land, upon which he erected a dwelling. He was a blacksmith, and about 1731 built iron works in East Kingston with William Whittier. He renewed the covenant in the First Amesbury Church, January 25, and was received in full communion, February 1, 1736. His wife Hannah was baptized November 23, 1735, at Kingston, and both were admitted to the East Kingston Church. October 4, 1739. He bought land on Powwow river in Kingston in 1735-36, and 1753. He sold one-eighth of the upper iron works at Trickling Falls, Kingston, in 1762; bought and sold land in Epping Parish, Exeter, 1747 and 1763, and in Nottingham in 1748 and 1753. He signed the association test in 1776. His will was made May 18, 1781, and probated January 29, 1782. He was a man of wealth and influence, was justice of the peace and filled other town offices. August 15, 1731, he married. in Amesbury, Hannah Jones. It was probably the children of this Jonathan who changed the spelling of the family name from Blesdale, to Blaisdell, as after this time the latter form appears exclusively in the records. The children of Jonathan and Hannah were: Henry, (died young), a child, Henry, a child, Mary, Jonathan, Abner, Ebenezer, Hannah (died young), Elizabeth and Hannah.

(V) Henry, third child of Jonathan and Hannah (Jones) Blaisdell, was born in East Kingston, about 1736. He was a blacksmith and resided in Kingston, East Kingston, Tamworth, and Eaton. He died in Tamworth about 1825, aged eighty-nine years. He married (first), November 22, 1758, according to the East Kingston church records, Mary Currier, daughter of John and Ruth Currier, of Kingston. She died July 17, 1770, aged twenty-eight years. Married (second), March 4, 1772, as stated in the Hawke church records, Sarah Dolloffe, of Hawke. She died in 1760. Married (third), December 20, 1778, Kingston church records, widow Hannah Ross, of Brentwood, who died December 20, 1788. Married (fourth), September 29, 1792, Hannah Nicholson. His children were: Rhoda. Abner (probably), James and others.

(VI) James, son of Henry and Hannah (Ross) Blaisdell, was born September 20. 1779, and died January 4, 1851. He settled in Tamworth, May 10, 1802, and married Abigail Stetson, who died May 28, 1846.

(VII) Stetson, son of James and Abigail (Stetson) Blaisdell, was born in 1810. He married Sally Emery, daughter of Rev. James Emery.

(VIII) Hannah, daughter of Stetson and Sally (Emery) Blaisdell, was born in Tamworth, July 15, 1835, and died March 9, 1906. She married Francis Hubbard Lord. (See Lord, VII).

(Preceding Generations on Pages 515-16.)

BARTON (VI) Albert G., youngest child of John and Achsah (Lovering) Barton, was born 1825, in Croydon, and was reared in that town. He became a farmer and was industrious and successful and accumulated a large estate. He married Zilpha Sherman.

(VII) Seth, only son of Albert and Zilpha (Sherman) Barton, was born January 29, 1859, on the homestead in Croydon, which is now a part of Corbin Park. He was educated in the public schools of Croydon, and at Colby Academy, New London. He was early accustomed to the labors of the farm, and made agriculture his occupation until twenty-eight years of age. On attaining his majority he purchased a farm of two hundred acres in Croydon, most of which he afterwards sold to form a part of Corbin Park. Having acquired the carpenter's trade he let the farm in 1887 and removed to Newport, where he was employed in building operations. Among the buildings in the erection of which he was engaged, was the popular summer hotel Grandladen, on Lake Sunapee. He has aided in the construction of a large number of buildings in and about Newport. He has taken an active part in the life of the town and has been a member of its fire department several years. While a resident of Croydon he was chairman of the school board of that town in 1887. He is an ardent Republican in political principle, and a very industrious man. A good mechanic, he has been able to secure a competency through his own labors. He was married, June 2, 1881, to Francelia. daughter of Elon and Polly Lovilla (Hardy) Cutting, of Croydon. (See Cutting, VII). She was born March 31, 1857, in Unity, New Hampshire. Seth Barton and wife are the parents of one daughter, Mary Barton, born December 7, 1885, who graduated from the Newport high school in the class of 1903, and subsequently pursued a course in a Boston business college. She was married, November 24. 1904, to Leslie Marshall, of Newport, and they have one daughter, Marion Francelia, born April 12, 1906, named after her two grandmothers.

(IV) Peter, youngest child of Bezaleel and Phebe (Carlton) Barton, was born after 1760, in Sutton, Massachusetts.

(V) Bezaleel (2). Barton. married Hannah Powers and resided in Croydon, New Hampshire.

(VI) Levi Winter, son of Bezaleel (2) and Hannah (Powers) Barton, was born in Croydon, New Hampshire, March 1, 1818, and died in Newport, New Hampshire, March 10, 1899. When he was a boy the advantages of even the common schools were beyond his reach, and his early education was restricted to the short terms of the winter season, and then with occasional interruptions until he was eighteen years old, after which for several terms he was a student in the academy at Unity, New Hampshire. After attaining his majority he determined upon a thorough collegiate training and education. and to that end took a preparatory course at Kimball Union Academy, later entered

very truly yours
Geo. W. Barton

Dartmouth College, and graduated from that institution in 1848. During his senior year in college he studied law with the Hon. Daniel Blaisdell, of Hanover, New Hampshire, and after graduating continued his law studies in the office of Jonathan Kittredge, of Canaan, New Hampshire, afterward chief justice of the court of common pleas of the state. In connection with his law studies in Canaan he taught school five terms, and after removing to Newport in January, 1851, he completed his course of law reading with Metcalf & Corbin, and in July of the same year was admitted to practice.

Having come to the bar, Mr. Barton at once entered actively into professional life and soon came to be recognized among the foremost lawyers of Sullivan county. He was law partner with Hon. Ralph Metcalf at the time of his election as governor of New Hampshire, in 1855; and like most of the lawyers of his day he took an earnest interest in political affairs, and from 1855 to 1858 was register of deeds of Sullivan county. In 1859 he became county solicitor and served in that capacity five years. In 1863-64-75-76-77 he represented Newport in the general assembly, and served as member of the judiciary committee, being chairman of the committee for five years. He served as state senator in 1867 and 1868. In 1863 he was a candidate for the office of attorney general of New Hampshire, and in 1866 was chairman of the board of commissioners appointed by the governor to audit and report the indebtedness of the several towns of the state growing out of the Civil war.

Mr. Barton was a member of the constitutional convention of 1876, and in the same year was a presidential elector on the Republican national ticket. He declined the office of bank commissioner of the state, to which he was appointed by Governor Harriman. In 1877 he was a member of the commission appointed to revise and codify the laws of the state, and performed the duties of that position. Twice he sought the Republican nomination for a seat in the national house of representatives, but each time was defeated in the convention. Throughout his entire professional career he was interested in farming pursuits, and devoted much of his leisure to stock raising, fruit growing and farming generally. Much of his time during the later years of his life was spent on one or other of his farms. In 1839 Mr. Barton married Mary A. Pike, of Newport, who died in 1840, leaving an infant son. He married (second), August 25, 1852, Elizabeth F. Jewett, of Nashua, New Hampshire. His children, by both marriages, were: Ira McL., Herbert J., Charles Fremont, Ralph Winter, Leander M., Florence Frances, Natt Lincoln and Jesse Marston Barton. More detailed stories of the career—as well as the genealogies—of Levi Winter Barton may be found in "Successful Men of New Hampshire," "The Granite Monthly" and "History of Cheshire and Sullivan Counties."

(VII) Ira McL. Barton, son of Levi W. and Mary A. (Pike) Barton, was born in Newport, New Hampshire, March 11, 1840, and died in that town January 19, 1876, after an active and honorable but all too brief career as a brave soldier and brilliant lawyer. He was given a good early education, and at the age of seventeen years began teaching and taught with excellent success in the towns of Newport, Claremont and Alstead, New Hampshire. He fitted for college at Kimball Union Academy, and in 1858 entered Dartmouth College for the class of 1862, but left before graduation and took up the study of law in his father's office. In 1863 he was admitted to practice.

At the outbreak of the Civil war Mr. Barton was the first Sullivan county man to enlist, and although only twenty-one years old at the time, he soon raised a company of volunteers for the three months' service, which was mustered in as Company E, First New Hampshire Volunteer Infantry, he being commissioned its captain, while the regimental command was given to Colonel Tappan. At the expiration of its term of service the company was mustered out, many of its men, however, re-enlisting, and at once afterward Captain Barton recruiting another company, of which he was captain, and which was mustered in as Company E, Fifth New Hampshire Volunteer Infantry, afterward known throughout the army as the "Fighting Fifth" of New Hampshire. After serving in the peninsular campaign under McClellan, during which he took part in the fight at Fair Oaks, the Seven Days' Fight and the subsequent retreat to Harrison's Landing, where he won the warm commendation of his superior officers, Captain Barton resigned his commission on account of sickness and disabilities, and returned to his home in Newport. However, as soon as he was again able to enter the service he recruited a company of heavy artillery—Company B—which he commanded and took to the front, being stationed first at Fort Constitution and later at Fort Foote, near Washington. During the summer of 1864 he was sent back to New Hampshire to recruit a regiment of heavy artillery, which he did with commendable promptness, and as promptly Governor Gilmore commissioned him lieutenant-colonel. This command was stationed at Fort Sumner, in the defenses of Washington, and was on duty there at the time of the assassination of President Lincoln and until the close of the war.

After the war Colonel Barton received an appointment as second lieutenant in the regular army, and while stationed at Pine Bluff, Arkansas, was promoted first lieutenant. At the end of two years he resigned his commission and accepted an appointment as district attorney for the tenth district of Arkansas, and afterward was appointed judge of the criminal court of Jefferson county in the same state. He served in the latter capacity two years, then resigned and took a partnership interest in and the editorship of the *Jeffersonian Republican*, a weekly paper published at Pine Bluff, Arkansas. However, having fought a good fight in a memorable gubernatorial campaign in Arkansas, Colonel Barton disposed of his newspaper interests in the west and returned to Newport. In December, 1875, he resumed the general practice of law in partnership with his father, which relation was continued until the death of the junior partner, January 19, 1876.

Colonel Barton married (first), in 1861, Helen M. Wilcox, of Newport, who died. He married, (second), Addie L. Barton, of Ludlow, Vermont.

(VIII) Jesse Morton, son of Colonel Levi Winter Barton and Elizabeth F. (Jewett) Barton, was born in Newport, New Hampshire, January 21, 1870, and received his earlier education in the public schools of that town. Like his father, he laid the foundation of his classical education at Kimball Union Academy, then entered Dartmouth College and graduated from that famous institution with the class of '92, and during this course he taught school to pay his way through college. After leaving college he began teaching and for the next several years filled a pedagogue's chair with gratifying success, first in the grammar school at Penacook, then three years as principal of the Simonds Free High School at Warner, New Hampshire, and afterward for a year in a select school in Chicago, Illinois. In the fall of 1897 he matriculated at Boston University Law School, and in connection with his course there studied law under the direction of A. S. Wait, Esq., of the Sullivan county bar, and also in the office of his own father. In March, 1899, Judge Barton was admitted to practice in the courts of New Hampshire, and since that time has been actively identified with the professional and political life of his native county. In 1901-02 he represented the town of Newport in the New Hampshire legislature, and in 1903 was a member of the state constitutional convention. In January, 1906, he was appointed probate judge of Sullivan county, which office he now holds. He is a member of the New Hampshire State Bar Association, and of the order of Free and Accepted Masons, a member of the Chapter, and also of the Independent Order of Odd Fellows. Judge Barton is one of the trustees of the Newport Savings Bank and Richard's Free Library. He takes an active interest in the work of the Methodist Episcopal Church of Newport and is one of its board of trustees.

(Preceding Generations on Page 711.)

MORRILL (III) Jacob, fifth child and third son of Isaac and Phoebe (Gill) Morrill, was born in Salisbury, Massachusetts, May 25, 1677. The date of his death is unknown. His will was dated December 1, 1750, and probated March 25, 1754. He was a soldier in Captain Henry True's company, which went to Exeter, July 5, 1710. He married (first), December 4, 1701, at Salisbury, Elizabeth Stevens, daughter of Lieutenant John and Joanna (Thorn) Stevens. She was born February 14, 1678, but the date of her death is also unknown. He married (second), January 5, 1723, Elizabeth Dalton. His twelve children, all by the first wife, were: Jonathan, Joanna (died young), Abraham, Samuel, Joanna, Ruth, Jacob, Jeremiah, Elizabeth, Isaac, Judith and Sarah.

(IV) Abraham, third child and second son of Jacob and Elizabeth (Stevens) Morrill, was born in Salisbury, Massachusetts, December 22, 1703. He was of the West Parish and is called "husbandman." He was baptized and signed the covenant in December, 1721, and was admitted to the second Salisbury Church, January 7, 1728, and signed himself senior after 1731. He died August 15, 1757. His will, executed August 6, was probated October 17, 1757. He married (first), May 15, 1729, at Salisbury, Eleanor True, who was born in Salisbury, November 4, 1705, baptized June 16, 1706, and died March 26, 1745. She was the daughter of William and Eleanor (Stevens) True, of Salisbury. He married, (second), June 30, 1747, Mary Currier, who died, perhaps July 2, 1788. The children were all by the first wife and named as follows: William, Abraham, Zebedee, Eleanor and Jabez.

(V) William, eldest son of Abraham (2) and Eleanor (True) Morrill, was born in Salisbury, April 21, 1735, and baptized in the Second Salisbury Church, May 4, 1735. He removed to Brentwood, New Hampshire, where he was a man of consequence and filled various official positions. He signed the association test in 1776. He was selectman of Brentwood, a justice of the peace for many years, and a deputy from that town to the fourth Provincial congress which met at Exeter, May 17, 1775. He married Lydia Trask and among his children was William.

(VI) Captain William (2), son of William (1) and Lydia (Trask) Morrill, was born in Brentwood, New Hampshire, and died August 27, 1838. He was a prominent citizen and business man of Brentwood, represented the town in the state legislature, and filled important local offices, including that of selectman. He married (first), Mary Gordon, of Brentwood, who died May 26, 1799, aged thirty-one years and six days. He married (second), Elizabeth Dudley, of Brentwood. His children were: Nathaniel, Dorothy, Zebedee, Mary, Sarah Dudley, Samuel, John Dudley, Ann, William and Frederick.

(VII) Mary, daughter of Captain William and Mary (Gordon) Morrill, was born April 25, 1798, and married, November 26, 1826, John Fifield. (See Fifield I).

(Preceding Generations on Page 771.)

LUND (IV) Jonathan, second son and third child of Thomas (3) and Elizabeth Lund, was married April 2, 1741, in Dunstable, to Jean Barnum, and evidently spent his life in his native town. His children were: Olive, Joanna, Mary, Oliver and Mehitable.

(V) Jonathan (2), elder son and third child of Jonathan (1) and Jean (Barnum) Lund, was born July 24, 1747, in Dunstable, and made his home in that town through life. He was known as Captain Jonathan, and probably derived his title from service in the state militia. He was married October 22, 1765, in Dunstable, to Olive Sargent, and their children (recorded in Dunstable) were: Nathaniel, Joseph, Olive Sargent, Elizabeth and James Taylor.

(VI) Joseph, second son and child of Jonathan (2) and Olive (Sargent) Lund, was born December 24, 1767, in Dunstable, and undoubtedly lived all his life in that town. There is authority for the statement that his wife's baptismal name was Betsey, but no record of their marriage appears in the vital statistics of the state, neither are their children on record, but the family record shows that they had a son, Joseph S.

(VII) Joseph S., son of Joseph and Betsey Lund, was born in Nashua, in 1800, and died in Concord, December 27, 1882, aged eighty-two years and ten months. He grew to manhood on a farm and acquired such education as he could in the common schools of his time. Soon after attaining his majority he bought a farm in the southeast part of Concord, where he remained the balance of his life. He was a man of rare shrewdness and financial acumen, and was prosperous in all he undertook. He added largely to his real estate by the purchase of woodlands. For a time after going to Concord he was engaged in boat building. After he had accumulated considerable property he had a large amount of money loaned out, and also had bank stock and interest in manufacturing concerns. In politics he was a Democrat, and in religion a believer in the Universalist creed. He died possessed of a handsome property, after a residence of sixty years in Concord. He married (first), Mary Swett, daughter of Stephen Swett. She died in 1840, leaving one child, Charles Carroll. He was married (second), in Manchester, November 23, 1846, by Rev. Cyrus W. Wallace, to Phebe C. Abbott, of Concord. He was married (third), in Manchester, April 21, 1877, by Rev. C. W. Wallace, to Widow Amanda J. Nutting, of Portsmouth, who survives him. She is the daughter of Moses and Betsy W. Allen, and was born in Hebron, Maine.

(VIII) Charles Carroll, only child of Joseph S. Lund and Mary (Swett) Lund, was born December 9, 1832, and died December 4, 1880. He prepared for college in Orford and Pembroke Academies, and in 1851 entered Dartmouth College, from which he was graduated with the class of 1855, after having completed a classical course. He was a member of the Kappa Kappa Kappa society. On returning to Concord he taught a year in the high school of that city, and also studied law, in the offices of Hon. L. D. Stevens and Judge Fowler, and was admitted to the bar in 1856. Soon after his admission he opened a law office in St. Paul, Minnesota, where he practiced eight years, having for partners John B. Sanborn and Theodore French, both New Hampshire men. The style of the firm was Sanborn, French & Lund. In 1864 he returned to Concord, and became the law partner of Hon. Lyman D. Stevens, his former preceptor, the firm being Stevens & Lund. This relation lasted until 1870. Notwithstanding Mr. Lund had entered the profession of law, which he did not like, at the instance of his father, he was very successful in it, patent office cases being favorite with him, as he was fond of mathematics and mechanical employment and things pertaining to machinery.

Before going to college he had studied civil engineering, in which he was deeply interested and highly proficient, and spent part of a season in actual work with Mr. Adams, the chief engineer of the Concord & Montreal railroad, which he greatly enjoyed. In 1870 he accepted the invitation of a friend, a civil engineer, to spend his vacation in the summer of that year with him in surveying the proposed railroad between Concord and Rochester. This employment afforded him so much satisfaction that he determined to abandon the practice of law, and he accordingly closed his office and went to the Pacific coast, where with a corps of forty men he surveyed a line for a railroad between Portland, Oregon and Puget Sound, which was afterward accepted and built upon in preference to several other lines which were subsequently surveyed by others. When this survey was completed he returned to Concord and was assistant engineer in chief of the construction of the Concord water works system. He also constructed the water works system in Leominster, Massachusetts. Later he was made chief engineer of the Concord & Montreal railroad, and as such had charge of the construction of various extensions of that road in the White Mountain region and above, including the Wing road to the base of Mt. Washington, the road to the Profile House, and the road to Lancaster, the successful and economical construction of which required engineering skill of a high order and the completion of which placed Mr. Lund in the front rank of engineers and brought him much deserved credit. Mr. Lund died at that comparatively early age of forty-eight years. Had he devoted himself to this profession earlier in life, or had his life been spared a few years longer, he would doubtless have attained great celebrity as an engineer. He was a member of the Masonic fraternity and the Knights of Pythias. He married, in Concord, June 17, 1860, Lydia French, who was born in Concord, March 26, 1838, daughter of Theodore and Lydia (Pollard) French, of Dunstable, Massachusetts. She was prepared for a higher course in private schools, and graduated from Mt. Holyoke Seminary in 1857. Three children were born to this union: Mary (died young), Fred B. and Joseph W.

(IX) Fred B., son of Charles C. and Lydia (French) Lund, was born in Concord, January 4, 1865, was prepared for college at Phillips Andover Academy, and entered Harvard University in 1884, and graduated *summa cum laude* in 1888. He is a member of the Phi Beta Kappa society. Following his graduation from the literary department of Harvard, he matriculated in the Harvard Medical School, where he completed the four years' course in three years, and became an interne in the Massachusetts General Hospital, and remained there three years. In 1893 he entered the general practice of medicine with offices in Boston, and immediately took high rank as a physician and surgeon. He now has a large and lucrative practice. He is a surgeon on the staff of the City Hospital of Boston.

(IX) Joseph Wheelock, youngest child of Charles C. and Lydia (French) Lund, was born in Concord, March 14, 1867, and attended the common and high schools of Concord, and subsequently graduated from Phillips Andover Academy in 1886, Harvard University in 1890, and Harvard Law School in 1893. Since the latter date he has been engaged in a successful law practice in Boston.

(For Ancestry see page 1011.)

HESSELTON Nathan Hesselton was probably the son of Nathan (or Nathaniel), whose name appears in the early records of Wilton, New Hampshire. He married Phebe ——, and the names of seven children are given: Phebe, John, Nathan, Samuel, Louis, Betty and Sarah. Nathaniel and Nathan Hesselton's names were signed to the resolve "to defend by arms," etc. Nathan Hesselton served four months in the Revolution by his son David (three years service). David Hesselton, son of Nathan, served in the war of the Revolution.

Nathan (1) Hesselton removed to Weston, Vermont, later to Andover, New Hampshire. He married Prudence, daughter of Timothy Baldwin, of Wilton. After the death of her husband she returned to Wilton. Their children were: Abel, Daniel, Joel, Nathaniel and Hannah. Daniel, son of Nathan and Prudence (Baldwin) Hesselton, was born November 11, 1807, and died June 24, 1877. He married Harriet Chandler. They lived in Vermont. Their three sons all served in the Civil war. Helen M. Hesselton, daughter of Abner, married Frederick G. Ellison. (See Ellison, III).

(For Ancestry, See Pages 914-15.)

HUBBARD (VI) Deacon Hezekiah, son of Nathan and Mary (Patterson) Hubbard, was born in Groton, Massachusetts, January 19, 1755. He came to Rindge, New Hampshire, about the year 1783, and settling on what has since been known as Hubbard's Hill he became a prosperous farmer, an eminently useful citizen and an active member of the Congregational Church, of which he was a deacon for many years. His death, which was sudden, occurred April 22, 1822. He married Rebecca Hutchinson, who was born at Billerica, Massachusetts, in 1762, and she died in Rindge, April 13, 1849. They were the parents of thirteen children, namely: Benjamin, Levi, Rebecca, Sally, Polly, Rodney, Harry, Hezekiah, Mersylvia, Eliphalet, Otis, John Hutchinson and Addison, all of whom were born in Rindge.

(VII) Harry, fourth son and seventh child of Deacon Hezekiah and Rebecca (Hutchinson) Hubbard, was born in Rindge, July 8, 1795. He began life as a farmer, but learned the shoemaker's trade and for a time resided in Burlington, Vermont. From Burlington he went to Shrewsbury, Massachusetts, and died in that town. His first wife, whom he married June 8, 1823, was Clarissa Fay, and on December 6, 1832, he married for his second wife Dorcas Whitney, daughter of Dr. Isaac Whitney. His first wife bore him two sons, Henry B., born August 28, 1825, became an extensive boot manufacturer in Worcester, Massachusetts. Appleton B., who is referred to at length in the succeeding paragraph.

(VIII) Appleton Burnham, youngest son of Harry and Clarissa (Fay) Hubbard, was born in Hopkinton, Massachusetts, May 29, 1829. He engaged in agricultural pursuits in Troy, New Hampshire, and was permitted to enjoy that independent life but a short period, as he died September 29, 1862, at the age of thirty-three years. On September 19, 1854, he married Betsey L. Clark, daughter of Howard and Dolly (Bemis) Clark. Of this union there are two sons, Charles A., who will be again referred to; and Harry, who is now a successful lawyer in New York City.

(IX) Charles Appleton, eldest son of Appelton B. and Betsey L. (Clark) Hubbard, was born in Troy, New Hampshire, June 7, 1857. He was graduated from the New Hampshire State College of Agriculture and the Mechanic Arts in 1877, and for the succeeding two years was employed as a clerk in the general store of E. P. Kimball & Sons, Troy. Removing to Boston in 1882 he was for a short time engaged in the electrical business, but destiny seems to have led him into other fields of usefulness, wherein his business ability has found more scope for development. Securing an advantageous position in the comptroller's office of the Union Pacific Railway Company in Boston, he worked up through the various ranks for several years, or until 1897, when he was appointed comptroller of the Oregon Short Line Railroad Company with headquarters in Boston. This company operates over fourteen hundred miles of railroad located in Utah, Wyoming, Idaho and Oregon, and Mr. Hubbard performed the duties of his responsible position with marked ability for two years. When the United Fruit Company was organized in 1899 Mr. Hubbard was chosen treasurer, and relinquishing the railway service he began the financial management of the new enterprise with a spirit of energy which has ever since continued unabated, and the expansion of the fruit company's interests and its present high standard in financial circles is in no small measure due to his ability and sound judgment. The United Fruit Company is the largest importer of fruit products in the United States, and the largest banana importing concern in the world, having handled during the past year thirty-five million bunches of this fruit. The company owns directly one of the largest sugar plantations in Cuba, which produced during its fiscal year ending September 30, 1907, forty-five thousand tons of raw sugar. It also has acquired practically all of the common stock of the Nipe Bay Co., giving the company control of a plantation of about one hundred and thirty thousand acres of land, of which some twenty thousand acres has been planted in sugar, and a mill erected and a railroad and other facilities constructed for producing large quantities of sugar. This new property produced over sixteen thousand tons of sugar in 1907. The company operates a line of steamships, some of which are named in honor of distinguished admirals of the United States navy, and it employs a force of twenty-seven thousand men. Mr. Hubbard resides in Newton and affiliates with the Masonic order of that city, being a member of the Blue lodge, the Royal Arch Chapter, Gethsemane Commandery, Knights Templar, and the Scottish Rite bodies of Boston up to thirty-second degree. On October 15, 1884, he was united in marriage with Mary Anna Stearns, daughter of Julius Augustus and Mary Anna (Wood) Stearns, of Rindge. Mr. and Mrs. Hubbard have two children, Harry Appleton and Marion.

(For Ancestry, see page 1031.)

THAYER (II) Nathaniel Thayer, seventh son of Richard Thayer, was born in 1658. He settled in Boston. In 1676 he married Deborah Townsend. His children were: Nathaniel, Zachariah, Cornelius, John, died young; John, Ebenezer and Deborah.

(III) Cornelius, third son and child of Nathaniel and Deborah (Townsend) Thayer, was born in Boston, November 14, 1684. He married Lydia Turell, of Medford, Massachusetts in 1706, and resided in Boston. He was the father of six children, namely: Lydia, Nathaniel, Samuel, Deborah, Cornelius and Turell.

(IV) Nathaniel, second child and eldest son of Cornelius and Lydia (Turell) Thayer, was born in Boston, July 17, 1710. He married Ruth Eliot, a sister of Rev. Dr. Andrew Eliot, of Boston. She became the mother of several children: Ebenezer, Catherine, Ruth, Lydia and Deborah.

(V) Rev. Ebenezer, eldest child of Nathaniel and Ruth (Eliot) Thayer, was born in Boston or Braintree, July 16, 1734. He graduated from Harvard College in 1753, prepared for the ministry, and was ordained September 16, 1766. For twenty-six years he was pastor of the church in Hampton, New Hampshire, and his death occurred September 6, 1792. He married, October 2, 1766, Martha Cotton, daughter of Rev. John and Mary (Gibbs) Cotton, and a descendant in the fourth generation of the Rev. John Cotton, who became the first minister of the First Church in Boston in 1633. His children were: Ebenezer, born July 16, 1767; Rev. Dr. Nathaniel, born July 11, 1769; Martha, born in April, 1771; John, born in July, 1773; Catherine, born September 1, 1775; and the late Rev. Andrew Eliot Thayer, of Nashua.

(VI) Rev. Andrew Eliot Thayer, youngest child of Rev. Ebenezer and Martha (Cotton) Thayer, was born in Hampton, November 4, 1783. In addition to the ancestors already mentioned he was a descendant of Sir Richard Saltonstall, one of the founders of Massachusetts and an assistant under Governor Winthrop; Nathaniel Ward, an early settler in Ipswich; and of Edward Rossiter, who was also an assistant to Governor Winthrop. Mr. Thayer was fitted for college in Exeter, New Hampshire, and was graduated from Harvard College with the class of 1803. He then studied theology and was ordained to the ministry in 1806, but owing to impaired health was obliged to postpone, for a time, active participation in pastoral work and seek a more temperate climate. Upon his recovery, in 1820, he came to Nashua, opened a book store and circulating library on the site of which is now the entrance of Thayer's Court. He supplied the pulpit of the Old South Church until 1824, also taught school and he assisted in establishing *The Nashua Constellation*, of which he was editor and one of the publishers. The name of that paper was subsequently changed to *The Nashua Gazette*, and in 1832 Mr. Thayer sold out to General Hunt, who changed it from a Whig to a Democratic organ. During Mr. Thayer's editorship of the *Gazette* it was published in a room in the rear of his bookstore, and the *Nashua Telegraph* began its existence in the same apartment. In November, 1838, his bookstore was destroyed by fire, and he resumed business in a building which stood upon the site of the present Whiting Block. Through his instrumentality Mr. Beard was induced to establish and edit *The Nashua Weekly Telegraph*, and in relation to this fact Editor Beard stated after Mr. Thayer's death that "a debt of gratitude, as well as a pecuniary debt, has been due him, and although we have been compelled to be a poor paymaster in regard to the latter we have never disowned the former." Mr. Thayer's interest in the general welfare of the town led him to accept various positions of trust, and he fulfilled his public duties with ability and faithfulness. His character was of a type well calculated to inspire confidence and admiration, and his death, which occurred January 31, 1846, was the cause of sincere regret.

Mr. Thayer married Lucy Flagg, daughter of John and Lucy (Curtis) Flagg, and she survived him. Her public-spirited generosity equalled that of her husband, and she was noted for her charity and benevolence. During the Civil war she aided much in relieving the wants of the soldiers, and otherwise providing for their comfort. She died at her home in Thayer's Court, June 24, 1874. Andrew E. and Lucy (Flagg) Thayer were the parents of several children, of whom are now living: Lucy F. and Katharine M. Thayer.

(For Ancestry See Pages 869-71.)

BARNARD (V) John, third son of Tristram (2) and Dorothy Currier Barnard, was born February 29, 1747, in Amesbury, and died in that town in 1794. His will was executed on the 19th of September of that year, and proved on the 27th of the following month. He had purchased a farm in Weare, New Hampshire, but died before his removal thither. His farm in Amesbury was sold to Daniel Barnard. The intention of his marriage to Dorothy Challis was published. and it is presumed that she became his wife. His children were: Moses, John and Eliphalet.

(VI) Moses, eldest son of Tristram and Dorothy (Challis) Barnard, was born in 1781 in Amesbury. He removed to Acworth in 1800, and in 1802 settled on a farm, where he resided with his wife sixty-two years. He married Polly Gove, who was born March 13, 1785, in Weare, daughter of Elijah and Sarah (Mills) Gove. Elijah Gove was born May 20, 1752, in Hampton, New Hampshire, and died in Weare. He was one of the signers of the association test in that town, and served two enlistments in the Revolutionary army. His first service was one month in a New York regiment, and he was later a private in Captain Samuel Philbrick's company, Colonel Moore's regiment, which marched from Weare to Charlestown, New Hampshire, on the Alarm in July, 1777. He was a son of Jonathan Gove, who was born in 1695, and married (first), Mary Lancaster; and (second) Hannah Worthen. He was a son of John Gove. (See Gove, III). The children of Moses Barnard were: Sarah, Dorothy, Mary, John (died young), Melvina, Squier Page. Emily M., Lucina, John M., George, William C., and an infant daughter deceased.

(VII) Dorothy, second daughter of Moses and Polly (Gove) Barnard, was born in 1803. in Weare, and was married (first), to Sylvanus Miller, and (second), became the first wife of Reuben Shepardson. (See Shepardson, VIII).

(For Ancestry See Pages 837-8.)

FOLSOM (VIII) Jeremiah, eighth child and third son of Deacon John (2) and Abigail (Perkins) Folsom, was born probably in 1685, and died in 1757. He settled about 1712 on a farm of one hundred acres which he inherited from his father, just south of Newmarket Village, where in 1719 he built a brick house which was standing in 1874. He was a good farmer and an enterprising business man and left much land to his children at his death. He married, probably in 1705, Elizabeth, whose surname is unknown. Their children were: Nathan, Jeremiah, Elizabeth, Susan, Abigail, Sarah, Ann and John.

(IX) Colonel Jeremiah (2), second son and child of Jeremiah (1) and Elizabeth Folsom, was born in Newmarket, July 25, 1719. and died in 1802, aged eighty-three years. In 1767 he was an innholder in Newmarket. He held very strong views on religion, was punctual in attendance at church, and a devoted follower of the Evangelist Whitefield. He married, March 28, 1742, Mary Hersey, and they had ten children: Jeremiah, John, Peter, Simeon, Josiah, Levi, Enoch. Jacob, Mary and Samuel.

(X) Levi, sixth son and child of Colonel Jeremiah and Mary (Hersey) Folsom, was born in Newmarket, July 12, 1753, and died June 21, 1844, aged nearly ninety-one years. He removed in 1779 to the new settlement in Tamworth. He married, in Newmarket, December 4, 1777, Joanna Weeks, of Greenland. She was born December 31. 1755, and was the orphan daughter of Dr. John and Martha (Wingate) Weeks, of Hampton, and was brought up and educated by her brothers and sisters. She died in Tamworth, July 17, 1826, aged seventy-one years. Both were born in affluent circumstances, but received scarcely anything from the estates of their parents, and found it hard in a new settlement to provide for their nine children. She was better qualified to instruct them in the knowledge of books than to provide for their material wants, and left them the influence of an intelligent christian mother. She was much loved and highly respected by those who knew her best. The children of Levi and Joanna were: Ward Weeks, Jeremiah, Elizabeth, John Weeks, Levi, Joanna, Mary. Martha Wingate and George Frost.

(XI) Colonel Levi (2), fifth child and fourth son of Levi (1) and Joanna (Weeks) Folsom, was born in Sandwich, April 11, 1788, and died December 9, 1841. He was a farmer and a lumberman, and erected mills on the Bearcamp river. In both civil and military life he was a leading citizen, and held various offices. He married Lydia, a daughter of Thorn Dodge, of Wenham. Massachusetts, (see Dodge, VIII). She died of fever, May 7, 1824. at the age of thirty, leaving six small children: Elizabeth, Joanna Weeks, John Thorn Dodge, Martha, Levi Woodbury and Lydia D.

(XII) John Thorn Dodge, third child and eldest son of Colonel Levi (2) and Lydia (Dodge) Folsom, was born in Tamworth, April 6, 1818. He married. April 14, 1842, in Wenham, Massachusetts, Asenath Whipple, and settled in South Tamworth, where for many years he was postmaster. Asenath Whipple was born February 27, 1822, in New Boston, New Hampshire, only daughter of Dr. Robert Whipple, and is still living. She has living four daughters, ten grandchildren and eight great-grandchildren. She had six children: Lydia D., Judith M. (died young), Judith Madeline, Elizabeth Ann, Helen Asenath and Joanna Weeks.

(XIII) Helen Asenath, fifth daughter and child of John T. D. and Asenath (Whipple) Folsom, was born in Tamworth. August 15, 1854, and married September 14, 1876, Charles H. Smart, of Ossipee Center, (see Smart second family, III), and has: Annie May, Charles Ellis and Harry Preston.

(For Ancestry See Page 832.)

ORDWAY (II) Edward, third son of James and Anne (Emery) Ordway, was born September 17, 1653, in Newbury, and resided there, where he was married December 12, 1678, to Mary Wood.

(III) Edward (2), son of Edward (1) and Mary (Wood) Ordway, was born about 1695, and passed his life in Newbury. He was married there August 1, 1728, to Katherine Hill.

(IV) Edward (3), son of Edward (2) and Katherine (Hill) Ordway, was born July 15, 1742, and died in 1834. He was a Revolutionary soldier, joining the ill-fated expedition against Canada under Benedict Arnold in the winter of 1775-6. In relating his experience of that terrible winter he used to say, "A man is hungry when he can eat his boots." He became totally blind before his derth, which occurred at his home in Sutton, New Hampshire, June 21, 1834, at the age of ninety-four years. He was a pioneer settler in Sutton, where he cleared up a farm. He was married December 29, 1776, to Elizabeth Eaton, who died on the same day that he did, at the age of eighty-two years. They were buried in a cemetery at Warner Village, near the present railroad station. Their children were: Giles, Joseph, Edward, Daniel, Betsey and Hannah.

(V) Giles, eldest child of Edward (3) and Elizabeth (Eaton) Ordway, was born October 4, 1777, in Haverhill, Massachusetts, and was an old-time carpenter and joiner, which in his day included painting and glazing, all the work being done by handicraft. He moved from Haverhill to Bow, New Hampshire, about 1820, and to Concord in 1821. He built a set of buildings on the east side of South street, near Bow line, where both he and his wife died. He was married December 2, 1802, to Elizabeth Webster, who was born January 29, 1779, a daughter of James and Mehitable (Rollins) Webster. (See Webster V). She died October 5, 1834, and he survived her more than twelve years, passing away May 31, 1847. Their children were: Eliza, Giles, Webster, Harriet and Albert.

(VI) Eliza, eldest child of Giles and Elizabeth (Webster) Ordway, was born December 11, 1808, in Haverhill, and was married September 18, 1826, to Benjamin (2) Wheeler, of Bow. (See Wheeler VII).

(For Ancestry See Pages 516-18.)

PICKERING (IV) William, eldest son of Thomas (2) and Mary (Janvrin) Pickering, was a farmer in Newington and Greenland. He was born in 1745, and died May 16, 1795. He showed the true stock and spirit of his ancestors, and though not a man who made a show in life he had a good property, and his children were brought up to do credit to the family name. He married Abigail Fabyan, of Newington, and had ten children, three of whom, John, Stephen and Daniel, became residents of Wolfborough.

(V) Daniel, son of William and Abigail (Fabyan) Pickering, was born in Greenland, November 22, 1795, and died in Wolfborough, February 14, 1856. The following excellent sketch of him is taken from the History of Carroll County, edited by Georgia Drew Merrill. He passed his early life in Greenland, and was educated at the Brackett Academy of Greenland, and Phillips Exeter Academy. On arriving at maturity he went to Wolfborough, where his brother John had previously located, and built a hotel, and there at once engaged in merchandising. He was successful, and soon erected the store at Pickering's Corner, opposite the "Pavilion," and continued in business as a merchant for thirty-five years. He carried the largest stock of goods in Carroll county, and drew trade from a territory of thirty miles in radius. At one time he had three stores in active operation: that at Wolfborough village, one at Goose Corner, and one at Tuftonborough. For many years much of the pay for goods was given in products of the farm and forests, and Mr. Pickering had many teams engaged in drawing these to Portsmouth and returning with the goods. He was a natural salesman. It is said that "He was the pleasantest man that ever waited on a customer," and he made the hearts of the children glad by his plenteous gifts of "goodies." He always gave a liberal allowance of the commodity sold, and the wealth he acquired was untainted with short weight or false measure, and the confidence of the community was secured by his fair dealing. About 1840 he formed a partnership with John N. Brackett, Ira P. Nudd and Moses Thompson to carry on the manufacture of shoes for Boston parties in connection with merchandising. The firm was Pickering, Brackett & Company for two years, when Freeman Cotton succeeded Mr. Brackett, and the firm name became Pickering, Cotton & Company. The amount of business transacted by Mr. Pickering as a merchant was very large, and he was also connected with every branch of commercial activity in the town. He carried on the manufacture of brick on a large scale. In connection with his brother Stephen he originated and was a large owner of the Pickering Manufacturing Company, whose woolen and satinet mills were located at Mill Village, now Wolfboro Falls.

He purchased wide tracts of timber land, and carried on extensive lumbering operations, was one of the incorporators of the Wolfborough Bank, and its president, and one of the stock company that built the steamer "Lady of the Lake." He did much to develop the growth of the village of Wolfborough and Mill Village. He owned a tract of land running from Pickering's Corner to the site of the Greendon House, and a large farm. He laid out his land in lots, was willing to sell one at a reasonable price, and built many houses. He lived to see a beautiful place spring up as the result of his public spirit. He erected a number of buildings in Mill Village, and aided others to build. He was the prime mover in the erection of the Pavilion Hotel. In 1820 he was one of the three persons named in the act of incorporation of the Wolfborough and Tuftonborough Academy. He sold the lot for its site at a very small price, and was later one of the trustees. The council that organized the Congregational Church met at his house, and he and his wife were of the first twelve members. He was devoted to religion, was a prompt and regular attendant at all meetings, and contributed freely to build up and sustain the church and its works. He gave the lot on which the church stands to the Congregational Society as long as it should be used for church purposes, and his house gave bounteous and open hospitality to its clergymen. He was an "old line" Whig in politics, and was postmaster for years, keeping the office in his store. In person he was somewhat above medium size, with dark hair and eyes, and while quiet and a man of few words in business he was very pleasant and social in society, and every one was at ease in his presence. He was a kind and considerate employer, a lenient creditor and benefactor to the poor, and in the circle of his home was the soul of kindness. A shrewd and far-seeing financier, he accumulated wealth. He was a valued adviser in business affairs, and the personification of punctuality, promptitude and system in all transactions. When the lamp of his life went out suddenly, while going from his some to his store, the poor lost a friend and the better element of the community one of its chief pillars.

Daniel Pickering married, June 26, 1822, Sarah C. Farrar, who was born March 3, 1801, and died November 12, 1867. daughter of Joseph and Mehitable (Dana) Farrar, of Wolfborough (see Farrar, VI). They began housekeeping and always lived in the building erected by John Pickering as a hotel. Three children were born of this union: Joseph W., Eliza M. and Caroline D. The first two died young. Caroline D., born August 10, 1824, married, January 11, 1848, Charles Rollins, of Boston. (See Rollins, VII). She died September 2, 1907, at Wolfborough, New Hampshire.

(Preceding Generations on Page 584.)

CARPENTER (XI) William (4), second son and child of William (3) and Abigail Carpenter, was born 1631. in England, and came with his father to Rehoboth. He was a man of much ability, a valuable counselor in the colony and had some educational attainments, as evidenced by his excellent writings and the good condition and form of the records kept by him. He was elected town clerk of Rehoboth, May 13, 1668, and with the exception of one year continued in that capacity until 1693. In 1668 he was deputy to the general court, and in the same year was made deacon of the church. He was on the committee to settle the boundary between Taunton and the North Purchase in 1670, and was one of the proprietors of the North Purchase and drew Meadow Lot, May 16, 1668. He was clerk to the community of the North Purchase in 1682, and was one of the committee appointed to sell the meeting house in 1683. In that year he was elected surveyor of the North Purchase and laid out eighty-three fifty-acre lots. By occupation he was a farmer. His house was located on a rise of land on the left of the road leading from the East Providence meeting house to Rehoboth, about fifty rods from the crossing of Ten Mile river. He died January 26, 1703, in Rehoboth, aged seventy-two years. His estate was valued at two hundred pounds. five shillings and four pence. He was married, October 5, 1651, to Priscilla Bonet, who died October 20, 1663, on the day her son, Benjamin, was born. William Carpenter was married (second), December 10, 1663, to Miriam Searles, who died May 1, 1722, aged ninety-three years. in Rehoboth. His children were: John, William, Priscilla, Benjamin, Josiah, Nathaniel. Daniel, Noah, Miriam, Obadiah, Ephraim (died young), Ephraim, Hannah and Abigail.

(XII) Nathaniel. fifth son and sixth child of William Carpenter, and second child of his second wife. Miriam Searles was born May 12, 1667, in Rehoboth, and lived most of his early life in Sekonk, Rhode Island, and died in 1713, at Attleboro, Massachusetts. He was representative to the general court in 1724-29-33-35. He was, evidently, a good business man and became possessed of considerable property. His will disposes of interests in Wrentham and Rehoboth, and Ashford. Connecticut. To the Rehoboth Church he left "a good tanker" (tankard) and another tanker to the church at Attleboro, to be purchased out of his estate. He was married September 19, 1693, to Rachel Cooper, who died July 9, 1694, aged twenty-three years. He was married (second), November 17, 1695, to Mary Preston, of Dorchester, who died May 25, 1706, aged thirty-one years. His third marriage occurred July 8, 1707, to widow Mary Cooper, who died April 9, 1712, aged thirty-six years. His fourth wife was Mary Baker. His children were: Nathaniel (died young), Ezekiel, Ezra, Elijah, Dan, Rachel, Nathaniel and Mary, twins; Nathaniel. died when twenty-seven days old; and Mary, died when one year old.

(XIII) Ezra, third son and child of Nathaniel and Mary (Preston) Carpenter, was born March 20, 1698, in Rehoboth, and graduated from Harvard College in 1720. He entered upon the christian ministry and was ordained at Hull, November 24, 1725, and was dismissed from the pastorate there November 23, 1746. He settled, as pastor, at Swanzey, New Hampshire. October 14, 1753, and was dismissed March 16, 1769. The same dates apply also to Keene, which would indicate that he was in charge of two parishes at the same time. Keene parish was then called Upper Ashuelot, and Swanzey, Lower Ashuelot. He died at Walpole, New Hampshire, August 26, 1785, in his eighty-eighth year. He was chaplain of the state troops from 1749 to 1763 in Massachusetts. He was married, November 28, 1723, to Elizabeth, daughter of Rev. Thomas Greenwood. She was born April 5, 1704, and died March 12, 1766, in her sixty-second year. Their children were: Elizabeth, Elijah, Theodosia, Greenwood, Preston, Olive, Content, married John Kilburn, and Rachel.

The following was taken from the cemetery in Walpole, New Hampshire, located on the south middle of the old lot, near where the old Kilburn stone used to stand:

"In memory of the Rev. Ezra Carpenter, Born Attleborou April 1st, 1698. Educated at the University of Cambridge—36 years pastor of ye church of Christ—21 at Hull and 15 at Swanzey. An able Divine. sound in ye faith, and a rational preacher of the gospel, respectable for his erudition of manners, easy and polite in his conversation. Pious and entertaining. A faithful shepherd. A kind husband, affectionate parent, a lover of good men, given to hospitality. As Christ was his hope of glory, so in the full assurance of ye mercy of God to eternal life, he died at Walpole Aug. 26, 1785, Aetatis 88 Dum Pulvis Christo Chartes, Huec dulce dormit, Expectaris Stellum Matutinam."

(XIV) Greenwood, second son and fourth child of Rev. Ezra and Elizabeth (Greenwood) Carpenter, was born March 31, 1733, in Hull, Massachusetts, and died February 3. 1809, in Swanzey, New Hampshire. He first resided in Charlestown, Massachusetts, and about 1756 removed thence to Swanzey, New Hampshire, where the remainder of his life was passed. He was taxed upon property in Charlestown in 1756 for the last time. He enlisted July 12, 1779, in the Continental army, for one year, from Swanzey. in the Sixth Regiment, and his compensation was recorded at five pounds per month. On March 21, 1781, he enlisted for three years, under Captain Ried, in the third company from Swanzey. He was married February 10, 1753, to Sally Leathers and (second), to Susan Hammond, who died February 3, 1809. Four of his children were born in Charlestown, and the remainder in Swanzey, namely: 1. William, born at Charlestown,

Massachusetts, married Lucy Sumner, of Swanzey, New Hampshire, died at Potsdam, New York. 2. Betsey, born at Charlestown, Massachusetts, married Sylvanus Hastings, of Charlestown, New Hampshire, she died in Lashute, Canada East. 3. Olive, born at Charlestown, Massachusetts, married Joseph Barrows, of Walpole, New Hampshire, she died in Ohio. Children of second marriage: 4. Theodosia, born at Swanzey, New Hampshire, October 24, 1774; she married Dr. John Jackson, of Lebanon, New Hampshire; she died at Swanzey, New Hampshire, August 7, 1822. 5. Hastings, born at Swanzey, New Hampshire, March 22, 1776; he married Maria Hooppole, of Schenectady, New York; he died at Canada, March 1, 1815. 6. Abigail, born at Swanzey, New Hampshire, October 7, 1777, married Eber Hubbard, of Glastonbury, Connecticut; she died at Fulton, New York, March 5, 1839. 7. Elijah, born at Swanzey, New Hampshire, December 23, 1779; he married Fanny Partridge, of Montague, Massachusetts; he died at Swanzey, New Hampshire, October 24, 1861. 8. Consider, born at Swanzey, New Hampshire, February 19, 1781, married (first), Thankful Belding, of Swanzey, New Hampshire; she died at Swanzey, New Hampshire, March 6, 1815. He married (second), Fanny Leonard, of Keene, New Hampshire. He died at Swanzey, New Hampshire, December 31, 1857. 9. Daniel, born at Swanzey, New Hampshire, October 26, 1782, married Roxana Crofford, of Potsdam, New York. He married (second), Sally Baker, of Potsdam, New York. He died at Potsdam, New York. 10. Ezra, born at Swanzey, New Hampshire, July 27, 1784, died at Schenectady, New York, August 23, 1805. 11. Susan, born in Swanzey, New Hampshire, September 10, 1786, died at Seneca Hill, New York, July 31, 1871. 12. Sophronia, born November 29, 1788, died in Swanzey, New Hampshire, April 18, 1810. 13. Preston, born May 3, 1782, died at Genesee, New York, September 5, 1814.

(XV) Elijah, son of Greenwood and Susan (Hammond) Carpenter, was born December 23, 1779, in Swanzey, and died October 24, 1861, in that town, where he was a farmer on the paternal homestead during all of his life. This farm consisted of one hundred and fifty acres, and by his industry and judicious management it was made to give him a good income. He was an extremely conscientious man, making the golden rule his guide in life, and he enjoyed the confidence and esteem of his fellows to a marked degree. He was possessed of considerable legal knowledge, and because of this and his natural ablity he exercised a wide influence. He was a member of the legislature several terms, was a state senator and served ten years as high sheriff, and was deputy sheriff until after he was sixty years old. He was spoken of as "Squire" Carpenter, and according to the custom of the times wore a sword while attending court in the capacity of high sheriff. Mr. Carpenter was married, December 11, 1815, to Fanny Partridge, daughter of Amariah Partridge. She was born November 1, 1787, in Montague, Massachusetts, and died March 10, 1876, in Algona, Iowa. Her children were: Thankful G., born February 14, 1817, married (first), Joshua Wyman; (second), Zebina Knights. Harriet R., born May 4, 1819, married Nathan Watkins. Julia A., died in infancy. Julia A., born May 15, 1823, married Cyril R. Aldrich. Elizabeth G., born December 20, 1825. George, mentioned below. Elijah P., born April 10, 1831, died in Keene, October 31, 1872.

(XVI) George, sixth child and elder son of Elijah and Fanny (Partridge) Carpenter, was born September 13, 1828, in Swanzey, where he still resides. He attended the common schools of his native town and Mount Caesar Seminary and academies at Ludlow and Saxton's River, Vermont. He engaged in roofing business at Springfield, Massachusetts, and continued there about two years, his work being distributed over a wide district in the vicinity of Springfield. In 1852 he went to California, and remained three years. In 1885 he returned to his native town and settled upon the paternal homestead, which is known as Valley View Farm, and located at Swanzey Centre. Mr. Carpenter has always been a student and has kept abreast of the progress of his time, through study and reading. With his wife he began the Chautauqua course in 1883, and graduated in the "Pansy Class" of 1887. He subsquently pursued a university course a number of years under able instructors. He has been much interested in questions of political economy, and has been identified with various movements calculated to promote reform in the national government. He was reared a Democrat and has been affiliated with the Greenback party, which nominated him for congress in 1882, and for governor in 1884 and 1886. In 1892 he was a candidate of the People's party for presidential elector, and continued his alliance with that organization and supported William J. Bryan for the presidency in 1896.

The Carpenter homestead is one of the most interesting points in Swanzey, being the location of an old Indian fort. It has been in the possession of the family since 1753, one hundred and fifty-four years, and has been handed down for four generations. Mr. Carpenter's water supply is obtained from the same spring which supplied the fort. The farm now contains about two hundred acres of land and in addition Mr. Carpenter has acquired about four hundred acres of outlaying timber land. The old farm is still divided into fields by the original heavy stone walls. Much of the ground is now permitted to grow up timber and but a limited amount is devoted to the growth of crops. The buildings are pleasantly located, surrounded with majestic pines and are indicative of the comfort and refinement which are characteristic of the best New England homes.

Mr. Carpenter is identified with Golden Rod Grange of Swanzey, as is his wife, and they have given time and effort to its work. They are also contributors to the support of Mount Caesar Library Association, which occupies the old seminary building. This building was purchased by Mr. Carpenter and donated for the uses of the association. He was married, June 14, 1864, to Lucy Jane, daughter of Colonel Carter and Lucy Baker Whitcomb (see Whitcomb VII).

(Previous Generations on Pages 1083-4.)

FISKE (X) Deacon Ebenezer, sixth son of Deacon William (4) and Sarah (Kilham) Fiske, was born in 1686, and died August 25, 1732. He married, December 1, 1733, Mrs. Martha Kimball, who died March 28, 1764. He died September 30, 1771, aged ninety-three years. He was the sixth son of his parents, executor of his father's will, principal heir of his estate, and lived at Wenham, where he was a substantial and quiet-living farmer. He was honored by election to various local offices, but was principally occupied with his private affairs and those of the church in which he was deacon from his election, May 16, 1739, until his resignation "by reason of age." in 1758. He was the father of nine children: Sarah, Jonathan, Ebenezer, Elizabeth, Jacob, Mary, William, Mercy and Lucy.

(XI) William, seventh child of Deacon Ebenezer and Elizabeth (Fuller) Fiske, was born at Wenham, Massachusetts, November 30, 1720. He married, 1749, Susannah Batchelder, of Wenham, born 1731, died 1810. She married a second time, the last husband being Benjamin Davis. William Fiske was the sole executor of his father's will. After settling the estate and disposing of the homestead and various tracts of land, he removed in 1773-74 to Amherst, New Hampshire, where he settled on a tract of land on the south side of Walnut Hill, and became the founder of the Amherst branch of the Fiskes. Of him personally little is known except that in his character and principles he was a staunch Puritan. His father and grandfather were successively deacons in the original Wenham church for upwards of seventy years, the same church of which the Rev. John Fiske was the original pastor. More remotely still the family had been identified with the great reformatory struggle in England. Mr. Fiske died in 1777, in the eighty-second year of his age. He and his wife were the parents of nine children: Jonathan, Elizabeth, William, David, Mary, Ebenezer, John, Susannah and Anne. (Ebenezer and descendants receive mention in this artcle.)

(XII) David, third son of William and Susannah (Batchelder) Fiske, was born at Wenham, Massachusetts, June 25, 1757. At the age of eighteen he enlisted for one year in the Revolution. In 1786 he married Edith Tay, of Chelsea, and settled in Merrimack, New Hampshire. In 1801 he moved to Amherst, New Hampshire, which was his home till his death at the age of eighty-six. The five children of David and Edith (Tay) Fiske were: Betsey, born September 12, 1788, died unmarried, August 25, 1876. Edith, born March 1, 1790, married John Sprague, of Bedford, New Hampshire, removed to Ohio and died there. David, who is mentioned below. George, born August 22, 1794, married Arinda Lane. Ardella, born December 18, 1803, died unmarried, September 30, 1828. David Fiske died at Amherst, New Hampshire, in 1843.

(XIII) Deacon David (2), eldest son and third child of David (1) and Edith (Tay) Fiske, was born at Amherst, New Hampshire, September 20, 1792. He was an enterprising, industrious farmer, and a man of sound integrity. He was deacon of the Congregational Church in Amherst from 1836 till he moved to Nashua in 1859. On January 19, 1823. Deacon Fiske married Abigail Nourse, daughter of Deacon Benjamin Nourse, of Merrimack, New Hampshire. She was born in 1800, and died in June, 1825. They had two children: Thomas Scott, born November 22, 1823, married Clara Isabel Pittman; and James Porter, born June 5, 1825, married Sarah C. Hill. In 1828, three years after the death of his first wife, Deacon Fiske married her sister, Harriet Nourse. She was born August 21, 1799, and died August 22, 1872, the same day as her husband. There were three children: George, born October 22, 1835, married Elmira F. Morrill. Abbie Arinda, born November 24, 1838, married, July 26, 1860, George W. Ordway, of Bradford, Massachusetts, and lived in Chicago. Mary Porter, mentioned below. Deacon David Fiske died in Nashua, New Hampshire, August 22, 1872.

(XIV) Mary Porter, the second daughter and youngest child of Deacon David (2) and Harriet (Nourse) Fiske, was born December 9, 1841, at Amherst, New Hampshire. She was married at Nashua, December 10, 1867, to George A. Marden, of Lowell, Massachusetts. (See Marden, VI). Mrs. Marden's maternal ancestry is traced back to Francis Nourse, who was born in England, and came to Salem, Massachusetts. His wife, Rebecca Nourse, was one of the victims hanged during the witchcraft craze.

(XII) Deacon Ebenezer, sixth child and fourth son of William and Susannah (Batchelder) Fiske, was born in Wenham, Massachusetts, November 11, 1762, and died in Wilmot, New Hampshire, May 8, 1838, aged seventy-six. He removed from Wenham to Amherst with his father when eleven years of age, and resided in the latter place until he attained his majority. Owing to the reduced circumstances of the family caused by the bankruptcies of of his father's brother-in-law, White, for whom the father had largely endorsed, Eben lost the opportunity of enjoying educational advantages. However, he inherited a remarkably strong physical frame and a strong intellect, and possessed good sterling qualities and an unbending will. Many and remarkable are the feats of strength recorded of him when in the prime of his powers, while his excellent common sense and well-known integrity made him a counselor among his fellow townsmen in Mont Vernon, where he subsequently resided, and for many years filled various local offices. After some years' residence in Mont Vernon he removed to Warner, New Hampshire, where he purchased a farm, and later located on a farm on "Wilmot Flat," in Wilmot, New Hampshire. Later in life he moved to the hills in the northwestern part of the town, called North Wilmot, and near where a meeting house afterward stood. Here he and his wife spent the remainder of their lives, their son Calvin caring for them. Ebenezer Fiske was a man a man of decided, conscientious, fixed and exemplary principles, and the resolute energy and courage which always rise superior to the difficulties of the occasion. During most of his life he was a member and deacon of the Congregational Church.

He married, at Mont Vernon, New Hampshire, in 1782, Abigail Woodbury, who was born in Beverly, Massachusetts, March 7, 1766, and died December 9, 1839, aged seventy-three years, second daughter of James Woodbury, of Mont Vernon. She was of an excellent family, and a relative of Judge Levi Woodbury, of Portsmouth, New Hampshire, a farmer of that state, and secretary of the United States treasury under President Jackson. Six sons and six daughters were born of this union, all of whom except a son who died in infancy, lived to mature age. All of these except the two youngest were born in Mont Vernon. Their names are: Abigail, John (died young), Ebenezer, James, Hannah, Desdemona, Luther, Calvin, John, Mehitable, Mary and Ploma.

(XIII) Mehitable, tenth child and fourth daughter of Deacon Ebenezer and Abigail (Woodbury) Fiske, was born in Mont Vernon, April 18, 1800. She married, March 14, 1819, James B. Straw, of Salisbury, and was the mother of Governor E. A. Straw (see Straw, V).

(VII) Nathaniel, second son and child of William Fiske, was born in South Elmham, and resided in Weybred, England. He is named in the wills of his father, uncle Eleazer, and cousin George. He married Mrs. Alice (Henel) Leman, and they had two children: Nathaniel and Sarah.

(VIII) Nathaniel (2), eldest child and only son of Nathaniel (1) and Alice (Henel) Fiske, was born in Weybred, Suffolk county, England, where he resided. There is a tradition in the family that he died on the passage to New England. He married Dorothy Symonds of Wendham, daughter of John. Their children were: John, Nathan, Esther and Martha.

(IX) Nathan, second son and child of Nathaniel (2) and Dorothy (Symonds) Fiske, was born in England, about 1615. He settled in Watertown, Massachusetts, as early as 1642, but his name does not appear on the list of proprietors of that year. He was admitted freeman May 10. 1643, and was selectman in 1673. His will was dated June 19, and he died June 21, 1676, aged forty-four years. In 1644 he was proprietor of one lot of nine acres which was his homestall. In his will he disposes of various pieces of land and a house and farm. His wife's name was Susanna. Their children were: Nathan, John, David, Nathaniel and Sarah.

(X) Lieutenant Nathan (2), eldest son of Nathan (1) and Susanna (Fiske) Fiske, was born in Watertown, October 17, 1642, and died October 11, 1694, aged fifty-two. October 1, 1673. he bought of Thomas Underwood and wife 220 acres of farm land in Weston for £10. He was selectman 1684-88-91. His inventory included house and twenty-two acres of land, valued at £45; six acres of land in Newton, £9, one hundred and twenty acres about Prospect Hill, £6, seven acres in Thatcher's Meadow, £5, and about two hundred and fifty acres of farm land £15; total £151. He married Elizabeth Fry, who died May 15, 1696. Their children were; Nathan, died young: Elizabeth, Martha, Nathan, Susanna, Abigail, William (died young), William and Anna.

(XI) Deacon Nathan (3), fourth child and second son of Lieutenant Nathan (2) and Elizabeth (Fry) Fiske, was born in Watertown, January 3, 1672, and died January 26, 1741, aged sixty-nine years. He was a man of note in his town and held office for many years. He was representative in 1727-28-29-32, and much confided in by his townsmen. He was selectman 1711-14-17-19-20-22-23-24-26-27; town treasurer, 1820-22-23; town clerk 1724-28-39; and was elected deacon as early as 1717. He married, (first), October 14, 1696, Sarah Coolidge, born about 1678. daughter of Ensign John of Watertown. She died November 27, 1723, and he married (second), May 22, 1729, Mrs. Hannah (Coolidge) Smith, born December 7, 1671, daughter of Simon and widow of Daniel Smith, Jr. She died October 4, 1750. The children of Deacon Nathan and Sarah were: Sarah, Elizabeth, Nathan, Josiah, Henry. Daniel, Samuel, Grace G. and Hannah P.

(XII) Nathan (4), third child and eldest son of Deacon Nathan (3) Fiske, was born in Watertown, February 25, 1701, and died in Weston, Massachusetts, January 4, 1769, aged sixty-eight. He resided in Weston, Massachusetts, and at his death left what in those days was considered a large estate. He married, (first), December 9. 1730. Anne Warren, born February, 1711, daughter of Deacon John of Weston. She died October 1, 1736, and he married (second), February 21, 1738, Mary Fiske, baptized June 30, 1712, daughter of Deacon Jonathan Fiske, of Lexington and Sudbury. After the death of her husband she was killed by a fall from a horse while on a visit to Sudbury on horseback. Nathan Fiske had three children by his wife Anne and eight by his wife Mary, viz: Anne, Nathan, Sarah, Jonathan. Ezra, Samuel, Thaddeus, Mary, Oliver, Mary and Hepzibah.

(XIII) Captain Jonathan, eldest child of Nathan (4) and his second wife, Mary (Fiske) Fiske, was born in Weston, December 15, 1739, and died in Medfield. He was captain of the Weston company in February, 1776, and was in the Revolutionary war. His company, with others, was in the regiment commanded by Colonel Eleazer Brooks, of Lincoln, Samuel Lawson, of Weston, major. This regiment with other troops was ordered to take possession of Dorchester Heights. He resided in Weston and Medfield. He married, April 30, 1760, Abigail Fiske, daughter of Thomas and Mary (Pierce) Fiske, of Waltham. Their children were; Nathan, Thaddeus, Micah, Ebenezer, Abigail. Jonathan, (died young), Jonathan, Abijah and Isaac.

(XIV) Major Jonathan (2), seventh child and sixth son of Jonathan (1) and Abigail (Fiske) Fiske, was born in Weston, January 19, 1774, and died in Medfield, June 19, 1864, aged ninety years. He was a tanner and farmer, a man much respected, and the holder of various town offices, a deacon in the church, and was at one time major in the Massachusetts Militia. A writer has said: "While none of this branch of the family or immediate ancestors have reached high positions of public honor, the family has been remarkably free from any who have in any way brought reproach or disgrace on the name. They have been upright and honorable and have been respected in the community in which they have resided; they have been intelligent and in several cases have received college educations." Jonathan married, in Weston, April 7, 1799, Sally Flagg, born July 8, 1773, daughter of Isaac Flagg; she died March 18, 1865, aged ninety-three years. He resided in Medfield, and he and his life lived together sixty-five years. Their children were: Sally, Clarissa, George, Amos Flagg. Abigail Lamson, Isaac and Charles.

(XV) Hon. Amos Flagg, fourth child and second son of Major Jonathan (2) and Sally (Flagg) Fiske, was born in Medfield, August 1, 1805, and died in Marlow, New Hampshire, January 6, 1873. In early manhood he settled in Marlow and opened a country store at what is known as Marlow Hill, where he conducted a thriving business. until what is now Marlow Village became the principal place in that town; his store and family were then removed to that village. There he continued to thrive and prosper and became the foremost citizen of the town, both in wealth and position. He held various town, county and state offices, the principal of which was state senator, to which office he was twice elected and served from 1863 to 1866. He was a man of strong character and sterling integrity. He died in Marlow, respected by all who knew him. He and his wife were both members of the Methodist Church in Marlow, and very active in its support. By his will he endowed this church, and after his decease, his widow contributed largely to its support. He married, in Marlow, October 30, 1830, Eliza Stone, of Marlow, who was born October 21, 1809, and died May 15, 1891, aged eighty-two. She was a most estimable lady. Their children were: Eliza (died young), Harriet Adelaide, Charles (died young) and Arthur W., Catherine, Henry and Eliza.

(XVI) Harriett Adelaide, second daughter and child of Amos D. and Eliza (Stone) Fiske, was born in Marlow, April 8, 1834, and married Dr. Marshall Perkins (see Perkins).

(Previous Generations on Pages 1144-5-6).

ROLFE (VII) Timothy Carter, second son and sixth child of Henry and Deborah (Carter) Rolfe, was born May 9, 1817, in the town of Concord, where he resided through-

CPSIA information can be obtained
at www.ICGtesting.com
Printed in the USA
LVHW081527110221
679066LV00004B/19

9 781296 527723